1915
2015

Kenneth Black, Jr.   Harold D. Skipper   Kenneth Black, III

Life Insurance

THE CENTENNIAL EDITION

1915
2015

Book composition and production by:
    { In a Word } www.inawordbooks.com

Publisher's Cataloging-in-Publication

Black, Kenneth.
    Life insurance / Kenneth Black, Jr., Harold D. Skipper, Kenneth Black, III. — The centennial edition, 1915–2015.
        pages cm
        Includes bibliographical references and index.
        LCCN 2015901430
        ISBN 978-0-9858765-1-7

    1. Life insurance. 2. Life insurance — United States. 3. Health insurance. 4. Health insurance — United States. I. Skipper, Harold D., 1947– II. Black, Kenneth, 1953– III. Title.

HG8771.B55 2015   368.32
                      QBI15-600037

1 2 3 4 5 6 7 8 9 10

To the memories of
George W. Skipper Jr. and Harold D. Skipper Sr.
&
Mabel Llewellyn Folger Black and Kenneth Black Jr.

CONTENTS

PART III. LIFE INSURANCE DUE CARE

PART IV. LIFE INSURANCE IN PERSONAL AND BUSINESS PLANNING

In Memoriam:
Past Authors

SOLOMON S. HUEBNER, the sole author of this text until 1958, is often called the "father of insurance education" in the United States. He taught the first courses ever given in insurance and established (1913) and chaired the nation's first academic department of insurance at the Wharton School, University of Pennsylvania. Although his Wharton doctoral thesis concerned foreign-trade aspects of marine insurance, he invited life insurance managers to lecture to his early Wharton students. He quickly realized the urgent need for uniformity, fairness, and honesty in the life insurance industry.

He authored several path-breaking insurance textbooks, including the first edition of this volume, published in 1915. Since that time, succeeding editions have been in continuous use both at the university level and in professional programs. He invited Dr. Kenneth Black Jr. to join him as coauthor of this text in 1958. Dr. Huebner was active in both academic and professional circles, serving as President of the American Risk and Insurance Association (ARIA). He was made a Laureate of The Insurance Hall of Fame, International Insurance Society, Inc. (IIS) in 1957, its inaugural year. Dr. Huebner retired from the University of Pennsylvania in 1953 and died in 1964.

KENNETH BLACK, JR. was the founder of the Department of Risk Management and Insurance (1959), Regent's Professor Emeritus, and Dean Emeritus of the Robinson College of Business at Georgia State University. He held the C.V. Starr Chair of International Insurance from its founding until 1993, and, in 1989, the Kenneth Black Jr. Chair of Insurance was founded in his honor. He held bachelors and masters degrees from the University of North Carolina, with a doctorate degree from the University of Pennsylvania where he studied as a Huebner Fellow.

Dr. Black was author or coauthor of 15 books and numerous articles and essays and served as the editor of the *Journal of Financial Service Professionals* for 42 years. He was also active in industry and government, serving as Vice Chairman of the President's Commission on Railroad Retirement. He served as President of both ARIA and of the IIS. Among the many honors and awards Dr. Black received are: the John Newton Russell Memorial Award (1999) presented by the National Association of Life Underwriters; Laureate, The Insurance Hall of Fame, IIS (1993); and the Solomon S. Huebner Gold Medal from the American College (1985). Dr. Black retired from the faculty at Georgia State University in 1992 and died in 2005.

ABOUT THE AUTHORS

HAROLD D. SKIPPER is Professor Emeritus of Risk Management and Insurance at Georgia State University. While at GSU, he chaired its Department of Risk Management and Insurance and held the C.V. Starr Chair of International Insurance from 1993 until he retired in 2005. He is past President of ARIA and founder of the Asia-Pacific Risk and Insurance Association (APRIA). His bachelors degree is from Georgia State University and his masters and Ph.D. degrees are from the University of Pennsylvania where he studied as a Huebner Fellow.

He is author or coauthor of four books and dozens of articles and serves on the advisory boards of several international educational institutions. His major non-academic experience includes work with the *United Nations Conference on Trade and Development* in Geneva, the Paris-based *Organization for Economic Cooperation and Development (OECD)*, the *World Bank,* as well as several major corporations and law firms. Among his professional recognitions are ARIA's *Kulp-Wright Book Award* (2009) for "Outstanding Original Contribution to the Literature of Risk and Insurance," the IIS's *John S. Bickley Founder's Award* (2009); establishment (2005) of the *Harold D. Skipper Award for Outstanding Risk and Insurance Research*, presented annually at the APRIA conference; and membership (1995) in Phi Beta Delta, Honor Society for International Scholars.

Harold D. Skipper can be reached at haroldskipper@gmail.com

KENNETH BLACK, III is a graduate of the University of North Carolina and received his Juris Doctorate from the University of Georgia School of Law. He has worked across a wide spectrum of insurance, life insurance, and health insurance-related activities serving both consumers and providers of financial services. These have included reinsurance brokerage at Lloyd's of London, both practice and systems design in personal financial and estate planning, investment counseling, third party administration of health care plans, and strategic planning for financial services providers. He was a participant in a multi-disciplinary independent marketing group that designed, arranged reinsurance, and marketed the first substandard annuity for smokers in the United States.

He has provided consulting services to major life insurers, national and international life insurance agency operations, and law firms. As an adjunct instructor for many years, he taught courses in business law, risk and insurance principles, life insurance, financial planning, and financial institutions management in the Department of Risk Management and Insurance at Georgia State University. He has also served as guest lecturer in the department's Munich Re International Visiting Fellows Program. He is a member of ARIA and APRIA. From 1993 to 2007, he organized and served as the founding president of a private life insurer affiliate of the former Fortis banking and insurance group.

Kenneth Black, III can be reached at kenblackiii@gmail.com

PREFACE

This 15th edition of *Life Insurance* is published in recognition of the 100th anniversary of this book's first edition. The first edition was published in 1915 and authored by Solomon S. Huebner. That edition was considered pioneering for its setting out *both* insurance principles *and* practices in a single, expansive treatise aimed explicitly at students of the business, whether students in the traditional collegiate sense or those undertaking professional development studies. This edition continues that legacy.

The book's simple title, *Life Insurance*, should be understood in its broadest context. It clearly encompasses insurance that promises to pay money on the death of an insured; that is, we address mortality risk. It also includes insurance that promises to pay while an insured is alive; that is, we address longevity risk. Finally, it encompasses insurance that promises payment or services to insureds in the event of incapacity, disability, or loss of health; that is, we address morbidity risks.

Revisions contained in this and the predecessor 14th edition were significant and sweeping. First, we have listened carefully to the book's users who have urged us to streamline the text by taking a more focused approach to topics, through crisper writing, by eliminating or reducing coverage of less essential topics, and by assuming a more knowledgeable reader. Consequently, the number of chapters is reduced from the 35 in the 13th edition to 24, with word count similarly reduced. In doing so, we curtailed somewhat the emphasis on social insurance programs, heath-care financing, group insurance, and some other areas, but believe that what remains provides a sound, reasonably complete treatment of these subjects within a life insurance context.

Second, we have also listened to users who expressed a preference for a greater emphasis on the fundamentals of economics and finance that underpin life insurance theory and practice. This continued stronger emphasis will be noticeable throughout the text, but especially within the chapters on life insurance company operations.

Third, we have attempted to make the book even more relevant to students and practitioners by including the latest innovations in products, their pricing, and their applications to individual, family, and business problem solving. Toward this end, we have considerably deepened the treatment of enterprise risk management over that contained in earlier editions, in accordance with the increased understanding and emphasis occurring over the past two decades.

Fourth, while the 14th edition represented a major revision and was published but a relatively short time ago, several factors compelled us to make further revisions to the text sooner rather than later. These included the perceived need to update information in several vitally important sections, such as the tax treatment of life insurance and the implementation of the *Patient Protection and Affordable Care Act of 2010.* We also discovered several portions of the significantly revised 14th edition that needed clarification and others portions that contained errors or were in need of more in depth treatment.

At the same time, we strove to retain those aspects of the book that our users told us were its strengths. Thus, we continue to give careful consideration of the external factors impinging on life insurer management and regulation. We also continue to approach our subject matter simultaneously from the viewpoints of the buyer, the advisor, the insurer, and the regulator. We have again presented what we believe are forthright appraisals of various life insurer products and suggestions for how they and the companies and agents that sell them can be evaluated. Further, while this edition retains its historical emphasis on U.S. practice, international practices and terminology are presented throughout.

We continue to devote entire chapters to explanations of how life insurance products (1) fit within a personal financial planning context, (2) are taxed, (3) are useful within estate planning situations, (4) assist in retirement planning, and (5) find helpful application in many business situations. Of course, each of these chapters is updated to reflect the latest applications, law, and tax treatment, but the reader will also find that theoretical and practical background provides a more stable learning platform. While these areas change continuously, an exposure to the topics is important to students and practitioners.

The authors benefited greatly from the help of many individuals. We note first our debt to the M Financial Group, Inc., for allowing us to draw from key portions of its *Advisor's Guide to Life Insurance* coauthored by Harold D. Skipper and Wayne Tonning. Several individuals at M Financial were instrumental in ensuring that the *Advisor's Guide* was a state-of-the-art treatment of life insurance from the perspective of those offering insurance advice, and we have captured some of this applied perspective within the 14th and 15th editions at relevant places.

Additionally, we benefited greatly from the constructive help, advice, and criticism of the following individuals: Joseph M. Belth, founder and former editor of *The Insurance Forum* and Professor Emeritus of Insurance at Indiana University; James M. Carson, The University of Georgia; Conrad S. Ciccotello and Bruce A. Palmer, Georgia State University; Cassandra R. Cole and Lorilee A. Medders, Florida State University; Paul D. LaPorte and James O. Mitchell, LIMRA International; Mary Bickley Naismith, Life Office Management Association; William G. Loventhal III, The Northwestern Mutual Life Insurance Company; Lawton M. Nease III, Nease, Lagana, Eden and Culley; W. Jean Kwon, St. John's University; Michael R. Powers, Tsinghua University; William H. Rabel, The University of Alabama; Robert D. Shapiro, The Shapiro Network, Inc.; Layne Sheridan; Phillip E. Stano, Sutherland Asbill & Brennan LLP; and Wayne Tonning, The M Financial Group, Inc. We carry forward our indebtedness to the many hundreds of individuals who provided constructive advice and criticisms with earlier editions. Their impact remains in this volume, and we thank them.

We wish also to thank Alexander Bukovietski of In a Word, LLC for his contributions to the design and production of this volume. Through his counsel and insight, the authors have developed an appreciation for the complex sequence of events that follows from manuscript to publication.

In addition, we also acknowledge with appreciation the superb electronic learning aids that David R. Lange, Auburn University Montgomery, has developed and made available at our web site. We are confident that his dedication to "learning by doing" will greatly enhance the students' mastery of the material.

Finally, we thank our long-time colleague, Deborah S. Gaunt, for her careful editorial review of the entire manuscript for the 14th edition. Her keen eye for detail and accuracy greatly improved the final product.

This volume will be published in two international editions, and we would like to acknowledge the important assistance we have received in these projects. In the People's Republic of China, we thank Dr. Qixiang Sun, Dean of the School of Economics, Peking University, for her long-time support of and instrumental involvement in securing a Chinese edition; and also the book's translator Dr. Wei Zheng, Chair, Department of Risk Management and Insurance, Peking University, and Weina Qi, Economic Science Press, Beijing, for their leadership and skill in preparing the Chinese edition. We also express appreciation to the Economic Science Press and to The China Life Insurance Company Limited for their support of this venture. In India, we are grateful to Professor B.S.R. Roa of the Disha Educom (India) Private Limited, for his long-time support of and leadership in arranging for an Indian publication of the volume; and to Professor R. Vaidyanathan of the Indian Institute of Management, Bangalore, for his assistance with the Indian market and publishing.

The present authors are grateful for the privilege that has been afforded us to continue the impressive legacies of Drs. Huebner and Black and hope that throughout this volume we have maintained the high standards of excellence and professionalism to which their entire careers were committed. Both built bridges of knowledge and understanding.

None of those who reviewed the manuscripts for the 14th or 15th editions bears any responsibility for the deficiencies that may remain in the completed work. Instead, any deficiencies remain those of the authors.

Harold D. Skipper
Kenneth Black, III

CHAPTER 1

The Economics of Life Insurance

"He is the happiest man who can see the connection between the end and the beginning of his life."

Goethe

Humans have always sought to reduce uncertainty.[1] This innate drive to reduce risk motivated the earliest formations of clans, tribes, and other groups. Group mechanisms ensured a less volatile source of life's necessities than that which atomized individuals and families could provide. The group provided greater physical security and helped their less fortunate members in times of crises.

People today continue their quest to achieve security and reduce uncertainty. We still engage in activities and rely on groups to help reduce the variability of income required to obtain life's necessities and to protect acquired wealth. The group may be our employer, the government, or an insurance firm, but the concept is the same. Wealth itself has communal origins: many historians consider the first cultural manifestation of wealth to be the production of grains by incipient agrarian societies in amounts exceeding requirements of current consumption and the emergence of the stockpile.

In some ways, however, we are more vulnerable than our ancestors. The physical and economic security formerly provided by the tribe or extended family diminishes with industrialization. Our income-dependent, wealth-acquiring lifestyles render us and our families more vulnerable to societal and environmental changes over which we have little control. Contemporary individuals are in need of more formalized means to mitigate the adverse consequences of unemployment, loss of health, old age, death, lawsuits, and loss of wealth. As extensions of human activity, businesses are similarly vulnerable.

A BRIEF HISTORY OF LIFE INSURANCE

Humans have long been concerned about the adverse effects on their families of their deaths. Indeed, the risk transfer aspect of life insurance dates back more than 2,500 years to Greek societies. An elaborate funeral ceremony was an important social and religious ritual of ancient times (and this view persists today to varying degrees in many cultures). The belief was that the soul of the departed could gain entrance into the special paradise of his or her faith only if the funeral was conducted with all required rituals, sacrifices, and feasts. The Greek societies assumed this risk for its members by assuring them of a proper burial.

The Roman collegia, patterned after the Greek societies, were numerous during the period of the Roman Republic. These collegia evolved into mutual benefit associations with stated benefits and regular membership contributions. The dissolution of the Roman Empire brought an end to these societies, although similar organizations continued to exist in the Byzantine Empire.

The need for mutual protection and security not only continued but increased after Rome fell. Guilds evolved to meet this need. These guilds, particularly in England, provided mutual assistance to their members as witnessed by the mentioning in most guild statutes of a host of perils for which members might qualify for relief, including death, illness, capture by pirates, shipwreck, the burning of one's home, and the loss of one's tools of trade. Craftsmen guilds evolved in Japan during the period 1699-1868. Guilds, however, were not organized primarily for benevolent or relief purposes. Their primary purposes were religious, social, and economic.

English friendly societies were true mutual benefit groups. Not concerned with trade, craft, or religion, they were operated by officers and a committee elected by members and governed by a set of rules adopted and amended by the membership. Hardly a hamlet in England did not have at least one friendly society. All societies had some form of death or burial fund benefit. Many societies provided benefits for a variety of other perils. Unlike the guilds, benefit payments did not depend on the member's need, although payments often were restricted by the funds available.

The beginnings of friendly societies predate, by some time, the first mortality tables, the laws of probability, and the mathematics of insurance. Society members were assessed as needed to provide the promised benefit payments. **Assessment basis** insurance contracts permit insureds (members) to be assessed retrospectively as claims occur, to provide promised benefit payments.

Contributions were not scaled according to the age or insurability of members, so a large share of the burden was placed on young, healthy members. As a result, many discontinued their memberships. Average mortality rates increased as the average age of the members increased, placing a still heavier burden upon those of advancing years who often were the ones least able to afford it. High failure rates were an inevitable result.

The earliest insurers were individual underwriters who either alone or in concert with others assumed various life insurance risks. Contracts were of short duration; seldom a year. Clearly, long term life insurance contracts could not be satisfactorily underwritten by individuals, for the insured could outlive the insurer! During this early time, the practice of individuals writing their names under the amount of insurance that they were willing to back arose. This practice gave rise to the term "underwriting," with the person making the contract being known as an "underwriter."

Some early underwriters apparently were not eager to meet their obligations. A 1584 dispute, the earliest on record, illustrates how the meaning of words can be critically important. A life insurance contract was issued on June 15, 1583 by the office of insurance within the Royal Exchange for £383 6s 9d on the life of William Gybbons for a term of 12 months. Thirteen individuals underwrote the contract. The premium was £75. The insured died shortly before the expiration of one year. The insurers refused to pay on the grounds that *their* intended 12 months were the shorter *lunar* months, not the more common *calendar* months. On this basis, the policy had expired. Mr. Gybbons' heirs prevailed on their suit against the underwriters.

Individual underwriting gave way over time to corporate underwriting. The first true mutual insurance company was *The Life Assurance and Annuity Association* established by the *Mystery of the Mercers of London* on October 4, 1699. It failed 46 years later. By 1720, two English insurers, *The Royal Exchange* and *The London* (both stock companies), had managed to receive a monopoly on British insurance. When the *Equitable* applied for a corporate charter to form a stock insurer in 1761, it was refused. Its founders, therefore, decided to form a mutual company, which did not require a charter. Thus, in 1762, *The Society for Equitable Assurances on Lives and Survivorships* was born. The *Equitable* is said to have been the first life insurer to operate on modern insurance principles, including relying on age-based premiums. While the *Equitable* legally remains in existence as the world's oldest life insurer, it is not selling new policies, with its existing business having been transferred to other insurers or placed in run off because of financial difficulties incurred during the 2000s.

The history of life insurance is intertwined with government in numerous ways. One of the most interesting was the effort to raise funds to support government expenditures through the sale of a type of life annuity. Box 1-1 highlights the best known of these schemes.

Box 1-1

France and Tontines

The right to receive rent from land and to transfer this right to others was well established before Roman times. A landowner, for a consideration, could transfer the rent or income from a designated farm or landholding to a beneficiary who might receive this rent in money or in kind for life or for a specified time. It was but a short step from life rents based upon land to annuities based upon the grantor's solvency. Governments as well as monasteries and other religious organizations used the sale of annuities as fundraising devices. The religious prohibition against usury made the annuity a favored device for borrowing large sums.

In fact, in 1689, Louis XIV of France used an annuity scheme devised by Lorenzo Tonti to raise needed funds for the state. Under what was to be known as **tontines,** amounts were paid into a fund by participants who received payments from the fund only for as long as they lived, with a portion of the forfeited funds of deceased participants being used to augment payments to survivors. When participants died, their annuity payments ceased. Portions of these former payments were then allocated among the survivors in what today are called *benefits of survivorship*. As more annuitants died, payments to survivors grew. Other governments and private promoters continued this scheme almost into the twentieth century, when it was outlawed.

The emergence of corporations in England in the late 17th and early 18th centuries, coupled with the availability of adequate mortality statistics and the development of sound actuarial principles, marked the birth of modern life insurance. The introduction of the agency system of marketing using commissioned salespersons gave further impetus to life insurance growth. Today, life insurance companies are found in almost every country and the products provided by these companies are important sources of family and national economic security and economic development.

THE LANGUAGE OF INSURANCE

Insurance is a vitally important risk management tool. From an economic perspective, **insurance** can be defined as a financial intermediation function under which insureds each contribute to a pool from which payments are made to them or on their behalf if specified contingencies occur. Insurance is a contingent claim on the insurance pool's assets.

From a legal perspective, **insurance** is an agreement (insurance policy or contract) by which one party (policyowner) pays a stipulated consideration (premium) to the other party (insurance company or insurer) in return for which the insurance company agrees to pay a defined amount or provide a specific service if specified contingencies occur during the policy term. The person whose life or health is the object of the insurance policy is the **insured**. In most instances, the insured is also the **policyowner** (also called **policyholder**) who is the person that can exercise all policy rights and with whom the insurer deals. The **beneficiary** is the person or entity entitled to insurance death or health benefits in the event of a policy claim.

Insurance can be examined from several perspectives. We offer three here:

- social versus private,
- life versus nonlife, and
- commercial versus personal.

SOCIAL VERSUS PRIVATE INSURANCE

Governments have determined that they, not the private sector, should or must provide some types of insurance. Thus, most countries have extensive social insurance schemes that provide survivor, retirement, disability, health, and unemployment benefits to qualified residents.

Social insurance possesses several characteristics. First, participation is compulsory and financing relies on government-mandated premiums (i.e., taxes). Second, income security is provided for well-defined risks (e.g., unemployment, retirement), and the recipient is not subject to an economic needs test. Finally, it emphasizes social equity (i.e., income redistribution), a characteristic that distinguishes it from private insurance which emphasizes individual actuarial equity (i.e., premiums reflect the expected payout for each insured).

Private insurance is offered by insurance firms in the private sector. Its purchase may be compulsory, as with auto liability insurance, but need not be. Premiums reflect insureds' expected losses. This book's main focus is on private insurance.

LIFE VERSUS NONLIFE INSURANCE

The private insurance sector divides itself between companies that sell insurance on the person, known as *life insurance, life assurance, personal insurance*, and *long term insurance,* depending on the country, and those that sell insurance to protect property, referred to as *nonlife insurance, property/casualty insurance,* or *general insurance,* depending on the country. The nonlife branch includes insurance to cover:

- property losses – damage to or destruction of property, including homes, automobiles, businesses, aircraft, etc.,
- liability losses – payments owed third parties resulting from the insured's negligence from automobile operation, professional care or advice, product defects, etc., and
- workers' compensation and health insurance payments in some countries.

This book is concerned with the life branch of the private insurance business. Life insurance, broadly defined, focuses on the following types of risks and the corresponding types of insurance:

- **Mortality risk** – possibility that one's death creates undesirable financial consequences for others; covered by life insurance (or life assurance),
- **Longevity risk** – possibility of outliving one's financial resources; covered by endowments, annuities, and pensions, and
- **Morbidity risk** – possibility that injury, illness, or incapacity creates unacceptable financial consequences; covered by health insurance, disability income insurance, and long term care insurance.

Definitions within the life branch can be inconsistent between countries and even within a single market. When referring to life insurance as a branch of private insurance, it often includes all three classes of insurance coverages listed above. The title of this book, *Life Insurance*, adopts this view. Similarly, a **life insurance company** is a corporation authorized under the law of its sovereign state to sell products that involve life and/or health contingencies. When referring to insurance coverage, the term **life insurance** usually means policies that pay benefits to named beneficiaries on the death of the insured. Even here, we encounter inconsistencies. In most markets, annuities and pension-related coverages are classified separately from life insurance policies.

Health insurance indemnifies an insured for costs incurred and/or wages lost because of illness, injury, or incapacity. Thus, **disability income insurance** is health insurance that pays a stated, usually monthly, benefit if illness or injury prevents the insured from working. **Long term care insurance** is health insurance that pays a stated, usually monthly, benefit if incapacity of the insured prohibits him or her from engaging in specified activities of daily living. Policies often provide for three levels of nursing home care: (1) skilled nursing care, (2) intermediate nursing care, and (3) custodial care. **Medical expense insurance** is health insurance that indemnifies the insured for costs incurred because of illness or injury.

Some markets, notably in Europe, classify health insurance as nonlife insurance. In the U.S., private health insurance commonly falls within the life branch.

This book's emphasis is on private insurance for the mortality and longevity risks, while offering limited treatment of morbidity risks.

PERSONAL VERSUS COMMERCIAL INSURANCE

Life insurance companies sell products and services both to individuals and to organizations; i.e., they sell personal and commercial insurance. In the U.S. insurance lexicon, **personal insurance** is any insurance purchased by individuals for non-commercial purposes. This can include individual life and health insurance, home insurance, and family automobile insurance.

The U.S. life insurance industry often classifies its personal insurance as being either industrial life and health insurance or ordinary insurance. **Industrial life and health insurance** is a type of personal insurance in which policies of modest benefit amounts are sold to individuals of low to modest incomes and whose premiums are collected weekly or monthly at the insured's residence or place of employment. **Ordinary insurance** is individually issued life, health, and retirement coverages, other than industrial insurance.

Commercial insurance is any insurance designed for purchase by organizations, such as businesses. Commercial life, health, and retirement coverages are more commonly referred to as group insurance in the U.S. **Group insurance** is a type of commercial insurance in which a group of persons who usually have a business or professional relationship to the contract owner are provided coverage under a single master contract.

Finally, **credit life insurance** and **credit health insurance** provide life and health insurance through financial institutions to cover debtors' obligations if they die or become disabled.

Government oversight is more stringent in personal insurance than in commercial insurance because commercial buyers are generally better able to look after their interests than are individuals. This book emphasizes personal life insurance.

Life insurance is of enormous importance throughout the world. The more economically developed a country, the greater the role of insurance as an economic security device. A United Nations' committee formally recognized that life insurance "can play an important role in providing individual economic security and in national development efforts, including the mobilization of personal savings."[2]

LIFE INSURANCE INTERNATIONALLY

The commonly accepted measure of insurance market size is gross direct written premiums. Globally, such premiums grew at an inflation-adjusted rate of a modest 0.7 percent, to US$2,608 billion, in 2013, after growing by 2.3 percent the previous year. Advanced market life premium growth has stagnated at an average annual rate of -0.2 percent, post-2008 financial crisis. Post-crisis growth has been particularly weak in North America (-2.9 percent), Oceania (-3.7 percent), and Western Europe (-0.6 percent). Advanced economies in Asia, led by Japan, realized average annual growth premium growth of 3.0 percent.

Overall, life premiums in emerging markets have grown more slowly post-crisis than before, but with significant regional variations. Thus, average annual premium growth fell from 16 percent during the 2003-2007 period, to 3.8 percent in 2009-2013. Swiss Re notes that this relative decline is due mostly to regulatory changes that dented growth in China and India, the two largest such life markets. In Latin America, the Middle East, and Africa, however, average growth post-crisis has been higher than that observed pre-crisis.

In general, the international life insurance industry's profitability improved marginally in 2013, according to Swiss Re, driven mainly by rising equity markets. It remained below pre-crisis levels. The industry is said to be well funded, its capital position having recovered alongside market strengthening and regulatory support in many countries. Swiss Re expects profitability to remain under pressure going forward because of some older, less profitable business and sluggish economic growth.

Long-term world growth in life insurance premiums has been driven by comparatively high growth rates in emerging markets, increasing life expectancy, and governments having to reduce the generosity of social insurance programs in the face of fiscal imbalances. The effects are to substitute private insurance for government insurance, increasing demand for the products sold by life insurers. The demand for products to protect against longevity risk, such as annuities, has driven premium growth. Figure 1-1 shows the regional distribution of life insurance premiums worldwide.

Regional Distribution of Life Insurance Premiums (2013)   **Figure 1-1**

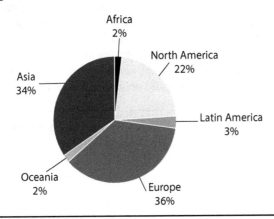

Europe was the world's largest life insurance market in 2013, accounting for 36.3 percent of total direct premiums written, up from the 33.4 in 2012. Asia slipped to second place worldwide, at 34.4 percent, roughly the same as 2012. North America's share fell to 22.4 percent from 23.7 percent in 2012.

The world's ten largest national life insurance markets and that of the European Union (E.U.) are shown in Figure 1-2.

Two measures are used traditionally to show the relative importance of insurance within national economies. **Insurance density** is the average annual per capita premium within a market. Values are usually converted from national currency to U.S. dollars. As such, currency fluctuations affect comparisons, and this fact can lead to distortions, especially over time. Even so, this measure is a useful indicator of the importance of insurance purchases within national economies.

Figure 1-2   Life Insurance Premium Income for 10 Largest National Markets and the
                      European Union (Millions of US Dollars, 2013)

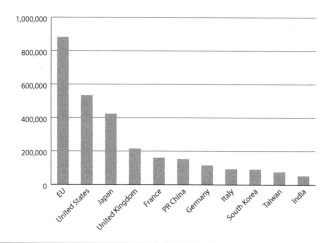

The U.S. remained the largest national life insurance market in the world, followed by Japan, with
the United Kingdom (U.K.), France, China, and Germany thereafter. Collectively, the member
states of the E.U. accounted for considerably more in premium income than any national market.

The other measure, **insurance penetration**, is the ratio of yearly direct premiums written to gross domestic product (GDP). It is an indication of the relative
importance of insurance within markets and is unaffected by currency fluctuations. Even so, it does not give a complete picture as it ignores differences in insurance price levels, national product mixes, and other market variations. Figures 1-3
and 1-4 show life insurance density and penetration for selected countries.

Figure 1-3   Life Premiums per Capita for Selected Countries, European Union, and
                      World (US Dollars, 2013)

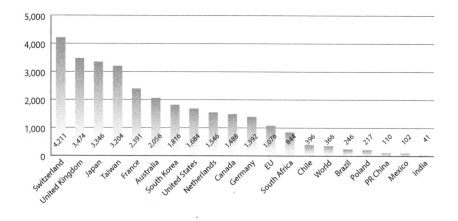

Life insurance density for selected countries, the E.U., and the world for 2013 are presented. The
Swiss per capita expenditure of $4,211 was second only to Hong Kong, at $4,445 (not shown in

the figure). The U.K. figure of $3,374 was the world's fifth highest (following Finland at $4,109 and Denmark at $4,093, neither shown), with Japan at sixth highest at $3,346. At $1,684, the U.S. per capita figure ranked 18th in the world. The average for the E.U. member states was $1,620, up in both nominal and real terms from 2012. Density figures for several other country groupings (not shown) were relatively low owing to low per capita incomes. Thus, Latin America and the Caribbean averaged $131, the ASEAN countries averaged $93, and Africa overall averaged $46.

Life Premiums as Percentage of Gross Domestic Product for Selected Countries, European Union, and World (2013)

Figure 1-4

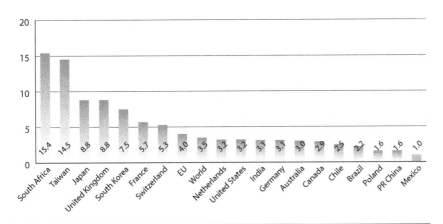

Life insurance penetration ratios for 2013 are presented for selected countries, the E.U., and the world. Taiwan had the world's highest ratio at 14.5 percent. South Africa ranked second at 12.7 percent. At 8.8 percent, Japan tied for fourth with the U.K. The U.S. tied with the Netherlands and Malaysia (not shown) for 19th worldwide, at 3.2 percent. The E.U. averaged 4.73 percent. The ASEAN countries averaged 2.37 percent, while Africa and Latin American and the Caribbean countries averaged 2.43 and 1.39 percent, respectively (not shown).

THE ROLE OF LIFE INSURANCE IN ECONOMIC DEVELOPMENT

Financial services are essential to economic development. As financial intermediaries, insurance companies perform similar functions and provide similar generic benefits to a national economy as other financial intermediaries such as banks. At the same time, the risks that insurers present to national economies differ in important ways from those of other financial intermediaries, including especially those of banks, as explained more fully in Chapter 9. Further, the benefits of insurance in individual and corporate risk management mean that their overall contributions to economic development differ from those of other financial intermediaries. The more developed and efficient a country's financial markets, the greater will be its contribution to economic prosperity. It is for this reason that governments strive to foster greater competition among financial service providers and ensure that markets are regulated appropriately and are financially sound.

It is wrong to view insurance as a simple pass-through mechanism for diversifying risk under which the unfortunate few who suffer losses are indemnified from the funds the insurer collects from the many insureds. Laudable though it is, this function masks other fundamental contributions that insurance makes to prosperity. Insurance:

- promotes financial stability,
- substitutes for and complements government security programs,
- facilitates and motivates savings, and
- fosters more efficient capital allocation.

Countries that are best at harnessing these contributions give their citizens and businesses greater economic opportunities. We examine each of the contributions below.

PROMOTES FINANCIAL STABILITY   All types of insurance help stabilize the financial situation of individuals, families, and organizations. Without insurance, individuals and families could become financially destitute and forced to seek assistance from relatives, friends, or the government. The stability provided by insurance encourages individuals and firms to invest and create wealth. Indeed, banks and other lenders often insist that key executives of firms carry substantial life insurance made payable to the firm.

SUBSTITUTES FOR AND COMPLEMENTS GOVERNMENT SECURITY PROGRAMS   Life insurance can substitute for government security programs. Private insurance also complements public security programs. It can thus relieve pressure on social insurance systems, preserving government resources for essential social security and other worthwhile purposes and allowing individuals to tailor their security programs to their own preferences. Studies have confirmed that greater private expenditures on life insurance are associated with a reduction in government expenditures on social insurance programs. This substitution role is especially important because of the current fiscal challenges faced by national social insurance systems.

FACILITATES AND MOTIVATES SAVINGS   The general financial services literature emphasizes the important role of savings in economic growth. Savings can be either financial or non-financial. Non-financial savings take the form of real assets such as land, jewelry and buildings for example. Financial savings are held in financial assets such as savings accounts, bonds, shares, annuities, and life insurance policies. Generally, the more economically developed a country, the greater the proportion of its total wealth is held as financial savings.

Life insurers offer the same advantages as other financial intermediaries in channeling savings into domestic investment. Insurers enhance financial system efficiency in three ways.

- First, insurers reduce transaction costs associated with bringing together savers and borrowers. Thousands of individuals each pay relatively small life insurance premiums, part of which typically represents savings. Insurers then invest these amassed funds in businesses and with government. In performing this intermediation function, direct lending and investing by individual policyholders, which would be time consuming and costly, is avoided.

- Second, insurers create liquidity. Insurance premiums are "borrowed" funds entrusted to insurers by policyowners, not only to pay claims but to make loans and investments. Both life and nonlife insurers stand ready to provide policyholders (and third parties) with instant liquidity if a covered event occurs. The creation of liquidity allows policyholders to have immediate access to loss payments and savings while borrowers need not repay their loans immediately. If all individuals instead undertook direct lending, they likely would find unacceptable the proportion of their personal wealth held in long-term, illiquid assets. Insurers and other financial intermediaries thereby reduce illiquidity inherent in direct lending.
- Third, insurers facilitate economies of scale in investment. Some investment projects are quite large, requiring correspondingly large financing. Such large projects often enjoy economies of scale, promote specialization, and stimulate technological innovations and therefore can be particularly important to economic growth. By amassing large sums from thousands of smaller premium payers, insurers can meet the financing needs of large projects and thereby encourage economic efficiency.

Well-developed financial systems have a myriad of financial institutions and instruments. Contractual savings institutions, such as life insurers and private pension funds, can be especially important financial intermediaries. In contrast with commercial banks, which specialize in collecting short-term deposits, contractual saving institutions usually take a longer-term view. Their longer-term liabilities and stable cash flows are ideal sources of long-term finance for government and business and, as the recent economic crisis confirmed, act as economic shock absorbers during recessions.

FOSTERS A MORE EFFICIENT ALLOCATION OF CAPITAL   Insurers gather substantial information to conduct their evaluations of firms, projects, and managers both in deciding whether (and at what price) to issue insurance, and in their roles as lenders and investors. While individual savers and investors may not have the time, resources, or ability to undertake this information gathering and processing, insurers have an advantage in this regard and are better at allocating financial capital and insurance risk-bearing capacity. Insurers will choose to insure and to provide funds to the most appropriate companies, projects, and managers.

Because insurers have a continuing interest in the companies, projects, and managers to whom they provide financial capital or risk-bearing capacity, they have an incentive to monitor managers and entrepreneurs to reduce the chances that they engage in unacceptable risk-increasing behavior. Insurers thus encourage them to act in the best interests of their various stakeholders (customers, stockholders, and creditors, etc.). By doing so, insurers tangibly signal the market's approval of promising, well-managed firms and foster a more efficient allocation of scarce financial capital and risk-bearing capacity.

THE COSTS OF INSURANCE TO SOCIETY

Insurance offers societies great economic and welfare benefits but not without costs. First, insurers incur sales, servicing, administration, and investment management expenses. These costs are an indispensable part of doing business but increase the price of insurance. Such expenses may average 10 percent or more of policy premiums, with the loss payment and reserving accounting for the balance. The higher are such expenses, the less efficient are insurers, other things being the same.

Second, the existence of insurance encourages moral hazard – the tendency of insureds to alter their behavior because they are insured (see below). Some insureds inflate otherwise legitimate health insurance claims. Each year, some insureds are murdered for life insurance proceeds. All such behaviors cause premiums to be higher than they would be otherwise, represent a deadweight loss to society, and are societal costs of insurance.

LIFE INSURANCE MARKETS

Insurance operations, practices, and regulation can be better understood if they are placed in a logical framework. Economics provides that framework. An understanding of the economic principles that underpin insurance and insurance markets will prove enduring.

ECONOMIC EFFICIENCY AS A SOCIAL GOAL

We begin with a review of the conditions under which markets operate at optimum efficiency. The objective that a market-oriented economy has for its insurance industry is the same as that which it has for other industries – an efficient allocation of society's scarce resources while maximizing consumer choice and value. At the same time, society desires a system that leads to continuous innovation and improvement. These objectives are most likely to be achieved through competitive markets. A **market** is a system of exchange where goods or services are bought and sold.

Competition not only leads to economic efficiency, it provides an automatic mechanism for fulfilling consumer needs and wants and for creating a greater variety of choices. Additionally, in an effort always to secure an advantage over rivals in the market, suppliers engage in efforts to improve their products and services, thus further benefiting buyers.

A **perfectly competitive market** is one with no imperfections and, therefore, societal welfare, as defined by economists, is maximized. The conditions under which a market exhibits perfect competition are shown in Box 1-2. Such a market requires no government direction or oversight to accomplish these desirable social goals.

Neither insurance nor any other market fully meets these conditions. Fortunately, a market can meet them partially and still function efficiently. The more removed actual market functioning is from these ideal constructs, the more imperfect the resulting competition and, therefore, the less efficient is the allocation of societal resources. Consequently, the poorer will be the industry performance and attendant consumer value and choice. Such market-based (as opposed to governmental) deviations from the conditions for perfect competition that cause an inefficient allocation of resources are referred to as market imperfections (or market failures).

Box 1-2
Conditions for a Perfectly Competitive Insurance Market
The following conditions are necessary for a perfectly competitive insurance market:

- *A sufficiently large number of buyers and sellers such that no buyer or seller can influence the market.* This condition means that all buyers and sellers are **price takers** – none can influence the price of the product as determined by its supply and demand. Underlying this assumption is that neither sellers nor buyers engage in collusive behavior.
- *Sellers have freedom of entry into and exit from the market.* This condition means that new competitors can enter the market if they see that existing firms are making higher than **normal profits,** which are the minimal profits that firms must acquire to remain in operation. Firms must not only respond to rivals after they enter the business, but they also must anticipate new competitors. If competitors know that entry barriers are low, they will automatically hold the line on price increases even if no new competitors actually enter the market. The mere threat of new entry can be sufficient to ensure that firms will make only normal profits. Conversely, competitors will exit a market if they cannot make normal profits or if they can make greater profits elsewhere.
- *Sellers produce identical products.* This condition means that no seller can differentiate its products from those of its rivals. Hence, buyers have no incentive to pay more than the market price for any firm's products.
- *Buyers and sellers are well informed about the products.* This condition means that all firms and consumers possess full knowledge about the product or service under consideration and that none has knowledge unknown to others.

IMPERFECTIONS IN INSURANCE MARKETS

Insurers exist to control the effects of market imperfections. If insurance markets were perfectly competitive – which they are not – there would be no need for insurers, and government oversight of insurance would be superfluous, as all customers would have complete information.[*] Each of the functional operations of insurers exists because of imperfections in insurance markets, as does insurance regulation. An understanding of these imperfections is necessary to a sound foundation. They fall into four classifications:

- market power,
- externalities,
- free rider problems, and
- information problems.

---

[*] No financial intermediaries would exist if financial markets were perfectly competitive or "complete." **Complete financial markets** are those in which users and providers of funds have complete information about each other, borrowing/lending functions are frictionless, and monitoring is costless. In such an idealized world, all risks can be exchanged at no transactions costs in financial markets in which both buyers and sellers possess all the information they need about possible future "states of the world."

MARKET POWER   The competitive model assumes that a sufficiently large number of buyers and sellers compete such that none is large enough to influence price. In fact, most sellers and some buyers can influence price, to some degree. **Market power** is the ability of one or a few sellers or buyers to influence the price of a product or service. Conditions giving rise to market power include: (1) barriers to entry or exit, (2) economies of scale or scope, and (3) product differentiation/ price discrimination.

Barriers to Entry or Exit   A market with entry or exit barriers and few sellers likely is one in which existing firms have market power. Firms already in a market prefer barriers to entry. Indeed, society can benefit from firms attempting to create *legitimate* barriers such as when products and services undergo continuous improvement, and firms become more attuned to that which satisfies customers. For example, if an insurer devotes great human, technical, and financial resources to developing highly skilled risk selection expertise, it may have created a barrier to entry for competitors because, to compete in their sophisticated lines of business, competitors must acquire this expertise – a difficult and expensive process. Indeed, any investment, marketing, product innovation, or other operation that requires substantial "learning by doing" can create barriers to competitor entry. This gives incumbent firms a (likely temporary) competitive edge but also provides greater consumer choice or value.

Not all market-created entry barriers are legitimate. For example, society does not condone life insurance companies agreeing to set prices or apportion geographic areas among themselves. Nor do we condone a firm making misleading statements about itself or its products to gain market share. In general, market power that arises from concerted actions of suppliers is suspect, whereas market power that arises from individual firm action is not, provided its effects are not to mislead or harm customers. Indeed, society benefits when businesses use their skill, foresight, and acumen to gain market power in this way.

Neither entry nor exit barriers appear to be great in the insurance markets of the U.S., Canada, the E.U., and an increasing number of other countries. Governmentally created entry barriers exist in all countries in the form of licensing requirements and minimum capital requirements, but they usually are not onerous. They are justified on consumer protection grounds. Barriers to exit are comparatively rare worldwide, although some U.S. states are known to discourage domestic insurers from attempting to re-domesticate to other states.

Reasonable freedom of entry does not exist in many of the world's life and health insurance markets. Several countries limit or have onerous requirements for the creation of new domestic insurers, and many restrict entry of foreign insurers in some way, although the trend is toward more liberal markets.

Economies of Scale or Scope   Economies of scale (size) or scope can afford a firm market power. **Economies of scale** are marginal costs savings that exist when a firm's output increases at a rate faster than attendant increases in production costs, holding product mix constant, so that average cost decreases. **Increasing returns to scale** are associated with the size of a firm that has economies of scale.

At a certain size – called the **minimum efficient scale** (MES) – firms' long-run average costs are at a minimum, with further growth yielding no additional efficiencies. If further growth neither adds to nor detracts from efficiency (i.e., average costs are constant), the firm is operating at **constant returns to scale.** If further growth diminishes efficiency (i.e., average costs increase), the firm is operating at **decreasing returns to scale** where further growth diminishes firm efficiency; i.e., average costs increase.

If, however, efficiency increases (i.e., average costs decrease) over an *industry's* entire relevant output range and fixed costs are high and cannot be recouped on exit, conditions exist for a **natural monopoly.** With a natural monopoly, the MES is so large relative to market size that only one firm can operate efficiently.

Studies on insurance scale economies generally find increasing returns to scale for small to moderate size firms and either constant, modestly increasing, or decreasing returns for larger firms. Thus, market power because of scale economies might be minimal in insurance, with no evidence of a natural monopoly. Even small insurers compete successfully with larger firms, usually as careful niche players.

Whether a firm possesses market power from scale economies depends on its size relative to its market rather than its absolute size. A small firm in a tiny market may wield market power. A large multinational corporation in an international market may have little such power. Also, even a monopolist may be unable to exercise market power if the market is *contestable*, meaning that entry barriers are low and exit is easy. In such instances, the mere threat of competition from possible new entrants may be sufficient to cause existing firms to behave as if the market were competitive.

Economies of scope exist when average production costs decline as a firm produces a greater number of different products or services. This too can give rise to market power. Research suggests that scope economies exist for the joint production of some insurance lines and that some economies also exist in the joint marketing of insurance and banking services.

Product Differentiation and Price Discrimination   The pure competitive model assumes **product homogeneity** – meaning that competing products are perfect substitutes in the minds of buyers. The model also assumes that all suppliers charge the same price for these products. **Product differentiation** occurs when, because of product quality, service, location, reputation, or other attributes, one firm's products are preferred by some buyers over rivals' products. **Monopolistic competition** exists when a large number of firms produce similar but not identical products, giving the firms an element of market power in the short run. In the long run, the market tends toward a perfectly competitive market.

As with other firms, insurers routinely try to differentiate their products from those of their competitors. They may do so, for example, by building a reputation for financial soundness. Some products – such as term life insurance – are more difficult to differentiate than others, such as cash value insurance. The more complex is a product or the more complex the product is perceived to be by customers, the greater the likelihood of a successful product differentiation strategy. Regulators are concerned about product differentiation only if the effect is to mislead purchasers. Otherwise, product differentiation can lead to enhanced consumer choice and value and to continuous product improvement.

Insurers often attempt price discrimination, although regulatory requirements may thwart this strategy. **Price discrimination** is the offering of identical products at different prices to different groups of customers. For example, an insurer may offer almost identical long term care insurance policies through its agents, brokers, and the Internet but with each carrying a different price. With increasing competition, insurers seek ways to segment their target markets to charge different prices in each. Insurance regulators may become concerned about price discrimination when the insurer's underlying loss experience and expenses do not justify price differences on otherwise identical policies.

Extreme price discrimination can, in theory, lead to **predatory pricing** – lowering prices to unprofitable levels to weaken or eliminate competition with the idea of raising prices after competitors are driven from the market. Although theoretically possible, no evidence exists of widespread predatory pricing in insurance. Predation is a viable strategy only if reentry barriers are high, which generally is not the case in competitive insurance markets.

EXTERNALITIES   The conditions for a perfectly competitive market presume that all production costs are fully included in each firm's costs. This is not always true. The manufacturing facility that pollutes the surrounding air with no penalty for doing so imposes costs on the neighboring population in terms of a less pleasant environment and poorer health. Conversely, providing jobs by opening a new business in an economically depressed area may decrease the incentive for criminal activities thereby providing a beneficial spillover effect to the local community.

The Nature of Externalities   The above are examples of **externalities**, which occur when a firm's production or an individual's consumption has direct and uncompensated effects on others. **Positive externalities** exist if others benefit without having to pay. **Negative externalities** exist if costs are imposed on others without their being compensated.

The competitive model does not accommodate externalities easily under circumstances for which property rights are weak or nonexistent. The price of goods and services that carry externalities fails to reflect their true benefits and costs. With the polluter, its direct *accounting* costs of production as measured by its expenses for labor, machinery, etc., fail to capture all *economic* costs of production, because the business imposes uncompensated costs on the surrounding community. Its production costs are thus understated, so its prices are lower than they should be, resulting in more sales and higher production and still greater pollution. If the facility were forced to compensate the community for its lessened enjoyment and poorer health, its direct production costs would align more closely to its true economic costs.

Herein lies the problem with allowing competitive markets to deal freely with goods and services that carry externalities when property rights are ill-defined. In general, with negative externalities, the price will be too low, too much will be produced and consumed, and too many resources will be devoted to the industry. Conversely, with positive externalities, the price will be too high, too little will be produced, and too few resources will be devoted to the industry.

Externalities and Insurance   Both negative and positive externalities exist in life insurance. Perhaps the most significant insurance-related negative externality is health insurance fraud. From 5 to 15 percent of all health insurance claims in some markets, such as in Europe and North America, are believed to involve fraud. An extreme example of a negative externality associated with life insurance occurs when an insured is murdered for the death proceeds. Fraudulent claims make premiums higher for everyone and can impose costs on concerned families and employers.

Another negative externality flows from the sensitive economic role played by financial intermediaries, as was demonstrated in the 2008-09 recession. **Systemic risks** exist if the difficulties of financial institutions cause disruptions elsewhere within an economy. Box 1-3 discusses systemic risks in insurance.

Box 1-3
Systemic Risks in Insurance Markets

Two types of systemic risks are cascading failures and runs. **Cascading failures** exist when the failure of one financial institution is the cause of the failure of others, with the result that harm occurs elsewhere within the economy. Cascading failures are precipitated by **contagion risk** that exists when financial intermediaries are highly connected. Banks are highly connected via the interbank market. No equivalent mechanism exists with life insurance companies. Unlike banks, insurers do not lend short-term funds to each other. While life insurers can be connected via reinsurance – insurance purchased from other insurers (called reinsurers) on portions of the insurer's portfolio of policies – the practice does not rise to a level sufficient to pose a threat to the insurance industry or financial system or economy as a whole.

Also, **runs** – depositors or policyowners demanding their money at once – can lead to systemic risk if customers lose confidence in financial institutions. Runs result from liquidity risk which can exist when financial intermediaries have illiquid assets and/or mismatches in the durations of their assets and liabilities. Banks have both problems. Insurers do not. While runs have occurred in insurance – policyowners of the two largest U.S. life insurer failures, Executive Life and Mutual Benefit Life, initiated runs – they have been limited to insurers already in financial difficulty and have not caused the failure of sound insurers and have not posed a threat to the soundness of the insurance industry or to the financial system as a whole or the economy.

Positive externalities also exist in insurance. For example, insurers only rarely seek protection under copyright law for their product, processing, and service innovations, thereby allowing others to copy the innovations. Consequently, a tendency may exist for firms to engage in less development than they would otherwise.

Finally, a society may determine that its interests are served best by ensuring that unemployed, sick, injured, and retired persons are provided a base level of economic security through social insurance programs. In providing this insurance, government reduces the likelihood that relatives may have to relinquish their jobs to provide care and that such individuals might impose other costs on society, such as resorting to criminal activities.

FREE RIDER PROBLEMS   Goods or services supplied to one person but available to others at no extra cost can cause **free rider problems**. Goods and services with free rider problems and that carry extensive positive externalities are called **public**

goods. Examples include public education, police and fire protection services, and national defense.

A competitive market will not provide public goods. Everyone has an incentive to encourage others to incur the cost to produce the service, which others can then enjoy for free, but each waits for the others to do so, anticipating a "free ride." Consequently, if they are to be provided, government must do so, and they are appropriately financed by societal revenues (taxes). Indeed, the existence of public goods is the primary justification for the existence of governments and for having a tax system.

Free rider problems exist in insurance as when individuals know or believe that others will make good any losses that they suffer. Individuals who believe that they will receive free emergency medical care have less incentive to purchase health insurance.

Insurance regulation is a public good. Persons and firms benefit from regulation, even if they pay little or nothing for it. The private market seems unlikely to provide the level of regulation that most countries' citizens seem to want.

INFORMATION PROBLEMS   The perfectly competitive model assumes that both buyers and sellers are well informed. As a practical matter, we know otherwise. Information problems abound in insurance and are the industry's most important category of market imperfections.

Asymmetric information problems arise when one party to a transaction has relevant information that the other does not have and can take advantage of that fact to the first party's benefit and the other party's detriment. Most life insurance company operations and practices exist to address asymmetric information problems. They also constitute the most challenging problems of life and health insurance customers and drive most regulation in insurance. Four classes of such problems are:

- buyer ignorance,
- adverse selection,
- moral hazard, and
- agency problems.

Buyer Ignorance   **Buyer ignorance**, commonly referred to as the **lemons problem** by economists, stems from information relevant to a transaction being known by the seller but not by the buyer and the seller uses the information to the detriment of the buyer. "Lemon" is U.S. slang connoting an automobile that appears sound to the buyer but is defective in some way. Individuals purchase policies in good faith, relying on the integrity of the insurance company, its contract, and its representatives. Few consumers are sufficiently knowledgeable to be able to assess fully the quality and value of an insurance contract or to assess adequately an insurer's financial solidity or the integrity of its representatives.

The lemons problem in insurance provides the rationale for the great majority of insurance regulation. Insurers and their representatives have little incentive to disclose adverse information to potential customers. For example, an insurer in poor financial condition is not keen to advertise that fact to potential customers. Doing so would hurt sales. Governments seek to rectify the unequal positions between insurance buyers and sellers by mandating certain disclosures by insurers, by monitoring insurer financial condition, by regulating insurer marketing practices, and through other means. Private market solutions exist as well, as with rating agencies that rate the financial condition of insurers.

Adverse Selection   **Adverse selection,** also called **antiselection,** is the tendency of self selected insurance applicants to exhibit average claim experience greater than that of a randomly selected group of insureds, representing an asymmetric information problem resulting from the fact that the customer knows more than the seller about the customer's situation and uses that fact to the seller's detriment.

It plagues insurers worldwide and is the principal reason that insurers seek extensive evaluative information about proposed insureds. They want to know as much as practical about the loss potential of those to whom they might issue insurance. In this way, they can charge premiums that more equitably reflect the expected value of the losses that a proposed insured adds to the insurance pool.

The insurance company cannot be certain that buyers disclose all relevant information. Proposed insureds have incentives to secure the most favorable possible terms, conditions, and prices. To do so, they may not disclose all that they know about their insurability. If some insureds withhold or misrepresent key risk-related information in the evaluative process, they may pay premiums that are lower than the expected value of their losses. Doing so imposes costs on other insureds in the insurance pool. The challenge for insurers is to obtain sufficient information to assess insurability properly but without incurring excessive expense or imposing undue burdens on proposed insureds.

Insurers try to minimize adverse selection in several ways. First, a central purpose of insurance underwriting is to deter and detect adverse selection. Also, insurance contract wording helps minimizes adverse selection. For example, some individuals contemplating suicide purchase life insurance policies in hopes of providing money to heirs. Most life contracts, however, provide that the insurer need not pay death benefits if the insured commits suicide within the first two policy years. Further, the law provides that the insurer may be able to rescind a policy if the insured misrepresented information to procure insurance. Adverse selection can be so severe that private insurers refuse to offer insurance.

Moral Hazard   **Moral hazard** results when the presence of insurance changes the loss prevention behavior – called ex ante **moral hazard** – or loss minimization behavior – called ex post **moral hazard** – of the insured or beneficiary. The effect of moral hazard is that the insured becomes less risk averse. Nonlife insurers are concerned with both types of moral hazard. Life insurers are concerned primarily with *ex ante* moral hazard, but the concern differs as between life insurance and health insurance. Insurers are not overly concerned that insureds for life insurance will engage in behavior that will shorten their lives just because they are insured. Also, they are not particularly concerned that those who purchase life annuities will engage in behavior to lengthen their lives just because they own annuities. For most of us, the desire to continue living is uninfluenced by whether we are insured!

On the other hand, insurers try to avoid selling life insurance whose beneficiary would gain more from the insured dying than from the insured living. They also try to avoid selling disability income insurance whose benefit payment would exceed the insured's wages. Failure to avoid such situations means that the insurance itself increases the likelihood of the insured event occurring; i.e., it creates moral hazard.

Insurers try to minimize the creation of moral hazard in several ways. In underwriting life insurance, insurers want to be satisfied that the proposed beneficiary designation is logical (what is the relationship between the beneficiary and the proposed insured?) and that the insurance amount bears a reasonable relationship to the financial loss that the beneficiary would suffer on the insured's death. Contract wording also addresses moral hazard. To collect disability income benefits, the contract requires the insured to demonstrate the extent of disability. The main rationale for insurer claims settlement departments is to discourage and identify incidents of moral hazard.

Agency Problems   **Agency problems** arise because the interests of one party (the agent) differ from those of the party that it represents (the principal). A person who acts for another is an **agent**. The person whom the agent represents is the **principal**. The agent's incentive is to maximize its personal gain, which is not always compatible with simultaneously maximizing the principal's gain.

Agency problems lurk behind innumerable insurance relationships, operations, and practices. How do the insurer's stockholders (principal) ensure that the board of directors (their agent) takes their interests fully into consideration? How does the board (principal) ensure that managers (agents) take the board's (and stockholder's) interest fully into consideration? How does the insurer ensure that its salespeople (agents) do not misrepresent or withhold required information about the company and its products from customers and misrepresent or withhold key information about the customer from the company? The insurance company cannot always depend on its agents being completely forthcoming to underwriters about applicants' insurability. After all, salespeople are interested in making the sale to secure a commission.

The issue of how to ensure that the insurance regulator (the public's agent) adequately protects the public (principal) is an agency problem. In these and a host of other situations, inefficiencies can arise when the interests of the agent and the interests of the principal diverge.

The key to minimizing the problem lies in arranging incentives (and disincentives) such that the interests of the agent align more closely with those of the principal. This can be done, for example, by tying compensation more closely to the principal's desired outcome or by requiring disclosure by the agent of potential conflicts between the agent's and principal's interests.

Asymmetric Information Problems and Tradeoffs   By definition, solutions to information asymmetry problems rest in securing additional information. In each of the above instances, the affected party could obtain more information to reduce the asymmetry. An ill-informed buyer can engage in deeper research about her insurance needs and the quality and prices of insurance policies. The insurer considering the issuance of a policy can always secure additional information about the proposed insured. Insurers can undertake deeper claims investigations to root out fraudulent or exaggerated claims. An insurer's board of directors can establish a stricter system of monitoring managers, and managers can tighten supervision of salespeople.

However, contrary to the costless information assumption of the competitive model, securing more thorough information imposes additional costs on transactions, either on the consumer in increased search costs or on the insurer in securing more or better monitoring or information. Tradeoffs are inevitable between (1) additional costs incurred to become better informed and (2) additional claim payments and other inefficiencies in making decisions with less information.

Because insurance is a financial future-delivery product tied closely to the public interest, governments judge this information imbalance to warrant substantial oversight of the financial condition of insurers. The widely accepted view is that the public, especially poorly informed consumers, should be protected. The market has some solutions to these problems. Rating agencies monitor insurers' financial condition, rendering opinions as to their solidity. Also, insurance agents and brokers often provide evaluations of insurers and shop the market on consumers' behalf.

Government often believes that it should provide or require that information be provided for the public good. Also, significant economies of scale and scope exist with respect to the consumption and production of regulatory services, further supporting a governmental role.

WHY PRIVATE MARKETS FAIL TO INSURE SOME EXPOSURES

Private insurers will not provide insurance for every risky exposure. Thus, virtually no private insurance exists against the financial consequences of unemployment. Individuals with no income and no assets generally cannot secure insurance or most other private sector financial services. Insurers voluntarily sell comparatively little individual health insurance, disability income insurance, and life insurance to those in poor health. No financial intermediary will guarantee a family's entire fortune against losses, home against a decline in market value, or computer against obsolescence.

In each of the above and many other instances, the failure of the private market to provide the service stems from one or more of four reasons:

- insurers cannot adequately address the information problems that they encounter, especially severe moral hazard or adverse selection,
- demand is insufficient because buyers have low incomes and/or wealth,
- risk aversion is insufficient to motivate individuals to pay high premium loadings, and/or
- positive externalities accompany the purchase, such as with certain social insurance benefits for some population segments.

An immediate question is: does the failure of a private insurance market to provide some demanded insurance service warrant government stepping in to provide the service? To economists, none of the first three reasons above provides a rationale for government doing so. Only the existence of positive externalities provides such a rationale.

DETERMINANTS OF INSURANCE CONSUMPTION

Insurance consumption has evolved to suit each country's particular environment. Price and innumerable economic, demographic, and cultural factors influence the demand for insurance. Insurance supply is molded by price and by a market's risk-bearing capacity and government regulation.

PRICE   Price is determined by the interaction of the forces of demand and supply. From the insurer's perspective, its prices are influenced by its cost structures, by the competitiveness of the particular line of insurance, and by government tax and other policy. Unfortunately, what constitutes the price of insurance is not easy to define. The policy premium is not the price as insureds receive value from the promises of claim payments and often cash values. We also have no satisfactory measure for quantity. Researchers who model insurance have used proxies for price and quantity that, while not completely satisfactory, nonetheless allow us to gain insight into their effect on quantity demanded.

To explore the effect of price on insurance consumption, we need to understand **price elasticity** of demand, which is the percentage change in demand for a good or service resulting from a given percentage change in price; in formula format:

$$\text{Price Elasticity} = \frac{\Delta Q}{Q} \div \frac{\Delta P}{P}$$

In theory, price elasticity can range from zero (perfectly inelastic) to minus infinity. In practice, price elasticities typically range from zero to about minus two. They ordinarily carry a negative sign as the quantity demanded decreases (increases) as price increases (decreases). A price elasticity of –1.0 means that a given change in price can be expected to evoke a precisely proportionate and opposite change in quantity demanded: a 1.0 percent price increase should lead to a 1.0 percent decrease in quantity demanded.

In life insurance, one researcher calculated a price elasticity of whole life insurance policies issued in the U.S., using various price measures.[4] New sales were negatively related to prices, as expected, with elasticities ranging from –0.32 to –0.92, depending on policy type and the price measure used. Another study, using a different approach, estimated an elasticity of –0.24.[5] A study that examined the price elasticity of group life insurance in the U.S. found it to be –0.7; meaning that a 10 percent increase (decrease) in price could be expected to cause a 7 percent decrease (increase) in quantity ($1,000 face amount units) demanded.[6]

ECONOMIC FACTORS   Numerous economic factors influence insurance consumption. The level of a country's economic development, as measured by income, has been the most consistently important factor but others also have been found to be significant.

Income and Wealth   The higher an economy's income, other things being equal, the more it spends on all types of insurance. Also, at the microeconomic level, the higher a household's income, the greater its insurance consumption.

If we assume that countries follow a similar developmental path, a reasonable conclusion from the studies is that the income elasticity of insurance premiums is greater than 1.0. The **income elasticity of insurance premiums** tells us the relative change in insurance premiums written for a given change in national income. One researcher found that life insurance consumption in Asia is three times more sensitive to changes in income than in the member countries of the *Organization for Economic Cooperation and Development* (OECD) – the economically advanced, private-sector oriented economies.[7]

Studies suggest that the elasticity itself varies with level of income. Figure 1-5 provides a conceptual way of visualizing this relationship.

Stylized Relationship between Insurance and Economic Development   **Figure 1-5**

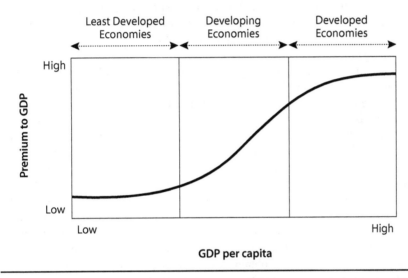

For the least developed countries, the ratio of premiums written to GDP is fairly low. For mid-income countries, the ratio begins to rise rapidly; that is, the income elasticity is higher. For economically advanced economies, the ratio of premiums to GDP seems to flatten out (and, therefore, the elasticity declines relative to mid-income countries) as consumers presumably have need for only so much insurance and, at higher incomes, have more alternatives to insurance. Also, several studies have shown that life insurance demand increases with increasing levels of insureds' wealth. These results are consistent with a belief that wealthier people have more to protect than the less wealthy, and they have greater financial resources with which to purchase insurance.

Inflation   Inflation rates influence insurance consumption. Inflation has long been considered as detrimental to life insurance supply and demand, and studies confirm this intuition. In times of high inflation and significant economic volatility, consumers seek shorter term, more liquid investments and avoid longer-term, fixed commitments. Traditional cash value insurance products are perceived as long-term, fixed commitments, and, therefore, demand for them shrinks during inflationary or volatile times. On the supply side, inflation causes uncertainty for insurers, negatively affecting long-term planning and investing.

Another interesting research finding is that inflation's affect seems to vary by region.[8] One study found that inflation's affect is about 2½ times more important to life insurance demand in Asian economies than in OECD economies.

DEMOGRAPHIC FACTORS   Demographics influence insurance consumption. We know that the age of first marriage for both men and women is increasing in many countries, while the years of higher education has lengthened. Dual income families are more common, as are single parent families. These and other demographic trends should be expected to affect insurance demand. Other factors include the following.

That much of the world's population is aging is well recognized. As a consequence, increasing proportions of individuals in many societies are elderly, with prospects for even greater population aging in the future. Increasing life expectancy is predicted to translate into a greater demand for savings-based life insurance products as well as for long term care insurance. Moreover, longer life is hypothesized to result in more affordable life insurance, which should stimulate sales in the segment of populations needing such coverage. Research results are mostly consistent with this hypothesis for developed economies but less so for developing countries.

The educational level of a population or of a household is believed to affect insurance consumption. The expectation is that the more educated or literate a population or household the greater the likelihood of understanding the need for insurance. Research findings are mostly consistent with this hypothesis.

The structure of households continues to evolve worldwide. The nuclear family accounts for a declining proportion of households in most developed countries. Research generally has found that life insurance demand is inversely related to the number of young children in the household and the dependency ratio.

By revolutionizing agricultural production, the plow altered societies worldwide. The production of goods and services thus grew in importance and with it arose ever-larger mining, manufacturing, and commercial enterprises. Business and employment specialization became more important, thus rendering individuals more reliant on trade to obtain that which they and their families no longer produced themselves. Specialization implies vulnerability.

Industrialization brings urbanization which in turn brings about a new social order where the predominant economic and social security formerly provided by family, friends, and acquaintances is replaced to varying degrees by formal public and private arrangements and a necessity for greater financial self-reliance. Research has revealed a positive relationship between industrialization and urbanization and insurance consumption.

SOCIAL FACTORS   Cultural perceptions of the role of insurance products can vary substantially. In many countries, especially in Asia, life products are sought primarily as savings instruments, and this is consistent with a high cultural propensity to save. In some countries, especially those that are predominantly Muslim, insurance is sometimes viewed as inappropriate because of religious beliefs (although products and insurer operations can be made to comport fully with these beliefs). See Box 1-4. Research has documented less insurance of all types is consumed in countries that are predominantly Muslim.

In some cultures and with certain relationships (as between close friends, for example), it might be socially unacceptable to refuse the offer to purchase insurance, because saying no is considered impolite. Too often, in such circumstances, a policy is purchased but is terminated shortly thereafter. This has been an issue in South Korea, for example.

Box 1-4
Islam and Insurance

For devout Muslims, the Koran is the source and guide for all social and economic decisions and institutions. The Koran was God's final revelation of His law to humankind. After the Prophet Mohammed's death, Islamic scholars built a body of law – the Shari'a – around the Koran. Among other things, the Shari'a sets out rules for the allocation of resources, property rights, production and consumption, the working of markets, and the distribution of income and wealth. The Shari'a is central to Islamic economic theory and lies at the base of all Islamic financial and commercial activity. For example, an ethic in Islam is that wealthy Muslims contribute (*zakat*) to the less fortunate.

The Koran proscribes the payment of interest (*riba*) and gambling. Like Western banking, Western-style insurance may be dismissed by devout Muslims as a form of usury or gambling. Additionally, some Islamic scholars have argued that insurance is an attempt to defy fate as predetermined by God. Other Islamic scholars respond that, even if life's harmful events are a certainty, preparing for the inevitable is no defiance, especially for one's dependents. Indeed, this is both ethical and economically sound.

To be compatible with Islamic principles, Islamic insurance must incorporate *Mudarabah* and *Takaful*. **Mudarabah** is a form of partnership for which one party provides the funds while another provides the expertise and management. The parties share any profits on a prearranged basis. Islamic insurers invest funds according to the Shari'a (no fixed-income securities; no investment in certain companies such as distilleries). By building a profit-sharing (rather than interest-paying) pooling arrangement, they fully respect the *riba* prohibition.

Islamic insurers establish a **Takaful** – a type of solidarity or mutual fund separate from the management operation, which relies on a pact among participants to guarantee each other. In this way, they respect the prohibition on gambling. The fund, as a collective rather than a one-on-one insuring arrangement, simply protects the investors and their heirs against events that would alter their economic status. The pooling arrangement is consistent with the *zakat* principle of helping those in need.

In a *Mudarabah* insurance contract, participants invest a fixed sum for a fixed term to be distributed between the investment fund and the *Takaful*. The insurer makes a clear distinction between shareholders and policyholders. They invest shareholder capital separately from policyholder funds. Underwriting is permitted to ensure fairness among participants, not to discriminate against or reject anyone. It would be unethical for *Mudarabah* participants to bear the risks of another without a contribution (*tabarru'*) that reflects equitably those risks.

Source: Harold D. Skipper and Tara Skipper, Chapter 16, in Harold D. Skipper, ed., *International Risk and Insurance.* Boston: Irwin/McGraw-Hill, 1998.

POLITICAL AND LEGAL FACTORS   Research has established that improvements in a country's political environment enhance insurance demand. Conversely, an unstable political environment depresses insurance demand. Such an environment means that private property rights, human rights, or both are less secure. The non-insurance related decisions made by public policymakers – regulatory agencies, the courts, the legislature, and others – have a profound impact on all financial services, including insurance.

Governments make decisions that directly affect insurance demand and supply. Some research has found an inverse relationship between private insurance consumption and the generosity of public economic security services; that is, the more important are public economic security sources, the less important are private-sector sources, other things being the same. Governments also determine what insurance products can be sold, who can sell them, and how they can be sold. Government often spurs insurance demand by making the purchase of some types compulsory or affording tax concessions for the purchase of some types of insurance.

Tax laws and the premium approval process greatly influence product design and value. For example, most countries' laws permit a tax deferred accumulation of interest on life insurance cash values and/or offer other tax preferences. Countries that have repealed such tax benefits have realized a decrease in sales of cash value insurance policies.

GLOBALIZATION The continuing globalization of financial services adds a new dimension to insurance consumption, especially for markets that have been highly restrictive. Increasing internationalization can attract increased capital from abroad, product and marketing innovations, and different ways of managing companies. Increased capital strengthens the financial capacity of insurance companies and can result in more competition and therefore consumption. Product and marketing innovations and different management styles can lead to greater consumer choice and value. The trend toward greater market internationalization has affected insurance consumption – as we have witnessed in many Eastern European countries and in China and India – although broad-based research on this issue is sparse.

ECONOMIC CONCEPTS OF LIFE INSURANCE CONSUMPTION

In this section, we explore economic concepts underpinning life insurance consumption. We first introduce the human capital concept. We then show how the human life value concept derives from human capital. We close this section with a discussion of how life insurance fits into the economic theory of lifetime consumption.

THE CONCEPT OF HUMAN CAPITAL

Sir William Petty, considered the "father of political statistics," is credited as the first economist to use the human capital concept, in 1699. Daniel Bernoulli, a famous Swiss mathematician, popularized the concept some 40 years later. **Human capital** is the productive capacity within each person and is considered to be the driving force in economic growth. The essence of human capital is that investments are made in oneself with an expectation of future benefits. Economic research in human capital gained substantial recognition when the 1991 *Nobel Memorial Prize for Economics* was awarded to Gary Becker for his pioneering research on the topic.

Investment in human capital – education, for example – has become one of the most cogent explanations for the differences in countries' rates of economic growth, as well as differences in wage rates between and within countries. Further, as Peter Bernstein wrote in his award-winning book on risk, despite the world's enormous wealth, human capital remains by far the largest income-producing asset for the great majority of people. Bernstein drew the logical connection between life insurance and human capital: "Why else would so many breadwinners spend their hard-earned money on life-insurance premiums?"[9]

THE HUMAN LIFE VALUE CONCEPT

The human life value (HLV) concept is a part of the general theory of human capital. Some semblance of HLV is expressed in the Code of Hammurabi, the Bible, the Koran, and early Anglo-Saxon law in which it was used to determine the compensation allowed to the relatives of an individual killed by a third party. In recent years, the valuation of a human life in connection with legal actions seeking recovery for wrongful death has gained prominence.

The HLV concept was first applied to life insurance in the 1880s through the efforts of Jacob L. Green, then president of the *Connecticut Mutual Life Insurance Company*, which merged into *Massachusetts Mutual Life Insurance Company* in 1996. **Human life value** is a measure of the future earnings or value of services of an individual – that is, the capitalized value of an individual's future earnings less self-maintenance costs such as food, clothing, and shelter. From the standpoint of one's dependents, the breadwinner's HLV is the value of the benefits that the dependents can expect. Similarly, from the viewpoint of an organization, an employee's HLV is the value added to the enterprise through his or her services to the firm. Thus, a person may have more than one HLV.

Not until the 1920s did the concept become widely accepted as an economic basis for life insurance. Solomon S. Huebner was one of the early and most effective proponents of the concept, helping to bring it into both the life insurance practitioner and academic communities. The first edition of this book, published in 1915, contained a section titled "Capitalization of the Value of a Human Life and Indemnification of That Value." In 1927, he published a volume titled *The Economics of Life Insurance* which dealt exclusively with the HLV concept. His five precepts or admonitions regarding HLV are as relevant today as they were almost a century ago. See Box 1-5.

Box 1-5
Huebner's Five Human Life Value Admonitions

1. *The human life value should be carefully appraised and capitalized.* The HLV is based on the fact that persons who earn more than is necessary for their self-maintenance have a monetary value to those who are dependent upon them. Thus, it is the present value of that part of the earnings of individuals devoted to family dependents and others who benefit from these individuals' economic earning capacity. Whenever continuance of a life is economically valuable to others, an economic basis for life and health insurance exists.

2. *The human life value should be recognized as the creator of property values.* HLV is key to turning property into a productive force. In other words, the HLV is the cause and property values are the effect.

3. *The family is an economic unit organized around the human life values of its members.* The family should be organized and managed, and its economic values finally liquidated, in the same manner that other enterprises are organized, operated, and liquidated.

4. *The human life value and its protection should be regarded as constituting the principal economic link between the present and succeeding generations.* The realization of the potential net earnings of the breadwinner constitutes the economic foundation for the proper education and development of children in the event of the breadwinner's premature death or incapacity and the protection of children against the burden of parent financial support.

5. *In view of the significance of human life values relative to property values, principles of business management utilized in connection with property values should be applied to life values.* Principles such as appraisal, conservation, indemnity, and depreciation should be applied to the organization, management, and liquidation of human life values. These principles have been applied to property values for decades.

One's HLV is subject to loss through (1) premature death; (2) illness, injury, or incapacity; (3) retirement; and (4) unemployment. Any event affecting an individual's earning capacity has a corresponding impact on her HLV. The probabilities of loss from death and incapacity are significantly greater than from the other commonly insured perils. Less than one building in every 100 ever experiences a significant fire or other loss throughout its history, whereas one of every seven workers dies before age 65. Moreover, the average property loss in well protected cities does not exceed 10 to 15 percent of the property value involved. Perhaps only one of every 30 fires results in a total loss. By contrast, the death peril always results in a total loss to the potential estate. The same is true of some health events.

Life insurance and health insurance make possible the preservation of an individual's HLV in the face of an uncertain lifetime. The HLV concept provides the philosophical basis for systematizing the insurance purchase decision.

ECONOMIC THEORIES OF CONSUMPTION AND INSURANCE

Individuals occupy their time either in activities that produce income (or its equivalent) or in those that do not. For the sake of simplicity, economists label these two states of nature as work and leisure. One's investment in self – in human capital – plus one's preferences, time, wealth, income, and a host of other factors, influence how time is divided between work and leisure. As Figure 1-6 illustrates, work gives rise to income, which in turn is spent on consumption or is saved.

Figure 1-6   **Work or Leisure**

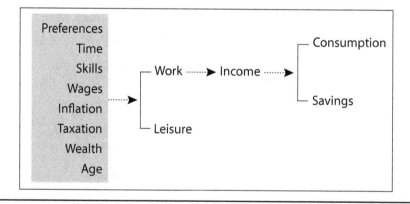

Economic theories of consumption seek to explain consumer consumption and saving behavior over one's lifetime. It will prove insightful to examine these theories.

ECONOMIC THEORIES OF CONSUMPTION Economic theories of consumption begin with the assumption that rational consumers seek to maximize their lifetime utilities. **Utility** is a measure of consumer satisfaction derived from economic goods. The theory holds that individuals seek to maximize their utility and minimize their disutility over their lifetimes – that is, to arrange their affairs to derive maximum enjoyment (and minimum discomfort) throughout their lives.

The maximization of lifetime utility, therefore, involves attempts by consumers to allocate their lifetime incomes in such a way as to achieve an optimum lifetime pattern of consumption. This means planning for the future and not living only for today. This concept is rational, but on what basis would we expect individuals to make allocations between now and the future or, stated differently, between consumption now and consumption (saving) for the future?

Some earlier theories suggested that current consumption was some function of a household's current income. More recent theories take a longer-term view, suggesting that individuals consider likely future income as well. The most widely accepted theory is called the **life cycle hypothesis**, which hypothesizes that individuals can be expected to maintain a more or less constant or increasing level of consumption over their lifetimes. Income will be low in the beginning and end stages of life and high during the middle stage of life.

In early life, families "subsidize" children. As the children enter the work force, they begin to contribute economically to their own maintenance, ideally no longer relying on parents for financial support. Incomes increase throughout most of one's working lifetime, with income exceeding expenditures to allow for saving. At retirement, incomes typically cease or diminish, with the retiree entering a period of dissavings as savings are drawn down to support maintenance.

CONSUMPTION THEORIES AND INSURANCE   In their earliest forms, no consumption theory allowed for bequests to heirs or for an uncertain time of death. In his seminal paper, Yaari extended the life cycle model by including the risk of dying. He showed conceptually that an individual increases expected lifetime utility by purchasing fair life insurance and fair annuities.[10] "Fair" means paying a premium equal to the expected value of payments to or on behalf of the individual, without charges for expenses or profits.

Pissarides extended Yaari's work by examining the joint motivation of saving for retirement and for bequests via life insurance.[11] He established that life insurance was theoretically capable of absorbing all fluctuations in lifetime income and, thereby, could enable consumption and bequests to be independent of the timing of income. As a result, the same effective consumption pattern could be achieved through the appropriate use of life insurance as could be achieved were the time of death known with certainty. Without life insurance, the lifetime consumption pattern would be different and involve less enjoyment (utility).

Lewis included the preferences of those dependent on the breadwinner's income.[12] His empirical estimates based on U.S. households were encouraging. He found that life insurance ownership was positively related to household income and to the number of dependent children. An important conclusion of his research was that social security substituted for privately purchased life insurance.

Past empirical research has not always found life insurance ownership to be consistent with the life cycle hypothesis. In recent research, Lin and Grace were able to disaggregate whole life and term life ownership and examine their relationship with financial vulnerability over the life cycle. They found the expected consistency. Interestingly, they also found that the more volatile is the financial situation of a household, the more life insurance it purchases and that life insurance is used to manage major financial obligations that were foreseeable in the near term, such as educational expenses and health care costs.[13]

Another dimension of the life cycle hypothesis relates to outliving one's assets. Life annuities offer insurance against this risk. Researchers have established theoretically that the purchase of actuarially fair annuities is welfare enhancing for risk averse individuals. For individuals with high mortality risk aversion, even high priced annuities may be attractive.

The market for individually purchased life annuities seems thin, however. One hypothesis for this result is the presence of substantial adverse selection. Individuals whose life expectancies are high seek annuities, using their superior knowledge about their expected longevity to secure good deals for themselves. As most insurers' annuity pricing schemes are not as refined as life insurance pricing, adverse selection problems would be more prominent with annuities than with life insurance.

For example, lower priced life annuities are not yet widely available for individuals with life-shortening health issues. Such persons, therefore, would be expected to shun life annuities in favor of holding greater proportions of their wealth in other assets – contrary to the expected utility-optimizing behavior implicit in the life cycle model. Such individuals are unable to maximize lifetime utility, because fairly priced annuities are unavailable to them.

CONCLUSION

Many of yesterday's insurance products, operations, and practices differ from those of today and will differ still more from tomorrow's products, operations, and practices. The fundamentals of risk and insurance, however, do not change, although our understanding of them deepens with time.

We should not study insurance as if we were examining sets of facts, figures, and operational details independent of their larger context. The economic fundamentals of risk and insurance provide this larger context as well as the foundation on which we construct our house of knowledge. The stronger that foundation, the more lasting will be our knowledge and the more easily we can add to it.

ENDNOTES

1   This chapter draws in part from Harold D. Skipper, Chapters 1, 3, and 4 in Harold D. Skipper, ed., *International Risk and Insurance*. Boston: Irwin/McGraw-Hill; 1998 and Harold D. Skipper and W. Jean Kwon, *Risk Management and Insurance: Perspective in a Global Economy*. Malvern, PA: Blackwell Publishing; 2007, Chapters 1, 2, 4, and 19.

2   *Resolution 21 (X), Life Insurance in Developing Countries*, Adopted at the tenth session of the Committee on Invisibles and Financing Related to Trade, United Nations Conference on Trade and Development, Dec. 1982.

3   All premium data are taken from "World Insurance in 2013," Sigma (2014), Zurich: Swiss Re.

4   D. F. Babbel, "The Price Elasticity of Demand for Whole Life Insurance," *Journal of Finance 4*, Issue 1 (1985), pp. 225-239.

5   M. J. Brown and Kihong Kim, "An International Analysis of Life Insurance Demand," *Journal of Risk and Insurance*, 60: (1993), pp. 616-634.

6   "The Effects of Price Adjustment on Insurance Demand," *Sigma* (1993), Zurich: Swiss Re.

7   D. Ward and R. Zurbruegg, "Does Insurance Promote Economic Growth? Evidence from OECD Countries," *Journal of Risk and Insurance*, 67: (2000), pp. 489-507.

8   *Id.*

9   Peter L. Bernstein, *Against the Gods: The Remarkable Story of Risk* (New York: John Wiley & Sons, 1996), p. 110.

10 Menahem Yaari, "Uncertain Lifetime, Life Insurance, and the Theory of the Consumer," *Review of Economic Studies* (Apr. 1965), pp.137-150. This finding was confirmed by Stanley Fischer, "A Life Cycle Model of Life Insurance Purchases," *International Economic Review* (Feb. 1973), pp. 132-152.

11 C.A. Pissarides, "The Wealth-Age Relation with Life Insurance," *Economica* (Nov. 1980), pp. 451-457.

12 F. D. Lewis, "Dependents and the Demand for Life Insurance," *The American Economic Review* (June 1989), pp. 452-467.

13 Y. Lin and M. Grace, "Household Life Cycle Protection: Life Insurance Holdings, Financial Vulnerability, and Portfolio Implications," *Journal of Risk and Insurance* (March 2007), pp. 141-173.

PART I

LIFE INSURANCE PRODUCTS

CHAPTER 2

An Overview of Life Insurance

This chapter begins Part I, which is a seven chapter sequence on life insurance products, with emphasis on personal products. In this chapter, we explore the various means by which survivors deal with the financial consequences of death, followed by the advantages and costs of life insurance in this regard. We then provide an overview of the main types of life and health insurance policies sold by life insurance companies. There follows a short explanation of the ideal requisites for the private sector to provide insurance and an introduction to life insurance pricing.[1]

Death can create profound emotional distress and equally profound financial distress for families. If a family's economic livelihood depends on the wages of one person, that person's death could be financially devastating for the family. Dual breadwinner families are not immune to the financial consequences of one death.

Businesses can be similarly devastated by the death of key employees, especially in smaller and closely held firms. Many key employees have special knowledge, skills, contacts, persuasiveness, or other attributes that are difficult, if not impossible, to replace completely without substantially higher costs. Additional problems can arise when the deceased is also owner of a closely held business. Heirs may inherit stock for which no ready market exists and thus no means to realize its value. Problems are created, not only for the heirs, but for any surviving owners, and the potential exists for personal discord, management problems, and a forced sale at a distressed price. All owners have a motivation to provide the means to avoid these situations.

When advisors help clients quantify the financial consequences of death, as discussed in Chapter 20, either the client's resources are sufficient to avoid adverse consequences or they are not. If resources are insufficient, additional resources must be located. These resources can come from:

- relatives,
- savings/investments,
- employer-provided death benefits,
- government-provided death benefits, and
- individual life insurance

MEANS OF DEALING WITH THE FINANCIAL CONSEQUENCES OF DEATH

RELATIVES

Many individuals rely explicitly or implicitly on wealth transfer from their relatives or their spouse's relatives to protect their families from a meaningful reduction in living standard brought about because of the individual's death. In some circumstances, reliance on family assistance might be rational. In others, it may not. Unless the timing and amount of family assistance is known with certainty, the financial risk of death is not completely eliminated. Reliance on this strategy places the financial well being of the individual's surviving family at risk and beyond the family's immediate control to a greater or lesser degree.

SAVINGS/INVESTMENTS

Loss exposures arising from the financial consequences of death can be retained or transferred. Meeting the death exposure via a savings program alone is tantamount to retaining the exposure in part until sufficient additional resources are accumulated. Retention is viable only to the extent survivors' financial requirements are satisfied. To the extent the savings program is incomplete, survivors must look to other resources. Other resources can be planned in conjunction with savings, and, as savings grow, reliance on other resources can be reduced.

We can think of this approach as having near term and longer term components. This approach is consistent with the view of those who advocate the purchase of term life insurance over cash value insurance, with the idea of saving the excess of the cash value policy's premium over the term premium. In practice, this approach requires financial discipline that many individuals lack.

EMPLOYER-PROVIDED DEATH BENEFITS

The employment relationship often is a source of death benefits. Most employer-provided death benefits are provided through group term life insurance at low or no cost to the employee. Such plans enjoy favorable income tax treatment for the first $50,000 of coverage. Supplemental life insurance is also sometimes made available. The employee usually pays the additional premium and is subject to the insurer's underwriting requirements. While available amounts may be larger than those provided under a tax-qualified group life insurance program, they ordinarily are not large.

Each of the above employer-provided death benefit plans can be important components for some individuals' financial plans; typically those in the lower income category. Because the death benefit is set by plan provisions, it does not necessarily address an individual's specific needs. For individuals with families or other substantial financial obligations, additional death benefit protection is almost always necessary.

Group term life insurance enjoys preferential tax treatment only if the plan provides nondiscriminatory coverage to all employees. Some highly compensated employees receive non-tax preferred benefits that are more generous. When cash value life insurance is used to fund the death benefit, cash values may also be used to provide retirement income. These plans are termed *nonqualified executive benefit arrangements*. While these plans do not enjoy the preferential tax treatment of group term plans, a different set of tax and other advantages accrues to the executive and the employer as discussed in Chapter 24.

GOVERNMENT-PROVIDED DEATH BENEFITS

Government-provided death benefits are important components of many individuals' financial planning. Social Security provides such benefits in the U.S., and similar social insurance programs are common worldwide. We provide a short overview here of the benefits afforded under the social insurance plan in the U.S.

Death benefit payments to qualified U.S. beneficiaries take two forms. First, the spouse or ex-spouse of a deceased worker is entitled to receive monthly survivor benefits if (1) he or she has not remarried and is at least age 60 and (2) the worker was fully insured. A widow or widower, regardless of age, may also qualify to receive monthly benefits if he or she is caring for an unmarried, dependent child of the worker. The child must be under age 16 or have a disability that began before age 22.

In addition, dependent children are entitled to a monthly benefit if they are unmarried and (1) under age 18 (or under 19 if attending a primary or secondary educational institution on a full-time basis) or (2) any age and were disabled before age 22. Dependent parents who are 62 and over are each entitled to a benefit as well.

In addition to income benefits, a lump-sum death benefit of $255 is paid on the death of the worker who was living with a spouse or who in death leaves a spouse or child entitled to monthly benefits. The Social Security law provides limitations on the maximum monthly benefits that can be paid to a family based on the earnings record of one person. It also requires that the decedent have worked in covered employment for certain minimum periods to qualify for the benefits. Finally, portions of the benefit payment are subject to income taxation for persons making more than specified maximums.

INDIVIDUAL LIFE INSURANCE

Perhaps the most widespread means of funding for the financial consequences of premature death is through the purchase of individual life insurance policies. Life insurance with a death benefit equal to the amount needed to fill any financial gap is a perfect hedge against the financial consequences of death. The event that gives rise to the need also gives rise to the solution. If purchased in adequate amounts, life insurance, in purely economic terms, replaces the deceased individual's future earnings, thereby protecting the family or business from the adverse financial consequences of death.

Insurance companies determine whether to issue the requested insurance policy based on an application submitted by the proposed insured – typically through an insurance agent – and, if the amount applied for is large, on results of one or more physical examinations, laboratory tests, and other information. The application contains questions of an administrative nature and questions relating to insurability. The insurer's underwriter needs sufficient information to determine whether the proposed insured qualifies according to health standards (see Chapter 11) and whether the amount of insurance requested bears a reasonable relationship to the financial loss that the beneficiary would suffer on the insured's death. The underwriter also wishes to know the purpose for the insurance, that the policyholder and beneficiary designations are logical, and that an insurable interest is present (see Chapter 18).

EVALUATION OF LIFE INSURANCE AS A FINANCIAL INSTRUMENT

In addition to its social advantages discussed in Chapter 1, life insurance offers several unique benefits to individuals relative to other financial instruments and means of dealing with the financial consequences of death. It also carries costs, but the costs of its utility to individuals are ordinarily reasonable when considered in the context of the potential consequences of death without insurance.

ADVANTAGES

First, as noted above, appropriately planned life insurance is a perfect hedge against the adverse financial consequences of death. The event that gives rise to the need also gives rise to the solution. Second, life insurance enjoys preferential tax treatment under the U.S. *Internal Revenue Code* (IRC) not enjoyed by other financial instruments. The tax that otherwise would be due on the interest earned on life insurance cash values is either avoided altogether or deferred, provided the policy qualifies as "life insurance" under tax law (see Chapter 21). The tax is avoided altogether if the policy is retained until death. Because interest accrues on a tax-deferred basis, the cash value is greater than the after-tax value of equivalent taxable savings media for a term-plus-side-fund arrangement.

If a qualifying policy is terminated during the insured's lifetime, income tax will be owed to the extent that the cash value and any other amounts received under the policy exceed the premiums paid, which is the policy's cost basis. However, tax will have been deferred for the holding period. Additionally, internal cost of insurance charges are paid with tax deferred earnings, and no adjustment to the tax basis is required if the policy is terminated.

Also, proceeds may be free of estate tax in well-planned situations. Thus, every dollar of such a policy's death proceeds in the beneficiary's hands could equal as much as two dollars of assets retained in the taxable estate (assuming a combined 50 percent federal and state tax rate). See Chapter 22.

Third, many life insurance policies today provide exceptional flexibility to address a client's changing financial and personal circumstances:

- They are tax-favored repositories of easily accessed, liquid funds if a need arises. Yet the assets backing these funds are generally held in longer-term investments, thereby earning a higher return than investments of comparable liquidity.
- The policyholder usually can deposit additional funds into the policy to enjoy further tax leverage, to lower internal mortality charges, and/or to extend the length of time that the policy will remain in effect without further premium payments. Likewise, premiums for many policies can be skipped or reduced to accommodate changed circumstances if sufficient policy value exists to sustain the policy.
- Face amounts can be decreased if a reduced insurance need develops, with corresponding reductions in internal mortality charges or premiums, or amounts often can be increased subject to satisfactory insurability.

COSTS

Life insurance is not without costs to individual purchasers. First, insurers necessarily incur operational expenses and taxes, and these must be paid via loadings in the policy. Such loadings vary over time, ranging, for example, from 100 percent or more of the first year premium to 5-20 percent thereafter, depending on the type of policy and its pricing.

Second, as with all savings media, purchasers of life insurance defer the utility of current consumption (by paying premiums) to accrue savings for future consumption for either themselves (with respect to cash value insurance) or their beneficiaries (for term and cash value insurance). Life insurance differs from other savings media in that it usually is purchased for the benefit of others and only indirectly for the benefit of the person whose life is insured.

Third, the life insurance purchase decision can be complex. Even the comparatively straightforward decision to purchase life insurance to cover one's family may not be simple. Is insurance needed and, if so, in what amount, what type, and from whom should it be purchased? The decision requires analysis at each stage, and the customer typically is not well versed in life insurance. Information problems, discussed in Chapter 1, are significant.

Complexity can increase by orders of magnitude if the purchase is for estate liquidity or is to be used in business situations or complex family situations as discussed in Chapters 22 and 24. The decision involves the same types of issues as the family purchase and others as well: How best to structure the arrangement? How do we minimize income, gift, and estate taxes? How to maximize the possibility of all heirs feeling that they have been treated fairly? How do we go about ensuring that the insurance amount remains adequate over time and that the policy being considered offers needed flexibility for changing circumstances?

POLICIES SOLD BY LIFE INSURANCE COMPANIES

Life insurance is purchased by either individuals or organizations. As we know from Chapter 1, we refer to insurance purchased by individuals as personal insurance. When purchased by organizations, we refer to it as commercial insurance, and, if related exclusively to a group such as employees or society members, as group insurance. The premiums and coverage of personal insurance sales dominate group insurance sales in most markets worldwide, including the U.S. market.

Insurance companies sell policies whose benefit payments are contingent on the happening of some event. Historically, policies sold by life insurers involved only *life contingencies*, meaning that payments to policyholders or their beneficiaries were contingent on whether insureds lived or died. **Mortality tables** show yearly probabilities of death by age and usually other variables such as sex and smoking status and are necessary for pricing these policies.

Life insurance companies also sell policies whose payments are contingent on whether insureds become incapacitated, sick, or injured. **Morbidity tables** show periodic probabilities and durations of incapacity, sickness, or injury by age (or age brackets) and often other factors, such as smoking status, and are necessary for pricing these policies.

Typical policies sold by life insurance companies worldwide can be classified as either mortality based or morbidity based. Recall from Chapter 1 that we classified the life branch as selling insurance to cover (1) death before a certain age, (2) survival to a certain age, (3) incapacity, and (4) expenses or lost income from injury or disease. We can see that the first two classifications are mortality based and the last two are morbidity based.

MORTALITY-BASED POLICIES

Mortality-based insurance policies can be considered as falling into two classes: life insurance and annuities. Policies that pay a prescribed death benefit if the insured dies during the policy term are commonly labeled as life insurance or, in some countries, as life assurance. The latter term is commonly used in the U.K. and other Commonwealth countries. **Annuity contracts** (or **pensions** in some countries) are policies that promise to make a series of payments through systematic liquidation of principal and interest and possibly benefit of survivorship for a fixed period or over an annuitant's lifetime. **Endowments** are life insurance policies that pay a stated sum if the insured dies before a prescribed time period and usually the same sum if the insured survives the time period.

LIFE INSURANCE   Life insurance policies pay a death benefit commonly as a stated sum of money – variously called the **face amount**, **sum assured**, or **death benefit** amount – on the death of the insured. As noted in Chapter 1, the insured is the individual whose death triggers payment of the face amount. The person who applies for the policy is the **applicant**. In most instances, the applicant is also the proposed insured, but sometimes the applicant may apply for the insured, as when a parent applies for a policy on a child's life. The applicant becomes the policyowner. Recall that the policyowner or policyholder is the person who can exercise all policy rights and with whom the insurer deals. The applicant names someone – the beneficiary – to receive the face amount on the death of the insured.

While thousands of different life insurance policies exist, all fall into one of two generic categories: term life insurance and cash value life insurance. **Term life insurance** pays the policy face amount if the insured dies during the policy term, which is a specified number of years, such as 10 or 20 years, or to a specified age, such as age 65. **Cash value life insurance** policies combine term insurance and internal savings – called the cash value – within the same contract; that is, they accumulate funds that are available to the policyowner, much as a savings account with a bank. Cash value life insurance is also sometimes referred to as **permanent life insurance**, meaning that it can remain in force for the whole of one's life (or to an advanced age).

All life insurance policies rely on the same pricing elements as we explore below. The details of how these elements function within a policy and the extent to which they are disclosed to the policyowner vary. The degree of disclosure or transparency within a policy depends on whether its pricing components are bundled or unbundled. With **bundled** policies, the policyholder is not informed as to how the premium is allocated to cover the insurer's operational expenses, taxes, and contingencies; to pay for the pure insurance component; to build cash values; or to support the scale of dividends for participating policies (discussed below). The policyholder pays an indivisible premium, receiving a bundle of benefits:

- a promise to pay a stated death benefit if the insured dies during the policy term,
- a promise to pay a stated value on policy surrender, for cash value policies,
- entitlement to receive (nonguaranteed) dividends declared by the insurer, for participating policies, and
- advice and administrative services of an agent and insurer.

Many contemporary policies are **unbundled**, meaning they disclose to the policyholder the portions of his or her premium that are allocated to pay for the costs of the internal insurance; to build cash values; and to cover the insurer's expenses, taxes, profits, and contingencies. Unbundled policies are also sometimes called **current assumption policies** as their values are derived from so-called current assumptions or more formally nonguaranteed policy elements, which are discussed below.

An insurance policy's stated annual cost of insurance rates, interest crediting rates, and loadings do not necessarily track its actual mortality, investment, and expense experience. Nonetheless, the policyholder is able to see how the premium is allocated among these policy elements.

Term Life Insurance Term life insurance policies **expire** if the insured survives the policy term, meaning that they terminate with no value. Term life insurance usually provides either a level or decreasing death benefit. Premiums either increase with age or remain level. Term policies with level death benefits and increasing premiums are commonly referred to as **renewable**, granting the policyowner the right to continue the life insurance policy for one or more specified periods merely by paying the billed premium. The premium ordinarily increases at each renewal. Thus, **yearly renewable term** (YRT) – also called **annual renewable term** (ART) – provides term insurance whose premiums increase yearly. These policies usually expire between ages 65 and 85 in the U.S. In Canada and other jurisdictions the term renewals may extend to age 100.

Initial premium rates per unit of coverage are lower for term life insurance than for other life products issued on the same basis. The increasing premiums, however, escalate at an increasing rate with policy duration. Term product prices are more easily compared than are prices of other life products, as term policies are usually structurally simpler than other policies. Term products usually have no cash values (i.e., internal savings) and often no dividends (see below), thus permitting policy price comparisons on the basis of premiums alone. As a consequence, buyer information problems are less with term insurance, thus rendering the term market more competitive.

Cash Value Life Insurance Unbundled cash value policies often distinguish between a policy's savings element before and after deduction of a surrender charge. The **cash value** is a life insurance policy's internal savings before deduction of any surrender charges or policy loans. With unbundled policies it is also called the **policy value, account value, accumulated value,** and the **gross cash value.** Unless stated otherwise, we will use these four terms as synonyms for a policy's cash value; i.e., the policy value before deductions. A **surrender charge** (also called a **back-end load**) is the amount assessed against a policy's cash (account) value as a type of penalty for early policy termination. The savings element after deduction of any surrender charge is called the **cash surrender value, surrender value,** or sometimes, simply **cash value.**

Any surrender charge usually declines over time, such as 10 to 15 years, and ultimately ceases such that the surrender value equals the cash or account value. A surrender charge allows the insurer to recover from owners who surrender their

policies some of the significant costs of policy issuance without penalizing policyowners who do not surrender their policies. Some unbundled policies also feature an explicit **front-end load** which is deducted from premium payments for
expenses, taxes, contingencies, and sometimes profits.

Bundled cash value polices feature no explicitly specified charges or loads,
with the cash value shown in the contract also equal to the cash surrender value, in
the absence of outstanding policy loans. Bundled cash value policies nonetheless
typically penalize early policy cash values and assess front-end loads; they simply
are not explicit as with unbundled policies.

All cash value policies can be considered as a combination of YRT insurance
and a savings account, such that the combination always precisely equals the policy's stated death benefit. Thus, for policies with level face amounts and increasing cash values, the amount of term insurance purchased each year decreases by
precisely the same amount of the cash value increase. The difference between the
policy death benefit and the cash value or policy reserve is called the **net amount
at risk** (NAR). (Some policies have a level NAR rather than a level death benefit,
as discussed in Chapter 3.) This concept is illustrated in Figure 2-1.

Figure 2-1	**Illustration of a Level-Premium Cash Value Policy Funded to Age 121, $1,000,000 Face Amount**

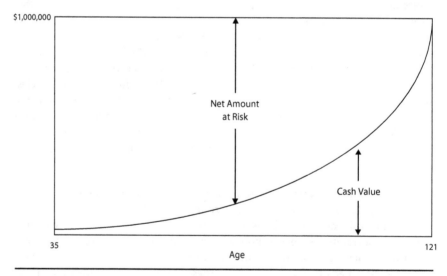

A cash value policy with a $1.0 million level death benefit and level annual premiums produces
increasing cash values each year and, therefore, a NAR that decreases each year by precisely the
same amount as the cash value increases.

Two types of internal charges are assessed annually under all cash value policies. The charges are explicit under unbundled policies but not under bundled
policies. First, a charge is assessed to pay for the policy's internal term insurance –
the NAR. This charge, called the **cost of insurance** (COI), is the internal age-based
rate assessed against each life insurance policy based on its net amount at risk,
to cover its share of mortality charges for the period. Second, a **loading charge**

is assessed to cover some or all of an insurer's future expenses, taxes, profits (or surplus accumulations), and contingencies. These charges also may be labeled as **expense charges, fees,** and/or **policy loads.**

Cash value policies typically contain guaranteed maximum COI and loading charges, either explicitly stated in the policy or implicit in the guaranteed cash values of bundled policies. Most insurers assess stated COI charges at less than the maximum permitted. As with other savings media, interest is credited yearly or more frequently to the cash value. In most non-variable (see below) policies, a minimum interest rate is guaranteed to be credited, but the insurer commonly credits a higher rate.

The gross premiums paid by policyholders for most bundled cash value life insurance policies are calculated using the maximum COI and loading charges and minimum guaranteed interest rates. In other words, the premiums are set conservatively. Because of conservative pricing, the policies as a group are expected to experience (1) lower mortality rates, (2) higher investment earnings, and/or (3) lower expenses than those built into policy pricing. The excess amounts from these expected favorable deviations of actual experience from that assumed in pricing can be returned to policyholders. These surplus funds are returned to policyholders in the form of **dividends**, the pro-rata share of divisible surplus paid by an insurer to the owners of its participating policies. They are also called **bonuses** in some countries.[1] These policies are classified as **participating** (par) or as being **with bonus** – meaning that they are entitled to receive dividends declared by the insurer.

Nonparticipating (nonpar) or **without bonus** policies are not entitled to receive dividends declared by the insurer. Traditionally, all nonpar policy elements (premiums, cash values, and death benefits) were fixed at issuance and never changed. Today, many nonpar policies provide some means of passing onto policyholders the insurer's favorable operating experience in a similar way that par policies allow participation in the insurer's results. We cover these issues in Chapters 3, 4, and 16.

Thousands of variations of cash value policies exist, consistent with insurers' product differentiation and market segmentation strategies to gain market power. To aggravate an already tough lemons problem for the customer (as discussed in Chapter 1), terminology is not always standard. We can, however, take a shortcut through this maze. Virtually every cash value policy falls into one of three categories, even if the policy is not labeled as such: (1) universal life insurance, (2) whole life insurance, or (3) endowment insurance.

Universal Life Insurance   **Universal life** (UL) **insurance policies** are characterized by flexible premium payments and adjustable death benefits whose cash values and coverage periods depend on the premiums paid. The policyholder, not the insurer, determines the magnitude of the premium payment. If premiums paid and interest credits exceed current policy charges, the cash value is increased by the excess inflow. If policy charges exceed the sum of premiums paid and interest credited, the excess charges are deducted from the cash value, leading to a cash value decline. Because of this premium flexibility and death benefit adjustability, policyholders effectively design their own policies to reflect their own needs and financial circumstances. The UL policy can be changed as those needs and circumstances change.

UL policies are usually nonparticipating (i.e., they are not eligible for policy dividends), but they routinely share in the insurer's operational results via nonguaranteed policy elements other than dividends. **Policy elements** are the pricing components of policies and include the premiums, benefits, values, credits, and charges under a life insurance policy. **Nonguaranteed policy elements**, also called **current assumptions,** are policy elements that are not guaranteed and that the insurer may increase or decrease as long as policy guarantees are respected and commonly include mortality and loading charges, interest crediting rates, dividends, and sometimes the policy premium.

Guaranteed policy elements are those that are fixed and guaranteed and that the insurer may not change. For example, an insurer may guarantee to credit an interest rate to policy cash values of not less than 3.0 percent (the guaranteed interest rate) but may currently credit 5.0 percent (the nonguaranteed interest rate). Because of lower interest rates experienced since the turn of the century, many companies have lowered current and guaranteed interest crediting rates on new policies and lowered current crediting rates on existing policies.

With most policies, the insurer may increase the interest crediting rate as it wishes, and policyowners expect increases as the insurer's investment returns increase. Similarly, the insurer ordinarily may decrease the interest crediting rate as it wishes but can never reduce it below the guaranteed crediting rate. It is worth noting that such a long interest rate guarantee – spanning the entire duration that a policy is in effect, potentially many decades – is almost never found in other financial instruments and legally impermissible for deposits with other financial intermediaries.

A UL policy's first year cash value is derived from the amount remaining after deducting charges for COI and loadings from whatever premium the policyholder decides to pay at policy inception. The insurer credits interest to the balance to yield the cash value at the end of the year. The internal operations of UL policies including the interest crediting rates and charges for COI and loadings are disclosed in periodic statements to the policyowner.

Whole Life Insurance   **Whole life** (WL) **insurance** typically requires the payment of fixed premiums and promises to pay a fixed death benefit whenever the insured dies and, therefore, is life insurance intended to remain in effect for the insured's entire lifetime. WL policies often are participating, but nonpar policies also exist. Most nonpar WL policies contain nonguaranteed elements similar to those found in UL policies. For some nonpar policies, all policy elements are guaranteed and fixed (i.e., the policies have guaranteed policy elements only), with no means of policy values being changed because of changing insurer operational results. For both universal life and whole life policies, the policy values are credited with interest based on the performance of underlying investments, typically investment grade fixed-income instruments managed by the insurance company, and supported by a guaranteed minimum credited interest rate.

Unlike UL policies, premiums for WL insurance policies (1) are directly related to the amount of insurance purchased, (2) must be paid when due or the policy will terminate, and (3) are calculated to ensure that the policy will remain in effect for the entire lifetime of the insured, which often is assumed to be age 100 or 121. If the insured does not die during the policy term and lives to the terminal age underlying policy pricing, the policy may endow, with the face amount paid as if the insured had died. With some whole life policies – called **ordinary life** or **level-premium whole life** – uniform premiums are assumed to be paid over the entirety of the insured's lifetime.

We can think of the necessary annual premium to fund an ordinary life policy as being equal to the level amount that would have to be paid into a UL policy over the WL policy term (e.g., to age 100) to cause the UL policy cash value to equal the face amount at age 100, relying only on guaranteed policy elements to derive that premium; i.e., using the guaranteed interest rate and guaranteed COI and loading charges.

Other whole life policies – called **limited-payment whole life** – provide that premiums will be paid over some period shorter than the insured's entire lifetime, such as to age 65 or for a set period such as 10 years. The necessary annual premium to fund the policy equals the level amount that would have to be paid into a UL policy over the premium-paying period to cause its cash value to equal the face amount at the end of the policy term (e.g., age 100), using the guaranteed interest rate and COI and loading charges. The shorter the premium-paying period, the higher must be each year's premium. The higher is each year's premium, the greater will be the cash value, other things being the same. In turn, the lower will be the policy's internal COI charges.

Of course, the policy remains in effect after all premiums have been paid – it is said to be **paid up,** meaning that no further premiums need be paid and the contract is guaranteed to remain in effect for the insured's entire lifetime. Thus, the WL policy with the lowest premium (and lowest cash values) is ordinary life as premium payments are stretched over the whole of life. The WL policy with the highest premium (and highest cash values) is **single premium whole life insurance** under which only a single (large) premium payment is made at policy inception.

Cash value policies are also available as variable WL and UL life insurance. **Variable life insurance** (also called **unit linked life insurance**) is either a bundled or unbundled life insurance policy under which the policyowner allocates premium payments to separate accounts offered by the insurer. **Separate accounts** are mutual fund-type accounts maintained by life insurers to hold investments backing the policy reserves; the cash values and death benefits are directly determined by the performance of assets held in those accounts. They are separate from the insurer's general account assets. The policyowner carries 100 percent of the investment risk, unlike the situation with non-variable policies.

Endowment Insurance   As noted above, most whole life policies endow at a very advanced age. In practice, policies endowing at earlier ages are termed **endowment insurance** and make two mutually exclusive promises: to pay a stated benefit if the insured dies during the policy term or if the insured survives the stated policy term. Historically, this benefit equaled the policy face amount and, if paid on survival, the policy was said to **endow.**

Thus, an endowment at age 65 policy pays the face amount if the insured dies before age 65 or pays the same amount if the insured survives to age 65. Very little endowment insurance is sold in the U.S. today because of adverse tax treatment, but it remains popular in many other markets worldwide. WL and UL policies can endow if the policy remains in force until the end of the mortality table used to calculate policy reserves, which is age 100 for older policies and age 121 for newer policies.

ANNUITIES   Life insurance has as its principal mission the creation of a fund. An annuity's function is the systematic liquidation of a fund. Most annuities sold by life insurers are also accumulation instruments, but this is the mechanism for developing the fund to be liquidated. The purpose of most annuities is to protect against the possibility of outliving one's income – the opposite of life insurance.

Technically, an **annuity** is any series of periodic payments. An annuity contract promises to make a series of payments through systematic liquidation of principal and interest for a fixed period or over a person's lifetime. A **life annuity** is any annuity whose payments are contingent on whether the annuitant is alive. The person whose lifetime is used to measure the length of time that benefits are payable is the **annuitant** who typically is also the income recipient. Thus, a **whole life annuity** is a life annuity payable for the whole of the annuitant's life, irrespective of how long that may be. In contrast, an **annuity certain** makes payments for a set period of time without reference to whether the annuitant is alive.

Each payment under a life annuity is a combination of principal and interest income and a survivorship element. Although not completely accurate, we can view the operation of a whole life annuity as follows: if a person dies precisely at his or her life expectancy, he or she would have neither gained nor lost through utilizing a life annuity. Those annuitants who die before attaining their life expectancies would not have received payments equal to the expected actuarial value of their contributions. The unpaid amounts are retained by the insurance pool to provide continuing income to those who outlive their life expectancies. As no one knows into which category he or she will fall, the arrangement is equitable and succeeds through the operation of the law of large numbers (see below).

Insurers offer a variety of options as to how annuity payments can be made. Most insurers also include a provision in their contracts to the effect that they will provide any other payment option that is mutually agreed upon by the insurer and the contract owner.

Annuity benefits can be expressed in fixed or variable units. Fixed annuities are much like bank savings accounts. The insurer guarantees to credit a minimum interest rate to the cash value during the accumulation period, but usually credits a higher rate. In addition, a minimum annuity payout is guaranteed.

Variable annuities feature separate account-backed cash values that are similar to mutual funds. With a **variable (unit-linked) annuity**, cash values and benefit payments vary directly with the performance of assets held in one or more separate accounts. In the absence of optional benefits, variable annuities do not contain minimum investment guarantees. The contract owner typically bears the investment risk and receives the return actually earned on invested assets, less charges assessed by the insurance company.

MORBIDITY-BASED POLICIES
Individuals face three broad categories of potential economic losses associated with the health risk. First, they can incur medical expenses when injured or sick.

Second, they may incur expenses to provide long term care if mental or physical illness, injury, or old-age frailty prevents them from engaging in the activities of daily living. Third, poor health or incapacity also can be so debilitating as to prevent employment – which means a reduction or even elimination of wages. Medical expense insurance, long term care (LTC) insurance, and disability income insurance policies, respectively, are designed to meet each of the three loss exposures.

MEDICAL EXPENSE INSURANCE

Healthcare expenses are most commonly financed by government programs, by employers, and by personal financial resources, as we discuss in Chapter 7. In many markets, individuals and families purchase individually issued medical expense insurance policies – commonly called simply health insurance – because no third-party financing is available or to augment or replace governmental or employer-provided coverage. Individuals in many markets can secure individual coverage from managed care organizations, such as health maintenance organizations, preferred provider organizations, and point-of-service plans, but most such coverage is employer-based. These are covered in Chapter 7.

Coverage under individually issued medical expense insurance policies may parallel that available through group health insurance. They may cover inpatient and outpatient hospital services, physician and diagnostic services, as well as specialty services such as physical therapy, radiology, and prescription drugs. More commonly, this coverage is more restrictive and, depending on the market, such policies usually are more expensive in comparison to employer-provided and subsidized health insurance. Deductibles and other co-payments often are higher with individual policies than under group insurance.

Individual health insurance policies can be issued on a guaranteed or nonguaranteed renewable basis. With **guaranteed renewable health insurance policies**, the insured has the contractual right to continue the policy by the timely payment of premiums, usually to a specified age, such as 65, but the magnitude of future premiums usually is not guaranteed. With **nonguaranteed renewable health insurance policies,** the insurer may unilaterally refuse to renew the policy, sometimes subject to restrictions.

LONG TERM CARE INSURANCE
The second major type of health risk faced by individuals and families stems from the possibility of becoming unable fully to care for oneself. Most often, such incapacity is associated with the aging process; illness or injury may also be a cause.

In most countries, substantial portions or the totality of such care is provided by family members or financed through the individual's or family's resources. The common external sources of LTC financing include (1) government, (2) group plans, and (3) individual insurance policies issued by commercial insurers. Coverage through the first two sources is common in many markets, although benefits may be limited. Government funding of LTC expenses accounts for the great majority of coverage in developed countries. Individual LTC policy coverage is not widespread in any market but is growing in many.

Private LTC insurance pays for services when the insured is unable to perform certain specified activities of daily living without assistance, such as bathing, eating, dressing, toileting, and transferring to and from bed. These policies also may pay benefits when the insured requires supervision due to a cognitive impairment such as Alzheimer's disease.

LTC insurance in some markets pays only for skilled care in a nursing home following a period of hospitalization. Generally, however, coverage extends to an array of services that promotes independent living, including personal care, assisted living, care management, support for family caregivers, home modifications, homemaker services, and hospice care, in addition to institutional care.

Coverage varies by market and also by the method of benefit payment. Some policies pay a fixed daily benefit for nursing home confinement. Others pay a fixed daily benefit regardless of whether the insured incurs LTC expenses, provided eligibility requirements are met. Still others reimburse for incurred expenses, up to the policy daily maximum.

Individual LTC policies typically are offered on a guaranteed renewable basis. Applications for individual LTC insurance are carefully underwritten by insurers. Long term care benefits often are also available as riders to life insurance policies, as discussed in Chapter 5 and annuity policies as discussed in Chapter 6.

Disability Income Insurance   Disability can seriously affect a worker's and a family's lifestyle and savings plans. For example, the U.S. *Department of Housing and Urban Development* estimates that 46 percent of foreclosures on home mortgage loans are caused by disability versus only 2 percent caused by death. The need for external sources of disability income typically declines with age, ideally disappearing at retirement when adequate non-employment income should be sufficient to maintain the individual or family. During the working years, most individuals require substantial external coverage.

The three major sources of external finance for the disability exposure – ignoring family and friends – are (1) government, (2) group plans, and (3) individual disability income insurance policies. The most common external sources of disability income in developed countries are social insurance programs. Additionally, many employers provide disability income benefits to employees who are unable to work because of sickness and injury, often funded via group insurance policies purchased from commercial insurers. Insurers also sell individual disability income insurance policies, although group coverages predominate.

Disability income insurance policies are designed to provide monthly benefits to replace lost income when the insured is disabled as a result of sickness or injury. Policies sold to individuals may be issued on a guaranteed renewable basis, with some policies issued on a basis that not only guarantees the insured the right to continue the policy but also guarantees future premiums – called **noncancellable and guaranteed renewable** – or simply **noncan** policies.

The benefit amount is typically stated in terms of a fixed monthly sum. The insurance usually is written on a valued basis, which means that it is presumed to replace the monetary loss sustained by the insured. Insurers limit the amount of insurance that they will sell to an individual such that disability income from all likely sources would replace a maximum proportion (e.g., 60 to 80 percent) of gross wages. This is the most important method of controlling the moral hazard problem discussed in Chapter 1. The benefit period is the longest period for which benefits will be paid. Typical benefit periods are two or five years or to age 65.

Insurers are in the business of assuming risks transferred to them by their insureds.[2] However, they do not accept all risks that individuals and corporations wish to transfer. A risk *should* meet several requirements for it to be considered insurable in the private market. The word "should" is emphasized, because exposures covered by insurers seldom meet all requirements perfectly. Generally, the more inconsistent is a given exposure class with the requirements, the less likely it is to be insurable in the private market. The requirements for an ideal insurable risk include:

- large number of independent and homogeneous exposure units,
- accidental losses,
- losses easily determinable as to time, amount, and type, and
- economically feasible premiums.

Large Number of Independent, Homogeneous Exposure Units

An **exposure unit** in insurance practice and theory is a person, place, or thing exposed to the possibility of loss. In life and health insurance, it refers to a life. Similar exposure units are grouped to form **insurance pools** (also called **risk classes**). Insurance companies specialize in forming insurance pools. Each insurance pool ideally should be composed of exposure units that are independent and homogeneous.

INDEPENDENT EXPOSURE UNITS   Two random variables (e.g., exposures units) are **independent** if the relationship between them is such that the occurrence of an event affecting one has no affect on the other variable. For example, two individuals located in different cities ordinarily are considered independent of one another. Events and activities affecting one person mostly have no effect on the other person. If, however, the two individuals were on the same flight to Singapore, a crash will affect both of them. For this exposure, they are interdependent.

Ordinarily insurers are able to diversify risk by forming large pools of exposure units that are statistically independent of one another thereby lowering the average risk per exposure unit in the pool. However, when the exposure units in insurance pools are all subject to the possibility of suffering losses due to a single catastrophic event, the risks are systematic and are no longer statistically independent. In this case, the exposure units are interdependent or correlated. When risks are correlated, the benefits of diversification across exposure units are reduced or eliminated, and private markets may not be able to accept such a risk transfer. Except for pandemics (and nuclear annihilation!), the death exposure largely meets the independence criterion within groups of insureds.

HOMOGENEOUS EXPOSURE UNITS   Random variables are said to be **identically distributed** or **homogeneous** if their probability distributions prescribe the same probability to each potential occurrence, which renders the distributions' expected values and variances equal. This condition is important because it allows insurers to charge each independent and identically distributed (IID) insured the same premium.

In reality, few exposure units are truly homogeneous, and insurers group similar exposure units into a class and charge pooled premiums. Life insurers are

Figure 2-2   **Relative Variations of Actual from Expected Claims as a Function of Number of Lives Insured**

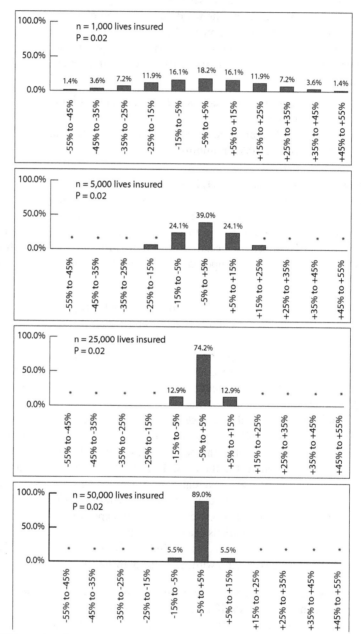

*Probabilities are less than 1.0 percent

When the numbers of lives insured are 1,000, 5,000, 25,000, and 50,000, the probability of actual claims being within 5.0 percent of expected claims is 18.2 percent if 1,000 lives are insured, 39.0 percent if 5,000 lives are insured, 74.2 percent if 25,000 lives are insured, and 89.0 percent if 50,000 lives are insured. Although not shown in the chart, the probability of actual claims being within 5.0 percent of expected claims is greater than 99.99 percent if 1,000,000 lives were insured.

largely able to accommodate this condition by creating insurance pools of insureds who are roughly of the same health and the same age, sex and smoking status.

LARGE NUMBER OF EXPOSURE UNITS   To function properly, private insurance must also have a sufficiently large number of exposure units to permit predictability. This predictability comes about because of the **law of large numbers** which holds that, as the number of units or trials taken becomes large, (1) the variation of actual from probable experience decreases and (2) each additional unit lowers the variation in outcome. Thus, the average loss for a pool of IID exposure units tends to fall closer and closer to the expected value of losses as more exposure units are added to the pool. It is the fundamental reason that insurance pools can spread, share, and reduce risk. Individuals acting alone cannot.

We can see this result easily in a simple example. Suppose that a hypothetical life insurance company insures the lives of a certain number of persons in a single year and that the probability that any one of the insureds will die that year is 2.0 percent. The expected number of claims is, therefore, 2.0 percent of the total number of insured lives. The actual number of claims may be more or less than the expected number. According to the law of large numbers, if the number of insureds is large enough, actual claims should show only a small relative deviation from expected claims. Using probability theory, one can calculate the probabilities of various deviations from expected claims, depending on the number of insureds. Figure 2-2 on the preceding page shows the probability of various deviations according to an increasing number of lives insured.

Thus, the law of large numbers allows insurers to pool IID exposures, which lowers the average risk contribution in the pool. Pooling IID exposures has a second effect that gives pools a comparative advantage in managing risk. This effect, known as **pooling of resources**, means the larger the number of fairly priced exposure units in an insurance pool, the greater the likelihood that the insurer's premium receipts and investment income will be sufficient to pay all claims that arise during the coverage period, *ceteris paribus*.

To show this effect, consider the following example.[3] Assume an insurer has established an insurance pool of IID exposures with a loss probability of 20 percent and so the probability of not having a loss of 80 percent. If a loss occurs, the insurer pays £5,000. Thus, the expected value of the loss (and the actuarially fair premium) is £1,000 [0.2 x £5,000]. Finally, assume the insurer charges a 40 percent loading, making a gross premium of £1,400. Figure 2-3 illustrates this concept graphically.

ACCIDENTAL LOSSES

Economic loss is caused by events that are either foreseeable or not. Ideally, exposure units should be subject to accidental or unintentional loss causing events. There are three reasons for this preference. First, when the insured has some control over either the likelihood of a loss occurring or its severity, problems of moral hazard may arise. Second, from a societal viewpoint, it is not good public policy to allow policyholders to collect insurance proceeds for losses that they cause intentionally.

Figure 2-3

Probability of Ruin and the Pooling of Resources Effect

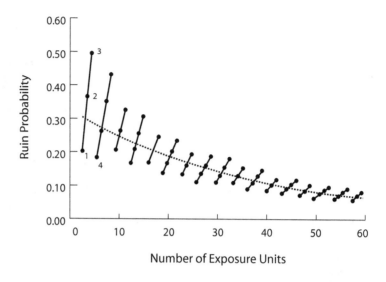

Number of Exposure Units

Figure 2-3 shows the probability of ruin for the insurance pool as a function of the number of exposure units in the pool. Ruin occurs when total insured losses exceed total premiums paid into the pool. With only one exposure unit in the pool, the probability of ruin equals 20 percent, which is exactly the probability of the insured suffering a loss. The reason for this result is that the pool contains only £1,400 and, if an insured suffers a loss, the loss will be £5,000 thereby bankrupting the pool. When a second exposure unit is added to the pool (shown as "2" on the left-most vertical line), pool resources increase to £2,800, but the probability of ruin actually increases. Of course, the pool cannot pay a full claim until its resources are greater than £5,000, which occurs when the fourth exposure unit is added to the pool and can be seen in Figure 2-3 by the discontinuity of the graph between the third (shown as "3") and fourth ("4" on the second line) exposure unit. This pattern continues until the positive effect of adding additional resources to the pool overwhelms the negative effect of adding an additional exposure unit to the pool. The ruin probability becomes closer and closer to zero as the number of exposure units in the pool becomes very large.

Finally, for losses that are not accidental and occur naturally over time, such as depreciation of a corporation's plant and equipment or wear and tear of a consumer's automobile, budgeting for eventual repair or replacement of the property is less expensive than the purchase of insurance. Such contingencies are not considered to be insurable as they are certain to occur.

The human body, as with all living things and like manufacturing facilities, equipment, and automobiles, has a limited useful life. In reliability theory terminology, the body follows a failure law that is a combination of an aging failure distribution that exhibits an exponential increase in failure rates and a non-aging failure distribution largely independent of age (see Gompertz discussion in Chapter 15).

Death is certain to occur, yet insurance is routinely provided against its adverse consequences. This is because death has both foreseeable and unforeseeable dimensions. We know that we will die, eventually. We just do not know when. We mostly insure against the "not knowing when" dimension. We also can make provision against the "eventually" dimension. Both (1) cash value life insurance and (2) term life insurance combined with a systematic plan of savings can address the unforeseeable risk of *untimely* death, as well as the certainty of death in the long run. In essence, the unforeseeable risk is insured via pure life insurance, either term or the net amount at risk with cash value insurance.

The foreseeable economic consequences of certain death are budgeted through the gradual increase in cash values and corresponding decrease in the net amount at risk within a cash value insurance policy or through systematically accumulating investment funds that gradually replace term insurance death benefits. The latter is a buy-term-and-invest-the-difference strategy. Both approaches can be viewed as sinking funds to replace the (economically) "failed" body.

PAYMENT AMOUNTS EASILY DETERMINABLE

An actuarially fair premium cannot be derived if losses cannot be defined precisely. Whenever a claim is filed, the details of the insured loss as to its time, place, and amount must be determinable and verifiable to establish whether the claim should be paid and its amount. Life insurance and annuity claims typically are simple, but claims for health, long term care, and disability income insurance are often complex. Further, any costs incurred by the insured or beneficiary, such as time away from work during this claims process, lowers the expected utility of insuring. Likewise, any direct costs incurred by the insurer during the claims settlement process is passed onto insureds as higher premium loadings.

ECONOMICALLY FEASIBLE PREMIUMS

The final characteristic of ideal insurable exposures is that the premium must be economically feasible. On the one hand, the **risk premium**, the additional amount that rational, risk-averse individuals will pay to purchase insurance in excess of the expected value of the loss, must not be too large. On the other hand, the owners of private insurance companies require that insurance rates be high enough to give them a competitive return on their investments. These two offsetting influences define the range of economically feasible premiums.

Many factors affect this range. For example, the degree of competition in an insurance market, the threat of new entrants, and the price and/or threat of alternative products and substitutes all have a direct effect on the insurer's ability to set prices. Likewise, the bargaining power of customers, the degree to which they face risks, and their attitudes toward risk affect customers' abilities to define the upper limit of the range of feasible premiums.

We follow the above overview of the policies sold by life insurance companies and requisites for their risks to be insurable with an introduction to life insurance pricing. Our purpose is to explain broadly the objectives that drive insurer pricing and to explore briefly the elements that constitute pricing. Detail is provided in Chapters 15 and 16.

INTRODUCTION TO LIFE INSURANCE PRICING

PRICING OBJECTIVES

All insurers strive to ensure that the rates charged for their products are (1) adequate, (2) equitable, and (3) economically feasible. Each is discussed below.

ADEQUACY   Insurance company rates must be sufficient to fund the benefits promised under its insurance products. Rate inadequacy can lead to financial problems and possible insolvency. Rate adequacy means that, for a given block of policies, total premium payments collected now and in the future by the insurer, plus the investment earnings attributable to any retained funds, should be sufficient to fund current and future benefits promised and related expenses, taxes, contingencies, and profits. A **block of policies** ordinarily constitutes all policies issued by the insurer under the same schedules of policy elements and on the same policy form.

An insurer cannot know with certainty the degree of rate adequacy until the last policy in a block has terminated. Because individually issued life insurance and health insurance may be issued at rates and on terms and conditions that may be guaranteed for many years, the issue of rate adequacy is especially important in establishing initial premium levels or pricing elements.

Life and health insurance rates are regulated to ensure adequacy in some countries, although the trend worldwide is toward deregulation of rates. Life and health insurance premium adequacy is regulated indirectly in the U.S. through the requirements of minimum reserves. Generally, life insurance rates are unregulated as long as they are sufficient to meet reserve requirements, but health insurance rates often are subject to control if regulators determine them to be too high.

EQUITY   Rates charged for life and health insurance should be equitable to policyowners. Equity means assessing charges and credits or premiums commensurate with the expected losses and other costs that insureds bring to the insurance pool. Stated differently, no expected *ex ante* subsidization should exist of any insured by any other insured.

The achievement of equity is a goal to be sought. In an imperfect world, it cannot be attained absolutely. Concepts of equity must give way to practical realities, and insureds are classified in similar, but not identical groups. These realities include the fact that the larger the number of insurance pools – also called classifications – the greater the expense in administering the pool. Also, a large enough group is necessary to permit reasonable prediction of losses within each classification. A precise assessment of the extra cost that each insured brings to the pool usually is not feasible.

As discussed in Chapter 11, the pursuit of equity is one of the goals of underwriting. **Underwriting** is the process by which insurers decide whether to issue insurance to a person and the terms and prices. Life insurers strive toward equitable treatment of insureds by varying life and health insurance rates by factors such as age, sex, plan, health, and benefits provided. Generally, a greater degree of refinement in rate classes – and therefore more actuarial equity – exists for life insurance than for health insurance. Actuarial equity is sometimes in conflict with concepts of social equity. For example, some persons believe it to be socially unacceptable to charge different life and health insurance rates to otherwise identically situated men and women, although they exhibit clear differences in expected mortality and morbidity.

ECONOMICALLY FEASIBLE   Life and health insurance insurers must establish rates that are judged by the marketplace as being economically feasible if they are to sell their policies. This criterion means that, among other factors, rates should not be excessive in relation to the benefits provided. If the rate adequacy criterion can be considered as establishing a conceptual floor for rates, this criterion can be considered as establishing a conceptual ceiling. Many countries and U.S. states define excessiveness with respect to some health insurance policies. These jurisdictions often provide that the insurer must reasonably expect to pay or actually pay in claims at least a certain minimum percentage (e.g., 80 percent) of the premiums collected.

Prices charged for life and health insurance in the U.S. and many other countries vary from company to company and, with some companies, prices are high. Even so, competition within insurance markets worldwide is keener than in times past, thus discouraging excessive prices. Simply put, in competitive markets life insurance companies are not likely to sell much insurance if the rates they charge or their charges and credits are uncompetitive.

PRICING ELEMENTS

Life insurance pricing involves numerous factors and decisions by company actuaries, but these four pricing components are key:

- mortality charges,
- interest credits,
- loading charges to cover expenses, taxes, profits, and contingencies, and
- persistency.

These policy pricing components will be more or less important in particular policies. For example, the interest component will be less relevant for term policies, whereas the mortality component will be highly relevant. Conversely, the interest component is highly relevant to high cash value policies, such as endowments and limited payment policies, with the mortality component usually less so.

The many variations of these components are mixed by actuaries in innumerable ways to develop different versions of the same generic policy types mentioned above as well as products with special attributes, thereby rendering them more relevant to certain target markets and uses. Each variation carries different opportunities for gain (and loss) by the insurer and costs and benefits for the policyholder.

The four pricing components, whether unbundled or not, are necessary to develop policy pricing. With bundled policies, while no allocation of the premium among policy elements is ordinarily provided to the policyholder and no disclosure typically is made of the current assumptions as to mortality, interest, and expenses underlying policy dividends, the components are there. With unbundled policies, the components are more evident. Neither bundled nor unbundled policies disclose how persistency influences policy pricing and values, for reasons explained below.

Each pricing component and its variations are based on actual experience, usually from the insurer itself but sometimes from actuarial consulting firms, public sources, industry-wide data, or reinsurers. The actual results experienced by an insurer as to mortality, investment returns, expenses, taxes, and persistency are called **experience factors** by actuaries and insurance regulators. From these experience factors, actuaries derive actual mortality charges to be levied against policies, interest rates to be credited to their cash values, and loading charges to be levied, irrespective of whether they are stated this way or are disclosed.

The gross premiums for many bundled par cash value policies are calculated using the maximum mortality and loading charges and minimum guaranteed interest rates, resulting in comparatively high, conservatively set premiums, as noted earlier. Some portion of the surplus resulting from lower mortality rates, higher investment earnings, and/or lower expenses than those built into the policy's premiums and values are paid to policyholders in the form of dividends.

Participating life insurance historically has been associated closely with mutual (i.e., policyholder-owned) insurance companies and nonpar has been associated more closely with stock (i.e., stockholder-owned) insurers. In fact, most par insurance is still sold by mutuals and most nonpar by stocks, although each may sell the other form in the U.S.

MORTALITY CHARGES   That mortality is a component of life insurance pricing is self evident. It is the job of actuaries to estimate the likelihood of paying death claims under policies each year and devise an equitable means of assessing each policy for its proportionate share of these claims via mortality charges. Mortality charges are assessed on each policy's net amount at risk, irrespective of whether they are disclosed or identified as such to the policyholder; i.e., whether the policy is bundled or unbundled. The total yearly (or monthly) charge is the product of that year's (or month's) NAR in thousands and the mortality charge COI rate per $1,000 for the insured's attained age, sex, and other rating and classification factors. We can think of this charge as paying for the policy's internal YRT insurance.

In the U.S., all UL and WL unbundled policies – both variable and not – contain a set of explicitly stated, guaranteed maximum mortality charges that may not be exceeded. Bundled policies do not contain a set of explicitly stated, guaranteed maximum mortality charges, but they can be constrained to assess charges no higher than those used to derive guaranteed cash values, depending on some technical operational details of the policy. Most insurers assess mortality charges at less than the maximum permitted, with the current charge explicitly stated with unbundled products and not so stated with bundled products.

INTEREST CREDITING RATE   The interest rate credited to policy cash values is another policy element in life insurance pricing. The ultimate cost of life insurance products can be highly dependent on the insurer's investment returns, which, in turn, drive the interest rate credited on policy cash values. Insurers that earn above average returns can price products more favorably than those that do not. Insurers that earn below average returns may not be able to retain customers in a competitive market.

LOADING CHARGES   Insurers incur expenses in the marketing, underwriting, and various other processes necessary for the successful prosecution of their business. They also must pay taxes to the federal government as well as to the states in which they conduct business. Finally, they wish to accumulate surplus to allow for unforeseen contingencies and must produce an economic profit for their owners. These elements are appropriately charged against the policies to which they relate. In determining the charges for these elements, actuaries make estimates of future expenses, taxes, profits (or surplus accumulations), and contingencies to develop the set of charges defined above – called variously *loading charges, expense charges, fees,* and *policy loads* – intended to compensate the insurer for some or all of these elements.

In the U.S., unbundled policies contain a set of guaranteed maximum loading charges that the insurer may assess. Insurers may charge less than the maximum permitted. Bundled policies contain no stated guaranteed maximum charges but are constrained as to how much they can assess policies by virtue of having guaranteed gross premiums.

PERSISTENCY   **Persistency** is the percentage of life insurance policies not terminated by lapse or surrender. A **lapse** is the termination of a life insurance policy and the insurer's obligations after expiration of its grace period (see Chapter 5) for failure to pay a premium necessary to maintain it in full effect. The premium not paid may have been that required on a scheduled basis, as with fixed premium contracts, or it may have been one that was needed to ensure an adequate account value to maintain a UL policy in force. A lapse also occurs when a policyowner ceases to pay premiums and allows some insurance to remain in partial effect under one of the so-called nonforfeiture options (see Chapter 5). A **surrender** is the voluntary termination of a life insurance policy by its owner for its cash surrender value.

Persistency is the measure of an insurance company's retention of its business. In general, the higher a company's persistency, the greater is the amount of surplus funds created over time as regards properly priced policies. These surplus funds can be used to enhance policyholder benefits, insurer profits, or both.

Persistency is not a policy element as are mortality charges, interest credits, and loading charges, but is important as assets that insurers accumulate from a block of policies do not precisely equal the liabilities that arise from those policies. When the accumulated assets arising from a group of policies are allocated proportionately among those policies, we get each policy's share of assets or what is called its **asset share**. The asset share is a conceptual segmentation of the insurer's general account investments accumulated on behalf of a group of policies; it does not affect individual policies or the insurer's obligations.

If a policy is surrendered and its asset share is less than its cash surrender value, the surrender imposes a cost on the insurer, directly reducing the insurer's surplus and is termed **surplus strain.** Conversely, if the asset share is greater than the surrender value, the surrender results in a gain – termed a **surrender gain.** For example, assume that a group of identical policies was issued exactly one year ago, and an annual premium of $1,000 was paid at that time by each policyholder. Assume further that the insurer incurred $1,200 in outlays for each policy's share of death benefits and acquisition expenses of selling, underwriting, administering, and issuing the policy last year. (Expenses after the first year are substantially lower.)

Thus, the insurer had a cash inflow of $1,000 per policy and an outflow of $1,200 (ignoring interest) per policy, resulting in a $200 drain on the insurer's assets during the first year of each policy. Stated differently, each policy's first year share of assets or asset share is a deficit: -$200.

Assume now that several policyholders surrender their policies at the end of the first policy year and each is paid $300 as its surrender value. This $300 must be paid from the insurer's assets. Thus, each of these policies has imposed a cost of

$500 ($200 + $300) on the insurer or, more accurately, on persisting policyholders of the group. The greater the number of first year policy surrenders for this block of policies, the greater the costs imposed on remaining policyholders, because the asset share ends up being less than the cash value by $500.

Our simple example reflects reality more closely than the reader may suspect. It is routine that policies' first year asset shares are less than their first year surrender values, and common for the asset share to be less than the surrender value for three or more years. All policies that lapse or are surrendered before the asset share deficit is recovered impose costs on persisting policyholders as reflected in the underlying product pricing. Similarly, in later years the asset share usually exceeds the surrender value and a surrender gain will benefit persisting policyowners, the insurer, or both.

ENDNOTES

1   This chapter draws in parts from Harold D. Skipper and W. Jean Kwon, *Risk Management and Insurance: Perspectives in a Global Economy* (Malden, MA: Blackwell Publishing, 2007), Chapters 19, 20, and A6 and Harold D. Skipper and Wayne Tonning, *The Advisor's Guide to Life Insurance* (Chicago; American Bar Association, 2011), Chapters 1 and 6.

2   This section draws from Richard D. Phillips, "The Economics of Risk and Insurance: A Conceptual Discussion" in Harold D. Skipper, ed. *International Risk and Insurance: An Environmental-Managerial Approach.* Boston: Irwin/McGraw-Hill, 1998, Chapter 3.

3   This example draws from M. L. Smith and S. A. Kane, "The Law of Large Numbers and the Strength of Insurance" in Gustavson, S. G., and S. E. Harrington eds., *Insurance, Risk Management, and Public Policy: Essays in Memory of Robert I. Mehr* (Boston: MA: Kluwer Academic Press, 1994).

PERSONAL LIFE INSURANCE PRODUCTS: I

This chapter and the immediately following one examine four types of personal life insurance products. This chapter covers term life insurance and universal life insurance. Chapter 4 covers whole life insurance and endowment insurance. Each chapter follows a similar format. The nature of the product is first presented, followed by its operational details and its uses and considerations applying to its possible purchase.[1]

TERM LIFE INSURANCE

We know from Chapter 1 that life insurance products are classified into one of four categories: ordinary, industrial, group, or credit. Ordinary and industrial insurance products are commonly called *personal insurance* worldwide and are distinguished by each proposed insured having to qualify for the requested insurance by meeting an insurer's underwriting requirements. About 57 percent of the amount of life insurance in force in the U.S. falls into the personal category, and term life insurance accounts for about three-fourths of this amount. Term life insurance accounts for somewhat over 40 percent of personal life insurance in force in the U.S. when measured by number of policies.

Group insurance is underwritten on the group as a whole, as with employees of a company or the members of an association. Group life insurance accounts for about 42 percent of the amount of all life insurance in force in the U.S. Almost the entirety of group life insurance is term insurance. While this chapter's focus is on personal life insurance products, we provide an introduction to group life insurance as well.

Credit insurance guarantees payment of a mortgage or loan debt to the lender/beneficiary at the debtor's death or disability and can be bought on an individual or a group basis. Credit life accounts for less than 1.0 percent of the total amount of life insurance in force in the U.S., all of which is term life insurance.

NATURE OF TERM LIFE INSURANCE

We already know that *term life insurance* furnishes protection for a limited number of years, at the end of which the policy *expires* meaning that it terminates with no value. The face amount of the policy is payable only if the insured dies during the stipulated term, and nothing is paid in case of survival. Term policies may be issued for as short a period as one year, but customarily provide protection for a set number of years, such as 10 or 20, or to a stipulated age, such as 75 or 80.

Initial premium rates per $1,000 of coverage are lower for term life insurance than for cash value life products issued on the same basis. The typical policy provides for no meaningful prefunding of mortality and thus no cash value. Premiums for term coverage, however, can escalate rapidly as the duration of the policy lengthens.

KEY FEATURES OF TERM LIFE INSURANCE

Three features applicable to many term life policies deserve special attention before discussing specific products. These are the renewability, convertibility, and reentry features.

RENEWABILITY Most one-year and five-year term policies and many 10-year policies are *renewable*, meaning the policyowner may continue the policy for a limited number of additional periods of protection merely by paying a higher renewal premium. This renewal option allows the policyowner, at each interim term period, to continue the policy without reference to the insured's insurability at renewal time. Companies often limit the age (generally to age 75 or 80 in the U.S.) to which such term policies may be renewed.

The premium, although level for each interim period, increases with each renewal and is based on the insured's attained age at renewal time. A scale of guaranteed future premium rates is contained in the contract, although some policies have **indeterminate premiums** that allow the company to charge rates lower than those guaranteed in the policy. From the policyowner's perspective, the term *renewability* means simply that the policy can be continued to the stipulated policy expiry age by paying the billed premium. Renewable term policies are increasing premium term life insurance.

As the premium rate increases with each renewal, mortality experience increasingly reflects adverse selection. Resistance to the higher premiums coupled with possibly lower cost product opportunities incent some insureds in good health to discontinue their policies in favor of new ones, whereas those in poor health tend to renew even in the face of higher premiums. Insurers try to accommodate this adverse selection problem through their pricing structure or other means, such as altering dividends, limiting renewability to stipulated maximum ages, use of reentry features (see below), or designing products that encourage (or require) conversion.

CONVERTIBILITY Most term insurance policies include a **conversion feature** that affords the policyowner the option to exchange the term policy for a cash value insurance contract, without evidence of insurability. The period during which conversion is permitted often is shorter than the maximum duration of the policy.

The conversion privilege increases the flexibility of term life insurance. For example, at the time a term policy was purchased, a policyowner may have preferred a cash value policy but, because of budget considerations, decided on low premium term coverage. After issuance, circumstances may have changed enabling the policyowner to purchase an adequate amount of cash value insurance.

The conversion feature permits the policyowner to exchange the term contract for a cash value policy that is more compatible with his or her present goals.

A significant percentage of insureds become uninsurable or insurable only at higher than standard rates. Under such circumstances, an expiring term policy may fail to protect the insured in the desired manner as the insured may not qualify for a new insurance policy or qualify only at a higher-than-standard rate. If the policy contains a conversion option, and if the time limit for making an exchange of the policy has not expired, the exercise of this option can be to the insured's advantage and thus protect against the possibility that no insurance would be in force on death. As with any option, its value stems from the holder's ability to exercise it on conditions most favorable to him or her. Insurers can be expected to embed the option price within the policy premium accordingly.

If the insured is insurable at standard rates, there may be no direct financial advantage to exercising the conversion privilege compared to reentering the marketplace and shopping carefully, although avoidance of the time and hassle of doing so has value. In effect, the value of the option is zero, because the option exercise (strike) price is no lower than the market (spot) price. Some insurers, however, offer a type of credit toward payment of the new policy's first year premium to encourage conversion. Conversion may be permitted on an attained age or original age basis. Box 3-1 discusses these bases.

Box 3-1
Attained-Age versus Original-Age Conversion

The **attained-age method** of conversion involves the issuance of a cash value policy of a form currently being issued by the insurer at a premium rate based on the insured's attained age on the date of conversion and is the rate the company offers to new insureds who qualify for standard rates at that time.

The **original-age method**, usually unavailable for universal life policy conversions and increasingly so for other cash value policies, involves a retroactive conversion, with the whole life or other cash value policy bearing the date and premium rate that would have been paid had the cash value policy been taken out originally in place of the term policy. Companies offering this option require that retroactive conversion take place within five years and many within six months of the issue date of the term contract. The policyowner is required to pay the difference between (1) the premiums (net of dividends or other credits) that would have been paid on the new policy had it been issued at the same time as the original policy and (2) the premiums actually paid for the term policy, with interest on the difference at a stipulated annual rate (e.g., 6.0 or 8.0 percent).

It has been said that the policyowner, in making a choice between the two bases of conversion, might prefer an original age conversion because he or she could obtain a lower premium rate and possibly more liberal contract provisions. However, with the trend toward lower premiums and better-valued products, it is far from clear whether either potential benefit would necessarily materialize. Even if the premium rate for the original age conversion were less than the rate for current issues, the wisdom of making an original age conversion could be doubtful because of the required payment of the difference in back premiums plus interest.

REENTRY Some insurers include a **reentry** feature in their term policies that allows policyholders to pay lower premiums than the guaranteed renewal premium if insureds can demonstrate that they meet continuing insurability criteria.

To understand the mechanics of reentry term, we must first understand the three types of mortality tables used by insurers:

1. **Select mortality tables** – show probabilities of death by age, sex, and duration of insurance for newly insured lives only. Other things being the same, these insureds exhibit lower death rates than others of the same age and sex, since they must have been in good health and otherwise insurable to qualify initially. The select period or benefit of selection usually lasts from 5 to 25 years.

2. **Ultimate mortality tables** – show probabilities of death by age and sex of insureds after the select period. The benefit of selection has faded from the mortality experience of the ultimate group. Thus, a select table represents very favorable initial experience, whereas an ultimate table excludes this experience and, therefore, exhibits higher average mortality rates, other things being the same.

3. **Aggregate mortality tables** – show probabilities of death by age and sex of insureds by combining both select and ultimate mortality. Mortality experience under this table falls between that of the select and ultimate tables.

Traditional term premiums are usually based on *aggregate* mortality experience. Reentry term premiums are based on a *select/ultimate* mortality split. This pricing results in a scale of premium rates that varies not only by age but also by the duration since the insured last demonstrated insurability. Figure 3-1 illustrates how an insurer might price a term policy with a reentry feature.

Knowing these results, the insurer can charge each group premiums that track their expected mortality rates. Thus, the insurer could be charging six otherwise similarly situated insureds a different premium, based on when they were first insured, for the same coverage under the same policy form. The 34-year-old woman who just purchased a term policy using reentry pricing would pay the lowest rate; another woman, at age 34, who purchased the same policy type the year before (at age 33 and now age 34) would pay a somewhat higher rate; a third woman, who purchased her policy two years ago (at age 32 and who is now 34), would be paying a still higher rate; and so on, depending on the duration of the select mortality table used as the basis for the rates. Even though each insured would now be aged 34, the select/ultimate dichotomy leads to a premium schedule that permits the person most recently insured to pay the lowest rate.

Such policies are referred to as *reentry* term because insureds may be able to reenter the select group periodically – in our example, once every five years – if the insured resubmits to the insurer evidence of satisfactory insurability. Thus, at the end of five years, insureds who can demonstrate continued insurability would be able to enjoy the much lower premium rates based on first year select mortality for their attained age.

For those insureds who fail to take advantage of the reentry provision or who fail to qualify for reentry because of insurability problems, ultimate rates are charged thereafter. These ultimate premiums are higher than the select premiums and usually considerably higher than traditional aggregate term rates as well. A person who cannot qualify for select rates usually will be unable to qualify for a new policy based on aggregate rates and, therefore, must pay the higher ultimate

Ultimate and Select Mortality Curves for a Term Product with a Reentry Feature

Figure 3-1

Insurer uses a five year select period. Its expected ultimate mortality experience for ages 30 to 40 is shown graphically in panel (a). The expected mortality rate is 1.35 deaths per 1,000 insured lives at age 30 and who have been insured for more than five years. The mortality rate for insureds at age 35 and who have been insured for more than five years is expected to be 1.65; and the age 40 expected mortality rate is 2.42.

Superimposed on panel (a) are the expected select mortality rates for newly insured lives at age 30. Their expected first year (i.e., age 30) mortality rate is 0.6 deaths per 1,000 insured lives. This rate is considerably lower than the rate that the insurer expects from those insureds who have been insured for more than five years but who are also at age 30.

The second year select mortality rate is 0.75 (versus the ultimate rate of 1.4), the third year select mortality rate is 0.9 (versus 1.45), the fourth year rate is 1.1, and the fifth year rate is 1.35 (versus an ultimate rate of 1.58). As from the sixth policy year, mortality rates for the two groups of insureds are expected to be identical.

Panel (b) superimposes on panel (a) the expected select mortality rates for new insureds at age 31. Their expected first year (i.e., age 31) mortality rate is shown as 0.65 deaths per 1,000 insured lives. Note that this rate is somewhat lower than the expected rate for those insured a year earlier who are at age 31 (i.e., who are exhibiting second year select mortality). The same relative relationship holds throughout the five year select period of this group of insureds, with their mortality rates grading into the ultimate curve at the end of their five year select period.

Finally, panel (c) superimposes on panel (b) the expected select mortality rates for new insureds at ages 32, 33, and 34, illustrating the expected mortality progression for each of these insured cohorts relative to the earlier groups. It can be seen at any given age that the insurer expects insured cohorts to exhibit as many different sets of mortality rates as there are years in the select period plus one for the ultimate mortality. At age 34, for example, the insurer expects six different sets of mortality experience. We anticipate those newly insured at age 34 to exhibit the lowest mortality. Those who are at age 34 but were insured a year earlier are expected to exhibit the next most favorable mortality, and so on.

Figure 3-1(a): Ultimate and 5-Year Select Mortality Curves

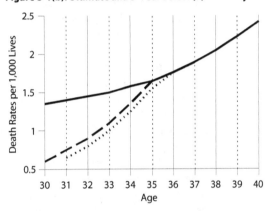

Figure 3-1(b): Ultimate and 5-Year Select (2) Mortality Curves

Figure 3-1(c): Ultimate and 5-Year Select (5) Mortality Curves

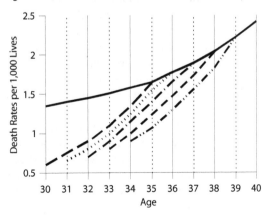

rates if he or she wishes to continue insurance coverage. The reentry feature, in effect, encourages insureds to self-declare their expected future mortality status, thus making for more refined risk classification.

TYPES OF TERM LIFE INSURANCE

Term life insurance provides a death benefit that either remains level, decreases, or increases over time. The great majority of personal and group term life insurance in the U.S. provides a level death benefit. Most credit life insurance provides a decreasing death benefit. Our discussion below centers on personal and group term insurance. We omit credit life because of its comparatively small presence in the U.S. and other markets.

PERSONAL TERM LIFE POLICIES   Some 99 percent of personal term life insurance sold in the U.S. provides a level death benefit over the policy period. Most policies in the remaining share provide a decreasing death benefit.

Policies that Provide a Level Death Benefit   We know that term policies with increasing premiums are commonly referred to as contracts that are *renewable*, a term that is synonymous with increasing premium. Thus, we find term policies whose premiums increase yearly – called *yearly renewable term* (YRT), *annual renewable term* (ART), or simply *increasing premium term*. Other term policy premiums increase every three, five, or ten years – called *three-year renewable term, five-year renewable term,* and *ten-year renewable term.* Whatever the renewal period, premiums increase at each renewal, more or less tracking the increase in mortality rates for the insured's attained age or an average of future such rates over the next term period. YRT policies were quite popular in the U.S., but less so in recent times as insurers have sought ways of minimizing the commodity aspect of term, with its low profitability. Ten-year renewable policies have become quite popular.

Traditionally, term policies expired not later than age 65, and this situation remains with some companies. Increasingly, however, we find term policies that extend coverage beyond this traditional cutoff age, to age 85 or higher. For example, one well known insurer's term-to-age-90 policy provides coverage to age 90, with level premiums for the first 10 years and YRT thereafter.

Renewable term product design has been toward (1) lower rates, (2) a greater number of rate bands (e.g., different rates at $100,000, $500,000, and $1 million death benefit bands), and (3) differentiated pricing categories. Differential pricing is accomplished in several ways. Some companies utilize reentry pricing, although this has become less common in the U.S. Almost all insurers use separate smoker/nonsmoker rates. Premium differences between smokers and nonsmokers can be substantial. Table 3-1 shows smoker and nonsmoker premiums for several companies' 10-year level-premium $1.0 million term policies.

Premiums for most term policies are fixed and guaranteed at policy issuance. Some term policies pay dividends but most do not. Additionally, some term policies provide that the insurer can unilaterally change premiums from time to time; i.e., they have indeterminate premiums based on changing insurer operational experience, subject always to the guaranteed maximum premiums set out in the contract.

Table 3-1

**Selected Companies' 10-Year Term Premiums
for Smokers and Nonsmokers, $1.0 Million**

	Premiums for:	
	Smoker	Nonsmoker
Company A	$1,675	$495
Company B	1,698	518
Company C	1,738	568
Company D	1,890	570

Other term policies have the same premiums each year. Such term contracts may be written for a set number of years or to cover the typical working lifetime. Contracts of the first type include *10-year* and *20-year term* policies that sometimes can be renewed for another term, or they become YRT thereafter. Contracts of the second type provide essentially the same protection but are not renewable include *life-expectancy term* and *term-to-age 65* (or to other ages), although comparatively few of these policies are sold today in the U.S.

Finally, while this chapter is concerned primarily with term policies, level death benefit term riders are also available to supplement the death benefit of a permanent policy. **Riders** provide additional benefits and features within a policy and usually are optional with the policyholder for an additional premium. These are discussed in Chapter 5.

Policies that Provide a Non-level Death Benefit   A comparatively minor amount of term life insurance sold in the U.S. and elsewhere involves policies whose face amounts decrease or increase with time. Decreasing term policies are commonly used to pay off a loan balance on the death of the debtor/insured in connection with a mortgage loan or a business or personal loan. Thus, **mortgage protection term** policies provide for face amount decreases that match the projected decreases in the principal amount owed under a mortgage loan. As the larger proportion of each early mortgage loan payment is applied to pay interest, the initial decrease in the mortgage loan's outstanding balance is slight, with later declines being substantial, as Figure 3-2 illustrates for a 30-year mortgage protection policy. Such policies' death benefits track this pattern and are available to cover a variety of mortgage loan durations (e.g., 10, 15, 20, 25, or 30 years) and amortization schedules. They usually provide for a conversion right. Level premiums are sometimes payable for a somewhat shorter period than the policy duration.

A type of decreasing term, called **payor benefit** and available as a rider to a policy insuring the life of a juvenile, pays a death benefit on the death of the premium payor (usually a parent) prior to the child's attaining a certain age, usually 21. The decreasing death benefit on the payor's life is exactly sufficient to pay all premiums that would be due from the payor's death until the insured's age 21. The benefit is designed to ensure that premiums due on the policy will be paid even if the premium payor dies (or becomes disabled).

Another type of decreasing term life insurance, the **family income policy** or **rider** is decreasing term that pays a death benefit to the beneficiary (usually the surviving spouse) as a monthly income until the beneficiary attains a certain age, or for a set period of from 10 to 20 years from the date of policy issuance. This policy or rider is often sold to protect the family during the childrearing years. Of course, if the insured lives beyond the specified age or beyond the set number of years from issue, no further coverage is provided by this benefit.

| Figure 3-2 | **Illustration of a Mortgage Protection (Term) Policy (per $1,000 Face Amount)** |

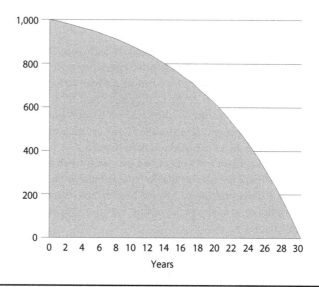

Increasing term insurance is also sold, but virtually never as a separate policy. Insurers offer increasing term coverage as a **cost-of-living-adjustment** (COLA) rider that provides automatic increases in a policy's death benefit in accordance with increases in inflation, as measured by a national cost-of-living index, such as the *Consumer Price Index* (CPI) in the U.S. The policyowner is billed with the regular premium notice for the additional coverage. No evidence of insurability is required for these annual increases provided the rider remains in force and is exercised fully each year. This requirement minimizes adverse selection. The amount purchased in the previous year is carried forward to the current year. Declines in the price index ordinarily do not result in declines in amounts purchased.

Another type of increasing term insurance is provided by a so-called **return-of-premium feature** (or rider) providing that, if the insured dies within a set number of years (e.g., 20 years) from the policy issue date, the death benefit will be augmented by an amount equal to the sum of all premiums paid to that point. Of course, the insurance company does not actually return the premiums paid and, in this sense, the feature's name can cause misunderstanding. Rather, the benefit is increasing term insurance whose annual death benefit is set to equal exactly the sum of the premiums paid to that year. The feature can be useful in certain business situations (see Chapter 24), but it is also sometimes included to gain market power by differentiating the underlying policy from other similar contracts (thus complicating comparisons) and to make the proposed policy seem more attractive to a prospect.

A recent and popular introduction to the term market is the **return of premium** (ROP) **term policy**, also sold as a rider to a base policy. Unlike the return of premium death benefit discussed above, this policy promises to pay an amount equal to the sum of premiums paid for the policy if the insured survives to a certain period, which may be from 10 to 30 years, depending on the insured's age and insurer's requirements. Of course, the insurer does not actually return the premiums. Rather, the policy provides for modest cash values such that the guaranteed cash value at the set policy duration equals the sum of premiums paid to that point. The policyowner can terminate the policy at that time and receive the "return of premiums" (cash surrender value) or allow the cash value to remain with the policy and effectively convert it to an increasing premium whole life policy that continues to build cash values to age 95 or later. If the policy is terminated prior to the set duration but after a specified number of years, such as six, surrender values are available, often in an amount equal to some multiple of the premiums paid to that point.

Premiums for the policy or rider are some 30 to 80 percent higher than premiums for comparable term policies without the feature. For example, one insurer's regular 30-year level premium term policy for $1.0 million carries an annual premium of $1,178. Its $1.0 million ROP policy issued on the same basis carries an annual premium of $2,570. The annual premium difference of $1,392 effectively provides for the cash value buildup; i.e., the "return of premium" feature, which would equal $77,100 ($2,570 x 30) payable in 30 years if the insured survives to that point. If the insured dies before 30 years, the $1.0 million face amount is paid.

Group Term Life Policies   Most group life insurance is provided as yearly renewable term insurance – the same generic insurance provided through individual policies. As in the case of individual coverage, the cost of the death benefit for each individual increases at an increasing rate from year to year. The employee may be unaware of this fact, however, because of the effect of using an average rate for the entire group. Some cash value life insurance is offered through the group mechanism, with most relating to post-retirement group coverage.

Group insurance programs are either contributory or noncontributory. A **contributory plan** is one in which both the employer and employees make contributions toward the plan's premiums. A **noncontributory plan** is one in which only the employer makes contributions toward plan costs.

Individual Eligibility Requirements   In general, only regular, active, full-time employees are eligible for group life (and health) insurance. All such employees or all such employees in certain classes determined by conditions pertaining to their employment (e.g., "all salaried employees" or "all hourly paid employees") must be included in the eligible group.

Another individual eligibility requirement is that an employee must be actively at work and must work no fewer than the normal number of hours in a work week at his or her job on the date when he or she becomes eligible for coverage. The requirement assures a reasonable minimum of health and physical well-being and protects the insurer against serious adverse selection.

A waiting period often is applied to new employees. This **probationary period** is the period of time (usually one to six months) after being hired that a new employee becomes eligible to participate in an employee benefit plan. The probationary period minimizes administrative expenses involved in setting up records for employees who remain with the employer for a short period. After completion of the probationary period, under a noncontributory plan, the employee automatically is covered. Under a contributory plan, the employee is given a period of time, known as the **eligibility period**, during which he or she is entitled to apply for insurance without submitting evidence of insurability. This period is limited, usually to 31 days, to minimize adverse selection. For the same reason, it is customary to require evidence of insurability from employees who have discontinued their coverage and desire to rejoin the plan. If the plan is written on a noncontributory basis, these rules do not apply, as all employees (or all employees within the designated classes) automatically are covered unless they specifically decline coverage.

Duration of Coverage   Once insurance becomes effective for a particular employee, the protection continues for as long as he or she remains in the service of the employer (assuming, of course, that the employer maintains the plan in force and the employee continues to pay contributory premiums required). The master contract usually gives the employer the right to continue premium payments for employees who are temporarily off the job provided that the employer does so on a basis that precludes individual selection. Upon permanent termination of service, the employee's coverage continues for 31 days beyond the date of termination. This extension of coverage gives the employee an opportunity to replace the expiring protection with individual insurance, to obtain employment with another firm with group insurance, or to convert the expiring term insurance to a cash value form of insurance. Many plans continue some coverage after retirement providing at least enough life insurance to cover the employee's last illness and funeral expenses.

Approaches to Benefit Amounts   Three approaches are common in determining the amount of coverage:

- *Compensation.* Most group life plans base the amount of insurance on a multiple of the employee's earnings. Multiples of 1, 1½, or 2 times earnings are common. The trend is to higher multiples.
- *Fixed Amount.* A fixed-amount benefit plan places all employees in the same category. This type of benefit is used principally in conjunction with union welfare funds.
- *Position.* The coverage amount may be set according to the position held by the employee. Thus, officers, superintendents, and managers may receive $50,000 each; foremen and salespersons $30,000 each; and all other employees $20,000 each.

Conversion Privilege   An insured employee has the option of converting his or her group life insurance protection to an individual cash value policy under certain conditions. Normally, the employee may convert within 31 days after termination of employment or cessation of membership in an eligible classification. The most significant potential advantage to the employee of the conversion feature lies in the fact that no evidence of insurability is required – in other words, the privilege constitutes an option that is an invitation to adverse selection. The death benefit provided under a group life insurance contract is continued during the conversion period.

USES AND CONSIDERATIONS OF TERM LIFE INSURANCE

Term life insurance has long been the subject of debate. Some advocate the use of term insurance to the virtual exclusion of cash value insurance, with others advocating the opposite viewpoint. Neither extreme position is tenable.

Term insurance can be useful for persons with modest incomes and high insurance needs, a common family situation. Risk management principles suggest that the family unit should be protected against catastrophic losses. If current family income does not permit the option of purchasing cash value life insurance in adequate amounts, the individual arguably should purchase term, if adequate financial protection is to be provided.

Those who have a career to establish and have temporarily limited income arguably should use their resources primarily to establish their careers and, therefore, opt for term insurance in preference to cash value insurance. Investment in oneself for self improvement, especially during the early career development years, should have high priority.

Term life insurance can also prove useful for persons who have placed substantially all of their resources in a new business that is still in its formative stages. In such instances, death could result in loss of the invested capital. New enterprises are particularly speculative and become stable only with time. Term insurance can also be appropriate to use as a hedge against a financial loss already sustained, when some time is required to recoup the loss.

Life insurance may also be needed to indemnify a business on the death of one or more employees whose contributions to the firm have been critical to its success. Also, owners of closely held businesses may wish to establish pre-death arrangements to ensure that their business interests will be sold at a fair price at their death so as to provide family liquidity. While cash value policies are usually sold in each of these situations, term life insurance also can meet the need, especially if funds available to pay premiums are inadequate to allow purchase of a sufficiently large cash value policy.

Term life insurance is naturally suited for ensuring that mortgage and other loans are paid on the debtor/insured's death and as a vehicle for ensuring that education or other needs are funded if death cuts planned savings short. Term insurance is a natural vehicle for any other situation that calls for temporary income protection.

Term insurance can also be the basis for a permanent insurance program through a so-called **buy-term-and-invest-the-difference** (BTID) strategy, under which an individual who has sufficient funds to purchase cash value life insurance instead purchases a lower-premium term policy and separately invests the difference between the two policies' premiums. The difference between the higher premium cash value policy and the lower premium term policy is invested separately in a mutual fund, savings account, annuity, or other investment media. The expectation is that the term policy plus separate investment will outperform the cash value life insurance policy.

Such programs can succeed if well conceived and well executed. A well-conceived program is one that recognizes the increasing premium nature of most term policies and devises a plan either to accommodate these increasing premiums or to minimize their impact (e.g., by planning for reducing insurance needs over time). A well-conceived program realistically assesses the policyowner's willingness, ability, and commitment to follow through with the plan. A well-executed program is one that includes high quality, reasonably priced coverage that provides the capability of adapting to changing circumstances. Similar care is needed with respect to the outside investment media.

Success requires the faithful execution – usually on an annual basis – of the BTID program. Thus, if the individual fails to set aside the planned amounts regularly, the program could be judged to have failed. Indeed, many observers suggest this possible failure to be a major practical detraction to BTID programs. Nonetheless, some insurers' and many agents' marketing efforts are oriented in this direction.

Term product prices are more easily compared than are prices of other life products, as term policies are usually structurally simpler than other policies. As a consequence, buyers suffer fewer information problems with term insurance, thus rendering the term market more price competitive than the market for cash value policies. Term products usually have no cash values or dividends, thus permitting policy comparisons on the basis of premiums.

UNIVERSAL LIFE INSURANCE

As we know, universal life (UL) policies are unbundled policies with premium flexibility and death benefit adjustability. As discussed in Chapter 2, all cash value policies are a combination of term insurance and a savings element. Because UL policies are transparent and unbundled in their operation, the resemblance to BTID is more apparent than with other forms of cash value life insurance. Their introduction in the late 1970s and early 1980s in North America surprisingly caused great debates and perhaps more news media attention than any life insurance policy introduced in the 20th century.

ORIGINS AND GROWTH

The concepts upon which UL is based are as old as the concepts underlying level premium payments and reserves; well over 100 years old. A key element – the use of the retrospective approach to cash value (and reserve) development – is analyzed and discussed, for example, in Spurgeon's 1922 authoritative book, *Life Contingencies*, long the standard for the study of this subject by North American actuarial students. Jordan's 1952 and 1957 editions of *Life Contingencies* continued the analysis.

The idea of UL as a product was mentioned by H.L. Riedner in 1946 and by Alfred N. Guertin in 1964. Ken E. Polk's 1974 article along with the accompanying discussion papers provided virtually all of the formulae needed for developing a workable UL policy. Polk referred to his hypothetical policy as variable premium life insurance.

It seems, however, that principal credit for conceiving of UL as a product goes to George R. Dinney of the *Great-West Life and Annuity Insurance Company*, a Canadian insurer. He appears to have conceived of the idea as early as 1962, although a written description of the product, which he dubbed *universal life plan*, apparently was made public only in 1971.

James C.H. Anderson, then president of what is now the actuarial consulting division of Towers-Watson, probably did more than anyone to publicize UL as a viable product and to stimulate serious thinking about the possible need and wisdom for developing such a product. His seminal paper, "The Universal Life Insurance Policy," presented at the *Seventh Pacific Insurance Conference* in 1975, is considered by many to be the most important step along the road to UL. Embedded in the UL concept as articulated by Anderson and others was a much lower agent commission schedule than those found with traditional life products, thus rendering policies more cost effective and easier to sell.

In 1976 one insurer, *American Agency Life*, in fact developed and sold a UL policy of the type described in Anderson's paper. Because of adverse taxation, the company soon discontinued sales. UL in its current form was not introduced and sold widely until its introduction by the *Life Insurance Company of California* in 1979. (Life of California and its successor incarnations were purchased by other financial groups, with the final entity being merged into *Pacific Mutual Life Insurance Company* in 1992.)

The UL concept was at first not welcomed by most persons in the North American life insurance business. It was perceived as a threat to the orderly development of the industry and not in consumers' or agents' best interests. Today, UL is considered simply as another life product.

NATURE OF UNIVERSAL LIFE INSURANCE

UL policies offer flexibility in premium payments and adjustability of death benefits. After deciding on the policy death benefit and pattern (see below), the applicant pays a certain minimum premium to get the policy issued. Thereafter, the policyowner pays as little or as much as he or she wishes into the policy, subject to insurer and tax prescribed maximums. The higher the premium paid, the greater is the cash value, other things being equal. The policy remains in force for as long as the cash value is positive, and the policy terminates (lapses) if the cash value goes to zero and no premium is paid within the policy grace period. Policyowners may increase (usually subject to evidence of insurability) or decrease their policies' death benefits (usually subject to tax considerations) as they deem appropriate.

UL policies are transparent in their operation, as noted in Chapter 2. The policyowner is able to see how funds are allocated to the various policy elements. An illustration usually is provided to prospective purchasers describing how these elements – premiums, death benefits, interest credits, mortality and other charges, cash values – interact and evolve over time. Each year the policyowner receives similar but abbreviated information in an annual report that details the actual policy cash flows over the previous policy year. Transparency does not mean that the policyowner can necessarily evaluate the adequacy of projected values; it means only that the policyowner will be able to see the disposition made of policy cash flows.

OPERATIONAL DETAILS OF UNIVERSAL LIFE INSURANCE

Figure 3-3 illustrates the operation of a typical UL policy. It shows the cash value, commonly called the *account value*, at the end of each of the first three months and at any month n in the future and the reconciliation of each month's cash flow. Thus, at policy purchase, the owner pays at least the minimum premium required to put the policy in effect. Thereafter, the owner may pay whatever premium he or she wishes – represented in the figure with a dashed line around the premium box. Perhaps most policyholders choose to pay a fixed amount monthly or annually. A premium or front-end load – typically expressed as a percentage of the premium paid, for example 10 percent – is subtracted from any premium paid. A load of 10 percent results in 90 percent of the premium being available to meet other charges and grow the account value.

Figure 3-3   Universal Life Funds Flow Illustration

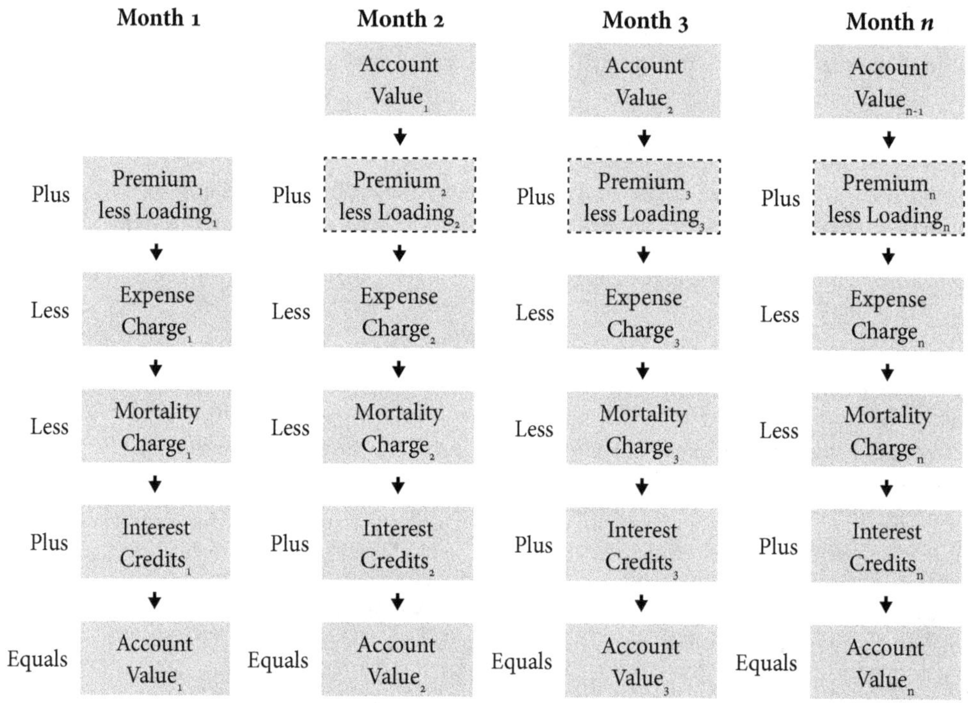

	Month 1		Month 2		Month 3		Month n
			Account Value$_1$		Account Value$_2$		Account Value$_{n-1}$
Plus	Premium$_1$ less Loading$_1$	Plus	Premium$_2$ less Loading$_2$	Plus	Premium$_3$ less Loading$_3$	Plus	Premium$_n$ less Loading$_n$
Less	Expense Charge$_1$	Less	Expense Charge$_2$	Less	Expense Charge$_3$	Less	Expense Charge$_n$
Less	Mortality Charge$_1$	Less	Mortality Charge$_2$	Less	Mortality Charge$_3$	Less	Mortality Charge$_n$
Plus	Interest Credits$_1$	Plus	Interest Credits$_2$	Plus	Interest Credits$_3$	Plus	Interest Credits$_n$
Equals	Account Value$_1$	Equals	Account Value$_2$	Equals	Account Value$_3$	Equals	Account Value$_n$

Expense charges, more commonly called **administrative fees,** are assessed periodically against an unbundled policy's account value, stated as a flat dollar amount such as $10, a charge per $1,000 of death benefit such as $0.10, and/ or sometimes as a percentage of the account value. Thus, at $0.10 per $1,000, a $1 million policy would be assessed $100 per month plus perhaps a flat $10.

The mortality or cost of insurance (COI) charge is also assessed monthly, based on the policy's net amount at risk (NAR). The NAR equals the total death benefit less the account value. Thus, if the COI charge is $0.35 per $1,000 of NAR for the month, a $1 million policy whose account value was $400,000 would be assessed $210 [($1,000,000 – $400,000) x $0.35/$1,000] for the policy's share of that month's death claims.

The monthly interest credit is the interest crediting rate applied to the account value on a daily basis, after other charges have been deducted. If the interest crediting rate is 5.0 percent per year, it would translate into a monthly rate of 0.407 percent. Thus, our $1 million UL policy whose end-of-month account value is $399,680 ($400,000 – $10 – $100 – $210) would receive an interest credit for the month of $1,627 ($399,680 x 0.00407), for an end-of-month cash (account) value of $401,307 ($399,680 + $1,627).

This process is repeated on a monthly basis using current assumptions, subject to the guaranteed maximum permitted expense and COI charges and minimum interest crediting rates. The same process applies to all UL and current assumption policies. If, at any time during the policy's existence, the cash value is insufficient to cover monthly mortality and other charges, the policy lapses unless additional funding is provided within a specified grace period, which typically is 31 or 61 days.

KEY FEATURES OF UNIVERSAL LIFE INSURANCE

Numerous UL product design variations exist. Here we present what we refer to as a generic UL product design. Variations of the generic design are presented later in this chapter.

DEATH BENEFIT PATTERN AND CHANGES   Universal life policies typically offer two optional death benefit patterns. In the absence of a change request, the selected pattern will be followed during the policy term. Under the first pattern, commonly called *Option A (or 1)*, the death benefit remains level. The net amount at risk decreases as the account value increases (and vice versa). The second pattern, commonly called *Option B (or 2)*, provides a level NAR, so that the death benefit equals what is sometimes called the *face amount* in UL parlance (which is the same as the death benefit in Option A) plus an additional death benefit equal to the account value.

Some policies also offer an *Option C (or 3)* in which the death benefit equals the face amount plus an additional amount equal to the sum of premiums paid. With Option C, the NAR is the difference between (1) the combination of the two death benefits and (2) the account value. The NAR will increase in years when the premiums paid are greater than that year's increase in account value and will decrease when the opposite result obtains. Other things being the same, COI charges will be higher under Options B and C than under Option A, which is logical as Options B and C are purchasing more insurance. Figure 3-4 illustrates the first two death benefit patterns.

Usually, the policyholder may change the death benefit option after policy issuance. If the change would result in an increase in future NARs, as for example would occur in moving from Option A to Option B, the insurance company usually will require satisfactory evidence of insurability.

As already emphasized, a UL policy's death benefit is adjustable – the policyholder may request that it be reduced or increased at any time. Underwriting is required for unscheduled face amount increases. Some insurers offer a guaranteed purchase rider (see Chapter 5) that provides an option for limited increases, and other policies provide for automatic, scheduled face amount increases, both without evidence of insurability. Unscheduled face amount decreases are always allowed but are constrained by the IRC definition of life insurance (see Chapter 21) and may be restricted by policy minimums.

Figure 3-4   **The Two Generic Universal Life Death Benefit Patterns**

Option A: Level Death Benefit

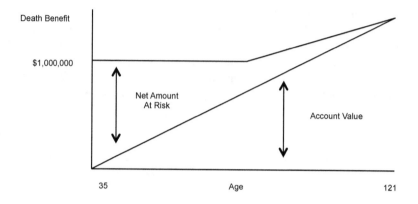

Option B: Level Net Amount at Risk

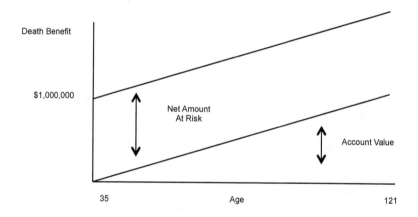

Option A and Option B illustrate that the cash value increases over time. It can be seen that, with Option A, the NAR decreases, whereas with Option B, it remains at a constant level. The NAR increases shown with Option A occur to ensure that the policy remains tax qualified.

GUARANTEED AND NONGUARANTEED POLICY ELEMENTS   UL contracts contain guaranteed maximum COI and loading charges, but insurers commonly charge less than the maximums permitted. For UL policies issued in recent years, COI rates may not exceed those derived from the *2001 CSO Mortality Table* (see Chapter 15). Minimum guaranteed interest crediting rates are also set out in the UL contract, but insurers routinely credit higher rates. Typical minimums are in the 2.0 to 4.0 percent range, with older policies sometimes having higher minimums.

UL cash surrender values must be at least as high as those mandated by state non-forfeiture laws (see Chapter 16).

Typically, loading charges in the early policy years are insufficient to cover the insurer's actual expenses, taxes, and desired profits. Insurers take one or both of two design approaches to recover these early net cash outflows not explicitly included in the loadings. First, as we know, UL policies often carry back-end loads, also called *surrender charges*, which ordinarily are a decreasing graded penalty applied against the cash value if the policy is surrendered within the first years (such as ten) of issue. Second, insurers usually build margins into the COI charges and interest credits that provide excess renewal year funds to recoup early-year losses.

As with all cash value policies, UL policies may be surrendered for their cash surrender values, which equals their account value less any surrender charges. The value received on surrender would be further reduced by any policy loans outstanding, for they must be repaid on policy surrender, thus yielding a policy's net cash surrender value. As explained more fully in Chapter 5, the right to borrow funds from the insurance company for an amount up to and secured only by a policy's cash value is a feature of all cash value policies.

In addition to accessing policy value via loans, UL policyholders also may make withdrawals from the account value at any time. Withdrawals reduce the account value, and thereby interest credits, as well as the policy face amount dollar for dollar. The NAR remains unchanged. The insurer may limit the number of withdrawals per year, such as to four, and may assess a modest fee for each withdrawal, such as $25.

More recently, specialized versions of UL have emerged. **Death benefit UL,** also called **protection UL,** products emphasize policies' death benefits and low premiums per $1,000 of face amount but typically offer low cash value accumulation and/or have heavy surrender charges. **Accumulation UL** products emphasize efficient cash value accumulation but are designed for higher premiums per $1,000 of face amount.

Many companies permit policyowners to attach cost of living riders and future purchase options to their UL policies. Chapter 5 discusses the operation of these features.

UL policyowners pay premiums of whatever amount and whenever they desire, subject to company rules regarding minimums and maximums. One of the potential disadvantages of UL is that policyowners might too easily allow their policies to lapse, as there are no required premiums. To overcome this concern, at least partially, companies often recommend that owners pay a regular **planned premium,** which is an amount set by the policyholder to be paid at regular intervals. At the agent's recommendation, the planned premium often equals the **target premium,** which is the maximum premium for which the agent can receive the standard commission rate and often is considered by the insurer to be an adequate "target" for funding the policy. Premiums amounts paid in excess of the target premium are commissioned at a lower rate. Thus, the agent is incented to recommend a payment of at least the target amount.

Because of policyowner concern about a possible lack of information and the uncertainty of future performance, many companies have introduced a guarantee that the policy will not lapse either for a stipulated period of time, commonly called a **guaranteed minimum death benefit** rider, or for life, commonly called a **no lapse guarantee** (NLG), provided at least a stipulated premium is paid, called the **minimum continuation premium.** If it is paid, the contract will remain in force with no (or even with negative) cash value. We discuss the NLG as a UL policy variation below.

USES AND CONSIDERATIONS OF UNIVERSAL LIFE INSURANCE

In thinking about how UL can fit into a financial plan, it is sometimes suggested that one think of UL not as a generic type of life insurance but as a flexible platform or shell that allows it to become whatever generic type of life insurance the customer wishes. As the policyholder, not the insurer, determines the magnitude of premium payments, the policyholder thereby determines the size and rate of the cash value buildup and so the policy's generic type. In fact, a UL policy *will* turn out to provide term life insurance, whole life insurance, or endowment insurance, depending on the premiums paid and other policy factors. The policyholder's actions determine the type prospectively, but this too can change with time. Because of this premium flexibility, policyholders can effectively design their own policies to reflect their own needs and changing financial circumstances.

For example, perhaps the initial premium paid is just sufficient with interest to meet all policy loads and COI charges for the balance of the year, so no further premiums are required during the year. The account value at year's end would be zero, based on current assumptions. The following year, a second premium is paid, again just sufficient to carry the policy through that year with no residual value at year's end, and so on each year thereafter. In this instance, the UL policy effectively provides YRT insurance (admittedly not usually a wise means of purchasing YRT insurance because of UL policy loadings being higher than YRT loadings). It builds no cash value – except for perhaps minor amounts during each policy year – and each year's premium payment must increase to cover each year's higher COI (YRT) rates.

Similarly, one can solve for the level annual premium that, if paid for 20 years, would maintain the policy in force for exactly 20 years, in which case the UL policy would be providing 20-year level premium term insurance. Theoretically, term insurance coverage for any duration and any premium payment pattern can be arranged. (Of course, the solution would be precisely correct only if future nonguaranteed policy elements were precisely as illustrated – an unlikely outcome.)

Consider the other extreme: a very large premium is paid at policy inception, such that future guaranteed interest credits alone would be sufficient to meet future internal policy charges (based on guaranteed policy elements) and allow the policy cash value to equal its death benefit at the end of the mortality table; e.g., insured's age 121. This is the definition of single premium whole life insurance. A still higher initial premium payment could cause the policy to endow at age 97, so the policy would be providing single premium endowment insurance to age 97.

Theoretically, any endowment period and any premium funding pattern could be created, although practically, endowments before age 95 are not desired as they lose their favorable income tax treatment. Subject to tax and insurer constraints, a UL policy can replicate any term, whole life, or endowment insurance benefit and premium payment configuration. In doing so, it provides great flexibility in planning both for its financing and for the adverse consequences of death. The ability to access its value via loans, withdrawals, and/or policy surrender provides another dimension of flexibility.

Several variations of generic UL have evolved over the years. Each is intended to address a specific need or concern. Here we cover:

- variable UL,
- no-lapse guarantee UL, and
- equity-indexed UL.

VARIABLE UNIVERSAL LIFE INSURANCE

A next logical step in life insurance product evolution was to combine the flexible characteristics of universal life with the investment flexibility of variable life. The result was **variable universal life** (VUL) – also called **flexible premium variable life** and **unit-linked life insurance** – which is variable life insurance configured as a universal life policy with its transparency, premium flexibility, and death benefit adjustability. It was first offered in 1985 in the U.S. by *Pruco Life*, a subsidiary of *Prudential Life Insurance Company of America*. (As discussed in the next chapter, variable whole life insurance predated VUL in the U.S.) With the strong North American stock market performance in the 1990s and early 2000s, VUL's market share rose substantially. It fell equally fast during the 2008-09 recession.

NATURE OF VARIABLE UNIVERSAL LIFE INSURANCE   Both VUL and variable whole life (see Chapter 4) insurance policies permit their owners to control their policies' investment allocations and, thereby, determine the levels of risk that they are willing to assume. They may select from a menu of funds from the insurer's separate account offerings for the investment of their account value. Recall that *separate accounts* are effectively mutual funds in which assets backing variable product liabilities are held separate from the insurer's general account assets, which back liabilities of all non-variable products.

Policyholders may change funds as they wish, altering the risk/return profile of their policies, subject to insurer administrative requirements. The policies' separate account investment risks are borne totally by the policyholder, a characteristic not found in generic universal and whole life insurance where the insurance company provides a minimum guaranteed interest crediting rate.

All variable products, their separate accounts, and related sales are subject to regulation by the U.S. *Securities and Exchange Commission* (SEC), in addition to state insurance regulators. Variable products are securities and, as such, potential purchasers must be provided with a prospectus. This lengthy booklet includes the identity and nature of the insurer's business, the use to which the insurer will put the premiums, financial information on the insurer, the fees and expenses to be charged, and policyowner rights.

Under laws administered mostly by the *Financial Industry Regulatory Authority* (FINRA) under the aegis of the SEC, securities must be distributed by registered broker-dealers. Life insurers usually maintain subsidiary registered broker-dealers but may also distribute through unaffiliated firms. Agents and home office

VARIATIONS OF UNIVERSAL LIFE INSURANCE

personnel involved with variable products must pass an examination intended to test their knowledge of variable products and related law and must become licensed to sell. securities. Additionally, specific requirements apply to advertising, annual reports to shareholders, shareholder proxies, and financial reporting.

OPERATIONAL DETAILS OF VARIABLE UNIVERSAL LIFE INSURANCE   VUL policies exhibit the same traits as generic UL policies as to transparency, premium flexibility, death benefit adjustability, death benefit options, and use of current assumptions as to mortality and loading charges. They differ in their investment flexibility and risk/return opportunity. The separate accounts backing the cash values are mutual funds (and must be registered as investment companies with the SEC) in which policyholders are permitted to invest in various bond, stock, balanced, international, and other funds. Funds must satisfy both securities and tax qualification criteria. Separate accounts are not subject to the restrictions applicable to an insurer's general account investments. Most separate accounts focus on equity investments, whereas an insurer's general account investments are mostly in bonds.

The VUL policy cash value is linked directly to and determined by the investment results of the separate account in which the policyholder has chosen to invest. If the separate account value increases after charges by 15 percent, the VUL policy account value increases 15 percent. If the separate account decreases by 15 percent, the policy account value suffers a corresponding loss. As future account values cannot be known, death benefits and surrender values are determined retrospectively. Renewal charges take place according to actual account values recorded on a specific date – usually monthly anniversary dates – often termed *monthly processing days*. Most VUL policies contain no guarantees as to minimum interest crediting rates. They also typically contain no guaranteed minimum death benefit, unless they contain a no lapse guarantee feature (see below) and required minimum premiums have been paid.

The VUL policyowner may hold investments in numerous accounts simultaneously to diversify his or her exposure. Increasingly, insurers allow policyowners to direct investment into funds not controlled by the insurer, such as those controlled by third party mutual fund companies.

The policyowner has the right periodically to transfer funds from one account to another. Most insurers allow up to four transfers per year at no charge. Some insurers charge a fee of $25 or so. Many insurers allow policyowners to establish automatic monthly transfers at no fee, usually from a money market (separate) account to one or several of the equity accounts. As all transfers are within a life insurance policy, no taxable gain (or loss) is realized because of the transaction – a distinct advantage over taxable mutual fund transfers.

USES AND CONSIDERATIONS OF VARIABLE UNIVERSAL LIFE INSURANCE   VUL policies require the same type of discipline as does generic UL. The prospective purchaser should commit to ensuring that the policy always has sufficient funds to be self-sustaining, ideally with investment income sufficient to cover all policy charges for a period with some residual to ensure cash value growth. VUL policies are potentially useful for those persons who desire to treat their life insurance policy cash values more as an investment than a savings account. Thus, the policy is more suitable to those with greater investment savvy who understand the volatility and long term nature of equity markets. At the same time, some VUL policies have been criticized because of having what some consider as excessive charges.

The owner assumes the investment risk. There is a danger if separate account investment results are not favorable; the policy's cash value could be reduced substantially and the policy could require additional unplanned premium payments. This risk should be considered most carefully. One of the strengths of the life insurance industry historically has been its investment guarantees. With variable insurance products, consumers are largely forgoing these guarantees.

On the other hand, as the assets backing the reserves of variable policies are held in separate accounts, they are not subject to the claims of the creditors of an insolvent insurer, unlike the situation with policies whose reserves are backed by the insurer's general account assets. This protection does not extend to the purely insurance elements of variable life, which are backed by an insurer's general account. Hence, the portion of any death benefit that becomes payable from the insurer's general account – a policy's NAR – is theoretically not shielded from creditors' claims. As a practical matter, death benefit claims of an insolvent insurer have usually if not always been paid by the available funds in liquidation, by another insurer who acquires the insolvent insurer, or by state guaranty funds.

Most VUL policies offer a **guaranteed minimum death benefit** (GMDB) feature or rider for an additional premium, which guarantees that a specified minimum death benefit will be paid irrespective of whether the policy account value is positive, provided benchmark premiums have been paid. The policyholder ordinarily selects both the minimum death benefit to be guaranteed (e.g., from 70 to 100 percent of the initial death benefit) and the duration of the guarantee, up to the entire lifetime of the insured. The higher the death benefit guaranteed and the longer the duration, the higher the premium for the feature.

Some VUL policies also offer an option for a no lapse guarantee. As with other NLG products, a minimum premium must be paid. These premiums typically are higher than those for non-variable NLG products, as the insurer's risks are greater, and there may be restrictions on fund allocations.

The usual withdrawal and loan privileges applicable to all cash value policies are available with variable policies as well. An important difference is that the insurer typically will permit loans for only 75 to 90 percent of the then cash value. Also, separate account assets equal to the loan amount are removed from the separate account and placed in a loan account that is credited with interest at a rate no higher than the loan rate and often a somewhat lesser rate.

Finally, while most variable life policyholders elect to invest in equities, other separate account investment options exist, including investing in the insurer's general account. Doing so gains the policyholder the normal general account crediting rate, but loses creditor protections. Some insurers provide for an enhanced general account yield if the policyholder commits to longer duration investing, but fund transfers from such arrangements are restricted, typically to no more than 10 percent per year.

No-Lapse Guarantee Universal Life Insurance
No-lapse guarantee (NLG) universal life policies guarantee a minimum death benefit to a certain age or for life, even if the account value becomes depleted before

that time, provided the minimum continuance premium is timely paid. Not all NLG policies are labeled as such but, if a UL policy provides this option, whether at an additional premium or not, it will remain in force to a certain age and the policy is a NLG contract.

The great advantage of these policies is that lifetime guaranteed insurance coverage can be purchased with a low premium outlay in comparison to that required for most other lifetime guarantee policies such as WL. There is a risk – because of their rigidity and complexity and perhaps because of policyholder naivety or ignorance – that the policyholder (and possibly agent) may fail to understand fully the purpose, nature, and risks of the policy – in other words, the product may be unsuitable for the customer.

NLG products are usually configured as UL policies, which means that premiums are flexible, but this very flexibility can put coverage at risk if inadequate premiums are paid. The required NLG premium results in slower cash (account) value development. Indeed, cash values typically taper to zero at about the insured's life expectancy based on current assumptions and guaranteed lifetime funding. Further, NLG policies typically have heavy surrender charges for the first 10 to 20 policy years. Because they have modest or nonexistent cash values, many advisors urge clients to think of NLG products as term insurance.

OPERATIONAL DETAILS OF NO-LAPSE GUARANTEE UNIVERSAL LIFE INSURANCE   As NLG products typically operate via a UL chassis, the observations about UL operation in general apply here as well, although practical limitations exist, as explored below. The main operational element within NLG products that differs from generic UL is the internal policy mechanism for determining whether the NLG promise is effective. Policies use one of two mechanisms: a specified premium test or a shadow account.

The **specified premium test**, the original NLG mechanism, provides that coverage remains guaranteed for as long as the minimum premium is paid such that actual premiums paid equal or exceed a cumulative premium to date. Some policies set a minimum annual premium. NLG premiums must be paid on time if the policyholder is to avoid loss of the NLG feature or a reduction in guarantee benefits (duration or amount).

Some specified premium products offer a **catch-up provision** that permits payment of additional premiums to restore the guarantee if the premium requirement is not met. Some products also include a **reset provision** that permits the guaranteed duration or the amount of guaranteed coverage to be reset based on adjusted future specified premiums.

Most NLG products offered today promise that the NLG remains in effect if either the policy's regular UL account value or what is called its *shadow account value* remains positive. The **shadow account** is derived from a modified universal life account value calculation using a set of guaranteed policy elements different from the set applicable to the regular account value calculation. If neither the regular account nor the shadow account has a positive value, the policy lapses.

The shadow account approach offers lower premiums and generally provides greater flexibility as regards premium payments and the duration and amount of the guarantee in comparison to the specified premium approach. For example, assume that actual premiums paid were less than the original premiums required to ensure a positive shadow account value for life (e.g., to age 121) and that these lower premiums result in a projected shadow account balance of zero at age 95. The duration of the NLG would then be reset to age 95. Alternatively, sufficient catch-up premiums (with interest) could be paid or the death benefit sufficiently lowered to re-establish the NLG for life. The shadow account determines the guarantee coverage only and is not available for cash withdrawals or policy loans.

USES AND CONSIDERATIONS OF NO-LAPSE GUARANTEE UNIVERSAL LIFE INSURANCE   Much has been written about NLG products, both positively and negatively. Below we provide an overview of its strengths and explain its risks. NLG strengths are said to include the following:

- *Simple promise.* The insurer's promise is simple: if the policyholder pays the requisite premium on time, the insurer guarantees the death benefit for life (or to a certain age).
- *Guarantees.* The NLG means the policyholder need not be exposed to or particularly concerned about the downside risks of decreased crediting rates or increased loads or COI charges that attach to other current assumption products (although cash values will be negatively affected by less favorable changes).
- *Lower cost lifetime guarantee of coverage.* NLG policies generally provide a lower-cost lifetime *guarantee* of coverage in comparison with other guaranteed lifetime policies (such as WL).

NLG products have raised concerns about the risks run by its purchasers, some of which are:

- *Little or no cash surrender value.* Low account and surrender values relative to other current assumption products afford little flexibility if policyholder needs change in the future (e.g., limited or no opportunity to use cash values for retirement income, collateral, short term cash, or tax-free policy exchanges). A NLG contract's use is largely limited to serving the purpose for which it was originally purchased.
- *Adverse liquidity consequences.* Within a NLG product, cash value withdrawals and loans decrease the strength of the guarantee, which defeats its original purpose. Thus, policy liquidity is effectively constrained.
- *Limited upside performance potential.* NLG products typically limit participation in favorable future experience such as higher interest earnings or mortality improvements. As these products provide protection from unfavorable deviations, insurers are not keen to share benefits arising from favorable deviations with policyholders. Other cash value products offer greater potential for improved policy performance, as favorable experience is more likely to be passed through.
- *Requirement of timely premium payments.* If the required premium is not paid on time, guarantee coverage may be terminated or reduced in duration or amount. Where catch-up premiums are an option, the amount needed includes both premiums and interest.
- *Potential for shadow account confusion.* The operation and function of the shadow account can be confusing to policyholders, especially with the passage of time. It could be misunderstood to be the cash value. Its

complexity could make it difficult for policyholders to make informed decisions.

- *Need for ongoing monitoring.* Ongoing monitoring of the policy and policyholder's circumstances is highly desirable to ensure that required premiums are paid on time or, if a payment is missed or late, to get the NLG back on track. Agent compensation for NLG products is typically low and may include no commissions after policy years 10 or 15, which reduces the incentive for agents to properly service the product.
- *Insurer insolvency risk.* Concern exists in the market that insurer reserves to support their NLG products may be inadequate and that lapse supported pricing is utilized (i.e., pricing subsidies are included from anticipated later year lapses, when projected asset shares are greater than surrender values – see Chapter 16). If lapse rates prove lower than anticipated, the subsidies will not materialize, leading to insurer losses.

Box 3-2 provides a comparison of key characteristics of NLG universal life and of generic UL policies.

As the preceding discussion makes clear, a NLG product may not be suitable for many customers. Ongoing monitoring is critical to the product's success. NLG products are appropriate for many individuals, especially older ones who have a demonstrated need for guaranteed cost, lifetime protection.

EQUITY-INDEXED UNIVERSAL LIFE INSURANCE

Equity-indexed universal life (EIUL), also called **indexed UL,** is a comparatively recent UL variation with the same operational characteristics and platform as generic UL products but with an interest crediting rate being either that which the insurer uses for its general account-based products or that determined by reference to one or more equity indexes, such as the S&P 500 index. The policyowner decides the account value amounts to be exposed to each crediting mechanism. While the equity index rate is determined by reference to an index, the policyholder does not participate directly in that index's market. EIUL differs from generic UL as well as VUL in this interest crediting mechanism.

OPERATIONAL DETAILS OF EQUITY-INDEXED UNIVERSAL LIFE INSURANCE As with other non-variable life products, the EIUL account value is backed by the insurer's general account assets, but it is divided into two or more policy accounts: a fixed account and one or more index accounts. The policyholder decides on the funds to be allocated to each account. The fixed account crediting rate is typically the same as that found with the insurer's other UL policies, being influenced by the investment returns in its general account. The **index account** is that portion of the EIUL cash (account) value for which the crediting rate is determined by changes in an equity index, subject to a guaranteed minimum crediting rate, called the **growth floor,** and a maximum crediting rate, called the **growth cap.** The growth floor limits the downside risk and the growth cap limits the upside potential.

The change in the index's market value is its **index performance rate.** Dividend income ordinarily is excluded in deriving this rate. Each transfer of funds into the index account creates a new segment of a specified duration, called the

segment term. The index performance rate is measured over this term. Common segment terms are one and five years.

The relevant index performance rate is then multiplied by each segment's **participation rate**, which is the proportion of the index performance rate that is counted in deriving the actual crediting rate, to yield the **growth rate**. A participation rate of 100 percent means that the entire index performance rate is considered and a rate of 80 percent means that 80 percent of the rate is considered. Other things being the same, a higher participation rate is preferred to a lower one. The crediting rate to be applied to the index account, called the **index crediting rate,** is the growth rate adjusted to take account of the segment growth floor and growth cap.

Box 3-2
Characteristics of No Lapse Universal Life and Generic Universal Life

Characteristic	No Lapse Guarantee UL	Generic UL
Provides a lifetime guaranteed death benefit at a guaranteed cost?	**YES** Death benefit is guaranteed for life if the required guaranteed premium is paid on time.	**NO** At NLG funding levels, coverage typically guaranteed to about life expectancy.
Future performance can be better than illustrated at issue?	**NOT LIKELY** NLG premiums are likely locked in and will not decrease based on improved emerging experience. Minimal upside cash value potential.	**YES** Better emerging experience can permit lower ongoing premium payments or higher cash values and death benefits.
Future performance can be worse than illustrated at issue?	**NO** Guaranteed premiums cannot be higher nor death benefits lower than originally illustrated if guaranteed premiums are paid on time; cash value performance can be worse.	**YES** Cash values can be lower and additional premium payments required to maintain policy in force if emerging experience is worse than originally illustrated.
Provides cash surrender values?	**MINIMAL** Little or no surrender values in early and later policy years. Some versions offer higher cash values but with higher premiums.	**YES** Particularly if well funded and minimal surrender charges. Actual values dependent on premiums paid.
Low premium outlay for death protection?	**YES** Among the lowest outlays for lifetime protection; most competitive at ages 65 and higher.	**YES** Current outlays may compare favorably with NLG, particularly at ages 65 and below; ultimate nets costs and outlays dependent on emerging experience.

The following example of three segment terms will clarify the interaction among these terms and factors. This policy has a growth cap of 12 percent, a growth floor of zero percent, and a 90 percent participation rate. The index performance rates for each of the three segments terms is 22.0, 9.0, and -19.0 percent, as shown in the table.

(1)	(2)	(3) [(1) x (2)]		(4)
Index Performance Rate (% change in index)	**Participation Rate** (% of growth rate used in calculation)	**Growth Cap**		**Index Crediting Rate** (applied to account value at segment maturity)
		Growth Rate *subject to ...*		
		Growth Floor		
22.00%	90%	Subject to 12% cap		12.00%
9.00%	90%	Within cap/floor range		8.10%
-19.00%	90%	Subject to 0% floor		0.00%

For the first segment term, the index increased by 22.0 percent yearly. Applying the 90 percent participation rate reduces this rate to 19.8 percent (0.22 x 0.9), but this policy has a 12 percent growth cap, so the actual index crediting rate applied to the policy's account value is 12 percent. The index performance of the next segment term is 9.0 percent. Taking 90 percent of that rate yields 8.1 percent, which becomes the actual index crediting rate for that segment, as this rate falls between the growth cap and floor.

Finally, the third segment realized a negative return, at -19.0 percent. Application of the participation rate reduces this loss to -17.1 percent. The policy contains a growth floor of zero percent, so this rate becomes the index crediting rate for this segment. Note that upside and downside returns are truncated by the growth cap and floor.

Upon maturity of each segment term, the index crediting rate calculation is restarted. The effect of this reset is to carry forward gains and avoid carrying forward losses, as the zero percent floor insulates the account value.

Index strategies are different from product to product, and some index products offer more than one index strategy. Differences occur in the growth cap rate, the floor rate, the participation rate, and the index itself. Other differences may include the method of performance rate calculation.

USES AND CONSIDERATIONS OF EQUITY-INDEXED UNIVERSAL LIFE INSURANCE   In addition to understanding the broad mechanics for deriving the interest crediting rate for the index account, the following can impact product performance:

- *Index returns omit dividends.* Dividends historically have accounted for an additional annual return of 1 to 3 percent.
- *Mid-term segment surrenders.* Surrender value within a segment term typically equals its value at the beginning of the term, less policy charges, plus any interim interest credited (see below) during the term. Index interest credit will be provided only for end-of-term segment surrenders. This is an issue more relevant for segment terms of greater than one year. For example, if the segment term is five years, and one year remains in the term at time of surrender, four years of index credit would be lost.
- *Interim interest credits.* Typically, EIUL products credit interim interest equal to the growth floor. Thus, if the floor is 1 percent, then 1 percent

is credited during the segment term. At the end of the term, the index crediting rate is determined, and a retroactive credit, net of the interim credit, is applied.

• *Minimum growth floor guarantee.* The growth floor may be guaranteed for life or it may be adjustable from term segment to term segment. Adjustable growth floors may or may not be favorable to the policyowner depending on the influence of the fee level charged and competitive pressures.

• *Minimum growth cap guarantee.* The growth cap is guaranteed for the current segment term only and can be changed for future segments. A guaranteed minimum growth cap establishes a minimum rate for the life of the policy.

• *Minimum participation rate guarantee.* Unless stated explicitly, the current participation rate is guaranteed for the current segment term only. A guaranteed minimum participation rate establishes a minimum rate for the life of the policy.

While the basic mechanics of an EIUL policy can be relatively straightforward, the proverbial "devil is in the details" – of which there are many. These policies can be misunderstood if not explained thoroughly, they require careful monitoring and service, and the details affecting the interest crediting rate can seem bewildering. Nonetheless, EIUL policies occupy an important place between traditional UL policies and variable UL policies. They can be considered as providing much of the downside protection of a traditional UL policy with some of the upside potential of a variable UL policy. Figure 3-5 illustrates this.

Risk/Return Profiles of Three Universal Life Policies   **Figure 3-5**

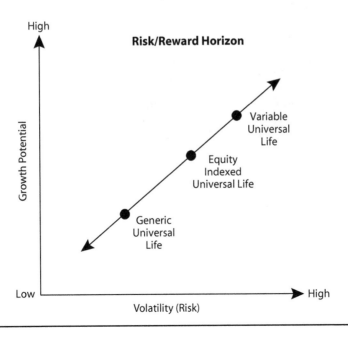

Some EIUL policies have been criticized as offering too little extra return because of the crediting limitations. Even so, as compared to variable UL, they offer substantial downside protection. Box 3-3 offers a comparison among generic UL, EIUL, and VUL relative to various characteristics of their approaches to crediting rates.

Box 3-3
Comparisons for Three Major Universal Life Policies

Characteristic	Generic Universal Life	Equity-Indexed Universal Life	Variable Universal Life
Funds held in general account or separate account?	General account. Funds not protected from creditors upon insurer insolvency	General account. Funds not protected from creditors upon insurer insolvency	Separate account. Funds protected from creditors upon insurer insolvency
Allocation of policyholder funds?	By insurer largely to fixed investments, called *fixed account*	Policyholder determines allocation between indexed account and fixed account	Policyholder determines allocation among available separate account investment options
Main investments?	Investment grade bonds and mortgages	Investment grade bonds and mortgages and equity index call options	Equity and bond mutual funds
Basis for valuing investments?	Book value, which provides more stable reported earnings than market value	Market value for indexed account. Same as UL for fixed account	Market value for separate account. Same as UL for fixed account (general account)
Degree of investment risk transferred to policyholder?	Marginal, only for crediting rates in excess of the guaranteed rate	Partial, for indexed account between the floor and cap. Same as UL for fixed account	100 percent of fund risk, including negative returns for the separate account. Same as UL for fixed account
How is crediting rate determined?	Book value investment return of entire investment portfolio or segments thereof less spread, subject to guarantee	Percentage change in index for indexed account, subject to participation rate, floors, caps. Same as UL for fixed account	Percentage change in market value of funds for the separate account. Same as UL for fixed account
Does the crediting rate include dividend income?	Indirectly, via book value investment return	No, for indexed account. Same as UL for fixed account	Yes for separate account. Same as UL for fixed account

Term life insurance and universal life insurance together account for about three-quarters of personal life insurance in force in the U.S. They are popular in many markets worldwide. Term life is comparatively simple to understand and to price. It suits the needs of many buyers, particularly those who need large amounts of insurance at low initial outlays.

Universal life insurance is transparent in its operation, which renders its internal operation more understandable to buyers and owners. It allows premium flexibility and death benefit adjustability, while its policy elements change with changing economic and other circumstances. The generic form and its variations make it the most popular selling cash value policy form in the U.S. As with all cash value policies, however, whether it proves to be low cost can be determined only with time. Insights can be gained at time of policy purchase through the analysis of illustrated values, a subject we take up in Chapter 19.

CONCLUSIONS

ENDNOTES

1   This chapter draws in parts from Harold D. Skipper and Wayne Tonning, *The Advisor's Guide to Life Insurance* (Chicago; American Bar Association, 2011), Chapter 7.

CHAPTER 4

PERSONAL LIFE INSURANCE PRODUCTS: II

This chapter is a continuation of Chapter 3, both chapters covering personal life insurance products. This chapter examines whole life (WL) insurance, insurance covering multiple lives, specialized life policies, and endowment insurance.

In contrast with term, whole life insurance is intended to provide insurance protection over one's entire lifetime. WL insurance policies have been the mainstay of the North American life insurance business for more than 150 years and continues to be significant in these as well as other markets worldwide.

WHOLE LIFE INSURANCE

NATURE OF WHOLE LIFE INSURANCE

As discussed in Chapter 2, the essence of whole life insurance is that it provides for the payment of the face amount upon the insured's death regardless of when death occurs. Its name describes its nature. As used in this text, a WL *policy* is generic and describes any type of life insurance policy that, by its terms, is intended to remain in effect to the end of the mortality table underlying the policy's pricing and whose premiums are required to be paid or the policy lapses. By this definition, UL policies can provide WL insurance but they are not WL policies.

The face amounts payable under WL policies typically remain level throughout the policy duration, although dividends are often used to increase the total amount paid on death, especially in Europe. The gross premiums also remain level throughout the premium payment period with most policies. Exceptions exist, as noted below, wherein future premium changes are stipulated in the contract or by the insurer.

Much WL insurance is priced on mortality tables that assume that all insureds die by a certain age. Age 100 has been common in North America, although the *2001 Commissioners Ordinary Mortality Table* is replacing this older mortality table, and its terminal age is 121. As all insureds do not die by age 100 or 121, but insurance companies price the insurance as if they did, it is only fair that the company pay the policy face amount to those few persons who live to the terminal age as if they had died. This fact is the reason that whole life policies have sometimes been referred to as *endowment-at-age-100 (121)* policies.

The age 100 "endowment" really is not an endowment in the usual sense, but rather it is paid by the insurer in recognition that the underlying reserve and cash value of the policy equal the policy face amount at age 100 and, therefore, no pure insurance protection exists beyond that point. Contemporary policies often permit the policyowner to defer receipt of the endowment if desired – usually for tax purposes.

Another equally valid viewpoint is that WL policies are also *term-to-age-100 (121)* policies, provided the underlying mortality table shows a probability of death during age 99 (120) of 100 percent. This view is justified by noting that the actuarial technique used for pricing WL is the same, in concept, as that used to price any term policy. The age-100 (121) payment, under this view, can be considered as a death benefit payment because the underlying mortality table assumes that all individuals surviving to age 99 (120) die during this year.

KEY FEATURES

The existence of cash values is a key feature of all WL policies sold in the U.S. Also, WL policies are either participating or not.

IMPORTANCE OF CASH VALUES All whole life policies involve prefunding of future mortality costs. The degree of prefunding is a function of the premium payment pattern and duration. Because of this prefunding, all WL policies sold in the U.S. and many other markets are required to have cash values, and the cash value must build to the policy face amount by the terminal age of the underlying mortality table. Many countries' laws, such as Canada and the U.K., do not require cash values, but insurers usually provide them by practice.

Whole life cash values are available to the policyowner via policy surrender. Alternatively, cash values can be used in other ways, providing flexibility to the policyowner, as discussed in Chapter 5. WL policies usually contain cash value schedules that show the guaranteed minimum amounts that the policyowner can receive on surrender of the policy.

Owners of WL insurance policies do not have to surrender their policies to have access to funds. As under other cash value policies, owners of WL normally can obtain loans from the insurer for amounts up to that of the policy's net cash surrender value. A policy's **net cash surrender value** is its gross cash value less surrender charges (or back-end loading) and the value of any outstanding loans plus the value of any dividends on deposit and the cash value of any paid up additions. It is the net amount that a policyholder would realize if he or she surrendered the policy.

Of course, interest is charged on any loan, and the loan is deducted from the gross cash value if the policy is surrendered or from the face amount if the insured dies and a death claim is payable. Policy loans may, but need not, be repaid at any time and are a source of policy flexibility.

PARTICIPATING AND NONPARTICIPATING WHOLE LIFE INSURANCE As we know, life insurance policies can be participating (par) or nonparticipating (nonpar). Par policies are more closely associated with mutual life insurance companies and nonpar policies are more closely associated with stock life insurance companies, although much nonpar UL is sold by stock subsidiaries of mutual insurers.

Most WL insurance sold worldwide is par. A significant proportion is nonpar but with nonguaranteed elements. The amount of nonpar WL sold that contains only guaranteed policy elements is small in most OECD countries, including Canada, the U.S., France, Germany, Japan, and Korea, although such remains popular in many developing countries. This small share is understandable as companies are unwilling to offer liberal pricing guaranteed for decades into the future. Conservatively priced products for which all policy elements are guaranteed do not compete well against those for which an insurer does not fix and guarantee all policy elements and may change them to reflect improved future experience.

Nature of Dividends   Participating policies are entitled to share via nonguaranteed policy elements called *dividends* in any distribution of the insurer's surplus funds that it decides to make under those policies. Insurers selling par policies typically price them conservatively. This conservative pricing means that the policies as a group are highly likely to generate profits – called *surplus*. Following each year's operations, the insurer's board of directors decides how much of these surplus funds – called **divisible surplus** – may be passed on to par policies in the form of dividends.

Actuaries then divide this divisible surplus among the par policies in an equitable manner, commonly following the **contribution principle** which holds that divisible surplus should be distributed to policies in the same proportions as the policies are considered to have contributed to the surplus. In implementing this principle, actuaries often use the so-called **three factor contribution formula** which recognizes that surplus derives from these three main sources, called *factors*:

1. **Gains from investment earnings:** actual investment earnings higher than the guaranteed minimum rate.
2. **Gains from mortality:** actual mortality experience more favorable than that implicit in policy pricing, meaning that death claims payments were less than priced into policies.
3. **Gains from loadings:** actual expenses lower than that implicit in policy pricing.

The sum of these three factors yields a policy's dividend. Historically, the gain from investment earnings has been the dominant factor in determining the magnitude of dividends. The actual gains from each factor historically have not been disclosed to policyholders; only the total. Some insurers now disclose some components. For example, one insurer illustrated how its dividend was derived for a 20-year-old whole life policy as follows:

Guaranteed cash value (BOY)	$65,217
+ Gross annual premium	+ 1,593
- Mortality & expense charge	- 191
= Balance	$66,619
+ Interest credit	+ 4,097
= Policy value	= 70,716
- Guaranteed cash value (EOY)	- 68,235
= Dividend	= $2,481

We do not know the actual gains from the mortality, loading, and interest components for the above policy, only the amounts assessed and credited to this policy. But we can see how the insurer made its calculation. Another insurer showed the actual gains by component. Below we show how its 20-year dividend per $1,000 of face amount was derived for a policy:

Interest credit	$9.21
+ Mortality gain	+ 5.33
+ Loading gain	+ (3.11)
= Dividend	= $11.43

Both insurers also disclose the rate used to calculate the interest credit, but no other underlying factors are disclosed. Note that the second insurer's gain from loading is negative, meaning that the allowance for expenses, taxes, and profits built into its original premium was insufficient to cover these charges by $3.11 per $1,000 in the year of this calculation. This deficit was made good from the gains from the other two factors.

Agents selling par policies typically provide prospective purchasers with a dividend illustration as part of the sales promotional material. A **dividend illustration** shows the dividends that would be paid under the policy if the investment, mortality, and loading factors implicit in the currently payable dividends were to remain unchanged in the future, which is unlikely.

Dividends actually paid, the schedule of which is a **dividend history**, are amounts actually paid as dividends in the past. Dividends actually paid usually exceed those originally illustrated if investment returns are higher than those prevailing at the time of policy issuance. They may be lower than originally illustrated if prevailing investment returns are lower than those at policy issuance.

Dividends are payable on a par policy's anniversary date. As par premiums are set in anticipation of paying dividends, the *Internal Revenue Service* (IRS) considers dividends to be a return of premium and not taxable income, unless the sum of dividends received exceeds the sum of premiums paid.

Nonparticipating policies are not entitled to share in any distribution of surplus funds by the insurer, but most nonpar cash value policies contain nonguaranteed elements other than dividends that ensure that policyholders share in the favorable (and unfavorable) actual or reasonably anticipated operational experience of the insurer. Other nonpar cash value policies – typically those of more modest face amounts – do not contain any nonguaranteed elements, which means that they do not share in the operational experience of the insurer. Nonpar policies in which all policy elements are guaranteed and fixed at policy issue are sometimes called **guaranteed-cost, nonparticipating life insurance.**

Dividend Options   Dividends may be applied or taken in one or more of several ways. The policyowner elects the desired option at the time the policy is purchased, but it can be changed at any time under most policies, although evidence of insurability may be required if the effect of the change would be to increase the policy's future net amount at risk. These options can be potentially important sources of flexibility. The five most common dividend options are:

1. *Cash.* The insurer pays the dividend in cash to the policyowner each year.
2. *Apply Toward Premium Payment.* Sometimes referred to inaccurately as *reduce premium,* the dividend is credited toward premiums due for the year, reducing the policyowner's current outlay.
3. *Purchase Paid Up Additional Insurance.* Commonly shortened to *paid-up additions* (PUAs), the dividend is applied as a net single premium at the insured's attained age to purchase as much paid up WL insurance as it will provide. Paid-up additions themselves may be par or nonpar. If they are par, annual dividends on the paid up additions further enhance the policy's total cash value and death benefit. On the insured's death, the policy's face amount plus accumulated PUAs are paid. On policy surrender the cash value of the paid up additions is added to the base policy's surrender value.

    Although PUAs is the most popular dividend option, some individuals do not wish to purchase single premium WL insurance, even if small in amount. Some consider it wiser to use dividends to reduce current premiums to permit the purchase of additional insurance. Even so, purchasing paid up additions can be a worthwhile approach to increasing insurance protection and offering flexibility because of their cash value.
4. *Accumulate at Interest.* Dividends are held by the insurer to accumulate at interest under the contract. The insurer guarantees a minimum crediting rate, although companies often credit higher rates. Accumulations can be withdrawn at will. On the insured's death, the policy's face amount plus dividend accumulations are paid, and, in the event of surrender, the cash surrender value plus dividend accumulations are paid.
5. *Purchase One Year Term.* Some companies make available an option to apply the dividend to purchase one year term insurance. The option takes one of two forms. One form applies the dividend as a net annual premium to purchase as much one year term insurance protection as it will buy. The other form purchases one year term insurance in an amount equal to the policy's cash value, with the excess dividend portion applied under one of the other dividend options.

Companies often permit dividends to be used in other ways. One is to have the dividend applied to shorten the premium payment period. Under this option, a cash value policy can be made self-sustaining at the time when the total policy cash value equals or exceeds the net single premium for the insured's attained age for an amount of insurance equal to the policy's face amount.

Another dividend option, the *add-to-cash-value option,* is similar to the paid up additions option in that it permits the dividend to accumulate as additional cash value but, unlike the additions option, involves no additional pure insurance protection. In other words, the option generates exactly a unit of additional death benefit for each unit of additional cash value.

Types of Whole Life Insurance

As a result of competitive pressures, many innovations have evolved in whole life insurance product design and pricing. Because of the vast array of WL products and the even greater number of company variations, the following discussion highlights only the more common policies.

ORDINARY LIFE POLICIES   Ordinary life insurance provides whole life insurance with premiums payable for the whole of life. This oldest form of WL may be referred to by several other names, including *straight life* and *continuous premium whole life,* and often the term whole life itself is used to denote ordinary life insurance.

Ordinary life policies are intended to afford permanent protection at a relatively modest annual outlay, as premiums are spread over the entire policy period. Premiums are always guaranteed for the duration of the policy, although some insurers charge less than the guaranteed premiums. Premium levels can vary significantly, depending on the competitiveness inherent in the insurer's target markets, whether the policy is par or nonpar, and a host of other variables. These variations complicate cost comparisons among seemingly similar policies.

Ordinary life policy cash values normally increase smoothly, reaching the policy face amount at age 100 or 121. As discussed more fully in Chapters 5 and 23, cash values can be a source of policy flexibility. Early cash values are typically low, as the high costs associated with policy sale and issuance are charged off during the first years. These high costs result from the commission paid to the salesperson, which often is 40 to 80 percent or more of the first year premium, as well as from underwriting and other administrative expenses.

Traditional ordinary life policies have lost market share in many countries to newer cash value products, particularly UL. Most UL and many variations of WL use variations of new money interest crediting rates. These current assumption products were introduced at a time when interest rates were comparatively high, which meant that illustrations showing potential future policy values were particularly attractive to prospective buyers. Many purchasers were not well informed about the risks inherent in policy illustrations or they chose to believe that high rates would continue. As interest rates fell, many discovered that new money rates could fall as fast as they rose. Actual results failed to meet policyholder expectations, with innumerable lawsuits ensuing.

At the same time, many insurers' par WL policies and some insurers' UL policies credited interest based on the investment return of their entire investment portfolios via the portfolio average method. New money rates change more quickly than portfolio rates. Thus, policies whose interest crediting rates are based on the portfolio average approach produce more attractive returns in a falling interest rate environment for the same reason that they produce less favorable returns – compared to new money products – in a rising interest rate environment. Thus, the advantage enjoyed by UL and other new-money-based products in a rising interest rate environment results in a disadvantage for them when interest rates fall, as occurred during and after the 2008-09 recession and during the late 1980s and the 1990s in several markets including Japan, Korea, and the U.S. As interest rates stabilize, new money and portfolio yields converge.

Table 4-1 shows a U.S. illustration for a traditional par $1,000,000 ordinary life policy issued to a 35-year-old male nonsmoker. Dividends are shown both as being netted against the premium payment and as purchasing PUAs. Of course, only one option would be selected. The negative impact on early cash values of the high front-end load is clear. The table shows that the guaranteed cash value at age 45 is $98,660 and at age 55 it will be $241,990. With PUAs, the total illustrated cash values are $133,515 and $415,771 at ages 45 and 55, respectively.

					If Nonguaranteed Dividends Used to Purchase Paid Up Additions		
End of Year	Gross Premium	Illustrated Dividend* (Year End)	Premium Less Dividend*	Guaran-teed Cash Surrender Value	Paid-Up Additional Insurance Purchased*	Total Cash Value* (Year End)	Total Death Benefit* (Year End)
1	$14,460	$1,060	$14,460	$0	$5,006	$1,060	$1,005,006
2	14,460	1,340	13,400	9,610	6,225	12,072	1,011,231
3	14,460	1,620	13,120	19,570	7,388	23,798	1,018,619
4	14,460	1,940	12,840	29,850	8,672	36,268	1,027,291
5	14,460	2,250	12,520	40,470	9,859	49,516	1,037,150
6	14,460	2,830	12,210	51,440	12,067	63,849	1,049,217
7	14,460	3,450	11,630	62,760	14,337	79,348	1,063,554
8	14,460	4,110	11,010	74,410	16,672	96,083	1,080,226
9	14,460	4,790	10,350	86,380	18,991	114,117	1,099,217
10	14,460	5,490	9,670	98,660	21,302	133,515	1,120,519
11	14,460	6,220	8,970	111,260	23,645	154,379	1,144,164
12	14,460	6,850	8,240	124,190	25,586	176,685	1,169,750
13	14,460	7,510	7,610	137,460	27,571	200,537	1,197,321
14	14,460	8,060	6,950	151,180	29,115	226,003	1,226,436
15	14,460	8,620	6,400	165,350	30,640	253,156	1,257,076
16	14,460	9,223	5,840	179,930	32,260	282,065	1,289,336
17	14,460	9,856	5,237	194,930	33,930	312,847	1,323,266
18	14,460	10,299	4,603	210,280	35,106	345,321	1,358,372
19	14,460	10,763	4,160	225,980	36,334	379,575	1,394,706
20	14,460	11,336	3,697	241,990	37,910	415,771	1,432,616

Illustration of Traditional Participating Ordinary Life Policy   Table 4-1

*Non-guaranteed illustrated values. Dividends assume no loans; loans may reduce dividends. Illustrated dividends reflect current (2011 scale) claim, expense and investment experience and are not estimates or guarantees of future results. Dividends actually paid may be larger or smaller than those illustrated. This illustration does not recognize that, because of interest, a dollar in the future has less value than a dollar today. 8% loan provision.

LIMITED PAYMENT WHOLE LIFE POLICIES   With limited payment whole life insurance, the policy remains in force for the whole of life, but premiums are payable for a number of years less than the whole of life, after which the policy becomes paid-up for its face amount, meaning that no further premiums are payable. The premium-paying period may be expressed as a set number of years, such as 10 or

20, or to a specified age, such as 65. A paid-up policy should not be confused with a matured or an expired policy both of which connote that the policy is no longer in effect. A policy **matures** when the face amount becomes payable as a death claim or when the policy terminates with the payment of an endowment amount. A policy expires when the policy term ends and no benefit payment is due, as in a term policy. A **paid-up** policy is one for which, according to the terms of the contract, no further premium payments are due but the policy is guaranteed to remain in effect.

Although potentially identical in practical effect, a paid-up policy differs in important ways from what has sometimes erroneously been called *vanish pay* policies. A paid-up policy is contractually guaranteed never to require premium payments beyond the stated premium payment period. No such guarantee exists with policies whose values *might* be such as to make them self sustaining.

Premium payments may be fixed at almost any number of years – from 1 to 30 or more. If premiums are limited to 20 years, for example, the policy is known as a 20-payment whole life policy. The greater the number of premium payments, the more closely the contract resembles the ordinary life form.

Companies also make available contracts that limit premium payments to a certain age, such as to age 65, 70, or even higher. The objective typically is to permit the owner to pay up the policy during his or her working lifetime. Thus, a policy that requires premiums to age 65 is known as a life-paid-up-at-65 policy (often abbreviated LP65). A 30-payment life and a LP65 policy both issued at age 35 (and based on the same pricing assumptions) would carry the same premiums and other policy elements, as they would be identical policies.

As limited-payment policies require the payment of premiums for a period less than the contract term, it follows that the annual level premium under these plans must be larger than that necessary if premium payments continued throughout the life of the policy. Theoretically, the premiums payable under a limited-payment policy are the actuarial equivalent of the premiums payable for the insured's entire lifetime under an ordinary life plan.

Because of higher premiums, limited-payment plans are not well adapted to those whose incomes are modest and whose need for insurance protection is great. Furthermore, many persons who may be able to pay premiums may choose an ordinary life policy, as it may afford greater flexibility via riders permitting additional premium payments, or they may be able to invest the difference in the premiums more profitably. Limited-payment policies fit many business insurance situations in which it is desirable to ensure that the policy is fully paid for within a certain time period and are popular in many countries, although less so in the U.S.

Of course, the disadvantage of higher premiums is offset to varying degrees by the availability of higher cash values. Other things being the same, the higher the premium for a policy, the greater the cash values (due to the greater prefunding of future mortality charges). All limited-payment policies contain the same nonforfeiture, dividend, and settlement options as well as other standard features of ordinary life policies that provide policyowner flexibility.

The extreme in limited-payment life insurance is the single premium whole life policy wherein the policy is paid-up from inception with a single payment. Such a policy has immediate, substantial cash value. The other extreme of WL is represented by the ordinary life insurance policy, for which the premiums are payable until the maturity of the contract. Limited-payment contracts vary between these extremes. Thus, five and 10-pay life policies are close to single-premium policies, whereas a LP85 policy or beyond is, for practical purposes, an ordinary life policy. Other things being the same, as the number of premium payments increases, the annual premium and, consequently, the rate of growth of cash values become correspondingly smaller. Limited payment whole life policies have become much less popular in recent years. Figure 4-1 shows a stylized illustration of cash values for various WL insurance policies for a male aged 40.

Stylized Illustration of Cash Values for Selected Whole Life to Age 100 Policies, Male, Age 40   **Figure 4-1**

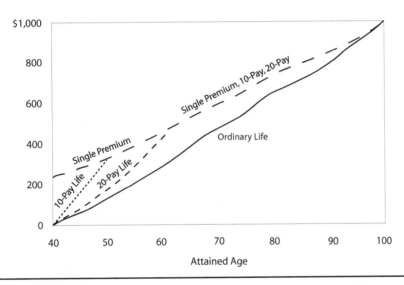

With whole life policies, the size of the cash value varies inversely with the length of the premium paying period. Thus, the ordinary life plan with payments for life has the lowest cash values, and the single-premium plan has the highest. After premium payments cease under the 10 payment and 20 payment WL plans, the cash values in each instance equal those under the single premium plan for policies using the same underlying pricing assumptions. This must be the case, as after the limited-payment period expires, the value to the company of future premiums is zero and all future mortality costs must be covered from existing funds and interest credited thereon.

CURRENT ASSUMPTION WHOLE LIFE POLICIES   **Current assumption whole life (CAWL) insurance** is unbundled, nonpar whole life insurance with nonguaranteed elements. These policies are also called **interest sensitive whole life** and **fixed premium universal life** policies. Many operate identically to UL policies except that premiums are set by the insurer and must be paid to maintain the policy in force. Some policies provide that favorable changes in current assumptions can result in lower premium payments rather than in higher policy values. The policy typically uses new money interest rates and current mortality charges in cash value determination. Their popularity has waned during the recent past.

Traditional WL relies on dividends as the mechanism for passing through deviations of actual operational experience from that implicit in the original policy pricing. CAWL policies are unbundled, meaning that an explicit allocation is made of premium payments and interest credits to policy loadings, mortality charges, and cash values. Although this allocation may not accurately reflect the company's actual internal pricing components, the owner can see the internal functioning of the policy in terms of how premium payments and interest credits are allocated. By contrast, bundled policies, such as traditional WL, provide little or no such transparency.

Variations in CAWL product design exist. For example, some insurers offer a death benefit equal to a level, stated amount plus an additional amount equal to the accumulation fund balance, duplicating the UL options A and B death benefit patterns. Some insurers make no premium redeterminations while others make them every year or every three or five years, and some versions contain even longer guarantee periods. Some CAWL policies make adjustments based on interest alone and some index the policy's current interest rate to interest rates on financial instruments, such as government securities or bond indexes.

VARIABLE LIFE POLICIES   Variable whole life insurance (VLI), also called *unit-linked life insurance* in many markets, provides WL insurance whose values vary directly with the performance of a specified investment fund, just as with variable universal life (VUL). VLI predates VUL, being first offered in the U.S. in 1976, after being developed and sold successfully in The Netherlands, England, and Canada. Its initial success in the U.S. was limited, with what is now known as *AXA-Equitable Life Insurance Company* involved in pioneering marketing efforts. Since that time, insurers worldwide have begun offering VLI or VUL or both.

VLI was introduced as a product that could help offset the adverse effects of inflation on life insurance policy values. It was believed that the long term investment returns of common stocks supporting the policies would increase at a rate faster than the inflation rate. While accurate historically over periods of many years, short term deviations were inevitable.

Nature   A variable whole life policy's death benefits and cash values vary to reflect the experience of a distinct pool of investments held in separate accounts, called *unit trusts* in some markets, which are distinct from the general account investments that back reserves on all of an insurer's non-variable contracts. Variable policies that carry fixed premiums are referred to as *scheduled premium* policies in many U.S. jurisdictions, just like traditional WL insurance.

As with VUL, VLI premiums net of expense loads and mortality charges are paid into the separate investment account. The policyowner may direct, within limits, where the assets backing the cash value are to be invested. Several options are available, as with mutual funds. Policy cash values and death benefits ordinarily are directly related to the investment performance. However, in the U.S. and Japan, regardless of the investment performance, the death benefit is guaranteed never to fall below a specified minimum. Cash values traditionally have not been guaranteed, although some newer VLI designs provide a guaranteed minimum return. The cash value at any point in time is based on the market value of the policy's share of the separate account's funds. Traditional VLI contracts pass all investment risk to the policyowner.

The death benefit is composed of two parts. The first part is a guaranteed minimum death benefit that corresponds to the basic plan of insurance underlying the VLI contract. The second part of the death benefit is variable. Any positive excess interest credits (i.e., the excess of the return on the underlying funds over an assumed investment return) is used to buy additional units of VLI insurance. These additional units are generally purchased at net premium rates on a daily, monthly, or annual basis. If the excess interest credits are negative, previously purchased units are surrendered and the total death benefit lowered. Regulation in the U.S. provides that the total policy death benefit may not fall below the minimum guaranteed.

Although it is relatively easy for insurers to describe how variable life insurance policy benefits vary to reflect the investment experience of the underlying separate account, to describe the specific method of determining benefit variation is a challenge. To supplement the narrative descriptions in the policy and prospectus, illustrations of policy benefits (assuming hypothetical rates of return in the separate account) are developed. Currently, applicable U.S. regulations permit illustrations based on (1) annual gross rates of return (after any tax charges and before other deductions) of 0, 4, 6, 8, 10, and 12 percent and (2) the Standard and Poor's 500 Stock Price Index with dividends reinvested.

Variable life policies may be par or nonpar. With par VLI, the dividend is a function of mortality and expense savings only and includes no element of excess investment earnings which are reflected in the separate account performance. Excess investment earnings less charges are credited directly to policy cash values.

Policy Provisions Unique to Variable Life In most respects, the VLI policy operates in the same manner as a traditional WL policy, including requirements that the policy contain the normal life insurance provisions discussed in Chapter 5. With traditional forms, fixed premiums are payable on regular due dates, and, if they are not paid, the policy lapses and goes under one of the nonforfeiture options on lapse. The policy may be reinstated subject to usual rules, except that past due premiums collected must not be less than 110 percent of the increase in cash value immediately available upon reinstatement. This condition is necessary because the reinstated policy reflects values associated with a policy that had never lapsed and thus would reflect any favorable investment experience during the period of lapse.

Policy loans must be made available in an amount equal to at least 75 percent of the cash value at a fixed (often 8.0 percent) or a variable interest rate. Loans against policy cash values have the effect of creating an additional investment fund. Under this approach, variable benefits are affected, as the return reflected in benefits is a blend of the separate account investment return and the net return earned on any policy loan. An interesting characteristic of this provision is that it presents an opportunity for a policyowner to influence the policy's variable benefits. In making a loan, the policyowner withdraws funds from the separate account making the policy less variable while the policy loan is outstanding.

The Appropriateness of Variable Life Traditional variable life insurance should be appealing to those who desire WL insurance at a fixed, level premium and the potential for important equity gains (and losses). Clearly, VLI is riskier than the more traditional forms of life insurance. As a result, regulations require greater disclosure than that required for other life policies, as discussed in Chapter 19.

Most financial plans have as one of their elements a savings program that is both highly liquid and relatively riskless. A VLI policy may not meet this objective. Its cash value might be more appropriately considered as an element in one's long term investment program.

OTHER WHOLE LIFE POLICIES   Several other forms of whole life insurance policies exist, some of which are covered here. While the market share of each of these policies is small in most markets, some of them were at one time relatively important in some markets and remain so in selected markets. Irrespective of their relative importance to a given market, they illustrate important concepts.

Modified Life Insurance   A **modified life insurance policy** provides WL insurance under which premiums are redistributed so that they are lower than an otherwise identical ordinary life policy during the first three to five years, and higher thereafter. Thus, one company's "modified 5" policy carries a premium during the first five years that is one-half of the premiums thereafter. During the preliminary period, the premium is more than the equivalent level term premium for such a period, but less than the ordinary life premium at date of issue. Logically, after the preliminary period, the premium is somewhat larger than the ordinary life premium at the issue date, but less than the ordinary life premium at the insured's attained age at the end of the preliminary period. Regardless of the redistribution arrangement utilized, the company expects to receive the actuarial equivalent of the regular ordinary life premiums, assuming that all underlying assumptions were equivalent.

Enhanced Ordinary Life Insurance   In the recent past, several mutual companies offered a par ordinary life policy that used dividends to provide some form of level coverage at a lower than usual premium. Under one approach, the face amount of a special ordinary life policy is reduced after a few years. However, before this period, dividends are used to purchase deferred paid-up WL additions, such that at the time the policy face amount is to be reduced, the deferred paid-up additions fill the gap, with the result that the total death benefit is (intended to be) at least equal to the original face amount (based on illustrated dividends).

Under another approach, the actual policy face amount may be 60 to 80 percent of the initial death benefit, with the difference made up by dividends purchasing paid-up additions and term insurance in such proportions that the total death benefit is intended to remain equivalent to or greater than the initial death benefit. It is hoped that paid-up additions eventually are sufficient to require no further purchase of term insurance.

A guarantee period is used to ensure that the total death benefit during the early policy years does not fall below the original level, even if dividends prove insufficient to meet the desired targets. With most companies, if dividends actually paid exceed those needed to purchase the requisite amount of additional coverage, the excess dividend purchases paid up additions. If dividends paid are lower than illustrated, the majority of plans require the purchase of one year term.

Graded Premium Whole Life Insurance   The traditional forms of **graded premium whole life** (GPWL) **insurance** provide that premiums begin at a level that is 50 percent or less than those for a comparable ordinary life policy. Premiums increase annually for a period of from five to 20 years and remain level thereafter. Cash values evolve much more slowly than do ordinary life values, often not appearing for five or more years. Policies may be par or nonpar and may have indeterminate premiums.

Many forms of GPWL are more akin to YRT policies than WL insurance. These types of GPWL begin with premiums that are comparable to those charged for YRT, and they have YRT-type increases for many years thereafter. The premium ultimately levels off. Typically, no cash values evolve until well after the tenth policy year. Premiums are often indeterminate and smoker/nonsmoker rates are typically used. A few companies also have reentry provisions.

Indexed Whole Life Insurance   Several companies offer **indexed whole life policies** whose face amount increases with increases in the inflation rate as measured by some national price index, such as the CPI in the U.S. These policies can be classified as to whether the policyowner or the company assumes the inflation risk. Under the approach where the policyowner assumes much of the risk, the death benefit increases each year in accordance with the price index and the insurance company bills the policyowner each year for the new, higher amount of insurance. The company agrees by contract not to require evidence of insurability for these increases provided each year's increase is accepted. If the policyowner declines in any year to purchase the increase, no further automatic increases are permitted because of concern about adverse selection.

The approach under which the insurer assumes much of the inflation risk is similar in effect to the preceding approach, except that the premium charged initially by the insurer anticipates future face amount increases. Thus, increases in face amount do not alter the premium level paid. Such policies often have a cap as to the maximum total increase permitted.

Special Purpose Whole Life Insurance   Insurers issue a wide variety of special policies and policy combinations. These special forms are based on the same principles that underpin all life insurance and typically rely on some type of whole life as the core insurance. They differ only in that they are typically oriented toward a particular, often lower income, market. The contracts were developed for specialized purposes and do not offer the same flexibility as do the more common forms of contracts.

Debit Insurance. Dating from the 1800s in the U.S. and with roots in seventeenth-century England, the debit insurance business was the backbone of the U.S. life insurance industry until early in the twentieth century. Originally, **debit insurance** was synonymous with industrial insurance – policies issued for small amounts, usually less than $2,000, with premiums payable weekly or monthly to an agent who called at the policyowner's home or place of employment. It was designed for low-income families who could not afford the amounts of protection and premium payments associated with ordinary life and health insurance.

The agent's assigned territory was referred to as the **debit** (derived from the agent's "debiting" the client's records for each premium payment). Industrial insurance today represents a tiny share of most country markets. Debit life insurance today in the U.S. encompasses **monthly debit ordinary** (MDO) insurance – ordinary policies typically written in the $5,000 to $25,000 range. In recent years, industrial life insurance and MDO have come to be known as **home service life insurance**.

Family Policy/Rider. Many companies issue a policy or, more commonly, a rider that insures all or selected members of the family in one contract, commonly called a **family policy** or **family rider**. When issued as a policy, it provides WL insurance on the father or the mother, designated as the principal insured. Term insurance is generally provided on the spouse and children. When coverage is issued as a rider, no underlying insurance is provided through the rider on the principal insured's life. Coverage on the spouse may be a stated amount or may vary in amount with age. Insurance on the children is term for a fixed amount. All children living with the family are covered, even if adopted or born after the policy is issued. Coverage is accorded children of more than a few days old (e.g., 15 days) and below a stated age, such as 18, 21, or 25, and it is usually convertible to any WL plan of insurance without evidence of insurability (and often for up to five times the amount of expiring term insurance). If the principal insured dies, the insurance on the spouse and children may become paid up.

Juvenile Insurance. Life insurance sold on the lives of children typically is some form of WL insurance (or endowment insurance in many Asian markets) on the application of a parent or other person responsible for the support of the child. Most companies permit the purchase of any reasonable amount of life insurance on a child's life subject to underwriting requirements as to reasonableness and adequacy of coverage on parents' and siblings' lives. Most companies require that the child be at least one month old. Because the insured under a juvenile policy is a minor, control of the policy typically vests in the applicant (usually a parent) until the child attains age 18. Many companies will issue regular policies to minors on their own application provided they are above the juvenile age limit set by the particular state involved.

Juvenile insurance is sold to provide funds (1) for last illness and funeral expenses, (2) for college education, (3) to start an insurance program for a child at a low premium rate, (4) to assure that a child will have some life insurance even if he or she later becomes uninsurable, and/or (5), with the addition of a rider to guarantee the right to purchase additional insurance, to assure the right to have a self-completing insurance program into adulthood. Whether any of these reasons is convincing to a parent or grandparent is a matter of judgment. Often, however, there is inadequate insurance coverage on parents' lives, and the primary objective should be to insure fully against loss of income brought about by the death of the breadwinners. The death of a child, as sad as it is, rarely causes major financial loss to the family, and therefore life insurance on a child's life is considered by many to be questionable.

Pre-Need Funeral Insurance. Whole life insurance benefits earmarked to prefund future funeral expenses are said to have first appeared in the U.S. in 1930. From a business that once evoked concerns about fairness and cost, it has evolved to what today is referred to as **pre-need funeral insurance** which pays death proceeds specified by the details of the goods and services to be delivered by the funeral provider. The typical buyer is 65 to 70 years old and purchases a $2,500 to $5,000 single premium WL policy.

Higher issue age limits, lenient underwriting (and accompanying higher mortality), and a small policy size result in comparatively high premium rates. Concern has been expressed in the U.S. that consumers (1) did not understand that life insurance was being used to fund the funeral, (2) were unaware of certain restrictions on delivery of the goods and services, and (3) were unaware that they were dealing with a life insurance agent in the form of the funeral home employee. As a result, many states now require greater disclosure with such policies.

USES AND CONSIDERATIONS OF WHOLE LIFE INSURANCE

Contemporary WL policies offer greater flexibility and value than did earlier versions. For persons whose life insurance need is expected to extend for 15 or more years and who are interested in accumulating savings via life insurance, WL can be an attractive option, as can UL. By leveling premium payments, WL outlays can be relatively modest. Interest credited on cash values enjoys the same favorable income tax treatment as other qualified cash value policies, rendering the policy a potentially attractive means of accumulating savings. Moreover, the importance of a conservative approach to investments backing par WL policy reserves – insurers invest heavily in long duration, high grade bonds – and use of the portfolio average method of investment income allocation have meant that many companies' WL policies' values held up well during the 2008-09 recession and afterward, especially in comparison to consumers' other investments and many UL policies.

Most WL policies prove costly for those who terminate them within the first 15 years or so and for whose life insurance need is less than 15 or so years, as the typically heavy frontend expenses penalize short- and medium-term values. For some persons, WL policies can serve as a quasi-forced savings plan due to the required high funding levels.

For many persons whose careers are just beginning, the premium payment required for an adequate amount of WL insurance may be too great, given other priorities. Rather than reduce the insurance amount to that which is affordable, good risk management principles argue for placing primary emphasis on the insurance needed to cover the potential loss, with secondary emphasis on product type. The only effective choice may be to purchase term insurance.

LIFE INSURANCE ON MULTIPLE LIVES

Life insurance most commonly insures the life of one person. It is theoretically possible to write a life insurance contract on any number of lives and to construct it to pay on the death of the first, second, third, etc., or last of the group to die. In practice, two important plans have evolved: (1) second-to-die life insurance and (2) first-to-die life insurance.

SECOND-TO-DIE LIFE INSURANCE

Second-to-die life insurance, also called **survivorship life insurance** and **last-to-die life insurance,** insures two (or sometimes more) lives and pays the death proceeds only on the death of the second (or last) insured to die. These policies can be in the form of WL, UL, VUL, or term insurance. NLG features are also available with some of these policies.

As the policy promises to pay only on the death of the second of two insureds, the policy's premiums are quite low relative to those that would be charged for a separate policy of the same type on each insured. If this year's probability of death is, say, 1.0 per thousand for one insured and 2.0 per thousand for the other insured, the probability of both insureds dying and, therefore, the policy face amount having to be paid is only 2 per million (i.e., 0.001 times 0.002). Premiums are based on such joint probabilities and are correspondingly low. The underlying mechanics and risk sharing (mortality, investment income, expenses) for single life and survivorship policies are identical, whether WL or UL, with the mortality charge rate being lower for survivorship. The policy options and riders offered for single life policies typically are offered for survivorship policies.

A so-called split option is available in many policies. The **split option** allows the survivorship policy to be split into two individual policies of the same generic type as the survivorship policy, one on each insured. Some insurers levy a separate charge for this option. The option can be elected only under certain conditions, such as on divorce. Also, some policies provide that a dramatic change in estate tax laws can trigger the option, as the usual reason for having purchased the policy (to cover estate taxes) may have disappeared.

Under U.S. estate tax law, assets bequeathed in a qualifying manner to a surviving spouse escape all federal estate taxation. At the death of the surviving spouse (and assuming no remarriage), any remaining assets are subject to estate taxation at potentially high rates. See Chapters 21 and 22. The second-to-die policy is well situated to meet the need for cash to cover these estate taxes and related expenses on the second death.

These policies are also commonly used to provide financial security for a disabled child or dependent relative in situations where one death would not necessarily result in financial disaster for survivors, but the deaths of both husband and wife (or other breadwinners) would. Many companies offer more flexible underwriting with survivorship life than with single life policies, such as when one of the individuals is uninsurable or highly rated.

FIRST-TO-DIE LIFE INSURANCE

In contrast to survivorship life insurance, **joint life insurance**, also called **first-to-die life insurance,** promises to pay the face amount of the policy on the first death of two (or more) insureds covered by the contract. The policy is often used to insure both a husband and wife, with each being the beneficiary for the other, and in business buyout situations involving multiple partners or major stockholders. The policy pays only on the death of the first to die and is terminated at that time.

Contracts usually provide that the survivor has the right to purchase a cash value policy on his or her life without providing evidence of insurability. Some contracts continue insurance temporarily, and most provide that if both insureds die in a common disaster, the insurer will pay the face amount on each death.

The premium for a given face amount is smaller than the total premiums paid for two individual life policies of the same generic type covering each individual. Joint life coverage is available as WL, term, or UL, with a NLG feature offered by some insurers. Joint life insurance is less popular today than in past times and is typically sold in comparatively modest amounts.

Highly specialized life insurance products exist in the form of proprietary and private placement life insurance products. Both types of products are targeted to individuals of high net worth, but the similarity mostly ends there.

PROPRIETARY LIFE INSURANCE

A **proprietary life** or **health insurance** product is a policy that is targeted and priced for a specific market and available to be sold exclusively by a cohesive group of agents. For example, one marketing organization offers proprietary products specifically targeted and priced for the ultra affluent market and sold exclusively by its agents whose target markets are high net worth clients. By targeting a specific market, the product can be priced to reflect more closely the actual and reasonably anticipated mortality, lapse, and other experience of that market. Thus, because ultra affluent individuals live longer on average than the insured population in general, proprietary products designed for that market can be priced with lower mortality charges than otherwise. Most proprietary life products are built on a UL chassis. These products may be distinguished from those intended to appeal to a broader or less favorable target market and sold via multiple distribution systems.

Captive life insurance agents (see Chapter 10) who have the exclusive right to sell the products of their insurers can be considered selling proprietary life insurance products if pricing reflects the characteristics of a specific market. Thus, if an insurer offers a class of policies with high minimum issue requirements (e.g., $1.0 million) and if these policies' mortality, persistency, and other experience is favorable and constitutes a separate experience class for purposes of pricing, they would be considered as proprietary products.

PRIVATE PLACEMENT LIFE INSURANCE

In the U.S., **private placement life insurance** (PPLI) products are individually tailored variable life insurance policies not subject to SEC registration requirements (although most other SEC regulations apply) and designed specifically for and available only to certain qualified investors. To purchase PPLI, individuals must qualify as accredited investors or qualified purchasers. An **accredited investor** is a wealthy investor who meets SEC requirements as to minimum net worth (in excess of $1.0 million) or annual income (in excess of $200,000). A **qualified purchaser** is any individual or family organization with net investments of $5.0 million or more.

PPLI is similar to retail VUL insurance in that:

- it must meet the IRC's definition of life insurance to retain favorable tax treatment,
- the underwriting process is the same,
- rating classifications are the same,
- the proposed insured must demonstrate a financial need for the requested insurance, and
- the mechanics of the PPLI policy itself are the same.

PPLI differs from retail life insurance in that:

- commissions and policy loads may be negotiated and are usually lower,

- neither the PPLI policy nor the separate account needs be registered with the SEC,
- no sales material or advertising is permitted,
- investment options are considerably broader, including private equity and hedge funds,
- the insurer need not be domestic, and
- the client can invest only after reading a private placement memorandum akin to a prospectus.

Some PPLI products are said to require minimum premiums as low as $1.0 million, but premiums in the $5.0 to $10.0 million and greater range seem more common, often with payments spread over some years. Buyers of PPLI are said to be less interested in the actual insurance component than in the tax and investment diversification benefits, although exceptions exist.

ENDOWMENT LIFE INSURANCE

Endowment insurance is popular in numerous markets (e.g., Germany, Japan, Korea, Taiwan, and Thailand), although no longer in the U.S. Even in the U.S., some endowment insurance is still found in qualified retirement plans, and many older endowment policies remain in force. An understanding of the concepts that underlie endowments is essential irrespective of the product's popularity in a given market.

NATURE OF ENDOWMENT INSURANCE

Term policies provide for the payment of the full policy amount only if the insured dies during the policy term. Endowment policies similarly promise to pay the policy face amount on the insured's death during the policy term but also to pay the face (or some other) amount if the insured survives the term. Whereas policies payable only in the event of death are purchased chiefly for the benefit of others, endowment policies, although affording protection to others against the insured's death during the fixed term, pay if the insured survives the endowment period. Endowment insurance can be viewed in two equally valid ways: (1) the mathematical concept and (2) the economic concept.

MATHEMATICAL CONCEPT   The insurer makes two mutually exclusive promises under endowment insurance: (1) to pay the face amount if the insured dies during the policy term or (2) to pay the face (or some other) amount if the insured survives to the end of the policy term. The first promise is identical to that made under a term policy for an equivalent face amount and period. An evaluation of the second promise requires introduction of the pure endowment concept. A **pure endowment** promises to pay a maturity amount only if the insured is living at the end of a specified period, with nothing paid in case of prior death. Pure endowment insurance is not often sold as a separate contract but often is embedded within policies that provide other benefits. In fact, most U.S. states prohibit the sale of pure endowment insurance policies, although a pure life annuity *is* a series of pure endowments (see Chapter 6). It is said that few people are willing to risk the *apparent* loss of all premiums paid in the event of death before the end of the endowment period.

Thus, to provide a death benefit during the endowment period, only term insurance for the same period need be added to the pure endowment. Pricing for the policy builds on this simple concept. Simply add the costs of providing term insurance for any policy duration, *n*, to the cost of providing the pure endowment benefit at the end of that duration, as follows:

$$Endowment\ Insurance_n = Term\ Life\ Insurance_n + Pure\ Endowment_n$$

ECONOMIC CONCEPT   The economic concept views endowment insurance as composed of two parts: decreasing term insurance and increasing savings. The savings part is available to the policyowner through surrender of the policy. This increasing savings feature is supplemented by decreasing term insurance, which, when added to the savings accumulation, equals the policy's face amount. This is the same analogy discussed in Chapter 2 with respect to WL insurance policies.

Insurance contracts have not always fit the increasing savings, decreasing term insurance model. In earlier times in the U.S. and in other countries today, no savings values existed in life insurance contracts. If an individual ceased premium payments, no return of any sort was available as a matter of contract. The contract promised to pay in the event of death or survival to a certain age, but if the contract was discontinued prior to the occurrence of one of these contingencies, all premiums were considered fully earned and any mortality pre-funding was forfeited. Of course, these forfeitures could be used to subsidize the persisting policies, making for lower premium payments than otherwise or enhanced dividends or other benefits.

TYPES OF ENDOWMENT POLICIES

Variations of endowment insurance are enormous worldwide. Many policies are for set durations of from 5 to 30 or more years, and others are arranged to mature at certain ages, such as at 60, 65, or 70. Endowment policies of from three to 10 years' duration are common in many Asian countries. Premiums often are due throughout the term, although limited payment plans, such as an endowment-at-age-65 paid up in 20 years, have been available. In several European countries, single premium endowment policies are popular. In the U.K., long term endowment policies are commonly purchased as a mortgage loan companion, the idea being that the endowment maturity value will pay off the outstanding loan balance at a preset time.

Besides the standard contracts, other applications of the endowment principle are sometimes made. With a **retirement income policy**, sometimes used for insured pension plans, the amount payable at death is the face amount or cash value, whichever is greater. The contract is used in insured pension plans utilizing individual contracts. A **semi-endowment policy** pays upon survival one-half the sum payable on death during the endowment period. **Modified endowment policies**, popular in some markets such as Thailand, provide for the payment periodically of a set percentage of the insured amount over the policy term, as well as a maturity amount.

Term life insurance riders are added to endowment policies in some markets, such as Japan. Within the U.S. in the 1970s, a popular form of term insurance, known by the misleading name of "deposit term," provided for payment of a modest endowment whose amount was set equal to a multiple of the difference between the first year and renewal premiums. (First year premiums on the policy were set to be higher than renewal premiums.) The marketing material suggested that this maturity amount was due to this premium differential, which was not correct.

Juvenile endowment policies insure the lives of juveniles and mature at specified ages or events associated with a child's education, marriage, or independence. These policies are popular in many markets, although not in the U.S. Educational endowment policies are particularly popular in several Asian countries, including Korea and Japan.

A company's liability under an endowment policy involves not only payment of the face amount upon death but also payment upon survival of the term. It follows that the annual premium on these policies must be higher than that for WL or term policies, except for very long endowment periods, in which the rate is only slightly higher than that charged on an ordinary life policy.

USES AND CONSIDERATIONS OF ENDOWMENT INSURANCE

At one time in the U.S., endowment insurance was considered an effective vehicle for accumulating savings. However, even before 1984 tax law changes effectively limited the endowment insurance market to qualified retirement plans, endowment insurance was having great difficulty competing against WL and term insurance. The high first-year expenses associated with policies sold at that time rendered many of them less-than-stellar savings vehicles.

While endowments remain popular savings instruments in numerous other markets, sales have declined in favor of WL, UL, and term life sales in most markets. Even so, favorable tax treatment coupled with a strong savings impetus has resulted in a continuing strong demand for endowments in many markets. Endowments can be effective savings instruments provided loadings are competitive with those of other savings media of equivalent risk.

SUMMARY OF ATTRIBUTES OF COMMON PERSONAL LIFE INSURANCE POLICIES

To close these two chapters on personal life insurance, we offer a summary of the attributes of the most common generic forms of such policies, shown in Table 4-2 for term life and the three most common generic cash value policies: WL, UL, and VUL. The appendix contains a more detailed summary of the attributes of these four generic forms plus other common cash value policies sold in the U.S.[1]

As shown in the table, life insurance death benefit payments ordinarily are received income-tax free, irrespective of the type of policy. (Specialized exceptions to this treatment are explained in Chapter 21.) The interest credited each year on tax-qualified policies' cash values – often called the **inside interest buildup** – is not included in the policyholder's taxable income for that year. If the policy is ultimately surrendered, some of this previously untaxed interest will be taxed in the year of surrender if a gain is realized on surrender, as discussed in Chapter 21. If the policy matures as a death claim, none of this previously untaxed interest ordinarily will be subject to income taxation, as the cash value (including the untaxed interest) becomes an indistinguishable part of the death proceeds. Tax-qualified policies are those whose funding in relation to their death benefits does not exceed limits laid out in the *Internal Revenue Code*, as described in Chapter 21. The great majority of life insurance meets these limits.

| Key Attributes of Generic Life Insurance Policies | | | | Table 4-2 |

Attribute	Term Life Insurance	Cash Value Life Insurance		
		Whole Life Insurance	Universal Life Insurance	Variable Life Insurance
Income tax free death benefit?	Yes	Yes	Yes	Yes
Accumulates cash values?	No	Yes	Yes	Yes
Income tax free or tax deferred cash value?	n.a.	Yes	Yes	Yes
Can borrow against cash value?	n.a.	Yes	Yes	Yes
Duration of coverage?	Fixed term	Lifetime	Depends on premiums paid	Depends on premiums paid
Adjustable death benefit?	No	No	Yes	Yes
Flexible premiums?	No	No	Yes	Yes
Guaranteed policy elements?	Death benefit and premium	Death benefit, maximum premium, and minimum cash values	Death benefit, maximum charges, and minimum interest crediting rate	Maximum charges
Nonguaranteed policy elements?	None, typically	Yes, commonly via dividends	Yes, via excess interest crediting rates and lower charges	Yes, via changes in account market value and lower charges

Other attributes of these generic policy forms are self explanatory, following from materials presented in this and the previous chapter. Thus, all cash value policies permit policy loans. UL policies' durations are a function of the premiums paid into them: too little and they lapse; enough and they can endow for the face amount, thus providing whole life insurance. UL has flexible premiums, and the death benefit can be adjusted.

The chapter appendix explores in detail the attributes that may distinguish one type of policy from another. The table starts with a short overview of each policy. It then examines each policy element in turn, starting with the death benefit then moving onto cash values, premiums, mortality charges, interest crediting rates, and policy loading charges.

The table shows each attribute that we examine within that heading. It also indicates how that attribute applies to term life insurance and to each of seven types of cash value insurance. As most term life policies sold today contain no nonguaranteed policy elements, our analysis assumes this position. Some par term policies are sold, but they tend to pay either no or low dividends. We omit survivorship life and joint life policies as they are generally available as any of the eight policies examined herein. They differ from the single-life policies discussed here only in a need for these contracts to deal with two deaths.

The seven types of cash value insurance policies examined comprise three types of WL and four types of UL policies. The three types of WL are (1) nonpar fixed WL, (2) nonpar CAWL, and (3) par WL. We label as nonpar fixed WL, policies for which all policy elements are fixed and guaranteed and cannot be changed. The four types of UL are (1) generic UL, (2) no lapse guarantee (NLG) UL, (3) equity-indexed UL (EIUL), and (4) VUL. We believe that these seven types of cash value policies encompass the great majority of permanent life insurance sold today in the U.S.

CONCLUSIONS

Whole life insurance accounts about one-quarter of personal life insurance in force in the U.S. After more than a century and a half of evolution, it remains popular in the U.S. and many markets worldwide. In its non-variable form, it offers a relatively conservative, long-term protection and savings package that has a demonstrated track record of performing well in both strong and adverse economic conditions. WL policies are found in several permutations intended to appeal to the needs of specific target markets.

First-to-die and second-to-die policies insure two or more lives, with the former paying a death benefit on the death of the first of two insureds and the latter paying on the death of the second of two insureds. Second-to-die life insurance has proven quite popular for estate conservation purposes in the U.S.

Endowment insurance is popular in many markets worldwide but not in the U.S. due to adverse tax treatment in comparison with other life insurance policies. The principles underlying the pricing of endowments are found in other products.

APPENDIX 4A:
ATTRIBUTES OF TERM AND CASH VALUE LIFE INSURANCE POLICIES[1]

Attribute	Term Life Insurance	Cash Value Life Insurance						
		Whole Life Insurance			Universal Life Insurance			
		Nonpar Fixed	Nonpar Current Assumption	Par	Generic	No Lapse Guarantee	Equity Indexed	Variable
Overview								
Primary Policy Appeal?	Guaranteed coverage for specific period and low premium outlay	Guaranteed lifetime coverage with all policy elements fixed	Guaranteed lifetime coverage, transparency, backed by conservative investments	Guaranteed lifetime coverage, backed by conservative investments	Flexibility, transparency, backed by conservative investments	Guaranteed lifetime coverage at low premium outlay	Flexibility, transparency, with limited equity-like returns and a guaranteed floor	Flexibility, transparency, with mutual fund returns
Bundled or unbundled?	Bundled	Bundled	Unbundled	Bundled	Unbundled	Unbundled	Unbundled	Unbundled
Contains nonguaranteed policy elements?	No, typically	No	Yes, via current interest credits and charges	Yes, via dividends	Yes, via current interest credits and charges	Yes, via current interest credits and charges for cash values; no for guaranteed coverage	Yes, via equity index changes and current charges	Yes, via market value changes and current charges
Death Benefits								
Guaranteed?	Yes	Yes	Yes	Yes	Yes	Yes	Yes	No
Duration?	Fixed term	Life	Life	Life	Flexible, including life	Flexible, including life	Flexible, including life	Flexible, including life

Attribute	Term Life Insurance	Cash Value Life Insurance						
		Whole Life Insurance			Universal Life Insurance			
		Nonpar Fixed	Nonpar Current Assumption	Par	Generic	No Lapse Guarantee	Equity Indexed	Variable
Adjusta-bility of duration?	No	Not easily	Not easily	Not easily	Yes	Yes	Yes	Yes
Death benefit adjustable?	No	No	Yes	Not easily	Yes	Yes	Yes	Yes
Choice of level or increasing?	No, typically	No	Yes	Yes, via riders or dividends	Yes	Yes	Yes	Yes
Cash Values								
Builds cash values?	No	Yes	Yes	Yes	Yes	Yes	Yes	Yes
Guaran-teed?	n.a.	Yes	Yes, if not relying on nonguar-anteed premium	Yes, except for illus-trated cash val-ues attrib-utable to dividends	Yes, if funded to guarantees	Yes, if funded to guarantees	Yes, if funded to guarantees	No
Location and nature of underly-ing invest-ments?	General account; bonds and mortgages	General account; bonds and mortgages	General account; bonds and mortgages	General account; bonds and mortgages	General account; bonds and mortgages	General account; bonds and mortgages	General account; bonds and mortgages and equity index call options	Separate account; fixed income and equity mutual funds
Increased likelihood of lapse with adverse develop-ment in current assump-tions?	No	No	No, unless relying on nonguar-anteed premium	No, unless relying on dividends to fund	Yes, but can be managed with additional premiums	No	Yes, but can be managed with additional premiums	Yes, but can be managed with additional premiums
Impact of changes in market value on cash value?	n.a.	None	Indirect and muted	Indirect and muted	Indirect and muted	Indirect and muted	Indirect and moderate	Direct

Attribute	Term Life Insurance	Cash Value Life Insurance						
		Whole Life Insurance			Universal Life Insurance			
		Nonpar Fixed	Nonpar Current Assumption	Par	Generic	No Lapse Guarantee	Equity Indexed	Variable
Policy-holder control of fund allocations?	n.a.	None	None	None	None	None	Allocations to index account	Total
Policy loans available?	No	Yes	Yes	Yes	Yes	Yes, but will impact NLG	Yes	Yes
With-drawals available?	No	No	No	Yes, indi-rectly via surrender of PUAs	Yes	Yes, but will impact NLG	Yes	Yes
Fixed rela-tionship to death benefit?	n.a.	Yes	Yes	Yes	No	No	No	No
High early cash values?	n.a.	No	Yes	No, typically	Yes, often	No	Yes, often	Yes, often
Protected from claims of insolvent insurer's creditors?	n.a.	No	No	No	No	No	No	Yes
Premiums								
Flexible?	No	No	No	No	Yes	Yes, but need to manage NLG	Yes	Yes
Ability to mimic any other pol-icy type?	No	No	No	No	Yes	Yes	Yes	Yes
Skipping premium payment possible?	No	Not easily	Not easily	Not easily	Yes	Yes, but will reduce NLG duration	Yes	Yes

Attribute	Term Life Insurance	Cash Value Life Insurance						
		Whole Life Insurance			Universal Life Insurance			
		Nonpar Fixed	Nonpar Current Assumption	Par	Generic	No Lapse Guarantee	Equity Indexed	Variable
Effect if premium not paid?	Lapse	Paid via policy loan if APL elected, o/w lapse to NFB*	Paid via policy loan if APL elected, o/w lapse to NFB*	Paid via policy loan if APL elected, o/w lapse to NFB*	Nothing, smaller policy value	Nothing, but will reduce NLG duration and policy value	Nothing, smaller policy value	Nothing, smaller policy value
How to resume premium payments and full coverage after premium nonpayment?	Pay past due premiums and re-qualify for insurance	If under NFB, pay past due premiums and re-qualify for insurance	If under NFB, pay past due premiums and re-qualify for insurance	If under NFB, pay past due premiums and re-qualify for insurance	Payments optional; full coverage remains if sufficient value	Payments optional; full coverage remains if sufficient value	Payments optional; full coverage remains if sufficient value	Payments optional; full coverage remains if sufficient value
Mortality Charges								
Guaranteed maximum mortality charges?	Yes	Yes	Yes, unless subsidized via other nonguar. elements	Yes, if mortality gains cannot be negative	Yes, unless subsidized via other nonguar. elements	Yes, unless subsidized via other nonguar. elements	Yes, unless subsidized via other nonguar. elements	Yes, unless subsidized via other nonguar. elements
Can actual charges differ from those at policy issuance?	No, typically	No	Yes	Yes	Yes	Yes for cash value; no for NLG	Yes	Yes
Who determines mortality charges?	Insurer	Insurer	Insurer	Insurer	Insurer	Insurer	Insurer	Insurer
Mortality charges disclosed to policyholder?	No, but premium may be near actual	No	Yes	No	Yes	Yes	Yes	Yes
Volatility of mortality charges?	None, typically	None	Low	Low	Low	Low for cash value; none for NLG	Low	Low

Attribute	Term Life Insurance	Cash Value Life Insurance						
		Whole Life Insurance			Universal Life Insurance			
		Nonpar Fixed	Nonpar Current Assumption	Par	Generic	No Lapse Guarantee	Equity Indexed	Variable
Crediting Rates								
Guaranteed minimum crediting rate?	n.a.	Yes	Yes, unless subsidized via other nonguar. elements	Yes, if investment gains cannot be negative	Yes, unless subsidized via other nonguar. elements	Yes, unless subsidized via other nonguar. elements	Yes, unless subsidized via other nonguar. elements	No
Can actual crediting rates differ from those illustrated at issue?	n.a.	No	Yes	Yes	Yes	Yes for cash value; no for NLG	Yes	Yes
Who determines crediting rate?	Insurer	Insurer	Insurer	Insurer	Insurer	Insurer	Insurer and index	Actual investment return
Rate disclosed to policyholder?	n.a.	n.a.	Yes	No, except for some insurers	Yes	Yes	Yes	Yes
Volatility of crediting rate?	None	None	Low to moderate depending on allocation method	Low to moderate depending on allocation method	Low to moderate depending on allocation method	Low to moderate for cash value; none for NLG	Low to high depending on allocation	Low to very high depending on fund choice
Crediting rate includes dividend income?	n.a.	n.a.	Yes, but modest	Yes, but modest	Yes, but modest	Yes, but modest	No	Yes
Policy Loading Charges								
Guaranteed maximum loading charges?	Yes	Yes	Yes, unless subsidized via other nonguar. elements	Yes, if expense gains cannot be negative	Yes, unless subsidized via other nonguar. elements	Yes, unless subsidized via other nonguar. elements	Yes, unless subsidized via other nonguar. elements	Yes, unless subsidized via other nonguar. elements

Attribute	Term Life Insurance	Cash Value Life Insurance						
		Whole Life Insurance			Universal Life Insurance			
		Nonpar Fixed	Nonpar Current Assumption	Par	Generic	No Lapse Guarantee	Equity Indexed	Variable
Can actual charges differ from those illustrated at issue?	No	No	Yes	Yes	Yes	Yes for cash value; no for NLG	Yes	Yes
Who determines loading charges?	Insurer	Insurer	Insurer	Insurer	Insurer	Insurer	Insurer	Insurer
Loading charges disclosed to policyholder?	No	No	Yes	No	Yes	Yes	Yes	Yes
Volatility of loading charges?	None	None	Low	Low	Low	Low for cash value; none for NLG	Low	Low

*APL = automatic premium loan. NFB = nonforfeiture benefits.

ENDNOTES

1   This discussion and the appendix draw from Harold D. Skipper and Wayne Tonning, *The Advisor's Guide to Life Insurance* (Chicago; American Bar Association, 2011), Chapter 8.

CHAPTER 5

LIFE INSURANCE POLICY PROVISIONS AND RIDERS

This chapter continues Part I on life insurance products by exploring the life insurance policy as a contract.[1] We first provide an overview of the physical format and content of life insurance policies. We next examine the major provisions commonly found in life insurance policies. These collectively define the scope of the insurer's promise to the policyholder. Thereafter, we explore common riders that may be optionally included in policies, typically for an additional premium charge.

State insurance laws require life insurance companies to include so-called *standard policy provisions* within their policies. The laws do not mandate actual wording for these provisions. Rather, they provide that policies must contain provisions whose language is at least as favorable to the policyholder as that of the statute. Certain other provisions may be included in life insurance contracts at the option of the insurer. We cover both types of provisions in the following section, noting whether each is required or optional. Provisions are sometimes also called *clauses*.

Policy forms proposed for use by insurers are required to be submitted to and often formally approved by the insurance department of each state in which the insurer wishes to sell the policy. In addition to including the standard policy provisions, forms may not contain certain prohibited or restricted provisions, and the policy language must meet certain minimum readability standards. Forms also must comply with specific administrative guidelines established by each state. See Chapter 12.

In general, life insurance policies may be physically arranged in whatever format the insurer chooses, with the exceptions of a few aspects of the first page and that the format may not be misleading. The first page ordinarily identifies the life insurer by its full name and address, may show the name of the insured and the policy number, and contains the contract insuring clause. Facsimile signatures of the insurer's president or CEO and secretary also appear.

The **insuring clause** or **insuring agreement** is the company's promise to pay the benefits due, subject to the policy provisions. It may describe in general terms that the company also agrees pay any benefits during the insured's lifetime. An illustrative clause is as follows:

OVERVIEW: POLICY CONTENT AND FORMAT

If the insured dies while this policy is in force, we will pay the sum insured to the beneficiary, when we receive at our home office due proof of the insured's death, subject to the provisions of this policy.

The owner's consideration for this promise is the truth of the statement made in the application and payment of the initial premium. These and other aspects of the formation and continuation of the insurance contract are covered in Chapter 18. The insurer's promise to pay policy benefits will remain in effect in accordance with the policy provisions as long as the required conditions are met.

States require that the first page include a summary description of the policy. Summary descriptions might be as follows:

FLEXIBLE PREMIUM UNIVERSAL LIFE INSURANCE POLICY
or

WHOLE LIFE INSURANCE POLICY

Immediately under these descriptions typically are short statements relative to the policy death proceeds (e.g., "Sum Insured Payable at Death"), the length of the premium payment period (e.g., "Premiums Payable for a Stated Period"), and whether the policy is participating or nonparticipating.

Also required to appear on the first page is a statement typically headed by:

RIGHT TO RETURN POLICY

This "free look" provision advises that the policy may be unconditionally returned to the insurer within a certain number of days (such as 10) of receipt, explains how to return it, and states that any premiums paid will be refunded promptly.

Immediately following typically will be a table of contents for the policy and policy specifications. The policy specifications will list relevant information specific to the policy, including the insured's name, age, sex, and underwriting classification; the policy type, number, face amount, premium (planned or otherwise) and payment period; policy date, maturity date, policyowner, and beneficiary (usually); death benefit; and dividend options, if applicable. Additional details about the policy sometimes are included. One or more pages of definitions of terms used in the policy might follow the specifications page, with some insurers including tables of relevant policy values at this point.

The balance of the policy's physical arrangement will follow no standard format but will contain the standard and optional policy provisions, presented and worded as the insurer wishes. Copies of the application (see Chapter 11) along with any supplemental application forms (e.g., aviation questionnaire) will be included, often near the end of the policy. Also commonly included at or near the end of the contract will be any policy amendments and optional riders.

LIFE INSURANCE POLICY PROVISIONS

A life insurance policy is a package of options. The death benefit is equivalent to a put option exercisable at death. The underlying instrument (asset) is the insured's economic value, which at death declines to zero, so the option holder (the beneficiary) is "in the money" and can be considered economically as selling the asset to the insurer at the agreed upon strike price (the policy face amount). The seller of such puts (the insurer) profits by selling many such options, comparatively few of which are exercised in any time period. Contract provisions that make the option more secure have value to the option holder (policyholder or beneficiary). Conversely, provisions that tend to make the option less secure lessen value. Policy provisions that accord policyholders additional flexibility are themselves embedded options that have value.

Our discussion of policy provisions is structured around those three classifications. Our terminology and provision titles will not necessarily follow that of any one insurer, and the provisions are unlikely to appear in any particular policy in the precise order presented here.

PROVISIONS THAT MAKE PAYMENT MORE SECURE

All of the provisions discussed in this section are required to be contained in all life insurance policies sold in the U.S. Each is intended to provide greater assurance of the policy benefit being paid.

ENTIRE CONTRACT CLAUSE   The **entire contract clause** provides that the policy itself and the application, if a copy is attached to the policy, along with amendments and riders, constitute the entire contract between the parties. A required provision, the clause protects the policyowner in that the company cannot, merely by reference, use its procedural rules or any oral or other statements made by the applicant or proposed insured, except for those contained in the application, as a basis for rescinding the policy. This clause also protects the insurer from claims that the agent orally promised additional or different benefits from those stated in the policy.

If the insurer believes that it has been materially misled in the application process, ordinarily it must look solely to the application attached to the policy to justify its attempt to reform or rescind the policy. A **material misrepresentation** is an inaccurate statement by a proposed insured or applicant that causes an insurer to issue a policy on terms or at a price more favorable than it would have, had the statement been accurate. See Chapter 18.

INCONTESTABLE CLAUSE   The **incontestable clause** provides that the validity of an insurance contract may not be contested after it has been in force for two years. A typical incontestable clause might read as follows:

> Except for accidental death or disability premium payment benefits, we cannot contest this policy after it has been in force for two years while the insured is alive.

The clause was originally introduced by life insurance companies on a voluntary basis to provide greater assurance to the public that insurers would not deny a claim because of relatively innocent misstatements by applicants. Its roots date back to the mid-1800s in England when insurers sought to allay public concern through inclusion of an *indisputable clause* that was intended to address the then ultra-technical application of the doctrine of warranties by many insurers. As English insurers sold life insurance in the U.S., this innovation and the resulting competition by the British soon forced U.S. life insurers to adopt the same practice. *The Manhattan Life*, using a five-year time limit, seems to have been the first U.S. insurer to have incorporated the clause into its contracts.

The use of the clause spread rapidly because it was perceived as a means of addressing the public's concern about the quality and trustworthiness of U.S. life insurers following a severe post-Civil War depression that precipitated numerous insolvencies. The depressed economic conditions of the 1870s saw insurers seeking new ways of gaining a competitive advantage through contract liberalization. The 1879 adoption of the clause by what is now *AXA Equitable Life Insurance Company* gave the clause its greatest impetus. The use of the clause is now common worldwide. In the U.S., as well as in Japan and several other countries, the maximum period of contestability is two years. In other countries, such as Germany and Spain, the time limit is one year.

The clause has been given a broad interpretation in the U.S. It prevents a life insurance company from declaring as void a life insurance contract after the passage of the specified time on grounds of material misrepresentation and, often, even fraud. **Fraud** is an intentional deception or misrepresentation made for personal gain. The rationale for this broad interpretation is the protection of beneficiaries. It removes the fear of lawsuits at a time – the insured's death – when it may be difficult for the beneficiary successfully to combat an insurer's charge of misrepresentation by a person who is no longer alive to present his or her side of the case. The company agrees not to resist claim payment if premiums have been paid and the company has taken no action to rescind the contract during the stipulated time period.

Even though the clauses have been accorded broad interpretation, some challenges to contract validity after expiration of the period of contestability have been successful. Certain fraudulent actions have been found to be so egregious that courts have allowed insurers to void such policies. In most cases, the incontestable clause has been held not to bar policy avoidance where the applicant was found to lack an insurable interest in the insured's life at policy inception, or for which another person substituted for the insured in a required physical examination. See Chapter 18.

PREMIUM PROVISION   Life insurance policies are required to contain a **premium provision** that explains the nature of premiums due or otherwise payable under the policy. For bundled policies, a statement as simple as premiums are due and payable in advance may appear. For unbundled, flexible premium policies, the provision may explain that premiums can be paid at any time, subject to insurer minimums and tax-constrained maximums. If loads are assessed against premiums paid, these too may be referenced in this provision.

The provision also may advise the owner that premiums can be paid monthly, quarterly, semi-annually, or annually by check, automatic draft, or electronic funds transfer. The provision itself ordinarily does not state the actual premiums due or premium loads. That information usually appears on the policy specifications page.

GRACE PERIOD PROVISION   The **grace period provision** requires the insurer to maintain the policy in force and to accept premium payments for a certain period after the premium due date or if the policy has insufficient account value to permit it to continue in force. State laws require a minimum grace period of 30 or 31 days. Universal life (UL) polices typically offer 61 day grace periods, with some states requiring this length. During this period, the insurer (1) is required to accept payment even though it is technically late (i.e., past the due date) and (2) may not require evidence of insurability as a condition of premium acceptance.

If the insured dies during the grace period, the company must pay the claim but is permitted to deduct any overdue premium or charges plus interest from the death benefit payment. The provision's purpose is to protect the policyowner from unintentional lapse.

REINSTATEMENT CLAUSE   Another required provision, the **reinstatement clause**, gives the policyholder the right to reinstate a lapsed policy under certain conditions. The two most important conditions are furnishing satisfactory evidence of insurability and paying past due premiums or charges.

The insured ordinarily is required to furnish evidence of insurability satisfactory to the company. Otherwise, those in poor health would routinely apply for reinstatement, as experience has shown. Most lapses are unintentional and are followed within a couple of weeks by a reinstatement application. Insurers usually take a liberal position in such cases, even though they have the contractual right to require a medical examination and other detailed evidence of insurability. The longer the time period since lapse, the more closely reinstatement requirements resemble those for new applications, as detailed in Chapter 11.

The term *evidence of insurability* is broader than the term *good health*. Insurability connotes meeting standards with regard to occupation, other insurance, and financial condition, as well as the physical characteristics and health status of the insured. The term *satisfactory to the company* has generally been held to allow the insurer to require evidence that would be satisfactory to a reasonable insurer.

An interesting issue in connection with reinstatement relates to how it interacts with the incontestable clause. The majority of courts in the U.S. have held that the period of contestability is reinstated but only with respect to statements made in the reinstatement application. A second view is that the original contestable period is effective, while a third and very much a minority view holds that the original contestable period is effective with respect to the policy as a whole, but that the reinstatement itself is a separate agreement that has no incontestable period and can be contested for fraud at any time. In contrast, the courts have been virtually unanimous in holding that the suicide clause (see below) does not run again.

The second condition for reinstatement is the payment of past due premiums or charges. With whole life (WL) and term policies, the usual terms require payment of the overdue amounts, less any dividends that would have been paid, with interest at 6.0 or 8.0 percent. The interest rate may sometimes be high relative to market rates but has the effect of not only compensating the insurer for the foregone time value of money assumed in policy pricing, but also for increased mortality resulting from adverse selection. Some jurisdictions limit the collection of past due amounts to any increase in reserve between the time of lapse and reinstatement.

For UL policies, a different approach is followed. The policyholder usually is not required to pay all back charges; only those applicable for the grace period during which coverage was provided plus enough to keep the policy in force for the next two or three months. Any outstanding policy loans under both WL and UL must be either repaid or reinstated through payment of past due interest.

The reinstatement provision was originally included voluntarily by companies to safeguard accumulated policy values. Under these older contracts, if the premium was not paid when due, the policy lapsed and any accumulated policy values forfeited. With the inclusion of nonforfeiture options, the value of the reinstatement option has declined.

Reinstatement ordinarily is not permitted if the policy has been (1) surrendered, (2) continued as extended term insurance and the period of coverage has expired, or (3) lapsed for five (sometimes three) or more years. If the extended term period has not expired and has several years to run, insurers often will reinstate the policy with little or even no evidence of insurability. At one time, reinstatement was more or less routinely preferred to purchasing a new policy. In today's competitive marketplace, such is no longer necessarily true. The considerations applicable to reinstatement are quite similar to those involved with replacement. See Chapter 19.

NONFORFEITURE PROVISION   Before the mid-1800s, insurance policies made no provision for cash surrender values. If a policy lapsed, the policyowner "forfeited" all contributions in excess of those necessary to cover current and past mortality charges and expenses. The states' *Standard Nonforfeiture Laws* prohibit such forfeitures today.

These laws set out the circumstances under which policies must have nonforfeiture values and minimum required values. The laws are not applicable to variable policies. In effect, they require cash values under all life insurance policies that involve substantial prefunding of future mortality charges. They also require that cash value life policies include **nonforfeiture provisions** that state the mortality table, rate of interest, and method used in calculating the policy's nonforfeiture values and the options available if the policy is terminated or lapses. These options provide policy flexibility so we cover them under that section below.

PARTICIPATION/POLICY VALUE PROVISION   Policies are required to state whether they are participating (par) or nonparticipating (nonpar). Par policies are required to contain what may be called a **participation** or **distributable surplus provision** which states that the policy will participate in any surplus that the insurer decides to distribute to policyholders. Nonpar policies will have a **nonparticipating provision** or equivalent that states simply that the policy does not share in any insurer surplus or perhaps that it does not pay dividends.

Nonpar policies containing nonguaranteed policy elements that permit excess interest credits and/or lower-than-guaranteed charges will contain a **policy value** or **account value provision** or equivalent that explains the nature of the nonguaranteed elements and how they are determined and applied within the policy. Cost of insurance (COI) charges, loading charges, and interest crediting rates will be explained, with guaranteed maximum charges indicated and, for non-variable contracts, the minimum crediting rate.

The provisions ordinarily stipulate that the insurer's board of directors will annually determine the dividend or other nonguaranteed policy elements, except for the crediting rates under variable policies. Subject to a few states' laws limiting surplus accumulation by mutual life insurers and to any regulatory (e.g., requirement for equitable treatment of policies) and policy (e.g., guarantees) constraints, the insurer's board of directors ordinarily has sole discretion to determine how these elements will be derived and applied to non-variable policies. Chapter 16 discusses how these nonguaranteed elements are derived for both bundled and unbundled policies. Dividend options, a source of policy flexibility, are covered below and in Chapter 4.

MISSTATEMENT OF AGE OR SEX PROVISION   States require that life insurance policies include a **misstatement of age provision** stipulating that if the insured's age is found to have been misstated, adjustment will be made in policy values to reflect the true age. Thus, if the misstatement were discovered at the insured's death, the amount of insurance will be adjusted to be that which would have been purchased by the premium or the then COI charges had the correct age been used at policy issue. Although not a standard provision, insurers often also include misstatement of sex within the same provision, whereby the amount payable is similarly adjusted if the application contains a misstatement of sex. Misstatements of sex are not common and usually occur because of a transcribing error, not because the proposed insured was unsure of his or her sex! Misstatements of age arise due to transcription errors also, but may be more common given the different definitions of age (age nearest birthday, age last birthday, etc.) used by different companies. Before the spread of computerized public birth records in the second half of the 20th century, mistakes and uncertainty as to an individual's actual date of birth were not uncommon.

If the error in age or sex is discovered while the insured is alive, the procedure followed for bundled policies depends upon the actuarial effect of the misstatement. If the age has been understated or the insured's sex incorrectly recorded as female, the owner of a bundled policy usually is given the option of paying the difference in premiums with interest or of having the policy reissued for a reduced amount. With an overstatement of age or an incorrect recording of the insured as a male, a refund is usually made by the insurer paying the difference in reserves. For unbundled policies, the account value is debited for age understatements (or incorrectly showing the insured as a female) or credited for age overstatements (or incorrectly showing the insured as a male) by an amount equal to the sum of the differences in the COI charges.

Without this provision, misstatements of age or sex could be interpreted as being material misrepresentations. With this provision, they cannot. Also, as the incontestable clause does not apply to age or sex misstatements, adjustments may be made in policy benefits after the period of contestability has expired.

PROVISIONS THAT MAKE PAYMENT LESS SECURE
Several life insurance contract provisions can be considered as rendering payment less secure in the sense that they protect the life insurance company from paying under conditions not contemplated in the pricing of the policy (put option). These include the suicide clause, the delay clause, and certain exclusion clauses.

SUICIDE CLAUSE   At one time, policies stated that no payment was due if death was by suicide. Yet, death by suicide is included in the mortality data used by insurers for pricing their products and so arguably should be covered as any other cause of death. An exception occurs when insurance is purchased in contemplation of suicide. It is for this reason that U.S. insurers may, at their option, include a **suicide clause** in their contracts that addresses this adverse selection possibility by excluding payment of claims if the cause of the insured's death is suicide occurring within the first two policy years. Virtually all insurers include this clause where permitted, although some limit the exclusion period to one year.

A typical suicide clause might read as follows:

For the first two full years from the original application date, we will not pay if the insured commits suicide (while sane or insane). We will terminate the policy and give back the premiums paid to us less any loan.

With regard to this exclusion, the question whether a death is suicide or due to other causes is almost always a question for a jury in the U.S. The legal presumption is that a person will not take his or her own life, so the burden of proof of suicide rests with the insurer. This fact, plus what is said to be a tendency of courts to seek ways of ruling for dependents, makes it exceedingly difficult to prove suicide. For example, some courts have held that an "insane" person, by definition, cannot commit "suicide," as suicide requires knowledge of right and wrong. This result has emerged even in the face of the "while sane or insane" policy language. Where death is determined to be by suicide and within the period of exclusion, the company will refund the premiums paid, with or without interest, depending on the contract.

Delay Clause   Life insurance policies in the U.S. must contain a so-called **delay clause** which grants the company the right to defer cash surrender value payments, withdrawals, and the making of policy loans (except for purposes of paying premiums) for up to six months after their request. This provision does not apply to the payment of death claims and is intended to protect the company against "runs" that could cause the failure of an otherwise financially sound company.

The clause had been primarily of historical interest until comparatively recent times. As the experience of more than one financially troubled insurer revealed in the 1990s, the clause is not always sufficient to protect a company.

Exclusion Clauses   The great majority of life insurance policies in North America and elsewhere contain but a single exclusion – for suicide – and even here, the exclusion is time-limited. States permit a few other, optional exclusions that can be applied on a case-by-case basis, the two most important of which are as follows:

Aviation Exclusion   Occasionally, an underwriter will add an **aviation exclusion** that excludes coverage if the insured dies in an aviation accident. It is rarely included in life insurance contracts today and usually only for insureds who are military pilots or fly experimental aircraft. This coverage restriction can be eliminated if the policyowner is willing to pay an extra premium.

All companies cover fare paying passengers on regularly scheduled airlines. Similarly, flights on unscheduled airlines usually do not result in any policy restrictions or an increased rate. Even private pilots and the pilots and crews of commercial airlines are insured with standard or with only slight extra rates.

War Exclusion   **War exclusion clauses** provide that the insurer need not pay a claim if the insured is in the military and his or her death occurs under certain conditions. The insurer returns all premiums paid with interest or refunds the policy's reserve. Companies have inserted war clauses in their contracts during periods of impending or actual war for policies issued to persons in or likely to join the military. Relatively few, if any, insurers presently include such clauses. Rather, they carefully screen military applicants at underwriting. War clauses are canceled at the end of the war period.

There are two types of war clauses: (1) the status type and (2) the results type. Under the *status clause*, the insurer need not pay the policy face amount if death results while the insured is in military service, regardless of the cause of death. Under the *results clause*, the insurer is excused from paying the face amount only if death is a direct *result* of war.

The distinction between the clauses resides in the significance of the cause of death. Under the status clause, the cause of death is immaterial if the insured dies while in the military even if he or she died from slipping on a bar of soap while taking a bath at home. Under the results clause, the cause of death must have resulted from military activity.

The validity of war clauses has not been the subject of much litigation, but the clause's interpretation has given rise to a large volume of cases. Much litigation has revolved around the question of whether a particular clause is a status clause or a results clause. Other litigation has related to the nature of death and the existence of war itself.

PROVISIONS THAT PROVIDE FLEXIBILITY

We now examine life insurance policy provisions that provide policyowners with greater flexibility. These provisions constitute a package of embedded options, thus enhancing the value of the contract.

RIGHT TO RETURN POLICY   As noted earlier, insurers are required to include a **right of return** (also sometimes called a **"free look"**) **policy provision** within their contracts, which gives policyowners an unconditional right to return a policy to the insurer within 10 days of its receipt. Some insurers extend the required period to 20 or more days. A full refund of premiums paid must be made on policy return.

DEATH BENEFIT PROVISION   UL policies contain what are sometimes called **death benefit provisions** or the equivalent in which the contract sets out the various death benefit options (see Chapter 3) and explains the method of determining the policy death benefit. The policyholder's rights to change the death benefit amount and option are set out, along with the operational details and procedures for effectuating any change. Thus, the policy advises that any change in the amount or option that could have the effect of increasing the net amount at risk will or may require evidence of insurability. Decreases require but a written request.

THE BENEFICIARY CLAUSE   The beneficiary designation is the core of a life insurance policy and warrants great care in selection and wording. The **beneficiary clause** typically states that the policyowner may have policy death proceeds paid to whomever and in whatever form desired, subject to contract terms and naming or referring to the designated person or entity entitled to receive death benefits.

The policyowner can prepare a plan of distribution in advance that accomplishes his or her personal objectives by allowing appropriately for future contingencies.

Nature of Designations   **Primary and Contingent Designations.** The person named as the first to receive policy death proceeds is called the *primary beneficiary.* More than one person may be designated as primary beneficiary. The person named to receive death proceeds if no primary beneficiary is alive at the time of the insured's death is called the *contingent* or *secondary beneficiary.* If no named beneficiaries are alive at the insured's death, death proceeds are paid to the insured's estate – a potentially undesirable outcome as proceeds will be included in the insured's gross estate for estate tax purposes and will incur probate costs. See Chapters 21-22.

Any contingent or later (called *tertiary beneficiary*) designation typically is made at the same time as the primary beneficiary is designated. A beneficiary designation with both primary and contingent beneficiaries might read as follows:

> *Proceeds to be paid to Christine B. Butterworth, wife of the insured, if living; otherwise to Bart B. Simpson, nephew of the insured.*

The importance of exercising care in the beneficiary designation cannot be overemphasized. If the policyowner's intentions are to be carried out effectively, the language must be precise and unambiguous. In the U.S., "to my children" is a designation that invites misunderstanding and possibly litigation. Courts have ruled that adopted children are included in the term "children," whereas stepchildren may not be included. Illegitimate children, if they are legally acknowledged by the policyowner, are generally included in the designation. However, if the policyowner fails to legitimize them, generally they will not be considered. The term "dependents" is limited to those actually dependent upon the policyowner for support.

The term "relative" has been held to include "those by marriage as well as by blood, but not an illegitimate child"; the term "heirs" refers to "those who take under the statutes of descent and distribution." Even if the intended persons finally receive the policy proceeds, litigation and delay can erode proceeds, and related aggravation can foster ill will and invites family discord. Too often, the construction of the beneficiary designation receives far too little care and attention.

Beneficiary designations should always carry the full given names of natural persons as well as their relationships to the insured so as to remove the possibility of any misidentification. They also should provide for the possibility that one or more beneficiaries may predecease the insured through use of contingent and, if needed, tertiary designations. If multiple beneficiaries are named at one level, the designation should indicate whether the share of any deceased beneficiary is to be shared among surviving policy beneficiaries, referred to as *per capita*, or among the deceased beneficiary's heirs, if any, referred to as *per stirpes*.

Insurers wish to avoid disputes involving beneficiary designations. The issue ordinarily is not whether policy proceeds are due but rather to whom they are to be paid. In situations where the insurer faces multiple claims for policy proceeds because of ambiguity in the beneficiary designation or otherwise, it will often **interplead** them – that is, pay the proceeds to a court for it to decide the rightful recipient.

Revocable and Irrevocable Designations. The partition of rights between the policyowner and the beneficiary depends upon whether the beneficiary designation is revocable. A **revocable designation** is one that may be changed by the policyowner without the beneficiary's consent. An **irrevocable designation** is one that can be changed only with the beneficiary's express consent.

Irrevocable designations are not commonly used. They find relevance in situations in which a policyowner may not or does not wish to retain the right to change beneficiaries, such as a divorce decree. Irrevocably named beneficiaries have a vested right in the policy that is so complete that neither the policyowner nor his or her creditors can impair it without the beneficiary's consent, including surrendering the policy or taking policy loans. See Chapter 18.

Changing the Beneficiary   When the right to change the beneficiary is reserved, the named beneficiary obtains no vested rights in the policy or in its proceeds while the insured is alive. The beneficiary possesses "a mere expectancy until after the maturity of the contract." The contract ordinarily states the method for accomplishing any beneficiary change. In the majority of cases, a change is a routine matter. Some policyowners have attempted a beneficiary change through their wills. In general, courts will not recognize a change via one's will if the policy sets forth an exclusive procedure for effecting a change.

If the policyowner has done all that he or she can to effect a beneficiary change but did not follow the procedure because of factors beyond his or her control, a beneficiary change will be deemed to have been accomplished under the **doctrine of substantial compliance**, notwithstanding the failure to comply fully with the policy requirements. Thus, when a policyowner/insured signed a change of beneficiary form and sent it to his wife to deliver to the company agent but the insured was killed before delivery to the agent, the change of beneficiary was held effective. In another case, the policyowner/insured requested change of beneficiary forms, signed them, but delayed forwarding them to the company, although there was ample time and opportunity. The forms were mailed after the death of the insured, but this was held to be an ineffective change of beneficiary.

Simultaneous Death of Insured and Beneficiary   The beneficiary's right to receive life insurance policy death proceeds is usually conditioned on his or her surviving the insured. If the insured and the beneficiary die in the same accident and no evidence shows who died first, the question arises as to whom to pay the proceeds. Most states have enacted the *Uniform Simultaneous Death Act* that provides that "where the insured and beneficiary in a policy of life or accident insurance have died and there is not sufficient evidence that they have died otherwise than simultaneously, the proceeds of the policy shall be distributed as if the insured had survived the beneficiary."

This resolves the question of survival, but it fails to solve the main problems facing policyowners. Specifically, if the proceeds are payable in a lump sum and no contingent beneficiary is named, no matter who is determined to have survived, the proceeds will be paid into the estate – of either the insured or the beneficiary – commonly an undesirable outcome. Related to this issue is the situation in which the beneficiary survives the insured by a short period of time.

Many companies allow use of a **survivorship clause** (also called a **time clause**) which provides that the beneficiary must survive the insured by a fixed period, such as 60 days, after the insured's death to be entitled to the proceeds. This clause, in conjunction with the naming of contingent beneficiaries, can prevent the proceeds from falling into the probate or tax estate of either an owner/insured or the original beneficiary.

SETTLEMENT OPTIONS   The majority of death claims are paid to beneficiaries as a single sum of money shortly after the insured's death. Beneficiaries may be ill-prepared emotionally and otherwise to make decisions concerning the disposition of what often are large sums. Poor investment and purchase decisions are too easily made during periods of great stress. Use of a trust as beneficiary or settlement options may be desirable. **Settlement options** grant policyowners (and beneficiaries) options other than a cash settlement as to how death proceeds will be paid. Most insurers also permit cash surrender values to be paid under settlement options. These can be particularly valuable options at retirement.

If the policyowner set up a settlement arrangement during the insured's lifetime, performance of that agreement after the insured's death is regarded by many U.S. courts as a continuation of the third party beneficiary arrangement. On the other hand, if a beneficiary elects to receive the proceeds under one of the settlement options, some courts have held that a new direct contractual relationship is established between the company and the beneficiary. In both instances, the beneficiary may enforce his or her rights under the life insurance contract or subsequent settlement agreement.

Settlement options are set out in the policy, and most contracts provide a choice from among the options discussed below and often other options. The policyowner may give the beneficiary as much or as little flexibility in designating the settlement option as he or she desires. Thus, a policyowner could fix absolutely the manner in which proceeds are to be paid, with the beneficiary having no right to alter the arrangement at the insured's death. Alternatively, the policyowner could design a settlement agreement that gives the beneficiary total freedom to alter its terms.

Cash   Most death proceeds are paid as a *lump sum* of cash (check, electronic fund transfer, or bank draft). In a strict sense, this is not an option, because life insurance contracts usually stipulate a cash settlement in the absence of any other direction by the policyowner or beneficiary.

In an effort to provide better service to beneficiaries and to retain more of the policy proceeds within the insurer corporate family, many insurers provide beneficiaries with the option of crediting proceeds to an insurer-sponsored **retained asset account,** which is an interest-bearing account on which drafts may be written. The beneficiary is free to leave proceeds in this account or to write checks to withdraw any or all of the proceeds.

The insurer often guarantees that a minimum interest rate is credited to the account balance and provides the option for the beneficiary to elect any other settlement option. This option meets the objective of providing the beneficiary with time to decide the disposition to be made of the funds, while permitting the beneficiary immediate access to the full proceeds if desired. The provision has become the subject of litigation as discussed in Chapter 18.

Interest Option Under the *interest option,* death proceeds remain with the company and only the earned interest is paid to the beneficiary. A minimum interest rate is guaranteed in the contract, although companies often credit higher rates. With most companies, interest may not be left to accumulate and compound. As legal limits restrict the length of time a principal sum may be kept intact, companies frequently limit the time that they will hold funds under this option to the lifetime of the primary beneficiary or 30 years, whichever is longer.

The interest option's main advantage is that, like the retained asset account, it assures the beneficiary freedom from immediate investment worries while guaranteeing both principal and a minimum interest rate. The rights of withdrawal and to change to another settlement option provide flexibility.

Fixed Period Option The *fixed period option,* as its name indicates, provides for the payment of proceeds systematically over a defined period of months or years, usually not longer than 25 or 30 years. It is one of two options based on the concept of liquidating principal and interest over a period of years without reference to life contingencies. The other is the fixed amount option (discussed below). The guaranteed interest rate in a given contract is usually the same for both options. Both options are annuities certain.

If the primary beneficiary dies during the fixed period, remaining installments (or their commuted value) are paid to a named contingent beneficiary. The amount of proceeds, the period of time, the guaranteed minimum rate of interest, and the frequency of payments determine the amount of each installment. Any interest in excess of the guaranteed rate is usually paid at the end of each year. The fixed period option is valuable when the most important consideration is providing income for a definite period, as in the case of a readjustment period following the insured's death or while children are in school.

As this option is based on the period of time selected, outstanding policy loans at the insured's death reduce the amount of each installment but do not affect the number of installments. For the same reason, any dividend accumulations, paid up additions, or other additional death benefit payments increase the beneficiary's income while the number of installments remains the same.

Fixed Amount Option The *fixed amount option* also systematically liquidates the death proceeds but with the income amount rather than the time period fixed. A specified amount of income is designated, such as $10,000 per month, and payments continue until the principal and interest thereon are exhausted.

Fixed amount options can be more advantageous than fixed period options, because they are more flexible. Most companies permit policyowners to specify varying amounts of income at different times, and beneficiaries may be given full rights of withdrawal or the right to withdraw up to a certain sum in any one year on a cumulative or non-cumulative basis. With both fixed period and fixed amount options, the commencement of installments can be deferred to a future time by holding the proceeds under the interest option until that time.

As the amount of each installment is the controlling factor under this option, dividend accumulations, additions payable, and additional death proceeds, together with any excess interest earned while installments are being paid, increase the number of installments but do not affect the installment amount. Conversely, loans outstanding at the insured's death or withdrawals of principal by the beneficiary decrease the number of installments.

Single Life Income Option   The several forms of single life income options represent the other broad class of settlement options – those that liquidate principal and interest *with* reference to life contingencies, that is, whether the insured is alive. The amount of each installment depends on the type of life income selected, the amount of the proceeds, the rate of interest being credited, and the age and sex (where permitted) of the beneficiary when the income commences. All life income options are life annuities. The most common forms are (1) pure life income option, (2) refund life income option, and (3) life income option with period certain.

With the *pure life income option,* installments are payable only for as long as the primary beneficiary (the income recipient) lives. No further payments are due to anyone when the primary beneficiary dies. The pure life income option provides the largest life income per $1,000 of proceeds. Most persons hesitate to risk forfeiting a large part of the principal on early death, particularly if there are others to whom they wish to leave funds.

The refund life income option may take the form of a *cash refund annuity* or an *installment refund annuity.* Both annuities guarantee the return of an amount equal to the principal sum less total payments already made. The difference in the two forms is that, under the cash refund option, a lump sum settlement is made following the primary beneficiary's death instead of installment payments being continued.

The *life income option with period certain,* the most widely used life income option, pays installments for as long as the primary beneficiary lives, but should this beneficiary die before a predetermined number of years, installments continue to a second beneficiary until the end of the designated period. The usual contract contains two or three alternative periods, the most popular being 10 and 20 years, but other durations may be obtained on request.

Joint and Survivorship Life Income Option   Under the *joint and survivorship life income option,* life income payments continue for as long as at least one of two beneficiaries (annuitants) is alive. As this option is a joint and survivorship annuity, it may continue payments of the same income to the surviving beneficiary or reduce the installments to two-thirds ("joint and two-thirds"), three-fourths ("joint and three-fourths"), or one-half ("joint and one-half") of the original amount and continue the payment of this reduced amount for the surviving beneficiary's lifetime. Some companies grant joint and survivorship options with a period certain of 10 to 20 years.

The joint and survivorship option can be particularly useful in providing retirement income for a husband and wife. The proceeds of a matured endowment or annuity or the cash values of any policy can be applied under this option.

Other Settlement Arrangements   In many instances, policyowners find that they can best provide for beneficiaries by selecting combinations of settlement options. Virtually any desired income pattern may be obtained by using the options either singly or in combination. Insurers ordinarily levy no charge for this service.

Notwithstanding the variety of settlement plans offered, situations arise for which the standard options do not fit well. Upon submission of the facts, companies usually are willing to develop special settlement plans, within reasonable limits. Where an individual desires still greater flexibility, consideration should be given to use of a trust (see Chapter 22). Such an arrangement is particularly appropriate if discretionary powers are indicated. Life insurance companies ordinarily will not accept any arrangement whereby they must exercise discretion in carrying out the terms of the agreement.

NONFORFEITURE OPTIONS   As noted earlier, cash value policies are required to contain **nonforfeiture options** that are activated automatically on policy lapse or can be elected by their owners if they choose to terminate their policies. The three options ordinarily provided are:

- *Cash.* On policy termination, its net cash surrender value is paid in cash (e.g., check) to the owner. Of course, protection ceases and the insurer has no further obligations under the policy. A policy's **net cash surrender** value is the gross account or cash value decreased by any withdrawals and surrender charges and the amount of any policy loans outstanding and increased by the cash value of any paid up additions, any dividends accumulated at interest, and any prepaid premiums.

  Benefits can, of course, be secured from cash value policies in ways other than policy surrender, including policy loans and cash value withdrawals under UL policies. Traditional par WL policies provide that any paid up additions may be surrendered, in whole or in part. Furthermore, as a matter of practice (usually not by contract), many insurers permit a partial surrender of traditional cash value policies.

- *Reduced Paid Up Insurance.* The policyowner may use the net surrender value as a net single premium to purchase a reduced amount of paid up insurance of the same type as the basic policy. All riders and supplementary benefits, such as premium waiver and accidental death, are terminated, and no further premiums are payable. The exchange is made at net rates, so it is based on mortality and interest only, with no explicit allowance for loadings.

- *Extended Term Insurance* (ETI). The policyowner may use the net surrender value as a net single premium to purchase paid up term insurance for the policy face amount less policy loans, for whatever duration that value will carry the policy. Policy loans reduce both the net surrender value and the face amount. Paid up additions increase both.

If the policyowner fails to pay a required policy premium by the end of the grace period and the premium is not paid under the automatic premium loan feature (see below), the policy's net surrender value will be applied automatically under either the reduced paid up or ETI option to continue coverage. Ordinarily, ETI is the automatic option.

UL policies need not offer nonforfeiture options as such, as they are not needed, although the termination of a UL policy for its net cash surrender value is always an option. The reduced paid up nonforfeiture option is duplicated under a UL policy by ceasing to pay premiums and reducing the face amount to that which the account value will support to the end of the applicable policy mortality table, with the calculation based on the guaranteed crediting rate and guaranteed COI and loading charges. The ETI option is duplicated under a UL policy by ceasing to pay any premiums and allowing the account value along with future interest credits to sustain the policy for as long as it can by covering internal charges.

POLICY LOAN PROVISION   All states require inclusion of a **policy loan provision** in cash value policies, under which insurers must make requested loans to policy-owners on the sole security of the policy's cash value, subject to certain limitations. The provision usually contains these key elements:

1. The insurer will lend to the policyowner an amount not to exceed the net policy cash surrender value less interest to the next policy anniversary (and, for variable policies, a further reduction typically of 10 percent) and, with UL policies, a deduction for charges for the balance of the policy year;
2. Loan interest is payable annually at a rate specified in the policy;
3. Any due and unpaid interest will be paid automatically by a further policy loan;
4. If total indebtedness equals or exceeds the cash surrender value, the policy will terminate, subject to the grace period;
5. The policyowner may repay the loan in whole or in part at any time; and
6. If the policy terminates by surrender or death, the indebtedness will be deducted from policy proceeds.

Policy loans can be a source of flexibility. No one need approve the loan, and it is confidential. The loan interest rate is favorable and contractually set (see below). The loan's automatic continuation is one of its unique features. From the insurer's point of view, the loan is fully secured.

Policy Loan Interest Rate   The policy loan interest rate or the procedure for determining it is stated in the policy. In the past, state laws required insurers to use a stated, fixed loan rate of 5.0, 6.0, or 8.0 percent, and many existing policies contain these rates. Under the NAIC's *Model Policy Loan Interest Rate Bill*, adopted by the majority of states, insurers now may use a fixed rate of not greater than 8.0 percent or use a variable rate approach that allows them to change the policy loan interest rate up to four times each year provided the rate does not exceed the greater of Moody's Composite Yield on seasoned corporate bonds two months prior to the determination date or the interest rate credited on cash values plus 1.0 percent. Companies are required to evaluate the need for a loan rate change at least once each year for variable rate policies.

When market interest rates decline, the law requires the company to reduce the loan interest rate whenever the ceiling rate has declined by at least one half of 1.0 percent below the rate currently being charged on policy loans. This requirement generally ensures that the loan interest rate will decline as market rates decline.

The NAIC model law does not make variable interest rates applicable to policy loans on existing policies. It is applicable only to new contracts issued with the variable interest rate provision. Several companies offered the variable loan interest rate provision in exchange for more liberal dividends on existing policies.

Automatic Premium Loans   Although not usually required, many companies include an **automatic premium loan** (APL) provision within their policies, which provides that, if a premium is unpaid at the end of the grace period and if the policy has a sufficient net surrender value, the amount of the premium due will be advanced automatically as a loan against the policy. UL policies, by their nature, have no need for APL provisions.

In some jurisdictions, the policyowner must specifically elect to make the provision operative. The purpose of the APL provision is to protect against unintentional lapse, as when a premium payment is overlooked. A disadvantage of the APL to the policyowner is that it may encourage laxity in payment of premiums; from the insurer's perspective, it encourages persistency.

DIVIDEND OPTIONS   Except for requiring policies to permit policyowners to take their dividends in cash, state laws ordinarily do not mandate the options under which dividends may be applied under par policies. Insurers, however, have long included options within their policies. As discussed in Chapter 4, dividends may be (1) received in cash, (2) applied toward payment of the premium, (3) used to purchase paid up additions, (4) left with the company to accumulate at interest, and (5) used to purchase one-year term insurance.

ASSIGNMENT/OWNERSHIP PROVISION   Ownership rights in life insurance policies, like other types of property, can be transferred by the owner to another person. Box 5-1 reviews the nature of property ownership, including insurance policies.

Box 5-1

The Legal Nature of Property

Legally, the term **property** refers not to the object itself but to the ownership rights associated with the property – i.e., rights of possession, control, and disposition. If the ownership rights are associated with land and objects permanently attached to land, such as buildings, the property is referred to as *real property*. If the ownership rights concern movable property, such as automobiles, furniture, stocks, and insurance policies, the property is classified as *personal property*.

There are two types of personal property: (1) choses in possession and (2) choses in action. **Choses in possession** are tangible objects (e.g., jewels). **Choses in action** represent intangible ownership rights evidenced by something tangible, which itself has no value. Thus, an insurance policy is a chose in action as the contract itself has no value; it evidences an intangible value. To recover value from a chose in action, legal action may be necessary.

Policies usually contain **ownership provisions** that state that the policyowner may exercise all rights under the policy without the consent of anyone else, unless a beneficiary is named irrevocably. Although the ownership of most policies can be changed in the absence of a permissive policy provision, the ownership provision gives the procedure for effectuating a change. Some policies show the change of ownership statement in a separate **assignment provision**. Although much variation exists in the wording, one company's provision reads:

> *You can assign this policy. We will not be responsible for the validity of an assignment. We will not be liable for any payments we make or actions we take before notice to us of an assignment.*

Assignment/ownership provisions do not prohibit an assignment/ownership change without the insurer's consent but provide that the insurer need not recognize it until it has received written notice of it and that it assumes no responsibility as to its validity. Assignments are of two types: absolute and collateral.

Absolute Assignments   An **absolute assignment** is the complete transfer by the existing policyowner of all rights in the policy to another person or entity. It is a change of ownership. In the case of a gift, the assignment is a voluntary property transfer involving no monetary consideration.

From time to time, life insurance policies are sold for a valuable consideration. As with a gift, these transactions are accomplished through an absolute assignment of policy rights, typically by using an absolute assignment/change of ownership form furnished by the insurer. A common situation calling for use of an absolute assignment is with life settlements whereby a policy, often no longer needed, is sold to someone. See Chapter 23.

Of course, an irrevocable beneficiary must consent to an assignment of the policy. A revocable beneficiary has no rights respecting the transfer. The question arises whether an absolute assignment, by itself, changes the beneficiary. Many courts have held that they do, while other courts have held the opposite. The new owner can change the beneficiary by following the customary procedures.

Collateral Assignments   A **collateral assignment** is a temporary transfer of only some policy ownership rights to another. Collateral assignments are commonly used to assign life policies as collateral for loans from banks and other lending institutions. Such assignments are partial in that only some (not all as with an absolute assignment) policy rights are transferred. They are temporary in that the transferred partial rights revert to the policyowner upon debt repayment.

The foregoing features of life insurance policies are either required to be included or optional with the insurer or policyholder. In each instance, their inclusion adds no explicit addition to policy premiums or charges.

COMMON LIFE INSURANCE POLICY RIDERS

Applicants who wish benefits or options beyond those provided by the routine provisions analyzed above often can secure them via policy **riders** which usually require additional premium payments. Our discussion here is of the most commonly found such riders. A given insurer may offer a greater or lesser variety of riders, with the details of operation and terminology differing from those explained below.

RIDERS PROVIDING LIFE INSURANCE COVERAGE

Several types of riders are available that provide life insurance coverage beyond that of the basic policy to which they are appended. We discuss four generic types below.

TERM RIDERS   Insurers have for decades permitted policyowners to attach term riders to basic policies to enhance the total death benefit. More recently, a modified application of this practice, known as term blending, has emerged. **Term blending,** also called **blending,** replaces portions of the cash value policy death benefit with term insurance. Some insurers' WL and UL policies are blended without giving the practice a name, but a reading of the illustration or policy will reveal the practice. Blending can improve policy performance by lowering commissions paid on the base policy and paying low or no commissions on the term insurance.

The face amount of blended policies is separated into two types of coverage, the base face amount and the term face amount. Thus, if a client wishes a $1.0 million cash value policy, he or she could purchase it all as WL insurance, as UL insurance, or as a combination of one of these policies and term insurance.

Consider examples of a $1.0 million UL policy and a $1.0 million WL policy, each with a face amount composed of a 50 percent term blend; in other words, each policy is composed of $500,000 of cash value insurance and $500,000 of term life insurance. For the 50 percent blended UL, the sales commission would be 50 percent lower than it would have been had $1.0 million of UL at the full target premium been paid. The term portion is non-commissionable or carries low commissions. The same concept applies to the policy loads deducted from the cash value, with higher premium loads deducted on premiums paid up to the target premium for the $500,000 UL base policy and lower loads on premiums in excess of the target. The net result is reduced overall internal policy loads, especially front-end loads, and higher cash values with the same premium outlay and death benefit.

A 50 percent blended WL policy functions in a different way. The premium paid is that required for the $500,000 WL base policy plus an excess amount. This excess first purchases the roughly $500,000 of the needed term insurance, with the remaining portion of this excess premium used to purchase paid up additions (PUAs). The actual initial amount of term insurance purchased is less than $500,000, because it is reduced by the death benefit of the PUAs. Each year thereafter PUAs are purchased in this way, reducing the amount of term insurance needed to be purchased each year, assuming a sufficiently high total premium is paid.

Also, dividends payable under the base policy are earmarked to purchase PUAs, further reducing the term amount purchased each year, assuming appropriate dividend growth and a sufficient paid premium. The commission rate applicable to the term premium may be the same or lower than the commission rate for the WL base, depending on the company. Purchased PUAs typically are commissionable at low rates. The net result is reduced overall policy loads and higher total cash values.

Blending is not available with every cash value policy or from every insurer. Depending on the situation, term blending often leads to better overall performance. However, if current assumptions are prospectively less favorable, term blending may adversely impact policy performance and increase lapse risk compared to a policy with no term blending. In addition, guaranteed policy elements may be less favorable with term blending, or the term face amount may terminate early. The policyowner's specific circumstances, objectives, and expectations play a critical role in the ultimate effectiveness of such term riders.

FAMILY RIDERS   Many insurers offer riders that provide insurance on the lives of one or more members of the family of the person who is the insured under the base policy to which the rider is attached. These riders are referred to by various names depending on the nature of the coverage, including *family rider, spouse rider, children's rider,* and *additional insured rider,* among others. A rider might provide coverage on the spouse and children, the spouse only, or the children only.

Coverage on the spouse usually is term life insurance to age 65 or so, either for a stated amount, such as $100,000, or varying in amount with age. The insurance is typically convertible without evidence of insurability to a cash value policy. Insurance on the children is ordinarily term to some age between 18 and 25 and for a modest fixed amount, such as $10,000. All children living with the family are covered, even if they were adopted or born after the policy is issued. Coverage usually is convertible without evidence of insurability, often for a multiple of the fixed amount, such as five times.

ACCIDENTAL DEATH BENEFIT RIDERS   An **accidental death benefit** (sometimes called **double indemnity**) rider provides that double (or other multiple) of the face amount is payable if the insured dies as a result of an accident. From a financial planning standpoint, there is seldom a reason why double or triple the policy face amount is needed because death was caused by an accident, as compared with death from other causes, but this rider is popular, perhaps because the premium is comparatively modest (reflecting a low probability of this type of death) and maybe because many people believe that they are most likely to die in an accident (which generally is inaccurate).

A typical clause includes a definition of accidental death akin to the following:

> *Death resulting from bodily injury effected solely through external, violent, and accidental means independently and exclusively of all other causes, with death occurring within 90 days after such injury.*

The expression **accidental means** insists that both the *cause* and *result* of the death must be accidental. The intention of this wording is to limit coverage to deaths that are purely and entirely accidental, although many U.S. courts have ascribed a more liberal interpretation to the terms. Payments from certain causes of death are explicitly excluded by the accidental death benefit provision. The numerous exclusions indicate the practical difficulties inherent in this form of coverage. Typically, deaths from the following causes are excluded:

- Certain illegal activities;
- In which illness, disease, or mental infirmity was also involved;
- Certain specified causes in which considerable doubt may exist about the accidental character of the death;
- War; and
- Aviation, except for passenger travel on scheduled airlines.

To be covered, death typically must occur within 90 days of an accident. The purpose of this restriction is to ensure that the accident is the sole cause of death. In general, the time limitations are enforced, although some serious problems can be created, with some courts holding that the 90-day requirement need not be strictly applied.

Accidental death coverage usually expires at age 65 or 70. Most insurers grade premium charges by age at issue, and a number of companies now offer multiple indemnity (two, three, or more times the face amount) coverage.

Guaranteed Insurability Option   The **guaranteed insurability option**, also known as the **additional** or **guaranteed purchase option,** permits the purchase of additional insurance on the insured's life without providing evidence of insurability, at periodic intervals and stated life events. It was developed to permit younger individuals to be certain that they would be able to purchase additional insurance as their circumstances changed, regardless of their insurability. The usual rider gives the policyholder the option of purchasing additional insurance at periodic, set intervals (commonly three years), provided the insured has not attained a specified age, such as age 40, at which age the rider expires. Option dates may be advanced for life events such as birth or adoption of a child and marriage.

In most cases, the amount of the additional insurance is limited to a multiple of the basic policy face amount or an amount stipulated in the rider, whichever is smaller. Insurers offer up to $100,000 or more per option date. The option requires an extra premium. The extra premium is payable to the last option date.

Insurers anticipate that the option is more likely to be exercised for insureds in poor health than for insureds in good health and otherwise insurable. In economic terms, the option can be viewed as being "in the money" for such insureds; buyers use their superior knowledge about their insurability status to secure good deals for themselves. Of course, the insurer is aware that option holders, as a group, will behave in this way. To cover the cost of this adverse selection by insureds in poor health, the premium for the option is calculated to cover the expected extra mortality incurred. Also, by designing the benefit to limit the age to which and times at which the options may be exercised, the insurer is minimizing opportunities for insureds to select against the company.

Living Benefit Riders

Living benefit riders (or provisions), also called **accelerated benefit riders,** promise to pay some or all of a policy's face amount prior to the insured's death if the insured suffers some specified adverse health condition. Under each, the policyowner must request that living benefit payments be made and the amount to be paid (determined by the policy limit), and proof must be provided that the insured's condition qualifies for the payments. Such coverage typically takes one of three forms.

Terminal Illness Coverage   Many insurers offer some type of **terminal illness coverage**, also called **accelerated death benefits,** that provides that a specified maximum percentage of from 25 to 100 percent of the policy's face amount can be paid if the insured is diagnosed as having a terminal illness, usually subject to a specified overall maximum payment, such as $250,000. A concern of many companies is that an unlimited benefit amount may create moral hazard in the form of more fraudulent claims. It is not unusual for the insurer to secure a release from all interested parties (e.g., beneficiary and assignee), not just the policyowner, to avoid any future misunderstanding.

Most provisions require that the insured have a maximum of one year to live, unless state law mandates otherwise. The insurer requires satisfactory evidence that the insured suffers a terminal illness, including (1) certification by a physician, (2) hospital or nursing home records, and, possibly, (3) a medical examination (paid for by the insurer). Some companies make no explicit charge for the coverage while others assess an administrative expense charge (e.g., $200) for processing the request and may reduce the amount payable to reflect lost interest. The benefit can be found in any type of policy.

CATASTROPHIC ILLNESS COVERAGE **Catastrophic illness coverage** provides benefit payments on approximately the same terms and conditions as terminal illness coverage, except that the insured must have been diagnosed as having one of several listed catastrophic illnesses. Also referred to as **dread disease coverage,** the rider or provision typically covers stroke, heart attack, cancer, coronary artery surgery, renal failure, and similar diseases.

Both terminal illness and catastrophic illness coverages provide that policy death benefits are reduced on a one-for-one payout basis. Cash values are reduced on either a one-for-one basis or in proportion to the death benefit reduction. According to the NAIC *Accelerated Benefits Guideline for Life Insurance,* prospective buyers of these coverages must be given numerical illustrations that reflect the effects of an accelerated payout on the policy's death benefit, cash values, premiums, and policy loans. Additionally, consumers must receive a brief description of the accelerated benefits and definitions of the conditions or occurrences triggering payment. Any separate, identifiable premium charge must be disclosed.

LONG TERM CARE RIDERS/COMBINATION PLANS A third type of living benefit – the **long term care** (LTC) **insurance rider** – promises to pay benefits if the insured is unable to perform the essential activities of daily living because of accident, illness, or frailty. Historically, LTC insurance was most commonly purchased as a standalone policy, but many observers believe that most LTC insurance will be purchased as riders to life insurance and annuity contracts in the future. See Chapters 6 and 8. This belief is fostered by changes in the federal tax law effective in 2010 that are favorable to what are called combination plans. **Combination plans** are life insurance or annuity contracts that include long term care insurance riders providing for an acceleration of a policy's death benefit payment in the form of monthly payments for qualified expenses. Insurers have sold versions of such plans for perhaps 15-20 years but with less favorable tax treatment and often different operational details.

LTC riders originally paid benefits to the insured in the form of accelerating a life policy's death benefit, as with terminal illness and catastrophic illness coverages. Both the cash value and death benefit were reduced dollar for dollar for benefit payments. Perhaps most riders continue this approach. Thus, a monthly benefit of up to 2 percent of the policy's face amount (subject to a further maximum monthly benefit amount) might be provided for a qualified health condition. Some insurers offered a LTC rider that was itself purely LTC insurance, like a standalone LTC policy, with benefit payments having no effect on the underlying life insurance policy.

Insurers specializing in this market began to combine the two approaches, offering various combinations. For example, a base life policy with a LTC acceleration rider might offer a 24 or 36 month payout period over which the policy's full death benefit could be paid out. Upon exhaustion of the policy death benefit, a further rider, called a **continuation rider** or **extension of benefits rider,** provides pure LTC insurance that picks up payments for whatever additional period (e.g., three to five years or more) was selected at policy issuance. Benefits might be inflation adjusted, and return of premium features might be included.

The base plan may be any type of insurance, but most often is WL, UL, or variable UL. Single premium plans are popular, especially with older, wealthy clients, but continuous premium plans are also available, often appealing to younger and less wealthy clients.

LTC benefits paid under qualified LTC insurance and from accelerating life insurance death benefits continue to be received income tax free. Prior to 2010, charges against a policy's cash value to pay for a LTC rider were treated as distributions under the policy. To the extent that the policy had undistributed gains, these charges were taxable income to the policyowner. As of 2010, these charges are still treated as distributions, but they are not considered taxable income, even if the policy has undistributed gains. Distributions still lower the policy's tax basis, but never below zero. Thus, a policy surrender or sale results in higher taxable gains, a potentially important implication for tax planning. This lowered tax basis is moot if the policy's full death benefits are accelerated or the policy terminates in payment of a death claim.

RIDERS PROTECTING AGAINST POLICY LAPSE

Insurers have incentives beyond the APL provision to help policyowners minimize the chances that their policies will lapse. We discuss two such riders, each aimed at addressing a different issue that can arise but with the common goal of minimizing lapse.

WAIVER OF PREMIUM/CHARGES RIDERS Insurers offer disability riders, called **waiver of premium** (WP) or **premium waiver** (PW) riders, which pay (waive) premiums otherwise due under fixed premium products if the insured becomes disabled. Parallel riders are available with UL policies that waive a specified premium amount – called **waiver of a specified premium** or the equivalent – or waive the monthly COI and expense charges – called **waiver of monthly charges** or the equivalent – if the insured becomes disabled. A supplemental premium ordinarily is levied for these riders, although a few companies levy no separately identifiable premium for the coverage, including its cost in the policy's gross premium.

The waiver benefit is an earmarked disability income payment in an amount set precisely equal to the referenced premium or charges. The benefit does not truly *waive* or *excuse* premium payments but provides a benefit that makes the payment on behalf of the insured upon his or her disability. Thus, dividends continue to be paid on par policies, cash values continue to increase, and loans may be secured. Such riders typically expire at age 60 or 65.

The question arises as to the meaning of disabled. Most policies state that the insured must be totally disabled or totally and permanently disabled to qualify for the benefit, often before age 60. **Total disability** commonly is defined in the policy as inability of the insured, because of illness or injury, to perform either (1) the duties of his or her own occupation or (2) the duties of any occupation for which he or she is reasonably suited by reason of education, training, or experience.

Insurers will use either definition or combine them to provide that the first, more liberal definition applies for the first few (e.g., two) years of disability, with the second definition applying thereafter.

The word permanent appearing in the definition is not as daunting as might seem. Any total disability lasting longer than the waiting period specified in the policy – typically six, but sometimes as little as three, months – is technically deemed to be a **permanent disability**, even though in everyday parlance it might not be.

How the WP rider interacts with the conversion feature in a term policy can be important. Assume that term premiums are being waived because of a qualifying disability, and the policyowner wishes to convert the term policy. Whether the premium for the new policy will be waived depends on the type of WP feature contained in the term policy. Three different term WP provisions are found. First, and most conservatively, the policy provides that premiums on any newly converted cash value policy will not be waived. Second, and most liberally, premiums on the new policy will be waived. Third, and middle of the road, some policies provide that premiums on the new policy will be waived, but only if the conversion is delayed until the end of the period during which conversion is allowed.

OVERLOAN PROTECTION RIDERS   Several companies offer **overloan protection riders** (OPRs) whose purposes are to guarantee that a policy will not lapse if policy loans equal or exceed the policy account value. If loans equal or exceed the policy value and the policy lapses, a significant income tax event may be created for its owner. This rider is intended to avoid this situation. Box 5-2 offers additional insight into this issue.

Box 5-2
When Overloan Protection Riders make Good Sense

Here is an example of the issue intended to be addressed by these riders. Assume that a UL policy was issued 15 years ago to Alain. He is now 55 years old. He paid a total of $1.0 million in premiums during the first ten policy years. Based on current assumptions, at age 65 Alain can institute a systematic program of annual withdrawals of $100,000 for 10 years followed by 10 annual policy loans of the same amount to provide retirement income. By age 75, when withdrawals cease, they would have totaled $1.0 million. As withdrawals reduce a policy's cost basis, his cost basis at that time would be reduced to zero. By age 85, policy loans totaling $1.0 million also have been taken.

Assume that the policy's account value at age 85 would be just slightly more than the loan totals. With no further premium payments, the policy would lapse before the end of the coming policy year, as the loan balance plus interest due would exceed the account value. If this were to occur, roughly $1,000,000 (in the form of the loan payoff) would be taxable to him as ordinary income. If the policy did not lapse because of an overloan protection rider and continued until Alain's death, no income taxable event would have occurred. See Chapter 21 on income taxation of policy proceeds.

The OPR permits the policyowner to elect to pay a one-time fee after a certain age (typically 75) and, subject to various conditions (e.g., the policy has been in force for at least 15 years; the loan balance must be in excess of 95 percent of the account value), all policy charges cease and the policy becomes paid up or frozen. It continues in this state until the insured's death or, unwisely, policy surrender. On death, the death benefit is received by the beneficiary income-tax free.

NO LAPSE GUARANTEE RIDERS   No lapse guarantee (NLG) riders guarantee that the policy to which they are attached will not lapse for a specified period or for life, even if the account value goes to zero, if a specified minimum premium is paid. When riders guarantee coverage for less than the whole of life, they are sometimes called *guaranteed minimum death benefit riders*. The details of NLG policies were discussed in Chapter 3 and apply equally to policies containing NLG riders.

ENHANCED CASH VALUE RIDERS

An **enhanced cash value rider**, offered by several insurers, eliminates or reduces surrender charges applicable to qualified policies during the first few policy years. The insurer may assess a one-time upfront charge for the rider, and/or the policy may provide for somewhat lower cash values at later durations. This feature can be important in situations for which premiums are financed via external loans and collateral is required. The greater a financed policy's cash surrender value relative to premiums paid, the less external collateral that the policyholder need tie up.

The feature also can be important for corporate owned life insurance. See Chapter 24. The usual accounting treatment for such insurance is that the difference between the yearly premium paid and yearly change in the cash surrender value (CSV) is recorded as an expense if the difference is negative (i.e., premium greater than change in CSV) and as income if the difference is positive. The greater the CSV increases each year, the less likely the corporation is to realize an expense charge. The rider ensures a higher CSV increase.

CONCLUSIONS

Life insurance policies are among the most secure types of insurance contracts and the simplest on which to collect. The policyowner and beneficiary can be assured that the insurance company will pay the agreed upon amount of money on the death of the insured occurring at least two years after the policy issue date if but two simple conditions are met: (1) premiums sufficient to keep the policy in force have been paid and (2) the simple process of filing proof of death is completed. If death occurs within the first two policy years, we add but two further conditions: (3) death was not caused by suicide and (4) the application questions were answered accurately. That's it (except for the insurer not having become insolvent, which is rare. See Chapter 17).

Although the conditions for collection are simple, the contract itself and, importantly, how it is structured and used can be complex. This chapter has introduced the life insurance policy as a contract, including supplemental benefits that can be included in it.

ENDNOTES

1   This chapter draws in parts from Harold D. Skipper and Wayne Tonning, *The Advisor's Guide to Life Insurance* (Chicago; American Bar Association, 2011), Chapter 9.

CHAPTER 6

RETIREMENT PRODUCTS

In financial terms, individuals not only face the risk of dying too soon (mortality), they also face the risk of living too long (longevity). They may outlive their financial resources. In this chapter, we examine the products offered by life insurance companies that protect against longevity risk. The first class of longevity products is the individual annuity. The second is comprised of products sold on a group basis, usually to retirement plans offered by employers. The life insurance industry also offers investment guarantees to support individual annuities and group retirement plans. Chapter 23 complements this chapter by discussing the importance of retirement income to society and to individuals in their personal financial planning. We begin this chapter with a brief discussion of the nature of the retirement risk

Longevity risk and the need for income to support individuals after their productive years are increasing dramatically. Retirement needs worldwide are usually addressed in four ways, often referred to as the *four pillars of retirement funding*:

THE NATURE OF THE RETIREMENT RISK

1. government benefits,
2. employer benefits,
3. individual savings, and
4. part-time employment.

The collective strain on the first three resources increases as world demographics change. Generous government-provided retirement benefits are deemed no longer sustainable. Employers have largely reached the same conclusion with regard to funding generous worker retirement benefits. At the same time, savings, especially within the OECD countries, seem unlikely to make good the expected gap created by shrinkage of the first two sources of income security in retirement. These observations suggest to many observers that the fourth pillar, part-time employment or what some have termed *phased retirement* – meaning a gradual withdrawal from the work force over time – is likely to figure more prominently in the future. The percentage of the world population reaching retirement age is increasing rapidly and retirees are living longer. Figure 6-1 shows the percentage of population aged 65 and over for selected countries in 1970, 2010, and the projected percentage for 2050.

Figure 6-1   Percentage of Population Aged 65 and Over in Selected Countries

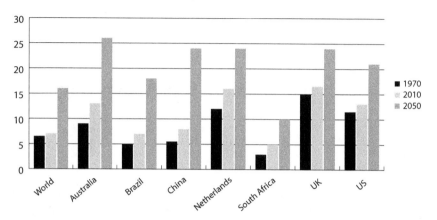

Source: OECD Fact Book 2009 Economic, Environmental and Social Statistics

The percentage of the world population over age 65 will increase dramatically over the first half of the 21st century. The risk of individuals outliving their financial resources will be an increasing concern.

The uncertainty in projecting longevity has been characterized historically in consistent overestimations of future mortality. Further, while *average* mortality has steadily improved, maximum life span seems to have been constant throughout human history at just over 100 years. At the same time as longevity is increasing, fertility rates are decreasing. Thus, the proportion of the working population able to contribute to the support of those beyond their working years is declining.

While the number of private employers providing retirement coverage to workers has remained relatively constant, employers have retreated from offering defined benefit plans that promise benefits to retirees based on their wages and often service. Under such plans, employers retain the risks of investment performance and retiree longevity. Defined contribution plans make no promises with regard to the magnitude of future benefits and have become more common. Under such plans, employers make specified contributions to the retirement plans and transfer subsequent investment and longevity risk to plan participants. Figure 6-2 presents the trend in the proportion of employers offering defined benefit plans and defined contribution plans.

After a long period of decline in the global savings rate, saving began to increase following the onset of the 2008-09 financial crises. The growing retirement funding need worldwide nevertheless remains a significant feature of global finance and demographics.

NATURE OF ANNUITIES

In general financial terms, an annuity is a series of periodic payments. As discussed earlier, the annuities that life insurers issue generally make periodic payments for as long as a designated person (the annuitant) is alive, termed a *life annuity* or *pure life annuity*. Also, life insurers issue simple annuities that do not depend on the annuitant's survival, called *annuities certain*. A temporary life annuity is a life annuity payable for a fixed period or until the death of the annuitant, whichever is earlier. A whole life annuity is a life annuity payable for the whole of the annuitant's life.

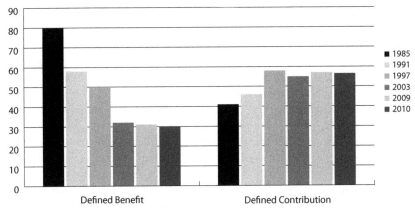

Employers Offering Retirement Plan Coverage 1985-2010

Figure 6-2

Source: Employee Benefit Research Institute

Employers historically provided significant longevity risk protection to workers through defined benefit retirement plans. Increasingly they have returned the risk to individuals by shifting from defined benefit plans to defined contribution plans.

PURPOSE OF ANNUITIES

Life insurance has as its principal mission the creation of a fund. The annuity, by contrast, has as its basic function the systematic liquidation of a fund. Of course, most annuities are also accumulation instruments, but this is the mechanism for developing the fund to be liquidated. From a *legal* viewpoint, a whole life annuity may be defined as a contract whereby for a consideration (the premium), one party (the insurer) agrees to pay the other (typically the annuitant) a stipulated amount (the annuity) periodically throughout the annuitant's life. In the absence of an explicit provision to the contrary, the understanding is that no portion of the consideration paid for the annuity need be refunded upon the annuitant's death after payments have commenced. The purpose of the annuity is to protect against the possibility of outliving one's income – just the opposite of that confronting a person who desires life insurance as protection against the loss of income through premature death.

Each annuity payment represents a combination of a liquidation amount supplemented by a survivorship element. The liquidation amount is derived from the orderly liquidation of the annuity's principal and interest credited thereon. The survivorship element is a prospective *pro rata* assignment to annuitants of the unliquidated funds of those annuitants who are expected to die before their life expectancy. Thus, surviving annuitants potentially receive more income than that produced by liquidation of their funds alone, and annuitants who die prematurely receive less than their contributions. The benefit of survivorship, however, becomes financially significant only at fairly advanced ages – at least the usual age of retirement. As discussed in Chapter 2, the arrangement is actuarially fair as annuity buyers face uncertainty as to their individual longevity, and the law of large numbers serves to allocate average results to all participants. Indeed the purpose of the annuity is to reduce financial uncertainty.

In most jurisdictions, only life insurance companies are permitted to sell contracts to the public that guarantee a life income over a person's life. Private individuals can make annuity agreements between themselves, termed *private annuities*, but they may not sell them commercially. For example, a private individual can sell a real estate interest in return for the buyer's agreement to pay the seller a life income. Because of the income recipient's concerns about the payor's reliability, these arrangements are usually made between family members.

Despite the difference in function, annuities are simply another type of insurance, and both life insurance policies and annuities are based on the same principles. Risk sharing and the law of large numbers underlie both, and premiums in each case are computed on the basis of probabilities of death and survival as reflected by mortality tables.

In Chapter 1, we noted the adverse selection problem in life insurance: those most likely to have claims are more likely to apply, to apply for larger amounts, and to maintain their policies in force. Adverse selection also exists with life annuities. Those with higher-than-average probabilities of a longer life would like to enter the risk pool at an average premium rate. Adverse selection with life annuities manifests itself in those in super standard physical condition being more likely to purchase them. Individuals in poor health will automatically shy away from them, as most companies do not offer a discount for those whose life expectancies are less than the average of the risk pool.

Insurers are aware of this phenomenon and, historically, have priced annuities on the assumption that the average purchaser will exhibit mortality superior to the population as a whole and superior to that found under life insurance policies. Experience confirms this tendency, for annuity mortality has been far superior to that under life policies and the population as a whole.

ANNUITY DEMAND

While the responsibility for retirement funding is increasingly becoming a larger responsibility for U.S. workers, retirees hold few annuities and annuity holders are unlikely actually to annuitize. Life insurers are largely competing ineffectively with other financial institutions and failing to capture the potential value of annuitization that follows the deferral period of annuities used primarily for savings. Retirees are failing to take advantage of the longevity risk reduction benefits of annuities for reasons explained below. Figure 6-3 presents the wealth of retiree households categorized by asset class. Annuities account for only 6.0 percent of the average retiree savings portfolio.

Figure 6-4 presents the rate of annuitization or conversion to life income for all U.S. annuity owners from 2003-2008. The rate is generally less than 1.0 percent.

Thus, the demand for annuities is weak, a term not synonymous with *unimportant*. Chapter 23 briefly discusses rational and behavioral reasons that have been proposed to explain the typical aversion to annuities. None of the reasons has gained wide acceptance as a complete explanation for weak demand.

The demand for **annuitization** – conversion of a savings annuity to a payout annuity that liquidates principal over the course of an annuitant's life or a stated period – is weaker still. Annuity features often cited to explain the weak demand for payout annuities include:

- the typical payout annuity purchase is irrevocable,
- consumers prefer to conserve liquidity,

- consumers prefer to conserve and control their capital,
- failure of insurers generally to offer life annuities priced for individual annuitant's expected longevity, and
- exposure to the risk of inflation and the creditworthiness of the insurer is irrevocable.

Financial Assets of *Fully Retired* Households   **Figure 6-3**

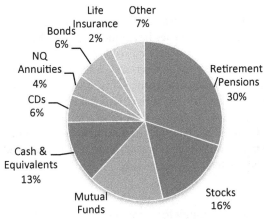

Source: LIMRA Analysis of 2010 *Survey of Consumer Finances,* Federal Reserve Board, 2012

U.S. Annuitization Rates   **Figure 6-4**

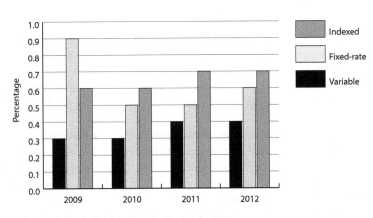

Source: LIMRA SRI, U.S. Individual Annuity Yearbook –2012

Three conclusions are readily apparent from these observations. First, there is a significant and increasing market for retirement savings products. Second, the market for annuitized life income is substantially underserved. Third, market development through innovation in product design and pricing is likely necessary to expand and transform the market from a savings dominated market to a longer term insured income market. As we see below, insurers have in fact responded with dramatic product design innovation in this century but much less so in pricing innovations.

The retirement risk structure of both the U.S. and the world is generally characterized as an evolving crisis. Solutions are generally believed to require the contributions of government, industry, and insurers. In this chapter, we explore the role of the life insurance industry in longevity risk reduction products. Chapter 23 examines the role of annuities and related longevity products in individual retirement strategies.

THE STRUCTURE OF FIXED ANNUITIES

Life insurers offer two generic types of individual annuities. **Fixed annuities** (FAs) credit investment returns to policies based indirectly on the performance of the insurer's general account investments or directly on changes in a specified inflation or equity index. In contrast, the performance and benefit of **variable annuities** (VAs) depend directly on the performance of separate account funds specified by the owner. We first discuss the structure of FAs, followed by a discussion of VAs.

Life insurers offer a wide variety of FA contracts. The owner is able to choose an annuity that features flexibility in the timing of premiums and benefit commencement, the manner in which invested funds earn returns, and the manner in which funds are liquidated.

PURCHASE BASIS

The purchase basis of an annuity incorporates an agreement between the insurer and the owner as to the timing of four events:

1. the payment of premiums,
2. the accumulation of investment returns,
3. the determination of benefits, and
4. the commencement of benefits.

Annuities may be purchased with a single lump-sum premium or premiums that are made periodically at the owner's discretion. Life income benefits may commence immediately or be deferred to a future date specified by the owner. Thus, the three basic purchase structures are the single premium immediate annuity (SPIA), the single premium deferred annuity (SPDA), and the flexible premium deferred annuity (FPDA).

The determination and commencement of benefits are simultaneous with the SPIA, SPDA, and FPDA. They both occur at the time of annuitization. The amount of the annuitized benefit payment depends on the insurer's expected mortality and interest earnings at the time of annuitization. In the interim, the guaranteed minimum benefit is the only contractual obligation the insurer provides to the owner. Insurers have also begun to offer **longevity annuities**, also called **deferred income annuities,** which are single premium deferred annuities that guarantee *future* income payments based on *current* rates, the income typically commencing a decade or more into the future and typically providing no death benefit or surrender value during the accumulation period.

The **single premium immediate annuity** begins to pay benefits one period, typically a month, after a single premium is paid. The premium often represents funds that have been accumulated through personal retirement savings, an individual retirement account, or a lump sum distribution from an employer-sponsored plan (see Chapter 23). The SPIA is purchased to provide a life income.

The **single premium deferred annuity** and the **flexible premium deferred annuity** are both deferred annuities, the difference being the former is purchased by a single premium and the latter with flexible periodic premiums. Both serve as savings accumulation vehicles until the owner elects to annuitize, thus converting to an immediate annuity. Deferred annuities feature two periods. The **accumulation period** is that period before annuity payments commence and during which premiums are paid and cash values accumulate. Premiums and cash values accumulate during this period at a rate determined by the accumulation structure of the annuity contract, as discussed below.

The **liquidation period** is that period during which annuity payments are made. The annuitant is said to **enter onto the annuity** at the time the accumulation period ends and liquidation via an income option begins. The owner is under no obligation to annuitize a deferred annuity and may elect to receive a cash settlement at any time (subject to limitations discussed below) prior to annuitization. Immediate annuities, by definition, are in liquidation at the beginning of the contract.

The purchase structure of an annuity generally does not constitute a permanent commitment. U.S. tax law permits the tax free exchange of any annuity contract for another annuity contract, so a fixed annuity can be converted to a variable annuity or a deferred annuity to a longevity annuity during the deferral period or at annuitization. See Chapter 21. Annuitization itself, while technically the exercise of a contractual option under the original contract, is effectively the·exchange of a deferred annuity for an immediate annuity. The right of exchange may be limited in some contracts.

SPDAs and FPDAs offer owners the option to purchase a life income at an unspecified future date. The amount of the income benefit depends on (1) investment performance during the deferral period; (2) mortality rates in effect at the time of annuitization; and (3) interest rates in effect at the time of annuitization. Thus, until annuitization, the contract owner knows only the guaranteed minimum benefit – which is the equivalent of stating only the guaranteed policy elements are known – and he or she retains future investment and mortality risks, except for the guaranteed values.

The longevity annuity exhibits features of both immediate and deferred annuities. It is like an immediate annuity in that the annual benefit is determined at the time the annuity is purchased. It is like a deferred annuity in that benefits commence at some point in the future. It is like neither in that the investment and mortality risks are borne by the insurer and not the owner during the deferral period. Its price is discounted significantly because it typically pays no death benefit if the owner dies prior to entering onto the annuity and offers no surrender value – unlike traditional deferred annuities.

The longevity annuity provides flexibility in two ways. It provides owners the ability to reduce the future benefit uncertainty through the purchase of a fully paid up life income – at current mortality and interest rates – to commence at some specified future date. It also provides planning flexibility. Consumers may wish to self-fund their retirement income to a target date and purchase a paid up income stream currently to fund future income requirements if they survive the target date. Many customers may consider this strategy the most attractive means of smoothing their lifetime consumption pattern.

Some insurers offer deferral periods as long as 50 years. The premium is thus minimized so the consumer is able to maximize the amount of retirement capital he or she retains while transferring the most uncertain portion of longevity risk. One 2010 published rate for a 55-year-old female would provide an annual lifetime income at age 85 of $40,632 for a current single premium of $50,000.

Figure 6-5 illustrates the agreed timing of events that define the nature of the annuity contract at purchase: the payment pattern of premiums, the accumulation of assets, the time of benefit determination, and the time of benefit commencement.

Accumulation benefits do not apply to immediate fixed annuities or to longevity annuities. Most fixed annuities credit interest at the discretion of the insurer and are based on the performance of the insurer's own general account assets, subject to a guaranteed minimum rate, such as 2.0 percent. Other fixed annuities may credit interest based on the performance of specified equity market, interest rate, or inflation indices. Insurers do not necessarily hold the specific assets associated with specific indices. The investment performance of all fixed annuities is backed indirectly by the performance of its general account assets and, therefore, by the general credit worthiness of the insurer.

In the U.S., Canada, and many other countries, interest credited on the cash values of personally owned annuities is not taxable to the contract owner as long as it remains with the insurance company. On liquidation, annuity payments are taxable as ordinary income to the extent that each payment represents previously untaxed income. The tax deferred nature of cash accumulations under such annuities represents a significant privilege that is rationalized on public policy grounds as an instrument for encouraging individuals to provide for their retirement needs. Tax laws impose certain restrictions on annuity withdrawals prior to retirement to ensure that this privilege is not abused. Additionally, the *Patient Protection and Affordable Care Act* of 2010 imposes a 3.8 per cent tax on distributions from non-qualified annuities for high income taxpayers. These and other tax provisions are discussed in Chapter 21.

GENERAL ACCOUNT FIXED ANNUITY   FPDA and SPDA contracts typically guarantee a minimum interest rate. Historical rates were often within the 3.0 to 4.0 percent range, depending on economic conditions at the time of issuance. The low interest rate environment of the U.S. this century led to significant reductions in typical guarantees on new products, such as to between 1.0 to 2.0 percent. While this rate may seem low, it must be recognized that the guarantee could easily span three, four, or more decades and, therefore, could prove to be exceedingly valuable.

For its part, the insurer would be foolish to guarantee high rates of such long durations. In any event, this type of long term guarantee is not found in other comparable savings media such as those offered by banks, thrifts, or money market accounts. Insurers increasingly offer short- to intermediate-term interest rate guarantees that are higher than the long-term contractual guarantee, such as 3.0 to 4.0 percent for the first 10 years

The Purchase Structure of Annuity Contracts   Figure 6-5

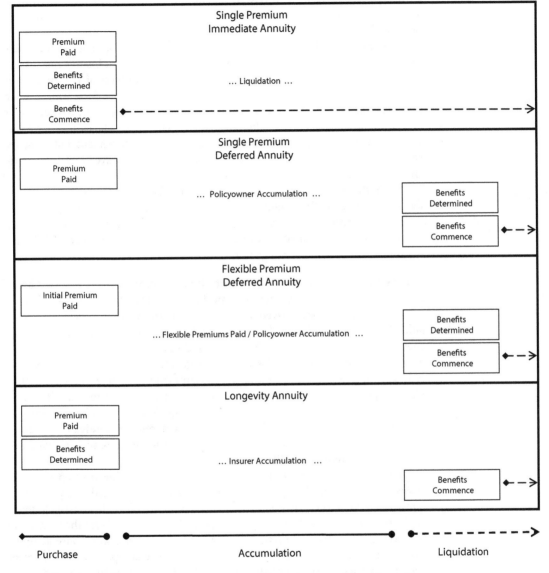

While the actual rate of interest credited to the FPDA cash value ordinarily is not linked directly with the insurer's earnings rate on its general account investments, that investment return, coupled with the insurer's desired competitive position, influences the determination of the actual crediting rate. Also, some insurers credit a **bonus** that pays extra interest (e.g., 1.0 percent credited to annuity cash values or deposits) over the standard crediting rate for an initial limited period. All rates are subject to revision by the insurer, subject to the minimum guaranteed rate, although most companies guarantee the current rate for at least the first contract year.

Most deferred annuities do not contain front-end loads. Rather, most insurers use a back-end load or surrender charge on policy termination. Most contracts permit a **free withdrawal corridor**, meaning that no surrender charge will be assessed on limited cash value withdrawals, such as those of less than 10.0 percent of the cash value.

The surrender charge is usually stated as a percentage of the total accumulation value and commonly decreases with duration. Thus, an insurer may assess a surrender charge of 7.0 percent on all withdrawals in excess of 10.0 percent of the fund balance during the first contract year, with this rate decreasing 1.0 percent per year, thereby grading to zero in the eighth contract year. No surrender charge would be applied thereafter. Surrender charge percentages and durations vary considerably; some first year charges are as high as 20 percent, but most are within the 5.0 to 10.0 percent range. A few policies do not have identifiable back-end or front-end loads.

The retirement income amount provided by a FPDA is a function of the accumulated cash value, the annuitant's sex (where permitted), and the age at which the contract owner elects to have payments commence. The usual range of benefit payout options is available, with each providing both a guaranteed minimum interest rate and a current nonguaranteed rate.

Equity-Indexed Annuities   An **equity-indexed annuity** (EIA) is a fixed annuity contract whose interest crediting mechanism is the greater of a guaranteed minimum rate or a rate derived directly from an external index, such as the *Standard & Poor's 500 Index* in the U.S. The minimum rate is usually 0 to 2.0 percent. EIAs contain elements of both fixed and variable annuities. The minimum guaranteed interest rate provides a downside guarantee. (Some insurers offer equity-index variable products with no minimum guaranteed rate.) Like VAs, they offer the potential for stock-market-like gains by tying the current crediting rate to equity indices, thus providing upside participation. Most EIAs are issued as SPDAs, although flexible premium varieties are emerging. An **index term** period of five to 10 years is specified, and the performance of the index and the guarantee determine the amounts credited to the account value.

EIAs function similarly to equity-indexed universal life insurance, as discussed in Chapter 3. The upside participation generally is stated as a percentage, often called the *participation rate*, of the increase in the index from issue to maturity. A few companies subtract a spread (e.g., 200 basis points) from the increase in the index each year and credit the difference to the contract. Some insurers cap the maximum return produced by the index performance and participation percentage. **Index-linked interest** credits are calculated over the index term and added to the policy's account value based on the indexing method, performance of the index, the participation rate, any cap, and the guarantee. The S&P 500 index does not reflect dividends and so they are excluded from index-linked interest; some companies may offer products whose index does reflect dividends.

There are three common indexing methods. The **annual reset method** determines index-linked interest annually by comparing the index value at the end of the contract year with the value at the beginning of the contract year. The **high-water**

mark method determines index-linked interest by retrospectively selecting the highest index value recorded at specified dates, usually policy anniversaries. The **point-to-point method** is based simply on the difference in the index value at the beginning and end of the index term.

As might be suspected, however, the product requires sophisticated design and asset-liability management by the insurer. Design decisions revolve around:

- the choice of equity index and guarantee,
- the indexing method and term,
- participation percentage or spread,
- administration, especially for FPDAs,
- surrenders and partial withdrawal provisions, and
- commissions.

At the end of the performance period, the owner may elect to surrender, continue the deferral under a new index term, or annuitize. Some companies allow contract owners who surrender before the maturity date to participate in a portion of any appreciation, but many do not. Annuitization options are generally the same as those for all FAs, discussed below. Some companies, however, offer annuitization payments that are also tied to the equity index.

EIAs are particularly attractive to insurers that do not offer variable annuities and to agents who are not licensed to sell variable products. As a general account-based product, it is subject to the same types of marketing and financial regulation as other fixed products. No special licensing, expense and investment management control, or disclosure requirements apply.

EIAs have been the focus of considerable negative publicity. Critics have pointed to high fees and the owner's incomplete participation in the index. The great variety of ways for calculating the equity return means that consumers might easily be confused and possibly even misled. Some have expressed the view that the products' risks and rewards might not be clearly and fully enough explained, thus possibly leading to market conduct difficulties for agents and insurers in the future.

INFLATION-INDEXED ANNUITIES   Annuities that offer payments adjusted for inflation offer significant protection for owners from one of the principal risks of retirement. Inflation-indexed annuities have been available in the U.K. market for some years due to the availability of inflation-indexed government bonds (*gilts*). The market for these annuities in the U.S. only began after the introduction of *Treasury Inflation Protected Securities* (TIPS) around the turn of the century.

One company offers a product that promises payments that are adjusted annually at January 1 according to the *Consumer Price Index-Urban* (CPI-U). Adjustments are subject to an annual limit of 10.0 percent. Increases are ratcheted so that a decline in the index will not cause a decline in the payment, although index declines accumulate and offset subsequent increases.

Initial benefits under the inflation-indexed annuity are substantially less than those of a comparable traditional SPIA. The payment benefit increases with increases in the CPI-U and the longevity of the annuitant. Another company offers an inflation protected subaccount as an investment option in its VA. The market for these annuities is still in a developmental stage and increased competition will likely produce increasingly attractive options.

LONG TERM CARE ANNUITY RIDERS   Some insurers have begun to offer annuities that apply part of the investment accumulation to charges for a rider that provides long term care (LTC) coverage, thus addressing two risks of retirement simultaneously. The mechanism for charges and the LTC coverage provided vary greatly in products in this developing market. The Chapter 5 discussion of combination plans applies here as well but without any death benefit protection as such.

The product possibilities became significantly more attractive with enactment of new tax treatment for policies under the *Pension Protection Act of 2006.* Previously, charges deducted from annuity cash values were treated as taxable distributions to the owner. The deemed distribution treatment no longer applies.

MARKET VALUE ADJUSTED ANNUITY   The **market value adjusted annuity** (MVA) (also referred to as a **market value annuity**) is a type of SPDA that permits contract owners to lock in a guaranteed interest rate over a specified maturity period, typically from three to 10 years. First introduced in the U.S. in 1984, the MVA is increasingly included as an option with variable annuities. If kept until maturity, its tax deferred value reaches the amount guaranteed at issue. However, unlike other FAs, if withdrawals occur, the cash value will be subject not only to possible surrender charges but also to a market value adjustment.

The adjustment may be positive or negative, depending on the interest rate environment at the time of withdrawal or surrender. If interest rates were higher than those at time of issue, the adjustment would be negative. Conversely, if rates were lower, the adjustment would add to the withdrawal or cash surrender value. The adjustment is intended to reflect the changes in market values of the assets – typically bonds – backing the annuities. Thus, as interest rates rise, the market values of previously purchased bonds decline.

Insurers may adjust interest or principal and interest under the market value provision. From a regulatory perspective, interest-only adjusted annuities are insurance products. If principal is also adjusted, the annuity is a security and must be registered as a variable product.

The theory for MVAs is that, if the actual available cash surrender value reflects its market value, the insurer, in effect, shifts much of the disintermediation risk to the contract owner. Insurers thus limit their disintermediation risk (i.e., the tendency to surrender during an increasing interest rate environment) and better match the duration of assets backing the MVA with its corresponding liabilities.

The MVA is less flexible than many other annuities, but it can offer advantages to buyers. For one thing, there is the possibility of a positive adjustment. For another, the typically longer duration guarantee can afford a greater sense of security.

CERTIFICATE OF ANNUITY   Another SPDA variation is the **certificate of annuity** (COA), first offered in the U.S. in 1983, which provides for a fixed, guaranteed interest rate for a set period of time, typically three to 10 years. It is similar to a bank issued certificate of deposit, except that, as an annuity, interest earnings are tax deferred. The COA differs from other annuities in that no unscheduled with-drawals are ordinarily permitted during the guarantee period. The full cash value is available on death and annuitization.

At the end of the selected guaranteed period, the owner can renew the COA for another period or select any of the standard annuity options, including surrender. Many insurers' products carry no identifiable front-end or back-end charges. As the contract does not permit early, unscheduled withdrawals, the interest rate credited should be higher than an otherwise similar SPDA, reflecting the insurer's reduced disintermediation risk. The contract is appealing to individuals who are near retirement, have little prospect of needing the funds during the guarantee period, and are interested in locking in a current market interest rate.

LIQUIDATION BASIS

When an immediate annuity is purchased or a deferred annuity is annuitized, the insurer begins payment of periodic benefits. Annuities may be liquidated with or without reference to life contingencies. With annuities certain, if the annuitant dies before the end of the annuity period, payments continue to a named beneficiary for the balance of the prearranged period. The annuitant may terminate the annuity during the liquidation period and receive the then cash value possibly net of surrender charges. Most annuity payments are, however, conditioned on the annuitant's survival. In addition to the age and sex of the annuitant, the amount and duration of life income benefits also depend on (1) the number of payees; and (2) refund provisions.

NUMBER OF LIVES   An annuity may designate one or more lives to determine the annuity paying period. Most annuities are **single life annuities** meaning that income payments are determined with reference to but a single life. The **joint and last survivor annuity** provides income payments for as long as *either* of two (or more) persons lives. The joint and last survivor annuity continues the same income until the death of the last survivor, and therefore requires higher premiums or lower payments than a single life annuity. A modified form known as a *joint and two thirds* (and *joint and one half*) *annuity* pays a reduced part of the initial payment to the survivor following the first death. Naturally, for a given principal, the modified form provides more income initially because of the later reduction. A limited market exists for the *joint life annuity* which provides for an income that ceases at the first death.

REFUND FEATURES   Broadly, life insurers offer annuitants two classes of *life* annuity payouts: pure and refund. We know that, with the pure whole life annuity, income payments continue for as long as the annuitant lives but terminate on the annuitant's death, and a temporary pure life annuity terminates at the earlier of the annuitant's death or the designated period. On the death of the annuitant under either annuity, no matter how soon that may occur after the commencement of income, no further amounts are payable to the annuitant's estate or to any beneficiary. The pure life annuity provides the maximum income for a given annuity purchase price.

Most persons seem to oppose placing a substantial sum of money into a contract that promises little or no return of the consideration paid if they should die shortly after income payments commence. Therefore, companies offer annuitants various refund options in the event that death occurs shortly after annuity payments have begun. In contrast to the pure life annuity, the entire purchase price is not used to provide income payments when a refund feature is present. Part of the purchase price is applied to meet the cost of guaranteeing a minimum benefit, irrespective of whether the annuitant lives to receive them. Thus, for a given premium outlay, a smaller periodic income payment will be available under a refund life annuity than would be available under an otherwise identical pure life annuity. The minimum benefit guarantee or refund feature may be stated in terms of a guaranteed minimum number of payments or as a refund of the purchase price (or some portion thereof) in the event of the annuitant's early death.

One class of life annuities with refund features, often named **life annuity certain and continuous** or **life annuity with installments certain**, calls for a guaranteed number of monthly (or annual) payments to be made whether the annuitant lives or dies, with payments to continue for the whole of the annuitant's life if he or she should live beyond the guarantee period. Contracts are usually written with payments guaranteed for five, 10, 15, or 20 years. Of course, lengthening the guarantee period reduces income payments. Remaining guaranteed payments are made to the named beneficiary if the annuitant's dies during the guarantee period.

Two important forms of annuity income promise to return all of the purchase price if the annuitant dies before that amount has been paid. The first form, the **installment refund annuity**, promises that payments will be continued to a named beneficiary on the annuitant's death, until the total payments equal to the purchase price. The **cash refund annuity** pays a lump sum amount to the beneficiary equal to the difference, if any, between the purchase price of the annuity and the simple sum of the installment payments made prior to the annuitant's death. For a given purchase price, the cash refund annuity provides a somewhat smaller income than the installment refund annuity, as the insurance company loses the interest it would have earned had the balance been liquidated in installments. In both cases, payments to the annuitant continue for as long as he or she lives, even after recovery of the guaranteed minimum benefits.

Annuities with refund features do not actually "refund" part of the consideration, although the economic effect is a type of refund. All refund life annuities can be thought of in two equivalent ways. First, we can consider them as a combination of (1) an annuity certain for the length of the guarantee or installment refund period plus (2) a deferred pure life annuity thereafter. Second, we can consider them as being a combination of (1) a pure life annuity for the entire period plus (2) term life insurance whose decreasing face amount is always just enough to provide income payments for the balance of the guarantee period or to provide the amount of the cash "refund." Figure 6-6 illustrates these two concepts, with the solid line representing an annuity certain and the dashed line representing a life annuity.

Two Equally Valid Interpretations of Life Annuities with Refund Features   **Figure 6-6**

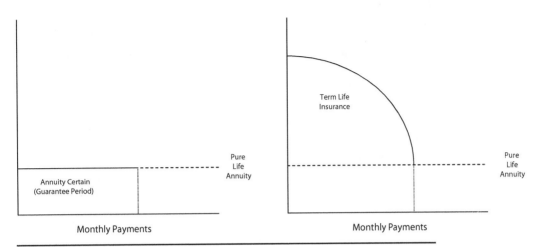

Table 6-1 provides a comparison of the income provided under some of the important forms of annuities for a given principal. The figures are shown on a guaranteed rather than a current basis and utilize the same rate basis. Variations demonstrate the impact that the form of annuity income, the age of the annuitant at the date of commencement of income, and the sex of the annuitant can have on the guaranteed monthly payments available from a $1,000 principal sum.

Immediate Life Annuity Monthly Incomes per $1,000 (Guaranteed Basis)   **Table 6-1**

Age Last Birthday	Pure		10 Years Certain and Continuous		Cash Refund	
	M	F	M	F	M	F
50	$5.00	$4.54	$4.91	$4.51	$4.68	$4.40
55	5.54	4.97	5.37	4.90	5.09	4.75
60	6.26	5.54	5.95	5.41	5.58	5.18
65	7.22	6.34	6.64	6.06	6.19	5.73
70	8.57	7.46	7.40	6.83	6.93	6.42
75	10.47	9.06	8.15	7.68	7.85	7.28
80	13.05	11.35	8.77	8.46	8.96	8.37

It is apparent from Table 6-1 that the cost of the refund feature is low at the younger ages, but becomes quite expensive at the higher ages. Not until about age 60 or 65 is any appreciable difference in income lost to add a refund feature. Consequently, many financial advisors recommend against the purchase of a pure life annuity when one is below age 60 or perhaps age 65.

Of course, at the time the annuity owner is about to enter onto the annuity, he or she could elect to surrender the annuity, withdrawing its full value as a lump sum. These funds could be invested elsewhere, including into another insurer's SPIA. The first insurer naturally prefers to retain the funds. Some insurers provide an incentive for the owner to annuitize rather than surrender or exchange. They may offer a one-time bonus or interest rate bonus, thereby increasing the annuitized amount; some offer an annuitization rate greater than that offered under their SPIAs; and most waive surrender charges in the event of annuitization. In an effort to encourage agents to recommend annuitization, a few insurers pay commissions at annuitization.

THE STRUCTURE OF VARIABLE ANNUITIES

As noted earlier, a variable annuity's cash values and benefit payments vary directly with the performance of the assets backing the contract. Assets backing variable annuities, as with those backing variable life policies, are maintained in separate accounts, and the variable annuities values directly reflect the account's investment results. In contrast, a life insurer's general account assets back FAs. (Optional VA living benefits discussed below are general account obligations, however.)

The contractual structure of VAs is similar to FAs in many respects. VAs may:

- be purchased with a single or flexible premium,
- be immediate or deferred,
- be surrendered for cash,
- pay benefits on a single or multiple life basis upon annuitization, and
- pay fixed benefits with or without refund features.

We focus on the significant investment and income provisions that distinguish VAs from FAs: (1) variable investment crediting based on separate account performance and (2) variable income benefits based on separate account performance. We close the section with brief notes on VA regulation and suitability.

SEPARATE ACCOUNT PERFORMANCE

VAs were first offered in the U.S. in 1952 by the *College Retirement Equities Fund*, a non-profit insurer specializing in the educational market. The rationale for variable annuities is that they should offer, over the long run, protection against the debilitating effects of inflation on fixed incomes – the kind of income provided by fixed annuities. The hope is that *long run* returns on common stocks and other investments will keep pace with inflation. Historical evidence suggests this is a reasonable expectation. As might be expected, sales of VAs tend to rise in rising stock markets and vice versa. Sales of FAs tend to move in the opposite direction of sales of VAs.

VA premiums paid to the insurance company are placed in a special variable annuity account. The separate account is a special purpose mutual fund generally available only through the insurer. The premiums, after deduction for any front-end loads, are applied periodically to purchase accumulation units in the account, the number of which depending upon the current unit value. A unit can be thought of as a share in the fund. Thus, if the net asset value of a unit is $10 on the purchase date, a premium of $100 after expenses will purchase 10 units. As the unit value changes with the market value of fund assets over time, the $100 premium would purchase more or less than 10 units. This procedure applies to all premiums paid until surrender or annuitization. (Paying constant premium payments produces a *dollar-cost-averaging* investment strategy.)

Under a traditional FPDA, SPDA, or other fixed-value annuity, the insurance company guarantees a minimum interest rate to be credited to the cash value during the accumulation period. In addition, a minimum annuity payout is guaranteed. In the absence of optional benefits discussed below, VAs do not contain such guarantees.

The general accounts of insurance companies are restricted as to the kind and quality of investments they may hold. As these investments support liabilities for products with interest guarantees, they should offer safety of principal and a predictable income stream. In contrast, comparatively few restrictions apply to separate account investments. Income, gains, and losses on separate account assets are credited to or charged against the separate account. Income, gains, and losses on the company's general account business and other separate account business have no effect on the separate account. Funds of VA contract owners are held in the separate account, and the contract owners participate fully in the investment results. Thus, in theory, the account value could fall to zero.

VAs permit simultaneous investment in multiple funds. After the 2008-09 financial crisis, some insurers began to require investors to hold minimum proportions (e.g., 30 percent) in bond funds. Transfers among funds are also permitted, usually at no charge for up to four transfers per year. Most insurers permit transfers during both the accumulation and liquidation periods. Most insurers include a general account option that owners may find attractive when they find market interest rates or stock market performance less attractive.

GUARANTEED MINIMUM DEATH BENEFIT   Most VAs provide protection against investment losses in the event of the annuitant's death during the accumulation period through a **guaranteed minimum death benefit** (GMDB), which guarantees that the amount paid on death will be the greater of the cash value or the amount invested in the contract. Some insurers offer a **ratchet GMDB** that establishes a new minimum death benefit periodically; alternatively the benefit may equal the premiums accumulated at a stated interest rate. The benefit can be viewed as contingent life insurance.

Thus, assume the owner pays a premium of $10,000 into the contract, and the cash value escalates to $12,000 over the next two years. Under the traditional GMDB, if the owner dies, his or her beneficiary receives $12,000. If, on the other hand, the cash value declines to $8,000 because of poor investment results, and the owner dies, his or her beneficiary would receive $10,000 – the amount invested in the contract.

The GMDB can be important to investors who are concerned about the riskiness inherent in VA investment returns. (Additional optional lifetime guarantees are also offered as discussed below.) The GMDB has a cost, however, in that the insurer must charge for the guarantee, thus depressing somewhat the effective yield under the policy. Most insurers establish age limits or time limits beyond which the guarantee does not apply in order to reduce these costs.

GUARANTEED MINIMUM ACCUMULATION BENEFIT   The **guaranteed minimum accumulation benefit** (GMAB), offered through an optional rider to VAs, guarantees that the annuity account value will not be less than the sum of premiums invested. Adjustments are made for withdrawals. A minimum holding period is usually required, along with a minimum period of no withdrawals.

VARIABLE INCOME BENEFITS

VA owners may take advantage of fixed annuity liquidation options if they desire (including exchanging their policies for a SPIA from another insurer if they find it attractive). Although comparatively few VAs have been annuitized to date, the product is designed to continue the presumed inflation protection of separate account performance by adjusting income benefits during the liquidation period.

At annuitization of the contract, the total units accumulated in the cash value account may be applied, according to actuarial principles and based on current valuation of a unit, to convert accumulation units to annuity units to be valued annually for the annuitant's lifetime. The number of annuity units purchased is a function of the assumed interest rate. The **assumed interest rate** (AIR) – also called the **benchmark rate** or **target return** – is the interest rate which, if earned uniformly throughout the liquidation period, would produce level annuity benefit payments. If the separate account earns a rate higher than the AIR, payments increase. If earnings are less than the AIR, payments decrease. Table 6-2 shows annual annuity payments under various fund performance scenarios assuming an AIR of 5.0 percent.

Table 6-2	**Annual Annuity Payments under Various Performance Scenarios (5.0 percent AIR, $1,000 First Payment)**

Time	Separate Account Net Earnings Rate				
	1%	**3%**	**5%**	**7%**	**9%**
0	$1,000.00	$1,000.00	$1,000.00	$1,000.00	$1,000.00
1	961.90	950.95	1,000.00	1,019.05	1,038.10
2	925.26	962.27	1,000.00	1,038.46	1,077.64
3	890.01	943.94	1,000.00	1,058.24	1,118.69
4	856.11	925.96	1,000.00	1,078.40	1,161.31
5	823.49	908.32	1,000.00	1,098.94	1,205.55
6	792.12	891.02	1,000.00	1,119.87	1,251.48
7	761.95	874.05	1,000.00	1,141.20	1,299.15
8	732.92	857.40	1,000.00	1,162.94	1,348.64
9	705.00	841.07	1,000.00	1,185.09	1,400.02

Thus, instead of providing for the payment each month of a fixed amount of dollars or other currency units, the VA provides for the payment each month or year of the current value of a fixed number of annuity units. The amount of each payment depends on the value of the annuity unit when the payment is made. The valuation assigned to a unit depends on the investment results of the separate account. For example, if an annuitant were entitled to a payment of 100 annuity units each month (as determined upon entering onto the annuity and using the AIR), and the dollar values of annuity units for three consecutive months were $10.20, $9.90, and $10.10, the annuitant would receive an income for these months of $1,020, $990, and $1,010.

A **guaranteed minimum income benefit** (GMIB) rider, which is purchased at issue, guarantees a minimum amount of retirement income based on assumptions in effect at purchase. The purchase price is a regular charge against the account value, perhaps 50 to 100 basis points. A GMIB is an attractive option because it protects the policyholder's investment against poor market performance during the accumulation phase. Payments can be more than projected if investment performance produces a rate of return higher than the guaranteed minimum rate of return. The GMIB essentially substitutes for the minimum benefit guaranteed under FAs while preserving the possibility of enhanced benefits when investment performance is superior.

Annuities are regulated at the federal and state levels, with emphasis on consumer protection via suitability and disclosure requirements. Federal regulation applies to variable annuities only, whereas state regulation touches both fixed and variable annuities.

As a security, variable annuities are subject to the same laws as variable life insurance, discussed in Chapter 4. Thus, requirements with respect to disclosure, sales loads, registration and financial standards, agent licensing, as well as other regulations apply to variable annuities. The *Financial Industry Regulatory Authority* (FINRA), in association with the *Securities and Exchange Commission* (SEC), regulates appropriate marketing practice for variable products through suitability and compliance standards. The suitability of VAs for seniors in particular has been questioned because of the limited investment time horizon of older owners. Surrender charges and investment volatility become more important considerations as potential buyers age. Regulatory Notice 07-43 mandates licensed sales professionals to take account of clients' age and life stage in light of an annuity's surrender charge period and amount.

At the state level, two NAIC model regulations are applicable.[*] The NAIC *Suitability in Annuity Transactions Model Regulation* (*Suitability Regulation*) sets forth standards and procedures for recommendations to consumers that result in a transaction involving annuity products to ensure the insurance needs and financial objectives of consumers are appropriately met at the time of the transaction. The NAIC *Annuity Disclosure Model Regulation* (*Disclosure Regulation*) establishes standards for the disclosure of certain information about annuity contracts to protect consumers and foster consumer education.

SUITABILITY

The NAIC *Suitability Regulation* sets standards for suitable annuity recommendations and requires insurers to establish a system to supervise annuity recommendations. This model regulation is patterned after similar FINRA requirements governing the suitability of variable annuity transactions. Compliance with the FINRA requirements is deemed to satisfy the requirements of the regulation. As of

SUITABILITY AND DISCLOSURE REGULATION OF ANNUITIES

---

[*]   The descriptions of these two regulations draws from the *Insured Retirement Institute* at www.irionline.org/government-affairs/annuities-regulation-industry-information/ state-regulation-of-annuities.

the date this book went to press, 45 states and the District of Columbia had adopted either the current version of the *Suitability Regulation* or one of the previous versions. Three states have suitability rules that do not follow the *Suitability Model*.

Among other things, the regulation requires an insurance producer, when making a recommendation to a consumer to purchase or exchange an annuity, to make reasonable efforts to obtain "suitability information," such as the consumer's age, annual income, financial objectives, and risk tolerance, that is "reasonably appropriate" to determine the suitability of the recommendation. It also requires the insurance producer to have "reasonable grounds" for believing that the recommendation is suitable for the consumer based on the suitability information and other facts provided by the consumer.

In addition, the insurance producer must have a "reasonable basis" for believing that (1) the consumer has been "reasonably informed" of the annuity's features; (2) the consumer would benefit from certain of those features; (3) the annuity as a whole, the underlying investment options selected by the consumer, and any riders or similar product enhancements are suitable for the consumer; and (4) in the case of an exchange or replacement of an annuity, the exchange or replacement is suitable. If no insurance producer is involved, these requirements apply to the insurer.

The *Suitability Regulation* also requires insurers to establish a supervisory system that is reasonably designed to achieve compliance with its requirements, including procedures for reviewing recommendations before issuing an annuity to ensure there is a "reasonable basis" to determine that a recommendation is suitable, as well as "reasonable procedures" for detecting recommendations that are not suitable. Finally, the regulation provides guidelines for separate account investments and requires that VA contracts state clearly the essential elements of the procedure for determining the amount of variable benefits. Other policy standards are laid down, including a requirement for mailing annual status reports to contract owners.

DISCLOSURE

The NAIC *Annuity Disclosure Model Regulation* requires that consumers be provided an Annuity Buyer's Guide and a Disclosure Document. As of the date of publication, one state had adopted the latest version of this regulation, but it was anticipated that states would soon begin to propose legislation to enact the latest version. Approximately 30 states had either previous versions of this regulation or different annuity disclosure rules.

The current version applies, with certain exceptions, to all group and individual annuity contracts and certificates, including to fixed, equity indexed, and variable annuities (except for non-registered variable annuities issued exclusively to accredited investors or qualified purchasers), while the previous version applied only to fixed and indexed annuities. For variable annuities, the Disclosure Document requirement applies, unless and until the SEC adopts a summary prospectus rule or FINRA approves for use a simplified disclosure form applicable to VAs.

The most significant aspect of the new regulation is that specific standards set forth the form and content of annuity illustrations. Previously, insurers were not required to follow uniform illustration standards. If the insurer decides to provide the purchaser with an illustration, the illustration has to comply with the detailed requirements of the regulation, and such illustration must reference the Buyer's Guide and the Disclosure Document. The regulation addresses the illustration of guaranteed and nonguaranteed elements, including that the rate illustrated may not be more favorable than that applicable to current nonguaranteed elements and may not include assumed future improvements in such elements.

For indexed annuities, carriers must show how a given index performed over the previous 10 years, as well as the index's best and worst historical performance over a decade. Insurers also have to include a description of the contract, its benefits, and how it works. For indexed annuities, the disclosure must also show the basis for caps, spread, and participation rates. Customers must also receive an explanation of the impact of any riders, along with information on the contract's federal tax status and the penalties that apply to withdrawals.

The Buyer's Guide and the Disclosure Document must be provided to the applicant at the time of a face-to-face sale. For other sales approaches, the Buyer's Guide and the Disclosure Document are to be sent no later than five business days after the insurer receives the completed application. There are separate guides for fixed, variable, and indexed annuities.

The revised model regulation also includes standards for fixed and indexed annuity illustrations that require, among other things (1) a narrative summary (unless the information is provided at the same time in a disclosure document); (2) a numeric summary; (3) for annuities with market value adjustment features (MVA), a narrative explanation of the MVA, a demonstration of the MVA under at least one positive and one negative scenario, and actual MVA floors and ceilings; and (4) for equity indexed annuity illustrations, specific requirements on illustrating nonguaranteed values. These illustration standards do not apply to variable annuity illustrations.

GUARANTEED MINIMUM WITHDRAWALS

This section discusses the most popular liquidity features, collectively called *guaranteed minimum withdrawals*, which are designed to provide a life income while allowing the owner significant withdrawal rights throughout the life of the annuity. These features may be offered as riders or as part of the base annuity contract and apply to FAs and VAs.

GUARANTEED LIFETIME WITHDRAWAL BENEFIT

The **guaranteed lifetime withdrawal benefit** (GLWB) guarantees the annuitant will receive a guaranteed stream of income payments, regardless of the contract account value, and provides complete access to a substantial part of the account balance throughout the deferral and liquidation periods. It may be a policy provision of or a rider attached to a fixed EIA or variable annuity. When activated, an annual charge is made against the account value, usually 50 to 100 basis points for the benefit provision or rider. The GLWB annuity or rider is characterized by two distinct phases in the deferral period and two phases in the liquidation phase.

DEFERRAL PERIOD   When the deferral period begins, the rider is inactive; at the time of the policyowner's election, the rider is activated and the withdrawal benefit determination process begins. (Some products eliminate the election and feature a withdrawal benefit determination phase that commences immediately and runs concurrent to the entire deferral period.) During the **inactive GLWB phase**, no fees are charged for the benefit provision or rider and premiums and investment income accumulate during the deferral period as with any deferred EIA or variable annuity. Fixed EIAs offer a minimum guaranteed return or a return based on the performance of an equity index. VA account values are a direct result of the gain or loss of separate account assets.

At the commencement of the **withdrawal benefit determination phase**, the rider becomes active, fees for the rider or provision are charged to the account, and the value of the *guaranteed lifetime withdrawal benefit base* develops. The **guaranteed lifetime withdrawal benefit base** is the amount that, together with a distribution factor, will determine the annual guaranteed withdrawal amount when the liquidation period begins. During the benefit determination phase, the insurer typically guarantees an attractive minimum return for 10 years, perhaps 5.0 percent or more. The benefit base will be the greater of the actual account value or an amount produced by the guaranteed return. The base may be determined as the sum of premiums paid and earnings accumulated to the date of determination (sometimes termed *premium roll up*). The base may also be determined periodically based on the account value at specified contract anniversary dates (sometimes termed *account value step up*); some insurers will restart the guarantee period when the account value exceeds the guaranteed amount at an anniversary.

Table 6-3 shows hypothetical benefit base determinations under two scenarios. The first assumes poor investment performance and no investment growth net of fees; the second assumes superior investment performance at 7.0 percent net of fees compounded for five years. The hypothetical guaranteed minimum return is 5.0 percent compounded annually. Note that only the account value is payable on the surrender of the annuity policy, the benefit base is used only to calculate annuitized withdrawal benefits. The two scenarios demonstrate the ability of the GLWB to provide downside protection from unfavorable market results while retaining the possibility of enhanced benefits if superior investment performance is achieved. Of course, the fee cost of the benefit limits the upside investment results that would have been captured in the absence of the benefit.

Table 6-3	**Hypothetical Guaranteed Withdrawal Benefit Base Results under Positive and Negative Investment Performance Scenarios**

Year	Guaranteed Benefit Base	Poor Investment Performance		Superior Investment Performance	
		Account Value	Benefit Base	Account Value	Benefit Base
1	$105,000	$100,000	$105,000	$107,000	$107,000
2	110,250	100,000	110,250	114,490	114,490
3	115,763	100,000	115,763	122,504	122,504
4	121,551	100,000	121,551	131,080	131,080
5	127,628	100,000	127,628	140,255	140,255

Liquidation Period   On liquidation, the GLWB does not pay a stated regular amount. It provides for the payment of the greater of (1) a stated percentage of the account value or (2) the **guaranteed withdrawal amount** – a dollar amount determined by multiplying the guaranteed lifetime withdrawal benefit base by the distribution factor. The distribution factor varies according to the age and sex of the annuitant and the pattern of distributions. For example, the distribution factor may be level for life or increase at a specified rate at the option of the owner. If the account value is depleted due to investment performance and/or longevity, the insurer continues payment of the guaranteed withdrawal amount.

During the liquid withdrawal phase, account assets in the amount of the guaranteed withdrawal amount are withdrawn regularly. The guaranteed with-drawal benefit base is reduced by the amount of each withdrawal to produce the **benefit base balance**. Excess withdrawals are typically permitted but discouraged by reducing not only the benefit base but the distribution factor as well. At each anniversary (or withdrawal), the benefit base balance can be compared to the account value. As long as the account value exceeds the benefit base balance, the guaranteed minimum withdrawal benefit does not apply. Payments reduce both the account value and benefit base balance, and the remaining account value continues to accumulate. Some contracts provide for a death benefit if the owner dies with a positive benefit base allowance.

The GLWB rider promises that a guaranteed amount is always available for withdrawal without regard to the account value. The **guaranteed withdrawal phase** begins when a withdrawal causes the account value to fall below the benefit base balance and payments are made by the insurer. The guaranteed withdrawal amount is paid by the insurer for the life of the annuitant or annuitants. During the guarantee period, excess withdrawal privileges and any death benefit typically come to an end. Some policies provide what is known as a **guaranteed minimum withdrawal benefit** under which withdrawals continue not for life but for a stated period or a stated total amount.

Contingent Deferred Annuities

During the 1990s, insurers began to offer **contingent deferred annuities** (CDAs) – also termed **stand alone living benefits** – that guarantee lifetime withdrawal benefits from the owner's mutual fund or managed investment account. CDAs effectively separate the investment and mortality guarantees from the underlying investments for individual owners. The terms of these contracts may provide as follows.

- Underlying assets remain with the mutual fund or investment account custodian.
- The risk of insurer default applies to the guaranteed benefits only.
- Withdrawal benefits are determined in accordance with terms similar to the GLWB annuity or rider.
- Fees are based on the age and gender of the annuitant and the risk properties of the portfolio.
- The contract is unilateral in that only the insurer makes promises, so the contract can be terminated at the option of the owner and without further charge.

If the account value is exhausted, the insurer continues the guaranteed withdrawals for the life of the annuitant. These products essentially ensure completion of a systematic withdrawal program from an investment account. At this writing, at least one state (New York) has ruled that CDAs are not annuities but an impermissible form of financial guarantee insurance. The IRS has recognized CDA arrangements as annuities for tax purposes as we discuss in Chapter 21.

IMPORTANCE AND SUITABILITY OF GUARANTEES

Product innovation in the form of accumulation, withdrawal, and income guarantees – collectively termed **guaranteed living benefits** (GLB) – have proven attractive to consumers who desire long term investment and mortality guarantees that provide guaranteed minimum performance while preserving the potential for enhanced performance. Whether these product innovations serve to increase insurers' market share in the retirement savings market and increase annuitization rates remains largely an open question. The LIMRA *Variable Annuity Guaranteed Living Benefit Election Tracking Survey* tracks the number of annuity purchasers electing GLBs quarterly. The election rate usually exceeds 50 percent.

The fees associated with VAs in general and GLBs in particular have been characterized as excessive by some. Other criticisms are similar to those associated with index annuities; the amount of potential gain sacrificed in return for the guarantees is too great relative to their underlying value. Guarantee performance during the global equity market declines of 2008-2009 do not support this view.

Figure 6-7 presents a summary of the contractual provisions that distinguish the many different varieties of annuities by their purchase, accumulation, and liquidation bases.

SUBSTANDARD MORTALITY ANNUITIES

Most life annuities are issued without underwriting or any evaluation of the annuitant's health. We know that adverse selection exists in the annuities market, and insurers generally price annuities to reflect this expected super-standard mortality. However, two classes of annuities are available for annuitants whose mortality experience is expected to be below average.

STRUCTURED SETTLEMENT ANNUITIES

A contemporary use of SPIAs has evolved from liability insurers' efforts to minimize their loss payouts. A **structured settlement annuity** (SSA) is a SPIA contract issued by a life insurer whereby the plaintiff (the injured party) receives periodic payments via a life annuity paid by the defendant (or the liability insurer) in a personal injury lawsuit instead of the more common lump sum payment. Typically, the defendant and the plaintiff, together with their attorneys and a structured settlement specialist, negotiate a settlement package intended to compensate the plaintiff for his or her losses, including future earnings.

The periodic payments are funded through an SSA purchased by the defendant or the liability insurer from a life insurer that guarantees to make the agreed upon payments to an intermediary settlement company, usually for the life of the injured person. The settlement company, in turn, makes payments to the plaintiff. The intermediary company is necessary to avoid constructive receipt by the plaintiff (and current tax) of the present value of all benefits at the time of the settlement. Settlement companies are specifically authorized in the tax law, but their use is limited to personal injury and wrongful death settlements. In a properly structured settlement, payments are included in the plaintiff's taxable income only at the time of actual receipt.

The Contractual Structure of Annuities   **Figure 6-7**

FIXED ANNUITIES

PURCHASE BASIS	ACCUMULATION BASIS	LIQUIDATION BASIS
Single Premium Immediate Annuity Single Premium Deferred Annuity Flexible Premium Deferred Annuity Longevity Annuity	General Account Credits Equity-Indexed Credits Inflation-Indexed Credits Market Value Annuity Credits Certificate of Annuity Credits Long Term Care Charges	Single, Joint and Survivor, Joint Life Refunds Enhanced Liquidity Withdrawals Guaranteed Minimum Withdrawals Guaranteed Minimum Lifetime Withdrawals Long Term Care Benefits

VARIABLE ANNUITIES

PURCHASE BASIS	ACCUMULATION BASIS	LIQUIDATION BASIS
Single Premium Immediate Annuity Single Premium Deferred Annuity Flexible Premium Deferred Annuity	Separate Account Credits Guaranteed Minimum Death Benefit Guaranteed Accumulation Benefit Long Term Care Charges	Single, Joint and Survivor, Joint Life Guaranteed Minimum Income Enhanced Liquidity Withdrawals Guaranteed Minimum Withdrawals Guaranteed Minimum Lifetime Withdrawals Long Term Care Benefits

---

Many SSA annuitants can be expected to exhibit substandard mortality experience if they have suffered some injury. To be competitive, the insurer must offer the lowest possible price to the liability insurer to win the sale. As the assessed likelihood of an early death increases, insurers can charge lower prices or pay higher benefits. The mortality evaluation is conducted on each case by an underwriter

Substandard Annuities

A few insurers have begun to offer life annuities that pay higher benefits to annuitants who present a life expectancy that is shorter than average. These annuities could help overcome the objections that many have to annuitization and permit more owners to acquire annuities that more accurately reflect their mortality risk.

Substandard annuities require medical underwriting similar to life insurance underwriting methods and may include attending physician statements, medical reports, and physical exams. Life insurance ratings, as discussed in Chapter 11, are usually expressed as a percentage surcharge to the standard rating at the age of the insured. Substandard annuities typically offer increased benefits by assuming for pricing purposes that the substandard annuitant's life expectancy will be that of an older annuitant. The annuitant, thus, receives the higher benefits applicable to an older person.

Competitive considerations make underwriting expertise especially important in the substandard market, and SSA writers may have an advantage as the market develops. If the market share of substandard annuities expands significantly, there may be upward pressure on rates in the standard market as average life expectancies increase.

RETIREMENT PLANS

In this section, we briefly identify group products provided to employers and retirement plan trusts that protect a retirement plan sponsor from the financial risk of plan participants living longer than average lives. Life insurers also provide investment products and services that do not incorporate mortality elements to retirement plans.

In the U.S., **qualified plans** are retirement plans that satisfy the requirements of the federal *Employee Retirement Income Security Act* (ERISA) and the federal *Internal Revenue Code* (IRC). Defined benefit (DB) and defined contribution (DC) plans receive favorable treatment under the federal provisions. **Defined benefit** plans specify the benefits required to be provided participant employees at retirement. Contribution requirements are implicit and vary according to plan investment performance and employee eligibility. **Defined contribution** plans specify the contributions that sponsors are required to make to each participant's account. Benefits are distributed in cash to the participant at retirement (or applied to an employer-sponsored postretirement option).

In the DC market, the plan assumes no longevity risk, but participants may elect life incomes by applying their DC account balances to products offered by insurers that guarantee life incomes. Life insurers also offer investment and administrative services to both DB and DC plans that sometimes are bundled with longevity protection.

DB plans create significant uncertainties for employer sponsors, hence the decline in the prevalance of DB plans. In addition to creating significant risks in coverage liability, investment, and mortality risk, DB funding obligations significantly complicate budgeting decisions. DB liabilities are usually quite large and also can have a significant impact on a sponsor's financial results. DB plans usually offer life income benefits for which insurers offer mortality protection products. Insurer longevity products and investment services can help reduce the uncertainty of the investment and mortality risks in DB plans. Also, the **Pension Benefit Guaranty Corporation** was established by the Federal government to provide insurance for plan participants whose plans have been terminated.

BENEFITS AND REQUIREMENTS

Private, employer-sponsored retirement plans are encouraged by ERISA and the IRC to promote private sector participation in the four pillars of retirement funding: social insurance through the Social Security system, personal savings, employer-provided benefits, and part-time employment. Thus, qualified employer plans feature:

- tax deductions for employer contributions,
- tax free accumulation of assets prior to distribution to participants, and
- no taxable income to participants until amounts are actually distributed during retirement.

Tax benefits are available only to sponsors of qualified plans: those that meet numerous and often complex technical requirements specified in the ERISA and tax laws. The overriding requirements are (1) the plan must be written, legally binding, and communicated to participants in accordance with regulations; (2) participants' benefits must be *vested* – they are not forfeitable upon termination of the employment relationship – according to schedules specifying the participants' length of service (participant contributions to contributory plans must vest immediately); and (3) plans must not discriminate in favor of highly compensated individuals. (For this reason, employers may offer nonqualified deferred compensation plans to highly compensated individuals – often funded with life insurance policies – as discussed in Chapter 23.)

DB plans may be self insured, partially self insured, or fully insured. Life insurers offer a variety of group products designed to protect qualified plan sponsors from the longevity risks associated with the benefits promised to plan participants. The most important of these is the group deferred annuity.

Under a **group deferred annuity** (GDA) plan, the employer purchases units of SPDAs each year to provide specified amounts of life income to be paid to participants at retirement. When used in conjunction with a DB plan, the annuity purchases are coordinated with the plan provisions. Typically, the employee's pension is separated into pieces that are associated with years of employment. Thus, for each year of service, the employee might be entitled to an annual pension of 2.0 percent of salary or a flat monthly amount, such as $50. Each year, the employer then purchases a single premium unit of deferred annuity, which becomes payable when the employee reaches retirement age. The employee's pension is the sum of the units purchased for him or her. GDAs are also used in terminal funding situations where the employer has no future obligations and wishes to transfer all accrued obligations to an insurer.

Insurers typically require a minimum number of participants, to maintain reasonable administrative costs. The employer is provided a master annuity agreement and employees receive **certificates of participation** that communicate the details of their benefits to be provided from the group deferred annuity plan. All administrative services are provided by the insurer, and the insurer assumes all investment and mortality risk. Thus, the only risk to the employer and participants is the risk of insurer insolvency.

Group annuity type products may also be offered to participants in DC plans both during and at the time of retirement. As employers assume no life income responsibilities under DC plans, these products are made available as options to participants.

SPECIAL INVESTMENT ARRANGEMENTS

Life insurers offer plan sponsors **guaranteed investment contracts** (GICs) that credit a specified interest rate for a specified period much like a certificate of deposit at a bank. Unlike banks, life insurers can offer a variety of terms and maturities to custom match plan sponsor needs. GICs are general account products that are backed by the general credit of the insurer.

Life insurers also offer non-insured investment services to qualified plan sponsors through separate accounts where the sponsor bears the risk of investment gains and losses. These separate account services may be provided to self insured DB plans along with plan administration services. Separate account fund options may also be offered as options to participants in DC plans.

In closing this section, we note that life insurers can offer a broad menu of retirement services that can be combined to suit the plan sponsor's needs in administration services, investment management, and participant longevity protection.

CHAPTER 7

HEALTH INSURANCE I: MEDICAL EXPENSE INSURANCE

As noted in Chapter 1, we classify health insurance into three categories. First, medical expense insurance – or simply health insurance – reimburses insureds or pays providers directly for hospital, medical care, and related services. Second, long term care (LTC) insurance pays stated benefits when insureds incur exceptional expenses because of their need for assistance arising from an inability to perform the essential activities of daily living. Third, disability income insurance usually provides stated periodic payments when an insured loses wage income because of injury or sickness. Chapter 8 covers these two latter types of health insurance.

This chapter focuses on medical expense insurance. We first examine the health care environment and the economics of health care. We then examine the basic mechanics and operation of the 2010 *Patient Protection and Affordable Care Act* (ACA). We next explore group and individual coverage with an overview of the properties of group underwriting and financing that distinguish the group product and market from the individual product and market. The individual and employer mandates of the ACA are emphasized. We close with a discussion of the basic features of selected government insurance programs.

THE HEALTH CARE ENVIRONMENT

Rising health care costs are a global phenomenon, constituting a major problem in both social insurance and voluntary employer-provided health plans, especially in developed countries. Many governments are exploring the possibility of shifting more medical expense costs to employers and individuals.

Most developed countries provide broad national health insurance coverage for individuals of all ages. In these countries, employers commonly offer supplemental medical expense plans to provide employees with more extensive medical care coverage than that provided under the national health insurance program. Table 7-1 presents an overview of health care benefits in selected countries.

Table 7-1   **Overview of Health Care Benefits in Selected Countries**

Country	Benefits Provided
Brazil	Basic health care services are provided by the government. Supplemental coverage typically is provided through prepaid groups (clinics, cooperatives, and preferred-provider organizations), with insured plans growing in popularity.
Germany	Universal, comprehensive health care insurance is mandated by the government and paid with compulsory employer and employee contributions. High-wage earners may opt out and select private insurance (employer must pay one-half of the insurance premiums) and/or may be provided supplementary insurance for high quality care (e.g., private accommodations).
Japan	The government regulates almost all aspects of the universal public health insurance system. The national government sets the fee schedule by developing consensus among stakeholders; gives subsidies to local governments, insurers, and providers to implement its policies; and establishes and enforces detailed regulations for insurers and providers. Government health insurance finances 80.5 percent of health care services.
Norway	Much of the health system is government-controlled. Norway's 429 municipalities, with additional funding from the Norwegian Health Economics Administration, are responsible for funding and delivering primary care services, including health promotion, preventive medicine, rehabilitative services, emergency care, and long-term nursing care. Private insurance plans represent about 5 percent of expenditures, primarily for elective care.
South Korea	Universal, comprehensive health care insurance is mandated by the government and care is provided through either government facilities or government authorized health care groups ("societies"). The government plan includes copayments (from 20 to 55 percent) and deductibles that may be financed through private insurance.
Thailand	The Universal Coverage Scheme (UCS) enrolls those not covered by existing government programs: the Civil Servant Medical Benefit Scheme and the Compulsory Social Security Scheme. About 74 percent of the entire population is covered. The UCS is financed through general tax revenues paid to local contracting units on the basis of population size.
United Kingdom	Universal, comprehensive health care services are provided by the government through the National Health Service. Redundant insured plans provided by employers are growing in popularity because of improved service over the government system.
Zimbabwe	Virtually no health care benefits are provided by the government or through employers. Workers' compensation coverage applies for work related injuries.

U.S. MEDICAL CARE COST TRENDS

The rate of increase in health care expenditures throughout the 1980s, 1990s, and 2000s was significantly higher than the increases in general inflation, population growth, and GDP. During much of this period, increases in health care costs were at rates twice that of overall inflation. After a period of relative stability in the early 1990s attributable to the first serious attempts at cost control, relatively high health care inflation has characterized the 21st century.

Health care costs are projected to account for 20 percent of U.S. GDP by 2021 according to the Centers for Medicare and Medicaid Services. One industry report (*2013 Milliman Medical Index*) calculates health care inflation at 6.3 percent and an average annual cost for a family of four of $22,030. While a practical impossibility, the scale of the health care inflation problem is often highlighted by noting that continuing high increases would result in health care costs consuming the entirety of U.S. GDP within the lifetimes of many Americans living today. All countries, including those with universal health care systems, spend less on health care than the U.S.

Additional factors that contribute to the increasing cost of health care and insurance include rising medical malpractice insurance rates, with its attendant practice of defensive medicine (see Box 7-1), an aging population with its attendant higher health care demand, the fact that many cost control efforts have achieved their maximum possible effect (for example most inpatient procedures that can be done on an outpatient basis are now done that way), and cost shifting and cost control efforts by major employers and Medicare have increased prices for plans that do not have the market power to negotiate prices. Figure 7-1 presents the annual rate of increase in employee costs for employer-sponsored plans.

Box 7-1
Medical Malpractice Lawsuits, Insurance, and Defensive Medicine

Medical malpractice suits are a factor in rising health care costs, particularly in the U.S. Patients have become increasingly likely to resolve disappointment with treatment outcomes through litigation. Others file fraudulent legal actions that are difficult to control. The litigious nature of the U.S. culture reinforces this avenue for conflict resolution. This increased incidence of medical malpractice claims has caused physician malpractice insurance costs to rise, and these costs are ultimately passed on to health insurers and in turn to consumers. An increasing number of established physicians have opted out of practicing medicine as a result of the litigious environment.

This increased willingness to sue is driven in part by a change in the relationship between patient and physician. Traditionally, a family practitioner treated a broad range of needs over an extended time, fostering a relationship of trust between physician and patient. Today, specialists outnumber general practitioners, and patients are less likely to know and trust these providers where their relationship is not continuing but occurs at critical times. When treatment fails or when unrealistic expectations are not met, patients, encouraged by attorneys or even greed, are more likely to sue providers.

Physicians may practice defensive medicine in an effort to avoid medical malpractice liability. They order tests and procedures that may not be medically necessary in an effort to reduce their liability in the event they are sued. These additional diagnostic procedures and treatments also drive up the total cost of health care.

Figure 7-1   **Annual Change in Total U.S. Health Benefit Cost per Employee**

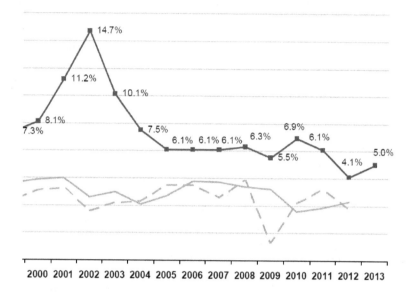

Source: 2013 Mercer National Survey of Employer-Sponsored Health Plans.

EMPLOYER RESPONSES TO RISING HEALTH CARE COSTS

Employers responded to rapidly increasing costs by raising the share of expenditures paid by employees or limiting the employer's contribution in other ways. These efforts included:

- increased employee co-payments (e.g., increased deductibles, higher coinsurance percentages, and greater use of internal limits on certain types of benefits);
- introduction of flexible benefit plans where the employee chooses from a variety of life insurance, medical care, and other benefits provided by a fixed employer contribution;
- termination of benefits entirely;
- redesigning benefits to create incentives for more efficient utilization of health care resources;
- improving the administration and financing of the plan; and
- using alternative delivery and reimbursement systems such as health maintenance organizations (HMOs), preferred provider organizations (PPOs), and point of service plans (see below).

Figure 7-2 illustrates the increased shifting of health care costs to employees through rising deductibles negotiated under contracts between employers and providers.

Average U.S. PPO Deductibles for Individual In-Network Coverage   Figure 7-2

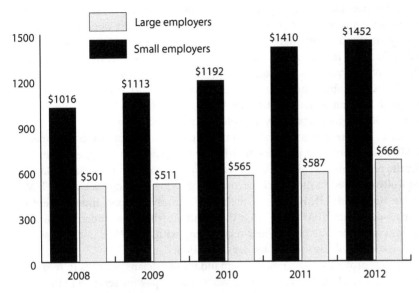

Source: 2012 Mercer National Survey of Employer-Sponsored Health Plans

HEALTH INSURANCE PROVIDERS

Private disability and LTC insurance are generally made available by life insurers. Private insurers are discussed in Chapter 9. Medical expense insurance arrangements are difficult to describe because the definitions of *provider* and *insurance* can vary according to context. Expense protection may be funded by insurance companies that indemnify insureds for expenses incurred, employers who fund cash benefit claims as an ordinary business expense, or organizations that provide services rather than cash reimbursement.

Health insurance in the U.S. is dominated by Blue Cross and Blue Shield Associations (Blues) and three commercial insurance companies (UnitedHealth Group, CIGNA, and Aetna), known collectively in the industry as "BUCA." Health care services are also provided through **health maintenance organizations** (HMOs), which are health care financing and delivery corporations that contract with physicians, hospitals, and others to provide services to beneficiaries, rather than cash reimbursement, and through **preferred provider organizations** (PPOs), which are health care intermediaries between sponsors and physicians and other health care providers who agree to provide services at discounted rates. Both HMOs and PPOs offer participant services via **provider networks**, which are affiliated health care providers, and through **out-of-network providers**, which are health care providers not affiliated with the HMO or PPO and which are compensated by cash payments for expenses incurred for services rendered.

Historically, employers and insurers have reimbursed participants in cash for cash expenses, and Blues and HMOs provided health services directly. With time, the distinctions have blurred somewhat and most organizations now employ features once exclusive to others.

The Blues have serviced the most significant number of participants since their inception. Originally, Blue Cross organizations were nonprofit entities organized by hospitals and Blue Shield associations by physicians to provide covered services for a prepaid fee. The organizations have generally operated together for a long time, and increasingly their operations have assumed insurer financing and administrative functions, just as insurers provide more service benefits. Many Blues have evolved into very large, for-profit organizations.

HMOs combine the financing and delivery of health care services by sharing risk with the plan sponsor and, hence, the risk of utilization intensity. Beneficiaries are usually assigned a primary care physician who acts as a "gatekeeper," and beneficiaries must receive a referral from the primary care physician to see a specialist. HMOs pay an amount per person or family to a physician and hospital in return for the provision of health care services to that person or family. Beneficiaries are typically required to make a co-payment (e.g., $25) for each visit. Many HMOs – called **staff model HMOs** – have their own staff. By contrast, **independent practice associations** (IPAs) are HMOs that contract with independent physicians to provide services. The practitioner relationship with the IPA is not exclusive, and the physician will also see fee-for-service patients.

PPOs provide an assurance of demand for physicians' services in return for a discounted fee. Beneficiaries of these plans usually pay for services to the limit of an annual deductible (e.g., $1,000) and a coinsurance payment (e.g., 20 percent). After the deductible has been paid, the beneficiary and insurer share the cost until an out of pocket maximum is reached, after which the insurer pays all fees. The beneficiary is thus protected from catastrophic health expenses.

Point of service (POS) preferred provider organizations are hybrid PPOs under which beneficiaries typically are treated by an in-network primary care physician who may make referrals to in-network or out-of-network specialists as the beneficiary chooses. Cost sharing increases with out-of-network specialists. Thus, if the beneficiary chooses to remain in the specified network and seek referrals to specialists, there may be a co-payment only. They retain the option of going outside the network, but they then are subject to deductibles and coinsurance.

THE ECONOMICS OF HEALTH CARE

As we know from Chapter 1, in a perfectly competitive market, buyers decide what to purchase based on full information about the quality and price of goods and services. Buyers, not sellers, determine the demand for goods and services, and demand for normal goods and services decreases with increases in prices, other things being equal. Price rationing occurs as buyers base purchasing decisions on the relative quality and price of the good as well as on their willingness and ability to pay. In a perfectly competitive market, no barriers to entry exist. In the real world, of course, the health care market has imperfections, and these imperfections shape health care financing.

Health care services may be financed (1) out of general tax revenues, (2) under a social insurance model, (3) through a voluntary private insurance system, (4) from an individual's or family's personal resources, and (5) a combination of these. Decisions at a national level about which approach to follow are rooted in how societies view themselves. Beliefs about the nature of health care and whether it is a right or a privilege or falls on a continuum between the two are important factors that shape the health care financing system of a given country. Many people believe that access to medical care should be a universal right rather than a privilege. For those who consider health care a right, everyone is entitled to all services equally.

Medical care is costly, however, and some tradeoffs in coverage are inevitable due to resource constraints; rationing must occur in some form. Thus, certain sub-groups of citizens may be uninsured (such as the poor or the unemployed), waiting times to receive care may be long (rationing through one's price of time), or access to state of the art technology or certain procedures may be restricted, especially for persons of advanced age.

The comparison of the health care market with a perfectly competitive market provides insight into how cost and quality problems arise and helps identify potential inefficiencies that can lead to service, quality, or pricing problems that negatively affect patients, health care providers, and insurers. Market imperfections also help explain the difficulty of health care reform. The more prominent such market imperfections are discussed in this section.

COST/BENEFIT MEASUREMENT PROBLEMS

Measurement of the marginal benefit of medical services on health status is difficult. Of course, individuals cannot purchase *health* from providers but instead purchase medical services to improve or maintain their health. From the standpoint of society, preventative medical services such as vaccinations provide a much greater marginal benefit than do more expensive, more technologically intensive interventions. Once vaccination and basic health services are provided, overall health is positively affected more by factors such as diet, exercise, and smoking than by the advancement of sophisticated technological procedures. Public policy relating to the optimal amount of medical care that should be provided to individuals is a complex question.

However, the health care market is characterized by rapid and continuing advances in medical technology requiring continuous capital expenditures. While the price of new technology declines over time, the constant invention of new medical products and the capital expenditures required to remain current and competitive are especially pronounced.

Cost/benefit analysis of medical technology can be difficult. Estimating their benefits requires consideration of factors such as improved morbidity and mortality rates, decreased lengths of hospitalization, and decreased recovery times. Estimation of the economic value of human life is also required. Cultural beliefs on prolonging life and quality of life also complicate benefit analysis.

INFORMATION PROBLEMS

The medical care market is characterized by substantial information problems. These problems take the form of buyer ignorance, adverse selection, and moral hazard.

BUYER IGNORANCE (THE "LEMONS" PROBLEM) Providers are well informed about the services they deliver, but consumers usually are not. For physicians, hospitals, and other providers to provide full information to consumers is costly, and providers tend to supply only essential information relative to a particular medical treatment.

When information on alternative treatments is available, consumers generally lack the technical expertise required for a full comprehension of the issues. Evaluating alternatives includes consideration of service quality, measured by criteria such as the success rate of the treatment, the degree of invasiveness of the procedure, or the length of recovery time. Further, the need to gather and analyze information usually occurs when the buyer is ill or injured, creating additional problems in comprehension and decision making. A partial solution to this is found in the general practitioner who serves as an advisor to patients who need non-routine medical treatment.

Information asymmetries also exist with respect to the price of medical services. Consumers generally have limited incentives to be well informed about the price of medical services, as third parties (government, employers, or private insurers) pay for most medical services. Even when consumers attempt to price and compare services, it is often difficult to determine in advance the total cost of services. Physicians themselves may not have financial incentives to be well informed about prices if their income is unaffected by the quantity or quality of services delivered (common with salaried physicians and when physicians order tests and services from third parties). Buyer ignorance, associated with understanding the nature of the medical treatment and comparing prices of alternative treatments, constrains price rationing and the efficient purchase of medical care. Further, the purchase of medical services often occurs in circumstances where the patient may have little or no interest in their prices, as with a severe illness or accident. As discussed below the ACA classifies plans and designates them as Platinum, Gold, Silver, and Bronze based on actuarial values in an attempt to minimize consumers' informational disadvantage with respect to insurance policies.

ADVERSE SELECTION   Whereas medical service providers have an information advantage over their consumers, these same consumers have an information advantage over health insurers. Individuals have a great deal more information about their individual health status and likely need for medical services than do insurers. Complicating the matter for insurers, information on an individual's health status is relatively expensive to obtain. This informational disadvantage to insurers frequently results in adverse selection.

As we know, adverse selection occurs when consumers use knowledge of their higher than average risk, which the insurer does not possess, to obtain insurance at lower-than-justified rates. Consequently, individuals with lower risks subsidize those with higher risks. Minimizing the impact of adverse selection underlies all contract design and company underwriting processes relating to health insurance coverage in a voluntary, private market.

These issues apply not only to medical expense insurance but also to disability income and long term care insurance which we discuss in the next chapter. The guaranteed issue requirement of the ACA minimizes adverse selection in medical expense coverage to some degree, but raises new issues in adverse selection; we specifically address adverse selection under the ACA in the discussion below.

MORAL HAZARD Third-party payment for medical services not only reduces incentives for consumers to seek price information but also increases the potential for moral hazard. Recall that moral hazard results when the presence of insurance changes the loss prevention or loss minimization behavior of the insured. The effect of moral hazard is that insureds become less risk averse, less inclined to minimize medical costs, and therefore inclined to demand more services for these and probably other reasons.

Individuals who have medical expense insurance do not pay market prices for services directly, but rather view the care as free or pay an amount significantly less than full price (such as the deductible or co-payment amount) for services. When the consumer's perception of cost is less than his or her perception of the price of services provided, consumers tend to demand more services than when they must pay the full price. The insurance changes the insured's incentives. Additionally, as insureds do not bear the full cost of medical care, they may be less careful about their health or wellbeing or engage in activities that can compromise their health status.

Another aspect of moral hazard in health insurance is what has been termed **supplier induced demand** in that providers treating insured patients have an incentive to recommend and perform more health services than they would in the absence of insurance. Medical professionals frequently disagree on the beginning or end of a particular episode of illness and on the health services needed to alleviate the condition. If insurance is present, they have a tendency to err on the side of more rather than less services. This incentive is enhanced as practitioners face the increasing likelihood of malpractice suits under the U.S. legal system.

Recommending services that may be of questionable value or even unnecessary but that benefit the provider economically has been identified as a related issue. In its worst manifestation, it can result in medical fraud, as in recommendations for services not needed and directing patients to a laboratory or other service facility in which a physician has an ownership interest.

To minimize the impact of moral hazard, insurers design contracts that transfer at least some cost of losses back to the policyowner by using deductibles, coinsurance, and co-payments. These provisions are included in an effort to discourage overuse of services and to reward the careful behavior of the insured.

MARKET POWER The medical services market is also characterized as having market power problems. These come in the form of barriers to entry and economies of scale.

Barriers to Entry Barriers to entry are prevalent in this market. Medical service providers must meet stringent capital, licensing, or other regulatory requirements that limit the number of market entrants. Hospitals require large capital expenditures for facilities and equipment and often a certificate of need from a state or federal jurisdiction in order to operate. Physicians and other health care professionals are required to obtain medical degrees, certifications, or other licensing to practice medicine. Obtaining the necessary credentials is itself a significant hurdle and constitutes an important major supply constraint.

Barriers to entry contribute to market power among providers, which can increase price and lower the quality of services provided. Similar barriers exist for health insurers.

Economies of Scale   Some argue that the production of health care services has large economies of scale. As a result, it is less costly to society to produce these services using a public utility model, rather than a competitive market model. The concept of economies of scale in health care may seem to be evident given the sheer number of physicians, hospitals, and other health care providers within most developed countries. However, the market for health care services is primarily local and not national in all but the very smallest countries.

Thus, the markets for health care services usually encompass a relatively small geographic area. As a result, competition in all but the largest cities may be insufficient for a workably competitive market. The question of scale economies is one of the factors underlying the continuing debate between those who believe that government is the most efficient provider and those who believe that the private market is the appropriate approach for the efficient financing and delivery of health care.

OVERVIEW OF THE PATIENT PROTECTION AND AFFORDABLE CARE ACT

The *Patient Protection and Affordable Care Act* (ACA), enacted in 2010, is the most extensive alteration ever of the U.S. health care financing system. It provides for a hybrid public/private financing approach to a comprehensive reform of the entire system. It retains private insurance coverage while attempting to create the mandatory participation feature of social insurance through an employer mandate requiring certain employers to provide coverage and an individual mandate requiring those not covered at work to maintain personal coverage. The act was controversial before and has been since its passage. The act's provisions are being phased in over a period extending to 2020, and many details remain to be determined.

Conflict of opinion exists between those who highly value fundamental principles of individual freedom and responsibility and those who highly value collective responsibility for social welfare. Despite the controversy, there seems to be a consensus that health care reform is necessary. The congressional opposition generally proposes significant amendments rather than a complete retreat from reform.

The *Affordable Care Act* in scale and scope is monumental, and its details are too voluminous and technical for a complete presentation. We provide a brief discussion of its major provisions and its expected impact on employer-sponsored and individual health insurance plans.

BASIC MECHANICS OF HEALTH CARE UNDER THE *AFFORDABLE CARE ACT*

The provisions of the act run thousands of printed pages. Many regulations that will govern its interpretation, implementation, and administration have yet to be written and will run to many thousands more. A wide range of grandfathering and transitional rules apply. Health care under the ACA includes continuing roles for government, industry, and individuals. It envisions a role for both private and social insurance coverage. The program is administered by the federal *Department of Health and Human Services* (HHS).

Perhaps the principal purpose of the ACA was to provide universal health care insurance coverage. All eligible individuals theoretically will be covered from one of four sources of financing:

- Approximately 160 to 170 million individuals are to be covered by mandated employer coverage.
- Approximately 50 million of formerly uninsured individuals will be required to carry qualifying coverage or face financial penalties.
- Approximately 40 million elderly individuals are to be covered under Medicare.
- Approximately 40 million individuals are to be covered under Medicaid and Children's Health Insurance Plans (CHIP) for the indigent.

The act authorizes the states to create what are called *American Health Exchanges* to provide coverage to individuals and small employer groups. States were given the option to establish exchanges or not. At this writing, 17 states have established exchanges and six are operated jointly with the federal government. The remaining states are serviced by a federally facilitated exchange. Exchanges (also called marketplaces) offer standardized health care plans for individuals, some of whom are eligible for federal subsidies.

The state- and federal-based exchanges are intended to operate as a public service to bring together buyers and sellers of health insurance. Internet web sites are the most important means by which the exchanges function. States are responsible for educating consumers and determining eligibility for the Medicaid and CHIP indigent care programs. They also are responsible for enforcing and monitoring plan designs and pricing of insurers offering coverage through the exchanges.

A variety of preventative care, wellness, and quality of care initiatives are included. The legislation also impacts long term care insurance as we discuss in Chapter 8. Figure 7-3 on the next page presents a flow diagram of health care financing under the ACA.

IMPACT ON THE PRIVATE HEALTH INSURANCE MARKET

The *Affordable Care Act* obviously affects the private health insurance market and providers significantly. Some provisions will change historical practices of insurance in private markets. Two of the most significant provisions of health care reform are the guaranteed issue/community rating requirements for health insurance, covered immediately below, and the employer and individual mandates, covered in later sections. Additionally, the act sets forth several other requirements, which will impact the value and extent of coverage.

GUARANTEED ISSUE   As from 2014, insurers were no longer allowed to underwrite individual insureds; no one could be declined. Together with community rating requirements discussed in the next section, individuals with pre-existing conditions became insurable at standard rates. The guaranteed issue requirement obviously creates an opportunity for many participants to acquire coverage with the knowledge that they will immediately file claims. This potential for adverse selection is mitigated by the requirement of mandatory coverage and fines for noncompliance.

The challenge for the system to continue to attract the participation of private insurers will be to ensure that high-risk insureds are distributed proportionately across all private providers. The ACA creates a temporary high-risk pool program for insureds with preexisting conditions. The sufficiency of the mandatory nature of individual coverage and the risk spreading of the pool remains to be seen.

Figure 7-3   **An Overview of Healthcare Financing under the *Patient Protection and Affordable Care Act* of 2010**

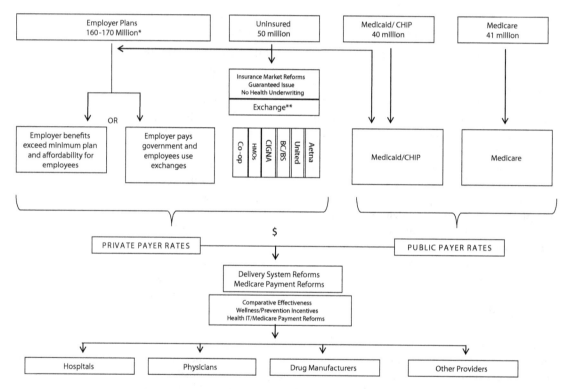

Source: Towers Watson based on US Census Bureau. Does not depict 15 million now with individual insurance expected to move to exchange or other sources.

*Employees may decline employer's plan in favor of exchange-based coverage, but they may obtain federal premium subsidies for exchange-based coverage only if the employer coverage does not meet minimum requirements or is "unaffordable."

**Low- and middle- income premium and out-of-pocket cost subsidies available up to 400 percent of federal poverty level.

NEW RATING CRITERIA   Historically, medical expense insurers based their premiums in large part on health status, health care use, and sex. Beginning in 2014, the ACA restricts premium rating practices for health plans for individuals and small groups. Rates may not be adjusted except for the following factors:

- individual versus family enrollment,
- geographic area,
- age (see below), and
- tobacco use.

Prior to the ACA, most states' health premiums reflected a 5:1 age band compression ratio, meaning the oldest insureds could be charged no more than five
times the rate of the youngest insureds. In an effort to make health care affordable
at later ages, the ACA requires an age band ratio of 3:1. Thus, a 64 year old can
be charged no more than three times the rate for a 21 year old. As a result, rates
for younger insureds will likely increase. Some critics believe rate increases will
overwhelm the savings effect of available subsidies (see below). Overall health care
costs are expected to increase after accounting for subsidies.[1]

An insurer's loss ratio is generally the percentage of premium income it pays
in claims. The ACA requires health insurance issuers (both insurers and self-
funded plans) to submit data on the proportion of premium revenues spent on
clinical services and quality improvement, called the **medical loss ratio** (MLR).
It also requires issuers to provide rebates to insureds if the MLR does not meet
minimum standards. The ACA requires insurance companies to spend at least
80 percent (individual market) or 85 percent (group market) of premium dollars
on medical care. If they fail to meet these standards, insurance companies are
required to provide a rebate to their customers to reflect amounts paid in excess
of these standards.

Insurers requesting rate increases greater than 10 percent can be required to
justify the request to the HHS. While the federal government can question such
increases, it cannot prevent insurers from implementing them. Presumably the
drafters expect this provision will constrain rate increases through a sort of public
shaming effect.

ESSENTIAL AND MAXIMUM BENEFITS   The ACA requires that health plans
offered in the individual and small group markets, both inside and outside of the
exchanges, offer a comprehensive package of items and services, known as **essential health benefits**. In general, these benefits are the types of care one needs to
prevent and treat sickness and do not include elective and non-essential treatments. Large group plans are not required to offer an essential benefits package,
but most already do, as these benefits were defined from the coverage typically
provided by large employers. Essential health benefits must include items and services within at least the following 10 categories: ambulatory patient services; emergency services; hospitalization; maternity and newborn care; mental health and
substance use disorder services, including behavioral health treatment; prescription drugs; rehabilitative and habilitative services and devices; laboratory services;
preventive and wellness services and chronic disease management; and pediatric
services, including oral and vision care..

Group and individual plans must provide coverage to adult dependents until
age 26. The same level of benefits and the same pricing must apply as is offered
other similarly situated dependents.

Health plans are prohibited from limiting the amount of benefits paid over
the course of an insured's lifetime. Beginning in 2014, annual limits are also

prohibited. The prohibition applies to essential benefits; nonessential benefits may continue to be limited.

ACTUARIAL VALUE PARAMETERS The ACA provides for four tiers of coverage based on the actuarial value of plans, i.e. the percentage of expected health care expense the plan will pay for a typical group of enrollees:

Platinum	90 percent
Gold	80 percent
Silver	70 percent
Bronze	60 percent

Amounts paid in excess of these actuarial values are to be borne by the insured through some combination of deductibles, co-pays, and coinsurance (see below).

The specified tiers are used for three primary purposes: (1) to set the minimum amount of coverage that qualifies individuals to avoid the penalty for not maintaining insurance (Bronze); (2) to facilitate the comparison of different plans by establishing standardized levels of insurance individuals and small businesses can buy in health exchanges or in the outside market; and (3) to serve as benchmarks for premium and cost-sharing subsidies provided to lower and middle income people buying their own insurance (see below).

MARKETING AND GRANDFATHERED PLANS It seems likely that the responsibilities and service opportunities for agents and brokers will be greatly reduced under the ACA. First, exchanges will replace much of the informational assistance provided formerly by intermediaries. Second, insurers will be pressured to minimize commissions to comply with the MLR requirements. HHS has said that it will participate in an agent-broker issues working group with the NAIC and may grant waivers to states in which the new MLR rules appear to be destabilizing the individual health insurance market.

Some group and individual plans existing before March 23, 2010 are exempt ("grandfathered") in part from ACA requirements. To remain grandfathered, plans may not make any major changes in coverage. Examples of changes in coverage that would cause a plan to lose its grandfathered status include:

- eliminating coverage for the diagnosis or treatment of a particular condition,
- any increase in coinsurance percentages,
- increasing deductibles or copays by more than the cumulative growth in medical inflation plus 15 percentage points, and
- reducing the share of the premium the employer pays by more than five percentage points.

Some provisions of the ACA do apply regardless of grandfathered status including the no-lifetime-maximum prohibition for group plans and the dependent-coverage-to-age 26 provision. But some ACA provisions do not apply to grandfathered plans, including:

- preventive services with no patient cost-sharing,
- federal or state review of rate increases of 10 percent or more for non-group and small business plans,

- appeal of claim denials to a third-party reviewer, and
- minimum essential health benefits. (This does not apply to large employers, whether or not they have grandfathered status.)

Grandfathered business is expected to diminish rapidly due to the introduction of guaranteed issue and the availability of premium subsidies both of which facilitate and encourage switching.

ADVERSE SELECTION AND RISK SELECTION UNDER THE *AFFORDABLE CARE ACT*

As discussed above, adverse selection occurs when consumers use knowledge of their higher-than-average risk, which the insurer does not possess, to obtain insurance at lower-than-justified rates. The ACA essentially imposes an asymmetrical information deficit on insurers by prohibiting medical questions and medical underwriting. Uncertainty about the health status of applicants would be expected to lead insurers to charge higher prices. The ACA seeks to limit adverse selection by limiting open enrollment periods, requiring most people to have insurance coverage or pay a penalty, and providing subsidies to help with the cost of insurance. Nevertheless, the tendency of individuals most likely to have claims to participate at a high rate must be expected.

Risk selection practices are also a concern. The ACA prohibits insurers from denying coverage or charging higher premiums based on health status. Insurers can be expected, however, to seek to attract healthier insureds by offering products that discourage those with expensive health conditions by limiting covered benefits. They might also compete for healthier insureds by offering products with high deductibles and so low premiums.

RISK ADJUSTMENT PROGRAM   To help mitigate the problematic aspects of adverse selection and risk selection, the ACA institutes a so-called risk adjustment program that redistributes premium income from individual and small group plans with low-risk participants to plans with high-risk participants. By doing so, the ACA drafters hoped to encourage insurers to compete on the value of the plans offered rather than by attracting healthier participants. The program is operated by the state if the state maintains an exchange, otherwise by the federal government.

Insurers with larger shares of low-cost enrollees pay into a fund that makes payments to insurers with larger shares of high-cost enrollees. The calculation of payments is based on the average actuarial risk of participants using a scoring system. The scores take into account age, sex, and diagnosed health conditions. Also, if a participant is receiving a federal subsidy, the score is increased to reflect the increased cost associated with induced demand.

The individual risk scores for the plan are then used to calculate the plan's average risk score. Adjustments to the average risk score are made based on actuarial value (i.e., taking into account deductibles and copays) and geographic cost variations. Plans with low average risk scores make payments into the risk adjustment program, and these payments are distributed to high average risk score plans, such that transfers into and out of the program net to zero.

REINSURANCE AND CORRIDOR PROGRAMS   Two temporary (2014-2016) programs also were created in an effort to mitigate potential transitional problems of adverse selection and risk selection: a reinsurance program and a risk corridor program. Whereas the risk adjustment program is designed to mitigate the effects of risk selection across plans, the reinsurance program is meant to reduce the incentive for insurers to charge higher premiums due to uncertainty about the health status of participants. Risk adjustment is based on expected costs while reinsurance is based on actual costs. Individual and small group plans are eligible for reinsurance payments.

Contributions are collected from all issuers and third party administrators on behalf of group health plans using a national per-capita rate announced in an annual HHS notice of benefit and payment parameters. Plans are eligible for reinsurance payments for each individual health claim that exceeds an *attachment point* ($70,000 in 2015). The reinsured payment amount is subject to a *cap* or maximum ($250,000 in 2015). Finally, a *coinsurance rate* applies, proposed such that eligible plans will pay 50 per cent of the amount between the attachment point and the cap in 2015.

The risk corridor program is designed to stabilize premium income and protect insurers from inaccurate pricing during the initial years of ACA reform (2014-2016). HHS collects funds from plans whose claims are lower than expected and makes payments to plans whose claims are higher than expected. If a plan's actual claims and quality improvement expenses are less than 97 percent of a specified target amount, it will be required to pay into the program. If a plan's claims and quality improvement expenses are higher than 103 percent of the target amount it is eligible for payments.

COMPREHENSIVE MEDICAL INSURANCE COVERAGE

Prior to the ACA, many medical insurance plans featured separate coverage for hospital services and surgical services, although the trend had been to comprehensive policies. With the essential benefits requirement of the ACA, virtually all plans are expected to be comprehensive. **Comprehensive medical insurance** plans cover a wide range of medical care charges, with few internal limits. They provide broad health care benefits including inpatient and outpatient hospital services, physician and diagnostic services, specialty services such as physical therapy and radiology, and prescription drugs. The scope of covered services has been expanded under the essential benefits provision of the ACA, particularly with regard to preventative services. Such plans are found in both individual and group markets and are offered by commercial insurers, the Blues, and HMOs.

Both life insurers and the Blues offer such coverage in the form of major medical expense insurance. HMOs offer comprehensive coverage as well, but their plans carry no special generic name; just HMO coverage. Both major medical and HMO plans cover usual and customary charges incurred for most medical care services, supplies, and treatments prescribed as medically necessary. Exact eligible charges and their descriptions vary from plan to plan. HMOs historically offered a broader range of preventive care services, but such services are mandated for all plans under the ACA. Coverage for confinement in skilled nursing facilities as well as home health care services and hospice care expense benefits are also covered.

Deductibles and Coinsurance

A **deductible** is a specified amount of medical expense that is paid by the insured before any costs are paid by the plan. **Coinsurance** is a specified portion of medical expense paid by the insured once expenses exceed the deductible and benefits are payable. The total amount paid by the insured is usually subject to a maximum limit, called an **out of pocket** (OOP) **maximum** or the equivalent. Major medical plans typically have all three of these features.

For example, covered claims amounting to $11,000 during one policy period would result in $9,000 of insurance payments for a plan with a $1,000 deductible, 80 percent coinsurance, and a $2,000 out of pocket maximum. The first $1,000 is paid by the insured, and 20 percent of the remaining $10,000 would be payable under the coinsurance provision for a total of $3,000 due to be paid by the insured in the absence of the maximum cap. The OOP maximum, however, limits the insured's responsibility to $2,000. The **accumulation period provision** determines the period of time during which multiple claims may be accumulated to satisfy the deductible and coinsurance provisions.

Deductibles may apply on an *all cause* basis where incurred expenses are accumulated toward the deductible without regard to the number or type of causes. Alternatively, a *per cause* deductible accumulates expenses from different causes separately. Some policies also provide a *carryover provision* that permits expenses incurred in the last three months to apply to the deductible for the next year. *Family deductible provisions* may also apply that waive the deductible for all family members after any two or three of them incur losses satisfying the individual deductibles.

The OOP maximum is subject to limits under the ACA and the limit correlates with the actuarial value of a Bronze plan. Higher actuarial value plans (i.e. Silver, Gold, and Platinum) have progressively lower OOP maximums. The OOP maximum for 2015 is $6,600 for an individual and $13,200 for a family of any size. The limit will be updated annually based on the increase in average per capita premiums for health coverage.

Maximum Benefits, Coordination of Benefits, and Subrogation

Historically, an overall maximum benefit was generally applied on a lifetime or a per cause basis. Lifetime maximums were usually at least $1 million although some were unlimited. The ACA now prohibits health plans from imposing annual or lifetime maximums.

Dual income families often have coverage under two group insurance plans. Such double coverage can result in individuals being overinsured, which would create the possibility of filing multiple claims for the same expenses. To avoid moral hazard, plans include **coordination of benefits** provisions designed to give insured individuals as much coverage as needed while at the same time eliminating overinsurance by setting forth limits and guidelines to determine the order in which two insurers covering the same claim will pay.

Major medical plans often include a **subrogation provision** that gives the employer or insurer that pays a claim the rights that a covered employee or insured might have against a third party. **Subrogation** is the transfer of one party's legal rights against a third party to another. Such a claim might arise when a covered individual is injured in a work-related accident. The employer or insurer could receive reimbursement if the worker or dependent received benefits under a workers' compensation statute.

GROUP HEALTH INSURANCE

THE EMPLOYER MANDATE

Beginning in 2015, the ACA requires employers with 100 or more full-time employees to maintain qualified coverage for their employees or pay a penalty. Beginning in 2016, employers with 50 or more full-time employees must offer coverage to at least 95 percent of full-time employees and dependents to age 26.

The coverage must meet specified definitions of *affordability* and *minimum value*. These definitions determine whether an individual qualifies for a premium tax credit (PTC), i.e., federal assistance toward the purchase of health insurance from an ACA exchange. In most cases, individuals who are offered health insurance coverage by their employer *will not qualify* for a PTC. Thus, employer coverage is considered *affordable* if the employee's share of the annual premium for self-only coverage is no greater than 9.5 percent of annual household income. Employer coverage is considered to offer *minimum value* if it is designed to pay at least 60 percent (the Bronze level) of the total cost of medical services for a standard population. The calculation takes into account deductibles, copays, and coinsurance. Starting in 2014, individuals who are offered employer-sponsored coverage that is affordable and provides minimum value will not be eligible for any premium subsidy (see below).

If an employer has at least one full-time employee who receives a federal premium subsidy in a federal or state exchange, the employer is subject to a penalty. If the employer fails to offer coverage, the penalty is $2,000 per full-time employee (excepting the first 30 employees). If an employer offers coverage that fails to satisfy either the affordability or minimum value specification, the penalty is the lesser of $3,000 per full-time employee receiving a premium subsidy or $2,000 per full-time employee (excepting the first 30 employees).

GROUP MEDICAL INSURANCE COVERAGE

As we know, group insurance is a means through which a group of persons who usually have a business or professional relationship to the contract owner are provided insurance coverage under a single contract. A sound understanding of group insurance and the scope of group products can be acquired only through a discussion of its distinguishing characteristics, its differences from and similarities to other forms of insurance, and a reasonably detailed examination of each of its components. Our context in this chapter is health insurance, but these observations also apply to group life insurance. Group life insurance is almost always provided as a companion benefit to group health insurance.

In a comparison of group insurance with other forms of insurance written by life insurance companies, several distinguishing features are evident: (1) the substitution of group underwriting for individual underwriting, (2) the use of a master contract, (3) lower administrative cost, (4) flexibility in contract design, and (5) the use of experience rating.

GROUP UNDERWRITING   The most important feature of group insurance is the substitution of group underwriting for individual underwriting. Group underwriting normally is not concerned with the health or other insurability aspects of any particular individual. Instead, the insurer seeks to obtain an aggregation of groups of individual lives that are expected to yield a predictable rate of morbidity (or mortality). If a sufficient number of groups of lives is obtained and if these groups are reasonably homogeneous in nature, the morbidity (mortality) rate will be predictable. The group becomes the unit of underwriting, and insurance principles may be applied to it just as in the case of the individual. As a practical matter, all underwriting with respect to qualified health plans is eliminated by the ACA.

GROUP POLICY   A second characteristic of group insurance is the use of a group policy (contract) held by the owner – most commonly, an employer. Booklets, certificates, or other summary evidence of insurance are held by participants that provide information on the plan provisions and the steps required to file claims. The use of certificates and a master contract constitutes a source of economy under the group approach.

The insured persons under the contract, usually employees and their beneficiaries, are not actually parties to the contract, although they may enforce their rights as third-party beneficiaries. The four-party relationship (employer, insurer, employee, and dependents) found in a group insurance plan can create unusual administrative and legal problems that are common only to group insurance.

LOWER COST   A third usual feature of group insurance is lower cost protection than that available in individual insurance. The nature of the group approach permits the use of mass distribution and mass administration methods that afford economies of operation not available in individual insurance. The larger the group, the more these economies are significant.

Specific areas of savings include sales commissions, which are far lower, as the total premium per group case is much larger than individual cases, and the time and effort of agents and brokers is less intensive. Fee based consultants may reduce the marketing (and other expenses) further. Also, larger employer plans are able to exercise market power in negotiating lower rates with service providers. Finally, administrative costs are reduced because a central organization (e.g., employer or association management) is willing and able to do much of the work, and further administrative savings result for contributory plans because premium collection is automated through payroll deduction.

FLEXIBILITY   In contrast to individual contracts that must be taken as written, larger employers usually have options in the design and preparation of the group insurance contract, although the contracts follow a similar pattern and include certain standard provisions. The degree of flexibility permitted is, of course, a function of the size of the group involved and applicable ACA requirements. The group insurance usually is an integral part of an employee benefit program, and, in most cases, the contract can be molded to meet the objectives of the contract owner, as long as the requests do not entail complicated administrative procedures, open the way to possibly serious adverse selection, or violate legal requirements.

EXPERIENCE RATING   Another special feature of group insurance is that premiums often are subject to **experience rating** under which the past financial results of the group are taken into consideration in adjusting the insurer's net charges for the plan. The larger and, hence, the more reliable the experience of the particular group, the greater the weight attached to its own experience in any single year. The knowledge that premiums net of dividends or premium rate adjustments will be based on the employer's own experience gives the employer a vested interest in maintaining a favorable loss and expense record. For the largest employers, insurers may agree to complicated procedures to satisfy the employer's objectives, as most such cases are experience rated and reflect the increased cost.

A special type of experience rating, called **retrospective premium arrangements**, provides for lower initial premiums than normal but with the insurer reserving the right to collect additional premiums at the end of the contract period to cover unexpected claims and expense. The additional premium is limited to the amount of the contingency component that would have been paid under the regular premium schedule.

ADVANTAGES AND LIMITATIONS OF GROUP MECHANISM

The group insurance mechanism has proven to be a remarkably effective solution to the need for employee benefits for a number of reasons. The utilization of mass distribution techniques extended protection to large numbers of persons with little or no life or health insurance. The increasing complexity of industrial/service economies has brought increasingly large numbers of persons together, and the group mechanism has enabled life insurance companies to reach vast numbers of individuals within a relatively short period and at low cost. The employer usually pays a large share of the cost. Moreover, in most countries, including the U.S., the deductibility of employer contributions and the favorable tax treatment of the benefits to employees make it a tax-effective vehicle to provide benefits.

From the viewpoint of the employee, group insurance historically had one great limitation – the temporary nature of the coverage. Unless an employee converted his or her coverage to an individual policy (which usually is more expensive and provides less liberal coverage), the employee lost his or her insurance protection if the group plan was terminated. Coverage is also often lost at retirement. (Minimum requirements for the continuation of terminated employees are discussed below.) These limitations are eliminated under the ACA.

Group life and health protection is continued after retirement in a significant proportion of cases today in the U.S., but the prevalence of this coverage is declining. Postretirement health benefits also often feature reduced coverage. When such continued protection is not available, the temporary nature of the coverage is a serious limitation. Retiree group health insurance is often provided as a supplement to Medicare.

ELIGIBLE GROUPS

The types of groups eligible for group insurance coverage have broadened significantly over the years. The *NAIC Model Group Insurance Bill* permits coverage on four specific categories of groups:

- employees of a single employer,
- groups based on a debtor/creditor relationship that can be issued group credit insurance that liquidates the obligations of the borrower in the event of death or disability,
- labor union groups where the policy is issued to the union and premiums are paid by the union or by worker contributions; coverage provided and premiums paid by employers under negotiated labor agreements must be implemented through a policy issued to a trust, and
- multiple employer trusts (METs) marketed by a sponsor representing multiple employers with a small number of employees.

In many states, other types of groups not specifically identified in the NAIC model bill are eligible for group insurance. These include trade associations, professional associations, college alumni associations, veteran associations, religious groups, customers of large retail chains, and savings account depositors, among many others.

ALTERNATIVES TO FULLY INSURED GROUP BENEFIT PLAN FUNDING

Self-funding and minimum premium plans are alternatives to fully insured plans and are discussed in this section. Employers are interested in alternatives to fully insured benefit financing programs for several reasons:

- to control and use reserve funds that would normally be available to the insurance company;
- to reduce or eliminate payment of premium taxes and insurer risk, profit, and contingency charges;
- to exercise more control over plan design by avoiding state insurance mandates and requirements;
- to participate more fully in their own favorable experience; and
- to enjoy improved cash flow via more immediate recognition of their own experience.

SELF-FUNDED PLANS   Insurance reduces risk through the operation of the law of large numbers. As the number of exposure units increases, average actual results converge toward average expected results. Some large employers provide health care to employee groups so large that the benefits of diversification through insuring are redundant. The plan itself is large enough to exhibit the benefits of diversification. Employers in this situation find it economical to have **self-funded plans**, also called **self-insured plans**, under which claims are paid in cash as they arise with no element of prefunding through commercial insurance. The intent is to avoid the administrative costs of transferring individual risks.

One of the principal advantages of self-funded plans arises because the federal *Employee Retirement Income Security Act* (ERISA) preempts state insurance law in all aspects of employee benefit plans. State group insurance laws typically specify mandated coverages and limits that are both broad and generous and include benefits that sponsors may prefer not to provide. Examples include psychiatric and substance abuse provisions that some employers believe are unproductive or are particularly susceptible to participant or provider moral hazard. Because self-funded plans have been determined to be employee benefit plans as opposed to group insurance, ERISA preemption permits employers to save costs by excluding some or all mandated coverages or providing limited benefits that need not meet the specifications of state law. Under the ACA minimum essential benefits must be provided. Self-funded plans also avoid state premium taxes, which average about 2.0 percent of premiums paid across the U.S.

With self-funded plans, the employer essentially must recreate the services of a small insurance company. Also employers must be mindful of the financial capacity to satisfy cash flow strain in the event of extraordinary losses. Self-funding employers usually respond to these concerns by (1) outsourcing administrative services and (2) purchasing stop loss reinsurance to cover extraordinary claims.

Administrative Services   The administrative management of a medical benefit plan is complex. It requires special technology and professional human resources. Life and health insurers that regularly offer group medical plans obviously have significant expertise in these areas. Required services include:

- actuarial and underwriting services,
- plan design,
- communication of benefits to employees,
- adjudication of claims for eligibility,
- managed care (see below) administration, and
- financial management (projecting and paying claims).

Self-funded plans often are administered under **administrative services only** (ASO) arrangements whereby the employer purchases specific administrative services from an insurance company or from an independent third-party administrator. There is no insurance and, therefore, no insurance contract is involved. The ASO agreement is a service contract between the insurer (or another third party) as administrator and the employer as buyer. It specifies the services to be provided, the rights and obligations of both parties, and administrative fees involved. Stop loss reinsurance is arranged separately, although, if an insurer provides the services, it may also provide the reinsurance.

Stop Loss Reinsurance   **Stop loss reinsurance** reimburses a self-funded employer for claims incurred above certain limits and is available on an individual or aggregate basis. *Specific stop loss reinsurance* reimburses the employer for the claims of an individual participant that exceed a specified deductible to a specified limit. *Aggregate stop loss reinsurance* reimburses the employer to a specified limit when aggregate claims during the policy period (usually annually) exceed a specified retention (e.g., 120 percent of expected claims). Employers may purchase either or both coverages, and the cost is a function of expected claims based on the benefits specified in the plan. The very largest employers are able to fund claims of any magnitude out of regular cash flow. They are fully self-funded.

Minimum Premium Plans   A **minimum premium plan** (MPP) provides that the contract owner assumes liability for all but the largest claims or very unfavorable total experience of the plan. MPPs create a partially self-funded arrangement that has premium tax savings for the employer as a primary objective. The employer/contract owner deposits funds as needed to a special bank account to cover claims funded by the contract owner. The insurer, acting as agent of the contract owner, pays claims from the special account first then from its own resources after a set limit.

The insurer continues to provide the same services, assumes the same risks, and, unless some special arrangement is made, holds essentially the same claim reserves as those under a conventional fully insured plan. The reserves must be maintained, as, on termination of the group plan, the insurer is still responsible, as under a fully insured plan, to pay all covered outstanding claims. In some minimum premium plans, the contract owner agrees to assume responsibility for all outstanding claims upon discontinuance of the plan, thus relieving the insurer of the need to maintain reserves (although the insurer may be at risk in the event of the bankruptcy of the contract owner).

Most states assess premium taxes only on premiums received by the insurance company for payment of claims under an insurance contract. Thus, by paying most of the claims directly from the contract owner to the covered individuals, an MPP makes it possible to avoid premium taxes on approximately 80 to 90 percent of claims costs.

MANAGED CARE   As health care costs have escalated and cost containment efforts have been emphasized, benefit redesign, alternative delivery systems, self insurance, and other developments led to the emergence of the concept of managed care, with a profound impact on health insurance. The U.S. National Library of Medicine describes managed care as programs that are designed to reduce costs and increase the quality of care by:

- providing economic incentives for providers and plan beneficiaries to choose less costly forms of care;
- implementing **utilization review** or **utilization management,** the determination and review of the medical necessity of procedures and treatments, including precertification and discharge planning;
- implementing cost sharing by beneficiaries;
- implementing **precertification** procedures that provide prior approval of procedures, hospital admission, and length of stay and stipulate benefits to be paid;
- implementing **discharge planning** procedures that limit the length of hospital stays to the medically necessary minimum. Patients may be discharged to their home or to alternative care facilities, and the complementary assistance of other professionals (e.g., social workers or psychologists) is sometimes offered or required;
- providing economic incentives for outpatient procedures;
- selective contracting with providers; and
- intensive management of high cost individual cases.

These objectives are pursued in several types of managed care plans. Some aspects of managed care plans are also featured in indemnity plans offered by insurers. Precertification and utilization review are common.

OTHER FEDERAL LAWS AFFECTING GROUP INSURANCE

Several other federal laws, in addition to Medicare, the ACA, and ERISA, affect group insurance plans. These must be considered in the design and/or administration of group health plans. How the ACA will affect these laws is unclear at this writing.

The *Age Discrimination in Employment Act,* enacted in 1967, prohibits age discrimination for most workers. In 1990, Congress explicitly brought employee benefits under the provisions of the act, requiring benefits to be continued for older employees. Under the act, medical expense coverage cannot be reduced. These restrictions apply only to benefits for active employees. There are no requirements under the act that any benefits be continued for retired workers. In contrast to other benefits, employees over age 65 cannot be required to pay any more for their medical expense coverage than is paid by employees under age 65.

A 1978 amendment to the *Civil Rights Act,* known as the *Pregnancy Discrimination Act,* requires, for all employment related purposes, that pregnancy be treated the same as an illness. The amendment applies only to the benefit plans (both insured and self funded) of employers with 15 or more employees. Although employers with fewer employees are not subject to the provisions of the amendment, they may be subject to comparable state laws.

Group medical coverage often terminates when the employment relationship ends. For employers with 20 or more employees, the *Consolidated Omnibus Budget Reconciliation Acts of 1985, 1986,* and *1990* (COBRA) require that group health plans allow employees and certain beneficiaries to elect to have their current health insurance coverage extended at group rates for up to 36 months following a qualifying event that results in the loss of coverage. The following are *qualifying events* if loss of coverage by an employee or the employee's spouse or dependent child results:

- the death of the covered employee,
- the termination of the employee except for gross misconduct,
- a reduction of the employee's hours so that the employee or dependent is ineligible for coverage,
- the divorce or legal separation of the covered employee and his or her spouse,
- the employee's eligibility for Medicare (for spouses and children), and
- a child's expiring eligibility as a dependent under the plan.

Under the act, any employee, spouse, or dependent child who loses coverage because of any of these events can elect to continue coverage identical to that provided to continuing employees and dependents, without providing evidence of insurability. The cost of the continued coverage may be passed on to the qualifying insured but cannot exceed 102 percent of the total cost to the plan for the period of coverage for a similarly situated, continuing active employee. The continuation of coverage is not automatic but must be elected by a qualifying beneficiary. COBRA does not apply to group life insurance.

The number of individuals who elect COBRA participation is likely to decrease substantially as many will find that the cost of acquiring individual coverage with federal subsidies more attractive than 102 percent of the employer's plan cost.

Congress determined that, despite the new guaranteed issue feature of the ACA, COBRA would remain in effect. Continuation of coverage would ensure that COBRA beneficiaries receiving treatment should be allowed to stay with their current health care providers. COBRA coverage for dental and vision care is not available on exchange plans and those expecting to find new employment may find it easier to continue existing coverage rather than going into an exchange only to exit upon finding new employment.

The *Family Medical and Leave Act of 1993* requires employers of more than five persons to allow eligible employees up to 12 weeks of leave during any 12-month period for personal illness, birth, adoption, or illness of spouse, child, or parent. Employers must provide the same health insurance coverage as during active employment.

The main focus of the *Health Insurance Portability and Accountability Act* (HIPPA) of 1996 is to make health insurance coverage portable and continuous for workers in small businesses (two to 50 lives). HIPPA lengthens the continuation period for employees who are disabled at the time of employment termination and their beneficiaries. Employees who change or lose jobs and meet eligibility conditions must either be accepted into a group plan or offered an individual policy. The act restricted the ability of insurers to refuse coverage for individuals with pre-existing conditions. The act also increased the deduction for health insurance expenses incurred as self-employed individuals.

INDIVIDUAL HEALTH INSURANCE

Fundamental differences exist between (1) the individual health insurance market, (2) the employer- or association-sponsored group insurance market, and (3) government-provided coverages. These differences make the individual health market complex in comparison to group and government-sponsored health insurance, which makes information problems even worse for purchasers of individual health policies than those typically found for the purchasers of individual life policies. The classification of policies as Platinum, Gold, Silver, and Bronze under the ACA is designed to mitigate information problems by making comparisons easier.

Individuals without government or employer-sponsored coverage usually access the individual health insurance market on their own and must choose from a variety of ways of doing so. Individuals are also faced with the complexity of determining their eligibility for premium subsidies under the ACA (see below). By contrast, individuals eligible for group or governmental coverage do not face the task of accessing the insurance market. The plan sponsor (employer or government) makes the determination. Because employers typically offer only one or a few health plans, the task of identifying and comparing products is greatly simplified or eliminated. Finally, the burden of selecting cost sharing options and paying for the products is significantly eased by employer contributions and payroll deduction.

Most consumers historically have purchased individual health insurance through agents. Some health insurance is sold directly to consumers by insurers, especially when insurers have high name recognition. Several U.S. Blue Cross/ Blue Shield plans and HMOs target the individual policy market. Another important access route is through business or social organizations, such as Chambers of Commerce, trade associations, unions, alumni associations, and religious organizations. Through pooled purchasing power, associations often can nego-tiate competitively priced products for their members. Finally, under the ACA, state and federal exchange websites are expected to become the most important method of access.

THE INDIVIDUAL MANDATE

As from 2014, individuals have been required to purchase individual insurance unless exempted or covered under a qualifying group or government plan. Cer-tain individuals are exempt from the requirement:

- individuals with religious objections,
- undocumented immigrants,
- incarcerated individuals,
- members of a native American tribe,
- an individual or family whose income falls below the threshold for filing an income tax return, and
- an individual or family who has to pay more than 8 percent of income for health insurance, after taking into account any employer contributions or tax subsidies.

Individuals who have coverage under any of these qualifying plans are also exempt:

- Medicare;
- Medicaid or Children's Health Insurance Program (CHIP);
- TRICARE for service members, retirees, and families;
- Veteran's health care program;
- a plan offered by the individual's employer; or
- certain grandfathered plans that existed before enactment of the ACA.

As discussed earlier, the ACA distinguishes different health care plans based on the actuarial value of the benefits provided. They are classified (in decreas-ing order of actuarial benefit) Platinum, Gold, Silver, and Bronze. To meet the requirements of the ACA mandate, individual policies must provide the specified essential benefits insured at the Bronze level.

Individuals who do not comply with the ACA individual mandate may be subject to an annual penalty tax that increases each year. In 2014, the penalty was the greater of (1) 1.0 percent of family income or (2) $95 for each adult and $47.50 per child, to a maximum of $285 per family. For 2016, the penalty has grown to be the greater of (1) 2.5 percent of family income or (2) $695 per adult and $347.50 per child up to a maximum of $2,085 for a family. People with very low incomes and others may be eligible for waivers. The fee is paid on the federal income tax form.

THE INDIVIDUAL/FAMILY SUBSIDY

Individuals and households with low or middle incomes may qualify for financial assistance to help pay for their health insurance coverage under the ACA. Sub-sidies are available for those whose incomes do not exceed 400 percent of the Federal Poverty Level (FPL). In 2014, the FPLs for an individual and for a family of four were somewhat more than $11,000 and $19,000 respectively.

The amount of the subsidy is determined by subtracting a percentage of individual or household income from the premium for a low-cost Silver plan offered in the relevant exchange. The contribution percentages increase as individual or household income increases relative to the poverty level for the household size. Individuals or households acquiring coverage with a higher benefit than the relevant exchange's low-cost Silver plan are required to pay the excess cost. These are the expected contributions as a function of household income relative to the FPL:

Income as Percentage of the Federal Poverty Level	Expected Contribution (as Percent of Income)
Up to 133%	2%
133-150%	3.0-4.0%
150-200%	4.0-6.3%
200-250%	6.3-8.05%
250-300%	8.05-9.5%
300-400%	9.5%

Under the ACA, households with incomes of less than the FPL may qualify for free coverage under Medicaid (see later in this chapter). The state, however must participate in the ACA-expanded Medicaid program. If it does not participate, and the individual does not otherwise qualify for Medicaid under the state's rules, the individual must pay the entire cost of any plan bought through the relevant exchange.

The Individual Health Insurance Contract
The basic structure of an individual health insurance policy is similar to that of a life insurance policy, as discussed in Chapter 5 and will be covered in more detail in Chapter18. The face of the policy identifies the insurer and provides sufficient information to identify the type of policy and the coverage contained in the contract. The policy identifies the insured and the beneficiary and contains an insuring clause and a consideration clause that identifies the premium payment and statements made on the application as the insured's consideration. As with life policies, a 10 or 20 day free look provision is generally included. Policies may be conditionally renewable, guaranteed renewable, or noncancelable. Policies also will contain any case management requirements such as utilization review and precertification as discussed above.

Health insurance contracts are more complex than life insurance contracts. Life insurance policy claims are usually straightforward: the death certificate is presented and the face amount of the policy is paid. Health claims are uncertain with respect to the number and time of losses and the certainty and amount of loss. Information and other economic problems abound in this field, including high rates of policyowner and provider fraud. Consequently, health policies are characterized by more technical definitions and a greater variety of optional coverages, coupled with specific notice and proof of loss time requirements.

All states have adopted the NAIC's model *Uniform Individual Accident and Sickness Policy Provisions Law* in substantially similar form. The model law contains 12 mandatory provisions and 11 optional provisions. Some provisions are relevant primarily to medical expense insurance, while others are relevant primarily to disability income and/or long term care insurance (discussed in the next chapter), and some are relevant to all types of health insurance policies.

REQUIRED PROVISIONS   The required provisions must be included in the contract. The wording need not be exactly as written in the model law, but provisions must be at least as favorable to the policyowner as those in the model law.

The *Entire Contract* clause provides that the policy, the application if attached, and any riders or amendments constitute the entire contract and that no changes made by an agent are valid; only changes approved by an executive officer of the company are effective. The *Time Limit on Certain Defenses* clause is a type of incontestable clause that prevents the insurer from asserting any defense based on a misstatement (except fraudulent misstatements) in the application including preexisting conditions. Given the guaranteed issue requirement and limited underwriting information permitted by the ACA, it would seem the only possibility of misstatement would involve smoking status and it is difficult to imagine the circumstances of a non-fraudulent misstatement.

The *Grace Period* clause grants an additional time period after the premium due date during which the premium may be paid without the policy lapsing. It varies according to the premium payment mode: seven days for weekly premium policies; 10 days for monthly premium policies; and 31 days for all other policies.

The *Reinstatement* clause provides for the reinstatement of a lapsed policy when the insurer or its agent accepts premiums; in some cases a new application will be required. Once the policy is reinstated, there is a 10-day waiting period for sickness coverage while accident coverage is immediate. Given the guaranteed issue requirements of the ACA, it may be simpler to acquire a new policy than to satisfy reinstatement requirements in the case of medical expense insurance.

The *Notice of Claim* clause requires the insured to notify the insurer of a loss within 20 days if reasonable. In the case of a disability income policy, the insurer can require the insured provide notice that a claim is continuing every six months. The *Claims Form* clause requires the insurer to provide claims forms for filing proof of loss within 15 days after receiving notice of a claim. If the forms are not provided, the insured can satisfy the proof of loss requirement with a written statement detailing the occurrence, the character, and the extent of the loss. The *Proof of Loss* clause requires proof of loss to be provided within 90 days of the loss if reasonable. In the case of a loss with periodic benefits the period is 90 days after the end of each period for which the insurer is liable.

The *Time of Payment of Claim* clause requires immediate payment of individual claims and at least monthly payment of periodic claims. The *Payment of Claims* clause requires the insurer to pay the named beneficiary, or if there is no named beneficiary, the insured while alive or the insured's estate. A *facility of payment* provision is optional under this required clause; it permits the insurer to satisfy its obligations for small sums (less than $1,000 perhaps) by making payment to any relative by blood or marriage who is deemed by the insurer to be equitably entitled to the payment. The *Change of Beneficiary* clause reserves to the insured the right to change beneficiaries unless a designation has been made irrevocable.

The *Physical Examination and Autopsy* clause permits the insurer to require, at its expense, a physical examination of a living insured or an autopsy of a deceased insured in the event of a claim. Some states may have non-insurance laws that prohibit autopsies; in those cases the prohibition will override this clause.

The *Legal Actions* clause provides that the insured may not bring a legal action to recover on the policy sooner than 60 days after filing proof of loss; the purpose is to allow the insurer adequate time to investigate the claim. No action may be brought by the insured after three years from the date of proof of loss have passed.

OPTIONAL PROVISIONS   The optional provisions are not required to be included in the contract. If they are included, the provision must be at least as favorable to the policyowner as the language in the model law.

The *Change of Occupation* clause allows the insurer to reduce the benefit under a disability income policy where the insured has changed to a riskier occupation. In those cases, the insurer will pay benefits based on what the premium charged would have purchased originally for the new occupation.

The *Misstatement of Age* clause adjusts the benefits under the policy to reflect what the premium paid at purchase would have bought at the correct age. We noted in Chapter 5 that this provision in a life insurance policy is mandatory in some states.

The *Other Insurance with this Insurer* clause allows the insurer to limit the total benefits it will pay under all policies it has issued to one insured. It may limit it by making void all coverage exceeding a stated amount and returning an appropriate part of the premium. It may also place a limit by requiring that insured or beneficiary select one policy for coverage with coverage under all other policies rendered void and the premiums returned. In a similar way, the *Insurance with Other Insurers* clause prevents overinsurance where the insured has policies with two or more insurers that cover the same expenses. The insurers will pay a proportionate share of any claim.

The *Relation of Earnings to Insurance-Average Earnings* clause provides that where the total monthly disability income benefit from all policies is greater than the insured's monthly income, each policy will pay only a portion of the lost income. We discuss this provision more fully in Chapter 8.

The *Unpaid Premium* clause allows the insurer to deduct the amount of any unpaid premium from the claim payment. The *Cancellation* clause allows the insurer to cancel a policy with five days written notice to the insured at the last address shown in the insurer's records. The insured may cancel by written notice to the insurer effective upon receipt or some later date specified in the notice. When the insurer cancels, it returns any unearned premium on a pro rata basis. If the insured cancels, the insurer is allowed to keep part of the unearned premium.

The *Conformity with State Statutes* clause automatically amends the policy to conform to state statutes with which it conflicts. In some states all insurance policies are required to include this provision.

The *Illegal Occupation* clause allows the insurer to avoid liability where the commission or attempt of a felony or the conduct of an illegal occupation is a contributing cause to the claim. Similarly, the *Narcotics* clause allows the insurer to avoid liability where a loss is "sustained or contracted in consequence of" the insured being under the influence of any narcotic not administered on the advice of a physician.

Specialized Individual Insurance Coverages

In addition to hospital/surgical and major medical insurance policies, many insurers offer specialized individual medical expense policies. These policies provide (1) hospital confinement indemnity; (2) specified disease coverage; and (3) Medicare supplemental insurance.

Hospital Confinement Indemnity Policies   In contrast with basic hospital expense insurance that is provided on a reimbursement basis, **hospital confinement indemnity** coverage pays a fixed sum for each day of hospital confinement. The benefit is most commonly sold as monthly amounts between $1,000 and $6,000 for continuous confinement of up to one year or more. The monthly amount is an aggregate of potential daily payments in any 30 day period of hospitalization. Thus, a policy that provides a $1,500 monthly payment will pay $50 for each day that the insured is hospitalized.

Specified Disease Policies   **Specified disease insurance** – sometimes termed **dread disease insurance**– provides individual health insurance that pays a variety of benefits up to substantial maximums solely for the treatment of a disease named in the policy, including most typically cancer and heart disease. Benefits usually are paid as scheduled amounts for designated events, such as hospital confinement, or for specific medical procedures, such as chemotherapy. Because insurance is limited to medical expenses associated with a single devastating disease, this coverage should be used only to supplement other health insurance.

Medicare Supplement Policies   Medicare is the U.S. government health insurance program for the elderly. It is covered later in this chapter. Medicare benefits are far from complete, and a private insurance market exists for policies – called **Medicare supplemental insurance** – that extend the benefits provided under Medicare. The term can apply only to a policy that meets specific minimum standards set out in state insurance law or regulation. Due to cost control provisions of the *Affordable Care Act*, premiums have increased and benefits are reduced under certain Medicare plans beginning in 2011, so Medicare supplemental plans may be more attractive.

Health insurers generally offer two basic types of policies: (1) the Medicare Wraparound policy and (2) the Comprehensive Medicare Supplement policy. The *Medicare Wraparound* policy provides coverage for eligible benefits not paid under Medicare, such as deductibles and coinsurance amounts that individuals must pay personally. These policies may continue to pay benefits for hospital and nursing home confinement after Medicare benefits are exhausted.

Comprehensive Medicare Supplement policies are similar to Medicare Wraparound policies except that they generally have significantly higher maximum benefit limits or are unlimited with respect to the duration of confinement in a hospital or skilled nursing facility. They also may provide benefits for a variety of health care expenses that Medicare does not cover.

The NAIC has specified standard coverages under Medicare supplement plans. The standards are set out in the NAIC's *Medicare Supplement Insurance Minimum Standards Model Act*. The plans have letter designations ranging from *A* to *N* and provide a set of basic and extra benefits. The combination of benefits in each plan may not be altered by insurers, nor may the letter designations be changed. Most states have enacted this or similar legislation or follow the standards.

The U.S. federal government operates or sponsors several health programs, the two most important and widespread being Medicare and Medicaid. Individual state laws also effectively require employers to provide work-related health and other benefits via workers' compensation laws. This section offers a short summary of these programs.

MAJOR GOVERNMENT-RELATED HEALTH PROGRAMS IN THE UNITED STATES

MEDICARE

Medicare is the U.S. social insurance program providing health insurance coverage for the elderly, defined as anyone age 65 and over. It is financed by a payroll tax on employers and employees and a parallel tax on self employed persons. The rate is 2.9 percent, shared equally by employers and employees. Self-employed persons pay the entire 2.9 percent. Effective 2013, the *Affordable Care Act* increased the payroll tax to 3.8 percent for high income employees. It also added a new 3.8 percent Medicare tax on the unearned net investment income of high-income taxpayers.

The ACA also sought to trim Medicare expenditures through:

- limiting annual payment increases for certain providers,
- reducing maximum Medicare Advantage payments,
- reducing payments to hospitals that serve a large number of low-income patients, and
- modifying the high-income threshold adjustment for Part B premiums.

Medicare offers four benefit plans, labeled Parts A, B, C, and D. Part A applies to all eligible participants, while Parts B, C, and D are optional. Medicare Parts C and D were defined by the *Medicare Prescription Drug, Improvement, and Modernization Act of 2003*. We examine the broadest benefit categories here while noting there are many specific coverages, exceptions, and exclusions that require careful study for any beneficiary's particular situation.

Medicare Part A covers hospital and nursing home care facility charges. It pays benefits for hospital stays of up to 90 days subject to cost sharing provisions. For up to 60 days, Medicare pays 100 percent after a deductible ($1,216 in 2014). For days 61-90, the beneficiary pays a daily co-payment ($304 in 2014). These costs and benefits apply to each hospitalization. Beneficiaries also have a **lifetime reserve** of 60 additional days that are available when stays extend beyond 90 days, but the extended benefits may be used only once by a beneficiary. Beneficiaries must pay a daily copay of $608 (2014) for each lifetime reserve day used.

Part A also pays for up to 100 days in a skilled nursing facility, subject to a daily co-pay ($152.00 in 2014) for stays longer than 20 days. There is no coverage for non-institutional care in the home or on an outpatient basis.

Medicare Part B pays for physician, nursing, and testing services as well as durable medical equipment such as mobility devices (e.g., canes or wheelchairs), prosthetic devices, and oxygen supply machines. There is an annual deductible ($147 in 2014) and a copayment of 20 percent of approved Medicare charges. Most laboratory testing is covered at 100 percent.

Medicare Part C provides the option of receiving Medicare benefits under private insurance plans known as **Medicare Advantage Plans.** These plans are available to beneficiaries with both Part A and B coverages. Insurers offering these products receive a capitation fee from the social insurance program. Benefits are more liberal than standard Medicare benefits and may require supplemental premiums by policyowners. These plans usually have managed care features and generally require the use of approved providers. Medicare Advantage Plans ordinarily incorporate the Part D prescription drug benefit. Extended coverage under Medicare Advantage usually incorporates extended benefits available under private supplemental plans.

Medicare Part D provides prescription drug benefits under stand alone plans that are distinct from Medicare Parts A, B, and C. Part D coverage is available only through private insurers. As with Part C, Medicare provides a capitation payment to Part D providers. Part D plans provide both basic coverage and catastrophic coverage, but there is a gap between the maximum basic benefit and the minimum catastrophic benefit that has required beneficiaries to pay 100 percent of costs while their out of pocket costs are in that coverage gap, known as the *donut hole.*

Some benefits are expanded under the ACA. Medicare prescription drug program enrollees will receive a 50 percent discount off the price of brand-name drugs during the coverage gap (the donut hole), and the gap will be phased out by 2020. Assistance for some low-income beneficiaries enrolled in the Medicare drug program is expanded, and beneficiary copayments for certain preventive care services are eliminated.

Premiums for Part A are not required for workers who have been *Federal Insurance Contributions Act* (FICA) participants for at least 40 quarters. Others pay a monthly premium based on the length of their FICA participation. Optional coverage under Part B requires a monthly premium ($104.90 in 2014) for most beneficiaries. Higher premiums are required of high-income taxpayers (ranging to $335.70 monthly).

Private insurers may or may not charge premiums under Parts C and D. If premiums are charged, benefits will be more liberal than the basic benefits provided for the Medicare capitation fee.

MEDICAID

Medicaid is a jointly funded federal/state health insurance program for certain low-income and needy people. It was created in 1965 through Title XIX of the *Social Security Act.* The states administer the program, with payments made for medical care on a traditional reimbursement basis or, increasingly, through managed care arrangements. Medicaid is the largest source of funding for medical and health-related services for people with low income in the U.S. Some 60 million individuals are covered under the program. It is jointly funded by the state and federal governments. The proportion of federal funding varies inversely with each state's per capita income. Thus, federal funding covers 83 percent of Mississippi's plan costs but only 50 percent of Connecticut's plan costs. States are not required to participate in the program, although all currently do. Medicaid recipients must be U.S citizens or legal permanent residents, and may include low-income adults, their children, and people with certain disabilities. Poverty alone does not necessarily qualify someone for Medicaid.

The ACA significantly expanded both eligibility for and federal funding of Medicaid. Under the law as written, all U.S. citizens and legal residents who did not qualify for Medicaid and with incomes up to 133 percent of the poverty level, including adults without dependent children, would qualify for coverage in any state that participated in the Medicaid program. The effect of this provision would have been to expand the Medicaid program to cover, not only those who were unemployed – as state plans generally did – but also to cover the working poor. The law provided that the federal government would pay 100 percent of the expansion cost for the program's first three years (2014 to 2017), 95 percent to 2020, and 90 percent to 2022. However, the U.S. Supreme Count ruled that states did not have to agree to this expansion to continue to receive previously established levels of Medicaid funding. Many states chose to continue with pre-ACA funding levels and eligibility standards. The result is that some 5.7 million poor people who otherwise would have been eligible for Medicaid are denied such coverage.

Workers' Compensation

State workers' compensation laws require employers to provide benefits to employees for losses resulting from work-related accidents or diseases. Based on the principle of liability without fault, the employer is held absolutely liable for the occupational injuries or diseases suffered by workers, regardless of who was at fault. Employees are not required to sue their employers to collect benefits. The full cost of providing workers' compensation benefits ordinarily is borne by the employer.

The key criterion for coverage under workers' compensation laws is that accidental occupational injuries or death must arise out of covered employment. Self-inflicted injuries and accidents resulting from an employee's intoxication or willful disregard of safety rules usually are excluded. Illnesses resulting from occupational diseases are covered in all states, with some states covering only specified diseases. Besides covering work-related medical expenses, these laws also provide disability income coverage, death benefits, and rehabilitation benefits. Benefit levels vary significantly from state to state.

Employers can comply with the law by purchasing a workers' compensation policy, by self-insuring, or by obtaining insurance from a monopolistic or competitive state fund. Most employers purchase workers' compensation policies from private insurance companies.

Endnotes
1   Kurt Giesa and Chris Carlson, "Age Band Compression Under Health Care Reform," *Contingencies*, January-February (2013).

CHAPTER 8

HEALTH INSURANCE II: DISABILITY INCOME AND LONG TERM CARE INSURANCE

As discussed in Chapter 7, medical expense insurance policies are *contracts of indemnity* meaning that insureds are reimbursed in cash for covered expenses or are paid in kind; i.e., needed medical services are provided. Illness and injury are sources of financial loss in other ways. They may prevent individuals from earning incomes or from being able fully to take care of themselves. Disability income insurance and long term care (LTC) insurance can provide funds to help mitigate the financial consequences of these morbidity conditions. As with life insurance policies, disability income and LTC policies are typically not contracts of indemnity but rather pay *stated sums* when the insured events occur.

DISABILITY INCOME INSURANCE

Most individuals seek and maintain medical expense insurance coverage to protect themselves from the financial consequences of medical expenses. Large proportions of the wage-earning population purchase group and individual life insurance. Much smaller proportions, however, protect themselves against the financial consequences of lost wages resulting from a disability. Indeed, in the U.S., only about one in four workers has private disability income coverage of any type. Consumers behave as if the possibility of losing one's income because of disability is not great or, if disabled, recovery will be swift and complete.

While the majority of disabilities are short term, lasting less than one month, the probability of a disability lasting three months or longer is quite high for individuals in their typical wage earning years. Figure 8-1 shows probabilities of disabilities lasting longer than 90 days for selected ages based on insured lives. We also show for comparison the probabilities of an individual death prior to age 65 based on the *2001 CSO Mortality Table*.

The probabilities of a experiencing a long term disability before age 65, defined as having a duration of at least three months, is substantially greater than the likelihood of death before age 65 throughout the typical working life. Additionally, if one is disabled for at least three months, the average duration of disability is in the 2.4 to 5.0 year range, as illustrated in Figure 8-2. Many disabilities are of considerably longer duration. Disabilities occurring before age 65 tend to have a significant impact that can last for the rest of life. Retirement savings can be depleted, savings plans can be disrupted, and working spouses may lose income and savings to the need to provide care for the disabled.

Figure 8-1   **Probabilities of Disability for 90 Days or Longer and Probabilities of Death Prior to Age 65**

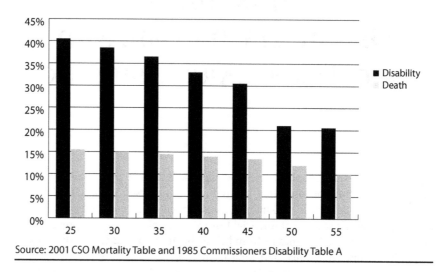

Source: 2001 CSO Mortality Table and 1985 Commissioners Disability Table A

Figure 8-2   **Average Duration in Years of Disabilities Lasting at Least 90 Days**

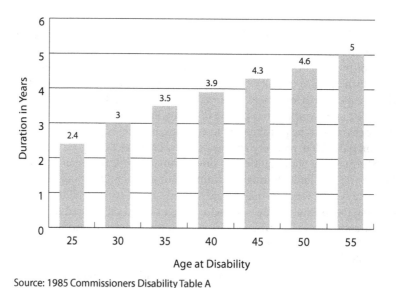

Source: 1985 Commissioners Disability Table A

The need for disability income coverage has increased in most countries. Informal support formerly provided by the family declines with economic development. Also, with a reduced sustainability of high government social insurance expenditures in many countries, there has been a shift of responsibility for disability income (and other coverages) from government to the individual. In the U.S. and other markets, we observe similar trends in some areas of employer-sponsored benefit plans, including disability income insurance. At the same time, advances in medical care and technology have turned many terminal diseases into disabling diseases. In effect, in many instances, medical advances have substituted disability for what formerly would have been death.

The financial consequences of a disability can be substantial; in some ways, even more financially debilitating on the family than death. With death, the deceased's income ceases but so too do expenses relating the deceased's personal maintenance. With disability, income ceases *and* expenses continue; in fact post-disability expenses can be higher than pre-disability expenses if skilled or intensive care is needed. Figure 8-3 illustrates this important financial planning concept. Adequate medical expense insurance should mitigate the rise in expenses and adequate disability income (and perhaps LTC) insurance would do the same for income.

Effect of Total Disability on Income and Expenses   **Figure 8-3**

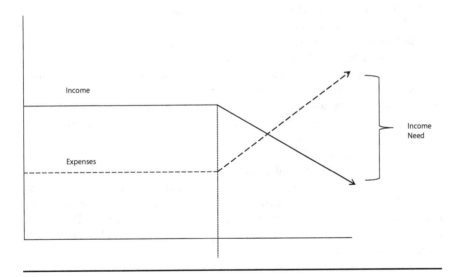

OVERVIEW OF DISABILITY INCOME POLICIES
Disability income policies are designed to provide monthly benefits to replace lost income when the insured is disabled as the result of sickness or injury and unable to work. Most disability income insurance is issued on a group basis, with a substantial portion issued to individuals, as well as sold through association plans, both of which ordinarily entail individual underwriting. Disability income coverage is also provided through social insurance, worker's compensation, and some state plans, as discussed at the end of this section. Our emphasis is on policies sold to individuals.

Such policies typically are issued on a guaranteed renewable or noncancelable basis. Recall that under a guaranteed renewable policy, the insured has a contractual right to continue the policy to a specified age, such as 65, and the insurer can change premiums but, as with individual medical expense insurance, only on a class basis and without regard to any particular insured's health. A noncancelable or noncan policy is one in which the insurer cannot cancel or refuse to renew the policy or unilaterally alter the premiums from those shown in the contract during the term of the policy. Clearly, a noncancelable policy provides greater price certainty in comparison to a guaranteed renewable policy, but it also is likely to have higher premiums.

The primary individual policy benefits usually are clustered together in the contract under a prominent heading, and any supplemental or optional benefits appear in rider forms attached to the policy. Many companies' systems integrate basic and optional coverages within an individually printed policy eliminating the need for riders. As with other group coverage, group disability income coverage is evidenced by a certificate or booklet that contains provisions similar, but usually less expensive, than those available under individual policies.

The basic benefit arrangement in the policies of the major insurers consists of a monthly benefit for total disability and a waiver of premium benefit. Supplemental coverages may include a monthly benefit for residual or partial disability (see below); a monthly benefit paid when certain social insurance programs fail to provide benefits; a cost of living benefit; and a guarantee for purchase of additional insurance at a later date. These provisions are augmented by a schedule that summarizes the available benefits and by a series of technical definitions that control and limit the way in which benefits are paid. The policy schedule shows a summary of the principal policy benefits, including any supplemental coverages, and it usually appears immediately after the policy cover page. The schedule shows the effective date of insurance, identifies the insured, and displays the benefit amounts and the premiums charged for them.

Of all insurance lines, individual disability income policies are the least amenable to generalized analysis and comparison. These contracts are designed to permit flexible adaptation to the individual needs of the insured through a broad range of interrelated benefit patterns and optional coverages. Probably no other type of insurance relies as heavily on subtle distinctions in benefits and the language used to describe them.

Contract design and language differ from insurer to insurer and, often, from policy to policy within the same company. Intense competitive pressures force insurers to find unique provisions or more precise definitions that will distinguish their policies in the marketplace. Companies constantly change contracts as they restate old concepts in new ways and introduce innovative coverages for the disability risk. Nonetheless, there are basic criteria to be used for thoughtful analysis and evaluation of all individual health insurance contracts.

Important Definitions

Technical definitions may be included in the benefit provisions, but more typically they form a separate part of the policy intended to define terms that are used to evaluate claims and control payment of benefits. The most important of these are the definitions of injury and sickness, preexisting conditions, and disability.

INJURY AND SICKNESS   The major North American insurance companies uniformly define **injury** to mean accidental bodily injury whose results were unforeseen or unexpected occurring while the policy is in force. This definition employs *results* language and has replaced an older provision that was known as an accidental means clause. The distinction between the two definitions is important, as not all accidental bodily injuries result from accidental means.

For an accident to be covered by a disability policy containing the accidental means clause, both the cause of the injury and the result (the injury itself) must be unforeseen or unexpected. For example, a person who deliberately jumps from a wall and unintentionally breaks his or her leg would not have a covered loss under an accidental means clause. Although the result – a broken leg – was unexpected, the cause – a voluntary leap – was not. The loss would be covered under the accidental bodily injury definition, as the broken leg was an unexpected result even though the precipitating act was intentional. Most U.S. jurisdictions now prohibit use of the accidental means clause in health insurance contracts.

Most insurers define **sickness** to mean sickness or disease that *first manifests* itself while the policy is in force. Some insurers use a less strict modification of the first-manifest language so that sickness means a sickness or disease that is *first diagnosed* and treated while the policy is in force. In either case, the intention is to control adverse selection by covering only sickness that is first contracted after the policy takes effect.

PREEXISTING CONDITION   Use of a preexisting condition limitation is customary in policies that contain a *first manifest* or *first diagnosed* definition of sickness. The **preexisting condition** limitation applies in the first two or three policy years to exclude benefits for any loss that results from a condition that the *insured misrepresented or failed to disclose* in the insurance application. In other words, if relevant health conditions were disclosed, no preexisting condition applies. The limitation varies from jurisdiction to jurisdiction, but the following is typical for the North American markets:

> *Preexisting condition means a medical condition which exists on the Effective Date and during the past five years either:*
> 1. *caused you to receive medical advice or treatment; or*
> 2. *caused symptoms for which an ordinarily prudent person would seek medical advice or treatment.*

DISABILITY   Traditionally, individual disability income policies have been called *loss-of-time* insurance because of the occupational definitions used to qualify the insured as disabled. A disabled person under these types of policies is presumed to have suffered a loss of income because he or she cannot work. The definitions of *total disability* and *partial disability* are premised on the inability of the insured to perform certain occupational tasks. In recent years, the concept of residual disability has largely replaced the partial disability provision as a means of paying proportionate benefits to an insured who works at reduced earnings as a result of sickness or injury. The residual concept differs from conventional stated value plans, as it emphasizes protection of income rather than protection of occupational performance.

Essentially, insurance companies define total disability in two different ways. One is an any gainful occupation definition, which is popularly, if somewhat inaccurately, called *any occ*. The other is an own occupation definition, which is usually referred to as *own occ*.

An **own occupation** clause deems insureds to be totally disabled if they cannot perform the major duties of their regular occupations. A regular occupation is the one in which the insured was engaged at the time disability began. Under this definition, insureds can be at work in some other capacity and still be entitled to policy benefits if they cannot perform the important tasks of their own occupations in the usual way.

Under an **any gainful occupation** clause, insureds are considered totally disabled if they cannot perform the major duties of any gainful occupation for which they are reasonably suited because of education, training, or experience. As the insured may be able to work at any of several suitable occupations even though he or she is incapable of working at his or her regular job, this clause is a more restrictive definition of disability than the own occupation definition. It can limit recovery of benefits under the policy.

Many insurers in the past further defined regular occupation as the recognized specialty (or recognized sub-specialty) in which a medical, dental, legal, or accounting professional was engaged at the time disability began. For example, an orthopedic surgeon would be totally disabled, even while at work in a general medical practice, as long as he or she could not perform the customary duties associated with orthopedic surgery. This practice has diminished as insurers experienced severe moral hazard problems with this generous definition.

The most common variation of the own occupation definition is the one that deems insureds to be totally disabled as long as they (1) cannot perform the major duties of their regular occupation and (2) are not at work in any other occupation. If insureds are disabled for their regular job, the insurance company can terminate disability benefits only if they voluntarily have chosen to work at some other job. If this provision is used, the company cannot insist that insureds resume work in some other suitable occupation.

Many disability insurers combine both occupation clauses in the same policy form to provide an own occupation definition for a specified period of time and an any occupation definition thereafter. The specified period will vary between two and 10 years in the policies of the major insurers. Many insurers allow own occupation coverage to age 65 for their most favorable classes of insureds, although recent trends are quite restrictive in use of this liberal definition.

The following example is taken from a leading insurer's policy, which is available only to its most favorable rating classes:

Total Disability, before age 55 or before benefits have been paid for five years for a period of disability, whichever is later, means that due to Injuries or Sickness:

1. you are unable to perform the duties of your occupation; and
2. you are under the care and attendance of a physician.

After you attain age 55 or after benefits have been paid for five years for a period of disability, whichever is later, Total Disability means that due to Injuries or Sickness:

> *1. you are unable to engage in any gainful occupation in which you might reasonably be expected to engage because of education, training, or experience, with due regard to your vocation and earnings at the start of disability; and*
>
> *2. you are under the care and attendance of a physician.*

Almost all insurers specify in the definition of disability or in a separate policy provision that an insured must be under the care and attendance of a physician to qualify for disability benefits. Most insurers do not interpret the medical care requirement literally, as common sense and various court decisions dictate that an insurer cannot deny benefits under this provision if medical care is not essential to the disabled insured's well being or recovery. The insurer cannot insist that an insured maintain a physician-patient relationship for the sole purpose of certifying a disability.

It is common to include a definition of presumptive disability in policies that provide benefits for total disability. Under the **presumptive disability** clause, an insured is always considered totally disabled, even if he or she is at work, if sickness or injury results in the loss of the sight of both eyes, the hearing of both ears, the power of speech, or the use of any two limbs. Usually, the insurer begins benefits immediately upon the date of loss and waives the medical care requirement. The insured can work in any occupation and full benefits will be paid to the end of the policy's benefit period while the loss continues.

BASIC COMPONENTS OF THE BENEFIT PROVISION

Three basic components establish the premium and define the payment of benefits under disability income policies: (1) the elimination period, (2) the benefit period, and (3) the monthly benefit amount. All other parts of the policy relate to these common elements and are used to limit or expand their value in meeting the specific needs of insureds at the time of loss. The value of a particular disability income plan to the insured lies in how liberally the insurance company permits these elements to operate within the policy provisions and its own administrative practices.

THE ELIMINATION PERIOD   The **elimination period**, sometimes called the **waiting period,** is the number of days at the start of disability during which no benefits are paid. It is a limitation on benefits that serves the same function as a deductible in medical expense and property insurance policies. It is meant to exclude the illness or injury that disables the insured for only a few days and that is more economically met from personal funds.

In general, insurers offer elimination periods of from 30 days to one year, with three months being common. As policy benefits are paid at the end of each month of continuing disability, a three month elimination period usually means that a disabled insured will not receive benefits for at least 120 days from the time sickness began or injury occurred. Premiums are lower for policies with longer elimination periods. Most insurers require that the elimination period be the same for sickness and injury. The elimination period is a significant determinant of cost;

premiums for a policy with a 30 day elimination period may be 300 percent or more of the premium for a 365 day elimination period.

The major insurers allow for a temporary break in the elimination period so that the insured will not be penalized for any brief attempt to return to work before the elimination period has expired at the start of disability. The brief recovery generally is limited to six months or, if less, to the length of the elimination period. If the insured is then again disabled because of the same or a different cause after the interruption, the insurer combines the two periods of disability to satisfy the elimination period.

THE BENEFIT PERIOD   The **benefit period** is the longest period of time for which benefits will be paid under the disability policy. Usually, the benefit period is the same for sickness and injury and generally is available for durations of two or five years or to age 65. Life benefits are also available but require continuous, total disability beginning before age 55, age 60, or (less commonly) age 65.

Most disabilities are of short duration. Roughly 98 percent of all disabled persons recover before one year has elapsed, and most disabled individuals recover within six months of the time disability began. If disability lasts beyond 12 months, however, the chances of a return to productive work diminish markedly, particularly at older ages. The effect of extended disability can be financially devastating. Long benefit periods are more consistent with sound personal risk management principles. Of course, the longer the benefit period, the higher the premium, other things being equal.

All insurers include a provision that is related to the benefit period and that deals with consecutive or recurrent episodes of disability and identifies whether the company is dealing with a new or continuing claim. The typical provision states that the company will consider **recurrent periods of disability** from the same cause to be one continuous period of disability unless each period is separated by a recovery of six months or more.

Among the major insurers, use of a 12-month recurrent provision is common in policies with benefit periods to age 65 or longer. The provision operates to the insured's advantage as a new elimination period is not required for disability that recurs more than six months, but less than a year, after a brief recovery during a long term claim.

This recurrence language protects the insured from multiple elimination periods, so that benefits for recurring loss due to the same cause become payable immediately for the unused portion of the original benefit period. The provision allows for a new benefit period and a new elimination period if loss results from a different cause at any time after an earlier disability or if loss recurs due to the same cause more than six months after recovery. This provision is designed to align the incentives of the insured and the insurer. Without it, an insured would be deterred from a return to work unless the ability to resume occupational duties permanently was completely doubt free.

THE BENEFIT AMOUNT   The benefit provided under the personal disability income policy is almost always payable as a fixed monthly amount. Like life insurance, the indemnity for total disability generally is written on a **stated value basis,** which means that the stated policy benefit is paid without regard to the actual economic loss suffered; it is presumed to equal or be less than the actual monetary loss sustained by the disabled insured. This amount is not adjusted to the insured's actual earnings or other insurance payments at the time of claim for total or partial disability. During a period of residual disability, however, indemnity may be reduced in proportion to lost earnings of the insured, as we discuss below.

Insurers limit the amount of disability income coverage they will sell to an applicant – termed the **issue and participation limit** – so that the total of all monthly indemnity does not exceed about 85 percent of earned income for insureds with low annual incomes, grading downward to about 65 percent or less for those in the highest income brackets. The income tax treatment of the requested disability income benefit will also be taken into consideration. If the premium is paid by the employer, benefits will be taxed as income to the employee, so the after-tax benefit will be less than if the insured paid premiums and benefits were not taxable. The benefit amount for corporate-paid policies, therefore, can be higher to cover the income tax the employee must pay.

The issue limits take into account other compensation that may be available to the disabled insured (e.g., employer sick pay plans, government programs, and other personal or group insurance). Insurers will also reduce these limits for individuals with significant unearned income or for those with high net worth. Thus, if unearned income exceeds a certain percentage of earned income, most insurers will treat the unearned income as if it were existing disability income protection.

The limits are intended to minimize the creation of moral hazard in the form of overinsurance, which occurs when benefits equal or exceed a disabled insured's pre-disability income. Experience demonstrates that overinsurance diminishes the incentive for a disabled insured to return to work, and, as a result, recovery often is delayed or does not occur at all. There are few effective mechanisms for controlling overinsurance after a claim is incurred – it is difficult to prove definitively that a person is *able* or that a disabled individual has recovered. In the absence of demonstrable fraud, companies must rely almost entirely on issue limits at the time of underwriting to minimize moral hazard.

Nevertheless, under the regular limits of the leading disability writers for personal insurance, an insured with adequate income in the more favorable risk classifications may acquire up to a maximum of $15,000 to $20,000 in monthly income benefit for total disability. This amount generally is separate from indemnity limits established for special business insurance policies, such as overhead expense insurance.

Basic Benefit Arrangements

The basic benefit arrangement of disability income policies consists of a benefit for total disability and a benefit for waiver of premium. These two components are common to all insurers, regardless of any additional coverages that may be included directly in the policy form. The benefit provision usually describes the circumstances of loss, the way in which the company will pay benefits, and at what point benefits may end.

The following is typical of the benefit provision for total disability:

When you are totally disabled, we will pay the monthly indemnity as follows:

1. You must become totally disabled while this policy is in force.
2. You must remain so to the end of the elimination period. No indemnity is payable during that period.
3. After that, monthly indemnity will be payable at the end of each month while you are totally disabled.
4. Monthly indemnity will stop at the end of the benefit period or, if earlier, on the date you are no longer totally disabled.

The waiver of premium benefit under disability income policies characteristically "waives" any premiums that fall due after the insured has been totally disabled for the shorter of 90 consecutive days or the elimination period. As noted in Chapter 5, this feature is itself a disability benefit equal to the premium amount. Any premiums paid during this period are refunded. Further premiums are waived while the insured remains disabled, until age 65. Some insurers also waive premiums that fall due within 90 days after recovery. The waiver of premium feature usually terminates when the insured attains age 65.

The basic provision often contains several minor but competitively necessary provisions that are not appropriate as optional benefit riders, as they do not carry a significant premium consideration. These supplemental benefit provisions include a transplant benefit, a rehabilitation benefit, a non-disabling injury benefit, and a principal sum benefit.

The **transplant benefit** provides that, if the insured is totally disabled because of the transplant of an organ from his or her body to the body of another individual, the insurer will deem him or her to be disabled as a result of sickness. This provision also includes cosmetic surgery performed to correct appearance or a disfigurement. The **rehabilitation benefit** generally allows a specific sum, often 12 times the sum of the monthly indemnity and any supplemental indemnities, to cover costs not paid by other insurance or public funding when the insured enrolls in a formal retraining program that will help him or her return to work. The **non-disabling injury benefit** pays up to a specific sum, usually one quarter of the monthly indemnity, to reimburse the insured for medical expenses incurred for treatment of an injury that did not result in total disability.

The **principal sum benefit** is a lump sum amount payable if the insured dies accidentally. This provision requires that death be caused directly and independently by injury and that it occur within a specified number of days, usually 90 or 180, following the date of the accident. The principal sum amount benefit also pays a single sum, usually 12 times the sum of the monthly indemnity and any supplemental indemnities, if sickness or injury results in dismemberment or loss of sight and the insured survives the loss for 30 days. The lump sum is in addition to any other indemnity payable under the policy, and it is payable for two such losses in the insured's lifetime. The principal sum benefit usually is limited to the irrecoverable loss of the sight of one eye or the complete loss of a hand or foot through severance above the wrist or ankle.

SUPPLEMENTAL BENEFITS

Among leading disability insurers, the most common optional or supplemental benefits are: (1) a residual disability benefit, (2) a partial disability benefit, (3) a social insurance supplement, (4) an inflation protection benefit, and (5) provisions for increased future benefit amounts. Although some insurers may include one or more of these benefits in the basic benefit provision, they are more frequently available for an additional premium as optional benefit riders that are attached to the policy. The benefits and the premiums of each optional rider generally are shown on the schedule page.

RESIDUAL DISABILITY BENEFIT   The **residual disability benefit** provides reduced monthly benefit in proportion to the insured's loss of income when he or she has returned to work at reduced earnings. In policies that provide for an own occupation definition of total disability, the residual benefit is payable only when the insured has returned to work in his or her own occupation. Most insurers allow the insured to be either totally or residually disabled to satisfy the elimination period of the policy and to qualify for waiver of premium.

The most common definition of residual disability employs a time and duties test that combines both occupational and income considerations, as follows:

> *Residual disability means that due to Injuries or Sickness:*
> *1. you are not able to do one or more of your important daily business duties or you are not able to do your usual daily business duties for as much time as it would normally take for you to do them;*
> *2. your Loss of Monthly Income is at least 25 percent of your Prior Monthly Income; and*
> *3. you are under the care and attendance of a physician.*

An alternative definition of residual disability is referred to as a *pure income test* and rests solely on loss of earnings:

> *Residual disability means that you are engaged in your regular occupation and your Income is reduced due to Accident or Sickness by at least 20 percent of your Prior Income.*

Most insurers do not require that an insured sustain a prior period of total disability before claiming residual benefits. In effect, a residual claim can begin on the occurrence date, and reduced benefits are payable at the end of the elimination period for the duration of the benefit period. From a practical standpoint, the vast majority of residual claims follow some period of total disability. Residual claims make up only a small portion of all disability claims, whether from occurrence date or as continuation following prior total disability.

The provisions for residual disability resemble those used for total disability, but they are accompanied by a series of technical definitions to define prior and current income and to describe the formula employed to compute the proportionate benefits. The customary benefit formula is:

> *Residual Indemnity = (Loss of Income/Prior Income) x Monthly Indemnity*

In this formula, *loss of income* means the difference between the insured's prior income and current income. Usually, loss of income in excess of 75 to 80 percent of prior income is considered to be 100 percent loss. In all cases, income refers only to earned income and excludes unearned income from savings or investments. *Prior income* is usually defined as the average taxable monthly income for the highest of the two or three years immediately before the date of disability. Most insurers index prior income at the end of each year of the claim to adjust for increases in the cost of living.

Current income means the insured's earned income in each month while he or she is residually disabled. Insurers differ in their treatment of current income, but they calculate it either on the basis of cash actually received or on an accrual method to exclude income that was earned but not collected before disability began. For example, assume that Jerry, who is residually disabled, is receiving current income of $1,000 per month but that he had a prior income of $3,000 per month. Assume also that the monthly indemnity is $2,000. Jerry could collect $1,333 under the residual benefit, which is calculated as follows:

$$Residual\ Indemnity = [(\$3,000\text{-}\$1,000)/\$3,000] \times \$2,000 = \$1,333$$

Some insurers apply the residual benefit formula strictly throughout the benefit period. Several insurers use the exact rate of current income to compute benefits for the first six months of payment and then average current income at six month intervals for the remainder of the claim. Other insurers guarantee a minimum benefit during the first six months of a residual claim by providing the greater of the residual indemnity from the formula or 50 percent of the monthly indemnity for total disability. The residual benefit is payable for the duration of the policy benefit period or until loss of income is less than 20 or 25 percent of prior income. Insurers usually do not renew residual disability provisions after the insured attains age 65.

Partial Disability Benefit   The residual disability concept generally has replaced the partial disability benefit for most professional and white collar occupations. Many insurers, however, provide a partial disability provision as an optional benefit for their less favorable occupational risks. The typical **partial disability benefit** is 50 percent of the monthly total disability indemnity and is payable for up to six months or, if less, for the remainder of the policy benefit period when the insured has returned to work on a limited basis after a period of compensable total disability. Partial disability customarily is defined in occupational terms with reference to time and duties. The following is typical of this definition:

> *Partial disability means that you are at work, but because of Sickness or Injury:*
> *1. you are unable to perform one or more, but not all of the major duties of your occupation; or,*
> *2. you are not able to be present at work for more than one-half of the time required in your usual work week.*

Social Insurance Supplement   The **social insurance supplement** (SIS) or **social insurance substitute** provides an additional disability income insurance benefit that approximates the amount an insured might reasonably expect to receive in disability benefits under a social insurance program, provided the insured qualifies for a disability benefit under the policy but does not qualify for a benefit under the terms of the social insurance program. It evolved as a response to the underwriting problem that is created by the existence of substantial benefits potentially available for disability under workers' compensation or for disability or retirement under U.S. Social Security. Most insurance companies take these substantial benefits into account and, to minimize the moral hazard of overinsurance at a later time, sharply limit the amount of conventional disability income insurance that they will issue to applicants with incomes below $35,000, particularly those in their less favorable occupational classes.

However, the insured may not qualify for the anticipated benefits of the social insurance plans. He or she may suffer a loss that is not covered by workers' compensation or that does not meet the highly restrictive definitions for total and permanent disability under Social Security, but does meet the insurer's definition of disability. If the insurance company has limited the amount of personal insurance, the individual will be underinsured each month by several hundred dollars or more.

The SIS benefit was developed to meet this potential coverage gap. The SIS benefit is paid when the insured meets the policy's definition for total disability but is not receiving benefits from any social service plan. It is payable as a fixed amount of indemnity that ceases when the insured begins to receive any income from a social insurance plan or it may be reduced by the amount of the benefit actually paid under the social insurance plan. If the offset method is used, the insurer usually specifies a minimum amount below which the SIS benefit will not be reduced while total disability continues.

RETURN OF PREMIUM RIDER   The **return of premium rider** pays a benefit amount at a certain time equal to the sum of premiums paid if no claims are made for benefits. A partial "return of premium" may be paid if total premiums paid exceed total benefits paid. The payment may be at a certain age (typically 65) or after a certain number of policy years. The rider is essentially an endowment at the specified date that pays no benefits or reduced benefits if the insured dies or becomes disabled. The policy and rider premiums are therefore much higher than the base policy premium. Purchasers should examine the economics of these riders carefully.

INFLATION PROTECTION BENEFITS   The **cost of living adjustment** (COLA) benefit under disability income policies provides for adjustments of benefits each year during a long term claim so as to reflect changes in the cost of living from the time that the claim began. Adjustments are computed by the rate of change shown in some price index, such as the *U.S. Consumer Price Index*. At one time, insurers marketed COLA riders offering fixed percentage increases. This practice resulted in some benefits outpacing the rate of inflation and led to moral hazard problems.

The method of adjustment is relatively complex, but generally it calls for a comparison of the index for the current claim year with the index for the year in which the claim began. If the index increased or decreased since the start of the claim, benefits for the next 12 months are adjusted by the percentage change in the index. The percentage change is limited to a specified rate of inflation, generally ranging between 5 and 10 percent compounded annually.

The adjusted policy benefits may increase or decrease each year as the index rises or falls, but the benefits cannot be reduced below the level specified in the policy on the date of issue. Some insurers apply a cap to limit increased benefits to a maximum of two or three times the original amount. Others place no limit on the maximum increase of adjusted benefits before the insured is age 65.

PROVISIONS FOR INCREASED FUTURE BENEFIT AMOUNTS   Insurers offer the flexibility of automatic increases in future benefits (prior to a claim) to accommodate inflation and increased earnings. Two supplemental provisions allow increases in future benefit amounts: the automatic increase benefit and the guarantee of future insurability. **Automatic increase benefit** provisions provide for scheduled increases in the monthly benefit amount, typically in each of five consecutive years at a fixed rate of 5 or 6 percent, with annual premium increases at attained age rates for the portion of increased indemnity. The insured has the right to refuse one or more of the automatic increases during the five year period and may, at the expiration of the schedule, apply to continue the automatic increases over another five year period. Some insurers incorporate this provision automatically without a specified premium charge while others use an optional benefit rider and additional premium.

The **guarantee of future insurability** or the **future increase option** allows an insured to purchase additional disability income insurance in future years without evidence of insurability. It is a call option that would be expected to be exercised with greater frequency among those whose insurability is questionable. The total increase that the insured may obtain under this benefit varies among insurers, but most often it cannot exceed twice the monthly indemnity that the insured has in force in all insurers on the original policy's date of issue.

The insured may exercise purchase options once a year, typically until age 50 or 55. The amount of additional monthly benefit that the insured can purchase each year is subject to the company's limits for insurance in relation to earned income, and, in some insurers, it may be further limited to a specific amount, typically $500. In other insurers, the insured can purchase all or part of the total increase option on any option date before age 45. After that, increases each year may not exceed one third of the original total.

If the insured is disabled on an option date, he or she can purchase additional insurance, but the additional amounts may not apply to the current claim, although many major insurers now include such amounts in existing claims. Income requirements are based on the earned income at the start of the claim, and immediate benefit payments are subject to an elimination period that begins on the date of issue of the additional insurance coverage.

It may prove useful to summarize the key differences between COLAs, automatic increases, and future increase guarantees. COLA adjusts benefits while the insured is receiving disability benefits to account for changes in the cost of living from the start of disability (when the claim lasts at least one year). Automatic increases are designed to keep insurance benefits current with changes in earned income or financial needs as a result of modest annual salary increases or the effects of inflation while the insured is not disabled. One insurer combines the automatic increase principle and COLA into a single benefit rider so that consistent adjustments occur annually whether the insured is healthy or disabled. Future increase guarantees are designed to adjust insurance benefits for individuals who anticipate substantial annual income growth that is above the average national rate for salary changes or who expect periodic substantial changes in income as they mature in their professional or business roles.

Extra-contractual Settlement Offers

Life insurers may make a settlement offer to a long term disability claimant, which is not a part of the policy provisions. A lump sum settlement of a disability claim is attractive to the insurer because the reserve for future benefits under the policy is released, and the administrative costs of active claim monitoring and management are avoided. If the expected present value of the reserve exceeds the amount of the lump sum settlement, there is an economic gain to the insurer.

The expected present value of the gain is a function of the periodic benefits owed and the duration of the claim. The duration of the claim, in turn, is a function of the probabilities of recovery and of death. If the claimant dies or returns to work, benefits cease. Thus, settlement offers are made generally to those claimants who exhibit longer than average expected lifetimes and a less than average probability of returning to work. An additional advantage to the insurer is a high average probability of death within the remaining portfolio of disabled insureds.

Settlement offers are less than the expected present value of claims because they are discounted for business risk. The insurer runs the risk of a renewed exposure if the claimant reopens the claim at a later date. The insurer also assumes the risk that the mortality and return to work assumptions incorporated into the offer are too conservative. Settlements may prove attractive to claimants who have more need for current capital than long term income. For example, proceeds might be used for business ventures or for the education of the claimant or the claimant's children. By contrast, lump sum settlements are inappropriate for many claimants.

Insurers are careful to ensure claimants have proper legal representation and an objective ability to manage the proceeds prudently. Psychological evaluations may be required by the insurer. Some insurers negotiate claims individually, while others seek to minimize the legal risk by making standard offers to all appropriate claimants. A standard offer reduces the risk of a successful legal reopening based on an allegation that the insurer unfairly exploited an advantage in negotiating with the claimant.

Governmental Sources of Disability Income Coverage

Besides individual and group disability income insurance sold by commercial insurers, disability income coverage also may be available through various government plans.[1] Three important sources are:

- Social Security disability benefits,
- workers' compensation, and
- state disability plans.

Social Security   The U.S. Social Security program provides benefits for qualified workers who become disabled. To qualify, the worker must meet three tests:

- be *fully insured*, meaning that he or she has either 40 quarters of coverage (i.e., has paid certain minimum taxes into the system each quarter) or at least one quarter of coverage for every calendar year elapsing after 1950 or after the year in which the worker attains age 21, if later,

- has at least 20 quarters of coverage out of the 40 quarters prior to disability, and
- has been disabled for at least five months.

The disability income benefit amount depends on the worker's past earnings, with higher earnings resulting in greater benefits. The formula used, however, is heavily weighted in favor of low wage earners, thus resulting in low income workers receiving a higher proportion of their wages replaced upon disability. Moreover, the system provides for certain maximum benefit payments, irrespective of past contributions to the system by the worker.

Disability is defined as the inability to engage in any substantial gainful activity by reason of any medically determinable physical or mental impairment that can be expected to result in death or which has lasted or can be expected to last for a continuous period of not less than 12 months. This definition is quite strict in comparison to the definitions used by commercial insurers, meaning that qualifying for benefits requires a truly substantial disability.

Rehabilitation is important in the disability program. Thus, a disabled beneficiary who performs services despite severe handicaps can continue to receive benefits for nine months. In addition, the law provides a three-month period of adjustment for beneficiaries who medically recover from their disabilities.

Monthly payments also can be made to certain dependent family members of a qualified disabled worker. An unmarried child of a deceased, disabled, or retired covered worker who has been disabled since before age 22 is eligible for a cash disability benefit at age 18 or after. The child's disability benefits are payable for as long as the disability continues and are the same as the benefit received by a dependent child of a disabled, retired, or deceased worker. Also, a mother's/father's benefit is payable to the parent who has in his or her care a disabled child receiving benefits. This applies if he or she is a spouse of a disabled, retired, or deceased worker. The rehabilitation features of the disability program also apply to a disabled child.

Workers' Compensation   As noted in the discussion on medical expense benefits, workers' compensation laws require employers to provide loss-of-wage benefits to employees for losses resulting from work-related accidents and diseases. Disabled workers are paid for their injuries according to a schedule of benefits established by each state's law. Benefit amounts vary by state and are subject to prescribed maximums that ensure somewhat limited benefits.

The key criterion for coverage under workers' compensation laws is that accidental occupational injuries or death must arise out of and be in the course of covered employment. Self-inflicted injuries and accidents resulting from an employee's intoxication or willful disregard of safety rules usually are excluded. Illnesses resulting from occupational diseases are covered in all states. Workers' compensation laws also provide rehabilitation benefits for disabled workers. Benefit levels vary significantly from state to state.

State Temporary Disability Plans   Five states – California, Hawaii, New Jersey, New York, and Rhode Island – and Puerto Rico have temporary disability benefit plans at the time of writing this chapter. Under these laws, employees can collect disability income benefits regardless of whether their disability begins while they are employed. These benefits are not provided for disabilities covered under workers' compensation laws. From a benefit standpoint, these laws (except in New York) generally are patterned after the state unemployment insurance law.

Employees contribute to the cost of the plans in all six jurisdictions. In California and Rhode Island, only employees contribute. Except for Rhode Island, which has a monopolistic state fund, an employee may obtain coverage from either a state fund or private insurers. The laws require that private coverage must provide benefits that are at least as liberal as those prescribed under the law. In effect, these plans are compulsory group disability income plans similar to the voluntary plans in effect in many businesses. Self-insurance generally is permitted.

LONG TERM CARE INSURANCE

Recall that long term care insurance promises to pay a benefit if the insured is unable to engage safely in selected activities of daily living (ADLs). As noted in Chapter 1, many societies are experiencing rapid population aging. While most elderly persons are able to care for themselves, many will require assistance at some point. Our discussion focuses on the elderly, but the LTC risk is not confined to them. Younger persons also may require assistance if injured or ill. Figure 8-4 shows the portion of the elderly population expected to require LTC as the population ages.

Percentage of Individuals Turning 65 Projected to have Needed Long Term Care, U.S., 2005, by Duration of Need   **Figure 8-4**

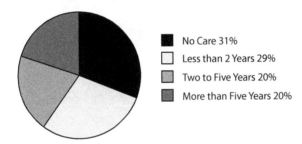

- No Care 31%
- Less than 2 Years 29%
- Two to Five Years 20%
- More than Five Years 20%

Source: Kemper, Peter, Harriet L. Komisar and Lisa Alecxih, 2005. "Long Term Care over an Uncertain Future." Inquiry Vol. 42, No. 4: 335-350.

Historically, any needed care was provided by family members through extended family living arrangements. Even today, families remain the primary source of care for the infirm, with the responsibility typically falling on females. But, the loss to caregiver families can be enormous. For example, according to the *MetLife Mature Market Institute*, the average lifetime loss in wages, pension, and Social Security benefits from taking time from work for caregiving is $324,044 for women and $283,716 for men. Moreover, the percentage of adults caring for a parent increased from 1994 to 2008 from 3 percent to 17 percent for men and from 9 percent to 28 percent for women. Even in the face of these figures, numerous factors continue to converge both to decrease the ability of families to provide care and to increase the demand for such care, including the following:

- a continuing decline in the importance of the extended family,
- a rise in single-parent households,

- a growing proportion of adult women working outside the home, now less available to render care,
- the increasing reliance by nuclear families on the incomes of both spouses, making both spouses less available to assist elderly parents,
- increasing life expectancy,
- a more mobile society with children less likely to live near elderly parents,
- reduced fertility rates and fewer children to provide care, and
- modern medicine's ability to prolong life, which does not always translate into physical independence.

Figure 8-5 presents the wide variety of diagnoses that cause nursing home and home care claims under LTC policies.

Figure 8-5   **Cause of Claim Percentage for Long Term Care**
by Nursing Home and Home Care

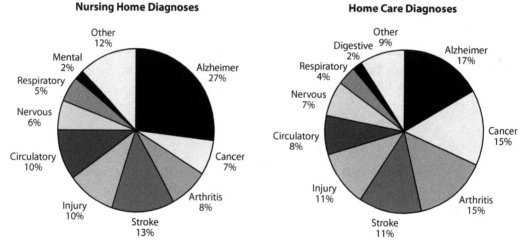

Source: Long Term Care Experience Committee Intercompany Study 1984-2004 (Society of Actuaries, 2007)

The need for LTC insurance can be expected to grow as more and more persons become aware of LTC's extraordinary costs. According to a survey reported by *John Hancock Life Insurance Company*, the average cost of a year's stay in a private room in a nursing home in the U.S., for example, exceeds $85,000, with some costing twice that amount. (Typical home-care costs are not much less.) The average confinement is between one and two years, with about one-fourth lasting more than three years. About 10 percent last more than five years. Of course, individual costs can be much higher than the averages suggest, causing an even more rapid dissipation of personal assets and possibly even impoverishment. Of even greater importance to many persons is the concern about possible loss of dignity and a loss of control that accompanies the depletion of wealth in old age.

As discussed below, demand for LTC insurance is not consistent with the need. Figure 8-6 presents the sources of financing for long term care and illustrates the relatively small role that private insurance plays in financing the LTC need.

Percentage of Funding Sources for Long Term Care   **Figure 8-6**

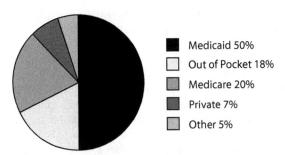

- Medicaid 50%
- Out of Pocket 18%
- Medicare 20%
- Private 7%
- Other 5%

Source: Komisar, Harriet L. and Lee Shirey Thompson, 2007. "National Spending for Long Term Care." Fact Sheet (February). Washington DC: Georgetown University Long Term Care Financing Project.

SOURCES OF LONG TERM CARE COVERAGE

Long term care insurance promises to pay expenses incurred if the insured is unable to engage safely in selected ADLs. The individual's inability to engage in these essential activities requires that someone provide the care, either in the home or in an institution such as a nursing home. Such care is financed in a few countries by the government but, in the majority of countries worldwide, LTC expenses are met from individual or family resources and, increasingly, through LTC insurance.

LTC insurance coverage is available through individual policies, employer-sponsored plans, association-sponsored plans, and riders to life insurance and annuity policies. See Chapter 5. About 70 percent of LTC policies are sold to individuals and through the group association market, with the remaining 30 percent sold in the group market. The group market, however, has been the fastest growing segment, having been only 8 percent of the LTC market in 1988.

In addition to the above sources of LTC coverage, the U.S. Medicare plan pays for about 20 percent of long term care costs, a small share as it is designed to cover medical expenses of the elderly (see Chapter 7) and not LTC. LTC benefits are paid under Medicare only for medically necessary care in a skilled nursing facility that follows a period of hospitalization for the same condition. Additionally, even this coverage is limited to 100 days, of which only 20 are covered in full.

Another potential source of LTC funding in the U.S. is the state-managed Medicaid program that is jointly funded by the federal and state governments. Medicaid, an important part of the U.S. welfare program, provides health benefits to qualified individuals and families with low income and assets. If individuals are impoverished and require LTC, Medicaid often will meet the costs. It, however, is far from an acceptable alternative for most persons. See Box 8-1.

Box 8-1
Eligibility for Long Term Care under the U.S. Medicaid Program
Medicaid is designed as a federal-state partnership. Three criteria must be satisfied to establish eligibility for LTC benefits under Medicaid. First, an applicant must meet federal requirements. Eligibility is established for those who are (1) age 65 or blind or permanently disabled; (2) pregnant women; (3) U.S. citizens or qualifying immigrants; and (4) residents of the state where the application is made. Second, applicants must satisfy a functional eligibility test. Generally, individuals must be unable to perform specified activities of daily living such as bathing, dressing, transferring from chair to bed, toileting, and eating.

Third, applicants must establish financial eligibility which involves evaluations of both income and assets. Eligibility limits vary from state to state, but annual income usually must not exceed $3,000 to qualify for home-based care and lesser amounts for institutional care. Most states allow the "medically needy" – those with large medical or long term care costs – to deduct these costs from their income for the purposes of this test. Assets limits vary from $1,000 to $8,000, but most commonly are $2,000. Home values and the value of an automobile may be excluded from the asset test. Program managers are careful to point out that, because of the first two criteria, poverty alone is not sufficient to establish eligibility.

Special rules apply for transfers of property made prior to the Medicaid application and to property in the estate of recipients at their death. If an applicant or representative gifts assets or sells them for less than fair market value, eligibility may be denied for a period of up to five years. When a recipient dies, Medicaid will seek to recover its costs from the beneficiary's estate. Technical exceptions to both rules apply.

Long Term Care Insurance Policies

Long term care insurance contracts necessarily contain language that both defines and limits coverage. This section explores the key elements of such policies.

Defining Long Term Care   In the past, long term care was synonymous with nursing home care and, for many people, this carried a somewhat negative connotation. Few elderly relished the idea of having to spend their last days in a nursing home. Many more elderly living options are available today that reflect different levels of care need. Today, LTC has taken on a broad meaning and may even carry a positive connotation. For example, one state insurance regulator offered this comprehensive definition:

> *Long term care (LTC) refers to a broad range of supportive medical, personal, and social services needed by people who are unable to meet their basic living needs for an extended period of time because of accident, illness, or frailty. LTC involves receiving the assistance of another person(s) to perform the essential activities of daily living (ADLs) when these tasks can no longer be performed independently. . . . ADL assistance may be provided at home by formal (paid) caregivers, such as home health aids, by informal (unpaid) caregivers, such as family members or friends, or in a nursing home.*

This definition makes clear that LTC is more than nursing home care. It includes home care and community care. Thus, the essential elements of LTC include:

- the need for medical, personal, or social services,
- the need results from an accident, illness, or frailty,
- services are provided by other persons, either paid or unpaid, at home or in an institutional setting, and
- services are to assist the individual in performing the essential ADLs.

As might be expected, the intensity of needed care typically increases with time. By nature, it is stressful and demanding. As such, the responsibility of caring for elderly parents or other relatives can have a significant adverse impact on caregivers and their families and on employee productivity, as stress increases. Recalling our discussion of economics in Chapter 1, LTC typically carries a negative externality – it imposes uncompensated costs on others (in this instance, employers, but also on family caregivers). Employers are increasingly investigating means of helping employees cope with the responsibilities of care giving.

COVERAGE   Most individual LTC policies are underwritten on the basis of an application and attending physician statements. Some insurers also interview the proposed insured by telephone, and some require a paramedical examination. Many companies utilize a single classification for all acceptable applicants, whereas others have preferred, standard, and rated classifications.

Nursing Home Care   Policies often provide for three levels of nursing home care: (1) skilled nursing care, (2) intermediate nursing care, and (3) custodial care. Each of these is described in Box 8-2. The first LTC policies, unlike those today, generally required a medically necessary hospital stay before admission to a nursing home.

Box 8-2
Levels of Nursing Care

Skilled nursing care is the highest level of nursing care and demands the greatest expertise. It is 24-hour care ordered by a physician and provided by a registered nurse, licensed practical nurse, or licensed therapist.

Intermediate nursing care is similar to skilled nursing care except that the patient neither receives nor needs 24-hour attention. Thus, it is effectively non-continuous skilled nursing care.

Custodial care, the most basic level of nursing care, typically takes the form of assistance with the activities of daily living. Individuals providing such non-medical care usually are not medical personnel, although the care must have been ordered by a physician and supervised by a nurse.

Policies pay benefits if the insured cannot perform basic living activities without assistance. Typical policies require that the insured be unable to perform two of five or six ADLs, depending on the policy. LTC policies contain a list of ADLs which typically includes five or six of the following:

- eating,
- bathing,
- dressing,
- toileting,
- continence,
- transferring (e.g., moving from a bed to a chair), and/or
- taking medicine.

Of course, some individuals can physically perform all ADLs yet cannot be left alone safely. Thus, LTC policies also include a *cognitive impairment* clause that permits benefit payments with respect to those who cannot safely perform essential ADLs.

Community Care   Most elderly are happier and healthier when they can maintain as much control over their own affairs and as much independence as possible. LTC policies usually provide benefit payments for insureds who require assistance but who are able to remain in their homes or communities. The benefits, usually stated as a percentage (e.g., 50 percent) of the full nursing home benefit, are available for a variety of programs and services:

- **Home health care** includes skilled nursing care, physical therapy, and related professional services as well as personal services such as assistance with ADLs. Care typically is on a part-time basis and may include payments to family members.
- **Adult day care** provides assistance with ADLs and also allows socialization. It might be available in a LTC facility or a community program facility.
- **Respite care** provides temporary relief for family members providing care in the individual's home by placing the individual in a LTC facility temporarily, such as a weekend, or having someone stay with the individual in his or her home temporarily.
- **Hospice care** involves special care and emotional support for persons diagnosed with terminal illnesses. The care may be provided in a facility or in the person's home.
- **Assisted living facilities** (ALFs) provide supervision, assistance, and limited health services to relatively healthy senior citizens. ALFs provide less medical care than nursing homes. They complement, not substitute for, nursing care.
- Therapeutic devices or equipment that help a person remain in the community are paid for under some policies.
- Modifications to retrofit the insured's home so that he or she can remain there, such as adding a wheelchair ramp.

Continuing care centers (CCCs), also called **life-care centers,** provide a range of sensitive living arrangements and services that reflect each person's level of needed care and assistance. They are an increasingly popular option for those who can afford them. Unfortunately, in many instances, these types of living arrangements are not covered by the LTC policy; rather, individuals purchase the right to live and receive support in the center. The payments typically take the form of an initial, large single amount plus monthly payments reflecting the level of care needed. An advantage of CCCs is that individuals can receive escalating levels of care while not having to move from the community.

BENEFITS   The benefit provisions in LTC policies set forth amounts payable by the insurer if a covered event occurs. These provisions relate to the types and levels of care for which benefits will be provided, any prerequisites for benefit eligibility, and the actual level of benefits payable. No policy covers all LTC expenses.

The policies offered by many companies provide a choice of elimination (waiting) periods before benefits become payable. The elimination period serves as a sort of deductible as it does with disability income insurance. Available elimination periods range from 0 to 365 days. Naturally, the longer the waiting period, the lower the premium, other things being the same.

The buyer is usually offered a choice from a schedule of maximum daily benefits and length of benefit periods. A typical LTC policy might offer the buyer a daily benefit schedule of $40 per day, increasing in $10 increments to a maximum of $250 per day. The schedule of the benefit periods offered might range from two to five years. Some insurers offer a lifetime benefit period, which carries quite high premiums.

Many policies today specify a maximum lifetime approach to defining benefit payments that is a function of the daily benefit and the benefit period. Thus, if the benefit amount is $100 per day and the benefit period is four years, the maximum lifetime payout would be $100 times 365 days times four years, for a total of $146,000. This $146,000 pool of money can be used for covered services in whatever way desired, subject to the daily maximum. In this way, the benefit period can extend beyond four years by using services costing less than $100 per day. Some policies pay a stated monthly benefit, as with disability income insurance. Thus, the policy may agree to pay $5,000 per month regardless of actual charges.

Community based care is less expensive than nursing home care, and it is typically preferred by the elderly themselves who seldom prefer to leave their home permanently. The maximum daily benefit is often 50 percent of the maximum daily benefit for nursing home care. The length of the benefit period is often the same for both coverages, but some policies require a different waiting period.

The majority of LTC policies offer some kind of **inflation protection** for an additional premium, which is designed to ensure that the benefit amount more or less increases with the cost of living. Many companies offer four options: (1) no inflation protection, with the benefit amount remaining at its original level; (2) increasing the original benefit amount by 5 percent or so per year; (3) increasing the benefit amount by 5 percent or so compounded annually; or (4) adjusting the benefit amount annually according to increases in a price index, such as the *Consumer Price Index* in the U.S. The differences in premiums among these options can be substantial, with, for example, the third option requiring a premium of about twice that of a policy with no inflation protection for persons in their 40s and early 50s.

It is increasingly common for contemporary policies to include bed reservation benefits, which continue to pay LTC benefits for a period, such as 21 days, should the insured become hospitalized during a stay in a nursing home or ALF. They also provide for care coordination/management services, caregiver training, coverage for homemaker services, and other miscellaneous benefits.

LTC policies most commonly insure one life, akin to the situation found with life insurance policies. There are also **shared benefit long term care** policies insuring two lives with the total benefit available for one or both lives, akin to a joint life insurance policy. Thus, a three year shared benefit period would provide three years of claims payments for each of two lives or could provide six years of coverage for one life or any other combination. Such policies are said to be about

15 percent more expensive than the purchase of two single-life three year policies, but afford stronger protection against the possibility of catastrophic LTC expenses.

PREMIUMS   LTC premiums are determined by the applicant's age, sex, medical condition and history, and, of course, the benefits provided. Issue ages vary widely by company. Some companies restrict LTC policies to the above-age-40 market. Actuaries remain uncertain about many aspects of LTC insurance pricing as they do not yet have a substantial enough body of experience on which to rely. The issue is further complicated because many LTC policies rely on lapse-supported pricing; that is, those who lapse early subsidize persisting policyholders. Higher persistency endangers profitability.

In the early 2010s, LTC premium rates were increasing rapidly – 10 to 40 percent at some companies. LTC insureds exhibited lower mortality, higher persistency, and unexpected claim rates.[2] The LTC policy is exceptionally complex for both insurer and customer. Information problems abound. As such, care must be taken in pricing and in purchase.

Premiums usually are level, although a few companies utilize increasing premiums based on attained age, either annually or at periodic intervals. As would be expected, annual premiums can differ greatly from one LTC policy to another, depending upon age at issue, waiting period, benefits, and other policy features. Box 8-3 presents representative premium rates for three companies' LTC policies.

OTHER CONTRACT PROVISIONS   In addition to the basic benefit provisions discussed above, LTC policies contain several other provisions that collectively define the quality of the policy. Thus, nearly all LTC policies provide for a waiver of premium, usually after 60, 90, or 180 days of confinement or days of benefits paid. Some companies provide a discount if both spouses purchase a contract.

Box 8-3
Monthly Premium for a Healthy Male, Age 55
90 Day Elimination Period, $200 Daily Benefit, Three Year Benefit Period
Nursing Home, Home Care, Assisted Living, and Community Care Benefits

	Basic Coverage	Comprehensive Coverage
Company A	$76	$214
Company B	183	238
Company C	129	447

Comprehensive Coverage includes Inflation Protection of 3 to 5 percent and nonforfeiture benefits
Source: *Office of Montana Commissioner of Securities and Insurance.*

Virtually all individually issued LTC policies are guaranteed renewable, meaning that the insured has a contractual right to renew the policy to some specified age, such as 79, but that the company retains the right to revise rates on a class basis. Some policies are guaranteed renewable for life. Very few, if any, policies are issued on a noncancelable basis.

Insurers in some U.S. states are required to offer individual LTC policies that contain nonforfeiture benefits. Such policies carry higher premiums than otherwise similar policies not containing such benefits. Typical nonforfeiture options include the right to cease premium payments and take a reduced paid up policy that provides benefits for a shorter period or receive a partial refund of premiums.

All LTC policies contain exclusions and limitations of coverage. Common exclusions include war, self-inflicted injuries, and chemical or alcohol dependency. Policies also exclude coverage for mental illness that is not organically based. In the past, policies did not cover senile dementia, Alzheimer's disease, or Parkinson's disease. Virtually all LTC policies now cover these conditions and all other mental illnesses that can be demonstrated to be organically based.

Most LTC policies restrict coverage of preexisting conditions – sickness that started or an injury that occurred prior to the issuance of the policy. The most common preexisting condition restriction is for six months (some policies use 12 or 24 months), although a few policies have no preexisting condition exclusions.

State Involvement in Long Term Care Insurance

The individual states regulate LTC insurance and most provide for what are termed *LTC partnerships*. As the long term care market developed, the NAIC wrote model legislation that has been adopted in most states. The *Long Term Care Insurance Model Act* specifies minimum standards that products must meet to be considered LTC insurance. The model includes the following major requirements:

- Insurers must summarize the coverages and features of the policy.
- The individual policyowner must have a free look period during which the policy can be canceled and the premiums returned for any reason.
- Waivers denying coverage for specific health conditions are prohibited.
- Insurers may not offer substantially greater benefits for skilled nursing care than for intermediate or custodial care.
- Policies must be guaranteed renewable, although state insurance commissioners may allow cancellation in limited circumstances.

At least 41 states participate in the Long Term Care Partnership Program, a joint federal-state policy initiative to promote the purchase of private long term care insurance. Under these programs, individuals who have purchased approved LTC policies can qualify for Medicaid to help pay their LTC bills once they have exhausted the LTC insurance coverage benefit, without having first to spend down their assets. See Box 8-1. Thus, if Joe's LTC policy provides for $200,000 in total benefits, this amount of his assets would be protected after Joe exhausted the LTC total benefit.

The Limited Demand for Long Term Care Insurance

After an initial period of strong demand and a growing market for LTC insurance in the U.S., demand in this century has flattened, with only slow growth. These observations emerge just as the need for care, cost of care, and aging of the population bring the consequences of the uninsured LTC risk to a nearer term focus. Some have predicted that the LTC market is unlikely to witness meaningful growth unless LTC coverage becomes a widespread employee benefit offering.

Explanations for the limited market penetration have emerged in the economics of both supply and demand. On the supply side, evidence suggests that premiums are perceived to be high relative to benefits and that the available coverage is limited relative to the typical LTC risk. Additionally, several large writers have recently withdrawn for the LTC market, citing higher-than-anticipated claims and fewer lapses. Also, they note the difficulty in securing what they believe to be needed premium increases from the states and the comparatively small LTC market.

Demand may be limited because of an underestimation of the need for coverage and the availability of unpaid family care. It appears that the existence of Medicaid coverage for LTC is also an important explanation for the relative market aversion to LTC insurance. Medicaid is a free public substitute for private health insurance, although not without important limitations, as noted earlier. Finally, as noted above, demand is negatively affected by recent significant price increases secured from and in process by state insurance regulators.

CONCLUSIONS

The probability of an individual becoming disabled or unable to care for him- or herself is greater than the probability of an individual's premature death. Disability income insurance can protect against the financial consequences of an individual's inability to work because of disability, and long term care insurance can protect against similar consequences arising from an individual's inability to perform certain activities of daily living. The cost of disability insurance is a function of the elimination period, the benefit period, and the amount of the stated monthly benefit. The cost of long term care insurance is a function of the elimination period, daily maximum reimbursement or monthly stated benefit, and the benefit period. Underwriting and policy provisions are designed to control moral hazard and adverse selection.

Aging populations represent a large and growing public exposure to these risks. Demand for disability income and long term care insurance is perhaps less than economic analysis would suggest. Thus, the markets for these products represent both opportunities and challenges for insurers and consumers.

ENDNOTES

1 This section draws from Harold D. Skipper and W. Jean Kwon, *Risk Management and Insurance: Perspectives in a Global Economy* (Malden, MA: Blackwell Publishing, 2007), Chapter A5.

2 Ann Tergensen and Leslie Scism, "Long-Term-Care Premiums Soar," *The Wall Street Journal*, October 16, 2010.

PART II

LIFE INSURANCE COMPANY OPERATIONS

CHAPTER 9

LIFE INSURER MANAGEMENT

This chapter begins Part II of the book, a seven-chapter sequence on *Life Insurance Company Operations*. This chapter presents an overview of the different providers of life insurance, their management structure, and the different departmental disciplines typically used to implement management policy. We follow with a description of the life insurance business including its character as a hybrid actuarial-financial intermediary; how insurers make money; a description of their assets and liabilities; and the importance and interrelated nature of risk, capital, and corporate value.

Our main purpose is to provide a framework for understanding life insurer management as an exercise in *risk management*. We close with a discussion of enterprise risk management. These concepts are necessary to understand the trends in financial regulation and reporting discussed in Chapters 12 and 13 and to understand the principles of life insurer capital and financial management discussed in Chapter 14.

LIFE INSURANCE PROVIDERS

Commercial life insurance policies are sold by companies that comply with the corporate formalities and license requirements in their states of domicile. The license is conditional – a failure to comply with the corporate formalities or insurance statutes and regulations can negate the company's right to sell insurance. The principal regulatory requirements dictate financial and operational standards that are designed to promote the solvency of companies and payment of claims to policyowners, an orderly insurance market, and fair conduct in insurance and investment practices.

COMMERCIAL LIFE INSURANCE COMPANIES
A viable life insurer requires both permanence and a high degree of financial security. Corporations and fraternal benefit societies can meet both of these requirements and, under many countries' laws (including those of the U.S.), are the only forms of business organization permitted to offer commercial life insurance to the general public. Thus, from a practical and legal viewpoint, the operation of a life insurance business requires the formation of a corporation. Both stock and mutual insurers sell life insurance. As we will discuss in Chapter 14, the largest source of capital for both stock and mutual insurers is policyowner premium

payments. One of the principal distinctions of stock and mutual insurers are the other sources of capital available to them.

A **stock life insurance company** is a limited liability corporation authorized to sell life insurance and which is owned by and operated for the benefit of shareholders who seek an adequate return on the capital they risk. Stock insurers may have access to capital to grow the business and support business risk through (1) the equity market, (2) a parent company, (3) internal accumulated surplus (profits/retained earnings), and (4) issuance of state-approved surplus notes – which are hybrid promissory notes that regulators allow to be counted as surplus capital or equity.

A **mutual life insurance company** is a limited liability corporation authorized to sell life insurance and which is operated for the benefit of its policyowners who have a quasi-ownership interest in the company. Mutual companies do not issue stock, which means they do not have direct access to the stock market to raise equity capital. Instead, to raise additional funds they must (1) grow it internally through accumulated surplus (profits/retained earnings), (2) form mutual holding companies thereby allowing indirect access to the equity market, (3) issue bonds, commercial paper, or other traditional debt securities, or (4) issue state-approved surplus notes. The substantial capital and large number of insureds required to constitute a viable life insurance company today makes organization of new insurers a difficult task. New stock companies are today generally organized mainly by existing insurers and other large companies, and mutual company formation is generally an historical oddity worldwide.

Of the 868 life insurers domiciled in the U.S. at the end of 2012, some 76 percent were stock companies and 14 percent were mutuals, with the balance being mostly fraternals. Stock companies held 71 percent of life insurance in force and mutuals held 26 percent in 2012. More than 11 percent of all U.S. insurers are foreign-owned (for a total of 99), with Canada (controlling 25 insurers), Switzerland (15), the Netherlands (13), Bermuda (9), and with France, Germany, and the United Kingdom controlling eight each.

Maximization of the value of shareholder equity or corporate value is the overriding objective of stock company management. Mutual insurers seek to maximize their claims paying ability and offer good value insurance. Mutual company policyowners also possess quasi-ownership rights in their insurer and the potential of literal ownership through demutualization, as discussed in Chapter 12. Management of the two company forms differs substantially in some respects, while in others distinctions are unimportant.

New stock life insurers, of which there are few worldwide today, are organized like all commercial companies. Initial shareholders subscribe to stock sales, the required amount of regulatory capital is raised by the subscription, and the company commences operations. To attract investment from capital markets, it is necessary for stock companies to provide competitive, risk-appropriate rates of return to investors.

Mutual life insurers were often organized by prominent citizens in communities where the need for safe, affordable life insurance was perceived to be underserved. Mutual companies were often formed initially as stock companies by organizers who subscribed for the initial shares with an expectation that the insurer would mutualize when it acquired sufficient financial stability, and the subscription capital would be redeemed to the organizers. Organizers were often bankers, lawyers, physicians, and others who expected to earn income by providing services to the new company.

The owner of a participating (par) policy in a mutual company is both a customer and, in a limited sense, an owner of the insurer. The right to vote for members of the board of trustees is the main practical ownership right. A policyowner's quasi-ownership rights expire when the contract terminates by claim, surrender, or lapse. By contrast, the policyowner in a stock company has no ownership rights merely by virtue of being a customer.

The principal historical distinction in insurance products offered by stock and mutual companies was participation by mutual policyowners in insurer operational experience. **Participation** is the retrospective allocation to policyowners of favorable experience that develops when mortality, investment, and expense assumptions used to calculate premiums are more than sufficient to provide policy benefits. Because of the policyowner-beneficial purpose of mutuals, par policyowners participate in the favorable performance of the insurer via receipt of policy dividends. Because of the profit rights of shareholders, policyowners of stock companies historically have not participated in the insurer's favorable experience via policy dividends.

Stock and mutual companies share the same fundamental long term imperative discussed above: the creation of corporate value, whether for the benefit of policyowners or shareholders. They have always competed strategically. Each type company's survival requires competitive products. Historically, their products were quite different but have become increasingly similar. Stock and mutual companies have always issued policies with fixed premiums, surrender rights, and death benefits. Mutual companies sold mostly par policies that featured generally higher premiums than stock companies, but the participation right returned some of the excess premium to policyowners through policy dividends in the event of favorable experience.

Stock companies traditionally sold nonparticipating (nonpar) policies with fixed premiums, surrender values, and death benefits that featured generally lower premiums than mutual company policies but that paid no policy dividends or other nonguaranteed benefit in the event of favorable experience. Favorable experience produced profits that historically were paid only to shareholders in the form of stock dividends. Par policies have often been thought of as safer, while nonpar policies have been thought of as carrying lower premiums because of stock company efficiency. Both mutuals and stocks may offer both par and nonpar policies.

With increasing competition, almost all contemporary cash value life policies feature some performance sharing mechanism, whether offered by stock or mutual insurers. The nonguaranteed elements for par policies remain chiefly in the form of dividends. The nonguaranteed elements for nonpar policies are segregated, often by policy pricing component, the most important of which are excess interest credits.

The life insurance industries in almost all developed countries are consolidating. Within the U.S., the number of stocks and mutuals now number less than

900, down from more than 2,300 in 1987, according to the *American Council of Life Insurers*.

LIFE INSURERS IN CONGLOMERATES

A **holding company** owns the outstanding stock of other companies and usually does not produce goods or services itself. Holding companies are often used as vehicles to combine businesses that exhibit scale and scope economies and diversification benefits. Life insurers may own or be owned by holding companies. Banking or investment companies may be acquired by insurers, and insurers may be acquired by other financial services companies. The largest and most visible U.S. financial services conglomerate was the *Citigroup* banking enterprise, which was composed not only of *Citibank* but also of the *Solomon Brothers/Smith Barney* securities broker and the *Travelers* insurance group. *Citigroup* has since exited the insurance underwriting business, although it remains active in insurance sales.

Financial services companies in general and insurers in particular may also diversify through the acquisition of industrial or service companies, and industrial companies may also acquire insurers and other financial services companies as evidenced by the evolution of *General Electric* into one of the largest financial services providers in the world. *General Electric* has since divested its insurance operations with its spin-off of *Genworth*.

The holding company structure presents special issues in regulation, which are discussed in Chapter 12. The special case of the mutual holding company is discussed below.

OTHER LIFE INSURANCE PROVIDERS

Other forms of insurers also sell life insurance, none of which hold important market shares in the U.S. A **fraternal benefit society** is organized as such under state law and operates under a lodge system that provides social and insurance benefits to members and their dependent families. Fraternals write less than 1.0 percent of the U.S. life insurance market total, but in some geographical areas they are important. Fraternal benefit societies had their genesis in North America around the turn of the last century at a time of significant immigration to the U.S. and Canada. Many ethnic and nationality groups sought means of preserving their cultural heritage and providing modest amounts of life insurance protection as their members assimilated into a new country and new economy. The fraternal benefit system was born in that environment, and many operating societies trace their origins to that time.

About one-half of fraternals are quite small and operate in only one jurisdiction. Larger societies are licensed in several jurisdictions, and the largest operate in all. While the importance of fraternals is declining, *Thrivent Financial for Lutherans* and *Knights of Columbus* are major commercial operations.

Savings bank life insurance (SBLI) is sold over-the-counter or by direct mail in savings bank institutions. In Connecticut, Massachusetts, and New York, savings banks historically had the statutory authority to underwrite and sell life insurance through insurance departments, which represented an exception to the general licensing requirements for insurance companies. These states authorized the sale of life insurance through their state savings banks largely as a result of the

Armstrong Investigation (1905) in New York and ensuing concerns about the high commission cost associated with life insurance offered by commercial companies. The purpose was to provide low cost, commission-free products. All three SBLI funds have been converted into life insurance companies; at least two now sell life insurance in many other states, and all market through agents. The Connecticut and Massachusetts companies are stock insurers while the New York company is a mutual.

In addition to life insurance, many life insurers also offer morbidity-based (health) insurance products. Other organizations also offer these products. The range of providers and products is discussed in Chapters 7 and 8.

CORPORATE MANAGEMENT

The most important features of a corporation are (1) liability for its obligations is restricted to its net corporate assets – if a corporation fails, its shareholders are not responsible for its obligations; (2) it generally enjoys all the commercial rights of a natural person in making, enforcing, and assuming responsibility for the performance of contracts; (3) the duration of its existence is perpetual; and (4) its management authority is centralized. In other jurisdictions, corporations are known by various designations in the language of their domiciles such as *Aktiengesellschaft* (AG) in German, *Societe Anonym* (SA) in French, *Sociedad Anonima* in Spanish, and *Kabushiki Kaisha* in Japanese, but the essential features of limited liability, perpetual duration, the right to contract, and centralized management are functionally the same. In the U.S., management authority vests in the insurer's board of directors (or the equivalent) and is executed through its officers. Responsibility in some countries is shared by an executive board chaired by the chief executive and a non-executive supervisory board where the company chairman presides. In the U.S., the chairman and chief executive offices may be occupied by the same individual.

THE BOARD OF DIRECTORS (TRUSTEES)

In common law jurisdictions, ultimate authority and responsibility for the management of a corporation resides with its board of directors or, in the case of mutual companies, its board of trustees. Unless otherwise noted, we will use *board of directors* to encompass both terms. In an economic sense, directors of stock insurers are agents of the shareholders, and trustees of mutual insurers are agents of the policyowners. (Problems implied by agency relationships were discussed in Chapter 1.) The authority of the board of directors is determined by the statutory law of its sovereign – the state or nation that grants its license – and by the corporation's articles of incorporation and by-laws.

Stock life insurer directors are elected by its shareholders, and mutual insurer trustees are generally elected by company policyowners. In both cases, the democratic nature of board elections is generally more apparent than real, because board composition tends to be perpetuated by existing directors and management. This perpetuation is a result of the typical control of the nominating committee of the board by existing directors and of the proxy system. Individual shareholders rarely vote their own shares, and policyowners rarely vote at all. What voting occurs is via proxies solicited by and transferred to existing board members who then vote large blocks of stock (or policies) in unison. The proxy system often protects incumbent management in mutual insurance companies to an even greater extent. Most mutuals do not automatically mail proxies. Policyowners must specifically request them.

As the nominees to board membership are first proposed by the board's nominating committee, boards tend to reelect themselves or their favored successors. In the case of stock companies, institutions such as pension plans and mutual funds often possess large shareholding and voting rights. There has been a movement toward shareholder activism in recent years whereby these voting aggregations and coalitions may exercise their rights outside the conventional nominating committee/proxy system and, in extreme cases, have led to hostility where attempts were made to remove incumbent management.

Both company employees (management executives) and outside, nonexecutive directors serve. Management directors are most familiar with the company's operations, while outside directors are expected to bring both a broader range of business experience and a level of independence that management directors cannot. Management directors generally do not receive additional compensation for serving on their boards. Outside directors usually earn an annual retainer, additional fees for meetings attended and committee service, and, in some cases, stock grants and other benefits.

Directors establish corporate management policy which is then implemented by the company's officers and other management. Directors also are charged with additional duties both by statute and by common law. Directors owe a fiduciary responsibility to the company that limits any conflict of interest or strictly limits the director's ability to transact business with the company for his or her own benefit or to pursue business opportunities that would be of natural interest to the company.

Directors are required to exercise proper care in the management of the company's affairs. Directors are shielded to a degree for liability arising from *bona fide* business decisions by the business judgment rule that generally protects directors from liability where decisions are based on reasonable care. Disregard for these duties or accusations of disregard can lead to personal liability for individuals serving as directors. Directors' and officers' liability insurance ordinarily is procured by the company to promote board service by qualified individuals.

The most important board committees for the typical life insurer are the executive or management committee, which has direct responsibility for the company's operations, and a finance committee or subcommittee focused on that aspect of operations. The audit committee, which certifies the financial results reported to shareholders and regulators, and the compensation committee, which establishes pay policy for officers and management, also address centrally important management issues. These committees are dominated by outside nonexecutive directors because of the obvious need for independence.

LEVELS OF AUTHORITY AND ORGANIZATIONAL STRUCTURE

Senior corporate officers including the chief executive officer are appointed by the board and charged with implementation of corporate management policies established by the board. Officers are usually full time employees and generally given broad discretion in the exercise of their day to day activities. Responsibility is further delegated from officers to senior and middle managers for day to day operations.

Life insurer organizational structures have changed in response to technological developments, increased competition, and the increasing demand for better customer service. In effect, the traditional hierarchical organization has evolved into a network organization. This organizational concept places less emphasis on hierarchy, while emphasizing task accomplishments and making use of networks of relationships involving employees and outside resources. Strategic alliances and outsourcing communication systems extend beyond the traditional corporate structure. Network organizations by definition are learning organizations in which employees continuously upgrade their knowledge bases and skill sets as part of their ongoing responsibilities to each other.

In a network organization:

- Fewer layers of management are feasible due to the increasing efficiency of the dissemination of information.
- Information efficiency also permits wider spans of control: ease of monitoring allows less direct supervision of employees.
- Small work groups and work teams are organized into strategic business units that focus on specific products or services. Insurers also organize service units for information, investment, and other services that compete with outside service providers.
- Insurers look outside the company for outsourcing, strategic alliances, and external communication systems in business operations.

AGENCY AND CORPORATE GOVERNANCE

The financial crisis of 2008-2009 developed in large part because of inappropriate management of the risks taken by financial institutions. One important risk management failure was insufficient monitoring of the risk associated with mortgages that were issued and securitized with systematic incentives that rewarded the issuers and securtitizers without recognizing the credit quality of the mortgages. Another element was the inadequacy of financial institution capital to reflect these and other risks. Important questions have emerged about management practice that failed to account for these risks. While the financial performance of life insurers during these events was less troublesome than the performance of banks, increased scrutiny of corporate governance prevails across the financial sector. **Corporate governance** is the set of factors that affect the direction, administration, and control of a corporation. An important theme of corporate governance is the nature and extent of accountability of management.

We discuss the related development of enterprise risk management practice below. In Chapter 13, we note new regulatory initiatives in corporate governance. In this section, we explore the central problem of risk and corporate governance, and some of the internal and external mechanisms that affect its control. We explore those that affect the practical discretion and accountability of management, and the results of research into the features of these mechanisms that are related to successful or unsuccessful governance practice.

In Chapter 1, we noted the economic problem of agency. The agent's incentive is to maximize its personal gain, which is not always compatible with simultaneously maximizing the principal's gain. Life insurer owners are principals who engage management as their agent. The personal incentive of management is often to expropriate insurer resources for its benefit, which destroys corporate value. A misalignment of incentives comes from several sources, but particularly from the facts that (1) corporate value is based on the creation of perpetual cash flow, while the relevant time horizon for a manager is only as long as his or her expected employment, and (2) managers' wealth is largely undiversified due to the concentration of their employment and compensation in one company, while owners are able to diversify their wealth across many companies. Thus, short-term, risky business practices can return disproportionately large rewards to management as compared to shareholders.

Expropriation can take the form of excessive compensation, benefits, and perquisites and of shirking behavior. Shareholders and other stakeholders must implement costly monitoring mechanisms to limit this behavior. Monitoring is undertaken for shareholders by the board of directors, auditors, rating agencies, and securities regulators and analysts. Additional monitoring is undertaken by other stakeholders, including the regulators who act on behalf of policyowners, the reinsurers that share risk with the insurer, and the company's agents and brokers who depend on the quality of its financial security and products.

Both internal and external mechanisms can be designed to constrain managers to pursue practices that *are* consistent with the creation of value for owners. Internal mechanisms include an effective board of directors coupled with rational compensation systems and debt and dividend policy. External mechanisms include the market for corporate takeovers, independent analysis by investment firms, and the existence and protection of minority shareholder legal rights.

Research into the internal mechanisms indicates that boards characterized by fewer members, relatively more nonexecutive outside directors, and a nonexecutive chairperson provide more independence, closer monitoring, and decreased incentives to expropriate corporate value. Equity-based compensation systems that pay managers more when their employer's stock prospers are effective, although expropriating behavior can nevertheless arise when management decisions are influenced by the system; as an example, decisions can be made that relate the timing of reported earnings to coincide with the timing of stock option exercise dates in a way that benefits managers. The amount of corporate debt and the need to remain current on its liabilities, as well as the need to satisfy a company's stock dividend policy have also been found to have a disciplinary effect on management practice. In this regard, a life insurer's interest crediting and dividend obligations on its policies are semi-obligatory requirements that constrain managers' discretion.

Active corporate takeover markets have been found to incentivize management to promote value-creating results. A failure to maximize corporate value can lead to the acquisition of companies by others and represents a threat to the job security and compensation of managers. Takeovers are a regular feature of equity markets in the U.S. and the U.K. but less so in other markets. Research also indicates that increased scrutiny and wide coverage by investment security firm analysts can lead to more transparent information in the market, higher value, and lower cost of capital. Finally, evidence suggests that a legal and regulatory environment that promotes the enforcement of minority shareholder rights tends to promote value oriented management practices.

In this section, we review the processes that are necessary to produce the insurer's products. We follow with a discussion of life insurers' departmental functions and ethical responsibilities.

THE PRODUCTION PROCESS

Although financial security is the principal service offered by insurers, benefit payments are the visible output of the insurance production process. The monetary inputs of premiums and investment earnings are combined with service inputs. The output requires five service operations. *Pricing and product design* are intended to ensure that benefits are well suited to policyowners and returns are satisfactory to shareholders. Promised benefits must be coordinated with feasible investment strategies to manage the insurer's asset and liability relationships. See Chapters 10 and 14-16.

Premiums paid by policyowners, together with investment income earned during the period commencing with the payment of premiums and concluding with the payment of claims, represent the raw materials of the benefit product. Premiums reflect the expected value of claims and expenses, as well as a margin or load for expenses and contingencies. The amount of the load reflects the insurer's capital costs, which, as we note below, are indicative of the relative risk assumed by the insurer and retained by the policyowner. See Chapters 14-16.

Distribution is the organized effort to sell policies. Commercial life insurers employ four methods: (1) personal sales by the company's agents; (2) personal sales by other producers who sell the company's products from time to time; (3) direct response sales through internet, mail, telephone, or media discourse; and (4) sales generated by institutional agents such as associations, banks, or other financial intermediaries. See Chapter 10.

Underwriting determines the acceptability of an applicant for insurance. The process determines whether the proposed insured is insurable and, if so, at what premium rate. Poor underwriting compromises the benefit of diversification. See Chapter 11.

Life insurers hold risk capital and reserve capital. **Risk capital** is an unencumbered amount set aside and expected to remain idle but available to pay unexpected claims and benefits, and is necessary to provide confidence to policyowners and their advocates (regulators and rating agencies) that an insurer will remain solvent under reasonably extreme circumstances. **Reserves** (or **reserve capital**) are actuarially determined investment funds dedicated to the payment of future policy benefits.[*] Depending on the context, the calculation of reserves may be based on regulatory statutory accounting principles (SAP reserves), generally accepted accounting principles (GAAP reserves), or best-estimate assumptions (economic reserves). Thus, risk capital (the difference in assets and reserve capital) may also be SAP, GAAP, or economic. The sources of risk and reserve capital are premium payments, retained earnings, and investor debt and equity capital.

A FUNCTIONAL OVERVIEW OF LIFE INSURER MANAGEMENT

---

[*]   In Chapter 14, we make finer distinctions among the types of capital *deployed* by insurers.

Reinsurance and hedging transactions, discussed in Chapter 14, may substitute for reserves and capital.

Investment management of collected premiums and accumulated assets backing reserves are designed to provide sufficient liquidity to pay benefits as they come due and to maximize returns. Consideration is also given to other portfolio constraints based on properties of an insurer's assets and liabilities, as discussed below and in Chapter 14.

Claim settlement procedures complete the promissory commitment of the insurer to the policyowner or beneficiary and are designed to exclude claims that are not a legal obligation of the insurer. The prompt payment of valid claims is the ultimate service provided by insurers. See Chapter 18.

The production process for insurance is distinct, because the inputs are determined *before* the outputs – claims and other benefits – are known. The inherent uncertainty in this method of operation is a source of significant risk and a central problem in life insurer risk management. Effective administration reduces the possibility of unexpected results at the departmental and line of business level and reduces life insurer risk.

DEPARTMENTAL STAFF FUNCTIONS

Life insurers organize themselves around various functions that must be performed by their staffs. We provide a quick summary of each major function.

The *marketing function* identifies the insurer's potential customers, manages the insurer's distribution channels, and assesses the demand for existing or new products. Ineffective marketing is a source of legal and strategic risk to a life insurer. Management of distribution channels is sometimes assigned to a separate but related *agency department*. Marketing is discussed in Chapter 10.

A life insurer's *actuarial function* is charged with analyzing and projecting actual and expected mortality, morbidity, and persistency experience and establishing investment specifications and constraints relative to product pricing. Actuarial staff directly manage or oversee a wide variety of other life insurer activities, such as compliance with financial regulations and financial reporting (with accounting managers). Specific activities are discussed in the actuarial Chapters 15 and 16 and also in Chapters 12 (regulation), 13 (solvency regulation and reporting), and 14 (capital and financial management).

The *investment function* incorporates the mechanics of the insurer's investment portfolio, including investment acquisitions, collection of dividends and interest, and the origination of corporate and real property loans. Investment portfolios are constructed in accordance with risk, return, and timing properties specified through an actuarial determination of both asset and liability requirements. Investment and asset-liability management are discussed below and in Chapter 14.

The *accounting function* collects, records, and reports data about the insurer's financial condition. It prepares financial statements and related reports in accordance with managerial, statutory, tax, and generally accepted accounting principles. Accounting staff must satisfy the requirements of internal and external auditors. Financial reporting is discussed in Chapter 13.

The principal risk management function of the *underwriting department* is to maintain the homogeneity of insureds so as to capture the benefits of diversification, reducing mortality and morbidity risks to predictable average results. Insuring lives that are actuarially underpriced destroys value. The underwriting department also arranges risk reinsurance, discussed in Chapter 11, to promote risk homogeneity and the ability of an insurer to diversify its mortality and morbidity risks. If a particular policy comes under the terms of a reinsurance treaty or if its size or the applicant's health are extraordinary and require a facultative (one-off) reinsurance transaction, regular premium, claim, and other cash flows between the insurer and reinsurer must be tracked.

The *treasury function* tracks the insurer's actual cash flows and accounts. Failures in this respect are a principal source of life insurer operating risk. The *legal function* serves all legal needs required by an insurer internally and/or through outside counsel. Routine compliance filings may be handled through specific departments but ultimately are a legal matter, as are financial reporting requirements, although they are performed primarily as actuarial and accounting concerns. In addition to routine matters, the market conduct litigation risk discussed in Chapter 18 is of particular importance. Life insurers establish compliance procedures specifically to monitor market conduct.

The *human resource function* is responsible for screening, hiring, and training of employees; administers employee benefit plans; and maintains employee records. It forecasts long term personnel needs and administers resignations, retirements, and discharges. Human resource management failures can be a significant source of legal liability.

The *information technology* (IT) *function* develops and maintains the life insurer's information systems and oversees information management throughout the company. Three principal areas of attention are the selection and maintenance of computer related hardware and application software, the maintenance of information databases, and the means to communicate data efficiently throughout the company. IT failures can be a significant source of operating risk.

Life insurers have a legal and ethical responsibility to pay valid claims promptly and to deny invalid claims. The payment of invalid claims raises the cost of insurance and is unfair to non-claiming policyowners. The *claims function* determines that a policy presented for claim was in force, the insured was covered, the death or other covered event occurred, and the policy was not contestable. The claim is paid together with any adjustments for withdrawals, outstanding policy loans, or supplemental benefits and must be made to the appropriate person.

Customer service encompasses a broad range of activities designed to maintain positive relationships with an insurer's existing and potential customers. Customer service employees represent a source of feedback that is indicative of service performance. In addition to premium payment details, customer service functions specific to the life insurance industry include executing policy provisions such as policy loans, change of beneficiary designations, assignment of ownership, dividend options, and investment instructions for variable products

Many life insurers make considerable use of outside resources to implement or supplement managerial practice. Outside advice is sought from law firms, actuarial consulting firms, accounting firms, independent marketing organizations, and management and technology consultants, among others. Outside consultation varies by size of company and depends on the expertise and time constraints of in-house personnel as applied to the required services.

LEGAL AND ETHICAL RESPONSIBILITIES

Life insurers also owe specific (although sometimes inexact and unpredictable) legal duties to their clients. Some are based on general principles of contract law (see Chapter 18) and some on specific policy provisions (see Chapter 5).

In addition, life insurers owe ethical duties to their customers. The *Life Office Management Association* proposes five ethical responsibilities that each insurer owes to its customers. First, insurers should apply underwriting decisions equitably to all applicants. Second, claims should be handled promptly and fairly. Third, customer service should be honest, objective, and fair. Fourth, the privacy and confidentiality of customer information should be preserved in the absence of written authorization from the owner/applicant. (For example, see Chapter 11 for disclosure to the Medical Information Bureau.) Finally, a life insurer should maintain adequate resources to pay claims and honor its obligations under the policies it issues.

FINANCIAL AND ACTUARIAL INTERMEDIATION

Individuals are subject to financial risk when they invest. They are also subject to the financial consequences of actuarial risk: they might die prematurely, become ill or disabled, or outlive their savings. Investors can reduce financial risk through financial intermediaries. Individuals can reduce the actuarial risk of life and health contingencies through life insurance companies.

The simplest example of financial intermediation is seen in banking. A bank pays interest to depositors, then loans the proceeds to credit-worthy borrowers at a somewhat higher interest rate. Interest is collected from borrowers and paid to depositors, and the difference is the **net interest margin**. This spread amount is employed to pay bank expenses and provide a return to its shareholders. Depositors benefit by reducing credit risk. They receive a *pro rata* share of a diversified average return.

The simplest example of actuarial risk intermediation through life insurers is seen in term life insurance (see Chapters 2 and 3). Policyowners pay premiums, contributing a *pro rata* share to the insurance pool for expected losses. Beneficiaries/owners then receive a disproportionate share of the pool in the form of either a comparatively large claim payment or a comparatively small "loss" in the form of premiums paid. Policyowners reduce personal actuarial risk by contributing a small, certain loss (the premium), thereby eliminating the possibility of a large loss. They receive a *pro rata* share of a diversified mortality experience.

LIFE INSURERS AS BOTH ACTUARIAL AND FINANCIAL INTERMEDIARIES

Life insurers are both actuarial *and* financial intermediaries. Financial intermediation was initially a by-product of level premium, cash value life insurance. In its basic form, term life insurance, the original life insurer product, is characterized by a fixed death benefit and increasing premiums as the insured ages. Because of adverse selection, healthy insureds tend to lapse their policies as premiums increase, the less healthy tend to persist, mortality rates rise, and premiums eventually become unaffordable.

The solution to the policyowner's affordability and insurer's adverse selection problems was the level premium policy that uses part of earlier premiums to fund mortality costs at the later ages (see Chapter 2). Lifetime coverage can essentially be acquired through an installment sale, not unlike a home mortgage. Regulators require that policyowners who have paid funds set aside for future mortality costs are entitled to a portion of those funds if their policies are surrendered, in the form of a cash value.

The prefunded mortality cost – the cash value – is the policyowner's economic equivalent of a deposit account. Nonforfeiture laws also require that interest be credited to cash values. In Chapter 13, we discuss the movement in regulation and reporting to explicitly treat cash value policies as a combination of a deposit and insurance contract, which is consistent with these economics.

Life insurers are therefore hybrid intermediaries that accept, diversify, and distribute both financial and actuarial risk. Insurers generate gross profits by adding a margin to mortality costs. They also generate gross profits by earning more on their investments than is credited to customers' cash value "deposits" thus creating a net interest margin just like a bank. Life insurer assets and liabilities are typically longer term than those of a bank and so are much more sensitive to interest rate changes.

The primary advantages of financial and actuarial risk intermediation are (1) risk reduction through *diversification*; (2) *informational efficiency* because individual savers/policyowners need not locate and qualify individual borrowers or others to share risk; (3) *scale efficiency* in reducing the cost of assembling, investing, and distributing funds and actuarial losses; and (4) *social efficiency* through the reduction of commercial and family economic uncertainty and from the direction of investment fund flows to the most suitable sectors of the economy.

While actuarial risk reduction is essential to the mission and existence of life insurers, and the availability and use of life insurance has significant and salutary social welfare benefits, in a profit-making and risk management sense, the actuarial risk intermediation function of the life insurance industry as compared to its financial intermediation function is comparatively small. Financial risk generally is more important than actuarial risk. Because mortality and morbidity risks are largely diversifiable, their contribution to a life insurer's risk is also comparatively small. The intermediation and reduction of risk associated with life contingencies is, nevertheless, the foundation of the industry on which the financial intermediation services are built.

REDEFINING RISK FOR FINANCIAL INTERMEDIARIES

The Capital Asset Pricing Model (CAPM), which we discuss in the appendix to Chapter 14, predicts that the share price of a company should reflect only the risk that does not affect all companies. **Nondiversifiable** or **systematic risk** is that risk applicable to an entire market or class of assets or liabilities. **Diversifiable** or **unsystematic** or **specific risk** is the risk particular to a given company, usually measured by the volatility or variance of its stock performance relative to the performance of the stock market as a whole, called *beta*. CAPM predicts that specific risk can be eliminated by diversification. The real world performance of the stocks of financial intermediaries in general and insurers in particular does not fully reflect the prediction of CAPM that stock price can be explained by the volatility of shares relative to the volatility of the market.

In accordance with these observations, theory predicts that a life insurer's capital structure, in addition to the volatility of its earnings and share price, is an important determinant of value reflected by (1) the covariablity of the insurer's different projects, (2) the marginal contribution of projects to the risk of insolvency, and (3) the possibility of extremely large losses without the possibility of extremely large gains; i.e., negative asymmetries of returns brought about by catastrophic losses due to epidemics, long term mortality trends, and other factors. Stock price is a function of both volatility risk as predicted by CAPM *and* the co-variability of each insurer's projects. Real world observations confirm this theory.

A simple and intuitive example can illustrate the principle of correlation and risk reduction. A life insurer that writes annuities only is subject to underwriting risk because of the possibility that general long-term mortality will improve over time increasing the cost of benefits. An insurer that writes annuities and life insurance, however, will see annuity losses offset by life insurance gains due to the longer lives of both classes of policyowners.

The amount and vulnerability of capital a life insurer holds is the principal concern of its policyowners: the primary source of its capital financing. To offer attractive policies, life insurers must address both volatility and solvency concerns. We discuss these issues in more detail in Chapter 14.

A SHORT HISTORY OF THE LIFE INSURANCE INDUSTRY AND RISK

The life insurance industry was profoundly affected by the unprecedented economic volatility of 1979-1982.[1] These years marked the end of a postwar era in which the industry was driven by a demand for income security and conducted on a near riskless basis (at least in a financial and underwriting sense). A convenient fit of consumer demand to industry advantage subsequently produced life insurer products optimized first for tax-free accumulation with minimum interest guarantees, and then for tax-free accumulation with interest, equity, and withdrawal guarantees. The risk management practice of the industry has evolved through the three periods from risk avoidance to risk transfer to risk assumption and management.

The life insurance industry after World War II was dominated by fixed-premium, fixed-benefit whole life (WL) insurance. Demand was continuously driven by a growing economy and population, and reflected the survivorship capital and income needs of single-income families and the spouses who typically outlived the family breadwinner.

As the postwar economy matured, demand for traditional life insurance products declined. Demographics changed as two-income families became typical and the baby-boom generation grew up. The industry's share of financial intermediation declined from 21.1 percent to 12.1 percent from 1950 through 1980 (*U.S. Federal Reserve*) with its disappeared share going mostly to expanding savings and security vehicles like private pensions and mutual funds.

Through diversification and the law of large numbers, life insurers avoided virtually all financial and underwriting risk:

- Mortality risk was largely eliminated by underwriting a large number of homogenous lives.
- Investment default risk was largely eliminated by the acquisition of a large number of highly rated bonds.
- Liquidity risk (which we discuss below) was largely inconsequential because policyowner demand for loan and surrender withdrawals reflected the large number of issued policies and were highly predictable.
- Asset/liability risk to capital was minimal because interest rates were stable. Duration mismatch was comparatively safe.

Mortality, investment, and asset/liability risks were treated as **silo risks**: each was segregated from the other and each had its own risk management methods. Each department considered risk only to the extent of unexpected results in its own performance, and took little account of results in other areas. There was neither communication nor even a common language for risk communication.

Beginning in 1979, rapid inflation and the deregulation of interest rates in the U.S. caused previously unknown volatility in financial markets. Consumers had paid little attention to the investment efficiency of WL policy cash values. The attraction and availability of double digit annual returns in bonds, certificates of deposits, and a booming 1980s stock market quickly marginalized the industry's staple offering because it caused disintermediation. **Disintermediation** is the withdrawal of funds from a financial intermediary for purposes of investing elsewhere, commonly for a higher expected return. Disintermediation occurred in two ways.

First, attractive alternative investments, dramatically declining mortality costs, and competition in term life insurance further depressed demand for WL insurance and increased demand for policy loans and surrenders. Second, some policyowners discovered the arbitrage opportunity embedded in the mandatory policy loan option. They could borrow on the security of the cash value at a low rate, invest at a higher rate elsewhere, maintain their insurance coverage at the same premium, and the premium itself could be borrowed. Liquidity demands soared, and the industry escaped massive cash flow insolvencies only because most policyowners failed to exercise their rights efficiently. The result was a shift in life insurance product demand from income security and protection to investment accumulation.

The industry responded with a wide variety of product options designed to meet the new investment-oriented demand and to mitigate insurer risk. Insurers enhanced policy performance with current interest-crediting mechanisms that paid competitive yields on policy values, and variable policy accounts whose value was tied directly to the value of a fund specified by the policyowner. The dominant products to emerge were current-interest universal life insurance, variable universal life insurance, and deferred fixed-interest and variable annuities.

However, even as life insurers responded to the demand for competitive savings components in their products, the savings demand was eroding among middle class consumers. Tax-deductible and expense-efficient options in the form of 401(k) and IRA plans, as well as the continuing importance of employer-sponsored plans, were enabled by the government and marketed by competing financial institutions. The statutory plan contribution limits were generous enough to absorb the capacity of most individuals to save.

Tax-preferred savings for high net worth consumers became the industry's growth engine. While premiums are not deductible, premium contributions and the tax benefits of life insurance and annuity savings accumulation are unlimited and prove attractive to consumers who have exhausted their tax-deductible savings options. Life insurance was sold for the purposes of both creating an estate and protecting it from estate taxation depletion. The life insurance savings element was also important due to the policyowner's right to access cash values through tax-free policy loans and withdrawals. At the same time, the sale of annuities through traditional and nontraditional distribution channels – banks and securities brokers – were so successful that, measured by premium receipts and assets, the life and health insurance industry became and remains predominantly an annuity industry.

The increased importance of investment performance demanded increased financial risk and altered insurers' risk management practice. Risk was transferred back to policy-owners in three ways: (1) contractual provisions such as market-determined policy loan rate features transferred the risk of interest rate fluctuations back to the policyowner, mostly eliminating any loan and surrender arbitrage; (2) losses in variable accounts were borne by the policyowner; and (3) insurers offered very conservative interest crediting guarantees while maintaining the flexibility to pay higher competitive market rates as economic conditions dictated. Nevertheless, little communication and still no common risk language were to be found.

Sales were driven by investment accumulation illustrations. The need for competitive returns became essential to life insurer prosperity. Insurers responded to the competitive pressure vigorously, boosting yields on general account products by intentionally mismatching assets (buying high-yield, long-term assets to fund ever shorter-term liabilities) and compromising credit quality.

Some insurers, most visibly *Executive Life*, invested largely in junk (below investment grade) bonds. When the junk market faltered, a "run on the bank" resulted as policyowners rushed to surrender their contracts, and another dimension of liquidity risk emerged. Life insurers had historically been able to satisfy all liquidity requirements through current cash inflows. An insufficient understanding of risk and risk management practice produced an alarming number of life insurer insolvencies: from 1988-1991, 103 life insurers became insolvent (*A. M. Best*). Box 9-1 gives an overview of some of the more prominent life insurer failures.

By the 1990s, the life insurance industry and its regulators became more interested in risk management. Cash-flow scenario testing, asset-adequacy opinions, and risk based capital (RBC) requirements (Chapter 13) were the first attempts to describe and control risk on a comprehensive, company-specific basis. Regulation historically had focused almost exclusively on industry average benchmarks without regard to a company's specific practices.

Box 9-1
Prominent Life Insurer Failures

Each of the following companies failed due to financial mismanagement, mostly as a result of unsuccessful management innovations motivated by the financial distress of 1979-1982. Each has also been the subject of study by regulators, economists, managers, and actuarial and accounting firms as the regulatory and management structure of the industry has evolved.

Executive Life

Executive Life was built by offering superior returns to policyowners. The returns were funded with high-yield, junk bond sales. A principal source was Drexel Burnham Lambert and financier Michael Milken. By 1983, the company had become the largest writer of annuities and one of the top 10 writers of life insurance in the U.S.; it was also a major issuer of guaranteed investment contracts. By 1985, more than 40 percent of the company's assets were invested in junk bonds.

Executive Life experienced catastrophic events in three areas. First, by the late 1980s, the junk bond market had begun to disintegrate, and the company was downgraded by the rating agencies. Its April 1991, financial statements presented a 44 percent capital loss. Second, Michael Milken was indicted for 98 securities law violations, Executive Life was investigated in the same area, and it settled a $30,000,000 law suit. Finally, changes in the tax treatment of annuities severely limited new annuity sales.

Executive Life was subject to exposures in market, credit, and operational risk. The company became the object of prolonged policy surrender runs by concerned policyowners, lacked the liquidity and assets to honor its obligations, and was seized by regulators.

First Capital Holdings Corporation

First Capital, like Executive Life, was heavily invested in junk bonds and developed liquidity problems when the junk bond market soured. Its problems were compounded due to an operational risk exposure: its financial reports.

The company recorded significant asset values in the form of deferred sales charges and the present value of future profits on existing policies. When liquidity demands increased, lapses exceeded assumptions by a considerable margin, and the company's capital was wiped out.

Baldwin United

Baldwin grew rapidly through the sale of single premium deferred annuities from 1977 through 1982. In March of 1982, it completed a major acquisition, but by late 1982 problems began to surface rapidly, and by September 1983 the company was bankrupt.

The source of the company's troubles was a classic case of asset/liability mismatch. Sales had been driven by high crediting rates issued in a high interest rate environment. Some policies credited an initial rate of 14 percent. A policy provision allowed policyowners to surrender policies without penalties if rates fell more than 75 basis points. When rates eventually fell, the company was left in an untenable position as it was forced to maintain a negative interest margin to avoid surrenders, and was seized by regulators.

Monarch Life

Monarch grew rapidly during the 1980s through the sale of variable life insurance to investors. When tax rules changed and the stock market crashed, the company's operations were severely affected. The company turned to a booming real estate market in an effort to recover; the real estate market soon collapsed as well.

By September 1990, the holding company had diverted nearly $165 million from Monarch Life to fund its real estate activities but could not fully repay the cash, which represented more than 110 percent of the insurer's reported capital and surplus. Monarch Life also lost $54 million in investments in affiliated real estate ventures and faced additional risk by acting as a loan guarantor for the holding company's real estate operations. The company was seized by regulators in 1991.

Life insurance and annuity policies have always contained embedded options and guarantees. Guaranteed minimum interest rates and the implicit mortality guarantee in annuitization options are examples. Historically these features were considered incidental, conservatively designed features that would not be material. Disintermediation experienced during the emergence of abnormally high interest rates first brought attention to the problem of options. Product design features discussed above have essentially eliminated the arbitrage opportunity that existed in the fixed policy loan interest provision. Yet, the current extended period of low interest rates is proving the minimum interest rate guarantee more material, and life insurers use increasingly more favorable product guarantees to distinguish their products from other financial companies.

Guaranteed minimum death benefits and living benefits in variable annuities first appeared in the 1990s. Index annuities offer policyowners significant upside potential in equities with downside guarantees. Today, guarantees also include guaranteed minimum income benefits (GMIB), guaranteed minimum withdrawal benefits (GMWB), guaranteed lifetime withdrawal benefits (GLWB), and guaranteed minimum accumulation benefits (GMAB). According to a *Life Insurance Marketing Research Association* (LIMRA) study, 88 percent of variable annuity buyers in 2011 elected a guaranteed living benefit rider.[2]

Unlike publicly traded options, the new guarantees, driven not by liquid markets but by policyowner behavior, are difficult to value and therefore to control. As a result of competitive pressure to guarantee minimum rates, to pay high rates on general account products, and to provide equity-based guarantees on variable products, the financial risk environment for life insurers has changed dramatically. The life insurance business is less about diversifiable life contingency risk assumptions and more about the assumption of option and guarantee risk influenced by the behavior of its policyowners. The guaranteed accumulation of assets now often includes a guarantee against investment losses.

Managers, regulators, and rating agencies have become increasingly aware of the consequences of historical developments such as the liquidity and asset quality crises of the past, the future implications of the new significance of options and guarantees in products, and emerging risks like climate change, epidemics, and long term changes in human mortality.

LIFE INSURER ASSETS AND LIABILITIES

In this section, we present an overview of the U.S. life insurance industry's assets and liabilities. Life insurers' investments are required to be divided between two accounts that differ in the nature of the liabilities for which the assets are being held and invested. An insurer's **general account** supports guaranteed interest-crediting contractual obligations, such as those arising from traditional and many contemporary life insurance policies, including WL and universal life. An insurer's **separate accounts** support liabilities associated with investment pass-through products or lines of business such as variable life insurance, variable annuities, and pension products for which all investment risk is borne by the policyholder. State laws allow assets in separate accounts to be invested without regard to the many restrictions of general account investments, due to their pass-through nature and policyholder control of asset allocations.

ASSETS

The most important asset classes held by life insurers are bonds, mortgages, stocks, and policy loans. Bonds are particularly well suited to funding general account liabilities because of their low default rates and their predictable, regular income features. Bonds achieve their return assumptions with a high probability thus increasing the insurer's probability of achieving its pricing assumptions.

A special class of corporate bond – the private placement – is important to life insurers and corporate borrowers alike. **Private placements**, in contrast to securities traded on public exchanges, involve loans where the terms of an offering are negotiated directly between the borrower and the buyer. Private placements are advantageous to both issuers and the life insurer buyer because (1) legal, accounting, and brokerage commissions associated with public offerings are avoided; (2) the issuer is certain that the entire offering will be acquired; and (3) the terms of the offering are negotiated directly, providing an opportunity for the parties to better define or customize their agreement.

Private placements are less liquid and marketable than public offerings; however, private placements normally pay increased yields to compensate for illiquidity. Liquidity concerns are further eased as an increasingly active secondary market evolves. Life insurers also benefit from negotiating investment terms in a way that helps control asset-liability matching risk. The cash flow properties of private placements can be tailored to meet the needs of both the issuer and the life insurer.

Other asset classes include:

- *Mortgages* and *collateralized mortgage obligations* (CMOs), which pay bond-like fixed income payments.
- *Corporate common* and *preferred stocks*, which feature volatile returns and risk not well suited to safely funding general account insurance liabilities. By contrast, variable contract owners had directed the investment of 80 percent of their assets into stocks.
- *Policy loans,* which are unique among life insurer investments for two reasons. First, they are not made as the result of an investment management decision. They are options exercised at the discretion of the policyowner. Second, because loans should never exceed policy cash values and unpaid principal amounts may be deducted from cash surrender or policy death proceeds, the safety of principal associated with most loans is absolute.
- *Risk management assets,* which are acquired to minimize the asset-liability risk exposure discussed in this chapter. Life insurers often enter into various types of hedging arrangements. **Hedging** is a strategy of acquiring securities whose gains and losses offset losses and gains in other securities or portfolios of securities. Hedging often is achieved through the purchase of derivatives. **Derivatives** are traded securities or contractual agreements whose cash flows depend on the value of other specified securities or indices. As reflected in their book value, derivatives do not constitute a significant asset class. They are essentially instruments of leverage, and a small investment controls a much larger potential cash flow. Their

importance and risks are understated in terms of a portfolio mix based on acquisition value.

Figure 9-1 illustrates the industry asset class mix in 2012.

Figure 9-1   **U.S. Life Insurer Asset Mix, 2012 Percentage**

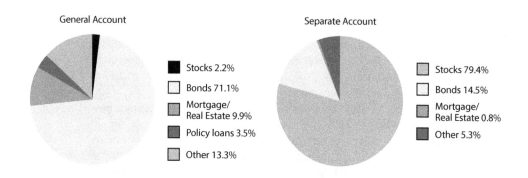

Source: 2013 ALCI Fact Book

LIABILITIES

Life insurer liabilities can be based on actuarial obligations or deposit obligations. Actuarial obligations are based on *mortality* results for life insurance and annuities and *morbidity* results for health insurance. Actuarial obligations are satisfied by the payment of claims. Like bank deposit liabilities, life insurer deposit liabilities are obligations based on funds held by the insurer that are not associated with mortality or morbidity. They may be in the nature of *demand* deposits like life insurance and annuity cash values or funds accumulated under a dividend option. They may also be *time* deposits like guaranteed investment contracts (GICs) that have no prematurity withdrawal right. (Life insurance and annuity account values subject to surrender charges can be considered time deposits with penalties for early withdrawal.) Deposit liabilities are satisfied by the payment of cash at the direction of the policy or account owner.

Most life insurer liabilities are associated with their major product lines:

- term and cash value life insurance,
- accumulating and liquidating annuities,
- medical expense insurance,
- disability income insurance,
- long term care insurance, and
- guaranteed investment contracts.

The estimation of the value of actuarial obligations is discussed in Chapters 11, 15, and 16. The most important risk management practices for actuarial obligations are careful underwriting to select qualified insureds and careful estimation of claim probabilities. These practices allow the insurer to capture the benefits of diversification and predictable claims. Figure 9-2 presents the 2012 U.S. life insurer liability mix for general and separate accounts.

CONSTRUCTING LIABILITY-APPROPRIATE INVESTMENT PORTFOLIOS

The investment portfolio construction process is designed to produce an investment program with cash flow properties that are consistent with an insurer's anticipated liability cash flows, pricing assumptions, and asset-liability risk management strategy. It is a fundamentally important risk management practice. Although the formal process varies from insurer to insurer, three general steps are essential to building a portfolio effectively.

U.S. Life Insurer Liability Mix, 2012 Percentage   Figure 9-2

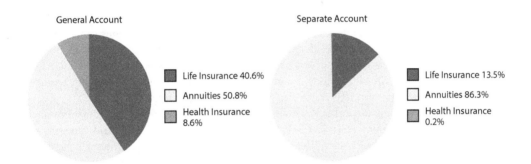

Source: 2013 ALCI Fact Book

First, it is necessary to establish proper control parameters. Selecting an appropriate benchmark reflecting the insurer's solvency and profitability constraints for the planning of the portfolio and the measurement of its success is the first step in portfolio construction. In most situations, a target or desired rate of growth will be established as a control parameter.

Second, portfolio constraints should be established. Certain aspects of the investment portfolio or of insurer operations are necessarily limited. Regulatory constraints are obvious. Less obvious may be the need of insurers operating internationally to invest in different currencies or limitations arising from the expected tax or financial reporting consequences of particular investment decisions. One element of an insurer's level of risk tolerance is established by the degree of variability in investment returns that is acceptable to management. The acceptable potential deviation of actual from expected results is a significant constraint. The objectives of dedicated bond portfolio management techniques are discussed in Chapter 14 and represent additional constraints for the typical life insurer.

Third, it is necessary to monitor and periodically adjust the portfolio. Monitoring the portfolio is accomplished by the periodic examination of two issues, a negative response to either signaling the need for a portfolio readjustment: (1) was actual performance during the measurement period within the distribution of acceptable outcomes and (2) does the distribution of possible future outcomes remain acceptable?

HOW LIFE INSURERS MAKE MONEY

We know that life insurers offer value to policyowners in the form of actuarial and financial intermediation services. Policyowners are thus able to benefit from both (1) actuarial intermediation services by transferring the financial risks of dying too young, living too long, losing the ability to work due to accident or illness, or incurring unexpected medical or care expenses and (2) traditional financial intermediation services of the kind offered by commercial banks, investment banks, mutual funds, and other intermediaries. Insurers make money when premiums, fees, and investment income exceed general expenses and the direct cost of providing actuarial services (i.e., maintaining reserves and paying claims) and the direct cost of providing financial intermediation services (i.e., cash value benefits).

It will be helpful to explain some of the terms used in the discussion below. As discussed above, policy reserves are actuarially determined investment funds dedicated to the payment of future policy benefit liabilities. **Changes in reserves** are the marginal amounts allocated each period to a life insurer's reserve. Depending on the context, the reserve may be *SAP* as required by regulation to maintain legal solvency, *GAAP* based on financial reporting conventions, or *economic*, based on realistic assumptions specific to the insurer's own business.

Surplus capital is the excess of a life insurer's reserves over the amounts of required policy reserves (SAP, GAAP, or economic) and RBC, and generally represents owners' equity. The **contribution to surplus** is the amount contributed each period to surplus capital after claims, expenses, and any required increase in reserves and RBC is satisfied.

To the extent an insurer's premium, investment, and fee income exceeds its claims, expenses, and reserve requirements, it can generally be said to make a profit. (Depending on the context again, profit can be SAP, GAAP, or economic.) Some profit is usually added to surplus to enhance the insurer's financial security, and the remainder is available to pay dividends to shareholders (or policyowners of participating products). The following means of viewing profit is stylized for the purpose of narrative convenience but generally follows the conceptual models required by state regulators and the U.S. federal income tax code. There is further discussion in Chapter 13.

Periodic Profit Statement
+ Premiums
+ Interest, Dividends, Rents, and Other Investment Income
+ Fees
- Claims
- Expenses
- Increase in Reserves
= Profit
- Contribution to Surplus (retained earnings)
= Distributable funds available to pay shareholder or policyowner dividends

At a given point in time, the net worth of an insurer is the following residual value:

Insurer Net Worth Statement
Total existing assets
+ Present value of future premiums
- Present value of liabilities
= Surplus (Net Worth or Owner's Equity)

A life insurer's measure of its periodic creation of corporate value is the sum of its contribution to surplus and its distributed profit. One measure of its social welfare value is savings and capital formation represented by its aggregate reserves and surplus capital.

We can consider that each of the functional areas discussed above exist to manage an insurer's risk. Indeed, risk management lies at the core of all insurance operations, for life insurers' principal purpose is to accept and redistribute the financial risks of life and health from their customers. Risk management originally referred to the identification, treatment, and alternative financing of mostly insurable risks. With the emerging importance of policyowner options, derivatives, and hedging strategies in the 1980s, it came to incorporate financial risk as well and evolved into what we today refer to as enterprise risk management (ERM).

Enterprise risk management comprises a range of processes and techniques designed to protect and create value by helping companies uncover all hidden risks, improve the stability of earnings, identify opportunities in assuming risk and risk arbitrage, and discovering natural synergies across business lines. The most important reason for the adoption of ERM, however, is the practical necessity of assuring stakeholders that the firm is aware of and managing its risks effectively. When effective, the transparency should reduce agency costs. Insurance and securities regulators, policyowners and rating agencies, shareholders and analysts, and managers themselves all have a significant interest in managing risk. Indeed, ERM is increasingly required in corporate governance and culture. In this section, we introduce an ERM framework for insurers and explore the risks they face, why risk management is important to them, and why risk and its management differ from that of non-financial companies. When successful, ERM identifies the mechanisms by which risk destroys value and how intervention can protect and restore value.

AN ENTERPRISE RISK MANAGEMENT FRAMEWORK FOR INSURERS

The *International Association of Insurance Supervisors* (IAIS) adopted a standard for the elements of effective ERM for insurance organizations. It calls for the incorporation of a framework into an insurer's governance at the board of directors' level and provides for the use of economic capital and stochastic financial analysis, important contemporary risk measurement and management tools discussed in Chapter 14. It identifies five key elements:

1. *Risk Identification and Measurement.* The framework should quantify a range of outcomes sufficient to adequately manage capital and solvency, documented to provide detailed descriptions of risks.

2. *Risk Management Policy.* The framework should include a policy that outlines the way in which the insurer manages each category of risk, both strategically and operationally. It should describe the linkages with the insurer's tolerance limits, regulatory capital requirements, economic capital, and the processes and methods for monitoring risk.

3. *Risk Tolerance Statement.* The insurer should establish and maintain a risk tolerance statement which sets out its overall quantitative and qualitative tolerance levels and defines tolerance limits, taking into account the correlation of risk categories. The risk tolerance limits should be embedded in the insurer's ongoing operations via its risk management policies and procedures.

4. *Risk Responsiveness and Feedback Loop.* The ERM framework should incorporate a feedback loop, based on appropriate information, management processes, and objective assessment to enable the insurer to respond to changes in its risk profile.

5. *Own Risk Solvency Assessments.* The board should determine the capital and other financial resources required to satisfy its regulatory obligations. It should incorporate an analysis of its medium and long term strategy and quantitative projections of its future financial condition.

RISKS FACED BY LIFE INSURERS

Life insurers are subject to a wide range of risks, many associated with their own internal operations, which we term **component risks**, with many others stemming from external social, competitive, and economic factors. Their overall or firm level risk is *not* the sum of component risks, because component risks are not perfectly correlated. Total risk is less than the sum of the diversified risk components.

It was the insight of H. M. Markowitz's portfolio theory that the risk of an individual investment, measured by the variance of its returns around its expected return, is relevant only when its variance is considered in conjunction with the covariance it exhibits to other assets in the investor's portfolio. (See the appendix to Chapter 14.) Only the asset's integrated contribution to portfolio risk is relevant. Similarly, when a life insurer executes a transaction – issuing a policy, buying a bond, acquiring another insurer – the component risk should be relevant only when its contribution to *firm* risk is considered, taking account of its correlation to other component risks and external factors.

Some component risks are common to all commercial firms; others, like some aspects of liquidity risk, are specific to financial intermediaries. Others, such as underwriting risk, are specific to all insurers, while still others, such as mortality and morbidity risk, are specific only to life insurers. A comprehensive means of classifying risk contributes to effective management by establishing a way of thinking about risk in a diversified, firm-level context.

The risk classification system devised and used by actuaries classifies risks into four *contingency* categories: **C-1** or **asset risk**, arising from defaults and changes in market values of investments; **C-2** or **pricing risk**, arising from inadequate risk and expense charges; **C-3** or **non-market interest rate risk**, arising from the correlation of asset and liability cash flows; and **C-4** or **miscellaneous business risks** that are not easily amenable to actuarial prediction. This classification system continues to be used by insurers and their regulators, but a broader classification system is coming into use for both financial and non-financial firms.

The international banking accords of the *Basel Committee on Banking Supervision* have been influential in bringing risk management to the forefront in banking, and its influence has spread to the insurance industry and risk management generally. The *International Actuarial Association/Association Actuarielle Internationale* adopted the broad categories specified by the Basel Committee: *market, credit, liquidity,* and *operational*. It adds an *underwriting* risk category for insurer purposes.

- **Underwriting risk** results from inadequate pricing arising from assumptions made with respect to claims and expenses and to policyowner behavior such as persistency and loan activity.
- **Market risk** results from volatile values and uncertainty in financial markets that can affect expected cash flows. For life insurers, its importance is generally relevant in its relationship to the value of liabilities (the asset-liability reflection of market risk discussed below).
- **Credit risk** results from the possibility that obligations due a life insurer may not be paid as due. The most important risks are bond default and reinsurer insolvency.
- **Liquidity risk** results primarily because policyowners and borrowers may make unexpected payments or withdrawals in response to changing interest rates; although more predictable, mortality and morbidity claims can also give rise to liquidity risk.
- **Operational risk** results from an internal or external failure of people, processes, or systems to function as intended.

Additionally, these fundamental risks are often decomposed into subcategories. It is important to note that we use such categorizations for convenience, but they are only informally related to the phenomena they describe. Different terms may apply to the same risks and definitions vary in usage. The risks and their interactions exist apart from the labels we apply, which is precisely the point of the ERM principle of looking beyond silo risk.

SPECIAL RISKS IN FINANCIAL INTERMEDIATION
In this section, we explore the special importance of capital and risk to financial intermediaries generally and to life insurers specifically. The relationship of risk to reward is known in all companies, and competition makes it compulsory.

LEVERAGE RISK   The nature of issuing life insurance policies causes the typical life insurer to finance its activities with extraordinary ratios of debt to equity as compared to non-financial firms and exposes them to special risks of financial intermediation. Life insurers place heavy reliance on debt financing for three reasons. First, life insurers are necessarily financed largely with customer liabilities in the form of policy reserves, a form of debt. The deposit-taking function and the discounting of risk charges for interest earned are essential to the cash value product form. Second, the tax treatment of financing costs reduces the relative cost of debt financing in the U.S. because interest credited to depositors' reserves and paid to bondholders is tax deductible, while stock dividends are not deductible.

Finally, the complexity of life insurer operations amplifies agency and information costs (see Chapter 1) of equity relative to debt and affects the time needed to arrange new equity financing under exigent circumstances. The nature and degree of debt financing has important implications for life insurer risk management, as we discuss next.

ASSET-LIABILITY RISK   Life insurers face investment risks associated with their assets and actuarial risks associated with their liabilities. They also are exposed to risk because of the systematic relationship of their assets and liabilities. Features of market risk affecting assets include:

- interest rate risk,
- credit risk, and
- equity market risk.

Underwriting risks include those related to:

- mortality,
- morbidity,
- longevity,
- catastrophes, and
- policyowner behavior such as policy borrowing or surrenders and premium payments or suspensions.

Asset-liability risk (ALR) arises because the same external factors can affect the value of assets and liabilities simultaneously and disproportionately. The most important of these factors is a change in market interest rates. **Intermediation** is the process of policyowners making payments to an insurer for investment. Payments may be premiums, policy loan interest payments, or policy loan repayments. **Disintermediation** occurs when policyowners exercise options to withdraw funds (surrenders, withdrawals, and loans) or reduce or suspend premium payments to invest these funds elsewhere. Unexpected disintermediation or intermediation develops when interest rates change unexpectedly, giving rise to the liquidity and reinvestment components of ALR.

Liquidity Risk   Liquidity risk due to disintermediation is associated with increases in interest rates that encourage policyowners to surrender polices, make withdrawals, or make policy loans to take advantage of other investment opportunities, thus increasing the insurer's cash outflows. Interest rate increases also affect the asset side of the balance sheet as bond holders and mortgagees delay the repayment of their loans as long as possible to take advantage of other investment opportunities, thus decreasing cash inflows. Insurers are forced to provide liquidity when net cash flow is down, potentially forcing them to sell fixed income assets to satisfy liquidity demands at the very time that the value of those investments has diminished due to the higher interest rates.

To illustrate elements of the above overview, consider how a life insurer's surplus capital is affected when asset values and liability values are determined in a net present value format, as follows:

$$PV\ (Assets) - PV\ (Liabilities) = Surplus\ Capital$$

Surplus capital is important in insurer risk management as a shock absorber for the financial consequences of unexpected events. Thus, the higher the level, other things being the same, the more secure are the insurer's promises to policyowners. It represents the shareholders' assurance to policyowners that the insurer will not default. However, policyowners must pay for the costs the insurer incurs to hold this excess capital – called *capital costs* – which in turn is driven by the return on capital required by investors. Simply put, more capital means higher premiums, as we explore in detail in Chapter 14.

The value of surplus capital is highly dependent on the discount rate employed, and the use of a single rate fails to reflect the reality that rates fluctuate, so we require a more robust approach. Duration offers one. **Duration** is the weighted average time to maturity of the cash flows of a fixed income asset or liability or portfolio of fixed income assets or liabilities, which we present more fully in the appendix to Chapter 14 for those who may need a refresher. When assets and liabilities are not matched in duration, they exhibit different sensitivities to changing interest rates. Long term asset values are typically impacted more than liabilities.

Consider an insurer whose present value of assets (PVA) is 110,000,000 and present value of liabilities (PVL) is 100,000,000, with an interest assumption of 4.0 percent and an average duration of eight years for liabilities (L) and 14 years for assets (A). Insurer assets are typically of longer duration than liabilities to take advantage of the higher yields associated with longer assets. The result is a duration mismatch. The resulting balance sheet is:

Assets	110,000,000
Liabilities	100,000,000
Net Surplus Capital	10,000,000
Ratio: A/L	110%

The A/L ratio is a measure of an insurer's financial strength; the higher the better. Of course, the 4.0 percent interest assumption is arbitrary. Actual interest earned will almost certainly be more or less, and any deviation produces a different capital result. Suppose the actual market interest rate environment moves to 5.0 percent. Because A and L have different durations, the reinvestment of cash flows at the unanticipated 5.0 percent interest rate will cause a deviation in results that produces a non-proportional impact to assets and liabilities and a dramatic deviation in the insurer's actual surplus capital and A/L ratio.

	4% Assumption	5% Reality*
Assets	110,000,000	96,207,571
Liabilities	100,000,000	92,630,140
Surplus Capital	10,000,000	3,577,431
Ratio: A/L	110%	103.9%

This liquidity risk is potentially significant. Indeed, under these assumptions, if the market interest rate environment moves to 5.67 percent or higher the insurer would become insolvent.

Liquidity Risk and Policyowner Behavior   As discussed in Chapter 5, life insurance policies offer options and guarantees in favor of the policyowner. Borrowers

---

*   The 4.0 percent present asset value of 110,000,000 is accumulated 14 periods at 4.0 percent and discounted 14 periods at 5.0 percent. The same method is applied to liabilities for eight periods.

also have options, although they are more predictable in the case of public market bonds. Predicting the behavior of liability option values in a life insurance policy context where no liquid market exists to observe market values is very difficult. It is further complicated by the simultaneous impact external factors such as interest rates have on both assets and liabilities. Their values are highly dependent on policyowner behavior relative to premium payments and surrenders and borrower behavior relative to loan prepayments.

Consider a company that issues a product that pays a contractual sum of 10,000,000 in 10 years. For simplification, we assume a certain sum both in amount and timing with no mortality element. A bullet GIC possesses these liability properties (see Chapter 6). We use this example to focus on customer behavior relative to the deposit function of life insurers.

The insurer invests the amount paid for the GIC in 10,000 zero coupon bonds purchased at 4.0 percent with a total maturity value of 10,000,000 in 10 years. The capital reduction found above is avoided because the company's assets and liabilities in this segmented portfolio are *duration matched*. The capital risk of the asset-liability component risk is controlled. Thus, even a dramatic move from an assumed 4.0 percent rate to an actual rate of 10 percent, as experienced during the 1970s and 80s, produces no net impact on the following year's balance sheet:

	4% Assumption	10% Reality
Assets	10,000,000	9,087,416
Liabilities	10,000,000	9,087,416
Surplus Capital	0	0

The same result would apply to *any* interest rate scenario. Life insurers are generally unable to match assets and liabilities so precisely. Competition compels them to seek higher returns through intentionally mismatching assets and liabilities. However, even in this example, the apparent immunity to a reduction in surplus capital under both scenarios is misleading if the contract owner has a right to terminate the contract prior its maturity.

In reality, bullet GICs generally do not possess such rights, but, for illustrative purposes, we assume that the policyowner has a right to withdraw based on a conservative 3.0 percent regulatory surrender right assumption. If interest rates move to 12%, the company faces a cash flow insufficiency and incurs a capital loss if the withdrawal option is exercised in year five. Bonds, while sufficient to pay the contractual amount at year 10, have dropped in market value at year five:

Source of Funds:	
Year Five Market Value Sale of Bonds	
(PV of 10,000,000 @ 10%)	5,674,287
Less: Use of Funds	
Year Five Contract Owner Withdrawal Payments	
(PV of 10,000,000 @ 3%)	8,626,088
Net Cash Flow	(2,951,801)

This cash flow insufficiency would require cash from other sources within the insurer and would also reduce the insurer's reported surplus. If the company were in financial distress, it may have to raise additional funds from external sources, such as equity. When policyowner behavior changes, capital and liquidity requirements are not accurately measured by a static determination of capital.

Dynamic financial analysis (DFA), as discussed in Chapter 14, accounts for the behavioral response of policyowners and borrowers to changing interest rates.

Reinvestment Risk and Policyholder Behavior   A related problem arises when interest rates fall. **Reinvestment risk** exists because policyowners will repay loans and increase flexible premiums when interest rates fall because the weighted investment portfolio of the insurer typically pays higher rates than they otherwise would earn. Similarly, bond issuers and mortgagees will repay their loans to refinance at lower rates. As a result, the insurer receives substantial cash inflows at precisely the time its investment opportunities are at low rates, and it may be unable to meet its product pricing assumptions.

Indeed, several major insolvencies in the 1980s and early 1990s occurred despite solid *appearing* statutory financial condition and high credit ratings, as alluded to earlier. Managers, regulators, rating agencies, and accountants failed to take proper account of the special aspects of interest rate risk attributable to deposits and the financial intermediation function; i.e., their asset-liability management was faulty. **Asset-liability risk management** (ALRM) is the process of preserving or enhancing a life insurer's surplus capital position as asset and liability values change in response to changing economic conditions and customer behavior.

Conclusions

Life insurers are typically large corporations that are amenable to general management practice in many areas. However, life insurers differ from most other commercial organizations because they are actuarial *and* financial intermediaries. They face special mortality and morbidity risks as actuarial intermediaries, and special credit, liquidity, and asset-liability risks as financial intermediaries. Because the values of their assets and liabilities are related to each other and to general economic conditions and must be managed concurrently, the holistic approach to risk embodied in enterprise risk management principles is particularly well suited to the industry.

Endnotes

1   This section draws on Narayan Shankar "A Strategic Analysis of the U.S. Life Insurance Industry," Parts I-IV, *The Actuary* (2005) and Kenneth M. Wright, "The Structure, Conduct, and Regulation of the Life Insurance Industry," in *The Financial Condition and Regulation of Insurance Companies,* Richard W. Kopcke and Richard E. Randall, Editors (Federal Reserve Bank of Boston) 1991.

2   "LIMRA Study: Guaranteed Living Benefit Riders Remain Popular With Variable Annuity Buyers," *Targeted News Services,* June 1, 2010.

CHAPTER 10

LIFE INSURANCE MARKETING

The term **marketing** is commonly used to encompass those activities of firms that are involved with the sales and distribution of products or services. The objective of marketing is to offer products that are well suited to the needs of consumers through effective, appropriate distribution channels at prices acceptable to both the seller and the buyer. While the typical person might think of marketing more in the context of attempts to enhance consumer perceptions of and desire for a firm's products or services, such promotion is the end stage of a more comprehensive process. For life insurance companies, that process involves decisions relating to the following:

- Development and maintenance of a marketing program,
- Product origination and development,
- Distribution,
- Compensation, and
- Promotion.

Different products require a different emphasis in each area. The application of these areas to a specific product and the relative emphasis attached to each is called a **marketing mix**. The successful insurer's marketing program is the effective aggregation and coordination of these elements. We cover each of these elements below, along with separate discussions on the international dimensions of life insurance marketing and on the future of life insurance marketing.

Life insurers sell mortality protection (life insurance), morbidity protection (health insurance), and longevity protection (annuity) products. The marketing of medical expense insurance is similar to the marketing of other indemnity insurance products like automobile or homeowner's insurance. The marketing of deferred annuities is similar to the marketing of other investment products like mutual funds. The marketing of the products most closely associated with human life contingencies – life insurance, life annuities, and disability income insurance – is driven by factors that are unlike those of any other products.

These are products of which it is said they are not *bought* but *sold*, as consumers rarely seek to acquire them. The lack of active consumer demand can be attributed to many factors. Perhaps the most important include the reluctance of individuals to confront their own mortality and physical frailty, the complexity and intangible nature of the product purchase decision compounded by information problems, and, in the case of life insurance, the fact that the individual who makes the purchase decision will not realize the financial reward of the death benefit.

As a result of consumer reticence, both life insurers and consumers rely heavily for advice on agents and brokers – collectively commonly referred to as *producers*. A life insurer's marketing strategy is closely bound up in its relations with its agents and brokers. Studies have indicated that consumers generally have negative perceptions of insurance producers, yet their opinion of the particular producers with whom they have chosen to work is much more favorable. The challenge for the life insurer is to find a marketing mix consistent with helping producers create trusted advisory relationships with customers, or by exploiting sales methods that bypass the traditional producer sales model through direct marketing methods or establishing relationships with financial institutions like banks or mutual fund companies.

THE MARKETING PROGRAM

A **marketing program** is a tactical plan that deals primarily with the product, price, distribution, and promotion strategies that a company will follow to reach its target markets and to satisfy their needs. The development and maintenance of a realistic marketing program is the primary responsibility of senior marketing executives. The elements of a marketing program include an analysis of the markets available to or desired by the insurer, identification of the nature of the perceived competition, and determination of the distribution techniques to be used. The plan must also include the design of a sales compensation system, a basic pricing strategy, and the special administrative systems and support needed by particular market segments or products. The marketing plan is then utilized to develop a product portfolio and project future production by product and amount.

Once the insurer's marketing program is initially documented, management evaluates its growth and profit goals and the capabilities and core competencies of the home office and marketing operations. The plan should reflect a realistic assessment of the company's strengths and weaknesses in relation to factors considered critical to the its success. This assessment leads to broad or narrow product portfolios, different distribution channel structures and geographic concentrations, and so on; that is, the search for a competitive advantage.

The results of this planning and development activity will be a quantification of what the company wants to achieve, reflecting a balance between long-term and short-term goals. With priorities established, specific goals set down, and a product portfolio established, the stage is set for selecting and utilizing one or more distribution channels to deliver products to the markets selected. Typically, however, the distribution channel comes first, and the tentative decisions regarding distribution significantly influence the process of developing a product portfolio. Below we discuss two elements that are especially critical to the success of a marketing program: (1) market segmentation and (2) the competition.

MARKET SEGMENTATION

As discussed in Chapter 1, rational consumers seek to maximize their lifetime utilities. The purchase of life insurance involves the conscious decision to defer current consumption for the purpose of addressing longer-term needs. An effective life insurance marketing program begins with an understanding of the factors that influence consumers to sacrifice current consumption and to purchase a particular product. Of course, these factors can be innumerable, but the very nature of the life insurance purchase dictates that certain factors or market characteristics are likely to be important in all market segments.

The most important of these ordinarily are wealth, age, gender, and family status, each of which arguably is highly correlated to the utility of any life insurance purchaser. When considered in light of other characteristics, these groups can be further differentiated: a 25-year-old couple with children will view a life insurance purchase more akin to a 40-year-old couple with young children than another 25-year-old couple with no children or child rearing plans.

Market segmentation is the process of identifying sub-markets with relatively homogenous product or marketing needs from a larger, more heterogeneous market. A focused product and marketing mix directed to a market segment's particular needs is generally more productive than an attempt to offer all things to all consumers. Ultimately, the life insurer addresses a specific marketing mix to a specific market segment to maximize the probability of purchase by consumers represented by that segment. Four sources of homogeneity can form the basis of effective market segmentation.

Geographic segments refer to the physical location of potential customers within that segment and may vary both by size and growth rates. Rural and urban areas generally demand different marketing mixes. Life insurers often target market segments by country, region, state, and postal codes. Geographic segments in the U.S. reflect differing life insurance needs due to differing populations: examples include the relatively large number of farming families in the midwest and retirees in Florida.

Demographic segmentation identifies consumers whose purchase behavior can be distinguished by similar demographic factors, including

- age,
- gender,
- marital status,
- education,
- financial situation,
- occupation, and
- life cycle status.

Psychographic or *lifestyle segmentation* is the process of identifying consumers with similar demographic characteristics who exhibit dissimilar purchase behavior based on their needs, attitudes, motives, and perceptions. These personality or lifestyle distinctions are revealed through their activities, interests, and opinions. This process has its origins in Abraham Maslow's hierarchy of needs.

Behavioristic segmentation segregates potential purchasers by the benefits that particular consumers seek. The same whole life insurance policy, for example, may provide different benefits to working families and to business purchasers. Consumers with similar demographic and psychographic profiles may also be distinguished by:

- Usage rate – the inclination to buy or not based on past behavior.
- Buyer readiness – the state of a purchaser's information regarding both needs and available products.
- Preferred distribution channel – the consumer's preference for dealing in an agent, direct response, or institutional sales context.

THE COMPETITION

Often, the most important long-term external consideration in developing and maintaining a marketing program is the competition. The program must offer some advantage in that it either serves an underserved market segment or captures and better serves some profitable portion of an existing market. Competition in the life insurance industry comes from other insurers and other financial institutions, and can have a significant impact on the marketing program.

Insurers compete for agents and brokers and offer price, product, underwriting, and/or policyowner service features that distinguish them from their competitors. If it is to remain competitive, an insurer ordinarily must respond to the introduction of innovative products by competitors when the insurer's position is threatened. It is equally important that the insurer anticipate the response of competitors to its own product introduction or innovation.

Finally, the competitive environment evolves. It is not sufficient to better the contemporary competition. It is essential that a product's position is defensible so that its profitability will persist when the behavior of the competition changes.

LIFE INSURANCE PRODUCT DEVELOPMENT

Products are created to facilitate the achievement of an insurer's goals, and the product line should reflect the company's character, culture, and long-range strategic plans. Obviously, the insurer's goals should be built around its perception of the needs of its customers. In addition, products must be designed and developed with concern for the needs of the marketing personnel, shareholders, and the public.

Product development is a continuous process. It includes the evolution of an idea, its refinement, and ultimately its implementation through a marketable product. Even then, the process is incomplete until the actual experience in marketing and managing the product has been reviewed and analyzed so that any necessary modifications can be made in a timely manner. The product development process includes both product design and product implementation.

PRODUCT DESIGN

Product design includes the generation and evaluation of a product idea, the clarification of the idea, and the assessment of its marketability. It requires an evaluation of the insurer's operating environment and screening of product ideas.

THE ENVIRONMENT   The product development process begins with an evaluation of an insurer's operating environment, both internal and external. The most important external environmental factors are *inflation,* the *business cycle, regulatory constraints, capital markets,* and *competition.*

During what might be termed normal inflationary times, consumer demand for life insurance usually increases as existing fixed-dollar coverages become inadequate and new coverage becomes more compelling for new consumers. The opposite is true for hyper-inflation as has occurred in some markets internationally. Variable insurance products, as well as complementary equity products such as mutual funds, are also usually more attractive to consumers when earnings and general prices are increasing.

The business cycle (the periodic expansion and contraction of a national economy) also affects demand for life insurance. Consumers generally have more discretionary income and assets as well as more comfort with a commitment to regular premium payments when economic times are prosperous.

The development of a life insurance product is feasible only when an insurer has the legal authority to do business in the geographic region contemplated, and its contractual provisions and sales practices conform to the statutes of the applicable regulatory authority. In the U.S., variable products also require conformity with both federal and state securities laws regarding the structure of the offering, disclosure of the material terms of the offering, and agent licensing.

In addition, critically important regulatory considerations in product development are the *de jure* mandate of insurer solvency. In the interest of maintaining solvency, life insurers are required to post minimum reserves based on each insurance contract's benefits and to maintain minimum levels of capital. Thus, a base minimum amount of premium is needed if premiums are to be sufficient to pay current benefits and to post the reserves required to secure future benefits, while maintaining adequate capital levels. As shareholder returns decrease with increasing capital, there is a practical maximum amount of capital that can be allocated to a product.

These twin financial mandates of solvency and profitability essentially dictate the minimum amount of capital that must be and the maximum amount that may be allocated to the development of a product. Capital is a limited resource, and the projected capital requirements and implicit returns of different products under consideration are fundamental threshold requirements for commitment to a new product. The impact on capital of product design and pricing are discussed in Chapter 14.

The insurer's internal environment and capabilities also must be consistent with the successful development of a product, both during its development and over the course of continuing sales and administration of issued business. If internal resources are inadequate in a given discipline or function, outsourcing should be considered.

SCREENING   Life insurance product ideas originate with management, actuaries, and distributors as well as from competitors' products. Ideas are screened initially to identify products that are feasible, likely to succeed, and consistent with the insurer's strategic plan, marketing strategy, and capital management constraints. Market size is important in this process. It reflects two complementary and somewhat counterintuitive concepts: (1) as market size increases, a small or decreasing share of larger target markets can be consistent with corporate objectives, and (2) a large and increasing share of smaller target markets may not be consistent with corporate objectives. Estimates of appropriate market size and share are designed to identify the economic feasibility of a product and its contribution to corporate value.

The distribution synergy of the product relative to the insurer's existing channels is evaluated during this phase as well. Products that are deliverable through existing channels to existing customers are most efficient. New distribution channels and new customers require larger scale investment of resources and may require the creation or acquisition of new distribution means or a joint venture strategy with nonproprietary distribution partners. A product's net income must reflect any new investment in distribution.

Product Implementation

Product implementation includes the final determination of rates, values, and other policy elements; the design of policy and application forms; the filing of these forms with regulatory authorities; the creation of supporting marketing materials and administrative systems that facilitate effective distribution and administration of the product; and the actual introduction of the product. The introduction and implementation of a new product requires the coordinated preparation across all functional processes of the insurer.

Final pricing determinations, investment policies, reserve compliance, and profitability goals and estimates are developed by the actuarial department. Promotion of the product to both purchasers and the distribution system is initiated. Departments responsible for policy issue and the administrative maintenance of policies (underwriting, customer service, claims) establish plans for the introduction and life of the product.

Product Life Cycles

Competition in life insurance almost always takes its toll on life insurance products, with demand ultimately decreasing over time. Product re-pricing and re-design can help, as explained below, but life insurance products are as subject to obsolescence as any others. A useful way of thinking about this process is the **product life cycle**, a theoretical marketing construct that describes the approximate key turning points and stages in the life of a product from introduction to decline. The four stages of the product life cycle are introduction, growth, maturity, and decline. These stages are represented stylistically in Figure 10-1, together with sales and profits.

During *introduction,* sales are low due to the consumer's unfamiliarity with the product, and profits are negative due to start-up investment and the negative cash flows associated with policy issue. Price competition is not typical of this stage, as competing products targeted at the same market with a similar marketing mix are usually nonexistent or few. As sales and profits increase, the product moves into the *growth* stage of its life cycle. Gross profits develop and increase. Unit profitability of the product line, however, begins to decline as competitors enter the market with more attractive prices or superior features.

In the *maturity* stage, sales growth slows or disappears and profits decline. In microeconomic theory, competition drives prices to an equilibrium level where extraordinary profits are unavailable, new competitors have no incentive to enter, and some competitors withdraw due to inefficiency or to pursue more attractive opportunities.

In the *decline* stage, sales and profits continue to decline due to new products and pricing or to changes in the regulatory or economic environment or both. Eventually insurers are faced with the decision whether to continue to offer the product, taking into account both the financial and reputational loss associated with a market exit. Of course, servicing a product that is no longer sold becomes more expensive. Resolution of both problems sometimes involves the sale of a product line to another insurer whose resources and target market are better suited to the product line.

Product Life Cycle   Figure 10-1

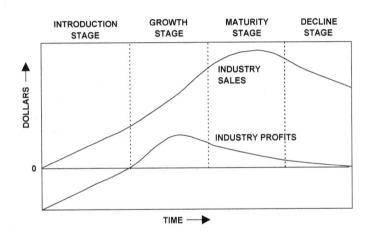

As an insurance product moves through its life cycle, as the external environment evolves, and as competitors' behaviors change, the product generally requires a regular and sometimes fundamental reconsideration of its pricing to maintain desired solvency levels and profitability results. Regular re-pricing occurs in the determination of dividends on participating products and non-guaranteed interest, expense, and mortality elements on unbundled policies. Changing competitive, mortality, economic, and regulatory conditions are considered in every redetermination.

Irregular re-pricing may be demanded when shifts in conditions are substantial. New fundamental premium structures can be required for an individual product or across an insurer's entire product portfolio. Unlike re-pricing strategies for some insurance products, substantial changes for individually issued life insurance policies typically can be made only with respect to newly issued policies or new products, as policies already in force permit changes only with respect to their non-guaranteed elements, if any. Where the difference between the guaranteed and non-guaranteed pricing components is great, substantial changes could in theory be made, but great care needs to be exercised in doing so. Policyholders in good health can easily terminate their now more expensive policies and secure new ones from competitors, leaving the insurer holding an insurance pool overrepresented with insureds who could not afford to terminate their policies; in other words, composed of those in poor health.

DISTRIBUTION CHANNELS

Life insurer products are sold by individual sales persons, by institutional sales agents, and by direct response marketing. This discussion presents distribution channels in these three broad categories.

Individual intermediaries *(producers)* are business persons who sell insurance products on an interpersonal level and are compensated by commission for each policy sold. **Institutional intermediaries** are deposit taking, investment intermediary, and other financial firms that sell insurers' products. Institutional sales in Asia and North America are not as important as in Europe. The **direct response** channel serves purchasers directly without the initial intervention of an individual or institutional intermediary.

Insurers maintain both proprietary and nonproprietary systems of individual intermediaries, called affiliated and independent distribution systems or channels. **Affiliated distribution channels** – also called **agency-building systems** – are insurer-owned or directed systems composed of individual intermediaries, called variously **captive agents, career agents, exclusive agents**, and **tied agents**, who are engaged full time in the sale of insurance exclusively or primarily for a single insurer or affiliated group of insurers.

Independent distribution channels – also called **non-agency building systems** – are not owned or directed by the insurer and rely on individual intermediaries, usually called **brokers**, who are independent salespersons, not required to sell insurance exclusively or primarily for a single insurer or affiliated group of insurers. Brokers are commonly former career agents who become independent, establish their own office and expense arrangements, and typically, although not exclusively, are among the most successful and knowledgeable intermediaries in the industry. In the U.S., life insurance brokers, as independent contractors, may be deemed to represent the insurer or the applicant, depending on the specific facts of a situation. Legal differences exist among the types of producers, as explained in Chapter 18. In the balance of this chapter and elsewhere, we refer to any individual intermediary as an *agent* or *producer* unless context requires a distinction.

AFFILIATED DISTRIBUTION CHANNELS
Four types of affiliated distribution channels exist:

1. Career agency
2. Multiple-line exclusive
3. Home service
4. Salaried

CAREER AGENCIES   Career agencies recruit, train, house, and supervise individual intermediaries and are operated on either a general agency or a branch office basis. The **general agency**, managed by a general agent, performs these functions as an independent business, while the **branch office** (also called **managerial system**), managed by an office manager, is owned and operated by the insurer. In both cases, the ultimate purpose is to implement the sales function of the insurer through successful career sales agents. General agencies possess more independence in their day to day business activities than do branch offices, but their contribution to the insurer's marketing strategy is functionally the same; general agents and branch managers undertake similar responsibilities and are compensated similarly as well.

The general agent's agreement with the insurer typically provides for payment of **override commissions** based on the agency's first-year premium production for new business. A separate override commission scale applies to premiums attributable to renewal business. Expense allowances are also paid as a function of first-year and renewal premiums, and bonus pay for performance may also be paid. Branch managers are generally paid a salary based on an incentive compensation formula that is generally not dissimilar to the general agent's compensation. Bonus pay for performance for both general agents and managers is likely to focus on similar objectives: persistency of in-force contracts, new premium growth, agent recruitment and retention, and agent productivity.

MULTIPLE-LINE EXCLUSIVE AGENTS **Multiple-line exclusive agents** (MLEAs) are commissioned exclusive agents who sell the life and health and property and casualty insurance products of a single group of affiliated insurers. Many multiple-line companies are among the largest and best known U.S. insurers, including *State Farm, Farmers,* and *Allstate.*

HOME SERVICE The **home service distribution system**, also known as the **combination** or **debit distribution system**, relies on commissioned exclusive agents who are assigned a geographic territory. The target market for home service distribution is lower income consumers. At one time, agents personally collected renewal premiums at the policyowner's home or business in their territory (or **debit**) on a weekly or monthly basis. This practice is disappearing as this market shifts from industrial life insurance to ordinary life, with premiums collected electronically or through the mail.

The home service system at one time was the principal distribution model of many of the largest insurers such as *Prudential* and *Metropolitan*. The cost of intense customer servicing and the widespread availability of checking accounts for those of modest economic means led to a de-emphasis of the home service system.

SALARIED There have been experiments, mostly unsuccessful, to employ individual life insurance agents on a salaried basis. Salary and bonus compensation, however, is common in the sale of group life and health insurance to employers. The **group sales representative's** purpose is to generate personal sales or to promote commissioned sales by others or both. Group representatives call on their company's own career agents, independent benefit consultants, third-party administrators, national and independent full service brokerage organizations, and agents of other companies. Group representatives are generally paid a salary and incentive bonuses based on production. The representative may also be involved in servicing group policyowners. Most small group cases are sold by individual career agents or brokers, and sales to larger employers or associations tend to be made through specialized brokers or specialized divisions of full service brokers.

In addition to group insurance as such, various forms of mass marketing have developed, frequently involving an agent. Association group, credit card solicitations, and worksite marketing are examples. Box 10-1 presents a short overview of worksite marketing.

Box 10-1
Worksite Marketing

Worksite marketing involves an agent selling personal insurance products to employees of a business or other employer, with the employer agreeing to collect the premiums through payroll deduction. Interest in worksite marketing has grown as employers attempt to reduce the cost of group benefits by shifting the costs to employees. Group life insurance is typically offered along with medical coverages. Forms of cash value life insurance and disability income insurance may also be offered on a voluntary payroll deduction basis to employees.

INDEPENDENT DISTRIBUTION CHANNELS

The other major classification of life insurance marketing channels relying on individual marketing intermediaries is the independent channel of which four are found in the U.S.:

- brokerage,
- personal-producing general agents,
- independent property/casualty agents, and
- independent marketing organizations.

Not all of these channels exist in every country, with some countries having no parallel to a truly independent distribution system. In markets where they exist, terminology may differ; e.g., the U.K. concept of independent financial advisors (IFAs) is akin to U.S. brokerage.

Insurers that market through nonexclusive agent strategies provide products and services to agents who are already engaged in life insurance selling. Thus, the key to success with this strategy is to gain access to the producer. The producer's loyalty is retained by quality service, good compensation, innovative and competitive products, and sound personal relationships.

BROKERAGE   Insurers typically gain access to the brokerage market through a company employee, often called a **brokerage representative** or **supervisor** or an independent **brokerage general agent**, who appoints brokers and promotes their efforts to sell the insurer's products. Brokers are also solicited through direct response methods. The life insurance brokerage market has three important intermediary segments: (1) career agents whose primary company does not or will not offer desired coverage either because of adverse underwriting or failure to offer a desired type of policy; (2) intermediaries whose principal business is not selling life insurance, such as financial planners, accountants, and institutional intermediaries, including the important institutions discussed below; and (3) independent life producers who have no primary affiliation with any insurer but specialize by product type or target an upscale market segment.

Historically, brokerage-oriented insurers specialized in low-cost term insurance and substandard business. The contemporary brokerage market features a broad range of products that includes almost all life insurance product lines.

Innovative products, pricing, commissions, and service are the competitive tools involved. In addition to specialty brokerage companies, many insurers that have traditionally relied on career agents now look to the brokerage market to supplement their distribution.

PERSONAL-PRODUCING GENERAL AGENTS   A **personal-producing general agent** (PPGA) is an independent commissioned insurance sales agent who generally works alone, is not housed in one of an insurer's field offices, engages primarily in the sales of new policies, holds contracts with several insurers, and usually focuses on personal production as opposed to the recruitment and management of career agents. (Some PPGAs employ subagents.) PPGAs are recruited through the same means as brokers: company employees, independent contractors, and direct response methods. Some companies seek PPGAs primarily to sell that company's full range of products, while other companies seek them to sell a specific product such as disability income insurance.

PPGAs are distinguished from brokers in two respects. First, broker production is generally intermittent and produces occasional sales, while PPGA production is expected to be considerable and continuing. Second, brokers earn commissions roughly equivalent to those paid career agents, while PPGAs receive not only sales commissions but general agent overrides and expense allowances. The typical PPGA is experienced and successful, does not need the supervision and maintenance expense typically devoted to career agents, and thus is able to command and earn the traditional general agent's additional compensation. Insurer support for PPGAs is usually limited to computer and advanced sales support.

INDEPENDENT PROPERTY/CASUALTY AGENTS   **Independent property/casualty agents** are commissioned agents whose primary business is the sale of property and casualty insurance for several insurers. Property and casualty companies that use independent agents often have life insurance affiliates, and they encourage the agent to take advantage of his or her customer relationships to sell life insurance for the affiliate. These agents may also participate in brokerage and PPGA distribution channels.

INDEPENDENT MARKETING ORGANIZATIONS   **Independent marketing organizations** (IMOs) are independent firms that specialize in specific products or target markets through which participating agents place their business with insurance companies that have contracted with the IMO. A few IMOs, called **producer groups**, are sponsored and owned by their member agents. Other IMOs are not so owned. Producer groups typically are self-supporting and represent a handful of high-quality insurers that may have agreed to develop special proprietary products and provide dedicated services for the group.

Producer groups believe that their clients require more sophisticated support services than those ordinarily provided by insurers, given the target market. Specialized software and other strong computer and research support are hallmarks of some producer groups. One producer group has created its own reinsurance company, to which its partner insurers cede portions of the underlying risk placed with those insurers. The group observes that favorable experience of its business is thus segregated, allowing insurers to develop and re-price in force proprietary products based on this experience. *M Financial Group* is the oldest and largest producer group in the U.S.

IMOs organized by non-producer groups focus on specific markets or products and undertake the same responsibilities and may enjoy many of the same benefits as producer groups. Independent distribution of sponsored products through various channels is managed by the IMO rather than the insurer.

FINANCIAL INSTITUTION INTERMEDIARIES

We classify insurance distribution via financial institutions into three categories:

- Deposit taking institutions
- Investment banks
- Other financial institutions

By **deposit taking institutions**, we mean any financial intermediary that takes deposits from and makes loans to consumers. Their significant asset base makes commercial banks the most significant of these institutions. Thrifts, credit unions, and other specialized institutions also take deposits, make loans, and sell insurance. **Investment banks** bring together investors and firms that issue securities; some investment banking activities involve the underwriting of securities and some are strictly sales intermediary activities. Other financial institutions include mutual funds, pension funds, as well as other insurers that do not manufacture a specific product but sell it on behalf of the manufacturing insurer that does.

DEPOSIT TAKING INSTITUTIONS   Banks are active in the sale of all areas of life and health insurance. Insurance products are distributed within the banking systems by bank staff, by commissioned agents employed by banks, and by independent third party marketers. **Third party marketers** are organizations that specialize in the bank sale of insurance products or affiliates of the more traditional agency system. Finally, some banks have purchased existing insurance agencies, typically focused on property and casualty business, that also incorporate life and health services. The manufacture or underwriting of insurance products by banks and other deposit taking institutions is discussed in Chapter 12

Traditionally, earnings from life product sales commissions have been particularly attractive to banks, because fee income can increase a bank's revenue and return on its existing capital structure without significant increases to a bank's required regulatory capital base. While the operating-risk component of bank risk-based capital does imply additional capital requirements for banks that sell insurance, most risk is borne and capital maintained by the insurer in such arrangements.

The primary area of success for deposit taking institutions has been in the sale of annuities. The central role of both banking and annuities in consumer savings makes the annuity success natural. More than 75 percent of banks engage in annuity sales, which collectively account for as much as 20 percent of the industry's total annuity sales. Many deposit taking institutions also promote the sale of life, medical, disability, and long term care insurance.

The sale of traditional life insurance products by deposit taking institutions was a relatively new phenomenon at the end of the last century, unlike the situation with credit insurance that has a much longer history. **Credit insurance** is a special class of life and health insurance that pays off a debtor's outstanding loan balance if he or she dies or becomes disabled during the loan term. Credit insurance is subject to regulation in specific statutory regimes that distinguishes it from other forms of life and health insurance.

Since the financial turmoil of 2008-2009, some banks have experienced new success in life insurance sales. Low interest rates and volatile market returns have reduced the demand for annuities and banks have begun to offer single premium whole life, which tends to be less interest sensitive. The sales process has become more routinely transactional than traditional life sales through simplified underwriting and enhanced customer service support.

INVESTMENT BANKS   Investment banks and their retail marketing divisions are important distribution channels for variable and fixed annuities as well as some non-variable life and health insurance. Stockbrokers typically sell for several insurers and are an important part of the life insurance brokerage channel.

In addition to traditional broker-dealer (BD) firms, life insurance sales are often important to commission-based independent financial planners who act as brokers for life insurers. These advisors typically are licensed by a securities firm that does not house or train them. Their relationship to their securities broker-dealer is thus economically the same as their broker relationship with the insurance companies they represent.

OTHER FINANCIAL INSTITUTIONS   Mutual fund companies have become an important intermediary distribution channel for life insurers. Sales are by traditional personal efforts or in a sponsored arrangement through direct response methods, as discussed in the next section. The savings nature of mutual funds, annuities, and life insurance is complementary. In some cases, simultaneous sales of term life insurance and mutual funds are made in accordance with a "buy-term-and-invest-the-difference" program.

Some mutual fund companies and investment banks are increasingly assuming the servicing functions that agents provided historically. An annuity application may be made at the mutual fund's web site, and the premium paid by a web-based transfer from the consumer's mutual fund account to the new annuity contract. A policyowner's online portal for annuity servicing may then be accessed through the fund or bank's web site, which then links invisibly to the insurer's information system. The consumer's unified account statement recites balances and transactions for both fund shares and insurance products. Mutual funds and investment banks are attracted not only to the fee income such arrangements provide but also to the tighter control of the customer relationship it affords. The identity of the actual manufacturing and obligation-bearing insurer may be relegated to fine print.

Life insurers increasingly act as distributors for the products manufactured by other insurers. These arrangements can prove attractive to the distributing insurer as it can provide a more complete product offering to consumers and a more competitive, comprehensive income base for producers. These ends can be furthered without the development and maintenance cost and capital requirements of a new product. Life insurers distribute both insurance products and investment products manufactured by other firms.

DIRECT RESPONSE CHANNELS

Direct response marketing can take many forms, but in a broad sense it means that the sale is made by the company, typically not involving an agent or commissions. The company solicits by mail, telephone, or media advertising (print, broadcast, or online), and the consumer's purchase response is made by phone, mail, or Internet communication. In some situations (e.g., some sales via telephone), the person with whom the consumer deals may be required to have an agent's license, but the consumer's purchase and all subsequent relations with the company are direct. Solicitation may also be made by point-of-sale kiosks, vending machines, and personal representatives.

From the consumer's perspective, the principal differences in policies bought directly and those bought through a personal or institutional intermediary usually are cost and service. Direct response products are delivered and serviced more efficiently, and cost savings usually are reflected in the purchaser's premium. The cost benefit is somewhat offset by reduced levels of personal customer service. Also, some life products sold via direct response entail little or no underwriting, which means that mortality costs are higher than with policies that are fully underwritten.

After a direct response sale, the client generally deals with the insurer on a direct basis. Premiums are paid electronically or by mail, and claims are made and paid through the mail or electronically. Although these procedures are usually common to sales made through any channel, in the direct response system, there is no agent to serve as an initial contact and facilitator.

As a result of the limited service and advice options associated with much direct response marketing, the historical emphasis has been directed to simple products, often sold as supplements to fundamental coverages delivered through agency channels. Beginning at the end of the last century, companies have experienced some success with more comprehensive direct response marketing programs across the full range of products targeted to life, health, retirement, and estate planning needs.

MEDIA CHANNELS Different direct response channels, like intermediary channels, reflect different intensities of market segmentation and targeting. The least segmented direct response methods are delivered through traditional mass media: mass mailings, newspapers, magazines, and broadcast. Target marketing is practiced in the mass media, as different magazines and cable networks, for example, attract different segments, but the primary attraction is the large number of readers, viewers, and listeners who can be reached simultaneously. Paid endorsements by media personalities are sometimes used, with critics claiming this sales technique can be misleading and expensive.

Telephone sales and targeted mailings are more focused than mass advertising. They are more expensive but produce higher response rates. Telephone and mailing lists are compiled by insurers internally and are also available from third party vendors who broker lists. These lists are the result of a filtering process that produces highly segmented and homogenous consumer groups.

Internet discourse and commerce are rapidly and radically changing the fundamental concepts of marketing and provide the means for the most efficient segmentation possible. Traditional marketing strategy was successful when the largest possible homogeneous consumer audience was reached. An Internet marketing strategy is successful when the smallest audience is reached. The purpose is to establish a one-on-one, personal relationship between seller and buyer.

The Internet marketer seeks consumers through revealed preferences. Consumers reveal their purchase readiness through (1) their historical viewing behavior reflected by an aggregate analysis of their web page views and responses to previous ads and (2) their immediate viewing behavior as reflected by the context of their currently viewed page. Given such precise targeting information, click-through ads can be custom designed and presented to the individual reader. The Internet is now used by all marketing intermediary and financial institution channels to promote themselves and their products and services. Web sites are universal and on-line premium quotes and applications are common.

ASSOCIATIONS AND COMMERCIAL FIRMS   Life and health insurance products (as well as property and casualty products) are distributed through direct response methods by insurers that seek the endorsement of sponsoring organizations. The organizations are paid fees for their sponsorship. In the U.S., the most important of these relationships are with professional organizations such as state bar associations and medical societies, or with voluntary associations such as the *American Automobile Association* and the *American Association of Retired Persons*. Indeed, the largest source of operating income of many associations is insurance fees.

Credit card companies also are a significant source of distribution for life and health insurance coverages, and premiums are billed to the consumer's credit card account and remitted to the insurer. Nonfinancial commercial firms also enter sponsoring relationships with insurers for fees. Credit and group life and health insurance have been offered through magazine publishers, and flight insurance offered through airlines.

TRENDS IN DISTRIBUTION

Individual life insurance sales production has shifted dramatically away from traditional, affiliated channels to independent channels. Figure 10-2 depicts individual sales personnel as a percentage of total producers and demonstrates a rough parity in participant numbers between affiliated and independent groups. In the early 1980s, the affiliated producer market share was approximately twice that of independent producers.

Figure 10-3 shows the associated trend in market share represented by different channels. In 1983, affiliated producers accounted for 62 percent of new annualized life insurance premium; by 2012, affiliated producers represented only about a third of production.

Figure 10-4 depicts market share by distribution channel for discrete life insurance and annuity markets. Traditional affiliated and independent life insurance producers account for a large majority of individual life insurance sales. Nontraditional production sources (banks, stockbrokers, financial planners, and advisors, among others) in the investment and retirement-oriented sale of annuities are of considerable importance. Traditional production sources account for less than one-half of total annuity production.

Figure 10-2   Total Life Insurance Sales by Affiliated and Independent Distribution Channels

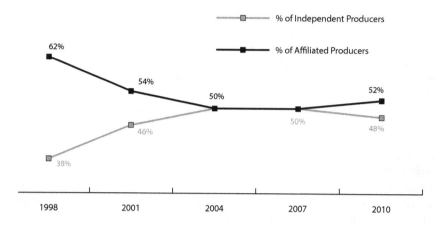

Source: LIMRA's 2012 Census of U.S. Sales Personnel. Affiliated includes agency-building, MLEA and home service agents. Independent includes brokers, PPGAs, and subagents.

Figure 10-3   Total Life Insurance Sales by Distribution Channel

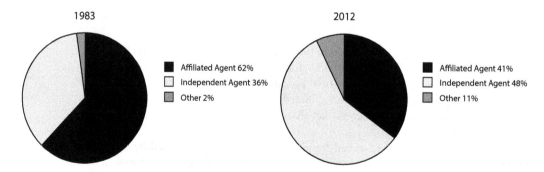

Source: LIMRA's U.S. Individual Life Sales Studies and Industry estimates. "Other" includes direct sales, financial institutions, and full service broker-dealers.

The impact of the 2008-09 recession on life insurance distribution has caused the affiliated agent market share to increase. The principal reason is the relative shift in demand from equity market-sensitive variable products to traditional whole life products offering guaranteed returns. Mutual companies in particular have promoted the relative safety of these products during turbulent economic times, and their sales are made primarily through affiliated producers.

Market Shares of Individual Life and Annuity Sales by Distribution Channel   Figure 10-4

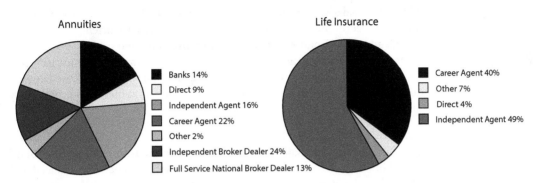

2012 Products and Distribution
U.S. Market – Individual Products

Annuities

- Banks 14%
- Direct 9%
- Independent Agent 16%
- Career Agent 22%
- Other 2%
- Independent Broker Dealer 24%
- Full Service National Broker Dealer 13%

Life Insurance

- Career Agent 40%
- Other 7%
- Direct 4%
- Independent Agent 49%

Source: LIMRA's U.S. Individual Life Sales Studies and Industry estimates. For annuities, "Career Agent" includes agency-building, MLEA and home service; "Independent" includes brokerage, PPGA and stockbroker/wirehouse; "Other" includes banks and savings institutions, worksite and channels other than those included in the previous categories. For life insurance, "Other" includes direct sales, financial institutions, and full service broker-dealers.

COMPENSATION IN MARKETING

The twin objectives of compensation in life insurance marketing are to encourage the sale of new policies and the continuation of existing policies, although commissions paid for new policy sales are routinely higher than those paid on policy continuation (renewal). This differential between commissions on new and renewal premiums is said to reflect the difficulty and complexity of making a new sale versus continuing to collect premiums on existing policies. Here we discuss the typical compensation arrangements found with respect to those involved in managing sales agents and to the agents themselves.

Management Compensation

The production of new and renewing premium income is central to management compensation philosophy. In the case of general agency management compensation, premium income is rewarded through direct percentage-based commissions. In the case of general managers, the goals are similar, but compensation arrangements are often more indirect. The principal reason for differing arrangements is agency expense. General agencies are often responsible for their own revenue and expense, while general managers' operational results are the responsibility of the insurer.

The typical general agent's contract is comprised of four principal elements:

1. management commissions or overrides based on the first-year premium production of each of the agency's sales agents;
2. additional overrides based on each sales agent's renewal premiums;
3. expense allowances on new and renewal premium income, also expressed as a percentage of paid premiums; and
4. a variety of bonuses designed to promote profitability, including new premium growth, persistency (due to the profitability of long term policies

and the unrecoverable costs of near term surrenders), and agent retention (due to the high cost of training new agents and active recruitment
of existing agents by competing insurers).

Although provisions vary from company to company, general managers typically are paid salaries, with their bonus compensation defined in terms of productivity in the recruitment and success of new agents. Agency efficiency is promoted
through additional bonuses for favorable expense ratios and profitability through
bonuses for persistency and agent retention. The trend in the U.S. and elsewhere
has been toward reducing management compensation, due to increased competition. The result mandates close management attention to increased productivity
at the sales agent level.

AGENT COMPENSATION

Individual agent compensation generally varies with the nature of the distribution
channel in which the agent works. We divide our discussion between affiliated and
independent channels.

COMPENSATION IN AFFILIATED DISTRIBUTION CHANNELS   The bulk of a career
agent's compensation is paid in commissions based on a percentage of premium
income. Percentages paid on new income are emphasized to drive new sales, but
additional, lower commissions are paid on renewal premiums to promote growing
stability in the agent's income and long-term customer service and satisfaction.
The typical agent contract for whole life policies might provide for payment of
a commission of 55.0 percent of first year premium, 5.0 percent of renewal premiums for a limited period, such as 10 years, followed by a service fee of 2.0-3.0
percent thereafter for the life of the contract. Commissions for term insurance,
universal life, and variable life are more variable but generally are less than those
paid on whole life policies.

Compensation paid for variable product sales is qualitatively and quantita-
tively different due to fuller disclosure of both product operation and compensation, less generous margins, and regulation. Variable products must be sold
through registered broker-dealers (BDs). Life insurers sell variable products
through proprietary BDs and independent investment bank BDs and BD affiliates
of commercial banks. Cash compensation usually comprises two components. A
cash sales commission – perhaps 2 to 10 percent of premium income – is paid
at the time of sale or premium payment. Additional compensation may be paid
based on the account value of the product. An **asset-based trail fee** is annual
compensation paid to the producer expressed as a percentage of the accumulated
account value. The percentage is usually a fraction of one percent, frequently 0.25
percent or 25 *basis points*. Agents are often provided an option to select between
specified combinations of commission and trail fee, thus allowing them to design
a personal compensation system that emphasizes or balances the near and long
term components. The asset-based component offers the theoretical advantages of
levelized commissions discussed below.

When an agent's contract terminates (due to a change in career or insurer affiliation), commissions generally terminate unless under the terms of the contract
commissions are **vested**, which means that the agent has a right to continue to be
paid commissions so long as the insurance policy remains in effect. Commissions

become vested when a contract is validated by some performance measure, such as a minimum level of production or service longevity. Not all agent contracts permit vesting.

Agents, like general agents and managers, may also receive additional bonus commissions for persistency and substantial production. Career agents typically also receive employee benefits generally available to workers in other industries, including life insurance, health insurance, disability insurance, retirement benefits, profit sharing, and thrift or 401(k) plans.

The extraterritorial influence of New York state regulation has a significant influence on agent compensation throughout the U.S. The commission schedules noted above were traditionally the maximum allowed under New York law. These rates applied, not only to companies domiciled in New York, but to the nationwide operations of any company licensed to operate in New York. These commission limits were increased slightly in 1998 and rules simplified, as competition among insurers rendered the consumer protection purposes of the original rules less compelling.

Companies not licensed in New York typically pay higher commission rates. Because of this extraterritoriality element of New York regulation, some companies avoid operating in New York entirely, while others have established subsidiaries licensed only in New York thus insulating the parent from the New York rules. Table 10-1 shows current commission limits for cash value life insurance contracts under New York law.

State of New York Commission Limits on Individual Life Insurance Policies by Policy Year and Distribution Channel   **Table 10-1**

Policy Year	Branch Office	General Agent
1	55.0%	63.0%
2	22.0%	27.0%
3	20.0%	23.0%
4	18.0%	20.0%
5-10	No limit	No limit
11-15	No limit	No limit
16+	No limit	No limit

New career agents are typically financed during their transition to fully commission-based compensation arrangements through a form of **training allowance**. The most prevalent forms are:

- Additional commissions beyond those provided by the standard contract schedule. (These plans do little to ease the transition for an agent who does not make immediate sales.)
- A fixed training allowance, paid regularly and in addition to sales commissions, that declines over the term of the training period specified in the contract.
- A line of credit that is accessed in specified amounts over a specified period. The outstanding balance is reduced as commissions are earned. Any balance still due at the end of the training period may or may not be offset against future commissions.

Multiple-line exclusive agent contracts apply to both property/casualty insurance as well as life insurance lines, although commission levels vary by line. Percentages and vesting provisions, if any, are generally less favorable than those enjoyed by career agents, although some may qualify for training allowance financing. Home service agent commissions are generally similar to those paid career agents. If the home service agent physically collects premiums, an additional percentage of the premium is paid as a service fee.

Group insurance commissions differ significantly from those for individual products, because premium amounts are much larger and many servicing functions are performed by the insurer, not the salesperson. They might grade from, say, 10.0 percent of premiums for relatively small groups, such as under 50 lives, to 0.5 percent or less for groups of 3,000 or more lives. Group representatives, as discussed above, are generally paid salaries and bonuses based on production.

Compensation in Independent Distribution Channels   Considerable variation exists in compensation in independent distribution channels, but some generalizations can be offered. Thus, basic broker compensation resembles that of the career agent. Depending on levels of production, brokers may receive little in the way of additional bonus commissions or benefits, or they may enjoy compensation equivalent to that of the same company's career agents. Compensation of PPGAs, like brokers, may depend on production. However, PPGAs, as noted earlier, generally receive general agent overrides as well as sales commissions.

Compensation, including benefits, to independent property/casualty agents is similar to that of career agents and may include additional expense allowances akin to those payable under PPGA contracts. Unlike MLEAs, independent agents generally are not offered financing plans. New agents in the property/casualty business usually begin their careers with an assigned or inherited book of business.

Producers at commercial banks and some other financial institutions – if not registered representatives of a securities broker-dealer – are most often compensated by the employer on a salary-plus-incentive basis for selling life and health products. Compensation is originally paid from the insurer to the institution. For annuity sales, they are compensated either by commissions with a draw or on a salary-plus-incentive basis. Some commercial banks rely on commissions exclusively, with a few relying exclusively on salary.

Life insurers sell significant sums of variable annuities through investment bank BDs and BDs affiliated with commercial banks. Compensation is paid to the BD who in turn pays its registered representatives – usually called *advisors* – according to its compensation policies. In addition to sales and trail commissions, compensation is paid to the BD for promotion, education, and training.

PROMOTION

Obviously, a life insurance product must be made known to consumers before they will purchase it; i.e., the product must be promoted in some way. The three principal methods of product promotion are (1) advertising and publicity, (2) personal sales, and (3) sales promotions. Promotion is designed to build a favorable image of or to shape the beliefs and impressions consumers have about a company or its products. General comforting terms such as "safe" and "caring" are characteristic of image building, terms with which any insurer would want to be associated. Promotion may also be designed to differentiate the company or its products from its competitors. Special product features or representations that the company was especially well suited for a particular target market, such as teachers or retirees, are examples of differentiation promotion.

Advertising and Publicity

Advertising is undertaken to deliver image-building or differentiation-themed messages to consumers. An advertising campaign should make clear the markets to be addressed and the results expected. For example, objectives are established to determine whether a particular advertising campaign is designed to enhance an insurer's general brand recognition or to create a specific purchase intention with respect to a specific product.

The advertising budget for a particular product is initially established as part of the capital budget for the product, and the media, frequency, and timing of publication are determined within the constraints of the budget. Because results are not easily predicted and experience produces valuable advertising expertise, programs are reviewed and adjusted regularly.

Publicity is a form of free or incidental advertising. Except in the case of product developments that are sufficiently novel that they are themselves news-worthy, publicity is generally designed to enhance a company's reputation in the market place. It may also be directed at an audience that is broader than the consuming public. The target audience may be regulatory authorities, consumer organizations, the capital markets, or other groups where a company's reputation is important. Publicity can include press releases, speeches by executives, charitable or other nonprofit sponsorships, funding of public service announcements or activities, and a host of other activities. Life insurers are naturally attracted to the support of causes that promote public health.

Sales Promotion

Sales promotions are incentive programs designed to improve sales at a particular time or of a particular product. Promotion incentives may be directed at either the distribution channels that sell products or, less commonly, to the consumers who buy them. Agents and brokers receive regular promotional support in the form of sales aids. These include brochures and other literature and may be made available both physically and online. The most important of these sales tools is access to illustration software that allows agents to show policy premiums, values, and benefits projected into the future. It is particularly important to the life insurance industry, as other financial institutions are generally not permitted to use similar projections in their sales materials.

Special agent incentives are offered periodically that are intended to boost sales of a particular product or general sales during a specific period. Rewards may include company novelty items or special recognition and awards for superior sales performers. The most important special incentives are supplementary bonus commissions and company-sponsored prizes for company convention or private vacation travel. Sales incentives offered to consumers are generally limited to inexpensive promotional goods such as t-shirts, coffee mugs, and the like. Anti-rebating statutes generally prevent more costly or direct financial incentives.

PERSONAL SALES

Life insurers use personal selling on two levels. At the wholesale level, companies use sales representatives to promote their products and services to their own agents, independent producers, and the other distribution channels they employ. At the retail level, most insurance sales are made by individual intermediaries.

Consumers do not ordinarily independently seek to purchase life insurance. Rather, the sale is usually the result of a proactive personal sales effort by an individual intermediary. Personal selling is most effective and most necessary, however, when the sale is complex and represents a significant financial commitment by the purchaser. Most cash value life insurance products are sold on this basis. The individual agent is widely considered as the most important sales tool for the industry.

IDENTIFICATION OF QUALIFIED CLIENTS   Personal sales efforts begin with an organized methodology for identifying potential buyers who possess the need, the financial means, and the inclination to acquire a life insurance policy. The agent intuitively seeks buyers whose subjective utility profile is a match for the agent's products and services.

The direct response methods used to sell products that are typically simple can also be employed to identify likely buyers of more complex products and services. A direct mailing, for instance, is unlikely to create a completed sale for any client's complicated, tax-oriented estate planning insurance needs, but may create an opportunity for the agent to begin a discussion about those needs that leads ultimately to a sale and a long-term relationship that the agent prefers and seeks.

A more important approach to the identification of qualified clients is the active development of personal relationships that lead to **referrals**, which are recommendations of the agent by one person to another. Referrals are generated in three ways. First, agents seek to establish professional relationships with **centers of influence**, who are persons who have an opportunity to recommend agents because of their status in a community or their role as an advisor, such as an attorney or accountant. Second, agents seek referrals from existing clients. Third, agents seek referrals from friends and acquaintances who may not offer professional advice to others but who are willing to recommend the agent in a favorable light because of their personal relationship with the agent.

Agents seek to be particularly attuned to individuals who are undergoing or about to undergo life-changing events that signal a change in their needs or means. Common life changing events include marriage, birth of a child, retirement, start or sale of a business, home purchase, or receipt of an inheritance.

IDENTIFICATION OF CLIENT NEEDS   One of the key components of an agent's job is to assist clients in identifying needs that could arise on their deaths. Death can give rise to the need for immediate liquidity and long-term assets. As discussed in Chapters 20 and 22, these can include:

- Replacement of a deceased wage-earner's income,
- Liquidation of a home mortgage balance and other outstanding debts,
- Completion of an educational savings program,
- Funeral and other final expenses, and/or
- Estate and inheritance taxes.

In what are sometimes called **program sales**, agents identify a limited, particular need that can be addressed with a particular product. For example, an agent may present a decreasing term life insurance policy whose face amount tracks the declining balance of a client's mortgage. An agent may also present a disability policy or deferred annuity to a potential client who is satisfied with his or her existing life insurance, or an agent may simply respond to a client who specifies a need for a certain amount of insurance and seeks advice only on the type of policy.

Many agents (and clients) prefer a more comprehensive approach that engages the client in a formal planning process that addresses the potential client's needs across the entire range of financial concerns, as we discuss in Chapter 20. A comprehensive relationship is more productive for the agent and generally results in more and larger sales and a closer relationship with the client. Agents also seek potential clients with a need to plan for the financial consequences of disability and for the accumulation of retirement funds. We explore these needs in Chapters 6, 8, and 23.

Business owners also may have death-related needs for life insurance, although they often differ from those of individuals and usually call for higher amounts of life insurance. Two of the most important of these are funding buy-sell agreements and key-employee insurance needs. These and other business uses of life insurance are discussed in Chapter 24.

CONTINUING CLIENT SERVICE   Most life insurers consider continuing client service to be a critical part of their mission, and agents devote considerable effort to maintain an ongoing relationship with policyholder clients. Among the important reasons for cementing client satisfaction after the sale are the opportunity for repeat sales, client referrals, and policy persistency.

Thus, continuing contact helps keep the agent apprised of a client's changing financial needs and of opportunities to make additional sales to the client. Client satisfaction is key to the client referral process. Most insurance products require periodic premiums, and maintaining an advantageous rate of renewal (persistency) is essential to the profitability of any product line.

THE INTERNATIONAL DIMENSIONS OF DISTRIBUTION

Having examined life insurance marketing with a strong emphasis on the U.S., it will be instructive to explore certain international aspects of life insurance marketing. Here we offer a selective overview of distribution, the role of multinational insurers in the U.S. and world markets, and the participation of U.S. insurers internationally.

LIFE INSURANCE DISTRIBUTION WORLDWIDE
Life insurance distribution in each national market is a reflection of its historical evolution, sophistication, philosophy as to the relative role of government and the private sector, and a host of other attributes. We provide an overview of markets in selected regions.

THE AMERICAS   Life insurance distribution in *Canada* has changed dramatically over the preceding two decades. Most distribution today is via brokers. The major Canadian life insurers had, until the late 1990s, relied heavily on career agency distribution. They began to dismantle these systems in favor of contractual arrangements with life brokerage firms, which became known as managing general agents (MGAs). A **managing general agent** is an individual, partnership, or corporation that holds at least one direct brokerage contract with a life insurance company registered to do business in Canada. It is a conduit that facilitates business between brokers and their clients and insurers by providing a range of services, akin to an IMO in the U.S.

In *Latin America,* most life insurance distribution historically has been through career agents. Recently, independent agents, brokers, marketing firms, and international brokers have appeared. Distribution practices vary widely. For example, in *Honduras* and *El Salvador*, career agents predominate, whereas in *Panama* and *Ecuador*, independent agents and brokers are the most prevalent. *Bancassurance* has grown rapidly in the region, with banks in many markets now controlling significant market shares. For example, in *Brazil*, banks control more than 80 percent of insurance sales. Life insurers are heavily involved in the pension business in many countries in the region, as the countries increasingly have adopted pension systems akin to that of *Chile,* which relies on mandatory savings via private-sector financial institutions.

EUROPE   The bancassurance movement continues to increase cost pressures on traditional insurers in many *European* countries. For example, banks are the main distribution channels in *France* (over 60 percent of the market share), in *Italy* (60 percent), and in *Spain* (70 percent). Banks also generate 25 percent of life business in *Germany*. As bancassurance becomes more widely accepted, it is proving increasingly difficult for conventional insurers to support costly career agency distribution systems. We discuss briefly three of the main life insurance markets in Europe

Distribution channels in the *United Kingdom* have been in flux since the late 1980s because of regulatory changes. The implementation of the *Financial Services Act of 1986* resulted in a clear distinction between independent financial advisors (IFAs) and appointed and company representatives. IFAs include insurance brokers, banks, building societies, lawyers, and accountants. These intermediaries are required by law to survey the market to find the best products to meet their clients' needs. Appointed and company representatives include tied agents, home service employees, and other types of career agents. They are limited to selling products of the company with which they are affiliated.

The role of independent brokers in the U.K. has traditionally been stronger than in other European countries, but they also are beginning to lose market share to banks and building societies. The traditional tied agent sales force has declined in relative importance. Most insurers have switched to IFAs. Premium volume via direct marketing comprises about 5 percent of the life insurance sector. By contrast, IFAs generate about 63 percent of regular premium business and about 70 percent of single premium business.

French life insurance distribution systems have changed markedly, particularly in terms of the bancassurance share of the market, as noted earlier. Several companies specialize in this business, including *Caisse Nationale de Prévoyance,* which has long held the right to distribute its products through Post Office and Treasury Office branches. Bancassurance insurers such as *Prédica* (subsidiary of the large French bank *Crédit Agricole*) and *SOGECAP* (subsidiary of the large French bank *Société Générale*) are both among the largest life insurers in France.

This unusual dominance of bancassurance in insurance marketing was fueled by the advantageous tax treatment accorded life insurance products in France. Other legal changes fostering growth were the elimination in 1990 of premium taxes for most individual life insurance contracts and the introduction of new individual pension plans in 2004 that allowed citizens to make tax-free contributions to individual accounts up to a defined limit.

Tied agents are the main distribution channels in *Germany*, accounting for about 35 percent of the premium volume. Independent (multiple-channel) agents and brokers together claim a 25 percent market share. The share by banks is about 25 percent. Interestingly, tied-pyramid sales forces claim a share of 6 percent.

ASIA-PACIFIC REGION   To many observers, the Asia-Pacific region offers the world's greatest life insurance potential. *Japan* was for years the global leader in life insurance premium volume. Life insurance also figures prominently in the financial markets of *Australia, Hong Kong, Korea, New Zealand, Singapore,* and *Taiwan,* to name the markets with per capita premium volumes of greater than US$1,000 in the region.

As other markets in the region have been deregulated and opened to international competition, they have seen significant premium increases, brought about because of competition that brings innovative products, distribution, and management processes. Two of the most promising markets, *China* and *India*, have yet to fully liberalize, but both seem committed to this path longer term, with the promise of enormous markets.

Distribution in *Japan* remains dominated by the industry's large network of part-time female agents. In 2011, some 250,000 agents were associated with sales branches of life insurers throughout the country. These operating units, which report to local branch offices, handle sales, premium collection, and policyholder service. The sales agents are required to be exclusive agents and generally transact business through house calls. During the past decade or so, the number of financial planners offering life insurance products as part of their services has risen. Many of them are employed by non-insurance financial institutions and by foreign-owned life insurers.

The *Korean* government actively promotes *bancassurance* and has expanded the scope for products in several phases during the early part of this century. The government expects bancassurance to capture more than 50 percent of life insurance and 36 percent of nonlife sales. Understandably, banks, through strategic alliances with life and nonlife insurers, dominate the *bancassurance* market, although security firms and credit card companies also offer *bancassurance* products.

As for other Asian markets, *Taiwan* uses distribution systems found in established life insurance markets, with the brokerage channel and *bancassurance* growing rapidly. As is the case in other Asian countries, many of Taiwan's life insurance agents are part-time. Distribution in *China* is via exclusive agents, while *bancassurance* distribution is said to be promising. *Hong Kong*, a special administrative region of China, has a sophisticated, well-developed life insurance market, dominated by career agents in terms of distribution, although brokerage is attracting great interest. Direct response marketing is becoming more common, as is distribution through banks. Whereas formerly the *Indian* regulatory authority allowed distribution via exclusive agents only, new channels are now allowed, including brokers and *bancassurance*.

THE ROLE OF MULTINATIONAL INSURERS

Mergers, acquisitions, strategic alliances, and new entrants have been changing the face of the life insurance industry across the globe. Until the late 1970s and 1980s, life insurance markets in North America and Europe were the world leaders in terms of premium volume, assets, and growth. As these markets matured and growth slowed, life insurance growth surged in many developing countries, particularly in Asia and, more recently, in Latin America and Eastern Europe. The shift resulted in increasing interest by life insurers from developed markets in the possibility of expanding operations internationally.

European insurers have invested enormous sums buying into insurance markets worldwide. Many have positioned themselves well within the European Union (EU) via mergers, acquisitions, and joint ventures. In Europe, insurance subsidiaries of banks are among the largest producers of new life insurance premiums. Prominent companies in the more advanced developing countries such as Korea, Singapore, and Taiwan have expanded outside their own borders.

As a global economy has emerged over the years, the relative stability of the U.S. economy and growth of the U.S. financial markets made the U.S. attractive to international investors. Many European and other international companies have significant investments in the U.S. life and health industry. In view of the size of the U.S. market, which represents somewhat more than a fifth of the world's life premiums, an insurer cannot be a true multinational without a meaningful U.S. presence. The U.S. market is relatively easy to enter, and merger activity has been significant. Naturally, acquisition activity tends to ebb and flow as currency exchange rates vary. As of year-end 2012, 99 of the 868 U.S. domestic life insurers were foreign-owned.

INTERNATIONAL PARTICIPATION OF UNITED STATES LIFE INSURERS

Relatively few U.S. insurers are truly multinational. No more than a few dozen of the 868 U.S. life insurance companies have any type of international operation at all. Furthermore, participation in the Canadian market represents the greatest part of most companies' international operations.

The primary reason that many U.S. insurers have not participated more substantially in international markets is their large, expanding domestic market. Few companies have felt a need to establish a presence abroad. Other reasons may include the historical insularity and cultural provincialism of the U.S., a centralized management organization in many large U.S. insurers, a lack of capital, and the tendency of U.S. companies to pursue short-term results.

THE FUTURE OF LIFE INSURANCE MARKETING

Life insurance marketing has changed and continues to change at a rapid rate. Companies continuously try to reduce distribution costs by making existing channels more efficient and exploring the possibilities in alternative channels.

THE PRODUCTION CHALLENGE

Life insurance executives consider distribution productivity the key component of success. On average, marketing activities account for one-half of total U.S. life insurer expenses. The development of competition from outside the industry, the demand for more transparent products like universal and variable policies, and the increasing sophistication of consumers all compel insurers to seek innovation in distribution.

Traditional compensation for agents is dominated by front-loaded or heaped first-year commissions, as industry belief and experience in the past have suggested that life insurance is *sold*, not *bought*. The importance of front-loaded first-year commissions raises issues about the appropriate alignment of interest produced between insurers, agents, and consumers. Specifically, **replacement**, the sale of a new policy in contemplation of the lapse of an older policy, and **churning** (repeated indiscriminate replacements) can significantly increase agent compensation without necessarily benefiting consumers. (These practices are discussed in Chapter 18.) Heaped first-year commissions may also deemphasize the importance of continuing policyowner service by the agent.

The creation and maintenance of a successful life insurance agent is an expensive proposition: development and training costs often exceed $100,000 and for every successful new agent there often are at least five who do not succeed and move on to other careers. Retention of successful agents is also difficult as the best producers are attracted to the enhanced compensation available to a PPGA or other independent environment. Box 10-2 lists many of the training and support needs and expectations of successful agents.

Box 10-2
Examples of Training and Support Needs of Successful Agents

SALES

- Administrative support
- Electronic application submission
- Lead generation
- Online access to application status
- Advanced sales support in tax and estate planning
- Sales and product training
- Sales and marketing material

SERVICE

- Administrative support
- Consolidated client statements
- Online access to client records
- Contact management software
- Sales and marketing material

Many insurers have explored and continue to explore the use of alternative distribution channels consistent with both their existing and new marketing strategies. Some insurers seek to enhance existing distribution channels, while others may make more fundamental changes, examining new direct response or financial institution channels.

POSSIBLE COMPENSATION ALTERNATIVES

Multiple costs are associated with distribution, including agent commissions, field manager compensation and expense, office expense, marketing support, and agent benefits. Agent compensation is the largest and most visible component of insurance distribution costs, however, and receives the most attention. Insurers consider nontraditional approaches to compensation in an effort to increase productivity and create a closer congruence of interest between agents and consumers and between agents and companies. New approaches can be effective, however, only when satisfactory sales volumes can be maintained. Among new approaches adopted by some insurers and being considered by more are:

- *Level Commissions.* Level commissions can increase consumer loyalty through a closer alignment of agent and consumer interest, promote a long-term relationship with the customer, enhance follow-on sales, and greatly diminish any inappropriate replacement incentive by the agent. These features also better align the insurer and agent by improving persistency, which in turn enhances profitability through policy renewals and a longer average policy life, thereby recovering more of the startup costs associated with new policies. They can also produce a more predictable, increasing income flow for the agent, permitting the agent a longer-term view of the client development process.

- *Salary and Bonus.* Under salary plus bonus plans, individuals responsible for the sale of life insurance receive a salary with an incentive bonus tied to performance. With the exception of wholesale representatives discussed above, these arrangements tend to be more effective in the financial institution context than in more traditional agent and broker sales.

These approaches have not enjoyed widespread adoption in the U.S. market. Agent compensation based on a percentage of assets under management rather than a percentage of first-year or renewal premiums offers substantially the same advantages as level commissions and has seen widespread adoption in variable product distribution. There are also additional advantages: the agent's compensation grows as client policy values increase with additional premium payments and favorable investment performance over time. Insurer profitability generally increases as client assets under management grow and persist.

MANDATORY COMPENSATION REFORM MOVEMENT IN INTERNATIONAL MARKETS

Compensation systems based on sales commissions are attractive to producers who can earn unlimited compensation and to life insurers whose marketing expense is largely variable and thus less risky. However, agency and information problems abound in the producer-consumer relationship. Commissions represent an incentive to the sale of expensive products, to the replacement of existing owned policies, and for producer biases toward life insurers that pay higher compensation and the purchase of insurance products to the exclusion of other financial products. Further, as we noted in Chapter 1, buyer ignorance is a prominent feature of life insurance markets.

As we have set forth in this and other chapters, compensation and replacements are currently regulated in some fashion in the U.S. Beginning in 2013, much stricter regulation in Australia, the Netherlands, and the U.K. limits or bans transaction-based compensation and asset-based trail commissions, and provides for negotiated fee agreements for specified services.

Major themes in international compensation reform include

- agreement between producer and customer as to remuneration,
- removal of the insurer from influence in how customers and producers agree to their compensation agreements,
- compensation based on work performed rather than products sold, and
- customer privilege to remove or replace advisors at any time.

Whether these changes will be implemented, or whether similar regulatory directions will develop in the U.S. remains to be seen. The evolution of distribution dominated by sales agents to distribution by producers as *advisors* has been well under way for several decades in advanced markets.

THE LIFE INSURANCE MARKET OF THE FUTURE

The development of the contemporary market for life insurance in the U.S. is characterized by both challenges and opportunities. Life insurance ownership declined in popularity in the U.S. over the last few decades, in part due to the increased availability of group life insurance to workers and to an increasing emphasis by ever more insurers on the affluent market segment with correspondingly less emphasis on the lower and middle income segments. More importantly, while the death benefits of life insurance remain important, the perception of cash value life insurance as a good savings and retirement vehicle has declined.

At the same time, the maturation of the baby boom generation is leading to an increased consumer need for accumulation products. As a result, life insurers have moved to establish securities broker/dealer vehicles for their distributors and to emphasize accumulation products like mutual funds and variable life insurance and annuities. Investment guarantees have proliferated. Overall prospects for the industry are nevertheless generally bright. Consider the following:

- government and industry funding of retirement security is declining in the U.S. (and all other developed markets) and individuals are assuming more personal responsibility for savings and savings planning;
- as employers reduce their commitments to the nonwage components of compensation, they are assisting employees in planning and saving with the employee's own funds;
- a major goal for many of the baby boom generation is said to be leaving a legacy for their children and grandchildren;
- as growing proportions of the population age, they become more security conscious;
- the next large demographic aggregation, the so-called baby boom echo, is entering its own age of affluence;
- Direct response marketing in the 21st century has become a significant distribution channel and continues to expand. Premium income and the number of policies sold through direct response channels have increased significantly in this century.
- The unbundling of investment and insurance product elements and account transparency of universal life and variable annuities are now reflected in a significant majority of industry sales. Interestingly, some products are rebundling protection around specific risks. Thus, with the LTC annuity rider discussed in Chapter 6, both the extraordinary personal care expense and asset depletion contingencies associated with an extraordinarily long life are addressed in the same product.

Although the ultimate scope and magnitude of the impact of Internet marketing is not yet known, its contribution to the landscape of life insurance marketing seems sure to be significant, as Internet access expands worldwide, and consumer concerns about financial transaction security and privacy decline. Industry efficiency is likely to increase, benefiting consumers. Economists have estimated that the result of moving from the high traditional search cost associated with life insurance to the lower search cost associated with Internet comparison shopping has led to significant premium reductions. Term insurance rate reductions of 8-15 percent are attributed to Internet cost search efficiency and the resulting price competition. Anytime, anywhere Internet communication is having and promises to continue to have dramatic effects for consumers in the area of customer service and education, for producers in the areas of training and technical support, and for insurers across the entire range of its operations.

LIFE INSURER PRODUCTS OF THE FUTURE

Life insurers' products have changed over time. The evolution of life insurer products from income security and replacement to investment accumulation to guaranteed investment accumulation and withdrawal is discussed in Chapter 9. Regulatory and demographic changes are likely to drive continued product innovation and development.

We discuss the developing changes in regulatory practice in Chapter 13. Economic principles-based reserving is replacing or supplementing the traditional formulaic reserve and risk-based capital requirements. U.S. federal tax liability, however, is defined by reference to the traditional reserves. The impact of this regulatory/tax discontinuity is not yet clear, but the potential for a significant tax effect arising from new reserves could constrain (or free) product design significantly.

Accumulation and withdrawal guarantees are characteristic of the industry and seem sure to continue to drive sales. Many of the guarantees now associated with annuities will spread to the life insurance product. Indeed, the distinction between life insurance and annuities may blur, as annuities with death benefits and life policies with accumulation and distribution features emerge.

Substandard underwriting and benefits are spreading into the annuity market, which traditionally was classified only by age and gender. As the baby boom generation ages, years of accumulated assets are becoming ready for liquidation, and differentiated pay-out options can be expected to develop. Life insurance features designed for seniors such as no lapse guarantees and geriatric underwriting also seem likely.

ENDNOTES

1   Dennis W. Goodwin, *Life and Health Insurance Marketing* (Atlanta: Life Office Management Association, 1989).

2   This section draws in part from Harold D. Skipper and W. Jean Kwon, *Risk Management and Insurance: Perspectives in a Global Economy* (Malden, MA: Blackwell Publishing, 2007), Chapter 21.

3   Ron Neyer, "Estimating the Impact of Direct Response Marketing," LIMRA Distribution Research monograph (2010).

4   Jeffrey R. Brown and Austan Goolsbee, *The Journal of Political Economy*, "Does the Internet Make Markets More Competitive? Evidence From The Life Insurance Industry," Vol. 110 (June 2002).

5   This section draws on Mike Brown and Keith Dall, "Product Trends in Life Insurance," *The Actuary* (June 2006).

CHAPTER 11

LIFE INSURANCE UNDERWRITING

Underwriting is the process by which an insurance company decides whether it is willing to issue any requested insurance – called *selection* – and, if willing, to determine of the terms, conditions, and rates to be applied – called *classification*. It is a core competency of life insurers' risk management programs. The individuals who practice underwriting are *underwriters*. They are the "gatekeepers" for insurers. The primary focus of this chapter is on life insurance, although the fundamentals and most of the practices set out in this chapter apply equally to health insurance.

Underwriters' jobs are to apply their knowledge of the relationships between (1) various health, lifestyle, and financial factors and (2) mortality (morbidity). They try to match the unique characteristics of each proposed insured with those equivalent factors in the underlying information and data on which they rely – if they can – and, thereby, derive an estimate for life expectancy (morbidity) for proposed insureds possessing those implicit characteristics. In effect, underwriters want to know that the deal that the proposed insured wants to enter with the insurance company is the same as the one that they believe the insurer is entering. To do so, they need to know as much as feasible to assess the risk they are undertaking, including everything that the proposed insured knows that might be relevant.

Underwriting, therefore, is as much about averages as about individual characteristics. Underwriters do not claim to be able to determine whether any of the specific characteristics of a given person will necessarily affect that person's life or health. They do strive to determine whether and the extent to which the health, lifestyle, and financial characteristics of a given person have been found to affect the lives of the universe of persons who possess those characteristics.

Underwriting is fundamental to all types of insurance purchases in a voluntary, private market. Without it, either government must provide (or subsidize) the insurance or only the simplest, low-value types of insurance would be sold. This section explores the reason for this truism.

RISK POOLING AND FAIR PRICES

In any insurance plan, each insured person contributes to a common risk pool from which amounts are paid to or on behalf of the insureds who suffer covered losses. If the plan is to function smoothly on a voluntary basis, each insured's contribution – called the **actuarially fair price** – to the pool should be based on the *expected* loss potential that he or she *ex ante* transfers to it.

Underwriting seeks to estimate that expected loss potential and select the price that most closely aligns with it. In this way, insureds with approximately equal expected loss potentials are classified equally and treated the same. Conversely, insureds whose expected loss potentials are different are classified differently and charged different rates. This process is consistent with the concept of **actuarial equity** – charging proposed insureds rates that reflect their expected loss potentials and having no *intentional* subsidy between rates classes.

GROUP VERSUS INDIVIDUAL INSURANCE   With group insurance, the group as a whole is the insured unit, so each group must contribute an amount sufficient to cover its expected loss potential. With individually issued insurance, each individual is the insured unit and should contribute an amount sufficient to cover the expected value of losses of insureds possessing the characteristics of the proposed insured.

Because the insured unit differs between group and individual insurance, underwriting similarly differs between them. With group insurance, the insurer is concerned with characteristics of the group as a whole, not with the characteristics of the individuals who compose the group. No *individual* underwriting is conducted or necessary, unless the group is composed of a few persons only. They qualify for the group coverages by virtue of the group itself having qualified. Conversely, with individual insurance, the insurer *is* concerned with the characteristic of the individual. We discussed group underwriting in Chapter 7.

SOCIAL VERSUS PRIVATE INSURANCE   If participation in an insurance pool is mandated by government for a given cohort of individuals and the pool must accept all such individuals, contributions to the pool need not reflect each insured's expected loss potential. Government simply mandates participation and requires contributions based on whatever criteria it deems appropriate. Insureds cannot exercise discretion as to whether they participate in the pool, nor can they influence the premium they pay by altering their loss characteristics. This is the essence of social insurance.

Underwriting is both unnecessary and irrelevant for social insurance. This distinction between voluntary private insurance markets and mandatory social insurance is crucial to understanding why underwriting is necessary in private insurance markets and not for social insurance, and why private markets can fail if the pool (insurer) is prohibited from pricing for risk.

FAIR PRICES AND SUBSIDIZATION   In a voluntary insurance market, if some insureds pay premiums that are insufficient to cover the expected value of their losses (and expenses), other insureds must make good the deficit. Insureds with low loss propensities would be subsidizing those with higher loss propensities. When dealing with hundreds and thousands of other insureds, each of whom is anonymous to us, we are not keen voluntarily and knowingly to subsidize any of them. Indeed, human nature being what it is, we are content to accept a subsidy from anonymous people (i.e., paying a price lower than the cost of production), but we are not happy about providing one to anonymous people (i.e., purposefully paying a price greater than the cost of production).

Of course, insureds who do not suffer losses always "subsidize" those who do. However, this type of *ex post* subsidy is fair, in the absence of a moral hazard problem and assuming fair pricing, because its occurrence is random. Ideally, each insured's *ex ante* likelihood of receiving this loss-payment subsidy from the insurance pool *is* the likelihood of his or her suffering a loss. This being true, contributions (premiums) from pool participants (insureds) should logically vary from participant to participant to reflect each participant's likelihood of collecting.

THE IMPORTANCE OF INFORMATION

In any group of individuals, some are near death, some have impaired health, some are exposed to unusual risks of death or ill health because of occupation or other activity, the great majority are in good health, and a few are free of even the slightest impairment. Knowledge and understanding of the way the various factors influence mortality and morbidity enable the company to classify insureds into groups that will give relative mortality and morbidity rates close to those that are anticipated. Classifications subject to a higher-than-average mortality or morbidity are said to be **substandard**.

If complete information were available to the underwriter on each proposed insured, underwriting would be a straightforward process. However, it is impractical and too costly for the insurer to acquire all possible information about each person's insurability. Moreover, it is not necessary to have such complete information. In fact, the pooling mechanism can function smoothly using even grossly incomplete information *if insureds do not possess important information about their insurability not also possessed by insurers.*

THE ADVERSE SELECTION PROBLEM Insurers cannot assume a natural symmetry of information between them and their proposed insureds. In a voluntary insurance market, a natural information asymmetry exists between buyer and seller in the absence of underwriting. Even with underwriting, some insureds do not reveal knowledge that would affect their insurability. This failure to reveal relevant information may be because the insurer did not ask the right questions or because of forgetfulness or misrepresentation or concealment on the part of proposed insureds, applicants, or others involved in the transaction. (In most instances, the proposed insured is also the applicant, but sometimes the applicant is someone else, as when a parent applies for insurance on the life of a child.

This information asymmetry encourages adverse selection. We know that adverse selection (also called *anti-selection)* can exist whenever an individual has freedom to buy or not to buy, to choose the amount or plan of insurance, and to persist or to discontinue as an insured. An important corollary to the general purpose of underwriting as discussed at the beginning of this chapter is that *underwriting is necessary to deter and detect adverse selection.*

Adverse selection is not limited to the buying process, although this chapter focuses on that. It occurs also when existing insureds perceive that their premiums are too high relative to their loss potential, and they have the option of discontinuing their insurance at little or no penalty. The accuracy of this statement is illustrated by the failure of the assessment form of life insurance in which premiums were *not* graded according to age. See Chapter 1.

An insurance pool can collapse because of an **adverse selection spiral,** which is the tendency of insureds who are charged premiums sufficiently greater than the expected value of their losses to withdraw from the insurance pool thereby precipitating premium increases for the remaining insureds, from among whom still more withdrawals occur, etc. This type of adverse selection is exacerbated by pricing and underwriting practices that fail to consider the major risk factors as understood by insureds.

If individuals know that an insurer will insure them without undertaking any underwriting, those in poor health and who otherwise can be expected to exhibit mortality (or morbidity) higher than average, will tend to apply for the coverage, hoping to secure a more favorable rate. As an example, consider the mortality experience under group term conversions. Figure 11-1 shows the mortality experience as reported in a study of group term conversions. The effects of adverse selection are obvious.

Conversely, if individuals know that the insurer will undertake an investigation of their insurability status, those in poor health might not apply at all or might be more forthright in answering underwriting queries – for they probably believe that the insurer may check on the veracity of their responses. Also, agents themselves engage in selection by seeking customers who are most likely to be insurable. Most have little interest in trying to sell life or health insurance to someone whom they suspect will be declined by the underwriters.

For these reasons, 90 percent of individuals who apply for life insurance in the U.S. are accepted at preferred or standard rates. This high percentage of acceptances is not representative of the insurability status of the U.S. population as a whole. Rather, it suggests that underwriting generally functions as we expect it to function, to both deter and detect adverse selection. By deterring and detecting adverse selection, insurance premiums are kept within a reasonable range, thereby preserving a private market. Without underwriting, the adverse selection spiral could, in the worst case, cause the complete collapse of an insurance market or, in the best case, cause such an escalation in premiums that all but the riskiest individuals would refuse to purchase insurance and withdraw from the market.

A British study, for example, found that premiums for term life insurance would be about twice as high if insurer mortality experience were the same as that for the population as a whole.[1] Stated differently, because of underwriting, premiums for the average U.K. purchaser of term insurance were one-half that which they would have been without underwriting. Of course, it is wrong to assume that an insurer's mortality or morbidity experience would mirror that of the population as a whole if underwriting did not exist. Without this gate-keeping function, adverse selection would ensure that the insured population would exhibit mortality experience far worse than that experienced for the population as a whole, as illustrated in Figure 11-1.

Ratio of Actual to Expected Mortality for Group Life Conversions, All Ages Combined   Figure 11-1

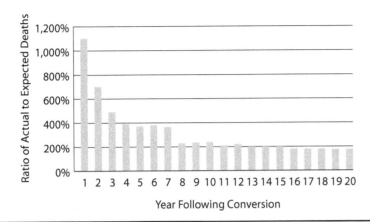

Insureds under group term life insurance plans typically have the right to convert this insurance to individual policies at standard rates if they cease to be eligible for the group insurance (e.g., because they lost their jobs). Individuals in good health tend not to convert whereas those in poor health tend to exercise this option (because the option's strike price – the group conversion rate – is less than its market price – the substandard individual rate).

THE ROLE OF COMPETITION   Clearly, voluntary private insurance markets cannot function efficiently and often not at all without underwriting to deter and detect adverse selection. However, even if adverse selection were no problem, insurers still would have to underwrite for competitive reasons. Competition drives businesses in general and insurers in particular constantly to seek advantages over rivals. These advantages may be in the form of new policies, special policy provisions, new ways of marketing, and hundreds of other means. One means of securing an advantage is through the application of superior information via the underwriting process. Thus, an insurer might be able to secure more complete information about its proposed insureds at little cost, enabling it to make better classification decisions.

Another means of securing a competitive advantage has been through mortality and morbidity studies and research that enable actuaries and underwriters to gain a better understanding of the factors influencing mortality and morbidity. The stronger this understanding, the more precise can be the insurer's pricing and underwriting. Precision requires greater classification refinement.

Consider, for example, how life insurers priced and underwrote life insurance prior to the introduction of separate rates for smokers and nonsmokers in the 1970s. Although actuaries had known for many years that smoking materially increased one's risk of dying, insurers had not incorporated this fact into their pricing. As a consequence, the rates for otherwise identical smokers and nonsmokers were the same. This situation changed in the 1970s when one life insurer, in seeking a competitive advantage over its rivals in the high-income market, began charging separate rates for smokers and nonsmokers. By doing so, it was able to offer significantly lower rates for non-smokers, thereby charging less than its competitors which charged pooled rates for smokers and nonsmokers.

In employing its knowledge of the adverse effects of smoking, it effectively split the traditional standard group into two groups. It began to "cream" the market – agents placed their nonsmoking clientele with this insurer and their smoking clients with other insurers. Smokers tended to seek insurance from the insurers that continued to use traditional pricing, as these smokers (more often, their agents) now understood that they were effectively being subsidized by the nonsmokers.

If the other insurers had *not* moved to differentiate between smokers and nonsmokers, the proportion of smokers in their insured groups would have grown as more smokers sought insurance from them while nonsmokers sought insurance from the insurers that recognized their more favorable loss propensities by offering lower rates. To compete successfully, other insurers had to adopt separate pricing for smokers and nonsmokers. Separate pricing is now commonplace in the U.S. and many other markets. Figure 11-2 offers a stylized view of this split of the traditional standard group into smokers and nonsmokers, assuming equal numbers of each type of insured.

Figure 11-2   **Anticipated Mortality Distributions: Traditional and with Tobacco Usage**

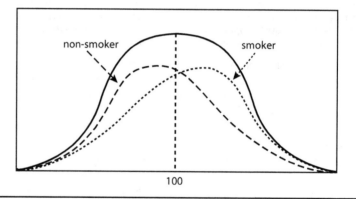

The upper distribution represents the traditional approach whereby smokers and nonsmokers were not charged differently. Average mortality for the combined group is represented by 100 percent. The figure reveals that the traditional distribution masked two other, distinct mortality distributions. The traditional distribution, of course, always included both smoker and nonsmoker mortality.

Most companies have now moved beyond the smoker/nonsmoker dichotomy. They have further split the smoker and nonsmoker classifications into preferred and standard categories, thus having four categories that they consider as falling within the "standard range." Some insurers offer even more categories.

GUIDING PRINCIPLES IN UNDERWRITING

Underwriting principles are the same for all life insurance companies. Standards of practice that flow from these principles are also broadly similar, but implementation details will vary from company to company and, within companies, even vary somewhat from underwriter to underwriter. Each insurer establishes it own underwriting policies and practices, often with the guidance of its reinsurers.

Differences between companies in underwriting are the result of different judgments as to what is the best overall policy.

EQUITY AMONG INSUREDS

The manner in which insureds are rated should be built on the principle of actuarial equity. Some grouping of insureds is desirable to yield a reasonable volume of experience within a given classification (pool) and because of expense considerations. On the other hand, to be satisfactory to the proposed insured and the company, the spread between the worst and best risks within a classification should not be so broad as to produce significant inequity or hinder a company in competition. In practice, the width of rating classes tends to vary directly with the degree of substandard rating. The width of each class is a function of the dependability of the available data on impaired lives and of competition.

An important means by which life insurers implement this principle is through the use of **underwriting guidelines** that provide recommendations and background for underwriting actions with regard to the majority of the health, lifestyle, and financial conditions and situations that underwriters are likely to encounter in conducting their risk management jobs. The insurer's guidelines may have been developed internally, or they may be those of one of its major reinsurers or some combination thereof.

While much – although by no means all – that underpins underwriting decision making is grounded in statistics, underwriting is not an exact science. Judgment plays a major role. Were it otherwise, we would have little need for a human underwriter, instead relying on computers to do the job. Of course, insurers' underwriting guidelines are designed to streamline and regularize the underwriting process and thereby make it more predictable and consistent across underwriters. However, guidelines constitute recommended procedures and practices; they are not edicts. Underwriters are still expected to use their professional judgment.

RECOGNITION OF UNDERLYING LOSS ASSUMPTIONS

Risk classification reflects the mortality (morbidity) levels assumed in determining the premium rate applied. If the proposed insured is to be considered at standard rates, the expected loss experience must be comparable to that used in determining these rates. In practice, some companies (especially large ones) continually study their morbidity and mortality experience and evaluate their classification rules. They review their experience on lives accepted as standard and compare their experience on impaired lives with the standard experience. Based on this study and analysis, each company adjusts its classification rules where indicated.

As insured experience is made up of selected lives, the underwriting that is to be exercised in the future should be at least as effective as that used in the past, if experience is to be similar to that provided for in the experience-based premium or cost of insurance (COI) rate structure. A situation of generally improving mortality or morbidity, however, might permit acceptance of some impaired lives without exceeding that assumed in the premium or COI calculations. Such action would adversely affect the company's competitive position if other companies continued to accept only standard risks at their standard rates.

SOCIAL ACCEPTABILITY

Underwriting factors used by insurers should be socially acceptable. This principle often has little or nothing to do with underlying risk characteristics and can prove inconsistent with the principle of actuarial equity. Historically, the practice of charging individuals according to their relative risks of dying or becoming disabled has been viewed as fair. This is because the actuarial (and economic) definition of fairness has been itself generally accepted; i.e., rates are fair if they reflect the expected value of each insured's losses.

Recent studies of public attitudes toward risk classification show that the U.S. public tends to accept as fair the use of those risk factors over which individuals have some degree of choice (e.g., hazardous hobbies and smoking). In contrast, the public tends to perceive as unfair the use of risk factors over which we have little or no control (e.g., heart attack history or cancer). This result is disturbing for insurers for many, perhaps most, diseases are beyond individuals' control. Yet, they can have a profound effect on mortality and morbidity. It also raises the important question as to how we determine what is within an individual's control.

The public seems also to believe that insurers make some adverse decisions with insufficient actuarial justification. This concern arose in public debates about the use of blindness as a classification factor and finds voice also in the debate about the extent to which insurers should be permitted to use genetic testing information. To the extent that the concern is valid, better research can mitigate it. To the extent that it is invalid, perhaps better explanations for underwriting decisions would help.

At the same time, insurers realize that some practices were, in fact, flawed. For example, in the distant past, U.S. life insurers routinely charged higher rates to black than to white persons. The justification for this differential was that blacks as a group did not live as long as whites of the same age and sex. Population and insured mortality statistics were cited in support of this practice; that is, the practice was considered to be "actuarially fair."

At about the same time that U.S. society concluded that the use of race as a rating factor was offensive, insurers realized that the observed differences in mortality between blacks and whites were driven not by race but by socio-economic and other factors. We know that poor people do not live as long as wealthier people. More blacks than whites are poor. Merely establishing a statistical relationship between a factor and mortality or morbidity does not also establish causation. Relevance can be important. Thus, it is wrong to consider the socially acceptable principle as being always in conflict with actuarial fairness – it can result in a more efficient insurance mechanism.

FACTORS AFFECTING INSURABILITY

In deciding whether to issue insurance (selection), and if so, on what terms and conditions and at what price (classification), life insurance companies examine several factors to guard against insureds being charged either excessive or inadequate rates. This section reviews the chief factors affecting a person's insurability for life insurance. We divide the discussion between rating factors and selection and classification factors.

Rating Factors

The underwriting process begins with a determination of the rating class into which the proposed insured's rating factors place him or her. This determination historically was based on the age and sex of the proposed insured. Most insurers today also base it on whether the proposed insured uses tobacco. For example, one set of premium rates applies to all 30-year-old, nonsmoking females and another set to the same aged females who smoke and yet another set to 31-year-old, non-smoking females, and so on.

Underwriting begins with the particular age-sex-tobacco combination applicable to each proposed insured. Each combination has its own set of premium or COI rates for each policy offered by the insurer. From here, the underwriter evaluates the proposed insured's other insurability factors to determine into which mortality classification (e.g., preferred, standard, substandard table 1, etc.) this particular (age-sex-tobacco) person falls.

Age   Expected future mortality is highly correlated with age (as is morbidity but to a lesser extent). Other things being the same, the older a person is, the greater the likelihood of death. Of course, chronological age is a proxy for biological age. Regrettably, science does not as yet offer sufficiently accurate, low cost means of determining one's biological age so chronological age is used as a convenient proxy. Age is a key factor in determining the *rate* an individual is to be charged for life insurance, but it is rarely a *selection* factor; that is, it generally is not used in determining whether to offer insurance, except for individuals who are of especially advanced age or, with some types of insurance, very young.

Furnishing proof of age is not required at the time of application, as (1) such a requirement could cause delay, (2) few persons misstate their age, (3) proof is usually easily obtained if needed, and (4) the misstatement of age clause (see Chapter 5) handles those situations where the problem arises. (An exception to this generalization can occur in the case of an immediate annuity, under which it would be impractical to adjust the amount of the benefits if a misstatement of age is discovered at the time of the annuitant's death, proof of age may be required at the time of annuity purchase.)

Sex   The sex of proposed insureds, like their ages, is not used as a selection factor but is routinely used as a rating factor with respect to individual life insurance. Yearly probabilities of death of females are less than the yearly probabilities of death of similarly situated males. As a result, most insurers worldwide charge lower life insurance premium and COI rates and higher annuity rates for females than for males. This was not always true. Several decades ago insurers charged women the same or higher rates because of the "frailty" of women and the "hazards of childbirth." Increasingly accurate statistics, competition, and a widening mortality gap between the two sexes caused insurers to alter this practice.

While mortality statistics clearly show a difference in death rates between men and women and, therefore, can be used *actuarially* to justify charging them different rates, other important considerations have arisen. The question now being debated is: Is it *socially* acceptable to charge men and women different rates?

TOBACCO USAGE   Use of tobacco in any form, whether chewing, dipping, or smoking cigarettes, cigars, or a pipe is an important risk factor by itself and now is commonly used as a differentiating rate factor in personal life and health insurance. In the past, smoking or other tobacco use was considered in underwriting, but only rarely as a factor of importance by itself. Insurers now understand that smoking and other tobacco use, even in the absence of any other negative factor, causes expected future mortality (morbidity) to be worse than the average.

Cigarette smokers experience mortality rates of more than twice those of nonsmokers. So important is this factor that the average female smoker can be expected to exhibit higher mortality than the average nonsmoking male of the same age. Tobacco use also aggravates other health problems.

SELECTION AND CLASSIFICATION FACTORS

No doubt, the great majority of proposed insureds, applicants, and/or others involved in the application process respond fully and accurately to insurers' underwriting inquiries. Unfortunately, insurers do not know *a priori* which ones are responding in this fashion and which ones are not. A not insubstantial number of individuals withhold or misrepresent information when they apply for insurance. Others seek insurance while knowing or suspecting the existence of an adverse condition that the company does not know about, in the hope that the condition will not be discovered. Therefore, for personal life insurance, underwriters want to learn whether an insured possesses characteristics that can affect his or her life and health. To do so, they ordinarily secure personal information that falls into three broad categories: health, lifestyle, and financial.

HEALTH CHARACTERISTICS   That an individual's health characteristics are essential for assessing likelihood of death and ill health is obvious. This category can be the most complex to assess and the most important and so usually entails the greatest amount of time, effort, and expense by the insurer.

Physical Condition   The physical condition of a proposed insured is of basic significance in underwriting. One of the determinants of physical condition is build. Build includes height, weight, and distribution of the weight. Overweight increases the likelihood of death and ill health at all ages. While moderate overweight may not have a ratable effect, it can magnify the significance of other physical ailments, such as cardiac conditions. Most companies use a table showing average weights according to height, age, and sex. The table is then extended to other weights, and expected extra mortality is shown as a percentage of standard. At the best weights (i.e., less than the average) the tables indicate a better than average expected mortality rate. Increasingly, insurers use the body mass index.

Other aspects of a proposed insured's physical condition also are considered. Companies know that future mortality experience will depend, in varying degrees, upon abnormalities in one or more of the important systems of the body – that is, the nervous, digestive, cardiovascular, respiratory, or genitourinary systems, and glands of internal secretion. The defects and disabilities that may be found in the organs of the body and the methods of ascertaining them are necessarily medical in character. It is beyond the scope of this book to explore them, but a few of the common ones that usually increase the risk may be mentioned.

Thus, an examination of the circulatory system may reveal elevated blood pressure, a heart murmur, or a high or irregular heart rate. An analysis of the urine may disclose the presence of albumin, sugar, or red blood cells. Indications of any of these or similar conditions necessitate further examination before the application can be accepted on terms satisfactory to both parties. Coronary risk factors are used by many companies in their overall assessment. Factors such as low blood cholesterol, optimal blood pressure, and nonsmoking contribute significantly to improved mortality from heart disease.

Mental Condition   The mental state of proposed insureds is particularly relevant with health insurance but also often for life insurance. Many persons suffer from mental disorders that can be material to the underwriting decision. These include anxiety, bipolar disorders, depression, neurosis, schizophrenia, suicidal tendencies, and others.

A surprisingly high proportion of the U.S. and other populations has thoughts of committing suicide, especially among those suffering mental disorders, but also among the elderly and alcohol abusers. The fact of a proposed insured having attempted to kill himself is obviously material to a decision whether to issue insurance to such a person. Similarly, the fact that an individual has made suicidal gestures or has thoughts about killing himself (*suicide ideation*) is also of obvious importance. Such individuals are more likely to act successfully on the gesture or idea, whether intended or not, than those who have made no such gestures or ideation. Ideation alone obviously requires a voluntary disclosure by the proposed insured.

Health History   A proposed insured's health history is especially important. If the individual has in the past suffered a serious illness or accident, an appraisal of its probable effects on future life and health will be made. The appraisal frequently will require that, in addition to the medical history given by the proposed insured, reports be obtained from personal physicians and other health care providers as well as from hospitals.

Insurance history also can be important. The proposed insured may have been refused insurance by some insurer or offered insurance under special terms. If so, this fact may imply an extra hazard that existed formerly and may still be present and should be investigated. In some jurisdictions, legal restrictions prohibit the basing of an adverse action solely on information of any previous such action by another company. In any event, sound underwriting practice dictates that the company makes every effort to establish for itself the proposed insured's insurability.

Family History   Family history is considered important by most companies because of the transmission of certain genetic characteristics by heredity. If the history shows that most members of the family have lived to old age without incurring heart disease, cancer, diabetes, and other serious diseases, it may be inferred that the proposed insured will be less susceptible to these diseases.

LIFESTYLE CHARACTERISTICS   We use the term "lifestyle" to encompass a range of factors, including occupation, avocation and sports, aviation, residence, military service, and drug use. Each of these factors can influence the underwriter's assessment of expected mortality. Lifestyle factors can be of great importance for a given proposed insured, but, on average, they usually are less so than health information in terms of time, effort, and expense to the company.

Alcohol and Drugs   Information is usually sought regarding the proposed insured's use of habit-forming drugs and intoxicating beverages. Excessive alcohol use is associated with higher than standard mortality. If the individual uses alcoholic beverages in large amounts, he may be declined or offered substandard insurance, depending upon the degree of use. Alcohol abuse is commonly associated with suicide, with the lifetime suicide risk of such persons found to range from 3.4 percent to as high as 15 percent. Use of alcohol in moderation seems to have no material impact on mortality rates, and some studies have found it to be beneficial.

Use of drugs not prescribed by a physician or drug abuse may call for a declination, depending upon the type of drug. A history of misuse or unsupervised use of over the counter or recreational drugs may require an extra rating, depending upon the length of time since the drug or drugs were used, the nature of the treatment given, and whether there has been participation in a continuing support program.

Occupation   Occupational hazards are less important today than in the past. They may increase the risk in at least three different ways. First, the occupation may present an environmental hazard, such as exposure to violence or a temptation to experiment with drugs or overindulge in alcohol. Second, the physical conditions surrounding an occupation can have a decided bearing upon health and longevity, as in the case of persons who work in close, dusty, or poorly ventilated quarters or are exposed to chemical toxins. Finally, there is the risk from accident, such as is faced by professional automobile racers, crop dusters, and professional divers. For example, fishermen and loggers experience death rates of almost 30 times those of average workers.

An individual who has recently changed from a hazardous occupation to a safer form of employment must be underwritten carefully, as he or she may still retain ill effects or the change may have been prompted by a health factor. Also, such a person is more likely than a person without such a history to return to the former occupation. The usual practice is to ignore prior occupation if the individual has been removed from it for a period of one or more years. Because of increased attention to job safety and working conditions, ratings have been reduced or eliminated for many occupations.

Hazardous Sports and Avocations   Activities such as scuba diving, mountain climbing, competitive racing, hang gliding, and skydiving can involve an additional hazard, and the individual may be charged a flat extra premium commensurate with the risk. A rider excluding death resulting from participation in the hazardous activity is employed occasionally.

Aviation and Driving   Flights as a fare-paying passenger on regularly scheduled airlines are not sufficiently hazardous to affect the risk. Where there may be a definite aviation hazard involving commercial, private, or military flying, the proposed insured may be requested to complete a supplementary **aviation**

questionnaire, which is a supplement to a life or health insurance application that elicits additional aviation information from a proposed insured who engages in commercial, private, or military aviation activities. The company may then charge an extra premium to compensate for the aviation hazard, or, infrequently, this cause of death may be excluded from the policy. If the risk is excluded and if death occurs because of aviation activities, the company is liable only for a return of premiums paid or the reserve accumulated on the policy, or, sometimes, whichever of the two produces the larger figure. Most scheduled airline and private pilots are issued standard insurance without aviation restrictions.

Insurers also recognize the high incidences of motor vehicle injuries and death, especially at younger ages. For this reason, they often secure a copy of the proposed insured's motor vehicle report. Excessive traffic citations – which are correlated with accident likelihood – can lead to an adverse underwriting decision.

Military Service   In the absence of hostilities, contracts are issued to U.S. military personnel with no exclusions or limitations. The adverse selection involved when individuals are engaged in or facing military service during a period of armed conflict can constitute an underwriting problem. Underwriting action taken in the past included outright declination, a limitation on the amount of insurance issued, or the attachment of a war exclusion clause (see Chapter 5) that limits the insurer's obligation.

War clauses were used extensively during World War II in policies issued to military personnel. They were also used by U.S. insurers during the Korean conflict, primarily for military personnel going to Korea or for members of particularly hazardous combat forces. War clauses generally were not used by U.S. insurers during the Vietnam, Iraqi, or Afghanistan wars. In any event, when hostilities cease, war clauses are routinely canceled and cannot be reactivated.

Residence   Mortality rates in most developing countries are higher than those in most developed countries, primarily because of differences in general living conditions. Individuals moving to a developed country from a developing country may already have been adversely affected by these conditions. When the proposed insured resides in a developing country, the possible increased hazards of climate, general living conditions, and political unrest will be included in the insurer's rate structure. Frequent travel to certain countries can also cause concern. Concerns for insurers located in one country and underwriting individuals residing or who have resided in other countries include the inability to develop full underwriting information and difficulties in investigating claims.

FINANCIAL CHARACTERISTICS   The purpose of financial underwriting is to ensure that the motivation for the insurance purchase is sound and that the amount of insurance applied for bears a reasonable relationship to the individual's insurable value. In advanced planning cases, trusts, trustees, trust grantors, donors, companies, and partnerships may serve as applicants, beneficiaries, or owners, and the insurer may consider the financial motivations and resources of all of them. The financial characteristics of proposed insureds are routinely considered by underwriters in deciding whether to issue insurance and the amount to issue. In other words, they are relevant only in the selection phase of underwriting. The underwriter wishes to know the rationale justifying the purchase of the requested insurance, including the rationale for the beneficiary designation and policyowner (if different from the insured), information about life insurance already in force and in process, and the proposed insured's net worth and income in relation to the amount of insurance requested, in force, and in process. As with lifestyle information, financial information can be of great importance in a given case, but, on average, usually is less so than health information in terms of time, effort, and expense to the company. It also tends to be more objective than medical information.

Determining Motivation   Determining the motivation for the proposed insurance is a primary element in financial underwriting. This is best demonstrated by a well-established purpose, logical beneficiary, and reasonable amount in relation to the insured's (and if different from the insured, the policyowner's) financial status.

Individuals have an insurable interest in their own lives to an unlimited extent, as discussed in Chapter 18. The logic for this treatment flows from the fact that life insurance policies are not contracts of indemnity (as with property and liability insurance) and because individuals are presumed to have a sufficient "love of life" such that no amount of money would cause them to agree to die solely for the money. While sound *legal* logic, it does not provide parallel *economic* logic for life insurers agreeing to issue policies in whatever amounts are requested – irrespective of how large. Nor does it provide *economic* logic for the insurer agreeing to accept just any beneficiary designation even if it is legally acceptable. Rather, in deciding whether to issue life insurance and the amount to issue, life insurance underwriters think in terms of the insurance being indemnification for a possible financial loss to the beneficiary, in much the same way as underwriters for property insurance think about the relationship between the requested insurance amount and the underlying building value and the payee under a fire insurance policy.

Determining Maximum Insurable Value   The most common reasons for the purchase of personal life insurance probably are to replace income lost to survivors and pay estate obligations occasioned by the death of the insured person. Much life insurance is also sold for business and charitable purposes. For underwriting the first category, insurers commonly use so-called *income multiples* as guidelines for the total amount of life insurance that they will agree to issue, taking into consideration life insurance already in force and applications in process or contemplated on the insured's life.

These multiples are gross estimates for the amount of income lost to survivors because of a person's death. Thus, one company's guidelines suggest that a 51-year old person with wages of $100,000 per year could qualify for a total amount of life insurance of up to 10 times the annual wage or $1.0 million. Younger ages have higher multiples; older ages lower multiples. These multiples are approximations of present value factors where the duration is roughly a person's remaining working lifetime. Table 11-1 presents multiples for one major insurer.

Another common reason for the purchase of personal life insurance is to provide liquidity to cover estate obligations. These obligations can be in the form of debts and estate settlement costs. Thus, many individuals purchase life insurance for purposes of paying off home mortgages and other debts on their deaths.

Determining the amount of insurance here is comparatively easy – the amount of the debt owed by the person.

Underwriting Guidelines for Maximum Insurance Amounts based on Earned Income		Table 11-1

Age	Multiple of Annual Gross Earned Income
20-35	20X
36-40	17X
41-45	14X
46-50	12X
51-59	10X
60-65	7X
66 and above	5X

Wealthy individuals often purchase insurance to cover their estate settlement costs, the most important of which are estate taxes. Their goal is to have life insurance death proceeds cover all or a good portion of these taxes rather than paying the taxes from the assets of the estate, thereby conserving estate assets for heirs. Determining the amount of insurance here is more complicated. A common approach is to estimate the future value of the gross estate (or net worth) by projecting today's value at a reasonable accumulation rate to the proposed insured's life expectancy or for set number of years less than life expectancy. The tax is then estimated on that projected value or some percentage of it. Other, less formal approaches are also sometimes used, such as assuming that estate taxes and settlement costs will be 50 percent of the value of today's estate.

The present and estimated future estate values are *the* determining factors for whether any insurance will be issued and, if issued, the maximum amount. If the amount of requested insurance is large, such as $2.0 million or so, insurers' underwriting guidelines commonly call for submission of a completed **financial questionnaire** which is a supplement to a life insurance application which elicits additional financial information about and from a proposed insured and/or applicant who applies for a comparatively large amount of insurance. If the amount of insurance is larger still, such as $5.0 million or larger, third-party verification of the proposed insured's financial status usually is requested in addition to the financial questionnaire, such as information from the insured's attorney or accountant.

Life insurance is also commonly purchased for business purposes. These purposes include (1) key person indemnification, (2) business continuation, and (3) nonqualified executive benefit plans. In each instance, the maximum insurable value will be that amount sufficient to (1) indemnify the business for the economic loss associated with the death of the key employee, (2) allow the business or others (commonly the surviving business owners) to purchase the business interest of a deceased owner, and (3) fund benefits at a reasonable level promised by the business to an executive. Chapter 24 explores these applications and life insurance amount determination in detail.

Finally, many individuals wish to leave funds to charities on their deaths. A common means of doing so is by purchasing a life insurance policy payable to their preferred charities. The charity usually is the policyowner and beneficiary, with the insured/donor paying (tax-deductible) premiums. Often the person has a history of making contributions to the charity, although this is not always essential. Where such a history exists, guidelines may suggest a maximum insurable value of 10 times or so of the amount of the average annual contribution.

Minimizing Adverse Selection and Moral Hazard   Applications involving questionable insurable interest or suspicious beneficiary designations immediately raise questions whether someone is speculating on human life with its attendant moral hazard. The underwriting cliché that insurers diligently seek to avoid situations where an insured would be "worth more dead than alive" harbors much insight into underwriting. Such situations are said to be associated with higher mortality because of moral hazard and adverse selection. Thus, underwriters are on alert for circumstances that might suggest that an individual is withholding or misrepresenting information for his or her or the beneficiary's benefit.

If a case does not "hold together" because of unresolved questions about financial characteristics, prudence results in a declination. The suspicions that arise naturally from such over insurance speculation in life insurance have proven justified, as they have in situations where someone tries to purchase fire insurance on another person's property or in amounts greatly in excess of the value of a building. Applications for life insurance for speculative purposes are rare when compared with the total insurance sold, but the cases are frequent enough to be of importance. Individual cases have involved millions of dollars. The importance of an income or wealth overstatement, of insurance understatement, or of intended short-term owner or beneficiary designations usually lies in the "hidden information" or "signal value" that they contain, rather than the offered information standing alone, as explained below.

SOURCES OF INFORMATION CONCERNING LIFE AND HEALTH INSURANCE RISKS

Insurers obtain information about proposed insureds from several sources, including (1) applications, (2) physical examinations, (3) laboratory testing, (4) agents, (5) attending physicians, (6) inspection companies, and (7) industry-sponsored data bases. Not all sources are necessarily used in connection with a given proposed insured. Also, the information from these sources often overlaps. Experience has proven this overlap to be beneficial. In many countries, especially in Europe and North America, laws establish procedures intended to ensure fair and equitable treatment of the consumer with regard to information confidentiality, accuracy, disclosure, and proper use.

THE APPLICATION

The life insurance application is the most important and critical source of information in the underwriting process. It typically is comprised of two parts. Part I elicits financial, lifestyle, and administrative information about the proposed insured and/or applicant including:

- past addresses,
- occupation,
- gender,

- date of birth,
- current coverage and current applications for life and health insurance with other insurers, any history of refused applications or policies issued with a rating, and whether existing insurance will be replaced,
- driving record,
- past and planned private aviation activities,
- avocations,
- foreign travel, and
- net worth and earned and unearned income.

Part II of the application is for recording the insured's answers to questions about his or her health. It is completed by a medical or paramedical examiner or, if the policy is applied for on a nonmedical basis, by the agent. Information is requested regarding:

- illnesses, injuries, diseases, and surgeries during the past ten or so years,
- physician consultations during the previous five or so years,
- alcohol, tobacco, and drug use, and
- the medical history of parents and siblings, including their current health and the causes and dates of any deaths.

Insurers seek to minimize the time required to complete an application to ease the process for the agent, proposed insured, and/or applicant. Thus, inquiries are limited to information essential to making an informed underwriting decision. The Part II medical questions may be condensed for younger insureds and for applications for smaller amounts.

PHYSICAL EXAMINATION

A medical exam is required if the requested insurance amount is comparatively large or if additional information is needed about the insured's health status. Results of the medical exam are reported to the insurer on special forms that augment Part II. The examiner may be a physician or, for lesser amounts of insurance and to minimize costs, a paramedic. The examination typically includes height, weight, chest, and abdomen measurements; a blood profile and test that measures exposure to the AIDS virus; and a urinalysis that includes testing for nonprescription drug and possible tobacco usage. A regular physical exam might include all of these items plus an examination of the condition of the heart, lungs, and nervous system. For larger life and health policies, more detailed information involving complete blood and urine testing, electrocardiograms, pulmonary functions tests, and chest x-rays often are requested.

The examination is not foolproof. Many serious medical conditions can be detected only through sophisticated tests or invasive procedures that are inappropriate for insurance underwriting and therefore they can pass undetected. Also, some individuals go to considerable effort to appear at their best through rest and diet and may deliberately or unintentionally not disclose important health issues.

LABORATORY TESTING

Blood and urine testing have become more prevalent and their scope broader in response to the excess mortality risk represented by AIDS and drug use. The cost is recovered in reduced claims. Claims are further reduced through the resulting availability of other useful underwriting information such as liver enzymes, lipids, and glucose levels.

Advances in genetic research mean that new information is becoming available on a variety of genetic illnesses. The life insurance industry's position is to treat genetic tests used by medical professionals in diagnostics, treatment, and preventive medicine no differently from any other medical tests used in clinical medicine. Presently, insurers do not order genetic tests.

THE AGENT

Insurers usually request information about the proposed insured and/or applicant via an **agent's report** in which the agent responds to queries such as for how long and how well he or she knows the proposed insured and/or applicant and whether he or she knows of any adverse information. The agent may also be asked to express an opinion about the individual's financial standing, character, and environment. For larger policies, the company may also request that the agent provide a letter explaining the rationale for the insurance and the requested amount.

Insurers know that agents have financial incentives to make the sale and, therefore, to present proposed insureds favorably. Reporting adverse information can harm the sale, but agents' ethical and legal duties call for them to report fully and accurately. This problem of incentive conflict is another example of the agency problem discussed in Chapter 1.

ATTENDING PHYSICIAN STATEMENTS

When the amount of insurance applied for is sufficiently large or if the individual application or the medical examiner's report reveals conditions or situations, past or present, about which more information is desired, the insurer may order attending physician statements (APS) that present physician reports of the proposed insured's condition and treatment. They may reveal additional health conditions or the names of additional physicians not reported in the application.

Physicians are not authorized to disclose patient information without a specific authorization from the patient. Thus, every application includes such an authorization to be signed by the proposed insured. The APS is considered by many to be an important source of information; securing multiple APSs can also be a source of significant delay in the processing of an application.

INSPECTION COMPANIES

For larger amounts of insurance, insurers obtain an **inspection report** which is an industry term for a consumer report – see below – used by underwriters and prepared by an inspection company, which is intended to verify and/or supplement mainly nonmedical information provided by a proposed insured and/or applicant. Most insurers obtain these reports from an independent **inspection company,** which is an industry term for a **consumer reporting agency** – see below – which is an organization that collects and sells information about individuals' employment history, driving record, financial situation, creditworthiness, character, personal characteristics, mode of living, and other possibly relevant personally identifiable information.

A significant part of the value of the report is its independence from the incentives of the applicant and agent to withhold or "interpret" information favorably.

Under U.S. law, inspection reports are called *consumer reports* and inspection companies are called *consumer reporting agencies*. A **consumer report** is defined by the U.S. *Fair Credit Reporting Act* (FCRA) as a written, oral, or other communication of any information by a consumer reporting agency that has a bearing on the consumer's creditworthiness, credit standing, credit capacity, character, general reputation, personal characteristics, or mode of living, and that is used or expected to be used in whole or in part to establish eligibility for credit, *personal insurance*, employment, or certain other purposes. An **investigative consumer report** is a consumer report in which information on a consumer's character, general reputation, personal characteristics, or mode of living is obtained from personal interviews with the consumer's neighbors, friends, or associates.

When the amount of insurance is not particularly large, the inspection company employee will make a rather general inquiry into the habits, character, financial condition, occupation, avocations, and health of the proposed insured, relying primarily on public records and the proposed insured and/or applicant. If the amount of insurance is large or if there is concern about possible adverse selection or moral hazard, a more careful and detailed report –an investigative consumer report – may be obtained, particularly regarding financial information, and more informants may be contacted. To obtain the necessary information for a more thorough report, the investigator may interview the proposed insured's and/ or applicant's employer, neighbors, banker, accountant, business associates, and others who may be able to contribute the information desired.

Insurers also utilize telephone interviews of insureds and/or applicants to replace or supplement inspection reports. A principal advantage is the discovery of inconsistencies between the interview and the written application.

INDUSTRY-SPONSORED DATA BASES

Another source of information regarding insurability in some countries is an industry-sponsored data base of personal information, such as the Medical Information Bureau in the U.S. and Canada. The **Medical Information Bureau** (MIB) is a membership-sponsored corporation that collects personally identifiable information about individuals who have applied for life or health insurance from member companies and who have certain medical and other conditions that might affect their insurability. Its purpose is to assist member companies in detecting adverse selection in the underwriting of individually issued life, medical, disability income, and long term care insurance. In addition to its traditional *Checking Service,* it also offers (1) a *Follow-up Service* that alerts members to new applicant information received within two years following the original Checking Service inquiry and (2) an *Insurance Activity Index* that provides members with an applicant's application activity for the previous two years.

The MIB also provides the dates of inquiries, alerting companies to the possibility that the proposed insured may be attempting to avoid certain underwriting requirements by applying for smaller amounts in several companies rather than for a large amount in one company. The *Disability Income Record System* provides information about applications for disability income insurance to assist insurers in recognizing situations involving potential overinsurance.

MIB procedures and some state privacy laws require that an individual be informed in writing before completing an application for insurance that the company may report information to the MIB and to secure the proposed insured's authorization for MIB to release information to the insurer about the proposed insured. The proposed insured is also advised how to obtain disclosure of his or her MIB file and dispute its accuracy. MIB disclosure and disputed accuracy procedures are set forth in the U.S. *Fair Credit Reporting Act* and state privacy requirements.

METHODS OF RISK CLASSIFICATION

Once underwriting information about a proposed insured has been assembled from various sources, it must be evaluated and a decision reached as to whether the individual is to be accepted at one of the preferred or standard rate classes, treated as a substandard but acceptable risk, or rejected entirely. Occasionally, a risk is postponed for a period of time until the effect of a condition or impairment is resolved. For instance, if the proposed insured is expecting to undergo imminent surgery, a decision could be postponed until after the surgery.

Ideally, the selection and classification system used by a company should (1) measure the effect of each factor affecting the risk, (2) assess the combined impact of interrelated factors including conflicting ones, (3) produce equitable results, and (4) be relatively simple and inexpensive to operate. Two systems have evolved to accommodate these concerns: the judgment method and the numerical rating system.

THE JUDGMENT METHOD

Originally, companies used the **judgment method** in life insurance underwriting, under which they relied on the combined judgment of those in the medical, actuarial, and other areas who are qualified for this work to make underwriting decisions. The method still finds applicability in health insurance underwriting and remains implicit in underwriting generally.

The judgment method of rating functions effectively when there is only one unfavorable factor to consider or when the decision to be made is simply whether to accept the proposed insured at standard rates or to reject him or her entirely. Where multiple factors (some possibly in conflict) are involved or a proper substandard classification is needed, it leaves something to be desired. Moreover, it requires the use of highly skilled personnel to achieve proper risk appraisal with consistency. To overcome the weakness of the judgment method of rating, the life insurance business developed the numerical rating system.

THE NUMERICAL RATING SYSTEM

The **numerical rating system** is a method under which an insurance company relies on a system of debits and credits representing adverse and positive expected marginal mortality rates, respectively, to derive an expected mortality classification for a proposed insured. It is based on the principle that a large number of factors enters into the composition of a risk and that the impact of each of these factors on longevity can be determined by a statistical study of lives possessing those factors. Under this method, 100 percent represents a normal or standard risk, one that is physically sound.

The numerical rating system is relevant in the classification phase of underwriting. It is used to assess a proposed insured's health characteristics and, to a lesser extent, lifestyle characteristics. It cannot capture extra mortality attendant to adverse financial characteristics, such as questionable motivation, overinsurance, or an illogical beneficiary, because these characteristics cannot be quantified. Either the underwriter resolves the adverse information at the selection phase of underwriting in the applicant's favor (and the application proceeds to the classification phase), or does not. If she does not, there is no way to quantify the extra mortality or other poor financial result expected from the perceived adverse selection and/or moral hazard that underlies adverse financial information. She, therefore, rejects the application; it never gets to the classification phase.

Most of the factors that might influence a risk in an unusual way are considered a debit or a credit. Values are assigned to the individual factors. For example, if the mortality of a group of insured lives reflecting a certain degree of overweight or a certain degree of elevated blood pressure has been found to be 150 percent of standard risks, a debit (addition) of 50 percentage points will be assigned to this degree of overweight or blood pressure.

Judgment still enters into the operation of the numerical system, primarily in the assignment of numerical values to each factor and, when it occurs, in determining the effect of two or more factors that are related to each other in some way. When two factors are so related that one affects the other, judgment and past experience may dictate an addition that is greater or smaller than the sum of the numerical factors. For example, if family history shows several early deaths from heart disease, this adverse factor may be nullified somewhat by good physical condition, good build, normal electrocardiograms, and similar favorable factors. On the other hand, this type of family history plus findings of obesity or elevated blood pressure would probably warrant a larger addition than the sum of the two adverse factors.

The system in practice is applied with common sense and has the advantages of greater consistency of treatment and of permitting lay underwriters to process all applications other than those requiring detailed medical analysis. This reduced reliance on physicians in underwriting helps minimize the expense of the underwriting process.

Numerical ratings range in most companies from 75 or less to a high of 500 or more. In most companies, ratings below 125 are considered preferred or standard. Proposed insureds who produce a rate in excess of the standard limit are either assigned to appropriate substandard classes or declined. The scale of ratings produced by the numerical rating system might be classified in a particular company as follows:

Preferred / Standard / Substandard . . . /Uninsurable

---

75   85   100   115   130   150   180 . . . 500   600

The illustration shown in Box 11-1 should help make clear the operation of the numerical rating system. Some companies' ratings extend to as high as 1000 percent. Generally, ratings of more than 500 percent are classified as experimental underwriting.

There can be wide differences in underwriting decisions among competing life insurance companies. These can be explained in two ways. First, the size of the numerical debits in their impairment manuals may differ. Second, their judgment in assessing debits and credits may differ. In addition, some numerical measures of impairments or variations of impairments do not appear in the manuals.

CLASSIFYING SUBSTANDARD RISKS

Substandard risks are insureds who are expected or do exhibit higher than average mortality or morbidity. In life insurance, higher than average expected mortality may be provided for by levying an extra premium or COI charge and by other methods. Companies have accumulated considerable statistics on impairments that aid them in estimating their influence on mortality. Similarly, the wide experience of reinsurers, especially with substandard risk appraisal, has assisted direct writing companies in establishing sound underwriting systems.

Box 11-1
Illustration of the Numerical Rating System

Jim Carson, aged 35, applies for a universal life policy. Information obtained by the company reveals the following:

Height – 5 feet, 9 inches
Weight – 205 pounds
Family history – better than average
Habits – good
Personal history – medical attention for slightly elevated blood pressure.

A paramedical examination is requested, and Jim's blood pressure is found to be 150/90. An attending physician's report provides details on the extent of the elevation and the response to treatment. The insurer first ascertains the basic rating for Jim, which depends on his build. According to the company's build table, Jim is overweight for his height. Expected mortality for such overweight persons is 25 percent higher than average mortality. According to the insurer's blood pressure table, this elevated blood pressure carries expected mortality of 75 percent higher than average. On the other hand, a credit of 10 is allowed for a favorable family history. The above is summarized below.

Factor	Debits	Credits
Build: overweight	25	
Personal history: blood pressure	75	
Family history		10
Total	**100**	**10**

Thus, to the average mortality of 100, we add the debits (100) and subtract the credits (10) to yield a numerical rating for Jim of 190. This puts him in the substandard category.

Companies use two types of statistics on past experience. Experience under insurance policies is useful, but often it is not available in sufficient quantity, particularly for impairments that occur infrequently, whose effects are poorly understood, or that are associated with mortality or morbidity so high that insurance is unobtainable at a reasonable price. Articles in medical journals are useful for these purposes.

Some companies use reinsurance extensively to seek standard insurance on risks that are substandard by their own underwriting standards. Some reinsurance companies pursue this business aggressively. They are willing to assume risks that a direct writing company, concerned about maintaining competitive pricing for standard risks, is not willing to assume. Doing so also assists them in developing reliable data on impairments.

INCIDENCE OF EXTRA MORTALITY

Many factors may cause a proposed insured to be declined or rated substandard. About three-fourths of all declined individuals in the U.S. have serious health impairments. Almost 90 percent of substandard ratings in the U.S. are related to various physical impairments such as heart murmurs, obesity, diabetes, and elevated blood pressure. However, rating systems for substandard insurance do not precisely follow over time the pattern of extra mortality of each impairment. This would be difficult and probably impracticable as such knowledge is insufficiently developed. The majority of companies, therefore, categorize substandard insured lives into three broad groups; *to wit*, those in which the number of extra deaths per 1,000 lives insured is expected to:

- remain at approximately the same level in all years following policy issuance,
- increase as insureds grow older, and
- decrease with time.

An example of the constant type of extra deaths is persons with hazardous occupations. An example of increasing extra mortality would be persons with diabetes, whereas individuals who had just undergone successful operations would be representative of the decreasing category. Such a classification permits companies to assess extra premiums or COI charges according to the incidence of the extra deaths. If companies expect the same number of extra deaths to occur in two groups over a particular period of time, but also expect the timing to be different, different types of extra ratings will be needed for the extra mortality in the group in which the extra deaths occur early (decreasing) compared to those needed for the group in which the deaths occur later (increasing).

METHODS OF RATING

Several methods exist for rating impaired lives. An effort is made to adapt the method to the type of exposure represented by the impaired individual, but departures from theoretically correct treatment are made for practical reasons. The objectives in establishing an extra premium or COI charge structure are that it be:

- Equitable between impairments and between classes,
- Easy to administer, and
- Easily understood by agents and the public.

MULTIPLE TABLE EXTRA   Most substandard life insurance pricing relies on the **multiple table extra method,** in which substandard risks are divided into broad groups according to their numerical ratings. Premium rates or mortality charges are based on mortality experience that corresponds to the average numerical ratings in each risk class. Most companies use the same nonforfeiture values and dividends as for standard risks. Some companies do not permit the extended term insurance option on highly rated cases.

Numerical ratings of up to approximately 125 are considered preferred or standard, and insureds with these ratings pay the lowest premiums and COI charges. The average rating of each additional substandard class is progressively higher than that for the preferred or standard class. Companies usually provide for at least four and sometimes as many as six or seven substandard classes when special nonforfeiture values are used, and as many as 16 classifications when standard values are used.

Proposed insureds are then placed in the appropriate class in accordance with their numerical ratings. The average numerical rating within these classes may range from about 125 to 500 or even higher. An example of a scale of substandard classifications is shown in Table 11-2.

Table 11-2   **Illustrative Scale of Substandard Mortality Classifications**

Table	Mortality (%)	Numerical Rating
1	125	120-135
2	150	140-160
3	175	165-185
4	200	190-210
5	225	215-235
6	250	240-260
7	275	265-285
8	300	290-325
10	350	330-380
12	400	385-450
16	500	455-550
Uninsurable	-	Over 550

Companies vary premiums for substandard risks on bundled policies by plan because the extra charge is levied effectively only on the net amount at risk. With most term policies, the net amount at risk is the same as the face amount. Thus, substandard premiums for term life policies typically increase in direct proportion to the degree of extra mortality involved. For example, a numerical rating of 200 is likely to result in about a doubling of the term premium. This same principle applies to COI charges for unbundled policies. For cash value policies whose net amounts at risk decrease over time, such as whole life policies, the substandard premium will not increase in direct proportion to the degree of extra mortality. Also, if policy loadings do not increase proportionally, because, for example, no commissions are paid on the extra premium, the additional charge will not be as large as otherwise.

Multiple table extra ratings do not differentiate among the various types of substandard risks with different incidences of extra mortality (i.e., increasing, decreasing, or constant). The assumption of a constant percentage of the standard mortality rates implies a number of extra deaths per thousand that increases with age for all types of cases rated on this basis. Although this method theoretically may not exactly reflect the incidence of extra risk, the method is justified on an expense basis, and, on the average, it is reasonably accurate. Many companies use the multiple table extra method for some impairments and flat (usually temporary) extras for others.

FLAT EXTRA PREMIUM   Under the **flat extra premium method** of substandard rating, a constant extra premium is charged to provide for the expected additional mortality. This method is used when the extra mortality, measured in additional deaths per thousand, is expected to be constant, either for a temporary period or permanently, and when it is largely independent of age. A regular policy is issued, with the policy treated as standard for the purpose of dividends and nonforfeiture values.

The method is appropriate for most hazardous occupations and avocations, as much of the extra mortality is of an accidental nature and independent of age. It is also appropriate for covering temporary extra mortality as when most of the extra risk falls in the early years after an operation, or when there is a particular event such as a coronary thrombosis. Coronary ratings are typically made up of a table rating plus a temporary flat extra premium.

OTHER METHODS Other methods of treating substandard risks include use of an **exclusion rider** under which an endorsement excluding from coverage any loss arising from the named peril giving rise to the additional risk is attached to the policy. While exclusion riders other than for suicide are not widely used, they find occasional application with certain lifestyle factors involving high risks, such as with certain types of aviation, avocation, occupation, and military exposures. See Chapter 5. Many jurisdictions will not approve use of life policy forms that provide for other exclusions.

Another method of treating substandard insureds is to provide a limited death benefit equal to a refund of premiums if death occurs in the first few (typically the first two) years. This limited death benefit, together with a higher standard premium, is used by some companies that offer direct response insurance with little or no underwriting, usually to older (over 50) age groups. Another form of limited death benefit contract is a graded death benefit, with the amount payable increasing in each of the first three to five years, after which the full death benefit is payable.

Usual underwriting practices are relaxed in several areas. In the process, special underwriting concerns are created. The following discussion is intended to explain how reasonable results can be obtained in these areas.

SPECIAL UNDERWRITING PRACTICES

NONMEDICAL INSURANCE

A substantial proportion of all new personal insurance is written without the benefit of a medical or paramedical examination – so-called **nonmedical insurance**. In one sense, the use of the term is unfortunate as it sometimes conveys the erroneous idea that the insurance is issued without any medical information. This is not accurate. Medical information is still sought, but it is gathered from the proposed insured through health-related answers to questions from the application and possibly from attending physician statements and other sources. The term *nonmedical* should be understood to be synonymous with *no physical examination ordinarily required*. The primary justification for nonmedical underwriting lies in expense saving. As long as expenses for a medical examination are greater than the cost of any extra mortality incurred because of its elimination, the process is economically sound.

Perhaps the most important risk management safeguard built into the nonmedical underwriting rules is a limit on the amount available on any one insured.

In the early days, this limit was $1,000. When experience proved to be more favorable than anticipated, the limits were gradually raised. Today some companies' limits are $500,000 or more at the younger ages (through age 30). A second safeguard built into nonmedical rules is a limit on the ages at which the insurance will be issued. Nonmedical insurance is not regularly available beyond age 50 or 60, except in special situations, such as a certain worksite marketing programs where the age limits might be higher. Other safeguards include the general limitation of nonmedical insurance to medically standard risks. Most companies impose no lower age limit, offering it down to age zero. Modifications are made on these safeguards from time to time as indicated by emerging experience, including the increasing costs of medical examinations in recent years.

In addition to the expansion of nonmedical underwriting, there has also been expanded use of simplified underwriting in which only a few health history questions are asked. For the cases in which adverse health information is developed from these or other sources, the company may request a physical examination. This occurs with an estimated 10 percent of nonmedical applications.

INSTANT-ISSUE UNDERWRITING

Life insurers have had expedited underwriting approaches for several years, labeled *expert* or *jet issue* systems, that relied heavily on computer-based underwriting. More recently, many life insurers have begun to combine the Internet and computer-based underwriting to offer what is sometimes called *instant-issue underwriting*. With this approach, an application is submitted via the Internet, often at specially designed locations, such as banks or brokerage offices, directly to the insurer. The application has comparatively few health questions and is processed within a matter of minutes, not hours or, more commonly, days. Policies are usually applied for and issued immediately.

Policies designed for instant issue tend to be mainly term or single premium insurance, targeted at healthy individuals and for comparatively modest maximum face amounts, such as $250,000. Some insurers involve their agents in the process but not all. Not only is the agent's and customer's time saved, but much paperwork is eliminated and the sale is closed immediately. A possible precursor of the evolution of instant-issue underwriting might be emerging, as Box 11-2 explores.

REINSTATEMENTS AND POLICY CHANGES

When a life insurance policy lapses, the policyowner has the contractual right to apply for policy reinstatement. To reinstate a policy, the owner must pay past-due premiums (or COI charges) plus provide evidence of insurability that is satisfactory to the insurer. Evidence of insurability is typically provided via a reinstatement application. This application is a shortened version of the original application, designed to be completed with minimal effort and time. Underwriting requirements commonly are less strict for recently lapsed policies. For policies that have been lapsed for a longer time and for which reinstatement is sought, the underwriting procedure often more closely resembles that for a new insurance policy.

Underwriting also may be required in connection with certain policy changes. In general, an insurer will require evidence of insurability on any policy change that increases the policy's net amount at risk, except when the change is one guaranteed by the contract (e.g., automatic face amount increases under a cost-of-living-adjustment rider). Also, if it is desired to add additional benefits – such as waiver of premium, accidental death benefit, or guaranteed insurability option – to an existing policy, the insurer typically requires evidence of insurability. Similarly, underwriting and additional requirements are necessary to reduce or remove an extra premium on a rated policy. In each case, the essential purpose is to avoid adverse selection.

Box 11-2
Use of Data Mining in Underwriting

Some insurers working with consulting firms are experimenting with the use of data mining as a partial substitute for traditional approaches to underwriting, especially as relates to medical information. Models developed by these consulting firms digest vast quantities of personally identified data collected by data gathering firms to make predictions about individuals' likely life expectancies. One of the consultancies has stated that insurers can save $125 per applicant by eliminating many conventional medical requirements through their process.

The data gathering firms sort details of online and offline consumer purchases, magazine subscriptions, leisure activities, and information from social networking sites in an attempt to discern individuals' lifestyles, including their physical activities, diets, transportation routines, financial status, reading and television viewing habits, travel activities, and others. The modelers claim that their results have consistently aligned with those of traditional underwriting.

An example offered by *The Wall Street Journal* from an actuarial seminar illustrates the concept. Sarah owns her own home, commutes one mile to work, runs, bikes, plays tennis, eats healthy food, watches little TV, travels abroad and has a premium bank card and good financial indicators. In contrast, Beth rents her home, commutes 45 miles to work, frequently buys fast food, walks for exercise, buys weight-loss equipment, watches a lot of TV, and has foreclosure/bankruptcy indicators. The consultancy model indicates that Beth appears to fall into the higher risk category based on indicators of long commute, poor finances, purchases tied to obesity, lack of exercise, and high TV consumption.

While this data-base marketing approach to underwriting is not widely practiced, it has great appeal for insurers because of its low cost and as a means to help secure the middle-income market – one that has shrunk greatly for life insurers over the past couple of decades. On the other hand, concern has been expressed about the use of information collected in this way and the possibility of unfair discrimination and whether existing consumer information protection law is being skirted.

Source: Leslie Scism and Mark Maremont, "Insurers Test Data Profiles to Identify Risky Clients," *The Wall Street Journal,* November 10, 2010, pp. A1 and A16.

REINSURANCE

Insurance sold to the public at large is classified as **direct insurance**. Insurers selling such insurance are called **direct (writing) insurers** or **primary insurers,** and attendant premiums are **direct premiums**. Insurance firms usually hedge their own portfolios of risks through the purchase of insurance on these portfolios, which is called **reinsurance**. Reinsurance involves a contractual arrangement between the direct insurer and the reinsurer. The party that assumes risk from a direct insurer is called the **reinsurer** or the **assuming company,** and attendant premiums are called **reinsurance premiums**. As a means of risk management, reinsurers typically seek their own reinsurance, called a **retrocession**. The insurer or reinsurer accepting the retrocession is termed a **retrocessionaire**.

Reinsurance remains one of the most important and flexible elements of enterprise risk management programs of insurers. Life insurers may transfer one or a combination of risks through reinsurance: mortality, surrender, and investment.[2] Reinsurance makes it possible for direct insurers to sell larger policies than would be possible otherwise. Reinsurance also can reduce the risks facing an insurer when policies with a high probability of lapse or surrender are issued, as in policies whose premiums rise sharply from one year to the next. Similarly, reinsurance may limit the investment risk inherent in high asset concentrations from single products, such as annuities. In 2012, 88 percent of U.S. life insurers purchased some reinsurance. Among insurers writing accident and health, 83 percent ceded accident and health premiums as reinsurance. In contrast, only 43 percent of insurers doing annuity business ceded annuity considerations, excluding deposit-type funds. More than a third of total U.S. life reinsurance premiums are paid to reinsurers domiciled in other countries.

Special Relationship

The reinsurer has no legal relationship with, nor any direct obligation to, the policyowner; the reinsurer's only obligation is to the ceding company and the policyowner may look only to the ceding company to enforce his or her rights. Because reinsurers and ceding companies share risks, but the reinsurer has no relationship with the insured or policyowner, the reinsurance business relationship is one of *uberrimae fides* or utmost good faith. The reinsurer relies on the insurer to issue the policy with the underwriting care that it would exercise were there no reinsurance and similarly for claims handling. As such, the relationship imposes special duties on both parties that are not present in typical commercial relationships:

- each must be vigilant and respectful of the interests of the other;
- each is required to disclose all material facts to the other;
- each must conduct its own business affairs with due regard for its impact on the other; and
- each must always act in good faith.

The parties agree to "follow the fortunes" of the other. The reinsurer is bound to indemnify the ceding company for any loss as long the reinsured acted in good faith and can provide proof of payment of loss. It is a mutual relationship, so that if the ceding company paid a fraudulent claim that could not be recovered, but acted in good faith and with due care, the reinsurer will share in the fraudulent loss.

Benefits of Reinsurance beyond Pure Risk Transfer   Direct writing insurers often look to their reinsurers for more than pure risk transfer. Reinsurance for financial management purposes is discussed in Chapter 14; insurers also seek to improve the efficacy of their underwriting through reinsurance. Reinsurers review and maintain policy and claim records on a large volume of risks from many ceding companies whose insureds are diverse and geographically distributed. The insurance pool from which they develop and provide underwriting knowledge is larger and wider than is normally available to a single primary insurer. Underwriting is further strengthened when risk is spread to more than one reinsurer or retrocessionaire because of exposure to an even broader range of policies and claims. Confidence that underwriters are competently and professionally meeting their underwriting needs allows a ceding company to concentrate on other activities to expand its business.

Further, reinsurance is regularly used by companies as a means of obtaining better underwriting offers for proposed insureds who do not qualify for a standard or a moderately substandard offer under their own underwriting standards. Some reinsurers with liberal underwriting philosophies aggressively seek this type of business. Typically, the ceding company retains only a small or no portion of the risk. Some reinsurers require a ceding company to maintain a portion of the risk on facultative cases (see below).

Reinsurance spreads the risk of loss between two companies. The risk can be spread even further if the ceding company uses more than one reinsurer or if the reinsurer in turn retrocedes some of that risk to another reinsurer. In the most elementary reinsurance arrangement, a single primary insurer cedes business to a single reinsurer, usually an independent firm operating in the open marketplace. The reinsurer also can be an affiliate of the ceding company when both companies are owned by a parent company, or of a specialized life insurance brokerage operation that has contracts with direct writing companies requiring them to cede business to the brokerage operation's reinsurer. This captive reinsurer reinsures risks exclusively from affiliated parties.

ESTABLISHING THE RETENTION   An insurer's **retention** is the amount or percentage of an insurance policy that it retains for its own account. A life insurer deals with a type of mortality risk that, in the aggregate and in terms of lives insured, can be measured and predicted with a remarkable degree of accuracy. On the other hand, its exposure from one insured may be $10,000,000 and the exposure from another may be $25,000. The probability of death for each may be the same, but the impact of the death of these insureds on the company's surplus would be dramatically different. Reinsurance can homogenize the size of retained risks.

With a recently organized or small company, a maximum limit on the amount of insurance it will retain for its own account on any individual is deemed prudent. In companies with a relatively small total number of insureds, mortality experience can fluctuate widely from year to year. In such companies, the surplus funds available to absorb unusual losses usually are small, and a single large claim or several significant claims might have a marked adverse effect on operations for the year. As a company increases in size because of an increasing total volume of insurance in force and increasing surplus funds, the chance of significant fluctuations in its overall experience decreases, thanks to the law of large numbers, and the company's ability to absorb losses increases, thanks to the pooling of resources concept as discussed in Chapter 2. It can thus gradually and safely increase its maximum retention on any one life.

Life retention limits range from $100,000 in smaller companies to $20,000,000 or more in the largest U.S. companies. With disability income and LTC insurance, retention limits usually are stated as monthly indemnity amounts, such as $2,000. There are usually various limits within a given company, depending upon age at issue, substandard classification, and, sometimes, plan.

AGREEMENTS   Reinsurance may be arranged on a facultative or an automatic basis. With **facultative reinsurance**, each application on which the primary insurer wishes to purchase reinsurance is submitted to and is underwritten separately by the reinsurer. When the direct writing company receives an application for a policy for more than the amount it wishes to assume, it negotiates with one or more reinsurers for a transfer of that part of the insurance that is in excess of the amount the company wishes to retain. The reinsurer then makes its own underwriting judgment and advises the ceding company of its decision.

The facultative method has advantages. It is flexible, and questions about the underwriting information can be discussed in the reinsurance negotiations. The original insurer also obtains the advice of the reinsurer with which it negotiates. The major disadvantages are the additional time required for completing the transaction, which may result in loss of business to competitors, and a higher cost per unit for such coverage.

With **automatic** (also called **treaty**) **reinsurance**, the direct writing company *must* transfer an amount in excess of its retention of each applicable insurance policy to the reinsuring company immediately upon payment of premium and the issuance of the policy, and the reinsurer *must* accept transfers that fall within the scope of the agreement. The treaty always provides that not more than a certain amount per policy may be transferred to the reinsurance company, and the agreement may provide for a distribution of the excess to more than one reinsuring company. Methods for allocating risk among a group of reinsurers include:

- *Quota share:* Each reinsurer receives a specified percentage of each risk ceded to the group.
- *Layering:* Risk is ceded in layers of insurance amounts. One reinsurer receives all reinsurance up to the limit of the first layer, a second reinsurer receives all reinsurance beyond the first layer up to the limit of the second layer, and so on.
- *Alphabet split:* Risk is ceded among reinsurers alphabetically based on insureds' surnames. Those whose last names begin with A–F go to the first reinsurer, and so on, until all reinsurance is allocated.

TYPES OF REINSURANCE

Various reinsurance plans are available based on ceding companies' needs and their reasons for reinsuring. Plans can be broadly classified as either **proportional reinsurance,** under which the assuming company and ceding company share risks on a per policy basis (i.e., a "portion" of each policy is shared), and **nonproportional reinsurance,** under which risks are not shared on individual policies but on aggregate losses attributable to a specified group of policies. Treaty reinsurance plans can be nonparticipating or they may be participating when the ceding company is given a right to some reimbursement of its premiums in the event of favorable experience.

PROPORTIONAL REINSURANCE Specified amounts or percentages are shared between ceding companies and reinsurers in proportional reinsurance. If sharing is via percentages, called **quota share,** the ceding company and assuming company establish the percentage of risk for which each will retain or assume responsibility. If sharing is via specified amounts, called **excess of retention,** the ceding company establishes a fixed amount for which it retains risk, and the assuming company assumes risk over this amount, up to its retention limit. Proportional plans in life insurance generally comprise four categories. The most common quota share plans are *coinsurance, modified coinsurance,* and *coinsurance with funds withheld.* The most common excess of retention plan is *yearly renewable term.*

Under **coinsurance,** the ceding company pays the assuming company a proportionate part of the gross direct premium less commissions and other allowances, premium taxes, and overhead allocable to reinsured policies, and the assuming company assumes a proportionate share of the risk according to the terms that govern the original policy. The reinsurer is liable for an amount determined by the size of the insurance assumed in relation to the original insurance amount. Thus, if the reinsurer has accepted one-half of the original insurance, it becomes liable for one-half of any loss. In return for this guarantee, the reinsurer receives a pro-rata share of the original premium less a ceding commission and allowance. These payments reimburse the direct writing company for an appropriate share of the agent's commissions, premium taxes paid, and a portion of the other expenses attributable to the reinsured policy.

Also, the reinsurer reimburses for a proportionate share of any dividends paid or other payments. In general, the reinsurance contract is a duplicate of that entered into between the direct writing company and the policyowner. The ceding company and the reinsurer share a risk – they effectively "coinsure" – according to agreed proportions, with reinsurance rates derived from the original rates charged the policyowner.

Companies often are interested in retaining control of the funds arising from their own policies. With **modified coinsurance,** the ceding company pays the reinsurer a proportionate part of the gross premium, as under the conventional coinsurance plan, less commissions and other allowances, premium taxes, and overhead allocable to reinsured policies; however, at year's end, the reinsurer pays to the ceding company a reserve adjustment equal to the net increase in the reserve during the year, less one year's interest on the total reserve held at the beginning of the year. The net effect of the plan is to return to the ceding company the bulk of the funds developed by its policies.

Another variation of coinsurance, sometimes called **coinsurance with funds withheld,** occurs when the ceding company keeps the premiums normally paid to a reinsurer, while the reinsurer keeps the allowances normally paid to the ceding company. This arrangement limits cash flow between the two companies, reinforcing the stability of their cash accounts. Both coinsurance with funds withheld and modified coinsurance enable a ceding company to take statutory credit in certain circumstances, reduce credit risk, secure credit, and retain control over investments.

Under a **yearly renewable term,** the reinsurer assumes the reinsured policy's net amount at risk in excess of the ceding company's retention. Unlike quota share plans, the reinsurance premium is not a function of the ceding company's direct premium to the policyholder. The ceding company pays premiums on a yearly renewable term basis, priced without regard to the original direct premium and so the relationship is not coinsurance. This plan is particularly appropriate for smaller ceding companies, as it results in larger assets for these companies and is simpler to administer than the coinsurance plan. Thus, for policies with declining net amounts at risk, a decreasing amount of reinsurance is purchased each year. If a loss occurs, the reinsurer is liable for the amount that it assumed that year, and the ceding insurer is liable for its retention plus the full reserve on the reinsured portion of the policy.

NONPROPORTIONAL REINSURANCE   Nonproportional plans apply to specified groups of policies rather than individual policies. There are three principal types. **Catastrophe reinsurance** is designed to protect against adverse results occurring from a specific event that affects multiple policies simultaneously. An example would be a plane crash that caused the death of several insureds of the same company at once; thus the attachment point (or deductible) for these policies is often expressed as the number of claims arising from the same event. **Stop loss reinsurance** is designed to protect against an adverse accumulation of unexpected claims, from whatever reason, during a particular period. The reinsurer reimburses some or all of a ceding company's aggregate claims above a fixed amount, a percentage of premium, or above some percentage of a predetermined measure of expected mortality. **Spread loss reinsurance** is designed to smooth reported results of ceding companies which believe their claims experience will be volatile; it is often more a financing vehicle than a risk vehicle, as the ceding company repays over time to the reinsurer the claim payments that it receives from the reinsurer.

Health reinsurance vehicles differ from life reinsurance vehicles because of the existence of partial claims. As discussed in Chapter 7, *specific stop loss* reinsurance reimburses the insurer when claims attributed to a single policy exceed a specified amount. *Excess of time* reinsurance is designed to protect against adverse results under individual disability income or long term care contracts whereby the reinsurer assume claims responsibility after a stated period. *Aggregate stop loss reinsurance* is designed to protect against an unexpected accumulation of claims from a specified group of policies during a specified period.

CONCLUSION

This chapter has covered two of a life insurer's most important risk management tools: underwriting and reinsurance. Both are concerned with ensuring that the insurer retains risks knowingly and with due regard for its financial capabilities. Underwriting is essential to a competitive market in personal life and health insurance, while reinsurance promotes competition by enabling insurers to expand the breadth and depth of their markets without undue risk concentration.

ENDNOTES

1   Association of British Insurers, 23 February 1995, as cited in André Chuffart, *Private Life Insurance: The End of an Era?* (Zurich: Swiss Reinsurance Company, 1995).
2   This section draws in part from *Life Insurance Fact Book* (Washington, D.C.: American Council of Life Insurers, 2013), chapter 6.

CHAPTER 12

THE REGULATION AND TAXATION OF LIFE INSURANCE COMPANIES

Governments worldwide intervene into their insurance markets. This intervention takes many forms; some direct, some indirect. The nature and the degree of government intervention vary with each country's socio-cultural and economic circumstances and its government's prevailing political philosophy. The hand of government is evident in insurance markets through regulation and taxation.

Whatever the nature and degree of intervention, the avowed purposes will always be noble – typically to protect consumers, to raise revenue to support worthwhile social objectives, or to ensure orderly, well functioning markets. This chapter examines the purposes, rationales, nature, and mechanism for insurance regulation and taxation. Our primary focus is on U.S. policies and practices.

We begin by examining the purposes of regulation and the reasons why regulation exists in its various forms. We follow with a review of regulatory practice in different international jurisdictions.

OVERVIEW OF REGULATION

THE PURPOSE OF GOVERNMENT INTERVENTION INTO MARKETS

There is widespread agreement among economists that the purpose of government intervention into private markets should be to maximize social welfare. Widely accepted economic principles suggest that an unregulated, perfectly competitive market promotes allocative efficiency in the sense that society's resources will be directed to areas that maximize social welfare. Rational government intervention, then, requires a determination that efficiency is not an exclusive objective or that insurance markets are not perfectly competitive. Both determinations are demonstrated.

First, resource efficiency has never been society's only goal: concern for fairness and compassion prevail to some degree in almost all societies. Many countries, for example, have long supported universal health insurance and, in the United States, *The Patient Protection and Affordable Care Act of 2010* represents a significant movement in that direction with a hybrid private/public approach. Likewise, most societies provide some form of collective or public assistance to its neediest members.

Second, beginning in Chapter 1, we have taken note of significant imperfections in insurance markets that distinguish them from perfectly competitive markets. We classified these imperfections into four broad categories:

- market power,
- externalities,
- free rider problems, and
- information problems.

The insurance business exhibits imperfections in all four categories. Examples abound: insurers seek market power (the ability to influence price) through market segmentation and product differentiation strategies; intentional losses, including murder, to collect insurance benefits is a negative externality. Public policy makers seem increasingly to consider health insurance as a public good. Insurers' product design, underwriting, and claim settlement operations are shaped by information asymmetry concerns: when the buyer knows more than the seller adverse selection and moral hazard problems can arise. The typical insurance buyer also suffers from information asymmetry by virtue of being poorly informed about insurance contracts, policy performance, and insurer financial solidity. These are some of the bases on which policymakers have justified government intervention into insurance markets to promote allocative efficiency and enhance social welfare.

Economists argue that government's intervention is justified when:

- Actual or potential market imperfections exist,
- The market imperfections do or could lead to meaningful economic inefficiency or inequity, and
- Government action can ameliorate the inefficiency or inequity.

Conversely, no government intervention should be warranted where (1) insurance markets exhibit no market imperfections; (2) imperfections exist, but they do not lead to important inefficiencies or inequities; or (3) meaningful market imperfections exist, but government's actions could not ameliorate the imperfection. Indeed, government regulation can make matters worse. Just as there is no perfect competition, there is no perfect regulation.

THEORIES OF REGULATION

The **public interest theory of regulation**, a normative (i.e., what "ought to be") theory, holds that government regulation exists to protect the public interest by correcting market imperfections and promoting allocative efficiency and social welfare. In a positivist sense, (i.e., what is observed in practice), regulation is thought by many to be less public minded and exists to protect private interests. Two important private interest theories of regulation exist.

One theory is that self-interested regulators engage in regulatory activities consistent with maximizing their political support. Under this theory, regulators might exhibit pro-industry biases to gain support from industry. Regulators might also engage in activities that appeal to consumers (voters) such as price suppression to gain their support, even if the long-term effects were detrimental. In theory, an equilibrium exists where attention to each constituency is optimal

A second theory – called the **capture theory of regulation** – holds that special interest groups, being well organized and well financed, influence legislation and regulation for their own benefit. Special interest groups in insurance include insurers, reinsurers, agents, banks, securities firms, brokers, and the firms that provide services to these industry participants. Thus, for example, U.S. banks complained about being denied full insurance marketing powers because agents had been able to unduly influence legislators and regulators. In effect, regulation is "captured" by the regulated industry and operated for its benefit.

Consumers are less informed and less well financed than the insurance industry, and the capture theory predicts regulation favorable to industry incumbents. Examples include restrictions on market entry by new (especially foreign) competitors, suppression of price and product competition, and control of inter-sector competition from other financial institutions. Empirical evidence in this area indicates that U.S. insurance regulation reflects features of both public and private interest theories of regulation.

INSURANCE REGULATION INTERNATIONALLY

With the increasing internationalization of insurance markets, the regulation of insurance has become more complex. The 2008-2009 financial crisis was a stark reminder of the interconnectedness of financial markets and the need for more effective cross-border coordination. The *International Association of Insurance Supervisors* (IAIS) has been an especially active player in this respect. This section introduces the IAIS and highlights regulation in a few large non-U.S. markets.

THE INTERNATIONAL ASSOCIATION OF INSURANCE SUPERVISORS
Established in 1994, the IAIS is the international standard setting body responsible for developing and assisting in the implementation of principles, standards, and other support for the supervision of the insurance sector worldwide. Its mission is to promote effective and globally consistent supervision of the insurance industry; to develop and maintain fair, safe, and stable insurance markets for the benefit and protection of policyholders; and to contribute to global financial stability. It provides a forum for members and observers to share their experiences and understanding of insurance supervision and insurance markets. In recognition of its collective expertise, the IAIS is routinely called upon by the G20 leaders and other international standard setting bodies to assist in resolving insurance-related issues.

The IAIS is a voluntary membership organization of insurance regulators from more than 200 jurisdictions in some 140 countries.[*] The NAIC and all U.S. regulatory jurisdictions are members. In addition to its members, more than 130 observers representing international institutions, professional associations, and insurance and reinsurance companies, as well as consultants and other professionals participate in IAIS activities.

Under the direction of its members, the IAIS conducts activities through a committee system, akin to that of the NAIC, designed to achieve its mandate and objectives. The committee system is led by an Executive Committee whose

---

[*]   This discussion draws from iaisweb.org.

members come from different regions of the world. It is supported by five committees established by the By-Laws – the Audit, Budget, Financial Stability, Implementation, and Technical Committees – as well as by the Supervisory Forum. Committees may establish subcommittees or working parties to help carry out their duties. These activities are supported by its Secretariat located in Basel, Switzerland and headed by a Secretary General.

OVERVIEW OF INSURANCE REGULATION IN SELECTED MARKETS

Insurance regulation is universal, but different approaches are followed worldwide. This section surveys insurance regulation in Canada, the European Union (E.U.), and Japan. Some 73 percent of life insurance worldwide is accounted for by these three markets and the U.S. Other life insurance markets are large (e.g., Korea and Taiwan), and numerous Latin American, Eastern European, and other Asian markets are growing rapidly.

Regulatory philosophies and practices have a profound effect on the performance, structure, and operation of a nation's life insurance industry. At one end of the international regulatory spectrum, some governments lightly regulate insurance – their primary emphasis being on insurer solvency. Competition is encouraged and relied upon as the primary consumer protection force. Hong Kong, the U.K., Ireland, and the Netherlands are examples of this approach. At the other extreme, government regulatory involvement can be extensive, covering not only solvency but also policy content and pricing. Germany, Japan, and Korea are traditional examples. Such heavy regulation is rationalized as conducive to a more orderly, stable market. Many markets (including the U.S. and Canada) fall between the two extremes.

REGULATION IN CANADA   Supervision of insurance in Canada is shared by the federal and provincial governments, with life insurers choosing to incorporate and be regulated at either the federal or the provincial level. The federal government is responsible for the solvency supervision of all non-Canadian companies operating in Canada on a branch basis and all federally incorporated insurers. These companies account for about 90 percent of the life insurance business in Canada. The *Office of the Superintendent of Financial Institutions* (OSFI) is the federal supervisory agency for insurance companies, banks, and other deposit taking institutions.

Provincial governments are responsible for the solvency supervision of all provincially incorporated insurers. In addition, provincial governments have exclusive jurisdiction over insurers' marketing practices such as contract wording and its interpretation, licensing of agents, and premium rates.

The Canadian life insurance market has become exceptionally competitive. The market is dominated by *Manulife Financial, Sun Life Financial,* and *Great-West Life Assurance.* The number of life insurers is dramatically lower in this than in the last century as consolidation has characterized the industry. Several Canadian life insurers have significant operations in the U.S., U.K., and other countries.

Canadian life insurance companies aggressively compete with deposit-taking institutions for savings through the issuance of deferred annuities. The main deposit-taking institutions in Canada are banks and trust and loan companies; this industry is far larger than the insurance industry. These companies own life insurers, although they are prohibited from distributing insurance directly through their retail branches. The Canadian banks make formidable competitors. Five Canadian banks dominate the scene with an extensive system of branch offices across the country.

The approach to supervising federally incorporated insurers and the Canadian branch operations of foreign companies is basically the same. The main difference is that Canadian branch operations of foreign companies must maintain sufficient assets to cover their Canadian liabilities, plus any required capital margins under the control of Canadian supervisory authorities.

Incorporation of a new federal insurance company requires at least C$10 million of capital, an acceptable business plan, and reputable owners and managers. Foreign insurers can choose to operate in Canada either by establishing a branch operation or by incorporating a new federal insurer. Companies wishing to establish a branch operation in Canada must have at least C$200 million in assets, adequate capital, and a track record of successful operations.

All federally incorporated insurance companies must submit an annual financial statement in a prescribed format, accompanied by an opinion from an auditor. On site financial examinations by OSFI examiners are carried out every two years and more frequently if needed. Subject to certain concentration limits and limits on real estate and share investments, previous quantitative tests for investments have been replaced by a prudent portfolio approach. Under this approach, the burden is on companies to develop prudent investment policies and implement appropriate control procedures.

To promote equity between generations of participating policyowners, regulations require some portion of unrealized gains and losses to be reflected in income. Another motivation of these regulations is to encourage the making of investment decisions for investment rather than income reporting reasons.

Canada requires use of an appointed actuary, similar in concept to that used in the U.K. Appointment is made and terminated by the insurer's board of directors, and the appointed actuary has access to the board. The actuary is responsible for determining the adequacy of actuarial reserves and for reporting to the board at least yearly on the insurer's financial prospects. If the appointed actuary becomes aware of circumstances that may have a material impact on the insurer's ability to meet its obligations, he or she must bring the matter to the attention of management and the board. If, in the opinion of the appointed actuary, satisfactory action is not taken within a reasonable time period, he or she has a statutory obligation to make the superintendent aware of the situation.

REGULATION IN THE EUROPEAN UNION The E.U. is a quasi-federal organization of its member nations whose constitutional basis springs from the treaties of the European Union. The union's constitutional system is characterized by two important features: (1) the objective of a single market and (2) governance by directive.

A principal existential purpose of the E.U. is the creation of a **single market** to present the union as a common entity externally and to maintain nondiscriminatory relations between its members. It is characterized by the free circulation of goods, capital, people, and services within the union. Legislation is disseminated through its member states not by statute but by directive. **Directives** are the legislation adopted by the European Parliament instructing member states to enact laws or regulations consistent with the directive to ensure harmonization of law and regulation throughout the union. They require consistency in the laws of member nations. A directive does not require specific forms or methods but requires minimum consistent standards in all E.U. nations' legislation and regulation. Thus, an E.U. domiciled insurer is able to underwrite and sell insurance in any member nations without authorization from the host nation, and insurers are regulated primarily by the domiciliary nation. The system thus shares some characteristics of regulation in the U.S., discussed below.

Member nations enjoy some measure of discretion and latitude in the regulation of their insurance industries, subject to the overarching requirements of the E.U. directives. Historically, member nations have exhibited significant variation in regulatory philosophy. As noted above, the U.K., the Netherlands, and Ireland have been characterized by less intrusive regulation, with a focus on insurer solvency. The regulation of other states has been more intense. Austria and Germany, in particular, have exercised the strictest regulation, with detailed oversight not only of solvency, but also policy terms, conditions, and prices. The trend in contemporary E.U. directives is to mandate less detailed prescriptive oversight.

Solvency II, greatly influenced by its international banking counterpart Basel II, is a new regulatory framework that is scheduled to take effect in 2016. It follows the Solvency I framework first developed in the 1970s and is designed to reduce the degree of variability in member nation regulation and so better to promote a single market. Solvency II will focus on risk management and emphasize the specific internal risks of individual insurers more than broad, average industry measures. Capital requirements will be consistent and risk-based. It will feature principles-based economic measures of assets and liabilities and contemporary stochastic risk measurement tools of enterprise risk management in setting capital requirements. Developments in financial reporting by the *International Accounting Standards Board* parallel the new approach and introduce performance measurement via embedded value.

Basel II and Solvency II are influencing U.S. and international regulation significantly. The uses of economic capital and embedded value in the convergence and harmonization of international financial regulation and reporting is addressed in Chapter 13.

REGULATION IN JAPAN   The Japanese life insurance market is the world's third largest, after the E.U. and the U.S. The industry is characterized by a small number of very large companies. Under the *Insurance Business Act* (IBA) the Prime Minister of Japan has overarching authority as insurance regulator. Except for certain important powers such as granting and cancelling insurance business licenses, most have been delegated to the Commissioner of the *Financial Services Agency* of the Japanese Government (FSA) and to the directors of the *Local Finance Bureau* and the *Local Finance Branch Bureau* of the *Ministry of Finance* (collectively LFB). The system favors insurer financial stability over other factors.

Japanese insurance regulation historically has been based on a so-called "convoy" philosophy. The convoy members (insurance companies) move no faster than the slowest ship (weakest or least innovative insurer), with price competition severely restricted. This practice – which is changing – ensured that the financially weakest insurer would survive. The MOF places a priority on insolvency prevention, although a mutual life insurer failed in 1997, the first such failure in recent Japanese history. Market stability is also of overriding concern. As in Germany, Japan historically has viewed unfettered competition as unstable and potentially ruinous.

The Japanese government has undertaken to deregulate and liberalize the nation's financial community, breaking down the walls that traditionally separated banking, securities, and insurance. Each of these sectors increasingly offers overlapping products, and this trend is expected to continue. Competition among sectors is rising.

U.S. FEDERAL REGULATION OF LIFE INSURERS

The insurance regulatory structure in the U.S. includes significant roles for both federal and state governments. The federal government has authority over all interstate commerce, while the states have authority over purely intrastate activities. Unlike other industries, insurance regulation remains largely the province of the states, first because of judicial decisions and subsequently because of legislative activity. From 1869, when the Supreme Court decided *Paul v. Virginia 75 U.S. 168 (1869)*, until 1944 when the court reversed itself in *United States v. South-Eastern Underwriters Association, et al. 322 U.S. 533 (1944)*, insurance was considered strictly a personal contract that did not constitute interstate commerce.

IMPORTANCE OF THE *McCARRAN-FERGUSON ACT*

In response to the 1944 decision, the *McCarran-Ferguson Act* (MFA) was passed by Congress in 1945 to maintain the central role of the states in insurance regulation. The MFA sets out the division of responsibilities between the federal and state governments with the intent that responsibility be shared. The primary responsibility for insurance regulation rests with the states. However, the act reserves to Congress the right to regulate insurance, but only where it expressly addresses insurance:

> No Act of Congress shall be construed to invalidate, impair, or supersede any law enacted by any State for the purpose of regulating the business of insurance, or which imposes a fee or tax upon such business, unless such Act specifically relates to the business of insurance.

Immunity from federal authority is thus granted where a federal statute *not specifically related to the business of insurance* would "invalidate, impair or supersede" state law that relates specifically to the "business of insurance." The "business of insurance" is not defined in the act. Court interpretations have held that it generally depends on whether the practice is related to the spreading and sharing of risk, whether it is an integral part of the relationship between insurer and insured, and whether the practice is relatively unique to the insurance business. In practice, the MFA also provides a limited exemption to activities that might otherwise be subject to the antitrust provisions of the *Sherman* and *Clayton Acts*, as long as the activity does not involve boycott, coercion, or intimidation. Thus, insurers may share underwriting and claim information, cooperate in standardizing policy forms, and participate in rate-making cooperation in reinsurance and other risk-sharing arrangements.

The MFA has been and is currently a source of controversy as some argue it permits collusion, tying arrangements, and price fixing and should be repealed, while others disagree and argue it is necessary to a safe and efficient industry. The possibility of a transfer of significant regulatory authority from the states to the federal government through adoption of an alternative optional federal charter and regulatory regime has been considered for some time and enjoys the support of most major life insurers. Companies that operate across state lines are burdened with numerous regulators and duplicative compliance duties. Some research indicates that the effect of the federal option would be to enhance competition, efficiency, and value to consumers, while producing a net positive economic result to most states.[1]

Box 12-1 sets out a summary of the arguments for and against primary regulation of insurance at the state level.

Box 12-1
Arguments for and Against State Regulation of Insurance

Some of the arguments for continuing state regulation include:

- State regulation already exists. It would be expensive to change and great uncertainty exists as to whether any other approach would be superior.
- Decentralization of government is a virtue in itself and consistent with U.S. citizens' views as to the appropriate locus of responsibility.
- States can be more responsive to local needs.
- There is no reason to believe that other regulation arrangements would be more effective or efficient than state regulation, especially given the unsatisfactory federal banking regulatory experience.
- Whatever uniformity is desirable can be achieved through the NAIC.
- The effects of ill advised insurance legislation are localized.
- States serve as laboratories for insurance regulation.

Arguments advanced in favor of some form of national, including federal, regulation include:

- The expense of having to file financial reports in and deal with each jurisdiction's insurance department is high and leads to insurer inflexibility, ultimately hindering U.S. domestic insurers in their competition with international insurers.
- Ill advised legislation can be passed easily in states where legislators cannot devote resources to studying legislation, as can the U.S. Congress.
- The political nature of the appointment or election of state insurance commissioners may produce poorly qualified regulators.
- Insurance commissioners and state legislatures are sometimes overly responsive to domestic insurance companies' pressures, to the point of placing extra burdens on non-domestic companies (e.g., discriminatory premium taxes).
- Conflicts arise between standard federal regulations and state rulings that adversely affect insurer operations.
- States find it increasingly difficult to solve regulatory problems involving non-U.S. insurers.
- Whereas U.S. insurers wishing to do business in other nations typically need deal with only one national regulator, non-U.S. insurers wishing to do business in the U.S. must deal with dozens of regulators.

Despite the restrictions of the MFA, many areas of life insurer operations are affected by federal regulations. We briefly cover some of the more important aspects.

The *Financial Services Modernization Act*

Until this act, the formation of financial conglomerates and the cross marketing of one financial sector's products by another (e.g., banks selling insurance) was greatly hindered by two federal statutes: the *Banking Act of 1933* and the *Bank Holding Company* (BHC) *Act* (1956). Sections 16, 20, 21, and 22 of the *Banking Act* collectively were referred to as the *Glass-Steagall Act* (GSA). The GSA stemmed from a belief in the early 1930s that banks' errant recommendations for and investments in stocks helped precipitate the Great Depression and led to the failure of more than 5,000 banks.

The other major impediment to integration and cross marketing was the BHC act and its 1970 amendments. They limited the ability of bank holding companies to engage in commerce, insurance, and other non-bank financial services activities, including prohibiting banks from marketing insurance. **Bank holding companies** are corporations that own banks and non-bank subsidiaries.

After more than two decades of trying to reform U.S. financial services regulation, success was achieved with the 1999 Congressional passage of the *Financial Services Modernization Act*, known more commonly as the *Gramm Leach Bliley Act* (GLBA). The act effectively eliminated restrictions on financial services integration in the U.S. Specifically, Title I repealed GSA and BHC restrictions on affiliations among banks, securities firms, and insurers. It allowed the creation under the BHC act of **financial holding companies** and authorized them to engage in a range of financial activities including insurance underwriting and distribution, securities underwriting, trading, and merchant banking activities, and banking. This title also provided for state regulation of insurance subject to prohibitions on discriminating against persons affiliated with banks, and clarified the role of the Federal Reserve as the umbrella holding company supervisor, with functional state or federal regulation for affiliates and subsidiaries.

The *Dodd–Frank Wall Street Reform and Consumer Protection Act*

The *Dodd–Frank Wall Street Reform and Consumer Protection Act*, enacted in 2010, was passed in response to the subprime mortgage crisis and related financial turmoil experienced worldwide in 2008 and 2009. The act and related legislation provided for little revision to the insurance regulatory scheme in the U.S. Also, no action was taken to adopt optional federal charter legislation as supported by the large U.S. life insurance companies or to repeal GLBA as some wished, believing that its relaxed inter-sectoral constraints contributed to the 2008-09 recession. Among other items, the bill provided for:

- The establishment of a *Federal Insurance Office* (FIO) that functions in an advisory role to the legislative and executive branches but has no direct regulatory authority. Its influence extends to efforts to develop international regulatory equivalency agreements, which suggests an important role in the convergence of international regulatory practice discussed in Chapter 13. The NAIC *Solvency Modernization Initiative*, discussed below, is such an undertaking. The FIO delivered in 2013 its report of recommendations to Congress on how to improve and modernize insurance regulation. The report stated that the goals of uniformity, efficiency, and consumer protection made continued and deeper federal involvement necessary to improve insurance regulation, although a hybrid federal/state model was still desired.

- The possibility of a federal role in the resolution or liquidation of insurers but only when (1) the *Federal Reserve Board* ascertains the liquidation has systemic importance potentially damaging to the national economy and (2) when states do not act effectively.
- The consumer protection elements of the act do not apply to life insurance and annuities.

Life insurers may be indirectly subject to the effects of new regulatory authority granted the *Securities and Exchange Commission* (SEC) and the *Commodities Futures Trading Commission* in the area of derivative securities. Wide discretion has been granted these authorities, and the extent of the impact will not be known until regulations under the law are promulgated. The life insurance industry believes that the long term nature of life insurer obligations makes derivatives indispensible, that insurers do not pose systemic risks, and that interest rate and other swaps can be traded safely without the intermediation of a regulated exchange.

OTHER AREAS OF FEDERAL INSURANCE REGULATION

Other important areas of federal regulatory oversight of the life insurance business are highlighted here.

Selling Securities. Life insurers that maintain separate accounts that support contracts for variable life insurance, annuities, and retirement plans must comply with federal securities laws. Variable products and the application of the *Securities Act of 1933, Securities Exchange Act of 1934*, and *Investment Company Act of 1940* are discussed in Chapters 3, 4, and 5. Life insurers that charge advisory fees to separate accounts or share advisory fees with unaffiliated advisers are also subject to the registration, disclosure, and other rules of the *Investment Advisers Act of 1940*. Life insurer agents who sell variable and related securities products are required to be licensed through the *Financial Industry Regulatory Authority* (FINRA). FINRA also maintains training and compliance standards as to variable product suitability.

Buying Securities. Federal securities regulation applies to many aspects of the acquisition and accumulation of securities in public markets as it does to all such acquirers. State blue sky laws may also apply. Additional rules related to the quality of securities are designed to promote solvency and are the subject of state insurance regulation. In addition to federal regulation of the accumulation of securities in amounts sufficient to acquire control of the issuer, there are additional constraints at the state level controlling the use of life insurance assets in the acquisition of corporate control of an issuer.

Issuing Securities. Stock life insurers may be subject to the *Securities Act of 1933, Securities Exchange Act of 1934*, and state blue sky securities laws. Public companies are further constrained by generally accepted accounting principles (GAAP), discussed in Chapter 13. The application of rules varies according to the private or public status of the insurer's securities, and additional nongovernmental regulation applies to all stocks traded on exchanges. The primary focus is on fair representation and disclosure of financial information and material risks; a company's failure in this area can lead to significant liability.

Lending. All U.S. financial institutions including life insurers are subject to constraints on their lending activities, particularly in transactions involving loans to consumers. Common law duties of good faith and fair dealing, as well as other contractual principles, can give rise to borrower claims and often involve oral representations of lender representatives. Fiduciary claims may also be made, particularly where an institution holds itself out as a financial advisor to the consumer. The offering of comprehensive financial services obviously creates factual circumstances more likely to give rise to these claims.

A broad range of statutory constraints also exists at both the federal and state levels including state consumer protection and usury laws. In real estate lending, life insurer lenders may also face legal liability under the *Fair Housing Act* and the *Real Estate Settlement Procedures Act* for unreasonable foreclosure and/or reselling of collateral property. Lender liability for environmental damage may also arise under regulations of the *Environmental Protection Agency*.

Taxation. In the U.S. and other countries, the taxing authority and rulemaking bodies exert considerable influence over the design of marketable products through the tax treatment of policyowners. Policyowner taxation is discussed in Chapter 21. In the U.S., general corporate income tax is applicable to life insurers, and a special federal tax applies to premiums paid to alien insurers and reinsurers that do not do business in the U.S. (See below.)

International Trade. Several agencies of the federal government are involved in insurance activities by virtue of their role in international trade and commerce. Thus, the *Department of Commerce, Department of State,* and *U.S. Trade Representative's* office are all involved in trade negotiations and other international actions, the effects of which are felt directly by U.S. insurers. Other countries' insurance markets may be more or less open to U.S. insurers depending on negotiations undertaken by these agencies. Their activities can also influence domestic regulation. For example, the *North American Free Trade Agreement* among Canada, Mexico, and the U.S. permits insurers of each country relatively free access to the others' markets and prohibits discrimination between national and non-national insurers.

U.S. STATE REGULATION OF LIFE INSURERS

In the U.S. (and in virtually all jurisdictions worldwide), regulation of insurance is shaped and influenced by the legislative, judicial, and executive branches of governments. Also, in the U.S., the *National Association of Insurance Commissioners* (NAIC) performs a vital role in the development of model regulations and laws and in the coordination of legislative activities and of state regulatory actions.

ROLES OF THE THREE BRANCHES OF STATE GOVERNMENTS
The legislative branch of government enacts laws – called **insurance codes** – that specify (1) the scope and standards that govern the administration of the law and (2) ordinarily, the requirements, procedures, standards, and enforcement mechanisms for

- the organization and operation of the insurance supervisory function,
- the formation and licensing of the various types of insurers for the various classes of insurance and reinsurance,
- the licensing of agents and brokers,
- the filing and sometimes approval of insurance rates,

- the filing and approval of policy forms,
- unauthorized insurers and unfair trade practices,
- insurer financial reporting, examination, and other financial requirements,
- complaint handling,
- the rehabilitation and liquidation of insurers,
- guaranty associations, and
- insurance product and company taxation.

Most jurisdictions also incorporate into their insurance law certain standards for life and health insurance contracts. Mandatory contractual provisions in the U.S. are discussed in Chapter 5.

The judicial branch in insurance regulation is primarily represented by federal and state courts that perform three essential functions in state insurance oversight:

- resolution of conflicts between insurers and policyowners,
- resolution of conflicts between insurers and regulators, and
- enforcement of applicable criminal provisions provided in insurance codes.

Legislatures and courts lack the experience to regulate a highly complex and rapidly changing industry like insurance in the detail necessary to achieve regulatory objectives. Legislation in many respects is based on broad principles, and the details of implementation are left to the executive branch of government, represented in the U.S. by the governors of the states. Legislatures provide for the delegation of executive authority to state insurance departments or commissions. The departments operate through the mechanism of administrative law and possess broad authority through the grant of quasi-legislative and quasi-judicial powers.

These state insurance departments usually are under the direction of a chief official who typically holds the title of *commissioner, superintendent,* or *director*. In a few states, the responsibility of direction is placed in a commission or board, which, in turn, selects an individual commissioner to carry out established policy. In 12 states, commissioners are elected (California, Delaware, Florida, Georgia, Kansas, Louisiana, Mississippi, Montana, North Carolina, North Dakota, Oklahoma, and Washington).

In the remainder of the states, they are appointed, usually by the governor. In many states, the state official who has this responsibility also has other duties, such as state auditor, comptroller, or treasurer. The insurance regulatory function may also be a part of a larger financial regulation agency, such as a department of banking or securities or, as with New York, a department of financial services.

In other countries, enforcement responsibility may rest within the ministry of finance (common), the economics ministry (e.g., Thailand), the ministry of industry and commerce (or a similar name), or the ministry of justice (e.g., Switzerland). The Canadian regulatory system resembles that of the U.S. with responsibilities split between the federal and provincial governments, except the option of a federal charter does not exist in the U.S.

A formal advisory body assists regulatory authorities in most countries. (In the U.S., the role of advisory groups generally is permissive and usually complementary to the NAIC model law process discussed below.) These bodies are typically composed of representatives of insurance companies, consumer groups, insurance experts, and others with an interest in insurance. The number of members varies from five to 60, depending on the country. The body advises the supervisory authority on important decisions. In some countries, the regulator must consult the advisory body before taking certain actions.

In the U.S., the right to conduct an insurance business, to represent an insurer in conducting an insurance business, or to represent the public in placing insurance are privileges granted only to those who qualify by obtaining a license. Mandatory compliance with the conditions of licensing is the source of regulatory authority, control, and supervision.

ROLE OF THE *NATIONAL ASSOCIATION OF INSURANCE COMMISSIONERS*

The NAIC is the most influential insurance regulatory body in the U.S. While it has no direct authority, its model laws significantly influence the laws of the states, and its state accreditation program creates a great deal of uniformity in state law.

STRUCTURE AND OPERATION   The NAIC is a voluntary association of the chief insurance regulatory officials of the 50 U.S. states, the District of Columbia, American Samoa, Guam, Puerto Rico, and the U.S. Virgin Islands. The NAIC (formerly the National Insurance Convention) was formed in 1871 to address issues concerning the supervision of interstate insurers within a state regulatory framework. The objectives of the association are as follows:

- fair, just, and equitable treatment of policyowners and claimants,
- the maintenance and improvement of state regulation of insurance in a responsive and efficient manner, and
- ensuring reliability of the insurance institution as to financial solidity and guaranty against loss.

The association operates through a committee structure wherein tasks are assigned by line of business (e.g., life, health, property/liability) and activity. Committees are composed of selected states that are represented by officials of the state's insurance department. To assist the committees, advisory or working groups, composed mostly or exclusively of insurance industry representatives, are appointed. They prepare background papers, conduct research, and draft tentative model bills and regulations. The NAIC has been criticized for relying heavily on industry-dominated advisory groups. In response, the NAIC began inviting consumer representation, although industry representatives remain more prominent in committee membership.

The NAIC's most important function is the development of model laws and regulations. In a legal sense, these laws are mere suggestions to the states; only laws and regulations enacted by the states have direct legal significance. Although adoption of the suggested models is not mandatory or universal, and some are enacted with variations introduced by the states, in practice they represent the essential structure of state insurance regulation. The NAIC has been successful in many respects and has served as a unifying and harmonizing force. Some of its more significant accomplishments include the following:

- adoption by all states of uniform annual financial reports (often called *blanks*),

- reciprocal recognition by most states of state solvency certification determined through each state's supervision of its domestic insurers,
- adoption of uniform rules for valuation of securities,
- establishment and revision of standard mortality tables,
- standard valuation and nonforfeiture laws,
- creation of a program that certifies state departmental solvency regulation, and
- coordination of activity with federal and state governments on insurance matters.

The NAIC has adopted more than 215 model laws, regulations, and guidelines applicable to virtually all aspects of insurance regulation. In addition, the NAIC has undertaken a number of major research projects and expanded its services to members.

The State Accreditation Program   The ability of the states to effectively determine the solvency of its domiciled insurers has been central to the debate over the efficacy of state regulation. In addition to models laws, the influence of the NAIC has expanded through the maintenance of a state accreditation program. NAIC accreditation requires:

- adequate solvency laws and regulations to protect consumers and state guaranty associations (discussed below),
- effective and efficient financial analysis and examination processes,
- cooperation and information sharing between states,
- timely and effective response to financially troubled insurers,
- appropriate organizational and personnel practices, and
- effective procedures for company licensing and changes in control.

The accreditation program is executed by the *Financial Regulation Standards and Accreditation Committee* of the NAIC, and its effect is the NAIC's most direct role in regulation. Because adoption of certain model laws are prerequisites to accreditation and states may refuse to recognize the solvency certification of insurers domiciled in non-accredited states, the accreditation program represents an indirect but effective enforcement mechanism. It also creates more homogeneity in regulation from state to state. The committee conducts preliminary reviews prior to a state's first accreditation and interim annual reviews and more extensive full accreditation reviews every five years for accredited states. With the accreditation of New York in 2009, all states have achieved accreditation.

Regulatory Modernization   In 2000, the NAIC put forth a *Statement of Intent – The Future of Insurance Regulation* and subsequently adopted an action plan to further the intent. The effort was in response to criticism from Congress and the *General Accounting Office* of the federal government and is related to the debate over the removal of insurance regulation from the states to the federal government. NAIC modernization is an ongoing, explicit attempt to address the issues that are necessary to upgrade and improve and ultimately to retain the state-based system of insurance regulation. The declared principles of the effort address seven areas of regulation:

1. consumer protection,
2. markets, market conduct, and interstate collaboration,
3. uniform interstate product filing and approval (a "speed to market" initiative),
4. producer licensing requirements,
5. insurer licensing,
6. solvency regulation, and
7. insurer control change.

AREAS OF STATE REGULATION

Insurance occupies a position of extraordinary trust in commerce. The policy-owner's commitment – the payment of premiums – is *current*, while the insurer's obligation – the payment of claims – is *future*. Market mechanisms and information available to the typical policyowner are insufficient to allow sound evaluation of the security of the insurer's promised future performance. In the absence of adequate regulation, if an insurer were unable to meet its obligations, policy-owners may become aware of a problem only upon an unacceptable event: *when their claims were not paid*. As a result, achievement of the objectives of regulation requires close supervision of insurers and their activities from organization to liquidation. Below we set out the broad areas of insurance regulation that are applicable to virtually all insurance markets worldwide, however, particular attention is given to the U.S. industry.

ORGANIZATION AND LICENSING OF INSURERS   Although the organization of insurance companies is governed to some extent by the law applicable to the organization of general corporations, states have supplanted most of their general corporation law with special acts pertaining only to insurance companies. State insurance laws prescribe specifically the requirements for the organization of a life company.

State insurance codes generally require specified amounts of minimum paid-in capital and minimum surplus funds. Additionally, ongoing requirements address prescribed minimums for *reserves* (based on the amount of insurance issued) and *risk-based capital* (based on each insurer's asset and liability portfolio characteristics). These requirements are discussed below and in Chapters 13 and 14. In addition to initial financial requirements, applications also generally require an examination of an applicant company's business plans as well as the fitness and competency of the incorporators.

The states recognize three types of insurers that operate under their dominion according to the charter of the corporate domicile:

- **domestic insurers** are domiciled (incorporated) in the state in which they are licensed to do business,
- **foreign insurers** are domiciled (incorporated) in a state different from that in which they are licensed to do business, and
- **alien insurers** are domiciled outside the U.S.

Licensing requirements for domestic and foreign insurers are similar and, from a solvency perspective, distinctions are less important after the NAIC grant of accreditation to all states. All insurers are required to make a substantial deposit of qualified securities into trust for the ultimate benefit of policyowners, guaranty associations, and creditors. Foreign-insurer trust funds deposited in their state of domicile are recognized in other states. Deposit requirements for alien insurers vary from state to state and are more stringent.

The NAIC is developing a *Company Licensing Model Act* to establish standardized filing requirements and standards for a license application. Company licensing requirements are the first instance of solvency protection, and the act will be coordinated with the state accreditation program.

DEMUTUALIZATION   At about the turn of the 21st century, **demutualization** – the conversion of a mutual life insurer to a stock insurer (or upstream holding company) – was a dominant feature of the strategic landscape of the industry. The quasi-ownership rights of a traditional mutual company (principally the right to appoint management, to receive divisible surplus, and, in the case of liquidation, to receive any residual corporate value) vest in its policyowners for as long as their policies remain in force.

While mutuals have converted throughout most of the history of the industry, after about 1990 the process became more extensive. Highly visible insurers such as *Prudential, Metropolitan,* and *John Hancock* completed demutualizations. Nevertheless, other major insurers such as *New York Life, Northwestern Mutual,* and *Mass Mutual* continue to operate as mutuals, and a reasonable speculation would suggest that the continuing commitment to mutuality is predicated on different market postures or management preferences.

Because of the demutualization trend, mutuals have declined in importance in the U.S. life insurance industry. The industry in Japan, long dominated by a relatively few mutuals, has also seen the number of mutuals decline, from 14 in 2000 to five at this writing, but the mutual form remains important. Elsewhere in the world, the life insurance industries of other major economies are principally comprised of stock company participants, and, wherever the mutual form has been historically important, that importance has declined.

One 2006 study of 11 converted companies found results that largely suggest demutualizations have achieved positive results.[2] It found

- increases in returns on equity and returns on assets,
- increases in revenues,
- increases in product diversification, and
- increases in overall risk through financial leverage, reflected in increased post-conversion debt, as shareholders prefer the increased risk and returns associated with higher leverage.

A short term review of the operational results of mutual companies during the 2008-2009 recession suggests less volatile results for mutuals than for stocks. Mutuals place more emphasis on capital and claims-paying conservation than on the capital efficiency emphasized by stocks. Because mutuals do not access traditional capital markets, turmoil in those markets has not had the same impact on them as it has on stock companies that respond to public equity markets demanding higher returns on less capital.

Also, rating agency downgrades of mutuals in this period have been comparatively fewer and less severe than those experienced by stock companies. Results indicate that more risk tolerant stock companies fare better in a positive economic environment, and less risk tolerant mutual companies fare comparatively better when the environment is less positive.[3]

The primary motivation to demutualize is access to capital. Mutual companies have no shareholders, and some state statutes in the U.S. restrict a mutual company's accumulation of retained earnings. Common and preferred stock offerings as well as debt instruments with equity conversion features are not available to mutuals. Because retained earnings are both limited and unpredictable in a competitive environment, there are restrictive consequences for mutual company managers.

Alternative but less attractive options to retained earnings are available to mutuals. Highly subordinate forms of reinsurance and surplus notes can be sources of investment capital, but each comes with both legal requirements and reinsurer/investor conditions that are more restrictive than public capital market financing. These alternatives are discussed in more detail in Chapter 14.

The demutualization process is costly. The initial process requires significant accounting, actuarial, legal, and regulatory investigation and compliance, and additional cost in these areas becomes a permanent and recurring expense after conversion. Further, management will be monitored by and must be responsive to the new shareholder constituency. The need for additional capital, therefore, must be compelling to warrant demutualization. Corporate objectives in the contemporary market that may require capital include:

- *Growth* The initial expense of new policy sales generally exceeds initial premiums (see Chapter 2), and this cash flow deficit requires capital in the short run.
- *New Insurance Product Diversification* The contemporary generation of life insurance policies with flexible premiums and adjustable death benefits, and in the case of variable products, separate accounts, requires a considerable investment in actuarial, legal, and marketing support. Sophisticated information technology is essential to these products from the agent's desk and initial presentation to periodic policyowner reports to regulatory compliance.
- *Complementary Product Diversification* Insurance companies increasingly find complementary financial services such as mutual fund and asset management services either attractive or competitively necessary, and they require additional capital support.
- *Competitive Capital Adequacy* Companies find that financial regulatory compliance is not sufficient to compete successfully. Fluctuating risk-based capital requirements, liquidity constraints associated with both traditional and contemporary products, and solvency demands in the market may dictate increased levels of capital.
- *Acquisitions* Growth by acquisition and consolidation has been a distinctive feature of the industry. Mutual company acquisitions are necessarily cash only, while stock companies can offer their own shares to sellers.
- *Management Compensation* Performance rewards for mutual company managers must be paid in cash and generally reflect short term results. Stock companies can reward managers with stock and option grant

incentives that generate future reward for long term performance and are more harmoniously aligned with the long term interests of shareholders.

Any demutualization process in any state requires the adoption of a plan by the board in the interests of policyowners, approved by regulators, and finally approved by policyowners. Where shares are offered to the public as part of the demutualization, compliance with state and federal securities laws and regulations is also required. The approval percentage varies from state to state. The investigation and preparation of the plan are developed with the assistance of independent actuaries, accountants, and investment bankers.

The most important aspect of any plan of demutualization is the protection of the converting company's policyowners. Fairness determinations that must be resolved before the plan is approved and executed include:

- the allocation of aggregate policyowner compensation among policyowners whose policy plans and policy holding periods vary,
- the allocation of shares in any equity offering to policyowners and to purchasing shareholders, and
- the protection of surviving policy participation rights. Regulators may require the use of **closed blocks** that allocate specific investment, expense, and mortality results to specific groups of policies for the purpose of policy dividends.

The establishment of a mutual insurance holding company (MIHC) represents a partial conversion. An upstream MIHC is established, and the mutual insurer converts into a stock insurer subsidiary of the MIHC. Policyholders of the stock insurer continue as members of the MIHC, with the holding company owning not less than 51 percent of the stock subsidiary. Policyowners' quasi-ownership rights vest in the holding company, and policy dividend rights continue, thus preserving mutuality. Policyowners receive no compensation. The MIHC may sell up to 49 percent of the subsidiary's shares, thus accessing the capital market. Management may receive stock incentives, and the company operates as any other stock insurer. The benefits of share ownership then accrue in part to new shareholders and in part to policyowners through their ownership of the MIHC.

The MIHC is controversial because of incentive misalignment and conflict at the holding company and subsidiary levels. Some maintain it is difficult to harmonize the interests of policyowners and shareholders in this fashion and that policyowner rights, controls, and protections are not adequate under the mutual holding company procedure. Proponents argue that the MIHC procedure permits a partial current realization of the benefits of demutualization while permitting a subsequent offering of stock to the public timed to propitious market conditions. (In full conversions, the capital markets have come to expect a concurrent offering.)

SOLVENCY SURVEILLANCE   The mission of the NAIC is "To protect the interests of the policyholder and those who rely on the insurance coverage provided to the policyholder first and foremost, while also facilitating an effective and efficient market place for insurance products." The importance of the supervision of insurers' solvency is paramount. According to the NAIC, solvency surveillance and maintenance are based on seven core principles:

1. *Regulatory Reporting, Disclosure, and Transparency.* Standard, regular financial reports are required of all insurers.
2. *Off-site Monitoring and Analysis.* The NAIC conducts detailed financial analysis of insurers' reports.
3. *On-site Risk-focused Examinations.* Corporate governance, management oversight, financial strength, risk identification, and mitigation are evaluated through regular in-office examinations.
4. *Reserves, Capital Adequacy, and Solvency.* Funds necessary to maintain solvency are specified and verified in form and amount.
5. *Regulatory Control of Significant Broad-based Transactions/Activities.* Major events potentially affecting solvency are subject to approval, including change of control, dividends, transactions with affiliates, and reinsurance arrangements.
6. *Preventive and Corrective Measures, including Enforcement.* Authority is granted to regulators to minimize the impact of risks identified during off-site and on-site examinations
7. *Exiting the Market and Receivership.* Regulators oversee and require an orderly liquidation or transfer of exiting insurer liabilities to ensure the payment of policyowner claims.

The NAIC *Solvency Modernization Initiative* (SMI) is an ongoing self-critical review process designed to maintain and improve solvency monitoring and effectiveness. One of the fundamental regulatory reforms planned by the NAIC is the introduction of an *Own Risk Solvency Assessment* (ORSA) requirement that essentially formalizes the enterprise risk management process described in Chapter 9. ORSA and the NAIC solvency framework and its implementation in conjunction with the financial reporting framework are discussed in Chapter 13.

UNAUTHORIZED INSURANCE   One of the more vexatious problems confronting state insurance regulation involves the question of control over the activities of unauthorized insurance companies. By refusing to apply for a license, the unauthorized insurer may attempt to escape regulation in all states except its state or country of domicile, on the basis that it has no representatives within the state and, consequently, it is not legally doing business there. Unauthorized insurers generally make no reports to the state insurance department. As their business may be conducted through the mail or the Internet, the state commissioner may be handicapped in rendering any service to the policyowner in a dispute with the insurer. States attempt to address this problem through a variety of means including regulation of advertising by mass marketers, permitting service of process on the commissioner of the home-state insurance department by home-state consumers, and making unauthorized insurance contracts voidable at the option of the insured.

The completion of the state accreditation program provides consumers an increased level of comfort with respect to insurer solvency, and some states have attempted to reach unauthorized insurers through criminal penalties by adopting a form of the *Unauthorized Transaction of Insurance Criminal Model Act*. Problems persist despite these efforts.

INSURANCE POLICY REGULATION   Insurers are required in most states to file policy forms and rates. Most states require life insurance policy forms be filed with and approved by the state insurance department before the policy can be sold in that state. The mandatory policy provisions discussed in Chapter 5 are necessary for approval. These provisions are required to protect consumers from unfair and deceptive trade practices and to address the information asymmetry problems discussed in Chapter 1.

Life insurance rates are not regulated directly and do not require approval. Regulators are generally more concerned with rate *adequacy* than with rates that are unfairly *excessive*. Competition has proven to be an effective regulator of excessive rates. By contrast, regulators believe that, in the absence of regulation, life insurance rates could be driven below prudent levels as insurers compete for business and assume increasingly risky investments to allow lower premiums that could threaten solvency. The system of mandatory reserves is intended to ensure rate adequacy.

Life insurance rates are retrospectively regulated in indirect ways under two circumstances: (1) some states limit the amount of surplus that mutual insurers can accumulate and require periodic dividends consistent with the limit and (2) some states limit dividend payments to shareholders that are attributable to profits arising from participating (par) policies, thus protecting policyholder dividends.

In the absence of direct regulation or approval, life insurance rates typically must be filed to establish a public record reference for misstatement of age adjustments and other provisions involving premiums prorated on the basis of age. By contrast, health insurance rates may be directly regulated under a provision in most states that requires benefits be fairly proportional to premiums. Also, the Affordable Care Act requires health insurers to pay at least 80 percent of premium income derived from the sale of medical insurance in benefits. As part of the NAIC modernization effort, the *System for Electronic Rate and Form Filing* (SERFF) was developed. All 50 states have adopted the uniform procedures of the system, which is designed to enable companies to send and states to receive, comment on, and approve or reject insurance industry rate and form filings over the Internet.

MARKETING PRACTICES   Broadly interpreted, state regulation of marketing practices includes control over the licensing of agents and brokers, and over unfair trade practices.

Licensing of Agents and Brokers   In all U.S. jurisdictions, insurers are permitted to appoint only agents and brokers who are licensed or in the process of becoming licensed. New agent licensing requires a conditional appointment and attestation of character by a licensed insurer subject to the individual's successful application to the state. In making the appointment, the insurer assumes responsibility for agent or broker conduct under the law of the state. This relationship is discussed in more detail in Chapter 18.

New producers are required to pass an examination of their knowledge of life and health insurance generally, of policy provisions, and of rules and regulations that apply to the sale of insurance. States typically require a minimum course of formal study (40 hours is common) prior to the examination, and some states require continuing education. Rules vary by state: some states issue perpetual licenses while others require periodic renewal. Licenses may be revoked for consistent or willful failure to comply with state law and for fraud, conversion, and other serious causes. Licensing is not universal internationally. Many national regulatory regimes rely on insurers to manage the conduct of their agents as the insurer is usually ultimately responsible for the agent's misbehavior

Unfair Trade Practices Impermissible marketing activity at the company level is discussed in Chapter 18 and includes disputes arising out of "vanishing" premiums, selling life insurance as a retirement plan without adequate disclosure, selling life insurance to tax-qualified plans, bonus annuities, and other practices. Insurer responsibility for these types of activities often is based in common law concepts of contract and tort and includes an allegation that the insurer aided or participated in the misconduct.

Insurers can also share responsibility for the market conduct of unsanctioned, improper sales practices by their agents, and some impermissible agent conduct has been codified. All states reacted to the MFA by adopting the *NAIC Model Unfair Trade Practices Act* to prevent the intrusion of the *Federal Trade Commission* (FTC) into their scope of authority, which would have otherwise had authority through the "not regulated by states" language of the MFA. The most important agent prohibitions are:

- **Rebating**, which is the practice by a producer (or insurer) of giving something of value (e.g., portion of the agent's commission) not specified in the insurance contract to an applicant in return for the purchase of a policy. Anti-rebating statutes evolved decades ago in response to perceived marketplace abuses. Traditional arguments against rebating have focused on concerns about insurer solvency, unfair discrimination, and the unique nature of insurance. Critics of anti-rebating statutes claim that the prohibition unfairly prevents buyers from negotiating fully with sellers – a result that is offensive in a competitive system. The states of Florida and California allow rebating, although many insurers still prohibit their agents' giving a rebate and guidelines generally require no unfair discrimination in the granting of rebates. Opponents consider rebate prohibition a form of regulatory capture.

- **Twisting**, which is the practice by a producer of inducing a policyowner through misrepresentation to discontinue an existing life insurance policy to purchase a new one. In contrast to simple *replacement* – discontinuing one policy to purchase another – twisting is illegal. The purchase of a life insurance policy can be a complicated transaction. The consumer easily could be misled, either intentionally or unintentionally, by an agent. The receipt of a new first year sales commission (which typically greatly exceeds the renewal commission) usually is the agent's incentive to twist or replace. In recognition of this fact, several states have promulgated versions of the NAIC *Model Replacement Regulations* that require the disclosure of certain information considered pertinent to the proposed replacement decision, as we discuss in Chapter 19.

- **Commingling and misappropriation of funds.** Producers are responsible for receiving money from the customer and remitting money to the insurer, often in large amounts. Misappropriation of funds, even for brief periods with an intention of repayment (or repayment in fact) and commingling of premium or claim funds with the agent's own funds are both impermissible. Recall that industrial insurance premiums were historically paid in cash to the agent at the insured's home or workplace. With modern bank checks and electronic funds transfers, these problems are no longer common.

Finally, life insurer advertising is regulated by the states. Many have adopted the NAIC *Model Life Insurance Advertising Regulation*. In addition, the FTC oversees direct mail solicitations.

ISSUES IN GROUP SUPERVISION

Special problems can arise when insurers operate as distinct units within groups of operating companies. Here we identify several issues that pose problems, as well as regulatory trends in group supervision. As we discuss in Chapter 9, however, in an enterprise risk management context, group risk can also be reduced through the benefits of diversified operating units.

As discussed in Chapter 1, contagion risk exists because of the possibility of cascading failures resulting from financial intermediaries being highly connected. The same risk exists within a financial group or conglomerate. Contagion or **financial infection** can arise when one unit of a financial services conglomerate becomes a source of distress throughout the group.

A bank with an insurance subsidiary might be compelled to transfer capital to the subsidiary, thus weakening the bank's capital position. Related group problems include transparency issues when funds are transferred between group units without a full accounting, often in an attempt to raise perceived capital levels through **double-gearing**, the double counting of subsidiary capital to prop up conglomerate capital.

Regulatory arbitrage, the shifting of activities within the group to take advantage of different regulatory approaches in different industries, can also change reporting and capital appearances with no real change in the group's economic risk. **Conflicts of interest** – situations where an individual or corporation may have an interest in promoting one product or service over another that does not align with the customer's interest – can arise when a financial institution offers multiple financial services and promotes proprietary products of subsidiaries through formal or informal coercion.

The recent global financial crisis taught regulators that they needed to be able to assess better the enterprise-wide risk of a holding company system and its impact or contagion on insurers within such a group. To improve the regulation of financial service conglomerates, the use of supervisory colleges was incorporated into the U.S. regulation. Supervisory colleges are intended to facilitate oversight of internationally active insurance companies at the group level. The IAIS defines a supervisory college as "a forum for cooperation and communication between the involved supervisors established for the fundamental purpose of facilitating the effectiveness of supervision of entities which belong to an insurance group...." The NAIC included the concept of supervisory colleges into its SMI by adopting revisions to the *Insurance Holding Company System Regulatory Model Act* and its companion regulation. State insurance regulators, following the lead of the IAIS, drafted a *Holding Company and Supervisory Colleges Best Practices* document as an appendix to its *Financial Analysis Handbook*. It includes standards for participating in international supervisory colleges and provides additional references to the IAIS guidance paper on supervisory colleges and how participation can work within the existing U.S. regulatory framework.

U.S. life and health insurers are taxed by the federal and state governments. Federal taxation is based on insurer's net income as defined in Subchapter L of the *Internal Revenue Code* (IRC). In addition to the general federal tax on income of individuals and corporations, special taxes apply to life insurance policies. All states impose a tax on premiums paid to life insurers, and a federal excise tax applies to premiums paid to alien insures not licensed in the U.S.

Theoretically, an efficient and fair tax system should be simple, equitable, and neutral. Life insurer taxation features compromises in each area as taxing authorities strive to raise revenue efficiently and fairly, while addressing different perspectives on fairness.

TAXATION OF U.S. LIFE AND HEALTH INSURERS

STATE GOVERNMENT TAXATION

The most prominent U.S. state taxation of life insurers takes the form of premium taxation. States also levy retaliatory taxes, and some states apply income taxes.

PREMIUM TAXATION   Many countries and all states in the U.S. impose a premium tax of some sort. In many countries, the premium tax takes the place of net income or related taxation. A complete premium tax system requires a tax base, tax rates, and any special deductions, credits, or exemptions provided for in the law. In the U.S., under the typical state premium tax structure, the tax base is the simple total of the insurer's premium revenue in the state with certain exceptions. Premiums received for assumed reinsurance are excluded, and dividends paid to policyowners are deductible. The former exclusion avoids double taxation, and the latter deduction is tacit recognition that dividends are considered a return of premiums.

Tax rates on life insurance premiums written by foreign insurers range from about 1 to 4 percent. Tax rates on domestic insurers vary from 0 to 4 percent. Some states tax health insurance premiums at a higher rate than that for life insurance premiums, while others do the opposite. Annuity premiums are not taxed in most states. Studies have found that the effective tax burden on insurers arising from premium taxation is consistently higher than that on other financial and nonfinancial institutions; where annuity premiums are taxed, banks and other savings institutions have a substantial and visible advantage.

The goal of tax neutrality is not achieved when selected forms of insuring organizations enjoy preferential treatment. Incidents of such failure include domestic and out-of-state fraternal life insurers being exempt from premium taxation. Also, Blue Cross/Blue Shield organizations and other nonprofit health care service plans, until recently, were exempt from premium taxation in most states. The trend is toward taxing them as any other health insurer. Self-insurance arrangements by commercial enterprises for health and other employee benefit coverages are generally exempted from premium taxation – a fact that encourages self insurance compared to group insurance. (See Chapter 7.)

The premium tax system has both desirable and undesirable attributes. Perhaps its greatest recommendation is simplicity: it avoids the complication of the income tax levied at the federal level. Administration, compliance, and enforcement are relatively easy, it provides regular revenue to the state that is generally increasing over any substantial time period, and it is established.

On the other hand, policyowner equity is compromised because (1) it constitutes a direct tax on savings that is applicable only to insurance products; (2) it is regressive in that it hits lower income persons who purchase life insurance relatively harder than higher income persons; (3) it discriminates unfairly against higher premium and cash value forms of life insurance that promote savings and capital formation; and (4) it discriminates unfairly against those who must pay higher premium rates, such as the elderly and those who are rated substandard.

Neutral treatment of insurers is sacrificed when premium taxes are higher for out-of-state insurers than for domestic insurers. In the absence of the MFA exemption, this discrimination would almost certainly be unconstitutional. It has the same negative effects on cross-border trade as tariffs and has been condemned by the NAIC for distorting competition and ignoring the national character of the U.S. market.

RETALIATORY TAXATION   **Retaliatory tax laws** require out-of-state insurers to pay the higher of the tax due using their home state's laws and the host state's law. Such laws are intended to promote the interstate business of domestic insurers by discouraging other states from imposing excess taxes.

These laws have been held to be constitutionally valid. All states except Hawaii have retaliatory tax laws.

INCOME TAXATION   Nine states subject foreign insurers to state income taxation. Three of these states provide that the income tax can be offset against the premium tax, and five provide that the premium tax can be offset against the income tax. Fourteen states subject their domestic insurers to state income taxation.

Six of these states exempt domestic insurers from premium taxation and, in essence, tax insurers as they do any other domestic corporations, with recognition for their special characteristics. Five permit offsetting premium taxes paid by domestic insurers against the state income tax obligation. Two states permit offsetting the income tax against the premium tax due, and New York provides that domestic insurers must pay both premium taxes and income taxes up to a stated maximum.

FEDERAL GOVERNMENT TAXATION

U.S. federal government taxation of life insurance companies is an important source of government revenue. Income taxation is the most important but other forms of taxation also exist.

INCOME TAXATION   The income taxation of life insurers is complicated by the same economics that complicate insurer financial reporting generally: the difficulty of determining "profit" and "income" when revenue is received currently for obligations to be performed later. Additional difficulties in life insurer income taxation arise due to (1) the tax treatment of investment income earned on policy reserves established for future policyowner benefits and (2) the consistent application of income tax concepts to nonprofit mutual companies and profit making stock companies.

The basic accounting equation for life insurer taxable income is:

$$Net\ Income =$$
$$Premiums + Investment\ Income - Operating\ Expenses - Net\ Change\ in\ Reserves$$

Several adjustments are made under the provisions of the IRC to arrive at a *life insurance company taxable income* (LICTI). The adjustments are discussed below.

Permitted Reserves   The permitted deduction for reserves is the largest permitted deduction in determing life insurer taxable income. Until 1984, the deduction was defined by the taxpayer company's domiciliary state statutory reserve. Under current law, a reserve for any contract is the greater of (1) the net cash surrender value of the contract and (2) the reserve for the contract as computed under federally prescribed standards. In no event may this amount exceed the statutory annual statement figure.

The deduction does not distinguish between premiums and interest, thus any premium and investment income that exceeds the net addition to reserves is taxable to the extent it also exceeds operating expense. Premium and investment income are effectively sheltered from taxation up to a ceiling defined by the permitted reserve. The reserve computed under federal standards uses the same methods and assumptions used for calculating statutory reserves, modified to take account of the following five federal standards:

- The *Commissioner's Reserve Valuation Method* must be used for life insurance contracts (see Chapter 16).
- The minimum valuation interest rate to be used is the greater of (1) a federal market interest rate determined using the average of the yields of midterm government bonds over the previous five years for the year in which the contract was issued and (2) the prevailing state interest rate.
- Mortality tables must be the most recent standard tables for mortality and morbidity prescribed by the NAIC that at least 26 states permit to be used in computing reserves for the type of contract involved at the time of issue.
- Reserves for any amounts in respect of deferred and uncollected premiums must be eliminated unless the gross amount of these premiums is included in gross income.
- Reserves for excess interest – interest exceeding the prevailing state assumed interest rate – and guaranteed beyond the end of the taxable year must be eliminated.

Dividends   The general rule is that policy dividends paid on par policies are deductible from gross income if they are not fixed contractual obligations but depend on company experience or discretion. This treatment is consistent with the IRS view that policy dividends are in whole or in part a return of premium for which no deduction was taken by the policyowner. Stock dividends are not deductible in accordance with general principles applicable to all taxable corporations.

However, unlike policy dividends paid by stock companies under their par policies, policy dividends paid by mutual companies do not exclusively represent a return of premium: they also represent earnings or income that is attributable to the quasi-ownership rights of the policyowner. Thus, policy dividends paid by mutual companies are treated as a hybrid: only 55 percent of dividends is deductible. The apportionment of the deductible/nondeductible shares was a congressional estimate designed to reflect both average stock company economics and a fair attribution of aggregate tax liability to the stock and mutual sectors.

The Small Life Insurance Company Deduction An additional life insurer deduction from gross income is the *small life insurance company deduction*. This deduction (applied primarily for political reasons and consistent with the general congressional policy of encouraging small business) equals 60 percent of the tentative LICTI, up to a maximum of $3,000,000. Thus, the small company deduction can never exceed $1,800,000 (i.e., 0.60 x $3,000,000). If tentative LICTI exceeds $3,000,000, the amount of the small company deduction is phased out by an amount equal to 15 percent of tentative LICTI in excess of $3,000,000. Thus, for an insurer with tentative LICTI of $15,000,000 or more, no small company deduction is allowed.

THE 1990 DEFERRED ACQUISITION COST (DAC) TAX Prior to 1990, first-year expenses incurred in selling policies were deductible from life insurer gross income in the same way they were expensed under statutory accounting. In 1990, Congress mandated a new provision known as the *DAC tax* that had the effect of capitalizing, deferring, and amortizing acquisition costs (e.g., commissions and underwriting expenses) in a manner similar to that found under GAAP accounting. The purpose was to achieve a better match of revenue to expenses.

In practice the tax was applied through a simplifying proxy for true capitalization, deferral, and amortization. A specified percentage of premium income (as opposed to specific reported items) is capitalized and amortized over 10 years, as follows:

- 1.75 percent of annuities,
- 2.05 percent of group life insurance, and
- 7.7 percent of other life and non-cancellable accident and health insurance.

Small companies are permitted to accelerate amortization of the first $5,000,000 over five years rather than 10. The DAC tax represented a significant increase in the industry's tax liability, ultimately borne by policyowners. While raising federal revenue, it also increased product prices and reduced interest credits, dividends, and other non-guaranteed benefits.

FEDERAL EXCISE TAX U.S. IRC Sec. 4371 imposes a 1.0 percent excise tax on premiums for life, health, and annuity premiums paid to alien insurers that are not taxed as U.S. companies. Such companies are taxed as U.S. companies if they (1) engage in a technically defined "U.S. trade or business" or (2) elect to be taxed as U.S. companies under code Sec. 953(d). The tax usually is avoided by alien insurers that are active in the U.S. but applies to offshore reinsurance transactions.

U.S. regulation of the life insurance industry is shared between the states and the federal government. The primary purposes are the promotion of solvency and the protection of policyowners. Important subsidiary purposes are the promotion of an orderly insurance market and fair dealing by insurers in the market. The largest part of insurance regulatory law is derived from NAIC model laws that are adopted, with some variation, by the states. Additional regulation is exercised by the federal government, largely in areas applicable to all companies. Life insurers are taxed on their premium revenue, on their net income, and on premiums ceded to alien reinsurers. **CONCLUSIONS**

ENDNOTES

1   Martin F. Grace and Robert W. Klein. "Insurance Regulation: The Need for Policy Reform," Monograph, Center for Risk Management and Research, Georgia State University, May 29, 2008.
2   J. W. Meador and L. Chugh. "Demutualization in the U.S. Life Insurance Industry," *Journal of the Academy of Finance*. Fall 2006.
3   "Revenge of the Mutuals: Policyholder-Owned U.S. Life insurers Benefit in Harsh Environment," *Moody's Insurance*, August 2009.

CHAPTER 13

LIFE INSURER FINANCIAL REPORTING AND SUPERVISION

Policyholders are interested in the *solvency* of a life insurer or its ability to satisfy its obligations. The principal purpose of regulatory supervision of life insurers is to mandate solvency. Regulators require insurers to maintain adequate capital and reserves. Shareholders are interested in the *profitability* of a life insurer or its ability to generate excess funds after paying benefits and expenses, and satisfying reserve and minimum capital requirements.

The purposes of external financial reporting for life insurers are (1) to demonstrate that the company is *solvent*; i.e., the policies it sells will be honored and claims will be paid and (2) to establish that the company is *profitable*; i.e., its resources increased more than its obligations during the reporting period. In this chapter, we explore the regulation and related reporting of life insurer solvency and the reporting of profit, as well as the future of regulation and reporting. This exploration occurs in a state of transition with rapidly evolving new methods driven by a failure of historical methods to fully describe and recognize risk. All of the principles and many of the practices enunciated here are relevant to other countries, although our focus is on the U.S.

FINANCIAL CONDITION, SUPERVISION, AND REPORTING

Most commercial enterprises undertake transactions that are primarily of short duration. In the sale of goods, for example, delivery and payment typically take place within a short period of time. Single-year results produce an accurate financial picture where the great majority of transactions are completed during the year. The unusual timing of life insurance cash flows, however, makes its single-year financial picture of its results problematic for three reasons:

- Life insurance transactions rarely commence and close during the same reporting period. Usually premiums are invested and benefits are paid years after policy inception.
- The cash valuation of future obligations always exceeds the cash amount of current assets.
- Future obligations and future resources available to satisfy them are *uncertain*: future premiums, investment earnings, and benefits are all subject to unknowable contingencies.

The concepts of solvency and profitability are discrete states: the basic accounting equations produce positive surplus and earnings or they do not. The degree to which an insurer exhibits solvency or profitability is a measure of its *solidity*; increasing amounts of surplus and profit imply increasing solidity. The concepts of solvency and profitability are also arbitrary in that the terms have no useful meaning apart from the accounting conventions used to define them.

The solvency representation is a necessary requirement of policyowners and the regulators who protect them, and the profitability representation is a necessary requirement of stockholders and the regulators who protect them. The two are related because short-term profitability is an implied condition of long-term solvency: continuing operating losses will eventually cause insolvency.

A basic accounting equation for the solvency determination of any company begins with a comparison of its total assets and total liabilities. If assets exceed liabilities, then the company is solvent and there is a positive element of *owners' equity*:

$$Owners'\ Equity = Assets - Liabilities$$

A basic equation for the profitability determination of any company begins with the comparison of revenue and expense:

$$Earnings = Revenues - Expenses$$

As noted, the determinations whether a life insurer is solvent and profitable are complicated by the economics of the life insurance business, and these basic equations are inadequate to describe financial condition. First, life insurer income is received *currently* as consideration for *future* claims and benefits. Second, premiums collected currently are invested for some time at some interest rate until a claim is made. Third, future claims are dependent on *contingencies* that also introduce uncertainty: an insured will die or not during a specific period, for example.

The value of assets should incorporate not only current cash and investments but future premiums and investment income as well, and the value of liabilities should incorporate not only the company's current obligations but future obligations arising from claims of unknown timing. Therefore, solvency and profitability determinations both require:

- an estimate of uncertain future revenues and expenses based on necessary assumptions about average results,
- the reduction to an expected present value of assets and liabilities from an assumption about average investment returns and an assumption about average probable claims, and
- the idea and funding of a reserve based on these estimates whereby premiums collected currently are set aside for the purpose of paying claims in the future.

The practice of estimating future revenues, expenses, and reserves is called a **valuation** and is central to the reporting of both solvency and profitability. After the assets and liabilities are valued, the basic accounting equations can better reflect the economics of life insurance. In the life insurance industry, owners' equity is known as *surplus* or *surplus capital,* thus:

$$Surplus\ (Capital) = Present\ Value\ of\ Assets - Present\ Value\ of\ Liabilities$$

And profitability is measured by:

Net Income = Premiums + Investment Income – Expenses – Net Change in Reserves

Assumptions used for valuations depend on the needs of the user and have produced different accounting methods. Three mandatory reporting methods are employed in the U.S. *Statutory Accounting Principles* (SAP) are promulgated by the state insurance regulators through the *National Association of Insurance Commissioners* (NAIC) via model laws. As discussed in Chapter 12, the state accreditation program generally guarantees that essential model laws are adopted in all states. SAP is used by regulators to determine solvency.

Generally Accepted Accounting Principles (GAAP), promulgated by the *Financial Accounting Standards Board* (FASB) and stated in *Financial Accounting Standards* (FAS), are used by the capital markets to determine profitability. Finally, accounting for income tax reporting, as discussed in Chapter 12, is prescribed by federal law and generally builds from SAP, with modifications.

Further, while they do not establish formal accounting systems, rating agencies also maintain somewhat different but important solvency, profitability, and claims-paying ability standards. Securities analysts in the capital markets also play an informal but important role with respect to profitability. Finally, many jurisdictions outside the U.S. employ *International Financial Reporting Standards* (IFRS), promulgated by the *International Accounting Standards Board* (IASB). IFRS methods differ significantly from U.S. SAP and GAAP. We discuss IFRS later in the chapter as part of the ongoing and expected convergence of U.S. accounting with IFRS.

The scope of life insurer supervision is broad. The NAIC, through its model laws and the state accreditation procedures, is the motivating authority behind most state law. The *Internal Revenue Service* (IRS) plays an indirect but important role in financial regulation in two directions. First, IRS results directly affect the creation of after-tax profits and corporate value. Second, IRS rules applied to the taxation of policyowners, discussed in Chapter 21, are a significant factor in life insurer product design.

Life insurer financial reporting is subject to the requirements of several organizations. Accounting rules also are a source of implicit regulation. In addition to the NAIC, FASB, and IFRS, the most important other U.S. organizations in financial reporting are:

- The *American Institute of Certified Public Accountants* (AICPA), which oversees the public audit process.
- The *American Academy of Actuaries*, which provides guidance to the NAIC in its formulation of *Statements of Statutory Accounting Principles* (SSAP) and which is the source of prescribed scenario and model requirements specified in cash flow testing regulations.
- The *Securities and Exchange Commission* (SEC), which mandates GAAP accounting, requires regular reports for publicly traded companies, and regulates the amount of *reported* profit (not actual profits). (Non-U.S. companies subject to regulation by the SEC may prepare their U.S. financial statements according to IFRS.)

LIFE INSURER ACCOUNTING CONVENTIONS

In this section, we delve more deeply into SAP and GAAP as practiced in the U.S. We omit discussion of the IRS-prescribed modifications of SAP for income tax reporting as these were covered in Chapter 12. An insurer's financial condition as determined under both SAP and GAAP rely on rules-based factors and formulae derived from average industry experience benchmarks, while an insurer's *economic* financial condition is determined in accordance with the properties of its own policies and investments and realistic economic assumptions.

Because the financial condition of a life insurer depends on unknowable future events such as mortality experience, earned investment income, expenses, and policyowner behavior, determinations of solvency and profitability necessarily depend on assumptions. Consumers of life insurer financial information require different assumptions that reflect their different views of risk and different views of what is ordinary or extraordinary and acceptable or unacceptable. SAP, GAAP, and economic evaluations of financial condition are founded on assumptions that reflect the needs of the user.

Shareholders and policyholders have different views of insolvency risk. Policyowners are risk averse; they seek to reduce it. Shareholders are risk tolerant; they decline risk-free investment opportunities to seek higher returns. While these consumers of life insurer financial information have different views of risk, they share an overall aversion to insolvency. In the event of insolvency, the full payment of claims without external assistance is unlikely, and profits are inconceivable. The degree of their aversion is measured by their tolerance for the *probability of ruin* or *default*. The management of a life insurer must consider these differing viewpoints. Table 13-1 shows the different objectives of different users of life insurer financial information and the accounting systems that address the different needs.

Table 13-1   Accounting Objectives and Approaches Required by Principal Users of Life Insurer Financial Reports

Accounting Objective	User	Accounting Approach
Solvency	State Regulators	SAP
Solidity/Profitability	Shareholders (SEC)	GAAP
Taxable Income	IRS	Tax-basis Accounting
Operational Information	Insurer Management	Managerial Accounting

AN ANALYSIS OF STATUTORY ACCOUNTING PRINCIPLES

SAP financial statements are intended to present an insurer's financial condition from the viewpoint of the regulator, providing a basis for solvency surveillance. The main purpose is to offer proof of an insurer's ability to meet its contractual obligations to policyowners.

The insurer must present financial statements annually that meet the statutory definition of solvency in terms of investments, reserves, capital, and surplus that are defined by law. Limitations of the statutory system are discussed below, and economic solvency does not necessarily imply statutory solvency. Perhaps more importantly, statutory solvency does not necessarily imply economic solvency.

Because life insurers hold large amounts of money for the benefit of their policyowners, SAP treatment required by state law is similar to the accounting required of a trustee or fiduciary. The insurer must demonstrate that its assets, together with future premiums and conservatively estimated interest income, will be sufficient to meet all promises to policyowners. Other sources of income, such as profits on existing or new lines of business, are not taken into account. In effect, the insurer is viewed as a trustee for the benefit of policyowners, and the insurer's ability to generate future profits as an operating business or going concern is ignored.

Statutory accounting principles limit the usefulness of statutory reports in solvency determination. One of the principal limitations of SAP solvency determination results from the "snapshot approach" that it utilizes. Results are reported at a specific point in time under a set of static assumptions that ignore the possibility (indeed certainty) of changing economic conditions in the future. We discussed the stochastic and systematic nature of life insurer asset and liability values in Chapter 9.

Bond values are recorded on the statutory statement at amortized value (discussed below) rather than market value. This valuation convention is based on the premise that most bonds held by insurers are held to maturity and that fluctuating market values would not significantly impact solvency. The simultaneous impact of changing market interest rates on asset and liability values makes this assumption unrealistic. During periods of relatively high interest rates, the artificial stabilization of asset values by the amortized value convention may cause an insurer's statutory statement to exhibit a state of solvency when in reality it would be unable to satisfy its cash obligations as they come due. Figure 13-1 illustrates the relationship of amortized values to market values in different interest rate environments.

The Relationship of Amortized Bond Values in Different Interest Rate Environments   Figure 13-1

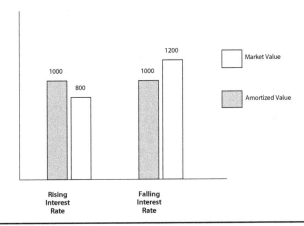

The economic value of bonds fluctuates when interest rates fluctuate. The difference in amortized value and economic value is not important if a bond is held to maturity, but if a bond must be sold to satisfy liquidity requirements when interest rates rise, a loss will be incurred. Thus the statutory balance sheet may present an unrealistic view of solvency.

Statutory accounting also proves to be inadequate for the needs of investors and creditors because of its balance sheet orientation. With the exception of asset valuation conventions discussed above, SAP treatment generally examines an insurer as if it were not an operating entity but rather a company in runoff or liquidation. This results from the conservative approach that requires accounting for all policyowner funds currently and ignores the long-term benefits to be expected from investing in the future of the company. Additionally, the conservative assumptions required in the valuation of an insurer's liabilities normally do not reflect the potential profit that can be generated by in-force policies.

Further, an increase in new business typically creates cash shortages in the first years of any block of new policies. Under SAP treatment, **surplus strain**, the impact on surplus of high expenses associated with the acquisition costs of new business, together with reserving requirements, reduces current earnings and surplus. Also, as cash surrender values generally are less than reserves set aside for a particular policy, the termination of a policy releases the excess reserves and produces a surrender contribution, which perversely has a positive impact on earnings and surplus. This result is counterintuitive.

Thus, earnings under SAP rules are penalized as an insurer grows, with faster growth producing a greater punitive impact on earnings. Conversely, earnings are exaggerated by the surrender contribution when an insurer is losing market share to competitors. The balance sheet focus of SAP is designed to prove an insurer's ability to pay future benefits that arise under its current policies. As such, it is an inadequate tool for measuring a company's ability to generate long-term profits or for comparing results with other insurers or its own past experience.

AN ANALYSIS OF GENERALLY ACCEPTED ACCOUNTING PRINCIPLES

While solvency is the primary focus of statutory accounting, the principal purpose of GAAP is to report financial results for a company in a manner that is comparable to that of other companies and other reporting periods for the purpose of evaluating profitability. This comparability is essential to investors who need to be able to evaluate the relative merits of alternative investments both in the insurance and other industries. Comparability is necessary when financial reports are used in any analysis designed to predict future financial results.

GAAP requires a presentation of assets, liabilities, and cash flows. While GAAP is designed to report consistently on revenues, benefits, expenses, and current operating profit, it is often found to be inadequate as a financial management tool. GAAP does not recognize potential future profits on existing and future policies, and therefore, it is not well suited for evaluating the long-term financial impact of current management action. Three aspects of GAAP accounting limit its usefulness as a financial management tool. These shortcomings are in large part the result of reporting the arbitrary, one-year profits of organizations that are engaged in an essentially long-term enterprise.

First, GAAP generally includes an accounting convention known as the *lock-in principle*, which prevents a restatement of assumptions regarding interest, expense, and mortality for traditional policies in force. The principle was designed primarily to deal with guaranteed-cost, nonparticipating policies. Today's product environment is dominated by policies that reflect actual operating experience. The accuracy of expected results for a block of policies can be considerably improved by periodic reevaluations, and FAS 97 (universal life policies) and FAS 120 (for mutual companies) now effectively exempt interest-sensitive products and participating (par) business from the lock-in principle. Lock-in continues to apply to other traditional life products.

Second, as with their treatment under statutory accounting, unrealized capital gains are not recognized in the GAAP income statement. As discussed in Chapter 14, capital gains and losses are an integral element of the total return generated by an actively managed investment portfolio.

Third, GAAP in many respects does not reflect the future impact of current events. As in statutory accounting, GAAP treatment of surrenders may produce increased current-period earnings without reflecting the loss of future profits on lapsed policies, and investment in distribution systems and other capital expenditures may produce decreased current earnings without a concurrent recognition of the insurer's increased capacity to generate future profits.

MANAGERIAL ACCOUNTING

While life insurer accounting practice is necessarily designed to accommodate regulatory reporting requirements, company management typically employs supplemental accounting procedures designed to promote operational efficiency. These procedures do not form the basis for any external reports but do play a role in the audit process.

Regulatory reporting systems are primarily historical in nature. While they certainly employ projective methods of reserving for future claims, the emphasis is on the change in financial condition from the previous reporting period to the current period. By contrast, **budget accounting** is employed by management for *future* expense planning purposes in both an operational or short-term context and a strategic context lasting five years or more. Budget accounting can be prepared in a *top-down* process where senior management sets parameters or a *bottom-up* manner with significant contributions by employees and junior management. Either process can begin with benchmarks from the results of the previous reporting period or from a *zero base* that requires justification for the first dollar of each expense. The results are an important element for planning the deployment of capital.

Cost accounting is employed to make discrete expense analyses across different product lines, services, and operations. Cost accounting can help identify more and less productive areas of operation, establish policy dividend scales for par products, and review the emphasis placed on different products and services from time to time.

Audit and control procedures are designed to limit the risk associated with mistakes, fraud, and other irregularities in the process of reporting and managing assets and liabilities. Internal audit procedures are executed by staff independent of the regular accounting staff and are designed to ensure that practices are consistent with management policies, records are kept that are consistent with conformity to SAP and GAAP reporting, and assets are properly monitored. External audits are required in all states and performed by public accounting firms in accordance with standards established by the *AICPA*. The auditing firm must confirm that the statements are free from material misstatements, are a fair representation of the financial condition of the company, and are consistent with the standards of SAP and GAAP. The methodology involves a sampling of individual transactions and an evaluation of the internal audit and control methods.

FINANCIAL REPORTING

Using financial statements and other relevant data, life insurers are required to make periodic reports to the insurance regulators of the states in which they are licensed and to shareholders and the SEC. While we cover both types of reporting, our primary emphasis is on reporting to the insurance regulators, given the focus of this book.

REPORTS TO STATE INSURANCE REGULATORS

Insurers are required to file detailed annual statements in their state of domicile and with each state in which they are licensed to operate. These statements are to be prepared using forms published by the NAIC, commonly called the *NAIC blank*. Use of the basic form is universal throughout the U.S., although some states employ modifications. While we noted the indirect authority of the NAIC in regulation in Chapter 12, several mechanisms make the NAIC authority in financial reporting a practical necessity:

- Through the 1990s, the NAIC undertook a codification project designed to simplify, harmonize, and reduce to writing what was perceived to be an unnecessarily diverse range of accounting practices across states and companies. One of the guiding principles was conforming statutory practice to GAAP practice as closely as feasible, while maintaining the public interest focus of SAP. The result was the *NAIC Accounting Practices and Procedures Manual* as well as a series of *Statements of Statutory Accounting Procedures*.
- The NAIC requires cash flow testing under a range of economic circumstances and requires an *Asset Adequacy Opinion* from a Qualified Actuary.
- The NAIC's *Securities Valuation Office* (SVO) in New York City is responsible for day-to-day credit quality assessment and valuation of certain securities owned by state regulated insurance companies and determines the permissible values of designated investments.

As discussed in Chapter 12, the NAIC accreditation process requires substantial compliance with these and other financial reporting methods and represents an implicit enforcement power. The annual statement is intended to demonstrate an insurer's solvency with a **Balance Sheet** showing its assets and liabilities and owners' equity by broad categories. If assets exceed liabilities, the insurer is solvent by statutory definition and excess assets represent, in general accounting terminology, the *owners' equity* in the company. Life insurance regulators designate owners' equity as *capital stock and paid-in surplus*, which represent funds paid into the company by shareholders, and as *surplus*, which is the remaining excess of assets over liabilities.

The **Summary of Operations** is the insurer's income statement for the reporting period and presents a company's current period profitability by providing a summary of the insurer's income and its disposition. The equation of net income was given earlier. The Summary of Operations also provides a reconciliation of beginning and ending surplus, as follows:

Ending Surplus = Beginning Surplus + Net Income + Surplus Adjustments

The **Cash Flow Statement** presents the net change in the company's cash position over the course of the reporting period, as follows:

Cash Flows from Operating Activities

+ Cash Flows from Investing Activities

+ Cash Flows from Financing Activities

= Net Change in Cash

ASSETS   Four important SAP measures of asset value are applied to life insurer assets. First, an asset's **book value** is the acquisition cost of the asset, less any accumulated depreciation. An asset's **market value** is the amount that the asset would realize in a current market sale. Next, **amortized value** is the difference between a bond's acquisition cost and par value, increased or decreased in successive stages until that value equals the bond's par value at maturity. The purpose of amortized value is to (1) smooth the balance sheet effect of changing market interest rates on bond market values and (2) reflect the assumed general intention of an insurer to hold a bond to maturity, thus trivializing the effect of changing market values during the holding period. As we have seen, this assumption has proven unrealistic. Amortized value remains important, but FAS 159 represents a permissive option for insurers to record assets at fair value. We discuss the increasing importance of fair value concepts below.

Not all of an insurer's assets are permitted to be counted toward its statutory solvency requirements; assets that are not so counted are called **non-admitted assets** and those that are so counted are called **admitted assets**. Some assets may be admitted in part and non-admitted beyond a specified limit. Thus, the recorded values of admitted assets are referred to as their **admitted values**. Most traditional investment assets are admitted assets, while assets of questionable value or liquidity such as office equipment are non-admitted values.

LIABILITIES   Statutory financial statements require the recording of several classes of liabilities, the most important of which are discussed here.

Policy Reserves   A life insurer's most important source of financing is premium income, and its most prominent liability is the policy reserve, which represents a segregation and dedication of premium and investment income to the payment of future claims. Reserves represent the net of the expected present value of future benefits and future premiums, both using interest and mortality assumptions defined in the applicable valuation statute. Reserves are calculated on a *seriatim* or policy-by-policy basis. The calculation methodology is discussed in Chapter 16.

As high first year expenses can cause surplus strain, SAP provides two reserve modifications to alleviate this strain. The Full Preliminary Term Method and the Commissioner's Reserve Valuation Method (CVRM) treat each policy, whether term or not, as a term policy in the first year and generally do not require a first-year reserve. Additionally, the CVRM limits reserve relief to a maximum. The mechanics are discussed in Chapter 16. Special rules apply to reserves for term life insurance and the mortality component of universal life products.

The Asset Valuation Reserve and Interest Maintenance Reserve   The **Asset Valuation Reserve** (AVR) and the **Interest Maintenance Reserve** (IMR) are statutory accounting mechanisms designed to prevent volatile fluctuations in reported surplus due to the changing market values of securities. They are based on the same unrealistic assumptions that underlie amortized valuation for bonds: that short-term value fluctuations are less important when insurers typically hold investments for long-term purposes. Further, while required to be shown as insurer liabilities, neither represents amounts owed to anyone and, economically, are earmarked surplus.

The IMR absorbs realized capital gains and losses attributable to changing market interest rates. The AVR absorbs both realized *and* unrealized capital gains and losses not attributed to interest rates. The AVR applies to real estate, mortgage loans, and short-term investments as well as to bonds and corporate stocks. Because the AVR does not reflect interest-related changes, its importance is limited to the asset quality of included investments. The IMR and AVR are allocations of surplus based on asset properties as opposed to conventional reserves based on liability values. They are intended to reflect the influence of asset quality on capital adequacy.

Debt Financing   Like other corporations, life insurers may issue bonds to raise capital. The bonds are repaid over time and pay interest at a stated rate. Life insurers also issue *surplus notes,* which possess both debt- and equity-like properties. Like bonds, surplus notes generally have a repayment and amortization schedule. Like common stock, the notes are unsecured and recorded in the capital and surplus portion of the balance sheet. As a debt and not true equity or surplus, surplus notes do not provide permanent surplus; they must be repaid.

Surplus notes were originally issued mainly by financially troubled mutual insurers, which had no access to the equity market. Today both stocks and mutuals rely on them to enhance their regulatory solvency. They can be issued by insurers only with the prior approval of their domiciliary regulator. Moreover, interest and principal payments on the notes may be made only with the regulator's approval. Holders possess only residual rights that are superior to common shareholder rights but inferior to all other debt financing. They are valued at the unpaid principal amount.

Reinsurance   Liabilities are generally reported net of amounts ceded to reinsurers. A separate liability is recorded for reinsurance in unauthorized companies. To the extent unauthorized reinsurance is properly guaranteed by cash, letters of credit, or other acceptable security, the unauthorized reinsurance liability does not apply.

Some insurers establish non-mandatory *special reserves* or *special surplus* for low-probability/high-loss contingencies such as epidemics and natural disasters. Most other insurance-related liabilities apply to deposit-like amounts such as policyowner account balances, prepaid premiums, and incurred but unpaid claims.

CAPITAL STOCK AND SURPLUS   The excess of a company's assets over its liabilities represents its **capital stock and surplus. Capital stock** represents the par value of all common and preferred shares issued and not owned by the insurer.

Surplus is recorded in several potential ways, depending on its source. **Contributed surplus** is the amount paid for shares in excess of their par value, if any. **Special surplus funds** are voluntarily earmarked surplus designated to meet general contingencies. They serve the same purpose as special reserves. **Unassigned surplus** consists of all other surplus amounts and represents the corporation's "free" capital. It is not legally earmarked for any particular purpose and may be used for distributions to policyowners or shareholders in the form of dividends or for the expansion or diversification of the insurer's operations.

The "free capital" nature of surplus is limited, however, because companies also are required to file an annual *Risk-Based Capital* (RBC) *Report* with the annual statement. This report shows the insurer's *total adjusted capital* and its *authorized control level RBC*, terms explained below, thus yielding an RBC ratio. The mandatory amount of RBC is a specified minimum, and the RBC ratio serves as a benchmark measure of surplus adequacy for the purpose of regulatory intervention.

SUPPLEMENTARY SCHEDULES AND EXHIBITS   Insurers are also required by statutory reporting requirements to provide further details of items that appear only in total in the primary financial statements. Among the exhibits, the more important are those that furnish details or classified information about (1) premium income; (2) investment income; (3) capital gains and losses; (4) expenses; (5) taxes; (6) policy reserves; (7) policy and contract claims; (8) life insurance issued, terminated, and in force (the "policy exhibit"); and (9) annuities issued, terminated, and in force (the "annuity exhibit"). General interrogatories and footnotes follow the exhibits.

The most important investment schedules found in the NAIC statement are those relating to real estate, mortgage loans, and securities (bonds and stocks). The schedules for real estate and securities show in considerable detail the amounts owned at the end of the year and the purchases and sales during the year. Somewhat similar information is given for mortgage loans but with less detail. Other important schedules show detailed information regarding (1) individual bank balances, month by month; (2) resisted claims; (3) premiums by state; (4) transactions with affiliates; (5) derivatives; and (6) reinsurance.

A statement of the company's business in the state in which the report is being filed is included. The statement shows the numbers and amounts of policies issued, terminated, and in force together with a statement of premiums collected and policy dividends and benefits paid in the state. Naturally, the necessity of furnishing this information by state requires that the insurance company maintain its records in such a way as to be able to report its business by state.

REPORTS FOR SHAREHOLDERS AND POLICYHOLDERS

The NAIC statement is complex and difficult to read. Condensed and simplified financial statements are included in the published annual reports issued by companies to their policyowners and shareholders. Any statutory figures in these reports are prepared from information in the NAIC statement. The scope of annual reports and the nature and detail of the information included in them vary greatly from company to company. Most of these reports contain supplementary information on the company's operations, plans, and other matters usually also found in the trade press. Among other things, there frequently is a narrative presentation of a promotional nature.

GAAP financial information often is included, with a reconciliation of the principal GAAP statement items with the corresponding statutory statement items. In both SAP and GAAP, "Management's Discussion and Analysis" is an important source of information reflected in the annual report. Most companies publish full SAP and GAAP statements under investor or policyowner information pages on their websites.

Publicly traded life insurers also file quarterly and annual reports prepared on a GAAP basis with the SEC. The most important of the required reports is Form 10-K, which sets forth an annual statement of the insurer's business properties and proceedings, its financial statements and supporting schedules, and exhibits and information regarding the insurer's officers and board of directors. Filings with the SEC are discussed more fully in Chapter 17.

SAP VERSUS GAAP TREATMENT OF ACCOUNTING ITEMS

The SAP statement in each state follows closely the form prescribed by the NAIC. In the past, GAAP statements were and many still are developed by adjustments to insurers' SAP statements. Increasingly, SAP and GAAP statements are developed independently. The differences in SAP and GAAP statements are produced by the differing treatment of items that are entered into each statement. We can group the differences into three broad categories:

1. valuation of assets,
2. valuation of liabilities, and
3. recognition of income and expenses.

VALUATION OF ASSETS

The primary differences in SAP and GAAP regarding the valuation of assets involve the classification of assets that may be listed as approved assets and the reporting of realized and unrealized capital gains and losses. Only the value of admitted assets may be shown on the statutory balance sheet. By contrast, all insurer assets, including non-admitted assets that do not meet regulatory approval (*e.g.,* furniture, vehicles) may be reported on the GAAP balance sheet.

The treatment of invested assets under GAAP and SAP differs. We have already discussed valuation under SAP. Under GAAP, FAS 115 requires investments to be classified into three categories, the effects of which are that many bonds amortizable under SAP are recorded at fair value under GAAP. Without the stabilizing effects of amortized value on *all* bonds, FAS 115 makes GAAP balance sheet equity more volatile. The three FAS 115 categories are:

- *Held-to-maturity securities* – reported at amortized values (e.g., private placements, public bonds, and mortgage-backed securities).
- *Trading securities* – reported at fair value with unrealized capital gains and losses included in earnings (e.g., treasury bonds).
- *Available-for-sale securities* – reported at fair value with unrealized capital gains and losses excluded from earnings (e.g., public bonds and mortgage backed securities).

FAS 157 provides guidance for the determination of fair value. It adopts the concept of "exit value," which is the price an asset would bring in an orderly transaction in an actively traded market or the price an obligor would pay to discharge or transfer a liability. The preferred determination is a quoted price in an active public market. Where there is no quoted public price but similar assets do trade, values can be inferred from the analogous information. Finally, where there is no such information or "observable inputs," use of internal practice and procedure is appropriate, with documented justification.

Special rules apply under GAAP (FAS 133) to the recorded values of *derivatives*, such as swaps, options, and futures. These risk-management hedging assets are valued at either cost or market value, generally depending upon the valuation applicable to the asset or liability being hedged. Additionally, insurers must disclose the risks and accounting procedures associated with their derivative positions.

When insurers acquire derivatives for hedging purposes, FAS 159 makes the reporting of related assets and liabilities at fair value optional to mitigate earnings volatility where assets and liabilities would be listed using the somewhat inconsistent standards set forth in FAS 133. It addresses hedging situations where derivative valuation standards differ from the primary asset and liability standards. The initial adjustment is applied directly to retained earnings without proceeding through the income statement.

VALUATION OF LIABILITIES

The principal differences in SAP and GAAP treatment of the valuation of insurer liabilities involve life insurance policy reserves and the payment of dividends. SAP requires the posting of reserves that are based on statutorily defined, conservative assumptions regarding mortality and interest. Under GAAP, more realistic assumptions are used with respect to mortality and interest. For interest sensitive life products covered by FAS 97 (e.g., universal life), GAAP policy reserves are equal to the policy's account value. For traditional life products, GAAP policy reserves are less conservative than statutory reserves.

In addition, a major difference between GAAP and SAP is the use of lapse rate assumptions in GAAP but not in SAP. This assumption can have a large effect on GAAP liabilities. An insurer uses assumptions that follow its own experience or industry-wide experience.

Policyowner dividends reported under SAP are limited to the anticipated liability for the insurer's following year. Because of the underlying assumption of continued company existence as a going concern, GAAP financial statements reflect, as a liability, policyowner dividends over the premium-paying periods of the contracts. As dividends are paid, the balance sheet liability is reduced accordingly.

RECOGNITION OF INCOME AND EXPENSE

One tenet of GAAP dictates that income is recognized when it is earned and not when it is received. This means that earnings should be recognized when the service (insurance protection) is provided. GAAP premiums are recognized as earned over the coverage period of policies in force, while SAP premiums are recognized as earned over the premium-paying period.

SAP rules are generally based on an implicit assumption that solvency should be demonstrable if the insurer were to be placed in runoff or liquidated during the current reporting period. GAAP assumes the continued existence of the insurer as a going concern. These approaches require a significantly different treatment of the high first-year acquisition expenses associated with new policies.

Although some statutory accounting relief can be provided through the use of the modified reserving techniques noted above, first-year acquisition expenses generally are charged in full to the current year's statutory income. Despite the fact that these first-year expenses are associated with policies that will generate future income, the conservative requirements of SAP do not allow for their amortization over the anticipated premium-paying period. GAAP, by contrast, assumes the continuing existence of the insurer and seeks to match the timing of expenses associated with the production of income to the period when the income is produced. GAAP thus recognizes that future income will be associated with first-year expenses and requires the deferral of those expenses in a way that reports the expenses ratably over a period of time. Costs related to future income are charged to future periods.

Under GAAP, acquisition costs are capitalized as a deferred asset. In traditional policies, deferred acquisition costs (DAC) are amortized in proportion to anticipated premiums and charged in future periods. With interest sensitive policies, in which premiums exceeding mortality and expense charges are considered deposits, these costs are amortized over the policies' life as gross profits emerge. As the expenses are charged, the capitalized DAC value is reduced accordingly.

Table 13-2 presents a comparison of SAP and GAAP treatment of important accounting items.

Table 13-2   Comparison of SAP and GAAP Treatment of Specific Accounting Items

	SAP	GAAP
Valuation of Assets		
Accepted Assets	Admitted Assets Only	All Assets
Valuation of Liabilities		
Reserves	Defined by law	Company and Industry Experience
Recognition of Income		
Premiums Earned Over:	Premium Period	Coverage Period
Recognition of Expense		
First Year Acquisition Expense:	Full Charge	Deferred and Amortized

FINANCIAL SUPERVISION

In this section we discuss the various solvency-related mechanics employed by the states to promote and monitor solvency, including procedures for dealing with the special problems of insurers that are not in compliance. The most important of these mechanics require insurers to charge sufficient prices and manage their cash flow; to invest in quality assets; to maintain prudent amounts of capital to cover unreserved, unexpected losses; and to report results in a consistent and conservative way. Box 13-1 presents a brief discussion of the NAIC's seven Insurance Financial Solvency Core Principles, many of which are explored in more detail below.

Box 13-1
U.S. Insurance Financial Solvency Core Principles
Core Principle 1: Regulatory Reporting, Disclosure, and Transparency

U.S. regulators receive required financial reports from insurers on a regular basis that are the baseline for continual assessment of the insurer's risk and financial condition. Standardized financial reporting is used in the financial statements to ensure comparability of results among insurers. To address concerns with specific companies or issues, supplemental data are requested in addition to the standardized data, and these data may be requested on a more frequent basis from specific companies. The standardized format is updated as necessary to incorporate significant, common insurer risks.

Core Principle 2: Off-Site Monitoring and Analysis

Off-site solvency monitoring is used to assess on an on-going basis the financial condition of the insurer as of the valuation date and to identify and assess current and prospective risks through risk-focused surveillance. The results of the off-site analysis are included in an insurer profile for continual solvency monitoring. Many off-site monitoring tools are maintained by the NAIC for regulators (such as FAST – see below).

Core Principle 3: On-site Risk-focused Examinations

U.S. regulators carry out risk-focused, on-site examinations in which the insurer's corporate governance, management oversight, and financial strength are evaluated, including the system of risk identification and mitigation. Through the examination, the reported financial results are assessed and a determination is made of the insurer's compliance with legal requirements.

Core Principle 4: Capital Adequacy and Solvency

To ensure that legal obligations to policyholders, contract holders, and others are met when they come due, insurers are required to maintain reserves and surplus at all times and in such forms so as to provide an adequate margin of safety. The most visible measure of capital adequacy requirements is associated with the RBC system. The RBC calculation uses a standardized formula to benchmark specified levels of regulatory action for weakly capitalized insurers.

Core Principle 5: Regulatory Control of Significant, Broad-based Risk-related Transactions/Activities

The regulatory framework recognizes that certain significant, broad-based transactions/activities affecting policyholders' interests must receive regulatory approval. These transactions/activities encompass licensing requirements; change of control; the amount of dividends paid; transactions with affiliates; and reinsurance.

Core Principle 6: Preventive and Corrective Measures, including Enforcement

The regulatory authority takes preventive and corrective measures that are timely, suitable, and necessary to reduce the impact of risks identified during on-site and off-site regulatory monitoring. These regulatory actions are enforced as necessary.

Core Principle 7: Exiting the Market and Receivership

The legal and regulatory framework defines a range of options for the orderly exit of insurers from the marketplace. It defines solvency and establishes a receivership scheme to ensure the payment of policyholder obligations of insolvent insurers subject to appropriate restrictions and limitations.

Source: The National Association of Insurance Commissioners.

PRICING SUFFICIENCY AND CASH FLOW TESTING

While consumers often complain of high premiums and regulators concern them-selves with containing premium costs in many lines of business, the first stated concern of U.S. regulators is to require insurers to charge premiums that are high enough to permit the insurer to pay claims as they come due. Because insurers collect premiums in advance for claims to be paid later, competitive pressure could lead insurers to charge current premiums based on unrealistically hopeful assumptions about investment results or future claims to win customers based on price competitiveness. If investment performance or claims assumptions are not achieved, the insurers could become insolvent and the policyowners financially damaged.

Price sufficiency is regulated indirectly through the maintenance of required policy reserves. The application of conservative mortality tables and interest assumptions in calculating policy reserves puts an implied floor underneath premium levels, as premiums must be sufficiently high, not only to pay current expenses and claims, but to maintain a conservative reserve for future claims.

Cash-flow testing incorporates pricing sufficiency at a broad level; it also cap-tures all other insurer inflows and outflows. Requirements related to cash-flow testing followed the 1991 adoption by the NAIC of the *Actuarial Opinion and Memorandum Model Regulation*. The regulation requires companies to appoint a valuation actuary to render a professional opinion as to the insurer's finan-cial condition. A primary intent of the regulation was to encourage responsible asset-liability management and to reflect the dynamic nature of life insurer finan-cial condition. Cash-flow testing is the principal tool associated with the actuary's opinion, although it is not required in all cases. The process projects and compares, as of a given valuation date, the timing and amount of asset and liability cash flows after the valuation date.

The required actuarial opinion by a qualified actuary is a public document that must be filed along with the annual statement and is supported by an *Asset Adequacy Analysis*. The law marked a significant change in the role of the actu-ary, following the lead of other countries. The appointed actuary is responsible by law for the liability reserves. The *Actuarial Standards Board* provides professional standards for the appointed actuary's work.

The opinion includes a professional representation by an independent, appointed actuary that an insurer's assets are adequate to satisfy its liabilities and is accompanied by a memorandum that describes the process used in arriving at the opinion. These requirements supplement the formula-based reserves and RBC by focusing on the specific properties of each insurer's assets and liabilities.

CAPITAL REQUIREMENTS

In addition to the mandatory reserves required for each policy, life insurers are required to maintain specified amounts of capital. Each state requires a fixed, spec-ified amount of *initial capital and paid-in surplus* (as opposed to surplus from oper-ations, or retained earnings). Historically, minimum capital and surplus were the only fixed capital requirements and, together with policy reserves, represented the aggregate requirement for statutory solvency. The static capital amounts did not reflect the significant divergence in risk existing across different sized companies and different product types. For example, a fixed amount of capital clearly provides relatively less financial safety for a large company than it does a small one.

An important new component of life insurer solvency regulation was added by the NAIC through its 1992 adoption of the *Risk-Based Capital for Life and/or Health Insurers Model Act* and of RBC factors and reporting requirements. The purpose was to establish a uniform standard margin related to risk in each state and to create the necessary authority for timely intervention. These actions have altered the means by which minimally acceptable capital and surplus levels are defined and applied in the U.S.

RBC requirements are calculated based on the size and cash flow characteristics of each product portfolio:

- **Total adjusted capital** (TAC) equals statutory capital, paid-in surplus, the Asset Valuation Reserve, and, in the case of mutual companies, 50 percent of any declared and unpaid dividend.
- **Authorized control level** (ACL) is derived by a formula that reflects the insurer's particular risks, including asset risk (affiliates) (C0), asset risk (other) (C1), insurance risk (C2), interest rate risk (C3), and business risk (C4). (See Chapter 9.)
- Specified ratios of TAC/ACL must be maintained to avoid regulatory intervention.

Table 13-3 shows specific ratio trigger points with required specific regulatory action, if any. Regulatory intervention ranges from submission and approval of a plan to restore RBC to appropriate levels, to special examinations, and to permissive and then to mandatory seizure of the company by the commissioner.

U.S. Risk-Based Capital Trigger Points and Required Regulatory Responses   Table 13-3

RBC Level	Trigger Point % TAC/ACL	Required Action
No action	200 or more	No action required
Company Action Level	150-200	RBC plan required
Regulatory Action Level	100-150	RBC plan and corrective orders required
Authorized Control Level	70-100	Possible regulatory control
Mandatory Control Level	Below 70	Mandatory regulatory control

Out of an expressed concern about misunderstanding and misuse of RBC data, the NAIC and many insurers supported inclusion of a "gag rule" within the RBC model laws that have been adopted by the states. This rule prohibits an agent or insurer from disclosing RBC data "directly or indirectly" to the public. As RBC ratios exhibit a poor relationship with the financial strength ratings of rating agencies, agents for lower-rated insurers might attempt to use RBC data to show their companies in a better light (see Chapter 17). Critics of this prohibition contend that the rule is unconstitutional and ineffective, as agents who wish to use the data will find a way to do so; it is better to educate people about RBC than to prohibit disclosure.

While RBC requirements introduce some variability in capital requirements based on each company's risk profile, U.S. RBC requirements generally are deterministic, factor-based rules. We discuss below the growing importance of principles-based capital that is stochastic, reflects a greater degree of professional judgment, and takes into account company-specific risk features.

INVESTMENT QUALITY

Life insurer investments are regulated to promote life insurer solvency and the security of policy benefits. Both consumers and the capital markets are attracted to higher yielding investments because they can result in lower policyowner premiums and higher shareholder return on equity. Competitive considerations constantly press insurers to increase returns by assuming more risk, and investment-quality regulation counteracts this pressure. Life insurer solvency is promoted by restrictions on both the credit quality of individual assets and the quantities of assets held by the insurer.

The threshold quality constraints for individual assets are the standards defining admitted and non-admitted assets, as discussed earlier. Other quality constraints vary from state to state. Variations include *legal list* requirements that specify eligible investments, *prohibited investment* requirements that specifically disallow certain investments, and *prudent person* requirements that apply standards of judgment to the eligibility of investments.

Some quantitative constraints limit an insurer's holdings of certain asset classes (bonds, stocks, real estate) to a specified percentage of the total portfolio. Additional quantitative restrictions limit the percentage of securities of any one issuer that can be held by an insurer.

Basket or **leeway clauses**, which are common, permit insurers to invest a limited percentage (10 percent is common) of its assets in any lawful investment. In the past, insurers have used this flexibility to invest in emerging investment media such as equipment leasing and oil and gas exploration and development. As hedging activities increased among insurers, the basket clause was the eligibility mechanism for options, futures, swaps, and the like. As we discuss below, regulatory reform now admits hedging activities explicitly.

Major life insurer insolvencies arose in the early 1990s in the U.S., driven mainly by investments in high-yield bonds and mortgages, as discussed in Chapter 9. The NAIC responded with three new model laws that supplement the asset-quality components of RBC:

1. *The Medium Grade and Lower Grade Obligations Act* limits the maximum percentage of admitted assets that can be invested in lower credit-quality assets as defined by the NAIC and requires a written plan to be adopted by the company's board of directors at a threshold level.
2. *The Investments of Insurers Model Act (Defined Limits Version)* assigns percentage limitations to specified categories of investments, defining both general issuer diversification and credit-quality percentages.
3. *The Investments of Insurers Model Act (Defined Standards Version)*, an alternative to the *Defined Limits Version*, is structurally designed so that an insurer first is obligated to fulfill a "minimum asset requirement." The minimum asset requirement is made up of an insurer's liabilities and what

is called the *minimum financial security benchmark*. This benchmark equals either the company's minimum capital as required by statute or the authorized control level risk-based capital that applies to the insurer as set forth in the risk-based capital law of the state, whichever is greater. After fulfilling the minimum asset requirement, the insurer is permitted to invest its excess assets in accordance with a prudency standard.

The NAIC *Securities Valuation Office* evaluates and classifies investments by credit quality, with each investment assigned a designation from 1 to 6 in decreasing credit quality. The NAIC generally uses the ratings of private rating agencies to assign an equivalent designation for publicly traded securities. The NAIC also develops internal valuations for private placements. The designations are incorporated by reference into asset quality provisions: (1) the eligibility of bonds for amortized value treatment depend on NAIC designations and (2) the model laws described in the previous section all link provisions to NAIC designations. NAIC designations also play a prominent role in the valuation of liabilities and capital as discussed below.

SOLVENCY SURVEILLANCE

State laws typically require that the insurance regulator examine domestic insurers at their offices at least once every three to five years, depending on the state. These examinations involve a detailed review of all important aspects of operations and supplement annual public audits.

Special exams can be and are conducted more frequently if RBC, IRIS, FAST (see below), or other circumstances dictate them and may not be limited to an insurer's financial operations, such as reserves, investments, or capital changes. Commissioners generally possess additional discretionary powers to conduct examinations when deemed warranted.

Besides on-site examinations, states also rely on the NAIC for certain internal financial analysis. The NAIC *Risk-Focused Surveillance Framework*, adopted in 2004, emphasizes company-specific risk and coordinates four functions: exams, regular examination of periodic organizational change, an annual supervisory plan produced by the domiciliary regulator, and offsite financial analysis. The offsite analyses are known as *IRIS* and *FAST*.

Annual statement data are captured by the NAIC and serve as the inputs for the two phases of the *Insurance Regulatory Information System* (IRIS) program's process. In the first stage, 12 financial ratios are used to flag companies that show unusual results. In the second stage, a detailed analysis of financial statements and flagged ratios is performed by state examiners assigned to NAIC duty, and insurers may be subject to subsequent review by the their domiciliary states.

The *Financial Analysis Solvency Tools* (FAST) *Scoring System* supplements the IRIS ratios by analyzing "nationally significant" insurers using an additional ratio structure, an *Analyst Team System* (ATS) review that prioritizes insurers for attention, an RBC trend test, and loss projection tools. The system screens selected companies for risk of insolvency. It does this by assigning different point values to 29 different ratios to develop a score for likelihood of insolvency. Researchers have found this system to be a better predictor of insolvency than RBC ratios. Unlike IRIS ratios, FAST results are not published.

CONSENT TO MERGERS AND ACQUISITIONS

As discussed in Chapter 9, merger and acquisition activity has been robust world-wide, and most countries require regulatory approval for any change of insurer ownership. In the U.S., virtually all state laws regarding mergers and acquisitions are patterned after the NAIC *Model Insurance Holding Company System Regulatory Act* or its predecessors. The purpose is to maintain the financial solidity of surviving combinations and to avoid undue concentrations of market power.

If control of an insurer is sought, the prospective acquirer must file a detailed disclosure statement – called a *Form A* – with the state insurance regulator. The Form A filing includes disclosure of (1) audited financial information concerning earnings and financial condition of each acquiring party; (2) the acquiring party's intentions as to material changes in the insurer's operations, assets, corporate structure, or management; and (3) a full disclosure of the terms and conditions of the proposed acquisition. In an acquisition of less than all shares, control is defined as the power to direct management and is presumed to exist if the transaction involves 10 percent or more of an insurer's voting shares.

The insurance department exercises broad discovery powers and holds hearings in the course of investigating the transaction. The department has the authority to approve or disapprove each transaction, and grounds for disapproval include circumstances suggesting:

- The domestic insurer, after the change, would be unable to qualify for a license.
- The merger or acquisition would substantially lessen competition or tend to create a monopoly within the state.
- The acquirer's financial condition might jeopardize the insurer's financial stability or prejudice policyowners' interests.
- Any plans of the acquirer to liquidate, sell assets, or make other material changes in the insurer are unfair and unreasonable to policyowners and not in the public interest.
- The competence, experience, and integrity of persons seeking control are such that the acquisition would not be in policyowners' and the public's interest.
- The acquisition is likely to be hazardous or prejudicial to the insurance buying public.

The *Hazardous Financial Condition Model Regulation* has been substantially adopted in all states, and grants authority to commissioners to address risky behavior exhibited by life insurers. Authorities may intervene and may require additional capital when a broad number of general factors indicate movement toward an imperiled financial condition.

DIVIDEND RESTRICTIONS

In the interest of protecting life insurer financial solidity, states impose restrictions on the ability of life insurers to transfer capital and surplus funds to their parent holding companies or other affiliated corporations. These regulations essentially create a wall between a life insurance subsidiary and its parent company and affiliates. Besides restricting capital and surplus fund transfers, the regulations require that all assets, reserves, and capital and surplus be maintained by the life insurance subsidiary separately from the group's other funds and obligations. Any transfers that exceed certain limits must be approved by regulators. Before approving such transactions, regulators are required to confirm that the transaction would not impair the life insurance company's ability to pay policyholder benefits.

These policyholder protections were especially notable in the 2008–2009 financial crisis with regards to AIG, one of the world's largest financial conglomerates. AIG's troubles stemmed from its financial products division and not from its traditional insurance subsidiaries. This division's credit default swaps suffered huge losses due to the credit crisis. The assets within AIG's life subsidiaries remained isolated and protected for the benefit of these subsidiaries. Even had AIG the conglomerate been allowed to fail, its life insurers would have been largely insulated financially.

Rehabilitation and Liquidation

When solvency mandates are contravened, regulators may seek **corrective orders** from the judicial system requiring an insurer to (1) obtain state approval before undertaking certain transactions, (2) limit or cease its new business writings, (3) infuse capital, or (4) cease certain business practices. The regulator also may revoke an insurer's license. Transfer of control of an insurer to the state becomes necessary when all other interventions, including corrective orders, have failed to restore the insurer's condition to regulatory compliance.

Rehabilitation (*conservation* in some states) and liquidation are state regulatory analogs to general corporate bankruptcy receivership, reorganization, and liquidation procedures. The commissioner assumes the analogous role of trustee in bankruptcy. Under an order of **rehabilitation**, the commissioner becomes the insurer's receiver and is granted title to the domestic insurance company's assets. The commissioner is given the authority to carry on its business until the insurer either is returned to private management after the grounds for issuing the order have been removed or is liquidated.

Grounds for a rehabilitation order include (1) a finding that further transaction of business would be financially hazardous to policyowners, creditors, or the public; (2) a determination that the insurer's officers or directors are guilty of certain acts or omissions; and (3) where a substantial transfer of assets, merger, or consolidation is attempted without the prior written consent of the commissioner. If the insurer's impairment is resolved, the commissioner makes a determination that the company can be returned to private management. Rehabilitation may be mandated when an insurer is impaired but technically solvent.

Liquidation is the complete and final termination of an insolvent insurer's operations under provisions of state insurance law that permit the insurance regulator under court approval to entirely dispose of all assets and liabilities in accordance with that law. It is based on a finding of any of the grounds associated with rehabilitation as well as a condition of insolvency. Notice is given to other insurance commissioners, guaranty funds, insurance agents, and all persons known or reasonably expected to have claims against the insurer. Priorities for the distribution of assets are established. Taxes, the cost of administration, employee salaries, and policyowner claims receive the highest priorities. The distribution of assets in all states is controlled by the statutes of the domiciliary state.

An insolvent insurer typically will have insufficient net assets to cover its liabilities to policyholders. In these instances, the state guaranty associations are often involved in making good some of what otherwise would be policyholder or beneficiary losses. The first U.S. insurance guaranty mechanism was introduced by New York in 1941. Following the introduction of Senate proposals in 1969 to create a federal mechanism, the NAIC responded with the adoption of a life and health guaranty association model law. It has been replaced twice, by the 1985 and 2009 NAIC *Life and Health Insurance Guaranty Association Model Acts*.

The model act creates a nonprofit legal entity in the state, termed the *Life and Health Insurance Guaranty Association*. All insurers, as a condition of their being licensed to transact any type of insurance covered by the act in the state, must be members of the guaranty association. Thus, if an insurer is licensed in 50 states, it must be a member of 50 guaranty associations. An assessment mechanism is specified for general administrative costs and for costs associated with settling the claims resulting from insolvent or impaired insurers.

Guaranty associations exist to protect the residents of the state sponsoring the association. Protection is not provided for insurers or for policyholders resident in other states in which the insurer is licensed. Policyholders residing in other states generally are covered by that state's guaranty association. Funds are made available for covered losses to residents suffered through the insolvency of any company domiciled in the U.S., although alien insurer policies are excluded. Beneficiaries are covered regardless of their residence.

Several coverage limits apply. Most states provide for a maximum of $300,000 for life insurance death benefits but usually not more than $100,000 in net cash surrender values. Coverage limits range from $100,000 to $500,000 for annuity cash values and payments, including tax-qualified annuities and structured settlement annuities, with most states having limits greater than $250,000. Health insurance maximum payments are $500,000 for medical expense insurance coverage, $300,000 for disability income coverage, and $100,000 for all other health coverages. These limits apply in the aggregate to an individual insured, not on a per-policy basis.

The guaranty association honors benefits in cash or by continuing coverage. Continuation of coverage is achieved by the guaranty association (1) providing benefits as an insurer would subject to the coverage, limits, and exclusions of the state act or (2) transferring policies to a solvent insurer through an assumption reinsurance arrangement. Guaranty associations are financed with the assets of the failed insurer and the proceeds of a retrospective assessment system funded by solvent insurers. Many states provide a premium, franchise, or income tax offset or credit for assessments, and, in these states, the associated cost is effectively transferred to the state and its taxpayers.

All 52 insurance guaranty associations are members of the *National Organization of Life and Health Insurance Guaranty Associations* (NOLHGA). Through NOLHGA, the associations work together to provide continued protection for policyholders affected by a multi-state insurance insolvency. NOLHGA establishes a task force of representative guaranty associations to work with the domiciliary state insurance commissioner to develop a plan to protect policyholders.

The main economic problem with a guaranty system is that it diminishes market discipline through the creation of moral hazard by both policyholders and insurer managements. Policyholders, knowing that they can be made whole were their insurer to become insolvent, have less incentive to carefully select and monitor the financial condition of the insurers with whom they deal. Similarly, management knows that it can essentially shift consequences of risky practices to the guaranty mechanism. As a subset of the insurer management agency/moral hazard problem, the system has been criticized as, in effect, penalizing financially secure insurers twice. Thus, such insurers assert that they must first try to compete on price with irresponsible insurers that underprice their products, making such insurers more likely to become insolvent. Then, when irresponsible insurers become insolvent and assessments are levied, the same financially secure insurers are required, in effect, to subsidize their irresponsible market behavior.

Additionally, as maximum annual assessments of member insurers typically are limited to between 1.0 and 2.0 percent of their yearly net premiums written in the state, there exists the possibility that insufficient funds will be collected fully to meet the state's promises, especially were a large insurer to become insolvent. Finally, even with the facilitating work of NOLHGA, the system has been criticized because of the absence of a mandatory program or procedure of collaboration among state associations.

THE FUTURE OF FINANCIAL SUPERVISION AND REPORTING

Historically, financial reporting and supervision procedures have shared the following properties:

- an indiscriminate "one-size-fits-all" application of methods to all companies,
- a general assumption that products and product risk are relatively homogenous from company to company,
- the use of external models and a reliance on industry benchmarks without regard to company-specific risk and risk practices,
- an emphasis on inflexible rules and factors and an aversion toward professional discretion, and
- static, current-condition evaluations that ignore future changes in an unpredictable economic environment.

The approach was adequate for its times. Products and asset and liability portfolios were relatively homogenous across the industry, regulations were conservative enough to produce acceptable results, economic conditions were stable, and the framework was easy to implement and monitor. Following the significant changes in industry structure discussed in Chapter 9, new products, more sophisticated options and guarantees, and hedging techniques emerged. Insurers exhibited pronounced heterogeneity in both their asset and liability holdings.

Consequently, life insurer supervision and reporting are now in a state of transition. The internal adoption of alternative economic approaches to solvency and profitability by life insurer managers has been a precursor to analogous developments in financial supervision and reporting. The major difference is the adoption of stochastic determinations of capital and reserves similar to the determination of economic capital (EC). Governance provisions from enterprise risk management

(ERM) are also becoming important. Ironically, the focus of solvency determination is shifting from a balance sheet comparison of the expected present value of assets and liabilities to an EC-like projection of revenues and expenses, while profitability determination is shifting from revenue and expense comparisons to period-to-period redeterminations of capital represented by a comparison of the expected present value of assets and liabilities.

HARMONIZATION OF INTERNATIONAL SUPERVISION AND REPORTING

The influence of international approaches to solvency supervision and reporting is becoming substantial. There is ongoing and increasing convergence of practice and procedure between the IASB and FASB and between the NAIC and the *International Association of Insurance Supervisors* (IAIS). Convergence is a global development, led by accounting and regulatory authorities in the U.S. and the European Union (E.U.). The shared themes of the developments in both reporting and supervision are (1) international collaboration and (2) reliance on a *principles-based approach* (PBA). A PBA incorporates economic assumptions fit for company-specific circumstances and professional discretion in solvency and profitability determinations.

The 1992 *Basel I Accords* were an important milestone along the way. *Basel I* established a new regime for minimum capital requirements as developed by the *Basel Committee on Banking Supervision* and adopted by the central bankers of the Group of 10 (G-10) leading economies (now composed of the G-20). In an effort to improve banking capital sufficiency, banks were required to maintain risk-based capital in specified, factor-based percentages of different asset classes to recognize the different levels of risk associated with those asset classes. Concurrent with *Basel I*, capital regulation of E.U. insurers began to be coordinated with bank regulations to avoid regulatory arbitrage and preserve fairness in inter-sector competition. *Basel I* influenced the implementation of factor-based RBC in the E.U. insurance industry and the adoption of the factor-based RBC requirements adopted by the NAIC in the 1990s.

Basel II Accords were adopted in 2004 just as financial innovation, multinational business practice, and sophisticated new ERM practices led to a belief that the factor-based approach of *Basel I* was outdated. *Basel II* moved financial regulation to a stochastic, principles-based scenario approach to banking capital sufficiency across the E.U.

European insurance supervisors and the industry adopted similar methods in a regulatory regime termed *Solvency II,* to take effect in 2016. *Solvency II* will use internal models and establish solvency capital amounts based on default probabilities relying, for example, on Value at Risk (VaR) and Conditional Tail Expectation (CTE), as discussed below. The NAIC made a formal announcement in 2008 that it was studying the *Basel II* approach, and its evolving approach to solvency reflects this.

The IAIS is playing an increasingly central role in facilitating regulatory convergence internationally. The IAIS's approach to solvency includes the ERM and EC approaches. The NAIC generally follows the core principles of the IAIS solvency approach (see Chapter 12). The IAIS also serves in an advisory capacity to the FASB/IASB insurance contracts project (see below).

An important dimension of the collaboration between the NAIC and the IAIS is the supervision of multinational groups. The IAIS began development of the *Common Framework for the Supervision of Internationally Active Insurance Groups* in 2010. The purpose is to establish mechanisms for identifying and controlling group-wide risk and to promote a convergence of international regulatory and supervisory practice. Groups with $50 billion of assets or $10 million in premium income will be the subject of international supervision if premiums are written in three or more jurisdictions and at least 10% of total premium is written outside the home domicile.

Closely related are the efforts toward accounting convergence. Public accounting worldwide is largely practiced according to principles established by the FASB in the U.S. and the IASB in the E.U. and other countries. Additional countries maintain standards usually derived from the principles of these two organizations. The FASB and the IASB have the intention of having their accounting standards converge, as stated in a joint *Memorandum of Understanding*. Importantly, the SEC expressed its support for the incorporation of IFRS into the financial reporting system for U.S. issuers. It supports a single set of global accounting standards and acknowledged that the IFRS is best positioned to serve that role.

A significant component project of convergence is the harmonization of the international treatment of insurance accounting. A joint project is under active consideration by the FASB and the IASB to develop comprehensive international accounting standards for insurance contracts (both issuer and policyowner) that would make reports of insurer financial condition comparable worldwide. The project enjoys the support of the IAIS and the NAIC. The most important endorsed change is the adoption of a principles-based, stochastic cash flow approach to the presentation of an insurer's financial condition. The approach is consistent with the *Basel* banking approach. Both boards have concluded that insurance accounting practice is unnecessarily vague in that it differs from practice used by other financial institutions and is exacerbated by a "patchwork" of different accounting models in use by different entities in different jurisdictions. Communication to capital markets is inefficient and results in a higher industry cost of capital.

An additional change under active consideration is a bifurcated treatment of cash value insurance policies. Consistent with the economics of the contracts, insurers would separately account for cash values as deposits and for policy charges as term insurance premiums. The hybrid nature of these policies was discussed in Chapter 9.

Another important aspect of this trend will be the required use of **market consistent embedded value** (MCEV): the present value of future profits attributable to in-force business and the value of surplus, based on market-derived asset and liability values (as opposed to statutory values). Because liabilities are generally not traded in a liquid market, actuarial judgment must be applied to their market value. The value of future business is not recognized. Guidance is being developed for appropriate liability discounting methods reflecting the insurer's actuarial and financial risk as well as the special problem of valuing options and guarantees attributable to both assets and liabilities. MCEV is a variation of embedded value concepts used for management purposes, as discussed in Chapter 14.

Reporting principles and guidance have been developed by a high-level discussion group of European insurance company chief financial officers, the *CFO Forum*. While the original intention was to have mandatory MCEV reporting for European member companies based solely on the *Forum's* format by the end of 2011, developments in insurance reporting under *Solvency II* and the IFRS led the group recently to withdraw its efforts at a mandated format. Nonetheless, MCEV efforts continue apace with regard to European insurers and increasingly with many U.S. insurers as well, although no disclosure or reporting requirements exist for U.S. companies at this time.

THE PRINCIPLES-BASED APPROACH TO ACCOUNTING

The traditional approach to corporate accounting focused primarily on the income statement. Earnings for a particular period were recognized by matching current period revenues and expenses, and prepaid, unearned, and accrued items accounted for timing mismatch. Assets were recorded at historical cost or book value, and the balance sheet was largely a byproduct of retained earnings. As inflation acted on asset values and as the economy produced more intellectual and intangible assets, book value diverged even more from economic reality.

To make financial reporting more consistent with economic realities, the FASB and the IASB intent is to increase the importance of fair value to measurement and recognition. Increasingly, the balance sheet is becoming the primary report, and income is represented by the movement of net balance sheet equity (as defined by MCEV) from period to period. In keeping with finance theory, assets and liabilities are recorded at market value by reference to an active market or, in the absence of an active market, by discounted cash flow analysis.

The FASB and IASB announced the completion of the first phase of the development of a conceptual framework for a PBA to the presentation of corporate financial condition in 2010. It focuses on broad principles implemented through professional judgment, with the objectives of fair presentation rather than narrow rules, internal consistency, and international convergence. In 2013 it issued a proposal for comment to improve financial reporting of insurance contracts.

The proposal sets forth a building-block approach for life, annuity, and long-term health contracts. (Short-term health contracts will be subject to an approach designed for property insurance). The value of an insurance contract will be measured each reporting period as the net expected (probability weighted) value of cash inflows and cash outflows. The estimates are made, incorporating all relevant information including all features of the contract, guarantees, and options.

The IAIS and the NAIC are moving away from the traditional rule-based and formulaic approaches to reserving and capital sufficiency to a PBA in accordance with the higher regulatory solvency objective. The object of a PBA is to capture the net effect of product risk, corporate risk, and risk control practices in solvency determination. The PBA essentially adopts the philosophies of ERM, EC, and MCEV, as well as the principles-based philosophy developing in the accounting profession. The new approach to valuation retains the mortality and interest rate foundation of reserving but supplements them through a principles-based approach that:

- captures all of the benefits and guarantees associated with insurance contracts and their identifiable, quantifiable, and material risks including options;
- utilizes risk analysis and risk management techniques to quantify the risks (VaR, EC, MCEV);
- incorporates all risk and risk factors included in the company's risk assessment and evaluation processes;
- permits the use of company experience based on its availability and degree of credibility to establish assumptions for risks over which the company has some degree of control or influence;
- provides for the use of assumptions, set on a prudent estimate basis, that contain an appropriate level of conservatism; and
- reflects risks and risk factors in the calculation of reserves and capital that may be different from one another and may change over time as products and risk measurement techniques evolve, both in a general sense and within the company's risk management processes.[1]

Under the PBA, a significant amount of judgment and experience from the reporting insurer is required. Both the company's report and an independent review require specific validation of models, assumptions, margins, and the diversifying effect of aggregating results.

STOCHASTIC MODELS

Internal, company-specific stochastic cash flow models are supplementing deterministic, prescribed formulae and fixed values. Deterministic reserving methods are discussed in Chapter 16. The NAIC's *2009 Standard Valuation Model Law* (SVL2009) overlays the traditional deterministic reserving methods with an alternative stochastic cash flow reserve test based on specified assumptions:

- conservative margins for uncertainty,
- mortality,
- expense,
- asset performance factors such as interest rates and equity values, and
- policyholder behavior such as premium persistency, lapse, and withdrawals.

Most assumptions are based on "prudent estimates" derived from the reserving company's experience, published tables, and appropriate margins for uncertainty. Interest rates and equity performance are modeled stochastically in scenarios prescribed by *Actuarial Standards of the American Academy of Actuaries*.

U.S. RESERVES   The SVL2009 changes valuation dramatically with a move from prescribed mortality tables and discount rates to reserves that reflect the dynamic and individual nature of a life insurer's risk and financial condition. The purpose is to recognize volatile markets and changing product risk profiles to produce more realistic economic reserving requirements. Internal models are adopted as an adjunct to rules-based models that establish a minimum amount of capital. The law defines the statutory reserve as the greater of (1) a deterministic reserve and (2) a stochastic reserve.

The *deterministic reserve* is based on a gross premium valuation method: the present value of future benefits less the value of future gross premiums. It follows the traditional reserving model presented in Chapter 16 through a single scenario calculation on a seriatim, policy-by-policy basis and aggregates the results. It differs from the traditional approach by using prudent estimate assumptions rather than statutory specifications of mortality and interest estimates.

The *stochastic reserve* is based on a probability distribution of cash flow results using multiple economic scenarios. It is the average of the worst losses above a prescribed level, called *conditional tail expectation 70*. See Box 13-2.

The required reserve under SVL2009, the greater of the deterministic and stochastic results, applies only to new business, and companies with riskier profiles will be required to maintain larger reserves. The deterministic reserve serves as a floor on required capital and is a constraint on the considerable judgment permitted in the stochastic reserve calculation. An important but unclear side-effect of the PBA to reserves will be its impact on U.S. federal income taxation. As discussed above, permitted reserve deductions make reference to the statutory reserves required under traditional state law without consideration of the new principles-based reserve. There is no existing guidance or interpretation.

The Standard Valuation Law has become an accreditation requirement. As of 2013, seven states had adopted it and ten had introduced legislation.

U.S. RISK-BASED CAPITAL   The NAIC is considering new flexibility in RBC requirements to reflect products and investment portfolios with greater interest rate sensitivities. These issues are under study and development by the *Life Risk-Based Capital Working Group*. A PBA would feature a stochastic cash flow scenario approach based on an internal model applied to the C-3 interest rate component

---

Box 13-2
Risk as Conditional Tail Expectation

Variance – the possibility actual results will deviate from expected results – is a commonly accepted measure of risk in financial theory. It strikes many as an inadequate measure of risk since the idea of unlimited gains does not fit with everyday usage of the word risky. A more intuitive definition could include a recognition of how much can be lost. Risk incorporates more than deviation of results from expected results, it also involves the exposure: both the probability and magnitude of potential financial harm. The insurance industry has always used the ideas of maximum probable loss and the probability of ruin or default. These concepts fit well with policyowner concerns for solvency and are also central to a more contemporary measurement of risk termed **Value at Risk** (VaR): maximum acceptable loss associated with an asset or liability or portfolio of assets and liabilities, over a specified time period with a specified probability or confidence level. VaR captures the combined effect of probability and magnitude in appraising risk.

Tail risk is the outlier risk associated with low frequency/high severity losses. It derives its name from the shape of the low probability segments of the VaR probability distribution plot. **Conditional tail expectation** (CTE) or **Tail VaR** is a refinement of the VaR and is the measure of risk adopted in PBA reserves and capital. VaR defines the sufficiency of the required stochastic scenario reserve at a specified maximum loss but does not address the potential severity of higher severity losses. CTE addresses severity by taking the average of the worst cases occurring outside the relevant group by the specified probability or confidence level. It is an estimate of loss given that the loss exceeds the VaR. (One method of presenting a cumulative probability distribution of expected losses, the Monte Carlo method, is given in Chapter 14.) Consider the following simplified loss presentation:

Example 1

Percentile Rank	10	20	30	40	50	60	70	80	90	100
Worst Scenario Loss	1	1	2	2	3	4	8	12	20	32

The VaR = 8 while the CTE (70) = 18 [(8+12+20+32)/4]

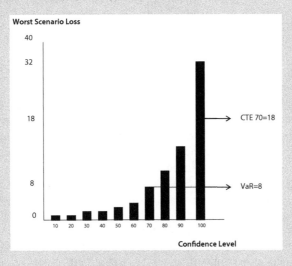

Example 2

Percentile Rank	10	20	30	40	50	60	70	80	90	100
Worst Scenario Loss	1	1	2	2	3	4	8	10	12	18

The VaR = 8 while the CTE (70) = 12 [(8+10+12+18)/4]

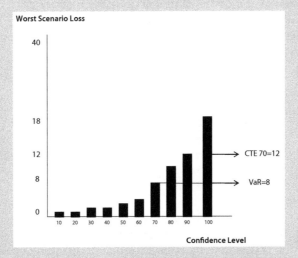

The scenario reserve set at the 70th percentile probability of default is eight in both examples, but tail risk in Example 1 considerably exceeds tail risk in Example 2. The PBA specification of CTE as the risk measure is designed to more accurately capture this tail risk.

of the RBC formula. (See Chapter 9 for the definitions of actuarial C-1, C-2, C-3, and C-4 risks.)

The RBC requirement is less stringent than the reserve requirement as reserves constitute the primary solvency constraint, the total asset requirement incorporates the reserve, and RBC represents a quasi fail-safe approach to extraordinary events. Unlike the reserve rules, the developing but as yet unspecified RBC requirements would apply to in-force business and new business. At this writing, the C-1, C-2, and C-4 risk rules remain factor-based, but stochastic approaches are planned.

LIMITATIONS OF THE PRINCIPLES-BASED APPROACH Questions about two important assumptions that have driven the move to a PBA have been raised by the NAIC.[2] First, the PBA assumes each insurer has an incentive to manage risk, although non-concurrent risk consequences exist between lenders and policyowners (who have fixed benefits) and shareholders (who have unlimited residual benefits): shareholders benefit from increased risk-taking while policyowners do not. The more thinly capitalized a company is, the more incentive shareholders and their management have to take on risk because intuitively they have less to lose. The existence of guaranty associations diminishes the incentive for policyowners to impose implicit market discipline on insurers through careful monitoring.

Second, deficiencies in internal model design may lead to results that do not accurately capture company risk or promote the appropriate risk management behavior that a PBA is designed to accomplish. Further, regulators may lack the considerable technical resources and expertise to monitor the consistency of model design and company implementation. U.S. regulators perceive a need to adopt "constrained regulatory discretion" by retaining traditional industry-standard deterministic rules as a supplement and backstop to a PBA.

CORPORATE GOVERNANCE AND RISK MANAGEMENT

The influence of ERM discussed in Chapter 9 is spreading rapidly from reserve and capital regulation to accounting and regulatory governance mandates. Here are some examples.

- The *Sarbanes Oxley Act of 2002* mandates board oversight of risk management practice.
- The *NAIC Model Audit Rule* incorporates the mandated risk management practice and disclosure provisions of *Sarbanes Oxley* and the SEC.
- The NAIC is examining risk management issues in its SMI. Under current consideration is the IAIS's "Guidance Paper on Enterprise Risk Management for Solvency Purposes" (February 2010).
- The *New York Stock Exchange* requires board-level risk oversight for listing eligibility.
- The SEC mandates disclosure of risk management practice (Rule 33-9089).
- All major rating agencies in the U.S. incorporate risk management governance concepts in their assessments of insurer financial condition.

The most important risk management regulatory initiative for life insurers is a concept known as *Own Risk and Solvency Assessment* (ORSA), the intent of which is to align insurance supervision with insurance business practice, with the common goal of improving the processes for understanding and measuring risks inherent in the business of insurance. The IAIS is promoting the concept as a key component of regulatory reform, which will require insurance companies to issue their own assessment of their current and future risks through an internal risk self-assessment process. The ORSA concept is now embedded in IAIS standards and is in various stages of implementation in the U.S., Europe, and other jurisdictions.

ORSA is an internal process undertaken by an insurer or insurance group to assess the adequacy of its risk management and current and prospective solvency positions under normal and severe stress scenarios. It requires insurers to analyze all reasonably foreseeable and relevant material risks that could have an impact on an insurer's ability to meet its policyholder obligations. Insurers and/or insurance groups will be required to articulate their own judgment about risk management and the adequacy of their capital position.

The *NAIC ORSA Guidance Manual,* adopted by the NAIC in 2012, provides information for insurers in performing their ORSA and documents risk policies and procedures. Pursuant to the *Guidance Manual* and the newly adopted *Risk Management and Own Risk and Solvency Assessment Model Act,* an insurer and/or the group of which the insurer is a member will be required to complete an ORSA "at least annually to assess the adequacy of its risk management and current, and likely future, solvency position." ORSA will apply to any U.S. insurer that writes more than $500 million of annual direct written and assumed premium, and/or insurance groups that collectively write more than $1 billion of annual direct written and assumed premium.

While the *Guidance Manual* is deliberately non-prescriptive, because each ORSA will vary depending on risks that are unique to that insurer/group, insurers are instructed to examine their own risk profile in three major sections.

1. *Description of the Insurer's Risk Management Framework,* which is a high-level summary of its own risk management framework, including its risk appetite, tolerance, and limits and internal controls.
2. *Insurer's Assessment of Risk Exposure,* which includes details showing the insurer's process for assessing risks (both qualitative and quantitative assessments) in both normal and stressed environments.
3. *Group Risk Capital and Prospective Solvency Assessment,* which demonstrates that current and future capital is sufficient to support identified risks.

Insurers must develop processes to perform a self-assessment in the stressed environment using either a stress test methodology or stochastic models. The NAIC expects jurisdictions to have adopted risk management and ORSA requirements into law by 2015.

CONCLUSIONS

The purpose of financial regulation of life insurers is to guarantee the solvency of insurers and thus the safety of policyowner assets and claim payments. The primary purpose of statutory financial reporting is to demonstrate solvency to regulators and policyowners. The primary purpose of GAAP accounting is to present an appropriate measure of a stock company's profit performance to investors. In the following chapter, we examine life insurer capital and financial management under the investor and capital market constraints discussed in Chapter 9 and the regulatory and reporting constraints discussed in this chapter.

ENDNOTES

1 "Principles for the NAIC's Adoption of a Principles-Based Reserving Approach," *Principles-Based Reserving (EX) Working Group* of the *National Association of Insurance Commissioners* (as of June 1, 2008).

2 This section draws on the 2009 Indiana State University Networks Financial Institute Policy Brief, Therese M. Vaughan "The Implications of Solvency II for U.S. Regulation."

CHAPTER 14

LIFE INSURER FINANCIAL MANAGEMENT

The objective of any firm, including a life insurer, is to maximize the value of its owners' interest in the firm. With stock insurers, this means maximizing shareholder wealth. With mutual insurers, it means maximizing policyowner wealth. While differences exist in some aspects of the financial management of mutual and stock companies – primarily due to different financing alternatives – the principles we examine serve to maximize the wealth of the owners of both stock and mutual companies. For ease of exposition, we limit our narrative to stock insurers.

In nonfinancial firms, general corporate finance practice tells us that value is created whenever a company undertakes a project with a positive net present value (NPV), with its positive and negative cash flows discounted at the company's cost of capital. Stated another way, a corporation creates value when the return on its investment exceeds the returns it must pay to those who provide its financing. The pertinent return to investors is the weighted average cost of capital (WACC), based on the principles of the Capital Asset Pricing Model (CAPM) for equity and of economic conditions and credit quality for debt.

We posit that life insurers also create value when they undertake a project with a positive NPV. However, financial intermediaries are fundamentally different than nonfinancial firms. Life insurers are distinguishable by the risks that are special or more important to them than for nonfinancial firms. We focus on two special dimensions of financial risk in this chapter.

The first dimension arises because some important principles of finance theory applicable to nonfinancial firms do not apply equally to life insurers, primarily due to the special nature of the insolvency risk. Those principles include (1) the Modigliana-Miller (MM) theorem that holds shareholder value is unaffected by how a firm's activities are financed, (2) the CAPM holding that risk is defined by the magnitude of the variance of a firm's earnings, and (3) the CAPM holding that the specific risk of a firm is irrelevant as investors can diversify and need be compensated only for systematic risk. Because of the special risk factors faced by life insurers, the assumptions underlying these principles do not hold and so the methods of value maximization as applied to nonfinancial firms require modification. This chapter builds on the preceding ones to explore life insurer financial management in detail, with an emphasis on issues and practices that differentiate life insurers from nonfinancial firms, particularly risk management.

The second dimension of financial risk arises because of the relationship of an insurer's assets and liabilities. **Surplus capital** (or simply **surplus**) is the difference between the values of an insurer's assets and liabilities as defined by a particular accounting convention and is synonymous with *equity* and *net worth*. Thus, growth in an insurer's expected net worth for one measurement period can be expressed:

$$E\big((A_1 - L_1)\big) = \big(A_0 - L_0\big)\big(1 + E(r)\big)$$

Where:

A = assets

L = liabilities

$E(r)$ = the expected return on surplus capital

Thus, surplus capital is a function not only of the expected return from insuring activities but also the *relative value of assets and liabilities*. There exists not only the risk of failing to produce the expected return, but also the risk that the values of A and L might change disproportionately. **Asset-liability risk** (ALR) arises from the possibility that the same external factors can affect the value of assets and liabilities simultaneously and disproportionately, the most important of which is a change in market interest rates.

We will see a tension throughout life insurer financial management between two inconsistent sets of solvency preferences. Shareholders are risk tolerant and prefer to invest *less* capital rather than more to produce higher investment returns; they can diversify the risk of insurer insolvency. Policyowners are risk averse, less able to diversify, and prefer *more* capital to reduce the risk of insolvency.

We will address three issues. First, we examine *capital and risk management* by asking three questions: Why do insurers hold capital? How does capital relate to risk? Why do insurers engage in financial risk management? Second, we examine *financial risk management* by examining some technical methods that life insurers use to maintain assets sufficient to satisfy their obligations under uncertain economic conditions. Third, we finish with an examination of *capital allocation* by exploring how insurers choose the activities they undertake to create value and how they measure the success of the expected and actual results that follow.

We include an appendix to this chapter that offers an overview of some finance fundamentals not covered in the body of this and other chapters and that explores some of the chapter concepts in more depth. The appendix is intended for those who may benefit from a refresher on some finance basics or who may desire a more detailed treatment of concepts presented here.

CAPITAL AND RISK MANAGEMENT

In this section, we discuss the importance of policyowner security, solvency, and the life insurer's need to hold capital for these purposes. We begin by clarifying some definitions that apply to the concept of capital and defining it in economic terms for this chapter. The next subsection discusses the importance of capital and the inadequacy of general financial theory to address its management in a life insurer's context, and the use of hedging to create contingent capital. We close the section with a description of the need to attribute capital and its costs consistently to each of an insurer's products, lines of business, or activities.

THE ECONOMIC VIEWS OF CAPITAL

In finance and economics, the term *capital* has many meanings that are not always consistent. In the context of corporate finance, **capital** generally refers to the financial wealth used to start or maintain a business. **Financial capital** generally means the funds provided to companies by investors either directly or through retained earnings, which are necessary to produce goods and services. This is its meaning in the context of the WACC. Thus, reserves, debt, and equity are the typical insurer's financial capital. In banking, the term *capital*, used alone, is taken to mean the difference between its assets and liabilities or, in terms of the above discussion, its net worth or owner's equity. Banks maintain capital to absorb unanticipated losses and provide a margin of security that inspires confidence in its customers and potential customers. The term *capital* is also sometimes used in the sense of owner's equity with insurers, but commonly the difference in assets and liabilities is referred to simply as *surplus*.

We can view the capital of a life insurer by its function. While different terminology and values apply to these functions according to the needs and customs of managers, regulators, accountants, and rating agencies, life insurer capital can be thought of as being allocated among these three basic functions:

- **Operating capital** is the amount of invested and accumulated nonfinancial assets, intangibles, and liquid working capital required to do business but not available to pay claims.
- **Reserve capital** is the amount of financial assets held by an insurer to pay its expected claims.
- **Risk capital** is the amount of financial assets held by an insurer to pay unexpected claims.

Operating capital generally suffices as the only needed capital for nonfinancial firms, but life insurers are required to maintain additional capital. A life insurer must maintain reserve capital sufficient to meet *expected* claims and other benefit payments. Risk capital is necessary to meet *unexpected* claims and benefits and is expected to remain idle. Risk capital is necessary to provide confidence to policy-owners and their advocates (regulators and rating agencies) that an insurer will remain solvent even under reasonably extreme circumstances. In this context, we can view expected claims and benefits as an expense and unexpected claims and benefits as losses.

Operating capital, reserve capital, and risk capital are defined, denominated, and measured by similar but somewhat different approaches according to the needs of those making the determinations. Table 14-1 provides an overview of relevant perspectives on life insurer capital. The reader will note that these perspectives generally follow the accounting conventions discussed in Chapter 13. Note that risk-based capital defines the required minimum amounts of statutory risk capital for purposes of regulatory intervention.

Table 14-1   Economic Functions of Capital and Stakeholder Perspectives

	Description	*Measurement*			
		Economic Capital	Regulatory Capital	GAAP Capital	Rating Agency Capital
Operating Capital	Nonfinancial Assets, Intangibles, and Liquid Working Capital	Fair Value of Marketable Assets (e.g., Product Lines, Distribution Channels)	No Value for Non-admitted Assets	Book Value or Fair Value	Derived from Rating Agencies' Proprietary Models
Reserve Capital	Financial Capital Held to Pay Expected Claims	Derived from Insurers' Proprietary Models	Statutory Reserves	GAAP Reserves	Derived from Rating Agencies' Proprietary Models
Risk Capital	Financial Capital Held to Pay Unexpected Claims	Derived from Insurers' Proprietary Models	Statutory Surplus: SAP Assets less SAP Liabilities (Sufficiency based on Risk-Based Capital Rules)	GAAP Surplus: GAAP Assets less GAAP Liabilities (Net Worth or Owners' Equity)	Derived from Rating Agencies' Proprietary Models
Principal Stakeholder Perspective		Managers	Regulators	Shareholders	Policyowners

THE IMPORTANCE OF CAPITAL AND CAPITAL STRUCTURE

CAPM principles are used to derive the value of risky stocks and the implicit returns investors require to bear that risk. Some risk is *specific* and arises from the volatility of returns associated with an individual company. Other risk is *systematic* in that all businesses are subject to broad societal influences and factors that have a tendency to move together. We know from modern portfolio theory (MPT) that specific risk can be eliminated through diversification. The capital structure irrelevancy principles of MM hold that the value of a firm is derived exclusively from the NPV of its cash flows and that its financing does not affect its value.

Two important implications of these principles (when certain assumptions hold) apply to nonfinancial companies. First, shareholders need not be concerned with specific risk (which can be eliminated) but require returns that compensate them for bearing only systematic, market risk (which cannot be eliminated). Second, owners will assemble their own investment portfolios based on their own preferences and risk profiles. They do not need management's help to do this. In fact, owners ordinarily do not want management to take their lifetime liquidity and risk preferences into consideration.

As a result, managers of nonfinancial companies need only to maximize net present values, acting as risk-neutral agents for the owners and undertaking every project whose net present value is positive. For a nonfinancial company, the risk of insolvency is an ordinary risk in that the important stakeholders – the owners – can eliminate it through diversification.

Managers of life insurers and other financial intermediaries that issue liabilities cannot ignore the specific risk of their companies. The specific risk of insolvency is the principal concern of several of their stakeholders: policyowners, regulators, and rating agencies. For a life insurer, insolvency is a special risk because policyowners realistically cannot eliminate it through diversification. Policyowners, regulators, and rating agencies must be intensely interested in the solvency of individual insurers.

Because of the importance of solvency to life insurer managers, two further implications make the CAPM and MM results less relevant. First, both CAPM and MM assume the relevant measure of risk is the volatility of earnings. Volatility is a proxy for risk where risk is defined in terms of uncertainty. Because solvency is so important to life insurers, the uncertainty associated with insolvency – e.g., when caused by extreme events – is more relevant than the uncertainty associated with the variance of reported earnings from period to period. The value at risk concept helps define these events. **Value at Risk** (VaR) is the maximum acceptable loss associated with an asset or liability or portfolio of assets and liabilities over a specified time period with a specified probability or confidence level.

Second, companies that experience financial distress incur unexpected costs due to bankruptcy costs and self-serving behavior by managers, customers, and suppliers. Additionally, life insurers are subject to significant liquidity risk as credit quality downgrades and negative publicity associated with financial distress can significantly affect policyowner lapses and surrenders. The demand nature of policyowner reserve financing exacerbates liquidity risk in the presence of financial distress.

While policyowners are implicit investors because their premiums give rise to insurers' reserves, they are ordinarily less motivated by investment considerations than by their desire for financial security in the presence of financial uncertainty. It is impractical for policyowners to purchase insurance from a sufficient number of carriers to eliminate insolvency risk. Regulators and rating agencies exist precisely for the purpose of enforcing and predicting, respectively, the solvency of individual companies.

Capital structure is therefore important to and affects the value of life insurers. Life insurers must maintain risk capital to address the needs of their customers, regulators, and rating agencies. From the policyowner's perspective, risk capital is the shareholders' assurance that the insurer will not default in the event of unexpected losses. From the shareholder's perspective, it is a form of insurance that guarantees (up to a limit) the company's expected returns. (If unexpected losses occur, risk capital funds restore the expected returns.) Policyowners and shareholders pay for these assurances in the form of capital costs.

Capital costs are the returns required by those who provide the capital plus the cost of hedging. (We discuss hedging in the next section.) Capital costs are an expense. More capital means that its higher costs must be reflected in higher premiums. Capital costs are central to the tension between the policyowner preference for security via higher risk capital, and the shareholder preference for superior returns via lower risk capital.

Thus, the amount of risk capital held by an insurer determines its default risk; less risk capital means a higher default probability. By **default** or **ruin risk,** we mean the possibility that an insurer will be insolvent and unable to perform its contractual obligations. As risk capital increases, the value of shareholder risk increases and policyowner risk decreases. Risk capital is the principal determinant of risk for both shareholders and policyowners. Thus, managing capital, managing value, and managing risk are closely related.

RISK CAPITAL, RISK MANAGEMENT, AND HEDGING

This subsection explores why and how life insurers manage financial risk. CAPM principles suggest specific risk is not important. MM principles suggest a firm's capital structure – its financing and risk capital position (surplus) – also is unimportant as it does not affect its value. Yet life insurers are heavily involved in the management of risk and capital. The insolvency risk is clearly the principal reason. While volatility-derived CAPM considerations do not tell the complete story of life insurer risk, because shareholders value moderate volatility and consistent earnings, there are other reasons to manage risk. Further reasons for managing risk include reductions in (1) earnings volatility over time, thus lowering tax liabilities; (2) agency costs as risk management signaling should reduce perceived agency problems; and (3) financial distress costs, which are important in the context of the financial security of financial intermediaries.

Recall that asset-liability risk management (ALRM) is the process of preserving or enhancing a life insurer's surplus capital position as asset and liability values change in response to economic conditions and customer behavior. It is the life insurer's special financial risk management practice of protecting the net value of assets and liabilities when interest rates and other economic factors change. The three most important ALRM practices in which a life insurer engages are asset-liability matching, capital allocation, and hedging. **Asset-liability matching** is the practice of designing policies and managing liability-matched asset portfolios to interact in a way that protects an insurer's net surplus position under changing economic conditions and customer behavior. A liability-matched asset portfolio is usually not a complete answer because it is impossible or impractical to anticipate and protect against all economic scenarios. **Capital allocation** is the practice of attributing operational and risk capital to projects that maximize value.

Hedging is the practice of holding risk management assets that pay cash flows to offset unexpected losses associated with a hedged asset or liability, a portfolio of hedged assets or liabilities, or the *net* relationship between assets and liabilities. **Hedge capital** is risk management asset cash flow that substitutes for and complements surplus capital. The two most important risk management assets for insurers are reinsurance and derivatives. We will examine examples of asset-liability matching, capital allocation, and hedging in subsequent sections.

As we noted above, managing risk, capital, and value are closely related for a financial intermediary. Risk capital is maintained in two ways. One method of managing default and other risk is simply to hold more surplus capital (equity), ideally in the form of liquid investments. Holding surplus capital in any form, however, is costly because it is heavily taxed (unlike earnings attributable to policy reserves which are essentially tax free) and holding *liquid* surplus capital imposes still other costs as it cannot be employed where the insurer has comparative and competitive advantages to produce excess returns, and is affected with agency problems.

The second alternative is hedging. Its principal advantage is the capital it frees up to be deployed in value-producing activities that would otherwise create a need to raise and hold additional equity (which is an insurer's most expensive form of financing) or prohibit the insurer from undertaking projects that create value. Hedging with risk management assets is usually more efficient than holding liquid assets.

Unexpected losses are the difference in expected losses and the VaR. If an insurer maintains risk capital exclusively in the form of liquid assets, it must fund the entire VaR. If it hedges, it shares the risk of unexpected losses with other insurers (via reinsurance) or capital market participants (via derivatives) in the same way policyowners share risk. It pays an actuarially fair share of the VaR plus a loading to the reinsurer and/or capital markets.

Hedging with risk management assets can also be an efficient complement to constructing a liability-matched asset portfolio. Managing assets to match liabilities is time consuming, requires dynamic portfolio reconstruction, and incurs administrative costs. Derivatives can be a cheaper and more flexible method of protecting the relationship of asset and liability values.

THE CAPITAL AND CAPITAL COST ALLOCATION PROBLEM

Financial capital has two economic purposes for life insurers: producing claims (operating and reserve capital) and producing confidence (risk capital). As discussed earlier, value is created whenever a company undertakes a project that produces a positive NPV discounted at the company's cost of capital. Discounting life insurer product cash flows at its WACC is a traditional capital budgeting exercise and fairly straightforward. Yet life insurers incur costs – the cost of holding risk capital to produce confidence – that is not accounted for in product cash flows.

Risk capital and its cost are difficult concepts to quantify because it is difficult to answer the question how much risk capital is required. Insurers use two reasonable proxies for required risk capital:

- **Regulatory capital**, which is the amount of reserves and risk-based capital (RBC) (and the implicit premium income necessary to fund them) required by law, and
- **Rating agency capital**, which is the amount of capital required to receive the quality rating an insurer desires. It serves as a reasonable proxy for policyowner confidence requirements.

Life insurers must explicitly satisfy the regulatory condition to remain solvent and licensed and implicitly satisfy the rating agency condition to sell marketable products. Thus, required capital is ordinarily the greater of regulatory and rating agency capital. Regulatory and rating agency requirements are based on artificially conservative assumptions because they are intended to promote solvency under reasonably extreme experience.

To determine whether life insurer projects create value, it is necessary to take account of the cost of holding risk capital. The cost of holding risk capital is a function of the amount allocated to a project and its cost. Thus, to identify and rank the value of projects, it is also necessary to ask how much operating, reserve, and risk capital is required to support each project to identify and rank the value of projects.

The two measures of required capital are artificially conservative when viewed from the perspective of a risk tolerant shareholder seeking returns. They are based on industry averages and do not necessarily reflect true economic risk. In the next section, we turn to the concept of *economic capital* to allocate capital (including risk capital) to projects based on more realistic assumptions that are specific to an insurer's own assets and liabilities. In a subsequent section on capital allocation, we discuss how to incorporate the cost of risk capital into the measurement of project value.

ECONOMIC CAPITAL

Life insurers are adopting financial management practices originating in the banking industry to address the limitations associated with managing to artificially conservative regulatory and rating agency capital requirements. This approach uses probabilistic measures of capital, called *economic capital*, based on realistic economic assumptions. **Economic capital** (EC) is the amount of capital required to absorb the maximum expected loss occurring with a specified probability over a specified time horizon. VaR is the related term for the amount of the maximum expected loss that EC is designed to absorb. Thus, EC incorporates both reserve capital to cover expected losses and risk capital to cover unexpected losses in one measurement; it does not distinguish accounting reserves and surplus.

VaR answers the question: what is the most that can be lost with X percent probability? EC answers the question: how much total capital (reserve and risk) is necessary to maintain solvency with a probability of Y percent? (If X and Y percent – the confidence levels – are the same, the two answers are the same.) EC represents a common risk language because its concepts and results can be applied to different insurance products and other products or lines of business. Thus, for example, the risk of a variable insurance policy can be compared to the risk of operating a third party administration subsidiary.

EC is established with the use of an insurer's realistic, best estimate assumptions specific to its own assets and liabilities as opposed to regulatory and rating agency determinations based on industry averages. EC has a variety of uses. As losses exceeding the EC amount will cause insolvency, the specified probability is also the ruin or default probability. It is a precise mechanism for stating an insurer's level of risk tolerance with respect to a product or line of business (LOB) and to its aggregate firm-level operations. Hence, the use of EC can bring more accuracy to methods that are sensitive to the cost of capital, such as:

- product pricing,
- capital allocation,
- financial performance measurement, and
- performance-based executive compensation.

As discussed in Chapter 13, there is a move to principles-based regulation and rating agency practice. These are based on VaR and EC concepts, so insurers familiar with EC practices are better able to communicate in the regulatory examination and rating agency review processes.

CALCULATING ECONOMIC CAPITAL FOR A LINE OF BUSINESS

In determining EC, a life insurer first defines its level of risk tolerance by specifying either a maximum loss it wishes to be able to survive or a probability of default it is willing to accept over a relevant time horizon. We know from the definition of EC that these are essentially simultaneous determinations as each element must be specified.

The determination of possible financial results – and thus the maximum acceptable loss – requires a projection of future results associated with a product or other LOB. The process begins with the construction of a deterministic financial cash flow model. Unlike other industries, cash flow testing has been central to life insurer management for decades. However, historically the most sophisticated cash flow testing simply added expense factors to the static interest and persistency assumptions of the asset share and accumulated book profit models (see Chapter 16) and perhaps took into account general expansion or contraction in the economy. These methods fail to capture the interconnected sensitivity of assets and liabilities to the same economic factors (such as interest rate changes and policyowner behavior) associated with net asset-liability value, disintermediation, and reinvestment. Examples were presented in Chapter 9.

While insurers use a variety of methods, we identify two financial analysis techniques that account for differing economic conditions. The **stress test** method applies a set of extreme assumptions to a deterministic model to determine financial results under a limited set of economic scenarios. The scenarios are designed to represent financial results under extreme circumstances and to test the limits of solvency. This method suffers from the weakness that a limited number of scenarios is useful only in the limited circumstances captured.

As computing has become more powerful and economical, insurers have begun to use a more complete (and complex) method of financial analysis based on probabilities and economic assumptions that evolve over the projected time horizon. **Dynamic financial analysis** (DFA) is the stochastic or probability-based projection of an insurance company's cash flows and financial condition over time, taking into account a full range of economic scenarios, asset and liability cash flows, the mutual dependences or interrelationships of the cash flows, and the factors that affect cash flows individually and collectively. Each scenario is referred to as a *path*. The simulation projects the earnings and balance sheet position (ending surplus capital result) under a wide range of assumed economic scenarios, while allowing the model's asset-liability management (ALM) strategy assumptions to change as management would expect to respond to economic conditions evolving along each projected path.

Stochastic simulation is usually a variation of a numerical method used widely in mathematics, statistics, physics, engineering, and finance. The **Monte Carlo method** applies randomly selected values to variables in a deterministic cash flow model that is repeated thousands of times to produce a range of possible results and their probabilities. As the number of simulations increases, the reliability of the range of results is expected to increase in accordance with the law of large numbers.

The increasing importance of policyowner and borrower options and guarantees in life insurer product design makes stochastic modeling especially useful.

The values of options and guarantees cannot be determined analytically because they are not deterministic but depend on unknown market and customer behavior. Stochastic modeling estimates how often and at what cost guarantees come into play. Monte Carlo simulation steps include:

- identifying the risks and variables to be incorporated,
- defining a domain or range of values that each variable can take,
- creating a deterministic mathematical model that identifies cash flow results and accounts for the important effects of correlation and diversification,
- incorporating dynamic assumptions about managerial responses to economic changes as each projected path develops,
- assigning random values (using a computerized random number generator) to each variable and simulating ending surplus produced by the randomly selected variable set,
- evaluating and storing the ending surplus capital value,
- repeating the process thousands of times, and
- assembling the stored ending surplus capital values into a cumulative probability distribution that ranks the present values of profits from worst to best.

Figure 14-1   **Determination of Economic Capital: Application of Risk Tolerance Specifications to a Ranked Probability Distribution**

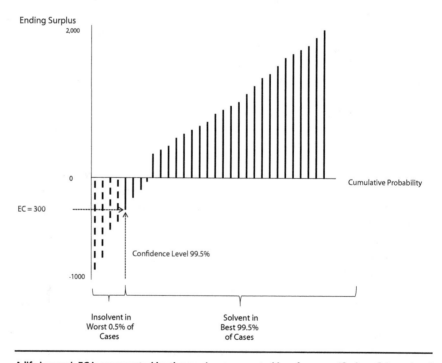

A life insurer's EC is represented by the maximum expected loss for a specified confidence level. The company remains economically solvent as long as actual losses do not exceed EC.

The simulation can be thought of as a probability-linked model of a real world future. The results are analyzed to (1) reveal the nature of cash flow interrelationships, (2) identify the likely causes of unfavorable as well as favorable results, and (3) ascertain an amount of EC that is consistent with the insurer's risk tolerance. Figure 14-1 shows the results of a hypothetical DFA result for one line of business. The projected results are ranked from worst to best. The results range approximately from a surplus capital loss of 900 to a surplus capital gain of 2,000. In this example, the insurer's risk tolerance level is defined by a default probability of 0.5 percent and an EC amount of 300. Thus, if the insurer maintains capital of 300 it can expect to remain solvent in all but the worst 0.5 percent of cases.

Figure 14-2 presents different confidence levels applied by two companies, *Conservative* and *Aggressive*, to the same product and set of economic scenarios. Company *Conservative* is prepared to tolerate insolvency in only the worst 0.3 percent of projected scenarios (99.7 percent confidence level), while Company *Aggressive*, as in Figure 14-1, is prepared to tolerate insolvency in the worst 0.5 percent (99.5 percent confidence level) of projected scenarios. By adopting a more cautious attitude toward risk, Company *Conservative* must maintain a higher level of capital (800) than Company *Aggressive* (300). The cost of maintaining capital support for Company *Aggressive* will be lower and thus its expected shareholder returns for a given premium will be higher, but it will prove less attractive to risk-averse policyowners. Adjustment of the confidence level redefines risk and EC while simultaneously affecting the insurer's premium.

Determination of Economic Capital for Insurers with Different Risk Tolerance Levels

Figure 14-2

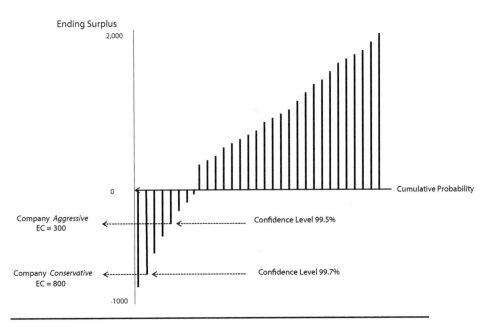

EC is an expression of a life insurer's tolerance for risk. In this example, Company *Conservative* holds 800 to protect against unexpected losses while Company *Aggressive* holds only 300.

CALCULATING ECONOMIC CAPITAL FOR THE FIRM

We know from portfolio theory that when an individual asset is added to a portfolio, the risk of the portfolio is reduced (unless the added asset is perfectly correlated to the existing portfolio). The portfolio risk reduction effect applies to a life insurer's product portfolio also. A simple example is the addition of an annuity product to a portfolio of life insurance products. Any deviations in mortality results due to changes in the longevity of the general population causing a loss in the life insurance portfolio will cause a corresponding gain in the annuity portfolio thus reducing the variability of results. (Of course, factors such as extreme adverse selection could cause both results to erode despite the general mortality trend.)

The results of MPT dictate the aggregate amount of EC required to support an insurer's entire operations. We know that this amount is the capital required to absorb the identified maximum adverse result expected to occur with a specified probability over a specified time horizon. It specifically is *not* the arithmetic sum of the EC amounts associated with each product. Because of the benefit of diversification, it must be less. Figure 14-3 shows a hypothetical accumulation of EC amounts by product line, a reduced amount of firm level EC, and the resulting diversification benefit.

Figure 14-3   **A Hypothetical Aggregation of Economic Capital by Line of Business**

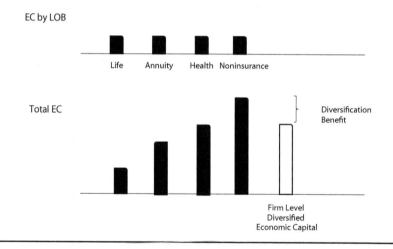

Thus, the total amount of EC held at the company level can be adjusted for the correlation of the risks of the various products. Several methods may be used for this purpose. One example is the construction of a correlation matrix analogous to the matrix constructed for stocks in the appendix to this chapter.

ATTRIBUTING FIRM LEVEL ECONOMIC CAPITAL AT THE LINE OF BUSINESS LEVEL

EC is used at the product level to estimate the cost of capital in a variety of ways, including product pricing and the rational allocation of capital to the projects that create the most value. Using the VaR attributable to the maximum probable loss of an individual product alone fails to account for any diversification benefit that the product brings to the insurer's portfolio. Thus, the determination of EC at the product level becomes a somewhat circular process comprised of (1) determining product VaRs, (2) calculating the aggregate diversification benefit and determining a firm-level EC amount, and (3) attributing a portion of the reduced firm level EC amount to each product. As the contribution of each individual product to portfolio risk differs from its own VaR determined without regard to diversification, the diversification reduction determined at the firm level is not attributable to each product *pro rata*.

The contribution of each product to portfolio risk can be estimated by calculating each product's marginal risk in these sequential steps:

1. determine each product's EC,
2. determine firm-level EC with all products,
3. determine firm-level EC separately without each product, and
4. take the difference between firm-level EC (1) with all products and (2) separately without each product to yield EC attributable to each product.

This sum of the allocated capital by this method will not equal the total diversified firm-level EC unless the products are perfectly correlated, an unlikely result. The unallocated capital can be viewed as a positive intra-firm externality in that each product in effect provides additional security to others.[1] Figure 14-4 presents a hypothetical decomposition of firm level EC by product line and the unallocated EC representing the intra-firm externality security benefit.

A Hypothetical Allocation of Economic Capital by Line of Business   **Figure 14-4**

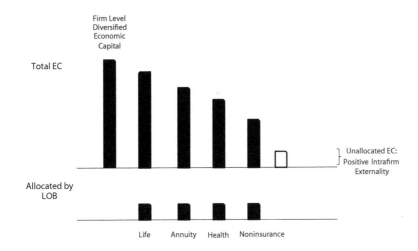

Here we examine some technical methods life insurers might use to manage financial risk. The presentation is intended to illustrate concepts of risk and risk management that show possible strategies to resolve important issues and not necessarily actual insurer risk management practice. We emphasize the holistic view of risk embodied by the enterprise risk management (ERM) principles discussed in Chapter 9.

FINANCIAL
RISK
MANAGEMENT

Some risk management techniques used by life insurers are common to all investors. The reduction of credit risk and equity market risk through the diversification of bond issuers and common stock holdings are examples. Of course, the diversification of actuarial liabilities is the essential tool that permits life insurers to bear actuarial risk. We focus on financial risk management as applied to the special risks that life insurers face.

The special risks of life insurer financial intermediation can be labeled as asset-liability risk (ALR). ALR is a special case of market risk that results from the possibility that changing economic conditions and customer behavior will erode or destroy the net of the value of assets less liabilities, whether we describe this net value as surplus capital, owner's equity, or risk capital. As discussed in Chapter 9, interest rate volatility creates the possibility of liquidity problems associated with disintermediation and reinvestment. ALR is usually associated with interest rates but may also arise when liabilities are based on equity returns.

Thus, a bond investor is exposed to interest rate risk because increasing market rates cause the value of bonds to decline. A stock market investor is exposed to equity market risk because the value of shares may fall. When interest rates rise or equity markets fall, the value of life insurer investments is likewise affected. Yet for a life insurer, interest rate risk and market risk are not completely described without reference to the insurer's liabilities. Risk is a substantively different exposure for a financial intermediary.

If rising interest rates cause the value of an insurer's liabilities to decline by at least as much as the value of its bonds, there really is no risk. If a declining equity market causes the value of an insurer's separate account investments to fall, the value of the reserve liability declines by the same amount. (Declining equity markets can be repugnant to life insurers for other reasons; e.g., its management fees are typically based on the value of separate accounts, the value of its own shares declines, and its cost of capital may be affected.) Thus, as discussed in Chapter 9, the creation and maintenance of a net interest margin in the general account are more important than achieving maximum absolute asset returns. Similarly, when liabilities are based on equity returns (as with variable products), assets that match corresponding liabilities are appropriate rather than assets designed to earn a maximum probable return.

The overriding risk for a life insurer and its principal financial management concern is the management of its ALR. ALRM is the process of preserving or enhancing a life insurer's surplus capital position as asset and liability values change in response to economic conditions and customer behavior. The three most important tools of ALRM are:

- asset-liability matching,
- hedging, and
- capital allocation.

We can view these as sequential steps in the same process. First, a life insurer seeks to design its policies and investment portfolios to interact in a way that reasonably protects the net surplus position under changing economic conditions. Second, because asset-liability matching is usually incomplete, insurers seek further to reduce ALR by hedging with risk management assets. Finally, insurers allocate an appropriate amount of their firm-level EC to projects that reflect the unmatched and unhedged ALR that remains. Risk remains because it is impractical to profitably match and hedge completely under all foreseeable economic conditions, and life insurers therefore intentionally retain a measure of risk consistent with their risk tolerance.

We proceed through this section by describing the exposure of the net asset-liability position to interest rate risk and then presenting examples of ALRM techniques. These include the concepts of (1) *duration* and *convexity*, which are useful in matching assets and liabilities subject to interest rate risk; (2) applying interest rate derivatives to the interest rate exposure; and (3) applying equity derivatives to an equity-indexed product. We begin with some essential financial background.

INTEREST RATE RISK AND THE SHORT STRADDLE POSITION

A **long straddle** position is established by an options speculator through the simultaneous purchase of a *put* (an option to sell) and a *call* (an option to buy) on the same asset. If the asset moves sufficiently – above the exercise price of the call or below the exercise price of the put – it is "in the money" and is said to possess a positive property of *moneyness*. The speculator gains as long as the price of the asset moves sufficiently in either direction. A **short straddle** position is established by simultaneously *selling* a put and a call. The speculator is in the money as long as rates *do not* move above the price of the call or below the price of the put.

Because life insurer surplus capital is at risk if market interest rates move significantly in either direction – due to liquidity and reinvestment risk – it is in a short straddle position.[2] It is analogously "in the money" as long as interest rates (and its asset and liability values and cash flows) do not increase or decrease significantly. Stable interest rates produce positive results; volatile interest rates destroy value. The insurer has effectively *written* – rather than bought – (1) a put option that allows policyowners and borrowers to give it cash that it must reinvest when rates have fallen *and* (2) a call option that allows policyowners and borrowers to withdraw funds when interest rates have risen. It is a short straddle taker because the policyowner and borrower options creating the short straddle are required either by law or by market forces.

Figure 14-5 presents the short straddle position of surplus capital, where r^* is the current market interest rate. As long as interest rates do not fall below point A or rise above point B, the insurer's surplus capital position is positive. Rates that move beyond points A or B put the surplus capital position "out of the money" and destroy value. ALRM can be thought of as a metaphorical strategy to manage the consequences of the short straddle position of surplus capital. The short straddle exposure of surplus capital applies at both the LOB and firm levels.

ASSET-LIABILITY MATCHING

Asset-liability matching in the short straddle context is accomplished by controlling the cash flow responses of both assets and liabilities to changing interest rate conditions. Controlling liability cash flows is addressed with product design, and controlling asset cash flows is addressed with a liability-matched asset portfolio whose duration and convexity properties match those of the liability portfolio.

Figure 14-5   **Life Insurer Surplus Capital in a Short Straddle**

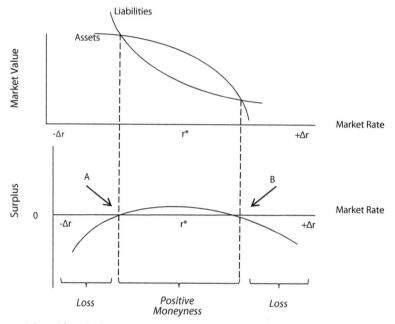

Source: Adapted from Anthony M. Santomero and David F. Babbel, Financial Markets, Instruments, and Institutions (Chicago: Irwin, 1997), p. 647

As long as interest rates do not rise above point B or fall below point A, the short straddle position is "in the money."

CONTROLLING LIABILITY CASH FLOWS: PRODUCT DESIGN   The most important product design mechanisms addressing disintermediation arising from policy loans, surrenders, withdrawals, and premium payment suspensions are the participation features that permit policyowners to share in positive investment performance. When interest rates rise, these features permit insurers to offer competitive earnings and reduce the incentives for policyowners to invest their funds elsewhere. Product design is also an exercise in liability control. The most important cash flow control features in product design are:

- use of variable policy loan interest rates that remove the disintermediation incentive to borrow on the cash value when interest rates rise because borrowing rates also rise,
- embedding of surrender charges,
- design and sale of variable (separate account) products that offer market rates of return and reduce incentives for loans, withdrawals, and surrenders, and
- use of flexible crediting rates under interest sensitive life insurance and annuity products that permit rates to be changed with changes in market rates.

These features control unexpected cash flow developments attributable to policyowner behavior. They are intended to limit cash outflows associated with policy options.

CONTROLLING ASSET CASH FLOWS: A DURATION MATCHED ASSET PORTFOLIO   In this section and in the chapter appendix, we discuss specific techniques designed to manage interest rate risk by calibrating a fixed income portfolio to the liabilities of general account products. Investment risk for life insurers incorporates not only the potential variability of investment return, but also the possibilities of inadequate product pricing and mismatched assets and liabilities. **Immunization** is the practice of structuring assets and liabilities so that a change in interest rates will affect asset and liability values equally such that surplus capital is unaffected.

Cash matching is a technique wherein a portfolio is constructed whose interest and principal payments exactly match a set of liability cash flows. Cash matching normally requires fixed and certain liabilities. As policyowner options have become widespread, life insurer liabilities have become far less fixed and certain, and thus the cash matching technique has become less useful.

With a bond dedication approach to ALM, an insurer maximizes the chances that investment yields are consistent with pricing assumptions and that solvency and profitability goals are achieved. **Bond dedication** is the informal allocation of the cash flows from a portfolio of bonds to the cash flows of a prescribed set of liabilities. The effect is that the relationship of asset and liability cash flows and values remains relatively constant through changing interest-rate environments. Ideally, future funds are locked in and fluctuating interest rates do not affect the expected cash flows.

Duration and convexity and their option-adjusted variants are discussed in depth in the chapter appendix. As noted there, duration can be thought of as the weighted average time to the cash flows of an asset or liability. Duration matching seeks to match the duration of the insurer's assets with the duration of its liabilities. It is used by many insurers to manage interest rate risk at the LOB level. It attempts to recognize and account for the fact that asset and liability cash flows are functions of interest rates and will not remain static as interest rates change over time.

Duration allows the financial manager to select assets and liabilities that immunize all or a portion of balance sheet surplus against interest rate risk by making the relative – although not absolute – values of assets and liabilities insensitive to interest rate changes. We begin with an examination of duration matching in the context of one product. We follow with a two-product case to illustrate the importance of product management in a portfolio context.

MATCHING AND IMMUNIZING A PORTFOLIO: ONE PRODUCT   Life insurers know that they face future cash payments to policyowners and beneficiaries. They want to match their asset cash flows to these payments. An example will illustrate the point. Assume XYZ Life's actuaries have concluded that its life insurance claims exactly five years hence will be $1,469,000. The company's chief financial officer (CFO) wishes to invest assets now so that XYZ will have exactly $1,469,000 in five years to honor its obligations to beneficiaries. The CFO calculates that, at 8.0 percent, the present value of those claims is $1,000,000. Current-issue five-year bonds pay an 8.0 percent annual coupon, and the current market yield for the bond is 8.0 percent. Thus, if $1,000,000 is invested in these bonds today, they should produce $1,469,000 in five years.

The total return on a bond is comprised of three components: (1) coupon payments, (2) interest earned on the coupon payments (reinvestment income), and

(3) proceeds from the redemption or sale of the bond. Thus, the three components of XYZ's income per $1,000 are as follows:

1. coupon payments equal to $400 (five annual coupons of $80 each),
2. reinvestment income equal to $69 (as the annual coupons are received, they can be reinvested at 8.0 percent, generating an additional $69 after five years), and
3. proceeds at redemption equal to $1,000, the bond maturity value.

If rates change, however, total return changes. Suppose that interest rates decline to 7.0 percent immediately after the bonds are acquired. What would be the total return? The $400 in coupons and the $1000 maturity value would be unaffected, but reinvestment income would fall to $60 from $69. Thus, if market interest rates fall, XYZ would find itself vulnerable. Because of reduced reinvestment income, total return would be about $9,000 less than expected ($9 x 1,000 bonds). This result would directly reduce XYZ's expected surplus capital by that amount.

Suppose XYZ's CFO applies the duration concept to the problem at hand: investing a sum of money whose total return over five years will be adequate to pay XYZ's fifth year claims while rendering the company invulnerable or immunized to a change in interest rates. If she invested XYZ's $1,000,000 in *six*-year bonds to fund the *fifth*-year claims, she would find that she could sell the bonds after five years with some confidence that the total return would be $1,469,000 whether there is an upward or downward shift in interest rates.

Consider the total returns produced by the six-year bonds (accumulated in five years) under different scenarios:

Cash Flows	Interest Rate Scenarios		
	Down to 7.0 percent	Stable at 8.0 percent	Up to 9.0 percent
1. Coupons	$400	$400	$400
2. Reinvestment Income	60	69	78
3. Bond Sale Proceeds	1,009*	1,000	991
Total Return after Five Years	$1,469	$1,469	$1,469

* At the end of five years, a cash flow of $1080 is due in one year (the last coupon of $80 and the redemption value). In other words, a cash flow of $1,080 is due in one year. With a market interest rate of 7.0 percent, the market value of the bond at year five is $1,080/1.07 = $1,009. Reverse logic applies to a rise in rates.

Thus, in every interest rate environment – down, stable, or up – the total five-year return should be $1,469. XYZ is immune from an upward or downward shift in market interest rates. (See, however, qualifications relating to convexity and the dynamic nature of duration below.)

MATCHING AND IMMUNIZING A PORTFOLIO: TWO OR MORE PRODUCTS   We now explore the immunization of two products.[3] The process provides insight into the interaction of different portfolios and how the risks in each portfolio are recognized together. Strictly matching each product fails to take advantage of one of the principal benefits of an ERM approach to financial management. The interaction is also one of the components of an economic capital model that can be tested stochastically.

The duration of a portfolio is the market-value weighted average of the duration of the individual assets and liabilities. In the formula below, w_{At} is the weighting (the value of asset t divided by the total value of assets), D_{At} is the duration of asset t, and D_A represents the duration of the portfolio of assets. Thus,

$$D_A = w_{A1}D_{A1} + w_{A2}D_{A2} + w_{A3}D_{A3} + ... + w_{An}D_{An}$$

$$= \sum_{t=1}^{n} w_{At}D_{At}$$

Similarly, w_{Lt} is the value of liability t divided by the total value of liabilities, D_{Lt} is the duration of liability t, and D_L represents the duration of the portfolio of liabilities. Thus,

$$D_L = w_{L1}D_{L1} + w_{L2}D_{L2} + w_{L3}D_{L3} + ... + w_{Ln}D_{Ln}$$

$$= \sum_{t=1}^{n} w_{Lt}D_{Lt}$$

Assume XYZ Life has issued two products: immediate annuities recorded as a $200 million liability with average duration of 6.3 years and guaranteed investment contracts (GICs) recorded as $1.4 billion with an average duration of 1.86 years. It has $1.0 billion of corporate bonds, $900 million of government bonds, and $200 million of mortgages with durations of 2.0, 4.73, and 7.2 years, respectively. The duration of the asset portfolio is calculated as follows:

Asset	Market Value (000s)	Market Value/ Portfolio Market Value	Asset Duration	Weighted Duration
Corporate Bonds	$1,000	0.4762	2.0	0.9524
Government Bonds	$900	0.4286	4.73	2.0271
Mortgages	$200	0.0952	7.2	0.6854
Total Portfolio	$2,100	1.0000		3.665 yrs

The duration of the liability portfolio is calculated as follows:

Liability	Market Value (000s)	Market Value/ Portfolio Market Value	Liability Duration	Weighted Duration
Annuities	$200	0.125	6.3	0.7875
GICs	$1,400	0.875	1.86	1.6275
Total Portfolio	$1,600	1.000		2.415 yrs

We can use the durations of the portfolios of assets and liabilities to estimate the effects of a change in interest rates on their values using the following formulae:

$$\Delta A = -D_A \left(\frac{\Delta r}{1+r} \right) A$$

and

$$\Delta L = -D_L \left(\frac{\Delta r}{1+r} \right) L$$

They measure the sensitivity of asset and liability values to changes in interest rates by applying D, the *duration* term, and the percentage change in interest rates to asset and liability values. D is an elasticity measure that predicts the dollar change in asset or liability values with respect to the interest rate change.

Recall that surplus capital equals assets less liabilities, so that estimates for changes in the values of assets and liabilities can be used to estimate the impact of a change in interest rates on the value of a company's surplus capital. The above two formulae can be combined to evaluate their joint impact on surplus capital. Thus,

$$\Delta S = -\left(D_A - D_L k \right) \left(\frac{\Delta r}{1+r} \right) A$$

where k is an adjustment term equal to total liabilities divided by total assets, reflecting the leveraging of surplus capital.

From the above formula, it can be seen that the effect of interest rate changes on the market value of an insurer's surplus capital decomposes into three effects:

1. *The leverage-adjusted duration gap [D_A - $D_L k$].* This gap is measured in years and reflects the degree of duration mismatch in the product portfolio. The larger the gap in absolute terms, the more exposed the insurer is to interest rate shocks.
2. *The size of the interest rate shock [$\Delta r/(1 + r)$].* The larger the shock, the greater the insurer's exposure.
3. *The size of the insurer [A].* The larger the scale of the insurer, the larger the dollar size of the potential net worth exposure from any given interest rate shock.

Thus, we can express the exposure of an insurer's net worth to interest rate movements as follows:

$$\Delta S = - \text{[Adjusted duration gap]} \times \text{[Interest rate shock]} \times \text{[Asset size]}$$

Where the duration of assets and the adjusted duration of liabilities are identical, the adjusted duration gap is zero, and a change in market interest rates will leave insurer surplus capital unaffected. A portfolio is said to be **duration matched** when changes in its asset values will be exactly offset by changes in liability values when market interest rates change.

Recall the balance sheet for XYZ Life:

Assets (000s)		Liabilities (000s)	
Corporate Bonds	$1,000	Annuities	$200
Government Bonds	900	GICs	1,400
Mortgages	200		—
		Total Liabilities	$1,600
		Surplus Capital (Equity)	500
Total Assets	$2,100	Total Liabilities and Surplus Capital	$2,100

Assume interest rates are at 9.0 percent and increase at all levels by 1.0 percent. In this situation, the assumed increase in interest rates will cause the value of surplus capital to fall by $35.18, calculated as follows:

$$\Delta S = -\left(D_A - D_L k\right)\left(\frac{\Delta r}{1+r}\right) A$$

$$\Delta S = -\left(3.67 - \left(2.42\right)\left(\frac{\$1,600}{\$2,100}\right)\right)\left(\frac{0.01}{1.09}\right)\left(\$2,100\right)$$

$$\Delta S = -\$35.18$$

Thus, the insurer would suffer a decline in its surplus capital of greater than 7.0 percent from such a change. XYZ is not immunized against changes in market interest rates. XYZ can move toward an immunized position by undertaking one of the following strategies:

- Decreasing the duration of its assets to equal the adjusted duration of liabilities (1.844). This could be accomplished, for example, by acquiring shorter term assets or variable rate assets.
- Increasing the adjusted duration of its liabilities to equal the duration of assets (3.67). This could be accomplished, for example, by issuing longer term GICs.
- Changing its capital structure to increase k. This could be accomplished by allowing surplus capital to decline, for example, by paying higher shareholder dividends.

Note that a combined immunization strategy can be accomplished by (1) managing the asset or liability duration of either product or both; (2) selling an entirely new product; or (3) adjusting its financing arrangements. The process reveals precisely the sort of information necessary to build an economic capital model that takes account of correlations and to manage a company in a holistic ERM manner.

In theory, the entire balance sheet of a company could be combined into one duration matching model. In practice, life insurer asset and liability portfolios are exceptionally complex. Balance sheet duration comparisons can be helpful as a rough measure of interest rate exposure, but using a deterministic duration matching model as the principal company-level risk management tool is usually impractical. Duration nevertheless is an important concept for measuring the sensitivity of surplus capital to interest rate changes at the LOB level for the purposes of financial simulation.

The simple duration model presented here describes the basic procedure for using duration to immunize an insurer's surplus capital. As discussed more fully in the appendix, duration changes dynamically, portfolios need to be rebalanced continuously, and the convexity property means surplus changes due to large interest rate changes are under-predicted by the duration model.

HEDGING: REDUCING ASSET-LIABILITY MISMATCH
The principal asset-liability mismatch risks are interest rate risk and equity market risk. Interest rate risk exists primarily in general account life and annuity products.

Equity market risk exists primarily in separate account variable life insurance and annuities with guaranteed minimum death benefit (GMDB) provisions that create a potential death benefit liability when policyowner accounts are less than premiums invested, and with guaranteed minimum withdrawal benefits (GMWB) that depend on policyowner account performance driven largely by stock fund investments. Equity market risk also exists in equity-indexed life insurance and annuity products.

Life insurers use hedging strategies to reduce ALR mismatch. Hedge capital generates cash flows to life insurers when specified events occur, reducing variance and substituting for and protecting surplus capital that otherwise would be lost. Hedging strategies can address the actuarial risks associated with mortality, morbidity, and longevity as well as financial risks. Derivatives generally are limited to capital market financial risks, while reinsurance can address both areas. (As we will see below with securitization, capital market opportunities in actuarial risk are developing.)

Hedging strategies include the purchase of reinsurance and derivatives. Reinsurance-provided capital market hedges are packaged and managed by the reinsurer, and the ceding insurer relies on its expertise and credit. Derivatives, available in several forms as discussed in Chapter 9, are packaged and managed in the capital markets. The use of reinsurance is equivalent to "buying" a complete hedging solution while derivatives are the components of a hedging strategy that is "built." The advantage of derivatives is the ability to customize hedge solutions; an advantage of reinsurance is simplicity in implementation and management. Counterparty risk exists in both cases: reinsurers, as with insurers, might become insolvent, and extreme economic conditions could affect actual performance in the derivatives markets.

Reinsurance and derivatives carry risks not present in ordinary investments. First, *basis risk* exists with all derivatives and with some reinsurance solutions. **Basis risk** arises because of the possibility that offsetting investments or reinsurance in a hedging strategy will not experience precisely identical inverse price changes because the notional amount or timing of cash flows of risk management assets are not precisely matched to the assets or liabilities hedged. This risk flows from the facts that derivative payoffs or reinsurance benefits may be based on market indices or other benchmarks, while the risks insurers hedge arise from their own assets and liabilities. The two ordinarily do not coincide perfectly.

Second, reinsurance and derivatives markets are not perfectly predictable. Derivatives costs vary with market forces so the future costs of hedging are uncertain, and longer term derivatives are relatively new and their developing markets introduce uncertainty not only as to their future cost but also as to whether they will actually be available. Reinsurance by contrast often can be acquired on a long-term basis at a relatively predictable cost, however some reinsurance solutions may not exist and the capacity and willingness of reinsurance companies to accept some risks – particularly variable annuities – has varied over time.

Accounting treatment of hedges can also differ. Under GAAP, liabilities are not recorded at fair value while capital market investments are so treated, resulting in volatility of reported surplus. Chapter 13 described optional provisions of FAS 159 that relate to the financial reporting of derivatives when used as hedging instruments. Reinsurance accounting is more stable. In practice, some companies find that the best solution lies in a combination of reinsurance and derivatives-based hedging.

HEDGING INTEREST RATE RISK WITH DERIVATIVES: INTEREST RATE OPTIONS This section presents a conceptually simple example of the use of interest rate options to expand the positive moneyness range of the short straddle position of a life insurer. These options substitute for risk capital by creating cash flows in the event of extraordinary interest rate movements, thus eliminating, within limits, some or all of the impact of short straddle losses on an insurer's surplus capital. The cash flows are calculated by reference to (1) a specified interest rate index and (2) the value of capital hedged, called the **notional amount**.

We examine results of the simultaneous purchase of an interest rate cap and an interest rate floor on the same interest rate index. An **interest rate cap** pays when an interest rate index exceeds a specified rate during a specified period. An **interest rate floor** pays when an interest rate index falls below a specified rate during a specified period. The specified rate is often the *London Interbank Offering Rate* (LIBOR). An interest rate collar's payoff mirrors the short straddle exposure. It expires without value if interest rates remain stable, but pays when interest rates move significantly up or down. They pay as a series of monthly options termed *caplets* and *floorlets*. Thus, with the following variables:

N = *the notional amount*
L = *LIBOR*
K = *the strike price interest rate*

the caplet and floorlet payoffs are:

$$P_{cap} = N\left(\frac{Days}{365}\right)\left(Max(L-K,0)\right)$$

$$P_{floor} = N\left(\frac{Days}{365}\right)\left(Max(K-L,0)\right)$$

An example will illustrate the concept. Assume that company *Good Life* wishes to hedge its interest rate exposure as presented in Figure 14-6. The market interest rate is 2.5 percent and *Good Life* believes that an interest rate range of 2.0 percent to 3.0 percent is consistent with its risk tolerance, management philosophy, and the liability properties of the portfolio. It is concerned about the impact to surplus capital of rate movements that reach beyond this range.

Good Life can effectively expand the positive moneyness range of its short straddle position from the segment A-B to the segment A'-B' by hedging. It purchases options with a cap strike price of 3.0 percent and a floor strike price of 2.0 percent. The expansion of the positive moneyness range is represented by the segments from A to A' and from B to B'. *Good Life* effectively expands the range of acceptable interest rate movements from the interval 2.0 – 3.0 percent to the interval 1.75 – 3.25 percent by substituting hedge capital for surplus capital.

Figure 14-6

**Expanding the Range of Acceptable Interest Rate Movements
with Interest Rate Options:
Current Rate 2.5%, Cap Strike Price 3.0%, Floor Strike Price 2.0%**

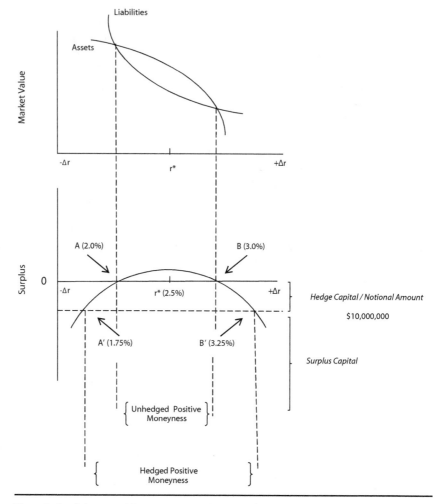

The unhedged short straddle position is "in the money" in the interest rate range from points A (2.0%) to B (3.0%). The hedging strategy expands positive moneyness to the range from points A' (1.75%) to B' (3.25%).

If LIBOR six months hence is 3.25 percent, the floor would expire without value and the payoff for the cap would be

$$P_{cap} = \frac{183}{366} \left(10,000,000\right) \left(Max\left(0.0325 - 0.03, 0\right)\right)$$
$$= 12,500$$

The $12,500 payoff to *Good Life* indemnifies it for what it would have lost without the options and protects its surplus capital to this extent. Recalling our earlier discussion, it effectively functions as risk capital to provide solvency assurance to policyowners and insures shareholders' expected returns in the presence of unexpected losses. The addition of hedge capital to surplus capital increases total effective capital and expands the range of interest rates that is suitable to *Good Life*'s liability portfolio. As with duration matching, hedging is a dynamic process and must be repositioned periodically.

Interest rate risk that cannot be controlled or hedged is retained. When the duration of assets exceeds the duration of liabilities, a company's surplus capital is vulnerable to a rise in interest rates. Conversely, when a company's adjusted liability duration exceeds its asset duration, falling interest rates could cause a loss of surplus. When a company's target market expects interest rates to rise, a company will be able to sell more attractive products if its asset duration exceeds its liability duration, and, the more severe the mismatch, the more attractive the products can be.

As a result, competitive pressures will normally require companies intentionally to mismatch the duration of their assets and liabilities and to assume some asset-liability matching risk to be competitive. In this example, *Good Life* projects a remaining exposure to surplus capital under scenarios where the market rate is less than 1.75 percent or greater than 3.25 percent. The interest rate risk that remains unmatched and unhedged requires an appropriate allocation of EC reflecting the retained risk.

HEDGING EQUITY MARKET RISK FOR AN EQUITY-INDEXED ANNUITY   Recall from Chapter 6 that an equity-indexed annuity (EIA) credits the policyowner account value with the greater of a minimum guarantee return and a guaranteed equity index return based on the performance of a stock market index. This section illustrates how hedging is used as a risk management tool for such a product. For simplicity, we assume a single premium EIA with no cap on its maximum performance credit. Determining returns to the account value requires the following:

- amount of the single premium,
- index term applied to the index-linked interest and guaranteed return,
- minimum rate of return,
- specified index, and
- participation rate (the percentage of the index gain credited to the account).

The account value is calculated then as:

$$AV_n = Max(Minimum\,Guarantee, Guaranteed\,Equity\,Index\,Return)$$

so

$$AV_n = Max\left[p(1 + gr)^n, p + p\left(\frac{Index_n - Index_0}{Index_0}\right)PR\right]$$

where:
p = the amount of the single premium
n = the guarantee period
gr = the minimum guarantee return
$Index_0$ = the value of the specified index at purchase
PR = the participation rate

The company can match its assets and its contingent liabilities by replicating the account value crediting obligation with a combination of a zero coupon bond (or bond portfolio) and equity index options. The premium is applied to three purposes as follows:

- *Minimum Guarantee:* To provide the minimum guarantee contract value, the insurer purchases a zero coupon bond whose proceeds at the end of the index term will amount to the minimum guarantee value. The guaranteed return offered will be less than market rates, so the purchase price of the bond will be less than the single premium.
- *Guaranteed Equity Index Return:* The insurer hedges future index increases by purchasing index call options to provide the guaranteed equity index return as stipulated in the contract. If the index does not increase, the options will be worthless, but the future value of the bond alone will exactly match the minimum guarantee crediting obligation.
- *Spread* The remaining amount of the premium is available to the insurer to pay expenses, capital costs, and earn a profit. Clearly, the amount of the single premium must exceed the cost of the bond and the equity options for the product to be viable.

As each guarantee period ends, the new guarantee period is hedged with a new zero coupon bond/equity index option position.

Hedging a VA with a GMDB is more complex than hedging an EIA because of basis risk. When the EIA is hedged, the insurer purchases options on the index specified in the contract; in the case of the VA, there is no perfectly matched option to buy, so there is always a risk that the assets hedged will not exactly match the policyowners' separate account assets. The potential VA liability is also more complex because the liability incorporates a mortality element: the VA liability arises only if the account value is down *and* the annuitant dies.

CAPITAL ALLOCATION

In this section, we evaluate the efficiency of an insurer's use of its capital by examining methods for identifying and ranking projects that create value. We identify a life insurer's sources of financing, its WACC, and the use of risk-adjusted return on capital to evaluate the financial performance of existing and proposed projects. We also explore the capital management possibilities in securitization.

EQUITY, DEBT, RESERVE, AND HEDGE FINANCING

As with all corporations, life insurers are financed with debt (e.g., funds borrowed from bondholders or banks) and equity (funds invested in the company by its shareholder owners). (Another potentially important source of external financing is surplus notes, as discussed in Chapter 13.) The essential nature of a life insurer is such that its most important source of financing is its customers via the establishment and maintenance of policy reserves, its largest liability. Thus, an insurer's product line largely determines its financing.

The nature of life insurer operations also creates other important sources of financing that we earlier termed hedge capital, the two most important being reinsurance and derivatives. We can think of hedge capital as insurance for insurers, which serves as a substitute for risk capital and reduces the variability of earnings. As discussed in the context of the short straddle hedge above, an interest rate option might pay a sum to the insurer if market interest rates move dramatically, or a reinsurance arrangement might reimburse the insurer for unexpected claims.

Hedging with risk management assets allows an insurer to leverage its existing capital. Derivatives in particular allow dramatic leverage. The high degree of leverage makes derivatives very risky when considered in isolation; however, when used as a hedging tool, their contribution to a portfolio usually reduces risk. However, hedging carries a form of credit risk. In both derivative and reinsurance arrangements, there exists counterparty risk – the possibility that the party or their guarantor (such as a bank or clearing company) on the other side of the transaction, the so-called counterparty, will default. It is analogous to the default risk of a bond.

THE COST OF CAPITAL

To identify and rank projects that create value for the firm, we must understand the firm's cost of capital against which project returns are assessed. We know that the cost of debt capital is the interest rate the market demands for purchasing the company's bonds or other obligations, and that the cost of equity capital is determined by the rate of return investors require to hold the company's shares. Generally, the total cost of capital to a firm is the weighted average of these two sources. Thus, the weighted average cost of capital is:

$$WACC = \frac{(Equity)(k_{equity})}{V} + \frac{(Debt)(k_{debt})}{V}$$

where k is the required market rate of return, and V is the total value of debt and equity.

Because insurers have additional sources of capital (e.g., surplus notes and reserves) at different costs, we expand and generalize the formula to:

$$WACC = \frac{\sum_i^n (k_i)(V_i)}{\sum_i^n V_i}$$

where n is the number of sources and, for the ith source, k_i is the required return and V_i the value of the financing. The cost of debt and surplus notes is straightforward and is measured by the interest rate payable. The cost of equity can be estimated with pricing models such as the CAPM or arbitrage pricing theory (APT), as discussed in the chapter appendix.

Measuring the costs of premium-financed reserves and hedge capital is more complex. Companies use a variety of methods. We use transfer pricing as a measure because it is simple and illustrative of the important concepts. **Transfer pricing** is the pricing of goods and services between related parties. We can consider this method as the insurer's investment division borrowing funds from the insurance division and paying interest for the borrowed funds. The rate paid must be sufficient to satisfy the insurance division's crediting obligations to policyowners and so the investment division must earn more than the crediting rate to produce a net interest spread.

The total value of financial capital is thus:

$$V = equity + debt + reserves$$

And the life insurer's weighted average cost of capital is:

$$WACC = \frac{(Equity)\,(k_{equity})}{V} + \frac{(Debt)\,(k_{debt})}{V} + \frac{(Reserves)(k_{transfer\,price})}{V}$$

An example will illustrate the concept. Assume ABC has a cost of equity of 20 percent and of debt of 10 percent; that its estimated transfer price of reserves is 7.0 percent. Further assume that ABC life is financed thus:

Assets (000s)		Liabilities (000s)	
Investments	$3,400	Reserves	$2,000
		Debt	400
		Total Liabilities	$2,400
		Surplus Capital (Equity)	1,000
Total Assets	$3,400	Total Liabilities and Equity	$3,400

The insurer's WACC is then:

$$WACC = \frac{1,000,000(0.20)}{3,400,000} + \frac{400,000(0.10)}{3,400,000} + \frac{2,000,000(0.07)}{3,400,000} = 11.18\%$$

As it costs ABC 11.18 percent to finance its activities, it must earn a return in excess of 11.18 percent on its projects to create value.

CAPITAL ALLOCATION

An important use of the WACC in corporate finance is the allocation of capital to projects that create value. **Capital allocation** is a procedure that assigns scarce capital to projects selected from among the set of all possible projects for purposes of maximizing shareholder value. It has special dimensions in the context of life insurer financial management. Industrial firms allocate the capital required to manufacture and sell their products. Similarly, a life insurer must allocate operating capital sufficient to cover the typical direct costs of manufacturing its projects: reserves, direct expenses, and an appropriate portion of general expenses. Life insurers must also take risk capital and its costs into account.

Capital allocation decisions should therefore take account of both external and internal costs of risk. External costs are reflected in the WACC; internal costs are reflected in EC. A risk-adjusted performance measurement approach is required. Risk-adjusted return on capital offers such an approach.

Risk-adjusted return on capital (RAROC) is a project's net economic income divided by its economic investment. Many interpretations and a variety of names attach to this concept, but the general theme is the same. RAROC takes account of risk, risk capital, and the costs of risk capital by (1) defining its investment as the attributed portion of firm level EC and (2) treating the cost of EC as an expense charge against income. For our purposes, we define a project's RAROC for a given measurement period as:

$$RAROC = \frac{p + i - l - e - (EC)(WACC)}{EC}$$

Where:

p = premiums
i = investment income
l = losses
e = expenses
EC = economic capital attributable to the product or project
$WACC$ = weighted average cost of capital

The term $(EC)(WACC)$ represents the cost of EC attributable to the project. If the RAROC of a proposed project exceeds its WACC, the project creates value and should be tentatively accepted. Alternative projects with greater RAROCs should be accepted first. If the RAROC is less than the WACC, proposed and existing projects should be rejected, repriced, sold, or abandoned.

As economic conditions and management decisions evolve over time, the issue may arise whether a life insurer should retain or dispose of a particular line of business. A principal motivation for converting existing business into current capital exists when its risk properties fit better and may be worth more in the product portfolio of another market participant than it is to the insurer. Portfolio choice theory can be applied to the insurer's product portfolio in a similar manner as it is applied to a portfolio of stocks. An insurer's business offerings may evolve in a way that the product's covariance properties relative to the rest of the product portfolio do not produce acceptable benefits of diversification. Also, new business opportunities may offer a better return so that capital from the disposition of an existing product line can be redeployed at a higher RAROC.

In such cases, the insurer might consider selling the line of business outright to another market participant. A line of business can also be divested via assumption reinsurance that transfers all assets and liabilities associated with a specific block of business to a reinsurer, which often requires policyowner approval.

SECURITIZATION IN CAPITAL MANAGEMENT

It is also possible to effectively dispose of business lines in parts. **Securitization** generally is the selling of asset-backed bonds that will be repaid regularly from the cash flows of specified assets backing the securities. Life insurers can sell securities or reinsurance obligations supported by the cash flows from defined blocks of business or other assets. It is a borrowing transaction for the insurer as in a bond transaction, but the security for the loan is limited to the specified asset cash flows rather than the general credit of the company

Securitization generally is the process of monetizing the present value of future cash flows. Life insurance transactions involve liability cash flows as well, so the asset being monetized is the excess of reserves over actual liabilities as they are realized; the asset therefore is the future profits or surplus "embedded" in the reserves. Life insurers may wish to monetize future profits, or embedded value (see below), to increase capital available for other projects or to reduce their overall cost of capital.

Embedded value securitizations are typically structured by (1) creating a special purpose vehicle reinsurer (SPVR) incorporated as a reinsurance company, (2) writing a reinsurance treaty between the securitizing insurer (or reinsurer) and the SPVR wherein the SPVR transfers funds to the insurer and the insurer agrees to repay the SPVR as the profits are realized, and (3) financing the SPVR with the purchase of its securities by investors (e.g., via surplus notes or preferred shares). Investors often are attracted to the opportunity to participate in an asset class whose risk is less correlated with interest rate risk of other fixed income investments. Because of the novelty of life insurer securitizations, transactions to date have usually required third party financial guaranty insurance. The proceeds of the securitization are available to the insurer for other investments. Figure 14-7 presents a visual representation of ebmedded value securitization. In practice, most value securitizations have been done with respect to aggregations of policies assembled by reinsurers from ceding companies.

Figure 14-7   Hypothetical Embedded Value Securitization Structure

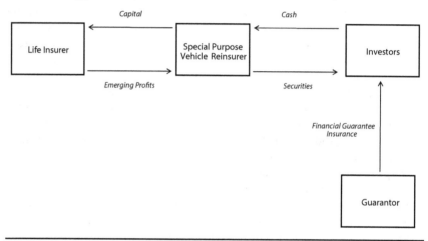

Life insurance related securitizations slowed at the onset of the 2008-2009 financial crisis but are originating again at this writing as capital markets become more familiar with them. In addition to securitizations based on cash flows from blocks of business, others have been based on the cash flows associated with:

- funding for reserves on term insurance and UL with secondary guarantees,
- mortality and longevity risk transfer,
- pure asset holdings such as mortgages and private placements,
- viaticals and life settlements.

RISK-ADJUSTED MEASUREMENT OF FIRM-LEVEL FINANCIAL PERFORMANCE

We discussed the risk-adjusted measure of financial performance for product lines (RAROC) above. In this section, we discuss risk-adjusted performance measurement at the firm level. Traditional measures of corporate performance such as *earnings, return on equity,* and *return on assets* are used in the financial analysis of corporate performance generally and in the life insurance industry. In the context of life insurer performance, however, these terms lack a rigorous meaning because they have no significance apart from the accounting conventions that define them, typically SAP or GAAP. These conventions are also of little value in terms of informing us about ALR and risk across different product and service lines (among other areas). We discussed the limitations of these accounting systems in the context of the movement toward risk-based, economic capital approaches by regulators and rating agencies in Chapter 13.

Market consistent embedded value (MCEV), a related EC-based performance measurement metric, measures the economic value of an insurer's present net worth and its in-force business based on the actual or estimated values of assets and liabilities, as follows:

MCEV = Net Worth + Value of In-Force Business

We define net worth as assets less reserves, with assets based on market values, if available, and with liabilities and other items whose values cannot be observed in liquid markets based on realistic economic assumptions. We define the value of in-force business as the discounted value of future profits on existing business less the economic cost of capital (including risk capital). A variety of discounting approaches is advocated by practitioners, but the important elements are the reflection of risk in the discount rate or cash flow projection and the clarity of assumptions.

MCEV is oriented to the viewpoint of shareholders and based on economic, real world assumptions as opposed to the industry benchmarks of SAP and GAAP. Thus, it is risk-based and reflects risk-based EC concepts in the valuation of reserves and the cost of capital. The full economic or enterprise value of a company also includes the value of future business – a function of distribution and other factors that are not easily valued from period to period.

MCEV can be helpfully decomposed into performance components as follows:

> Beginning MCEV
> +   any changes due to refinement of the EC model
> +   any changes due to restated economic assumptions
> +   expected return on the previous year's in-force value
> +   value of new business
> -   shareholder dividends
> +   new financing capital
>
> =
>
> Ending MCEV

By observing changes in MCEV, insurers can capture important indicators of performance during the measurement period as well as future directions. Figure 14-8 presents a graphical representation of a hypothetical movement in MCEV.

MCEV was widely adopted by European life insurers several years ago and often is reported to shareholders via annual reports. Its adoption in the U.S. and other countries has been slower but continues to grow.

CONCLUSIONS

The financial management of non-financial companies is driven by the compensation of shareholders for bearing risk in the capital markets according to CAPM concepts. Life insurers are different. Their financial management requirements cannot be completely derived from CAPM concepts. Solvency is the primary concern of customers and regulators, so the relevance of the reduction of specific, individual company risk is limited. Life insurers must hold surplus capital explicitly required by regulators (regulatory capital) and implicitly required by market forces (rating agency capital) as well as the insurer's own tolerance for risk (economic capital). Specific risk incorporates asset-liability risks and is managed with asset-liability matching and hedging methods. The costs of capital (operating, reserve, and risk) should be accounted for in evaluating the financial performance of a life insurer and its projects.

Figure 14-8   **Hypothetical Decomposition of Movement in MCEV and Value Added in One Measurement Period**

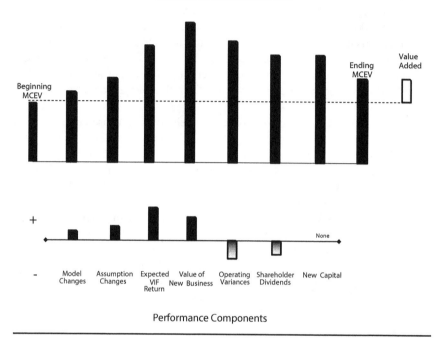

Performance Components

ENDNOTES

1   Robert C. Merton and Andre Perold, "Theory of Risk Capital in Financial Firms," *Journal of Applied Corporate Finance,* Volume 6, Issue 3 Fall 1993.

2   This section draws from Anthony M. Santomero and David F. Babbel, *Financial Markets, Instruments, and Institutions* (Chicago: Irwin, 1997), pp 646-647.

3   This discussion draws from and follows partially that presented by Anthony Saunders, *Financial Institutions Management,* 2nd ed. (Chicago: Irwin, 1997) Chapter 7.

Appendix 14A:
Principles of Finance

This appendix offers background information for aiding understanding of the concepts presented in this and other chapters. It also presents additional information that extends understanding of those concepts. In many cases, we provide endnote references to some historically significant, trailblazing papers. All the concepts and developments are discussed and explained in standard finance texts.

An **arbitrage** opportunity exists when an investor can simultaneously buy an asset at one price, sell it at a higher price, and earn a risk-free profit. The buy and sell transactions may not involve the same asset – assets or combinations of assets with identical cash flows offer the same arbitrage opportunity. Finance theory asserts such opportunities cannot endure in public financial markets – a **no arbitrage condition**.

The **efficient markets hypothesis** asserts that all public information is available to all investors, the market price is the best estimate of true value, and no individual investor can earn superior risk-adjusted returns.[1] Any arbitrage opportunities immediately disappear as all rational investors would seek "free lunch" returns. The buy and sell behavior of the arbitrageurs impacts price so that an equilibrium price obtains in all markets.

Valuation theory is based on the assumption that there are no arbitrage opportunities and that the **law of one price** holds: an asset (or assets with identical cash flows) will trade at the same price in all markets. Despite some evidence that markets are not entirely efficient and that arbitrage opportunities do occasionally arise, the one price assumption is useful most of the time.

The present value concept is based on the simple observation that any sum received in the future is less valuable than the same sum received currently because, if received currently, the sum can be invested at interest. The fundamental principal of valuation is *discounted cash flow* (DCF) analysis and the determination of net present value. *Net present value* (NPV) is the sum of the values for all cash flows (CF_t), both positive and negative, discounted to the date of valuation. In this manner, the cash flow properties of any asset, project, or company can be reduced to a current value. The pricing methodologies for assets and liabilities discussed below are adaptations of DCF analysis.

For most commercial corporations, the appropriate discount rate is the weighted average cost of capital (WACC) reflecting the returns investors demand for a corporation's stock and bonds, as discussed in the main body of this chapter. The discount rate reflects two properties associated with each cash flow: (1) a time value of money component or the *risk free rate* typically associated with the

FUNDAMENTAL ASSUMPTIONS OF FINANCE

government bond of similar maturity and (2) a *risk premium component* reflecting the uncertainty associated with the cash flow. The general formula for NPV is:

$$NPV = \sum_{t=1}^{N} \frac{CF_t}{(1+i)^t}$$

DCF forms the basis for the valuation of bonds, stocks, options, mortgages, and real estate. The following sections present the application of DCF analysis to these assets and explore the sensitivity of their values.

CASH FLOWS WITH OPTIONS

The uncertainty of future cash flows is accounted for in the selection of the discount rate in the basic DCF model. Another aspect of uncertainty is exhibited when parties to a contract have optional rights, and in these cases a simple adjustment of the discount rate is less useful. Of particular importance to life insurers are (1) the cash surrender, policy loan, flexible premium, and benefit rights granted to policyowners; (2) the prepayment rights of bond issuers and property owners whose mortgage loans are pooled in mortgage-backed securities; and (3) the value of derivatives acquired by insurers to hedge risk.

Two prominent methods are used for valuing options on traded securities. The *binomial tree pricing option* model values an option in succeeding periods under different stock price assumptions. The *Black-Scholes* model gives a differential equation that the price of an option must satisfy for an underlying asset.[2] Each makes use of the law of one price by creating cash flows equivalent to the option cash flows through the theoretical purchase of a combination of the underlying stock and the risk free asset (a *replicating portfolio*).

The mathematics of option pricing theory are beyond the scope of this text. However, the required inputs reveal the important determinants of value:

- probability the option will be "in the money,"
- time to maturity,
- current price,
- strike price,
- risk free rate, and
- volatility of the underlying security.

Insurance liabilities generally are not traded like securities, and trading transactions that do take place are generally private reinsurance transactions. Nevertheless, actuaries do make use of option pricing theories in estimating the value of liabilities. Policyowner and borrower option behavior is estimated in probabilistic economic capital models and in option adjustments to duration and convexity measurements (discussed below).

MODERN PORTFOLIO THEORY

As noted in Chapter 9, the benefits of diversification apply in many aspects of life insurer management. **Modern portfolio theory** (MPT) asserts the important *relevant risk* of any one asset or liability is the incremental risk (due to positive or negative covariance) that it brings to a diversified portfolio of other assets or liabilities.[3] If the incremental risk is not perfectly correlated to the risk of the portfolio, total portfolio risk is always less than the risk of the asset or liability considered in isolation. The concepts apply to the diversification of mortality and morbidity risk, to the diversification of credit risk in a bond portfolio, and to the risk of various products or services in an insurer's line of business portfolio. It is most prominently applied to portfolios of stocks. The theory was first proposed in Harry Markowitz's seminal 1952 article "Portfolio Selection."

THE RISK-RETURN TRADE-OFF

All financial intermediaries seek an adequate return on equity.[4] To do this, management focuses on two features of performance: return and risk. The expected return of an investment increases as its expected risk increases. The financial success of the firm is dependent on how well management balances these conflicting goals; they seek an adequate return on equity while limiting the insurer's exposure to risks that might destroy equity.

Behind this well understood maxim resides a host of finance concepts. We explore some of them here. Note that the focus is on *expected* returns, for no one can know what *actual* returns will be. Figure 14A-1 illustrates the concept.

The Relationship between Risk and Expected Return   **Figure 14A-1**

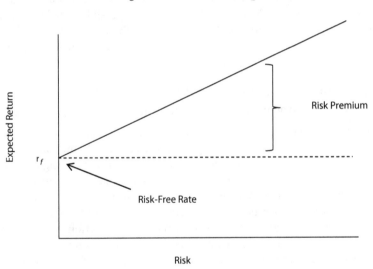

The expected return of an investment can be decomposed into the **risk free rate** associated with an asset assumed to be default free such as a government bond and a **risk premium** that reflects the unique risk of the investment.

EXPECTED RETURN DEFINED AND MEASURED

To achieve acceptable returns, management must be concerned with both the asset and liability sides of the balance sheet. For life insurers, liabilities arise principally in the form of deposit liabilities (policy reserves), which, in turn, flow from selling insurance policies. Premiums are the largest component of life insurer financing. If prices are set too low, the insurer, in effect, is paying too much for its financing, thus depressing returns. On the asset side, loans and other primary securities similarly must be acquired at a price that achieves an adequate return, taking into consideration the possibilities of defaults. The key to acceptable financial performance is, therefore, the spread between what the insurer earns on its assets and what it must pay for its funds (equity, debt, and insurance liabilities).

Expected benefits or returns come in the form of cash flows. Accurately measuring expected future cash flows is not easy in a world of uncertainty. To illustrate: assume ABC Life Insurer is considering offering a new annuity product that will cost $10 million to launch, with future cash flows depending on the state of the economy, as estimated in Table 14A-1.

Table 14A-1	Measuring ABC Life's Expected Returns			
State of the Economy	Probability of State	Project Cash Flow (000s)	Percentage Returns (CashFlow÷Investment)
Recession	20%	$1,000	10%
Moderate Growth	30%	$1,200	12%
Strong Growth	50%	$1,400	14%

In any given year, the investment could produce any one of three possible cash flows depending on the state of the economy. The expected value of the cash flow is simply the sum of the weighted average of the possible cash flow outcomes multiplied by the probabilities of the occurrence of the various states of the economy $[P(state_t)]$. Thus, the expected cash flow, ECF, may be calculated as follows:

$$ECF = P(state_t)(CF_t)$$

For this simple example, therefore, the expected cash flow is:

$$ECF = (0.2)(\$1,000,000) + (0.3)(\$1,200,000) + (0.5)(\$1,400,000) = \$1,260,000$$

In addition to computing an expected cash return from an investment, we can also calculate an expected rate of return earned on the $10 million investment. Similar to the expected cash flow, the expected rate of return is a weighted average of all the possible returns, weighted by the probability that each return will occur. The last column in Table 14A-1 shows the rate of return for each state of the economy. The reader might verify that the weighted average is 12.6 percent.

If we were investigating the expected return of a portfolio of investments, we would simply weight each investment's expected return by its share of total investment. Thus, assume that an insurer held one-third of its portfolio in the above investment whose expected return was 12.6 percent, one-sixth in a bond whose return was 6.0 percent, and the balance in a security whose expected return was 10.0 percent. The portfolio's expected return, therefore, is 10.2 percent – the weighted average of the individual returns – calculated as follows:

$$[(1/3 \times 0.126) + (1/6 \times 0.06) + (1/2 \times 0.10)] = 10.2 \text{ percent}$$

The general formula for n securities is

$$r = \sum_{i=1}^{n} (w_i)(r_i)$$

where

r = the expected return on the portfolio,
w_i = proportion invested in security i, and
r_i = expected return on security i.

RISK DEFINED AND MEASURED

As we saw in Chapter 9, risks can be classified and managed in several ways. Additionally, risk carries multiple meanings. For purposes of financial management, we limit our attention to the financial meaning of risk, which is variability of future cash flows. As discussed in the chapter text, other concepts of risk may be more relevant to life insurers. The wider the range of possible events that can occur, the greater the risk. A common quantitative measure of risk is standard deviation. The **standard deviation** is the square root of the variance. **Variance** is the weighted average squared deviations of each possible return from the expected return. Thus, we calculate the standard deviation as follows:

$$\sigma = \sqrt{\sum_{i=1}^{n} (r_i - \bar{r})^2 P(r_i)}$$

Where:

n = number of possible outcomes or different rates of return on an investment,

r_i = the value of the ith possible rate of return,

$\bar{r}$ = the expected value of the rates of return, and

$P(r_i)$ = the probability that the ith outcome or return will occur.

The standard deviation is a useful measure of risk, especially for distributions of returns that are normally distributed. With normal distributions, we know that two-thirds of the time an event will fall within one standard deviation of the expected value. We know also that it will fall within two standard deviations 95 percent of the time and within three standard deviations 99 percent of the time. Thus, as between two investments or projects having the same expected returns, we would prefer the one with the lower standard deviation (risk). Similarly, as between two projects with the same standard deviations, we would select that with the higher return.

RISK AND DIVERSIFICATION

While the standard deviation is a useful measure of risk for an individual security, measures of variability also can be calculated for portfolios of securities. Returns on portfolios of securities are generally less volatile than returns for individual securities because diversification reduces risk. Diversification works because prices of different securities do not move exactly together. Stated differently, security prices are less than perfectly correlated.[5]

HOW DIVERSIFICATION REDUCES RISK   Figure 14A-2 illustrates how portfolio variability decreases as we add securities to a portfolio of common stocks. The decrease occurs because some of the volatility of the expected returns of each stock is unique to that stock, called **unique risk**. The unique risk of each stock is countered to some extent by the unique risk of other stocks, thus reducing overall risk. Unique risk derives from the uniqueness of each firm, perhaps including its (and its competitors) unique environment. However, in practice, it is almost impossible to eliminate portfolio risk completely, as stock prices tend to move together.

There is some risk – called *market* or *systematic* risk – that cannot be avoided, regardless of diversification. **Market risk** stems from the fact that all businesses are subject to broad societal influences and factors that have a tendency to move together. Investors, therefore, will be exposed to some risk irrespective of the number of securities held. Market risk is also called **undiversifiable risk**.

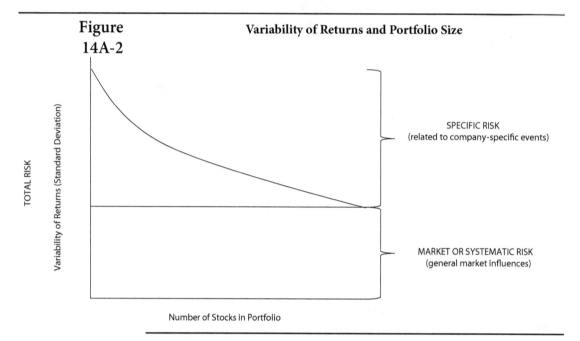

Figure 14A-2

Variability of Returns and Portfolio Size

SPECIFIC RISK
(related to company-specific events)

MARKET OR SYSTEMATIC RISK
(general market influences)

TOTAL RISK

Variability of Returns (Standard Deviation)

Number of Stocks in Portfolio

For a portfolio holding only one or a few securities, unique risk is quite important. As the number of securities held in a portfolio increases, however, diversification eliminates the great portion of unique risk. For reasonably well-diversified portfolios, therefore, only market risk matters.

MEASURING MARKET RISK   We now explore more explicitly how the risk of a portfolio depends on the risk of the individual securities. Suppose that 60 percent of an insurer's investment portfolio is held in the shares of Company A, with the remainder in Company B. Expected returns for the coming year are 15 percent and 21 percent respectively. The portfolio's expected return, therefore, is 17.4 percent [(0.60 x 0.15) + (0.40 x 0.21)] – the weighted average of the individual returns.

Assume that we know from past experience that the standard deviation of returns has been 18.6 percent and 28.0 percent for Companies A and B respectively. We believe that these figures are a fair measure of the spread of possible future returns. To calculate the portfolio's overall risk, we cannot simply take the weighted average of the standard deviations of the individual securities. This would be correct *only* if the two securities' returns were perfectly correlated. In any other case, diversification will reduce the risk below this figure.

The procedure for calculating the risk of a two-stock portfolio correlation matrix is shown in Table 14A-2. To complete the top left cell, we weight the variance of the returns of Company A (i.e., σ_A^2) by the *square* of the proportion invested in it (i.e., w_A^2). Similarly, to complete the bottom right cell, we weight the variance of the returns for Company B (i.e., σ_B^2) by the *square* of the proportion invested in it (i.e., w_B^2).

Calculating the Risk in a Two Stock Portfolio

		1	2
A	Company A's Stock	$w_A^2 \sigma_A^2$	$w_A w_B \sigma_{AB} = w_A w_B \rho_{AB} \sigma_A \sigma_B$
B	Company B's Stock	$w_A w_B \sigma_{AB} = w_A w_B \rho_{AB} \sigma_A \sigma_B$	$w_B^2 \sigma_B^2$

The entries in cells A1 and B2 depend on the variances of the securities issued by Companies A and B. The entries in cells A2 and B1 depend on their **covariance,** which is a measure of the degree to which two values vary in tandem. The covariance can be expressed as the product of the correlation coefficient $r_{A,B}$ and the two standard deviations $\sigma_A \sigma_B$.

Stock returns tend to move together. In this example, therefore, we assume a positive correlation coefficient and therefore a positive covariance. If the prospects of the two stocks were wholly unrelated, both the correlation coefficient and the covariance would be zero; if the stocks tended to move in opposite directions, the correlation coefficient and covariance would be negative. (A simple example of negative correlation is selling sunglasses and umbrellas on the beach. Each depends on the weather: whenever the sale of one prospers, the other suffers.) Just as the variances were weighted by the square of the proportion invested, so we weight the covariance by the product of the two proportionate holdings in w_A and w_B.

Once the values of each cell are computed, we simply add the four entries to obtain the portfolio variance. Taking the square root yields the portfolio's standard deviation, our preferred measure of risk. Using past experience as a guide, we find that the correlation between the two stocks is 0.2. Portfolio variance is thus calculated as follows:

$$\text{portfolio variance} =$$
$$[(0.60)^2 \times (18.6)^2] + [(0.40)^2 \times (28.0)^2] + 2(0.60 \times 0.40 \times 0.2 \times 18.6 \times 28.0) = 300$$

The square root of 300 is 17.3. Thus, at a 17.3 percent standard deviation, the risk of the two is less than the risk of either security measured separately.

The method of calculating portfolio risk can easily be extended to portfolios of any number (n) of securities. The matrix simply enlarges to nxn cells, with the individual security variances on one diagonal weighted by the square of the proportion invested in each, and the other cells containing the covariance between each pair of securities, weighted by the product of the proportions invested.

With just two securities, the number of variance cells equals the number of covariance cells. With a portfolio of many securities, the number of covariances is much larger than the number of variances. Thus, the variability of a well-diversified portfolio reflects the covariances much more than individual security variances. An investor's portfolio is tied together by a web of positive covariances that set the limit to the benefits of diversification; that is, they collectively constitute market risk. The risk of a well-diversified portfolio, therefore, depends on the market risk of the securities included in the portfolio.

Expected Return and Risk Values for Different Combinations of Two Stocks

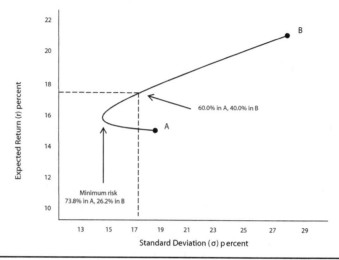

An investor can select from an array of possible risk/return combinations. In this example, if maximum expected return is the objective, irrespective of risk, a portfolio composed solely of Company B securities is called for. A minimum risk portfolio, irrespective of return, would be composed 26.2 percent of B's securities and 73.8 percent of A's securities. Any portfolio composed of more than 73.8 percent of A's securities is dominated by some other portfolio, in the sense that a higher return can be expected for the same risk.

Expected Return and Risk Values for Entire Market of Securities

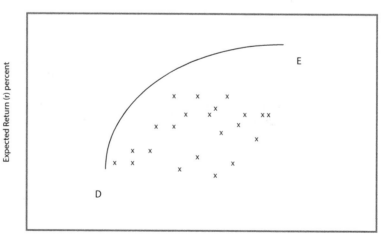

Each "x" represents a combination of risk and return for individual stocks. By mixing securities in different proportions, an even wider range of combinations can be obtained. The curved line DE is called the *efficient frontier* because it represents the set of efficient portfolios that dominates all other portfolios below and to the right of the line. From this set, the investor would select the portfolio that best matches his, her, or its risk/return preferences.

CONSTRUCTING EFFICIENT PORTFOLIOS   Using mean-variance analysis, Markowitz showed that it was possible to construct a set of portfolios that dominated all others; that is, portfolios that yielded the highest returns for a given risk. We illustrate this concept using the earlier example of Companies A and B. Recall that the expected returns were 15 and 21 percent and that standard deviations were 18.6 and 28.0 percent, respectively. Company B offers a higher expected return but at considerable additional risk.

There is no reason, however, to limit our portfolio to a single stock only. We noted above that a portfolio composed of 60 percent Company B stock and 40 percent Company A stock would have an expected return of 17.4 percent with a standard deviation of 17.3 percent. Figure 14A-3 shows expected return and risk values for different combinations of the two stocks. Figure 14A-4 shows this same principle applied to the entire market of securities.

In 1958, James Tobin extended the Markowitz model to include the possibility of investor borrowing and lending at the same rate.[6] The result was surprising: all investors would hold the same portfolio of securities. We explore this result briefly. Assume that our investor puts some money in risk-free Treasury bills (i.e., lends money) and the remainder in common stock portfolio S as shown in Figure 14A-5. Any combination of expected return and risk is possible.

The Effect of Lending and Borrowing on Expected Risk and Return Values   Figure 14A-5

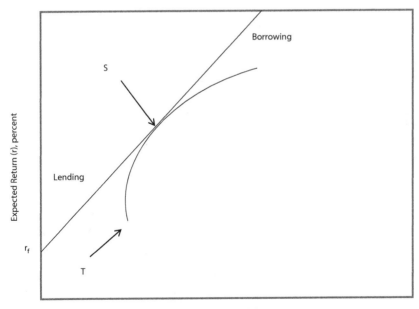

Any combination of expected return and risk is possible along the straight line joining r_f and S. As borrowing is simply negative lending, we can extend the range of possibilities to the right of S by borrowing funds at an interest rate of r_f and investing them along with other funds in portfolio S. (The model's validity is unaffected when borrowing and lending rates differ; only the slope of the line changes.)

Thus, the investor can lend money and end up somewhere between r_f and S or borrow and extend the range of risk/return choices beyond S. Regardless of the level of risk chosen, the highest expected return is achieved by a mixture of portfolio S and borrowing or lending. There would be no reason ever to hold portfolio T or any other portfolio along the efficient frontier except S.

The investor, therefore, faces two decisions. First, find the optimum portfolio of securities, S in our example. Under certain rigorous conditions, it can be proven that this portfolio will be the market portfolio that, as we know, has a *beta* of 1.0. Second, decide how much to borrow or lend to achieve the desired balance between risk and return.

THE PRICE OF EQUITY CAPITAL

In this section, we explore the cost of equity – the return investors demand for the risk they assume by investing in an issuer's stock.

THE CAPITAL ASSET PRICING MODEL

The capital asset pricing model (CAPM), first developed in the 1960s as an important extension of MPT, is widely used by securities analysts to value securities.[7] CAPM connects market risk to the investor's required rate of return and provides an intuitive way of thinking about the return an investor should require from an investment, given the asset's systematic risk. Risk is important, after all, only to the extent that it affects expected return. Security prices can be expected to reflect their risk, so we are also investigating the valuation of securities.

The minimum rate of return required by investors to acquire or hold a security depends on the opportunity cost of funds; that is, the return available from alternative, equivalent assets. As we have seen above, we can think of this return (r) as being decomposed into two basic components: the risk-free rate of return (r_f) plus a risk premium (r_p); thus,

$$r = r_f + r_p$$

DETERMINING THE MARKET RATE OF RETURN   The risk-free return typically is measured by the U.S. Treasury bill rate. The risk premium rate is the additional return expected for assuming the security's risk.[8] The higher the risk, the greater the expected incremental return. But what is an appropriate risk premium? We can rearrange the above equation to solve for the risk premium as follows:

$$r_p = r - r_f$$

which simply indicates that the risk premium for a security equals the required return less the market's risk-free return. For example, if the required return of a security is 15 percent and the risk-free rate is 5 percent, the risk premium is 10 percent. Also, if the required return for the *market* portfolio (r_m) is 12 percent, the risk premium for the market would be 7 percent. This 7 percent risk premium would apply to any security having market or systematic risk equivalent to that of the general market. Such a security is said to have a *beta* of 1.0. **Beta** is a measure of the sensitivity of a security's return to the market return in a well-diversified portfolio.

Thus, in this same market, a security with a *beta* of 2.0 should provide a risk premium of 14 percent or twice the 7 percent risk premium existing for the market as a whole. Hence, in general, the appropriate required rate of return for the *j*th security, r_j, should be determined by the following formula:

$$r_j = r_f + \beta_j\left(r_m - r_f\right)$$

This formula is the CAPM. The equation designates the risk-return trade-off existing in the market where risk is defined in terms of *beta*. Figure 14A-6 is a graph of the CAPM.

Expected returns are linearly related to *betas*. If asset A has a return of 18 percent and a *beta* of 2.0, asset B has an expected return of 10 percent and a *beta* of 1.0, and asset C has an expected return of 12.0 percent and a *beta* of 1.5, an investor could invest 50 percent in A and 50 percent in B to produce an expected return of 14 percent and a *beta* of 1.5. As a result, investors would avoid asset C having the same risk but a lower expected return. Investors would not acquire C unless its price dropped to the point where its expected return is 14.0.

MEASURING A PORTFOLIO BETA   Portfolio theory is interested in the contribution of an individual security to the risk of a well-diversified portfolio. Such a contribution depends on how likely the security is to be affected by general market movements; i.e., its *beta*. It is the amount that investors expect the stock price to change for each change in the price aggregate of the market. This is the only risk that matters for investors with diversified portfolios.

In statistical terms, a stock's *beta* is calculated by taking the ratio of (1) the covariance between the stock's and the market's returns to (2) the variance of the market return. The formula is as follows:

$$\beta_i = \sigma_{im} \div \sigma_m{}^2$$

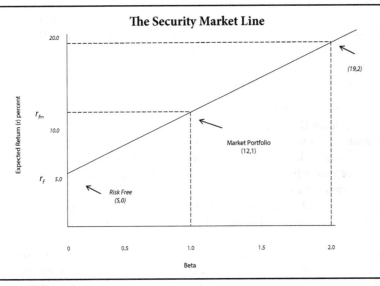

The Security Market Line

Figure 14A-6

This graph shows the appropriate required rate of return given a security's systematic risk and is called the security market line. For this figure, assuming a risk-free return of 5.0 percent and an expected market return of 12.0 percent, securities with betas equal to 0.0, 1.0, and 2.0 should have required rates of return as follows:

If $\beta_j = 0$: $r_j = 5.0\% + 0.0(12.0\% - 5.0\%) = 5.0\%$
If $\beta_j = 1.0$: $r_j = 5.0\% + 1.0(12.0\% - 5.0\%) = 12.0\%$
If $\beta_j = 2.0$: $r_j = 5.0\% + 2.0(12.0\% - 5.0\%) = 19.0\%$

Of course, the market is the portfolio of all stocks, so the average *beta* for all stocks is 1.0. Securities with *betas* of zero have no systematic risk. One-year treasury notes are assumed to have zero *betas*; their values are unaffected (if held to maturity) by changing market conditions. Securities with *betas* of greater than 1.0 exhibit market risk greater than the typical stock. Stocks with *betas* below 1.0 tend to move in the same direction as the market but not as far. The *betas* for most stocks fall between 0.6 and 1.6.

Investors are interested in whether their portfolios as a whole are more or less sensitive to market changes; i.e., whether their portfolio *betas* are greater or lesser than 1.0. To calculate the *beta* for a given portfolio, we take the weighted average of the individual stock *betas*. The weights equal the proportion of the portfolio invested in each security. Thus, if 50 percent of a portfolio is held in stocks with *betas* of 1.3 and the other one-half is held in stocks with *betas* of 1.1, the portfolio *beta* is 1.2. We expect this portfolio, on average, to realize a 1.2 percent change in value for each 1.0 percent change in the market.

CAPM suggests that investors need not worry about the market portfolio; they need only decide how much systematic risk they wish to accept. Market forces will ensure that any stock can be expected to yield the appropriate return for its *beta*. Thus, if a stock is "overvalued" for its risk, fewer investors will hold it, thus depressing its price and increasing its expected return. Conversely, if a stock is "undervalued," increased demand will drive up its price, thus lowering its expected return.

Assumptions underpinning all of modern portfolio theory are that transaction costs and taxes are negligible, that market participants have full information, that the information has been reflected in the security's price, and that no individual investor can influence market prices. These assumptions clearly do not comport with reality. However, the usefulness of a theory lies in its prediction accuracy, not the validity of its underlying assumptions, and most studies of CAPM suggest that it works reasonably well. CAPM is the widely accepted basis for calculating a corporation's cost of capital and establishing a benchmark to judge whether corporate products and projects create or destroy shareholder value.

Arbitrage Pricing Theory

Arbitrage pricing theory (APT) assumes the price of a financial asset is based on its relationship to many macroeconomic risk factors and that assets subject to the same risks will trade at the same price.[9] It is an alternative to the CAPM, a single-factor model that predicts the price of a stock based solely on its market *beta* – the relationship between a security's return and the market return. APT is a more general model based on the assumption that return may be a function of more than one factor. If two assets with the same risk exposures did not trade at the same price, an arbitrageur could buy the investment with the higher expected return (lower price), sell the investment with the lower expected return (higher price) short, and earn a risk free profit when the values converged. Such a situation would violate the no arbitrage and law of one price conditions of finance theory.

APT, like the CAPM, disaggregates the risk of an investment into firm-specific and market risks. Unlike the CAPM – which assumes that all of the market risk is captured in the market portfolio – APT accounts for multiple sources of market risk. A *beta* can be calculated for each of these factors similar to the market *beta* of the CAPM. (CAPM can be viewed as a special case of the APT, which allows for one factor only.)

The basic APT model assumes that the expected return for stock *j* will follow:

$$E(r_j) = r_f + \beta_{j1}F_1 + \beta_{j2}F_2 + \ldots + \beta_{jn}F_n + \epsilon$$

where r_f is the risk free rate, F is an influential factor, β is the *beta* measure of the sensitivity of the return to each influential factor, and ϵ is firm specific risk.

APT does not identify the factors that influence returns. A statistical procedure, *factor analysis*, is used to develop the APT parameters. The factors that influence the market component of unexpected returns usually include gross national product and inflation, but the model allows the use of many factors. *Betas* for the various factors are usually calculated by regression analysis of historical data. Like the CAPM, APT concludes that a portfolio will eliminate firm specific risk. Also like the CAPM, APT can be used to derive a firm's cost of capital.

THE PRICE OF STOCKS

The **dividend discount model** applies the cost of equity capital derived from CAPM, APT, or other models to discount the dividend cash flow of common stocks to derive a DCF value.[10] It assumes the meaningful return is the dividend distributed to shareholders and calculates the present value of dividends. The basic formula is:

$$\text{Value} = \sum_{t=1}^{\infty} \frac{\text{Expected Dividends in Period } t}{(1 + \text{Cost of Equity})^t}$$

Values can also be derived using earnings per share or measures of cash flow.

In its basic form, the model requires the estimation of dividends in perpetuity. To make the model more conceptually manageable, the **Gordon growth model** divides the value into two components: the present value of dividends during a specified extraordinary growth period and a terminal value based on the final dividend of the extraordinary growth period. This multistage approach recognizes that high growth companies cannot sustain their high growth rates forever. Thus:

$$\text{Value} = \sum_{t=1}^{n} \frac{(\text{Expected Dividend})_t}{(1+r)^t} + \frac{(\text{Terminal Value})_n}{(1+r)^n}$$

where *r* is the cost of equity and terminal value is:

$$\text{Terminal Value}_n = \frac{(\text{Expected Dividend})_{n+1}}{(r_n - g_n)}$$

where *g* is the expected perpetual growth rate of the dividend after year *n*, the end of the assumed extraordinary growth period.

THE PRICE OF BONDS

The value of a bond is the discounted value of its coupon and maturity cash flows. The cash flows are a function of its stated contractual interest rate. The discount rate is a function of the current interest rate environment and reflects a risk-free component (for a similar maturity) and a risk premium.

The general formula for the price of a bond is:

$$P = \frac{C}{(1+i)} + \frac{C}{(1+i)^2} + \ldots + \frac{C}{(1+i)^n} + \frac{M}{(1+i)^n}$$

or:

$$P = \left(\sum_{t=1}^{n} \frac{C}{\left(1+i\right)^t} \right) + \frac{M}{(1+i)^n}$$

Where:

C = coupon or periodic interest payment
n = number of coupon payments
i = market interest rate
M = maturity value

An understanding of bond pricing further requires an understanding of two important finance concepts: duration and convexity, which measure changes in a bond's price as interest rate changes. These concepts measure price elasticity with respect to market interest rate changes. We explore them in detail.

DURATION

The concepts of diversification fit nicely with the *credit risk* associated with bonds. As securities are added to a portfolio, the average risk of default due to issuer-specific factors decreases. However, the concepts of MPT – based on the relationship of an individual security's volatility to market volatility – have limited application to the *interest rate risk* associated with bonds because of the asymmetric nature of returns. Like a stock, a bond may become worthless, but a bond will never return more than its coupon and maturity cash flows. Further, its prematurity price volatility arising from market interest rates is shared with all other bonds – a systematic risk.

Intuitively, **duration** can be thought of as the average life of an asset or liability.[11] A way of visualizing duration is to imagine future cash flows as discreet weights on a plank, with the maturity value usually being the heaviest. The fulcrum that just balances the plank is analogous to the duration. Technically, duration is the weighted-average time to maturity using the relative present values of the cash flows as weights. Figure 14A-7 presents the visualization of this concept.

THE DURATION FORMULA   The calculation of duration begins with cash flows discounted at the current market interest rate.[12] These DCFs are used as weights applied to each time period to derive the weighted average maturity. The weighted average maturity is the duration. The formula for the calculation of duration is:

$$\text{Duration} = \frac{\displaystyle\sum_{t=1}^{n} \frac{CF_t}{(1+r)^t}(t)}{\displaystyle\sum_{t=1}^{n} \frac{CF_t}{(1+r)^t}}$$

where

CF_t = cash flow at end of period t
n = the last period in which cash flow is received
r = the market yield to maturity

Note that the denominator is the present value of the asset or liability cash flows; in other words, its economic value.

Conceptual Presentation of Bond Duration

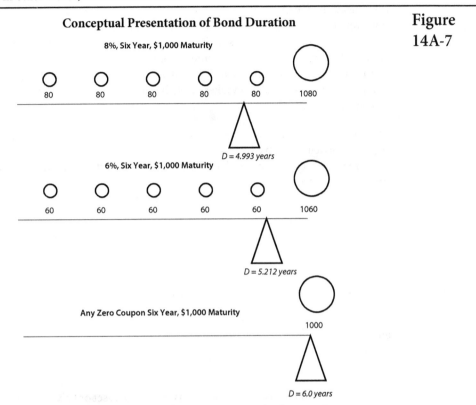

Duration is inversely related to interest rates. At any interest rate, the duration of a zero coupon bond is equal to its time to maturity.

Calculation of duration for a six-year bond with a face value of $1,000, an annual coupon of 8.0 percent, and a market interest rate of 8.0 percent

Table 14A-2

T	CF_t	$\dfrac{1}{(1+r)^t}$	$\dfrac{CF_t}{(1+r)^t}$	$\dfrac{(CF_t)t}{(1+r)^t}$
1	80	.9259	74.0741	74.0471
2	80	.8574	68.5871	137.1742
3	80	.7938	63.5066	190.5197
4	80	.7350	58.8024	235.2096
5	80	.6806	54.4467	272.2333
6	1,080	.6302	680.5832	4,083.4990
Sum			$1,000.00	$4,992.71

$$\text{Duration} = \frac{4,992.71}{1,000} = 4.993 \text{ years}$$

Several important characteristics of duration are worthy of note. First, it should be clear that *duration increases with increases in the maturity of fixed-income assets or liabilities.* Because duration relies on a present value calculation, however, duration does not increase as rapidly as does maturity.

Second, *duration decreases with increases in the yield to maturity.* This makes sense as later cash flows are discounted more heavily at higher yields (r) so their relative importance declines. Third, *the higher the coupon or interest payment, the lower the duration.* This also makes sense because the larger early payments are discounted fewer periods.

THE ECONOMIC MEANING OF DURATION   Duration directly measures the sensitivity or elasticity of a fixed-income asset or liability to small interest rate changes. The larger the value of an asset's or liability's duration, the more sensitive it is to interest rate changes. Thus,

$$Duration = -\left(\frac{\frac{\Delta P}{P}}{\frac{\Delta r}{1+r}} \right)$$

or

$$\frac{\Delta P}{P} = -D\left(\frac{\Delta r}{1+r} \right)$$

and

$$\Delta P = -D\left(\frac{\Delta r}{1+r} \right)P$$

Thus, duration measures the price elasticity of an asset or liability with respect to changes in interest rates. Consider the six-year bond presented above. If interest rates decline by 1 basis point (0.0001), the percentage change in price is predicted to be:

$$\frac{\Delta P}{P} = -(4.993)\left(\frac{-.0001}{1.08} \right) = .0462\%$$

and the predicted change in price is:

$$\Delta P = -(4.993)\left(\frac{-.0001}{1.08} \right)(\$1,000) = \$4.62$$

and

$$P' = P + \Delta P = \$1,004.62$$

Were market yields to fall by 25 basis points, the expected price change in the bond would be:

$$\Delta P = -(4.993)\left(\frac{.0025}{1.08} \right)(\$1,000) = \$11.56$$
$$P' = \$1,001.56$$

It is important to note that duration changes dynamically. The model predicts the change in values of the asset and liability portfolios *for a one-time change in interest rates.* When the interest rate changes, so does the duration of the portfolio.

Similarly, each instrument in the portfolio comes closer to maturity as time transpires, and the duration of the portfolio changes. Consequently, portfolios need to be continuously rebalanced because of constantly changing durations.

CONVEXITY

The price/yield relationship ordinarily is curved, not linear. **Convexity** or **positive convexity** is the property of a *non-callable* bond (or other cash flow stream) in a normal, *positive* yield curve environment such that, for a given interest rate shift, its potential increase in value due to a drop in rates exceeds its potential decrease in value for the same magnitude rate increase. (We will discuss callable bonds and inverted yield curves below.) As rates fall, price rises at an increasing rate, and as rates fall, price declines at a decreasing rate. Convexity is thus a desirable property of these bonds. The convex curve *EAC* in Figure 14A-8 represents the price/yield curve for a six year, 8.0 percent, $1,000 bond at market rates from 6.0 to 10.0 percent.

The Price Yield Curve for a Six Year, 8%, $1,000 Bond Price/Yield Points at Par, 6%, and 10%	Figure 14A-8

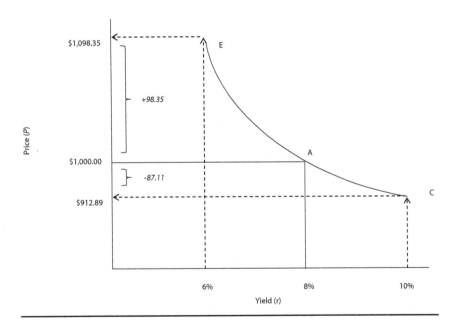

Because the price/yield curve is convex, the potential gain in a bond's value due to a decrease in market interest rates exceeds the potential loss from an interest rate increase of the same magnitude.

Convexity also limits the accuracy of duration calculations. The accuracy of the price sensitivity predicted using duration degrades with the magnitude of the interest rate change. Conceptually, duration is the slope of the price/yield curve and convexity is the change (derivative) of the slope. Because duration is the measure of the slope of the yield curve at the instantaneous current price/yield point, it is linear. For small changes in interest rates, duration is reasonably accurate. Figure 14A-9 shows the yield curve (curve *EAC*) and prices predicted by the duration model (line *DB*). **Duration convexity error** is represented by the difference between the actual asset or liability value following a given shift in interest rates and its value as predicted by duration. As the interest rate change becomes greater, the duration error due to convexity also becomes greater. Duration error is inherently conservative when convexity is positive: the duration model overestimates losses when rates rise and underestimates gains when rates fall.

To understand the importance of convexity, consider the six-year bond with an 8.0 percent coupon and yield, discussed above.[13] Recall that its duration was 4.99 years and that its price was $1,000 at an 8.0 percent market rate. If market rates increase to 10 percent, the duration model predicts a change in price as follows:

$$\Delta P/P = (-4.99)(0.02/1.08) = -9.2457\%$$

which translates into a price change from $1,000 to $907.54. These prices are shown as points A and B (exaggerated), respectively, in Figure 14A-9.

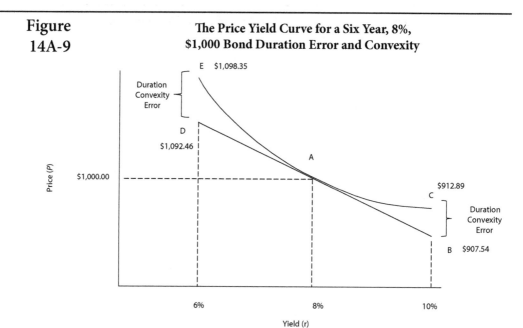

Figure 14A-9

The Price Yield Curve for a Six Year, 8%, $1,000 Bond Duration Error and Convexity

For a life insurer using the simple duration model, error due to convexity is a conservative error because decreases in surplus are overestimated when interest rates rise and surplus increases are underestimated when rates fall.

We know that the price of a security is the discounted value of its cash flows. The actual price of this bond at a 10 percent market rate, therefore, is:

$$P = \$80/(1.1) + \$80/(1.1)^2 + \$80/(1.1)^3 + \$80/(1.1)^4 + \$80/(1.1)^5 + (\$80+\$1,000)/(1.1)^6$$
$$= \$912.89$$

This is point C (exaggerated) in Figure 14A-9. It exceeds the price as predicted by duration by $5.35 or just over 0.5 percent.

The reader can verify that a fall in market rates to 6.0 percent results in a duration-predicted price of $1,092.46, shown as point D. By comparison, the actual price is $1,098.35, as calculated based on the discounted value of the bond's cash flows. It is shown as point E (exaggerated). Again the duration model has under-predicted the bond price increase, in this instance by $5.89 or 0.5 percent. Results of this type will occur for any fixed-income security.

NEGATIVE CONVEXITY   As we noted above, convexity is a desirable property when it is positive. **Negative convexity** exists when, for a given interest rate change, a bond's (or portfolio's) potential decrease in value exceeds its potential increase at any point on the yield curve. As rates fall, price increases at a decreasing rate, and as rates rise, price declines at an increasing rate. Negative convexity is observed when the yield curve is inverted or when a bond is callable.

Inverted yield curves – observed when long term market interest rates are less than short term rates – occur periodically. A more common situation occurs because of borrower options. Some bonds are callable at a defined price – when interest rates fall, the issuer has an option to prepay the bond principal to issue another bond at a lower rate. Similarly, mortgage-backed securities are subject to prepayment by mortgagees who can seek a new mortgage at a lower rate.

Because of convexity – whether positive or negative – the yield curve is essentially asymmetrical in that potential gains and potential losses are not normally equal. In the presence of options, the asymmetry is exaggerated considerably. Figure 14A-10 shows yield curves for a straight (non-callable) bond and a bond callable at price P* and rate r*. As rates fall, the price of the callable bond increases gradually, but the shape of the curve becomes concave (inverted) as rates approach r*. The bond should never be worth more than P*. Thus as the graph shows, the risk/return relationship of a callable bond is not symmetrical – the potential for price appreciation is limited by the call option, while the potential for price depreciation is the same as a non-callable bond as revealed by the shape of the yield curves as rates rise.

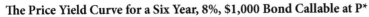

The Price Yield Curve for a Six Year, 8%, $1,000 Bond Callable at P*   **Figure 14A-10**

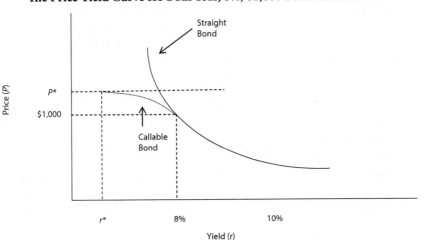

When a bond is callable, the shape of the yield curve is concave or inverted as rates fall but remains convex as rates rise. Potential gains and losses are asymmetrical.

When negative convexity exists – as it regularly does – duration error due to convexity is the opposite of the conservative error produced under positive convexity. The potential gains to an insurer's surplus are overestimated when options exist and when the yield curve is inverted, and potential losses are underestimated in the case of an inverted yield curve.

Convexity principles affect both the asset and liability portfolios of a life insurer. In the next section, we discuss the interrelated nature of assets and liabilities as well as techniques used to adjust duration for the convexity of assets and liabilities with options.

OPTIONALITY AND THE DEPENDENCE OF ASSET AND LIABILITY CASH FLOWS   The duration model assumes that both asset and liability cash flows are independent of interest rate changes. In fact, a high degree of correlation exists between interest rate changes and cash flows. This is a result of the financial options embedded in both assets and liabilities. For example, policyowners may surrender their policies when interest rates rise, and bonds may be called and mortgages repaid (via refinancing) when interest rates fall, disrupting expected cash flow patterns.

Continuing the example from the chapter narrative about XYZ Life, assume that its CFO forecasts the need in five years of $1,469,000 to fund anticipated cash surrenders and policy loans rather than death claims. If interest rates were to rise from 8.0 percent to 9.0 percent, the demand for policy loans and surrenders likely would increase. If we assume a 10 percent increase in demand, then XYZ's investment strategy to develop a fund of $1,469,000 in five years will be insufficient to fund its cash flow need of $1,615,900 ($1,469,000 x 1.1), and its surplus capital will decline.

Predicting the results of the behavior of option holders requires addressing at least two difficult issues. First, what will be the pattern of future interest rates? Second, what will be the reaction of option holders to future interest rate changes? Bond issuers may have a right to prepay or *call* their bonds before maturity and policyowners usually have options via withdrawals, loans, and surrenders. Further complicating the issue is the fact that no market for life insurance liabilities, other than limited reinsurance contracts, exists.

When assets, liabilities, or both contain embedded options, ideally both duration and convexity should be adjusted to take account of these options. This is done by application of the concepts of *option-adjusted duration* and *option-adjusted convexity* (also called *effective duration* and *effective convexity*), which are measures of duration and convexity that have been adjusted for the risk of options embedded in asset or liability contracts. While beyond the scope of this text, the process involves the adaptation of option pricing theory to immunization theory to recognize and account for the fact that assets and liability cash flows are themselves influenced by interest rates and will not remain static as rates change over time. Commercial software is available to measure option-adjusted duration and convexity.

THE MODIGLIANI-MILLER THEOREM

The **Modigliani-Miller theorem** (MM) is a theory in finance asserting that, under certain assumptions, the value of a firm is unaffected by its capital structure or dividend policy; i.e., how it is financed.[14] It assumes an efficient market and that there are no:

- bankruptcy costs,
- taxes,

- agency costs, and
- asymmetric information.

The theorem proves theoretically that the value of a firm is reflected entirely by the positive cash flows of its assets. Before MM, the prevailing view had been that the risk associated with financial leverage reduced the value of a firm. MM asserts that the risk associated with leverage does not change the value of the firm, but reallocates risk and value to the different classes of security owners; i.e., bond holders and shareholders. It is also called the *capital structure irrelevance principle*. A related theorem, called *MM with taxes,* finds that the tax benefits associated with leverage add value but are offset by bankruptcy, agency, and asymmetric information costs. It also concludes that a leveraged firm has a higher cost of equity, which again does not change the value conclusion but does shift risk bearing between debt and equity holders.

Endnotes

1   Fama, Eugene F. "Efficient Capital Markets: A Review of Theory and Empirical Work," *Journal of Finance*, Vol. 25, No. 2, May, 1970.

2   Fischer Black and Myron Scholes, "The Pricing of Options and Corporate Liabilities," *Journal of Political Economy* Vol. 81 No. 3 (1973) 637–654.

3   H. W. Markowitz, "Portfolio Selection," *Journal of Finance*, Vol. 7, No. 1 (Mar., 1952), 77-91.

4   This section draws on A. J. Keown, J. W. Petty, D. F. Scott, Jr., and J. D. Martin, *Foundations of Finance* (Upper Saddle River, NJ: Prentice-Hall,1998), Chapter 8.

5   This and the following section draw on Richard A. Brealey and Stewart C. Myers, *Principles of Corporate Finance, 5th Ed.* (New York: McGraw-Hill, Inc., 1996), 153-156.

6   James Tobin, "Liquidity Preference as Behavior Towards Risk," *Review of Economic Studies*, Vol. 25, No. 67 (1968) 65-86.

7   William F. Sharpe (1964). "Capital Asset Prices: A Theory of Market Equilibrium under Conditions of Risk," Journal of Finance, Vol. 19 No. 3, 425-442.

8   This presentation follows Keown, et al., *Foundations of Finance*, p. 242.

9   Stephen Ross, "The arbitrage theory of capital asset pricing," *Journal of Economic Theory* Vol. 13 No.3 (1976) 341–360.

10 This section draws on Eugene F. Brigham and Louis C. Gapenski, *Financial Management Theory and Practice* 6th ed., (Fort Worth : The Dryden Press, 1991), 232-246.

11 Myron J. Gordon, "Dividends, Earnings and Stock Prices," *Review of Economics and Statistics* (The MIT Press) Vol. 41 No. 2 (1959) 99–105.

12 Frederick R, Macaulay, "Some theoretical problems suggested by the movements of interest rates,: Bond yields and stock prices in the United States since 1856," *National Bureau of Economic Research*, 1938.

13 This discussion draws from and follows partially that presented by Anthony Saunders,, *Financial Institutions Management*, 2nd ed. (Chicago: Irwin, 1997) Chapter 7.

14 This example follows Saunders, *Financial Institutions Management*, p. 121.

15 F. Modigliani and M. Miller, (1958). "The Cost of Capital, Corporation Finance and the Theory of Investment," *American Economic Review* Vol. 48 No. 3 (1958) 261–297. "Dividend Policy, Growth, and the Valuation of Shares," *Journal of Business* Vol. 34 No. 4 (1961).

CHAPTER 15

LIFE INSURANCE ACTUARIAL FUNDAMENTALS

We cannot truly understand life insurance until we have a sound appreciation for its underlying principles and mathematics. Chapters 1 and 2 provided key elements. This chapter begins a more detailed, mathematical examination of life insurance pricing. We present the raw materials of life insurance and introduce net premium computations of life insurance pricing. The following chapter completes our analysis with actuarial applications of these concepts. Both chapters focus on more traditional pricing approaches to ensure mastery of fundamentals.

To establish the economically feasible premium, we must have some means of measuring risk. The measurement of risk lies at the foundation of any system of life insurance and relies on the application of probability, mortality, and interest concepts.

MEASUREMENT OF RISK IN LIFE INSURANCE

PROBABILITY CONCEPTS

First, we know that **simple probability** is calculated as the ratio of (1) events that satisfy a stipulated condition (e.g., death) to (2) the total number of events or exposures (e.g., lives). The corollary that the sum of all the separate probabilities equals one is based on the assumption that the events are mutually exclusive and exhaustive. Events are **mutually exclusive** if the occurrence of one event precludes the possibility of the occurrence of others. For example, a person who dies at age 35 cannot die at age 36. **Exhaustive** means the events under consideration cover all possibilities. A person will either live or die during a given year.

The **compound probability** that two independent events will occur equals the product of the simple probabilities that the events taken separately will occur. Suppose that two coins are tossed, and one wants to know the chance that both will fall heads up. As the chance that each separate coin will fall heads up is one-half, the probability that both will fall heads up is one-quarter (½ x ½). However, only when two events are independent will the product of simple probabilities equal the probability that both events will occur. We know from Chapter 2 that two events are independent if the occurrence of an event affecting one has no affect on the other.

MORTALITY CONCEPTS

Insurance is all about estimating the likelihood of the occurrence of future events. An underlying assumption for making such estimates with most types of insurance is that what has occurred in the past will occur again in the future, if the same conditions are present. Thus, from data showing ages at death in the past, probabilities of death and of survival in the future are estimated.

ESTIMATING FUTURE EVENTS AND THE LAW OF MORTALITY   This prediction is based on the assumption that a law of mortality exists. Benjamin Gompertz suggested the existence of a **law of mortality** in 1825 when he asserted that the death rate increases exponentially with age, as the body at first slowly then more rapidly deteriorates or fails. Indeed, innumerable mortality tables have conformed to this shape, as does the widely used *2001 Commissioners Ordinary Standard (CSO) Tables of Mortality.* The data for one of these appear in Table 15-1A at the end of this chapter. Figure 15-1 is a graph of the probabilities of death of this table, which reveals the exponential nature of mortality in relation to age.

Figure 15-1   *2001 CSO Mortality Rates,* **Ages 0-121, Males**

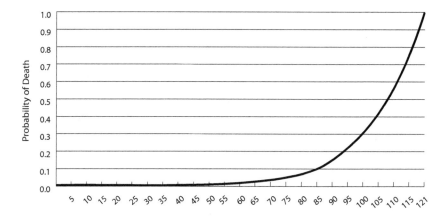

A more recent variation of the Gompertz approach, called the **Gompertz–Makeham law of mortality,** states that the death rate can be considered the sum of two components: (1) Gompertz's age-dependent component and (2) a component that works independent of age (the Makeham part). This latter component includes life shortening situations such as poor sanitation, malnourishment, and poor health or health care. Together, these two components seek to explain how mortality changes over time. In general, with economic development, the Makeham component becomes less important as a major driver of mortality rates. Thus, the overall decline in human mortality rates during the early part of the 20th century was due mostly to a decrease in the Makeham component, as economic progress allowed for healthier living standards and improved health care. It is said that the Gompertz component has been surprisingly stable over many decades.

It is not necessary to know all of the Makeham causes to predict with reasonable accuracy the rates of mortality within groups of persons in comparable environments. By studying the rates of death within large, reasonably homogeneous groups and noting all the circumstances that might, according to our best knowledge, affect those rates, it is possible to anticipate that any future group of persons with approximately the same set of circumstances will experience approximately the same rates of death. This is the function of underwriting, as discussed in Chapter 11.

APPLICATION OF THE LAW OF LARGE NUMBERS TO MORTALITY   The accuracy with which the theoretical estimates approximate actual experience has important bearings on the success of any method of insuring lives. This accuracy depends on two factors: (1) the accuracy of the statistics underlying the estimates and (2) the number of units or trials taken. With reference to the first factor, it is obvious that accurate data are a fundamental requirement if an accurate measure of mortality rates is to be obtained. Mortality statistics, from whatever source, should be scrutinized carefully for possible inaccuracies in the original data. Another dimension of accuracy is the presumption that future mortality experience can be reasonably approximated by past mortality experience. As we see below, this presumption is useful but cannot be accepted without qualification.

The second factor that determines accuracy of the estimates is the number of units or trials taken. We know from the law of large numbers that, as the number of trials is increased, the relative variation of actual from the probable experience decreases, and, if a very great number of trials is taken, actual and probable experience should converge.

With reference to the prediction of future mortality rates, the law of large numbers has a double application: (1) to the data base from which the statistics were drawn and (2) to the cohort to which the rates will be applied. Future mortality is estimated on the basis of past mortality data. We know the importance from Chapter 2 of random variables being independent and identically distributed (IID) in relation to each another. The statistics used for mortality estimations must include a sufficiently large group of IID individuals to ensure the operation of the law of large numbers. Assuming that the collected data are accurate and based on a large enough sample, they may be used to estimate future mortality, provided the group from which the data were drawn is representative of the group to which the data will be applied. Again we return to the importance of underwriting in ensuring this match.

MORTALITY STATISTICS   The establishment of any plan of insuring against death requires knowing probabilities of death, which is accomplished through the application of probability concepts to mortality statistics, resulting in a mortality table. A mortality table is a chart that displays yearly mortality rates by age and often by sex, tobacco use, and possibly other variables. It shows a hypothetical group of individuals beginning with a certain age and tracing the history of the entire group year by year until all have died.

The two main sources of mortality statistics are (1) population statistics showing deaths from census enumerations and returns from registration offices and (2) insurance statistics showing deaths of insured lives. Both census enumerations and death registration records can contain significant error. Census data, collected by a large number of individuals through personal interviews, are particularly susceptible to error. Misclassification is frequent, inaccurate information often is provided by respondents, tabulation errors creep in, and, not infrequently, ages are reported as unknown. Public records of death are frequently incomplete or inaccurate.

On the other hand, the mortality statistics of insured lives tend to be quite accurate. The nature of the insurance process leads to a careful recording of the date of birth, sex, and date of death of insured individuals. This facilitates the derivation of accurate death rates for the various age and sex classifications. As discussed in Chapter 11, experience among insured lives is significantly better than that of the general population because most insured lives have been subjected to an insurer's underwriting process. Virtually all mortality tables used today by life insurers are based on the experience of insured lives.

MORTALITY TABLE CONSTRUCTION   It will prove helpful to introduce some standard actuarial notation to simplify later discussion. These include:

x = age
l_x = number of individuals living at age x
d_x = number of individuals age x dying within one year
$\quad = l_x - l_{x+1}$
q_x = probability of individuals age x dying within one year
$\quad = d_x \div l_x$
p_x = probability of individuals age x surviving one year
$\quad = l_{x+1} \div l_x$

A person of any age will either die or survive that year. Thus, it can be seen for any age,

$$q_x + p_x = 1$$

Moreover, each d_x and l_x is related as follows:

$$l_{x+1} = l_x - d_x$$

Derivation of Death Rates   Insurance mortality tables are usually derived from an insurer or group of insurers collecting data showing (1) the ages at which persons come under observation and (2) the number of each sex dying at each age. Suppose that the following data have been collected for female lives:

Age	Number of Life-Years Observed	Number Dying during Year
0 to 1	10,000	80
1 to 2	30,000	90
2 to 3	150,000	600
3 to 4	80,000	360

From these figures, death rates may be computed for the respective ages as follows:

Age	Rate of Death Expressed as a Fraction	Rate of Death Expressed as a Decimal
0	80/10,000	0.0080
1	90/30,000	0.0030
2	600/150,000	0.0040
3	360/80,000	0.0045

The rate of mortality (q_x) at any given age is the quotient of the number of deaths by the end of one year (d_x) and the corresponding exposure at the beginning of the year (l_x).* The rate represents the probability that a person who has just attained a given age will die before he or she attains the next age. The rate of mortality is often expressed in terms of the number of deaths per thousand.

A mortality table may be constructed by using an arbitrary number of persons, known as the **radix**, assumed to be alive at a given starting age, usually the youngest age for which death rates are available, and successively applying the mortality rates at each higher age. Applying the death rates developed above to an arbitrary radix of 10,000,000 illustrates the process:

(1)	(2)	(3)	(4)	(5)
Age (x)	Number Living at Given Age (l_x)	Mortality Rate for Given Age (q_x)	Number of Deaths before Next Age [(2) x (3)] (d_x)	Number Living at Next Age [(2) – (4)] (l_{x+1})
0	10,000,000	0.0080	80,000	9,920,000
1	9,920,000	0.0030	29,760	9,890,240
2	9,890,240	0.0040	39,561	9,850,679
3	9,850,679	0.0045	44,328	9,806,351

As the probability of dying at age 0 is assumed to be 0.0080, 80,000 deaths are expected during the year among the 10,000,000 starting at age 0. This leaves 9,920,000 of the group to begin age 1. These die at the rate of three per thousand (0.0030), yielding 29,760 deaths during the year, leaving 9,890,240 to begin age 2. In this way, the original 10,000,000 are reduced in number by deaths year after year until all have died. This is the basis for the statement that a mortality table represents "a (hypothetical) generation of individuals passing through time."

As the radix of the table is arbitrary, the numbers in the columns headed "Number Living" and "Number of Deaths" are not significant in themselves. They simply reflect the series of death rates (q_x). Sometimes a mortality table has an additional column showing the "expectation of life" or "life expectancy" at each age. The figure in this column opposite any age is the average number of *full* years of life expected to be lived by persons attaining that age and is calculated from the following formula:

$$e_x = \sum_{t=1}^{\omega-x-1} \frac{l_{x+t}}{l_x}$$

where
e_x = life expectancy for an individual age x, and
w = terminal age of the mortality table being used.

The intuition for the above formula is straightforward. Beginning with l_x lives, after one year, there will be l_{x+1} survivors, each of whom has contributed one year to life expectancy. After two years, there will be l_{x+2} survivors, each of whom has

---

*   The distinction between "mortality rates" and "probabilities of death" is one of preciseness of attained age. For purposes of simplification here, mortality rates and probabilities of death are assumed to be identical. For the construction of a mortality table, probabilities of death are necessary; they refer to rates of dying among a group of persons who have just attained a certain age of life.

contributed two years to life expectancy, and so on. Thus, the total lifetime for all l_x lives is expected to be (based on the mortality table):

$$l_{x+1} + l_{x+2} + l_{x+3} + ... + l_{w-1}$$

and dividing by l_x yields e_x, the number of years expected to be lived on average by persons obtaining age x. This so-called *curtate life expectancy* formula requires living a full year after attainment of age x + t. Insureds who fail to live the full year are ignored by it or, stated equivalently, implicitly assumed to have died at the beginning of the year.

On average, this error amounts to ½ year of life, so a more accurate life expectancy calculation – called the *complete life expectancy* – adds ½ year to the results from the above formula. Expectation of life can be a misleading term as it has no necessary significance for any individual. The probable future lifetime of any person depends on many factors, including his or her state of health, and is highly unlikely precisely to equal life expectancy for that age.

Adjustments of Mortality Data   Mortality tables used by life insurers in calculating premium rates and policy values often do not reflect the precise mortality rates developed from the underlying mortality data. Because the volume of experience is not uniform at all ages and often insufficient to provide completely creditable statistics, two types of adjustments are commonly made to the derived rates: (1) the rates are smoothed into a curve, and (2) a security margin may be added to the rates in the derived curve.

This smoothing of the mortality curve or **graduation** is performed to eliminate the irregularities in the observed data that are believed not to be true characteristics of the universe from which the sample experience was extracted. One of several methods of graduation is used, depending on the data involved and the purpose of the computation. The objective in all cases is to introduce smoothness and regularity, while preserving the basic characteristics of the observed values.

When derived rates will be used in establishing policy reserves and cash values (see Chapter 16), mortality rates may be increased for life insurance reserving (valuation) and decreased for annuity valuation by a percentage called a **margin**. Thus, as a life insurance valuation table, the *2001 CSO Table* was built with margins averaging about 15 percent of the underlying mortality rates. Margins may also be provided by adjusting the underlying data prior to the derivation of the basic rates themselves. The insertion of these margins enhances the security of life insurance contracts by introducing conservatism and is considered sound practice.

TYPES OF MORTALITY TABLES   Mortality tables are classified in many ways. We have already mentioned the important difference between population mortality tables and those of insured lives. Here we explore classifications of insured lives tables.

Valuation versus Basic Tables   A **basic mortality table** reflects the actual experience of the population from which the data were drawn. Graduation typically will be applied to the data, but no margins are added to such tables. Basic tables are commonly used for:

1. calculation of gross premium rates.
2. development of current mortality charges for unbundled life policies.
3. development of dividend scales and dividend payments on participating (par) policies.
4. mortality studies of the insurer's own experience, especially in identifying trends.
5. financial statements prepared under generally accepted accounting principles.
6. asset share, model office, and other financial studies and projections.

A **valuation mortality table** is used as the basis for calculating reserves and cash values. These tables usually contain margins. The use of such tables is prescribed by law in many countries, including the U.S.

Valuation tables are also used by some insurers to calculate gross premiums, especially for par whole life policies.

Select, Ultimate, and Aggregate Tables   As we know from Chapter 3, mortality tables may be classified as select, ultimate, and aggregate. These terms relate to the extent to which the data used have been affected by the underwriting process. We know that recently insured lives, having passed the necessary requirements before becoming insured, show a lower rate of mortality than lives not recently subject to such scrutiny. Thus, the number of deaths occurring among 10,000 insureds aged 40 who have just passed a physical examination is expected to be lower than among 10,000 persons aged 40 who were first insured at age 30 and have been insured for 10 years. It is important for an insurer in estimating probable mortality experience to know whether it has a large number of newly selected lives.

Select mortality is based on data of newly insured lives only. **Ultimate mortality** excludes these early data – usually the first 5 to 25 years following entry – and is based on the mortality among insured lives after the benefit of selection has passed. The *2001 CSO Table* shown in Table 15-1A is an ultimate table. As insurers and their regulators are usually interested in establishing conservative reserve estimates, it is generally considered safer for an insurer to compute reserve liabilities on the basis of ultimate mortality. An **aggregate mortality table** includes all the mortality data, both the early years following entry and the later ones.

A **select and ultimate mortality table** shows rates of mortality by both age and duration of insurance. As the effects of selection generally wear off within 25 years or less, the mortality rates are differentiated by duration only for such a period. An example of a five year select and ultimate mortality table is presented in Table 15-1. The blocked ages show how the mortality rates vary by duration even though each insured is aged 30. The rates shown in column "6 and above" constitute the ultimate mortality level and can be used to develop an ultimate mortality table.

Table 15-1   Select and Ultimate Mortality Table Rates per 1,000 Lives

Age at Issue	Year of Insurance						Attained Age
	1	2	3	4	5	6 and above	
25	0.71	0.82	0.88	0.93	0.97	1.01	30
26	0.72	0.82	0.89	0.96	1.00	1.06	31
27	0.73	0.83	0.92	0.99	1.05	1.12	32
28	0.74	0.84	0.93	1.03	1.11	1.21	33
29	0.74	0.84	0.97	1.08	1.20	1.32	34
30	0.74	0.86	1.02	1.16	1.31	1.44	35

Select and ultimate tables are used for purposes of analysis and comparison. The basic tables prepared by the U.S. *Society of Actuaries* and the *American Academy of Actuaries* are derived from data supplied by a group of established insurers to show select and ultimate mortality to reflect mortality trends. The mortality used in determining par life insurance premiums usually are from ultimate tables. Select and ultimate mortality tables are frequently used in profit studies, in dividend and other non-guaranteed element calculations, and in the calculation of nonparticipating gross premiums.

Tables for Annuities   A mortality table based on life insurance experience is not suitable for use with life annuities. One reason is that annuities generally are not purchased by individuals in poor health. At the higher ages (particularly in the case of annuity contracts purchased by single premiums for immediate income), the rates of mortality experienced among annuitants are lower than among insureds under life insurance policies. A life insurance mortality table would overstate expected mortality rates.

Another important reason is that a more or less consistent improvement in general population mortality rates provides a gradually increasing margin of safety for life insurance but has the opposite result for life annuities. In fact, it is recognized that no annuity mortality table based solely on past experience can be used safely.

Static Tables versus Tables with Projection   Most life insurance mortality tables are **static tables**, meaning that changes in their mortality rates do not depend on the calendar year to which they apply. As the secular trend toward mortality improvement continued, these static tables have periodically been replaced by other static tables based on more recent experience. In recent years, many companies made some provision for their expectation that underlying mortality improves with time and are not using static tables. The improvement in mortality has led to increased margins in life insurance premiums, as the postponement in death payments enables insurers to earn additional income on their invested funds and to collect additional premiums. In par policies and all other policies with non-guaranteed elements, these gains can be credited to policyowners via enhanced dividends or reduced COI charges.

The situation has been just the reverse with life annuity contracts, in which improving mortality has led to smaller margins. Postponement of death has led to

additional annuity payments. To avoid the large expense of frequently constructing new static tables, the traditional practice was to make an allowance for the
decrease in mortality rates by using *age setbacks*; that is, the static table was still
used, but the rates shown in the table were assumed to be those that apply to lower
actual ages. For example, a 65-year-old person may be assumed to be subject to
the mortality rates of a person of 64 or 63, thus increasing the premium for a given
amount of annuity income. Setbacks of from one to four years are used.

Annuity tables used today – commonly called **mortality tables with projections** – contain **projection factors** on different bases that can be applied to the
basic table to make allowance for future reductions in mortality rates. For example,
suppose that the mortality rate for 65-year-olds is expected to improve at the rate
of 1 percent per calendar year. The projected mortality rate for 65-year-olds in
some future calendar year, say $CY + N$, can be calculated from the mortality rate
in an earlier calendar year by the following formula:

$$q_{65}^{CY+N} = q_{65}^{CY}(1-0.01)^N$$

The importance of providing for mortality improvement in annuity mortality
tables is significant because annuity business constitutes a majority and growing
proportion of many life insurance companies' total business. (Annuity business
includes, in addition to individual annuities, group annuities and settlement
option arrangements.) The need is particularly critical in the case of variable annuity products because of the growing proportion of such business, and no interest
margin exists to help offset mortality losses that may develop.

Smoker versus Nonsmoker Tables   Because smoking and other tobacco usage
has such profound negative effects on mortality rates, separate basic and valuation
mortality tables have been developed for tobacco users and non-users, commonly
titled simply smokers and nonsmokers. The *2001 CSO Tables* include separate
select tables by smoking status. Except for the very old and young, for most ages
and durations, the death rates of smokers is at least twice that of nonsmokers,
resulting, according to one study of population data, in a 10 year shorter life
expectancy for smokers in comparison to nonsmokers.

Specific Tables in Use Today   A multitude of mortality tables remain in use today.
The ones discussed below are used chiefly for purposes of valuing U.S. insurers'
policy liabilities and establishing cash values.

Life Insurance Tables. The *Commissioners 1941 Standard Ordinary Table of
Mortality* (*1941 CSO Table*) was used extensively for U.S. policies issued between
1948 and 1966. For many years prior to the advent of the *1941 CSO Table*, the
American Experience Table of Mortality was widely used. Until the mid-1980s, the
Commissioners 1958 Standard Ordinary Mortality Table (*1958 CSO Table*) was
required to be used as the basis for minimum reserves and nonforfeiture values in
all states. The *1958 CSO Table* was replaced by the *Commissioners 1980 Standard
Ordinary Mortality Tables* (*1980 CSO Tables*), with separate versions for males
and females.

A family of *2001 CSO Tables*, in turn, replaced the family of *1980 CSO Tables* as
the regulatory standard for reserves and nonforfeiture values. As with past tables,
these were developed by the U.S. *Society of Actuaries* and the *American Academy*

of Actuaries at the request of the *National Association of Insurance Commissioners* (NAIC). In addition to sex-distinct tables as well as gender-blended tables, 25-year select tables were included for the first time. The *1980 CSO Tables* included only a 10-year select period. The *2001 CSO Tables* also extended the final maturity age to 121 from age 100 of its predecessors. It offers smoker/nonsmoker tables as well as **composite mortality tables**, which combine smoker and nonsmoker experience. Table 15-1A is a composite table. As with its predecessors, the *2001 CSO Tables* were constructed to reflect more recent, mostly lower mortality rates for males and females. The improvement in mortality rates averages about 30 percent and generally is larger for males than for females.

In 2008, the SOA developed a set of valuation basic tables, called the *2008 Valuation Basic Table* (VBT). These sets of tables have significantly broader contributions from more life insurers, greater insurer contributions at ages above 60, and shorter select periods above age 65. Also, unlike the *2001 VBT*, the 2008 tables reflect both standard and preferred underwriting results and policy size. The tables have not formed the basis for new *CSO valuation* mortality tables.

Finally, the SOA and the AAA have developed *2014 VBTs* and *2014 CSO Mortality Tables*. These tables will replace the *2008 VBTs* and the *2001 CSO Tables*, although the timing for this change was not known at the time this book went to press; it was anticipated to be soon, however. The *2014 VBTs* are based on a significantly greater amount of business and exposures than the *2008 VBTs*, as well as materially more experience with preferred risks, older issue ages, and females. The new *VBTs* will be used for stochastic reserve purposes within a principles based reserving system, as discussed in the following chapter. The *CSO* tables will be used for reserves, nonforfeiture values, and tax purposes. Also, special tables for guaranteed issue, simplified issue, and preneed insurance are being developed. The tables show significant variation and improvement over the 2008 tables.

For example, the figures below show the ratio of actual to expected (A/E) mortality based on selected face amount bands and selected issues ages, where actual is that of the *2014 VBT* and expected is that of the *2008 VBT*, which itself showed improved mortality relative to the *2001 VBT*. Note the substantial differences for higher face amounts and higher issue ages. The differences result from more intense underwriting for larger amounts, advances in the care of age-related disease, and more late-age data in recent mortality tables. It is not expected that the 2014 tables' mortality rates will be shown as varying by face amount.

Face Amount Band ($)	A/E Ratio by Amount (percent)	Issue Age	A/E Ratio by Amount (percent)
50,000 – 99,999	105.6	40–49	100.1
250,000 – 499,999	88.6	60–69	95.1
1,000,000 – 2,499,999	81.9	80–89	61.6
5,000,000 – 9,999,999	74.1		
Aggregate	92.7		

Annuity Tables. The *1937 Standard Annuity Table* formerly was used extensively for U.S. individual annuity business. The steady improvement in mortality led to the development of the *Annuity Table for 1949*, which introduced projection factors to reflect continued improvement in mortality rates. The *1955 American*

Annuity Table was developed to provide reasonable rates for annual premium deferred annuities and life income settlement options. The *Group Annuity Table for 1951* was the first table based on the experience of group annuitants and was widely used in computing rates and reserves for group annuities.

In 1971, two new mortality tables, the *1971 Group Annuity Table* and the *1971 Individual Annuity Table*, were developed. In 1983, two further annuity mortality tables were adopted by the NAIC and remain in use in the U.S. The *1983 Individual Annuity Mortality Table for Males* (*1983 Table-a*) is used for reserve and non-forfeiture purposes on individual annuity business and the other applies to group business (the *1983 GAM Table*). The so-called *Annuity 2000 Mortality Table* was adopted by the NAIC for use by the states and most have done so for individual annuity contracts issued after date of state adoption.

Finally, the SOA and the AAA have developed new individual annuity basic and reserve mortality tables. These tables, the *2012 Individual Annuity Mortality Basic Table* and the *2012 Individual Annuity Reserve Mortality Table,* are effective in 2014. They are included for reserving purposes in the 2012 NAIC *Model Regulation for Recognizing New Annuity Mortality Tables,* which is being adopted by the states. The new tables apply to annuities in liquidation and likely will apply as well to settlement options in life insurance contracts. The reserve mortality table contains projection factors but is also a generational table, meaning that it contains a set of mortality rates that decrease for a given age from one projection year to another; i.e., rates vary from one year to the next.

The new tables result in an increase in statutory reserves for most ages, with increases being significant for some ages. Interestingly, the underlying experience exhibited significantly lower mortality – and thus greater adverse selection – for pure life annuities and higher annuity benefit payouts, although reserves are not expected to be required to vary accordingly.

APPLICATION OF PROBABILITY TO MORTALITY   Suppose that it is desired to estimate the probability of a man's death within one, two, and five years from age 35. We will use mortality rates from the *2001 CSO Table* to make these calculations. The probabilities are the ratios of the numbers dying within one, two, and five years to the number living at age 35. Thus, from Table 15-1A, 9,744,792 men are alive at age 35 and 11,791 of these are expected to die before the end of the year. Hence, the probability of death within one year is:

$$q_{35} = \frac{d_{35}}{l_{35}} = \frac{11,791}{9,744,792} = 0.00121$$

During the two years following the stated age, there are 11,791 + 12,458 deaths for a total of 24,249. Therefore, the probability of dying within two years (represented by $_2q_{35}$) is:

$$_2q_{35} = \frac{d_{35} + d_{36}}{l_{35}} = \frac{24,249}{9,744,792} = 0.00249$$

Similarly, the total number of deaths within five years is 66,182 (11,791 + 12,458 + 13,026 + 13,979 + 14,928). Thus, the probability that a man entering age 35 will die within five years is:

$$_5q_{35} = \frac{d_{35} + d_{36} + d_{37} + d_{38} + d_{39}}{l_{35}} = \frac{66,182}{9,744,792} = 0.00679$$

This last expression can be simplified as follows:

$$_5q_{35} = \frac{l_{35} - l_{40}}{l_{35}}$$

Probabilities of survival can also be easily calculated. The chance of living at least one year following age 35 (p_{35}) will be a fraction the denominator of which is the number living at age 35 and the numerator is the number that have lived one year following the specified age, thus,

$$p_{35} = \frac{l_{36}}{l_{35}} = \frac{9,733,001}{9,744,792} = 0.99879$$

The discussion in this and the following chapter utilizes the *2001 CSO Table* in illustrating the principles involved in rate-making. The *2001 CSO Table* is not, however, used by most life insurance companies as the primary basis for establishing premium rates. They use tables reflecting up-to-date experience, as discussed in Chapter 16.

INTEREST CONCEPTS

Prefunding for life insurance via fixed, level, or flexible premiums leads to the accumulation of large sums of money that are held by insurers for many years before being used to pay benefits. The funds are invested in income-producing assets whose earnings permit life insurers to charge lower premiums than otherwise would be the case. Interest plays a vital role in actuarial calculations and the operations of life insurance companies. Given its importance, we provide a short refresher on key interest concepts.

Interest is the price paid for the use of money. The original investment, referred to as the **principal amount** or simply **principal**, accumulates by the end of a specified term to an accumulated value. The interest earned for this particular period is the simple difference between the accumulated value and the principal.

Abbreviations commonly used are:

i = interest rate, often expressed as the rate for one year,

I = interest amount,

S = accumulated value,

A = principal amount or present value, and

n = number of compounding periods, often expressed in years.

Interest credited or paid only on the original principal is described as **simple interest**. In many instances, as with life insurance pricing calculations, interest earnings remain with the original principal also to earn interest. Interest not distributed but used to earn additional funds is described as **compound interest**. Here we are concerned with four compound interest functions.

ACCUMULATED VALUE OF 1   The future value of a principal amount accumulated at interest is its **accumulated value**. The first-year value is expressed as $S_1 = A(1 + i)$. If this amount were accumulated for an additional year, the interest for the second year would be i times S_1. The accumulated value at the end of the second year would be expressed as:

$$S_2 = S_1 + iS_1$$
$$= S_1(1+i)$$
$$= A(1+i)^2, \text{ where } S_1 = A(1+i)$$

By continuing to use simple algebra, the accumulated value of A at the end of n years may be expressed as $S = A(1 + i)^n$. Figures for $(1 + i)^n$ are shown in interest tables and easily derived on computer spreadsheets.

PRESENT VALUE OF 1   The value today of a future payment (or series of payments) discounted for interest is its **present value**. As $S = A(1 + i)^n$, it is only necessary to divide both sides of this equation by $(1 + i)^n$ to determine the expression $A = S/(1 + i)^n$. Thus, to determine the present value of the amount – that is, the principal – it is only necessary to divide the amount S by $(1 + i)^n$.

Of course,

$$\frac{S}{(1+i)^n} = S\left[\frac{1}{1+i}\right]^n$$

The symbol v is commonly used for $\left[\frac{1}{1+i}\right]$. Thus,

$$v^n = \left[\frac{1}{1+i}\right]^n$$

Values for v^n are easily derived via spreadsheets and are available in table format as well. The figures given in these tables are commonly referred to as the present value of 1 rather than $1/(1 + i)^n$ or v^n.

ACCUMULATED VALUE OF 1 PER YEAR   Suppose that an investment of 1 is made at the beginning of each year for three years. To determine the accumulated amount at the end of three years, it is necessary only to add the amounts to which each of the payments will grow. The first 1 will grow to an amount of $(1 + i)^3$. The second 1 will grow to an amount of $(1 + i)^2$, and the third 1 will grow to an amount of $(1 + i)$. The total amount at the end of three years may be expressed as:

$$\ddot{s}_{\overline{3}|} = (1 + i) + (1 + i)^2 + (1 + i)^3$$

where $\ddot{s}_{\overline{n}|}$ is the actuarial symbol for the accumulated value at the end of n years of 1 invested at the *beginning* of each year for n years. This notation is commonly read as "s double-dot angle n." The two dots above the s mean that payments are made at the beginning of each period. An s without the two dots means that the payments are made at the end of each period.

In general,

$$\ddot{s}_{\overline{n}|} = \sum_{t=1}^{n} (1 + i)^t$$

PRESENT VALUE OF 1 PER YEAR   Another common compound interest problem is to determine what principal (i.e., present value) should be invested now to provide equal annual payments at the *end* of each year for the next n years. The total present value of the payments is the sum of the present value of each individual payment. For example, suppose that we wish to find the present value of 1 payable at the end of each year for three years. The present values of the first, second, and third payments are v^1, v^2, and v^3, respectively. The total present value may be expressed as:

$$a_{\overline{3|}} = v^1 + v^2 + v^3$$

where $a_{\overline{n|}}$ is the symbol for the present value of 1 paid at the end of each year for the next n years. The $a_{\overline{n|}}$ notation is commonly read as "a angle n." The absence of the two dots above the a indicates that payments are made at the end of each period.

In general, then

$$a_{\overline{n|}} = \sum_{t=1}^{n} v^t$$

ANNUITIES An **annuity** is a series of payments or receipts (a series of payments by a payer is a series of receipts to the recipient or payee). Usually, the payment is a constant amount and the intervals are regular, such as, 100 payable at the end of each month for 10 years, or 5,000 payable at the end of each year for 20 years. The annuity payment may be certain to be paid, in which it is an **annuity certain,** or it may be contingent on a particular person being alive, in which it is a **life annuity.** A life annuity for a set term of years but terminating if and when the individual dies during the set term is a **temporary life annuity**. An annuity that pays for as long as either of two persons is alive is a **joint and last survivor annuity**.

When the annuity payments are assumed to be made at the *beginning* of each period, the annuity is an **annuity due.** Using actuarial notation for an annuity due:

$\ddot{a}_{\overline{n|}}$ = an n-year annuity certain
$\ddot{a}_x$ = a life annuity beginning at age x
$\ddot{a}_{x:\overline{n|}}$ = an n-year temporary life annuity beginning at age x

Annuity theory plays an important role in actuarial calculations, both in pricing annuities and in premium payments to life insurance companies, as they constitute an annuity due to the insurer.

OVERVIEW OF INSURANCE PRICING

The calculation of life insurance premiums and values requires information and assumptions regarding:

1. The mortality table to be used (usually divided between males and females and often between smokers and nonsmokers),
2. The benefits to be provided,
3. A rate of interest, and
4. The amounts needed to cover the insurer's expenses of operation, taxes, profits, and a margin for contingencies, called the **loading**.

As we know, insurance pricing relies on insurance (risk) pools that require the accumulation of a fund from amounts paid by insureds to provide benefits to those pool members who suffer loss. To establish the amount to be charged, the life insurer must start with some idea as to the likelihood of losses for the group; in other words, a mortality table.

As persons purchasing life insurance are not the same age and, generally, younger persons are less likely to die within the next year than are older persons, equity requires that premium rates charged be graded upward with increasing age. Similarly, as females on average live longer than do males, life premiums for males should from an actuarial perspective be correspondingly higher than for similarly situated females. The same relationships exists between smokers and nonsmokers and persons in poor health and those in good health.

Life insurance companies collect premiums in advance of providing insurance coverage. In longer-term coverages, that portion not needed immediately to provide promised benefits and loadings is invested and produces earnings that are used to supplement premium income to fund future expected benefits and ongoing expenses. In such cases, insurers can discount premiums in advance in recognition of the fact that they will invest the accumulated funds.

Premium computation must take account of the coverage period, the level of coverage, as well as all other factors related to the benefits promised under the contract. Included here is the likelihood of policyholders lapsing (i.e., voluntarily terminating) their policies. Our focus in this chapter is predominantly on fixed-premium, bundled life insurance policies. We take up pricing of unbundled contracts in the next chapter.

Life insurance typically provides a definite benefit amount in the event of death or survival. It is essential, therefore, that an accurate determination of the expected benefit cost be made and that an adequate amount be charged – an amount that is equitable as to claim likelihood, types of coverage, and other relevant factors. This is especially important because, unlike most other types of insurance, life insurance contracts can provide cover for decades and cannot be canceled by the company.

One means of determining premiums to be charged is to calculate net rates then add loadings. **Net rates** – called the actuarially fair rates in economics – are insurance rates calculated to recognize (1) the probability of the insured event, (2) the time value of money, and (3) the benefits promised. They make no allowance for loading to cover the expenses incurred by the insurer in selling, issuing, and maintaining the policy or for taxes, profits, or contingencies. When the net premium is loaded for these items, we obtain the **gross premium** – the amount charged policyowners.

This procedure for deriving gross premium rates, followed in principle by many insurers, is used here as it illustrates well the interaction of policy pricing elements and concepts. However, other methods are more commonly used today in deriving gross premium rate structures. One is for the insurer to select gross rates (based on market and competitive considerations) and then to test these rates against its objectives and expectations as to a range of possible future experience. If the test rates do not produce the profit and other desired results, rates (or other policy elements) are changed until acceptable results are obtained.

Another approach is to calculate gross premium rates directly through the use of realistic interest, mortality, expense, taxes, and lapse assumptions, and a specific provision for contingencies and profit (or contribution to surplus). With cash values and a dividend scale assumed, the gross premium rate structure is determined by solving a mathematical equation.

NET PREMIUMS

With the preceding principles as a base, we now begin the process by illustrating one method for calculating gross premiums. The balance of this chapter examines net premiums, with the following chapter completing the gross premium examination. This study begins by first determining net single premiums from which net level premiums are derived.

NET SINGLE PREMIUMS

A **net single premium** (NSP) is the present value of future benefits promised under a life insurance policy. Its computation requires information as to (1) the age and sex of the insured, (2) the benefits to be provided, (3) the mortality rates to be used, and (4) an interest rate. The computations that follow assume mortality of the *2001 CSO Table* as shown in Table 15-1A; an interest rate of 4.0 percent; a policy face amount of $1,000; and a male insured. As Table 15-1A is a composite table, tobacco use is not a factor in this illustration. The age of the insured will be stated in each instance. As do many life insurers in their rate computations, we make two simplifying assumptions: (1) premiums are paid at the beginning of each policy year, and (2) claims are paid at the end of the policy year in which death occurs.

TERM LIFE INSURANCE   Term life insurance, the simplest type of life insurance, covers a set period and promises to pay the sum insured if the insured dies within this period, with nothing being paid if death does not occur during the designated term. Yearly renewable term (YRT) policies, discussed in Chapter 3, are the simplest forms of term life insurance and offer an excellent opportunity to explain the elements of rate making.

Suppose that we seek the NSP on a one-year term life insurance policy of $1,000 on a male aged 45. In other words, we wish to know the amount of money that must be paid at the beginning of the year by policyowners to enable the insurer to pay $1,000 at year-end for each insured who dies during the period, ignoring loadings. The insurer is interested in the probability of having to pay the death claim – in other words, the chance of a 45-year-old male dying during the year.

We know from Table 15-1A that, for 45-year-olds, 25,394 of the 9,582,785 living at the beginning of the year are expected to die within that year. If we assume an insured pool of the number living and further that actual mortality experience will coincide with that expected under the mortality table, there would be 25,394 deaths during the year. Because each of these deaths represents a liability of $1,000 to the insurer and because the claims are assumed to be payable at the close of the year, the insurer must have $25,394,000 on hand at that time to pay claims.

This total amount need not have been collected at the beginning of the year, as the insurer is able to invest the premiums paid at that time and earn interest on them. A value of 1 discounted for one year at 4.0 percent interest is 0.962. Therefore, the insurer need have collected only $24,429,394 (0.962 x $25,394,000) in premiums at the beginning of the year to have at year's end sufficient funds to pay

$1,000 for each of the 25,394 deaths. To obtain the premium that each individual should pay, we divide the total fund needed at the beginning of the year by the initial number in the insurance pool:

$$\$24{,}429{,}394 \div 9{,}582{,}785 = \$2.55$$

The net single premium for our one-year term insurance policy at age 45 is $2.55, or, stated equivalently, it is the amount of money that must be contributed to the pool by each IID exposure unit. This method of determining individual net single premiums has been termed the *aggregate approach*, as it emphasizes the total fund necessary to meet death claims.

The same problem may be approached using the mathematically identical *expected value approach* which derives the result from an expected value calculation. The probability of death for 45-year-old males is shown in the table as 0.00265 (25,394 ÷ 9,582,785). The expected value of a death claim for an insured is, therefore, $1,000 x 0.00265 or $2.65. This value is needed at the end of the year, so we discount it at 4.0 percent or $2.65 x 0.962 = $2.55. In actuarial notation, it is:

$$(1{,}000)(q_x)(v)$$

To continue, suppose that we wish to know the NSP for a five-year term life insurance policy issued to males age 45; that is, the amount of money that, paid in a single sum at age 45, will purchase insurance against death were it to occur at any time within the next five years. Two facts are apparent: (1) the premium is paid only once, in a single sum at policy inception, and (2) death claims will be paid at the end of the year in which death occurs, not at the end of the five-year period. This latter fact has an important bearing on the interest earned and, therefore, on the method of computing the premium.

Manifestly, the cost cannot be correctly determined by multiplying the total probability of dying during the five years by the face amount of the policy and discounting this amount in one operation because some of the money collected will draw interest for one year only, another part will earn interest for two years, and so on. It is necessary to compute each year's mortality costs separately.

Nor can the cost be correctly determined by use of each year's q_x as shown in the mortality table. This is because q_x is the probability of death *for persons who have attained age x*. In the instant case, we need the probabilities that males *now age 45* will die during ages 45, 46, 47, 48, and 49. Thus, we face a compound probability. For example, the likelihood of our 45 year old dying during his 47th year equals the likelihood of living to age 47 multiplied by the likelihood of dying during that year. To die during age 47, the 45 year old must live to age 47! This likelihood is

$$(_2 p_x)(q_{47}) = \left(\frac{l_{47}}{l_{45}}\right)\left(\frac{d_{47}}{l_{47}}\right) = \left(\frac{d_{47}}{l_{45}}\right)$$

The actuarial notation for this relationship is

$$_{n|}q_x$$

It signifies the probability that a person age x will die during a deferred year n. Thus, the likelihood of our 45 year old dying during each of the next five years is:

$$q_{45} = \left(\frac{d_{45}}{l_{45}}\right) = \left(\frac{25,394}{9,582,785}\right) = 0.00265$$

$$_{1|}q_{45} = \left(\frac{d_{46}}{l_{45}}\right) = \left(\frac{27,716}{9,582,785}\right) = 0.00289$$

$$_{2|}q_{45} = \left(\frac{d_{47}}{l_{45}}\right) = \left(\frac{30,209}{9,582,785}\right) = 0.00315$$

$$_{3|}q_{45} = \left(\frac{d_{48}}{l_{45}}\right) = \left(\frac{31,633}{9,582,785}\right) = 0.00330$$

$$_{4|}q_{45} = \left(\frac{d_{49}}{l_{45}}\right) = \left(\frac{33,327}{9,582,785}\right) = 0.00348$$

Each of these figures must be multiplied by the insurance amount and by the present value of 1, discounted in each instance by the length of time the money is held. The money available to pay the first year's claims will be held for one year; for the second year's claims, two years; and so on, with the funds for the last year's claims being held for five years. The relevant discount factors for one, two, three, four, and five years at 4.0 percent interest are 0.962, 0.925, 0.889, 0.855, and 0.822. The net single premium for the five-year term insurance, therefore, can be calculated as shown in Table 15-2.

Table 15-2	Illustrative Net Single Premium Calculation for Five-Year Term Insurance (Male, Age 45, *2001 CSO Mortality*, 4.0% Interest, $1,000)

Policy Year (t)	Age (x)	Calculation	Present Value of Year's Cost of Insurance
1	45	$(\$1,000) \, (q_{45}) \, (v) \quad = (\$1,000) \, (0.00265) \, (0.962)$	= $ 2.55
2	46	$(\$1,000) \, (_{1|}q_{45}) \, (v^2) = (\$1,000) \, (0.00289) \, (0.925)$	= 2.67
3	47	$(\$1,000) \, (_{2|}q_{45}) \, (v^3) = (\$1,000) \, (0.00315) \, (0.889)$	= 2.80
4	48	$(\$1,000) \, (_{3|}q_{45}) \, (v^4) = (\$1,000) \, (0.00330) \, (0.855)$	= 2.82
5	49	$(\$1,000) \, (_{4|}q_{45}) \, (v^5) = (\$1,000) \, (0.00348) \, (0.822)$	= 2.86
		Total (Net Single Premium)	$13.70

Thus, if each insured paid $13.70 to the insurer and if the insurer earned at least 4.0 percent on resultant investments, this aggregate sum would furnish enough money to pay all expected death claims under these five-year term policies. By simply continuing this yearly process, the net single premium for a term insurance contract of any longer duration can be determined.

WHOLE LIFE INSURANCE   Whole life (WL) insurance provides coverage for the whole of life as defined by the mortality table used to calculate premiums, promising to pay the face amount whenever death occurs. It is like the term insurance just considered with the exception that, instead of being limited to a number of years less than the whole of life, it continues to the end of the mortality table. Because the *2001 CSO Table* assumes that everyone dies by attained age 121, the maximum possible age for which the cost of insurance against death needs to be calculated is 120. The NSP on WL insurance issued at male age 45 must, therefore, provide against the possibility that the insured will die during his 45th year, 46th year, 47th year, and so on, continuing for each year thereafter through his 120th year. The total annual probabilities insured against number 76; that is, for ages 45 to 121.

As with the term policy, the likelihood of dying in each separate year is multiplied by the face amount of the policy ($1,000), and each amount is discounted for the number of years from policy issuance. Table 15-3 illustrates the calculation.

Illustrative Net Single Premium Calculation for Whole Life Insurance (Male, Age 45, *2001 CSO Mortality*, 4.0% Interest, $1,000)   Table 15-3

Policy Year (t)	Age (x)	Calculation	Present Value of Year's Cost of Insurance
1	45	($1,000) (q_{45}) (v) = ($1,000) (0.00265) (0.962)	= $ 2.55
2	46	($1,000) $(_{1\mid}q_{45})$ (v^2) = ($1,000) (0.00289) (0.925)	= 2.67
3	47	($1,000) $(_{2\mid}q_{45})$ (v^3) = ($1,000) (0.00315) (0.889)	= 2.80
⋮	⋮	⋮	⋮
74	118	($1,000) $(_{73\mid}q_{45})$ (v^{74}) = ($1,000) (0.00000*) (0.055)	= 0.00**
75	119	($1,000) $(_{74\mid}q_{45})$ (v^{75}) = ($1,000) (0.00000*) (0.053)	= 0.00**
76	120	($1,000) $(_{75\mid}q_{45})$ (v^{76}) = ($1,000) (0.00000*) (0.051)	= 0.00**
		Total (Net Single Premium)	$291.16

* Less than 0.000005
**Less than $0.005

Thus, $291.16 is the net single premium based on the stated assumptions or, stated differently, $291.16 is the present value of the policy's share of each year's expected death claims beginning at age 45 and ending at age 121. While a handful of men may outlive their 120th year, the computation assumes that the insured will not have survived this age. Additionally, because sufficient money will have been accumulated to pay the claim at the close of the 121th year of life, the policy may be terminated for its full face amount at that time.

The net single premium calculation for a WL policy, in essence, apportions the probability of dying (a certainty) over the various years remaining in one's life. Thus, the death probabilities in the preceding WL NSP computation sum to

1.0. By contrast, a summation of the yearly death probabilities in Table 15-1A has no meaning.[*]

ENDOWMENTS We know from Chapter 4 that an endowment promises to pay a stated amount if the insured dies within the term of the policy or (usually) the same amount if the insured survives the term. We mentioned that it can be considered as a combination of term life insurance and a pure endowment. Thus, a five-year endowment insurance policy issued to a male age 45 will pay the face amount if the insured dies during the first, second, third, fourth, or fifth years, or the same amount if the insured survives the endowment period. The net single premium for these two promises can be found by summing the NSP for five years of term life insurance coverage and the NSP for a five-year pure endowment.

We know that the NSP for five years of term life insurance is $13.70. We have but to add to this figure the NSP for the pure endowment feature. As the maturity value is paid only if the insured survives the endowment period, the expected value of the maturity value is the product of the face amount ($1,000) and the probability of surviving the period. From Table 15-1A, we know that the probability of a male age 45 surviving for five years is:

$$_5 p_{45} = \frac{l_{50}}{l_{45}} = \frac{9,434,505}{9,582,785} = 0.98453$$

Stated differently, the probability of the occurrence of the insured event is 0.98453. Because the money paid as a single premium for a five-year pure endowment would be held for five years before the policy matures, the formula for determining the net single premium for a $1,000 pure endowment policy (at 4.0 percent interest) is:

$$NSP = (\$1,000)\,(_5 p_{45})\,(v^5) = (\$1,000)\,(0.98453)\,(0.822) = \$809.28$$

Thus, the NSP for our five year endowment policy is $822.98 ($13.70 + $809.28).

The maturity value of a pure endowment can be considered as comprising two components: an investment fund and a benefit of survivorship element. The investment fund component equals the value of the net single premium accumulated at interest only, thus, in our example:

---

[*] In explaining the differences between YRT and WL insurance, many commentators and publications show a graph of the premium rates for each policy against age. These graphs are intended to illustrate how YRT rates become prohibitively high with age in comparison with the level premiums of ordinary life. Such graphs are actuarially incorrect. The YRT rates are predicated on the probabilities of death for insureds *having attained that age* (i.e., they represent q_x) and not the probabilities of an insured *at age of issue dying in each future year* (i.e., the derived $_{n|}q_x$ figures, apportioning the probability of death over all future years). To have an actuarially accurate graph, either the YRT rates should be discounted for probabilities of survival to each year – thus causing each rate after the first year to be lower – or the face amount of the YRT insurance should be adjusted downward each year, as in a buy-term-invest-the-difference analysis. See Robert E. Cooper, "The Level Premium Concept: A Closer Look," *Journal of the American Society of Chartered Life Underwriters*, Vol. XXX (July 1976).

$$S = (A)(1.04)^5 = (\$809.28)(1.217) = \$984.89$$

The benefit of survivorship component results from the fact that those who die during the endowment period and, therefore, do not collect the policy's pure endowment, nonetheless contribute to the pure endowment risk pool by virtue of their having paid a NSP for this feature. As with any insurance policy, those who do not have a claim contribute in the risk pool to provide the funds to pay those who do have claims.

Thus, the needed $15.11 amount in excess of the investment fund to ensure a total endowment amount of $1,000 is contributed from the pure endowment portion of the NSPs paid by those who died during the endowment period. This benefit of survivorship is the survivors' share of the amounts left by those insureds who died before their policies endowed. Of course, the beneficiaries of the insureds who died before the policy endowed received their payments from the funds contributed for the term insurance portion of the NSPs paid by those who survived the endowment period – a sort of benefit of not surviving, to use parallel, if unpleasant-sounding logic.

Other types of endowment contracts exist: partial endowments, semi-endowments, educational endowments, and double endowments. They differ from the preceding policy in that the pure endowment element is not the same amount as paid on death. One has but to adjust the NSP calculation for the different pure endowment amount.

LIFE ANNUITIES   Life annuities promise to pay the possessor a stated income periodically during the annuitant's lifetime. An **immediate life annuity** is a life annuity for which payments begin one period hence. A **deferred life annuity** is a life annuity for which payments begin more than one period hence. (Most deferred annuities discussed in Chapter 6 are not deferred *life* annuities as those contracts do not become true life annuities until the policyowner elects to annuitize the policy values, except the longevity annuity.)

Immediate Life Annuities   An immediate 10-year temporary life annuity of $100 per year, purchased, say, at age 70 promises to pay $100 per year for 10 years provided the annuitant lives. The first payment is made at the end of the first policy year. The cost of this contract will be the net single premium (present expected value) at age 70 for the 10 promised payments. Because a payment is made at the end of each year, each year's cost must be determined separately and these amounts summed to obtain the NSP. This annuity to a series of 10 pure endowments, the first maturing in one year from date of purchase, the second in two years, the third in three years, and so on, until the 10 payments have been made.

Although the formulaes are equivalent to those for insurance, the mortality tables used for annuity computations are different, as noted earlier. The process for calculating the NSP for this annuity is illustrated in Table 15-4. Were we actually to run the math, we would use a mortality table for annuities, such as the *Annuity 2000 Mortality Table*, a widely used table in U.S. annuity valuation.

Table 15-4   **Net Single Premium Calculation for a 10-Year Immediate Life Annuity**
(Male, Age 70, $100 per year)

Policy Year (t)	Age (x)	Calculation
1	70	$(\$100)(p_{70})\,(v) = (\$100)\left(\dfrac{l_{71}}{l_{70}}\right)(v)$
2	71	$(\$100)(_1p_{70})\,(v^2) = (\$100)\left(\dfrac{l_{72}}{l_{70}}\right)(v^2)$
3	72	$(\$100)(_2p_{70})\,(v^3) = (\$100)\left(\dfrac{l_{73}}{l_{70}}\right)(v^3)$
$\vdots$	$\vdots$	$\vdots$
8	77	$(\$100)(_7p_{70})\,(v^8) = (\$100)\left(\dfrac{l_{78}}{l_{70}}\right)(v^8)$
9	78	$(\$100)(_8p_{70})\,(v^9) = (\$100)\left(\dfrac{l_{79}}{l_{70}}\right)(v^9)$
10	79	$(\$100)(_9p_{70})\,(v^{10}) = (\$100)\left(\dfrac{l_{80}}{l_{70}}\right)(v^{10})$

If the contract issued at male age 70 promised to pay an annuity for the whole of life, the computations must continue throughout the annuity mortality table, which in the case of the *2000 Table* is through age 115. If this same life annuity guaranteed that the first 10 years' payments were to be certain – that is, unaffected by the death of the annuitant before their completion – this fact must be taken into consideration in computing the net cost.

The probability of payment of the first 10 payments is a certainty. Therefore, they would be discounted for interest only. The 11th and all subsequent payments would depend on the probability of survival, and their net cost would be computed in the same manner as above for the pure life annuity.

Deferred Life Annuities   Immediate life annuities are usually purchased by persons of advanced age, and they contemplate the payment of benefits at periodic intervals following the date of issue. Some persons are interested in a deferred life annuity. Such annuities usually are purchased by annual payments during wage-earning years. It is also possible to pay for such a contract by a single premium paid at the date of purchase of the contract, with annuity payments beginning years later.

Assume that it is desired to find the NSP payable for a male, age 40, that will purchase the right to receive a whole life annuity of $100 beginning at age 70. We can analyze this problem through two steps. First, determine the amount of money that must be accumulated by the insurer at the time the annuity begins. This is equivalent to asking how much money must be available at age 70 to furnish $100 annually for life, the first payment to be made when the annuitant reaches age 70.

This problem is identical to that of the immediate whole life annuity just discussed above, with the exception that the first $100 payment is made at age 70, whereas in the former case, the first payment was made at age 71. Therefore, the insurance company must have on hand at the time the annuitant becomes 70 years of age the amount of money necessary to purchase an immediate life annuity, the first payment being at age 70. We merely add $100 to the figure to determine the net cost *at age 70* of a whole life annuity *due*, the first payment of which is made at that age.

Second, we must determine the value at age 40 that will grow to this sum at age 70. The problem is a simple present value calculation:

$$A = (S) \text{ x } (v^{30})$$

Most deferred annuities are purchased on a basis whereby payments (single or periodic) made during the accumulation period are not forfeited in the event of death. The foregoing calculation is based on this premise. With most longevity annuities, the cost at age 40 – were the product available at that age, which is doubtful – would be computed on the assumption that the single premium paid then would be forfeitable (i.e., the purchaser relinquishes any right to his or her contributions in case he or she failed to survive to age 70). In this situation, the above premium values would be discounted as well for the probability of surviving to age 70.

NET LEVEL PREMIUMS

We know that life insurance policies can be purchased with a single premium or by payment of periodic payments made monthly, quarterly, semiannually, or annually, and, with flexible-premium contracts, as often or infrequently as desired. Our focus here will be on traditional fixed-premium term, whole life, endowment, and annuity contract pricing.

If policyowners are given the choice of payment for insurance by single or annual premiums, the amounts must be determined on such a basis that the insurer will receive equivalent value under each method of payment. We know how to compute NSPs. We now have but to find the **net level premium** (NLP), the periodic premium equivalent to the NSP annualized over a specified premium payment period. Such premiums will be paid during the life of the insured or for a limited number of years, but always *cease upon the insured's death*. Note that this is the definition of a life annuity.

It is helpful to view annual premiums as life annuities. They differ in four important respects from the annuities thus far considered. First, they are paid *by* the policyowner *to* the insurer, whereas regular annuities are paid *by* the insurer *to* the annuitant. Second, annuities are ordinarily purchased by single or annual premiums. If annual premiums are analogous to annuities, what does the insurer offer the policyowner as consideration for the series of annuity (premium) payments? It promises a cash payment (the policy face amount) upon the happening of the insured event.

Third, annuitant mortality is considerably lower than insurance mortality. This consideration does not apply to the annuities represented by the annual level premiums, and regular insurance mortality tables are used in the calculations regarding life insurance annual level premiums. Obviously, life insurance purchasers will have the mortality experience of insureds, not that of annuitants. Fourth, the time when annual level premiums and annuity payments begin is different. An immediate life annuity pays the first annual income installment one year from the date of contract issue. In practice, the first annual premium is payable when a life insurance policy is issued and not one year later as is the case with annuities. Thus, a series of premium payments is a *life annuity due*.

The NLP cannot be obtained simply by dividing the net single premium by the number of agreed-upon installments. The NSP is a discounted expected value, and the net annual level premium must reflect (1) the possibility that the insured may die and not pay future premiums and (2) the smaller sum invested by the insurer with correspondingly smaller investment earnings. The series of NLPs will be a life annuity due that is equivalent at issue to the NSP.

TERM LIFE INSURANCE   In computing net annual level premiums, one begins by ascertaining the NSP. The second step is to define the premium payment period over which annual premiums are to be paid and for which the value of life annuity due is to be ascertained. An example will help to clarify the issues. Assume that we seek the NLP for a five-year term insurance policy of $1,000 at male age 45 using the *2001 CSO Table* and 4.0 percent interest. We do not use the *Annuity 2000 Table* because the calculation is required for a life insurance policy.

We found earlier that the NSP for this policy was $13.70. Beginning at date of issue, an annual level premium will be paid over a five-year period or until prior death and is, therefore, a five-year temporary life annuity due. The calculation for the present value of the five-year life annuity due is shown in Table 15-5. Note that the annuity due of 1 for this policy equals a temporary immediate annuity for four years plus 1 paid initially (making it an annuity due).

Table 15-5		Illustrative Five-Year Annuity Due Calculation (Male, Age 45, *2001 CSO Mortality*, 4.0% Interest)		
Policy Year (t)	**Age (x)**	**Calculation**		**Year's Present Expected Value**
1	45	1 due immediately		= 1.000
2	46	$(_1p_{45})\,(v) = \left(\dfrac{l_{46}}{l_{45}}\right)(v) = \left(\dfrac{9{,}557{,}391}{9{,}582{,}785}\right)(0.962)$		= 0.959
3	47	$(_2p_{45})\,(v^2) = \left(\dfrac{l_{47}}{l_{45}}\right)(v^2) = \left(\dfrac{9{,}529{,}674}{9{,}582{,}785}\right)(0.925)$		= 0.919
4	48	$(_3p_{45})\,(v^3) = \left(\dfrac{l_{48}}{l_{45}}\right)(v^3) = \left(\dfrac{9{,}499{,}465}{9{,}582{,}785}\right)(0.889)$		= 0.881
5	49	$(_4p_{45})\,(v^4) = \left(\dfrac{l_{49}}{l_{45}}\right)(v^4) = \left(\dfrac{9{,}467{,}832}{9{,}582{,}785}\right)(0.855)$		= 0.845
		Total		4.604

If the present value of the preceding annuity due is divided into the NSP on this policy, we obtain the NLP, the present value of which equals the NSP. Thus, the general rule for determining the net annual level premium on any policy is that we *divide the net single premium by the present value of a life annuity due of 1 for the premium paying period* or

$$NLP = \frac{NSP}{PVLAD \ of \ 1 \ for \ PPP}$$

Thus the net annual level premium on five-year term insurance policy of $1,000 for male age 45 is computed as follows:

$$NLP = \frac{NSP}{PLVLAD \ for \ 5 \ years} = \frac{\$13.70}{4.604} = \$2.98$$

WHOLE LIFE INSURANCE   The NSP for a WL policy of $1,000 issued at age 45 is $291.16, according to the earlier calculation. To find the NLP for an ordinary life policy, this sum must be divided by the present value of a life annuity due of 1 for the whole of life if premiums are paid annually through the life of this policy. The calculation of the present value of the whole life annuity due of 1 is shown in Table 15-6.

	Illustrative Whole Life Annuity Due Calculation (Male, Age 45, *2001 CSO Mortality*, 4.0% Interest)			Table 15-6

Policy Year (t)	Age (x)	Calculation	Year's Present Expected Value	
1	45	1 due immediately	=	1.000
2	46	$(_1 p_{45})\,(v) = \left(\frac{l_{46}}{l_{45}}\right)(v) = \left(\frac{9,557,391}{9,582,785}\right)(0.962)$	=	0.959
3	47	$(_2 p_{45})\,(v^2) = \left(\frac{l_{47}}{l_{45}}\right)(v^2) = \left(\frac{9,529,674}{9,582,785}\right)(0.925)$	=	0.919
⋮	⋮	⋮		⋮
74	118	$(_{73} p_{45})\,(v^{73}) = \left(\frac{l_{118}}{l_{45}}\right)(v^{73}) = \left(\frac{0^*}{9,582,785}\right)(0.055)$	=	0.000**
75	119	$(_{74} p_{45})\,(v^{74}) = \left(\frac{l_{119}}{l_{45}}\right)(v^{74}) = \left(\frac{0^*}{9,582,785}\right)(0.053)$	=	0.000**
76	120	$(_{75} p_{45})\,(v^{75}) = \left(\frac{l_{120}}{l_{45}}\right)(v^{75}) = \left(\frac{0^*}{9,582,785}\right)(0.051)$	=	0.000**
		Total		18.430

* Less than 0.5
** Less than 0.0005

Thus, the NLP for an ordinary life policy of $1,000 issued at male age 45 with *2001 CSO Table* mortality and on a 4.0 percent basis is:

$$NLP = \frac{NSP}{PVLAD \ of \ 1 \ for \ WL} = \frac{\$291.16}{18.430} = \$15.80$$

With limited payment whole life insurance, the premium payment period is less than the whole of life. The temporary life annuity due of 1 is calculated over the payment period, whatever it may be. Thus, to calculate the NLP for a five-pay WL policy, we divide the same WL NSP of $219.16 by the present value of the five-year temporary life annuity due as derived in Table 10-5, yielding a net level premium of:

$$NLP = \frac{NSP}{PLVLAD \ for \ 5 \ years} = \frac{\$291.16}{4.604} = \$63.24$$

In all instances examined here, the NSP for the WL policy is the same irrespective of the premium-paying period selected. This fact is true because the NSP measures the present value of future expected policy benefits and is blind to the actual premium payment mode.

ENDOWMENTS   Derivation of the NLP for endowments of any premium payment period follows the same formula as above. Derive the NSP for the endowment; i.e., NSP term plus NSP pure endowment. Then divide the result for the PVLAD for the premium payment period.

DEFERRED ANNUITIES   Deferred annuities often are paid with flexible, periodic premiums or, less commonly, by fixed, periodic premiums. Even when premiums are flexible, the contract holder often chooses to pay a level amount with the idea of building to a future target sum. Premiums may continue through the entire period of deferment or for a shorter period. Of course, annual level premiums are paid only while the annuitant is alive.

The calculation for this NLP is identical to that with life insurance with the exceptions noted earlier and the fact that, unlike a life insurance NLP calculation, the divisor for such annuities ordinarily is not a *life* annuity due, because few deferred annuities involve life contingencies during the accumulation period. In other words, except for longevity annuities, premiums paid for deferred annuities during this period are not "forfeited" to provide survivors with a benefit of survivorship were the annuitant to die during the accumulation period.

APPENDIX 15A:

2001 COMMISSIONERS STANDARD ORDINARY (CSO) TABLE OF MORTALITY, MALES, COMPOSITE SMOKER/NONSMOKER

Age (x)	Probability of death during age x (q_x)	Number living at age x (l_x)	Number of deaths during age x (d_x)	Probability of living through age x (p_x)
0	0.00097	10,000,000	9,700	0.99903
1	0.00056	9,990,300	5,595	0.99944
2	0.00039	9,984,705	3,894	0.99961
3	0.00027	9,980,811	2,695	0.99973
4	0.00021	9,978,117	2,095	0.99979
5	0.00021	9,976,021	2,095	0.99979
6	0.00022	9,973,926	2,194	0.99978
7	0.00022	9,971,732	2,194	0.99978
8	0.00022	9,969,538	2,193	0.99978
9	0.00023	9,967,345	2,292	0.99977
10	0.00023	9,965,052	2,292	0.99977
11	0.00027	9,962,760	2,690	0.99973
12	0.00033	9,960,070	3,287	0.99967
13	0.00039	9,956,784	3,883	0.99961
14	0.00047	9,952,901	4,678	0.99953
15	0.00061	9,948,223	6,068	0.99939
16	0.00074	9,942,154	7,357	0.99926
17	0.00087	9,934,797	8,643	0.99913
18	0.00094	9,926,154	9,331	0.99906
19	0.00098	9,916,823	9,718	0.99902
20	0.00100	9,907,105	9,907	0.99900
21	0.00100	9,897,198	9,897	0.99900
22	0.00102	9,887,300	10,085	0.99898
23	0.00103	9,877,215	10,174	0.99897
24	0.00105	9,867,042	10,360	0.99895
25	0.00107	9,856,681	10,547	0.99893

Age (x)	Probability of death during age x (q_x)	Number living at age x (l_x)	Number of deaths during age x (d_x)	Probability of living through age x (p_x)
26	0.00112	9,846,135	11,028	0.99888
27	0.00117	9,835,107	11,507	0.99883
28	0.00117	9,823,600	11,494	0.99883
29	0.00115	9,812,106	11,284	0.99885
30	0.00114	9,800,822	11,173	0.99886
31	0.00113	9,789,650	11,062	0.99887
32	0.00113	9,778,587	11,050	0.99887
33	0.00115	9,767,537	11,233	0.99885
34	0.00118	9,756,305	11,512	0.99882
35	0.00121	9,744,792	11,791	0.99879
36	0.00128	9,733,001	12,458	0.99872
37	0.00134	9,720,543	13,026	0.99866
38	0.00144	9,707,517	13,979	0.99856
39	0.00154	9,693,539	14,928	0.99846
40	0.00165	9,678,610	15,970	0.99835
41	0.00179	9,662,641	17,296	0.99821
42	0.00196	9,645,345	18,905	0.99804
43	0.00215	9,626,440	20,697	0.99785
44	0.00239	9,605,743	22,958	0.99761
45	0.00265	9,582,785	25,394	0.99735
46	0.00290	9,557,391	27,716	0.99710
47	0.00317	9,529,674	30,209	0.99683
48	0.00333	9,499,465	31,633	0.99667
49	0.00352	9,467,832	33,327	0.99648
50	0.00376	9,434,505	35,474	0.99624
51	0.00406	9,399,032	38,160	0.99594
52	0.00447	9,360,872	41,843	0.99553
53	0.00493	9,319,028	45,943	0.99507
54	0.00550	9,273,086	51,002	0.99450
55	0.00617	9,222,084	56,900	0.99383
56	0.00688	9,165,183	63,056	0.99312
57	0.00764	9,102,127	69,540	0.99236
58	0.00827	9,032,587	74,699	0.99173

Age (x)	Probability of death during age x (q_x)	Number living at age x (l_x)	Number of deaths during age x (d_x)	Probability of living through age x (p_x)
59	0.00899	8,957,887	80,531	0.99101
60	0.00986	8,877,356	87,531	0.99014
61	0.01094	8,789,825	96,161	0.98906
62	0.01225	8,693,664	106,497	0.98775
63	0.01371	8,587,167	117,730	0.98629
64	0.01524	8,469,437	129,074	0.98476
65	0.01685	8,340,363	140,535	0.98315
66	0.01847	8,199,828	151,451	0.98153
67	0.02009	8,048,377	161,692	0.97991
68	0.02185	7,886,685	172,324	0.97815
69	0.02364	7,714,361	182,367	0.97636
70	0.02577	7,531,993	194,099	0.97423
71	0.02815	7,337,894	206,562	0.97185
72	0.03132	7,131,332	223,353	0.96868
73	0.03462	6,907,979	239,154	0.96538
74	0.03808	6,668,825	253,949	0.96192
75	0.04191	6,414,876	268,847	0.95809
76	0.04608	6,146,028	283,209	0.95392
77	0.05092	5,862,819	298,535	0.94908
78	0.05656	5,564,285	314,716	0.94344
79	0.06306	5,249,569	331,038	0.93694
80	0.07014	4,918,531	344,986	0.92986
81	0.07819	4,573,545	357,605	0.92181
82	0.08654	4,215,940	364,847	0.91346
83	0.09551	3,851,092	367,818	0.90449
84	0.10543	3,483,274	367,242	0.89457
85	0.11657	3,116,033	363,236	0.88343
86	0.12891	2,752,797	354,863	0.87109
87	0.14235	2,397,934	341,346	0.85765
88	0.15673	2,056,588	322,329	0.84327
89	0.17188	1,734,259	298,084	0.82812
90	0.18766	1,436,174	269,513	0.81234
91	0.20244	1,166,662	236,179	0.79756

Age (x)	Probability of death during age x (q_x)	Number living at age x (l_x)	Number of deaths during age x (d_x)	Probability of living through age x (p_x)
92	0.21783	930,483	202,687	0.78217
93	0.23404	727,796	170,333	0.76596
94	0.25114	557,462	140,001	0.74886
95	0.26917	417,461	112,368	0.73083
96	0.28564	305,093	87,147	0.71436
97	0.30318	217,946	66,077	0.69682
98	0.32188	151,869	48,884	0.67812
99	0.34185	102,986	35,206	0.65815
100	0.36319	67,780	24,617	0.63681
101	0.38008	43,163	16,405	0.61992
102	0.39806	26,758	10,651	0.60194
103	0.41720	16,106	6,720	0.58280
104	0.43756	9,387	4,107	0.56244
105	0.45921	5,280	2,424	0.54079
106	0.48222	2,855	1,377	0.51778
107	0.50669	1,478	749	0.49331
108	0.53269	729	388	0.46731
109	0.56031	341	191	0.43969
110	0.58964	150	88	0.41036
111	0.62079	61	38	0.37921
112	0.65384	23	15	0.34616
113	0.68894	8	6	0.31106
114	0.72618	3	2	0.27382
115	0.76570	1	1	0.23430
116	0.80761	0*	0*	0.19239
117	0.85207	0*	0*	0.14793
118	0.89923	0*	0*	0.10077
119	0.94922	0*	0*	0.05078
120	1.00000	0*	0*	0.00000

*Less than 0.5.

CHAPTER 16

LIFE INSURANCE ACTUARIAL APPLICATIONS

This chapter continues the more detailed examination of the actuarial dimensions of the management of life insurance companies by focusing on the actuarial applications to life insurance product development. Specifically, we cover (1) life insurance reserves, (3) life insurance cash values, (3) premium rate structures, and (4) surplus distribution. Our emphasis is on non-variable life products.[1]

RESERVE DERIVATION

Policy reserves are liabilities that represent the present amount that, with future premiums and interest earned, is expected to be needed to pay future benefits under existing policies. More than 80 percent of the total assets held by U.S. life insurance companies represent funds held to support their policy reserve liabilities.

DEFINITION OF POLICY RESERVE

We noted earlier that life insurance policies may be purchased by a single payment, by fixed annual premiums paid over a period of years, or by flexible premiums. It was also pointed out that mortality rates generally increase with increasing age. Thus, in the early policy years, fixed, level premiums and (often) flexible premiums paid exceed the annual cost of insurance. The excess funds not used immediately to pay policy claims and expenses must be recognized by the insurer as liabilities and backed by assets that must be preserved for the benefit of policyowners until needed at some future date. In a similar manner, when a policy is purchased by a single premium, this premium becomes the policyowner's only contribution toward that policy's share of claims to be paid from the insurance pool and expenses incurred under contracts of the class, and a large share of this single premium must be held by the insurer to meet future obligations.

A **net level premium reserve** is a policy reserve under these policies established for certain policies in recognition that early net level premiums are intended to prefund future insurance charges. We know from the previous chapter that a net level premium is that amount at policy issue that, if paid in accordance with policy provisions, is intended to fund future policy benefits, net of expenses, based on an assumed interest rate and mortality table. Traditionally in the U.S., statutory reserve calculations ignored insurer expenses and lapse rates, being based solely on state-mandated mortality and interest assumptions and on the nature of policy benefits and method of calculation. The reserve as required to be calculated by U.S. regulators has no necessary relationship with the insurer's actual past or expected future experience.

METHODS OF CALCULATION

Reserves can be viewed (and calculated) in two ways: prospectively or retrospectively. The retrospective and prospective approaches are merely different ways of viewing the same issue and, therefore, with the same assumptions will always yield identical results.

RETROSPECTIVE METHOD   The retrospective method "looks back" at a policy's *past* premiums and benefits to determine policy reserves. Under this approach, the policy reserve is defined as follows:

$$\text{Policy Reserve} = \text{Accumulated Value of Net Premiums} - \text{Accumulated Cost of Insurance}$$

The retrospective method may be explained in terms of either a group or individual approach. Under the *group approach*, premiums more than sufficient to pay the death claims that are assumed in the early policy years create a fund to be used in later policy years when death rates rise and premiums alone may be insufficient to meet the then current claims. The retrospective reserve can be thought of as an unearned net premium reserve. It represents the provision in early premiums for prefunding of the benefits of surviving insureds.

Under the *individual approach*, the retrospective terminal (i.e., end-of-year) reserve for any particular policy year can be obtained by adding the net premium for an individual policy for the year in question to its terminal reserve of the preceding year, then (1) increasing the combined sum (called the *initial reserve*) by one year's interest at the assumed rate and (2) deducting the cost of insurance for the net amount at risk for the current year utilizing the rates from the valuation mortality table. Consideration of the process by which this reserve is built involves an understanding of the cost of insurance concept, which was introduced in the Chapter 2 discussion of life insurance pricing.

When an insured dies, the reserve held for the policy is, of course, no longer required. The assets corresponding to that reserve are considered to be freed to help pay the claim. The balance of the claim (the net amount at risk) is paid through charges against all policies in the group, including those that mature as a death claim. The contribution each insured must make as his or her pro-rata share of death claims in any particular year – the cost of insurance – is determined by multiplying the net amount at risk at the end of such year by the tabular probability of death during that year. Of course, this procedure is identical in concept to that used to determine the mortality charges with universal life (UL) policies.

PROSPECTIVE RESERVE   Although the retrospective method of computation offers a clear exposition of the policy reserve, it traditionally has not been used, in favor of the prospective approach. To consider it, we observe that the present value of future expected benefits (PVFB) is identical at policy inception to the present value of future expected net premiums (PVFP). Thus,

$$\text{PVFB} = \text{PVFP} \quad \text{(at date of issue)}$$

As soon as the contract is put into effect, the PVFB ordinarily exceeds the PVFP. This is apparent for any fixed premium policy with a maturity benefit as fewer premiums remain to be paid and the present value of future benefits is greater because the policy is nearer to maturity. The insurer is required to hold reserves such that, together with future premiums, are sufficient to fund all future benefits. Thus,

PVFB		**PVFP**		**Terminal Reserve**
(age of valuation)	=	**(age of valuation)**	+	**(age of valuation)**

Thus, the policy's terminal reserve at any future age at which the valuation is taking place is derived by taking the difference between the PVFB and PVFP,

Terminal Reserve		**PVFB**		**PVFP**
(age of valuation)	=	**(age of valuation)**	−	**(age of valuation)**

We know that the net single premium (NSP) for a given policy is the present value of future expected benefits, so the above equation may be written as

Terminal Reserve		**NSP**		**PVFP**
(age of valuation)	=	**(age of valuation)**	−	**(age of valuation)**

The present value of future net premiums necessarily must equal the net level annual premium (NLP) for the contract under consideration, multiplied by the present value of a life annuity due (PVLAD) of 1 for the remaining premium-paying period. Thus, the equation may be written in word form as

Terminal Reserve		**NSP**		**NLP**		**PVLAD of 1**
(age of valuation)	=	**(age of valuation)**	−	**(issue age)**	x	**for remaining PPP**

This same approach may be illustrated more analytically and concisely as follows:

$$_t V_x = A_{x+t} - (P)(\ddot{a}_{x+t})$$

where $_t V_x$ is the net level terminal reserve for a policy issued at age x at the end of any number of years t, P is the net level premium, and the other variables have the same meanings as discussed in Chapter 15. For whole life (WL) and endowment policies, the PVFP declines each year whereas the PVFB increases. To ensure that the insurer has sufficient funds to meet its future obligations, it must have funds on hand at each age sufficient to fill the gap created by this divergence.

For a policy not yet paid up, consider the 10th year reserve on a 20-payment WL policy issued at age 25. It would be formatted as follows:

Terminal Reserve$_{35}$	=	**NSP**$_{35}$	−	**(NLP**$_{25}$**)**	x	**(PVLAD**$_{35}$ **of 1 for 10 years)**

For a paid up policy, consider the 20th year terminal reserve on a 15-payment WL policy issued at age 35:

$$\text{Terminal Reserve}_{55} = \text{NSP}_{55} - (\text{NLP}_{25}) \quad \text{x} \quad (\text{PVLAD}_{55} \text{ of } 1)$$

$$_{20}V_{35} = \text{NSP}_{55} - (\text{NLP}_{35}) \quad \text{x} \quad (0)$$

$$_{20}V_{35} = \text{NSP}_{55}$$

The result illustrates the principle that, as no further premiums are due on a paid up policy, the reserve must equal the PVFB, which can be measured by the net single premium of the policy at the attained age. Further, with identical pricing assumptions, a single premium WL policy issued at male age 35 would produce a 20th year reserve identical to that of the 20th year reserve on the 15-pay WL policy, both of which would equal the net single premium for a WL policy at male age 55. The reserves at a given attained age on all paid up policies of the same type and amount and calculated under the same assumptions must be equal to each other at the age of valuation, and they all must equal the net single premium for that generic type of policy.

TYPES OF POLICY RESERVES

Reserves derived for different purposes are calculated differently. Here we summarize some of the key variations of policy reserves.

TERMINAL, INITIAL, AND MEAN RESERVES   Reserves may be classified as terminal, initial, or mean depending on the point of time within the policy year when valuation occurs. The calculations illustrated earlier concerned primarily the **terminal reserve** – that is, the present value of future expected benefits less the present value of future expected premiums as of the *end* of any policy year. The **initial reserve** is the reserve at the *beginning* of the policy year and equals the terminal reserve for the preceding year increased by the net level annual premium (if any) for the policy year. The **mean reserve** is the arithmetic average of the initial reserve and the terminal reserve for any year of valuation.

The initial reserve is used in connection with the interest component of dividend determination under participating (par) policies. The terminal reserve is used in connection with dividend distributions, as mortality savings are allocated on the basis of the net amount at risk, and the terminal reserve is used to determine the net amount at risk. The terminal reserve concept also is used to determine nonforfeiture values, although an adjusted premium is used rather than the net level premium in such determinations. Finally, the terminal reserve is used in connection with the form of reinsurance based on yearly renewable term insurance for the net amount at risk.

The mean reserve is used in connection with the annual statements of life insurance companies. As policies are written at different points throughout the year and insurer annual statements are prepared as of December 31, it has historically been complicated and expensive to attempt a precise calculation for each individual policy, although no longer so. For purposes of the annual statement, it is generally assumed that policy anniversaries are uniformly distributed throughout the calendar year of issue, and the mean reserve is used for such valuation purposes.

MODIFIED RESERVES   Ideally, each class of policies should pay its own costs. A principal difficulty is that the expenses of the first policy year usually greatly exceed those of any subsequent year and frequently exceed the entire first year premium. That first year expenses are high can be seen by considering that selling expenses, such as agents' first year commissions and expenses of physical examinations, of approving applications, and of preparing policies for issue, as well as the expenses of setting up records for new policies, are all incurred in the first policy year.

The major problem of the incidence of expense is that early policy expenses exceed contemporaneous income, resulting in a reduction of reported surplus under statutory accounting, called *surplus strain*. These expenses must be met when incurred, yet the insurer faces the necessity of maintaining a reasonable premium level, of paying death claims during the year, and of holding in reserve the remainder of the net premium. If the insurer has a strong enough surplus position, it may choose to meet this strain from this source. Many insurers, especially smaller ones, do not have strong surplus positions and must explore alternatives, such as reliance on reinsurance, but this comes at a cost. Regulations provide another way of dealing with this problem through some modification of the system of valuing reserves, whereby the policy reserve of the first year or of the first few years can be reduced. Two such methods are the full preliminary term method (FPTM) and the commissioners' reserve valuation method (CRVM).

Full Preliminary Term Method   The **full preliminary term method** assumes that the first year's premium under any form of policy pays only for (preliminary) term insurance for the first policy year and that the actual policy for reserve purposes comes into operation one year later than the age of issue and will be one year shorter for premium payment and coverage periods. By this means, the insurer need not earmark any portion of the first year premium to a reserve, with the entire premium being available for payment of first year claims and expenses. As the amount required for first year claims is the net premium for one year term insurance (typically a relatively small amount), the amount available to cover expenses is the excess of the gross premium over the one year term net rate.

The policy reserves for the second and later years are based on the net level premium for the insured but at one year older than the issue age. Thus, an ordinary life policy issued at age 35 would have a reserve at the end of the first year of zero. The reserve at the end of the *second* year would equal that of the *first* year terminal reserve for an ordinary life policy issued at age 36. The renewal (age 36) net premium equals the net level premium for age 36, and it is sufficient to provide benefits for an ordinary life policy issued at age 36 with level net premiums. The remainder of the gross premium is available each renewal year for expenses.

The net effect of the FPTM compared to the net level method is to defer funding the first-year reserve and amortize this amount over the remaining premium paying period of the contract. This method of valuation makes no distinction between various types of cash value contracts. The FPTM, conceived in Europe and once prominent in U.S. valuation law, remains prominent in many markets but is not found in contemporary U.S. law, except as a part of the Commissioner's Reserve Valuation Method (CRVM).

Commissioners' Reserve Valuation Method   The **Commissioner's Reserve Valuation Method** makes the 20-payment WL policy the maximum basis on which deferred reserve funding is permitted, and, in doing so, divides policies into two groups:

1. Those for which the net level premium for the second and subsequent years of the plan do not exceed the corresponding modified net premium for a 20-payment WL plan, in which case the FPTM is used, and

2. Those with higher premiums, in which case the additional amount for expenses is limited to the same amount as is permitted under the FPTM for a 20-payment WL policy. It is not exactly the same as the 20-payment life amount in the case of policies that require more or less than 20 years' premiums because the amount "borrowed" is "repaid" by a level premium payable for each year of the premium paying period, including the first.

For example, for ordinary life at male age 35, the CRVM calls for the FPTM, because the net premium at male age 36 is less than the corresponding 20-payment life preliminary term basis premium for the second and subsequent years. In the case of the endowment at age 65 issued at male age 35, the modified method applies, as the rate at male age 36 for an endowment at age 65 exceeds the 19-payment life rate at male age 36.

PREMIUM DEFICIENCY RESERVES   In the past in the U.S., if gross premiums charged by a life insurance company for a particular class of policies were less than the valuation net premiums, the insurer was required to maintain a supplemental reserve, called a **deficiency reserve**. Deficiency reserve requirements (or their equivalent) are founded on the theory that the use, in the prospective reserve formula, of a valuation net level premium larger than the actual gross premium overstates the PVFP and, consequently, understates the amount of the reserve. The deficiency is represented by the present value of the expected excess of the valuation net premium over the gross annual premium.

U.S. law no longer requires the establishment of deficiency reserves, as such. Rather, the law defines a new minimum required reserve as the PVFB less the present value of expected future valuation net premiums calculated by the method (CRVM or net level) actually used in computing the reserve for the policy, but using the minimum valuation standards of mortality and rate of interest. The gross premium on the policy is substituted in this reserve calculation at each contract year in which it is less than the valuation net premium. If the reserve calculated in this way is larger than the reserve otherwise required, it becomes the minimum reserve for the policy. In practice, the term deficiency reserve is still used to denote these special situations.

GAAP AND STATUTORY RESERVES   In the U.S., statutory minimum reserves are calculated on the basis of the *National Association of Insurance Commissioners* (NAIC) model *Standard Valuation Law* (SVL), which each state has enacted. The law specifies the mortality table and other factors that must be used by companies in calculating minimum policy reserves for their statutory financial statements. Policy reserves calculated under generally accepted accounting principles (GAAP) differ in several respects from statutory policy reserves, as explained in Chapter 14. For unbundled products, GAAP policy reserves are equal to the account value.

GAAP policy reserves for bundled products generally are less conservative than statutory policy reserves because of the following factors:

1. **Mortality Rates**. Insurers may use mortality rates that approximate their own mortality expectations. They generally assume mortality rates based on basic tables, but they often use a higher percentage of the rate shown in the basic table than they use for pricing, adding a margin for adverse results.

2. **Interest Rates**. Insurers may use interest rates that reflect their best expectations for future rates but also with a margin for adverse results.

3. **Lapse Rates**. Insurers may use lapse rates that approximate their expectations in this regard. Under statutory reserve computation, insurers may not take lapses and withdrawal rates into consideration.

The assumptions used for GAAP reserves generally must be used for the life of the policy, even if the insurer's expectations at issue turn out to be wrong. In contrast, under certain conditions, insurers may be permitted to strengthen or de-strengthen their statutory reserves. After business has been in force for some time, statutory assumptions may be changed but remain subject to the minimum standards in the *Standard Valuation Law*.

Another important difference between GAAP and statutory reserves involves the definition of the PVFB. For statutory reserves, the PVFB includes only the present value of future death benefits. Under GAAP, the PVFB for traditional products includes four elements:

- the present value of future death benefits,
- the present value of future surrender benefits,
- the present value of all expected policy dividends, and
- the present value of the insurer's expected maintenance expenses for the business.

Of course, the present value of future surrender benefits is a factor only for products that offer a surrender benefit, and the present value of future policy dividends is involved only with par policies. The present value of future level maintenance expenses generally influences the size of policy reserves only for single premium and other limited payment WL plans. GAAP reserves contain a safety margin to allow for unfavorable variations from actuarial assumptions. Even so, GAAP reserves are generally considerably smaller than statutory reserves.

Modified reserving may not be used with GAAP. Instead, GAAP limits surplus strain indirectly through its requirement that insurers amortize excess first year expenses, as discussed in Chapter 13. While insurers must still pay all first year expenses, only a portion of these expenses is charged to income in that year, with the balance amortized, usually over the premium-paying period, consistent with the matching principle.

To keep their books balanced, insurers create an asset account called **deferred acquisition costs** (DAC) representing that portion of first year policy expenses incurred by an insurer not charged against income in that year and amortized via a charge to income in those later years. Each year a portion of the expenses being amortized is charged to current income, and the DAC account is reduced accordingly. The effect of this process is that an insurer's first year acquisition expenses reduce surplus over a period of years, minimizing the strain on surplus. Thus, in examining GAAP reserves, it is necessary to deduct the DAC account from the GAAP policy reserves resulting in **net GAAP reserves**. Net GAAP reserves are similar to modified statutory reserves, both reflecting the need to ease the strain on surplus of excess first year expenses.

SIGNIFICANCE OF ACTUARIAL ASSUMPTIONS

In valuing its liabilities under outstanding contracts, a life insurance company must make assumptions as to the rate of mortality among its insureds and the rate of earnings on the assets backing the reserves. These assumptions are reflected in the mortality table and rate of interest assumed in making the valuation and the purpose for which the valuation is made, all of which may themselves be constrained by regulatory, tax, and other laws. Each assumption has an important impact on the valuation.

- **Mortality**. It usually is not possible merely by reviewing the mortality rates of two tables to determine which will result in the larger reserves at a given age and duration. Under the net level premium method, the effect of a change in mortality is somewhat spread over the premium paying period. The simplest way to analyze the effect of a change in mortality table is to calculate the reserves on both mortality bases for representative plans and issue ages. Without actually calculating the reserves, the determination of the effect on reserves of a change in mortality assumptions is a complex mathematical problem beyond the scope of this volume. In general, however, we observe that each move to a new valuation mortality table over the past decades has resulted in a decrease in required reserves for most ages, other things being equal.
- **Interest**. The impact on reserves of a change in the interest assumption can be easily visualized. If the assumed interest rate is decreased, the reserve will increase, as smaller anticipated earnings must be offset by a larger reserve at any point in time. The impact of the change in interest assumption in terms of the conventional prospective and retrospective methods of calculation is less clear as both the assumed earnings on the assets backing the reserve and the net premiums are affected by the change, and the net effect on these modifications leads to the final reserve level. Even so, because the prospective approach utilizes a present value calculation, we know that the higher the interest rate used in any present value calculation, the lower the present value, *ceteris paribus*. Thus, with reserve (and cash value) derivation, the higher the interest rate used, the lower the values, other things being held constant.
- **Lapse Rates.** Life insurance statutory policy reserves are calculated on the assumption that no policies will withdraw from coverage. This requirement makes the PVFB for statutory reserves considerably greater than the insurer's actual present value of future benefits. Withdrawal rates are considered in pricing and in calculating reserves based on GAAP and will be allowed under the proposals of the NAIC with respect to principles-based reserving, as discussed in Chapter 13 and below.

REGULATION OF POLICY RESERVES

Each U.S. state's laws stipulate the requirements that insurers must meet in calculating policy reserves for purposes of complying with statutory accounting requirements. In other countries, such as Canada and the U.K., the actuary has latitude in determining reserves, and a recently revised NAIC model *Standard Valuation Law* will grant U.S. insurers similar latitude. This new standard will allow principles-based reserving (PBR) but will not be effective country-wide until the year after (1) states representing at least 75 percent of 2008 total direct premiums written and (2) 42 of the 55 applicable jurisdictions have enacted the model law or the equivalent. At the time this book was going to press, it was expected that the new law would take effect not earlier than 2015 or 2016. As insurers have three years to implement the changes, we could witness widespread use of PBR only in 2018 or later.

Until that time, existing state SVLs must be followed. These laws have the effect of establishing minimum reserves for each life insurance policy sold in the U.S. The basis for reserve computation is stated in terms of the mortality table to be used, the maximum rate of interest to be assumed, and the method to be applied. The requirements differ as between life insurance and annuities and as among ordinary, group, and industrial life insurance. Supplementary agreements relating to proceeds left with the insurance company are subject to special rules. Additional aspects of the new SVL were discussed in Chapter 13.

REQUIREMENTS   Prior to 1948, some states had SVLs, but the laws were not uniform and applied only to policies issued in that state. As from January 1, 1948, states began following the 1948 version of a model SVL law, with current laws still based largely on that 1948 logic. The law required use of the *1941 CSO Mortality Table*. The *1958 CSO Table* was made mandatory on policies issued on or after January 1, 1966, with revised maximum interest requirements enacted at the same time.

Existing valuation laws still stipulate (1) the mortality table to be used, (2) the maximum interest rate to be assumed, and (3) the method to be applied. The SVL of the state in which the policy was issued applies. The maximum interest rates permitted vary as between annuities and life insurance, and, within each of these categories, based on duration and plan types. The longer the policy duration, the lower the maximum permissible interest rate, *ceteris paribus*.

The permissible maximum interest rate changes periodically based on whether significant changes occur in the *Moody's Corporate Bond Yield Average-Monthly Average Corporates*, as published by Moody's Investors Service, Inc. The maximum interest rates themselves depend on the type of insurance contract, and they may be much smaller than this composite yield rate. These maximum rates are recalculated at 12-month intervals. The maximum rate for a particular life insurance policy (or individual annuity contract) is fixed at its date of issue. A change in the maximum interest rate applies only to newly issued life insurance policies (or individual annuity contracts) – not to those already in force.

The 1980 model SVL introduced a new family of mortality tables, the *1980 CSO Mortality Tables*. The model law also permitted the substitution of new NAIC-approved mortality tables by regulation, not by amendment to existing law. Thus, as from 2009, the laws required use of the *2001 CSO Mortality Tables*. Finally, the law stipulates that the method used for calculating minimum reserves can be the CRVM. The net level premium method is not required but may be used as it develops higher reserves than the CRVM.

An important update to the NAIC model SVL adopted in 1990 was the requirement of the annual filing of an actuarial opinion. The **actuarial opinion** is a certification of "whether the reserves and related actuarial items ... are computed appropriately, are based on assumptions which satisfy contractual provisions, are consistent with prior reported amounts and comply with applicable laws of this state." The person who is to render the actuarial opinion is designated as the **appointed actuary**. Larger insurers and insurers that do not meet certain financial tests must also file their appointed actuary's opinion as to whether reserves and related actuarial items, in light of the insurer's assets, make adequate provision for the anticipated cash flows required by the insurer's contractual obligations and related expenses.

While specifying minimum reserve standards, the law further requires insurers to maintain aggregate reserves sufficient for the appointed actuary to be able to render the required opinion. This requirement means that insurers should maintain greater reserves than those resulting from the minimum reserve standards if, in the actuary's opinion, they are necessary. Numerous countries, including the U.K., Canada, and Australia, have a history of reliance on the accounting and actuarial professions for insurer financial monitoring.

The SVLs permit state insurance commissioners to promulgate special reserve (and surrender) requirements for policies whose cost and benefit structures do not fit easily into the classical mold. Some commissioners have taken advantage of this legislative opportunity by stipulating special requirements for unbundled products. These special requirements usually are patterned after the NAIC *Universal Life Model Regulation*.

In viewing reserve requirements for UL policies, it should be recognized that the UL account value mechanism is the cost structure of the policy. The guaranteed interest rate and mortality and loading charges take the place of the premium rate in more traditional forms of insurance. The flexible premium aspect of UL policies means that future premiums and policy benefits are not determinable at issue or at date of valuation, so the traditional methodology of "present value of future benefits minus present value of future premiums" is impractical.

The regulation defines a future premium to use for calculating policy reserves based on the level premiums needed at issue to cover guaranteed death benefits and to endow the contract at its maximum maturity date. The reserve calculations require that a projection of future benefits be made, using the fund value at the valuation date and assumed future premiums. Numerous issues remain concerning UL reserve derivation, including the appropriate means of calculating them when the policy has so-called secondary guarantees, such as a no-lapse guarantee.

PRINCIPLES-BASED RESERVE REQUIREMENTS   As mentioned above and in Chapter 13, a new SVL is expected to come into force in the near future, after many years of analysis and debate and with critically important work by the *American Academy of Actuaries*. The heart of this new law is replacement of the historical mandate to use static formulae and prescribed deterministic values in deriving reserves with a PBR approach using risk analysis techniques, such as modeling and simulation, and each insurer's own experience in an effort to capture better the various risks inherent in specific life insurance contracts. Provisions would be required for adverse deviations of actual from expected results. The new law will also add reserves for certain benefits, options, and guarantees that involve significant risks but that previously required little or no reserves under state laws, such as surrender benefits and no-lapse guarantees.

The approach would be much like that used in Canada but with more regulation. Those supporting the new approach have noted that U.S. life insurers have had to comply with multiple regulations influencing product design, which usually emphasize details with which regulators seemingly should have little concern. Insurer interpretations of regulations and regulatory guidance in design sometimes have been confusing or skewed, leading to expenditure of enormous time and effort by both the regulatory and business communities in an attempt to "get it right." The new approach would shift the burden to qualified actuaries, which does not require the great number of regulations and actuarial standards of practice presently found in the U.S. Those opposing use of the new approach contend that the practical effect will be another step in weakening life insurer reserves and so life insurer financial solidity.

CASH VALUE DERIVATION

Whether the reserve is for a level premium or a flexible premium policy, the result is the same – prefunded mortality charges. What is an appropriate, fair disposition of these prefunded charges if the policyowner surrenders his or her policy? The insurer no longer requires the assets to back the policy reserve, as its future liability under the policy ceases. Although the practice of allowing a cash surrender value in some form is old, for many years doing so was entirely optional on the part of U.S. insurers and remains optional in many markets, including in Canada.

CONCEPTS OF EQUITY

The actual treatment of withdrawing policyowners can be based on at least three possible concepts of equity. They are that terminating policyowners should receive:

1. Nothing,
2. A surrender value equal to the policy's net level premium reserve, or
3. A surrender value based on the policy's asset share.

The first view is that insurers should be permitted to design life insurance policies that promise nothing on policy termination. Of course, most term policies operate in this fashion, and many countries allow WL and other long-duration policies to be sold without offering a surrender value. For example, level premium term to age 100 has been an important product in the Canadian market.

Arguments for this view are that (1) many consumers purchase life insurance primarily or solely for the death benefit and care little about accumulating funds through a life insurance policy and (2) premiums for such a policy could be lower than those offering surrender values, by some estimates between 10 to 30 percent lower, depending on other factors. Under this approach, the policyowner bears the primary risk of loss associated with policy termination.

Further support for this view comes from the increasingly active secondary life insurance market wherein existing policies can be sold through life settlements.

If a policyholder no longer wants his or her policy, in theory, it often can be sold to others willing to, in effect, wager on the insured's life, especially if the insured's health has deteriorated. See Chapter 23. In fact, a WL policy without any cash values but a lower premium than another with cash values, likely would be worth more in the secondary market than the cash value policy. When the first *Standard Nonforfeiture Law* was widely adopted in the U.S. in 1948, a secondary life insurance market did not exist.

Discussions have taken place at the U.S. regulatory level about the possibility of permitting long term policies with no cash values, but they have not led to a meaningful relaxation of past nonforfeiture standards. Critics of current nonforfeiture requirements assert that the laws hinder creativity and innovation in product design. They further point out that the existence of surrender values encourages policy lapse, both because premiums are higher than otherwise and because the financial penalty for lapse is at least partially mitigated. Adverse selection – those in poor health are unlikely to lapse – ensures that ultimate mortality will be worse. Those opposed to eliminating requirements for cash values note that many buyers are not well informed about what they are purchasing and its risks and that buyers' beliefs and expectations often prove wrong, so the additional charge for having cash values, in effect, protects policyowners against their own ignorance or myopia.

At the other extreme, it has been argued that the withdrawing policyowner should be entitled to the return of all premiums paid (less dividends) plus interest at the contractual rate, less a pro-rata share of assumed death claims – that is, to the full net level reserve under the contract, irrespective of the policy year in which the surrender occurs. This view ignores the incidence of expense and assumes that unamortized acquisition expenses under policies surrendered during the early years after issue should be borne by persisting policyowners or charged to the insurer's general surplus or the agent's commission.

Proponents of this view note that a substantial proportion of purchasers of cash value policies terminate their policies within the first few policy years, even though it is accepted wisdom that these policies should be purchased only for long term needs. A high rate of early policy termination results in substantial consumer loss – loss that arguably is traceable to a large extent to the policy not having been suitable for the customer in the first instance. This lack of suitability could have stemmed from improper or incomplete counseling during the sales process, from the policy offering poor value, or from a host of other reasons. Thus, under this view, insurers and agents, having a greater financial stake in whether a policy terminates early and superior insurance knowledge, would be incented to do a better job of matching policy to customer needs and a better job of disclosure.

Critics of this view note that not all or perhaps even most early lapses result from unsuitable policies. Unforeseen changes in the consumer's circumstances also undoubtedly increase the rate of early policy termination. Further, they note, this approach encourages early lapse (and attendant adverse mortality selection) and could lead to an increase in overall premium rates, thus resulting in fewer sales.

The third concept of equity and the one that most closely tracks the intent of current state nonforfeiture laws is that withdrawing policyowners should receive a surrender value that is closely equivalent to their contribution to the funds of the insurer less (1) the cost of protection received, (2) any expenses incurred by the insurer in establishing and handling the policy, and (3) perhaps a contribution to insurer surplus or profit. The objective is that the withdrawal of an insured should neither benefit nor harm the continuing insurance pool in a substantial way. Under this concept, the amount received by the withdrawing policyowner would be based on the pro-rata share of the assets accumulated by the insurer on behalf of the classification of policies to which his or her policy belongs – that is, the asset share – although further deductions from the asset share can be justified.

The asset share value reflects the incidence of expense and its relationship to policy duration. It has been argued that the actual cash surrender benefit may be somewhat less for several reasons including the following:

- **Adverse Financial Selection.** In normal times, life insurance companies enjoy an excess of income over expenditures that is more than sufficient to meet liquidity demands. During difficult economic times, as well as in a rising interest rate environment thanks to disintermediation, demand may be so great that insurers must liquidate assets at depressed prices. The policyowner's option to demand the policy's cash surrender value at any time also necessitates a more liquid investment portfolio than would otherwise be required. Many insurers believe that policyowners who surrender their policies should be charged with the risk of loss of investment earnings (including capital losses), and they take this into account in establishing the surrender value.

- **Adverse Mortality Selection.** A life insurance policy is a unilateral contract to which the insurer always must adhere but which the policyowner has the option of terminating at any time. Whenever the payment of premiums seems a hardship, healthy insureds, not feeling the immediate need for insurance, may discontinue coverage. By contrast, insureds in poor health are more likely to appreciate fully the value of their insurance and can be expected to exert themselves to pay the premium. Hence, policies on the good risks are more likely to lapse if surrender values are liberal, while impaired risks are less likely to terminate their policies. This adverse (mortality) selection argues for terminating policyowners receiving less than the pro-rata share of their policies to provide funds to meet the higher death rate among the poorer risks that remain.

- **Other Reasons.** Some insurers believe that each contract should make a permanent contribution to the insurer's surplus or profit both to absorb adverse fluctuations and to enhance the insurer's overall financial security. To the extent that such a permanent contribution is required, the surrender allowance should be reduced. Further, a certain amount of expense is incurred in processing the surrender of a policy. Some insurers adjust the surrender value to reflect this factor rather than taking it into account in their premium loading formula.

REGULATION OF CASH VALUES

As with reserve requirements, all U.S. states have enacted *Standard Nonforfeiture Laws* (SNLs) that mandate the assumptions and method by which minimum cash surrender values are to be derived. Insurers may have surrender values higher than those required by the nonforfeiture laws, but values cannot be lower. As with reserves, the basis for surrender value computation is stated in terms of the mortality table to be used, the maximum rate of interest to be assumed, and the method to be applied.

The historical discussion about the mortality tables required to derive reserves applies to deriving surrender values as well, including use of the *1948, 1958, 1980, and 2001 CSO Tables*. While the same family of tables is used, different individual tables from that family may be used for calculation of reserves and cash surrender values. For example, an ultimate table is sometimes used to derive cash values, while a select and ultimate table is used for reserve derivation.

Past and present nonforfeiture laws also mandate maximum interest rates, but these are higher than the mandated maximums for deriving reserves, in the interest of promoting solvency. In each instance where there was an update to the SVL, so too was there a parallel update to the SNL. As we know, the surrender values required to be returned have been called *nonforfeiture values*, and the form in which these values may be taken are referred to as *nonforfeiture options*. As with the regulation of reserves, the SNL of the state in which the policy was issued applies.

REQUIREMENTS   Current SNLs stipulate that the nonforfeiture interest rate cannot exceed 125 percent of the reserve interest rate. Of course, insurance companies are free to use rates lower than the maximum permitted in law and many do so. The minimum nonforfeiture value at any policy duration is the present value of the future benefits under the policy less the present value of future *adjusted* premiums. This definition is essentially the prospective reserve formula utilizing an adjusted premium in lieu of the valuation net level premium. The **adjusted premium** is the level premium necessary to pay the benefits guaranteed by the policy (the net level premium) *plus* the level equivalent of a defined special first year expense allowance.

The maximum **first year expense allowance** is recognition that companies incur high initial costs that can be taken into consideration in deriving nonforfeiture values and presently is defined as the sum of (1) 1.0 percent of the average amount of life insurance over a policy's first 10 years (or $10 per $1,000) and (2) the lesser of 125 percent of the nonforfeiture net level premium or $40 per $1,000. The maximum first year expense allowance per $1,000 face amount is, therefore, $60 (1.25 x $40 + $10). If application of the formula to a specific policy results in an allowance of less than $60, the lesser figure must be used. Only by chance does this rule-driven allowance approximate a policy's actual acquisition costs. Further, it fails to recognize that costs vary by type and size of policy (beyond certain small sizes), in addition to many other variables. In an era before computers, one size was made to fit all and remains largely so today.

Calculation of the adjusted premium may be made in either of two actuarially equivalent ways. It may be regarded as the net annual level premium required to amortize a principal sum equal to the present value of the benefits under the policy and the special first year expense allowance. The second way of considering the adjusted premium is that it is the sum obtained by adding to the regular net annual level premium the annual amount needed to amortize the special acquisition expenses over the premium paying period.

The final step in determining the minimum surrender value is to substitute the adjusted premium for the regular net level premium in the formula employed in the computation of prospective reserves. In actuarial notation, this would be written:

$$_{t}CV_{x} = A_{x+t} - (P^{A})(\ddot{a}_{x+t})$$

where, $_{t}CV_{x}$ is the minimum cash surrender value for the policy issued at age x at the end of any number of years t, P^{A} is the adjusted net level premium, and the other variables have the same meanings as discussed in Chapter 15. The adjusted premium can be easily derived from the following formula:

$$P^{A} = (A_{x} + E) \div \ddot{a}_{x}$$

where E is the expense allowance calculated as described above.

For UL nonforfeiture values, the *Universal Life Model Regulation* breaks with the methodology required in the SNL and bases minimum values on a retrospective accumulation. Minimum required cash surrender values equal the accumulation at interest of premiums less acquisition and administrative expense charges, mortality and other benefit charges, service charges, and deductions for partial withdrawals. Acquisition expense charges are limited to the allowance provided in the SNL for a fixed premium, fixed benefit plan that would endow for the specified amount at the UL policy maximum maturity date.

Surrender charges are permitted and may not exceed any unused, unamortized acquisition expense allowance plus any excess interest credited in the previous 12 months. There are no limits on administrative, benefit, or service charges and no minimum interest rate. For fixed-premium unbundled products, the regulation basically is a restatement of the nonforfeiture law, with an explanation that future guaranteed benefits include those not depending on the policy account value, such as no-lapse guarantees.

Regulators and many industry executives have been concerned with nonforfeiture values in UL policies because the lack of limits on charges and interest credits produces no meaningful minimum cash surrender values. Some prefer to have explicit maximum benefit charges and minimum interest rates or a minimum interest rate of 3.0 percent or both. Proposals to place these limits in the regulation have met resistance from companies selling UL policies.

Many companies provide surrender values in excess of the minimums implicit in SNLs. This may be accomplished by (1) assuming lower first year expenses than the maximum permitted, (2) assuming the maximum expenses and amortizing them over a shorter period or at an uneven rate over the premium paying period, (3) assuming a lower rate of interest than that permitted by law, or (4) a combination of the above. If lower first year expenses are assumed, the adjusted premium will be smaller, making the present value of future adjusted premiums smaller and resulting in larger surrender values.

Similarly, in the case of amortizing the maximum permitted excess first year expense allowance over a shorter period or at an uneven rate, the adjusted premium is itself adjusted, this modified adjusted premium being known as a **nonforfeiture factor**. Where larger values are derived through the use of nonforfeiture factors, the term **standard nonforfeiture value method** is applied. The term **adjusted premium method** refers to the derivation of minimum values only.

Not all life insurance policies are required to have cash values according to SNLs. The laws exempt certain level term policies and all decreasing term policies provided they expire before age 71. The law also exempts reinsurance, group insurance, and policies for which the above formula would produce cash values of less than 2.5 percent of the beginning year insurance amount.

EVOLUTION OF MORE FLEXIBLE NONFORFEITURE STANDARDS   The forthcoming change underway in the U.S. from formulaic reserving to PBR represents a fundamental shift in U.S. regulatory solvency protection philosophy. A parallel process is underway with respect to SNLs, although developments lag the SVL work. A work group of the *American Academy of Actuaries* was charged by an NAIC task force in 2010 to "study the feasibility of a new nonforfeiture law for life insurance and annuities to replace the existing nonforfeiture standards." The work group has stated that reform is needed because of:

- Competition in the financial services industry,
- Advances in technology,
- Increased consumer awareness and access to information,
- Rigidity of the current formulaic approach to nonforfeiture minimums,
- An existing regulatory framework that tends to lead companies to use complex and difficult to understand product designs to ensure compliance,
- Current laws and varying interpretations that result in inconsistent regulatory treatment of products with similar benefit guarantees, and
- Current laws that fail to recognize relationships between the value of pre-funded benefits and a product's gross premiums.

They noted that a new approach offers several potential benefits for consumers, companies, and regulators. It could increase the number of product choices available to consumers, while offering potentially lower cost products. It could enable companies to simplify their designs, rendering them more understandable to consumers, while making available new and innovative products. It could enhance regulatory oversight through greater transparency and flexibility in SNL mandates.

The group's proposed approach provides specific guidance with respect to minimum nonforfeiture methodologies but only general guidance with respect to the establishment of assumptions, and not explicitly define values or parameters, as with current law. In other words, they embrace some of the same concepts as found in the PBR approach, allowing qualified actuaries to set mortality and other necessary inputs. The group's proposal to the NAIC would have newly issued policies after some effective date follow their less prescriptive approach to value determination, called the *Gross Premium Nonforfeiture Method* (GPNM). This method embeds three key elements: (1) a new actuarial methodology to determine required nonforfeiture values, (2) enhanced consumer reporting and information access process, and (3) an enhanced regulatory information system and feedback loop to facilitate oversight.

The proposed GPNM approach is based on a set of *Guaranteed Nonforfeiture Basis* (GNFB) factors selected by the insurer, subject to certain guidelines and guardrails. These GNFB factors are applied to the actual gross premiums paid and any resulting prefunding values are used, along with any declared and credited nonguaranteed elements, in the determination of what is defined as the *Required Policy Nonforfeiture Account* (RPNA). All policies with any prefunding must have an RPNA value, subject to "de minimis" exceptions. An unresolved issue at the time this book was going to press was whether contracts would be required to have cash surrender values when an RPNA was present. Regardless of whether required, any cash value made available must be actuarially related to the RPNA amount but not necessarily equal to it. The approach, in other words, is quite similar to that of the account value mechanism within UL policies.

We now examine how insurers develop the actual gross premiums that they charge policyholders or, in the case of UL policies, the rate structure. We use the term gross premium rate structures to encompass both gross premiums and a UL policy's account value mechanism. As noted in Chapter 15, one approach to developing gross premiums is to add to the net premium a loading to cover insurer expenses, taxes, profits, and contingencies. The more contemporary approach is to solve an equation for the amount necessary to provide the package of options that is a life insurance policy.

We first introduce the four key components or elements of rate structures. We then provide an overview of the calculation of rate structures. We close this section emphasizing the critical role of profitability and testing in the entire process.

DERIVATION OF GROSS PREMIUM RATE STRUCTURES

ELEMENTS OF GROSS PREMIUM RATE STRUCTURES

Once the particulars of the product being considered in terms of the benefits and their pattern are settled on, derivation of a gross premium rate structure relies on these four elements: (1) the expected amount and incidence of claims, (2) an appropriate rate of investment return, (3) amounts to cover expected expenses, taxes, profits (or surplus), and contingences, and (4) withdrawal rates and amounts withdrawn. All calculations in this and the previous chapter are made on the assumption that premiums are paid annually. In fact, most premiums are not paid annually and adjustments of the annual premium are required, as discussed in Box 16-1.

Box 16-1
Other-than-annual Premiums

Premiums paid other-than-annually are called **fractional** or **modal premiums**. When premiums are paid in this manner, a carrying charge is added to the fractional premiums, based on the company's experience. The purpose of the carrying charge is to reimburse the insurance company for the additional expense associated with more frequent premium collection, to offset the loss of interest stemming from the deferment of part of the year's premium, to compensate for the higher lapse rates that often arise when premiums are paid other than annually, and to compensate for fractional premiums not paid in the year of death. The carrying charge is sometimes viewed as including an element of life insurance protection as companies disregard any remaining fractional premiums due in the year of death.

A fractional premium often is calculated by multiplying the annual premium by a specified factor and sometimes adding to the result a flat amount. Common factors for semiannual premiums are 0.51, 0.515, and 0.52; for quarterly premiums, 0.26, 0.2625, and 0.265; and for monthly premiums, 0.0875, 0.0883, and 0.09. See Chapter 19 for a discussion of the lack of consumer disclosure in connection with modal premiums.

Under traditional policy forms, assumptions as to each of these elements can be selected, a formula embodying all of them derived, and a premium rate calculated. Under unbundled product forms, assumptions are still required, but such policies offer the ability to explicitly tailor the margins on each element to meet specific competitive or profitability objectives. In any event, with both bundled and unbundled product forms, tentative gross premium rate structures are tested and refined through profit studies to ensure they are consistent with insurer objectives, as examined later.

Each of the above four elements is explored below. As background for this discussion, the reader may wish to review the introductory pricing discussion contained in Chapter 2.

MORTALITY   Small to medium-sized insurers often rely on the mortality rates from studies by the *Society of Actuaries* or obtained from reinsurers or consulting firms, making adjustment in the data as they believe appropriate. Larger insurers usually develop internal policy mortality charges for their life insurance products from a study of their own recent mortality experience. This experience will have been determined by the characteristics of the cohort of insureds from which the experience was drawn. A host of factors influences mortality, including age, sex, health, body mass, occupation, avocations, lifestyle, smoking status, wealth, and drug and alcohol usage. Ideally, the study will have categorized mortality across as many of these characteristics as feasible, permitting their use to form both rating categories and underwriting classifications. In making these categorizations, two interrelated factors must be considered: (1) the market from which the experience was gathered and (2) the nature and degree of underwriting applicable to the experience group.

Insurers develop products to be relevant and appeal to certain target markets. These markets can vary enormously in their composition and so too can their mortality experience. For example, we know that individuals with low incomes and wealth do not live as long on average as those of moderate incomes or wealth, and that individuals of still higher incomes and wealth live longer still. It is, therefore, important that the target market from which mortality experience underlying a product's mortality charges was drawn be similar to the target market for the new product or that appropriate adjustments be made in the data.

Second, the degree and rigor of underwriting applied to the experience group has a strong influence on the mortality experienced. For example, the mortality experience under guaranteed issue ("take all comers") life insurance, which involves no underwriting, and under simplified issue ("accept or reject") life insurance, which involves minimal underwriting, results in comparatively high mortality rates. Mortality experience under life insurance policies issued on a nonmedical basis – meaning without a physical exam but with health questions and reports from the proposed insured's health care professionals – would be better but still not superior. Policies issued with rigorous underwriting tend to result, unsurprisingly, in superior mortality experience. Further, the larger the policy face amount, the more rigorous generally is the underwriting.

These two factors are interrelated and can be mutually reinforcing. For example, high-income individuals purchase larger policies (and undergo greater underwriting scrutiny) than do low-income individuals, other things being equal.

Simplified issue policies of modest amount appeal more to low- and middle-income individuals than do regular underwritten policies purchased most frequently by higher-income individuals.

After determining the most relevant mortality experience, actuaries use this information as the basis for setting the charges to be assessed different insureds. These charges can be viewed as falling into two categories. First, sets of standardized mortality charges will be established for each age and sex combination and usually subdivided further into smoking status. Second, sets of optional mortality charges will be established to be added to the standardized charges for those proposed insureds whose characteristics suggest a shorter life expectancy than that implicit within the standardized charges.

In developing standardized mortality charges, underlying mortality experience will be sorted (if possible) according to the various rating categories intended for use. Either implicitly with bundled products or explicitly with unbundled products, **mortality margins** are added to the underlying mortality rates to develop the actual mortality charges to be assessed within the policy. Here is the procedure:

> **Procedure for Setting Actual Mortality Charges**
> Estimate relevant historical mortality experience rates
> + Mortality margin
> = Mortality charges

Mortality (and other) margins are a part of an insurer's overall pricing structure and are not necessarily intended to represent mortality and its risk only. They can provide a cushion against adverse developments and can be a source of insurer profits, surplus accumulations, and/or expense recovery. For bundled products, the set of internal current mortality charges typically is not revealed to prospective applicants. For unbundled products, the set of current mortality charges either is explicitly stated in the policy illustration or can be obtained on request, with the guaranteed maximum rates stated in the contract itself.

As we know, mortality charges for unbundled products typically are called *cost of insurance* (COI) rates. Whether bundled or unbundled, all life insurance policies are assessed mortality charges to pay for the policy's pure (YRT) insurance component or, stated equivalently, each policy's fair share of yearly death claim benefits paid. Hence, a specific set of premium or COI rates is developed for each age-sex-smoking status combination. Increasingly, insurers also provide even lower premium and COI rates for proposed insureds who exhibit "preferred" characteristics (e.g., low weight in relation to height, no family deaths from cancer or heart disease before age 60, no adverse personal health history).

Of course, the older the proposed insured, the higher the mortality charges, other things being equal. Males are charged higher rates than similarly situated females, as females live about eight years longer than males on average. Smokers are charged more than nonsmokers for the same reason. Individuals having preferred characteristics live longer than do those who do not, all else equal. These differences manifest themselves in COI rates that vary by these characteristics, as the table below for one insurer with four rating categories shows:

Monthly COI Rates for a Life Insurer with Four Rating Categories							
Age 55							
Females				Males			
Nonsmoking		Smoking		Nonsmoking		Smoking	
Preferred	Standard	Preferred	Standard	Preferred	Standard	Preferred	Standard
[$1.18]	[$1.75]	[$5.10]	[$5.10]	[$1.38]	[$2.00]	[$5.56]	[$6.17]

The chart shows that the lowest annual rates, $1.18 and $1.38 per $1,000 of net amount at risk, are for nonsmoking, preferred-class females and males respectively. Note the substantial rate differences for nonsmokers and smokers, reflecting higher probabilities of death for smokers than for nonsmokers and probably other pricing considerations as well.

Continued mortality improvements are likely to have an impact on future product pricing and, to a lesser extent, repricing. Most mortality experts believe that mortality rates will decline further in the future because of continuing medical advances, aided by research. Actuaries and other insurance industry experts are also generally optimistic about future improvements in insured mortality experience. They believe the insurance industry will develop an even better understanding of the risk factors affecting mortality and, in turn, will develop more refined underwriting tools and techniques.

Other researchers are not as optimistic. They believe that sedentary lifestyles and the continuing rise in obesity will take their toll. They also observe that the smoking cessation rate might be ending or even reversing. The high cost of health care itself is an additional deterrent to access.

INVESTMENT RETURNS   Determining the rate of interest to be used in pricing calculations involves estimates of investment returns over the next 20 or more years. These estimates must be made with knowledge that the long-range impact of interest on life insurance pricing is great. The interest rate selected normally falls within a range of possible rates, the upper limit of which (during a period when interest rates are increasing) is the rate being earned on new investments and the lower limit the valuation rate of interest for policies currently being issued. Furthermore, recognition can be given to the possibility of changes in earned interest rates in future years. For example, a higher interest rate might be assumed for policy years 1 to 10, with a lower rate assumed thereafter.

The crediting rate will be a function, first, of the insurer's investment returns. The difference between the insurer's actual investment return and its interest crediting rate is called variously the **interest margin,** the **investment margin,** or the **spread,** as shown here. The importance of the spread to life insurer financial performance was discussed in Chapter 9.

> **Procedure for Setting Current Interest Crediting Rate**
> Current investment return
> <u>− Interest margin</u>
> = Interest crediting rate

Spreads typically range from 50 to 200 basis points. Insurers' target spreads are influenced by numerous factors. The product's target market can affect the margin. Thus, if the product is aimed toward customers who wish to accumulate higher cash values, the insurer may seek to build in a comparatively thin spread, especially if the target market is highly competitive. Also, the larger the average policy size, the lower can be the spread because of size economies.

Some insurers design products with the intention of varying the current crediting rate by the time policies remain in force, in recognition that investments accumulated on behalf of different generations of policies will earn different yields. A variation of this approach is the **investment generation method** in which insurers artificially segment their investment portfolios, allocating the segments to the blocks of policies that are considered to have given rise to those investments. Investment returns can vary across different generations.

Other insurers base their current crediting rate on the average investment return of their entire investment portfolio, called the **portfolio average method**. This method does not segregate policies into generations; instead it uses the same interest rate for all policies. This method produces a more stable interest crediting rate than the approaches discussed earlier.

As we know, investments backing the liabilities arising from variable insurance products are managed through accounts separate from an insurer's general account assets that back the liabilities of its non-variable products. The cash values of variable products are determined by and linked directly to the market values of the underlying investments in the separate account. No minimum interest rate is guaranteed to be credited to cash values.

The cash values of most non-variable products do not change with the market performance of any specific underlying investments, and the contracts guarantee to credit a specified minimum interest rate; e.g., 2.5 percent. The cash values of these UL and WL policies are neither determined by nor linked directly to the market values of investments in the insurer's general account. The interest rate credited to these cash values is significantly *influenced* by but not directly *determined* by the insurer's investment returns.

POLICY LOADS   Policy loads are intended to cover expenses and taxes incurred and usually to provide for profits and contingencies. Insurer expenses may be classified in many ways. Generally, they fall into two broad categories: investment expenses and operating expenses. **Investment expenses** are the costs of making, processing, and protecting the insurer's investments. As they relate directly to the production of investment income, they are usually deducted from the gross investment income. They are, thus, taken into account in determining the interest crediting rate or calculation of a bundled policy's gross premium and dividends and are not ordinarily considered explicitly in connection with policy loads.

Operating expenses are the costs incurred in normal business operations, other than investments. Insurers usually record such expenses as falling into one of four categories:

1. *Acquisition expenses,* sometimes called *first-year expenses,* are those costs relating to the procurement and issuing of new business, including underwriting.

2. *Development expenses* are those costs incurred in developing a new product line.
3. *Maintenance expenses,* also called *renewal expenses,* are those costs incurred to maintain and service policies after they are in force.
4. *Overhead expenses,* also called *administrative expenses,* are those costs incurred that are not directly related to a specific product, such as executive salaries, rent, utilities, etc.

Insurers also separate operating expenses as to whether they are direct or indirect. **Direct expenses** are those directly attributable to a specific product (e.g., agent's commission). Most acquisition expenses are direct. Identifying direct expenses and allocating them to a particular product line is relatively straightforward. All product pricing systems include direct expenses in a product's pricing structure.

In contrast, **indirect expenses** are those applicable to general insurer operations that cannot be attributed to a specific product line only. Expenses such as senior management compensation, accounting expenses, utilities, and information systems exist and continue irrespective of whether the insurer offers a particular product. Development, maintenance, and overhead expenses are mostly indirect. Identifying and allocating indirect expenses to a product line during the pricing process is complex and often arbitrary.

For purposes of determining a proper amount of loading, operating expenses often are assigned to one of three major groups:

1. Expenses that vary with the amount of premiums – for example, agents' commissions and premium taxes.
2. Expenses that vary with the amount of insurance – for example, underwriting costs.
3. Expenses that vary with the number of policies – for example, the cost of preparing policies for issue and establishing the necessary accounting records.

Each of these three allocations results in a cost per some measured unit and is called a **unit cost**. In view of the arbitrary and difficult nature of allocating indirect expenses, some companies allocate only direct expenses to a specific product, called **marginal costing**. In contrast, traditional **full costing** allocates both direct and some indirect expenses to each product. In the case of marginal costing, indirect expenses may be allocated to each overall product line rather than to particular products.

Taxes and fees are omnipresent. U. S. federal income taxes apply across the board based on insurer profitability, so their impact on insurers varies with profitability. As with all other employers, insurers must pay Social Security taxes on behalf of their employees, representing a surprisingly large outflow because of the labor-intense nature of the business. Another surprisingly high effective tax for life insurers is the tax on premiums that each insurer must pay to each state from which it receives premiums. This tax averages about 2 percent of all life insurance premiums received by insurers. State premium taxes are often passed on directly to the policyholder.

The foregoing suggests that loadings ideally would consist partly of a percentage of premium charge, partly of a charge for each $1,000 of insurance, and partly of a charge per policy. In fact, the loadings of many bundled products are structured in this tripartite manner. Many unbundled products omit one or more of the three elements in their loads, with a few having no identifiable loads. In the latter situation, of course, the insurer's expenses must be met from mortality and interest margins.

After conducting studies as to past operational expenses and taxes and making adjustments for reasonably anticipated future changes including inflation, actuaries develop unit costs based on expense categories, as alluded to above. The determination of unit costs involves both the amount of expenses incurred, as shown by cost evaluations, and the timing of their occurrence. From these unit costs, final loading charges and fees to be assessed policies are derived by adding expense margins, as shown here:

> **Procedure for Setting Current Loading Charges**
> Estimate historical expenses and patterns
> <u>+ Expense margin</u>
> = Loading charges

The **expense margin**, also called **safety margin**, is intended to provide for contingencies, for profits or surplus accumulation, and/or to cover losses associated with early policy lapses. Of course, mortality margins and interest margins can cover the same elements, although we tend to associate each particular margin with its policy element.

Once all unit costs are developed and appropriate expense margins added to these costs, actuaries typically combine them to yield explicit loading patterns for unbundled policies of a (1) flat annual (or monthly) amount per policy or as a percentage of the account value (commonly called an *administrative charge*), (2) a percentage of the first year premium and a lower percentage of renewal premiums (called *front-end loads*), and, sometimes, (3) a charge per $1,000 of face amount. Additionally, some policies assess back-end loads against cash values withdrawn in early policy years.

Bundled policies accomplish their loading goal through a different process. One common means is to solve for the gross premium necessary to equal the present value of all durational benefits, unit costs assigned in various ways (see above), and taxes and adding a percent of premium and per-unit margins for profit, desired permanent surplus contributions, contingencies and, where applicable, dividends. In all instances, such tentative premiums are tested under various scenarios.

For most unbundled products, the identifiable loading charges assessed against a particular policy typically will be determined by the magnitude of the premiums paid and sometimes the account value and death benefit amount. For bundled products, loading will be embedded as an indivisible component within the premium (and usually cash value) but will likely have been derived as a percentage of first year and renewal premiums as well as flat policy charges and possibly an assessment based on the face amount. Unlike mortality charges, individual insured characteristics have no effect on loading charges, although loads may be banded by policy size.

Loading charges for variable life insurance are typically configured somewhat differently. As variable products are subject to the rules and regulations applicable to other securities, all charges and fees must be disclosed. Most meaningful charges are expressed as a percentage of the account value, such as investment management fees and mortality and expense (M&E) charges. M&E charges typically are not intended to cover routine death claims (mortality) but to provide mortality and expense margins akin to and for the same reason as those applicable to general account policies.

PERSISTENCY   Recall that persistency is the percentage of life insurance policies not terminated by lapse or surrender during a specified time period, often yearly. We defined a lapse in Chapter 2 as the termination of a policy for nonpayment of premiums or, in the case of variable life or universal life policies, the depletion of the account value below that required to maintain the policy in force. A surrender is the voluntary termination of a policy by its owner for its cash surrender value. In general, the better a company's persistency for a group of policies, the larger the surplus funds that arise from that business. The use of policy termination rates is necessary in life insurance pricing because of the disparity between surrender values and asset shares. Terminated policies whose surrender value exceeds their asset shares impose costs on the insurer.

Terminated policies whose asset shares are greater than their surrender values result in a gain for the insurer by the amount of the difference between the two figures. First impressions could be that life insurers, therefore, would like policies to lapse or be surrendered during periods wherein the asset share was greater than the cash surrender value. Ordinarily, this is not true, as the insurer would be foregoing even larger future gains if the policies remain in force. Some insurers, however, have engaged in **lapse-supported pricing**, which is the practice of pricing a product such that gains from lapses and surrenders are allocated to subsidize later policy benefits. State regulations limit this practice.

Predicting future termination rates is difficult. The difficulty is caused by extreme fluctuations over the years, largely as a result of economic conditions. Although for many insurers lapse rates may not be as important in pricing as are the other three factors, for other insurers, the financial implications can be significant.

Actual persistency rates experienced by an insurer are a function of many factors, several of which are within its control. Some of the key factors include the following:

- **Target market.** Each of an insurer's policy forms ordinarily is aimed at a particular market segment. Policies aimed at individuals of low or modest means tend to experience the highest lapse rates and, therefore, incur higher loadings for this fact and vice versa for high income markets. Markets can be segmented by factors other than income or wealth. For example, policies targeted to certain professions or affinity groups often experience better persistency than otherwise would be found for that group's income or wealth characteristics.

- **Nature of policy sale or service.** Related to policy suitability issues is the situation in which a policy is inappropriately sold or serviced. A policy can be sold inappropriately for many reasons, some of which are that the customer did not truly understand what he or she was purchasing, the recommended premium to be paid was either too small or too large in relation to the goal for the policy, and so on. Poor customer service falls into the same category. When customers believe that they have not been advised or otherwise dealt with fairly or appropriately, the tendency is to terminate the relationship.
- **Policy cost.** A not uncommon situation arises when an individual purchased a policy only to discover that it does not offer good value in relation to its premiums. A policy may have seemed to have been reasonably priced at time of purchase, but the insurer could not or did not continue such favorable pricing over time. Expensive policies tend to experience higher lapse rates than less costly policies.
- **The economy.** Policy lapse rates vary with the performance of the economy. In economic downturns, lapse rates tend to rise. In good times, they tend to be lower.
- **Surrender charges.** Policies that provide for higher penalties – surrender charges – for early termination often experience better persistency than those providing smaller or no such penalties.
- **Commission charge-backs.** If a policy is terminated by the policyholder during the first year, many life insurers require the agent to repay some or all of the commission paid. This practice gives the agent a greater financial incentive to ensure that the policy is sold and serviced appropriately.

Actuaries will have conducted studies of the persistency experience of the various policies that the insurer has sold over time. In developing a new product, they will use these experience studies to inform them as to the most likely persistency rates to use in new product development, assuming that the product characteristics and target market are similar to past experience. If they differ, appropriate adjustments would be made in the data. Additionally, the actual rates used in pricing are influenced by the insurer's pricing goals and projected cash flows associated with the block of policies. In practice, termination rates usually are differentiated by plan of insurance, age of issue, and frequency and method of premium payment. Under most plans, lapse rates are highest in the first policy year, diminishing significantly thereafter.

CALCULATION OF GROSS PREMIUM RATE STRUCTURES

The preceding discussion makes clear that life insurance pricing components can be and are mixed in different ways by insurers to accomplish different marketing and profit objectives. The precise mix will be driven by the competing interests of policy performance and profitability, coupled with the insurer's underlying mortality, investment, expense, and persistency experience. Strong results in each category can lead to good policy performance and sound profitability for the insurer.

Profitability is essential for insurer long-term viability. Precisely how expected profitability is embedded into product pricing will be a function of product and market factors. Profits will be built into some or all of the preceding four key pricing components, depending on the product target market and competition within that market. Just as the pricing elements can be mixed in different ways, so too can expected profits be allocated in innumerable ways.

In deciding on this mix and the premiums needed to fund the insurance package, considerations such as adequacy, equity, legal limitations, competition, and specific insurer objectives all enter into the process. Adequacy clearly is the most important requirement, because insurer solvency can be jeopardized by inadequate charges. Equity in premiums and charges is primarily for the benefit of policyowners, although there is a practical limit to the degree of equity that can be attained.

Of course, charges must not be in conflict with any law. Competition will naturally affect an insurer's premium rate structures. In setting growth and profit goals, other objectives, such as markets selected, products emphasized, or compensation philosophy can all affect the pricing structure finally adopted.

Contingencies can cause adverse deviations from underlying assumptions. They can arise from adverse mortality, investment, termination rate, and/or expense deviations. The expense, mortality, and interest margins – collectively called **product margins** – help ensure that the insurer will be able to meet its contractual obligations even under adverse circumstances. These product margins also are intended to be sources of profits or surplus accumulation. For par insurance, it is customary to insert a specific allowance in the margins for the purpose of creating additional surplus from which dividends can be paid.

Margins within life products are commonly described as being thin or wide; thin meaning relatively small margins and wide being relatively large margins. Whether product margins are thin or wide for a given life insurance policy is influenced by a policy's risk characteristics. Table 16-1 shows the general relationships between various characteristics and the magnitude of product margins, as enumerated by the *Life Office Management Association*.

Table 16-1	Likely Effect of Selected Risk Characteristics on Product Margins		
Policy Characteristic		**Assessment**	**Degree of Product Margin**
Mortality and expense charge guarantees		Weak	Thin
		Strong	Wide
Guaranteed minimum interest rate		Low	Thin
		High	Wide
Magnitude of surrender charges		Low	Thin
		High	Wide
Who bears investment risk?		Policyholder	Thin
		Insurer	Wide
Nonguaranteed policy elements present?		Yes	Thin
		No	Wide
Level of early anticipated lapse rates		Low	Thin
		High	Wide

Policy Characteristic	Assessment	Degree of Product Margin
Market competitiveness	High	Thin
	Low	Wide
Insurer profit objective	Low	Thin
	High	Wide

The table is largely self-explanatory, if highly simplified. The lower the insurer's perceived risks, the thinner can be product margins and vice versa.

TESTING THE GROSS PREMIUM RATE STRUCTURE

Life insurance pricing is built around profits. It is important to undertake profit testing to determine whether it appears that a tentative rate structure is likely to result in acceptable profitability. It is not unusual for the first such tests to reveal profit margins that miss the company's targets. Moreover, even if initial results appear to be acceptable under the "most likely" scenario – meaning the actuary's best estimate for actual future investment, mortality, expense, and persistency experience – we know that this particular scenario will almost certainly *not* occur. Actuaries are not *that* good at estimating future experience.

In Chapters 9 and 14, we discussed enterprise risk management and the application of portfolio theory to financial management. We noted the importance of the marginal contribution of individual product performance to risk and return results for the insurer's aggregate product portfolio after taking account of correlations across product lines. Before results can be aggregated, the performance of individual products is usually examined without reference to portfolio factors, which we do here. Thus, in this and following sections, we focus on standalone or *silo* performance at the line-of-business product level. While these performance features are the most fundamental components of life insurer financial performance, they should nonetheless later be considered in a portfolio context.

Profit testing inevitably involves sensitivity analysis, which tests the product under many different possible future scenarios by making a series of small changes in the underlying assumptions. Insurers will use one or more of several modeling techniques in testing the gross premium rate structure. Before introducing these models, we first need to understand the key sources and measures of insurer profit.

SOURCES OF PROFIT   For an insurance company to manage effectively to its anticipated and actual profits, it should understand the sources of those profits. To do this in a life insurance context, actuaries consider three main sources of profits: (1) investment gains, (2) mortality gains, and (3) expense gains. Sometimes, surrender gains are also considered. The classical formula for the three sources of gain on a yearly basis is as follows:

$$B_t = I_t + M_t + E_t$$

where,

B_t = book profit per \$1,000 payable at the end of policy year t
I_t = investment gain for policy year t
M_t = mortality gain for policy year t
E_t = expense gain for policy year t

Each of the three sources of gain can be determined by the following formulae:

$$I_t = (i'_t - i_t)(_{t-1}V_x + {}_tP_x)$$
$$M_t = (q_{x+t-1} - q'_{x+t-1})(1{,}000 - {}_tV_x)$$
$$E_t = ({}_tG_x - {}_tP_x - {}_te_x)(1 + i'_t)$$

where,

x	=	age of issue
i'_t	=	actual investment return earned in policy year t
i_t	=	reserve interest rate in policy year t
${}_tV_x$	=	t^{th} policy year's terminal reserve per \$1,000 for a policy issued at age x
${}_tP_x$	=	t^{th} policy year's valuation net premium per \$1,000 for a policy issued at age x
q_x	=	reserve mortality rate at age x
q'_x	=	actual mortality rate at age x
${}_tG_x$	=	t^{th} policy year's gross annual premium per \$1,000 for a policy issued at age x
${}_te_x$	=	t^{th} policy year's actual expenses incurred per \$1,000 for a policy issued at age x

Each of the three main sources of profitability are summarized here.

- *Gains from Investment Earnings.* The interest or investment element in the equation derives the gain by multiplying the policy's initial reserve by the difference between the company's actual investment return and the interest rate used for reserve calculation. As life insurance policies are often written for long durations, insurers assume conservative rates of interest for their net premium and reserve computations to assure its being earned throughout the life of the contract.

- *Gains from Mortality.* The mortality gain arises from the difference in the insurer's actual from its reserve mortality, applying that difference to the policy's net amount at risk. Because the reserve mortality table is deliberately made conservative, it is common for a gain to result from operations.

- *Gains from Loading.* An expense gain arises to the extent that the loading in the premium exceeds actual expenses incurred. This gain is accumulated to year's end to comport with the timing of the other two sources of gain. Sound insurance company management dictates that the gross premium should be more than sufficient to meet normal requirements, so that the insurer and its policyowners may be protected against exceptional conditions. The loading on par policies frequently includes an amount for policyowner dividends together with gains from other sources. Competitive conditions – especially in the matter of agents' commissions – as well as inflationary pressures on expenses have at times caused expenses to exceed loadings in the aggregate.

The financial results from application of this formula to an existing or anticipated product will reveal the three most important sources of profit for that product. It is possible, of course, that overall profitability for the product may be acceptable but that profitability by component is not. For example, the expense component might reveal losses that were being made good by the mortality component. Perhaps this result is acceptable as the insurer intentionally included generous mortality margins but inadequate or even negative expense margins. Conversely, perhaps the result is unacceptable as expenses incurred (or expected to be incurred) are excessive because of a new, higher commission scale for agents that was being advocated by marketing.

Many actuaries will add an additional component to the above formulation to account for gains from surrenders. The additional gains from surrenders (SG) component would be as follows:

$$SG_x = (r' - r)\,({}_tV_x - {}_tCV_x)$$

where r' is the actual yearly surrender rate, r is the surrender rate assumed in pricing the policy, and ${}_tCV_x$ is the tth policy year's cash surrender value.

Components of the above equations are illustrated as relying on statutory values, rather than GAAP values. In fact, either or both statutory accounting principles (SAP) and GAAP values can be and often are used, each having a different purpose and each providing a different perspective on the sources of profitability. Of course, the differences are ones of timing of profitability, as SAP generally produces smaller early duration profits.

MEASURES OF PROFIT   Profits are essential to the financial health of any enterprise, and life insurers are no exceptions. Actuaries seek to maximize the chances that newly developed products provide an acceptable profit. (Mutual and fraternal companies sometimes prefer the term "surplus" to profits, but they mean the same as used here.) Expected and actual emerging profits are also important to the determination of the most appropriate allocation of an insurer's limited capital base and yearly comparisons of the financial health of blocks of policies.

In Chapters 9, 12, 13, and 14, we discussed the importance of the emerging concepts of enterprise risk management, economic capital, and economic profit to the reporting, regulation, and financial management of life insurers. We also noted that SAP and GAAP measures of financial performance are found lacking in reflecting life insurer risk realistically. The techniques discussed there reflect the merging of actuarial science and financial management theory. In this section, we describe the more traditional actuarial methods of profit performance measurement. While these methods are less refined in incorporating risk and other contemporary financial concepts into profit management, they remain important for companies – including those undertaking new methods – because of their familiarity, existing capabilities, and ease of comparison with past performance.

Further, as noted in Chapter 14, statutory and GAAP accounting results remain important constraints on management techniques, and thus traditional actuarial profit measures based on these results can be thought of as inputs to more contemporary practice. Economic capital and profit concepts, financial reporting, and regulation are converging but, as long as they are not identical, companies will find a variety of measurement tools valuable as they address the requirements of different stakeholders.

Profit commonly is thought of as the excess of receipts over disbursements. With life insurance policies, we know that the timing of receipts (e.g., premiums and investment income) and disbursements (e.g., death claims, expenses, and surrender values) do not coincide. Measures of profit used by life insurers attempt to adjust for these differences. Thus, profit in a life insurance context is defined as receipts less disbursements less the increase in reserves.

Because of the importance of reserves in insurer profits, the means by which they are calculated can have an important bearing on an insurer's profitability from year to year. Of course, in the long run, total profits will be unaffected by the means by which reserves are calculated, as all reserves ultimately are released for each block of policies. The timing of the emergence of profits, however, is affected and so too will be the present value of such profits. Thus, profit derived from reliance on SAP typically will differ from that derived from GAAP. This is because, among other factors, statutory reserves usually are higher than GAAP reserves, as discussed earlier, so profitability in the early years of a block of policies is likely to be shown as greater under GAAP than under SAP.

Nonetheless, many parties that have reason to analyze insurer profitability rely on SAP measures of profit, sometimes instead of or in addition to GAAP measures. Plus, statutory profits add to insurers' statutory surplus, which is the basis on which an insurer's solvency is assessed. Early year strains on this surplus because of negative statutory profits can be a particularly important factor in insurer pricing. GAAP measures of profits tend to be more important for stock insurers than for mutual insurers. Some of the more common measures of insurer profit include the following:

- **Profit margin** is the present value of profits divided by the present value of premiums. It informs management of that proportion of each premium composed of profit, on average. Its calculation requires not only the selection of appropriate discount rates but also of expected mortality and persistency. The result can be quite sensitive to these assumptions, as can the other measures discussed here.
- **Return on investment** (ROI) is the ratio of the present value of expected profits to the initial surplus employed to support the product for a set number of years, such as over the life of the product or sometimes yearly. *Investment* is understood to refer to funds the company has advanced to support the product, including initial acquisition expenses and risk-based capital requirements applicable to the product. Companies often strive for an ROI of 15 percent or so.
- **Internal rate of return** (IRR) is that rate of interest that causes the present value of profits to be zero.
- **Return on equity** (ROE) is the ratio of annual expected profits to equity for a product for a set period of time, usually for a single year. Equity is understood to refer to each year's net funds that the company has advanced to support the product. Thus, equity initially would be the same as investment in the ROI discussion. At the beginning of the next year, the equity denominator would be increased (or decreased) by the amount of the previous year's profit (or loss).
- **Return on assets** (ROA) is the ratio of profits to the assets that result from a product for a set period of time, often for a single year. This ratio is commonly used for products that develop large amounts of assets.
- **Break even** is the number of years that will have passed before earnings equal disbursements. It is not a measure of profits as such but is useful in

assessing whether a product (investment) meets an insurer's objectives. It often is analyzed using the insurer's target or **hurdle rate**, which is the minimum acceptable investment return an insurer expects from a new product. The rate might vary by the nature of the product with riskier products (e.g., variable life) expected to meet a higher hurdle rate than traditional products (e.g., par whole life).

ROI and ROE are used for all types of insurance products but are especially relevant for products that require large initial surplus. Most companies seek an ROE that exceeds that which it could earn by merely investing the surplus allocated to the product in fixed income instruments.

There is a trend toward new performance measures based on enterprise risk management and economic capital concepts. Risk adjusted return on capital (for product performance) and market consistent embedded value (for firm performance) are discussed in Chapter 14.

TESTING PROCEDURES   We cover two traditional procedures used by insurers to model product performance. Each procedure develops yearly profit figures that are then used to yield some measure of overall profitability.

The Asset Share Model   One means of testing a tentative gross premium rate schedule and other policy elements relies on the **asset share model**, which is a simulation of the anticipated operating experience for a block of policies, using the best estimates of what the individual factors will be for each future policy year. The purpose of this calculation is to determine, for a block of policies, whether the insurer's profit, reserving, and other objectives can be met based on the anticipated operating experience.

The calculation derives an expected fund (per $1,000 of insurance) held by the company at the end of each policy year after payment of death claims, expenses, dividends, or other nonguaranteed benefits or credits, cash surrender values, and allowance for actual investment earnings. The accumulated fund at the end of each policy year is divided by the number of surviving and persisting insureds to produce each policy's "share of assets" or asset share. Usually the test is for a maximum of 20 or 30 years. Netting each year's change in reserves against each year's change in assets yields annual profit.

Asset share calculations for newly proposed policies are made before the fact. As future experience is not known, estimates must be made that are thought to be reasonable representations of future experience. Asset share calculations seek to determine whether the individual elements of a policy result in a competitive product that is well balanced and produces acceptable results for both the insurance company and policyowners. If the asset share results are deficient in light of company objectives, increases may be made in premiums with respect to bundled products or in mortality or loading charges in unbundled products.

Alternatively some specific policy element benefit (e.g., death benefit, dividends, cash values, interest crediting rate) can be decreased. Perhaps the insurer might decide to forgo changes in policy elements, instead focusing on operational economies to reduce expenses, change investment philosophy to allow riskier and thus higher yielding investments, or make other operational changes. If the fund accumulation appears excessive, especially in light of competitive considerations, the premium rate or policy charges could be reduced or benefits increased.

The asset share method accumulates profits within the calculation based on the same assumptions as other aspects of the calculation. In other words, each year's profit or loss is carried forward at the same assumed investment returns, survival rates, lapse rates, etc., as applied to other cash flow items. Increasingly, insurers rely on testing procedures other than asset shares.

Accumulated Book Profits Model   The **accumulated book profits model** is identical to the asset share model with the exception that profits and losses are not retained within the calculation but are assumed to be maintained separately in a **profit account** that accumulates the values at a selected hurdle rate. The hurdle rate selected is set to reflect the company's cost of capital for the product being evaluated or the **risk discount rate,** which is the rate that market investments of comparable risk command. The hurdle rate normally will be higher than the rate embedded within the asset share calculation.

Hurdle rates commonly fall within the 10-15 percent and higher range. They tend to be lower for mutual than for stock life insurers. Thus, a profit goal for a product using the accumulated book profits approach might be that the product is expected to achieve a break even by 10 years at a 15 percent hurdle rate.

There is a trend toward the use of probabilistic models and risk measurement in financial models. Dynamic financial analysis and Value at Risk are discussed in Chapter 14.

SURPLUS AND ITS DISTRIBUTION

Guaranteed life insurance premiums are calculated conservatively in the interest of the long-term viability of the insurer. Consequently, insurers anticipate realizing a gain from operations over time. The immediate result of such gains is an increase in the insurer's surplus. The size and disposition of this surplus depend, among other factors, on whether the business generating it is guaranteed cost nonparticipating (nonpar) insurance; nonpar insurance but with nonguaranteed elements; or par insurance.

Surplus arising from guaranteed cost nonpar insurance is available to the insurer to use in whatever legitimate manner it wishes. Policyholders have no contractual right to any portion of it or to have any pricing elements of their policies adjusted either favorably or unfavorably. Nor do owners of nonpar policies containing nonguaranteed elements commonly have any contractual right to any portion of insurer surplus arising from profits originating from their policies. However, the contracts allow insurers to make pricing element adjustments.

Pricing adjustments for such nonpar policies ordinarily are made in response to changes in current and anticipated insurer operational experience, both favorable and unfavorable, while being certain to respect all guaranteed policy elements. Any time the insurer assesses mortality or expense charges at rates less than those guaranteed, we can think of the insurer, in effect, as discounting mortality and expense charges in advance, in anticipation of future surplus that otherwise would have arisen had they not done so. Likewise, any time the insurer's interest crediting rate is greater than the guaranteed rate, we can think of the insurer, in effect, crediting investment gains in advance, in anticipation of future surplus that otherwise would have arisen. However, these pricing adjustments are not made by paying present accumulated insurer surplus to such policyholders, as with par business.

Only par policies contractually grant their owners the right to participate in an insurer's accumulated surplus in the form of dividend payments, even if the practical effect of the two differences in providing nonguaranteed value to customers might not be very meaningful. Thus, discussions of surplus and its distribution via dividends apply solely to par business. As Box 16-2 discusses, terminology in this respect differs in other countries from that followed in the U.S.

Box 16-2
Surplus Distribution Terminology in the United Kingdom
In the U.K. and other Commonwealth countries, par policies are referred to as **with-profits policies** and divisible surplus (dividends) are called **bonuses.** Bonuses are declared at the insurer's discretion or as required by law at fixed intervals often greater than a single year. A special type of bonus, called a **reversionary bonus,** is commonly found, under which divisible surplus is used to increase the policy's face amount (commonly called the **sum assured**) and its surrender value. The amount is often calculated as a percentage of the face amount without regard to the insured's age or the time that the policy has been in force. Sometimes an additional or **terminal** (or **capital**) **bonus** is paid on policy maturity, the intent of which is to allow the policyowner to share more equitably in the favorable operations of the insurer.

DIVISIBLE SURPLUS

Following each year's operations, an insurer with par business typically determines how much of the total surplus (previously existing surplus plus additions for the year) should be retained as a contingency fund or other special surplus appropriation and how much should be distributed to policyowners as dividends. No fixed relationship need exist between the surplus gain in a particular calendar year and the dividends distributed to policyowners on the next policy anniversaries. The directors or trustees of the insurer, as a matter of business judgment, make the decision. The amount earmarked for distribution is designated as *divisible surplus* and once set aside by action of the directors or trustees, loses its identity as surplus and becomes a liability of the insurer.

In deciding the portion of the total surplus that should be retained as contingency funds, a balance must be maintained between the need for a general contingency fund and the competitive advantages of a liberal dividend scale. When the surplus earned for any given year is insufficient to permit the insurer to maintain its current dividend scale, management may decide to use a portion of the general contingency fund for this purpose. Conversely, if, during a temporary period, additions to surplus are more than adequate to support the existing dividend scale, the excess often is added to the general contingency fund to avoid the expense and complications involved in changing the scale. If the excess or insufficiency is substantial or is expected to continue over a reasonable period, competitive consideration usually leads to a change in the scale.

In the interest of security of benefits and good management, surplus and general contingency funds should increase as policy reserves increase through new business and the natural accretion under older policies. With many insurers, each policy is expected to make a permanent contribution to the insurer's surplus.

These contributions enable insurers to fulfill their contractual obligations even in the face of catastrophes or severe economic downturns that occur only occasionally. Thus, over the lifetime of a class of policies, aggregate dividend distributions made often will be somewhat less than the contributions of the class to surplus. On the other hand, some insurers' dividend practices result in substantially complete liquidation of each generation's contributions to surplus by the time that generation of policies goes off the books.

Although insurers may use their discretion in determining the amount of surplus to be distributed, some governments regulate this matter by statute. New York limits the amount of surplus an insurer can retain on its participating business to an amount not exceeding $850,000 or 10 percent of its policy reserves and other policy liabilities, whichever is the greater amount. The U.K., France, Germany, Singapore, and many other countries have similar limitations. Their purpose is to prevent insurers from retaining more surplus than is judged necessary. Many commentators today question whether such limitations serve the public interest and are warranted, especially given the concern over insurer solvency and need for growth.

FREQUENCY OF DISTRIBUTION

In the U.S., surplus is distributed annually on par policies. This annual distribution is required by statute in many states. In the past in the U.S. and in Canada and other countries still, deferred dividends are paid. **Deferred dividends** are those payable only at the close of a stipulated number of years, such as 5, 10, 15, and 20. The deferred dividend plan lost favor with policyholders in the U.S. and with many state legislatures many years ago. Annual distribution, it is argued, is well adapted to the policyowner who wishes to keep his or her net annual outlay to the lowest possible amount, and it also serves to encourage managerial economy, the lack of which precipitated the 1905 Armstrong investigation of the industry and its practices. The laws limiting deferred dividend plans in the U.S. date largely from that time.

Policies that provide for payment of deferred dividends are commonly called *deferred dividend, accumulation, distribution,* or *semi-tontine* policies. According to the underlying principle of the plan, they should encourage persistency. Policyowners who fail to continue premium payments to the end of the designated period (because of death, surrender, or lapse) lose the dividends they would have received under the annual dividend plan. The lost dividends revert to those policyowners who continue their premium payments throughout the deferred dividend period. This fact is the reason why they are sometimes referred to as semi-tontines. See Box 16-3 for what might be a close economic equivalent of deferred dividends.

Box 16-3
Interest Rate Bonuses

In an effort to encourage good persistency, many insurers offer unbundled policies that provide for interest rate bonuses. They are similar in effect to deferred dividends under par policies. **Retroactive bonuses** provide that, after a predefined time period (e.g., 10 years), a bonus interest rate will be retroactively applied to all previous periods. **Prospective bonuses** provide that, after a predefined time period, future interest credits will be augmented by a bonus rate.

THE CONTRIBUTION PRINCIPLE

The allocation of divisible surplus among policyowners is a complex matter. Equity is the basic objective, but consideration must be given to competition, flexibility, and simplicity. That the allocation should be competitive is self-evident. Flexibility can be viewed as a facet of equity, as adaptability to changing circumstances is essential if equity is to be attained. Simplicity is desirable both from an expense viewpoint and from the viewpoint of understanding by agents and policyowners.

One way of obtaining reasonable equity is to follow the **contribution principle,** which holds that *each class of policyowners should share in divisible surplus in proportion to its contribution to surplus.* The principle, introduced in Chapter 4, does not require the return of all or even most surplus. It merely requires that whatever the amount of divisible surplus, it be allotted to policyowners in the approximate proportion in which they contributed to it. This principle underlies the equity implicit in participating insurance. While the contribution principle provides the underlying philosophical base for surplus distribution, the question arises as to its application. The most widely used approach for applying the principle is the **three factor contribution method,** which apportions divisible surplus to par policies based on mortality, investment, and expense gains associated with those policies.

We know from earlier discussion about the main sources of insurer profitability that surplus arises from favorable deviations of actual mortality, investment, and expense experience from that originally assumed in premium calculation. These three profit sources underpin the three-factor contribution method. The only meaningful difference between the basic three sources of profit calculation and the basic three-factor contribution calculation is that the primed values in the profit calculation, i', q', and e', which represent the insurer's *actual* investment return earned, mortality rate experienced, and expenses incurred, are replaced in the dividend calculation by values that actuaries determine will yield the surplus that the insurer's board has decided will be distributed and not the total surplus. Divisible surplus is typically less than total yearly earned surplus, so one or more of the mortality, interest, and expense values used for dividend derivation ordinarily are less than that actually realized by the insurer.

Application of the formula in this way usually results in dividends that vary with (1) the plan and amount of insurance and (2) age at and years from issue. When special benefits are involved, such as disability and accidental death, an additional factor sometimes is included for these features. Also, some par policies make special dividend payments, as Box 16-4 describes.

Box 16-4
Special Forms of Surplus Distribution

Some insurers pay a **terminal dividend** when a policy terminates by endowing, death, or surrender. These dividends typically are payable only if the policy has been in force for a minimum length of time (e.g., 15 years). In theory, the purpose of terminal dividends is to return to terminating policyowners part of the general surplus to which they have contributed or adjust for a guaranteed cash value that is less than the asset share.

A **postmortem dividend** is payable at death, but either it is paid in proportion to the part of the policy year of death for which premiums have been paid or represents a one-time distribution of surplus, mainly on term insurance, in lieu of dividends on each policy anniversary while the insured was living.

For most WL plans, the annual dividend under the contribution plan increases with duration. This is aside from a possible increase in the scale itself. The normal increase of dividends with duration occurs because the interest gain normally increases with duration. In the usual case, this more than offsets the tendency for the mortality and expense factors to decrease with duration, but this is not always so. An unfavorable investment market may cause the opposite to occur. Also, the fact that many insurers have switched to the investment generation method of interest allocation renders dividend patterns less stable.

ENDNOTES

1   This chapter draws in parts from Harold D. Skipper and Wayne Tonning, *The Advisor's Guide to Life Insurance* (Chicago; American Bar Association, 2011), Chapters 6 and 13; and from Albert E. Easton and Timothy F. Harris, *Actuarial Aspects of Individual Life Insurance and Annuity Contracts* (ACTEX Publications, 2007), Chapters 4 and 11.

Life Insurance Due Care

CHAPTER 17

LIFE INSURANCE ADVISOR AND COMPANY EVALUATION

Insurance purchasers want well-suited, low-cost insurance with favorable contractual terms, from financially secure, well-managed insurers that will deal fairly with them over the years. Putting the pieces of this puzzle together is not simple. This chapter begins Part III of the text, a three-chapter sequence on life insurance due care, which is intended to help put the puzzle together.[1] These chapters plus portions of the chapters in Part IV address the broad area of life insurance due care. **Due care** requires that those offering life insurance advice conduct their business affairs with diligence, prudence, and competence, such that recommended insurance is suitable for the individual's circumstances, reasonably expected to offer good value, and procured from insurers that are financially sound.

This chapter begins by exploring the life insurance purchase decision. We then note the persons who offer life insurance advice and include a short discussion of how to evaluate agents. We also explore the importance of selecting a financially sound company. In doing so, we discuss the conflicting incentives that life insurer managers have to maintain financial strength while avoiding holding excess capital. We next offer an overview of insurers' financial operations that determine financial strength, then delve into the importance and role of rating agencies and other information sources in evaluating life insurer financial strength.

THE LIFE INSURANCE PURCHASE DECISION

Some individuals shop carefully before deciding on the type and amount of insurance to buy and from whom to buy it. Regrettably, most buyers do little or no comparison shopping and may make unsound decisions regarding the insurance or the insurance company or both. Insurance products today are more complex than ever, and most persons are not well enough informed to make wise purchase decisions without advice. Stated differently, use of an advisor can help rectify the information imbalance between buyers and insurers.

In the minds of consumers, the life insurance "product" is the policy contract on which thousands of words of insurance jargon are printed. The policy form is not really the product. The product is intangible. It is the set of promises that the insurer makes. We explore these in Chapter 18. Moreover, on what basis does the consumer assess whether the premiums paid are reasonable in light of the package of promises? A proper assessment of likely benefits versus premiums to be paid is prudent both at the time consideration is being given to policy purchase and after the purchase, on an ongoing basis. We explore this dimension of due care in Chapter 19.

In summary, the life insurance purchase decision is complex, and the typical consumer is ill-equipped to deal with its many intangible elements. The purchase is based on trust that the agent and other advisors are giving informed, sound, unbiased advice and that the insurer will offer good product value and ultimately deliver on its promises, perhaps decades into the future.

EVALUATING LIFE INSURANCE ADVISORS

In this section, we introduce the main categories of individuals who offer life insurance advice and discuss how to evaluate agents.

LIFE INSURANCE ADVISORS

Many individuals offer life insurance advice – some for a fee and most for a commission. Competent, informed, trustworthy insurance advisors often are a consumer's best assurance of making a wise purchase decision. The most common insurance advisors include:

- Insurance producers
- Personal financial planners
- Financial institution employees
- Accountants and attorneys

INSURANCE AGENTS **Insurance producers** – called agents and brokers – are salespeople licensed by the state and under contract to sell at least one insurer's products, typically for a commission and on a face-to-face basis. For most individuals, the producer is the source of both advice and the policy. Indeed, producers account for more than 90 percent of new individual life insurance sales and virtually all cases in which planning is complex, as with estate and business planning.

Many life insurance agents hold professional designations. The oldest and most widely recognized life insurance oriented designation is the *Chartered Life Underwriter* (CLU®), granted by *The American College* (www.theamericancollege. edu/). To earn the CLU® designation, a candidate must (1) pass eight examinations touching on life insurance fundamentals, planning, and uses; (2) have three years of qualified, fulltime experience; (3) meet an ethics requirement; and (4) agree to comply with the *College's* Code of Ethics. Individuals holding this designation can be presumed to be knowledgeable about life insurance and its uses. As with all professional designations, the CLU® is no guarantee of competent or unbiased advice.

Individuals holding the CLU® designation often affiliate with the *Society of Financial Service Professionals* (SFSP) (www.financialpro.org/). Originally, only individuals holding the CLU® designation could be members, but membership was considerably broadened several years ago to include a diversity of financial practitioners, from fee-only financial planners, estate planning attorneys and accountants, to asset managers, employee benefits specialists, and life insurance agents. The *Society* provides qualified continuing educational opportunities to its members, including those required for the CLU®, CFP® (see below), the *American Bar Association*, and state accountancy boards. Members agree to be bound by the *Society's* Code of Professional Conduct.

PERSONAL FINANCIAL PLANNERS   Personal financial planners also offer advice on insurance. Most planners also sell insurance for a commission, which means that they are insurance producers. As such, they are subject to the producer evaluation criteria discussed later. Some planners do not sell insurance, instead offering advice on a fee-only basis, on the theory that having no financial stake in the sale leads to more unbiased advice. In most states, the term "personal financial planner" or equivalent is largely unregulated, so no assurance of competency or being impartial necessarily attaches to the term.

Many planners hold the *Certified Financial Planner*™ (CFP®) designation, the most widely recognized designation in personal financial planning. It signifies that the individual has (1) met minimum educational requirements (applicable course work or other professional designations plus a bachelor's degree), (2) passed 10 hours of comprehensive examinations, (3) at least three years of qualified fulltime experience, and (4) met standards of fitness and passed a background check. While the CFP® program includes the study of life insurance and its uses, it is broader than life insurance alone, so the study program can allot only so much time to its mastery. Also, as with all professional designations, the CFP® is no guarantee of competency and fair-mindedness.

The American College also offers the *Chartered Financial Consultant*® (ChFC®) professional designation. This designation requires candidates to pass nine examinations and meet the same requirements that apply to those seeking the CLU® designation. Six of the ChFC® exams qualify the individual to take the CFP® exams. In addition to insurance education, the ChFC® curriculum includes income taxation, retirement planning, investments, and estate planning.

FINANCIAL INSTITUTION EMPLOYEES   Life insurance is sold by the employees of many financial institutions, including commercial banks, investment banks, thrifts, credit unions, and mutual fund organizations. Any employee of a financial institution who sells life insurance must hold an agent's license from the relevant state, so the discussions later about producer selection apply to them.

Financial institutions are important distribution channels in some markets, especially in Europe, but less so in North America. Banks' share of the overall U.S. life insurance market is less than 5 percent, although their share of new individual annuity sales exceeds 14 percent. Such institutions hope to increase insurance sales by leveraging their existing customer base. No professional designation exists that is oriented specifically toward stock brokers or employees of noninsurance financial institutions giving life insurance advice.

ATTORNEYS AND ACCOUNTANTS   Many accountants leverage their existing client base by offering insurance advice, most of them for a fee and some of them on a commission basis, which means that they are insurance producers and should be evaluated on that basis in addition to their profession's standards. Attorneys often are involved in more complex insurance cases and offer their services for a fee as insurance advisors from a legal and tax viewpoint. Because accountants and attorneys are thought of by clients as fee-only advisors and not agents, those who are agents and receive commissions in connection with the sale of policies to clients should disclose this fact to clients.

Accountants and attorneys will have met formal education requirements in their fields, but nothing in their ordinary courses of study would have provided extensive knowledge about life insurance. Accountants and attorneys typically will have developed such expertise through experience in estate and/or business planning and by taking specialized professional development programs. Such programs are offered by the *American Accounting Association* and the *American Bar Association* as well as by other professional bodies, such as local chapters of the SFSP and of *Estate Planning Councils* (www.naepc.org/).

Evaluating Life Insurance Producers

If a customer chooses to work with a producer, it is important that he or she work with one whose business practices meet high standards of fairness, competence, integrity, and diligence – in other words, who conduct themselves according to professional precepts. An evaluation of producers against these tenets can minimize the chances of dealing with someone whose advice may be suspect or even wrong. We explore each of these tenets below and offer means of securing evaluative information.

Tenants of Professionalism   Each profession has codes of conduct to which its members subscribe. The discussion below draws from *The Advisor's Guide to Life Insurance* referenced at the beginning of this chapter, which builds on several organizations' codes but relies most heavily on the *Code of Professional Conduct of the Society of Financial Service Professionals.*

Fairness   The codes of conduct for innumerable professional organizations routinely cite fairness as a key tenet. For example, the first canon of the SPSP Code states: "Fairness requires that a professional treat others as he/she would wish to be treated if in the other's position." The tenet has multiple dimensions. *First,* the agent should not misrepresent or conceal material information. Besides the obvious admonition of not purposefully misrepresenting or concealing relevant information, it means also that policy illustrations and other sales material should be constructed to avoid unintentionally misleading or leading to incorrect interpretations, and should not omit information that might ordinarily be useful as an aid to understanding. Chapter 19 explores this mandate.

A *second* implication is that the advisor should disclose to the client all information material to the professional relationship, especially as relates to actual or potential conflicts of interest. Of course, producers have a financial stake in the sale of life insurance in the form of commissions and possibly other benefits. Only the state of New York requires disclosure by agents of their commissions to prospects, so agents are not compelled to disclose them in other states. Agents who are SFSP members, however, agree as follows:

> *A potential conflict of interest is inherent in the relationship between the client and the financial service professional when the professional is compensated by commissions on the sale of financial products. In such circumstances, if asked by the client or prospect, the professional should disclose, to the best of his/her knowledge, all forms of compensation, including commissions, expense allowances, bonuses, and any other relevant items.*[2]

In other words, SFSP members agree to disclose to the prospect – if asked by the prospect – their commissions and other financial interests in connection with a potential life insurance sale. Agents who are not SPSP members should be willing to disclose commissions as well.

A *third* implication is that the agent should offer his or her best advice as to product suitability. Thus, the producer should take care to ensure that the recommendations as to insurance amount, policy funding, type of policy, and the way the policy is structured (e.g., ownership and beneficiary) are appropriate to the specific needs, circumstances, and goals of the client. Clearly, compliance with this tenet requires the agent to be competent to make an appropriate assessment. In turn, this requires that the agent help the client to understand the available options to meeting his or her needs and goals. Chapters 20-24 explore this mandate.

Fourth, in offering advice and recommendations, the producer should maintain professional independence. This mandate constrains the agent to offer best advice concerning policy illustrations and policy value, in the client's interest. Is the policy credibly illustrated and does it offer good value based on all available information? Compliance with this mandate also requires the advisor to be competent to make such an assessment. Chapter 19 explores this mandate.

While insurance agents are under no legal obligation to provide "best product" advice (unless they profess otherwise), this fourth mandate would hold them to a higher standard than that which exists in law. This can pose problems for exclusive agents, as a given insurer is unlikely to have the best products in all categories and client circumstances. As noted in the SFSP Code:

> *The requirement of professional independence ... presents a special challenge for Society members who are contractually bound to sell the products of only one company, or a select group of companies. In such cases, the member must keep paramount his/her ethical duty to act in the best interest of the client, even if this means foregoing a sale.*[3]

Fifth, the agent should take care to ensure that the recommended insurer is financially sound. (See below.) Again, compliance with this mandate presumes competence to make such an assessment. Further, the same special circumstances faced by exclusive agents regarding "best product" advice applies here as well.

Competence   Like fairness, competence lies at the very core of professionalism. Competence is a synthesis of education and experience. It begins with mastery of a common body of knowledge required for the market served by the agent. The maintenance of competence requires a commitment to learning and professional improvement that must continue throughout one's professional life. Competence represents the attainment and maintenance of a level of understanding and knowledge that enables the producer to render services with facility and acumen. Competence also has several dimensions.

First, an agent should have mastered the body of knowledge necessary to provide competent advice to clients within his or her target market. This mastery ideally would have its foundation in formal education, such as a bachelor's degree. One or more advanced degrees directly relevant to the agent's business (e.g., MBA, MS, JD, etc.) suggests a deeper commitment and understanding of the relevant body of knowledge. Of course, even individuals without college degrees could have achieved the necessary mastery of the body of knowledge required for his or her target market, but most such agents focus on lower-to-middle income market segments. Evidence of mastery of the relevant body of knowledge for a life insurance agent often is demonstrated through holding appropriate professional certifications and membership and active participation in relevant professional societies. As noted earlier, common designations include the CLU®, CFP®, and ChFC®.

Second, as a complement to the above mandate, an agent should refrain from giving advice in areas for which the agent lacks requisite training and competence, including unauthorized areas. This mandate limits the scope of an agent's advice to that which is compatible with the body of knowledge mastered by the agent, which, most commonly, should comport with his or her target market. Most agents focus their sales efforts in simple family situations. They usually lack the knowledge and training to be confident of offering sound advice in more complex estate, family, professional, and business circumstances. This mandate dictates that agents should refuse, seek consultation on, or refer to others those professional engagements that exceed the personal competence of the agent.

Third, the agent should have had a meaningful amount of business experience within his or her target market. Many observers recommend a minimum experience of five years. Of course, an agent with less experience may have support services or colleagues who can provide reasonable assurance that a lack of experience will not be detrimental to the client. Also, not every situation requires a highly trained agent.

Fourth, producers should enhance their knowledge in all relevant areas in which they are engaged including participation in continuing education activities. At a minimum, this tenet requires the producer to meet the continuing education standards set by the state and all professional societies and associations in which the agent is a member. For example, the SFSP requires 30 hours of qualified study every two years, as does the CFP® Board of Standards. One would hope to find relevant activities beyond these minimal requirements.

Integrity   Integrity requires the agent to conduct him- or herself with candor, honesty, and trustworthiness. The producer is to observe the principles of objectivity and independence. This tenet also embeds several elements.

First, producers should respect the confidentiality of their clients' business, professional, and personal information and not disclose it except as business necessity or law dictates. In the course of offering advice and helping clients qualify for needed life insurance, agents ordinarily learn sensitive information. Agents and others with whom the agent works or is responsible should work under clearly established confidentiality safeguards and guidelines.

Second, an agent's business affairs should be conducted with the greatest emphasis on ethical behavior. Ethical responsibilities flow from society's unwritten standards of moral conduct and are not defined solely or entirely by either law and regulation or codes of professional conduct. One test of ethical behavior is whether the producer's peers would find his or her conduct above reproach if they were fully aware of all aspects of that conduct. As with confidentiality, agents and others with whom they work or are responsible should work under clearly established ethical guidelines.

Third, agent communication with existing and prospective clients and the general public should be objective, truthful, candid, and not have the tendency to mislead. The SFSP Code comments on this element as follows:

Financial service professionals will not use words or make statements in brochures or advertising materials or in any client communication that create false impressions or have the potential to mislead. For example, products salespersons should not refer to themselves as financial/estate planners/consultants, if they do not provide these services. Words such as deposits or contributions should not be used to describe life insurance premiums. Life insurance policies should not be referred to as retirement plans.... Financial service professionals must avoid creating the impression that they represent a number of companies when they place business with only a few companies.[4]

Diligence   Diligence imposes the responsibility to conduct one's business affairs with thoughtfulness, patience, timeliness, thoroughness, and consistency. Several tangible aspects of diligence include the following.

First, recommendations to clients should be made only after acquiring a thorough understanding of the client's financial needs, goals, and circumstances, followed by appropriate research and documentation. This mandate lies at the heart of due care, which requires an agent to conduct his or her business affairs with diligence, prudence, and competence, including investigation of the quality, value, and suitability of recommended insurance. (As applied to variable products and other securities, the roughly equivalent term is **due diligence** – the process by which a broker/dealer ensures that an investment is as represented. The terms carry different legal connotations, with the latter carrying weightier legal consequences.)

An increasingly important aspect of an agent's responsibilities stems from common law standards of conduct. Generally, advisors must exercise at least that degree of care exhibited by a reasonably prudent person of their peer group. Thus, the conduct of an attorney expert in tax law will be judged against that of other tax attorneys. Similarly, a life insurance agent's conduct will be judged against that of other, reasonably prudent insurance producers.

Second, agents should cooperate fully with other professionals in the client's interest, where relevant. A track record of the agent having done so helps minimize concern by clients that their interests may fall victim to others' faulty communication or worse.

Third, agents should act with competency and consistency in promptly discharging their responsibilities to clients. Implicit in this mandate is a requirement to deliver superior service. One of the most important elements in this requirement is that the agent monitor and ensure that periodic information is provided to clients concerning their policies' performance and any material changes in insurer financial solidity and that clients understand the information. Unfortunately, state unfair trade practices laws prohibit the dissemination of derogatory information as to the financial condition of an insurer, *even if the information is accurate.* The law can create a dilemma for the agent in that his or her professional responsibility is to keep clients informed about any deterioration in insurer financial solidity whereas the agent can be accused of violating state law in doing so.[5]

Fourth, and related to the third mandate, agents should be committed to and have a demonstrated record of effectively serving their clients' interests not only at time of sale but on an ongoing basis. A proxy for overall client satisfaction with agents is the lapse rate on their business. A high first-year voluntary policy termination (lapse) rate by the agent's policyholders suggests that something is likely amiss. Maybe policyholders discovered that the policies sold by the agent did not offer good value, contrary to his or her assertions, or that the policies were ill suited in light of the client's needs, goals, and circumstances. Either conclusion does not speak positively about the agent's diligence and general professionalism. Reasons external to the agent could explain high lapse rates, such as the insurer changing the underlying pricing of newly issued policies (but why didn't the agent know of this possibility?) or the agent's target market experiencing economic turmoil (was such reasonably foreseeable?) or the agent's target market exhibiting high lapse rates, as with low income households (is the agent attempting to sell in other market segments for which he or she is unqualified?).

SOURCES OF INFORMATION ABOUT AGENTS   The agent often is the main source of information about him- or herself. Inevitably, the demeanor of the person will influence opinions as will the attitude and professionalism exhibited. *The Advisor's Guide to Life Insurance*, a book for attorneys advising clients about life insurance, recommends use of a questionnaire if the attorney does not know the agent. Box 17-1 shows the questionnaire. Its answers can provide greater insight into an agent's professional experience and conduct.

In addition, inquiries about the agent can be made with the state insurance regulatory authority. The insurance department can provide information about any complaints and the nature of the licensing of the individual, although detailed information about individual complaints is often deemed to be confidential. For agents licensed to sell variable policies, information can be sought from the *Financial Industry Regulatory Authority* (FINRA) about the individual. FINRA's web site (www.finra.org) under "BrokerCheck Reports" provides a range of information about registered firms and brokers. It shows the person's credentials, current registrations, exams passed, and previous employment. It also shows information about client disputes with the individual as well as any regulatory actions taken against him or her. While potentially useful individually, a condition of use is that the information not be published or otherwise disseminated.

The *Securities and Exchange Commission* (SEC) also maintains an Investment Adviser Public Disclosure website (www.adviserinfo.sec.gov) that gives information about advisers' employment and regulatory histories. Regrettably, no services equivalent to those offered by FINRA or the SEC seem to exist for agents not involved with variable products.

EVALUATING LIFE INSURANCE COMPANIES' FINANCIAL STRENGTH

It is important to assess a life insurer's financial strength. Doing so, however, is not easy, especially for those not schooled in finance and insurer operations.

WHY ASSESSING LIFE INSURER FINANCIAL STRENGTH IS IMPORTANT

The life insurance industry is heavily regulated. In an effort to protect policyholders, as we know from Chapters 12 and 13, life insurance companies are subject to conservative rules and requirements that involve, among other factors, how companies manage their finances and support the products they issue to customers. However, life insurance companies can and sometimes do fail. Because the failure

Box 17-1
Life Insurance Agent Questionnaire

Agents are expected to conduct themselves with fairness, competence, integrity, and diligence. Please respond to the following questions that touch on each of these four areas.

1. **Fairness**
   A. What is the justification for your recommendation regarding the:
      i. Amount of insurance?
      ii. Type of policy?
      iii. Policy funding technique?
      iv. Beneficiary?
      v. Policy ownership arrangement?
      vi. Insurance company?
   B. Did you review multiple insurers and products, including policy performance comparisons? Which ones and why did you eliminate them?
   C. With what life insurance companies do you place most of your business and why?
   D. Are you free to place business with insurers not affiliated with your primary insurer? If not, explain why the client should be satisfied with your primary insurer.

2. **Competence**
   A. What is your educational and professional background, including professional designations?
   B. What do you consider your area of expertise?
   C. For how many years have you worked fulltime in the life insurance business, and for how many years have you devoted most of your time in your area of expertise?
   D. What are the qualifications and experience of your support staff?
   E. What continuing professional development activities have you undertaken in the past three years, including pursuit of any professional designations?
   F. To what professional organizations do you belong? What positions have you occupied within them?

3. **Integrity**
   A. Do you or your firm have a written and enforced confidentiality policy and accompanying guidelines?
   B. Do you or your firm have a written and enforced ethics policy and accompanying guidelines?
   C. Has any client ever sued you or registered any complaints against you with any professional society, government regulatory agency (including any state insurance department), or the *Financial Industry Regulatory Authority* (FINRA) and, if so, explain the circumstances?

4. **Diligence**
   A. What is your understanding of the client's financial needs, goals, and circumstances?
   B. What is your policy regarding working with other professionals? With how many have you worked in the previous year and what is their expertise?
   C. What is the platform/administrative set up on which you provide ongoing policy service and how do you monitor policy and insurer performance, including treatment of in-force policies and insurer financial strength?
   D. Explain the source of any leverage that you have with insurers in connection with policy negotiation and pricing and re-pricing.
   E. What have been the first-year lapse rates on the business that you have written in each of the preceding three years?

Source: Harold D. Skipper and Wayne Tonning, *The Advisor's Guide to Life Insurance* (Chicago; American Bar Association, 2011), Chapter 2.

of a life insurance company can have far graver consequences for its customers than can the failure of most other corporations, greater scrutiny is warranted.

THE SPECIAL NATURE OF LIFE INSURANCE   Embedded within life insurance policies are long-term, intangible financial promises not found with other financial or consumer products. These promises differ from those of most other products in at least three important respects.

- First, the promises embedded within a life insurance policy usually are of considerably longer duration than those found with other financial instruments and consumer products. The insurer states, essentially, that it intends to fulfill all of its obligations under the insurance contract whenever it is called upon to do so, whether today or 60 or more years from now.
- Second, in insurance, the guarantee *is* the product. There is no inherent value in the pieces of paper called an *insurance policy*. Only the *promises* embedded in the policy have value, and they can be no more secure than the financial security of the entity that makes them.
- Third, because of the great information asymmetry between life insurance buyers and sellers, buyers cannot easily assess the financial strength of the insurer and, hence, cannot easily assess the value of its promises.

For these three reasons, the financial strength and integrity of a life insurance company are more vital to its customers than is true of most other enterprises.

LIFE INSURERS IN FINANCIAL DIFFICULTY: LESSONS FROM THE PAST   While far fewer life insurance companies than banks got into financial difficulty in the recession that began in 2008, life insurers are not immune to financial difficulty, with some 616 having become financially impaired in some way since 1976. We follow the A.M. Best definition of a **financially impaired insurer** as one for which its:

- ability to conduct normal operations is impaired,
- capital and surplus have been determined to be insufficient to meet legal requirements, and/or
- financial condition has triggered regulatory concern.

Figure 17-1 shows the number and relative frequency of impairments per year since 1976. Almost 92 percent of financially impaired insurers have been comparatively young and small, with capital and surplus of less than $20 million. The average annual Financial Impairment Frequency (FIF) for small insurers was 2.3 percent whereas the average for large insurers was only 0.03 percent. Additionally, most have gotten into difficulty because of adverse results from writing accident and health insurance.

Lest we leave an erroneous impression, several large, well known life insurers have also become financially impaired. As Figure 17-1 shows, the year 1991 was an *annus horribilis* for the industry, especially with regard to large insurers. More than 80 life insurers became financially impaired that year, accounting for somewhat less than 3 percent of industry premiums written. Unlike most other years, several large insurers are included in the 1991 total. The failures of 146-year-old *Mutual Benefit Life* and of *Executive Life*, California's largest domestic life insurer, were especially shocking. These two failures sent shock waves through both the insurance industry and the entire financial community. Only one year prior to their failures, both insurers were rated in the "secure" category by several rating agencies, demonstrating those agencies' fallibility.

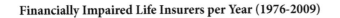

Financially Impaired Life Insurers per Year (1976-2009)

Figure 17-1

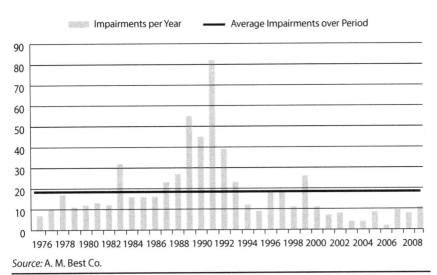

Source: A. M. Best Co.

At first glance, the number of impairments since 1976 may seem large, but it represents an average annual impairment rate of somewhat less than 19 companies per year, representing an annual average financial impairment frequency (FIF) of less than 0.9 percent. This amounts to less than one in 114 life insurers having become financially impaired annually over this study period.

A comment is in order regarding the world's most infamous financial impairment of an insurance group – *American International Group* (AIG). AIG remains well known for its many insurance companies worldwide, including a major presence within the U.S. life and nonlife insurance sectors, although it continues to sell units. Less well known was AIG's many financial activities outside of mainstream insurance. Its financial products division was heavily involved in selling **credit default swaps** – financial instruments bought by investors to protect against defaults on bonds. When the financial crisis hit in full force in 2008, the credit ratings of innumerable bonds declined, resulting in calls on AIG to post massive amounts of additional collateral. Reserves were grossly insufficient. Because of concern that the failure of AIG could precipitate a domino-like failure of other major financial institutions, the federal government agreed to bail out AIG. AIG's insurance subsidiaries, including its life subsidiaries, ultimately were not directly affected by the impairment of the holding company. AIG's financial impairment was neither precipitated by nor related to its mainstream insurance operations.

INSURER MANAGEMENT OF FINANCIAL STRENGTH

The managements of life insurance companies, including their boards of directors, are responsible for knowing their companies' financial strength and determining the best course of action relative to it. Although it might seem that the natural inclination would be for insurers to aim to become and remain exceptionally strong financially, the incentives impinging on management are ambiguous, as alluded to in Chapters 13 and 14.

INCENTIVES TO HAVE STRONG FINANCIALS   Life insurance executives have natural motivations to ensure insurer financial strength and profitability. They and their employees have good jobs for which they are well compensated, and they would like to keep them. Executives and boards of directors also understand the importance of their companies being sufficiently strong financially to garner decent ratings from rating agencies and to avoid undue attention and criticism from state insurance regulators. Low ratings can be discouraging to agents and can penalize sales. Unusual attention or criticism by regulators is bad for any business but can be especially damaging to businesses that rely on trust, as with life insurance.

To secure decent ratings, a life insurer must have sound financials, meaning that it operates profitably and has a strong balance sheet. A strong balance sheet is one in which assets exceed liabilities by a sufficient margin to enable the insurer to weather adverse operational and economic conditions with minimal disruption to operations and without provoking regulatory concern about the insurer's financial condition. The excess of assets over liabilities, commonly called *net worth*, is referred to in insurance parlance as *capital and surplus* or sometimes as *surplus*, sometimes as *capital*, and sometimes as *owners' equity.*

INCENTIVES TO AVOID HOLDING EXCESS CAPITAL   We noted in Chapter 14 the inconsistent solvency preferences of policyowners (who seek security and desire more surplus) and shareholders (who seek high returns and so want to minimize surplus). Holding surplus is expensive, and the cost of an insurer's products must reflect this. The need to provide affordable products and to provide adequate returns to investors mitigates incentives to holding excess surplus for stock insurers. In the contemporary U.S. market, mutual companies are subject to the same market imperatives.

Nevertheless, because mutual companies in the past accumulated surplus for unjustifiable reasons – management perquisites primarily – at least one state (New York) maintains limits on the amount of surplus that mutuals may accumulate on behalf of participating policyholders.

Thus, as noted in Chapter 14, shareholders are risk tolerant, whereas policyowners are risk averse. Shareholders prefer to invest less capital to produce higher investment returns, whereas policyowners prefer more capital to provide greater policy security.

ASSESSING INSURER FINANCIAL STRENGTH

An assessment of an insurer's financial strength is essential but not simple. Neither the typical life insurance advisor nor certainly the average life insurance buyer is technically capable of making a reasoned, independent assessment of an insurer's financial strength. Doing so requires mastery of specialized and sometimes confusing insurance terminology and, importantly, requires a high level of accounting, actuarial, and financial competence by those conducting the analysis.

This section explores some of the financial elements of insurers that make up an assessment. Our purpose is not to expound on the full panoply of tools essential for such an analysis – although the ones discussed below would be included. Rather, we seek to promote a better understanding of the significance of financial information about insurers provided by rating agencies, state insurance regulators, insurers themselves, and others.

Insurance companies' financial solidity depends greatly on the nature and quality of their investments. Assets held by life insurers back the liabilities that arise from in-force policies. Asset growth occurs when cash inflows exceed cash outflows. As noted in Chapters 13-14, life insurers' investments are divided between two accounts that differ in the nature of the liabilities for which the assets are being held.

An insurer's general account supports guaranteed interest crediting contractual obligations, such as those arising from traditional and many contemporary life insurance policies (including whole life and universal life). An insurer's separate accounts support liabilities arising from variable products for which investment risk is borne by the policyholder, as with variable life insurance. State laws allow assets in separate accounts to be invested without regard to the many restrictions of general account investments. Most separate account investments are in equities in contrast to general account investments that are predominantly in more conservative fixed instruments such as bonds and mortgages.

Importantly, variable policyholders must look mainly or solely to the assets held in the separate account were the insurer to fail. Other than the guarantees relating to death benefits and withdrawals within the contract – which make it important for variable policyholders also to consider the financial strength of the insurer, not solely the security of the separate account investments – the insurer itself ordinarily has no obligation toward variable policies' cash values. The separate account assets are not subject to the creditors of the life insurer were it to become insolvent.

In contrast, the insurer itself and all general account assets back policies whose liabilities are required to be held in the general account. The general account assets are not specifically earmarked for these liabilities, although policyholders have priority over general creditors. It is for this reason that we are primarily concerned here about the financial solidity of the insurer in relation to its general account obligations and attendant policies.

As discussed in Chapter 13, publicly available financial data on life insurers are, for the most part, based on statutory accounting principles (SAP), the accounting conventions laid down by insurance regulators and required to be followed by life insurance companies. This approach can be contrasted with more widely used generally accepted accounting principles (GAAP), which are predicated on the notion of a business as a going concern. As SAP is more conservative and geared towards the ability to meet current financial obligations, analyses of life insurers' financial strength typically rely on SAP data.

The traditional elements of financial analysis include (1) capital and surplus adequacy, (2) leverage, (3) asset quality and diversification, (4) liquidity, and (5) operational performance. We discuss ratio analysis exclusively. A problem with ratio analysis is that it fails to consider interrelationships among values, so it omits some potentially important information, of the type discussed in Chapters 9 and 14. Additionally, while our focus is on financial strength, elements of an insurer's operations can have bearings on strength, including market position and brand, distribution, product focus and diversification, and competence of management. These elements are included in the insurer reports prepared by rating agencies, but omitted here. This overview gives a flavor for why certain relationships can prove of vital importance. Each ratio would be assessed against prevailing industry values at the time of an evaluation and further considered in light of the insurer's pattern of assets and liabilities.

CAPITAL AND SURPLUS ADEQUACY   The relative level of an insurer's capital and surplus is the most important factor in assessing an insurer's financial condition. Insurers need surplus to absorb unanticipated fluctuations in asset and liability values and operational results. The greater an insurer's surplus relative to its obligations, the more secure it is, other things being the same.

In evaluating the adequacy of an insurer's surplus, certain adjustments must be made in the values shown on their regulatory balance sheets. SAP requires the establishment of certain liabilities for the purpose of minimizing fluctuations in the value of insurer *reported* surplus, such as the Asset Maintenance Reserve and Interest Maintenance Reserve, discussed in Chapter 13. These are not true liabilities, as they do not represent amounts actually owed to anyone. As such, they should be excluded from liability values and added to capital and surplus figures. All references to surplus in this section should be understood to have been so adjusted.

As an absolute figure, the amount of an insurer's capital and surplus has little meaning. Two surplus ratios, however, offer insight into financial solidity. The first ratio is:

$$\textbf{Surplus adequacy = Surplus} \div \textbf{Liabilities}$$

The higher the ratio, the greater the financial strength, although surplus and reserve levels can vary substantially with an insurer's mix and age of business. The ratio ignores the degree of conservatism that may be inherent in one insurer's reserve calculation but not found in the calculation of another's. For this reason, it is interpreted with care and ordinarily compared only with similarly situated insurers.

A second useful measure of surplus adequacy is the rate of surplus formation:

$$\textbf{Rate of surplus formation = Growth rate of surplus} \div \textbf{Growth rate of liabilities}$$

Calculated over a reasonable time period, such as five years, this ratio ideally should be positive. A consistent, substantial increase in surplus relative to liabilities suggests that the insurer's financial security is increasing. The higher the ratio, the better, *ceteris paribus*. Other measures of surplus adequacy are sometimes used. Most are variations or refinements on the above two ratios.

LEVERAGE   Leverage is a measure of how intensively a company uses its debt versus capital and surplus. Leverage increases return on equity, but it also increases risk due to required interest and principal payments. In the context of insurance, four measures of leverage are commonly used. The first is the ratio of liabilities to surplus. The lower the ratio, the less the leverage. This ratio is the reciprocal of the surplus adequacy test discussed above and is simply another way of viewing the same thing. Either ratio is used in financial evaluations.

The second ratio measures the intensity of surplus use in premium writings:

Net premiums written ratio = (Net premiums written + Deposits) ÷ Surplus

The ratio measures an insurer's exposure to pricing errors, a major cause of life insurer failures. The higher the ratio, the greater the exposure, *ceteris paribus*. Ideally, this ratio should be used to compare insurers with comparable product mixes.

The third ratio measures the ability of an insurer to cover its recurring interest and dividend obligations without stress.

Earnings coverage ratio = Net gain from operations ÷ (Interest expense and preferred dividends)

Net gain from operations is the approximate SAP equivalent of earnings under GAAP. It is calculated on an after-tax basis and ordinarily includes realized capital gains if taken directly from an insurer's SAP annual statement. Ideally such gains would not be included as insurers can determine their timing thereby potentially masking what is otherwise poor operational performance in a given year or two. Because capital gain treatment can vary from year to year and because of the natural volatility of NOG, this ratio ideally would be calculated as an average or a trend over a reasonable period of time, such as five years. The higher the ratio, the better able is the insurer to meet its ongoing obligations.

A final leverage measure reveals the extent to which an insurer relies on reinsurance. Almost all insurers purchase reinsurance to reduce claims fluctuations. Some insurers rely on reinsurance to reduce the strain on their surplus caused by the insufficiency of funds collected to cover liabilities established under SAP. Financial problems can arise from undue reliance on such reinsurance. Additionally, if the insurer continued to rely heavily on reinsurance to relieve the strain, profitability could suffer. After all, reinsurers themselves must make a profit.

Further, excessive reliance on reinsurance may introduce an additional solvency risk for the direct writing insurer. If the reinsurer were to default on its obligations, the direct writing insurer's solvency could be undermined. (Worth recalling is that the policyholder must ordinarily look solely to the direct writing insurer in the event of its insolvency. Thus, a low-rated direct writing insurer that touts its reinsurer's high rating could be engaging in a deceptive sales practice.) A commonly used measure of the extent to which an insurer relies on surplus relief reinsurance is:

Surplus relief = Reinsurance commissions and expense allowances ÷ Surplus

QUALITY AND DIVERSIFICATION OF ASSETS   The lower the quality of an insurer's assets, the greater the surplus needed to absorb adverse fluctuations, *ceteris paribus*. Indeed, an insurer can appear to be in a strong surplus position yet, because of the riskiness of its assets, may be vulnerable. Asset diversification is also important. Assets back an insurer's liabilities. Recall that admitted assets are those that may be included in determining an insurer's solvency under SAP; i.e., counted in measuring the excess of assets over liabilities. Non-admitted assets are not recognized by regulatory authorities in assessing solvency. Further references to assets refer to admitted assets only, unless stated otherwise.

Bonds of average or below average quality (noninvestment grade) can yield higher returns, but the principal and payment of interest are at higher risk. Some portion of an insurer's bond portfolio also can be in or near default, thus risking loss of both principal and interest. Investment prudence is the key. Limited investment in bonds of average or below average quality is considered prudent.

The ratio of noninvestment grade bonds to surplus reveals the extent to which an insurer's surplus could cover those bonds were a severe economic downturn to affect its performance. Therefore, the first asset quality ratio is:

**Investment in noninvestment grade bonds ratio =
Noninvestment grade bonds ÷ Surplus**

Noninvestment grade bonds is taken here to mean the sum of an insurer's investments in below investment grade bonds and bonds in or near default. The lower the investment in such bonds the better, *ceteris paribus*. This ratio also includes any below investment grade mortgage backed securities.

Next to bonds, mortgages are insurers' most prevalent general account investment. The trend in recent years has been toward commercial mortgages. In adverse economic times, insurers may experience adverse mortgage performance, as in the 2008-09 recession. The ratio of mortgages in default to surplus indicates the extent to which an insurer's surplus can cover mortgage defaults. Thus:

Mortgage default ratio = Mortgages in default ÷ Surplus

Mortgages in default is taken here to be the sum of an insurer's mortgages on which interest is overdue by more than three months, mortgages in the process of foreclosure, and properties acquired in satisfaction of debt. The lower the mortgage default ratio, the better. This ratio does not capture mortgage backed securities in default.

Another potentially important asset quality ratio is:

Investment in common stock ratio = Investment in common stock ÷ Surplus

Common stock value can fluctuate greatly from year to year. This ratio is an indication of the extent to which an insurer's surplus could be affected by these fluctuations.

LIQUIDITY Adequate liquidity should be maintained to meet an insurer's expected and unexpected cash needs. Otherwise, assets may have to be sold at disadvantageous prices. One useful measure of liquidity is:

**Current liquidity ratio = Unaffiliated investments, excluding mortgages and
real estate ÷ Liabilities**

Unaffiliated investments refers to assets other than bonds, stocks, and other investments held in affiliated enterprises, less property occupied by the insurer, typically its home office. The current liquidity ratio measures the proportion of net liabilities covered by cash and unaffiliated investments other than mortgages and real estate. Mortgages and real estate are excluded as they are not always readily convertible into cash. The lower the ratio, the more vulnerable is the insurer to liquidity problems.

Three other useful liquidity ratios of importance are:

Affiliated investments ratio = Investments in affiliated companies ÷ Surplus

Investment in real estate ratio = Investment in real estate ÷ Surplus

Non-admitted assets ratio = Non-admitted assets ÷ Surplus

These three ratios measure the extent to which an insurer's investment portfolio may be illiquid. Also, these asset classes often produce no income, and excessive investment in them may result in financial difficulty. The lower these ratios, the better, *ceteris paribus.*

OPERATIONAL PERFORMANCE   Sound operational performance is essential for an enduring, strong insurer. It reflects the ability and competence of management. Insurers with comparable product mixes provide a more relevant basis for comparison. More than a single year should be examined to detect unusual trends and variations, as many factors may distort results. We include five useful operational performance ratios. The first is:

Return on equity = Net gain from operations ÷ Surplus

Net gain from operations is calculated in the same manner as discussed earlier. This ratio reflects the return on an insurer's capital and surplus from insurance operations and investments. The higher an insurer's return on equity, the more effectively it uses owner funds. On the other hand, a high ratio can reflect excessive leverage or low capitalization.

An insurer's investment yield is a potentially important operational performance factor as well as a potential indicator of product performance. The ratio is:

Yield on investments = Net investment income ÷ Invested assets

This ratio reflects how well investments are being managed. It does not include realized and unrealized capital gains (losses). The higher the yield, the better, other things being the same. Unfortunately, other things rarely are the same. A higher yield may reflect higher risk. This is another reason why the asset quality evaluation is important.

Realized and unrealized capital gains and losses can be important components of insurers' investment performance. The following ratio includes such gains (losses):

Total return on investments = (Net investment income + Capital gains) ÷ Invested Assets

The rough insurer counterpart to return on sales is measured by the ratio of net operating gain to total income. That is:

Net operating gain ratio = Net gain from operations ÷ Total operating income

Net gain from operations is calculated in the same manner as discussed earlier. *Total operating income* is the sum of premium and investment income. This ratio is a measure of the average profitability within each dollar of revenue. Clearly, the higher the ratio, the better. Again, results should be interpreted with caution and only over time because of the use of SAP data.

Finally, we are interested in how much an insurer spends in commissions to procure and maintain business and on overall expenses, as a percentage of premium and deposit income. The ratio is:

$$\text{Expense ratio} = (\text{Commissions and expenses}) \div$$
$$(\text{Net premiums written} + \text{Deposits})$$

Commissions and expenses include all commissions paid through the sales channels and all other insurance expenses, taxes, and fees. The lower the ratio, the better, other things being the same – which is rarely the case.

THE ROLE OF RATING AGENCIES

Rating agencies play a prominent role in the assessment of life insurer financial strength. In this section, we first explain why rating agencies are so important and provide an overview of four major life insurer rating agencies. We then examine the nature of rating agency reports and rating systems.

THE IMPORTANCE OF RATING AGENCIES   Neither the typical life insurance advisor nor certainly the average life insurance buyer is technically capable of making a reasoned, independent assessment of an insurer's financial strength. Rather, those giving advice about life insurance usually rely on secondary sources in counseling clients concerning life insurer financial strength. The most important of which are rating agencies. **Rating agencies** are businesses that provide commentary and opinions about the ability of firms to meet their obligations. Several rating agencies offer opinions about life insurers' financial strength and their ability to meet ongoing obligations to policyholders. They express their opinions in the form of commentaries and ratings. Rating agencies employ analysts capable of conducting necessary in-depth analyses.

As the ratings of *Executive Life* and *Mutual Benefit Life* suggest, rating agencies are not infallible. Also questions have been raised about conflicts of interest related to rated entities having to pay for ratings, although many changes have been made in this respect. Rating agencies have been found to be the most consistent and best predictors of insurers' financial condition. After all, this is their business, and their financial success and livelihood depend on their being right far more often than they are wrong.

FOUR MAJOR RATING AGENCIES   We offer a short overview of four rating agencies that offer opinions about the financial strength of life insurance companies. While a few other rating agencies also offer opinions, our discussion is limited to those agencies that have been designated by the *Securities and Exchange Commission (SEC)* as *Nationally Recognized Statistical Rating Organizations* (NRSROs). They are A.M. Best, Fitch Ratings, Moody's Investors Service, and Standard and Poor's.

- **A.M. Best.** A.M. Best (www.ambest.com) has been publishing financial information about insurance companies for more than a century – longer than any other rating agency. It published ratings briefly in the 1930s and has since 1976. It also rates more U.S. life insurers than any other rating agency, numbering about 1,000. If an insurer requesting a rating disagrees with Best's analysis, no rating is assigned. A previously assigned rating may be withdrawn on request, but Best announces that fact publically and also what the rating would have been. Ratings are reviewed periodically, but not less frequently than once a year and can be changed at any time. Insurers pay an annual fee to Best to be rated.

- **Fitch Ratings.** Fitch (www.fitchratings.com) rates more than 300 U.S. life insurers, each for a fee. If an insurer requests a rating, Fitch will make the rating public even if the insurer disagrees with the rating. The insurer may later request that the rating be withdrawn, in which case Fitch exercises its discretion whether to withdraw it. Also, insurers may request a tentative assessment based on less-than-complete information and may, thereafter, choose to abort the process, in which case Fitch makes no public announcement.

- **Moody's Investor's Service.** Moody's (www.moodys.com) rates about 200 U.S. life insurers. Ratings are reviewed frequently and can be changed at any time. Moody's states that it reserves the right to decide whether and when to issue and publish ratings and related information, except in rare instances where disclosure has been contractually limited. It also reserves the right to rate entities even if a rating has not been requested, if the market has sufficient interest in it and relevant information is available. Insurers pay an annual fee to be rated.

- **Standard & Poor's** (S&P). About 350 life insurers requesting ratings are rated by S&P (www.standardandpoors.com/ratings). A few dozen life insurers not requesting ratings are also rated based solely on publically available information, with the rating designated as "pi". If an insurer requesting a rating disagrees with S&P's analysis, no rating is assigned. A previously assigned rating may be withdrawn on request, but S&P announces that fact publically and may assign a pi rating. S&P does not suppress the ratings of pi-rated insurers.

THE NATURE OF RATING AGENCY REPORTS   Individual company ratings are available at no charge from each rating service's website. Full reports may be purchased from the rating agency either via subscription to their services or on a case-by-case basis from their websites. Reports also are available from insurance agents and insurance companies.

Rating Agency Reports   While the content and format of each rating agency's reports differ, they include similar types of information. They identify the insurer and provide its contact information. The agency's rating is provided along with an indication whether the rating outlook for the insurer is negative, stable, or positive, although terminology varies. A rating outlook is important as it offers the agency's opinion about the likely trend in the insurer's rating. The agency's justification for its rating outlook is provided within the report.

There follows key financial data and ratios, discussions of the insurer's strengths and weaknesses as perceived by the rating agency, and the rationale for its rating of the insurer. The order of these items is not the same with each agency nor are they labeled precisely in this way. The insurer's current and likely future competitive position in its various target markets is often discussed. Management and corporate strategy usually are covered in some way, along with comments about its risk management capability. Quantitative and qualitative analysis and remarks are included about the insurer's investments, liquidity, capitalization, profitability, financial flexibility, and other related financial and operational elements. Various financial data and ratios are also provided.

Rating Categories   Each rating agency has its own rating categories, and this fact leads to noncompatibility of ratings. For example, an A+ rating from Best is its second highest rating, but it is Fitch's and S&P's fifth highest rating. Table 17-1 lists each of the four rating agencies' categories along with a rank number that indicates where each rating ranks among those of each rating firm. Equivalent rank numbers *do not* mean equivalence of ratings. Insurers receiving ratings shown in the shaded area fall into the rating agencies' "vulnerable" category. Insurers receiving ratings not appearing in the shaded area are considered "secure."

Table 17-1   Rank Orders of Ratings and Categories for Four Rating Agencies

Rank Number	Best	Fitch	Moody's	S&P
1	A++	AAA	Aaa	AAA
2	A+	AA+	Aa1	AA+
3	A	AA	Aa2	AA
4	A-	AA-	Aa3	AA-
5	B++	A+	A1	A+
6	B+	A	A2	A
7	B	A-	A3	A-
8	B-	BBB+	Baa1	BBB+
9	C++	BBB	Baa2	BBB
10	C+	BBB-	Baa3	BBB-
11	C	BB+	Ba1	BB+
12	C-	BB	Ba2	BB
13	D	BB-	Ba3	BB-
14	E	B+	B1	B+
15	F	B	B2	B
16		B-	B3	B-
17		CCC+	Caa1	CCC+
18		CCC	Caa2	CCC
19		CCC-	Caa3	CCC-
20		CC	Ca	CC
21		C	C	R

A possible annoyance with securing and using ratings from multiple agencies is their noncompatible rating scales and possible confusion as to the meanings of the ratings themselves. Many advisors secure the Comdex number for the insurers that they are reviewing. *Comdex* is a composite index of ratings, expressed as the average percentile of a company's rating; i.e., the proportion of rated insurers that are rated lower (www.ebixlife.com/vitalsigns/). While not itself a rating, it gives an insurer's standing on a scale of 1 to 100, in relation to other rated insurers. Thus, a Comdex of 90th means that the composite of the insurer's ratings places it in the 90 percentile of rated companies; i.e., 10 percent are rated higher and 90 percent lower. While the Comdex system seems logical, concern exists that its use can lead to unfair comparisons because not all insurers are rated by the four major agencies – which means that rankings can be skewed – and the use of its numerical index may suggest a degree of accuracy that does not exist.

USING RATING AGENCY REPORTS AND RATINGS   Many advisors follow the practice of reviewing reports from more than one agency. Doing so sometimes reveals differences in opinions, which might favor one insurer over another. The narrative and data will reveal the insurer's target markets, including whether the insurer specializes in products that the client is considering. Reports also may identify whether the insurer's financial results in the lines of business most relevant to a consumer might be suffering adverse development and the reasons for such. Finally, reports often identify areas that may demand additional investigation.

Clearly, higher ratings are preferred to lower. Regrettably, other things are not always the same, and it is worth remembering that ratings are opinions and not guarantees or assurances of financial strength. A lower rated insurer may offer better underwriting or more flexible or competitive products or superior advice and ongoing service. As the rating agencies themselves often point out, small differences in ratings, especially between adjacent categories, mean only slight perceived differences in financial strength. For example, an insurer that relied on more than five distribution channels and offered five or more distinct product lines, could be rated higher than an otherwise identical insurer that had fewer distribution channels and product lines.

Great caution should be exercised in dealing with life insurers whose ratings from one or more agencies fall within the vulnerable category or that have no rating from any of the major agencies. A vulnerable rating or no rating does not mean that the company necessarily is about to fail or that it is in financial difficulty. However, the failure rate of companies having vulnerable or no ratings has been considerably higher than those rated in the secure category. Insurers in financial difficulty often withdraw their ratings.

Rating agencies may place a company's rating "under review" for a variety of positive, negative, evolving, or developing implications of any potentially meaningful sort. For example, an acquisition by the insurer of another insurer or the pending sale of the company would be expected to cause a rating review. Likewise, either adverse or positive internal financial developments or senior management turnover may provoke a review.

OTHER SOURCES OF INFORMATION ABOUT INSURERS

In securing information about a specific life insurer, care should be taken to ensure that one is using the insurer's correct name and, ideally, state of domicile. Affiliated life insurers often have similar names. *American General Life Insurance Company* and *American General Assurance Company* are both AIG affiliates, although only the former is heavily involved in individual life insurance sales. Even unrelated life insurers have names that can be easily confused – *American General Life Insurance Company* and *General American Life Insurance Company* are unrelated.

While rating agencies are the most common sources of information on life insurer financial strength, other sources of information are available as well. They include the *National Association of Insurance Commissioners* (NAIC) and state insurance departments, the SEC, insurance companies and agents, and publications. These sources are not substitutes for rating agencies' analyses and opinions.

THE NAIC AND STATE INSURANCE DEPARTMENTS   State insurance regulators are charged with protecting and assisting insurance consumers and are logical sources of information about insurers. Individual states are more or less effective in carrying out this mandate, so varying degrees of usefulness exist. To cite but one example, reports of the financial examinations of their domestic insurers are readily available on some insurance department web sites, but others do not make their reports so easily accessible.

Nonetheless, individual state insurance departments and the NAIC house much potentially useful information about life insurers' financial condition. Recall that the NAIC is the trade association to which all state insurance regulators belong and that it helps to coordinate state insurance regulation (see Chapter 12). The information that it houses on life insurers is derived from each state's insurance regulatory official. Often there is an advantage in securing needed information from the NAIC as opposed to the insurer's state of domicile as the NAIC often makes the information available electronically via its website whereas many states do not. Indeed, states rely on the NAIC to perform this function for them. Three types of regulatory information can prove potentially useful: financial statement information, complaint data, and risk-based capital ratios, each of which is discussed briefly below.

Financial Statement Information   As discussed in Chapter 13, life insurers are required annually to file detailed financial information with state regulators, called the *financial statement*. These financial statements are public record information. As such, they should be accessible at the state insurance departments of the states in which the insurer is licensed, but this is not always the situation. Some states provide the statements of domestic insurers only, referring any inquiry about licensed, non-domestic insurers to the NAIC website.

Annual statements can run to hundreds of pages in length, going so far as to require the listing of every individual investment in an insurer's portfolio. Consequently, the majority of the information therein is of little interest to most consumers. On the other hand, some important nuggets reside therein. For example, the financial data allow the calculation of the financial ratios discussed earlier. It also permits a double check of financial data provided by agents and others with a financial interest in the transaction.

One of the most interesting and potentially insightful elements of the annual statement filing is *Management's Discussion and Analysis* of the insurer. Management is required to set out the company's background and organizational structure, discuss the likely effects of adverse economic events, and summarize its financial operations and liquidity and capital resources. The section wherein management explains the company's principal risks and uncertainties can be especially insightful, although the discussions can appear as laundry lists of everything that could go off its mark.

Few, if any, states make the statements available on their websites. Instead, the states authorize the NAIC to make them available to the public electronically. Selected financial information can be found at https://eapps.naic.org/cis/index.do. One can learn from this same site the states in which the insurer is licensed. More detailed financial information, including annual statements, can be obtained from the NAIC Store at https://eapps.naic.org/insData/index.jsp. Registration is required but is free, as are the first five reports.

A strange characteristic of this facility is that users are required to acknowledge that the information is copyrighted by the NAIC and that the information cannot be used for commercial purposes. These two characteristics are strange in that they seemingly could not be applied to the same information in the hands of individual states – where the information legally resided before the states authorized the NAIC to house it. It appears that the NAIC can convert public record information into copyrighted private information that otherwise could be used for commercial purposes, because the NAIC is not a government entity. Finally, a few states make the reports compiled from on-site financial examinations of their domestic insurers available on their web sites. While these exam reports can be interesting and revealing, too often they are dated.

Complaint Data Insurers that are tending toward financial difficulty often provoke higher levels of consumer complaints about poor quality service, claims handling, and marketing activities than they did formerly or more than their peer companies. Independent of whether high complaint frequency hints at financial difficulty, who wishes to deal with a life insurer for which its insureds and beneficiaries lodge an excessive number of complaints?

State insurance departments compile data on the nature and frequency of closed complaints lodged against licensed insurers. Such data typically are not available from the departments' websites directly, but the NAIC compiles such data for the states that wish to participate in the NAIC system. State participation is voluntary, so the NAIC complaint data are not necessarily complete, although it appears sufficiently so as to provide useful information.

The NAIC website at https://eapps.naic.org/cis/index.do allows the user to compile various reports, including the following:

- *Closed Complaint Counts by State.* Displays the total number of closed complaints for the selected company in each state.
- *Closed Complaint Counts by Code.* Displays the total number of closed complaints by type of coverage, reason the complaint was filed, and disposition of the complaint.
- *Closed Complaint Ratio Report.* Displays the ratio of the company's U.S. market share of closed complaints compared to the company's U.S. market share of premiums for a specific policy type.
- *Closed Complaint Trend Report.* Displays total closed complaint counts by year with the percent change of counts between years.

The Closed Complaint Ratio Report and the Closed Complaint Trend Report ordinarily are the most informative. The Ratio Report normalizes the number of each company's complaints to its market share. Insurers with larger market shares can be expected logically to garner more complaints than insurers with smaller market shares, other things being the same. Complaint ratios of insurers with similar products and target markets should be compared. A national median complaint ratio is also provided, allowing for a comparison of the specific insurer's complaint ratio to the national median. The Trend Report highlights whether claims are increasing meaningfully, but this should be considered in relation to market share or increases in business.

Risk-Based Capital Ratios We know that insurers are required to calculate and provide their risk-based capital (RBC) ratios to state insurance regulators. These ratios are not made available to consumers by regulators. The RBC system was created to provide a standard for insurer capital adequacy intended to reflect each insurer's unique risks. The higher are a life insurer's asset, insurance, interest, and business risks – as measured by a formula – the greater its required capital level, *ceteris paribus*. This required capital level is measured by taking the ratio of an insurer's total adjusted capital to an RBC level.

Individuals and companies within the insurance business are prohibited from disclosing insurers' RBC ratios. Presumably, individuals and businesses *not* engaged in the business of insurance are not. Thus, an advisor who is not engaged in the business of insurance can secure these ratios, they can be utilized to inform him- or herself and clients about insurers' relative risk. Further, rating agencies provide to the public their own risk adjusted capital ratios, which factors into their overall insurer financial strength ratings.

SECURITIES AND EXCHANGE COMMISSION Public companies above a certain minimum size must annually file with the SEC a report of the company's performance on **Form 10-K**. This annual report is far more detailed than the similarly named glossy annual report provided to shareholders. The 10-K includes detailed information related to the company's history, nature of its business, organizational structure, risk factors, equity, subsidiaries, and audited financial statements, among other information. Stock life insurers are required to file these reports. Relevant accounting data in these reports are based on GAAP not statutory accounting principles.

Every annual report must be composed of four *Parts*, each of which is divided into *Items*. These reports can run into hundreds of pages in length, with resulting information overload akin to that which can occur with the financial statements filed with state insurance regulators. Typically, the most relevant items within a 10-K for a life insurance company are:

- *Item 1 – Business.* This item describes the nature of the company's business, the subsidiaries that it owns, and the markets in which it operates. It also includes discussions of effects that are significant to particular industries, as with competition and regulation in an insurance context.
- *Item 1A – Risk Factors.* In this item, the company is required to state the risks that it faces; i.e., anything that reasonably could go wrong. This includes likely external effects, possible future failures to meet obligations, and other risks sufficient to ensure that current and potential investors are adequately warned. This item is especially relevant for life insurance companies, with a litany of possible negative effects typically discussed and, to some degree, analyzed.

- *Item 7 – Management's Discussion and Analysis.* Within this item, management is required to discuss the operations of the company in detail and usually to compare the current period to prior periods. It provides an overview of the company and a summary discussion of the key issues that it faces; the company's outlook; and results from operations. A related item here is a discussion of market risk. These comparisons provide an overview of the operational issues and the causes of increases and decreases in business.

In addition to the 10-K, a company is also required to file abbreviated quarterly reports on **Form 10-Q**. If significant material events occur, such as the sale of an affiliate or change of independent auditors or CEO, between filings of the 10-K and 10-Q, companies are required to report them on **Form 8-K**. Form 10-K, as well as other SEC filings, can be searched at www.sec.gov/edgar/searchedgar/companysearch.html.

Insurance Companies, Agents, and Publications   Insurers being considered by clients are logical sources of information about their financial health. They can provide copies of their annual reports which contain summary financial data and commentary about their strategic directions, plans, and operations. Such information is also commonly available on insurers' web sites. They also have brochures and/or other promotional material. While such materials can be expected to be self-serving, they can provide a useful perspective as to how the company views itself and its relationship with its customers.

If potentially adverse financial information is revealed about an insurer that is being considered, through rating agencies and/or other sources, the insurer can be invited to respond to the negative information. In some instances, the information may be of minor consequence, but the onus ordinarily is on the insurer (or its agent) to make such a case.

Insurers can also be a source of useful information about their competitors. Insurers are understandably reluctant to criticize competitors directly, in part because doing so can run afoul of state insurance regulation. But they often will have conducted their own financial analyses of competitors and may make them available to prospective customers. Care should be taken in interpreting these analyses, especially when they are supported by simple comparisons of financial ratios, as such ratios cannot provide the in-depth insight that rating agency evaluations entail.

Life insurance agents often maintain or have access to resources of the type mentioned. Additionally, experienced, successful agents ordinarily have an "ear to the ground" that enables them to pick up the latest "chatter" about insurers against which they compete regularly. Many agents were at the vanguard of suspicions concerning the financial strength of *Executive Life Insurance Company* before its collapse.

Major business publications such as *The Wall Street Journal, Fortune, Bloomberg Businessweek,* the *Financial Times,* and others carry news about life insurers, just as they do about other major corporations. Monitoring news and archival research can reveal information that may be helpful. Publications whose focus is insurance in general and life insurance in particular generally are more relevant, such as *Best's Review* and *The National Underwriter,* among others.

IMPLICATIONS TO POLICYHOLDERS OF INSURER FINANCIAL DIFFICULTY

Individuals owning policies with life insurance companies that are encountering financial difficulties often find themselves involved in a world of uncertainty. The implications to such policyholders differ as between those circumstances in which there has not been regulatory intervention and those in which the state regulator has become involved.

WITH NO REGULATORY INTERVENTION

Managers of insurance companies almost always know when their companies are trending towards financial difficulty and usually before the regulator, their agents, rating agencies, and certainly policyholders know it. They are keen to reverse the trend if they can and ordinarily undertake voluntary actions to try to do so. These actions might entail reducing operational expenses, changing the pricing factors for new policy sales, and/or changing pricing on existing policies (where they can do so). More drastic actions could involve seeking new infusions of capital; selling business units or blocks of business; purchasing surplus relief reinsurance; issuing surplus notes; exploring merger possibilities; trying to sell the company to a financially sound insurance group; and other actions.

Any of these actions can have an impact on existing policies. Unsuccessful actions could mean that the insurer becomes financially impaired and requires regulatory intervention. Even successful voluntary actions are likely to have a cost, and these costs could be passed on to future or existing policyholders or both. For policies not yet issued, the insurer could decide to undertake increases in the premium rates or the loadings and cost of insurance charges. Obviously, such a strategy is fraught with competitive implications.

With regard to existing policies, the insurer faces a more challenging situation when contemplating price increases to restore profitability. All policy contracts have some form of contractual guarantee(s) that must be respected. Recall that guaranteed policy elements are those that cannot be changed unilaterally by the insurer. Nonguaranteed policy elements are those that the insurer can change unilaterally. An insurer may not unilaterally increase premiums or lower cash values for in force par life policies, although it can lower or even eliminate dividend payments. Even forms of life insurance that allow premiums to be increased unilaterally by the insurer contain ceilings beyond which the premiums may not be increased. Policy face amounts may not be decreased unilaterally.

Additionally, all universal life (UL) type policies, including variable UL, contain guarantees. Neither current policy loadings nor cost of insurance charges can exceed guaranteed maximums specified in the contract, and the current interest crediting rate on cash values cannot fall below specified contractual guaranteed minimums for general account-backed policies. Collectively, these guarantees mean that the insurer can increase costs under existing policies to a limited extent only.

In each instance, pricing increases can lead to increased policy terminations as insureds in good health replace their insurance with policies from more competitive insurers. The result can be that the original insurer is left with a group of insureds in overall poorer health and, thus, experiences proportionately more death claims. An in-force price increase can result in decreased profits for the insurance company, which is why price increases require careful consideration.

WITH REGULATORY INTERVENTION

The dynamics of financial difficulties change dramatically when the insurance regulator becomes involved. Through informal actions, he or she may seek a friendly merger but with uncertainties for continuing policyholders about future coverage and pricing treatment. If blocks of life insurance are unprofitable, the regulator may allow or insist on changes to nonguaranteed pricing elements.

If the company is placed in receivership, losses are far more significant, and there will be greater incentives to enhance profits through adverse changes in nonguaranteed policy elements. If the underlying product line is profitable, there is also an incentive for the block to be maintained. Even guaranteed policy elements are not immune to change if the receiver believes changes are essential (and a relevant court agrees). Liens may be placed on policies, the guaranteed minimum interest rate may be reduced, and other guaranteed elements altered. While a receiver would view changing guarantees as a last resort, logic may dictate enactment of a discounted guarantee in preference to impairing the company further.

What happens in the worst case? While the state-based guaranty associations provide important protections to policyholders of failed companies, they do not offer the same types of assurances as those provided to bank customers via the *Federal Deposit Insurance Corporation*. Guaranty associations are not backed by any government and do not necessarily have immediate access to needed funds, having to rely on a post-event assessment system. Further, the nature and degree of protection varies by the policyholder's state of residency.

Each state guaranty association pays claims in accordance with the limits established by that state's statute. To ensure coverage by the association, policyholders must continue to pay premiums on their policies, even if the insurer is insolvent – not a pleasant experience. Despite the existence of guaranty associations, policyholders of failed companies face uncertainty, delays, aggravation, and possible losses.

Further, as each state's guaranty association relies on post-event assessments of the state's licensed insurers, the association may face liquidity problems between the time claims are submitted and funds collected. If statutory maximum assessments for a year have been levied and are insufficient to cover losses, the association cannot levy further assessments until the following year. Claimants may have to wait until additional funds become available. In past insolvencies, claims have taken six months and more to be paid.

Claims not paid by the guaranty association because they exceed the state limits become claims against the estate of the liquidated insurer. General creditors have no rights to assert a claim on the separate account assets held by insurers to cover liabilities under variable insurance contracts.

CONCLUSIONS

Advice by agents can be of enormous significance to customers. Most agents undeniably offer sound advice, but not all are capable of doing so, especially for more complex situations. Even if an insurance policy offers good value and the insurer is financially sound, poorly conceived beneficiary designations, policyowner arrangements, policy funding, policy options, and a host of other elements can wreck the policyholder's financial plans. Conversely, the most logically conceived policy arrangements can fall apart if the policy proves to be unnecessarily costly or the insurer suffers financial reverses.

The solvency record of the life insurance industry is impressive, especially in comparison to that of banks. The average policyholder is highly unlikely ever to be required to deal with the insolvency of a life insurer. But this very fact can lead to unwarranted complacency and lack of due care. Some, mostly small life insurers fail each year, but from time to time failures occur of insurers with household names. If a policyholder's life insurer fails, it makes no difference to her whether failures are rare or whether the insurer is large or small or purple.

The assessment of an insurer's financial strength is of critical importance to the purchase decision. Such an assessment, even by knowledgeable persons, remains a complex, daunting task. Advisors and insurance buyers necessarily place the greatest weight on rating agencies' opinions. While rating agencies are not perfect, their ratings have been found to be useful predictors of insurers' financial health.

ENDNOTES

1 This chapter draws in part from Harold D. Skipper and Wayne Tonning, *The Advisor's Guide to Life Insurance* (Chicago; American Bar Association, 2011), Chapters 2-5.
2 *Code of Professional Responsibility of the Society of Financial Service Professionals*, at http://www.financialpro.org/About/CodeOfProfResp.cfm, A1.3a.
3 *Id.* at A1.6a
4 *Id.* at A4.4a.
5 See "Life Insurance: An Industry Built on Secrecy," *The Insurance Forum.* May/June 2004.

CHAPTER 18

LIFE INSURANCE POLICY EVALUATION I: LEGAL ASPECTS

An insurance policy is a commitment by an insurer to indemnify an insured for a covered loss or to pay a defined sum or provide defined services if a specified event occurs during the term of the policy, but only so long as the policyowner has paid necessary premiums. A seemingly simple concept is revealed to be quite complex through generations of legal interpretation. Our focus is on U. S. law.

LIFE INSURANCE AND THE LAW OF CONTRACTS

ECONOMICS AND THE LAW

We noted in Chapter 1 that the market for life and health insurance is imperfect. Information asymmetries produce problems on both sides of the life insurance contract. For consumers, the main problem is they lack the information and expertise to understand the insurance as well as the company that offers it. Highly technical contracts offered by complex financial institutions can be bewildering to consumers and provide the potential means for companies and agents to take unfair advantage of their customers. For insurers, the main problems are the opposite: consumers may take unfair advantage of companies through their superior knowledge of their own risk properties (adverse selection) and self-interested behavior (moral hazard).

General contract law, statutory provisions, and judicial decisions regarding life and health insurance are designed to minimize the opportunity and/or incentive for either party to take advantage of the other. A written document or policy is required to minimize misunderstanding. In economic terms, the purpose is to (1) minimize information problems and (2) create an enforceable agreement.

REGULATORY CONTROL OVER POLICY PROVISIONS

U.S. states and most countries do not mandate required policy forms but exercise considerable control over insurance contracting by requiring prior approval of policy forms that must contain specific provisions. Regulatory disapproval can be caused by provisions that are assessed to be unfair, inequitable, or misleading.

Statutes usually do not prescribe the exact wording for standard provisions; rather, they stipulate that actual policy wording must be at least as favorable to the policyowner as that of the statute. Standard provisions touching on some or all of the following are generally required: (1) entire contract clause, (2) incontestable clause, (3) grace period, (4) reinstatement, (5) nonforfeiture provision, (6) policy loans, (7) annual dividends, (8) misstatement of age, (9) settlement options, (10) loan and nonforfeiture provisions, and (11) policyowner's right to return the policy for a refund. Mandatory policy provisions are intended to protect the policyowner, the beneficiary, and the company, as well as to provide flexibility to policyowners. These provisions were discussed in Chapter 5.

Requirements vary from state to state: minor differences or additional provisions may be required, and states establish individual filing and approval procedures. New procedures are being developed, the intent of which is to avoid the common and confusing practice of insurers drafting one principal policy and attaching different endorsements in each state to reflect special state requirements.

Life and health insurance policies are required to be written in simplified language in most U.S. jurisdictions. Most of these laws and regulations are based on the NAIC *Life and Health Insurance Policy Language Simplification Model Act*. The laws and regulations require that policy language meet an ease of readability test and that policies be printed in at least a minimum type size with an accompanying table of contents or index.

As an adjunct to insurance laws, court decisions have important effects on the way that life and especially health insurance contracts are written, interpreted, and enforced. These judicial opinions may create new law through new interpretations to prevailing insurance principles or may restate existing insurance law. Also, the structure of insurance contracts is indirectly influenced by laws on taxes, social insurance, human rights, and employment benefits.

THE INSURANCE POLICY AS A CONTRACT

A life insurance policy is a contract and must comply with all relevant laws to be enforceable. We provide background in this section about the policy as a legal instrument and how it comes about. We first reintroduce some key definitions from Chapter 1. First, recall that the insured is the person whose life or health is the object of the insurance contract. Except in some health insurance policies, the insured usually has no rights in the policy in his or her capacity as insured. The policyowner, also called the policyholder or simply owner, is the person who owns the contract and can exercise all rights under the policy. In most instances, the insured is the owner of a life insurance policy, but this usually is not required. When the owner is not the insured, a different basis for insurable interest must exist for a valid contract. (See below.)

The applicant is the person who applies for the insurance policy. Most commonly, the applicant is the proposed policyowner (and proposed insured). Unless noted otherwise, we will use the term applicant to mean proposed owner. Finally, the beneficiary is the person entitled to receive benefits under a life insurance, health insurance, or annuity policy. In the absence of an irrevocable beneficiary designation (Chapter 5), the beneficiary's interest is an expectancy interest, which provides no rights in the policy prior to the maturity of claim. If the insured is not the policyowner, it is common for the policyowner to be the beneficiary. Courts and legislative bodies are not as precise as we are here and do not use these terms in a consistent way; the same can be said for insurance agents and employees. For example, the term *insured* is often incorrectly used as a synonym for *policyowner*.

For this reason, care should be taken in reading and interpreting court decisions and laws.

DISTINGUISHING CHARACTERISTICS OF INSURANCE CONTRACTS

The life insurance relationship is unique. Several features of life insurance contracts distinguish them from other commercial agreements. First, the insurance contract is one of **utmost good faith** *(uberrimae fidei)*: each party is entitled to rely in good faith upon the representations of the other, and each is under an obligation not to attempt to deceive or withhold material information from the other. In economic terms, each party is supposed to avoid using its superior knowledge arising from information asymmetry to take unfair advantage of the other. The rule of *caveat emptor* – let the buyer beware – does *not* generally apply. The company must depend to a great extent on the statements of prospective policyowners/insureds/applicants in assessing the insureds' acceptability for insurance, and buyers must rely upon the insurer's good faith because the insurance contract is intricate and highly technical.

The insurance contract is characterized as one of **adhesion,** meaning that its terms and provisions are fixed by one party (the insurer) and, with minor exceptions, must be accepted or rejects *in toto* by the other party (the prospective policyholder). Thus, ambiguities or unclear elements in the contract are construed against the party which drafted the contract wording (insurer).

Life insurance contracts as well as most disability income and long-term care policies are **valued policies**, meaning that the insurer agrees to pay a stated sum of money irrespective of the actual economic loss. Most property and liability and medical expense policies, in contrast, are contracts of indemnity. Under a contract of **indemnity**, insureds suffering a covered loss are entitled to recover an amount not greater than that which would be necessary to place the insured in the same pre-loss financial position. Under a life insurance and some health insurance contracts, the insurer promises to pay a definitive amount of money that does not purport necessarily to represent a measure of the actual loss. This fact can easily give rise to moral hazard, and insurers carefully consider in the underwriting process the extent of the applicant's likely economic loss in the event of the insured's death, incapacity, or illness.

The contract is **conditional** in that the insurer's obligation to pay a claim depends upon the performance of certain acts, such as payment of premiums and furnishing proof of death. This conditionality is designed to protect the insurer from moral hazard. Further, the life insurance contract is **unilateral** in nature, meaning that only one party, the insurer, gives a legally enforceable promise. The owner of the contract makes no promise to make premium payments, but, if he or she chooses to make them in a timely manner, the insurer is bound to accept them and meet its obligations under the contract. This fact creates some adverse selection in that insureds most in need of insurance will make every effort to pay premiums.

Finally, insurance contracts are classified as **aleatory** meaning that their outcomes are governed by chance and that one of the parties may obtain more than the other. By contrast, most contracts are **commutative,** which means that they carry an approximately equal exchange between the contracting parties. As discussed below, this distinction has important implications.

FORMATION OF INSURANCE CONTRACTS

The agreement between a life insurance company and a person seeking insurance must meet all requirements prescribed in law for the formation of a valid contract:

- The parties to the contract (applicant/policyowner and insurer) must be legally capable of making a contract.
- There must be a definite offer made by one party and an acceptance of the offer by the other party on the same terms (mutual assent).
- Valuable consideration must be exchanged.
- The purpose of the agreement must be lawful.

CAPACITY OF THE PARTIES   **Legal capacity** exists when a party to a contract has the legal ability to make it. An insurer is competent to contract when it is in compliance with all relevant law of the jurisdiction where the contract is made; insurer capacity is rarely an issue. Capacity issues usually involve the age or mental condition of a policyowner or beneficiary. In some jurisdictions, where compliance is incomplete, the contract may be void entirely. In others it may be voidable. A **void** agreement has no legal force or effect, whereas a **voidable** agreement is one that can be made void at the option of the innocent party. In the majority of U.S. jurisdictions, the contract remains binding on both parties in the absence of **repudiation**, which is the express act of voiding a policy.

With few exceptions, the minimum age at which a person can enter into contracts (the **age of majority**) in the U.S. is 18. Contracts made by minors are generally voidable at the option of the minor. The insurance company remains obligated to perform the contract until the minor elects to void or repudiate it. If the minor repudiates the contract the insurer is obligated to return all premiums paid. Some states make age exceptions (1) where the minor is married and/or (2) the contract concerns **necessaries**, which are those things reasonably necessary for the condition in life of a minor, including necessities such as food, clothing, and shelter but also items appropriate for the minor's social position and financial status.

Although life insurance is not a necessary, it has important values to the insured and his or her family. To enable and encourage insurance companies to provide insurance for older minors, without the risk and obvious moral hazard involved in unilateral repudiation, many U.S. jurisdictions have statutes that give minors who are older than a specified age (15 is common) the legal capacity to contract for insurance. These statutes, in some cases, limit a life insurance beneficiary designation to spouses, children, and parents.

A person who is unable to understand the nature of the transaction in which he or she is engaged because of the influence of intoxicating liquor or drugs at the time of application lacks legal capacity. The effect is to make such contracts voidable, and the individual, with some exceptions, may be able to repudiate the contract within a reasonable length of time after he or she recovers sufficiently to understand the consequences of his or her actions.

Contracts made by a person whose mental incompetency precludes an understanding of the nature of the transaction are voidable and are treated in the same manner as are contracts made by minors. If a person has been declared legally incompetent and a guardian has been appointed, all agreements made by the incompetent person (ward) are void. As in the case of minors, an incompetent person may be held liable for the reasonable value of necessaries.

Trade with companies or persons legally defined as an enemy alien hostile to the U.S. is illegal and no valid contract with them can be made by U.S. persons. Prior to 1977, during times of declared war or national emergency, enemy aliens were defined by the *Trading with the Enemy Act* of 1917. In the absence of a declared war, the emergency declaration is now made under the *International Emergency Economic Powers Act of 1977*. At any given time, a number of nations may be the subject of a presidential declaration of a state of emergency that threatens the U.S. national security, foreign policy, or economy.

Contracts already in force between domestic citizens and enemy aliens are either suspended or terminated by declaration of war. Court decisions in regard to life insurance contracts under such conditions are not uniform. A particularly troubling issue for insurers, especially those in Europe, relates to the holocaust during World War II. Box 18-1 briefly explores this issue.

Box 18-1

Life Insurance and the Holocaust

Many Jewish and other citizens insured under life insurance policies during World War II were unable to pay premiums because their possessions were confiscated, and they were interred in concentration camps. Surviving beneficiaries of the thousands that were murdered either did not know of the death or had no means of filing a death claim. From the insurer's viewpoint at the time, such policies lapsed or went under nonforfeiture options that later expired. Could (and should) death claims be denied because of war exclusions, a failure to comply with policy conditions such as premium payment or claim filing conditions, or prohibitions relating to contracting with enemy aliens?

From the point of view of beneficiaries and their heirs, amounts are due them because many policies were in force at the time of death, and circumstances beyond their control prevented the timely filing of death claims. Other policies lapsed because of morally repugnant acts by governments at the time. In many instances, no one having knowledge of the policies survived. Victims of the holocaust and their families note they were neither "at war" nor "enemy aliens."

However, reconstructing records and tracing families of insureds is exceptionally complex. Issues being addressed 65 and more years after the end of World War II are (1) what should be done to make right this troubling and complex matter; (2) what amount of money should be paid; (3) who is entitled to the money; and (4) who should pay it?

Contracts against public policy and those with an illegal purpose are also unenforceable. As was mentioned earlier, a contract with an enemy alien is held to be against public policy and void. Any contract is illegal and void (and the insurer is relieved from paying a claim) when it is negotiated with intent to cause a loss, or when a court determines the contract creates an intolerable incentive to cause loss. These issues relate to murder and insurable interest, as are discussed below.

MUTUAL ASSENT AND THE INCEPTION OF INSURANCE   As with other contracts, an offer and an acceptance must exist before an insurance contract is created. In the insurance context, these concepts receive special interpretations. Most applicants for individually issued life and health insurance do not approach an insurance company seeking insurance. Instead, the applicant is usually first contacted by an producer who solicits an application that is submitted to the insurance company. The existence of the contract depends on the circumstances.

The insurance contracting process is initiated either by payment of the first premium with the application or by submitting the application without payment. The latter situation is deemed to be an invitation to the insurance company to make an offer to insure. The insurer can make the offer by issuing the policy. The applicant can accept the insurer's offer by paying the premium at the time the policy is delivered and, commonly, certifying that the answers to the health, lifestyle, and financial questions as recorded in the application have not changed.

Often, a premium is paid with the application. In most instances, a premium receipt is given. Much less frequently, no receipt is issued: in such cases, most jurisdictions hold that no contract is in force until the policy is issued and delivered. Here the applicant is considered to have made an offer that he or she may withdraw at any time before acceptance by the company.

Three types of premium receipts are found in the U.S. Each provides some form of temporary coverage. The **insurability conditional premium receipt** provides that the insurer is considered to have made an offer conditional upon the proposed insured's insurability and the applicant accepts the conditional offer by payment of the premium. The insurance becomes effective as of the date of the conditional receipt or, if later, the time of the physical examination, provided that the proposed insured is found insurable. The delivery of the policy itself is not essential. Most U.S. insurers use this type of receipt.

Under this arrangement, if the proposed insured died after the application and other essential information was completed, but before the insurer made its underwriting decision, and the proposed insured otherwise would have been insurable according to the company's underwriting standards, the claim would be paid. Insurers routinely pay such claims. The purpose of this type of receipt is to provide protection between the date of the conditional receipt (or physical examination, if later) and the time of policy delivery, but only for those proposed insureds who were insurable at the time of the application or exam.

Most U.S. courts interpret the conditional receipt language as written, in the absence of an ambiguity. A minority of courts has adopted the view that this receipt provides unconditional temporary or interim coverage that continues until the insurer takes affirmative action to terminate it.[1] Many such courts rely on the reasonable expectations doctrine (see below) to establish coverage; i.e., applicants reasonably expect interim coverage for premiums paid.

The **binding premium receipt** provides insurance that is effective from the date the receipt is given. It provides immediate, unconditional coverage. The agent is instructed to issue the receipt only if the applicant's answers to selected health questions are satisfactory. Usually, both the conditional and binding receipts stipulate a maximum amount payable if death occurs during the period of coverage under the receipt. The coverage is provided for a stipulated, fixed time period or until the insurance company renders an underwriting decision on the application, whichever is sooner. A minority of life insurers use binding receipts.

Finally, the **approval conditional premium receipt** provides that insurance will be effective only after the application has been approved by the company. The period of protection – from the date of approval until the date the policy is issued or delivered – is typically minimal. The approval premium receipt has largely been replaced by the insurability conditional premium receipt.

The **effective date** of a policy is the date that the insurer becomes legally obligated to perform under the contract. Ordinarily, for the contract to be put in force (i.e., effective), the policy must be delivered – typically evidenced by a signed delivery or acceptance receipt – and, if no premium was paid with the application, the initial premium paid, while the insured is alive.

Backdating is the practice by which an insurer calculates premiums or COI charges under the policy based on an earlier age for the proposed insured. Premiums charges are thereby lower than they otherwise would be. Backdating beyond six months is sometimes prohibited by law. Although backdating does not alter the effective date of the protection, it does raise two important questions. First, when is the next premium due? Second, from what date do the incontestable and suicide periods run?

A few courts have held that an annual premium provides coverage for a full year. However, the majority of U.S. decisions have held that the **policy date** (i.e., the date appearing on the contract) or other date specified in the contract determines the date on which subsequent premiums are due, even though this means that less than one full year of protection is effective during the first year.

With regard to the suicide and incontestable clauses, the general rule is that the earlier of the effective date or the policy date establishes the point of measurement. Thus, with a backdated policy, the clauses generally run from the policy date. When the policy date is later than the effective date, the clauses are held to run from the effective date. When the clauses themselves specify a certain date, this date usually controls.[*]

CONSIDERATION   The consideration by the applicant for the promises of the company consists of the statements in the application and the payment of the first premium. Premium payments subsequent to the first are not part of the legal consideration but are conditions precedent that must be performed to keep the contract in existence.

The insurer may agree to accept a check, note, cash, money order, electronic funds transfer, or, in the absence of a prohibitive statute, services in payment of the first premium. Although a check is customarily considered cash, payment by check is usually accepted only as a conditional payment. This means that, if a check is not honored by the bank, no payment is considered to have been made, and the insurer's promise is no longer binding, regardless of the policyowner's good faith.

All life and health insurance policies contain a **consideration clause** that summarizes the factors that led the insurer to issue the policy and represents the applicant's consideration for the insurance agreement. It generally is a simple statement that the applicant has completed an application and paid a premium in exchange for the company's promise to provide insurance.

Most companies use the consideration clause to make the application a part of the policy. Unless a copy of the application is attached to the policy, the insurer

---

[*]   Some insurers also include an **issue date** in their contracts, which is the date the policy was issued. The policy date and issue date often are the same. Such policies usually specify from which of these two dates the suicide and contestable periods run.

ordinarily cannot contest the validity of the insurance contract because of any misstatements or misrepresentations made in the application. The following example is typical of the consideration clause:

> *We have issued this policy in consideration of the representations in your application and payment of the first premium. A copy of your application is attached and is a part of this policy.*

LEGAL PURPOSE AND INSURABLE INTEREST   Contracts for an illegal purpose or contrary to public policy are void *ab initio.* They have no legal effect at any time. Thus, a life insurance contract entered into as part of a murder plot is clearly unenforceable. Courts will not enforce such contracts because they are deemed to be void as contrary to public policy. In some cases, insurers may voluntarily pay a claim to avoid the cost of litigation and the risk a court might determine the contract was *not* entered into as part of a murder plot.

Contracts formed legally but becoming payable as a result of a murder are not paid to a beneficiary who is the murderer. These payments are generally prohibited by common law precedent, or *slayer statutes* that prohibit the murderer from acquiring any property interest or benefit resulting from the murder. Payments may be made to innocent contingent beneficiaries, specified relatives, or the victim's estate. Insurers may use a legal procedure known as **interpleader** in the case of murder or possible murder: payment is made to a court that determines the appropriate disposition of the death proceeds.

In many jurisdictions, gambling transactions are illegal and, therefore, unenforceable at law. We know that gambling transactions and life insurance contracts are both aleatory, as opposed to commutative, in character. For example, the sale of property involves an exchange of approximately equal values, and so is commuative in character. We know that under an aleatory agreement, each party recognizes that one of them may obtain more than the other, with each also knowing that the outcome is governed by chance.

The distinction between a contract of insurance and a wager is vitally important. One enters a wager in hopes, through chance, of gaining at the expense of others. One enters an insurance contract to avoid a financial loss and transform uncertainty into certainty.[*] A gambling contract creates a risk while an insurance contract transfers an existing risk. The requirement of an insurable interest in insurance removes the transaction from the gambling category. Statutory definitions of **insurable interest** commonly include something akin to it being a lawful and substantial economic interest in the continued life, health, or bodily safety of the insured person or, for persons closely related by blood or law, a substantial interest engendered by love and affection. Note that a *legal* determination that insurable interest exists is a necessary condition to a valid life insurance contract but is not alone sufficient for the issuance of a policy; as discussed in Chapter 11, life insurers have *economic* insurable value requirements designed to satisfy the company that the insurance is motivated by reasonable financial considerations.

---

[*]   The law of large numbers removes, to a great extent, the speculation on the part of insurance companies. They are not gambling either. Also, when all policyowners are viewed as a group, there is an exchange of approximately equal value between them and the insurer.

Background and Rationales for Insurable Interest   The requirement for the existence of an insurable interest traces its origins to a 1774 law enacted by the British Parliament in response to the widespread practice of speculators taking out insurance policies on the lives of celebrities and other strangers. The law declared that policies procured without a valid insurable interest were null and void. Insurable interest requirements became widely adopted in the early U.S., often not via statute but by judicial enforcement of the public policy against wagering contracts.

Two cases established firmly both the context and scope of insurable interest requirements in the U.S. In *Warnock v. Davis,* the U.S. Supreme Court set out in its 1881 opinion the necessity for and parameters regarding insurable interest when it observed:

> It is not easy to define with precision what will in all cases constitute an insurable interest, so as to take the contract out of the class of wager policies.... But in all cases there must be a reasonable ground, founded upon the relations of the parties to each other, either pecuniary or of blood or affinity, to expect some kind of benefit or advantage from the continuance of the life of the assured. Otherwise the contract is a mere wager, by which the party taking the policy is directly interested in the early death of the assured. Such policies have a tendency to create a desire for the event. They are, therefore, independently of any statute on the subject, condemned as being against public policy.[2]

The Court, in objecting to wagering on human life, placed insurable interest requirements in the wider realm of public policy. The Court insisted on an expectation of "some kind of benefit or advantage from the continuance of the life of the assured." The issuance of a life insurance policy was to be "condemned" if it were for purely commercial purposes independent of such an expectation.

The Court's later opinion in the landmark 1911 case of *Grigsby v. Russell,* authored by Justice Oliver Wendell Holmes, Jr., confirmed the underlying insurable interest standard set out in *Warnock,* while establishing clearly that a life insurance policy should, "so far as reasonable safety permits," be treated as any other property as concerns the transfer of ownership of an otherwise valid policy to someone with no insurable interest in the insured.[3] The Court said: "To deny the right to sell except to persons having such an interest is to diminish appreciably the value of the contract in the owner's hands."

Justice Holmes qualified the ruling by noting that it applied only where "an honest contract is sold in good faith" and that it expressly did not apply to situations in which "a person having an interest lends himself to one without any as a cloak to what is in its inception a wager." Thus, the existence of an apparently valid insurable interest at contract inception is not determinative if a later transfer of beneficial interest was for the purpose of vitiating the initial insurable interest requirement.

Public Policy Rationales   At least two different but mutually reinforcing public policy justifications exist in support of insurable interest requirements. The first justification is that wagering on human life is objectionable to society, independent of any other factor. Thus, contracts entered for the purpose of creating such a wager should not be enforceable, precisely because they are offensive to societal norms. The U.S. Supreme Court, in objecting to wagering on human life, seemed to place the insurable interest concept squarely in the public policy domain.

The second public policy justification for the existence of insurable interest is that its absence can create an incentive to murder. The law requires that the applicant have an interest in preserving life in spite of the insurance, not taking it to gain from the insurance. While the incidences of policies being acquired for this purpose are rare in comparison to the total number of policies issued each year, they are, nonetheless, of sufficiently large number to fill pages of a Google search of "murder and life insurance."

Economic Rationales Independent of the public policy rationales underpinning insurable interest requirements, at least two economic rationales support them. First, the absence of an insurable interest is likely to create a moral hazard. The lack of any economic (or other) interest by a beneficiary in the continued life of an insured has, as the U.S. Supreme Court observed, "a tendency to create a desire for the event."

In noting this tendency, economists would argue that the Supreme Court was embracing the concept of moral hazard. This tendency can manifest itself, not only in murder, but also in failing to do all that one reasonably could to keep the insured alive. Of course, this economic rationale reinforces the public policy rationale against allowing contracts that might increase the likelihood of murder. The difference is that insurance companies have natural economic incentives to try to detect and deter incidences of moral hazard, even in the absence of the public policy rationale, but they are not always successful in doing so.

The second economic rationale for a requirement for an insurable interest is that its absence can create negative externalities. From an economic perspective, murder imposes uncompensated costs on both survivors and society, and contracts that might increase the incidents of murder or hasten death place economic costs on both survivors and society, irrespective of any criminal penalties imposed.

Another potential negative externality for insurers rests in its reputational effects on the life insurance industry as a whole. Without insurable interest standards, life insurance could come to be viewed more as a commercial undertaking than as a means of providing for one's family on death. The *Warnock* Court's admonition that the issuance of a life insurance policy was to be "condemned" if it were for purely commercial purposes seems on point. The economic effect of this possible alteration in public perception could be to dampen the industry's reputation and, thereby, reduce the appeal of life insurance as an instrument for providing family security. This reduced industry reputation and reduced demand for life insurance might spill over to other economic security products offered by life insurance companies such as annuities, pensions, and health insurance.

From an economic viewpoint, individuals who acquire life insurance policies possessing a legitimate insurable interest at inception ordinarily may treat their policies as they treat any other property, subject to the Court's admonitions. If the policies were, however, acquired at inception by a person with an apparently valid insurable interest but with the intent and for the purpose of later transferring them to persons without such an interest, the transaction would suffer from the same adverse economic consequences identified above. It is economically the same as someone with no insurable interest at inception acquiring a policy on a person's life.

Consequences of not having an Insurable Interest   In the absence of a valid insurable interest, life insurance policies are unenforceable at law. Consequently, life insurance policies procured without a valid insurable interest are usually held to be illegal and void. Most U.S. jurisdictions, in fact, incorporate this interpretation into statutory law, and provide that such contracts are void unless the benefits are payable to the individual insured or his personal representative or to a person having, at the time of such contract, an insurable interest in the life of the individual insured. This doctrine evolved out of regard for public welfare rather than for the protection of insurance companies.

Sometimes the question arises as to whether the incontestable clause can preclude an insurable interest challenge. The public policy argument for insurable interest would seem to lead to the conclusion that the clause is irrelevant, as the policy containing it never existed, so neither did the clause. The same public policy logic would seem to lead to the conclusion that no actions taken by the policy owner or the insurer after policy issuance could mend a defective insurable interest such as to resurrect a contract otherwise void *ab initio*.

While many states have no case law on this issue, the majority of states having examined the issue judicially have held that the incontestable clause does not bar insurable interest challenges to contract validity. This position is consistent with the logic that the mere passage of time should not, in itself, be capable of curing what at policy inception was a defective contract because of a lack of an insurable interest. A prominent Delaware case, PHL Variable Insurance Company v. Price Dawe 2006 Insurance Trust, 28 A.3d 1059 (Del.2011) recently affirmed this view. Two states take the opposite view, with New York's position announced in Kramer v. Phoenix Life Ins. Co 15 N.Y.3d 539, 914 N.Y.S.2d 709 (Nov. 17, 2010)

An insurer has both a strong financial motivation and a legal duty to ascertain that an insurable interest exists. Although the insurer may be relieved from paying the death proceeds under a policy issued with no insurable interest, it nonetheless incurs substantial expenses in such an arrangement and runs the great risk of encouraging early death. The latter problem gives rise to additional mortality costs to the company, as not all insurable interest deficiencies are uncovered.

Of greater importance, the insurer becomes exposed in tort for a breach of its duty to use reasonable care to avoid creating an incentive for the beneficiary to murder the insured. Thus, in one well known case, three life insurers issued policies on a child's life, with the child's aunt-in-law as applicant and beneficiary. The jury held that the insurers' failures to ascertain whether an insurable interest existed represented the motive for the aunt-in-law's murder of the child. The $100,000 wrongful death judgment in favor of the child's father against the insurers was substantially greater than the life policies' face amounts.[6]

Insurable Interest in One's Own Life   A fundamental principle in law is that every person possesses an insurable interest to an unlimited extent in his or her own life, and that he or she, in the absence of a statute to the contrary, may make the insurance payable to whomever he or she wishes. An alternative, yet functionally equivalent view is that questions of insurable interest do not arise in such circumstances.

In the context of legality, the pecuniary measure of an applicant's insurable interest is unlimited. When the contract is taken without collusion and without intent to violate any laws, the natural love of life is held to constitute a sufficient insurable interest and to support a policy for any amount. In an economic context, insurers routinely decline otherwise legal applications for amounts that they consider imprudent relative to the insured's financial status.

A few states require that the beneficiary have an insurable interest in the insured/applicant's life or be related to him or her in a stated degree of kinship. Beneficiaries not falling within the designated classes are barred from collecting policy proceeds, with the insurer usually required to pay proceeds to the insured's estate. The rationale for this requirement is that the beneficiary who has no insurable interest may be more interested in the insured's early death. Most states, however, apparently disagree with this logic, noting that the insured/owner is highly unlikely to name such a person as beneficiary.

Insurable Interest in another Person's Life   One person insuring another's life must have an insurable interest in that life. Even in cases where the interest exists, a policy obtained without the knowledge and consent of the insured may be contrary to public policy and void. Insurable interest may arise in four classes of relationships.

Family and Marriage Relationships U.S. courts seem to exhibit some uncertainty as to whether someone has an insurable interest in another's life solely because of being related by blood or marriage. Spouses and persons with close blood relationships seem to support an insurable interest, although most cases do not base the decision on the relationship alone. Rather, they have held that, in view of the relationship, it is proper to presume that a pecuniary benefit or gain would have inured to the survivor had the insured lived.

Some jurisdictions have based insurable interest solely on close relationships, such as between husband and wife, parent and child, grandparent and grandchild, and siblings, but have generally refused to extend it further. As regards other relationships, the courts hold that the interest should be based upon a reasonable expectation of deriving pecuniary benefit from the continuance of the insured's life.

Creditor-Debtor Relationships The rule is clear that creditors have an insurable interest in the lives of their debtors to the extent of the debt and interest thereon. Results are not uniform where the insured amount exceeds the debt and interest. The U.S. Supreme Court in one interpretation of state law placed an indefinite restriction upon the creditor's insurable interest by providing that the relationship between the amount of insurance and the amount of the debt must not be so disproportionate as to make the policy take on the appearance of a wagering contract as distinguished from its legitimate purpose – security for the indebtedness. In *Cammack v. Lewis*, for example, the court declared that a policy of $3,000 taken out by a creditor to secure a debt of $70 to be a mere wager without any legitimate claim to secure a debt.[7]

This decision has made the relationship between the debt amount and the insurance amount an important factor to be considered, but this relationship has never been defined precisely. Various theories have been used by courts to make the insurance proceeds in excess of the debt payable to the debtor's estate or other beneficiary designated by the debtor. Where the law was not explicit and the terms of the transaction not clear, the most popular theory for making such payments is that the creditor is legally construed to be a trustee for the benefit of the debtor's estate.

Business Relationships Non-credit based business relationships can also support an insurable interest. The insurable interest must be based on a substantial pecuniary interest existing between the parties.[8] Thus, an employer may insure the life of an employee and the employee the life of an employer; a partner the life of a copartner and the partnership the life of each partner; and a corporation the life of an officer or director.

Less formal relationships have also been found to support an insurable interest: a corporation holding a property interest contingent upon another person reaching a certain age may protect itself against the loss of that contingent right by the death of that person before the person has attained the prescribed age; those who furnish funds for corporate enterprises may have an insurable interest in the lives of the managers and promoters of the corporations; and certain stockholders have purchased life insurance on the lives of prominent financiers who were instrumental in financing and promoting the corporations whose stock they held. In all cases, the insured's consent to the transaction has been required.

Nonprofit Organizations Most states have amended their insurable interest laws giving nonprofit organizations an explicit insurable interest in the lives of donors. Thus, such organizations may purchase life insurance policies on their lives, with their consent, provided it is the beneficiary under the policy. Some states require that the beneficiary be named irrevocably while others require the charity to be both owner and beneficiary.

The Time and Continuity of Insurable Interest In property insurance, the general rule is that insurable interest must exist at the time of the loss. An insurable interest is not necessary at the time the property insurance contract is made. In life insurance, by contrast, insurable interest generally need exist only at contract inception, unless the policy itself or statute provides otherwise. The fact that insurable interest need exist only at the inception of the contract is a corollary to the view that life insurance policies are not contracts of indemnity but agreements to pay a stated sum on the occurrence of a stated event.

This view is also reflected in the fact that, when an insured is executed for a crime, the proceeds are payable to an appropriate beneficiary. Similarly, if a beneficiary murders the insured, proceeds still must be paid, but, of course, to an innocent beneficiary – assuming as noted above that the policy was not acquired with an intent to commit murder, which in most states would make the contract void *ab initio*.

GOVERNING LAW

Generally speaking, contract validity is governed by the law and usages of the place where the contract is made. This is held to be where the last and essential acts necessary to formation of the contract took place. The laws of several jurisdictions, including those of other countries, may appear to apply, and where provisions conflict the general rule becomes subject to special interpretation.

In a case where an insured was a citizen of Kansas and made application for insurance in Missouri, the state of the insured's domicile was held to have had a more significant relationship to the parties, and, therefore, Kansas law applied.[9]

Similarly, assignments and other matters relating to contract performance are governed by the law of the place of performance, regardless of the place where the original contract was made.

THE APPLICATION AND ITS INTERPRETATION

An **application** for life or health insurance is the applicant's offer to the insurer for insurance and represents the beginning of the contractual relationship. The proposed insured is required to give accurate answers to questions relating principally to his or her personal and family health history, habits, employment, insurance already in force, financial status, and other applications for insurance that either are pending or have been postponed or refused. The policy usually stipulates that insurance is granted in consideration of the application, which is declared to be a part of the policy, and generally contains a clause to the effect that the policy and the application (a copy of which is attached to the policy when it is issued) "constitute the entire contract between the parties." Most laws require that a copy of the application be included as a part of the policy; if not the insurer is *estopped* from denying the correctness or truth of information in the application. **Estoppel** is the principle that prevents one from denying or asserting any position contrary to that established by the individual's own conduct or by previous legal determinations.

Insurers place great reliance on information furnished by the proposed insured in deciding whether to issue the requested policy. The company is entitled to have all relevant information that may influence its decision, especially given the natural information advantage that the buyer has over the seller at time of underwriting and the aleatory nature of the life insurance contract. As a result, the applicant should act in good faith, and, if the information given is false or incomplete, the insurer may be in a position to rescind the contract. We discuss this important topic below through discussions of misrepresentation, concealment, and warranties.

MISREPRESENTATIONS   A **representation** is a statement made to an insurer for the purpose of giving information or inducing it to accept a risk. A **misrepresentation** is the giving of a false statement. Generally, representations are construed liberally in favor of the applicant and need be only substantially correct. The tendency in U.S. court decisions has been to protect the applicant by giving him or her the benefit of the doubt when the misrepresentation is innocent or immaterial. A material false representation can render a policy voidable at the option of the company, even though there was no fraudulent intent on the part of the insured. It has been modified in many jurisdictions, as well as in other countries (such as France and Japan) either by court decision or by statute.

Within most U.S. jurisdictions, as well as in the U.K., the materiality of a concealed or misrepresented fact determines the validity of the contract. A misrepresentation is **material** if it has "a natural tendency to influence, or [is] capable of influencing, the decision of the decision making body to which it was addressed."[10] Thus, if the insurer would have denied the application, charged a higher premium, or issued a more limited policy, the fact concealed or misrepresented is material and can affect the validity of the contract. If the insurer had known the actual facts and would have issued the insurance nonetheless or would have issued it with terms and premiums as favorable, concealment or misrepresentation is immaterial and the policy remains valid. In some countries, such as Australia, and in a few U.S. states, the law provides that the test of materiality is whether a reasonably prudent person would have believed the information to have been material.

Intent is a state of mind, and, in effect, French, Japanese, and some U.S. courts require that the insurer show not only that the representations in the application were false but also that they were fraudulently made. In most jurisdictions that provide that misrepresentations only need be material, a rescission is permitted without regard to intent or even knowledge. Some jurisdictions provide that the policy will not be invalidated unless the misrepresentation is made with intent to deceive; others, that the misrepresentation must have contributed to the loss. The general purpose of such laws is to prevent a forfeiture of the policy unless the company has been deceived to its detriment.

CONCEALMENT   **Concealment** is the withholding of information, and courts have repeatedly relied on the concept of utmost good faith to invalidate policies where it is deemed the withholding of material facts by either party rendered the risk actually insured different from that intended. The validity of the policy, therefore, depends on the full disclosure of all material information.

The doctrine of concealment, which was developed in connection with marine insurance, is primarily for the protection of the insurer and, at one time, was applied to all branches of insurance. As the business developed, most U.S. courts concluded that some relaxation of the rule should be made. With respect to life and health insurance, many courts now follow the finding in the case of *Penn Mutual Life Insurance v. Mechanics' Savings Bank and Trust Company*. In that case the court held that failure to disclose a fact material to the risk in the absence of intent to deceive (fraud) does not void the policy.[11] The concealment doctrine still applies in some states, the U.K., and other countries.

WARRANTIES   The doctrine of **warranty** requires that a warranted statement must be absolutely and literally true. A contract can be rescinded or canceled if the falsehood of the statement can be shown, irrespective of its materiality; a party need prove only that a warranted statement is incorrect.

Because of the hardship and injustice that a technical enforcement of the common-law rule pertaining to warranties sometimes caused, and also because a few insurance companies took undue advantage of warranties in their policies in earlier times, many jurisdictions enacted statutes protecting insureds against technical avoidance of life and health insurance contracts because of breach of warranty. These statutes differ widely, but, in effect, provide that all statements made by the insured shall be deemed representations and not warranties. Effectively, therefore, warranties are of mainly historical interest in North American life and health insurance.

RULES OF CONTRACT CONSTRUCTION   Insurance contracts are to be interpreted to effectuate the meaning of the parties when they entered into the agreement.[12] The contract language should clearly and unambiguously express the intentions of the parties. The rules of insurance contract construction (interpretation) take into account the distinct relationship between the insurer and the policyowner, which differs substantially from most other contractual relationships. The great information asymmetry existing in insurance creates unequal bargaining power between (1) expert agents, underwriters, and claims and service personnel and (2) relatively unsophisticated, inexperienced applicants, policyowners, insureds, and/ or beneficiaries.

Moreover, life and health insurance policies are typically written using standard forms containing much technical language. The insurance contract of adhesion is proposed by the insurer on a take-it-or-leave-it basis with no practical opportunity for the applicant to negotiate modifications, and the policyowner usually sees the contract for the first time only after paying the premium. The special nature of this relationship has led jurisdictions to adopt special rules of insurance contract construction that favor the policyowner. Three common rules of interpretation are presented here.

The **contra proferentum** doctrine emanates from the notion that insurance policies are contracts of adhesion, and, therefore, any ambiguities in contract language are construed strictly in favor of the policyowner/insured. The corollary of this doctrine is that the contract will be construed precisely as written, in the absence of any ambiguity. This rule still applies in some form in the majority of U.S. courts.

The **implied covenant good faith and fair dealing** that requires insurers to make prompt and full settlement with insureds and beneficiaries and to consider the insured's interest in settling claims. It requires that neither party may do anything that could injure the right of the other to receive the benefits of the agreement. Allegations of bad faith are almost always raised by insureds in disputes with their insurer.

The **reasonable expectations doctrine**, viewed by many legal authorities as an extension of the *contra proferentum* doctrine, was set forth succinctly by Professor Robert Keeton in a famous 1970 article:

> The objectively reasonable expectations of applicants and intended beneficiaries regarding the terms of insurance contracts will be honored even though a painstaking study of the policy provisions would have negated those expectations.[13]

The doctrine has been used to grant coverage when the express language of the policy does not grant coverage. A majority of states recognize the doctrine in some form. Variations range from (1) using it only to resolve ambiguities or to fill gaps created by ambiguities (the majority view) to (2) applying the doctrine to justify contract construction at odds with policy provisions even though no ambiguity exists. The doctrine does not deny an insurer the opportunity to make explicit contract qualifications effective, but to do so the insurer must call the qualification to the attention of the applicant at the time of contracting. The insurer will not be allowed to use contract provisions or clauses to limit coverage in ways that are inconsistent with the reasonable expectations of an insured with an ordinary degree of familiarity with the insurance coverage at issue.

One important interpretation of the reasonable expectations doctrine suggests that marketing patterns and general practices of an insurer can shape a policyowner's reasonable expectations.[14] Thus,

> An individual can have reasonable expectations of coverage that arise from some source *other* than the policy language itself, and... such an

extrinsic expectation can be powerful enough to override any policy provision no matter how clear.[15]

Some observers contend that insurers help create policyowners' reasonable expectations. Indeed, the insurance industry works diligently to improve its and its agents' images. Advertisements proclaim the insurer's financial soundness, expertise, and professionalism. Prospective applicants are repeatedly reminded of the reliability and dependability of the insurer. Insurers spend enormous sums of money in agent training to support professionalism. Therefore, it should come as no surprise that the courts have taken the insurers at their advertised word.

When we make a payment, we expect to receive something for value given. To suggest that this is not true strikes a discordant note, especially with U.S. courts. They have used strong language to condemn restrictive language in policies, receipts, and literature given to the applicant as well as aggressive sales promotions to acquire new customers. Thus, in a case dealing with conditional receipts, Judge Learned Hand, said:

> An underwriter might so understand the phrase, when read in its context, but the application was not to be submitted to underwriters: it was to go to persons utterly unacquainted with the niceties of life insurance, who would read it colloquially. It is the understanding of such persons which counts.... To demand that persons wholly unfamiliar with insurance shall spell all this out in the very teeth of the language used is unpardonable.[16]

The reasonable expectations doctrine probably arose because the remedies available to insureds and third parties for breach of contract are limited in comparison to those available with respect to products under tort law, which offers an array of possible damages, including punitive damages in many instances. The distinction between contract and tort law continues to blur, aided by the reasonable expectations doctrine.

PRESUMPTION OF DEATH AND DISAPPEARANCE

Life insurance policies understandably require proof of the insured's death as a condition for paying a claim. Doing so is difficult or impossible in circumstances where the insured has disappeared leaving no trace or hint of his or her whereabouts. A well settled rule in U.S. law – taken from English common law – is that when a person leaves his or her usual place of residence and is neither heard of nor known to be living for a term of seven years, the person is presumed to be dead. Therefore, if (1) an insured disappears for a period of seven years and (2) the absence is unexplained, the insurance company may be required to pay the policy death proceeds. The issue usually revolves around the second of the two conditions.

Thus, the beneficiary usually seeks to establish that the absence is unexplained by proving that the insured was happy and financially solvent with no reason to leave home. In contrast, the insurer might seek to establish that there were good reasons for the insured to leave home such as marital or financial difficulties. The burden typically falls on the insurer to rebut the presumption of death.

The only presumption in most jurisdictions, however, is the fact of death; not the time of death within the seven year period. A minority view is that the insured died on the last day of the seven year period. However, if evidence is presented that the absent person, within the seven years, encountered some specific peril, or, within that period came within the range of some impending or immediate danger that might reasonably be expected to destroy life, the court or jury may infer that life ceased before the expiration of the seven years. In such cases, the insurer must pay the face of the policy plus interest thereon from the date of the presumed death.

If the presumption of death applies, the claim is paid if the policy is in force, if there is a death benefit applicable under a non-forfeiture provision, or if the presumed death must have occurred prior to the lapse of the policy. The time of death may become important if a primary beneficiary dies during the seven year period and there is a contingent beneficiary. In the absence of an agreement between the parties, a court may have to decide on the distribution of policy proceeds.

Although rare, situations arise in which the insurer has paid the death proceeds to the beneficiary on the presumption that the insured died, and the insured reappears. What rights, if any, does the insurer have to recover proceeds in such instances? The general rule is that, if the insurer paid the full death proceeds in good faith, the insurer has the right to recover the amount paid on the basis that it was paid under a mistake of fact. If, however, payment by the insurer was less than the full policy amount, as in a compromise settlement, it cannot be recovered.

EFFECT OF FAILURE TO READ APPLICATION AND POLICY

General contract law imputes to the parties knowledge of the terms and conditions of any contract entered into freely and fairly, in the absence of fraud or mistake, as suggested earlier. This general rule does not seem fully applicable to contracts of adhesion, such as insurance. The information imbalance between the applicant/policyowner and the insurer is significant. As stated by one authority:

> The insured [applicant] buys protection very much as he would any other commodity. Indeed, in business life, he no more thinks of examining the policy delivered to him by an expert manufacturer of such commodities than he does of taking apart the automobile … to discover possible defects in its manufacture. And for the ordinary purchaser it would be easier … to detect defects in … an automobile … than in [an insurance policy]. It is now generally recognized by the public at large, and by some courts as well, that it is only rarely that even careful businessmen [and women] do in fact read insurance policies.… The prevailing business custom is for the insured to rely upon the accuracy, skill, and good faith of the person who acts for the insurer in filling out the application, delivering the policy, and collecting the first premium.[17]

To a great degree, neither applicants nor policyowners read the materials or policies presented to them. The suggestion that they should know their contents is, at one level reasonable but, at another level is perhaps contrary to human nature. This reality has led some courts to declare that the policyowner is entitled to assume that the policy provides protection in accordance with his or her reasonable expectations. Other courts exhibit a more traditional view, imputing knowledge of terms, conditions, and limitations. Thus, the question of the responsibilities of the applicant and, later, the policyowner to read relevant material seems confused at this point, with court rulings on both sides of the issue.

INSURER'S LIABILITY FOR DELAY, IMPROPER REJECTION, OR FAILURE TO ACT
Many courts have held that when an insurer retains an applicant's premium but
has not issued the insurance policy, elementary justice dictates that a contract of
insurance is in existence or else the company is liable for damages resulting from
its delay or failure to insure. The insurer's liability may derive from the contract
because of a receipt or otherwise or it may be in tort for damages generally. A tort
claim succeeds through a finding that the insurer had a duty to accept or reject
the application in a timely fashion and that it acted negligently or unreasonably
in delaying. In most cases of the insured's death, these damages will be the face
amount of the proposed policy.

In addition to negligence, other conduct by the insurer may justify coverage. For example, the failure to return the premium promptly with the rejection
has been held to be unconscionable and thus justifies interim coverage. In other
cases, the courts have not been concerned with the relationship between the
insurance company and its agents. Instead, they have viewed the company and its
agent from the standpoint of the applicant; i.e., they have applied the reasonable
expectations doctrine.

The amount of delay giving rise to liability varies with the circumstances.
Often, either the agent or the company or both may be aware of circumstances
that require an acceptance or rejection within a definite time limit. One example
involved a case wherein an individual made an application for insurance with the
intention of replacing existing insurance. It was clear to the court that the insurer
should have recognized the need for a decision before the existing policy lapsed.
This was particularly true in the court's view in cases in which the individual
insured was no longer insurable.

LIFE INSURANCE AND THE LAW OF AGENCY

We noted in Chapter 1 that one of the four classes of asymmetric information
problems is that of principal-agent. In that discussion, we made clear that our
use of the terms principal and agent was to be taken in their broadest sense; i.e.,
one person acting for another. The principal-agent problem arises because the
interests of the principal and the interests of those whom it engages to act for it do
not always align perfectly; in fact, they rarely align perfectly. This misalignment
occurs because the incentives that motivate the agent usually differ from those
that motivate the principal.

In the discussion here, we take a purely legal view of the principal-agent relationship. The incentive incompatibility mentioned above between the principal
and agent applies to this subset of principal-agent problems. Indeed, in response
to this information problem, an entire body of law has evolved that attempts to
establish clear rules of authority and conduct in connection with this relationship

Legal agency is a central concern to life insurers because the actions of the
insurer's employees and other agents can cause the insurer to be responsible for
contracts they make (normally an expected and desirable result) and the wrongs
they commit (an unexpected and undesirable result). (Civil wrongs are termed
torts and can arise through negligence or intentional actions such as fraud or def-
amation.) Because of the typical life insurer business model, agents and employees
who make sales – which we refer to as *producers* – are most often involved when

agency issues arise. However, life insurers may be responsible for the conduct of agents and employees in non-sales situations as well.

Here we focus on the insurer's responsibility to the applicant/policyowner for the actions of its agents. Principals and agents also have duties and responsibilities as to each other. Thus the unauthorized conduct of an agent that gives rise to an insurer's liability to an applicant/policyowner may at the same time cause the agent to be liable to the insurer.

Overview

Two classes of agents exist in law: (1) general agents and (2) special agents. A **general agent** has powers identical to those of his or her principal within the limit of the particular business or territory in which the agent operates. A **special agent** has more limited powers, extending only to acts necessary to accomplish particular transactions for which he or she is engaged to perform.

Our discussion is complicated by the widespread use of the term *general agent* in the life insurance industry, which is not synonymous with the same term in the context of agency law. A life insurance general agent in the industry sense has limited powers that are not identical with the insurer and so the "general agent" is a special agent under agency law.

Further complications arise from the widespread use of the industry term *agent* to refer to all producers. Some producers are employees and some are independent contractors. Exclusive agents may be employees or may be independent contractors, while independent agents are independent contractors by definition. Life insurers are bound to contracts executed by and liable for the torts committed by employees and other agents *acting within the scope of their actual, apparent, or implied authority.* The **scope of authority** extends to "all actions an agent would reasonable believe to be designated or implied and necessary or incidental to achieving the principal's objectives."[18] Of course, not all acts of an agent fall within the scope of authority.

Whether a life insurer's liability for the conduct of a producer rests on an employment or agency relationship does not in itself affect the nature or extent of the insurer's liability. If either relationship is established, the life insurer is responsible as if it had itself executed a contract or committed a tort, provided the agent was acting within the scope of authority. An employee is essentially an agent by definition.

The attribution of liability to an insurer for the conduct of an independent contractor producer depends on the identity of the producer's principal. If the producer represents the insurer, insurer responsibility follows. If the producer represents the applicant/owner, insurer responsibility does not follow and the applicant/owner may look only to the executed contract for the insurer's responsibility. Responsibility for promises made by or any wrongful conduct of the producer is the producer's alone.

As discussed elsewhere in this text, the term broker in the property and liability insurance industry generally is understood to mean an independent contractor who represents the insured in acquiring insurance. In the life insurance industry, the term may, but does not necessarily, carry this same meaning. Independent of its legal meaning, it also refers to an agent who represents more than one company. A life insurance producer – by whatever descriptive term he or she may be described – is not always the agent of the insurer, especially if the producer is an independent contractor licensed to sell the products of many insurers and has been engaged by the insured to procure insurance on his or her behalf.

While inconsistent industry terminology confuses the discussion, it does not confuse the issue of whether an agency relationship exists. The *Restatement (Third) of Agency* § 1.02 provides "Whether a relationship is characterized as agency in an agreement between parties or in the context of industry or popular usage is not controlling." Thus, usage of the terms *exclusive agent, captive agent, independent agent,* or *broker* in the industry are not in themselves relevant to the determination of the existence of an agency relationship; the determination turns on the facts of each situation.

AUTHORITY AND POWERS OF THE AGENT

Agency law defines the powers of agents in accordance with the type and scope of authority granted by the principal. **Actual authority** exists "when, at the time of taking action that has legal consequences for the principal, the agent reasonably believes, in accordance with the principal's manifestations to the agent, that the principal wishes the agent so to act." *Restatement (Third) of Agency* § 2.01. Actual authority may be express when written, spoken, or communicated by action, or it may be implied. **Apparent authority** is created by "a person's manifestation that another has authority to act with legal consequences for the person who makes the manifestation, when a third party reasonably believes the actor to be authorized and the belief is traceable to the manifestation." *Restatement (Third) of Agency* § 3.03. Apparent authority is based on the principle of estoppel. That is, if the principal clothes another with certain vestiges of authority, such as receipt books, application forms, specimen policies, sales literature, and similar items that lead a person to reasonably believe that an agency relationship exists, the principal will be prohibited from declaring later that no agency existed.

Implied authority extends to acts necessary or incidental to achieving the principal's objectives, as the agent reasonably understands. A combination of implied authority and express and/or apparent authority define the scope of an agent's authority. Although an insurer is not liable for the acts of an agent acting outside the scope of actual, implied or apparent authority, insurers as a practical matter are potentially liable for transactions with any reasonable connection to the sale or servicing of a life insurance policy if *any* legitimate indications of agency exist. This liability can extend to former agents. The termination of actual authority does not by itself end any apparent authority held by an agent. **Lingering implied authority** exists as long as it is reasonable for a third party with whom an agent deals to believe that the agent continues to act with actual authority.

While industry terminology does not affect the determination of the existence of an express agency relationship, as a practical matter it does bear on appearances. Appearances are fundamental to the concepts of *apparent authority* and *scope of authority.* Thus, plaintiffs will find it easier to establish these elements of a claim based on the insurer's vicarious liability in the case of an exclusive producer who is housed in an office maintained by the insurer and sells only that insurer's products. Substantial ties between an exclusive producer and the insurer are also much more easily established than between an independent producer and any individual company since the independent producer usually represents multiple companies all of whose identities are not necessarily disclosed.

Laws require that insurance agents possess certain minimum levels of knowledge about insurance and, in some cases, a certain amount of training before a license will be granted. Agents (and insurers) are further required to observe certain laws and regulations relating to how they conduct themselves in the market. Practices associated with agents' and insurers' sales, counseling, and servicing activities are collectively referred to as **market conduct**. As noted below, insurers and agents in several countries, including the U.S., encountered substantial market conduct difficulties in recent decades.

Besides market conduct rules established by government, insurers have their own rules. Indeed, it is in their own best interest to establish and maintain management policy and practice to ensure that all market conduct is consistent with law and regulation. A failure to do so exposes them to liability. Beyond rules necessary to comply with the law, however, insurers establish rules to define, limit, and clarify agents' authority and to try to create incentives for agent behavior that is compatible with the insurer's goals and objectives. Unless such rules are known to applicants, however, they may not be binding on them. By placing responsibility for the agent's acts solidly with the insurer, the insurer has a strong incentive to ensure that its agents are well trained and comply fully with all legal and other requirements. Much litigation has arisen, beginning during the 1990s, from what may be termed agents' untoward zeal and from insurers' failure to establish and enforce clear rules of market conduct to guide agents.

To guard against this, most insurers try to call attention to the limitations of the agent's authority by the use of larger type size or color in receipts or other documents or literature provided to the applicant. They also include various policy-value disclaimers in policy illustrations. If applicants fail to read these warnings, they may have difficulty claiming that they were misled despite the less strict view of the policyowner's reading responsibility noted above.

In insurance, it is a common and often necessary practice for agents to employ others to assist them in their work. Although no unanimity exists on the subject, the weight of authority seems to suggest that, in the absence of restrictions, the company can be liable not only for the acts of its agents, but also for the acts and knowledge of subagents and employees to whom the agent has delegated authority.

In the course of their daily business, agents are frequently asked to express opinions on the reliability of dividend and other nonguaranteed illustrations and on the meaning of policy provisions. It is important that a clear understanding exist between the company and its producers regarding this expression of opinion. In the field of automobile sales, courts have decided that automobile manufacturers should not be permitted to advertise the virtues of their product and at the same time insist on standing on the terms of a sales contract disclaiming warranties. For the same reason, neither should an insurer be allowed to advertise the expertise of its agency force and then deny these very qualities after the product has been purchased.

The concern is that to ignore the disparity of the bargaining positions brought about by information asymmetries between the average insurance purchaser and the more knowledgeable insurance agent is to invite overreaching on the part of insurers. Accordingly, when an insurance agent renders an opinion that is contrary to the written contract or marketing materials and the proposed policyowner relies on such an opinion, the insurer may be bound. The courts may, in effect, apply the principles of estoppel, at least implicitly if not explicitly.

NOTICE OF LIMITATIONS IN APPLICATIONS AND POLICIES

Insurers are aware of the powers granted to their agents and of the potential for abuse because of the impossibility of eliminating all incentive incompatibility between them and their agents. Accordingly, they take measures to place applicants on notice of the limitations of the powers granted their agents and to minimize market conduct difficulties. Nonetheless, agency related market conduct difficulties can arise despite plain disclosures to policyowners.

As a general practice, life insurance companies insert a provision in their policies or application forms prohibiting their agents from altering the contract in any way. Although the wording of such clauses is not uniform, the following is representative of the usual provision:

> *A change in this policy is valid only if it is approved by an officer of the Company. The Company may require that the policy be sent to it for endorsement to show a change. No agent has the authority to change the policy or to waive any of its terms.*

Despite the apparent reasonableness of these policy provisions, court decisions on the matter are not uniform, with various rules having been formulated.[19] One such rule provides that policy limitations upon any agent's authority operate as notice to the applicant of the limited extent of the agent's powers and thus protect the company.[20] In another group of cases, the courts have adopted a position that is more favorable to the policyowner by holding that such policy restrictions upon an agent's authority are not conclusive as to those matters involved before the contract is completed, but relate only "to the exercise of the agent's authority in matters concerning the policy after its delivery and acceptance, the theory in the main being that no presumption can reasonably attach that the insured [policyowner] was cognizant of such provisions or could anticipate that they would be incorporated into the policy".[21] Still another rule holds, in effect, that restrictions in the policy relate only to acts before a loss has occurred.[22]

Some courts have prohibited companies from rescinding insurance in case of policy violation where (1) the company or any agent clothed with actual or apparent authority has waived, either orally or in writing, any provision of the policy; or (2) where the company, because of some knowledge or acts on its part or on the part of its agent, is estopped from setting up as a defense the violation of the terms of the contract. Courts generally are reluctant to allow parole (oral) evidence to alter the interpretation of a written document. However, whether the courts rely on an oral waiver of policy provisions or upon the doctrine of estoppel, the company is held bound. This holds even where some provision of the contract has been violated and the policy contains a provision limiting the agent's power to make policy changes.

AGENT'S LIABILITY TO PRINCIPAL FOR MISCONDUCT

When an agent exceeds or violates his or her authority, there is personal liability to the principal for any resulting damage. Any loss or damage to the principal must be indemnified by the agent. Examples of agents' misconduct include exceeding specific authority, binding unacceptable risks, failure to transmit information concerning risks, collusion with the applicant, incorrect statements concerning the proposed insured, failure to transmit funds collected on behalf of the principal, and failure to follow explicit instructions issued by the principal. In practice, however, most cases involving serious violation of agency agreements are resolved by the agent's discharge and a revocation of license rather than litigation and damages.

MARKET CONDUCT, PRODUCT SUITABILITY, AND CONSUMER LITIGATION

The conduct of insurers and agents in marketing life and health insurance is subject to statutory and common law standards. They are subject to various disclosure and related requirements and to *Unfair Trade Practices Acts* that prohibit them from engaging in any activities that could mislead consumers. Consumer litigation in these areas has become a major concern of life insurers.

AN OVERVIEW OF CONSUMER LITIGATION

The courts in numerous countries, including the U.S., U.K., Australia, and Japan, have been taking a more aggressive position regarding life insurance market conduct. Within the U.S., allegations of unfair and misleading marketing practices led to an explosion of litigation since 1990. An active plaintiff's bar, aging population, flexible but complex new products, and new distribution systems have all contributed to a litigious operating environment of unprecedented dimension and importance. Consumers allege injury from both sales agent zealotry and flawed product design. Legal theories of liability abound:

- breach of contract,
- negligence,
- bad faith,
- emotional distress,
- fraud,
- defective products,
- consumer protection law violations,
- *Racketeer Influenced Corrupt Organization* (RICO) claims,
- *Employee Retirement Income Security Act* (ERISA) claims, and
- securities law claims.

In addition to private litigation, enforcement action has come from state attorneys general, state insurance regulators, the *Financial Industry Regulation Authority* (FINRA) and the *Securities and Exchange Commission* (SEC). A comprehensive legal analysis of these issues is not possible in this volume, but we introduce one of the most prominent sets of lawsuits – so-called *vanishing premium* cases – to illustrate but one major issue. We follow that discussion with a listing of other, less prominent market conduct and product cases that, nonetheless, could prove important.[23]

"Vanishing" Premiums During the high interest rate environment of the 1980s, life insurance policy sales materials illustrated future premiums and policy values that were predicated on the prevailing high nonguaranteed interest rates being credited on the policies. It was quite common for agents to show applicants that they could pay as few as five to seven annual premiums and their policies would be self-supporting in the sense that internally generated interest (via dividends or excess interest credits) would be more than sufficient to cover all policy charges for the duration of the contract (typically, age 100). Of course, this so-called vanishing premium or vanish pay option did not guarantee that no further premiums would be due because the plan's success lay in the insurer being able and willing to continue to credit high interest rates – rates that sometimes were 12 percent or even higher.

By the early 1990s, many policyowners who expected that their policies would be self-sustaining or even paid up found that premiums were due. Interest rates had fallen to their more modest pre-1980s levels, and policy premiums and values reflected this changed reality. Insurers were inundated with consumer lawsuits complaining that they were misled.[24] Many insurers settled claims for hundreds of millions of dollars,[25] and disputes continue at this writing. The success of consumers and the plaintiff's bar in the vanishing premium cases seems to have encouraged an array of new legal claims, astonishing in its breadth. Here is a sampling of those cases:

Replacement and Churning Related, but not limited to, the vanishing premium situation is the issue of unsuitable replacement of life insurance policies driven by the agent's incentive of a heaped first year commission (see Chapter 10). Replacement is discussed in Chapter 19.[26]

Life Insurance as an Investment or Retirement Product Successful suits have been filed on the claim that consumers were misled about the nature of the product they purchased. Agents and companies were found to have led consumers to believe that they were acquiring a retirement or investment savings product rather than a cash value life insurance policy.[27]

Annuity Suitability for Seniors The typical policy holding period for seniors is shorter than the period for other consumers. Plaintiffs allege that variable annuities are inherently defective for senior policyowners due to surrender charges, surrender charge periods, and tax laws. Several suits have been unsuccessful.[28]

Bonus Annuities Bonus annuities are products that pay an increased interest credit in the first year. Complaints allege that there is no disclosure that the bonus is recovered during the withdrawal penalty period through increased charges and that policyowners would be better served by traditional annuities. Several cases have been dismissed,[29] but a class action suit is pending.[30]

Fixed Annuity Crediting Rates Insurers discriminate between annuity classes by crediting different interest rates based on the policy issue date. Plaintiffs receiving lower rates unsuccessfully maintained the practice was not disclosed and that it was unfair, impermissible discrimination.[31]

Qualified Plans Plaintiffs successfully complained that annuities and life insurance fees are an unsuitable and unnecessary cost when purchased inside a qualified retirement plan because plan assets are not taxable to begin with, making the tax qualification of life insurance and annuities redundant.[32]

Retained Asset Accounts Many insurers either offer to or automatically deliver checkbooks to beneficiaries to draw against a retained account in lieu of cash death benefit payments. (See Chapter 5.) Plaintiffs alleged that the funds do not represent payment according to the terms of the policy and that fund interest spreads earned by the insurer should inure to the benefit of the beneficiaries.[33]

Structured Settlements Life insurers receive lump sum payments from defendants in personal liability law suits, which are disbursed periodically to the plaintiff through settlement assignment companies. A plaintiff's complaint that fees and commissions not credited to benefit payments represent a reduction in the plaintiff's original settlement resulted in a $72.5 million class action cash settlement.[34]

Revenue Sharing Plaintiffs alleged that revenue-sharing agreements between investment managers, custodians, trustees, plan sponsors, and broker/dealers in the context of 401(k) retirement plans and other arrangements administered by life insurers may constitute a breach of fiduciary duty to the plans on the part of the insurer.[35] Litigation continues at this writing. Life insurers who administer these plans routinely receive payments from mutual fund companies that provide investment services to separate accounts.

Universal Life Policy Design Plaintiffs unsuccessfully complained that universal life policies were designed to lapse before the "maturity date" of the policy – at each insured's "life expectancy" – by intentional manipulation of interest credits and expense charges.[36]

Long Term Care Insurance Plaintiffs alleged that products were defectively priced and misleading by failing to fully disclose the extent of premium increases under the guaranteed renewability policy provision. Some cases have failed,[37] but an insurer settled claims in at least one case.[38]

Non-Smoking Child Discrimination Parents of juvenile insureds have unsuccessfully alleged that insurers unfairly discriminate against non-smoking juveniles by failing to classify and insure juveniles as smokers and non-smokers with respective smoker and non-smoker mortality charges.[39]

INDUSTRY AND REGULATORY RESPONSES

The litigation situation represents a significant business risk for life insurers such that the actuarial profession has referred to the litigation as a technical "catastrophe" or "disaster."[40] In many instances, defenses based on statutes of limitations and policy and illustration disclaimers have failed. Many claims have succeeded in spite of clear and unambiguous language that would seem to exculpate insurers. Some claims seem trivial. Yet in other cases, insurer and agent conduct arguably has been excessive. The NAIC and FINRA have responded with closer regulatory attention to market conduct and marketing practices.

The NAIC conducts regular market conduct examinations and began publication of the *Market Conduct Annual Statement* in 2002 to collect and monitor uniform market conduct related data. It has also promulgated the *Suitability in Annuity Transactions Model Regulation*. Its *Market Conduct Examination Standards Working Group* recently developed an updated *Market Regulation Handbook*.

FINRA, in association with the SEC, promotes appropriate marketing practice for variable products through suitability (Rule 2310) and compliance (Rule 2320) standards. Regulatory Notice 07-43 reminds licensed sales professionals to take account of clients' age, life stage, and surrender charge period and amount provisions in considering variable product sales.

These results continually remind insurers of the information problems of its customers and of how courts often will craft their own solutions to this information asymmetry. Liability issues arising from selling policies over the Internet will undoubtedly be another area where information asymmetry will be a concern for insurers. The case law is unclear, but such issues will certainly arise.

CREDITOR RIGHTS IN LIFE INSURANCE

The historical treatment of debtors was often harsh. Governments increasingly found such harsh treatment objectionable, recognizing that it resulted in negative externalities to families and society as a whole. Thus, laws were enacted to provide for an equitable distribution of the assets of debtors, while giving them an opportunity for rehabilitation. These laws came to have particular relevance for life insurance because of its special relationship to family economic security. This section explores the rights of creditors and debtors in life insurance policies. We first examine the rights of the policyowner's creditors, then the rights of the beneficiary's creditors. The focus is on U.S. law. It is important to note that state law provisions vary considerably in this area and a definitive survey of state law is outside the scope of this text.

RIGHTS OF THE POLICYOWNER'S CREDITORS

Insolvency is not the same as bankruptcy. **Insolvency** is the inability to pay one's debts. **Bankruptcy** is the application of bankruptcy laws to a debtor who may or may not be insolvent. An insolvent debtor becomes bankrupt through the application and protection of the bankruptcy laws. Federal law generally applies, although state law may apply in some circumstances where Federal law fails to speak or expressly defers to state law.

THE FEDERAL BANKRUPTCY LAW   Title to a bankrupt person's property vests in a trustee appointed by the bankruptcy court to manage the bankrupt's financial affairs. **Exempt property** is property excluded from the claims of creditors. The debtor has the choice of either state or federal exemptions under the federal *Bankruptcy Reform Act*. The act provides for, among other things, a modest homestead exemption. To avoid discrimination against non-homeowners, the act provides an equivalent exemption of other property if the homestead exemption and certain other exemptions are not used.

Under the law, creditors of the policyowner have no interest in insurance policy proceeds if (1) the beneficiary is other than the policyowner, his or her estate, or his or her legal representatives and (2) the beneficiary is named irrevocably.[41] Thus, if the policy is made payable to the policyowner, his or her estate, or legal representatives, it is subject to the claims of creditors in case of bankruptcy, except where other exemptions apply. If the policyowner names a beneficiary not in the classes listed above, but reserves the unqualified right to change the beneficiary, the policy will pass to the trustee in bankruptcy for distribution to creditors to the extent of its cash surrender value. Except for the application of either federal or state exemption statutes, the courts can be expected to interpret a revocable beneficiary designation as giving the trustee in bankruptcy the power to distribute a policy's cash surrender value among creditors.

The courts have held that the trustee has no interest in policies without cash values. In *Morris v. Dobb, trustee*, a husband took out a policy payable to his legal representatives and subsequently transferred it to his wife four months prior to filing a bankruptcy petition. The policy had no cash value, and the court ruled that the trustee had no interest in the policy.[42]

Cases arise where shortly following the filing of a petition in bankruptcy a policy payable to the insured/policyowner/bankrupt or his or her representatives matures through the death of the insured/policyowner/bankrupt. According to federal law, the trustee in bankruptcy obtains title only to the net cash surrender value of the policy at the time of the filing of the bankruptcy petition. The trustee's interest does not extend to any other policy values, such as life insurance death proceeds. The *Bankruptcy Reform Act* also reserves to the bankrupt an aggregate interest of $12,250 in 2014 (indexed every three years for inflation) in life insurance policies on his or her life. Amounts in excess of this are payable to creditors unless they are exempted by state laws.

The federal bankruptcy law presents policyowners with a dilemma. To protect cash values from creditors, an irrevocable beneficiary designation is generally required. The designation, however, limits the usefulness and flexibility of the policy. The relative importance of the cash value to the policyowner's total assets should be considered, and both the cash value and its importance may change over time. An alternative to the irrevocable beneficiary designation is a change of ownership, which could similarly limit the usefulness of the policy.

STATE EXEMPTION STATUTES   The U.S. Congress has consistently deferred to the states in bankruptcy matters. Some state exemption statutes, optional under the federal act, are more favorable in protecting policy values from the claims of the policyowner's creditors. Almost all states provide protection for a policy's cash values. Previously, many statutes limited protection to the spouse and children, but most states no longer follow this practice.

Amounts due the policyowner from the insurer are protected until the policyowner exercises applicable policy options.[43] Any payments made to the policyowner, such as cash surrender values or dividends that have been deposited to the debtor's account, typically are not exempt. Many states also exempt annuity cash values.

Some of the laws providing exemption are applicable only if the named beneficiary is in a certain class, such as the individual's spouse or children or a dependent relative. Some provide the exemption to any beneficiary who has an insurable interest in the insured's life. Few require an irrevocable beneficiary designation. A few states limit the amount of the annual premiums payable for exempt insurance. Under other statutes, the limitation is based on the total amount of insurance proceeds, although such policy amount limitations are becoming less common.

Many states exempt payments made under disability income insurance policies from the claims of the insured's creditors. Even payments in possession of the insured may be exempt.

RIGHTS OF THE BENEFICIARY'S CREDITORS

Creditors of a revocable beneficiary have no rights to policy values during the insured's life, as the beneficiary has no property rights in the policy. Even with an irrevocably named beneficiary, creditors cannot reach the cash value of the policy, as the beneficiary does not possess the right to obtain the cash value without the consent of the owner.

The rights of a beneficiary in life insurance death proceeds, whether designated revocably or irrevocably, vest absolutely at the insured's death. In the absence of an exempting statute, the beneficiary's creditors are entitled to the insurance proceeds as soon as that right vests in the beneficiary.

Some state laws exempting life insurance proceeds from claims of creditors expressly refer only to creditors of the policyowner. However, most states have broad statutes that exempt insurance proceeds, even in the possession of the beneficiary, against the creditors of both the policyowner and the beneficiary. Several statutes extend this protection to proceeds payable to the insured's estate provided the proceeds inure to the benefit of certain designated relatives or dependents.

Most such statutes limit the exempt insurance to a stated amount, and a few apply the beneficiary's exemption only to group life insurance proceeds. State statutes frequently provide that proceeds payable to beneficiaries under fraternal benefit policies are exempt from claims of creditors.

Many statutes also protect annuity income from the claims of creditors. Some afford this protection only to annuities purchased by someone other than the annuitant, but many apply the protection to annuities owned and purchased by the policyowner. These statutes sometimes limit the amount of exempt annuity income to a stated monthly amount. These rules about creditors' rights do not apply to federal tax liens and situations involving misappropriated funds.

UNPROTECTED POLICIES

There are two important exceptions to the protection of life insurance and annuity policies from the creditors of policyowners and beneficiaries. First, policies acquired with misappropriated funds are clearly not protected. A somewhat more complicated analysis is required when policies are acquired as part of a plan designed to protect assets from creditors.

Under the *Uniform Fraudulent Transfer Act*, adopted in most states, a **fraudulent transfer**, sometimes referred to as a **fraudulent conveyance**, is a payment made with the actual intent to hinder, delay, or defraud a creditor. If life insurance or annuity premiums are determined to have been made with such intent, creditors may access the policy cash values. Even in the absence of intent, a transfer may also be *constructively fraudulent* if the debtor is insolvent, becomes insolvent, or as a business is left with an unreasonably small amount of capital to continue its operations. Transfer of an existing policy with a cash surrender value may also constitute a fraudulent transfer. Transfers of policies that are exempt to begin with; i.e. those that would be exempt if still owned by the debtor, are not recoverable by creditors.

The definition of *creditor* clearly includes present creditors and usually applies to future creditors whose claims were reasonably foreseeable at the time of the transfer but usually not to potential future creditors whose claims arise after the transfer but were not foreseeable. Thus purchases of life insurance and annuities can be used as effective asset protection strategies as against future creditors whose individual claims are not foreseeable at the time premiums are paid.

The Spendthrift Clause

In addition to the broad statutes that exempt life insurance proceeds from creditor claims, most states allow policyowners to include in the policy settlement provisions a clause that provides further protection of the proceeds from claims of the beneficiary's creditors. The somewhat offensively named **spendthrift trust clause** provides that the beneficiary has no power to assign, transfer, or otherwise encumber the installment payments to which he or she is entitled under the settlement option. Installments payable made under a settlement option that contains such a clause are not subject to any legal process, execution, garnishment, or attachment. In most states, the provisions extend only to beneficiaries other than the policyowner. Otherwise, such a device could be used by a policyowner to defraud creditors.

If the mode of settlement is selected by the beneficiary, the payments received may not be secure from the claims of the beneficiary's creditors. The spendthrift clause protects only the money being held by the insurance company. Once money is paid to the beneficiary, it loses its distinction as unpaid life insurance proceeds.

In most states in which no statute exists, the courts have upheld the use of spendthrift clauses. A discretionary trust may be used to accomplish the same thing in the few states where the clauses have been held invalid.

Conclusions

The law of life insurance is in a continuously evolving state. The law derives from general legal principles that take on highly specific interpretations in the context of the life insurance contract and the business practices of its participants. These interpretations are found in statutes, regulations, and legal decisions. The evolution of business practice in the information age seems certain to perpetuate the evolution of applicable legal principles. Litigation grounded in claims of consumer protection is an ever present and significant risk.

Endnotes

1 See, *Metropolitan Life Ins. Co. v. Wood,* 302 F.2d 802 (9th Cir. 1962), and Jill M. Crumpacker, "Temporary Life Insurance Under A Conditional Receipt," 32 Washburn L.J. 104 (1992).
2 104 U.S. 775, 779 (1881).
3 222 U.S. 149, 156 (1911).
4 *New England Mut. Life Ins. Co. v. Caruso,* 135 A.D.2d 129, 130 (N.Y. App. Div. 1988).
5 *PHL Variable Ins. Co. v. Price Dawe 2006 Insurance Trust* and *Lincoln National Life Ins. Co. v. Joseph Schlanger 2006 Insurance Trust,* Delaware Supreme Court, Nos. 174 and 178 (2011).
6 *Liberty National Life Insurance Co. v. Weldon* 267 Ala. 171, 100 So 2d (1957).
7 82 US 643 21 L.Ed. 244 15 Wall. 643.
8 The special case of Corporate Owned Life Insurance (COLI) is discussed in Chapter 23.
9 *Mutual of Omaha Ins. Co. v. Russell* 402 F. 2d 339,344 (10th Cir. 1968).
10 *Kungys v. United States,* 485 U.S. 759, 770 (1988).

11 72 Fed. 413 (C.C.A.), 1986; *Blair v. National Security Insurance Co.*, 126 F.2d 955 (1942). *Haubner v. Aetna Life Ins. Co.*, 256 A.2d 414 (D.C. App. 1969) (insured has affirmative duty to disclose material information).

12 This section draws in part from T. Richard Kennedy and Michael A. Knoerzer, "Freedom of Contract and Choice of Law in Insurance," *AIDA Quarterly Update*, Vol. 1, No. 3 (Summer 1995), pp. 12-16.

13 Robert Keeton, "Insurance Law Rights at Variance with Policy Provisions," 83 *Harvard Law Review* 961, 967 (part 1) and 1281 (part 2) (1970).

14 Stephen J. Ware, "A Critique of the Reasonable Expectations Doctrine," 56 *University of Chicago Law Review* 1461, 1463-75 (Fall 1989).

15 Mark C. Rahdert, "Reasonable Expectations Reconsidered," 18 *Connecticut Law Review* 323, 334 (1986).

16 *Garnet v. John Hancock Mutual Life Insurance Co.*, Conn., 160 F 2nd 599 at 601 (1947), quoted by dissent in *Morgan v. State Farm Life Insurance Co.*, 400 P 2nd 223, 240, One. 113 (1965).

17 Buist M. Anderson, *Anderson on Life Insurance* (Boston, Mass.: Little, Brown and Company, 1991), pp. 255-257, citations omitted.

18 *Restatement (Third) of Agency* § 2.02.

19 George James Couch, *Couch Cyclopedia of Insurance Law*, 2nd ed. (Rochester, N.Y.: Lawyers Cooperative Publishing Co., 1959–1968), 26:82.

20 *Id.*, 26:83.

21 *Id.*, 26:86.

22 *Id.*, 26:88.

23 "Significant Trends In Financial Services Litigation," Phillip E. Stano, Steuart H. Thomsen, Brian C. Spahn, Christopher W. Hammond, and Natanyah Ganz. Presented at Annual Meeting of The Association of Life Insurance Counsel, May 5, 2009 at www.sutherland.com.

24 *In re New England Mutual Life Ins. Co. Sales Practices Litigation*, 183 F.R.D. 33 (D. Mass. 1998); *In re Jackson Nat.l Life Ins. Co. Premium Litigation*, 183 F.R.D. 217 (W.D. Mich. 1998).

25 See, e.g., "Principal Settles Class Action," *Insurance Journal*, Dec. 9, 2000. www.insurancejournal.com, Heather Williams, "Lincoln National settles vanishing premium lawsuits for $28.3 million," *Insure.com*, Jan. 3, 2001, Cybulski, Mark, "New England Life Insurance Co., settles lawsuits for $172 million," *Insure.com*, May 25, 2000, Cybulski, Mark, "Provident Mutual settles lawsuits for $45 million," *Insure.com*, Sept. 8, 2000.

26 *Willoughby v. John Hancock Mut. Life Ins. Co.*, No. 96.00307, slip op. (N.Y. Sup. Ct. . 3, 1997); *Banks v. New York Life Ins. Co.*, 722 So.2d 990 (La. 1998); *Cope v. Metropolitan Life Ins. Co.*, 82 Ohio St. 3d 426; 696 N.E.2d 1001 (1998).

27 See, e.g., *Banks v. New York Life Ins. Co.*, 722 So. 2d 990 (La. 1998); *Duhaime v. ohn Hancock Mut. Life Ins. Co.*, 177 F.R.D. 54 (D.C.Mass. 1997); *Kirkham v. American Liberty Life Ins. Co.*, 717 So. 2d 1226 (La. App. 2d Cir. 1998).

28 See, e.g., *In re Am. Investors Life Ins. Co. Annuity Marketing & Sales Practices Litig.*, MDL No. 05-01712 – MAM (E.D. Pa. filed Oct. 26, 2005).

29 See, e.g., *Sayer v. AmSouth Inv. Servs. Inc.*, No. 05-cv-1423- RDP (N.D. Ala. Oct. 12, 2006); *Delaney v. Am. Express Co.*, No. 3:06-cv-5134, 2007 WL 1420766 (D. N.J. May 11, 2007); *Phillips v. Am. Int'l Group, Inc.*, No. 1:07-cv-00802 (S.D.N.Y. May 30, 2007); and *Cirzoveto v. AIG Insurance Co.*, No.2: 06-cv-02534-BBD-egb (W.D. Tenn., March 30, 2009).

30 See, e.g., *Mooney v. Allianz Life Insurance Co.*, No. 06-cv-00545-ADM-FLN, (D. Minn., Feb. 26, 2009).

31 See, e.g., *Avritt v. Reliastar Life Ins. Co.*, No. 09-2843 (8th Cir. Aug. 12, 2010).

32 See, e.g., *Cooper v. Pacific Life Insurance Co.*, No. 2:03-cv-00131-AAA-JEG (S.D. Ga. filed Aug. 18, 2003).

33 See, e.g., *Mogel v. UNUM Life Ins. Co. of Am.*, 547 F.3d 23 (1st Cir. Nov. 6, 2008).

34 See, e.g., *Spencer v. Hartford Financial Services Group, Inc.*, No.3:05-cv-01681-JCH.

35 See, e.g., *Haddock v. Nationwide Fin. Servs.*, 419 F. Supp. 2d 156, 169-72 (D. Conn. 2006).

36 See, e.g., *Blumenthal v. New York Life Insurance and Annuity Corporation*, Case No. CIV-08-456-F (W.D. Okla.) (Friot, J.).

37 See, e.g., *Alvarez Insurance. Co. of North America. ("INA")*, No. 07-1102, 2008 WL 647784. (3d Cir. Mar. 11, 2008) *Rakes v. Life Investors Insurance Co. of America*, 2008 WL 2518717 No. 06-cv-99- (N.D. Iowa June 20, 2008).

38 See, e.g., *Shaffer v. Continental Casualty Co.* No. 2:06-cv-CV-06-2235-PSG-PJW (C.D. Cal. Filed Apr. 12, 2006).

39 *Alleman v. State Farm Life Insurance Company*, 508 F. Supp. 2d 452 (2007).

40 "Enterprise Risk Management Specialty Guide," Society of Actuaries, August 30, 2005, www.soa.org.

41 *Central National Bank of Washington v. Hume*, 128 U.S. 195 (1888); *Morse v. Commissioner of Internal Revenue*, 100 F.2d 593 (1939).

42 110 Ga. 606, quoted *In Re Buelow*, 98 Fed. 86 (1900); *Burlingham v. Crouse*, 228 U.S. 459 (1913).

43 R.C.W.A. 48.18.410. *In re Elliott*, 446 P.2d 347, 72 Wash.2d 600 (1968).

CHAPTER 19

LIFE INSURANCE POLICY EVALUATION II: PERFORMANCE COMPARISONS

This chapter, the last of Part III on due care in life insurance selection, explores life insurance policy performance comparisons.[1] In doing so, we first explain the regulation, nature, and content of life insurance policy illustrations, which are commonly used in insurance selection. The sections that follow then discuss the means of assessing the sustainability of policy values shown in illustrations and how illustrated policy values are used in competitive situations. The importance and nature of policy reviews are covered next, along with a discussion of options to be undertaken when emerging values depart from those illustrated. We close the chapter with an examination of cost and benefit disclosure requirements.

The prospective life insurance buyer often desires a competitive evaluation of a recommended policy. This evaluation usually involves an illustration of possible future policy values. Illustrations can serve other purposes as well. They show prospective buyers how the various policy elements work together, how different funding and coverage levels might affect future policy values, and how the proposed policy fits into financial plans. By altering the assumptions underlying illustrations, they also can be used to gain insight into a prospective buyers' risk tolerance. Finally, they can be used to provide a baseline for ongoing policy reviews. This section explores illustrations within the context of regulatory requirements, focusing on the use of illustrations in competitive situations.

The majority of policies sold today contain nonguaranteed policy elements, also called current assumptions. Illustrations prepared for such policies, therefore, contain both guaranteed and nonguaranteed values. Illustrations containing nonguaranteed values do not suggest or promise that those values will be realized. These facts remind us that policy selection should not rely solely on illustrated performance. Other factors to be considered include insurer financial strength and agent quality and integrity, underwriting, policy service, insurer historical treatment of in-force policies, and insurer intentions of managing future policy performance, among others.

LIFE INSURANCE POLICY ILLUSTRATIONS

NON-VARIABLE LIFE INSURANCE ILLUSTRATIONS

Because of past market conduct misdeeds (see Chapter 18) related to policy illustrations and their uses, the *National Association of Insurance Commissioners* (NAIC) promulgated the *Life Insurance Policy Illustration Model Regulation* in an effort to ensure that illustrations do not mislead purchasers of life insurance and to make illustrations more understandable. Regulations are now in effect in most states and are followed by most life insurers even in the states that have yet to adopt it. The standards established by the regulation demanded sweeping changes in the way policy illustrations were calculated, prepared, and presented to customers. The regulation applies to all life insurance except variable life, credit life, and life policies of less than $10,000. This section provides an overview of the regulation's requirements. The NAIC issued the Annuity Disclosure Model Regulation in 2010 for similar purposes. As of this writing only one state has adopted it, but widespread adoption is expected.

REQUIREMENTS The regulation does not require the use of policy illustrations in sales, but, if an illustration is used, it and its use must comply with the regulation's standards. The illustration must be clearly labeled as a life insurance illustration and must contain such essential information as the name of the insurer; the name and address of the agent; the name, age, sex, and underwriting class for the proposed insured; the initial death benefit; and the dividend option or other nonguaranteed elements applied.

The regulation's required **basic illustration** must follow a specified format intended to ensure consistency and completeness and is composed of a narrative summary, a numeric summary, and tabular detail. The **narrative summary** contains valuable information about the illustrated policy including descriptions of its benefits and mechanics, available riders and options, and identification and descriptions of column headings and key terms used in the illustrations. It is useful in aiding a prospect in understanding important policy differences that extend beyond the numbers. Narrative summaries typically are several pages in length.

Table 19-1   Example Universal Life Numeric Summary

| | | | Guaranteed 3.00% | | Nonguaranteed | | | |
| | | | | | Intermediate | | Illustrated 5.45% | |
Yr.	Age	Cumulative Premium Outlay	Cash Value	Death Benefit	Cash Value	Death Benefit	Cash Value	Death Benefit
5	55	$106,565	$22,591	$1,000,000	$56,200	$1,000,000	$91,558	$1,000,000
10	60	213,130	35,805	1,000,000	123,139	1,000,000	218,480	1,000,000
15	65	213,130	0	1,000,000	0	1,000,000	324,437	1,000,000
20	70	213,130	-	-	-	-	451,046	1,000,000

The **numeric summary** is a one-page synopsis of illustrated policy values for at least policy years five, 10, and 20 and at age 70, if applicable, based on (1) guarantees alone, (2) current nonguaranteed assumptions, and (3) a midpoint set of assumptions. Both the agent and the customer must sign this summary indicating that they have discussed and understand that nonguaranteed values are subject to change and can be higher or lower than those illustrated. Table 19-1 shows a numeric summary for a universal life (UL) policy issued to a 50-year-old male for which premiums are illustrated as being paid for the first 10 years only. Under this policy illustration, insurance coverage ceases in policy year 20 based on guaranteed elements as well under the intermediate assumption. Although not shown, coverage would remain in force through age 120 based on current assumptions.

The **tabular detail** must include policy values on a guaranteed basis for at least each policy year from one to 10 and for every fifth year thereafter, ending at the policy's terminal age. Nonguaranteed values may be shown if they are described in the contract and must be shown for the same years as are guaranteed values. When advisors and agents speak about life insurance illustrations, most consider the tabular detail – also called **ledger pages** – as primary. The tabular detail is used for policy performance comparisons and to show how insurance fits into a financial plan. It is also used for determining appropriate policy design and for showing downside risk potential via less favorable assumption changes. Insurers are also permitted to provide **supplemental illustrations**, which are intended to augment the data and information contained in the basic illustration. Such illustrations are subject to the same standards as other illustrations.

Finally, insurers are to provide a report annually on policies designated by the insurer as ones for which illustrations are used. This **annual report** – also called an **annual statement** – shows the status of the policy and relevant transactions that have taken place under it during the preceding policy year. Previous and current year values must be shown. The report must disclose if the policy would lapse, based on guaranteed values, during the next reporting period. The policyowner must be notified of any change in pricing elements during the preceding year that negatively affects policy values. The insurer must either provide an updated illustration or notify the policyowner of the availability of such an illustration.

PROHIBITIONS   The regulation prohibits several practices. Insurers and agents may not represent a policy as other than life insurance or describe nonguaranteed elements in a misleading manner, such as suggesting that they are guaranteed. They cannot represent that premium payments will not be required unless factual and are prohibited from using the terms "vanish" and "vanishing premium."

Insurers may not project mortality gains in their illustrations, and they may not illustrate a lapse-supported policy. A **lapse-supported policy** is one in which later policy values rely on gains from policy lapses and surrenders to support those values. No illustrations may show nonguaranteed values more favorably than the lesser of those currently payable by the insurer or those derived from use of the disciplined current scale (see below).

THE ILLUSTRATION ACTUARY   One of the most important requirements of the model regulation is that life insurers must appoint an **illustration actuary** who must make certain annual certifications to the insurance regulator and the insurer's board of directors regarding the insurer's practices and compliance with the regulation. The practical effect of this requirement is to place much of the responsibility for ensuring reasonable illustration practices on the actuarial profession – the logical place. The actuarial profession received its share of criticism for not being more diligent in policing insurers' past illustration practices.

The actuary must certify that illustrations rely on a **disciplined current scale** (DCS), meaning that each set of assumptions implicit in an illustration is based on the insurer's actual recent experience, defined by the *Actuarial Standards Board* as "current, determinable and credible." Additionally, the actuary must disclose:

- Whether nonguaranteed policy elements illustrated for both new and in-force policies are inconsistent with nonguaranteed elements actually being paid.
- Whether, since the last certification, a currently payable scale issued within the previous five years has been reduced for reasons other than changes in the experience factors underlying the DCS.
- Whether nonguaranteed elements illustrated for new policies are inconsistent with those illustrated for similar in-force policies.
- Several other aspects as to the nature and practices followed in illustrations.

The regulation also requires that a "responsible officer" of the insurer, other than the illustration actuary, certify annually to the state insurance regulator that the insurer has complied with the regulation. If the insurer changes its illustration actuary, it must notify the regulator promptly, providing the reasons for the change.

VARIABLE LIFE INSURANCE ILLUSTRATIONS

The NAIC illustration model regulation does not apply to variable life insurance. At the time this book was published, the NAIC was in the process of developing illustration regulations for variable life. However, variable life illustrations are subject to FINRA (*Financial Industry Regulatory Authority*) standards and guidelines. FINRA regulates securities firms and is dedicated to investor protection, as explained in Chapter 17. FINRA's guidelines regarding variable life insurance (VLI) illustrations are as follows:

- Hypothetical illustrations using assumed rates of return may be used to demonstrate the mechanics of a VLI policy and how the performance of the underlying investment accounts could affect policy cash values and death benefits.
- Illustrations may use any combination of assumed investment returns up to a gross rate of 12 percent, provided that one of the returns is a 0 percent gross rate. The purpose of the 0 percent rate of return is to demonstrate how a lack of growth in the underlying investment accounts could affect policy values and to reinforce the hypothetical nature of the illustration (although concern has been expressed that use of a 0 percent rate implies, wrongly, that it is the worst possible situation).
- Illustrations must reflect the maximum (guaranteed) mortality and expense charges of the policy for each assumed rate of return. Current charges also may be illustrated.
- Preceding any illustration must be a prominent explanation that the purpose of the illustration is to show how underlying investment performance could affect policy cash values and death benefits. The explanation must also state that the illustration is hypothetical and is not to be used or interpreted as a projection or prediction of investment results.

Actual policy values are almost certain to differ from illustrated values. Thus, the policyowner faces uncertainty as to the sustainability of policy values. This uncertainty has two dimensions. First, factors wholly external to the insurer will shape future values. Future investment yields will be higher or lower than those prevailing at the time the policy was illustrated. Inflation will be higher or lower, and epidemics and other mortal calamities will occur or not. All will affect insurer operational results likely affecting nonguaranteed policy elements and, therefore, policy values. Management, unable to influence these exogenous factors, seeks to ensure that its risk management program maximizes the chances of successfully managing through them.

Second, factors internal with the insurer will also influence future policy values. The quality of the insurer's underwriting will influence mortality experience. The quality of agent advice and insurer service and the competitiveness of the insurer's policies will influence lapse rates. Expenses and investment returns, while shaped by external factors, also are within the insurer's control to a certain degree.

It is desirable to have some means of assessing the possible effects of these external and internal factors on currently illustrated values. We provide one such approach in this section. Before doing so, it will prove useful to review the experience factors that will influence the direction of future nonguaranteed policy values.

ASSESSING THE SUSTAINABILITY OF ILLUSTRATED POLICY VALUES

FACTORS AFFECTING SUSTAINABILITY

Recall that life insurance pricing focuses mainly on four experience factors:

1. Mortality,
2. Investment results,
3. Expenses and taxes, and
4. Persistency.

Chapter 16 emphasized that one of the ways that actuaries devise policy pricing from these four building blocks is by (1) adding margins to the actual or expected experience as to mortality and expenses and taxes and (2) deducting a spread from realized or expected investment returns. Actual or expected persistency is accommodated indirectly and affects each of the first three building blocks. Figure 19-1 summarizes this process.

Insurer Experience Factors Adjusted to Show Policy Pricing   **Figure 19-1**

Insurer Perspective		Policyholder Perspective
Experience Factor	Adjustment	Individual Pricing Element
Mortality	*+ Mortality Margin*	*= Mortality (COI) Charges*
Investment Returns	*- Investment Spread*	*= Interest Crediting Rate*
Expenses & Taxes	*+ Expense Margin*	*= Loading Charges*
Persistency		***Yields: Gross Premium (or Combined Pricing Elements)***

The first three experience factors are adjusted to account for expected profit, contingencies, persistency, and market competition to yield a policy's pricing elements. These elements are used to derive a policy's gross premium in the case of bundled contracts such as par whole life (WL), or a schedule of cost of insurance (COI) and loading charges and interest crediting rates in the case of unbundled policies such as UL and VUL. Both par WL and UL policies embed a set of guaranteed maximum charges and minimum crediting rates, but each may assess lower charges and credit higher interest rates than those guaranteed in the policy.

Most par WL and UL policies do not assess maximum permitted charges or credit only the minimum required interest rate. The difference between the charges actually assessed and the maximums that could be assessed plus the difference between the interest rate actually credited to the cash value and the minimum that must be credited to it are a policy's nonguaranteed pricing elements or current assumptions. These component differences are evident with UL policies. They are bundled to form dividends with par policies, with the component differences usually not shown.

These current assumptions form that portion of policy illustrations that are subject to change over time and that we wish to understand in more depth to be able to assess the sustainability of an illustration. In accordance with state regulations, these nonguaranteed values are to be based on the insurer's current experience, but there is leeway in terms of how insurers define such experience. (We need not concern ourselves with the sustainability of those illustration values derived exclusively from the guarantees contained in the policy, except for the need to deal with insurers whose chances of not being around to honor those guarantees are high. See Chapter 17.)

After a policy has been issued, its nonguaranteed elements can be expected to change as the insurer's mortality, investment, expense, and persistency experience changes over time. If the time-of-sale policy illustration was based on the insurer's then current experience, future positive or negative experience deviations logically can affect future nonguaranteed policy values. We say "can" advisedly as most policies do not require insurers to enhance policy values because of favorable experience deviations or to penalize policy values because of unfavorable experience deviations. Most policies reserve the decision whether to alter such values solely to the insurer's board of directors. It is for this reason that an initial investigation of insurer intentions can be important.

Therefore, an exploration of the sustainability of the values shown in a policy illustration should focus on the current and possible future trends of each of the three main experience factors that drive a policy's pricing. We note an important caveat: many insurers build in cross subsidization between pricing elements and this fact complicates analysis. For example, many companies cover some of their expenses by embedding within their mortality margins amounts greater than that needed purely for mortality purposes. This fact is a reminder that a policy's entire package of loadings and credits determines insurer profitability and policy performance, not necessarily any one pricing element.

MORTALITY EXPERIENCE   We expect insurers to base their illustrations on their actual, recent mortality experience, with no projections of future potential mortality improvements. Mortality charges are intended to cover policies' proportionate share of death claims. For unbundled policies, these charges are the product of the unit COI rate times the policy net amount at risk (NAR) – the policy death benefit less the account or cash value. The mortality charges for par WL policies are bundled into the guaranteed premiums and nonguaranteed dividends.

Other things being the same, the higher are the premium payments under UL policies, the lower will be the total COI charges under the option A death benefit pattern. This logic follows as account values will be higher with higher premium payments and thereby will generate lower NARs, and vice versa. This same principle applies to any cash value policy whose NARs develop slowly, and vice versa, and to all term policies. Thus, we observe that the nonguaranteed mortality charge component of nonguaranteed values is often more important the higher is a policy's relative NAR, *ceteris paribus*.

An insurer's mortality experience for a particular product line – which affects its COI rates – depends on the target market for that line and on the depth and quality of underwriting associated with the line, among other factors. While all insurers follow common underwriting principles, each company has its own practices, and these practices typically vary by product line. Pricing should reflect actual underwriting practices. Strict underwriting should result in better (i.e., lower) mortality experience and thereby lower mortality charges (and vice versa). However, strict underwriting also entails higher expenses and reduces the volume of business as fewer individuals may qualify for coverage. This dynamic drives insurers' continual quest to find the right balance.

Over the last 50 years, mortality rates have decreased at an annual rate of 1 to 2 percent. More recently, mortality experience continued to improve but at a slower pace. A 2010 *Society of Actuaries'* mortality study of the experience of 39 insurance companies for the period 2003 through 2007 showed an annual mortality improvement rate of approximately 3 percent per year for males and 1 percent for females.

Most mortality experts believe that mortality rates will continue to decline in the future, albeit at slower rates, thanks to continuing advances in the science of aging, better medical technology, and, in general, the application of greater human and financial resources. Other researchers are not so optimistic given more sedentary lifestyles, the rise in obesity and diabetes, and the high cost of health care, among other reasons.

Insurance industry observers generally are optimistic about future improvements in insured mortality experience. They believe that insurers will develop an even better understanding of the risk factors affecting mortality and, in turn, will develop more refined underwriting tools and techniques. These observers also believe that future insurance applicants will be more affluent, on average, than in the past, leading to lower mortality experience. More affluent insureds live longer, on average, than less affluent insureds. Two factors drive this lower mortality: (1) access to better health care and more health care options and (2) greater awareness of risk factors that affect longevity.

How emerging mortality experience affects nonguaranteed mortality charges depends somewhat on product type. For UL, a distinction often is noted between new and in-force policies. History suggests that insurers reduce mortality charges for new policies to ensure that they are competitive. Most insurers, however, have not passed on better mortality experience to in-force policies, instead retaining such mortality gains. Some insurers have a track record and stated intention of passing on such favorable gains to in-force policies. For this reason, an insurer's historical practice and future intent can yield insight into likely future practice. Of course, historical experience and practices and statements of good intentions are no guarantees of future practice.

For par WL, emerging mortality experience, in theory, should be reflected in the dividend, but the bundled nature of traditional WL does not usually permit a determination whether underlying mortality assumptions have been appropriately adjusted. For unbundled products, the COI charges are explicit, so mortality charge changes can be verified. The above observations about mortality apply equally to variable and non-variable life insurance policies. The mortality charge component of both types of policies often contains a nonguaranteed element.

INVESTMENT EARNINGS   As with mortality, we expect insurers to base illustrated values for their non-variable policies on interest rates that are supportable in light of the insurer's actual investment yields. Variable contracts are different in that credited investment earnings are based on asset allocations, including equities, chosen by the policyholder and are not guaranteed. The remainder of this section focuses on the crediting rates for non-variable contracts.

Historically, the interest crediting rate is the nonguaranteed policy element most likely to change, as it is dependent on investment earnings that fluctuate. More than 80 percent of most life insurers' investment portfolios is comprised of investment grade bonds and mortgages. As the 2008-09 financial crises revealed, returns on such investments have been comparatively stable, if declining. Indeed, new money bond yields have been declining since the early 1980s. As a result, insurers' portfolio earnings have been under downward pressure, resulting in declining interest crediting rates. Figure 19-2 shows this relationship for one prominent insurer.

Most interest crediting rates are based on the investment earnings of a seasoned portfolio. Because of the comparatively long maturity dates of most bonds and mortgages, a lag exists between a change in new money rates and the resulting change to portfolio earnings and the interest crediting rate. Of course, some crediting rates are based on new money rates, comparatively new portfolios, or the investment generation method of allocation, resulting in a crediting rate that reacts more quickly to changes in new money rates.

Given that new money fixed income interest rates and resulting portfolio earnings change frequently, it should be anticipated that interest crediting rates will change frequently as well, as Figure 19-2 suggests. If new money rates increase, portfolio earnings should increase eventually, which should lead to an increase in the crediting rate (and vice versa). The extent to which portfolios have allocations to other investments, such as equities, will impact portfolio earnings and crediting rates, although the effect typically is minor owing to their relatively small allocations. We provide analytical tools for assessing interest crediting rates later in this chapter.

EXPENSES AND TAXES   Loading charges are intended to cover insurer expenses, taxes (unless they are shown separately, as with some UL policies), contingencies, and/or profits. Expenses incurred by insurers to issue and administer policies have been falling for some years, thanks to efficiencies. Expense efficiencies are expected to continue.

Expenses usually are predictable and manageable, but changing a schedule of loading charges on in-force UL policies is uncommon. Changing such charges with par WL, including increasing them (see Chapter 4 WL dividend sample), might be more common. The comments regarding mortality and its impact by policy type and policy status (new versus in-force) apply here.

Loading charges typically have a smaller impact on policy performance than either mortality charges or interest crediting rates. Also, expense efficiencies have not been as significant as mortality improvements. If historical trends continue, future expense efficiencies may be included in new policy pricing, but it seems unlikely that in-force UL products will see loading reductions. Even so, as with mortality, some insurers have a track record of reducing loads on in-force policies. In theory, expense efficiencies should be included in deriving current dividends for par WL, but verifying such usually is not possible.

Historical Bond Yields and Sample Crediting Rates   **Figure 19-2**

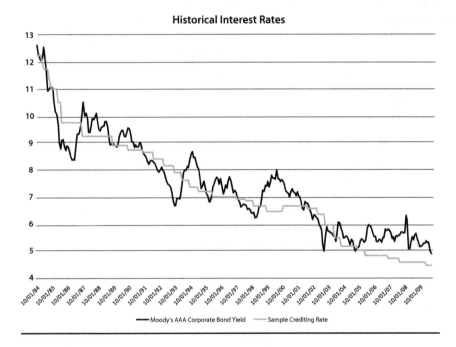

LAPSE EXPERIENCE   Insurers should use lapse rates based on their recent experience. If they use lower lapse rates, the effect can be that actual policy values will not grow as fast, even if all other pricing factors were as originally illustrated. This is because the insurer is likely to adjust charges or the crediting rate to make good any cash flow deficit caused by use of the lower lapse rate.

At the other extreme, some lapse-supported pricing has been observed, although illustration regulations should significantly limit its practice. If actual policy results would be negatively affected by persistency being *better* than that assumed in the illustration, the policy may be lapse supported. This imposes an additional risk on the customer and makes the policy illustration less comparable with others.

AN ILLUSTRATIVE ASSESSMENT PROCESS

Due to the complexity of life insurance pricing, assessing whether illustrated policy values are sustainable is correspondingly complex. In addition to the basic pricing elements discussed earlier, insurance pricing typically deploys other tools to finance and manage the insurance risks, including various reserve methodologies, reserve financing, reinsurance, and production quotas. Further, an assessment of the reasonableness of individual pricing elements can be difficult due to cross subsidization among policy elements, so comparisons of specific elements may not be as revealing as one might hope.

Thus, as adjusting mortality and loading charges on in-force policies is uncommon and adjusting interest crediting rates is common, a focus on the interest crediting rate is more likely to be informative about policy value sustainability. Following is an overview of a suggested process for assessing the sustainability of illustrated policy values based on current assumptions.[2]

Figure 19-3   **Historical Five-Year Rolling Average of Moody's Bond Yields and Sample Crediting Rates**

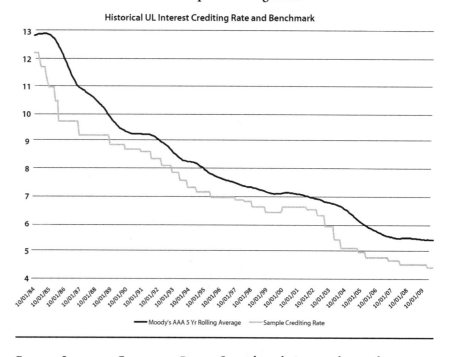

REVIEW INTEREST CREDITING RATE   Several analytics can be used to assess interest crediting rates. One approach relies on use of interest rate benchmarks. As invested assets backing life insurance products are typically investment grade bonds and mortgages, crediting rate movements have tended to track corporate bond benchmarks. UL portfolios, for example, have closely tracked movements in the five-year rolling average of Moody's AAA Corporate Bond Yield. See Figure

19-3. The five-year rolling average represents a portfolio of seasoned investments maturing and rolling over with the purchase of new investments.

Likewise, the seven-year rolling average of Moody's AAA Corporate Bond Yield has served as a good benchmark for WL dividend interest rates. The longer rolling average represents the longer duration of investments that historically back WL portfolios, which is likely due to better policyholder persistency. A complication that is said to exist with crediting rates used within some insurers' dividend calculations is that they may incorporate some positive mortality and/or expense experience to support the rate. For example, if investment earnings have declined, an insurer may offset the decline with better mortality experience, resulting in smaller reduction to the interest crediting rate. The motivation for doing this would be tied to disclosure of the dividend crediting rate in marketing. If no rate is disclosed, there is no motivation to subsidize the rate in this way.

Crediting Rate Comparison   Our first interest crediting rate analytic is to compare crediting rates to the Moody's benchmark. Table 19-2 offers an example. The crediting rates for Policies B-D are lower than the benchmark, while the Policy A crediting rate exceeds the benchmark and is 90 basis points (bps) higher than the next highest crediting rate. The Policy A rate appears suspect and would call for an investigation as to how the insurer can offer such a rate and whether a rate reduction might be in the offing. If so, realized policy values will be lower than those illustrated. Whether the insurer uses a portfolio average or an investment generation crediting approach can affect the rate of change in crediting rates, with the former changing more slowly.

Current Crediting Rate Comparison   Table 19-2

Moody's Benchmark	Policy A	Policy B	Policy C	Policy D
5.50%	6.25%	5.05%	5.35%	5.25%

Crediting Rate Change Indication   An analytic useful for indicating the likely direction of near-term investment returns (and so crediting rates) involves a comparison of current new money rates to the rolling average rates. If the current new money rate is less than the rolling average, there is likely downward pressure on portfolio earnings and therefore on interest crediting rates. Conversely, if the current new money rate is greater than the rolling average, there is likely upward pressure on portfolio earnings and so on crediting rates. Table 19-3 compares new money rates versus the seven year rolling average as of June 2010. It shows that there was some pressure for a reduction in crediting rates post-June 2010, as the new money rate was 60 bps less than the rolling average. Stress testing, as described later, might be useful in such cases.

Dividend Interest Rate Change Indication   Table 19-3

(A) Moody's New Money AAA Corporate Bond Yield	4.88%
(B) Moody's 7 Year Rolling Average	5.48%
Future Dividend Rate Change Indication: (A)-(B)	-0.60% (-60 bps)

Also, an examination of insurer reactions to past changes in benchmarks can give hints at how the insurer might react in the face of future changes. For example, if a benchmark has risen in the not-too-distant past and the insurer did not or was slow to change the crediting rate, the reason for this action might be informative as to future insurer actions.

REVIEW ILLUSTRATED PERFORMANCE   Another approach to assessing the sustainability of illustrated policy values is to perform an illustration performance comparison. One or more of the performance measures presented later in this chapter are used to evaluate the competitiveness of products being considered or solely to juxtapose the policy being considered against others. The idea here is to obtain a sense of the relative performance of the policy. Illustrated performance that is "too good to be true" often begs for further inquiry as to how the insurer is able to support such an illustration.

Consider the policies in Table 19-4. The premiums for Policies A, B, C, and D are determined using what the industry refers to as premium solve. **Premium solve** refers to the practice of setting a death benefit amount, pattern, and duration and, if applicable, attainment of a target cash value by a specified policy year then *solving* for the premium necessary to support that package of benefits typically based on illustrated nonguaranteed values. This example employs a 10-pay premium solve, which *does not mean that the policies are paid up in 10 years, only that, if current or superior nonguaranteed assumptions continued, no further premiums need be paid to sustain the policies.*

Table 19-4   **Illustration Performance Review**

	10-Pay Premium Solve (Current Assumptions)			
	Policy A	Policy B	Policy C	Policy D
Annual Premium	$20,000	$22,000	$22,150	$23,000
Difference from Policy A		10.0%	10.8%	15.0%
Surrender Charge Duration	20 years	10 years	10 years	None

Note that the latter three policies carry premiums that are at least 10 percent greater than that of Policy A. Is the Policy A insurer operating so much more efficiently than the insurers for the other policies? Do the policies differ in some meaningful way? Is there a serious question whether the Policy A illustration values are sustainable? Each question requires greater exploration. In reviewing illustrated performance, the entire package of outflows and inflows should be considered. For example, consider the policies' surrender charges shown in Table 19-4. It is not uncommon for policies with low premiums also to carry higher surrender charges. Policy A has surrender charges for 20 years, while the other policies have them for 10 years or less. From a pricing standpoint, a policy's very low premiums may be subsidized by surrender charges. In other words, illustrated values may indeed be sustainable if current experience continues but at a tradeoff of lower premiums for lower surrender values.

Other Illustration Assessment Considerations   Advisors recommend that all illustrations be stress tested. A stress test involves running illustrations with reduced crediting rates and/or at less favorable charges to provide an idea of potential downside policy performance. It is useful for managing policyholder expectations. One should be wary of a highly competitive policy illustration based on current assumptions that experiences meaningful performance deterioration under slightly less favorable assumptions.

The track record, reputation, and intentions of an insurer often provide the greatest comfort regarding illustrated policy value sustainability. Seasoned advisors and producers who service in-force policies should have an understanding of which insurers treat their policyholders well. Some insurers have a questionable reputation regarding in-force policy performance and service, while others have quite positive reputations.

In addition, it can be insightful to secure a sense of an insurer's intentions in managing future policy performance. If emerging experience were similar to recent experience, would the insurer maintain current assumptions or would unfavorable adjustments be needed because of earlier aggressive insurer pricing? Even though illustration regulations limit the use of experience improvements, insurers still may deploy pricing practices that provide some level of experience improvements while complying with the regulations.

The above types of analyses inevitably lead to questions about insurer pricing practices. A book published by the *American Bar Association* for use by attorneys in offering insurance advice suggests that answers to the questions shown in Box 19-1 on the next page by relevant insurers can be insightful.[3]

Using Illustrated Policy Values for Policy Performance Comparisons

An important and common use of policy illustrations is in comparing the costs and benefits of competing policies. While important limitations accompany such comparisons, they have value. In setting out below various means of making competitive comparisons, we note that the buyer should not necessarily seek that mirage called the "best buy." Rather, he or she should seek a policy that seems to offer good value in relation to other policies available from sound life insurance companies.

The Need for Comparisons

Life insurance policy costs can vary greatly. Variations result from differences in the competitiveness within different market segments and in company operational efficiency, investment performance, underwriting policy, profit objectives, marketing costs, and a host of other variables. A seemingly higher cost policy may reflect either superior benefits or simply poor value.

Although insurance awareness is rising, so is product complexity. Earlier chapters highlighted how information asymmetries between buyers and insurers continue to influence the evolution of the market and of its regulation. Consumers often erroneously equate a policy's cost with its premium. The premium is a measure of the annual outlay for a policy, not its cost. Cost includes all elements of a policy (premiums, death benefits, cash values, and dividends), not just premiums. The true cost of life insurance to any individual can be determined only *ex post*; i.e., only after the contract terminates by death, maturity, or surrender.

Its cost is dependent on each individual's unique circumstances and the actual cash flows experienced under the policy. However, it is virtually impossible to estimate a policy's competitiveness *ex ante* – before policy termination – without relying on current illustrated values and comparing them with competing policies, particularly for policies containing nonguaranteed policy elements – and the great majority of cash value policies fall into this class, as do many term policies. Illustrated policy performance can vary greatly depending on the insured's characteristics (gender, age, and risk classification), premium funding (amounts and duration), and policy type. The only way to determine if a policy illustrates competitively is to conduct a comparison.

Box 19-1:
***American Bar Association* Life Insurance Policy Questionnaire**

General Pricing

- What superior pricing factors drive this policy's competitive illustrated performance? (Sample answer: Policy is targeted and priced for the high net worth market that has exhibited superior mortality experience.)

Investment Earnings

- Is the current crediting or dividend interest rate sustainable if future new money bond yields remain at today's level? If not, please comment.

Mortality

- Will the current dividend scale or schedule of mortality charges need to be adjusted if emerging mortality experience remains consistent with current mortality experience? If yes, explain why.
- Do the underlying mortality charges for the current dividend scale or schedule of mortality charges cover the mortality pricing assumption in all durations? If not, how does the insurer cover the negative mortality margins?
- Has the insurer increased mortality charges or the mortality charge component of the current dividend scale on any in-force life insurance policy in the last 10 years? If so, provide examples and reasoning.
- Has the insurer decreased mortality charges or the mortality charge component of the current dividend scale on any in-force life insurance policy in the last 10 years? If so, provide examples and reasoning.
- If emerging mortality experience is better than the pricing mortality, will the insurer pass on the better experience to in-force policyholders through a reduction in the schedule of mortality charges or increases in the mortality component of the dividend scale?

Expenses

- Do current policy charges or the policy charge component of the current dividend scale fully cover the insurer's actual expenses for issuing and administering this product? Explain.
- Has the insurer increased any policy loadings or policy charge component of the current dividend scale on any in-force life insurance policy in the last 10 years? If so, provide examples and reasoning.
- Has the insurer decreased any policy loadings or policy charge component of the current dividend scale on any in-force life insurance policy in the last 10 years? If so, provide examples and reasoning.
- If emerging expense experience is better than the pricing expenses, will the insurer pass on the better experience to in-force policies through reduced policy loads or increases in the expense component of the dividend scale?

FACTORS TO CONSIDER IN PERFORMANCE COMPARISONS

Policy comparisons should be based on as many identical characteristics of the policies and the proposed insured and scenarios as feasible. In an ideal world, one would compare only policies of the same or similar type (e.g., whole life); death benefit amount, duration, and pattern; premium amount and duration; and target cash value (if applicable). The real world seldom presents itself in these ideal terms. When searching for policies that seem to offer good value, WL policies often must be compared to UL policies and both are sometimes compared to term policies. Further, policy mechanics relative to death benefits, premiums, cash values, and dividends inevitably differ among insurers.

All illustrations should be run assuming the same insured characteristics. Thus, the same sex, age, and smoking and health status should be assumed for each, although doing so sometimes can be challenging as insurers may use different definitions of terms such as age, smoker status, and preferred risk. If a policy has riders or special benefits, the same or similar riders should be illustrated for all policies, if possible.

Variable life insurance and equity-indexed UL do not have an interest crediting rate as such. Policy illustrations for variable life are prepared using hypothetical earning rates and current mortality and loading charges. The earned rate can be specified as either a gross rate or a net rate. A net rate is the gross rate net of investment management fees and expenses. The net rate for some companies is also reduced for the mortality and expense (M&E) charge. All variable comparisons should be prepared at the same net and gross rate assuming similar asset allocations and the same treatment of M&E charges. Similarly, equity-indexed UL comparisons should be based on similar assumptions about the index performance.

MEASURES OF ILLUSTRATED POLICY PERFORMANCE

All methods of comparing illustrated policy costs rely on holding some elements constant across policies and solving for the value of the policy element(s) not held constant or for a proxy for some measure of policy cost. The value being sought is the dependent variable or value, as its amount is derived from or depends upon other selected values.

Often, no single performance measure provides a definitive answer as to which policy seems to offer the best value. For this reason, common practice is to examine several measures with the purpose for which the insurance is being purchased dictating which measures seem most relevant. Below we examine three categories of the most commonly observed performance measures: (1) value solve, (2) internal rate of return, and (3) interest adjusted net cost. We separately explore briefly four other, less commonly used measures.

VALUE SOLVE MEASURES **Value solve measures** is the term for a category of three performance measures commonly used within the life insurance industry that involve the production of policy illustrations that solve for a dependent policy element by setting the other major policy elements equal to each other. The three measures are premium solve, death benefit solve, and cash value solve. While these measures reveal similar if not identical performance rankings among policies, their utility varies with the purpose for which a policy is being considered. For simplicity in the discussion and examples below, we assume nonpar policies or par policies whose dividends are applied to augment cash values or accumulate at interest. The use of other dividend options would necessitate adjustments in relevant policy elements of the illustrations of competing policies.

Premium Solve   As noted earlier, premium solve involves setting a death benefit amount, pattern, and duration and, if applicable, attainment of a target cash value by a specified policy year then *solving* for the premium necessary to support that package of benefits. It may be the most widely used illustrated performance measure. It can be used with flexible-premium and fixed-premium policies in most instances. This measure is commonly used when a client is especially interested in the amount of the annual cash outlay.

To solve for the premium, the number of annual payments must be specified. Premiums typically are level. Common premium payment periods are one year ("single-pay"), 10 years ("10-pay"), to age 65, and to age 95 or 100 (older cash value policies) or 121 (newer policies), with the latter two payment durations referred to as "level pay," "full pay," or "life pay." Common cash value targets are to have the cash value equal the death benefit (CV=DB) or $1.00 at ages 95, 100 or 121. Table 19-5 provides an example. We assume an age 55 male, best nonsmoker class, level $1.0 million death benefit, 10-pay, and CV=DB at age 121. Policy A provides the lowest premium solve for the specified death benefit and cash value target, with the other three products requiring premiums that are 1.0 percent, 5.0 percent, and 10.0 percent higher.

Table 19-5   **Premium Solve Example**

Policy	Premium Solve (Annual)	Difference from A
A	$20,000	
B	20,200	1.0%
C	21,000	5.0%
D	22,000	10.0%

Death Benefit Solve   Typically the amount of coverage has been determined and known. Sometimes funds to pay premiums are limited, so the individual is interested in purchasing as much insurance as those funds will buy. Solving for the amount of death benefit that a specified funding level and pattern will purchase is called **death benefit solve**. Table 19-6 shows results for the same parameters as used in Table 19-5 but assuming a cash value target of $1.00 at age 121 and a premium of $20,000 (and removing policy D from consideration). Policy A provides the highest death benefit, with the other policies solving for a death benefit that is 5.0 to 10.0 percent lower than that of Policy A.

Table 19-6   **Death Benefit Solve**

Policy	Death Benefit Solve	Difference from A
A	$1,000,000	
B	950,000	-5.0%
C	900,000	-10.0%

Surrender Value Solve   The last value solve measure uses the surrender value as the dependent policy value. **Surrender value solve** sets the death benefits and premiums equal and solves for the cash surrender values. This measure is commonly used for sales wherein accumulating high cash values is important.

INTERNAL RATE OF RETURN MEASURES   Two internal rate of return (IRR) measures solve for a rate of return that causes accumulated scheduled premiums (net of dividends, if appropriate) at selected policy durations to equal the death benefit and cash surrender value at that duration. The two measures are commonly referred to as death benefit (DB) IRR and surrender value (SV) IRR.

Death Benefit Internal Rate of Return   DB IRR is perhaps the most common death benefit performance measure. **Death benefit internal rate of return** is derived by solving for the interest rate that causes accumulated premiums (net of dividends, if appropriate) at selected policy durations to equal that duration's death benefit. No allowance is made in the measure for the portion of premiums that builds cash values, so the IRR is understated. In the early years, a cash value policy's DB IRR is quite high, but declines steadily with time. The DB IRR can be interpreted as the yield that the beneficiary would have realized if the insured died at the set duration, assuming no changes in the policy or its elements. It is an intuitive measure, as DB IRRs can be compared to the returns of other financial instruments such as stocks and bonds.

Ideally, in comparing returns on other financial instruments with DB IRRs, both are on a tax equivalent basis. Life insurance death proceeds ordinarily are income tax free and premiums are not tax deductible, so the returns on other instruments should be evaluated on the same after tax basis. Table 19-7 provides an example of DB IRRs, with the same assumptions as the Table 19-6 example.

Death Benefit Internal Rate of Return Example   Table 19-7

Policy Year	Age	Policy A Premium=$20,000	Policy B Premium=$20,200	Policy C Premium=$21,000
10	65	28.21%	28.04%	27.36%
20	75	10.64%	10.58%	10.31%
30	85	6.45%	6.41%	6.25%
45	100	4.04%	4.01%	3.91%
66	121	2.69%	2.67%	2.61%

For this example, the policy with the lowest premium (Policy A) naturally produces the highest DB IRR in all policy years as the death benefit for all policies is an identical level $1.0 million, and Policy A has the lowest premium. From this logic, a ranking of policies using premium solve is the same as a ranking using DB IRR. IRRs tend to decrease over time, reflecting a longer period until payment of the death benefit and more premium payments.

A stronger focus or weighting often is placed on the DB IRR at life expectancy (around age 85 for this example). For this example, the 1.0 percent higher annual premium for Policy B translates into a reduction of only 4 basis points (bps) in the IRR by age 85, whereas the Policy C IRR at that time is 20 bps lower. Small differences in performance measurements usually are interpreted cautiously, if not ignored completely, given the number of years involved and the nonguaranteed nature of illustrated policy values.

Surrender Value Internal Rate of Return   The companion **surrender value internal rate of return** solves for the interest rate that causes accumulated premiums (net of dividends, if appropriate) at selected policy durations to equal that duration's cash surrender value. No allowance is made in the calculation for the value of the death benefit promise, so its value is understated to that extent. Table 19-8 provides an example of SV IRR calculations for the same policies and assumptions as in Table 19-6.

Table 19-8			**Surrender Value Internal Rate of Return Example**		

Policy Year	Age	Policy A Premium=$20,000	Policy B Premium=$20,200	Policy C Premium=$21,000
1	55	-100.00%	-60.00%	-22.00%
10	65	1.05%	0.43%	0.49%
20	75	2.32%	2.61%	2.65%
30	85	2.29%	2.87%	2.68%
45	100	2.10%	2.23%	1.59%
66	121	2.69%	2.67%	2.61%

Some observations are in order. First, note that the policy illustrated as performing the best at each year, indicated by shading, varies over time. Policy A, the lowest premium policy, which performed best with the DB IRR, lags by the SV IRR measure. This is unsurprising as its lower premiums results in lower cash surrender values. Second, SV IRRs are typically negative in the early policy years due to high front end policy loads, including surrender charges, and then become positive as the account (cash) value grows. Third, had we run SV IRRs for a term policy, it would have been -100 percent for all years, as a term policy typically has no cash values, but its DB IRR would have been the highest at every duration.

Fourth, note that the IRRs for these sample policies are comparatively low. They are depressed because the COI charges are levied over the entire policy durations, and the insured is not young, so COI rates are high. These policies are not pure savings instruments. This fact reveals an *economic* shortcoming of the two IRR measures. An insured who surrenders his policy at age 75 has an apparent IRR of 2.32 percent for Policy A, assuming the original nonguaranteed values were realized precisely. In fact, he would have had death protection for these 20 years, and this protection has economic value. Its economic value can be viewed as the sum of all mortality charges over the period. Were we to reduce each year's premium by those charges and run our calculation anew, the IRRs would be uniformly higher. The same principle applies to the DB IRR in which a portion of each year's premium is applied to build cash values.

The SV IRR will be less than the interest crediting rate (or earning rate for variable life) due to policy loads and COI charges. The difference between the crediting rate or earning rate and the SV IRR provides an idea of the amount of charges levied under the product, expressed as an annual asset based charge. For example, if the crediting rate is 5.0 percent and the SV IRR is 2.6 percent, the illustrated charges could be expressed as 240 bps of annual asset charges.

These IRR measures have shortcomings. First, the two measures are jointly relevant for cash value policies only. SV IRRs for term policies are uninformative as such policies are not purchased for their internal savings feature and typically have no cash values. Second, DB IRR has been criticized as being no more logical than making the same calculation for any other insurance product; who uses IRR to evaluate a fire insurance policy assuming fire occurs at various times? Third, as noted above, each IRR measure fails to take the value of an important policy element into account, so understates a policy's true *economic* IRR. Finally, the IRR terminology is considered by some to be misleading as it is not a "rate of return" as that term is understood and used in the context of savings and investments. Yet, except for the final shortcoming, the same types of criticisms apply to the two interest adjusted cost measures mandated by state regulators (discussed next), which are also intended as measures of policy value on death and on surrender.

INTEREST ADJUSTED NET COST MEASURES The NAIC *Life Insurance Disclosure Model Regulation* (see below) mandates the disclosure to prospective buyers of two sets of interest adjusted net cost (IANC) indices, which are intended to assist buyers in selecting a comparatively low-cost policy. Most advisors do not use these indices, and it is not known whether their mandated disclosure has meaningfully assisted buyers generally. Even so, as they routinely appear on illustrations, they should be understood.

The two required sets of indices are the net payment cost indices and the surrender cost indices. **Net payment cost indices** (NPCIs) are intended to inform the prospective buyer of the estimated average annual net payment or outlay per $1,000 of insurance over selected time periods (ordinarily 10 and 20 years), taking into consideration only the policy's premiums and illustrated (nonguaranteed) dividends, if any, while adjusting them for the time value of money. They are death benefit measures of illustrated policy performance. They answer the question: "what would have been the average annual net *payment* per $1,000 of death benefit under this policy if money is valued at the discount rate used, premiums were paid as planned, dividends (if any) were paid as illustrated, and the insured died at the end of selected time period?"

Surrender cost indices (SCIs) are intended to inform the prospective buyer of the estimated average annual net cost per $1,000 of insurance over selective time periods (same as NPCIs) taking into consideration the policy's premiums, illustrated dividends or other nonguaranteed policy values (if any), and surrender values while adjusting these values for the time value of money. They are surrender-based measures of illustrated policy performance. The SCI calculations are identical to the NPCI calculation except that they include credit for the surrender value at the specified year. They answer the question: "what would have been the average annual net *cost* per $1,000 of death benefit under the policy if money is valued at the discount ratio used, premiums were paid as planned, dividends or other nonguaranteed values (if any) were realized as illustrated, and the policy was surrendered at the selected time period?"

The indices are not useful standing alone. They are relevant only in relation to those of other policies and, even then, many question their value to prospective purchasers. Regulations make clear that they are to be used for comparing similar policies only, which means that they should not be used for comparing policies with greatly different funding patterns or amounts of coverage. A further drawback is that they presume that everyone values money at 5.0 percent per year. This assumption might be reasonable for some buyers, but certainly not for others. It is for these reasons that other measures, such as internal rates of return on death and surrender, are more commonly used in many market segments.

OTHER MEASURES   Several other measures of policy performance occasionally are used. These methods can provide insight into policy performance and competitiveness.

Equal Outlay Method   One method used by some planners to compare the costs of two or more policies is what the authors have named the **equal outlay method** (EOM), which involves observing differences in resulting cash surrender values or accumulations for two or more policies by setting cash outlays and initial death benefits to the same level for all policies. This method assumes that equal amounts of money are expended under each of two or more proposed insurance arrangements. The differences in the cash values (or accumulations) between the policies are then observed over time. The policy yielding the highest value would be preferred, other things being equal. The EOM can be used to compare both similar and dissimilar policies, although not without some problems.

Table 19-9 illustrates a buy-term-and-invest-the-difference (BTID) calculation between WL and yearly renewable term (YRT) policies, both with an initial death benefit of $100,000. Equaling outlays for the two plans is accomplished by assuming that annual differences between the two policies are accumulated each year at some reasonable interest rate. Illustrated dividends under the WL policy are illustrated as purchasing paid up additions (PUAs). Table 19-9 shows that hypothetical side fund values are projected to be greater than the surrender values of the WL policy through policy year 12. As from policy year 13, the WL's illustrated surrender values are greater than the side fund's projected balance. The WL surrender values are composed of the guaranteed surrender value for the WL base policy plus the nonguaranteed surrender value of the PUAs. The analysis is not unbiased, as the YRT arrangement provides a higher death benefit in the early years for the same outlay.

The analysis suggests that, if the need for insurance is, say, for 10 years or less, the YRT arrangement seems superior based on illustrated values and the stated assumptions. On the other hand, this WL policy's relative position appears to improve continuously from a cost standpoint (based on these assumptions) as time passes. If a UL policy is being compared with another UL or a WL policy, the EOM functions identically to the cash value solve measure. If fixed-premium term or cash value policies are being compared, results can be more challenging to interpret unless the identical outlays can be made to support identical death benefits under the policies for the selected duration.

Cash Accumulation Method   The **cash accumulation method** (CAM) often is used for comparing a term life insurance policy with a cash value life insurance policy, which involves observing differences in resulting cash surrender values or side fund accumulations for the policies after setting cash outlays and death benefits to the same levels for all policies. It functions similarly to the EOM in that (1) outlays for two plans being compared are set at equal levels, (2) annual premium differences are accumulated at some assumed interest rate, and (3) one observes the cash value/side fund differences over time in an effort to draw meaningful cost based conclusions. However, unlike the EOM, (4) the lower premium policy's face amount is hypothetically adjusted each year so that the sum of the side fund and the adjusted face amount exactly equals the death benefit of the higher premium policy. The CAM corrects for the unequal death benefit bias of the equal outlay method. At least in the early policy years, the lower premium policy's face amount will be declining.

Example of Equal Outlay Method: **Table 19-9**
Whole Life (WL) versus Yearly Renewable Term (YRT)

End of Policy Year	WL Premium	YRT Premium	Difference between Premiums	YRT Side Fund: Accumulated Difference at 6 percent	WL Surrender Value: Base + PUAs	YRT Death Benefit: $100,000 + Side Fund	WL Death Benefit: Base + PUAs
1	$1,533	$145	$1,388	$1,471	$ 15	$101,471	$100,078
2	1,533	148	1,385	3,028	1,195	103,028	100,550
3	1,533	154	1,379	4,671	2,515	104,671	101,410
4	1,533	162	1,371	6,405	3,991	106,405	102,655
5	1,533	172	1,361	8,232	5,634	108,232	104,285
6	1,533	185	1,348	10,154	7,456	110,154	106,286
7	1,533	200	1,333	12,177	9,476	112,177	108,661
8	1,533	219	1,314	14,300	11,704	114,300	111,393
9	1,533	242	1,291	16,526	14,163	116,526	114,491
10	1,533	268	1,265	18,859	16,870	118,859	117,938
11	1,533	288	1,245	21,310	19,843	121,310	121,743
12	1,533	333	1,200	23,861	23,100	123,861	125,869
13	1,533	373	1,160	26,522	26,664	126,522	130,325
14	1,533	417	1,116	29,296	30,534	129,296	135,033
15	1,533	466	1,067	32,185	34,733	132,185	139,997
16	1,533	521	1,012	35,189	39,287	135,189	145,215
17	1,533	581	952	38,309	44,224	138,309	150,700
18	1,533	646	887	41,509	49,571	141,548	156,454
19	1,533	716	817	44,907	55,359	144,907	162,486
20	1,533	791	742	48,388	61,621	148,388	168,807

Applying the CAM to the policies in Table 19-9 and using the same assumptions, we would observe that the side fund values were larger in the earlier policy years because the YRT premiums for those years would be slightly less (because of a lower YRT face amount). While not shown here, these augmentations make a slight difference but, by policy year 13, the illustrated surrender value of the WL policy again exceeds the projected side fund balance. The interest rate assumption in all performance measures that require one can be critically important, including the IANC method, the EOM, the CAM, and others not presented here. In general, advisors recommend using conservative after-tax rates.

Comparative Interest Rate Method   Another method used to compare the relative costs of two policies is the comparative interest rate method, also known as the **Linton Yield** method after M.A. Linton of the *Provident Mutual Life Insurance Company,* who devised the method. The **comparative interest rate** (CIR) method is a special case of the CAM in that it solves for the interest rate that causes the accumulated value of the annual differences in policy premiums (the side fund) to be equal to the higher premium policy's surrender value at the end of the period of analysis. Stated differently, the CIR is the rate of return that must be earned on a hypothetical side fund in a BTID plan so that the value of the side fund will exactly equal the illustrated surrender value of the higher premium policy at the designated point in time. The higher the CIR, the less expensive the higher premium (e.g., WL) policy relative to the alternative plan (e.g., term plus side fund).

As with the CAM, outlays and death benefits are held equal. In the preceding BTID example, the 20-year accumulated differences exactly equal the 20-year illustrated surrender value at an interest rate of 7.93 percent; the example's 20-year CIR. Its five-year CIR is -6.65 percent and 10-year CIR is 4.0 percent. The CIR method requires a computer, as the solution interest rate is found by an iterative trial and error process.

Yearly Prices of Protection and Rates of Return   Some aspects of the identified shortcomings of the SV IRR and DB IRR measures are overcome by the yearly price of protection and yearly rate of return methods. The **yearly price per $1,000 of protection** (YPT) method derives year-by-year measures for a policy's implicit mortality charges per $1,000 of net amount at risk. The **yearly rate of return** (YRR) method derives year-by-year measures for the implicit rate of return on the savings component of a cash value policy. Each method requires an assumption about the value of the other. Thus, the derivation of YPT figures requires an assumption about a YRR, which is the rate of return deemed applicable to savings instruments displaying risk comparable to that of a life insurance policy. The YPT formula is as follows:

$$YPT = [(P + CVP)(1 + YRR) - (CV + D)] \div (DB - CV)(0.001)$$

where

YPT	= yearly price per $1,000 of protection
P	= annual premium payable at beginning of policy year
CVP	= cash value at end of the preceding policy year
YRR	= assumed yearly rate of return expressed as a decimal
CV	= cash value at end of policy year
D	= illustrated (or actual) dividend payable at end of policy year
DB	= death benefit payable at end of policy year

For example, consider a par whole life policy. It has a $100,000 death benefit and a $1,500 level annual premium. Its cash value is $10,000 at the end of year nine and $11,000 at the end of year 10. A dividend of $300 is payable at the end of the tenth year, and the assumed YRR on the savings component is 2.0 percent. One may verify that the YPT is $4.83.

After the high-loads of the first few policy years, YPTs typically increase as one would expect along with the increasing likelihood of death. The first few YPTs can be high, thus revealing the high front loads. Generally, they should exhibit a fairly smooth progression after the first few policy years. If not, certain types of actuarial manipulation may be the reason.

The YRRs for a policy can be found using the above formula, rearranged to solve for YRR. The derivation of YRR figures requires assumptions about a schedule of YPT figures. Both YPT and YRR are part of a broad system of life insurance disclosure long advocated by Joseph M. Belth, professor emeritus of insurance at Indiana University. Dr. Belth's system also includes mandatory disclosure of an estimate of the present value of the amount that a life insurance company retains to cover expenses and profits as well as the annual percentage rates associated with paying non-annual premiums. See the next section.

Evaluating Premium Payment Modes

Besides allowing the payment of premiums annually, insurers give policyholders the option of paying premiums semiannually, quarterly, or monthly. The values shown in policy illustrations almost invariably assume that premiums are paid annually, yet the great majority of policyholders do not pay annually. For those who intend to pay premiums other-than-annually, performance evaluations can mislead them into purchasing policies whose performance is illustrated as good when using annual premiums but whose performance would be poor if the actual mode of premium payment were used. This is because insurers assess additional charges for payment modes other than annual as discussed in Chapter 16. For some insurers, these charges are quite large.

Prospective buyers should understand how large. To do so, they should obtain the annual percentage rate (APR) equivalent of the charges. The APR is the implicit amount of interest being charged by the insurer on deferred premium amounts. Use of APRs is important as it is easy to misinterpret the dollar figures for each mode of payment. For example, assume that a policy's annual premium is $1,000 and its semiannual premium is $530. One might too quickly believe that the additional charge amounted to 6.0 percent; i.e., ($30 + $30) ÷ $1,000. In fact, the APR is 25.5 percent.

APRs vary greatly among insurers and even within the same insurer for different policies. In one survey, for example, they ranged from 0 to 54 percent, with more than a quarter of the surveyed companies having APRs of greater than 20 percent. Regrettably, no state requires insurers to provide this important information to perspective policyholders, and only a handful of insurers provide APR information voluntarily. Indeed, at least one state (Utah) prohibits insurers from providing it.

One can calculate APRs for a policy by inserting the policy's modal premiums into web-based calculators (e.g., www.insuranceforum.com). Alternatively, APRs can be calculated using the formulae shown in Box 19-2.

Box 19-2:
Estimating APRs for Non-annual Premium Payments

Annual percentage rates for various modes of premium payment can be approximated closely using the following formulae:

Semiannual: $APR = 2 (2S - A) \div (A - S)$

Quarterly: $APR = 12 (4Q - A) \div (5A - 2Q)$

Monthly: $APR = 36 (12M - A) \div (13A + 42M)$

where APR is the annual percentage rate expressed as a decimal, A is the annual premium, S is the semiannual premium, Q is the quarterly premium, and M is the monthly premium.

POLICY REVIEWS

The actual performance of a policy containing nonguaranteed elements inevitably varies over time from that which was illustrated originally. Additionally, policyholder actions, such as not paying planned premiums, adjusting death benefits, or taking unanticipated loans can cause a policy to deviate from its original projection. Policy reviews can determine whether actual and emerging policy values seem likely to enable the policy to accomplish its owner's financial goals. Policy reviews are intended to reveal whether some policyholder action is needed get a policy back on track and, if so, what action. Further, policy reviews are important audit devices.

NATURE OF POLICY REVIEWS

Policy reviews typically are of two types: annual and detailed. Annual reviews are typically simple. Detailed reviews are more in depth and usually occur less often than annual reviews.

ANNUAL REVIEWS   Insurers provide policy reports to policyholders annually on the policy anniversary. An annual report contains the beginning and ending policy year values, including the surrender value, account (cash) value, and death benefit. Transactions affecting any policy cash flows and values also are shown, including premium payments, withdrawals, loans, and loan interest due and paid. Dividends paid are shown for par WL policies. For UL policies, they show actual policy COI and loading charges assessed and interest credited to account values during the policy year. Relevant interest crediting rates are also typically shown. For variable policies, the statement also shows policy value detail by fund or account.

Annual reviews consist of comparing the current policy values and elements against those illustrated in the most recent policy illustration. That illustration may be the one provided at the time the policy was sold – called *as-sold illustrations* in industry jargon – or an updated illustration at some later period – called an *in-force illustration*. The objective of the comparison is to determine whether the policy remains on track to meet the policyholder's insurance goals.

Annual policy reviews can differ by policy type. Annual reviews of WL policies can be less technical than those for unbundled policies because of the fixed relationship between policy values and premiums and the bundling of policy charges and credits (which also can make it difficult to identify the reason for any performance deviation). Table 19-10 offers an abbreviated sample of a par WL policy annual report.

Abbreviated Example of Whole Life Annual Report　　　　Table 19-10

Policy Information

Plan:	Whole Life AA
Policy Date:	July 1, 2014
Premium Payment:	$121,250
Billing Cycle:	Payable Annually

Benefit Summary

	Death Benefit as of July 1, 2014	Cash Value as of July 1, 2014	Cash Value as of July 1, 2013
Guaranteed Values	$5,500,000	$720,000	$600,000
Dividend Additions	350,000	170,000	120,000
Total	$5,850,000	$890,000	$720,000

Your current annual dividend of $35,000 was applied to purchase $72,000 of dividend additions.

Policy values are audited by comparing each annual report to the previous year's annual report and to the most recent policy illustration. If the dividend scale has not changed since the policy was issued or the last obtained illustration, current values should match those illustrated at that time. If they do not match, the reason for the deviation should be discovered. If the dividend scale has changed, the guaranteed values shown in the current statement still should match the guaranteed values from the most recent illustration.

Annual reports for UL policies are more detailed than those for bundled policies due to the unbundling of policy charges and credits and premium flexibility. In addition to providing beginning and ending year policy values, UL annual statements include a summary of the year's policy activity. Table 19-11 shows an example of UL policy activity. In addition to the sum of the annual activity, some annual statements also provide policy activity by month. A UL annual report also includes the current and monthly crediting rates for the policy year.

Example of a Universal Life Summary of Policy Activity　　　　Table 19-11

Account Value as of July 1, 2013	$ 58,000
Premiums Received	+ 60,000
Premium Charges	- 3,600
Interest Credited	+ 5,600
Sum of Monthly COI and Expense Charges	- 23,000
Account Value as of July 1, 2014	= $97,000

As with WL, current UL policy values are compared to those of the previous annual statement and to those of the most recent illustration. Beginning values from the current statement should match the ending values from the previous year's statement. Whether current policy values deviate from the values of the most recent illustration should be noted. The summary of policy activity can reveal which policy credits or charges caused any change in values.

In addition to the information already described for WL and UL, annual reports for VLI include policy value detail by fund allocation. The fund value equals the number of shares times the share value. Shares are bought each time a premium is paid and sold to cover monthly charges, based on that day's share value. The summary by account allows for an assessment of policy performance by account. Earned rates can be negative, thereby causing substantial changes in policy values. For this reason, ongoing policy reviews for variable products are even more important than reviews of non-variable products.

A VLI annual statement should also include a one-year projection based on planned premiums, guaranteed charges, and a 0 percent gross annual rate of return on the variable investment option. The projection provides an idea of the amount of cushion inherent in existing policy value to be able to weather an adverse scenario. Of course, the policy will lapse if the account value goes to zero (in the absence of a no lapse guarantee). Even a 0 percent assumption has proven to be too high for some years.

DETAILED REVIEWS   Detailed periodic policy reviews are needed to assess the impact on illustrated future policy performance of actions by policyholders and of changes by insurers in current assumptions. Detailed reviews rely on current performance benchmarks and on security and comparing up-to-date illustrations of a policy's possible future performance. The objective of the review is to determine whether illustrated future policy performance would fulfill the policyholder's life insurance goals and, if necessary, to make appropriate adjustments in policy funding or other policy elements.

Many advisors recommend conducting a detailed review if an examination of an annual policy report or other material reveals that any of the following has occurred:

- Premiums were not paid as scheduled or planned, either as to amount or timing.
- Distributions inconsistent with the original schedule were made.
- Any policy changes were made that could affect future performance.
- The interest crediting rate or, for variable life, the actual earned rate deviated from that shown in the most recent annual report or illustration.
- The premiums for indeterminate premium policies, the COI rates for unbundled policies, or mortality charges for par WL for which such charges are disclosed differ from those shown in the most recent annual statement or illustration.
- Expense loadings for unbundled policies or, if disclosed, for par WL policies differ from those shown in the most recent annual statement or illustration.
- Dividends actually paid deviated from those in the most recent illustration.

Additionally, detailed reviews are recommended periodically, such as every five or so years, even if none of the above actions occurred. The reason for a periodic review of this type is not so much to ensure that the policy remains on track to accomplish its goals as to determine whether the existing policy continues to offer good value relative to other comparable policies. A life insurance policy that offers poor value can remain on track because, for example, general investment returns increased but the insurer chose to pass on little or none of that increase. The techniques discussed earlier would be applied to the existing and one or more possible replacement policies.

OPTIONS TO ACHIEVE INSURANCE GOALS

Deviations of actual from illustrated policy values are all but certain under current assumption policies. Policyholders are more concerned about negative than positive deviations, but both types can warrant action.

WHEN POLICY VALUES ARE INSUFFICIENT   When reasonable illustrations of current plus future policy values suggest that values are insufficient to allow a policy to meet insurance goals, some policyholder action may be needed. Such actions can include the following.

- **Doing Nothing.** The policyholder always has the option of doing nothing about an illustrated negative deviation. This may be the wise course of action if:
  - The insured's health has deteriorated and the expectation of his or her living past the projected date of policy lapse is remote. For WL policies, consideration might be given to allowing the policy to go under the extended term nonforfeiture option.
  - The review is taking place early in the life of the policy, and sufficient time remains for future nonguaranteed policy elements to move in a favorable direction, allowing policy values to get back on track.
  - The policyholder is unable to pay additional premiums. If the policy being reviewed is par WL, paying additional premiums may not be a viable option anyway. If dividends were earmarked to allow a policy to become self-sustaining, and they are now illustrated to be inadequate to accomplish that goal, the WL policyholder's problem is more or less the same as that of the UL policyholder in the same position.
- **Making Additional Payments.** For UL, an in-force illustration can be run that solves for the additional premium needed to achieve the funding goal. For par WL, the additional payment alternatives will vary depending on the dividend option elected. For example, if the dividend option was to reduce premium outlays, the policyholder has but to change to another option, such as purchasing PUAs.
- **Reducing Future Death Benefits.** If the policyholder cannot or chooses not to make additional payments, reducing the face amount could be considered. For UL, an in-force illustration can be run that solves for a reduced face amount based on a specific cash value goal at a set age, such as age 121. For WL policies, insurers typically will allow reductions in the death benefit, thereby reducing the required premium.
- **Replacing the policy.** If a policy's actual and/or illustrated future performance is disappointing relative to that of other policies in the market, consideration may be given to replacing it with a policy that illustrates superior performance, although care should be exercised when comparisons are based on values illustrated for many years into the future.

WHEN POLICY VALUES ARE GREATER THAN NECESSARY   Policy values can evolve to be greater than those shown in an earlier illustration. Certainly, policyholders prefer over- to underfunded policies, but one should not conclude that a policy offers good value solely because of the fact of overfunding. Even with overfunding, advisors often recommend that periodic policy replacement reviews be performed, particularly if the insured's health has not deteriorated.

A policy can be considered as being overfunded if current and future illustrated values exceed those needed to allow the policy to accomplish the policyholder's insurance goals. The policyholder can consider several options in response to this condition, including the following:

- **Doing Nothing.** Making no changes may be the most logical response to overfunding, especially when inflation is likely to produce a need for additional insurance or policy value in the future.
- **Reducing Future Payments.** For par WL policies whose dividends are earmarked to reduce premium payments, having greater-than-illustrated dividends means that out-of-pocket payments automatically are reduced below those anticipated formerly. Payments also can be reduced at some point in the future by changing the PUA option to reducing premium outlays. For UL policies for which planned premiums are being paid, the policyholder can reduce future planned premiums by solving for the lower premium that would allow the policyholder's insurance goal to be obtained.
- **Increasing Future Death Benefits.** As explained above, "doing nothing" can be the equivalent of increasing future death benefits. This course of action may be appropriate for planning purposes either because future death-related needs are expected to increase due to inflation or other reasons.
- **Taking Policy Distributions.** Distributions (withdrawals, partial surrenders, and loans) can be taken from the policy to get it back on track. Distributions under WL policies ordinarily would be taken first from PUAs in the form of surrenders and dividends on deposit. Further distributions likely would be via policy loans and, thereafter, via partial policy surrenders, but only if essential or if the surrendered insurance was no longer needed. Distributions under UL policies are more direct but can result in low cash values and an increased risk of lapse.

COST AND BENEFIT DISCLOSURE

Most U.S. and many other jurisdictions require certain information disclosures to prospective life insurance buyers. These disclosures are intended to help the consumer become more informed thereby rectifying, to some extent, the information imbalance between buyer and seller. The hope is that buyers will make better purchase decisions.

BACKGROUND
Although recommendations for improving life insurance disclosure were made as early as 1906 via the Armstrong Investigation in New York and in 1908 by the Wisconsin insurance commissioner, significant activity on the issue did not occur until

the 1960s. Following a threat of federal legislation, the NAIC adopted an interim model life insurance disclosure regulation in 1973 and revised versions later.

Important U.S. congressional subcommittee hearings on life insurance marketing and disclosure were held in 1973 and 1978, both of which raised questions about existing disclosure and marketing practices. The *Federal Trade Commission* (FTC) staff also investigated life insurance marketing. Its 1979 report identified several consumer problems and offered detailed recommendations for how it believed the problems should be solved, differing in important respects from the approach recommended by the NAIC. The life insurance industry testified vigorously against the report and was able to get the U.S. Congress to bar the FTC from undertaking future such investigations without explicit congressional authorization. Since then, the NAIC's efforts have been directed toward discipline in whatever disclosures were made.

NAIC NON-VARIABLE LIFE INSURANCE DISCLOSURE REQUIREMENTS

More than 40 U.S. jurisdictions require disclosures to prospective life insurance purchasers as recommended in the NAIC *Life Insurance Disclosure Model Regulation* or one of its predecessors. The regulations do not apply to annuities, credit life insurance, group life insurance, variable life insurance, and life insurance policies issued in connection with pension and welfare plans, although the NAIC has adopted parallel regulation for annuities, as discussed in Chapter 6. The life model regulations require that a prospective purchaser be supplied with

- a **Buyer's Guide** that is intended to assist prospective purchasers in deciding how much and what type of life insurance to buy and comparing the costs of similar policies and
- a **Policy Summary** that is intended to help prospective purchasers understand the specific policy being considered for purchase and that contains illustrated and guaranteed policy values along with other policy information.

The insurance company is required to ensure that all prospective purchasers receive a Buyer's Guide and a Policy Summary prior to accepting the applicant's initial premium, unless the policy for which application is being made or the Policy Summary contains an unconditional refund provision of at least 10 days' duration. In these cases, the Buyer's Guide and Policy Summary may be delivered with or prior to delivery of the policy. Most states mandate a 10-day "free look" requirement, and many insurers allow a 30-day period. A Buyer's Guide and a Policy Summary are also to be provided to any prospective purchaser who requests them.

The Disclosure Regulation requires the agent to inform prospective purchasers of the company he or she represents. Terms such as financial planner, investment advisor, financial consultant, and financial counseling may not be used in such a way as to imply that the agent is generally engaged in a fee-for-service advisory business, unless that is the case. The use of cost comparison methods that fail to take the time value of money into consideration is prohibited except to show a policy's cash flow pattern.

Several provisions in the latest model regulation are not found in most states' regulations. For example, the model regulation requires that the method of investment income allocation (i.e., new money or portfolio average) be shown on the Policy Summary, and, if an insurer fails to follow the contribution principle, a statement to that effect must also be included. Any change from one investment income allocation method to another requires that affected policyowners be notified.

A further modification of the disclosure regulation, which is not in effect in any state, would substitute a Life Insurance Yield Comparison Index for the surrender cost comparison index. This yield index, akin to the CIR, is calculated by using a standard, prescribed set of term (mortality) rates that are applied to the policy's net amount at risk (rather than to the difference between the policy's death benefit and a hypothetical side fund, as in the CIR method).

THE BUYER'S GUIDE   The Buyer's Guide is intended to help prospective purchasers (1) decide how much life insurance to buy, (2) decide what kind of policy to buy, and (3) compare the costs of similar life insurance policies. The language of the guide is mandated by the regulation. The suggestion in the Buyer's Guide for choosing an appropriate amount of life insurance to buy is general; it advises the consumer to figure out how much cash and income would be needed if the insured died. The guide explains briefly the principal types of life insurance and points out positive and negative aspects of each. The Buyer's Guides used in many jurisdictions contain an explanation of the distinction between par and nonpar life insurance, although the Buyer's Guide in the latest model regulation focuses on guaranteed and nonguaranteed values.

The Buyer's Guide includes a general description of the Surrender Cost Comparison Index and the Net Payment Cost Comparison Index, and advice on how to use them. The consumer is admonished that: "a policy with smaller index numbers is generally a better buy than a similar policy with larger index numbers. . . ." These IANC indices are contained in the Policy Summary.

THE POLICY SUMMARY   The Policy Summary contains information and data on the specific policy being considered by the consumer. The name and address of the insurance agent (if any) and the insurance company must appear on the summary, along with the generic name of the insurance policy (e.g., whole life insurance).

The Policy Summary must contain certain policy data (premiums, death benefits, cash surrender values, and illustrated dividends) for the first five policy years and for representative policy years thereafter sufficient to show the pattern of premiums and benefits. These years must include the tenth and twentieth years and at least one age from 60 through 65 and policy maturity.

In addition to the above policy data, the effective policy loan interest rate must be stated and 10- and 20-year surrender cost and net payment cost indices provided. The procedure for calculating the indices is mandated by the regulation. A 5.0 percent interest assumption is to be used. There is no requirement that the APR for modal premium payments be calculated and disclosed.

Additionally, these model disclosure regulations do not require the disclosure to prospective buyers of the fact and extent of agents' commissions. Only the state of New York requires that agent commissions be disclosed to prospective buyers. Many persons believe that consumer disclosure should include information on commission payments to alert the prospective buyer as to the nature and extent of an agent's interest in the sales transactions. Commission disclosure is required in several countries, including Australia, Norway, and the U.K.

VARIABLE LIFE DISCLOSURE REQUIREMENTS

As discussed in earlier chapters, variable life and annuity contracts are subject to both federal and state disclosure requirements. The intent of these requirements is to allow the prudent investor to be able to make an informed decision whether to purchase the security (variable product); i.e., to rectify some of the information asymmetry between buyer and seller.

STATE-MANDATED DISCLOSURE   Disclosure in connection with the sale of VLI typically follows the provisions the NAIC's *Variable Life Insurance Model Regulation* or an earlier or similar version of the regulation, in effect in most states. The regulation requires insurers to provide to the applicant for a variable life policy a summary explanation of the principal features of the policy, including a description of the manner in which the variable benefits will reflect the separate account investment experience and factors that affect the variation. Further, disclosure must include statements of the investment policy of the separate account, of the net investment return of the separate account for the lesser of each of the last 10 years or each year the account has been in existence, and of the charges levied against the separate account during the previous year.

Additional information must be provided in terms of summaries of the method to be used in valuing assets held by the separate account and of the federal income tax aspects of the policy applicable to the insured, the policyowner, and the beneficiary. Finally, illustrations of benefits payable under the contract may be provided, which may not include projections of past experience but may use hypothetical assumed rates of return to illustrate possible levels of death benefits.

The regulation does not require disclosure of agent commissions, unlike federal rules. Compliance with the regulation can be achieved by delivery to the applicant of a prospectus containing effectively the same information as that above. In addition to this initial disclosure, the regulation mandates that insurers provide annual policy status reports to policyowners, which summarize policy and separate account activity for the preceding policy year.

FEDERALLY MANDATED DISCLOSURE   Federally mandated disclosure follows the requirements of the *Securities Exchange Act of 1933*. Applicable to both variable annuity and life contracts, disclosure must be full and accurate and is accomplished through two mechanisms. First, the securities issuer must file a registration statement with the SEC that contains detailed information on the security, the issuer, the officers, and security holdings. Details of the underwriting arrangement and financial statements also must be included.

Second, the act requires that each potential buyer be given a prospectus. This detailed booklet includes the identity and nature of the insurer's business, the use to which the insurer will put the premiums, financial information on the insurer, the fees and expenses to be charged, and policyowner rights. It contains most other information included in the registration statement. The prospectus is to be highly readable, easily understandable, and kept current.

In common parlance, a replacement occurs when a new life insurance policy is purchased and, in connection with that purchase, an existing policy is terminated or values extracted from it. State insurance regulations (see below) extend this definition to include discontinuing premium payments and other acts that have the effect of reducing the value otherwise provided under that policy.

Many within the life insurance industry have strong views whether replacements in general are good for consumers, with advocates on both sides of the debate. Many agents and executives, as well as many state insurance regulators, argue that replacements generally are not in the consumer's best interest. For reasons enumerated later in this section, they believe that a new policy is unlikely to be better for the policyholder than an existing policy. Many others contend that so many life insurance policies have performed poorly over time, were needlessly costly at time of purchase, and/or are ill-suited for customers that the presumption should be reversed: replacements generally *are* in the consumer's best interest. Still others take a neutral position that replacements are neither inherently good nor bad for the consumer and that each case should be judged on its merits.

Some readers may view this intra-industry debate with detached amusement. "And why *wouldn't* one take a position of neutrality?" In fact, most agents probably are reluctant to recommend replacement because either their views place them into "replacements are bad" category, they wish to avoid the hassle associated with complying with replacement regulations, or they prefer to avoid having to imply that an existing policy, perhaps sold to a client by a friend, does not offer good value or is not suitable.

On the other hand, some agents probably "never met a policy that shouldn't be replaced." Indeed, some agents and insurers had a marketing strategy based on replacement of existing insurance. Many have been accused of engaging in **churning**, which is the systematic and indiscriminate replacement of existing insurance for purposes of securing new commissions.

REPLACEMENT PROCEDURES

While individual life insurers and agents have their own procedures for replacements, these will have been dictated to a great extent by state insurance replacement regulations, which set out the requirements that all agents and insurers doing business in the state must follow with respect to replacements. They are patterned after the NAIC *Life Insurance and Annuities Replacement Model Regulation* or one of its predecessors.

The model regulation establishes minimum standards of conduct to be observed by insurers and agents in life insurance and annuity replacements. It is intended to ensure disclosure of material information to purchasers and to reduce opportunities for misrepresentation and unfair business practices. The regulation expands and clarifies information that must be communicated by an agent to a purchaser at the time an application is completed and provides disclosure notice formats to ensure uniformity.

The regulation's definition of replacement is broad:

> *"Replacement" means a transaction in which a new policy or contract is to be purchased, and it is known or should be known to the proposing producer, or to the proposing insurer if there is no producer, that by reason of*

the transaction, an existing policy or contract has been or is to be lapsed, forfeited, surrendered or partially surrendered, assigned to the replacing insurer or otherwise terminated, converted to reduced paid-up insurance, continued as extended term insurance, or otherwise reduced in value by the use of nonforfeiture benefits or other policy values, amended so as to effect either a reduction in benefits or in the term for which coverage would otherwise remain in force or for which benefits would be paid, reissued with any reduction in cash value, or used in a financed purchase.

All versions of the NAIC's model replacement regulations impose sales-related obligations on both insurers and agents. The latest obligations apply to almost all individually issued life insurance policies, including variable life. First, agents are required to submit to their insurers, with or as part of the application, the applicant's signed statement whether the applicant owns existing policies. If the applicant does not have existing policies, the agent's duties regarding replacement are satisfied.

If the applicant has existing insurance, the regulations require the agent to present and read to the applicant, not later than at the time of taking the application, a "Notice Regarding Replacement." The reading requirement can be waived by the applicant. The notice cautions the policyowner that he or she should carefully consider whether a replacement is in his or her best interest, then offers some reasons why it might not be and sets out a series of statements and questions intended to cause the owner to consider many aspects of the prospective transaction.

The notice also inquires whether a replacement is being considered. Both the applicant and agent must sign the notice, irrespective of whether replacement is being considered, attesting to the accuracy of the responses. A copy of the notice is to be left with the applicant. If a replacement is being considered, information is to be provided about the policies to be replaced and the reason for the replacement.

The regulation establishes duties for both replacing insurers and existing insurers. For example, replacing insurers using agents are required, among other things, to:

- Establish and maintain a system of supervision and control to ensure compliance with the regulation.
- Monitor and maintain records of each agent's replacement activity.
- Determine that required sales materials and illustrations used in connection with a replacement are complete and accurate.
- Promptly notify the existing insurer of the replacement and, if requested, also mail a copy of the illustration, policy summary, or disclosure document for the proposed policy.
- Notify the policyowner of the right to return the policy or contract within 30 days of delivery and receive a full refund of all premiums paid.
- Maintain records of required notification forms and illustrations.

Existing insurers are required, among other things, to:

- Establish and maintain a system of supervision and control to ensure compliance with the regulation.
- Promptly inform its replacing policyholder of the right to receive information regarding his or her existing policy values. The information must

include an in-force illustration or a policy summary if an in-force illustration cannot be produced and must be provided promptly if requested by the policyowner.

- Upon receiving a request to borrow, surrender, or withdraw policy values, notify the policyholder that the release of policy values may affect guaranteed and nonguaranteed policy elements.
- Maintain records of notifications received.

REPLACEMENT ANALYSIS

Arguments as to whether replacements are "good" or "bad" provide the individual buyer little guidance. The policyowner considering replacement should weigh several factors. Box 19-3 highlights the more common considerations as contained in the model regulation. Thus, the notice observes that most cash value life insurance policies have their initial costs charged, one way or another, against early cash values. These initial high costs would have already been met under an older policy. However, a performance analysis such as discussed earlier in this chapter can help determine whether this argument is persuasive, just as a performance analysis can help reveal whether a higher premium rate for a new policy seems justified financially.

It should always be considered that incontestable and suicide clauses begin anew under new policies, but this fact is rarely persuasive by itself to forestall a replacement, unless the proposed insured intends to kill himself or lie on the application! Moreover, some companies will waive these clauses on new policies to the extent that they had elapsed under the older policy.

If an older policy is not perceived as serving the consumer's needs, the existing insurer may be willing to make an internal exchange on more beneficial terms than those that a new insurer may be willing to offer. Also, older policies sometimes can be adjusted to meet new circumstances through changes in dividend options or through policy loans and other alterations.

CONCLUSIONS

This chapter introduced how one can understand and use life insurance policy illustrations in policy performance comparisons. It also explained the importance of understanding underlying pricing assumptions and how to assess their sustainability. We explored the importance and nature of annual and periodic policy reviews, along with options to take when realized policy values deviate from those illustrated. The chapter closed with an examination of life insurance policy disclosure requirements in connection with policy sales that both do and do not involve replacement of existing life insurance.

ENDNOTES

1   This chapter draws in parts from Harold D. Skipper and Wayne Tonning, *The Advisor's Guide to Life Insurance* (Chicago; American Bar Association, 2011), Chapters 13-17.
2   This process builds on that used by M Financial Group. Special thanks are due Wayne Tonning and his associates.
3   Skipper and Tonning, page 328.

Box 19-3
Life Insurance Questions from the NAIC "Notice Regarding Replacement"

You should discuss the following with your insurance producer [agent] to determine whether replacement or financing your purchase makes sense:

Premiums:
- Are they affordable?
- Could they change?
- You are older – are premiums higher for the proposed new life insurance policy?
- How long will you have to pay premiums on the new life insurance policy? On the old life insurance policy?

Life insurance policy values: New policies usually take longer to build cash values and to pay dividends.
- Acquisition costs for the old life insurance policy may have been paid, and you will incur new costs for the new one.
- What surrender charges do the policies have?
- What expense and sales charges do the policies have?
- Does the new life insurance policy provide more insurance coverage?

Insurability: If your health has changed since you bought your old life insurance policy, the new one could cost you more, or you could be turned down.
- You may need a medical exam for a new life insurance policy.
- Claims on most new policies for up to the first 2 years can be denied based on inaccurate statements.
- Suicide limitations may begin anew on the new coverage.

If you are keeping the old life insurance policy as well as the new life insurance policy:
- How are premiums for both policies being paid?
- How will the premium on your existing life insurance policy be affected?
- Will a loan be deducted from death benefits?
- What values from the old life insurance policy are being used to pay premiums?

If you are surrendering an annuity or interest sensitive life product:
- Will you pay surrender charges on your existing contract?
- What are the interest rate guarantees for the new contract?
- Have you compared the contract charges or other policy expenses?

Other issues to consider for all transactions:
- What are the tax consequences of buying the new life insurance policy?
- Is this a tax-free exchange? (See your tax advisor.)
- Will the existing insurer be willing to modify the old life insurance policy?
- How does the quality and financial stability of the new company compare with the exiting company?

Source: NAIC Life Insurance and Annuities Replacement Model Regulation.

PART IV

LIFE INSURANCE IN PERSONAL AND BUSINESS PLANNING

CHAPTER 20

PERSONAL FINANCIAL PLANNING

This chapter begins Part IV of the text, which examines the use of personal life insurance in personal and business planning. We explore both the theory and practice of personal financial planning (PFP) and, thereby, set the context for the other chapters in this part.

As noted in Chapter 1, a person's income stream flows from his or her productive capacity, referred to in economic theory as his or her human capital. For PFP purposes, we operationalize this economic definition so as to define **human capital** as the present value of an individual's future earnings. At an individual's retirement, human capital will be exhausted, and income from financial and real assets – called **investment capital** – are required to support the individual through the end of life. The sum of human and investment capital at any point in life yields an individual's **economic wealth**.

Both human capital and investment capital losses can be hedged by the purchase of personal insurance products, which can be viewed as call options. Thus, life and disability income insurance hedge against loss of human capital; i.e., they are options that pay when an individual's income stream is interrupted by death, illness, or injury. Life annuities and long term care (LTC) insurance hedge against loss of investment capital; i.e., they are options that pay when investment capital is depleted as a result of a longer than expected life (annuities) and because of loss of investment capital occasioned by additional expenses incurred because of incapacity or frailty, usually associated with aging (LTC insurance). They provide liquid assets at precisely the times they are needed.

We present PFP in a context that integrates the investment and insurance aspects of financial planning by considering economic wealth and associated risks. The primary focus of this chapter is on human capital (the accumulation phase of life) and relevant insurance products, while Chapter 23 covers investment capital (the liquidation phase of life) and relevant insurance products. The two are interrelated. The results of the retirement planning process in Chapter 23 indicate whether the preretirement financial plan has been realistic and useful or, stated equivalently but differently, the results of the financial planning process of this chapter dictate whether the retirement plan will be realized.

WEALTH AND THE LIFE CYCLE

The objectively measured demand for life, disability income, LTC, and annuity insurance is weak compared to what normative life cycle theory suggests it should be, resulting in consumers being exposed to more risk than is theoretically necessary because of underinsurance. (Recall the distinction between *normative* issues – what ought to be – and *positive* issues – the way things are – as noted in Chapter 1.) Thus, in an objective context, the lifetime utility maximization hypothesis – that consumers seek to maximize their utility and minimize their disutility over the course of their lives – fails to describe actual behavior accurately for great proportions of consumers.

Nonetheless, we take a normative view in addressing PFP as we are interested in "best practices" in PFP and do not assume that individuals' and families' actual planning practices are necessarily optimal. We note differences in normative and actual practices along the way, being certain to point out how market imperfections work against best practices. Thus, we presume individuals wish to maximize utility by balancing savings and consumption to satisfy preretirement needs but also to maximize retirement income possibilities subject to lifetime necessities, all the while insuring both human and investment capital against the personal risks that can disrupt the progress of a life cycle financial plan. In this way, the investment capital available at retirement becomes the benchmark or bellwether of the success of a financial plan.

To achieve this life cycle balancing act, it is necessary to spread consumption from the economically productive years to the nonproductive years. Some type of smoothing is necessary because of the **economizing problem** – unlimited wants and limited resources. Some interpretations suggest that utility is maximized when consumption is a constant percentage of the present value of an individual or household's wealth to be consumed over the life cycle. We assume utility can be maximized in this and other ways as well. For example, intuition suggests that many individuals and households save and sacrifice for a lifetime to undertake expensive activities like travel during leisure or retirement. Additionally, research indicates that many individuals sacrifice current consumption to provide both lifetime gifts and testamentary or other bequests to heirs or philanthropic organizations.

THE FINANCIAL LIFE CYCLE

The economically productive period of life ordinarily begins when a young person leaves the family and its authority (legally called **emancipation**), enters the work force, and begins to save – and ends at retirement. What is called the *economically nonproductive* period of life is thought of as beginning at retirement and ending at death (although many retirees secure part-time employment). We refer to the preretirement economically productive years when both financial and real assets are acquired as the **asset accumulation phase** of life and the economically nonproductive postretirement period during which assets are liquidated as the **asset liquidation phase** of life.

Theoretically, utility will have been maximized over the financial life cycle – emancipation to death – when assets accumulated through retirement age are just sufficient to be liquidated through the date of death. As individuals enter the work force, their most significant, if not only, economic wealth is in the form of their human capital. As retirement approaches, human capital is exhausted so that accumulated investment capital becomes the sole source of economic wealth and income to complete their lives in financial security.

Thus, a principal concern of PFP should be a savings plan to create, manage, and protect both human and investment assets to provide for a comfortable retirement. The purpose of risk management with insurance products is to provide the financial means to complete (1) a preretirement savings program even if interrupted by death or disability and (2) a postretirement plan of asset liquidation that lasts a lifetime. Of course, most people have important preretirement goals; a college fund for children is typical. We will rank these goals by subjective priority to evaluate the impact of satisfying them on long term retirement possibilities. Figure 20-1 illustrates the accumulation and liquidation of assets over the life cycle.

The Expected Value of Human and Investment Capital over the Life Cycle   **Figure 20-1**

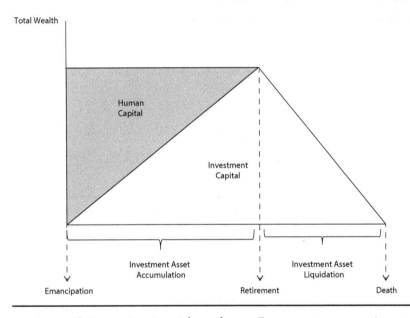

Accumulating savings is a risky endeavor. Expenses, taxes, poor investment performance, inflation, and intemperate spending represent impediments to asset accumulation. Institutions and academicians have developed a variety of theoretically and practically advanced approaches to the accumulation and liquidation of assets. Most institutions are able to invest over a time horizon that is either precisely determined or perpetual, unlike the human life cycle. In addition to investment uncertainty, individuals face the uncertainties of life and health. They die at and live to unexpected ages. An untimely death or disability destroys human capital and can unnecessarily leave a lifetime savings plan unfinished. An extraordinarily long life can deplete an individual's assets and ability to maintain financial independence, but planning for an extraordinarily long life also can lead to an unnecessarily low level of consumption and satisfaction.

We term these consequences *unnecessary* because the risks of death, disability, incapacity, and longevity can be reduced through insurance. Life insurance and disability income insurance can substitute for human capital, thus ensuring the accumulation of needed investment capital. LTC insurance and life annuities protect the individual and family from the possibility of an extraordinarily long life or a damaged life that prevents an individual from caring for him- or herself, thus ensuring the sufficiency of a planned liquidation of investment capital. (LTC insurance is generally thought of as a product for the elderly, and we use it in that sense in this chapter. After retirement, health issues are not a human capital risk. They are a risk to the sufficiency of accumulated capital to fully fund retirement. As we point out in Chapter 8, while less probable, young people too are sometimes unable to care for themselves, and LTC coverage applies in these cases also.)

Figure 20-2 presents the insurable exposures of death, disability, personal care, and longevity in conjunction with the accumulation and liquidation of capital over the life cycle.

Figure 20-2   **Insuring the Value of Human and Investment Capital over the Life Cycle**

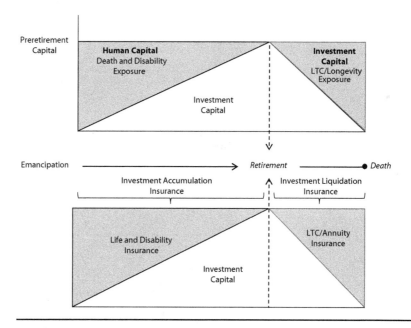

LIFE CYCLE RISKS AND MANAGEMENT TOOLS

For purposes of setting PFP in a risk management context, we identify the eight most important risks faced by all but the wealthiest individuals and households. Six are specific to individuals (wage, mortality, health, savings, care, and longevity), and two are environmental and apply to all individuals (inflation and investment). Recall that risk can be avoided, treated (reduced or controlled), or transferred through insurance.

Wage risk is the possibility that an individual's earnings from employment are less than expected. It has two dimensions. The first is volatility – compensation for some occupations can vary widely from period to period. The second is unemployment – a sort of income default risk when income disappears entirely. Despite the fact that many individuals suffer unemployment at some point and that many do during recessionary times, in the long run – the relevant time horizon for most of the PFP period – most individuals are at work most of the time. Human capital is therefore generally less risky than many investments.

In addition to successful career management, two other methods exist for treating wage risk. The first is to accelerate the conversion of human capital to investment capital through accelerated savings. The second, disability income insurance, transfers the risk associated with a loss of wages arising from an inability to work because of illness or injury (discussed in Chapter 8).

Mortality risk is the possibility that a budgeting and savings program designed to support an individual or family to and through retirement is not completed due to the death of a breadwinner during the working life. Mortality risk is transferred via life insurance (discussed specifically in Chapters 3, 4, and 5 and throughout this text). **Health risk** is the possibility that individuals lose their ability to work or incur medical expense because of illness or injury. Medical expense and disability income insurance address this risk, as discussed in Chapters 7 and 8. **Savings risk** is the possibility that unexpected expense, a lack of planning, or carelessness impedes or interrupts the planned conversion of human capital to investment capital.

Care risk is the possibility that individuals are unable to care for themselves due to a physical or mental impairment. LTC insurance addresses this risk, as discussed in Chapter 8. (During the working life, care costs arise apart from and usually in addition to wage interruptions.) **Longevity risk** is the possibility that an individual will live to an unusually old age and that his or her financial assets will be insufficient to complete an orderly plan of investment asset liquidation designed to last a lifetime. Longevity risk is transferred via life annuities (discussed in Chapters 6 and 23).

Inflation risk is the possibility that the cost of living will exceed that anticipated during life. During the working life, inflation risk is largely hedged through a competitive wage. Inflation risk is especially important in two other respects. First, health care inflation has been even greater than the general rate of inflation. Second, during retirement, the competitive wage hedge ends, thus exposing the retiree to additional inflation risk in both general living and health costs. Inflation risk can be addressed with asset allocation in general savings, through variable annuities and life insurance, and in the relative amounts allocated to insurance and noninsurance products. It can also be addressed with inflation-indexed bonds and annuities (see Chapter 6).

Investment asset risk is the possibility of poor relative investment performance. Performance can be poor due to (1) suboptimal (or negative) returns for a given level of risk, (2) an inappropriate level of risk, and (3) negative real returns when the earned rate does not exceed the rate of inflation. Investment asset risk is treated through rational asset allocation and portfolio construction.

Unlike the individual risk management treatment of wage, mortality, health, savings, personal care, and longevity, investment asset risk treatment tools are the same for individuals and institutions. However, because of the uncertainties associated with human health and mortality, the appropriate level of risk for individuals is not constant – it varies over the life cycle. Life style, life cycle, and target date investment funds offered by mutual fund and insurance companies address this risk (discussed in Chapter 6). PFP requires the effective management of human and investment capital risk while taking account of each in a portfolio context.

PERSONAL

FINANCIAL

PLANNING

IN A RISK

MANAGEMENT

CONTEXT

In the years before retirement, individuals are able to influence the value of their investment capital accumulation through their spending behavior: the more saved, the more capital accumulated. The value of investment capital becomes essentially fixed at retirement, and the postretirement component of utility over the life cycle is thus a residual function of the preretirement conversion of human capital to investment capital through savings (income less consumption). In short, individuals and couples retire on what's left. At retirement, they become essentially *price takers* – market prices of consumption, investments, and longevity insurance dictate the satisfaction to be derived from what is usually a fixed and limited resource base.

The elements that the individual can influence – preretirement savings and consumption – are the most important determining factors. The accumulated asset base at retirement can be compared to a set of retirement opportunities to judge the sufficiency of the financial plan. Retirement planning is essentially incomplete until an idea of the expected retirement asset base is developed.

We also unrealistically assume that individuals successfully maximize their human capital. We do see below that an individual's career flexibility should be considered in the financial plan, but the most obvious means of increasing human capital – increased labor and career management – are beyond the scope of this chapter.

HUMAN CAPITAL RISK MANAGEMENT

During the accumulation phase of life, the principal risks relate to wages, health, and mortality. Wage risk is managed with career management and a maximum savings rate. Because it offers no savings or investment benefit, we consider medical expense insurance as a pure insurance product similar to property and liability coverage of automobiles and homes. In this section, we discuss the insurable risks and the products that can help complete an incomplete savings program for a disabled individual or a deceased breadwinner's family.

As we discuss in Chapter 8, the likelihood of a disability interrupting or ending an individual's ability to earn a living is greater than the likelihood of death. Contributions to retirement plans are suspended more often than not in both employer and voluntary employee funding of defined contribution (DC) plans. Further, while the demand for life insurance is less than the theoretical ideal, the demand for disability income insurance is weaker still. From the normative perspective, disability income insurance is no less important than life insurance in the protection of human capital.

Important considerations include the definitions of disability (own occupation versus any occupation) and the interaction of the elimination period and benefit levels with available savings and premium costs. Product options for addressing inflation risk – additional benefit purchase options and inflation indexed benefits – are also important considerations.

We saw in Chapter 8 that the potential moral hazard associated with disability income insurance – potentially fraudulent claims and delayed career resumption – is significant. As a result, insurers limit the purchase of benefits to amounts less than 100 percent of earnings. Together with the fact that an individual's expenses may rise in the event of disability, disability income insurance generally provides an incomplete – albeit significant – solution to the disability risk. Thus, personal savings is an important element in the treatment of the disability risk.

The importance of protecting human capital from the financial consequences of death is the dominant theme in this text, and its discussion constitutes the greater part of the closing half of this chapter. We emphasize the use of life insurance in the role of protecting human capital during the accumulation phase of life. However, as cash value life insurance incorporates both an insurance element and an investment element, we also cover some of the investment aspects of life insurance in this chapter, as well in Chapter 23. In later chapters, we also discuss the complementary roles of life insurance in estate (Chapter 22) and business planning (Chapter 24).

INVESTMENT CAPITAL RISK MANAGEMENT

A full treatment of the investment portfolio selection and management process is beyond the scope of this text. Most of the theory in this area focuses on a static asset allocation designed for certain or perpetual holding periods without regard to taxes. In personal financial planning, the investment objectives of individuals change substantially over the course of the life cycle, and taxes have a dramatic impact on the financial performance of individual savings. This section examines portfolio issues closely related to human capital. We discuss the importance of the protection of investment capital by minimizing taxes, by planning for the LTC contingency, and by reducing longevity risk through life annuities. We also address the role of investment guarantees in the protection of investment capital.

TAXES AND THE INDIVIDUAL INVESTMENT PORTFOLIO
It is a well accepted premise of financial economics that benefit derives not from what is earned but what from is kept: after-tax results are the only complete measure of financial performance. Qualified plans and life, health, and annuity insurance products provide a variety of tax benefits. Strategies to reduce taxes protect investment capital throughout life by accelerating the value of savings during the accumulation stage of life and retarding the depletion of assets during the liquidation phase. Our discussion is based on tax law in the U.S.

Importance of Considering Taxes
Figure 20-3 shows a conceptual comparison of distributable after-tax funds for hypothetical accumulation accounts featuring the impact of the deductibility of contributions, the deferral of tax on product and plan accumulation, and the inclusion or exclusion of distributions in taxable income. Each of these features may sometimes apply to life and health insurance premiums, earnings, and benefits and to tax qualified retirement plans. The illustration demonstrates the significant economic impact of taxation on the future after-tax value of $1,000 of pretax earnings.

Figure 20-3   **$1,000 Pretax Income Taxed, Contributed, Accumulated and Distributed Under Different Tax Treatment Assumptions, Hypothetical Accumulation Accounts, 40% Marginal Tax Rate, 10 Year Accumulation, 5% Pretax Interest**

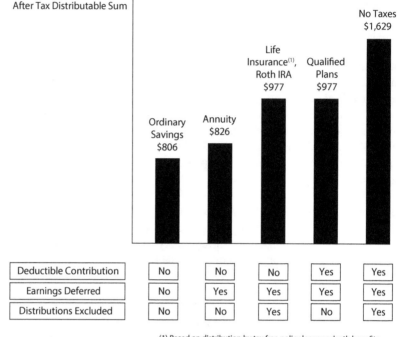

Deductible Contribution	No	No	No	Yes	Yes
Earnings Deferred	No	Yes	Yes	Yes	Yes
Distributions Excluded	No	No	Yes	No	Yes

(1) Based on distribution by tax free policy loans or death benefits.

The values in the figure are derived by taking the after-tax value of the $1,000 contribution as the starting point. Thus, if the contribution is tax deductible, its after-tax value *is* $1,000. If the contribution is not tax deductible, its after-tax value is $600 – $1,000 less the 40 percent tax paid on the $1,000 of taxable income. Hence, for an individual whose maximum tax bracket is 40 percent, the ultimate economic benefit of a $1,000 contribution to a product or plan invested for 10 years at 5.0 percent produces an ultimate distributable after-tax amount ranging from $806 for nonqualified savings to $1,629 for a product or plan that features premium or contribution deductibility, deferral of current income tax on accumulations, and tax free distribution of proceeds.

The taxation of insurance products is discussed in detail in Chapter 21, and qualified plans are discussed in Chapter 23. Briefly, the tax treatment of the following plans and products are:

- Ordinary fixed-income savings do not feature deductibility or deferral of income tax.
- Long term capital gain assets feature deferral of taxable income and a favorable tax rate on sale.
- Ordinary nonqualified annuity premiums and Roth Individual Retirement Account (IRA) contributions are not deductible and earnings are tax deferred (or, with Roths, can be tax free). Distributions under

annuities in excess of total premiums are taxable proportionately over the distribution period beginning at age 59½ and under Roth IRA distributions can be tax free if certain conditions are met.

- IRAs, qualified retirement plans (both defined benefit [DB] and defined contribution [DC]), and qualified annuities feature deductible contributions and the deferral of tax during the accumulation period. Distributions are taxed as ordinary income.
- Individual medical expense insurance premiums are deductible to the extent total medical expenses exceed 10.0 percent of adjusted gross income. Benefits are paid income-tax free.
- Individual disability income insurance premiums are not deductible, earnings during the accumulation period are effectively tax deferred via the insurer's discounting of premiums for expected interest (although no pre-claim distribution is possible), and benefits are income-tax free. Employer-paid disability income premiums are deductible to the employer or business owner, earnings during the accumulation period are treated effectively the same as under individual policies, and benefits are subject to ordinary income tax. Any premiums paid by the employee are not deductible, but benefits proportional to the employee's premium are received tax free.
- Long term care insurance premiums are deductible to the extent total medical expenses exceed 10.0 percent of adjusted gross income. Premiums are discounted by the insurer so accumulation is effectively tax free. Benefits are received income tax free, subject to limits.
- Premiums paid for qualified individual life insurance policies are not tax deductible, earnings are tax deferred, and distribution via the death benefit is income tax free to beneficiaries. Lifetime distributions via withdrawals are income-tax free up to the policy's tax basis, and policy loans are income tax-free to the policyowner provided the policy is not a modified endowment contract (see Chapter 21).

Tax Efficient Portfolios The preceding discussion of taxation provides a theoretical justification for the construction of a savings program that takes maximum advantage of tax benefits. While the justification may be ideal from a tax perspective, other considerations play an important part. These include the gross costs of qualified plans and insurance products, including sales commission and administrative charges. Additional considerations are the individual's subjective opinion of his or her own mortality, tolerance of risk, available economic resources, bequest motives, and liquidity requirements.

The first consideration in savings usually should be the creation and maintenance of an emergency fund. Investment return and tax considerations are less important than liquidity for emergency funds. Thus, the emergency fund is usually invested in cash or other highly liquid short term instruments (sometimes termed *cash equivalents* or *near cash*). Some practitioners believe that too much importance is attached to liquidity for emergency funds and that increased yields secured by sacrificing some liquidity are justified. Life insurance and annuity cash values seem an appropriate compromise.

For longer-term savings, generally, the most tax efficient investment vehicles are qualified plans because they feature both deductibility of contributions and the deferral of taxation during the accumulation period. The amount that can be contributed, however, is limited by the statutes that authorize the plans.

Premiums for life insurance and nonqualified annuities are not deductible. Like qualified plans they feature tax deferral, and, unlike qualified plans, they provide for an *unlimited* amount of contribution and subsequent accumulation free from income tax.

Passive nonqualified fixed income investments generally feature no tax benefits. Long term capital gain assets feature the deferral of current tax and favorable tax rates on sale. *From a tax perspective only*, therefore, individual savings would be prioritized into a hierarchy of savings plans and products:

- First, an emergency fund composed of cash or equivalents or suitable substitutes should be established or identified.
- Maximum permitted contributions to qualified plans should be made.
- While qualified plan limits will accommodate the savings plans of most individuals, the balance of savings should be devoted to annuities or cash value life insurance, if death benefit protection is otherwise needed. If the insured survives the accumulation phase of life, life insurance cash values can be converted to investment assets.
- Taxable investments should be made only when liquidity or other required considerations cannot be addressed with qualified plans or products. Long-term capital gain assets should be emphasized.

Figure 20-4 presents a graphical illustration of tax efficient accumulation and distribution of investment capital over the course of the life cycle.

The most tax efficient portfolio is not necessarily the most practical or best portfolio. Nevertheless, other considerations aside, the contribution of tax benefits to the financial performance of individual savings dominates the marginal benefits of careful product selection, asset allocation, and portfolio management. The reasons for any departure from a tax efficient paradigm, therefore, should be compelling.

PROTECTING INVESTMENT CAPITAL   As retirement approaches and the value of an individual's human capital declines, the investment portfolio should ideally become less volatile and more liquid. **Volatility** is the deviation of actual from average returns. Asset allocation commonly should reflect a declining tolerance for risk by an increased emphasis on fixed-income investments.

Dynamic asset allocation can be accomplished by active portfolio management in a professionally or self-managed portfolio. As discussed in Chapter 23, life style, life cycle, and target value funds provide dynamic asset allocation with professional management and the other benefits of mutual fund intermediation. These funds are available from mutual fund companies; life insurers also offer these fund types in variable annuities, life insurance, and qualified defined contribution plans.

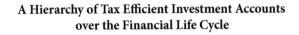

**A Hierarchy of Tax Efficient Investment Accounts
over the Financial Life Cycle**

Figure 20-4

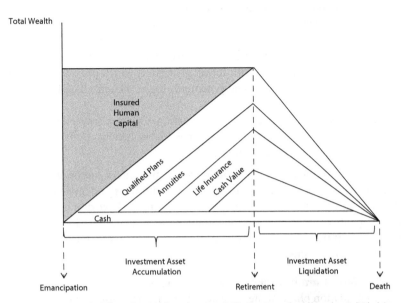

Note: The magnitude of plans and products is not drawn to scale. The importance of each depends on individual circumstances.

Use of Investment Guarantees   As discussed in Chapters 3, 4, 5, and 6, life insurers offer investment guarantees that protect investment capital from loss during both the accumulation and liquidation phases of life. These guarantees accelerate the accumulation of assets and retard the depletion of assets being liquidated. General account (non-variable) life insurance and annuity products offer minimum long-term guarantees for life that are not available from other financial institutions. Life insurance products can offer equity index options and no-lapse guarantees that protect cash values and death benefits from capital loss; annuities offer equity and inflation index options with similar benefits. While fees are charged for these guarantees, equity index products offer the potential for investment gains based on superior market performance, and inflation index products protect inflation adjusted, real returns (within limits).

Variable annuities offer a variety of tax-free account guarantee options. Only life insurers offer investment guarantees in a tax-deferred environment in unlimited amounts for the whole of life. Certain guarantees protect capital from premature depletion due to investment performance or inflation, including:

- The guaranteed minimum accumulation benefit, which provides that the annuity account value will not fall below the amount invested.
- Equity index annuities, which provide for participation in the gains of an equity market index with a guarantee of no principal loss.
- Inflation index annuities, which provide for investment credits tied to an inflation index up to certain, reasonably liberal limits.

Other guarantees protect capital from premature depletion by bundling longevity and investment guarantees, including:

- The guaranteed minimum withdrawal guarantee, which provides for minimum withdrawals of a maximum percentage each year with the total equal to an amount not less than the sum of premiums paid and potentially higher benefits based on investment performance.
- The guaranteed lifetime withdrawal guarantee, which provides for minimum withdrawals for life and potentially higher benefits based on investment performance.
- The guaranteed minimum income benefit, which guarantees a minimum rate of return and payment and can pay higher benefits if market performance exceeds the minimum guarantee.

Some aspects of the investment and longevity guarantees can be attached to mutual funds and managed private account funds with the stand alone or contingent deferred annuity discussed in Chapter 6. In Chapter 23, we discuss the diversification benefits of fixed and variable annuities with guarantees in a portfolio context, as well as the costs (fees and opportunity costs in a rising equity market or low inflation environment).

Use of Long Term Care Insurance   Care risk represents a significant exposure during the liquidation phase of life, when disability income insurance is generally not available. Care expenses can disrupt the orderly liquidation and sufficiency of investment capital by depleting an individual's investment assets quickly. LTC insurance is designed to reduce this risk and to protect the sufficiency of investment capital after retirement. Medicare provides only limited benefits for long term care.

As discussed in Chapter 21, LTC insurance offers deductible premiums when premiums and other medical expenses total more than 10.0 percent of adjusted gross income. LTC riders attached to annuities (Chapter 6), by contrast, effectively make premiums fully deductible because charges assessed in the tax deferred account are not treated as taxable distributions. (Because the annuity basis is reduced by the charges, in the event the policyowner/insured never incurs a long term care claim, the charges are effectively recaptured in whole or in part during the liquidation of the annuity.)

Use of Life Annuities   The final challenge in managing financial risk over the life cycle is ensuring that the individual's investment capital lasts as long as the individual's life. Chapter 6 discussed life annuities that protect investment capital from premature depletion due to an extraordinarily long life. Chapter 23 discusses the role of life annuities in retirement decisions.

Longevity risk management options designed to protect investment capital have become numerous in this century. The spectrum includes guarantees of life incomes through:

- investment guarantees,
- lifetime withdrawal benefits,
- inflation index annuities,
- equity-indexed annuities,

- contingent deferred annuities that attach lifetime withdrawal and minimum return benefits to stand alone investment portfolios, and
- longevity annuities that provide guaranteed income at significantly advanced ages in return for significantly discounted current premiums.

INVESTMENT CAPITAL RISK AND LIFE INSURANCE   When a life insurance program is needed, it should be implemented in the most appropriate cost efficient structure. The requisite insurance should be acquired on a basis that minimizes the conversion of investment capital to insurance costs, subject to sound mortality risk management. Chapter 19 discussed the buy-term-and-invest-the-difference strategy, in which investment and insurance elements of cash value policies can be replicated through a combination of the purchase of term insurance and a systematic savings program. For the purposes of this discussion, however, we assume a life insurance need for which cash value insurance is appropriate.

Cash value life insurance is a long-term financial instrument. Its financial performance affects both the death benefit and the potential use of cash values during life. Death benefits may increase over time with the performance of cash values or separate accounts, and dividends can be used to supplement the death benefit of par whole life (WL) policies. If the insured survives the accumulation phase of life, cash values may be available to fund retirement during the asset liquidation phase, as discussed in Chapter 23.

The most fundamental investment consideration in cash value life insurance is the decision whether to purchase a traditional general account policy or a variable, separate account product. Each has advantages and disadvantages. The general account policy offers minimum guaranteed returns that resemble the less volatile, lower risk, and stable income qualities of a bond fund as compared to the higher risk associated with equity investments. The investment returns are paid exclusively in the form of regular current interest credits to policy value, so the tax deferral benefits of the policy are maximized as compared to fixed income investments made in a taxable account. The fixed income nature, however, exposes policy performance to the risks of inflation and higher market interest rates. (Interest credits may rise over time with market interest rates, but the insurer's portfolio returns and its ability and willingness to increase interest credits generally lag the market because of the long term nature of most of its investments.)

Variable policies offer potentially superior inflation-adjusted real returns. Because life insurance is long term, the increased volatility of equity investments is better tolerated. Variable policies also offer the options of bond funds or the insurer's general account during times of market uncertainty, thus offering the flexibility to largely replicate the benefits of traditional general account policies. The tax benefits of deferral when accounts are invested in equity funds are somewhat less important as a significant portion of equity returns may be attributable to long-term capital gains. As discussed above, long-term capital gains themselves feature deferral and ultimate taxation at low rates.

While it is impossible to determine in advance that any life insurance structure will definitively produce the best result for any individual, it is important to understand the taxation, risk, return, and time horizon of the structure. The options of term insurance, taxable investment funds, traditional WL, variable universal life, etc., can be considered in the context of investment capital management and its interaction and correlation with human capital. The goal is to minimize the cost of protecting human capital while optimizing the risk and return relationship of both human and investment capital.

CORRELATION BETWEEN HUMAN CAPITAL AND INVESTMENT CAPITAL

Portfolio theory takes account of the relative weights, volatility, and correlations of individual securities.[1] In PFP, the relative weight, volatility, and correlation of the human capital component of the economic wealth portfolio should be considered in the allocation of the investment capital component of the economic wealth portfolio.

Volatility can be measured historically or applied prospectively as the *expected* volatility of the *expected* return. More volatility is usually associated with the higher returns of equity investments compared to bond investments. Volatility is more tolerable in longer investment holding periods as the deviations from expected returns become smaller relative to the long term average; it is less tolerable as the need for liquidity increases. Diversification among uncorrelated investments reduces volatility. As a general rule, then, the investment portfolio should be devoted increasingly to less volatile, more diversified, and more liquid investments as retirement and the asset liquidation phase of life approaches.

Like investment capital, human capital can exhibit volatility. Some occupations feature a high probability of job security and salaried compensation that is predictable. Teaching positions are often associated with these properties. Human capital in low volatility occupations exhibits bond-like properties: a stream of predictable income. These occupations also feature a measure of inflation protection as compensation can be expected to increase with the general rate of inflation.

Other professions exhibit volatility akin to equities. Examples might include commissioned insurance salespersons, investment brokers, and property developers. Compensation in these occupations can vary widely from period to period. (Workers who have the flexibility to change jobs can effectively reduce the risks of income volatility and job security.)

The volatility of economic wealth is the weighted volatility of human and investment capital volatility. The volatility of human capital can be correlated with the volatility of investment capital. The allocation of investment assets should be decided with consideration for the interaction of human and investment capital. Thus, during the preretirement accumulation of investment assets, those with low wage income volatility should be able to tolerate the higher expected returns and volatility of a portfolio devoted significantly to equity investments. By contrast, high volatility earners should be more interested in low volatility investments, such as bonds.

The correlation of human and investment capital volatility and performance should be considered in two respects. First, the compensation of stockbrokers, portfolio managers, investment bankers, senior corporate executives, and many others can be closely correlated to the performance of the stock market. An objective analysis suggests diversification through an investment portfolio devoted largely to bonds and other non-equity instruments.

In addition to the correlation of human capital to the equities market in general, human capital is often highly correlated to the performance of individual securities when employees are invested in the securities of their employer. Executive stock options and 401(k) matching programs are sources of correlation. Negative events can become catastrophic when they affect both human and financial capital simultaneously.

Some individuals in the finance profession may feel that they have superior knowledge of the equity markets that overrides their need for diversification, yet few would have predicted that the U.S. stock markets would have posted no significant gains for the first decade of this century. Thousands of employees at Enron and WorldCom lost their jobs and much of their life savings at the same time when the firms became insolvent, and virtually all would have viewed as unthinkable the sequence of events that led to their situation just months before the troubles played out.

Diversification away from employer securities can be difficult. Stock options and matching programs typically require minimum holding periods. Senior executives face a further potential constraint as the sale of their employer securities is publicly reported, and the sale itself can sometimes affect the value of shares. The employer contribution to the employee's value in these plans certainly mitigates some of the increased risk of the mandatory investment concentration. Nevertheless, diversification should be considered whenever it is possible.

In summary, younger workers, workers with stable income and job security, and workers with the flexibility to change employment easily should be more tolerant of the higher returns and volatility associated with equities. Workers with volatile incomes or incomes highly correlated to the equities markets should be invested more in bonds and like securities. Finally, employees should reduce their holdings in employer securities when possible.

PERSONAL FINANCIAL PLANNING ADVICE

PFP advice is available to individuals from a variety of specialists: attorneys, accountants, stock brokers, insurance agents, and others.[2] PFP advice is also available from financial planners who offer generalized financial advice and often coordinate the services of other professionals. Some financial advisors are independent and compensated exclusively with fees. They are perhaps more objective, but they are few in number and can be expensive. Most PFP recommendations tend to reflect the source of advice. Those whose primary attachment is to investment companies focus more on investments, and those whose primary attachment is to insurance companies focus more on insurance. Financial advice is further complicated because many institutions provide both investment and insurance services and products.

The individual chooses between two PFP delivery models: assimilating and coordinating the services of many specialists (the specialist model) or delegating that responsibility to a financial planner (the planner model). Figure 20-5 presents an organizational flow chart of each model.

PFP is complex. Both the planning process and the products and services required to implement a successful plan are not completely understood or accessible to most consumers. As a result, individuals typically rely on the advice of others. While we focus on professional advisers, intuition suggests the most important financial advice for many individuals is solicited from trusted and respected relatives and acquaintances. (Life insurance agents have long sought referrals from these types of individuals, termed *centers of influence*.) The complexity of PFP appears to increase in our contemporary environment as employers abandon DB retirement plans for DC plans, and government is perceived to be a less important source of benefits (see Chapter 23). More responsibility thus rests with individuals.

Figure 20-5   **Personal Financial Planning Delivery Models**

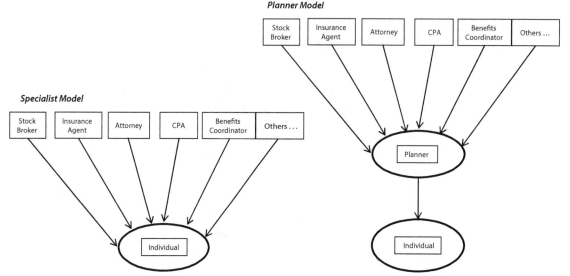

Source: Kenneth Black, Jr., Conrad S. Ciccotello, Harold D. Skipper, Jr., "Issues in Comprehensive Personal Financial Planning," Financial Services Review, Vol. 11 (2002).

Whether intentional or not, individuals who do not seek the services of a financial planner adopt the specialist model, which requires them to assimilate and coordinate the advice of many advisers. These individuals look to insurance agents for insurance advice, stock brokers or mutual fund representatives for investment advice, attorneys for estate planning, etc. While specialists certainly can be expected to offer superior advice in their respective professions, three distinct disadvantages attach to the specialist model.

The first is the conflict of interest arising from agency problems. Despite the insistence of the primacy of the client interest in the formal standards of conduct for virtually every profession and the good faith efforts of individual practitioners to subscribe to this principle, economic incentives are often inconsistent with the client's best interest. Insurance agents earn more when the client purchases more insurance than stocks; brokers earn more when the client purchases more stocks and bonds than insurance. Commissions are not the sole source of agency problems: a fee-based adviser like an attorney earns more when an estate plan is more complex and requires more documents.

The first problem is exacerbated by the second: asymmetric information problems. The complexity of financial products and services makes both the superior knowledge of the specialist adviser (having perhaps spent a career learning the profession) and his or her information advantage relative to the client inevitable.

The final problem we discern in the specialist model is the lack of coordination (or stated differently, the difficulty of self-coordination) of the various products and services. Investment decisions ideally should not be made without regard to insurance ownership and possibilities. Estate plans should not be implemented without an understanding of the liquidity properties of the estate. In the context of this chapter – taking account of the importance of the interrelationship of the risks of human and investment capital – the coordination of insurance and investments takes on special significance. (Among specialists, insurance agents should have a natural affinity for this set of issues as their products alone address the protection of both the human and investment capital components of personal wealth.)

The planner coordination model, by contrast, *theoretically* should offer (1) economies of scope in product and service consumption, (2) reduced information costs, and (3) lower monitoring costs. When agency, information, or competency problems arise, however, these costs can be exacerbated because the effect may be systematic, extending to multiple facets of the financial plan.

Economies of scope exist if multiple products and services can be procured at a lower cost than the sum of the costs of the individual products and services procured separately. A comprehensive view of products and services – and human and investment capital – can offer economies of scope in the consumption of products and services. As an example, efficient planning avoids the duplication of benefits. A planner, for example, may offer the best available independent advice for most individuals to coordinate their life insurance plans with employment related group insurance and retirement plan death benefits.

An effective planner model should reduce information costs. The planner deals with the various professional advisers regularly and usually should be better able to screen both their qualifications and their advice for an appropriate application to the client's requirements. In this context, the planner's expertise should reduce the informational advantage of the specialists. Further, planner referrals result in the supervision of selected specialists; horizontal referrals from specialist to specialist are less likely to result in supervision.

In the specialist model, the individual is required to screen and monitor multiple advisers for their qualifications and continuing advice. By retaining a planner, the individual's qualification efforts are focused on one adviser. The benefit of reduced monitoring costs in the planner model, however, is linked to the potentially systematic effect of agency and information costs incurred in the planner relationship.

Like specialist advice, planner advice is not disinterested. Planners who sell products for commissions are clearly subject to the same conflicts of interest and other issues as commission-based specialists, and most planners sell financial products. Planners who are compensated by fees only may not have an economic interest in particular products or services, but they do earn more as the complexity of a client's position increases along with the time required to devise and maintain the plan, and they are in a position to influence the complexity of the plan. Further, because professionals rely on each other for referrals as a principal marketing strategy, a fee-based planner may in fact have an implicit interest in particular products or services provided by favored specialist colleagues.

The benefits of the planner model remain theoretical unless and until the individual identifies an appropriate planner. We also note the importance of specialist advice in the planner paradigm. First, even the professional planner is unlikely to possess the same level of competence in each discipline as a full time specialist professional. Second, many specialists are extraordinarily competent in areas outside their specialty, and an outstanding specialist can substitute for a less able generalist.

One of the important screening tools in choosing advisers is their professional qualifications. Earned designations such as the *Certified Financial Planner* (CFP®), the *Chartered Life Underwriter* (CLU®), the *Chartered Financial Consultant* (ChFC®), the *Chartered Property and Casualty Underwriter* (CPCU®), and the *Chartered Financial Analyst* (CFA®) can be important considerations (although not exclusively important). These and other issues in the selection of professional advisers are discussed in more detail in Chapter 17 with an emphasis on life insurance advice.

THE PERSONAL FINANCIAL PLANNING PROCESS

In this section, we set out a paradigm for the financial planning process. In doing so, we make the following assumptions:

1. Individuals seek to maximize lifetime utility through a rational accumulation of assets during the productive working years and a rational liquidation of assets during a self-sufficient retirement.
2. Individuals are price takers in the investment, insurance, and labor markets – they have no market power. Markets dictate the price consumers pay for financial returns and insurance and the price they receive for their labor.
3. The four important determinants of retirement resources are earnings, the price of insurance, the return on investments, and the continuing savings/consumption choice over the entire life cycle.
4. At retirement, the value of assets accumulated during the productive years and the prospective prices of investments and insurance are fixed.
5. The savings and consumption behavior of individuals is the only meaningful determinant of retirement resources that are a matter of the individual's choice.

As a result of these assumptions, we take the view that the set of opportunities that can be realistically expected at retirement is the rational measure of the success of a lifetime financial plan. The principal independent variable is savings behavior, and the principal dependent variable – and the principal indicator of utility viewed over the course of the life cycle – is the set of retirement possibilities that results at retirement. Because savings determines retirement, we view establishing rule-based objectives for either as incomplete.

The process set out below offers a road map to maximizing utility over the course of the financial life cycle. It provides an orderly, systematic approach to planning. It involves five sequential steps. While the steps are presented below as discrete actions to be taken, each step in fact blends into and complements those steps that precede and follow it.

GATHER INFORMATION

The first step in the financial planning process is to assemble relevant quantitative and qualitative information. Relevant financial information varies from situation to situation but usually includes the compilation of cash flow and asset/liability statements. Together these constitute the initial asset base that will grow both by investment performance and the conversion of human capital to investment capital through savings over the course of the accumulation phase of life. Additional information is assembled about existing investments; life, health, and other insurance protection; employee benefits; and the client's tax situation and current estate plans, including documents such as wills and trusts and inheritance prospects. Practitioners usually proceed through a questionnaire or check list.

In addition to quantitative information, qualitative information is sought concerning the individual's interests, lifestyle, attitudes and desires, family situation, risk tolerance, and health and related information that will underlie the individual's objectives. In fact, often at this stage the financial advisor assists the individual in establishing his or her objectives – the second step in the financial planning process.

ESTABLISH OBJECTIVES

We assume that the ultimate objective of planning is to provide for the nonproductive years of retirement while maintaining an appropriate standard of living during the working phase of life. Most households also establish intermediate objectives, in the following priority:

1. provide for food, clothing, shelter, current educational costs, and an acceptable standard of living,
2. provide an emergency fund,
3. insure the value of human capital,
4. establish a fund for future educational costs,
5. establish purpose funds for preretirement goals, e.g.:
   - automobiles
   - new home
   - second home, etc., and
6. add residual free cash flow to retirement savings.

Retirement savings thus becomes a residual function of preretirement consumption and saving choices.

MODEL POTENTIAL FINANCIAL OUTCOMES

The third step in the PFP process involves analyzing the relevant data and objectives to discern ranges of possible financial outcomes under different conditions. This is done most commonly through development or use of some type of financial analysis or model. This process is not simple. The present and future financial condition of individuals and households is highly complex and subject to a wide and nonstandard array of factors. The number of variables and the range of values they can take in the future make any effort to construct a one-size-fits-all model a difficult if not impossible undertaking.

A detailed discussion of PFP modeling is beyond our scope, but we set forth a basic algorithm for PFP. In practice, the algorithm can be implemented with financial spreadsheets adapted to the individual's current financial position and projected into the future. Commercial software packages and online services offering their own algorithms are also available. A planning model is an iterative process. It provides the necessary inputs and assumptions to proceed in sequence to:

- construct asset/liability and expected cash flow statements at the time of planning. In a PFP sense, liabilities include the present value of income needs in addition to mortgages, automobile loans, and the like,
- identify items of recurring income and expense, including the costs of insuring human capital,
- identify contributions to purpose funds,
- model the investment and accumulation of remaining cash,
- project the cash flow and asset/liability statements to retirement age, and
- evaluate the projected retirement cash flow possibilities including the costs of insuring the sufficiency of accumulated investment capital (LTC and annuity insurance). We consider these elements in more detail in Chapter 23.

The process is repeated to grasp the range of results produced under various scenarios. Testing the sensitivity of results to different economic assumptions such as inflation and investment returns is a measure of the realism of the plan; testing the savings and consumption assumptions is a measure of the realism of the individual's resources and expectations. Viewing the effect of changes in the independent variable – savings – on the dependent variable – the set of retirement possibilities – provides insight into the one lifetime determinant that the individual can choose to influence.

THE COMPLEXITY OF FINANCIAL MODELING   Planning for the future necessarily makes the estimation of the future an integral part of PFP. Yet projecting a financial position many years into the future is subject to considerable uncertainty. First, future economic conditions are unknowable. Wages, interest rates, investment returns on various classes of investments, inflation, and other variables affect the value of both human and investment capital and the impact of unemployment, death, or disability. A wide range of possible scenarios could reasonably be anticipated.

Additionally, if annual projections are made over a reasonable range of economic assumptions and variables through, say, age 100 for each spouse, the resulting data would literally be beyond human comprehension. It is therefore impractical and ultimately unnecessary to project all possible results. Several factors mitigate the importance of information lost due to the impracticality of examining all scenarios.

First, because of correlations, assumptions about inflation, wages, interest rates, and equity returns can be made with some consistency. Choosing one inflation rate scenario is unrealistic, but because of the correlation, if the inflation assumption proves to be too low, it is likely that the unexpectedly high cost of living expense that results will be offset by unexpected high wages and investment returns. As the natural inflation hedge that competitive wages provide disappears after retirement, the importance of planning for inflation during the liquidation period is magnified. Most inflation, interest rate, other investment, and wage assumptions can reasonably be expected to be positively correlated.

Second, because of the uncertainty involved in projecting human and economic conditions many years into the future, much of the information that is not captured by an incomplete projection would be of questionable value anyway. The reader is reminded of the multiple scenarios faced by life insurers and the discussion in Chapters 9 and 14 of the application of value at risk and Monte Carlo concepts to risk management. The application of probability concepts to individuals is less helpful because (1) unlike an insurer, the individual cannot average mortality, morbidity, longevity, and wage results and (2) most individuals prefer to eliminate rather than minimize the probability of extreme results.

TESTING SCENARIOS WITH THE FINANCIAL MODEL   The financial model should produce a future estimated asset/liability position that defines the individual's set of retirement opportunities. These opportunities should be tested against the retirement financial model. (We discuss the environment for retirement planning in Chapter 23. The financial environment in retirement differs considerably from the working life environment.)

Test results help the individual evaluate the quality of life that can be expected at retirement. To the extent the results are unsatisfactory, different expectations about the standard of living, the education fund, and any special purpose funds should be examined. The impact to lifetime utility of savings and consumption choices undertaken during the asset accumulation phase of life can be evaluated by judging the effect on the set of retirement possibilities. The process is repeated until a satisfactory balance of consumption, spending, and retirement possibilities is identified.

Testing does not necessarily produce a satisfactory lifetime result. An unsatisfactory result, however, describes the economizing problem with some precision. The individual is able to see the limits of his or her expected resources. The amount of consumption that can be reduced and the amount of free cash flow that can be generated are limited by the minimum costs of daily living and the value of human capital.

Options to improve the individual's lifetime utility in these circumstances are outside the scope of PFP. They do not exist in the area of savings or careful investment and insurance management. The only options really are to increase the value of human capital or increase investment returns. More free cash flow can be created through a career change or devoting more time to labor through increased hours, second jobs, or the entry of a nonworking spouse into the labor force. Increased investment returns should be available only by assuming increased risk; caution is advisable in this direction as increased risk by definition may be as likely to reduce the retirement asset base as it is to increase it.

DEVELOP AND IMPLEMENT PLAN

Once consumption and savings parameters have been established through the modeling effort, the sequence of events required to implement the plan should be developed. After the budget is established, the most important components are the implementation of the insurance, investment, and legal arrangements.

Life, health, and property insurance in appropriate amounts should be arranged through the services of qualified specialists. As we discuss below, life insurance may be required for purposes in addition to the protection of human capital as determined in the financial model. Business, estate, debt, and bequest needs may be essential to the plan.

An investment plan should be implemented that takes account of issues discussed earlier in this chapter, including:

- the correlation of the volatility of human and investment capital,
- a decreasing exposure to risk as retirement approaches,
- maximizing the tax efficiency of investments, and
- subject to these constraints, the application of professional portfolio management skills to accumulating investments with appropriate risk.

Finally, documents such as wills, trusts, and powers of attorney should provide for legal contingencies. If the services of a financial planner are used, the planner likely will be closely involved in identifying specialist advisers and coordinating their activities. The planner will also manage the implementation process in conjunction with his or her client.

MONITOR AND REVISE PLAN

The final step in the PFP process is that results should be monitored to ascertain the extent to which they are compatible with initial expectations. If they are not, changes may be needed. In addition to the need for revisions occasioned by results deviating from expectations, revisions also will be necessitated by tax and other environmental changes and by the client's changing financial fortunes, family situation, and goals and objectives.

DETERMINING THE TOTAL PERSONAL INSURANCE NEED

The death or permanent disability of an individual destroys the value of human capital. Because human capital is required to maintain an expected standard of living and complete a life cycle savings plan, life and disability insurance capital usually are required as standby substitutes for human capital. Additional capital may be required at death for other purposes.

An individual's total life insurance need is the sum of the amounts needed to (1) substitute investment capital for human capital, (2) satisfy cash requirements at death, and (3) provide capital for desired bequests. We cover each below. Additionally, addressing the first need also may require disability income insurance.

HUMAN CAPITAL REQUIREMENTS AT DEATH

The human contingencies of life and health can produce a staggering proliferation of situations that impact household income, household expense, and the value of human capital. In a two-income family, for example, when one spouse dies, multiple succeeding scenarios must be considered. The surviving spouse will (1) work or not, (2) become disabled or not, and (3) die or not. Further, the first spouse may die immediately or at some point in the future, and the surviving spouse's succeeding situations may arise immediately or at some point in the future. These multiple scenarios exist also in the event of the death of the other spouse. Finally, because spouses spend much time together, it is reasonable to examine the possibility that both die or become disabled in the same accident immediately or at some point in the future.

As with economic scenarios, there are reasons that the value of information lost through the use of a simplified examination of human capital scenarios is mitigated. First, some scenarios naturally disappear; it is clearly unnecessary to consider the disability of an individual after her death! Second, objectives are likely to be reevaluated after a dramatic life event such as death or disability. Third, as projections extend further into the future, results become less credible.

However, an individual's death or disability is not generally correlated to economic conditions. Anticipating the loss in human capital resulting from these events is made easier because of the changing natural value of human capital over time. Because (1) the real (inflation adjusted) value of human capital generally declines over time, (2) the real value of remaining lifetime expenses generally also declines over time, and (3) the real value of the unfunded purpose funds declines as contributions are made each year, estimating insurance protection based on assumptions of immediate death and disability may produce a current year real value that exceeds the need in future years. (This observation is limited to the life insurance need respecting human capital; other needs, particularly estate taxes, typically increase over time. They are also more easily estimated. See Chapter 22.)

When inflation is high, however, the present value of human capital can increase in nominal terms. Inflation must be taken into account in determining the nominal amount of insurance coverage and in planning for contingent means to maintain adequate coverage under conditions of increasing prices. The most obvious means are (1) conservatism in the estimation itself and (2) the inflation protection features offered by life and disability insurers. Coverage can also be reduced when less nominal coverage is required.

HUMAN CAPITAL EXPOSURE AND COVERAGE   The present value of an individual's future earnings represents the value of his or her human capital. The present value of the funds required to maintain an appropriate standard of living, complete the funding of purpose funds, and provide for the survivor's retirement years may not be the same as his or her human capital. In Chapter 1 we defined human life value (HLV) as a measure of the future earnings or value of services of an individual – that is, the capitalized value of an individual's future earnings less self-maintenance costs such as food, clothing, and shelter. The HLV concept provides the philosophical basis for systematizing the insurance purchase decision. As an individual's self-maintenance costs including retirement saving needs disappear at death, the value of human capital generally exceeds the HLV. Similarly, both may exceed the capital needs of survivors. Should the amount of insurance coverage address the HLV, the human capital value, or the needs of survivors?

The value of human capital can be segregated into a needs-based component that should be insured and a component that need not be insured. However, individuals often wish to purchase more than the insurable component; when they do, the excess amount by this measure takes on the essential nature of a benevolent bequest. We discuss bequests below.

When the PFP financial model incorporates an estimation of the unfunded living expense and life cycle savings plan, it can form the basis for estimating personal insurance needs. It also reveals the impact of its inflation assumptions on life and disability income insurance needs. The maximum amount of protection indicated between the planning date and the retirement date can reasonably be expected to suffice.

CALCULATING THE HUMAN CAPITAL NEED   Having defined the human capital exposure and the practical precision that can be brought to modeling it in the previous sections, the determination of the insurable amount is straightforward. It is the sum of the present values, discounted at a realistic interest rate, of:

- funds required to maintain an appropriate standard of living,
- unfunded purpose funds whose purposes survive the death of the insured, and
- funds required to complete an appropriate life cycle savings and liquidation program.

CASH REQUIREMENTS AT DEATH

Death gives rise to the need for cash to settle the decedent's affairs. Some cash requirements are inevitable: funeral expenses, estate administration, and, possibly, estate taxes. Other requirements, primarily the liquidation of debts and bequests, are discretionary and functions of individual preference.

Life insurance is commonly used to meet these cash requirements if other sources are unavailable or insufficient. Life insurance also is used to create needed funds when assets are insufficient to address other postmortem requirements. Liquidity is a particular concern in estate and business planning, as we discuss in Chapters 21, 22, and 24. Liquidity needs arising at death can cause the sale of illiquid assets under exigent circumstances. Assets may have to be sold at less than optimal prices because of time constraints.

The most typical cash needs required at the death of an individual are:

- final medical and other illness expense,
- funeral costs,
- probate costs,
- reconstitution of a depleted emergency fund,
- family adjustment funds (e.g., moving expenses or vocational or professional training for a surviving spouse), and
- estate tax and business needs (Chapters 22 and 24).

Cash requirements at death change over time and financial models should accommodate the dynamic properties of these changes. For example, estate taxes, if applicable, usually increase (or appear) over time.

CONSIDERATION OF BEQUESTS AT DEATH

In determining the need for life insurance, we began above with the theoretical object of substituting investment capital for human capital. In the absence of a bequest motive, the amount of life insurance acquired on a breadwinner's life should be just sufficient to satisfy child-rearing responsibilities and provide a life income for the spouse (taking account of his or her earnings). This focus on a utility maximizing objective implies that, in a well planned estate where consumption has indeed been smoothed, the surviving spouse's last dollar of assets will have been consumed at death, with nothing left to bequeath. Under this scenario, any property transferred to heirs would be an accidental bequest, occurring because the individual died before his or her assets were fully consumed.

Yet, individuals routinely die with a positive net worth, thereby leaving a bequest. For some, the bequest is certainly "accidental." For many others, the bequest is intended and even planned. In other words, individuals often desire to preserve parts of their wealth to be able to provide funds to heirs beyond that which is necessary for human capital replacement purposes. They also often wish to provide funds for others, including charities, educational institutions, friends, and relatives.

Evidence for presumably intentional bequests via life insurance is abundant. As individuals age, both their human capital and their need for life insurance to replace it decrease. Yet, many people do not decrease the amount of their life insurance as they age, or terminate it at the time that their human capital and cash needs would objectively be fully funded via their investment assets. By continuing such insurance, these individuals are sacrificing current consumption to be able to provide bequests in the form of life insurance death proceeds.

As we have seen in previous chapters, individuals do not purchase annuities in the amounts that the utility hypothesis suggests. In the absence of a desire to provide support for survivors or bequests, rational individuals theoretically would invest 100 percent of their assets in life annuities. This is so for two interrelated reasons. First, the individual is thereby assured of not outliving his or her assets. With other financial instruments, the only means by which the individual can be assured of not outliving his or her wealth is to risk "wasting" some of it in the form of an accidental bequest.

Second, the life annuity payout will be greater, other things being the same, than that which could be realized with any other financial instrument, because some of each annuity payment is composed of a benefit-of-survivorship element, which is not found with other instruments (see Chapter 6). This is true at any age (albeit only marginally so at younger ages) and is also true no matter how long the annuitant lives. The level of consumption during life is higher despite the fact that the present value received by an annuitant who dies soon after the annuity purchase is small relative to the amount invested. The unconsumed wealth that remained with the insurer would not have been consumed in the absence of the annuity either. It would have been an accidental bequest had it been retained.

Several theories have been suggested to explain the bequest motive. Some have suggested strategic motives – individuals use the promise of life insurance or other benefits to influence the behavior of beneficiaries during the benefactor's life. Some suggest beneficiaries themselves are an important determinant of demand by influencing the life insurance purchase decision. Affection and devotion to one's heirs are perhaps the most intuitive explanations. The law has long referred to family beneficiaries under a will as the "natural objects of the testator's bounty." Finally, many people are motivated by a desire to contribute philanthropically. (Some life insurance agents specialize in charitable life insurance sales, and most philanthropic organizations incorporate a planned giving function designed to encourage contributions through life insurance and other estate plans.)

In the context of the life cycle utility hypothesis, we must conclude that the bequest motive, in addition to the human capital motive, is a source of utility. Individuals derive satisfaction from preserving part of their wealth for their heirs or philanthropy. Thus, the bequest motive is an important consideration in PFP.

For individuals whose life cycle utility is promoted by bequests, life insurance can be used in two ways. First, policies can be purchased for the benefit of specified individuals, charities, or other beneficiaries. Second, an amount of life insurance greater than that necessary to substitute for human capital can be purchased. Agents often follow one of two approaches in recommending the amount of life insurance to purchase, and different approaches apply to each with regard to bequests.

First, the **capital liquidation approach** to the life insurance need determination derives a needed life insurance amount by assuming that both the life insurance death benefit (capital) and interest earned thereon are liquidated to complete the surviving household or spousal life plan. (The purchase of a life annuity is an example of complete liquidation.) With this approach, an identifiable amount can be added to the determined insurance amount to account for the bequest.

Second, the **capital retention approach** derives an amount of life insurance to satisfy the income objective for a surviving spouse and family by assuming that the interest earned on life insurance death proceeds will alone be sufficient to meet the objective, with the life insurance death benefit retained and ultimately transferred to heirs when its income-producing role has been fulfilled. This transfer on later death becomes the bequest.

Of course, the segregation of capital from income can be adjusted to partially retain capital. Also, a life insurance purchase for an amount exceeding the human capital substitution requirement can serve as a margin for conservatism, adding additional security to the surviving spouse and a provision for heirs can be considered a contingent or subsidiary purpose to be satisfied if the additional capital is not required during the surviving spouse's life.

The cost of the total life insurance need (human capital protection, cash requirements at death, and bequests) is an input to the individual's budget. The PFP model is necessarily circular. It is impossible to determine a budget without the cost of insurance, and it is impossible to know the insurance need without a budget.

Because of the inherent uncertainty in the assumptions driving the PFP model, no practical value is added by a precise mathematical solution. The best practical result is realized when the insurance need is determined approximately and conservatively as with the assumptions used to calculate it.

Conclusions

Personal financial planning is a multidisciplinary approach to systematically converting the individual's human capital to investment capital and protecting both from the risks that could preclude the realization of utility maximization over the life cycle. Life and health insurance products are the only means of protecting human capital during the accumulation phase of life and the sufficiency of investment capital during the liquidation stage of life. Risks should be evaluated in a portfolio context, taking account of the interrelationship of human and investment capital. The process itself promotes a rational organization of the individual's financial management.

Endnotes

1   This section draws on Roger G. Ibbotson, Moshe A. Milevsky, Peng Chen, and Kevin X. Zhu, "Human Capital, Asset Allocation and Life Insurance," *Financial Analysts Journal,* Vol. 62., No.1 (2006).

2   This section draws on Kenneth Black, Jr., Conrad S. Ciccotello, Harold D. Skipper, Jr., "Issues in Comprehensive Personal Financial Planning," *Financial Services Review,* Vol. 11 (2002).

CHAPTER 21

LIFE AND HEALTH INSURANCE PRODUCT TAXATION

Chapter 20 emphasized the importance of taxation to financial instruments within a personal financial planning context, including taxation of life and health insurance products. It also offered a short overview of such taxation to emphasize this key point. This chapter begins a two-chapter sequence that explores in detail the tax treatment of life and health insurance contracts relating, as appropriate, to their premiums, cash values, and amounts paid during life and at death. In this chapter, we explore the U.S. federal income tax treatment attaching to such policies. Chapter 22 explores the estate and gift taxation of life insurance and its uses in an estate planning context. While the focus is on U.S. tax law, the underlying tax and economic principles and many of the practices apply internationally. As will be seen, the design of life and health insurance products is greatly influenced by their taxation, and products designed to comply with federal income tax law enjoy favorable tax treatment.

In 1895, the United States *Supreme Court* ruled the federal taxation of certain types of income – which presumably encompassed income related to life insurance and annuity contracts – to be unconstitutional and unlawful.[1] In response, Congress passed and, by 1913, the states ratified the Sixteenth Amendment to the U.S. Constitution, which broadened the powers of the Congress to tax income "from whatever source derived. . . ." A later Court ruling made clear that Congress had the authority to tax *any increase in wealth* from whatever source derived unless it was specifically exempted – as the Congress has done with regard to life insurance death proceeds and other aspects of life, health, and annuity taxation.[2]

U.S. income tax is executed under the provisions of the *Internal Revenue Code* (IRC or Code). The *Internal Revenue Service* (IRS) is responsible for the administration and collection of the income tax. Three important features distinguish the taxation of income associated with life and health insurance products. First, because of what Congress has judged to be significant contribution of life and health insurance products to social welfare, they are accorded favorable treatment under the IRC. Financial returns from insurance policies in the form of benefits in particular are afforded special treatment as Congress intends to provide incentives

BACKGROUND

to those who wish to use their personal means to protect their financial security from the risks of life, health, and longevity.

Second, Congress generally intends to extend the favorable tax treatment to funds that are saved for the purpose of purchasing insurance protection, although, interestingly, not to the direct purchase of coverage via term policies. Thus, the interest credited – the so-called *inside interest build-up* – on prepaid mortality costs within life insurance and prepaid morbidity costs within health insurance policies enjoy favorable taxation. Congress has largely intended to extend the favorable tax treatment *only* for the prepayment of insurance protection.

Third, the industry has long been characterized by entrepreneurial innovation that seeks to expand the sale of insurance products that satisfy the letter of the tax law while promoting investment benefits unintended by Congress, often through the conversion of tax-preferred prefunded insurance costs into disposable investment income. While the Code sanctions this conversion in some respects, the challenge before the Congress and the IRS has been to limit tax preferences to those product features that promote the intended incentives to insure and to distinguish insurance products from other taxable investments.[3]

LIFE AND HEALTH INSURANCE PRODUCT TAXATION FUNDAMENTALS

Several fundamental concepts are necessary to understand the income taxation of life and health insurance products. The Code begins by applying the income tax to the concept of *gross income* and defines it as all income "from whatever source derived." *Taxable income* is generally defined by certain adjustments to gross income in the form of exclusions, deductions, and deferrals.

Some income is referred to as *exempt* income based on the character of the income – e.g., municipal bond interest – or the status of the recipient – e.g., a qualified nonprofit or charitable organization. Other items of income are effectively exempt because they can be excluded or deducted from gross income.

Exclusions are income items specified in the Code that need not be included in deriving gross income, as well as income items that are not *received* as that term has been interpreted. Life insurance death benefits are an important exclusion. *Deductions* are expenditures as denoted in the Code that may be subtracted from gross income, such as business contributions to qualified retirement plans. *Income deferral* is the permissible delay allowed by the Code in including otherwise taxable income in gross income with regard to certain tax favored instruments, such as qualified retirement plans, life insurance policies, and annuities. (Income may also be deferred through planning strategies such as nonqualified deferred compensation plans where the employee defers actual or constructive receipt of income as discussed in Chapter 24.) Deferred income is not taxed currently but is generally taxed at the time of distribution. Investment earnings compound and accumulate tax free during the deferral period and significantly increase the after-tax amount that can be distributed in the future.

The greatest tax advantage is captured, therefore, when contributions toward the purchase of a financial instrument are *deductible*, the earnings on it are *deferred,* and distributions are *excluded* from income. As noted in Chapter 23, qualified plans generally enjoy both deduction and deferral privileges. Personal life insurance, annuity, and health insurance premiums are generally not deductible, but enjoy deferral. (In some cases, as we see in Chapter 23, a savings instrument can be both a qualified plan and an insurance policy; e.g., a 403(b) retirement annuity.)

Distributions are taxed as received, with two exceptions. First, as we see below, life insurance proceeds paid at the death of the insured are received by the beneficiary income tax free. Second, qualified benefits paid under long term care policies are excluded from gross income. Qualified plans and life insurance and annuity products share the deferral privilege, but each has a distinct advantage relative to the other. Qualified plan contributions are deductible while insurance and annuity premiums generally are not. By contrast, qualified plan deductibility and deferral privileges are restricted to limited amounts, while life insurance and annuity contributions and deferral are unlimited. The unlimited aspect of these privileges has been an important factor in the life insurance industry's success in marketing its products to wealthy clients.

In addition to taxing income, the Code also imposes a tax on the net gains resulting from the sale of assets such as stocks, bonds, mutual funds, and real estate. Long term capital gain (LTCG) income is taxed at a lower rate than ordinary income. To qualify for LTCG treatment, assets must have been held for longer than one year; short term capital gains are taxed as ordinary income. Because their internal earnings are deferred from taxation, life and health products generally do not enjoy capital gain treatment if they are terminated prior to maturity – any net gain generally is treated as ordinary income.

Tax rules can cause one form of income to be re-characterized as another form of income. This is a significant advantage to the beneficiaries of life and health insurance policies because many benefit payments are excluded from gross income. Thus, the accumulated interest earnings – the inside buildup – in policy cash values (or implicit earnings in discounted premiums funding future benefits) are effectively converted to an excluded form of income when death benefits are paid tax free. Conversely, when distributions from life insurance and annuity policies are made in the form of cash surrender benefits, conversion can work partially to the disadvantage of the policyowner. Whatever policy earnings might have been attributable to LTCGs are converted to ordinary income. On the other hand, as explained below, the policyowner is allowed to include cost of insurance (COI) charges in his or her tax basis, thereby converting what otherwise should be ordinary income into excluded income.

Withdrawals from life insurance and annuity policies often can be made free from income tax if certain rules are respected. When withdrawals are taxable, they generally are taxable to the extent they exceed the policyowner's basis in the contract. Generally **basis** (also referred to as the **cost basis, tax basis,** and **investment in the contract**) is defined as the sum of premiums and other contributions paid into a contract, reduced by the amount of refunds, dividends, cash surrenders, or other withdrawals that were not included in taxable income.

Taxation in the U.S. is a highly complex and technical subject. Its interpretation and implementation is also highly complex and technical. Important features of tax law come from all the forms of law discussed in Chapter 12: legislative, administrative, and judicial. The number of sources and the inconsistent applicability to all taxpayers in all situations is daunting. A full understanding of the tax law is impossible without a reading of all of them. While the full detail is impossible to provide in this text, Box 21-1 offers an overview of sources of U.S. tax law to aid understanding.

Box 21-1:
Sources of U.S. Life and Health Insurance Tax Law

The legislative source of the U.S. tax law is the *Internal Revenue Code* and amendments to it passed by Congress and executed by the President. The two main purposes of the income tax are to (1) raise revenue to finance the activities of government and (2) create incentives for economic behavior that Congress deems prudent. Life and health insurance tax provisions reflect both purposes.

Some aspects of the law are not clear as written, so advisors often turn to the **legislative history** – testimony and documents considered by Congress during its deliberations in enacting a law – in attempting to interpret the law. Legislative history materials are published in so-called *bluebooks*. The Code §7702 bluebook dealing with life insurance product taxation is used as a guide to Congressional intent; its importance is due to the failure of the *Treasury Department* to provide complete regulatory direction under the law in many technical aspects.

The source of administrative interpretations and implementation of tax law is the *Treasury* generally and the IRS in particular. We describe below the various tools used in their administration of the law.

- **Regulations** are issued in response either to a Congressional mandate contained in legislation or to a perceived need by *Treasury* for it to provide an interpretation for the proper implementation of a law. Regulations generally are presented in three stages. *Proposed regulations* are circulated for comment by interested parties. *Temporary regulations* have immediate effect but are subject to amendment following a period of comment from interested parties. *Final regulations* are adopted permanently under a *Treasury Decision* (TD).
- **Revenue rulings** are issuances that apply to specific fact situations the department considers to be of general interest. They are valid until revoked and may be relied on by taxpayers.
- **Private letter rulings** (PLRs; also referred to simply as *Letter Rulings* or *LTRs*) are interpretations of fact situations that are not deemed to be of general interest. They may be relied on only by the taxpayers who receive them but serve as an indicator of *Treasury* views.
- **Technical advice memoranda** (TAMs) are statements prepared after the fact in response to tax issues, usually in connection with a taxpayer audit. They may not be relied on by taxpayers but serve as an indicator of *Treasury* views on the considered situation.
- **General counsel memoranda** (GCMs) are detailed analyses prepared to explain the reasoning underlying regulations, revenue rulings, and LTRs.
- State insurance laws and judicial interpretation are an indirect source of federal tax law. The Code incorporates relevant state regulatory requirements in many of its own sections.

Original judicial decisions can come from three different federal courts: the *Tax Court, District Courts*, and the *Federal Court of Claims*. Decisions may be appealed to the federal *Circuit Courts of Appeal* and ultimately to the *Supreme Court*. In addition to the staggering multitude of different tax law sources, the situation is further complicated by the fact that the IRS is not bound by any court decision unless it comes from the *Supreme Court*. When any lower court decision is issued, the IRS generally follows with a statement of *acquiescence* or a statement of *non-acquiescence* indicating its intention to honor or ignore a court decision, respectively.

FEDERAL INCOME TAX LAW AFFECTING POLICY DESIGN AND OPERATION

To master the details of the income tax treatment of life and health insurance products, it is essential to understand some of the intricacies of important IRC requirements that must be met for life insurance policies to qualify for many of its favorable tax aspects. These requirements have a major effect on the design of life insurance policies and on their ongoing operations. In this respect, two Code definitions are of critical importance: (1) life insurance and (2) modified endowment insurance. Both are covered here.[4]

Code Section 7702 Definition of Life Insurance

IRC §7702 contains a definition of life insurance for purposes of determining whether a policy qualifies for certain aspects of favorable tax treatment. The favorable tax treatment afforded life insurance may be vitiated in whole or in part if a policy fails to meet the definition.

BACKGROUND   As noted in earlier chapters, the design of life insurance policies in the U.S. underwent substantial change during the late 1970s and early 1980s. Sales presentations emphasized the high potential tax preferred savings that individuals could accumulate through their life insurance policies, using illustrations predicated on the then high interest crediting rates. These new products raised significant questions among taxing authorities as to the propriety of applying tax preferences to policies that were clearly oriented to investment accumulation rather than death protection. In response, the *Tax Equity and Fiscal Responsibility Act of 1982* (TEFRA) provided a definition of life insurance for flexible premium products. The taxation of annuities was also modified to reduce incentives for their use as short term investment vehicles.

The *Deficit Reduction Act of 1984* (DEFRA) greatly expanded and refined the provisions enacted by TEFRA. Specifically, the new law added Section 7702 to the IRC, which provided for the first time a federal, statutory definition of life insurance. (It also modified the annuity taxation rules enacted by TEFRA to further limit the use of annuities as short term investment vehicles.) Failure of a policy to meet the definition generally results in the policy being treated as a combination of term insurance and a taxable side fund. The law generally applies to policies issued after December 31, 1984.

Traditional fixed premium/fixed benefit whole life (WL) policies contain an established actuarial relationship among premiums, cash values, and death benefits. Fixed premiums generally were calculated to be just sufficient, *and no more*, to cause the policy to endow at age 100 and to cover all mortality and expense charges through that age. Flexible premium policies began to offer cash values that were far more than sufficient to accomplish these purposes: they created significant *excess* cash values designed primarily as investment accumulations.

Most early universal life (UL) policies were designed simply with a corridor of pure life insurance protection between the policy's cash value and death benefit rather than incorporating a specific actuarial relationship designed to fund the policy to the maturity age. The sufficiency of the dollar amount of the net amount at risk (NAR) – the difference between the face amount and cash value – was not addressed, and as the IRS General Counsel noted, taken to a logical extreme, the corridor of protection under the old rules could have been reduced to as little as one dollar. These policies functioned more as tax preferred investment accounts than as life insurance.

THE DEFINITIONAL TESTS   To address this situation, Congress mandated that life insurance policies must meet one of two tests to qualify as life insurance for income tax purposes. Whichever test is chosen, that test must be met for the entire life of the contract.

The Cash Value Accumulation Test   The first test applies mainly to traditional cash value policies. The §7702 **cash value accumulation test** (CVAT) requires that a policy's cash surrender value cannot at any time exceed the net single premium that would be required to fund future contract benefits (defined to be mainly death and maturity benefits) provided under the policy. Recall that a policy's net single premium is the expected present value of the future death and maturity benefits promised under the policy and does not include amounts for policy loadings (see Chapter 15). The net single premium is calculated using interest at the greater of 4.0 percent or the rate guaranteed in the contract. The mortality charges are based on those specified in the contract, or, if not specified, the mortality charges used in determining the contract's statutory reserves. For contracts issued after October 20, 1988, the mortality charges must be reasonable and cannot exceed those of the prevailing mortality table required by the state insurance regulators, currently the *2001 Commissioners Standard Ordinary Table of Mortality* (*2001 CSO Table*).

For example, consider a $1 million WL policy with a cash surrender value of $300,000. Under the test, the single premium for $1 million of WL insurance at the insured's attained age and based on the required assumptions and net of loadings must not be less than $300,000. In other words, if this policy's present cash surrender value, $300,000, were more than necessary to fund its future death benefits, the policy would be considered "overfunded." If the policy fails the test, it loses much of its tax preferred status.

The Guideline Premium and Cash Value Corridor Tests   The second test is a two-pronged test, intended for UL and other unbundled life policies, and requires the policy death benefit to be the greater of an amount determined according to a guideline premium test and a cash value corridor test (GPT/CVCT). The former represents a minimum level of premium that must be paid for qualification, while the latter represents a maximum level of cash value accumulation. Figure 21-1 is a visual representation of the operation of the two tests that we discuss in this section. Note that the initial face amount, determined by the guideline premium test, applies until the growth of policy cash values causes the amount determined by the cash value corridor test to exceed the initial amount and become operative. In the next paragraphs, we define and explain the mechanics of the two tests.

The **guideline premium test** (GPT), also a two-pronged test, is met if the cumulative premiums paid under the contract do not at any time exceed the greater of a guideline single premium or a guideline level premium. These tests effectively limit the amount of premiums that can be paid into a contract for a specified amount of coverage. The **guideline single premium limitation** (GSP) is the gross single premium that would be required to fund future insurance benefits (defined to be mainly death and maturity benefits) provided under the contract at the insured's attained age and based on certain required assumptions. It is computed using interest at the greater of 6.0 percent or the rate guaranteed in the contract. Mortality charges are based on the same standard as applies to the cash value accumulation test discussed above.

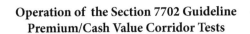

Operation of the Section 7702 Guideline   Figure 21-1
Premium/Cash Value Corridor Tests

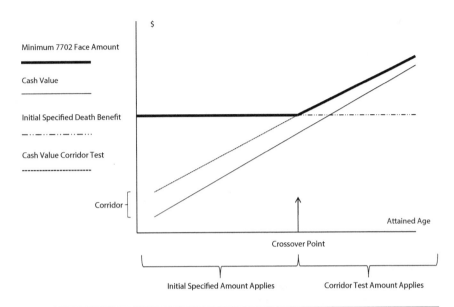

The **guideline level premium limitation** (GLP) is the level annual amount payable over a period ending not before the insured's age 95 for the contract benefits, based on the same assumptions as the GSP except the interest rate is 4.0 percent rather than 6.0 percent. The actual cumulative gross premiums paid into a contract may not exceed the greater of the cumulative GLP or the GSP. The cumulative GLP equals the simple sum of GLPs to each policy year.

For example, assume that a policy's GSP is determined to be $420,000 and that its GLP is $36,000. Assume further that the simple sum of the actual gross premiums paid through policy year 10 totals $400,000. The guideline premium limitation would be met as it permits gross premiums of the greater of $420,000 or $360,000 to have been paid into the contract through policy year 10. Had the sum of the GLPs been more than $420,000, the policy would have failed the guideline premium limitation, would be considered overfunded, and would have lost some of its tax favored treatment. The death benefit amount determined under the guideline premium test is that at policy inception and is often referred to as the *initial specified amount*.

The **cash value corridor test** is met if the policy's promised benefits at all times are at least equal to certain percentage multiples of its cash value. The test effectively limits the amount of cash value that can be accumulated over time for a given face amount. These percentages range from 250 percent for insureds of attained ages up to 40, stepping down to 100 percent for attained age 95. Table 21-1 shows applicable percentages for various ages. Thus, if a 75-year-old owns a policy whose cash value is $10,000, the policy death benefit must be at least $10,500 ($10,000 x 105 percent) for the policy to meet the corridor requirement.

Table 21-1   **IRC Section 7702 Corridor Requirements at Selected Ages**

Insured's Attained Age at Beginning of Contract Year		Percentage Decreases Ratably	
Greater Than	Not More Than	From	To
0	40	250	250
40	45	250	215
45	50	215	185
50	55	185	150
55	60	150	130
60	65	130	120
65	70	120	115
70	75	115	105
75	90	105	105
90	95	105	100

The law requires that the policy maturity age must be assumed to be between ages 95 and 100. Thus, policies endowing *before* age 95 do not qualify as life insurance under the IRC. (This requirement effectively ended endowment insurance sales in the U.S.) Policies endowing *after* age 100 also seemed to pose a problem for policy designers and policyowners. Recall from Chapters 15 and 16 that the mortality table commonly used in life insurance reserving and cash value calculation for new policies – the *2001 CSO Table* – has a terminal age of 121, not age 100 as with its predecessor table, on which the §7702 requirements were patterned. In Rev. Proc. 2010-28, the IRS indicated it would not challenge contracts under 7702 or 7702A after age 100 if certain technical requirements were met.

CONSEQUENCES OF FAILING TO MEET THE DEFINITIONAL TESTS   Failure to meet the IRC definition affects the taxation of both a policy's cash value build-up and its death benefit. Section 7702 excludes the cash value portion of a life insurance policy from the favorable IRC §101(a)(1) treatment (see below); that is, the cash value is excluded from treatment as *death proceeds* which are received free of income tax.

Prior to the enactment of §7702, the deferral of taxation on cash values was based on the constructive receipt doctrine that excluded increases because access to the funds required surrender. Courts ruled that the surrender constituted a forfeiture of a substantial right – the insurance benefit – and as such the income in the contract was not constructively received.[5] Section 7702 overrides the constructive receipt doctrine and causes the inside build up or income on the contract – the current-year increase in cash value and COI charges less the current year premium – to be included in taxable income.

A §7702 failure has serious adverse consequences for both the policyowner and insurer. If a contract failure is not discovered for some time, the policyowner faces the possibility of back taxes and penalties for any prior gains. The NAR in such policies does, however, qualify for Section 101(a)(1) treatment. Draconian penalties also apply to insurers – a 28 percent tax on the gain in all failed policies – although there are procedures for correcting unintentional violations, and penalties can be waived by the IRS.

The Cash Value Accumulation and Guideline Premium Tests in Operation   As discussed in Chapter 3, a UL policyowner typically chooses between a level NAR or a level death benefit. Policies following the second approach usually also provide that the death benefit will not be less than the minimum tax-qualified amount. The option to qualify under either the CVAT or GPT/CVCT may also be provided.

Under §7702, the death benefit of a UL policy cannot be determined in advance as the amount must be the greater of the guideline premium test and the cash value corridor test, and the cash value corridor test can be determined only on the date of death. It is defined as a function of the policy cash value that varies over time according to interest credits or, in the case of variable products, the separate account value, and the charges are calculated as if the insured had died on the processing day. Thus, the procedure is complex. A conditional death benefit is determined at specified dates (often called *processing days*) for the purpose of calculating monthly or annual COI charges. The actual death benefit paid is determined as of the date of death. Most polices specify these dates to be the nearest business day. To avoid §7702 failure through a faulty policy design or clerical error, most policies include an overriding provision that defines the death benefit to be no less than the amount necessary to qualify under §7702. The policy thus qualifies by its own terms.

The policy specification page of a type B death benefit pattern indicates an initial specified amount or face amount based on initial and planned premiums for the purpose of calculating COI charges. The CVAT and level NAR death benefit options cause the death benefit to track the cash value in a mostly linear relationship until advanced ages. The type A death benefit pattern, under the GPT/CVCT test, is the greater of the two guideline premium tests and the cash value corridor test. In operation, the death benefit remains level, with the net amount at risk changing to result in the level death benefit; when the corridor amount exceeds this total amount, the death benefit becomes the corridor amount.

The choice of the GPT/CVCT or CVAT affects the future amount of premiums, death benefits, and face amounts. Generally, the CVAT allows future premiums to be increased to a degree, while the GPT/CVCT does not. The face amount and COI charges are lower during the initial years of the CVAT policy, but higher than the GPT/CVCT at later ages. Decreases in face amount for GPT/CVCT qualified policies generally require a distribution of cash value (and attendant tax consequences) while some CVAT decreases will not. The CVAT provides more flexibility while the GPT/CVCT permits more lifetime cash value accumulation for the same death benefit.

Code Section 7702A   Definition of Modified Endowment Contracts

The other critically important IRC definition related to life insurance taxation is that of a modified endowment contract (MEC), as defined in the *Technical and Miscellaneous Revenue Act of 1988* (TAMRA). MEC requirements were enacted as Congress believed that the definition of life insurance in §7702 had not sufficiently discouraged the use of life insurance primarily as an investment instrument. Single premium policies were a particular concern. A **modified endowment contract** is a life insurance policy entered into after June 20, 1988, that meets the IRC §7702 definition of life insurance as discussed above but that fails to meet a technical premium test termed the *seven-pay test*. A MEC is subject to tax rules that differ from non-MEC life insurance.

A life insurance policy fails to satisfy the **seven-pay test** if the cumulative amount paid under the contract at any time during the first seven contract years exceeds the cumulative amount that would have been paid had the policy's annual premium equaled the net level premium for a seven-pay life policy of the same type, using certain required assumptions. The seven level premiums are determined at policy issue, and the policy death benefit is taken to be that of the first contract year, without regard to any scheduled benefit decreases. The test does not require seven literal premiums; other premium patterns may qualify. Thus, if the net level premium for a seven-pay WL contract is $50,000, cumulative premiums actually paid into the contract may not exceed $50,000 in policy year one, $100,000 in policy year two, etc., and $350,000 by policy year seven.

If a policy's death benefit is reduced during the first several policy years, the policy is subjected to a new seven-pay period and test based on the reduced insurance amount. Also, any policy – regardless of its date of issue – that undergoes a material change in future benefits is subjected to a new seven-pay period and limit. Material changes include increases in face amount, reductions in a substandard rating, change of non-smoker status, or substitution of an insured. Material changes cause a loss of any policy grandfathered status.

The principal difference in the tax treatment of non-MECs and MECs involves lifetime distributions. For non-MEC policies, distributions in the form of dividends, withdrawals, and partial surrenders are based on first-in, first-out (FIFO) tax treatment – meaning any distributions are deemed to originate first from the policy's cost basis; that is, amounts paid into the policy, on which taxes were already paid. Thus, such distributions are not taxed as income, up to the cost basis of the policy, which usually equals the cumulative premiums paid. Only after distributions exceed the cost basis are they taxed. Distributions in the form of policy loans ordinarily have no taxable component provided the policy is in force, irrespective of their magnitude.

All distributions under MECs, including dividends and policy loans (and pledges of the policy for third party loans), require last-in, first-out (LIFO) treatment – meaning they are deemed to originate first from any untaxed gains within the policy, and only after all gain is taxed are distributions considered as coming from the cost basis and therefore tax free. This treatment is dictated in IRC §72. Section 72 also provides for a 10 percent penalty tax on distributions before age 59½. (Section 72 imposes the same penalty for pre-age-59½ distributions from qualified plans and annuities.) Thus, when MECs are used as investment instruments – e.g., withdrawals are taken – they are treated approximately the same as annuities and retirement plans.

If MEC policies are held until maturity, they are treated as any other life insurance policy: cash values increase tax free and death proceeds are received income tax free. As a result, despite the fact that MECs generally impose lower total mortality charges for a given level of premium than a non-MEC, MECs are especially unattractive if withdrawals before age 59½ are expected.

Table 21-2 shows the tax treatment of non-MECs and MECs under cash withdrawal and policy loan transactions and the resulting after-tax proceeds for a policy whose cost basis is less than the distribution. It shows two important features of distributions of life insurance cash values. First, policy loan proceeds are more attractive than withdrawals, as well as partial surrenders, for non-MECs in this situation. Second, the LIFO treatment of both loans and withdrawals, as well as the penalty tax for withdrawals before age 59½, significantly reduces the after-tax proceeds of both transaction types.

Tax Treatment of Policy Loan and Cash Withdrawal Proceeds for Non-MECs and MECs, 40 Percent Income Tax **Table 21-2**

	Non-MEC	MEC age 59	MEC Age 60
Total CSV	20,000	20,000	20,000
Basis	5,000	5,000	5,000
Cash Withdrawal	10,000	10,000	10,000
Taxable Income	5,000	10,000	10,000
Tax @ 40%	2,000	4,000	4,000
Penalty Tax @ 10%	0	1,000	0
Net Proceeds	8,000	5,000	6,000
Policy Loan Proceeds	10,000	10,000	10,000
Taxable Income	0	10,000	10,000
Tax @ 40%	0	4,000	4,000
Penalty Tax@10%	0	1,000	0
Net Proceeds	10,000	5,000	6,000

In examining the income taxation of life and health insurance and annuities, it will prove convenient to examine the tax treatment by relevant policy elements.

LIFE INSURANCE POLICYOWNER TAXATION

PREMIUMS
Premiums for life insurance policies are generally not deductible for individuals or for businesses. Exceptions exist when:

- the policy is owned by and for the benefit of a qualified charity or charitable trust;
- the policy is owned by an employer, the policy is payable as an executive bonus, and the executive includes the value of the premium in taxable income; and
- the policy is payable to an ex-spouse or children under an alimony agreement.

DEATH BENEFITS
IRC Section 101(a)(1) establishes the general rule that life insurance death proceeds are excluded from taxable income. Proceeds must be paid by reason of the

death of the insured; i.e., the insured's death must have caused the maturity of the contract. Thus, term life insurance death proceeds are received free from income tax. Also, as noted above, the NAR under §7702-failed cash value policies paid by reason of death also qualifies for exclusion. Other amounts paid at the time of death under such policies, such as annuity cash values or other proceeds that would have been payable during the insured's lifetime, do not qualify as death proceeds.

Thus, if an insured under a $100,000 *qualified* life insurance policy died after premiums of $3,000 had been paid, the entire $100,000 would be received income tax free by the beneficiary. With the exception of transfers for value noted below, this result applies irrespective of the cash value or the amount of premiums paid and irrespective of who was the policyowner, insured, beneficiary, or premium payer. Death proceeds include the policy face amount and any additional insurance amounts paid by reason of the insured's death, such as accidental death benefits and the face amount of any paid-up additional insurance or any term rider.

Special rules apply in several situations. These include transfers of life insurance policies for a valuable consideration, employer owned life insurance, and selected other less common situations. Additionally, death proceeds payable under life insurance settlement options have their own tax rules. Each of these situations is discussed below.

TRANSFER FOR VALUE RULE   The **transfer for value rule** [IRC Section 101(a)(2)] provides that death proceeds under a life insurance policy are included in gross income to the extent of the excess of gross policy death proceeds over the policy's cost basis if the policy or any interest in it was transferred to another person for a valuable consideration. The excess of the gross death proceeds over the cost basis would be taxable to the beneficiary as ordinary income. The basis would be recovered income-tax free on death. Thus, if Barbara sold (i.e., transferred ownership of) her $100,000 policy to Nancy for $3,000 and if Barbara died ten years later with Nancy having paid $12,000 in premiums (net of dividends), the beneficiary would receive $15,000 of the death proceeds free of tax as a recovery of cost basis ($3,000 consideration plus $12,000 premiums paid), but the $85,000 balance would be taxable as ordinary income.

The rule applies to any transfer for value of a right to receive all or a part of the death proceeds of a life insurance policy, with exceptions noted below. The most common situation in which the rule is invoked involves sales of policies. Thus, death proceeds collected by a viatical settlement firm are subject to this rule (but see below also). The rule, however, is not limited to sales. It applies generally to all situations in which a life insurance policy, by virtue of its transfer for a valuable consideration, takes on the characteristics of other financial instruments. Consequently, only those transfers in which the policy more or less retains those original purposes for which policies are purchased are exempt from the rule. Such transfers include those in which:

- The transfer is to the insured (for example, a corporation sells its key person policy to the insured/key employee who resigned),
- The transfer is to
  - a partner of the insured,
  - a partnership in which the insured is a partner, or
  - a corporation in which the insured is an officer or shareholder.

- The transfer does not involve a tax basis change, including
  - a tax free corporate organization or reorganization or
  - a *bona fide* gift.

EMPLOYER OWNED LIFE INSURANCE   *The Pension Protection Act of 2006* added several preconditions to the income-tax free receipt of death benefits under life insurance owned by employers on the life of their employees. The general rule today is that life insurance death benefits received under insurance payable to the employer – called **employer owned life insurance** (EOLI) under the IRC – are subject to income taxes to the extent that the benefits exceed the employer's cost basis in the policy. Fortunately, the law also provides that death benefits payable under EOLI policies meeting either one of two exceptions and for which certain notice and consent requirements are met will not be treated as taxable income. These notice and consent requirements are detailed in Chapter 24; a brief introduction suffices here.

The requirements are, first, that the insured employee must be a director or highly compensated employee when the policy was issued and must have been employed within the 12 months preceding the claim. Second, before the policy was issued, the employer must have notified the employee of its intent to insure, the amount of insurance, and the fact that the employer would stand as beneficiary. Finally, the employee must have given his or her consent to the arrangement. Additionally, employers are subject to annual information filing requirements on these policies.

TAXATION OF DEATH BENEFITS FOR OTHER REASONS   Several other highly specific reasons can cause life insurance death proceeds to be subject to income taxation. These include situations in which death proceeds were received:

- under a policy issued without a valid insurable interest and so were considered wagering income,
- under a qualified pension or profit sharing plan,
- by a creditor from life insurance on the debtor/insured's life,
- as corporate dividends or compensation,
- as alimony, and
- as restitution of embezzled funds.

Additionally, death proceeds payable to a corporation can incur ordinary income taxation due to the corporate alternative minimum tax (AMT). Corporate and individual taxpayers must pay the greater of the AMT or regular tax. The AMT is intended to ensure that no taxpayer avoids liability entirely by taking extreme advantage of certain tax provisions termed *tax preference items*. They are, in general, amounts that accrue to the corporation but are not included in its regular taxable income, such as incentives like stock options and intangible drilling costs. For corporations, life insurance death proceeds and cash value increases are also tax preference items. (These items are not tax preference items for individuals.)

Alternative minimum taxable income (AMTI) is determined by adding tax preference items back to regular taxable income. The AMT tax rate of 20 percent is applied to AMTI after an exemption of $40,000 (phased out with increasing income). The AMT applies when (1) a policy's yearly cash value increase exceeds that year's net premium or (2) death proceeds paid exceed the policy's cash value.

If life insurance death proceeds or cash values are expected to incur the AMT, consideration should be given to having the insurance owned outside the corporation.

SETTLEMENT OPTIONS   The favorable income tax treatment of life insurance death proceeds is unaffected by the election of a settlement option, although income taxes usually will be due on any interest paid on the death proceeds following the payment of the claim. Thus, under the interest option, interest received by the beneficiary is taxable as ordinary income. Interest retained by the insurer also is taxable unless the beneficiary cannot withdraw either principal or interest for a stated time period. At the end of the time period, all accrued, untaxed interest is taxable.

Under the installment or fixed period option, each payment is deemed to be composed of part principal and part interest. The portion deemed to be a return of principal is not taxed. The procedure for deriving this portion is to calculate an amount held by the insurer (usually, the lump sum amount payable at the insured's death) and prorate this amount over the actual or expected payment period. Amounts in excess of the annual prorated principal are treated as interest and are taxable income to the recipient. The principal is *not* amortized in a financial sense. The portions attributable to principal and interest remain constant over the installment period. Thus, if $100,000 of death proceeds is paid over a ten year fixed period and the payments are $15,000 per year, $10,000 ($100,000 divided by ten years) is excluded from yearly taxable income as a return of principal.

The procedure to derive the excludable amount of each payment under the fixed amount option divides the amount held by the insurer by the number of payments required to exhaust the principal at the guaranteed interest rate. The amount of each payment in excess of this figure is deemed to be taxable interest. Payments made beyond the guaranteed period are considered to be interest only and, therefore, fully taxable. Payments under the life income option are taxed as any life annuity. Annuity taxation is discussed below.

DIVIDENDS

Dividends payable under participating life insurance policies normally are considered a nontaxable return of excess premiums. This result is unaffected by the dividend option selected. If dividends are left on deposit to accumulate at interest, the interest credited on the accumulation is, of course, taxable. Unless used to purchase paid-up additional insurance, dividends reduce a policy's cost basis.

Two exceptions exist to this general rule. First, if the policy is a MEC or fails to meet the IRC definition of life insurance, dividends taken as distributions (i.e., received in cash, credited against the premium, or accumulated at interest) are taxable. Also, dividends paid under a MEC may be subject to an additional 10 percent penalty tax if distributed prior to age 59½. Second, if the total of the dividends received as distributions under a non-MEC policy exceeds the total of the premiums paid, all dividend amounts received in excess of the sum of premiums paid constitute ordinary income. MECs, however, are almost always nonparticipating policies, wherein dividends are not a feature.

CASH VALUES

Life insurance policy cash values can involve tax consequences in the context of increases, surrenders, loans, and policy exchanges.

INTEREST ON CASH VALUES   The interest credited to a life insurance policy's cash value is not currently taxable if the policy meets the IRC §7702 definition of life insurance. This favorable tax treatment also applies to MECs. If a policy fails to meet the IRC definition, a portion of the year's cash value increase will be subject to ordinary income taxation if the year's benefits under the policy exceed the premiums paid during that year. Benefits for tax purposes are the sum of (1) the year's cash value increase, (2) the value of pure life insurance protection, and (3) dividends received. The value of the pure insurance protection is determined by multiplying the NAR by the lesser of (1) the applicable IRS uniform premium rate or (2) the COI charge, if any, stated in the contract.

If a life insurance policy passes the test originally but later fails, all prior years' deferred income is included in the policyowner's gross income in the year when the policy first fails to meet the test. The policyowner relies on the life insurance company to ensure that this does not occur.

Debate continues over whether sound public policy should permit the tax-advantaged inside interest build-up within life insurance policies. Proponents of the *status quo* argue that the tax favoritism accorded life insurance constitutes sound social policy in that it encourages families to make provision for their financial security. They further point out that current tax law provides reasonable safeguards against abuse while still encouraging worthwhile social application. Finally, they note that the interest income is not actually received by the policyowner unless the policy is surrendered, much as the homeowner does not actually receive his or her home's appreciated value without selling the home. Policy loans and home equity loans are similarly analogous.

Critics claim that favorable tax treatment is unjustified as it distorts the savings market, making life insurance products artificially more attractive than other savings instruments. They also note that the government loses tax revenues (estimated by the Congressional Budget Office in 2009 at $265 billion over ten years on the inside interest buildup) because of this tax favoritism and that the homeowner analogy is flawed for several reasons, among them that tax theory would not extend tax preference to either the homeowner or the policyowner. Finally, they point out that the social benefits that are supposed to accrue because of the tax favoritism accrue overwhelming and increasingly to the wealthiest segments of the population and less and less so to those who are poor or of modest wealth. They cite 2007 Federal Reserve survey data reporting that 22 percent of assets accumulated tax-free in cash value policies were held by the wealthiest 1 percent of U.S. families and that 55 percent were held by the wealthiest 10 percent of families, with the bottom 50 percent by net worth holding only 6.5 percent.

CASH SURRENDER PAYMENTS   The general rule for taxation of lump sum cash surrender value payments under life insurance policies is the **cost recovery rule,** under which the amount included in the policyowner's gross income upon policy surrender is the excess of the gross proceeds over the cost basis. **Gross proceeds** are the amounts paid on surrender, including the cash value of any paid up additions and the value of dividends accumulated at interest.

For example, assume that Rebecca's $100,000 ordinary life policy issued 20 years ago carries an annual premium of $1,300 and has a cash surrender value of $30,000. The sum of all dividends received in cash over the 20-year period is

$7,000. If Rebecca surrendered the policy, the amount subject to ordinary income tax treatment would be calculated as follows:

	sum of premiums paid:	$26,000
Less:	*sum of dividends received:*	7,000
Equals:	*cost basis:*	19,000
Gross proceeds:		$30,000
Less:	*cost basis:*	19,000
Equals:	*taxable income:*	$11,000

Premiums paid for supplementary benefits such as the waiver of premium and accidental death benefit features are not a part of the basis. Although premiums waived under a waiver of premium feature logically should be included in the cost basis as the benefit is economically equivalent to disability income benefits, apparently the tax court disagrees.[6] If policy loans are outstanding on surrender, the net surrender value (cash surrender value less loan) constitutes the gross proceeds, but the cost basis is lowered by the loan amounts previously received.

The cost basis of a life insurance policy includes the pure cost of insurance. Theoretically, yearly COI charges, which exist with every life insurance policy, should be excluded from the basis as representing current expenditure and not an investment. Thus, taxable income to the policyowner technically is understated by the value of these mortality charges, representing an additional tax benefit.

Losses on surrender of a life insurance policy in the hands of the original policyowner or subsequent donee normally cannot be recognized for income tax purposes. The rationale for disallowing a deductible loss is that the method for computing taxable gain (and loss) makes no allowance for mortality charges. Therefore, any loss is assumed to be composed, in whole or in part, of such mortality costs. Losses on policies that have been transferred for value are deductible in the hands of the buyer.

The cost recovery rule generally applies to life insurance cash value withdrawals and partial surrenders. Thus, using our previous example, assume that Rebecca withdraws $5,000 in cash value from her policy while continuing the policy. As the cost basis is $19,000, the entire $5,000 is received income-tax free. The withdrawal lowers her basis to $14,000. As noted above, distributions under MECs are subject to special treatment. LIFO treatment and premature distribution penalties apply.

POLICY LOANS   Personal loan interest is not deductible, and the rule applies to policy loan interest. Policy loan interest paid on policies owned by a business and covering the lives of key persons, defined as officers and 20 percent owners, may be deductible, subject to certain conditions. Deductions are allowed only for loans on policies covering key persons and for loan amounts of less than $50,000 per individual insured. The $50,000 limitation does not apply to policies purchased prior to June 21, 1986. To obtain the deduction, the interest actually must be paid. The total number of key persons within a business for whom policy loan interest can be deductible may not exceed the greater of (1) five or (2) the lesser of 5.0 percent of the total officers or 20 individuals.

This business related deduction is not allowed when policy loans are used to finance life insurance after August 6, 1963 under a systematic plan of borrowing, with four exceptions. The most important exception is the four-in-seven exception, under which a deduction is allowed if no part of at least four of the first seven annual premiums due on a policy is paid through borrowing, either from the policy or other sources. If borrowing in any year exceeds the premium for that year, the excess is considered to be borrowing used to finance the previous year's premium. Thus, the four-in-seven test is failed if policyowner borrowing during the seven year period exceeds an amount equal to three years' premiums, irrespective of when the borrowing takes place during the period. The four premiums can be paid in any order. It appears that, once the seven year requirement has been satisfied, borrowing beyond that period is unrestricted for tax purposes.

As a general rule, taking a loan under a life insurance policy does not, in itself, constitute a taxable distribution. If the contract is a MEC, however, policy loans are treated the same as withdrawals. They are taxable as income to the extent that the cash value of the contract immediately before the payment exceeds the contract's cost basis. The 10 percent penalty tax also applies if the loan is made before the insured reaches age 59½.

Finally, non-MEC life insurance policies with outstanding debt carry potential tax liability in the event of surrender. Recall that policy loans reduce a policy's cost basis. For policies carrying large loans, the net cash surrender value can be quite small. At surrender, the owner would receive a check for the small net cash value. At the same time, the owner could face significant taxable income and a tax bill exceeding the amount of the net surrender because of a low or even negative cost basis. This phenomenon is known as *phantom income*.

POLICY EXCHANGES   Code §1035 permits what has become known in the industry as a **Section 1035 exchange** or simply a **1035 exchange** under which a policyowner undertaking a replacement can avoid an otherwise taxable gain on surrender if he or she simultaneously exchanges the policy for another one meeting §1035 qualifications. To qualify, the exchange must be of

- a life insurance policy for another life insurance policy or endowment or annuity contract,
- an endowment for an annuity contract or another endowment of no greater maturity date than the replaced endowment, or
- an annuity for another annuity.

Gain in the original policy is rolled into the new contract and not recognized on replacement. The new policy assumes the cost basis of the original policy. The distinction between (1) an exchange and (2) a surrender and purchase is not always clear. Several IRS private letter rulings suggest that, in general, the contract to be replaced should be assigned to the replacing insurance company without the policyowner actually receiving any surrender value proceeds.

Note an annuity *may not be exchanged* for a life insurance policy without the recognition of any gain in the annuity contract under §1035. Otherwise the accumulated tax-free earnings in an investment oriented annuity would have a tax-free exit strategy through the acquired life policy death benefit.

POLICY SALES

The tax treatment to the owner of a policy sold in the secondary market is more complex than that found with most other lifetime transactions involving life insurance. If a policy is sold to an unrelated third party, the policyowner must take any gain into taxable income. Part of any taxable gain may be taxed as ordinary income and another part as capital gains under IRS Revenue Ruling 2009-13.

The portion of the gain considered ordinary income is the difference between the cash surrender value and the aggregate premiums paid under the policy, which is the same as the taxable amount for a cash surrender. The portion of gain considered capital gains is the difference between the policy sale price and the adjusted basis *minus* any amounts subject to ordinary income tax. The *adjusted basis* equals the sum of premiums paid less the cost of pure insurance protection during the years of policy ownership before sale.

To illustrate: Cathy owns a UL policy with a cash surrender value of $78,000 on which she has paid a total of $64,000 in premiums. If she surrenders the policy, she would realize an ordinary income tax gain of $14,000 ($78,000 – $64,000). Assume that a life settlement company offers to purchase the policy from her for $80,000. Assume also that she paid COI charges totaling $10,000 in the past. Her adjusted basis, therefore, would be $54,000 ($64,000 – $10,000). Hence, if she sells the policy, she will recognize $14,000 ($78,000 – $64,000) as ordinary income and $12,000 ($80,000 – $54,000 – $14,000) as capital gains.

MATURED ENDOWMENTS

Living proceeds received from a matured endowment are taxed the same as proceeds received on policy surrender; i.e., the cost recovery rule – assuming, of course, that the policy qualifies as life insurance (or is grandfathered) and is not a MEC. The cost basis is subtracted from the gross proceeds to derive taxable income.

Almost all endowment maturities occur because the insured has survived to the maximum possible attained age assumed in pricing the policy, historically age 100, until adoption in this century of the *2001 CSO Table*. (Other endowment policies are almost never sold, and remaining policies issued prior to the enactment of §7702 are fewer each year.) The forced distribution under an endowment provision can cause a hardship for policyowners who have no need for the distributed funds. As more and more insureds survive to age 100, many companies offer riders or other provisions that allow the policyowner to maintain the policy in force without further payment of premium, although the tax consequences of such a strategy have never been tested or verified. Also, with the increasing use of the *2001 CSO Table*, very few insureds survive to the table's terminal age (121).

ACCELERATED DEATH BENEFITS

As discussed in earlier chapters, some life insurance policies permit payment of a portion or all of the death benefit if the insured is terminally or chronically ill. The general rule is that accelerated death benefits payable in connection with a terminally ill insured are deemed to be amounts *paid by reason of the death* of the insured and, therefore, are received income tax free under Code §101(a)(1). To qualify, a physician must certify that the insured's illness or physical condition can reasonably be expected to result in death within 24 months.

The same tax treatment and conditions apply to amounts received by life settlement firms in connection with their purchase of a policy on a terminally ill insured, except that the transfer for value rule applies to benefits. Benefits do not qualify for §101(a)(1) treatment if the policyowner is a business and the insured is a director, officer, or employee of that business or has some other financial interest in the business. In this situation, accelerated benefit payments will not be treated as tax-free death benefits.

SPECIAL VARIABLE PRODUCT TAX ISSUES

The IRS has exhibited an antagonism toward variable life insurance and particularly variable annuity products since their inception. There has been a persistent effort to treat the policyowner as the economic owner of the separate account assets underlying these policies. Because of perceived control of the underlying assets, the Service has not viewed the insurer as the owner of the assets for tax purposes or the policies as insurance. Such an interpretation would subject investment gains in separate accounts to treatment as current income taxable to the policyowner.

The Service's position has rested on the degree of control retained by the policyowner. Three lines of analysis expressed at various times by the Service represent unacceptable levels of control. Revenue Rulings 2003-91, 2003-92, and 81-225 are the important statements on the "investor control" doctrine. They are based on:

- the ability to control acquisition, disposition, and management of separate account assets,
- the use of publicly available pools of assets, and
- the use of *de facto* publicly available pools of assets.

As a result, variable products today offer investment options that are available only through life insurers to purchasers of variable insurance contracts. Many mutual fund companies offer products available only through insurers that closely resemble their publicly available funds.

In 1984, Congress passed Code §817(h) for the purpose of limiting the primary use of variable contracts as investment vehicles. It requires "adequate" diversification of assets for variable products to receive the tax benefits of insurance treatment. It provides that separate accounts are adequately diversified only if:

- not more than 55 percent of the account is invested in one asset,
- not more than 60 percent is invested in two assets,
- not more than 80 percent is invested in three assets, and
- not more than 90 percent is invested in four assets.

Section 817(h) did not address the investor control issue, so it has not disposed of the Service's objections. As a practical matter, publicly available variable products easily satisfy the statutory diversification standards as well as the Service's stated position on investor control in publicly available products. Investor control and some technical aspects of diversification remain as issues in private placement and corporate-owned life insurance policies where investment options are customized.

ANNUITY POLICYOWNER TAXATION

Annuity tax rules have become more stringent over the years in an effort to discourage the use of annuities as short term tax deferred investments rather than as long term retirement funding vehicles. No specific tax law definition of an *annuity* equivalent to the §7702 definition of life insurance exists. A definition has evolved over time through a combination of implicit Code provisions, judicial decisions, and IRS guidance. Annuities that meet the *de facto* definition enjoy the privileges of:

- deferral of taxation on accumulation,
- exclusion ratio tax treatment during liquidation,
- tax free exchanges under §1035 (annuity for annuity but not annuity for life insurance), and
- qualification under IRC §403(b) and other qualified plans (see Chapter 23).

Under accepted definitions, an annuity is any periodic payment resulting from the systematic liquidation of a principal sum. Both annuities certain and life annuities are included in this definition. Tax treatment varies depending on whether living proceeds are paid during the accumulation or liquidation period.

DURING THE ACCUMULATION PERIOD

In general, interest credited to the cash values of personally-owned annuities is tax deferred. With the exceptions noted below, the contract owner does not include this interest income in his or her gross income until annuity liquidation begins or at contract surrender. Dividends paid, cash value withdrawals, loans, and amounts received on partial surrender of an annuity, however, are taxable as ordinary income to the extent that the contract cash value exceeds the cost basis; i.e., the LIFO rule applies, as with MECs. The balance is received as a recovery of investment and is tax free.

The 10 percent penalty under Section 72 also applies. There are exceptions to the penalty, the most important of which are (1) a series of substantially equal lifetime periodic payments is taken so that annuitization prior to age 59½ is excepted, (2) payments are made to a taxpayer who is at least 59½ years old, (3) payments are made under tax qualified retirement plans, or (4) payments are attributable to the taxpayer's disability or death.

DURING THE LIQUIDATION PERIOD

During annuitization, a portion of each annuity payment represents a return of non-taxable investment in the contract and the balance of each payment is considered taxable income. (As noted above, the same procedures apply to life insurance proceeds received under income settlement options.) The taxable and non-taxable portions of the payments are determined by an exclusion ratio. The ratio is multiplied by the amount of each guaranteed payment to yield the amount of each annuity payment excluded from gross income. The remainder of the payment represents taxable income.

The **exclusion ratio** for an annuity is the ratio of the investment in the contract to the expected return under the contract:

$$Exclusion\ Ratio = \frac{Investment\ in\ the\ Contract}{Expected\ Return}$$

The *investment in the contract* is the *basis* as discussed earlier, reduced by an amount prescribed by the IRS that represents the value of any refund feature. The **expected return** is the amount of the annuity payment multiplied by an IRS scheduled expected return multiple for life annuities, or by the number of certain payments in the case of an annuity certain. The IRS expected return tables specify for each age a multiple based on the gender, number of lives, and temporary or whole life nature of the payments.

As an example, assume $100,000 of premium has been paid into a life annuity. There have been no withdrawals or dividends. Thus, the investment in the contract is also $100,000. The guaranteed minimum annual payment is $5,500. The beneficiary is a 60-year-old male and the life annuity guarantees at least 10 years of payments if the annuitant dies before 10 years' payments have been made. The investment in the contract is first adjusted for the refund feature. The percent refund value for a male age 60 with a 10 year certain feature is 8.0 percent. Thus, the investment in the contract adjusted for the return feature is:

$$(1 - Percent\ Refund\ Value)\ x\ Investment\ in\ the\ Contract =$$
$$0.92\ x\ \$100,000 = \$92,000$$

The expected return in the contract is:

$$Payment\ x\ Expected\ Return\ Multiple =$$
$$\$5,500\ x\ 24.2 = \$133,100$$

The exclusion ratio is:

$$\$100,000 \div \$133,100 = 0.751$$

The amount excluded from taxable income is:

$$0.751\ x\ \$5,500 = \$4,131$$

And the taxable amount is:

$$\$5,500 - \$4,131 = \$1,369$$

The taxable amount of $1,369 is derived from the minimum guaranteed payment. The actual *nonguaranteed* payment almost certainly will be more than this amount. The excluded amount will not change each year, but the taxable amount will change as the insurer adjusts the nonguaranteed payments for changing investment returns and other factors.

DEATH OF THE ANNUITANT

If the owner dies during the liquidation period and the annuity calls for continued payments, the beneficiary is generally taxed according to the same exclusion ratio that applied to the deceased. If the owner dies before annuitization, deferred earnings will be treated as ordinary income to a non-spousal beneficiary and the surviving beneficiary is required to make an election to:

- take an immediate lump sum payment,
- withdraw the entire amount in one or more distributions within five years, or
- begin annuitization within one year of death, over the life of the new owner.

If the owner at the annuitant's death is a trust established by the annuitant, an immediate total distribution is mandatory. If the owner is a spouse, the spouse may continue the contract to preserve tax-preferred growth.

SPECIAL ANNUITY TAX ISSUES

The tax treatment of two specialized and new forms of annuities is not yet known with certainty. Additionally, new taxes levied on investment income in connection with the *Patient Protection and Affordable Care Act of 2010* seem to be applicable to at least one aspect of annuities.

Contingent Deferred Annuities   Contingent deferred annuities (CDAs) are guarantees issued by an insurer that attach the equivalent of guaranteed minimum withdrawal benefits to a separate mutual fund or managed account (see Chapter 6). The unprecedented properties of such an arrangement raised issues for both issuing companies and policyowners. Two private letter rulings have addressed these issues and thus give some indication of the IRS view on the status of CDAs as annuities for tax purposes.

The tax treatment of insurers depends on whether a CDA arrangement is treated as an annuity. The IRS indicated to one taxpayer in an LTR that the arrangement would be treated as an annuity. Insurers in New York, however, face some uncertainty as the *New York State Department of Financial Services* did not consider a CDA arrangement to be an annuity, thus creating a potential conflict, although legislation has been introduced that effectively overturns the Department's position. Some tax definitions of annuities make reference to state law.

The treatment of policyowners under CDA arrangements has been addressed favorably by the IRS in four LTRs (200949036, 20101016, 201117012, and 201117013). Private letter rulings can be relied upon only by the requesting tax payer. The interpretations indicated that the IRS will:

- apply the exclusion ratio to benefit payments,
- consider the taxpayer to be the owner of the underlying investments,
- permit the policyowner to deduct losses, receive capital gain treatment, and receive qualified dividend treatment attributable to underlying investments in the mutual fund or managed account, and
- not treat the CDA arrangement as a straddle under Code §1092; a contrary position would have denied long term capital gain treatment.

Longevity Annuities   As we know from Chapter 6, longevity annuities are deferred single premium annuities that provide a lifetime income commencing at a date years into the future, based on interest and mortality assumptions at the time of purchase. The policies typically have neither surrender value nor death benefits during the deferral period, so death during this period results in a "forfeiture" of premiums paid. As annuity distributions must generally begin at age 70½, there was a question as to whether a longevity annuity deferred past that age would violate the minimum required distribution requirement. (Nonqualified annuities are not subject to minimum distribution rules.) The Treasury responded to the issue with Regulations (1.401(a)(9)-6) that resolve the conflict. Longevity annuities meeting certain requirements will be deemed "Qualifying Longevity Annuity Contracts" (QLAC) and automatically be deemed to avoid the minimum required distribution rules. Qualification requires:

- No more than 25 percent of any employee retirement plan (or 25 percent across all pretax IRAs aggregated together) can be invested into a QLAC,
- The cumulative dollar amount invested into all QLACs across all retirement accounts is limited to the lesser of (1) $125,000; or (2) the 25 percent

limit. The $125,000 dollar amount is indexed for inflation, adjusted in $10,000 increments,

- The limitations are specified for each spouse with his or her own retirement accounts,
- The QLAC must begin its payouts by age 85 (or earlier),
- The QLAC must provide fixed payouts (not variable or equity-indexed), although cost-of-living adjustments are permitted,
- The QLAC cannot have a cash surrender value and must be irrevocable, and
- A return-of-premium death benefit payable to heirs as a lump sum or a stream of income is permitted.

UNEARNED INCOME MEDICARE CONTRIBUTIONS TAX AND ANNUITIES The *Patient Protections and Affordable Care Act of 2010* provides for a new tax on net investment income – the *Unearned Income Medicare Contributions Tax* – to help fund Medicare. It is in addition to ordinary income taxes due. Beginning January 1, 2013, a tax of 3.8 percent is levied on interest, capital gains, dividends, rents, royalties, and certain other investment income. The tax rate is applied to the lesser of the taxpayer's (1) net investment income or (2) adjusted gross income above $250,000 for married taxpayers filing jointly (or $125,000 for married taxpayers filing separately) and $200,000 for all others.

Qualified plans and their annuity distributions are excluded. Nonqualified annuity benefit payments are subject to the tax, while investment income during the deferral period is not. The treatment of withdrawals other than benefit payments is not clear.

The income tax treatment to the policyowner of medical expense insurance, disability income insurance, and LTC insurance is covered in this section.

HEALTH INSURANCE POLICYOWNER TAXATION

MEDICAL EXPENSE INSURANCE

Premiums paid by individuals for medical expense insurance are deductible only to the extent that all unreimbursed medical expenses, including the premiums, exceed 10 percent of adjusted gross income. Insurance premiums paid or health care benefits provided by employers are not taxable to the employee. Amounts provided by employers that are available to pay health insurance premiums, but not *required* to pay health insurance premiums, are generally not deductible except for qualified contributions to a health savings account, often an option under a cafeteria plan (see Chapter 7).

The income tax treatment of amounts paid under individual or group health insurance policies is straightforward. Generally, amounts received under such policies are amounts received for personal injuries and sickness and so are treated as a tax-free reimbursement for expenses incurred.

DISABILITY INCOME INSURANCE

The taxation of disability income insurance is uncomplicated. Premiums paid by an individual are not deductible and benefits are received tax free. Premiums paid by an employer are deductible as a business expense and benefits are taxable to the employee in the event of a claim. If the employee contributes toward the premium, his or her premium is not deductible but benefits attributable proportionately to that premium are received tax free.

LONG TERM CARE INSURANCE

Long term care insurance is granted significant tax advantages under the Code. These advantages are consistent with the tax treatment of insurance products that promote personal financial security. This section follows on our discussion of LTC in Chapter 8. In some respects, LTC contracts receive the most generous tax treatment of any insurance: subject to some limitations, premiums are deductible, prefunding of future insurance costs accumulate tax free, and benefits are not includible in taxable income.

CODE SECTION 7702B DEFINITION OF LONG TERM CARE INSURANCE   IRC §7702B defines long term care insurance as §7702 does life insurance and 7702A does modified endowments. Tax benefits granted under the Code apply only to *qualified long term care insurance* (QLTCI) contracts. The most important qualification criteria are:

- The policy must pay benefits only for qualified services.
- The policy must provide benefits under both an activities of daily living and a cognitive impairment test.
- The policy must offer inflation protection and nonforfeiture options. Qualified nonforfeiture options include:
  - reduced paid up insurance,
  - extended term insurance,
  - shortened benefit period, and
  - additional options approved under state law.
- Cash surrender value is not a permitted nonforfeiture option. Cash benefits at death or lapse are limited to a return of premiums paid.
- Minimum consumer protection provisions are mandated.

PREMIUMS AND BENEFITS   The Code provides for a deduction from taxable income in the amount of annual premiums paid for QLTCI. For individuals, deductibility applies only if total medical expenses for the year, including LTC premiums, exceed 10 percent of adjusted gross income. Self employed individuals may deduct the entire premium from business earnings.

Only prescribed maximum amounts of premium are deductible. The deduction limit increases with the age of insured and is indexed to inflation. Limits for 2014 are:

- Age 40 or less $ 370
- More than 40, less than 50 $ 700
- More than 50, less than 60 $1,400
- More than 60, less than 70 $3,720
- More than 70 $4,660

While LTC policies do not offer a cash surrender value, level or stepped premiums are discounted for interest and for future morbidity costs. Implicitly, then, the interest discount is not taxed and ultimately may be converted to a tax free benefit.

Reimbursement benefits paid under a QLTCI contract are excluded from gross income. In 2014, per diem benefits are excludable to the extent they do not exceed the greater of $330 (indexed for inflation) or actual qualified LTC expenses. Benefits that exceed these limits are includible in gross income. In other words, per diem benefits that exceed actual expenses but are less than $330 per day are received tax free.

Benefits are qualified if the insured is (1) receiving care pursuant to a plan prescribed by a licensed health care practitioner, and (2) certified *chronically ill* by the practitioner, as unable to perform at least two of the activities of daily living or requires substantial supervision due to cognitive impairment.

QUALIFIED LONG TERM CARE INSURANCE RIDERS   The *Pension Protection Act of 2006* modified Code §7702B to enhance the tax advantage applied to QLTCI riders under life insurance policies and made coverage possible as annuity riders. Charges attributable to LTC riders and deducted from the cash value of the base policy had been considered distributions from the base policy and includible in taxable income.

The Code now treats riders as separate contracts for tax purposes (under state law, they remain parts of the base contract) if the base contract complies with the §7702 life insurance and §72 annuity requirements. Charges for riders paid from policy value that satisfy the criteria for QLTCI are not taxed as distributions. Charges reduce the policyowner's basis in the base contract. These provisions do not apply to qualified annuities.

CONCLUSIONS

Life and health insurance products are afforded special tax privileges under the *Internal Revenue Code*, as the U.S. Congress has for many years sought to promote personal financial responsibility. Although subject to highly technical rules and interpretations, the savings elements accumulate and the benefits are generally received free from income tax. The tax advantages, in addition to the economics of the insuring agreements, make these products useful tools in individual financial, retirement, and estate planning as well as in the financial management of businesses.

ENDNOTES

1 *Pollock v. Farmers' Loan & Trust Company*, 157 U.S. 429 (1895), *affirmed on rehearing*, 158 U.S. 601 (1895).

2 *Commissioner v. Glenshaw Glass Co.*, 348 U.S. 426 (1955).

3 For a discussion of this "tug of war" between industry entrepreneurs and taxing authorities see Christian D. DesRochers, John T. Adney, Douglas N, Hertz, and Brian King, *Life Insurance and Modified Endowments Under Internal Revenue Code Sections 7702 and 7702A*. Society of Actuaries (2004), Chapters VIII and IX.

4 This section draws in parts from Harold D. Skipper and Wayne Tonning, *An Advisor's Guide to Life Insurance* (Chicago; American Bar Association, 2011), Chapters 7 and 18.

5 See Cohen v. Commissioner, 39 T.C. 1055 (1963), acq. 1964-1 C.B. 4, Nesbitt v. Commissioner 43 T. C. 329 (1965), Griffith v. Commissioner 35 T. C. 882 (1961).

6 *Estate of Wong Wing Non v. Comm.*, 18 TC 205 (1952).

CHAPTER 22

LIFE INSURANCE IN ESTATE PLANNING

This chapter explores how life insurance can be helpful in estate planning.[1] We begin with a short exposition of the general nature of the estate planning process. We then present overviews of the U.S. federal estate, gift, and generation skipping transfer taxes. We next discuss how property passes at death, some common estate planning instruments, and how life insurance fits into estate planning.

As estate planning is driven by the many details of each nation's laws relating to the above subject areas and, therefore, varies widely from nation to nation, we are unable to embed an international perspective in this exploration, instead focusing on U.S. law and practice. Of course, some elements of the U.S. situation will be similar if not identical with selected elements of other countries' laws and practice, so, to that extent, the material herein can be relevant to other nations.

THE ESTATE PLANNING PROCESS

The purpose of estate planning is to develop a post-death plan that will enhance and maintain the financial security of individuals and their families. Estate planning is concerned with the distribution of property at death and is intimately intertwined with lifetime financial planning. Indeed, the estate planning process is identical in principle to the financial planning process. As we explore more fully later in this chapter, data first must be gathered and objectives established. This normally is done as a part of fact finding in personal financial planning. A plan is then designed for the individual. After review and approval, the plan must be implemented, including the execution of necessary legal documents and any transfers of property. Finally, the individual should be made aware that a periodic review of the plan is desirable to determine if changes in financial positions, family relationships, goals, laws, or other circumstances necessitate changes in the estate plan.

An estate plan reflects the values of the individual. It may evidence his or her cares and concerns for other human beings as well as for him- or herself. The plan also may reflect his or her self-interest, grievances, and grudges. Much will be revealed about the individual's character, philosophy of life, and attitudes by the types of planning options selected and the reasons for which he or she selects them.

Estate planning usually involves one or more of the following: an attorney, an accountant, a bank trust officer, an insurance specialist, and a financial planner. An attorney is crucial because plans usually cannot be executed properly without knowledge of the law; plus only attorneys may practice law. The attorney provides legal advice and prepares needed instruments assuring that the individual's intentions are expressed in legally enforceable language that serves as the basis for carrying out the plan. These instruments may include wills, trusts, buy-sell agreements, and others.

An accountant is the advisor most likely to have annual contact with the client and to be familiar with the details of individual's assets, liabilities, and income. The accountant also is most likely to prepare the estate tax return. If a trust is needed, a trustee will be necessary. Trust officers will be familiar with estate planning and various estate planning tools. The long term nature of the relationship between the trustee and beneficiaries argues for great care in trustee selection. Bank trust departments are often trustees.

A life insurance specialist commonly plays an important role in estate planning, often instigating such planning, as he or she can secure the products to provide the estate with needed cash to pay estate tax and other liabilities and to fund other estate planning goals, including providing funds for the future income needs of surviving family members. Life insurance is the primary asset of many estates.

A personal financial planner also may have initiated the individual's interest in estate planning or may have already been involved as a financial or investment advisor. Many financial planners, as noted in Chapter 19, are licensed life insurance agents and may sell the needed insurance coverages.

UNITED STATES FEDERAL TRANSFER TAX LAWS AFFECTING ESTATE PLANNING

The U.S. *Internal Revenue Code* (IRC) provides a unified system of taxation on the transfer of property by gift during life and upon death. The estate and gift tax provisions are also important in a life insurance context because the cash proceeds of life insurance are often used to pay the estate tax attributable to other property in a decedent's estate, and the transfer of policy ownership during life can be a valuable estate planning tool. The presentation here provides a foundation for the discussion of estate planning.

ESTATE TAXATION

The federal estate tax is a tax on a person's right to transfer property on his or her death. The federal gift tax, discussed in the next major section, is a tax on a person's right to transfer property during life. Although not a tax on the property itself, it is calculated on the value of such property. Since 2000, the rules have changed dramatically and erratically. The most recent changes apply to estates and gifts for the years 2013 and later.

The tax, introduced at a modest level in 1916, can be substantial in very large estates, but some 99.8 percent of estates pay no estate tax. Generally, a federal estate tax return must be filed and any estate taxes paid within nine months of the death of any U.S. citizen or resident who leaves a gross estate of more than a specified effective exempted amount. For decedents dying in 2014, the effective exempt amount is $5,340,000, indexed for inflation. Property valued in excess of this amount is taxed at a 40 percent rate. The number of estates subject to the estate tax has declined dramatically, with only about 0.14 percent of estates subject to the estate tax. An extension of up to 10 years for payment of the taxes may be granted by the *Internal Revenue Service* (IRS) for "reasonable cause," including for taxes associated with certain closely held businesses.

The first step in calculating the federal estate tax is to measure the value of the decedent's gross estate. The **gross estate** generally is the value of all property or interests in property owned or controlled by the deceased person. Next, allowable deductions are subtracted from the gross estate, resulting in the **taxable estate**. **Allowable deductions** include funeral and administration expenses, debts of the decedent, as well as bequests to charities and the surviving spouse. The gross estate less all allowable deductions except bequests to the surviving spouse and to charities is referred to as the **adjusted gross estate**.

Adjusted taxable gifts are added to the adjusted gross estate to yield the **tentative tax base**. **Adjusted taxable gifts** are those made after 1976, net of annual exclusions taken, for which a gift tax return was filed and that are not otherwise included in the decedent's gross estate. The reason for this addition is that the estate tax law is part of the unified transfer tax law that applies to transfers made at death and during life. It is necessary to add the value of lifetime taxable transfers (gifts) back to the tax base to derive the appropriate marginal tax bracket.

The appropriate tax rate is then applied to the tentative tax base to derive the **tentative federal estate tax**. Certain tax credits (the most important is the *unified credit* applicable to total gifts and bequests) are subtracted from the tentative tax to arrive at the estate tax. The **unified credit** is a tax credit that can be applied to offset estate and gift taxes. It is indexed for inflation as from 2011. For deaths occurring in 2013, the credit was $2,045,800 and for those occurring in 2014 the credit is $2,081,800. The practical effect of the unified credit is to eliminate transfer taxes on total lifetime and testamentary transfers up to a **unified credit equivalent** of $5,340,000 in 2014. After applying all applicable credits against the tentative federal estate tax, we have the amount of **federal estate taxes owed**.

In summary, the procedure is:

> *Gross Estate*
> – *Allowable Deductions*
> = *Taxable Estate*
> + *Adjusted Taxable Gifts*
> = *Computational Tax Base*
> x *Applicable Tax Rate*
> = *Tentative Tax*
> – *Credits*
> = *Federal Estate Tax Owed*

The relevant items that compose each of the adjustments are summarized in Table 22-1. The balance of this section presents more detailed information regarding the federal estate tax, beginning with an elaboration of the gross estate.

THE GROSS ESTATE The gross estate, the starting point for estate tax computation, is composed of the value of the decedent's interest in all property. The gross estate is derived by summing the values of each of the categories shown under the heading *Gross Estate* in Table 22-1. Some are reviewed briefly below. Outright ownership of property is not required for its value to be included in the gross estate. The value for estate tax purposes is the fair market value of the property at the date of death or, if a lower estate value would result (e.g., because of investment losses), six months after death – the **alternate valuation date**. A penalty of from 10 to 30 percent of the amount of tax owed can be imposed by the IRS for under-valuation. Special valuation rules are available for real property used for farming and other business purposes.

Table 22-1   **Federal Estate Tax Computation**

Gross Estate	Allowable Deductions	Adjusted Taxable Gifts	Credits
Owned property (§2033)	Funeral expenses (§2053(a)(1))	Gifts made after 1976 that are not otherwise includable in the gross estate, net of annual exclusions taken (§2001(b))	Unified credit (§2010)
Dower and curtesy interests (§2034)	Administration expenses (§2053(a)(2))		Gift taxes paid (§2012)
Gifts within three years of death (§2035)	Claims against estate (§2053(a)(3))		Federal estate taxes on previous transfers (§2013)
Gifts with life interest retained (§2036)	Mortgages and other debts (§2053(a)(4))		Foreign death taxes paid (§2014)
Gifts taking effect at death (§2037)	Unreimbursed casualty and theft losses (§2054)		
Revocable gifts (§2038)	Charitable, public, and religious bequests (§2055)		
Annuities (§2039)	Bequests to surviving spouse (§2056)		
Joint interests (§2040)	State estate and inheritance taxes paid (§2058)		
Powers of appointment (§2041)			
Life insurance death proceeds (§2042)			
Transfers for insufficient consideration (§2043)			
Certain marital deduction property (§2044)			

Property Owned by the Decedent   Property owned by the decedent includes all property of the decedent passing by will, by the applicable state's intestacy laws if the decedent died without a valid will, or by any other legal transfer at death including joint property with right of survivorship. Thus, the values of all personal property, financial assets and investments, and real property are included within this category.

For most persons, this is the largest category of the gross estate. If the decedent owned a life insurance policy on someone else's life (i.e., the decedent was *not* the insured), its interpolated terminal reserve (see below) plus any unearned premiums for the policy would be included in the decedent's gross estate.

Certain Gifts   The Code provides that the value of certain classes of gifts also must be included in the gross estate. They fall into four categories.

First, the value of certain gifts (Section 2035) made by the decedent within three years of his or her death is added to the gross estate. These include transfers in which the donor/decedent had retained certain interest in or power over the gifted property and gifts of life insurance policies. Gift taxation is discussed below.

Second, the value of gifts with a life interest retained (Section 2036) is added to the gross estate. These are gifts where the decedent gifted property to someone but retained the right to receive income from the property for life, the right to use the property, or the right to designate who ultimately receives the property or income. For example, if Sarah gave her house to Blake but retained the right to live in the house for the rest of her life, this IRC section requires that the value of the house be included in Sarah's gross estate.

Third, the value of gifts taking effect at death (Section 2037) are included in the gross estate. A gift taking effect at death occurs when property is given to someone (in trust or otherwise) but with the stipulation that he or she may take possession or enjoyment of it only upon the donor's death. If the likelihood of the gift reverting to the donor immediately before death is greater than 5 percent, the entire value is included in the gross estate. For example, assume that Claude established a trust for his granddaughter, Celie, with the trust corpus (assets) to be paid to her on his death, but if she predeceased him, the corpus is to revert to him. If the chance that he would survive Celie were greater than 5 percent, the value of the entire gift would be included in his gross estate. Finally, gifts wherein the decedent retained the power to alter, amend, revoke, or terminate the gift are revocable gifts (Section 2038) and their value is included in the gross estate.

Annuities   If a decedent was receiving annuity payments at his or her death and the payments ceased at the annuitant's death, no property interest exists to include in the gross estate. If income or lump sum payments are to be made to another person on the annuitant's death, the present value of those survivor benefits might be included in the estate. Survivor benefits are included in a decedent's gross estate to the extent that the decedent paid for the contract. Thus, if the decedent paid *no* part of the contract purchase price, the entire value of the survivor benefits is *excluded* from the gross estate. If the decedent paid the full contract purchase price, the opposite result occurs. If the decedent paid only a portion of the purchase price, that proportionate share of the survivor benefit is included in the gross estate.

For example, if Martin contributed the full $50,000 toward the purchase of a joint and last survivor annuity and the value of the survivor benefit on his death was determined to be $40,000, the entire $40,000 is included in his estate. If Martin had paid one fourth of the purchase price, $10,000 is included. Also, the cash value of an annuity during its accumulation period is included in the decedent's estate under this code section if, and to the extent that, the decedent made contributions toward its purchase.

Joint Interest Property   Property owned jointly during lifetime by the deceased person and someone else is referred to as **joint interest property** and is included in whole or in part in the decedent's gross estate. The extent to which this property is included is a function of the nature of the ownership interest. Although state variations exist, four types of joint ownership are commonly found.

Property is held in **joint tenancy with right of survivorship** (JTWROS) when it is owned by two or more persons and, on the death of any owner, his or her ownership interest passes automatically to the surviving owners. Ownership is not vested in any individual but in the owners as a group. As such, 100 percent of the property's value is included in the decedent's gross estate, except to the extent that the survivors contributed to the property's purchase. Thus, if Luke's estate, on whom the burden rests, can prove survivors contributed $800,000 toward a $1.0 million property purchase price, only 20 percent of the property's current value would be included in his estate. Under a JTWROS, the decedent's heirs have no claims against the property; the surviving owners continue to be the sole owners as a group. Ownership interest arising from a JTWROS cannot be passed by will.

A **tenancy by the entirety** is a joint ownership of property created between spouses in which a decedent's interest passes automatically to the surviving spouse. Unlike the joint tenancy, the property is deemed to be owned 50 percent by each spouse, irrespective of who contributed the purchase price. Thus, 50 percent of the property value is included in the gross estate of the first spouse to die. Ownership interest does not pass by will but by the nature of the ownership.

A **tenancy in common** is a joint ownership arrangement wherein each member owns his or her share outright and a decedent's ownership interest passes to his or her heirs. On the death of a member of a tenancy in common, his or her proportionate share is included in the gross estate.

The fourth form of joint ownership, **community property**, establishes property acquired during marriage as property of the marriage community. On the death of one spouse, one half of the property value is included automatically in the decedent's estate, irrespective of the proportion of the purchase price paid by the decedent. Rules pertaining to community property law vary greatly from state to state. Eight U.S. states (Arizona, California, Idaho, Louisiana, Nevada, New Mexico, Texas, and Washington) have community property laws. Wisconsin adopted a marital property system in 1986 that is similar to community property in many respects.

Power of Appointment   If a decedent held a general power of appointment over property on his or her death, the value of the property is included in the gross estate. A **general power of appointment** exists when an individual has the right to dispose of property that he or she does not own, including giving it to him- or herself. For example, Leonard may be receiving a lifetime income under a trust and have the power to withdraw all or a portion of the trust corpus during his lifetime. This right to invade the trust funds or **corpus** is a general power of appointment and will cause the entire value of the trust to be included in Leonard's gross estate on death, even though he may never have actually exercised the withdrawal right.

Property over which an individual has a general power of appointment will not be included in the gross estate if the holder's right to consume or invade the property is limited by certain defined standards, such as those relating to his or her health, maintenance, education, or support. Also, a **special power of appointment**, wherein the individual has the power to appoint anyone *but* himself or herself or his or her estate or creditors to receive property, does not cause property to be included in the gross estate.

Life Insurance   IRC Section 2042 provides that life insurance death proceeds are included in a decedent's gross estate for federal estate tax purposes if either of two conditions applies:

1. the proceeds are payable to or for the benefit of the insured's estate or
2. the insured possessed any incidents of ownership in the policy at death.

Thus, even if the insured did not own the policy, death proceeds are included in the gross estate if the estate is the beneficiary. Also, proceeds payable, not *to*, but *for the benefit* of the decedent's estate are included in the gross estate. For example, if Russell, as the owner and beneficiary of a $250,000 policy on Sydney's life, collaterally assigns the policy to a bank to cover her loan of $100,000, the $100,000 death proceeds utilized to extinguish the estate's debt is included in Sydney's estate even though Russell was both owner and beneficiary of the policy.

If the deceased insured possessed no incidents of ownership in the policy and if proceeds are not payable to or for the benefit of the estate, proceeds escape inclusion in the gross estate under this IRC section (although other sections occasionally result in their inclusion). Incidents of ownership include the right to change the beneficiary, the right to surrender or otherwise terminate the policy, the right to assign the policy, the right to obtain a policy loan, and, in general, the ability to exercise any important right of the policy. Complete policy ownership certainly will cause death proceeds to be included in the estate, but possession of only one important policy right alone might cause the entire proceeds to be included in the gross estate.

A policy can be removed from the gross estate, even though the insured was the owner, if it is given or sold to someone else via absolute assignment (and provided proceeds are not payable to or for the benefit of the estate). If the ownership transfer is via gift and occurs within three years of the date of death, however, the policy proceeds will be included in the gross estate as a gift made within three years of death (IRC Section 2035).

Miscellaneous   Certain other interests are included in the gross estate: (1) dower and curtesy interests (Section 2034) and (2) certain marital deduction property (Section 2044). A dower (for the wife) or a curtesy (for the husband), also called a *forced share*, is a statutory requirement directing that a surviving spouse must receive at least a certain minimum proportion of the estate of the deceased spouse.

Transfers for insufficient considerations (Section 2043) are included in the gross estate. They are transfers wherein the amount paid for property was below fair market value. The excess of the fair market value over the consideration received is included.

The Taxable Estate   After deriving the gross estate value, the next step is to derive the taxable estate: the gross estate less deductions. IRC Sections 2053 to 2058 define these deductions. Each of these sections is discussed below.

Expenses, Debts, and Claims   Deductions are permitted for the cost of the decedent's funeral and for the expenses associated with the administration of the estate. These latter expenses include items such as appraisal fees, attorney's fees, and executor's commissions.

Claims against the estate – such as those arising from unpaid property, income, and other taxes owed prior to death – are deductible. Indebtedness of the decedent can be deducted provided the asset, if the debt is secured, is included in the estate. Thus, mortgage and auto loan balances at the time of death are deductible. Other debts such as those arising from consumer loans and charge card balances are also deductible provided the decedent is legally responsible for their payment.

Unreimbursed Losses   Casualty and theft losses incurred during estate settlement are deductible from the gross estate. If the loss is indemnified by insurance or otherwise, only the net loss is deductible.

Charitable and Related Transfers   Property left to qualified religious, charitable, scientific, literary, and educational organizations, as well as property left to foster amateur sports competition and the prevention of cruelty to children or animals is deductible. Additionally, bequests to qualified veterans' organizations are deductible.

Family-Owned Business Interests   Enacted in 2003, IRC Section 2057 eases the estate tax burden for qualified family-owned businesses, making it easier for heirs to retain the business. The purpose is to prevent a forced sale to satisfy estate taxes. To qualify for this special deduction, the decedent must have materially participated in and owned the business and a family member must do likewise afterward. Certain minimum time periods apply. The executor must elect the additional deduction. The deduction is available for up to $675,000 of qualified family-owned business interests. If the deduction is taken, the estate tax unified credit exemption equivalent is equal to the lesser of the regular unified credit exemption equivalent or $1,300,000 minus the deduction.

To qualify, the business interest must comprise at least 50 percent of the adjusted gross estate. A **qualified family-owned business interest** is defined as any trade or business with its principal place of business in the U.S. that is owned at least 50 percent by one family, 70 percent by two families, or 90 percent by three families provided the decedent's family owned at least 30 percent.

Transfers to Surviving Spouse   The value of any property left to a surviving spouse – called the **marital deduction** – may be deducted from the gross estate in determining the taxable estate. The deduction is *unlimited*. If all property is left to the surviving spouse, the taxable estate is zero. For most married decedents, this deduction is the most important. Generally, only property that would be included in the surviving spouse's estate qualifies for the marital deduction. This requirement means that certain terminable interests in property left to the spouse will not qualify, such as a life-only interest in property. The IRC, however, in Section 2056, provides certain exceptions to the terminable interest rule. The most important exception relates to **qualified terminable interest property** (QTIP), which is property passing from the decedent that meets these conditions:

1. the surviving spouse is entitled to a lifetime income payable at least annually from the property,
2. no one can appoint (e.g., by gift) any part of the property to anyone except the spouse during the spouse's lifetime, and
3. the executor makes an irrevocable election to have the marital deduction apply.

Thus, a surviving spouse can be given a lifetime only interest in property and have the value of the property taken as a deduction from the gross estate if the specific conditions are met. The spouse must receive income at least annually from the property and no one must be able to divert property ownership away from the spouse during his or her lifetime. The purpose is to further a decedent's wishes by preventing a surviving spouse from transferring the property to anyone other than the decedent's ultimate intended beneficiaries without disinheriting the spouse entirely.

Finally, a deduction may be taken for estate and inheritance taxes paid to states. In the past, these taxes could be credited against the federal estate tax, but no longer. Although most states no longer levy such taxes, they can be an important part of planning for those that continue to levy them, such as New York.

TENTATIVE TAX BASE   Adjusted taxable gifts are added to the adjusted gross estate to derive a tentative tax base. The U.S. estate tax law is part of a transfer tax law that applies to both living and testamentary (i.e., death) transfers. This unified approach means that it is necessary to add back, for estate tax computational purposes, the value of property gifted during life and that did not qualify for the annual exclusion. This permits the calculation of a transfer tax based on all taxable transfers, both living and testamentary. A credit is permitted (as discussed below) for previous gift taxes paid. This recalculation is necessary because transfer tax rates are progressive: higher rates apply to larger taxable amounts.

In 2014, individuals are permitted to give away annually up to $14,000 per donee (gift recipient) and not pay any gift tax or file a return. If a spouse joins in the gift – termed **gift splitting** – up to $28,000 per donee annually may be given without incurring any gift tax. These figures are indexed for inflation. Moreover, one spouse may give the other any amount and incur no transfer tax liability, as the unlimited marital deduction is also available for marital gifts.

The value of adjusted taxable gifts is the sum of all post 1976 gifts, net of exclusions and deductions. Also, unlike the taxes on incomplete gifts included in the gross estate, gift taxes paid on these adjusted gifts may be excluded from the gross estate. The value included in the tentative tax base is the property value at the time of the gift, not its fair market value at date of death.

TENTATIVE AND FINAL FEDERAL ESTATE TAX   The appropriate federal estate tax rate is applied to the tentative tax base to derive the tentative federal estate tax. The maximum federal rate is 40 percent. The actual federal estate tax owed is obtained by netting permissible credits against the tentative federal estate tax. Typically, the most important is the unified credit, $2,081,800 in 2014, that can be applied against estate (and gift) taxes otherwise due. It is applied on a cumulative basis to all lifetime and testamentary transfers. It applies as a direct offset against the tax. The credit is the equivalent of exempting $5,340,000 from taxation for 2014.

Three final credits include, first, taxes paid on previous gifts. This treatment is consistent as the value of previous gifts is added back into the estate. Second, occasionally a decedent leaves property and the heir dies within a short time of the first person's death. If estate taxes were paid on the property left to the heir, a part or all of that tax may be available as a credit against the estate tax of the second decedent. The permissible credit is a decreasing percentage of the estate tax paid on the first death transfer; thus,

- 100 percent if deaths occur within two years,
- 80 percent if deaths occur within three or four years,
- 60 percent if deaths occur within five or six years,
- 40 percent if deaths occur within seven or eight years,
- 20 percent if deaths occur within nine or 10 years, and
- 0 percent if deaths occur 10 or more years apart.

Third, to prevent double taxation, a credit is allowed for death taxes paid to another country or U.S. possession if (1) the value of the property is included in the gross estate and (2) the property is situated in that other country or possession.

The latest (2013) tax reform makes permanent the concept of portability, which effectively makes the federal estate tax exemption amount (or, equivalently, the unified credit) "portable" between spouses. **Portability** allows any unused exemption amount following the death of the first spouse to be added to the exemption amount of the second spouse on his or her death. This avoids the former necessity to set up special trusts that to accomplish the same goal.

AN ESTATE TAX ILLUSTRATION   An example can illustrate the operation of the estate tax and its impact on an estate. Mike is a real estate developer who is exploring with his attorney what his likely estate tax obligation would be on his death. Mike's personal balance sheet showing assets and liabilities consists of the following:

Assets

Residence	$1,000,000
Real Estate Investments	14,000,000
Financial Investments	1,240,000
Total Assets	$16,240,000

Liabilities

Mortgages	$4,000,000
Consumer Debt	100,000
Total Liabilities	$4,100,000
Net Worth	$12,140,000

Mike also owns a $1,000,000 term life insurance policy, payable to Dawn, his wife, thus qualifying for the marital deduction. His current will provides that the balance of his estate is to be passed to his children. He has made no taxable life-time gifts. His attorney estimates funeral expenses at $10,000 and estate adminis-tration expenses to be $130,000. The value of his gross estate would be:

Total Assets	$16,240,000
Plus: Life Insurance	1,000,000
Gross Estate	$17,240,000

Subtracting *allowable deductions* yields his estimated taxable estate, as follows:

Gross Estate		$17,240,000
Less: Allowable Deductions		
Mortgages	4,000,000	
Consumer Debt	100,000	
Funeral Expenses	10,000	
Administration Expenses	130,000	
Marital Deduction	1,000,000	
Total Deductions	$5,240,000	
Equals: Taxable Estate	$12,000,000	
Plus: Adjusted Taxable Gifts	0	
Equals: Computational Tax Base	$12,000,000	
Tentative Tax from Tax Table	$4,745,800	
Less: Credits		
Unified Credit	$2,081,800	
Federal Estate Tax Owed	$2,664,000	

The *computational tax base* is the taxable estate, as Mike has made no lifetime taxable gifts. Thus, applying the lower tax rates to the first $1,000,000 of the estate and 40 percent to the $11.0 million balance yields a *tentative tax* of $4,745,800. Reducing this amount by his unified credit of $2,081,800 results in an estimate of $2,664,000 for *estate taxes owed* were he to die in 2014. (Alternatively, one can reduce the computational tax base of $12 million by the $5.34 million tax credit exemption equivalent, and apply the 40 percent rate to the $6.75 million balance to derive the same $2.664 million tax.)

Two important observations can be made about Mike's potential estate tax situation. First, the tax owed at his death can be substantially reduced or even eliminated by increasing his bequest to Dawn via the marital deduction. Second, he requires liquid funds of $2,804,000 to pay funeral and administrative costs and federal estate taxes. Yet his liquid funds (financial assets and life insurance) are only $2,240,000. Thus, in the absence of an increased bequest to Dawn, perhaps some part of Mike's real estate must be sold to provide the liquid funds needed at an inopportune time for Dawn – soon after Mike's death. The liquidity problem is exacerbated if the mortgage loan must be paid off. These potential problems can be addressed before Mike's death through proper estate planning and life insur-ance, as we discuss later.

GIFT TAXATION
As with the federal estate tax, the federal gift tax is imposed on the right to trans-fer property to another person. The estate tax reaches those transfers that take

place when a property owner dies, whereas the gift tax reaches those transfers that take place during the property owner's lifetime. Despite the imposition of this tax, there can be advantages to making gifts. To understand these, we first examine the general provisions of the gift tax law. Next we consider the gift tax treatment of life insurance and annuities.

A lifetime gift to an individual incurs a federal gift tax generally at the same rate as the federal estate tax. As in the estate tax situation, the unified credit is applied directly to reduce the tentative gift tax. The amount of gift tax payable in a specific taxable period is determined by a three step process:

1. Determine the sum of all of the donor's lifetime taxable gifts, including prior gifts and current gifts. (Taxable gifts do not include gifts qualifying for the annual exclusion ($14,000 in 2014) per donee for present interest gifts.

2. Apply the unified rate schedule to the total taxable gifts to derive the tentative tax.

3. Subtract the unified tax credit to yield the gift tax payable in the current period.

GIFT TAX EXCLUSION   The federal gift tax law is not aimed at the usual exchange of gifts associated with birthdays, holidays, and similar occasions. Consequently, the law provides that gifts valued at or less than an **annual exclusion** are exempt from gift taxation and from filing a federal gift tax return. In 2014, the exclusion is $14,000. This exclusion applies to gifts made to each recipient, irrespective of the number. Moreover, it is available year after year. This means that an individual could give $14,000 – or $28,000 if gift splitting is elected – to each of a large number of recipients each year without incurring any gift tax liability.

The exclusion is indexed for inflation. The IRC provides that the indexed exclusion is rounded to the next lowest multiple of $1,000. Because the inflation adjustment occurs in multiples of $1,000, it can be several years between adjustments.

The annual exclusion is available only when the gift is one of a present interest. A **present interest** exists where the donee has possession or enjoyment of the property immediately rather than at some future date. The exclusion is not available for gifts of **future interest** in property; that is, any interest in property that does not pass into the donee's possession or enjoyment until some future date. (Future gifts can be made legally, but they do not qualify for the gift tax annual exclusion.)

DEDUCTIONS   As with the federal estate tax marital deduction, the **gift tax marital deduction** permits tax free transfers between spouses. This deduction is available without limit. Further, the IRC permits full deduction for gifts to qualified charities of the same types as those mentioned in the discussion of the estate tax charitable deduction. Gifts to private individuals can never qualify for the charitable deduction, no matter how needy or deserving the beneficiaries may be.

GIFTS OF LIFE INSURANCE   A life insurance policy is especially well suited as a gift. The death benefit, which subsequently passes estate tax free, normally greatly exceeds the value of the gift. Gifts are also made of annuities. Gifts of life insurance and annuities include gifts of the contract itself, gifts of premium payments, and gifts of policy proceeds. Each of these is dealt with individually, as the valuation of each differs.

Gifts of Life Insurance and Annuity Contracts   If a policyholder irrevocably assigns all of his or her rights in an existing insurance contract for less than an adequate consideration, he or she has made a gift of the contract and gift taxes may be due. Of course, if the owner receives an adequate consideration for the transfer, it is not a gift. If the owner gives an existing contract upon which premiums remain to be paid, the value of the gift is the policy's **fair market value**, which is the market value of a comparable contract or, if a comparable contract is not ascertainable (a likely result), the interpolated terminal reserve (an amount equal to the policy reserve interpolated to the date of the gift) plus the value of unearned premiums and any accumulated dividends, and less any policy indebtedness. The reserve value, not the cash surrender value, is considered, although the difference often is negligible except in the early policy years. If the policyowner gives a single premium or paid up life insurance policy or annuity, the value of the gift equals the **replacement cost** of the contract, which is the single premium that an insurance company would charge for a comparable contract issued at the insured's/annuitant's attained age. A comparable contract is one providing payments of the same amount.

The following example illustrates the computation of a contract's fair market value using its interpolated terminal reserve. Assume that a gift is made today of a contract issued 10 years and eight months ago. This year's annual premium of $1,800 was paid on its due date, eight months ago. The 10th and 11th year's terminal reserves are shown below, along with the amount of the year's increase in reserve.

	11th year terminal reserve	*$16,000*
Less:	*10th year terminal reserve*	*13,900*
Equals:	*Increase in reserve* *$2,100*	

The value of the gift is composed of the reserve at the time of the gift plus the unearned premium. The reserve at the time of the gift equals the reserve at the beginning of the year ($13,900) plus the pro-rata increase in the reserve (8/12 of $2,100 or $1,400) for a total of $15,300. The unearned premium is $600 (4/12 of $1,800), that portion of the premium paid that is applicable to insurance protection *not* already provided. The value of the gift, therefore, is $15,900.

Gifts of Premiums   When an individual makes the premium payments on a life insurance policy or annuity contract that he or she does not own, the individual has made a taxable gift to the owner in an amount equal to the premium paid, subject to the annual exclusion. Thus, if Larry makes a premium payment on a policy owned by Kelley on her own life and under which Jay is the beneficiary, Larry has made a gift to Kelley in the amount of the premium payment.

Similarly, premiums paid by an insured are gifts if the insured has no incidents of ownership in the policy and proceeds of the policy are payable to a beneficiary other than his or her estate. Premiums paid by a beneficiary on a policy that he or she owns are not gifts.

Gifts of Insurance Proceeds   Under ordinary circumstances, life insurance death proceeds are not gifts. In some extraordinary instances, however, they may be a taxable gift. When one person owns a policy, a second is the insured, and a third is the beneficiary, a gift is made from the policyowner to the beneficiary at the insured's death. The amount of the gift equals the full amount of the insurance proceeds.

Thus, if Becky owns a policy of life insurance on her husband's life, with their children named as revocable beneficiaries, Becky will be deemed to have made a gift to the children in the full amount of the proceeds when they are paid at her husband's death. There is no intent to make a gift in the literal sense, but a taxable gift has been made nevertheless. A gift of endowment insurance proceeds likewise occurs when, upon the maturity of an endowment policy, the proceeds are paid to a revocable beneficiary of the policy who is not the owner.

GENERATION-SKIPPING TRANSFER TAXATION

The IRC provides for a **generation skipping transfer tax** (GST) to be levied when a property interest is transferred to persons who are two or more generations younger than the transferor. The **transferor** for property subject to the federal estate tax is the decedent and, for property subject to the gift tax, the transferor is the donor. The GST tax is intended to ensure that transfer taxes are paid by wealthy persons who might otherwise avoid a generation of transfer taxes by passing their property to heirs (**skip persons**) beyond those of the immediately following generation. The tax is in addition to any federal estate or gift taxes owed because of the transfer.

For example, a grandmother may gift property directly to her granddaughter rather than to her son. In the absence of the GST, this gift could avoid all transfer taxes that otherwise might have been incurred if the transfer were first to her son and then by the son to the granddaughter.

The amount of the GST tax is a function of the property value transferred and the applicable tax rate. In 2014, each person may transfer up to $5.34 million during his or her lifetime free of the GST tax. If the spouse joins in the transfer, a $10.68 million lifetime exemption applies. These exemption amounts are indexed for inflation.

The value of transferred property in excess of the exemption is subject to the maximum prevailing transfer tax rate, currently 40 percent. The GST tax is of little importance to most persons, but those with great wealth could incur substantial taxes under this provision.

Life insurance death proceeds, irrespective of the manner in which they are paid, can attract the GST tax if they are paid to a skip person. This unpleasant result can be avoided by ensuring that the death proceeds are not included in the insured's estate and through appropriate use of life insurance trusts, as discussed later in this chapter.

HOW PROPERTY PASSES AT DEATH

Property is transferred at death through different mechanisms. First, property is transferred under the specific provisions of wills and trusts. Second, property may pass by operation of law. Examples include joint tenancy with right of survivorship where property passes automatically from the deceased joint owner to the surviving joint owner(s), benefits mandated under Social Security and other statutes, and contractual provisions such as life insurance, annuity, or qualified plan beneficiary designations. Finally, if there is no will, all other property – all not specifically provided for elsewhere – is transferred under the laws of intestacy to familial heirs of the deceased. (In the rare event no statutory heirs are alive, the property passes – **escheats** – to the state.)

Property that passes by will (or state intestacy laws, see below) is sometimes referred to as **probate property**. The probate process can be expensive. Property transferred under other legal mechanisms – particularly trusts, life insurance, annuities, and qualified plans – escapes probate and so its costs. The rules requiring the inclusion of property in probate and the inclusion of property in the gross estate for estate tax purposes are entirely different.

Several estate planning instruments may be used to ensure that (1) assets are sufficient to meet objectives, (2) beneficiaries receive assets in the proportion and manner desired, (3) minimum income, estate, gift, and state death taxes and other transfer costs are paid, subject to accomplishing the desired objectives, and (4) sufficient liquidity exists to cover transfer costs.

WILLS

A **will** is a legal declaration of an individual's wishes as to the disposition of his or her property on death. It is the principal means by which most estate plans are implemented. A person who dies without a valid will or without having made a complete disposition of his or her property is said to have died **intestate. Intestate succession statutes** determine the identity of heirs and their shares of distributed property. The distribution is based on the degree of individuals' **consanguinity** (blood relationship) to the decedent rather than the decedent's intentions. Without a will, property cannot be left to charity or to a friend. The state, rather than the individual, appoints the person to administer the decedent's estate, called an **administrator,** and the state, not the individual, chooses guardians for any minor children. For these and many other reasons, a will is an essential element of in estate plan.

A will affords the opportunity to declare beneficiaries and to name an **executor** – the individual or institution (bank or trust company) responsible for the execution of the will's provisions and the administration of the estate. The typical will calls for the payment of the deceased person's debts and all estate expenses. The will can provide for gifts to charities and other persons including those who are "natural objects of the deceased's bounty." Wills can also create trusts and name trustees and guardians for minor children. Wills permit the implementation of plans to save income, estate, and gift taxes and to minimize estate expenses. As with the overall estate plan, the will should be reviewed periodically and revised as needed.

Wills are particularly important tools for owners of closely held businesses. The will can authorize the executor to continue the business to avoid a forced sale, or it can direct its sale. Children or others with an interest or aptitude for the business can inherit the business directly thereby possibly avoiding family discord.

A will is an **ambulatory instrument**, meaning that it does not take effect until the death of the **testator**, the person making the will. Therefore, it can be changed at any time during life. A new will should expressly revoke any prior wills. The existence of multiple wills is a costly administrative burden, likely causing confusion as to the intentions of the deceased. A **codicil** is an amendment that adds provisions or changes a part of a will but does not replace the will. A will also can be revoked by physically destroying or mutilating it.

A will must meet technical and legal requirements. The testator must be competent to make a valid will. Competency means that the testator is of legal age, understands that he or she is making a will, knows the extent and nature of the property being disposed of, and knows the natural objects of his or her bounty. The will must be free from fraud, duress, and undue influence. The will also must be in writing and properly executed, according to applicable state law. Oral wills generally are not valid, with some exceptions. The will must be signed, indicating an intent to make a will, and generally attested to by an appropriate number of witnesses.

In many states, a surviving spouse is entitled to what is called a *statutory* or *forced-heir share* of the deceased spouse's property, usually a one-third share. If the decedent's will leaves a lesser amount to the surviving spouse, the survivor can elect against the will and receive the same amount that would have been received had the testator died without a will. In some states, the right to elect against the will extends to children as well.

ADVANCE DIRECTIVES

Advance directives are legal documents that provide one's family and physicians with written instructions regarding one's preferences regarding medical treatment in the face of serious medical conditions. As has been said, "these documents speak for you when you're unable to speak for yourself." Four types of advance directives have become common.

- A **living will** is an advance directive setting forth the individual's wishes as to the use of life sustaining measures in case of terminal illness, prolonged coma, or serious incapacitation. An estate's value can be substantially reduced because of extraordinary, end-of-life medical measures intended to extend life. Indeed, an average of about 15 percent of *lifetime* medical expenses is incurred in the last six months of life. In response to this potential situation, an increasing number of individuals execute living wills. Older people with a living will spend only about one-third as much on their final hospital stay as those without one.

  Living wills offer some clear advantages in this age of impressive life prolonging technology, which may, unfortunately, not translate into improving quality of life. A living will is intended to ensure that the individual's (as opposed to some well intentioned family member's) wishes are being carried out. A living will also can ease the anguish that family members may suffer in making what could be excruciating life-or-death decisions.

- A **medical power of attorney** (POA) is an advance directive that designates an individual, referred to as the individual's health care agent or proxy, to make medical decisions for the person if he or she is unable to do so. A medical POA is sometimes called a *durable power of attorney for health care*. However, it is different from a durable power of attorney authorizing one person to make financial transactions for another.

- A **durable power of attorney** is an advance directive allowing individuals to protect themselves financially after they have become incapacitated or been declared incompetent to conduct their own affairs. Many financial planning experts consider this instrument to be among the most important in connection with planning for the elderly. It allows the holder of the power to make and execute financial decisions such as completing and signing tax returns and paying bills on behalf of the incapacitated or incompetent individual. Obviously, the person named to hold the power should be one in whom the individual has the utmost trust. A spouse or an adult child often holds the power. Upon recovery by the individual, full legal control reverts to him or her. Upon death, the power is terminated.
- A **do not resuscitate** (DNR) **order** constitutes a request not to have cardiopulmonary resuscitation (CPR) if a person's heart stops or if he or she stops breathing. A DNR order may be included in other advanced directives. One need not have another advance directive to have a DNR order. A physician can place a DNR order in a patient's medical chart.

State requirements for advance directives vary, but most statutes require the inclusion of an express statement that the individual is "of sound mind" and is voluntarily making the declaration. The details of the desired or undesired treatment are spelled out to the extent feasible, although no document can address all possible scenarios. State laws typically define key terms, such as "life sustaining procedure" and "terminal illness" and require that the documents be signed, dated, and witnessed in the manner of a will. No witness may have any interest in the individual's estate.

GIFTS

As noted earlier, a gift is the transfer of property ownership for less than an adequate consideration. The difference between the property's fair market value and its sales price, if any, is the value of the gift. For a gift to be complete, the donor (gift giver) and donee (gift recipient) both must be competent, and the donor must have a clear intent to make a gift. Furthermore, the donor must give up ownership and control, and the gift must be delivered and accepted by the donee. A gift is not considered complete for tax purposes if it is delivered and then borrowed back for an indefinite period of time.

As mentioned above, as of 2014, $14,000 (indexed for inflation) can be given away in property or cash each year to any number of persons regardless of relationship, without incurring gift tax liability, and gifts can be split between spouses, irrespective of which one owns the property. By making gifts (in property or cash) within the annual exclusion, the value is removed from the estate for tax purposes. In other words, $14,000 ($28,000 if a split gift) per year can be given to any one person, with no gift tax liability incurred, and the gifted property will be removed from the estate. If a gifting program is started early and continued, a series of annual exclusion gifts can substantially reduce estate taxes.

If a gift of more than the exclusion amount is made to any one person during a calendar year, a **taxable gift** has been made. A federal gift tax return is to be filed, and gift tax assessed according to the tax rate schedule. It is not necessary actually to pay tax until the unified tax credit has been exhausted. Some of the tax-based reasons for making gifts include the following:

- Individual gifts up to the amount of the annual exclusion are not added back to the estate for purposes of calculating federal estate tax. Thus, the estate is reduced by the amount of the annual exclusion.
- A credit is allowed against any federal estate tax due equal to the amount of any gift tax paid during lifetime.
- The gift tax is tax exclusive whereas the estate tax is tax inclusive. In other words, the assets used to pay gift taxes are not themselves subject to tax, yet assets used to pay estate taxes are included in calculating that tax. Box 22-1 illustrates the potential importance of this advantage.
- The appreciation of the value of the gift from the date of gift to the date of death is excluded from the estate.
- If a gift is made to someone other than the spouse, federal income tax can be saved if the property transferred would have otherwise produced taxable income to the donor.

Box 22-1
An Important Tax Advantage of Gifts: Tax Exclusiveness

The U.S. federal transfer tax system generally is tax *inclusive*. This means that estate taxes are levied on the total value of property in an individual's taxable estate, including property used to pay estate taxes. Property transferred during life, however, is generally tax *exclusive*. That is, transfer taxes do not apply to the taxes themselves. This difference can profoundly affect the total transfer taxes paid.

For example, Manfred wishes to transfer property valued at $5.0 million to Dagmar. He has exhausted his unified credit and is in the 40 percent marginal transfer tax bracket, so gift taxes would be about $2.00 million ($5.0 million x 0.40). Thus, Manfred needs $7.00 million to transfer $5.0 million to his daughter via gifting.

If Manfred chose to retain the property and transfer it to Dagmar at his death, the estate would need $8.57 million to make the transfer and pay related estate taxes. The estate taxes on $8.57 million would be $3.57 million (at the 40 percent rate), netting the $5.0 million to Dagmar. Thus, Manfred would require $1.57 million more property to achieve his objective at death than to do so during life. Of course, this treatment ignores the fact that transfer tax payment is made earlier with a lifetime rather than a testamentary transfer.

There are also many non-tax advantages in making taxable gifts. Box 22-2 lists some of the common non-tax reasons.

A life insurance policy can be an excellent type of property to gift. The value of the gift is the fair market value, as discussed above. Were the policy included in the estate at the time of death, the estate tax value would be the amount of the death proceeds. If the face amount of the policy were $1,000,000 and the value for gift purposes were no more than $14,000, the policy could be transferred by gift within the annual exclusion, and there would be no gift tax consequences. The donor must live for more than three years from the date of the gift to avoid inclusion of the policy proceeds in his or her estate under IRC Section 2035.

Greatly appreciated property can make an appropriate gift. If sale of the property is anticipated, a gift to a person in a lower income tax bracket can make good financial sense. The donee would then sell the property and pay less in taxes on the gain. The gift tax consequences should be compared with the income (or capital gain) tax consequences to determine which approach is expected to yield the lower tax bill.

Box 22-2
Non-tax Reasons for Making Gifts

Motivations for making gifts often are either unrelated or only indirectly related to saving on estate or income taxes. Non-tax reasons for making gifts include the following:

- Individuals derive satisfaction from giving to others.
- The expense of administration and other costs associated with processing the estate can be minimized or avoided by giving the property away during life.
- Anyone can review the public records of a probate court. By making a gift, the property is removed from probate and confidentiality retained.
- By giving property away, management responsibilities are shifted to the new owners.
- Should a person believe that he or she is no longer able to manage assets properly, the assets might be given away to protect their value.
- Making gifts to children can provide the opportunity for them to learn how to manage money or property.
- If an individual has assets that he or she wishes to pass to a particular individual and anticipates the possibility of family disharmony, making a gift during lifetime might avoid or minimize problems. If a will does not exist or is declared invalid because of a will contest, property that passes through the estate could ultimately be passed to unintended individuals. By giving the property away, this risk is eliminated.

If the property will be sold after death, it often may be smarter to retain it rather than give it away. This is because appreciated property receives a step-up in tax basis if included in the estate, whereas property that is given away carries over the donor's tax basis. If property is given away and the donee sells it, income tax must be paid on any difference between the amount received on sale and the donor's tax basis. If the property is retained and its value included in the estate, an estate tax may have to be paid on the fair market value of the property. The value of the property included in the gross estate becomes the new tax basis.

Thus, suppose Larry owns only one piece of property. He paid $10,000 for it, and it is now worth $200,000. If he gives the property away and the donee sells it, the donee must pay tax on the $190,000 gain. If he does not give away the property but retains it until his death, naming the person to whom he would have given it during lifetime as the beneficiary, the value of the property ($200,000) will be included in his estate for estate tax purposes but also becomes the new tax basis. If the property is then sold for its $200,000 fair market value, there is no gain and no income or capital gains tax need be paid by the beneficiary.

There are other potential disadvantages to making taxable gifts in excess of the equivalent exemption amount. One disadvantage, of course, is the loss of control. Moreover, the transfer tax is paid earlier than would otherwise be the case if the assets were held until death.

JOINT OWNERSHIP OF PROPERTY

Various types of joint ownership were presented above. Joint ownership can be a means of bypassing the probate estate and, thus, avoiding probate costs. This can be helpful in some situations. A potential disadvantage of joint ownership is that under a tenancy by the entirety (right of survivorship between spouses), the tax law requires that 50 percent of the fair market value of the property be included in the gross estate of the first joint tenant to die. Although this form of ownership avoids estate tax on one-half of the total property value in the first estate, 100 percent of the fair market value at the time of the death of the surviving spouse would be included in his or her estate. This is true because he or she would receive the first decedent's interest through survivor's rights, assuming that the surviving spouse did not sell or give away the property during his or her lifetime.

As only 50 percent of the value of the property was included in the first spouse's estate, the stepped-up basis for income tax purposes would apply only to that part of the total value. The excluded 50 percent would not receive a stepped-up basis. If the property might be sold during the surviving spouse's lifetime, this area should be examined carefully. It might be better if the entire property value were included in the gross estate to obtain a stepped-up basis on the total value of the property.

Trusts

Trusts are effective, common estate planning tools. They often supply elements that are impossible to obtain through gifts, provide flexibility, and can save on income, estate, and gift taxes. A **trust** is a legal arrangement whereby one party transfers property to someone else who holds the legal title and manages the trust property for the benefit of others. Property held in a trust is called the trust *corpus*. The person who establishes the trust is the **grantor** (also called the **creator** or **settlor**). The person who receives the legal title and manages the property is the **trustee**, and persons for whose benefit the property is held are the **beneficiaries**. (While we defined beneficiary narrowly in Chapter 1 in the context of a life insurance policy, the recipients of property distributed by wills and trusts are also termed beneficiaries.) As the word *trust* implies, faith and confidence are placed in the trustee to act solely on the beneficiary's behalf – a **fiduciary** responsibility. Legally, the trustee must act in accordance with the law and the provisions of the trust instrument.

Generic Types of Trusts   Many types of trusts exist, each designed to meet specific objectives. A trust created during life is an **inter vivos** or **living trust**. A living person creates the trust and transfers property to it. A trust created at death through a person's will is a **testamentary trust**. Property is transferred to the trust at death. It allows a testator to "control property from the grave" in that he or she can specify the post-death form and timing of distributions to children and others. This type of control can be useful in protecting property from being squandered and to ensure effective property management.

A living trust can be revocable or irrevocable. With a **revocable trust**, the grantor can terminate or alter the trust as he or she wishes and regain ownership of the property. With an **irrevocable trust**, he or she permanently relinquishes ownership and control of the donated property. A revocable trust might be desirable as a device for transferring assets directly to beneficiaries outside of the probate estate, avoiding related costs, and allowing the trust's business to be conducted on an uninterrupted, confidential basis. A revocable trust, however, provides no income, estate, or gift tax savings as the grantor retains effective ownership of the trust corpus. The value of the trust corpus will be included in the taxable estate, and trust income is taxable to the grantor. Administration and management charges often must be paid, offsetting some of the savings from not having the property pass through probate.

Control and ownership are relinquished over property placed in an irrevocable trust. This loss of flexibility could be a high price to pay should conditions change. When property is placed in an irrevocable trust, generally a complete gift has been made that may have gift tax consequences. Of course, income and estate tax savings applicable to any gift of property or cash may result.

TRUSTS FOR MINOR CHILDREN   Many persons make gifts from time to time to their minor children or grandchildren to accumulate funds for education or other use when they are old enough to handle the responsibility. A trust can be useful in such situations. As the annual exclusion is available only for gifts of a present interest, it may be unavailable for a gift to a minor in trust if the funds are not presently available to that minor. One way to avoid this problem is to establish a trust for minors known as a **Section 2503 trust** whereby a gift of a future interest can be made to minors without the loss of the annual gift tax exclusion. To qualify for the annual exclusion, IRC Section 2503(c) mandates the trust must provide that:

1. the trustee has discretion to distribute both principal and income,
2. the beneficiary is entitled to receive the trust corpus at age 21, and
3. should any beneficiary die before reaching maturity, his or her share of the assets is included in his or her gross estate.

By meeting these requirements, income can be accumulated until the minor reaches age 21, and the annual exclusion per beneficiary can be used. This type of trust is popular but can be costly to set up and maintain. Grandparents who wish to establish an educational fund for their grandchildren often use it. A generation skipping transfer tax could be imposed in such situations if the amounts involved were substantial.

With a Section 2503(c) trust, gifts of life insurance policies in trust for minors should qualify as those of a present interest if (1) policy value may be used for their benefit, (2) policy ownership vests at age 21, and (3) policy proceeds or value are included in the child's gross estate were he or she to die prior to age 21. Any premiums paid by the grantor should also qualify as present interest gifts. (A 2503(b) trust does not automatically vest at age 21.)

Gifts also can be made to minors under the *Uniform Gifts to Minors Act* or under the *Uniform Transfers to Minors Act*. These approaches are less expensive. Under these acts, an adult is named custodian for the minor and manages the property through a custodian account. The property is distributed to the minor at age 18 or 21, depending on state law.

CRUMMEY TRUSTS   In spite of its name (which is that of a successful litigant), the Crummey trust is a useful device. With a **Crummey trust**, also referred to as a **Crummey provision** or a **Crummey power** (within an irrevocable trust), gifts to the trust qualify as present interest gifts and thus the annual exclusion, provided the trust beneficiaries have a reasonable opportunity to demand distribution of amounts contributed to the trust. Otherwise, if trust beneficiaries do not have the right of their immediate enjoyment, they are gifts of future interest and do not qualify for the annual exclusion.

A Crummey provision ordinarily works as follows. The grantor makes a gift to an irrevocable, living trust. The trust beneficiaries often are the grantor's children, grandchildren, or both. The beneficiaries are notified by the trustee that they have the power for a defined period (e.g., 15 to 60 days) to withdraw some portion of recently gifted property. The simultaneous acts of the grantor transferring property to the trust and the beneficiaries being permitted to withdraw the same property from the trust are tantamount to the grantor giving the property to the beneficiaries outright, thus qualifying for the annual exclusion.

Of course, it is not anticipated that the beneficiaries will withdraw any property from the trust during the defined period. By not executing their powers, the beneficiaries permit their powers to lapse, such that the gifted property continues to be held by the trust under its distribution terms.

IRREVOCABLE LIFE INSURANCE TRUSTS   **Irrevocable life insurance trusts** (ILITs) are irrevocable living trusts created to own and be beneficiary of life insurance that is not part of the grantor's gross estate, yet with proceeds available to provide estate liquidity. If the grantor owns a life insurance policy that would otherwise be included in his or her estate, gifting of such a policy to the ILIT can be advisable. The full face amount is removed from the estate, yet it is valued at its much lower fair market value for gift tax purposes. If the grantor lives more than three years from the date the policy is gifted, death proceeds should not be a part of his or her taxable estate. If the policy is applied for and owned by the trustee from its inception, policy death proceeds should be excluded from the gross estate even if death occurs within the first three years, provided the purchase of the insurance was at the discretion of the trustee.

The trustee pays policy premiums from either trust corpus or annual gifts to the trust from the grantor. The latter is the more common approach, although the gifts must not be designated for premium payments. The trustee will have been given the authority (at his or her discretion) but not a mandate to purchase insurance and, if desired, to use trust funds – including those gifted annually by the grantor – to pay premiums.

Figure 22-1 illustrates the functioning of an ILIT for a death that occurred in 2011. At that time, the exemption amount was $5.0 million and the highest tax rate was 35 percent. After paying debts, covering administrative expenses of settling the estate, and meeting the decedent's charitable bequests, her remaining estate was composed almost exclusively of timberland valued at $25 million, which was in the family for decades, and neither she nor her two adult children wished to sell it. After taking the $5.0 million exemption from this amount, the taxable estate was $20 million. At a flat 35 percent tax rate, estate taxes of $7 million were due to the government.

The widow's will provided that her two children were to share equally in her estate. She had wisely and accurately estimated her estate taxes at $7 million and had created an ILIT whose trustee had elected to purchase a $7 million policy insuring her life. On her death, the life insurance company paid the $7 million death proceeds to the trust.

The trust agreement authorized the trustee to purchase property from the estate, which the trustee elected to do, thus acquiring family land valued at $7 million and simultaneously providing the executor with cash to pay estate taxes.

The ILIT trustee distributed the land valued at $7 million to the two children in equal proportions. After paying the IRS, the executor distributed the remaining $18.0 million of family land equally to the children. We can see that the life insurance, which was not included in the gross estate thanks to sound estate planning, enabled the family to retain ownership of the land and to meet estate settlement obligations.

Illustration of Irrevocable Life Insurance Trust   Figure 22-1

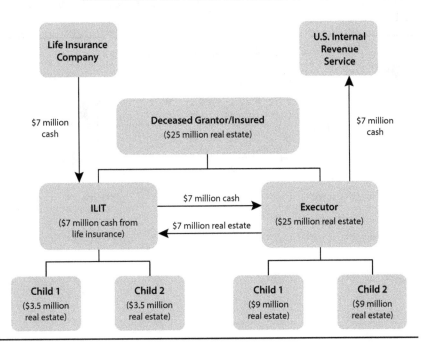

CHARITABLE REMAINDER TRUSTS   A **charitable split-interest gift** is shared by charitable and non-charitable beneficiaries according to the wishes of the donor. A **charitable remainder trust** (CRT) is an irrevocable trust funded with a split-interest gift by a grantor under which the trust (1) pays an income to a named non-charitable beneficiary for life or a specified term of up to 20 years; and (2), at the end of the trust term, pays the remaining assets to the charity beneficiary. If it is a living trust, the grantor may receive the income (often the case), and his or her property rights are termed a *retained interest*. The charitable beneficiary's interest is termed a *remainder interest*.

The CRT can be an effective means of helping a charity and of saving on transfer taxes. Many estate planners consider the CRT to be one of the best, simplest, and most underutilized estate planning tools.

As an example, an individual with highly appreciated assets, such as stock, real estate, or interests in a closely held business, can transfer the property to the trust for the exclusive benefit of the charity. Often, the property has provided a low income in relation to its value. The trustee promises to make a stream of income payments to the income beneficiary. The trustee often will sell a part or all of the donated property, investing the proceeds to provide some or all of the needed income to the beneficiary. Because the charitable trust is tax exempt, any sale is free from taxation. Thus, more money is available to fund a higher income than if the grantor had sold the property and paid taxes.

Because a charity is entitled to the remainder interest, the grantor is entitled to an income tax deduction immediately in an amount equal to that interest. The amount of the deduction is determined actuarially in accordance with IRS procedures. In general, the more distant the remainder interest and the higher the retained interest, the less the deduction, and vice versa. Figure 22-2 illustrates the CRT process.

Figure 22-2

Charitable Remainder Trust Process

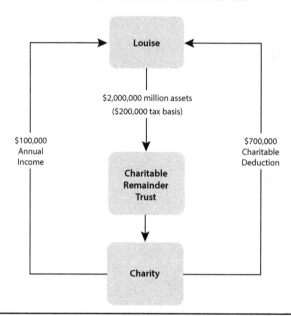

This CRT illustration assumes highly appreciated property valued at $2 million and a tax basis of $200,000 is donated to the charity via a trust. Here, Louise is the grantor and is to receive a lifetime income of 5 percent of the initial trust value or $100,000 per year. The remainder interest is valued at $700,000 by IRS procedures and is deductible immediately by Louise as a charitable contribution.

Of course, the grantor loses ownership and control of the property transferred to the CRT. The CRT, thus, saves estate taxes but the transfer deprives heirs of the value of the property, a dissatisfying result for many individuals. To overcome this problem, many donors establish **wealth replacement trusts**, which are ILITs containing insurance whose death benefit roughly equals the value of the property transferred to the CRT and is ordinarily made payable to those who otherwise would have been heirs to the donated property. The life insurance premium might range from 1 to 3 percent of the policy face amount, likely less than the income from the CRT. Of course, such trusts can prove attractive in other circumstances, as when property is given for non-charitable purposes. Death proceeds should not be included in the grantor's gross estate.

Thus, Louise might create a wealth replacement trust with her children as trust beneficiaries. The trust would purchase a $2 million life insurance policy on her life, and she would make annual gifts to the trust in the amount of the policy premium, funded from the CRT income stream.

Advanced Planning Concept:[4] Intentionally Defective Irrevocable Trusts An **intentionally defective irrevocable trust** (IDIT), also called an **intentionally defective grantor trust,** is a deferred sale arrangement between a grantor and an irrevocable trust that allows the grantor to make transfers of appreciated income producing property to junior generations, free of gift tax. The individual sells assets to the IDIT in exchange for an installment note, freezing the current value of appreciating and income producing property and removing future appreciation from his or her estate.

Traditionally, individuals creating irrevocable trusts wished to avoid running afoul of the so-called grantor trust rules, as doing so made the grantor the effective owner of trust assets for income tax purposes. An IDIT purposely runs afoul of these rules. The grantor is personally liable for all income (ordinary income and capital gains) attributable to trust assets and must take it into his or her taxable income. By paying all income taxes incurred by the IDIT, its assets grow unreduced by such taxes, thereby increasing the value of assets available to trust beneficiaries. In effect, the payment of income taxes by the grantor is a gift to trust beneficiaries that is not subject to gift taxation, and they reduce the grantor's gross estate. Even though the grantor is considered the owner of trust assets for income tax purposes, he or she should not be treated as the owner for estate tax purposes, as separate tax rules govern each determination.

Implementation involves the following steps:

- The grantor establishes an IDIT.
- The grantor sells income producing and highly appreciating assets to the IDIT in exchange for an installment note payable over time bearing an interest rate equal to the appropriate applicable federal rate. As the grantor is treated as the owner of trust assets, the sale should produce no income or capital gain taxes.
- Prior to the execution of the sale, the grantor seeds the IDIT with at least 10-15 percent of the value of the installment note to adequately fund the IDIT and avoid the entire transaction being challenged by the IRS as a transfer to a trust with a retained interest. This should be the only gift to the trust that is taxable.
- The IDIT uses income generated from the trust assets to make payments on the note to the grantor. Any income remaining in the IDIT after payment may be used by the IDIT trustee to pay premiums on a life insurance policy insuring the life of the grantor. This allows the grantor to fund a life insurance policy outside the estate without the imposition of gift taxes on the premium payments.
- At the end of the installment note period or on the grantor's death, all property held in the IDIT, including life insurance death benefit proceeds, should pass to the IDIT beneficiaries free of estate taxes. If the grantor dies during the term of the installment note, only the balance of the note should be included in the grantor's estate.

IDITs also should appeal to individuals wishing to pass wealth to their grand-children and great-grandchildren without incurring the GST tax, as the GST tax is a tax on gifts, not sales. Only amounts used to seed the trust should be considered to be a GST.

LIFE INSURANCE ANALYSIS FOR ESTATE PLANNING

Life insurance is often the most efficient and effective means of providing needed estate liquidity and of meeting other estate planning goals. Chapter 20 pointed out that the objective in financial planning is, among other purposes, to guide the client toward a sound insurance outcome. In guiding the customer, agents, brokers, planners, and other advisors in the estate planning arena will cover the same generic elements: the *identification* of the client's post-mortem financial objectives, *assembling and analyzing* relevant information, and *development and implementation* of a plan to accomplish the client's objectives.

IDENTIFY OBJECTIVES

Much life insurance is sold to meet estate planning objectives, the most common of which is estate conservation. **Estate conservation**, also called providing **estate liquidity,** involves using death proceeds from life insurance on the decedent's life to cover some or all of the estate obligations due on his or her death, the most important of which typically are estate taxes.

Life insurance is useful in other estate planning situations as well. For example, life insurance may be used for charitable purposes via a CRT or an outright gift of a policy to a charity. With an outright gift, the policyowner donates a policy on the insured's life to a charity or authorizes the purchase of a policy on his or her life. The charity becomes the policyowner and beneficiary. The value of the gift is the lesser of premiums paid or the interpolated terminal reserve. The value would be deductible for income tax purposes as a charitable donation. Future premium payments by the donor on the policy would also be tax deductible donations. In addition, some people use life insurance to replace the value of wealth given to others or donated to non-profit organizations, which otherwise would have been left to heirs.

Life insurance also can be useful in estate planning to help achieve a more equitable distribution of wealth on death. For example, if grandfather Randall wants to leave his deceased wife's $5 million necklace to Caroline and only $8 million in other assets is available to be left to his other grandchildren, Camden and Connor, he could purchase a $2 million policy payable one half to each to equalize the value of assets left to each grandchild. This type of use can arise whenever it is desired not to liquidate high value assets, and the assets are by nature or preference indivisible, as for example a family business in which only one of three children is interested and capable of running.

GATHER INFORMATION

In general, the same types of asset, liability, and income information discussed in Chapter 20 will be needed here as well, along with certain other information. Thus, the advisor will have gathered data about the nature and value of the assets owned by the individual, but also as to other property that he or she controls (yielding the gross estate) and the nature and value of the individual's liabilities plus anticipated charitable and spousal bequests (yielding the deductions). If a spousal bequest is anticipated, information gathering and planning ordinarily would be conducted for both spouses.

If the estate planning use to which life insurance may be put is other than estate liquidity, necessary information will have been gathered to permit an analysis to be conducted. For example, for wealth replacement, the advisor will have determined not just the magnitude of the desired replacement but also information about the person or persons to whom the life insurance would be paid and whether a trust seems desirable.

Finally, the advisor ideally will have learned important financial characteristics about the individual that will help guide the advisor toward the most suitable policies. These characteristics include the individual's ability and willingness to pay premiums along with his or her financial discipline and risk tolerance.

ANALYZE INFORMATION

For estate liquidity purposes, an estimate is made of the individual's and, if applicable, his or her spouse's likely federal estate taxes owed were either to die immediately. Other scenarios are also examined, such as simultaneous death and projections of values should death(s) occur at certain ages. Admittedly, such projections are speculative, not just because of changing values of assets and liabilities but also because of the possibility of changes in the federal estate tax law. Nonetheless, such projections are desirable both because they can be informative and because they can be useful to the agent in convincing life insurer underwriters as to the reasonableness of the amount of requested insurance. Other estate planning purposes typically involve less qualitative analysis.

Whatever the estate planning purpose, existing liquid assets and cash coming into the estate as a result of prearranged asset sales, such as interests in a closely held business (see Chapter 24), may be netted against the goals to derive a residual amount to be covered by insurance. Analyzing estate planning related information serves two purposes:

1. to determine figures for the amounts of taxes due or to fund other estate goals, and
2. to select the policy type that will most closely track the goal over time.

DEVELOP AND IMPLEMENT THE PLAN: MATCHING POLICIES TO GOALS

The next step is to develop and implement a plan to accomplish the stated objectives. This step commonly involves the amendment or creation of trusts and related estate planning legal documents.

NATURE OF INSURANCE NEED INFLUENCING SELECTION OF POLICY TYPES   Selecting among the various types of life insurance policies for purposes of achieving estate planning goals often is simpler than doing so for family income and related purposes of the type discussed in Chapter 20. This is because the nature of the insurance need for estate planning purposes is oriented toward accomplishment of very few specific, quantifiable goals. These are the characteristics of the typical estate planning need for life insurance that drive most policy choices.

- **Coverage needed for the entirety of life.** The life insurance coverage is purchased to meet a need or goal that does not ordinarily diminish with age, remaining for the individual's entire life. For this reason, the selected policy ordinarily will be a cash value variety that will remain in force for the entirety of life, either whole life (WL) or universal life (UL)

- **Death benefit oriented.** The life insurance policy purchased for estate planning purposes ordinarily is intended to be a source of funds at the insured's death and not to provide or make available funds for the insured or others during his or her lifetime. For this reason, cash value development may be of less or even no importance in the policy selection process, so WL, UL, or no-lapse guarantee (NLG) UL are often the policies of choice. Even so, advisors often recommend that consideration be given to cash value accumulation as it provides flexibility for changing circumstances and cash needs (emergencies, retirement, or value applied for a policy replacement).

- **Motivated to minimize premium outlay.** If cash value development is of less importance and as the payment of premiums often involves gift tax considerations, the insured's motivation is to pay premiums at the lowest feasible level that will still meet his or her estate planning goals. For this reason, recommended policies typically will require comparatively low premiums per $1,000 of face amount.

POLICY OPTIONS FOR FAMILIES   For married couples, the marital deduction coupled with the unified credit may eliminate or greatly reduce estate taxes at the death of the first spouse, focusing the need for liquidity to meet estate taxes on the second spouse's death. Several types of policy structures can provide the desired cash, each approach being a matter of personal preference, including the following:

- Purchase individual policies on the life of each spouse in a total amount sufficient to meet the projected need, with each policy held in a separate ILIT. On the death of the first spouse, the death proceeds would be paid to its ILIT, with investment income thereon used to augment the surviving spouse's income or to accumulate, thus providing additional estate tax-free wealth to trust beneficiaries on the surviving spouse's death. Suitable policies commonly are NLG UL or some form of par WL or UL. This approach usually requires higher premium outlays than other options and, for this reason, is not the approach of choice for most people.

- Purchase a low-premium joint life permanent policy that provides for payment of the face amount at the first death. As with the two-policy approach, proceeds from the first death can be used to augment the survivor's income or to pass additional wealth to heirs. Special care should be taken in designating ownership of joint life policies. If the surviving spouse/insured is owner of the policy, the proceeds will be included in the estate of the second to die. This approach usually requires a lower premium outlay than the two-policy approach.

- Purchase an appropriate WL or UL policy on the life of one spouse only. If the insured is the first to die, the proceeds would be retained as above for ultimate liquidity needs. This may be the only feasible solution if one spouse is uninsurable, and it is a reasonable one even if both are insurable. Proceeds would be invested, augmenting the surviving spouse's income.

- Purchase a second-to-die policy that pays the face amount when the second insured dies. Assuming both spouses are insurable at reasonable rates, this approach should involve the smallest premium outlay, other things being the same. This approach may also be an option in the event one spouse is uninsurable, as some insurers will issue a survivorship policy with only one insurable life.

In large estates and with large amounts of insurance, the insurance is ordinarily owned by someone other than the insured or spouse. An ILIT may be the most common alternative. An adult child can be another. Use of an ILIT as owner can be especially wise if the insurance is not to be liquidated at the first death, but instead retained for meeting estate liquidity needs on the second death and only one policy or a joint life policy is to be purchased.

POLICY OPTIONS WITH OTHER FAMILY AND HOUSEHOLD ARRANGEMENTS   Family and household arrangements not composed of a married couple cannot benefit from the unlimited marital deduction. Rather, they must rely on the other estate planning tools and the unified credit only, to minimize estate settlement costs. The nature of the insurance need as discussed above ordinarily would not be affected by the family structure, so emphasis usually will be on lifetime coverage with minimal premium outlay and less emphasis on cash values, suggesting the same low-cost, death-benefit oriented products as with married households. Certainly, second-to-die policies find less relevance here.

POLICY OPTIONS FOR OTHER ESTATE PLANNING GOALS   Situations arise for which estate planning calls for additional life insurance for wealth replacement, charitable purposes, or other goals in addition to estate liquidity. The most suitable types of policies ordinarily will track those used for estate liquidity but be owned by and payable to separate trusts. Other arrangements may also be appropriate.

While most estate planning situations place a low priority on cash value accumulations and their availability, not all do so. Some family situations may suggest a desire to allow the non-insured spouse to be able to access future cash values for family emergencies or other purposes. This goal can be accomplished through another advanced planning technique called a spousal access lifetime trust, as discussed in Box 22-3.

Box 22-3
Making Cash Values Available using a Spousal Lifetime Access Trust

Some married couples with likely estate tax obligations wish to retain the option of accessing a policy's cash value for possible future needs, such as unforeseen adverse financial developments or children's educational costs. Of course, they wish to keep policy death proceeds out of the gross estate, so an ILIT may be the approach of choice, except that ILITs ordinarily do not provide for access by either spouse to policy cash values without endangering the favorable estate tax status of the death proceeds.

A **spousal lifetime access trust** (SLAT), a special type of ILIT, can preserve the favorable estate tax treatment of the death proceeds while allowing indirect access to the policy cash values. As with an ordinary ILIT, the SLAT trustee is permitted but not required to purchase a life insurance policy on the life of one of the spouses, with premiums commonly paid via grantor gifts to the trust. The terms of the SLAT provide that the trustee may, at its discretion, make policy loans and withdrawals, which should be free of income tax to the SLAT, subject to IRS rules. If the SLAT has no taxable income, the trustee may, at its discretion, then make distributions to the non-insured spouse that are free of income and gift tax.

LIFE INSURANCE AND THE GENERATION-SKIPPING TRANSFER TAX

Life insurance can become involved in a generation-skipping transfer and, thereby, incur a GST tax, as discussed above. In general, a GST can evolve from (1) the payment of premiums, (2) the transfer of policies, and (3) the payment of death proceeds. Generally, funds transferred to a skip person to pay premiums on a life insurance policy or an annuity are considered a GST. Additionally, a transfer to a trust for which a skip person is a beneficiary may result in a GST when the property is transferred to the trust, such as amounts to pay premiums on a policy owned by an ILIT. The annual gift tax exclusion and the $5,340,000 (2014) lifetime GST exemption (double if a spouse joins in) may be available to reduce or eliminate any GST tax.

A GST generally occurs also when a life insurance or annuity contract is transferred to a skip person. Additionally, such an insurance contract transferred to a trust with a skip person as beneficiary may result in a GST. Again, the annual exclusion and lifetime exemption would be available.

Finally, regardless of the manner of payment of life insurance or annuity proceeds, a GST will have been made if policy benefits are transferred from an insured or annuitant to a skip person. Thus, if a grandparent is the insured and owner of a $8,340,000 life insurance policy and a grandchild is beneficiary, a GST will have occurred on the grandparent's death, and about $1.20 million of GST tax [($8,340,000 – $5,340,000) x 0.40] would be due on the transfer.

Leveraging of the GST lifetime exemption can be accomplished by allocating the exemption against the premium dollars (or against the value of the policy on transfer) versus the higher ultimate value of the death proceeds. Leveraging of the exemption can also be accomplished for premiums on policies in an ILIT or for policy transfer to such a trust.

CONCLUSION

Individuals of all levels of wealth should make plans for the orderly distribution of their property at their deaths. If they do not do it, the government will do it for them! One of the biggest obstacles to making plans is the unpleasantness inherent in the subject of death and the awkwardness of discussing it.

As a subset of financial planning, effective estate planning provides the structure for implementing one's post-death wishes at minimal costs. We might routinely think of life insurance as an effective, efficient mechanism for providing financial support to families. However, many people seem surprised to learn of the important role that life insurance can and does play in providing the liquidity necessary to meet estate planning objectives. Life insurance is unique among financial service products in that the event that creates the need can simultaneously cause generation of the funds to meet the obligation. As long as death itself causes additional expenses and taxes, life insurance can be expected to play this vital role.

ENDNOTES

1   This chapter draws from Harold D. Skipper and Wayne Tonning, *The Advisor's Guide to Life Insurance* (Chicago; American Bar Association, 2011), Chapter 11.

2   The Emeloid Co. v. Comm., 189 F. 2d 230 (3rd Cir. 1951).

3   http://www.massmutual.com/mmfg/pdf/MM_Success_Plan.pdf

4   The authors acknowledge M financial Group for the advanced planning techniques presented in this chapter.

CHAPTER 23

RETIREMENT PLANNING

This chapter continues our Part IV exploration of the uses of insurance products in personal and business planning. We focus on retirement planning, building on the material on personal financial planning from Chapter 20 and on income taxation from Chapter 21. We examine the situation in the U.S., although the principles and many of the practices apply universally.

Recall that Chapter 20 described the life cycle in two stages: (1) the accumulation or working life phase when assets are accumulated and (2) the retirement or liquidation life stage when assets are spent down. During the accumulation stage, the individual relies on *human capital* – earned income – for living expenses and retirement savings. During the liquidation stage, the individual must rely primarily or exclusively on *investment capital*. That chapter focused on the accumulation stage of life.

This chapter emphasizes the liquidation phase of life and the savings vehicles available to fund it. It is again worth reminding ourselves of the enormous complexity inherent in planning in general and retirement planning in particular, for we confront the economizing problem of trying to satisfy unlimited wants with limited resources and the difficulty of planning many years if not decades before retirement.

Recall from Chapter 1 that the life cycle hypothesis suggests that risk-averse individuals will maximize their lifetime utilities by smoothing their lifetime consumption pattern. This smoothing is accomplished through a program of saving during the productive working years and spending down those savings during the retirement years. But how is this smoothing accomplished in practice? As with other risk exposures, retirement has two dimensions: frequency (the likelihood of reaching retirement age) and severity (the amount needed in retirement). Each is a function of longevity: will retirement income be needed and for how long? Upon reaching retirement, severity of the risks of retirement is a function of income requirements.

Our focus in this chapter is on longevity risk and the use of insurance products to reduce it. In a financial sense, the severity dimension (potential income needs) of longevity risk is the sum of the costs of a variety of considerations. Box 23-1 lists the important factors identified by the *Society of Actuaries* (SOA) in its *Retirement Risk Chart*.

THE UNCERTAIN ENVIRONMENT FOR RETIREMENT PLANNING

Box 23-1
Retirement Risk Issues

The SOA *Risk Retirement Chart* is assembled as a public service to raise awareness of the challenges that individuals face at retirement. It reveals an extraordinarily broad scope of uncertainty associated with a wide variety of potential risk issues and emphasizes the need for planning. These risk issues include:

- Longevity
- Inflation
- Interest Rates
- Stock Market
- Business Continuity
- Employment
- Public Policy
- Unexpected Health Care Costs and Needs

- Lack of Available Facilities and Caregivers
- Loss of Ability to Live Independently
- Change in Housing Needs
- Death of a Spouse
- Other Changes in Marital Status
- Unforeseen Needs of Family Members
- Bad Advice, Fraud, or Theft

DEMOGRAPHIC AND ECONOMIC DIMENSIONS OF RETIREMENT PLANNING

Individuals today live longer than at any time in history. The German Chancellor Otto von Bismarck established the world's first formal public retirement program in 1889, at which time age 65 was set as that country's national retirement age. With a life expectancy at birth of 45 years, few Germans actually lived long enough to collect anything. It is perhaps surprising that 125 years later, age 65 remains synonymous with retirement.

At the beginning of the 20th century in the U.S., life expectancy at birth was 45 years for males and just short of 50 years for females. People typically worked until death, and few lived long enough to retire. Indeed, the very notion of "retirement" was foreign to most citizens. By the beginning of the 21st century, life expectancy at birth had increased by 30 years to almost 76 years for males and 81 years for females. Today in the U.S., the typical worker retires at age 62 and can expect to live another 21 years or so in retirement (and at least another five years beyond that for individuals in the highest socio-economic categories).

Another important factor in the retirement environment is inflation, the archenemy of retirement planning. Figure 23-1 demonstrates that even a 2 percent inflation rate will reduce the purchasing power of retirement savings by one-half over 30 years. Inflation in the U.S. has actually averaged about 4 percent over the last 50 years, doubling prices in 18 years. If inflation were to average 6 percent, the retiree would need $32,071 in income in year 20 to have the same purchasing power as $10,000 today.

During a worker's career, inflation risk, in fact, usually is less important than commonly believed, as wages and inflation generally move together creating a natural inflation hedge. At retirement, however, the worker's ability to earn in an inflationary environment comes to an end, and income from savings and retirement plans must rise over time to maintain living standards.

The environment for health care planning is also uncertain. U.S. health care inflation, averaging about twice that of the *Consumer Price Index* (CPI) since the turn of the century, hits retirees particularly hard given their higher-than-average consumption of health care services. While surveys of the *Employee Benefit Research Institute* (EBRI) reveal that large proportions of workers expect to have access to employer-provided health care in retirement, much smaller proportions of actual retirees report having such coverage. Indeed, many employers are eliminating health care coverage for future retirees, so workers' expectations seem likely to be unrealistic. Further, while the 2010 *Patient Protection and Affordable Care Act* ensures coverage for the great majority of individuals, it has not yet been fully implemented and its ultimate impact on Medicare (government health insurance for the elderly) is unclear.

Amounts Necessary to Maintain $10,000 of Purchasing Power at Various Durations and Rates of Inflation

Figure 23-1

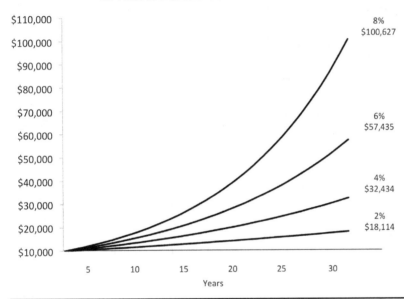

In addition to illness and injury rates increasing with age, so too does the need for assistance with the activities of daily living. For example, whereas 6 percent of those aged 65 to 74 require assistance with bathing, this percentage increases to 31 percent for those aged 85 and greater. Such care is expensive in terms of both compensation of caregivers and time and attention of helpful friends or relatives.

A primary concern of retirees is the ability to maintain an acceptable standard of living in retirement. Government social insurance programs in general and the U.S. Social Security benefits in particular are skewed in favor of lower income workers. Those with moderate to high incomes cannot depend on Social Security retirement benefits to provide as significant a share of their retirement income. This fact is illustrated in Figure 23-2. It shows the results of a *Georgia State University* study of retiree income replacement ratios in the U.S. The figure shows the percentage of pre-retirement salary necessary for retirees to maintain their standards of living.

Figure 23-2   **Income Replacement Ratios in the United States Necessary to Maintain Preretirement Living Standards**
(Married Couple, One Wage Earner, Age 65 Worker, Age 62 Spouse)

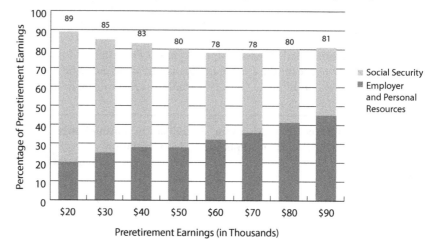

Source: Bruce A. Palmer, 2008 *GSU/AON RETIRE Project Report*, Georgia State University Center for Risk Management and Insurance Research RESEARCH REPORT SERIES: Number 08-1, June 2008.

The **income replacement ratio** is a person's gross earned income after retirement, divided by his or her gross income before retirement. By taking into consideration changes in a person's post-retirement taxes, expenditures, and savings, it can serve as a benchmark target for retirement savings. Conventional wisdom suggests that retirees need a minimum retirement income of about 80 percent of their pre-retirement wages to maintain a standard of living in retirement equivalent to the one enjoyed before retirement. There is also a wide-spread belief that future Social Security retirement benefits will not be as generous as those enjoyed by past and current retirees, another source of uncertainty. Figure 23-3 shows that among the three major sources of retirement income – Social Security, private savings, and employer-provided benefits – employer-provided (non-Social Security) benefits are the least prevalent.

Further, a clear trend is observed in employers shifting from offering defined benefit (DB) plans that eliminate investment risk for workers to defined contribution (DC) plans that transfer the investment risk associated with maintaining retirement income to workers. For example, according to the *U.S. Department of Labor* and EBRI, while the number of DC plans increased by more than 10 percent from 1991 to 2008 (latest year), the number of DB plans decreased by more than 50 percent over this 16 year period, and observers believe a significant further decline has occurred since 2007 and will continue. The prolonged period of low interest rates since the turn of the century has significantly increased the cost of defined benefit plans. These facts emphasize the importance of personal savings in retirement planning.

PSYCHOLOGICAL DIMENSIONS OF RETIREMENT PLANNING
While we offer techniques below for deriving estimates of desired retirement savings, sound retirement planning is as much about its psychological as its purely

economic dimensions. Here we offer results from the latest survey of worker perceptions about retirement planning and explore briefly the evolving understanding of behavioral finance on planning.

PERCEPTIONS   The attitudes and behavior of U.S. workers regarding retirement are characterized by inattention to planning and saving and pessimism following the global financial stress that emerged in 2008-2009, according to EBRI's 2013 *Retirement Confidence Survey*. The number of people with no substantial savings at all is increasing. The number surveyed who have less than $1,000 in savings and investments rose from 20 percent in 2009 to 30 percent in 2013. Additionally, as many as 34 percent have not saved at all, and 43 percent of workers over 55 are not currently saving. Finally, Americans are expecting to work longer. The percentage expecting to retire after the traditional age of 65 has increased steadily and dramatically from 11 percent 1991 to 25 percent in 2006 to 36 percent in 2013. The unexpected increase in the aggregate years of service and compensation of workers retiring at later ages is another source of increasing retirement costs.

American confidence in institutions generally is weak. A substantial number have lost confidence in government (62 percent), insurance companies (45 percent), banks (32 percent), and employers (23 percent). Confidence in government retirement benefits specifically is very weak. Some 70 percent of workers are not confident their Social Security benefits will equal the benefits participants receive today, and the same percentage hold that belief about Medicare.

Percentage Age 65 U.S. Retirees Receiving Income from Specified Sources, 2012   **Figure 23-3**

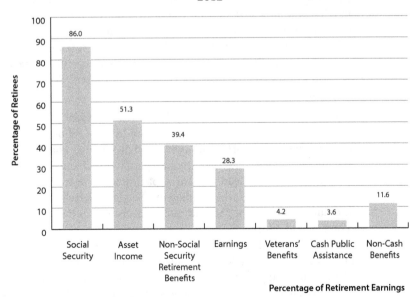

Source: 2012 *Income of the Aged Chartbook*, Social Security Administration

---

Workers are largely ignorant of their retirement income needs. Only 42 percent of those surveyed have made an effort to calculate their retirement needs.

A perceived lack of control may help to explain the pessimism and lack of planning. A majority of older adults reports that they are afraid that their financial resources will be insufficient to meet their future financial needs. This perception seems largely unrelated to objective levels of financial resources, with high-income retirees being as likely as low-income retirees to be worried about the adequacy of their resources.

Underlying this fear is the issue of personal control. We desire to control the major elements of our lives, and, for events that we cannot control, we want to control how they are resolved. Financial assets are a control-enhancing and control-preserving resource. The emotional intensity associated with the fear that financial assets will be inadequate for future needs is more than concern about money; it is concern that we will lose control, personal autonomy, and ultimately independence. Awareness and understanding of these and other psychological dimensions of retirement and retirement planning will aid both the individual and his or her counselor in making better suited decisions.

BEHAVIORAL ECONOMICS   Utility maximization by rational investors in efficient markets has dominated the traditional analysis of financial markets and individual investor and saver decision-making. Recall from Chapter 1 that utility maximization is a prescriptive or normative concept that describes the way rational individuals should be expected to behave. It has been known for a long time that, in fact, investor and saver behavior does not conform to the predictions of expected utility theory. **Behavioral economics** is a positive or descriptive discipline that seeks to understand how psychological factors such as cognitive bias can influence how investors, savers, and other economic actors make economic decisions. This discussion focuses on some of what has been learned and predicted about how people think in relation to financial matters. The observations and predictions of behavioral finance are central to retirement planning for individuals.

Observers began to question why expected utility failed to correctly predict behavior when economic and finance research disclosed behaviors and anomalies that did not conform to the expected behavior of utility maximizers. Some of the important behaviors include:

- *Anchoring,* the tendency to act in accordance with a reference point that may not be reasonable. One example is the tendency to follow a rule of thumb: retirement plan participants will often divide their contribution equally among the plan's choices without regard to the character of each fund. This tendency can lead to a participant being invested mostly in stocks or mostly in bonds – depending on the plan offerings – without much thought given to the fact that such a decision can have a drastic effect on risk and return.
- *Overconfidence,* which can lead people to invest in that which is most familiar. This can quickly lead to inadequate diversification in a number of ways. Investing only in local companies, for example, exposes a portfolio to systematic microeconomic factors that would be avoided with a geographically diverse portfolio. As discussed in Chapter 20, large holdings of employer stock by employees is risky.
- *Framing,* which causes people's decisions to vary depending on how an issue is presented. More people will choose to make an investment

presented as "a 70 percent probability of winning" than one presented with "a 30 percent probability of losing" even though the expected outcomes are identical.

- *Herd behavior,* which exists because individuals have a tendency to mimic the behavior of larger groups. Prime examples are market bubbles, such as the overvaluation of Internet stocks at the turn of the century.

Planners and individuals should be aware of these human tendencies, none of which are consistent with rational utility maximization. For workers who participate in retirement plans sponsored by their employers, perhaps the most important pitfall to avoid is too passive an approach to retirement plan options.

Behavioral research indicates that default options (particularly the default contribution rate in 401(k) plans and investment choices) incorporated into retirement plans tend to be the most frequently selected. Participants choose the path of least resistance. Underlying causes have been explained as procrastination, complexity, and choice overload. Even though the default options may not be designed into plans to be optimal for workers, participants often interpret default options as recommendations.

Plan sponsors, designers, and administrators effectively pave the path of least resistance when they design retirement plans, particularly the default provisions chosen by passive participants. Plan designers are beginning to recognize the importance of default provisions as simplified and automatic enrollment plans become more common. When active decisions affecting participation and contribution rates are required, participant savings rates tend to increase.

THE RETIREMENT PLANNING PROCESS

Retirement planning is an integral subset of financial planning and should incorporate the same comprehensive steps discussed in Chapter 20: (1) gather information, (2) establish objectives, (3) develop a plan, (4) construct a financial model, and (5) implement and monitor the plan. This section focuses on the features of the process important to retirement planning. Many of the general observations in Chapter 20 are equally applicable here.

Information related to both death and retirement needs is usually gathered at the same time. The needed information includes existing investments that could be used to provide retirement income, likely benefits from employer-provided and government retirement plans, and any other sources. If the time to retirement is long, estimates will be gross approximations only.

Retirement income objectives usually are couched in general terms, such as being able to maintain one's current standard of living during retirement. Of course, expenses related to work and savings for retirement cease on retirement. Also, Social Security, federal income, and state and local taxes typically are lower.

Computer-assisted retirement planning is routine today. Sophisticated programs are available from commercial software vendors and numerous web sites. Financial advisors as well as consumers rely on these programs, both to guide them through the process and to conduct the analysis. As discussed in Chapter 20, however, caution is advised in the application of generalized, stock software analyses as any "one size fits all" approach is likely to miss important information relevant to a particular individual's circumstances.

After available resources are determined, additional resources required to meet retirement goals are represented by the present value of future income needs netted against the present value of present and future available resources. Calculations should use reasonable interest rates, considering historical and current trends, and should take inflation into account in determining the level of income desired at retirement age, often based on a projection of the current income. The result is a measure of the net present value of the shortage of resources to meet the desired income objective.

The three common expected annual income sources are (1) government benefits, (2) employer-provided income, and (3) income from individual sources. First, as to government resources, Social Security estimation is more complex for retirement planning than for death planning because the Social Security survivor benefit is a known, calculable product, and near-term projections probably are reasonable. For persons not near retirement, projecting Social Security retirement benefit levels decades into the future is speculative. Consequently, these calculations typically are viewed as providing gross estimates only.

Employer-sponsored retirement benefits are also problematical. Individuals change employers, and employers change their retirement plans. Therefore, estimates for retirement income from employer-sponsored sources should be conservative. Finally, current and projected savings and investments are determined. While the savings rate is theoretically the determination of the saver, unexpected expenses, uneven adherence to a plan, and other factors mean these assumptions are characterized by uncertainty just as government and employer benefit assumptions. The difference in the desired income and the income available from government, employer, and personal resources represents the additional personal savings required to achieve the targeted replacement ratio.

In this section, we use a simplified methodology to illustrate key elements found in the comprehensive methodology suggested in Chapter 20. We assume that Helen, aged 45, plans to retire at 65.

I. **Make Inflation Assumption**

Helen believes a 4 percent long term inflation assumption is reasonable.

II. **Project Income to Retirement Age**

Her annual salary is $75,000 today, and she anticipates that future raises will average 6 percent per year. In other words, she expects her wages to rise at a real rate of 2 percent after inflation. We determine her expected retirement wage:

$$\$75,000 \times (1.06)^{20} = \$75,000 \times 3.2071 = \$240,532$$

(Actual purchasing power of the $240,000 in today's dollars would be about $110,000: $75,000 x (1.06 ÷ 1.04)^{20} = $75,000 x (1.01923)^{20} = $109,777.)

III. **Determine Income Replacement Ratio**

She anticipates retiring at age 65 at 70 percent of her then pre-retirement salary.

IV. **Determine Social Security Wage Replacement Ratio**

Helen estimates her Social Security benefit will provide an inflation-adjusted retirement income equal to 20 percent of her pre-retirement salary.

V.   **Determine Employer-Provided Wage Replacement Ratio**
Helen estimates that her employer-sponsored plan will provide a retirement income of an additional 30 percent of her pre-retirement salary and
that her salary will increase in step with inflation.

VI. **Determine Additional Annual Required Income**

Additional Required Income =

Income Ratio	(70 percent)
less Employer Ratio	(20 percent)
less Social Security Ratio	(30 percent)
=	(20 percent)

Additional Income Requirement = $240,000 x 0.2 = $48,000

VII. Determine Present Value of Annual Required Income Need
Helen wishes to fund the additional retirement income need via a life
annuity. If she wanted to purchase an annuity to provide this amount, the
probable cost at age 65 might be $700 to $1,100 for each $100 of annual
income desired, according to her agent. She wishes to be conservative,
and uses the higher figure to account implicitly for assumption errors.
Thus, Helen should aim to have accumulated about $528,000 ($48,000 x
$1,100)/$100) by age 65.

VIII. Determine Funding Plan and Vehicle
To accumulate this sum through level contributions to savings, Helen
must make annual payments of about $12,000 if the savings medium
earns 7 percent. If Helen would like her annual retirement savings contribution to grow with her expected 6 percent salary increases, she could
begin saving about $5,500 and increase it by 6 percent per year. This
steadily increasing contribution would also grow to the needed $528,000
amount if all assumptions were realized. As Helen has decided to purchase an annuity, the interest assumptions reflect tax-free rates earned in
a deferred annuity net of policy expense.

Helen's results are highly dependent on assumptions, the validity of which
changes over time. Important life events and environmental changes can materially affect results. This necessitates periodic fine tuning and, occasionally, a
complete overhaul. The key to sound plan implementation is less the mechanics
and more a firm commitment by the individual to make the necessary contributions regularly. More retirement plans fail from lack of commitment than for any
other reason.

The principal risk in retirement is living longer than resources are sufficient to satisfy objectives. "Sufficient" is a relative term, necessarily defined by each individual
and which relates directly to our Chapter 1 discussion about rational individuals
seeking to maximize their lifetime utilities. Generically, resources are sufficient
if they are capable of supporting a desired standard of living for as long as life
continues while protecting against unexpected changes in the cost of living. The
components of sufficiency are related. For example, accepting a lower standard

**RETIREMENT
PLANNING RISK
MANAGEMENT**

of living can mean that limited resources available at retirement can support that standard of living for a longer time.

Prior to retirement, workers are able to control the amount of resources that they will have/need at retirement through: (1) their personal savings behavior for retirement (and, so, their consumption behavior); (2) selection of their age of retirement; and (3) their chosen standard of living in retirement. We explore these three factors below. Workers are unable to control: (1) future rates of inflation or (2) how long they live.

The risk associated with having sufficient resources, therefore, is a function of three factors: (1) the subjective preretirement choices made by workers, (2) inflation, and (3) the length of life. We can think of this risk as being that part of an individual's possible life span that cannot be funded through resources available at retirement, which we call **retirement tail risk**. Figure 23-4 is a stylized plot of retirement tail risk that compares the present value of income needs with the funded and unfunded parts of a retiree's possible life span under two living standards that we label as *higher* and *lower* to reflect life income possibilities for a given set of resources at retirement.

| Figure 23-4 | Unfunded Longevity and Retirement Tail Risk |

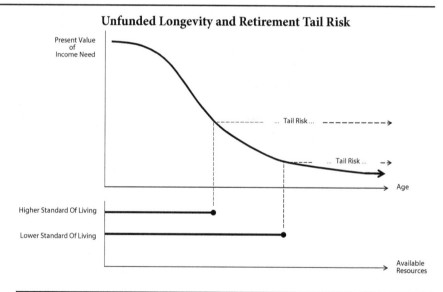

The figure illustrates the effect of living standards on the period that can be funded with available assets and on the period and amount of the retirement tail risk or unfunded longevity. Annuities offer substantial advantages in reducing the two risks retirees cannot influence: inflation risk and longevity risk. Annuities are also attractive preretirement savings vehicles with tax advantages and investment risk control options. However, annuities are not risk-free products. The risks associated with annuities are discussed in detail later in this chapter.

PERSONAL SAVINGS FOR RETIREMENT

The retirement planning process outlined above provides estimates for amounts needed to be saved for a given retirement income and other assumptions. However, the actual amounts saved during the working years to fund income during the retirement years are personal decisions reflecting a myriad of often conflicting factors and considerations. In this section, we discuss available means of funding these savings via both qualified plans and nonqualified programs. Qualified plans and nonqualified programs possess different tax and economic advantages and limitations and each can be used in conjunction with the others. Retirement funding should use feasible savings combinations that best approximate the ideal tax characteristics for investments:

- tax-deductible contributions,
- tax-deferred accumulation, and
- tax-free distributions.

SAVINGS THROUGH QUALIFIED PLANS   The number and provisions of employer-sponsored retirement plans that are provided to workers is daunting. Each plan variety has been the subject of multiple volume-length expositions. The Appendix to this chapter summarizes some of the salient characteristics of the most common types. In this section, we discuss the role that voluntary employee contributions make in retirement planning.

Qualified Employer-Sponsored Plans   We know from Chapter 6 that qualified pension plans come in two generic types: (1) defined benefit plans wherein the employee is promised a certain periodic benefit at retirement and (2) defined contribution plans wherein the employer (and often employee) contributes to a retirement account for the employee. With DC plans, contributions are invested and accumulate on a tax-free basis to be made available to employees at retirement or other service separation if the employee's plan interests are vested. Also, plans are either (1) noncontributory – only the employer contributes – or (2) contributory – the employee also contributes.

Three types of defined contribution plans are especially distinct. **Profit-sharing plans** are noncontributory DC plans that do not require but allow annual contributions by employers. **Employee Stock Ownership Plans** permit shares of the employer-sponsor stock to be contributed to the plan and assets of the plan to be invested in the stock of the employer-sponsor. Finally, **401(k) plans** permit employees to defer some of their compensation on a pretax basis; these plans may also allow employers to make qualified matching contributions.

Voluntary contributions to employer plans are personal savings in the sense that they depend on the exercise of the employee's discretion. The employee should coordinate contribution decisions with his or her personal financial and retirement plans. Employer-sponsored DC plans offer different distribution options at retirement, the effect being to convert employer-provided benefits to personal savings with the distribution option becoming a personal savings decision.

Contributory DC plans feature separate accounts for employees, with varying investment options. Except as noted below, contributory DC plans share some or all of the following investment and distribution options that bear on retirement planning:

- employees generally are able to direct their investments (and implicitly establish their own level of risk tolerance) and choose from a variety of investment options including brokerage accounts, mutual funds, group annuities, and individual annuities;

- distributions at retirement may be in a lump sum, paid periodically, or annuitized for life (based on the account value and not on a benefit formula);
- some plans now offer *personal pension plans* that permit participants to purchase paid-up life income benefits that commence at retirement;
- plans may also offer *lifecycle* or *target date* funds designed to match participant investment portfolios to their expected retirement ages;
- distributions prior to age 59½ are subject to a 10 percent penalty tax;
- distributions must begin by age 70½;
- employer contributions on behalf of employees must vest – become owned by the participants – at some plan-specified or determined future date;
- employee contributions are never forfeitable – they vest immediately – and distributions due to employment separation may be rolled into an Individual Retirement Account (IRA) (see below) for further tax deferral; and
- catch up provisions may permit contributions in excess of those normally permitted to the extent that prior contributions were less than permitted.

When an employee retires or otherwise ends an employment relationship, the employee's vested interest in any qualified plans may be transferred via what is termed a *rollover* to an IRA or other qualified plan. Rollovers can also be made from one type of IRA to another. Rollovers may be indirect, where the employee receives the distributed funds and is required to redeposit the funds into a qualified IRA within 60 days, or direct, where funds are transferred directly from the employer to the IRA custodian.

Rollovers to qualified annuities can be an attractive option when an immediate or future life income is desired. Deferred annuities can also be attractive savings vehicles when the retirement date is in the future. An IRA rollover effectively converts employer-sponsored or provided benefits to personal savings. In the case of both DB and DC plans, the employee's interest at retirement becomes personal to the retiree. Funds generally can be taken as a life income or lump sum under either type plan. (A life income under a DC plan is acquired through purchase of an individual or group annuity with some or all of the retiree's account balance.) At retirement, these plan assets along with personal savings become "available resources" for the planning purposes discussed above.

Tax-advantaged Plans for Individuals   Personal savings that are not made through employer-sponsored or funded plans may be tax-qualified or nonqualified, the latter discussed below. Tax-qualified plans, termed **Individual Retirement Accounts** (IRAs), were created to encourage retirement savings by persons who were not participating in qualified pension, profit-sharing, or Keogh plans. Anyone can set up an IRA, irrespective of whether he or she is covered by a qualified plan. However, only if the person is not covered by a qualified plan are IRA contributions fully deductible. In addition to the deductibility of contributions, taxation on the asset investment returns is deferred. A **Roth IRA** does not provide for the deductibility of contributions, but distributions are tax free, subject to certain limitations. The maximum deductible contribution to IRAs in 2014 is the lesser of $5,500 or earned income. (The limit is an aggregate limit for individuals who maintain both traditional IRAs and Roth IRAs.) If the person is covered by a qualified plan, a portion of the contribution may be deductible, depending on the individual's earnings level and marital status. Investment earnings on all contributions (irrespective of whether they are deductible) accumulate tax free until distributed.

ERISA authorizes two funding instruments for IRAs: (1) individual retirement accounts and (2) individual retirement annuities. Individual retirement accounts are the more popular, accounting for more than 90 percent of all IRAs. They take one of three forms. First, IRAs may be established as bank trust or custodial accounts in which contributions usually are invested in one or more of a bank's interest-bearing instruments or, in some cases, self-directed securities accounts. This form generally is offered by all types of deposit-taking institutions. Second, a trust or custodial account may be established whereby investments generally are made exclusively in mutual fund shares, usually within a specific family of funds. Third, stock brokerage firms offer a trust arrangement, called a *self-directed account*, under which the owner may select and manage his or her own investments from a range of available stocks, bonds, mutual funds, and direct participation programs. Mutual fund and brokerage accounts technically use a bank as a trustee, but the bank's role is purely custodial.

Individual retirement annuities are either fixed or variable contracts issued by insurance companies. As they are restricted and nontransferable so as to meet the necessary IRA requirements, no trustee or custodian is required. When the participant or beneficiary reaches retirement age, the contract can be surrendered for its cash value or used to provide a regular income payment. The laws governing IRAs specifically prohibit IRA investment in life insurance.

SAVINGS THROUGH NONQUALIFIED APPROACHES When tax-qualified savings opportunities have been exhausted, the balance of personal savings must come from after-tax income. While nonqualified savings are generally less economically productive than qualified savings, they come without the limitations on contributions and liquidity associated with tax-qualified plans. Further, qualified plans must meet numerous nondiscrimination and other requirements.

Nonqualified Non-insurance Savings Vehicles A full discussion of the many nonqualified, non-insurance savings and investment options available to investors falls outside the scope of this treatise. Suffice it to say that the range extends from relatively conservative saving instruments – such as passbook savings accounts and certificates of deposits at banks, money market funds, and short-term government securities such as 3-month treasury bills – to somewhat riskier investments – such as government and corporate bonds, houses, and land – on to still riskier investments such as diamonds, gold, artwork, common stock, and mutual funds.

Each of these investments will have its own expected risk/return profile and, importantly, its own tax treatment on deferrals and distributions. Most of them do not carry the favorable tax treatment of nonqualified insurance products.

Nonqualified Insurance Products: An Overview Insurance products can be especially attractive nonqualified savings vehicles. Here we provide an overview of their usage in this manner. We provide a more detailed analysis of both annuities and life insurance later in the chapter.

The tax benefits of accumulation in annuities and life insurance are an attractive feature of these nonqualified savings instruments. Accumulated earnings in an annuity are deferred until the policyowner elects to receive funds, and undistributed funds continue to enjoy tax deferral. These tax benefits subsidize annuity and life insurance longevity and death protection costs, respectively. In some cases, policyowners find the tax savings benefits alone justify the acquisition of a policy. Life insurance cash values can be accessed tax free throughout the life of the insured, and any deferred tax liability is eventually extinguished if the policy is held until the death of the insured. While limited adverse tax consequences can exist when lifetime values are accessed under certain circumstances, the tax advantages in an uninterrupted savings plan are particularly attractive.

Highly compensated employees often are entitled to proportionately lower Social Security and employer-sponsored retirement benefits than are other workers. Also, many owners of small businesses do not offer extensive retirement benefits to their employees, but they would like to provide for themselves, for their families, and often for particularly valuable employees. These facts have led increasing numbers of businesses to offer special, nonqualified retirement benefits instead of or as a supplement to qualified retirement plan benefits. As nonqualified plans, the employer need make no effort to meet the qualification requirements under the *Internal Revenue Code* or the *Employee Retirement Income Security Act* for tax-favored treatment of plan costs or benefits. (We cover these and other business uses of life insurance in Chapter 24.)

Not only does the tax treatment of insurance products differ from that of most other nonqualified investments, so too in many instances does the investment risk. Recall from earlier chapters that general account insurance products credit nonguaranteed interest to policyowner cash values based roughly on the earnings of the investments held in that account and, so, such products have their own unique investment properties. The cash values of variable products are based directly on the investment performance of the separate accounts that policyowners have chosen to back such products and, so, have their own unique investment properties. Whatever the savings medium or asset, risk is common to all. We can classify investment risk by market, credit, and liquidity exposure. Of course, life insurance and annuities also reflect mortality and longevity risk.

Credit risk, also called **default risk,** is the risk of loss of principal or interest when a borrower (usually bond issuers) fails to make contractually promised payments. In the case of general account insurance and annuity products, this risk is the possible insolvency of the insurer. Life insurance companies have an excellent solvency record – far better than banks – and are supported by guaranty associations, as discussed in Chapter 13. Variable products generally eliminate the insurer's credit risk, except for the pure insurance elements of such contracts. This is because policyowners have a protected interest in the separate accounts backing their policies, although the credit risk of funds selected by the policyowner pass directly through to the policy.

Market risk is the possibility that investments will decrease in value due to changes in market risk factors. The four standard market risk factors are stock prices, interest rates, foreign exchange rates, and commodity prices. Market risk directly affects the value of most separate accounts supporting variable products and indirectly affects other policyowners due to the market risk exposure of the insurer's general account.

Liquidity risk is the possibility that a security or asset transaction cannot be completed quickly enough in the market to capture a gain or prevent a loss. Life insurance and annuity cash values are generally very liquid. Important exceptions exist when surrender charges are applicable and for annuities with guarantees that apply only after minimum holding periods. As with market risk, general account policyowners are indirectly affected by liquidity risk and management of the insurer. Liquidity increases in importance as the planned retirement date nears.

Policyowners are able to reduce investment risk in life insurance and annuity contracts through the acquisition of specialty policies or policies that contain guarantees that explicitly minimize these risks. These were discussed in Chapters 4 and 6 and are summarized later in this chapter.

RETIREMENT AGE

The retirement age a worker chooses affects both available and required resources for retirement. As retirement is deferred, the length of retirement shortens by an unknown amount (thus reducing the amount of required resources) and available resources increase (as benefit contributions and accumulation continue during the longer accumulation period). Thus, postponing retirement almost always reduces retirement risk. Of course, a shorter retirement period may not be consistent with all of a worker's life objectives.

Annual EBRI surveys reveal that the typical worker expects to retire at age 65, not at age 62, which is the actual median reported retirement age. This difference between expectations and reality is enlightening for planning purposes. Only 7 percent of workers say they plan to retire before age 60, yet 30 percent retired that early. Sixteen percent of workers report that they plan to retire at age 60–64, although 38 percent of retirees report actually retiring at these ages.

A major reason for these differences is that a surprisingly large proportion (45 percent for 2011) of retirements is unexpected. Of those who retired earlier than planned, 63 percent cited health problems or disability as a primary reason, with 23 percent citing downsizing or closure of their employer, and 18 percent citing the need to care for a spouse or other family member. Retirement planning, therefore, should address the possibility that unanticipated circumstances will force a change in the expected retirement age.

Additionally, while financial considerations always play an important role in retirement decisions, we should also be attuned to their social, health, and psychological dimensions. When workers see their peers retiring, they may feel that it is time to do likewise. Moreover, the degree of satisfaction we derive from our jobs and the demand for our services influence the timing of retirement. Regrettably, the impact of these influences on the retirement decision is not easily appreciated when we are young.

STANDARD OF LIVING IN RETIREMENT

In addition to the length of retirement, the retiree's chosen standard of living in retirement is the other determinant of the retirement tail risk exposure. As represented in Figure 23-3, longevity determines the length of retirement tail risk and the income requirement determines the magnitude or "fatness" of the tail.

Wealthy retirees with sufficient wealth to support their standard of living indefinitely have no retirement tail risk.

PENSION MAXIMIZATION STRATEGY   One way that some retirees who have life income benefit payments under DB plans may be able to increase income is through use of life insurance. DB plans are required to offer the participant the option of either a single life annuity payout (benefits paid as long as the retiree lives) or a joint and survivor life annuity payout (benefits paid as long as either the retiree or another designated person, usually spouse, lives). If a life income for two is consistent with the retiree's financial plan, a more attractive option than simply selecting the survivor life income option may exist via a so-called **pension maximization strategy**, which involves the election by a retiree of a single life income option in lieu of a joint and survivor life income option, using the income difference to purchase life insurance on the annuitant's life for the benefit of the survivor.

With this strategy, retirement benefits for both income recipients might be enhanced. The proceeds of the life insurance at the retiree's death can be used to commence a new life income for the survivor. If the premium for the life insurance is not more than the difference between the amounts paid under the single and survivor income options and if survivor income via the life insurance is projected to be at least as great as the survivorship annuity payment, this strategy can be superior to the joint and survivor income option.

A retiree's goals may also include both income and a bequest for heirs. In such situations, the retiree could elect a lump sum distribution and use the proceeds to purchase both an annuity for income and a life insurance policy for heirs. This strategy is equally applicable to DB and DC plans.

DELAYING SOCIAL SECURITY RETIREMENT BENEFITS   Another means of ensuring adequate retirement income and protecting against tail risk is to delay receipt of Social Security retirement benefits. Of course, this option ordinarily is reasonable only for those whose retirement income from other sources prior to age 70 will afford an acceptable standard of living. Annual Social Security retirement benefits are 76 percent greater for individuals who delay receiving benefits until age 70 compared to those who claim benefits at age 62, the earliest possible age to receive benefits, and 33 percent greater compared to those who claim benefits at age 66, the present normal retirement age. The increase in benefits is due, respectively, to avoiding reductions for early retirement and maximizing the increase for delayed claiming. No further increase occurs for delaying claiming of retirement benefits beyond age 70.

As Social Security retirement benefits are guaranteed by the government to the end of life, there is no chance of outliving the income. Of course, life annuities backed by insurers and pension plans offer the same promise, but both of these has varying degrees of credit, market, and investment risk. Social Security benefits have none of these risks. In addition, as Social Security benefits are indexed to inflation, the recipient avoids inflation risk as well. Because spouses may receive a spousal benefit ordinarily equal to the greater of 50 percent of their spouses' full retirement benefit or their own benefit, delay in taking Social Security retirement benefits provides higher benefits to a surviving spouse as well.

This section explores the use of nonqualified annuities in personal savings programs in more detail. Reasonably priced and designed annuities can offer several advantages for their owners. They also offer some potential disadvantages.

POSSIBLE ADVANTAGES OF ANNUITIES
Nonqualified annuities offer tax deferral benefits to their owners, as alluded to above. They also provide unique longevity protection, can provide inflation protection, and can provide unique investment guarantees. We explore each below.

TAX DEFERRAL   Each year, individuals purchase thousands of annuities unrelated to employment and not qualified under any plan for deductibility of contributions. Annuity owners face no contribution limitations yet enjoy unlimited tax deferral of investment income. Besides deferring taxes on investment earnings, they can provide contemporary investment returns. Figure 23-5 illustrates this concept.

PERSONAL
SAVINGS
THROUGH
NONQUALIFIED
ANNUITIES:
AN EXTENDED
ANALYSIS

The Benefits of Tax Deferral: An Illustration

Figure 23-5

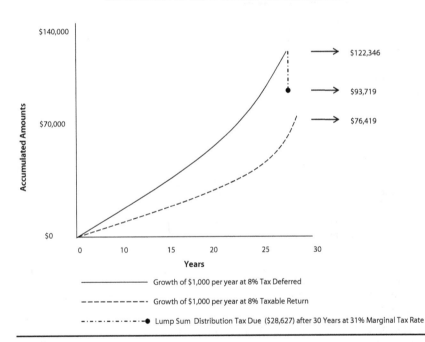

- —————— Growth of $1,000 per year at 8% Tax Deferred
- — — — — — Growth of $1,000 per year at 8% Taxable Return
- — · — · — · —● Lump Sum Distribution Tax Due ($28,627) after 30 Years at 31% Marginal Tax Rate

---

A $1,000 per year contribution is assumed to be made to an annuity crediting 8 percent on the gross contribution (on a tax deferred basis) and to another savings instrument earning 8 percent but on a taxable basis. A marginal tax rate of 31 percent is assumed for both instruments. The annuity fund builds to $122,346 at the end of 30 years whereas the taxable fund grows to $76,700. For a fair comparison, the assumption is made that the annuity value is taken as a lump sum distribution at that time, resulting in all deferred interest earnings being subject to the 31 percent tax. (Amounts paid on a periodic basis would receive more favorable tax treatment, as discussed in Chapter 21.) Even after paying $28,627 in taxes, the annuity purchaser would still be $17,000 ahead of the taxable investment.

LONGEVITY PROTECTION   As we know, investors are assumed to maximize their lifetime utilities. Too much consumption at an early age creates the risk of a large drop in consumption at later ages. Too much saving causes the consumer to live below an otherwise affordable level of current consumption. We also know that annuities can eliminate the financial uncertainty associated with living too long.

Evidence suggests that investors should choose an annuity for at least part of their retirement funds. Figure 23-6 shows the income that would be available to a 65-year-old with $100,000 available to provide lifetime income under three strategies, each with market-consistent assumptions appropriate for the year of the study (2004): (1) purchase a life annuity, (2) self-annuitize by drawing down an amount equal to the annuity benefit, and (3) draw down level amounts that amortize the available fund from age 65 to 100.

Figure 23-6   **Income from Alternative Payout Strategies $100,000 Sum at Age 65**

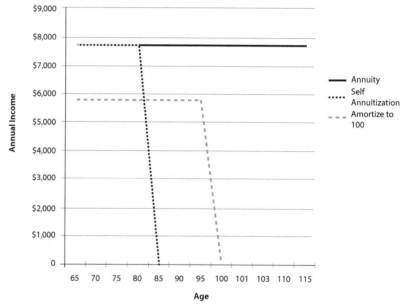

Source: Jeffery R. Brown, *Rational and Behavioral Perspective on the Role of Annuities in Retirement Planning*, Working Paper 13537, National Bureau of Economic Research (October 2007). *Uninsured options based on an interest rate of 4.58 percent, 10-year U.S. Treasury Strip, and contemporaneous annuity market rates.*

The annuity produces significantly more potential lifetime income than either of the uninsured options and eliminates retirement tail risk. The self-annuitization option produces the same level income for about 20 years only. The amortized-to-100 option produces significantly less income without completely eliminating longevity risk. Considered in this light, investor behavior is paradoxical because so few investors choose the annuity option. We noted in Chapter 6 that annuities make up but a small portion of retiree wealth and that few deferred annuities are actually annuitized.

We know that Markowitz portfolio theory remains the accepted mechanism for optimizing asset allocation decisions in retirement savings (see Chapter 14, appendix). The standard approach, however, does not take into account retiree longevity, so it ignores products (annuities) that can eliminate longevity risk through diversification and insurance. A more helpful approach incorporates not only asset allocation but asset allocation between uninsured liquidation and insured annuity liquidation approaches, and asset allocation within variable annuities. Annuity markets offer a variety of investment and longevity guarantee options.

Researchers have examined the asset and product allocation issues of variable annuities with guaranteed minimum withdrawal benefits (GMWB) – see Chapter 6 – that guarantee a minimum life income while preserving the possibility of increasing benefits with superior investment performance. Figure 23-7 illustrates the hypothetical performance of variable annuities with and without GMWB. During the generally rising market for equities from 1979 through 1999, the account balance and the benefit base (the guaranteed withdrawal amount) grow at the same pace. During the falling markets of 2000 through 2008, the benefit of the guarantee is substantial. The benefit base is more than twice the account value. These results, of course, are particular to the periods presented and different periods would produce different results. Further, variable annuities and associated guarantees generate fees that reduce equity performance during increasing markets.

Hypothetical Equity Performance: Variable Annuity with Minimum Guarantee 1979-2008   **Figure 23-7**

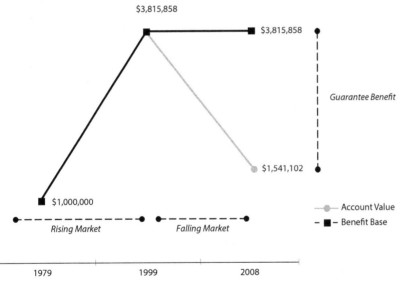

Source: Chen, Peng and Milevsky, Moshe A., *Merging Asset Allocation and Longevity Insurance: An Optimal Perspective on Payout Annuities*, Journal of Financial Planning (February 2010).

No portfolio plan can eliminate all risks completely, but this research indicates the potential benefit that variable annuities with GMWB can bring to a retirement portfolio. Researchers also identified the important factors at issue when allocating retirement assets between uninsured and insured segments of the portfolio.

- As the owner's aversion to risk increases, so should the allocation to annuities.
- Retiree's whose wealth significantly exceeds their income needs should be less attracted to annuities.
- Existing life income resources should affect the need for annuitization.
- Subjective expectations about life expectancy may be an appropriate consideration. While an individual's intuition is certainly not determinative, we know that annuity purchasers do live longer on average than others.
- Significant variations exist in fees and terms of variable annuities and associated guarantees. Critical consideration of these fees and terms is important to maximize benefits.
- Potential buyers expecting a significant probability of exceeding the maximum withdrawal amounts specified in the annuity contract should find annuities less attractive. Excess withdrawals are penalized.
- Retirees with bequest intentions will find annuitization less attractive.

As discussed in Chapter 6, the life insurance industry now offers two options that may substitute for a variable annuity with GMWB. Each addresses the annuity market's apparent aversion to the irrevocable transfer of asset control and continuing exposure to insurer credit risk associated with traditional annuities. Each represents a tool for new approaches to retirement planning.

The longevity annuity allows the purchase of a forward commitment to a future life income at current rates. Income commencement can be deferred for many years so the price of the income is discounted heavily for both interest and mortality. Purchasers can retain assets in a managed portfolio and confidentially take income from it during the annuity deferral period. The annuity effectively protects against tail risk by capturing the insurer's guarantee only for the least likely longevity scenarios: those at the most advanced ages. A longevity annuity can be purchased at age 65 for income commencing at 85, for example, at a price representing a small percentage of a portfolio. Thus, the purchaser retains ownership and control of the assets that might have been transferred in total to a traditional annuity.

The contingent deferred annuity – or stand alone guarantee – attaches a GMWB to a purchaser's mutual fund or managed account. The purchaser acquires the withdrawal guarantees associated with variable annuity terms and riders while retaining title and control of assets. The contract can be terminated by the owner at any time, providing additional flexibility.

INFLATION PROTECTION   Inflation expectations are reflected in the rates of return paid on fixed income investments. However, an increase in financial market expectations of inflation causes interest rates to rise. Fixed income investments lose capital value, and the income produced loses purchasing power. General-account-based fixed annuities are essentially long term fixed income investments. The suitability of fixed annuities depends on the portfolio properties of individuals' other investments and can be appropriate in a diversified strategy as they provide a floor of guaranteed life income. Considered individually, however, they are subject to considerable inflation risk.

Life insurers offer three individual annuity strategies designed to reduce inflation risk. First, variable annuities permit their owners to invest in stocks through separate accounts whose performance is directly reflected in annuity values. Second, the values within equity-indexed annuities are tied directly to the performance of the stock market. Long term stock returns historically have exceeded both inflation and long term bond returns. Third, life insurers now offer inflation-indexed annuities whose benefits increase with increases in an inflation index, usually the U.S. CPI. These are discussed in Chapter 6.

These annuities by no means provide complete protection against inflation, and they come at a cost. Stock performance becomes more volatile as holding periods shorten. Inflation-indexed annuities pay a lower initial benefit and thus may never provide the intended protection. Further, maximum yearly benefit increases may be capped for both inflation- and equity-indexed products so they will not provide complete protection in the event of high inflation.

INVESTMENT GUARANTEE   The reasons for relatively weak demand for annuities may also explain the popularity of annuities with investment guarantees. Recall from Chapter 6 that the annuity industry is largely driven by buyers who elect investment guarantee options that prevent significant losses while retaining the opportunity for investment gains. These include guarantees as to minimum withdrawal, income, and/or accumulation and as to lifetime withdrawals. Equity-indexed and inflation-indexed annuities also provide guarantees.

Of course, guarantee options are not free. Insurers charge for them, thereby, reducing benefits. Savers may find guarantees more attractive than pure annuities, because they are perceived to be less of a gamble, reduce the possibility of regret, and/or maintain increased liquidity.

POSSIBLE DISADVANTAGES OF ANNUITIES

Each annuity advantage comes at a cost. Some considerations that can render annuities unsuitable or otherwise unattractive savings and income options include:

- The fixed nature of the typical annuity benefit exposes the annuitant to inflation risk.
- The irrevocable nature of the traditional annuity commitment limits an annuitant's spending flexibility, particularly for large purchases such as real estate.
- The annuity commitment runs counter to many consumers' preferences to conserve and control their capital.
- The irrevocable nature of the commitment exposes annuitants to the credit risk of the insurer, somewhat mitigated by the protection of state guaranty associations.
- The traditional annuity liquidates principal completely and thus limits the annuitant's ability to provide bequests.
- The failure of insurers generally to offer life annuities priced for individual annuitant's expected longevity renders many payout annuities unfairly (actuarially speaking) expensive.

As discussed in Chapter 6 and above, there has been considerable development of the annuity market that now features products and options designed to mitigate some of these disadvantages while preserving the benefits of a guaranteed life income. Also, a secondary market for retirement and structured settlement annuities in liquidation is emerging – akin to that for life insurance policies (see below) – and could mitigate some of the above concerns. Information on the market is limited, but regulatory oversight has been characterized as weak or nonexistent. Concern has been expressed over the use of high discount rates and the lack of proper disclosure to the annuity owner given that, among other issues, this can substantially lower the amounts paid to the owner.

PERSONAL SAVINGS THROUGH LIFE INSURANCE: AN EXTENDED ANALYSIS

Previous discussions have focused primarily on the role of life insurance in managing the financial risk of untimely death. In this section, we see that lifetime savings benefits are an important adjunct to actuarial risk reduction. As the need for death protection declines over the course of a lifetime, the savings set aside in cash value policies to fund death benefits can be converted to lifetime use.

POLICY WITHDRAWALS, PARTIAL SURRENDERS, AND LOANS

The most common means of accessing life insurance policy values when death protection is no longer needed is a simple surrender of the policy for its cash surrender value. Taxable income may be incurred with surrenders, as discussed in Chapter 21. However, other strategies exist for converting cash values to disposable income while preserving many tax benefits.

Policy withdrawals, partial surrenders, and policy loans are each means of using policy cash values as the basis for securing cash under a policy (1) without having to terminate the policy and lose its death benefit coverage in the process and (2) which minimize the incidence of taxable income. Policy withdrawals occur when the policyowner removes cash value from a life insurance policy with no effect on the policy's net amount at risk. Withdrawals are commonly associated with unbundled policies such as universal life and not with bundled whole life (WL) policies. The withdrawal decreases the total death benefit and cash value by the amount of the withdrawal. Another form of withdrawal occurs with participating (par) WL policies when the policyowner, having elected the accumulate-at-interest dividend option, withdraws some of those dividends.

A partial surrender is associated with bundled life insurance policies. Not all bundled cash value contacts give the owner a right of partial surrender, but most insurers allow it. Cash value withdrawals, as such, ordinarily are not permitted with bundled policies, except for withdrawals of dividends accumulating at interest. Rather, as discussed in Chapter 5, to obtain cash values the policyowner must surrender portions of the policy. For example, assume that Bettie owns a bundled policy having a $1.0 million face amount and a $400,000 cash surrender value. She wants to secure $200,000 or one-half of the policy's cash surrender value. To do so, she must execute a partial surrender of one-half of the policy, reducing not just the cash surrender value but the death benefit, the net amount at risk, and the policy premium by one-half as well.

Another form of partial surrender occurs with par WL policies when the policyowner, having elected the paid-up addition (PUA) dividend option, surrenders portions of those PUAs. For example, assume that Dean elected the PUA option when he bought a par WL policy 20 years ago. These PUAs now provide an additional $60,000 of life insurance and have a cash surrender value of $30,000. Dean wants $20,000 cash from the PUAs, so he executes a two-thirds surrender of them, reducing not just their cash surrender value by two-thirds but their death benefit and net amount at risk by two-thirds as well.

Finally, policyowners may exercise the contractual right to secure a loan under their cash value policies on the security of and in an amount up to the policy's net cash surrender value. Interest is due on policy loans and is paid either in cash or by a further policy loan.

We know from Chapter 21 that non-MEC life insurance policies enjoy first-in-first-out (FIFO) tax treatment on withdrawals and partial surrenders, meaning that they are not included in taxable income until the sum of such distributions equals the policy's cost basis. We also know that ordinarily loan transactions are not taxable. Combining these two types of distributions can yield a tax efficient strategy for securing retirement (or other) income under a life insurance policy. Such a strategy can replicate the tax advantages of a Roth IRA but without limits on annual contributions. See Figure 20-3. Periodic withdrawals are taken until they equal the policy's cost basis, whereupon they cease. These are not taxable. Thereafter, a series of monthly or annual policy loans is initiated which also are not taxable events. Ideally, the difference between the policy loan rate and the interest crediting rate on the cash value is not great, thereby allowing for many years of loans. When the insured dies, the loans are repaid from death proceeds, and no taxation should occur. This strategy is illustrated in Chapter 24.

ANNUITIZATION

If the need for death protection under a cash value policy becomes unnecessary, and a life income is desired, two tax efficient options exist for converting cash values into a life income. The first is the life income settlement option discussed in Chapter 5. The second is the tax free exchange of the life insurance policy for an annuity policy under a Section 1035 exchange as discussed in Chapter 21. In both cases, tax deferral continues over the course of life on undistributed amounts. Immediate annuitization of the annuity is not necessary; the exchange can be for a deferred annuity. If immediate annuitization is desired, the guaranteed rates under the settlement option should be compared to available market rates for annuities.

SALE OF A POLICY IN THE SECONDARY LIFE INSURANCE MARKET

The market in which new life insurance policies are purchased from insurance companies is called the **primary life insurance market**. The market in which existing life insurance policies are bought and sold is called the **secondary life insurance market**. The HIV/AIDS crises of the 1980s gave impetus to the secondary market for life insurance where infected insureds could sell their policies for amounts greater than the cash values; such sales were labeled **viatical settlements** or simply **viaticals.**

As the viatical market declined with improvements in HIV/AIDS treatment, entrepreneurs then shifted from buying policies on terminally ill insureds to buying policies on those whose health had become merely impaired or on which investors believed they would make money because of insurer mispricing. Sales of such policies in the secondary market are commonly known as **life settlements** to distinguish them from viaticals. Except for tax and regulatory matters, the dividing line between viaticals and life settlements is arbitrary, and both terms today are understood to refer to sale of an existing life insurance policy in the secondary market.

In the past, a policyowner deciding to terminate his or her life insurance policy because insurance was no longer needed or affordable surrendered the policy to the insurance company under one of its nonforfeiture options or simply allowed it to lapse. The life settlement market represents a new option. If a policy is marketable, policyowners may be able to realize greater value by selling their policies than they would realize by surrendering them. Policyowners should proceed with caution, however, as this market is still evolving, is controversial, and associated with considerable fraud. Concerns about fraud and inappropriate sales practices led the NAIC to amend its 1993 *Viatical Settlements Model Act* in 2007 and the *National Conference of Insurance Legislators* to adopt its own model act, also in 2007, the *Life Settlements Model Act*. One of the chief concerns relates to so-called *stranger originated life insurance*. See Box 23-2. Also, life insurers increasingly are inserting accelerated benefit riders in their policies, allowing greater benefits to be paid under certain circumstances. See Chapter 5.

Box 23-2
Stranger-Originated Life Insurance

Life insurance policies may come onto the secondary market via two separate and distinct avenues. First, the policyowner may wish to sell an existing policy, originally bought for bona fide purposes, because of changed circumstances. We know from Chapter 18 that a policy so acquired originally for legitimate purposes is freely transferable at any time. Second, a policy may have been acquired for the express purpose of being sold in the secondary market. Such policies are purchased from life insurers at the behest of stranger investor/promoters whose motivations solely are to earn commissions on the original purchase and to sell policies for a profit in the secondary market. These policies are known as **stranger-originated** (or **owned**) **life insurance** or **STOLI**. They are purchased at the behest of stranger/promoters on the life of an elderly person for the purpose of being sold. The policies are not purchased for family, business, charitable, or any other legitimate purpose, so are inconsistent with insurable interest requirements.

The elderly person typically is convinced to participate in the scheme for some type of economic inducement, such as an offer of immediate or future cash, free insurance for a period of time, and/or a piece of the expected profit when the policy is sold. The intent is to have the STOLI policy be owned directly or indirectly by stranger-investors who have no preexisting family or business relationship with the insured.

A deliberate illusion is presented to the insurer to make it appear that the proposed insured (or a trust or business entity carrying the insured's name) will be the owner of the policy. In fact, the proposed insured (or trust) is only posing as the policyowner on behalf of the stranger-investors who typically finance all or most of the premium. Life insurance companies will not knowingly issue STOLI. To get around the obstacle of insurance companies discovering that an application seeks insurance benefiting a stranger/investor, the conspirators disguise their involvement via misrepresentations. A common technique is to structure the transaction to appear to company underwriters as a purchase for estate liquidity purposes. To convince insurers to issue such large policies, the proposed insured's net worth and income are commonly exaggerated.

The secondary life insurance market, as all markets, relies on willing buyers and sellers arriving at agreeable prices. The sales process usually involves a life insurance agent or broker, often called a *producer* in the model laws, locating owners willing to sell their policies and negotiating the sale on behalf of the owners with life settlement firms, often called *providers*. Producers are paid commissions by the firms that purchase the policies. Commissions can be quite high, with one long-time knowledgeable observer labeling them "obscene."[5] Policies sold in the secondary market are sometimes said to have been *settled*.

The typical target insured is age 65 and older. The minimum eligible policy face amount is in the $250,000 – $500,000 range or greater, and the insurance typically is no longer needed or wanted. The objective of the settlement firms (or the investors to whom the policies are then sold) is to realize attractive investment returns based on the purchase price and future premiums paid relative to the benefits paid at the insured's death. Settlement firms expect to make profits when a disparity develops over time in life insurance policies between their cash values and their economic or actuarial values. The disparity can arise because the health of the insured has deteriorated or the policy was mispriced.

Mispricing can occur if an insurer underestimates the magnitude of future mortality rates or overestimates future lapse rates involving certain types of pricing. The economic values of these policies should be greater than their cash values. Taxes are due on any gain, but where the market price of a policy maximizes its value to the policyowner, a decision to sell may be advisable. There is no escaping the fact, however, that strangers ultimately have an interest in the early death of the insured.

CONCLUSIONS

In Chapter 20, we noted retirement as the key economic life cycle event when individuals' human capital is depleted and accumulated capital becomes the means of support. Because of the uncertainty of human life spans, retirement planning for individuals must address the risk of outliving their assets. The three most important sources of retirement income are Social Security, employer-sponsored retirement plans, and personal assets. Social Security and some employer plans – although increasingly less so – provide lifetime benefits. To the extent individuals rely on personal assets for their retirement, only annuities can eliminate longevity risk.

ENDNOTES

1   This section draws in part on "Behavioral Finance and Retirement Plan Contributions: How Participants Behave, and Prescriptive Solutions," *Employee Benefit Research Institute Issue Brief* 301 (January 2007).

2   See, *2011 Retirement Confidence Survey: Confidence Drops to Record Lows, Reflecting "The New Normal,"* EBRI (March 2011).

3   James Xiong, Thomas Idzorek, and Peng Chen, "Allocation to Deferred Variable Annuities with GMWB for Life," White Paper, Ibbotson and Associates Inc. (2010).

4   This section draws from Harold D. Skipper and Wayne Tonning, *The Advisor's Guide to Life Insurance* (Chicago; American Bar Association, 2011), Chapter 18.

5   See, Joseph M. Belth, "Obscene Commissions for Intermediaries in the Secondary Market for Life Insurance Policies," *The Insurance Forum* (January 2008), pp. 1-3.

	Payroll Deduction IRA	SEP	SIMPLE IRA Plan	Safe Harbor 401(k)	
Key Advantage	Easy to set up and maintain.	Easy to set up and maintain.	Salary reduction plan with little administrative paperwork.	Permits high level of salary deferrals by employees without annual discrimination testing.	
Employer Eligibility	Any employer with one or more employees.	Any employer with one or more employees.	Any employer with 100 or fewer employees that does not currently maintain another retirement plan.	Any employer with one or more employees.	
Employer's Role	Arrange for employees to make payroll deduction contributions. Transmit contributions for employees to IRA. No annual filing requirement for employer.	May use IRS Form 5305-SEP to set up the plan. No annual filing requirement for employer.	May use IRS Forms 5304-SIMPLE or 5305-SIMPLE to set up the plan. No annual filing requirement for employer. Bank or financial institution handles most of the paperwork.	No model form to establish this plan. Advice from a financial institution or employee benefit adviser may be necessary. A minimum amount of employer contributions is required. Annual filing of Form 5500 is required.	

An Overview of Important
Employer-Provided Retirement Plan Features

	Automatic Enrollment 401(k)	Traditional 401(k)	Profit Sharing	Defined Benefit
Key Advantage	Provides high level of participation and permits high level of salary deferrals by employees. Also safe harbor relief for default investments	Permits high level of salary deferrals by employees.	Permits employer to make large contributions for employees.	Provides a fixed, pre-established benefit for employees.
Employer Eligibility	Any employer with one or more employees.	Any employer with one or more employees.	Any employer with one or more employees.	Any employer with one or more employees.
Employer's Role	No model form to establish this plan. Advice from a financial institution or employee benefit adviser may be necessary. Annual filing of Form 5500 is required. Some plans require annual non-discrimination testing to ensure they do not discriminate in favor of highly compensated employees.	No model form to establish this plan. Advice from a financial institution or employee benefit adviser may be necessary. Annual filing of Form 5500 is required. Some plans require annual non-discrimination testing to ensure they do not discriminate in favor of highly compensated employees.	No model form to establish this plan. Advice from a financial institution or employee benefit adviser may be necessary. Annual filing of Form 5500 is required.	No model form to establish this plan. Advice from a financial institution or employee benefit adviser would be necessary. Annual filing of Form 5500 is required. An actuary must determine annual contributions.

	Payroll Deduction IRA	SEP	SIMPLE IRA Plan	Safe Harbor 401(k)	
Contributors to the Plan	Employee contributions remitted through payroll deduction.	Employer contributions only.	Employee salary reduction contributions and employer contributions.	Employee salary reduction contributions and employer contributions.	
Maximum Annual Contribution (per participant)	$5,500 for 2014. Additional contributions up to $1,000 can be made by participants age 50 or over.	Up to 25% of compensation not exceeding $260,000 but no more than $52,000 for 2014.	Employee: $12,000 in 2014. Additional contributions up to $2,500 can be made by participants age 50 or over. Employer: Either match employee contributions 100% of first 3% of compensation (can be reduced to as low as 1% in any 2 out of 5 yrs.); or contribute 2% of each eligible employee's compensation.	Employee: $17,500 in 2014. Additional contributions can be made by participants age 50 or over up to $5,500. Employer/ Employee Combined: Up to the lesser of 100% of compensation not exceeding $250,000 or $50,000 for 2012 Employer can deduct (1) amounts that do not exceed 25% of aggregate compensation for all participants and (2) all salary reduction contributions.	
Contributor's Options	Employee can decide how much to contribute at any time.	Employer can decide whether to make contributions year to-year.	Employee can decide how much to contribute. Employer must make matching contributions or contribute 2% of each employee's compensation.	Employee can decide how much to contribute pursuant to a salary reduction agreement. The employer must make either specified matching contributions or a 3% contribution to all participants.	

	Automatic Enrollment 401(k)	Traditional 401(k)	Profit Sharing	Defined Benefit
Contributors to the Plan	Employee salary reduction contributions and maybe employer contributions.	Employee salary reduction contributions and maybe employer contributions.	Annual employer contribution is discretionary.	Primarily funded by employer.
Maximum Annual Contribution (per participant)	Employee: $17,500 in 2014. Additional contributions can be made by participants age 50 or over up to $5,500. Employer/Employee Combined: Up to the lesser of 100% of compensation not exceeding $250,000 or $50,000 for 2012. Employer can deduct (1) amounts that do not exceed 25% of aggregate compensation for all participants and (2) all salary reduction contributions.	Employee: $17,500 in 2014. Additional contributions can be made by participants age 50 or over up to $5,500. Employer/Employee Combined: Up to the lesser of 100% of compensation not exceeding $250,000 or $50,000 for 2012. Employer can deduct (1) amounts that do not exceed 25% of aggregate compensation for all participants and (2) all salary reduction contributions.	Up to the lesser of 100% of compensation not exceeding $52,000 or $57,500 for employee 50 and older for 2014. Employer can deduct amounts that do not exceed 25% of aggregate compensation for all participants.	Annually determined contribution.
Contributor's Options	Employees, unless they opt otherwise, must make salary reduction contributions specified by the employer. The employer can make additional contributions, including matching contributions as set by plan terms.	Employee can decide how much to contribute pursuant to a salary reduction agreement. The employer can make additional contributions, including matching contributions as set by plan terms.	Employer makes contribution as set by plan terms.	Employer generally required to make contribution as set by plan terms.

	Payroll Deduction IRA	SEP	SIMPLE IRA Plan	Safe Harbor 401(k)	
Minimum Employee Coverage Requirements	There is no requirement. Can be made available to any employee.	Must be offered to all employees who are at least 21 years of age, employed by the employer for 3 of the last 5 years and had compensation of $550 for 2014.	Must be offered to all employees who have earned income of at least $5,000 in any prior 2 years, and are reasonably expected to earn at least $5,000 in the current year.	Generally, must be offered to all employees at least 21 years of age who worked at least 1,000 hours in a previous year.	
Withdrawals, Loans, and Payments	Withdrawals permitted anytime subject to federal income taxes; early withdrawals subject to an additional tax (special rules apply to Roth IRAs).	Withdrawals permitted anytime subject to federal income taxes, early withdrawals subject to an additional tax.	Withdrawals permitted anytime subject to federal income taxes, early withdrawals subject to an additional tax.	Withdrawals permitted after a specified event occurs (e.g., retirement, plan termination, etc.) subject to federal income taxes. Plan may permit loans and hardship withdrawals; early withdrawals subject to an additional tax.	
Vesting	Contributions are immediately 100% vested.	Contributions are immediately 100% vested.	Employee salary reduction contributions and employer contributions are immediately 100% vested.	Employee salary reduction contributions and most employer contributions are immediately 100% vested. Some employer contributions may vest over time according to plan terms.	

	Automatic Enrollment 401(k)	Traditional 401(k)	Profit Sharing	Defined Benefit
Minimum Employee Coverage Requirements	Generally, must be offered to all employees at least 21 years of age who worked at least 1,000 hours in a previous year.	Generally, must be offered to all employees at least 21 years of age who worked at least 1,000 hours in a previous year.	Generally, must be offered to all employees at least 21 years of age who worked at least 1,000 hours in a previous year.	Generally, must be offered to all employees at least 21 years of age who worked at least 1,000 hours in a previous year.
Withdrawals, Loans, and Payments	Withdrawals permitted after a specified event occurs (e.g., retirement, plan termination, etc.) subject to federal income taxes. Plan may permit loans and hardship withdrawals; early withdrawals subject to an additional tax.	Withdrawals permitted after a specified event occurs (e.g., retirement, plan termination, etc.) subject to federal income taxes. Plan may permit loans and hardship withdrawals; early withdrawals subject to an additional tax.	Withdrawals permitted after a specified event occurs (e.g., retirement, plan termination, etc.) subject to federal income taxes. Plan may permit loans and hardship withdrawals; early withdrawals subject to an additional tax.	Payment of benefits after a specified event occurs (e.g. retirement, plan termination, etc.). Plan may permit loans; early withdrawals subject to an additional tax.
Vesting	Employee salary reduction contributions are immediately 100% vested. Employer contributions may vest over time according to plan terms.	Employee salary reduction contributions are immediately 100% vested. Employer contributions may vest over time according to plan terms.	May vest over time according to plan terms.	May vest over time according to plan terms.

CHAPTER 24

LIFE INSURANCE IN BUSINESS PLANNING

Life insurance is most often purchased for family or other personal reasons, as noted in the preceding chapters. Much individually issued life insurance is also purchased to foster business purposes. In closing Part IV on life insurance in personal and business planning, this chapter explores common business-related applications.[1] As background to discussion of these applications, we first introduce the major forms that business enterprises may take in the U.S. and offer short discussions of potential problems of each form in terms of business continuity. While this discussion is U.S.-centric, the concepts apply to many other markets. We then present tax considerations applicable to business uses of life insurance, followed by analyses of how life insurance can be useful in helping business address several important issues.

FORMS OF BUSINESS ORGANIZATIONS

Businesses in the U.S. have traditionally operated as sole proprietorships, partnerships, and corporations. Each of these forms continues to be important, but a new form of statutory business organization developed at the end of the last century, the limited liability company (or LLC), is perhaps the most popular form of new small business venture. Variations of each form exist, although a detailed discussion of all variations is outside the scope of this text.

SOLE PROPRIETORSHIPS

A **sole proprietorship** is an unincorporated business owned by an individual who usually also manages it. No legal distinction exists between the proprietor's personal and business assets and liabilities or income. In the absence of work in professions or trades that themselves require licensing or other documentation, the sole proprietor may establish himself or herself in business by the mere declaration that he or she is in business. More than 22 million sole proprietorships exist in the U.S., accounting for about 4 percent of total U.S. business revenue. The great majority of sole proprietorships are small, having fewer than ten employees.

A sole proprietorship is a fragile business enterprise because of its dependence on a single individual. Upon the death of the proprietor, his or her personal representative generally is obligated to liquidate the business, thus possibly losing its value as a going concern.

Partnerships

A **partnership** is a voluntary association of two or more individuals or entities for the purpose of conducting a business for profit as co-owners. Business assets and liabilities are owned by the partnership. Almost 3 million partnerships exist in the U.S., accounting for about 13 percent of all U.S. business receipts. Most engage in commercial activities, in contrast with professional activities such as law or medicine.

Partnerships are of two basic types. A **general partnership** is one in which partners are actively involved in the management of the firm and fully liable for partnership obligations. A **limited partnership** is one having at least one general partner and one or more limited partners who are not actively engaged in partnership management and who are liable for partnership obligations only to the extent of their investment in the partnership.

The partnership form of business has several advantages, but it is subject to the general rule that any change in the membership of the partnership causes its dissolution. On the death of a general partner, the partnership is dissolved and, in the absence of arrangements to the contrary, the surviving partners become liquidating trustees. They are charged with the responsibility of winding up the business and paying to the estate of the deceased a fair share of the liquidated value of the business. From the viewpoint of remaining partners and the deceased partner's heirs, liquidation not only may produce losses to them by shrinkage in asset values but, more important, may destroy their source of income.

The seriousness of the consequences often leads surviving partners to attempt to continue the business by buying out the interest of the deceased partner and reorganizing the partnership. This procedure may not be practicable for two reasons. First, it may be impossible quickly to raise the necessary cash. Second, even if the surviving partners can raise the cash, they must prove that the price paid for the interest is fair – a tough call given their fiduciary status. The record of litigation indicates that, in the absence of advance agreement among the partners, attempts to continue the business are fraught with legal and practical complications.

Corporations

A **corporation** is a business legally separate and distinct from its owners and possesses these characteristics:

- owners' liability for corporate obligations is limited to their investments in the corporation,
- easy transfer of owners' interests in the corporation by sale of their shares of stock, and
- owners' deaths have no effect legally on the corporation's continued existence.

Some 5.8 million corporations exist in the U.S., accounting for 83 percent of all U.S. business receipts. Most corporations are **closely held corporations**, also referred to as **close corporations** and **closed corporations,** meaning that they typically are owned and managed by a small number of investors, often family members, with their shares of stock not listed on any organized exchange. Although a shareholder's death legally has no effect on a corporation's continued existence, the nature of a closely held corporation can lead to practical problems. Shareholders are often also important managers. The practical difficulties encountered in attempting to continue operation of such a business following an actively involved shareholder's death stem from the very characteristics of a closely held corporation.

PROBLEMS ASSOCIATED WITH THE DEATH OF A MAJORITY SHAREHOLDER   Consider the situation of typical majority shareholders of close corporations. They likely run the business as its chief executive, being paid a handsome income that their families enjoy. On their death and in the absence of a legally binding arrangement to dispose of their interest at death, the family inherits that interest, but all income ceases as closely held corporations typically do not pay dividends. Of course, as majority owners (and voters), the family has options. It can:

1. insist that another family member already employed in the firm or that the firm will hire be paid a sufficiently high income;
2. insist that the corporation begin paying dividends of sufficient amount to enable the family to continue its former lifestyle;
3. sell their stock to persons with no existing ownership interest in the firm; or
4. sell their stock to persons with an existing ownership interest in the firm.

The viability of these options will vary depending on circumstances. With the first option, a family member with no previous meaningful involvement in the business normally would be unable to contribute much to it and might be a source of disruption and even conflict. Existing owner/managers may conclude that their best interests are served by leaving, perhaps beginning their own competing business. All parties could lose economic value were this to happen.

The second option likely would be unpalatable to the other owners. They would, in effect, be taxed twice on dividend income that they would prefer not to have in the first place, at least not in that form. If they were expected to take over the former responsibilities of the deceased CEO/owner in addition to paying high dividends, resentment could be expected, perhaps leading to resignations. Of course, if the minority owners could somehow block the efforts of heirs to have the company pay high dividends, dissatisfaction by the heirs could lead to other challenges.

The third option, selling to outside interests, could be feasible in appropriate circumstances but also could be viewed by potential purchasers as a "fire sale" opportunity. This is particularly true as outsiders are likely to recognize that the principal value of the business is in the remaining employees, who could resign. Further, associates in a close corporation, as in a partnership, typically join forces because they work well together and each makes a certain contribution that, taken together, produces a vigorous, profitable combination. Outsiders may not fit well into this corporate family, leading to disruption of the business or, in extreme cases, even to liquidation. Perhaps of greater importance to the minority shareholders, they would know that compensation and dividend policy would be in the hands of the new majority shareholders. Again, they may find leaving the firm the best option, allowing the new folks to fend for themselves.

The final option is likely the most efficacious provided agreement can be reached as to a fair price and the minority owners are able to raise the necessary cash. The heirs may perceive themselves to be in the superior bargaining position and insist on a high price or simply refuse to sell their interests.

The disabled majority shareholder is also in an unenviable position. Indeed, he or she may insist on continuing to collect a salary, which has the easy potential to lead to disgruntled minority shareholders.

PROBLEMS ASSOCIATED WITH THE DEATH OF A MINORITY AND 50/50 SHAREHOLDER

The minority and 50/50 shareholder situations likely pose even more formidable problems. The minority shareholder's heirs, while they may not be able to exercise control, nonetheless may be able to render life miserable for the majority shareholder/managers. All shareholders have rights, such as being entitled to a proportionate share of dividends, to examine the corporate records (with legitimate reason), and generally to participate in all shareholder activities. Lawsuits by disgruntled minority shareholders are not uncommon.

A majority shareholder's beneficiaries can enforce their wills on the surviving shareholders; a minority shareholder's beneficiaries generally cannot. The minority shareholder's heirs are potentially in a most unenviable position. They own stock that was possibly subject to substantial federal estate taxes yet the stock may have little or no marketability. Additionally, they receive no income from their investment, as closely held corporations rarely pay dividends. The disabled minority shareholder likely will be in a worse position still.

Similar circumstances apply to the death or disability of one of two 50/50 shareholders. In fact, such circumstances often are worse for all concerned, as deadlocks are possible in which no business decisions can be made.

LIMITED LIABILITY COMPANIES

The **limited liability company** (LLC) is a relatively new form of business combining features of partnerships and corporations, whose governance and owners' rights are defined more by an *operating agreement* of its members than by statute, and which features limited liability and flexibility in the tax status of participants. It has seen widespread adoption worldwide in recent decades. Rather than partners or shareholders, LLCs are owned by *members* whose ownership interests are represented by *membership units*. Management is delegated to managing members or independent managers.

The creation and operation of an LLC is a streamlined and less administratively burdensome undertaking than that of a corporation. In the U.S., the LLC is an entity disregarded as such for tax purposes, and it elects to be taxed as any of the traditional business entity forms: proprietorship, partnership, or traditional corporation. The standard statutory governance and owners' rights differ from partnership and corporations. However, these factors are variable in all cases due to LLC operating agreements, partnership agreements, and corporate by-laws and shareholder agreements. Thus, most of the business succession and other issues and strategies associated with corporations or partnerships exist in identical or analogous ways for an LLC.

In general, the tax treatment of individually issued life insurance used for business purposes follows that of personally owned life insurance, with one important exception. The general rule is that life insurance death benefits received under insurance payable to the employer – called **employer owned life insurance** (EOLI) under the U.S. *Internal Revenue Code* (IRC) Section 101(j)(3)(A) – are subject to income taxes to the extent that the benefits exceed the employer's cost basis in the policy. Fortunately, the law also provides that death benefits payable under EOLI policies meeting either one of two exceptions and for which certain notice and consent requirements are met will not be treated as taxable income. The two exceptions are:

TAX CONSIDERATIONS IN BUSINESS APPLICATIONS OF LIFE INSURANCE

1. Insureds are present or former directors or highly compensated employees. A highly compensated employee is one who, at the time of policy issuance, meets one of the following conditions:
   - owned 5.0 percent or more of the corporation's shares at any time during the preceding year,
   - earned compensation of $110,000 (indexed) during the preceding year,
   - was among the five highest paid officers, or
   - was among the highest paid 35 percent of all employees.
2. Life insurance death proceeds are paid to the insured's heirs (or a trust for the heirs) or used by the employer to redeem stock owned by the insured in the employer.

In addition to meeting one of the preceding exceptions, the insured must have been given notice prior to the insurance purchase that such insurance was to be purchased and consented to its purchase. The notice must state that the employer intends to be the owner and beneficiary of a life insurance policy on the executive's life and that the employer may choose to continue the coverage beyond the executive's employment. The notice must also state the maximum amount of life insurance that could be placed on the executive's life.

Finally, employers must annually report any such life insurance arrangements to the IRS. The report must include the number of employees insured by the employer and the number of employees for whom valid consent was obtained. It is exceedingly important that all requirements be met if the policyholder is to avoid having death proceeds subject to income taxation.

Here we cover four business applications of life insurance:

BUSINESS APPLICATIONS OF LIFE INSURANCE

- key person indemnification,
- business continuation arrangements,
- nonqualified executive benefit plans, and
- group term carve outs.

KEY PERSON INDEMNIFICATION

Many businesses have been built around one or more individuals whose capital, energy, technical knowledge, experience, or power to plan and execute makes them particularly valuable to the organization and a necessity to its successful operation, at least in the early stages of the organization's existence. Where would Microsoft have been without Bill Gates, Apple without Steve Jobs, or Berkshire

Hathaway without Warren Buffet? And how many thousands of firms today, particularly small to medium size firms, are similarly dependent on one or two key employees for their continued success or even viability? In each instance, the death of the key employee could have profoundly adverse financial effects on the firm.

As with insurance that indemnifies the firm for property and liability losses, so too can life insurance mitigate losses caused by the death of key individuals. **Key person insurance**, also called **key employee** (and **key man)** insurance, is purchased to help compensate a business for the decrease in earnings brought about by the death of one or more key persons. This generic term encompasses individuals who are employees as well as those who might not technically be employees but whose death could adversely affect a business, such as the author who received a multi-million dollar advance, or the award-winning actor whom the studio landed to make a movie. The financial planning process provides a framework for exploring key employee insurance

IDENTIFY OBJECTIVES The first step in the financial planning process is to identify objectives; in this instance to determine whether anyone's death, commonly that of an employee, might lead to a material deterioration in the firm's financial situation, precisely paralleling the effort undertaken with families. What is material to one firm will not necessarily be so with other firms.

A firm's financial position could deteriorate in several ways. Gross revenues may deteriorate meaningfully on the death of the firm's star saleswoman, innovative biologist, brilliant CFO, best-selling author, world-class soccer player, etc. Compounding any of these declines in gross revenue could be meaningfully higher expenses because of a need to replace the key person. The financial health of a firm may also depend on less visible and more modestly compensated administrative personnel whose participation is similarly important to the firm.

One area sometimes overlooked in thinking about the financial effects on the firm of the death of key persons is the loss of a firm's high credit rating. Insurance on the lives of key employees can assure banks and other lenders as well as suppliers that the business will have a financial cushion if one or more of them were to die. Similarly, if prospective lenders or other creditors are assured of the firm's continuation as a going concern in the event of the death of key owner/manager(s), the firm usually will be able to obtain a larger line of credit on better terms. These types of assurances can be especially important to small and medium size firms.

Another issue can arise in connection with bonds. If a firm's financial success lies chiefly with the efforts of one or two individuals, and it seeks to raise substantial funds via bond issues, buyers may demand a premium or even refuse to purchase the bonds if they know that the death of the key employees might impair the concern to such an extent that the liquidation of its assets might prove insufficient for the full redemption of the bonds.

GATHER AND ANALYZE INFORMATION Businesses purchase all types of insurance to stabilize their financial position. Usually, we think of stabilization in terms of protecting the value of the firm. One widely recognized measure of the value of a business is the present value of current and future net cash flows. The market establishes this value for businesses whose stock is publicly traded. The market will penalize the stock price if it perceives that any major operational, property, liability, or personnel loss could negatively affect cash flows. Property, liability, business interruption, key person, and other insurance can be thought of as the business hedging this possibility, such that any loss will be indemnified, thus shoring up share prices. Publicly traded firms might establish the risk management objective that no insurable loss to the firm – whether a property, liability, business interruption, or personnel loss – should cause the share price to fall by more than a certain percentage.

Establishing value for businesses not publicly traded on an organized exchange poses challenges. While the value of such a business is the present value of current and future net cash flows, this value is not established by a market and must be estimated. Some advisors estimate this figure by taking some multiple of the business's net worth as shown on its balance sheet or by estimating the present value of future profits. Thus, a closely held business might want to ensure that no loss to the firm would cause the net worth or future profits to fall by more than a certain percentage.

As applied to key person insurance, consideration must be given to questions such as how to estimate the actual impact on the firm's finances of that key person's death, whether the loss would be temporary or permanent, and the appropriate discount rate to use. The degree of accuracy inherent in these and other factors used to estimate the value of the economic loss produced by the death of a key person varies according to the type of business, particular function of the key person, and other circumstances.

DEVELOP AND IMPLEMENT PLAN   After deciding that the death of one or more key individuals could have unacceptable financial repercussions for the firm and quantifying those repercussions, a plan for dealing with them must follow. Succession planning comes into play here, but it takes time and there is no guarantee of success. Life insurance is a common financial response. The importance of key person life insurance was recognized in a well known 1951 tax court case. The court stated:

> What business purpose could be considered more essential than key man [or woman] insurance? The business that insures its buildings and machinery and automobiles from every possible hazard can hardly be expected to exercise less care in protecting itself against the loss of two of its most vital assets – managerial skill and experience.[2]

For insurance on key executives, the business provides written notice to the key executive that it intends to buy life insurance on his or her life. The notice must state (1) that the employer will be the beneficiary of the policy and may remain so even after the executive is no longer employed by the business and (2) the maximum amount of insurance to be purchased on his or her life. Written consent to proceed with the purchase must be obtained. Other requirements for EOLI as discussed earlier also must be met.

The business then applies for the policy for which it will be the owner and beneficiary. It also pays the premiums. Key person insurance is not a type of policy but a special application of the usual types of insurance. Thus, the policy type should be selected based on the expected nature of the insurance need including its magnitude, duration, and pattern, as well as the financial characteristics of the

726 PART IV: LIFE INSURANCE IN PERSONAL AND BUSINESS PLANNING

firm, including its ability and willingness to pay premiums and its risk tolerance and discipline. The latter two items are more relevant to small than to large firms.

Another consideration is whether it is desirable to have cash values available for other purposes (e.g., as loan collateral or to informally fund a deferred compensation arrangement – see below). If a cash value form of life insurance is used, the firm's liquidity is enhanced through the accumulation of cash values. Cash values are balance sheet assets.

Whole life (WL) and universal life (UL) policies are most often recommended for key employee indemnification. Term life insurance is commonly recommended to cover short term needs, as arise with individuals under performance contracts or if funds can be put to better use outside the life insurance policy. Specialized disability income policies are also available to cover business overhead expenses and for key employee disability. See Boxes 24-1 and 24-2.

Box 24-1
Business Overhead Expense Insurance

Business overhead expense (BOE) **insurance,** also called simply, **overhead expense insurance,** covers the monthly business expenses of business owners and professionals in private practice if they become disabled. A reimbursement benefit is paid during total disability, defined in occupational terms. Benefits begin after 30 or 60 days of disability and pay up to a specified amount each month while disability continues, until an aggregate benefit amount has been paid. The aggregate amount generally is a multiple of 12, 18, or 24 times the monthly benefit, rather than a specifically limited duration of months. The policy waives any premiums due during disability.

Covered expenses usually are those that the IRS accepts as deductible expenses for federal income tax purposes. They include rent or mortgage payments for the business premises, employee salaries, installment payments for equipment (but usually not inventory), utility and laundry costs, business insurance premiums that are not waived during disability, and any other recurring expenses that the insured normally incurs in the conduct of his or her business or professional practice.

The major insurers pay benefits on a cumulative basis, so that if the full monthly benefit has not been paid in a given month because of lower than expected covered expenses, any unpaid benefit is carried forward and is available to be paid in any month in which expenses exceed the designated monthly benefit. Benefit amounts of up to $30,000 or so per month are generally available.

Premiums paid for overhead expense insurance ordinarily are deductible by the business as a necessary business expense, whether the business is a sole proprietorship, partnership, or corporation. Benefits received are considered ordinary income, but they may be offset in whole or in part by the business expenses that the policy benefits are designed to cover.

BUSINESS CONTINUATION ARRANGEMENTS

Businesses whose ownership interests have no ready market are referred to as **closely held businesses,** of which closely held corporations are an important component. The problems of business continuation are particularly acute for closely held businesses of all types. These problems stem from the typical characteristics of such businesses, as alluded to earlier:

- *Unity of ownership and management.* The owners typically manage the firm, receiving a salary. Indeed, in a survey of families having any business interests, 92 percent reported having an active role in the business;
- *Small number of owners.* The great majority of closely held businesses are owned by fewer than ten individuals.

- *Ownership interest not readily marketable.* Because ownership interests in closely held businesses are not traded on organized exchanges, there typically is no ready market for that interest. The only persons ordinarily interested in purchasing such an interest are the other owners and possibly competitors.

Box 24-2
Key Employee Disability Income Insurance

Key employee disability income insurance provides for payment of a monthly indemnity to a business entity during the total disability of an essential employee who is the named insured under the policy. Funds may be used to attract a replacement for the key employee or to reimburse the firm for a portion of profit lost due to the key employee's disability. Benefits begin after a specified period of disability and continue while the insured is disabled for up to 12 or 24 months.

The amount of indemnity is typically high, reflecting the employee's value to the business, and generally it is issued independently of any limits that the insurance company may have set for personal insurance. Although the payment of benefits depends on the disabled status of the insured, the policy itself is owned by the business entity and all benefits are paid directly to the business. Key employee disability insurance is offered by a few insurers only. The income tax treatment of key employee disability income insurance and disability buy/sell insurance is the same as that for personal coverage. Premiums are not deductible, and benefits are received income tax free.

Closely held businesses are a major source of U.S. economic activity and employment. Almost 20 percent of nonfinancial assets held by U.S. households was composed of privately held business interests, a larger proportion than that which households held in shares of public corporations. Nine of every 10 businesses are family run.

Problems of business succession are, by definition, particularly acute for privately held firms, yet owner/managers more often than not fail to address them. In one survey, only 45 percent of family business owners who planned to retire within the next five years had identified a successor.[3] Apparently, no question was asked in the survey about having identified a successor in case of death, but the percentage almost certainly would have been even lower.

Moreover, even business owners who plan for succession often overlook critically important issues. Survivors often find themselves facing creditors who doubt their business abilities and, therefore, reduce credit lines and call loans. Many customers try to take advantage of successors, as do many employees. Every ownership transfer involves some difficulty, with the U.S. *Small Business Administration* reporting only 30 percent of family businesses succeeding into the second generation and only 15 percent into the third. The greater the care and thought exercised in business continuation planning, the greater the likelihood of business survival for the benefit of all stakeholders. Yet, in the majority of situations, those who built and control the business do no meaningful planning.

The problems of business stability and continuation following the death of one or more of the owners of a closely held business are critically important to both the family of the deceased owner and surviving owners and employees. While the essential issue is the same irrespective of business organizational form, the details for addressing the issue will vary based on form, so our discussion below is structured around each of the three major forms.

SOLE PROPRIETORSHIPS   Sole proprietorships are fragile, usually quite small operations. In seeking to preserve any going concern value of the firm following the death of the proprietor, either a family member steps in or purchasers must be identified. The time for planning for either eventuality is well before death, for, if a sale is contemplated after death, heirs are unlikely to be in a strong bargaining position.

If a sale is desirable, the owner ideally would have both identified the purchaser and made pre-death arrangements to effectuate a buyout on his or her death via a one-way buy/sell agreement. A **one-way buy/sell agreement** obligates the estate of a sole owner of a business (including a corporation) to sell and another party to purchase that owner's interest. A binding buy/sell agreement between the proprietor and a friendly competitor could be negotiated. The agreement could be funded by insurance purchased on the proprietor's life by the competitor and under which the competitor is owner and beneficiary. Premiums would be paid by the competitor.

Alternatively, one or more key employees, dependent perhaps on the business for their livelihood, might find the prospects of acquiring the business to be attractive. A buy/sell agreement funded by insurance on the proprietor's life could guarantee their eventual ownership while acting as an inducement for these key employee(s) to remain with the business. The policy could be owned by and payable to the employee or owned by and payable to a trust that collects the proceeds and supervises execution of the agreement.

Premiums for such insurance are not tax deductible, but policy proceeds should be received free of income tax and not taxable in the proprietor's estate. If the key employee(s) have insufficient funds to pay the required premiums, the proprietor could assist the employee(s) financially, for example through a split dollar arrangement (see later in this chapter). The nature of the insurance need commonly suggests the purchase of some form of WL or UL insurance, with the precise details being influenced by cash flow issues.

PARTNERSHIPS   To avoid the difficulties noted earlier when one partner dies, members of a partnership commonly enter into a buy/sell agreement. This agreement binds the surviving partners or the partnership to purchase the partnership interest of the first partner to die at a prearranged price set by the agreement and obligates the deceased partner's estate to sell that interest to the other partners. The value of the partnership interest is determined at the time the agreement is entered into and periodically revalued, or a formula for value determination is included in the agreement.

Types of Business Continuation Arrangements   Most buy/sell agreements are of one of two types: entity or cross purchase. Under an **entity buy/sell agreement**, the business entity itself is obligated to buy the ownership interest of any deceased partner, with each partner having bound his or her estate to sell if he or she were to be the first to die. Under a **cross purchase buy/sell agreement**, each owner binds his or her estate to sell his or her business interest to the surviving owners, and each surviving owner binds himself or herself to buy the interest of the deceased owner. The agreement is among the business owners themselves, not between the business enterprise and its owners. Other forms of less frequently found buy/sell agreements exist. For example, under an **option buy/sell agreement**, an owner of an interest in a business obligates his or her estate to sell and another party has the option but not obligation to purchase that interest on the owner's death.

The business continuation arrangement of a professional partnership (e.g., for attorneys or physicians) usually differs from that discussed above. Provision usually is made for a continuation of income to the deceased partner's estate or heirs for a specified time period, with the income amount possibly based on a profit sharing agreement. A separate agreement might provide for the purchase and sale of the deceased partner's tangible business assets.

Use of Life Insurance   Life insurance commonly is used to fund such agreements. Under the entity approach, the partnership itself applies for, owns, and is beneficiary of a life insurance policy on each partner's life. The face amount of each policy usually equals the value of the insured partner's ownership interest. Under the cross purchase approach, each partner applies for, owns, and is beneficiary of a life insurance policy on each of the other partners' lives. The face amount of each policy usually equals the agreed upon value of the interest that the surviving partner/policyowner would purchase from the deceased partner's estate.

Agents and planners commonly recommend cash value life insurance for partnership buy/sell agreements because of the nature of the insurance need. Participating (par) WL, UL, and no lapse guarantee UL policies can each fit the need, depending on other circumstances. Joint life and multiple life policies are also sometimes suggested, each requiring careful consideration for necessary arrangements after the death of the first partner.

Figures 24-1 and 24-2, shown below in the discussion on corporate buy/sell arrangements, apply also to partnerships. As illustrated in the two figures, upon the first death among the partners, the operation of the plan is straightforward. The life insurance proceeds are used by the partnership or surviving partners, as the case may be, to purchase the interest of the deceased from his or her estate. The partnership is reorganized by the surviving partners and continues in operation, and the heirs of the deceased receive in cash the going concern value of the involved partnership interest. All parties benefit by the arrangement, and the problems of liquidation obviated. The surviving partners can enter into a new buy/sell agreement or amend the original agreement to account for changes in the value of their respective interests.

Use of Disability Income Insurance   The same principles discussed above apply to disability-based buyouts, although policy options are more limited. Such insurance is offered by a few insurers only. Such policies provide cash to a business or professional partnership or small corporation to purchase the business interests of a totally disabled partner or shareholder. Policies are arranged so that benefits are not payable until after 12, 24, or 36 months of disability. The duration is chosen to correspond to a **trigger point**, which is the date designated in the formal buy/sell agreement at which the healthy persons must buy out the totally disabled insured/owner's interest.

Insureds generally are considered totally disabled if, because of sickness or injury, they are unable to perform the major duties of their regular occupations and are not actively at work on behalf of the business or practice with which they are associated. Benefits may be paid as monthly indemnity to a trustee, who then releases the total payment at the trigger point. More commonly, benefits are paid as a lump sum or under a periodic settlement arrangement in reimbursement for the actual amount paid by the buyers to purchase the disabled insured's interest. The maximum benefits of buyout policies are established at the time of underwriting and are based on the value of the business entity as determined by one or more generally accepted accounting methods.

Taxation of Life and Disability Insurance in Partnership Buy/Sell Agreements The income tax treatment of life insurance and disability insurance purchased to fund a cross purchase agreement is the same as that for personal insurance. Premiums are not deductible whether paid by the partnership or a partner. Death proceeds and disability benefits normally would be received free of income tax. The cost basis of each surviving partner's interest is increased by the amount paid for the deceased partner's interest under a cross purchase plan. The tax treatment of life insurance purchased to fund an entity plan ordinarily will be the same as that for a cross purchase plan provided the EOLI exceptions and requirements are met.

Life insurance death proceeds are excluded from the gross estate of the insured unless the insured possessed any incidents of ownership or the proceeds are payable to or for the benefit of the insured's estate. Any death proceeds payable to the partnership normally would increase the value of the partnership for estate tax purposes.

CORPORATIONS Numerous complexities and uncertainties can accompany managing and/or selling the ownership interest in a closely held corporation after the death of an owner. These issues can be largely avoided by having made advance arrangement for the orderly continuation of the business via a buy/sell agreement. The agreement generally requires the estate of the deceased shareholder to sell and either the corporation or other shareholders to buy the decedent's interest in the business at an agreed upon price. Additionally, the plan can allow for continuity in business management, provide income for the deceased owner's family, and offer direction for future ownership of the business.

Establishing a fair value for the business is of enormous importance not only to the buyers and sellers but also for estate tax valuation purposes. Many advisors counsel their clients to engage a business valuation specialist to assist in establishing the value, ideally following methods acceptable to the IRS. Accountants often assist their clients in identifying such specialists. Also specialists can be found at the *National Association of Certified Valuation Analysts* (www.nacva.com) and *Institute of Business Appraisers* (www.go-iba.org).

Business continuation plans usually are structured in one of three ways: entity (more commonly called a stock redemption in a corporate context), cross purchase, or wait-and-see buy/sell. The essential difference among the three structures is in the process for determining who will purchase the shares. In a **stock redemption,** the business is obligated to purchase the shares and the decedent's estate is obligated to sell them. In a cross purchase, individuals, usually other shareholders, will purchase the shares. A **wait-and-see buy/sell agreement** allows the shareholders and the business to postpone the decision between a cross purchase and stock redemption agreement until the death of a stockholder. The corporation has the right of first refusal to purchase stock under the agreement, with individual stockholders obligated to purchase the stock if the corporation refuses.

In some instances a buy/sell arrangement is undesirable, perhaps because the principal shareholder wishes to pass his or her interest to family members or because no willing buyer can be located. A not mutually exclusive but alternative means of selling some of the stock and securing cash for the estate is a **Section 303 stock redemption** through which an income-tax-free redemption is permitted for qualifying estates in an amount to cover federal and state death taxes, funeral expenses, and estate administration expenses. To qualify, the value of the stock must represent more than 35 percent of the decedent's adjusted gross estate. The redemption must be made within four years of the filing of the estate tax return.

Use of Life Insurance   These buy/sell agreements are commonly funded by life insurance. Each shareholder is insured for the value of his or her stock interest owned, the insurance being owned by either the corporation or the other shareholders. Upon the first death among the shareholders, the life insurance death proceeds are used by the corporation or surviving shareholders, as the case may be, to purchase the stock of the deceased person from his or her estate. The ownership future of the survivors is assured, and the estate beneficiaries receive cash instead of what could prove to be a speculative interest.

Wait-and-see agreements funded by life insurance follow the cross purchase approach with each shareholder owning policies on the lives of the other shareholders. If the corporation elects to purchase the stock on an owner's death, surviving shareholders contribute the necessary cash to the corporation from the insurance proceeds, as either capital contributions or interest bearing loans.

Life insurance is also used to fund Section 303 redemptions. The corporation applies for, owns, and is the beneficiary of a policy whose face amount is sufficient to provide the corporate funds needed to effect the redemption.

Figure 24-1 illustrates the workings of an insurance-funded stock redemption plan and Figure 24-2 illustrates the operation of an insurance-funded cross purchase plan. The wait-and-see approach will function as one of these two plans.

As the purpose of the life insurance is to provide funding for the buyout of a deceased business owner's interest, irrespective of when death occurs, some form of cash value insurance is most commonly recommended by agents and planners, usually par WL or generic UL. If a succession plan involving a lifetime buyout is in place and is to take place within the next few years, term life insurance might be recommended.

Factors Influencing Type of Agreement   Many factors will influence the decision involving which of the three business continuation approaches seems most appropriate, some of which are discussed here.

Taxation. If the corporation is in a lower tax bracket than the shareholders, a redemption plan may be preferred and vice versa. This is because premium payments would take a smaller share of the corporation's after tax income than it would of the shareholders' after tax income and vice versa.

Ease of Administration. Administration of a cross-purchase plan becomes complex quickly as the number of involved shareholders increases. Under a stock

Figure 24-1   Entity Buy/Sell Agreement

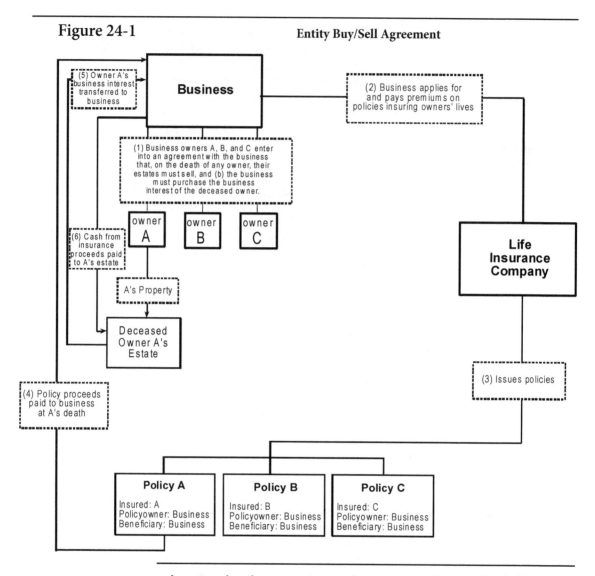

redemption plan, the corporation purchases but one policy per shareholder. Under a cross purchase plan, the total number of policies needed is n(n - 1), where n is the number of shareholders. Thus, with five shareholders, 20 policies would be needed. Trustee cross purchase agreements can mitigate this issue.

Effect on Cost Basis. With a stock redemption plan, the purchased stock becomes treasury stock. The other shareholders retain their original stock with no increase in cost basis. Upon subsequent sale, their taxable gain could be substantial. With a cross purchase plan, the purchased stock acquires a cost basis equal to the purchase price of the new shares. Upon subsequent sale, this higher basis reduces the amount of any realized taxable gain. (If shareholders are likely to retain their stock until death, the cost basis issue may be moot, as the stock will obtain a stepped up basis equal to its fair market value at time of death, *assuming future changes in the estate tax law follow the historical pattern.*)

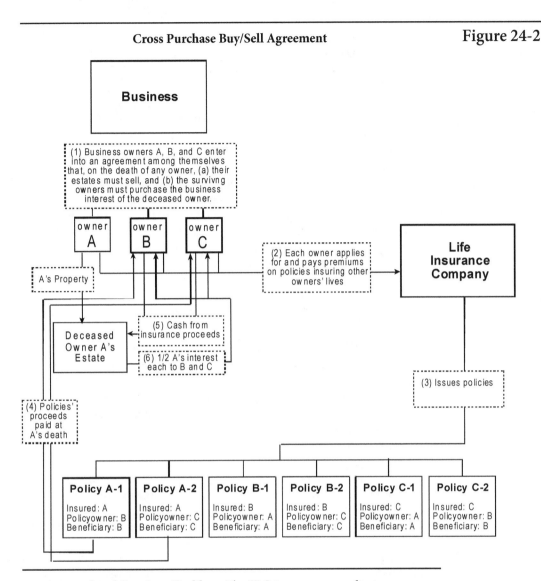

Cross Purchase Buy/Sell Agreement   Figure 24-2

Accumulated Earnings Problem. The IRC imposes a penalty tax on corporations that accumulate earnings beyond that needed for legitimate business purposes, to avoid the amounts being taxed to shareholders. Life insurance owned by a corporation to fund a stock redemption buy/sell agreement could attract such taxation. The tax is tied to the maximum tax rate applicable to dividends, currently 20 percent. The tax is in addition to the corporation's regular tax liability. A cross purchase plan avoids this concern altogether.

Corporate Creditors. Under a stock redemption plan, any policy cash values and death proceeds are subject to attachment by the creditors of the corporation, as the policy is a general corporate asset. This issue is not encountered under a cross purchase plan.

State Law Restrictions. The laws of most states provide that corporate redemptions can be made only from available corporate surplus; hence, insufficient surplus, no redemption. Insurance proceeds and contributions to capital can help alleviate this problem under a stock redemption plan. The problem does not occur under cross purchase buyouts.

Loan Limitations. Many closely held corporations operate on credit. The loan agreements used by most banks contain restrictions on the payment of dividends or redemption of stock without the bank's consent. A stock redemption agreement could fail unless fully funded and any indebtedness satisfied, so that creditors would not object to the redemption. This issue does not arise with a cross purchase agreement.

Attribution Rules. A complete redemption of a shareholder's stock by a corporation ordinarily results in capital gains treatment. Redemption of only a portion of a shareholder's stock generally invokes dividend treatment. For this reason, most stock redemption plans are complete redemptions. A problem can arise, however, in certain family-owned and other corporations because of the IRC's **attribution rules**, the effects of which are to attribute the stock owned by family members or estate beneficiaries to a decedent. Fortunately, the family attribution rules can be waived under certain circumstances.

Cash Flow. Shareholders often prefer a stock redemption approach because they prefer to spend the corporation's funds on life insurance premiums rather than their own, even if doing so might be inferior to using other approaches.

Taxation of Life Insurance in Corporate Business Continuation Agreements Premiums paid for life insurance to fund corporate buy/sell agreements and Section 303 redemptions are not tax deductible. Death proceeds in excess of the policy's income tax basis – ordinarily, premiums paid – will be subject to income taxation as EOLI unless the exemption and notice and consent requirements are met, as discussed earlier. Ordinarily, these conditions will have been met, and death proceeds will be received by the beneficiary free of income tax. Interest credited to policy cash values similarly will not usually generate taxable income.

Life insurance death proceeds paid under cross purchase arrangements will not ordinarily be included in a deceased shareholder's gross estate. Proceeds payable under stock redemption plans could cause the value of the business to increase, thus increasing the estate value of the deceased's stock.

Another consideration in using life insurance to fund general stock or Section 303 redemption agreements is whether cash value increases or policy death proceeds would invoke the alternative minimum tax (AMT) applicable to corporations. This tax may be imposed on tax preference items. The AMT could apply if (1) a policy's yearly cash value increase exceeds that year's premium or (2) death proceeds paid exceed the policy's cash value. Small corporations, generally those with gross receipts not in excess of $7.5 million, are exempt from the AMT.

If corporate ownership of a life insurance policy would trigger the AMT, consideration would be given to the cross purchase approach. The AMT could be triggered by key person life insurance as well as other instances involving corporate owned life insurance (see below). For the majority of corporations, however, cash value increases are unlikely to cause an AMT problem.

Nonqualified Executive Benefit Plans

Nonqualified executive benefit plans can be structured to provide a wide range of benefits and can provide them to whomever the business wishes. Indeed, the very purpose of nonqualified benefit plans is to favor select employees. These plans are "nonqualified" in the sense that they do not meet the requirements of the IRC and the *Employee Retirement Income Security Act* (ERISA) for qualified plans, as to nondiscrimination. We explore three types of nonqualified benefit plans:

- Executive bonus plans,
- Split dollar life insurance, and
- Nonqualified retirement plans.

Life insurance policies often are used to fund these plans. The insured employees typically are those whose skills, talents, and experience make them particularly valuable to the business.

EXECUTIVE BONUS PLANS An **executive bonus plan**, also called a **Section 162 plan**, is an arrangement under which the employer pays the premiums on life insurance policies for selected executives who own the policies. Par WL, generic UL, variable UL, and equity-indexed UL policies often are recommended plans. The employer is free to discriminate among employees benefitted by this plan. The premium payments by the business are compensation and, therefore, ordinarily tax deductible. To claim this deduction, the death proceeds cannot be payable to the business.

The executive must include the amount of the premium payment in his or her taxable income. Because the plan provides nonqualified life insurance, no portion of the premium paid by the employer may be excluded for the executive's taxable income. Some employers pay an additional bonus to cover this income tax obligation.

As the owner of the policy, the executive may name the beneficiary and exercise all other policy rights. Death proceeds will be included in the executive's gross estate if he or she retains any ownership interest or if proceeds are payable to or for the benefit of the estate, which typically is not the case.

SPLIT DOLLAR LIFE INSURANCE **Split dollar life insurance** is a funding arrangement under which one party, commonly an employer, pays portions of the premiums of a life insurance policy insuring another party, commonly an employee, with policy benefits shared between the two parties. In a business context, it is intended to help an employee obtain life insurance at a lower outlay than otherwise would be possible, by splitting premium payments and policy benefits between the two parties. It is a funding method, not a type of policy. The objective of split dollar plans is to join together the needs of one party with the premium paying ability of another. Specifically, the parties purchase an insurance policy on the life of the employee and agree in writing to split the premium payments as well as the policy's death proceeds and cash value. The concept works with any cash value policy, including WL, UL, equity-indexed UL, and second-to-die policies.

Choice of Split Dollar Plans Split dollar plans commonly take one of two forms: endorsement or collateral assignment. Under the **endorsement approach**, insurance on the employee's life is applied for and owned by the employer, which is primarily responsible for premium payments. The employer is beneficiary for that portion of the proceeds equal to its premium payments. The policy is endorsed to provide that the employee designates the beneficiary to receive the remainder of the death proceeds. The employer is considered by the IRS as providing a taxable *economic benefit* to the employee equal to the economic value of the death proceeds plus the cash value (if any) to which he or she has access that was not taken into income in prior years. Any portion of premiums paid by the employee is netted against these taxable amounts.

If the plan is terminated prior to the death of the insured employee, the employer recovers the equivalent of its premium outlay directly from the cash value that it controls as owner of the policy. This may be accomplished by surrendering the policy or giving the insured employee the option to purchase it for an amount equal to its cash surrender value.

Under the **collateral assignment approach**, the insured employee applies for the policy and is primarily responsible for premium payments. The employee designates his or her own personal beneficiary. In a separate agreement, the employer obligates itself to lend the employee the agreed upon amount of each premium. This loan may be interest free, but income taxes will be due on the loan interest foregone, based on the applicable federal interest rate. The employee is responsible for additional premiums, if any. The employee collaterally assigns the policy to the employer as security for the loan. At the insured employee's death, the employer recovers the amount of its loan from the death proceeds, not as a beneficiary of the policy, but as a collateral assignee.

The recommended approach will be influenced by several factors. A fundamental issue is whether the employer or employee controls the policy. If the employer wants the cash value available for use in its business, the endorsement approach is preferable. If the employee is not an officer or shareholder, the endorsement method may be preferable to the employer as a means of retaining key employees. Also, the endorsement approach is ordinarily recommended if the parties intend the policy to fund a nonqualified retirement arrangement (see below).

Tax Consequences of Split Dollar Plans   Split dollar life insurance plans are subject to complex tax rules, the totality of which is beyond the scope of this short overview. As noted above, the typical split dollar plan results in a taxable economic benefit to the employee. This benefit is determined by reference to a set of IRS-prescribed rates, called the *Table 2001 rates* or, if lower, the insurer's rates for term policies that it sells. Premiums paid by an employer on insurance covering the life of an employee and for which the employer is directly or indirectly a beneficiary under the policy are not tax deductible. Death proceeds ordinarily are received income tax free provided EOLI exceptions and requirements are met with respect to endorsement split dollar.

Insurance death proceeds are included in the gross estate of a decedent/insured if he or she possessed any incidents of policy ownership or if proceeds are payable to or for the benefit of the insured's estate. Under the usual endorsement system, the employer is the sole owner of the life insurance policy. To protect the insured employee's rights under the agreement, the ownership rights of the employer are modified by an endorsement that provides that the insured employee's personal beneficiary cannot be changed without the insured employee's consent. This is an incident of ownership. This ownership right might be avoided if the agreement provides that the beneficiary cannot be changed without the consent of the beneficiary, rather than of the insured. Even if the death proceeds are included in the insured's gross estate, they should qualify for the unlimited marital deduction if they are paid to the surviving spouse.

Under the collateral assignment system, the insured employee often is the policyowner, so full policy death proceeds less amounts owed to the employer via the collateral assignment would be included in his or her gross estate. If the employee wishes to avoid inclusion of the proceeds in his or her gross estate, the beneficiary for the insured/employee's share of the proceeds commonly applies for and owns the life insurance policy. The owner/beneficiary may be a trust, the insured's spouse, or any other third party.

Any split dollar plan between a corporation and a majority shareholder/ employee/insured can be expected to result in death proceeds payable to a beneficiary other than the corporation being included in the gross estate of the insured. This result is based on an estate tax regulation that imputes the incidents of ownership possessed by a corporation in an insurance policy on the life of a majority shareholder to that shareholder to the extent that the proceeds are not payable to or for the benefit of the corporation. There are ways to avoid this result, but their examination is beyond the scope of this short discussion. Proceeds payable to the corporation are not included in the shareholder's estate but are considered in establishing the value of the decedent's stock.

Split Dollar Plan Variations   Several split dollar arrangements are found, with varying premium splits. Additionally, split dollar plans are commonly recommended in situations other than as a nonqualified benefit for important employees. Other split dollar uses are shown in Box 24-3.

Box 24-3
Split Dollar Life Insurance Variations

In addition to the traditional use of split dollar life insurance as a nonqualified executive benefit, it also has been found effective in the following situations:

- *Sole Proprietor Buyout.* A sole proprietor may not have any family members to whom he or she wants to leave the business at death and no outsider is interested in purchasing it. In such a situation, the business owner may offer to sell the business to an interested employee at the business owner's death. To solve the problem of the employee having insufficient funds, the employer may enter into a split dollar plan with the employee, with insurance on the life of the employer and the employer paying the premium.

- *Split Dollar in a Cross Purchase Buy/Sell Agreement.* One drawback to the use of a cross purchase buy/sell agreement is that the shareholders are personally responsible for the payment of premiums on insurance used to fund the plan. An alternative is to have the corporation help finance the purchase of needed insurance through a split dollar plan. The arrangement proceeds as usual with the exception that each shareholder collaterally assigns the policies that he or she owns on other shareholder's lives to the corporation as security for the corporation's loans.

- *Split Dollar in a Nonqualified Retirement Plan.* A split dollar arrangement can provide the mechanism for informally funding a nonqualified retirement plan (see below). Policy values provide the means from which payments ultimately are made or the employer reimbursed.

- *Family Split Dollar.* Parents or grandparents wishing to assist a family member in the purchase of life insurance and not wishing to reduce the share of their estates to be passed on to others may find a split dollar approach appealing. As this is not an employer/employee arrangement, there should be no taxable income.

Nonqualified Retirement Plans   Life insurance is often recommended as a form of informal funding for nonqualified retirement plans. These plans offer employers advantages and disadvantages relative to qualified plans. Advantages include being able to select the key employees who will participate in the plans without fear of running afoul of ERISA nondiscrimination requirements. Additionally, administrative expenses of nonqualified plans should be less than those of qualified plans. The main disadvantage from the employer's perspective is the inability to take immediate tax deductions for plan funding. Two common such plans are:

- Nonqualified deferred compensation plans, and
- Supplemental executive retirement plans.

Nonqualified Deferred Compensation Plans   A **nonqualified deferred compensation plan** is a contractual arrangement under which compensation for services rendered is postponed, usually until retirement. The employee ordinarily will not be taxed on these deferred amounts until they are received (e.g., at retirement), when the individual may be in a lower marginal income tax bracket. The employer does not obtain an income tax deduction for these payments until such time as payments actually are made.

The plan may be either employer- or employee-initiated. In both instances, the idea is to postpone some portion of present compensation, raises, or bonuses, in return for which the employer agrees to pay an income in the future, often at a rate augmented by interest. If the plan is employee-initiated, the employer and employee agree to postpone compensation to which the employee otherwise is entitled to avoid present income taxation to the employee and to save for retirement. (Deferring income is consistent with the life cycle hypothesis discussed in Chapter 1.) Employer-initiated plans often are intended as a supplemental benefit to encourage retention of highly valued employees. They function in the same way as employee-initiated plans.

Life insurance is often recommended as the informal funding device. The employer applies for, owns, and is beneficiary of the policy. The employee or employer will have selected a specific amount or percentage of the executive's compensation to be deferred. The employer may view premiums paid for the policy as flowing from these deferred sums. Policy cash values accumulate on a tax deferred basis.

At retirement, the employer makes withdrawals, initiates policy loans, and/or surrenders portions or the entirety of the policy to fund its retirement income obligation to the employee. If the employee dies while employed, life insurance death proceeds would be received by the employer income tax free, provided EOLI exceptions and requirements were met, and could be used to fund any death-related obligations under the plan, to reimburse the employer for premiums paid, or to fund retirement benefits for other executives.

A deferred compensation plan variation – a **death benefit only** (DBO) **plan** – promises to pay an income benefit to the employee's survivor on the employee's death. No retirement benefit is promised, often because the employee will have an adequate retirement income from a qualified plan. DBO plans are less costly than other forms of deferred compensation plans and usually are intended to help retain employees. Life insurance is a natural funding medium.

Supplemental Executive Retirement Plans   A **supplemental executive retirement plan** (SERP) is a nonqualified retirement plan that provides retirement benefits to selected employees only. Some SERPs provide a flat amount per year to participating employees. Other SERPs – called **excess SERPs** – provide a benefit amount equal to the difference between (1) the full amount under the employer's qualified retirement benefit formula that would be paid to the executive but ignoring any ERISA-imposed limits and (2) the actual retirement benefits payable to the executive under the qualified retirement plan *and* Social Security. Another popular SERP – called a **target SERP** – is intended to replace retirement benefits lost by ERISA-imposed limits *and* counteract the bias in Social Security retirement benefits that favors low income workers.

Life insurance is often the recommended informal SERP funding device. As with nonqualified deferred compensation plans, the employer applies for, owns, and is beneficiary under the policy. The policy death benefit and premiums are determined by the retirement benefit promised to the executive. Otherwise, the policy payout options on death and in life are the same as with deferred comp plans, with taxation also being the same.

Funding Nonqualified Retirement Plans   Nonqualified retirement plans may be funded or unfunded. A **funded nonqualified retirement plan** is an arrangement under which the employer establishes and maintains assets in an escrow account or trust fund as security for its promise to make future payments. The employee is said to have a beneficial interest in such plan assets. These plans are uncommon as the employee is taxed currently on the funded value of a non-qualified plan.

An **unfunded nonqualified retirement plan** exists when the employer has not formally earmarked assets to fund the plan, or, stated differently, when the employee must rely exclusively on the employer's unsecured promise to make payments. A plan is not considered funded merely because an employer establishes **informal funding** via a reserve fund to meet future obligations under the plan, provided the fund is not formally linked to the obligation and remains a general asset of the business subject to attachment by its general creditors.

Tax Treatment of Nonqualified Retirement Plans   Prior to 2005, nonqualified deferred compensation plans simply relied on the constructive receipt doctrine – see below – to avoid current taxation to the employee. In 2005, IRC Section 409A "Inclusion in gross income of deferred compensation under nonqualified deferred compensation plans" became effective, and since then nonqualified plans must qualify under 409A. This section applies to a very broad array of plans, including those discussed in the preceding paragraphs with elective deferrals and supplemental plans under which the employee has no option to receive current cash. (Some split dollar plans are also covered.)

The consequences of a 409A violation are draconian and fall directly on the employee rather than the employer: the employee is taxed immediately on the amount of income that has vested; the employee is subject to an immediate 20 percent penalty tax; and the employee is liable for interest from the time of the violation until the payment of taxes, which could be years in the case of an undiscovered violation.

To avoid taxation of deferred amounts under 409A both the documents creating the plan and the operation of the plan must be consistent with the statute. There are four classes of expressly prohibited provisions.

1. Payments can only be made on the employee's separation from service, disability, death, a fixed payment date or schedule, a change in control of the business or the occurrence of an unforeseeable emergency.
2. Deferred compensation payments may not be accelerated.
3. Elections to defer compensation must be made irrevocably in the year before the services are performed to which the compensation relates.
4. Methods to secure the payment of nonqualified deferred compensation are not permitted and there must be a "substantial risk of forfeiture."

Payments will be treated as ordinary income to the employee when they are actually or constructively received. There is **constructive receipt** of income if it is made available to the employee or if he or she could have taken it but chose not to. Income is not constructively received if it is subject to a **substantial risk of forfeiture**, that is if (1) employees' rights are subject to the claims of employer's creditors or (2), even if the employee's rights are nonforfeitable, the agreement was entered into before the compensation was earned and the employer's promise to pay is unsecured.

If the promise to pay is secured in any way, such as the employee being given an interest in assets or other financial instruments (e.g., life insurance) used to fund the agreement, the employee will be taxed on the economic benefit of the security interest. To minimize the chance of taxation under the economic benefits doctrine, these agreements provide that rights to payments may not be assigned or transferred.

Contributions by an employer to an appropriately established irrevocable trust from which deferred compensation payments will be made are not taxable to the employees at the time the contributions are made. Generally, the employer is not entitled to an income tax deduction until such time as amounts are received by the employee. Under these so-called **rabbi trusts**, trust assets remain subject to the claims of the employer's general creditors if the employer becomes insolvent, but, in the absence of such claims, trust assets must be used solely to provide deferred compensation benefits. Named after the first such arrangement established for a rabbi, these trusts are intended to provide assurance to participating employees that they will receive benefits even when there has been a management change or a hostile takeover. The employer remains obligated under all but the most distressed circumstances.

Under a **secular trust**, trust assets are not subject to the claims of the employer's general creditors. Thus, employees enjoy an even greater degree of security, but trust contributions are taxable to employees as a substantial forfeiture risk does not exist. These trusts are typically used when the employee is in a lower tax bracket or otherwise wants to recognize income currently.

The present value of remaining payments under a nonqualified retirement plan is included in the deceased employee's taxable estate if the employee was receiving or was entitled to receive payments at his or her death and if the agreement provided that payments were to continue after death. If payments are continued to the employee's spouse, they usually qualify for the marital deduction. If payments ceased on death, there clearly would be nothing to include in the gross estate.

Example Table 24-1 offers an example of how life insurance can be used to fund nonqualified retirement compensation, whether in the form of nonqualified deferred compensation or a SERP. In this example, a variable universal life policy is purchased on the life of Lorilee Strother, a brilliant 45-year-old architect with Pitts Innovative Group. PIG applies for and is owner and beneficiary of the policy. The death benefit could serve both as key employee insurance and/or to fund a promised death benefit for Lorilee's family. The policy is also intended as the vehicle for informally funding a promised $100,000 per year retirement benefit to Lorilee for 20 years, beginning at policy year 22.

Example of Life Insurance to Provide both Death and Retirement Benefits **Table 24-1**

(Variable Universal Life at 6.0 percent Net Return, 45-F, Nonsmoker, Non-guaranteed Values and Charges)

Policy Year	Age	Premium Outlay	With-drawal	Policy Loan	Net Account Value	Net Cash Surrender Value	Death Benefit
1	45	$33,675	0	0	$30,152	$28,083	$2,280,029
5	49	33,675	0	0	168,758	167,609	2,280,029
10	54	33,675	0	0	394,580	394,580	2,280,029
15	59	33,675	0	0	702,636	702,636	2,280,029
20	64	33,675	0	0	1,124,282	1,124,282	2,280,029
21	65	33,675	0	0	1,227,138	1,227,138	2,280,029
22	66	0	$100,000	0	1,196,749	1,196,749	2,180,029
23	67	0	100,000	0	1,164,325	1,164,325	2,080,029
24	68	0	100,000	0	1,129,738	1,129,738	1,980,029
25	69	0	100,000	0	1,092,854	1,092,854	1,880,029
26	70	0	100,000	0	1,053,521	1,053,521	1,780,029
27	71	0	100,000	0	1,011,467	1,011,467	1,680,029
28	72	0	100,000	0	966,502	966,502	1,580,029
29	73	0	7,175	$92,825	918,426	918,426	1,477,476
30	74	0	0	100,000	867,042	867,042	1,372,103
31	75	0	0	100,000	812,158	812,158	1,263,833
32	76	0	0	100,000	753,568	753,568	1,152,585
33	77	0	0	100,000	691,087	691,087	1,038,277
34	78	0	0	100,000	624,531	624,531	920,826
35	79	0	0	100,000	553,748	553,748	800,146
36	80	0	0	100,000	478,608	478,608	676,146
37	81	0	0	100,000	399,097	399,097	548,737
38	82	0	0	100,000	315,213	315,213	417,824

Policy Year	Age	Premium Outlay	With-drawal	Policy Loan	Net Account Value	Net Cash Surrender Value	Death Benefit
39	83	0	0	100,000	226,724	226,724	302,538
40	84	0	0	100,000	132,455	132,455	210,465
41	85	0	0	100,000	31,694	31,694	111,767
42	86	0	0	0	30,495	30,495	112,667
60	104	0	0	0	14,988	14,988	41,421
76	120	0	0	0	1,158	1,158	41,739

Policy illustrations are prepared at several interest rates and scenarios, in accordance with common practice and legal requirements. See Chapter 4. The PIG CFO believes that a net return of 6.0 percent (gross return of 6.75 percent) represents a reasonable long term return on the separate account, so our abbreviated table shows only that return for selected years. An annual premium of $33,675 is illustrated as being paid for 21 years, with none payable thereafter for a total of $707,175. Tax free withdrawals of $100,000 begin at policy year 22 and continue until withdrawals equal the policy's income tax basis of $707,175, at Lorilee's age 73. (Withdrawals thereafter would be taxable income to PIG.)

Income-tax free policy loans of $100,000 per year are executed thereafter to fund benefit payments. At the 6.0 percent assumed net return, the policy could sustain these loans and the interest thereon until Lorilee's age 85, *and* then the policy would remain in force for the balance of her life; i.e., through age 120. Were the policy to be terminated for reasons other than death after policy loans were taken, the sum of the loans would be taxable to PIG, as the policy's tax basis would be zero. See Chapter 21.

GROUP TERM CARVE OUTS

Group term life insurance is a popular if largely ignored tax qualified employee benefit. Premiums are deductible to the employer, and the employee is not taxed on the first $50,000 of employer-funded coverage. The value of employer-funded amounts in excess of $50,000 is taxable income to employees. The value is determined by applying the IRS's *Premium Table* rates to these excess amounts.

Premium Table rates increase with increasing age, which means that older employees face ever increasing taxable income from their employer-provided group term life insurance in excess of $50,000. The amount of group insurance for which an employee is eligible often is some multiple of his or her salary, such as three times. Executives, who tend to be both older and more highly compensated than other employees, may be required to take substantial amounts into their taxable income from this employee benefit. Further, as rates are pooled for group life insurance, the cost to the employer of including even a small number of older, highly paid employees can have a significant effect on overall plan costs.

These factors led to the development of the **group term carve out** (GTCO) concept. The process is simple. The amount of group term coverage on highly paid executives is reduced to $50,000. At a minimum, what the employer would have paid for the group term coverage in excess of $50,000 is applied toward the premiums for a permanent policy owned by the employee, not the employer. The payment is still deductible to the business and now taxable to the employee as direct compensation, instead of *Premium Table* compensation.

Advantages of this approach include the fact that the increasing amounts that executives must take into taxable income now go toward premiums to purchase insurance that builds cash values. Alternatively, the employer can set a level premium payment, thus insulating the group term program from the high cost of providing large amounts of life insurance on highly paid employees. For owner/employees, the insurance becomes a source of both death protection and cash value buildup that can be important for retirement and other living purposes.

Individually issued life insurance policies have been used creatively and effectively in businesses for decades. They are used to hedge the business against financial loss occasioned by the death of individuals whose services are essential to its success. Life insurance is routinely used also to facilitate the smooth transition of closely held business ownership interests through buy/sell agreements while (1) sparing heirs the angst of deciding how to deal with that interest and (2) providing certainty to surviving owners. Life insurance also is often recommended to informally fund various nonqualified executive benefit programs, allowing the business to provide executives with tangible proof of their perceived worth to the business. These and other business applications of life insurance seem likely to continue and perhaps to gain even more prominence as both regulation and tax rates grow.

CONCLUSIONS

ENDNOTES

1   This chapter draws from Harold D. Skipper and Wayne Tonning, *The Advisor's Guide to Life Insurance* (Chicago; American Bar Association, 2011), Chapter 12.

2   *The Emeloid Co. v. Comm.*, 189 F. 2d 230 (3rd Cir. 1951).

3   http://www.massmutual.com/mmfg/pdf/MM_Success_Plan.pdf

GLOSSARY

1035 exchange See **section 1035 exchange**.

401(k) plan Qualified defined contribution retirement plan permitting employees to defer some of their compensation on a pretax basis; plans may also allow employers to make qualified matching contributions.

Absolute assignment Complete transfer by a policyowner of all rights in a policy to another person or entity.

Accelerated benefit rider See **living benefit rider**.

Accelerated death benefit See **terminal illness coverage**.

Accidental death benefit Rider to or a provision of a life insurance policy and sometimes other policies that promises to pay a specified additional death benefit if the insured dies as a result of an accident. Often called **double indemnity** when the additional benefit is twice the face amount of the base policy.

Accidental means Definition of accidental death that requires both the cause and result of the death being accidental.

Account value See **cash value**.

Account value provision See **policy value provision**.

Accredited investor Wealthy investor who meets requirements of the *Securities and Exchange Commission* as to minimum net worth (in excess of $1.0 million) or annual income (in excess of $200,000).

Accumulated book profits model Simulation of anticipated operating experience for a block of policies using the best estimates of what the individual factors will be for each future policy year with profits and losses carried forward at a selected hurdle rate and maintained separately in a profit account.

Accumulated value (1) Future value of a principal amount or amounts accumulated at interest. (2) See **cash value**.

Accumulation period Time before annuity benefits commence and during which cash values accumulate and one or more premiums are paid.

Accumulation period provision Under medical expense benefits, specified period of time during which multiple claims may be accumulated to satisfy the deductible and coinsurance provisions.

Accumulation universal life Universal life policy that emphasizes cash value accumulation but requires higher premiums per $1,000 of face amount.

Actual authority That authority granted to an agent by a principal in specific language or terms. Also called **express authority**.

Actuarial equity State achieved when each participant in an insurance pool pays an actuarially fair price.

Actuarial opinion Annual certification required of an insurer's appointed actuary by state insurance laws as to whether reserves and related actuarial items are computed appropriately, are based on assumptions that satisfy contractual provisions, are consistent with prior reported amounts, and comply with applicable state laws.

Actuarially fair price Value of the *ex ante* expected loss of each participant in an insurance pool that is paid to the pool.

Additional purchase option See **guaranteed insurability option**.

Adhesion Characteristic of personal insurance contracts providing that their terms and provisions are fixed by one party (the insurer) and, with minor exceptions, must be accepted or rejected word for word by the other party (the prospective policyowner).

Adjusted gross estate Under federal tax law, gross estate less allowable deductions except bequests to the surviving spouse and to charities.

Adjusted premium Under the *Standard Nonforfeiture Law*, the level premium necessary to pay guaranteed policy benefits (the net level premium) plus the level equivalent of a defined special first year expense allowance.

Adjusted premium method Descriptor indicating derivation of minimum nonforfeiture values.

Adjusted taxable gifts Under federal tax law, those made after 1976, net of annual exclusions taken, for which a gift tax return was filed and which are not otherwise included in the decedent's gross estate.

Administrative fee Expense charge assessed periodically against an unbundled policy's account value, stated as a flat dollar amount such as $10, a charge per $1,000 of death benefit such as $0.10, and/or sometimes as a percentage of the account value.

Administrative services only Contractual arrangement under which an employer-sponsor of a self-funded benefit plan purchases specific administrative services from an insurer or other entity.

Administrator Individual or institution responsible for the administration of an estate of a person who dies without a valid will.

Admitted asset Asset recognized and accepted on the annual statement of an insurer for the purpose of satisfying an insurer's statutory solvency requirements.

Admitted value Value recorded on an insurer's balance sheet for its admitted assets.

Adult day care Provides assistance with the activities of daily living and allows socialization in a long term care facility or community program facility. Commonly covered by long term care insurance policies up to a percentage (e.g., 50 percent) of the full nursing home benefit.

Advance directive Legal document that provides one's family and physicians with written instructions regarding one's preferences regarding medical treatment in the face of serious medical conditions.

Adverse selection Tendency of self selected insurance applicants to exhibit average claim experience greater than that of an otherwise identical randomly selected group of exposure units, representing an asymmetric information problem resulting from the fact that the customer knows more than the seller about the customer's situation and can use that fact to the seller's detriment. Also called **antiselection**.

Adverse selection spiral Tendency of insureds who are charged premiums sufficiently greater than the actuarially fair price to withdraw from the insurance pool thereby precipitating premium increases for the remaining insureds, from among whom still more withdrawals occur, etc., leading to a continuing spiral of withdrawals and premium increases that can result in the pool collapsing.

Affiliated distribution channel Insurer-owned or directed system composed of individual intermediaries, called variously **captive agents, career agents, exclusive agents**, and **tied agents**, who are engaged full time in the sale of insurance exclusively or primarily for a single insurer or affiliated group of insurers. Also called **agency-building system**.

Age of majority Minimum age at which a person can enter into contract, typically 18 in the U.S.

Agency problem Asymmetric information problem in which the incentives and interests of one party (the agent) differ from those of the party that it represents (the principal).

Agency-building system See **affiliated distribution channel**.

Agent Person who acts for another. See also **insurance agent.**

Agent's report Report providing supplementary information about a proposed insured and/or applicant and his or her relationship to the agent, which is prepared by the agent and submitted to the underwriter in connection with a life or health insurance application.

Aggregate mortality table Mortality table showing probabilities of death by age and other possible criteria such as sex of insureds within both the select and ultimate mortality groups.

Aleatory Characteristic of insurance contracts providing that outcomes are governed by chance and that one party may realize more than the other.

Alien insurer In U.S. terminology, an insurance company organized in another country.

Allowable deductions Under federal estate tax law, items that qualify for deductibility from the gross estate to derive the taxable estate, which include funeral and administration expenses, debts of the decedent, as well as bequests to charities and the surviving spouse.

Alternative minimum taxable income Alternative calculation of taxable income determined by adding tax preference items to regular taxable income.

Alternative valuation date Under federal tax law, option to use the fair market value of the estate property at a date six months after death.

Ambulatory instrument One taking effect only at death.

Amortized value Difference between a bond's acquisition cost and par value, increased or decreased in successive stages over time until that value equals the bond's par value at maturity.

Annual exclusion Value of yearly gifting exempt from gift taxation and from filing a federal gift tax return.

Annual renewable term See **yearly renewable term**.

Annual report Required by the NAIC *Life Insurance Policy Illustration Model Regulation* to be provided annually on policies designated by the insurer as ones for which illustrations are used, shows the financial status and relevant transactions that took place under the policy during the preceding policy year. Also called **annual statement**.

Annual reset method Equity index annuity indexing method that determines index-linked interest annually by comparing the index value at the end of the contract year with the value at the beginning of the contract year.

Annual statement See **annual report**.

Annuitant Person whose lifetime is used to measure the length of time that benefits are payable under a life annuity. Sometimes used also to mean the recipient of annuity payments.

Annuitization Election to liquidate as an annuity accumulated savings from a fixed or variable annuity or other savings media.

Annuity Series of periodic payments or receipts.

Annuity certain Annuity payable over a set period without reference to whether the annuitant is alive.

Annuity contract Insurance policy that promises to make a series of payments through systematic liquidation of principal and interest and possibly benefit of survivorship for a fixed period or over an annuitant's lifetime.

Annuity due Annuity whose payments are made at the beginning of each period.

Antiselection See **adverse selection**.

Any gainful occupation With disability income insurance, clause that deems an insured to be totally disabled if he or she cannot perform the major duties of any gainful occupation for which he or she is reasonably suited because of education, training, or experience.

Apparent authority That authority which a third person believes an agent to possess by virtue of circumstances made possible by the principal and upon which the third party is justified in relying.

Applicant Person or entity applying for a life or health insurance policy.

Application Instrument by which an applicant provides answers to insurer's questions used to determine proposed insured's insurability. Applicant's offer to an insurer for insurance.

Appointed actuary Person designated by an insurer's board of directors to render the actuarial opinion required by state insurance law.

Approval conditional premium receipt Formal acknowledgement that the applicant has tendered the first policy premium and which provides insurance coverage only after the application has been approved by the insurer.

Assessment basis Insurance contracts that permit insureds (members) to be assessed retrospectively as claims occur to provide promised benefit payments. In the past, used by fraternal organizations whose contributions were not scaled according to the age or insurability of members thus resulting in adverse selection.

Asset accumulation phase Preretirement economically productive years of life when both financial and real assets are acquired.

Asset liquidation phase Economically nonproductive postretirement years of life during which assets are liquidated.

Asset share The conceptual segmentation to individual policies of an insurer's general account investments accumulated on behalf of a group of policies.

Asset share model Simulation of anticipated operating experience for a block of policies, using the best estimates of what the individual factors will be for each future policy year.

Asset Valuation Reserve Accounting mechanism required by regulators designed to minimize volatility in an insurer's statutory surplus by earmarking portions of it to absorb realized and unrealized capital gains and losses not attributable to interest rates.

Asset-liability management Practice of matching the sensitivity of the net of asset and liability values to interest rate changes.

Asset-liability matching Asset-liability risk management practice of designing insurance policies and managing liability-matched asset portfolios to interact in a way that protects an insurer's surplus capital position under changing economic conditions and customer behavior.

Asset-liability risk Possibility that the same external factors can affect the value of assets and liabilities simultaneously and disproportionately, the most important of which is a change in market interest rates.

Asset-liability risk management Process of preserving or enhancing a life insurer's surplus capital position as asset and liability values change in response to changing economic conditions and customer behavior.

Assignment provision Policy provision stating that the policyowner has the right to transfer ownership of the policy and advising that the insurer need not recognize a transfer unless the insurer is notified of it.

Assisted living facility Provides supervision, assistance, and limited health services to relatively healthy senior citizens as an alternative to nursing home care. Commonly covered by long term care insurance policies up to a percentage (e.g., 50 percent) of the full nursing home benefit.

Assumed interest rate Under a variable annuity during annuitization, the interest rate that, if earned uniformly throughout the liquidation period, would produce level annuity benefit payments. Also called the **benchmark rate** or **target return**.

Assuming company Reinsurer or direct writing insurer that sells reinsurance.

Assumption reinsurance Total transfer of assets, liabilities, and risk from one insurer to another under which the assuming company legally replaces the ceding company in transactions on sections or books of business, and issues assuming certificates to affected policyholders.

Asymmetric information problem Situation in which one party to a transaction has relevant information that the other does not have and can take advantage of that fact to the first party's benefit and the other party's detriment.

Attained-age conversion Exercise of a conversion feature with the premium cost of insurance for the new policy based on the insured's attained age as of the date of conversion, being the same as that which the company offers to new insureds who qualify as standard.

Attribution rules *Internal Revenue Code* provision that attributes the stock owned by family members or estate beneficiaries to a decedent for estate taxation purposes.

Audit and control procedures Protocols designed to limit the risk associated with mistakes, fraud, and other irregularities in the process of reporting and managing assets and liabilities.

Authorized control level Under the state-mandated risk-based capital system, the minimum amount of total adjusted capital that must be held to avoid possible regulatory intervention, its value derived by a formula intended to reflect the insurer's particular contingency risks.

Automatic increase benefit Feature of some disability income policies and riders providing for scheduled increases in the monthly benefit amount, typically in each of five consecutive years at a fixed rate (e.g., 5 percent or so), with annual premium increases at attained age rates for the portion of increased benefit.

Automatic premium loan provision Cash value life insurance policy provision, usually at the policyowner's option, stating that the amount of a premium due and unpaid will be advanced automatically as a loan against the policy at the end of the grace period if the policy has sufficient net cash surrender value.

Automatic reinsurance Reinsurance under which the direct writing company must transfer an amount in excess of its retention of each applicable insurance policy to the assuming company immediately upon payment of a direct premium and the issuance of the policy, and the reinsurer must accept transfers that fall within the scope of the agreement. Also called **treaty reinsurance**.

Aviation exclusion Policy provision occasionally included in life insurance policies insuring pilots that excludes coverage if the insured dies in an aviation accident.

Aviation questionnaire Supplement to a life or health insurance application that elicits additional aviation information from a proposed insured who engages in commercial, private, or military aviation activities.

Backdating Practice of establishing a policy date before the application date to enable premiums or COI charges to be based on an earlier age of the proposed insured.

Back-end load See **surrender charge**.

Balance sheet Financial statement showing assets, liabilities, and owners' equity or surplus.

Bankruptcy Application of bankruptcy laws to a debtor who may or may not be insolvent.

Basic illustration Required in a specified format by the NAIC *Life Insurance Policy Illustration Model Regulation* to be provided to applicants on policies designated by the insurer as those for which illustrations are used, includes a narrative summary, a numeric summary, and tabular detail.

Basic mortality table Tabulation that displays yearly probabilities of death drawn from records of the actual experience of the population from which the data were drawn.

Basis With regard to life insurance and annuities income taxation, the sum of premiums and other contributions paid into a contract, reduced by the amount of refunds, dividends, cash surrenders, and other withdrawals that were not included in taxable income. In the case of an annuity, may be further reduced by a prescribed proportion if the payout includes a refund feature. Also called cost basis, investment in the contract, and tax basis.

Basis risk Possibility that offsetting investments in a hedging strategy will not experience precisely identical inverse price changes because the notional amount or timing of cash flows of risk management assets are not precisely matched to the assets or liabilities hedged.

Basket clause Provision in state insurance law that permits insurers to invest a limited percentage (e.g., 10 percent) of its assets in any lawful investment. Also called **leeway clause**.

Behavioral economics Positive or descriptive discipline that seeks to predict how investors and savers actually behave.

Benchmark rate See **assumed interest rate**.

Beneficiary In an insurance context, person or entity entitled to insurance death or health benefits in the event of a policy claim.

Beneficiary clause Life insurance policy provision stating that the policyowner may have policy death proceeds paid to whomever and in whatever form desired, subject to contract terms and naming or referring to the designated person or entity entitled to receive death benefits.

Benefit base balance Under a guaranteed lifetime withdrawal benefit, the benefit base after reduction due to withdrawals.

Benefit of survivorship. (1) Survivors' share of the unliquidated funds of those annuitants or insureds who die before their expected age of survival or before their policies endow. (2) Contributions remaining in the insurance pool of those who had no claims or whose claims were less than their contributions to the pool, thus providing funds to other claimants.

Benefit period With disability income insurance, the longest period of time for which benefits will be paid, usually the same for sickness and injury and generally available for durations of two or five years or to age 65.

Beta Measure of the volatility or variance of a stock's performance relative to the performance of the stock market as a whole.

Binding premium receipt Formal acknowledgement that the applicant has tendered the first policy premium and which provides insurance coverage from the application date.

Blending See **term blending**.

Block of policies Set of all policies issued by an insurer under the same schedules of policy elements and on the same policy form.

Bond dedication Informal allocation of the cash flows from a portfolio of bonds to the cash flows of a prescribed set of liabilities.

Bonus (1) Extra interest (e.g., 1.0 percent) credited to annuity cash values or deposits, paid over the standard crediting rate for a limited initial period. (2) In U.K. and Commonwealth terminology, policy dividend.

Book value Acquisition cost of an asset less accumulated depreciation.

Branch office Office owned and operated by an insurer and its general manager that recruits, trains, houses, and supervises individual producers.

Break even Measure of profitability calculated as the number of years until earnings equal disbursements.

Broker Independent salesperson who does not sell exclusively or primarily for a single insurer or group of insurers. Also called a **producer**.

Brokerage general agent See **brokerage representative**.

Brokerage representative Insurer's salesperson who appoints brokers and promotes their efforts to sell the insurer's products. Also known as a **brokerage supervisor** or **brokerage general agent**.

Brokerage supervisor See **brokerage representative**.

Budget accounting Employed by management for future expense planning purposes in both an operational or short-term context and a strategic context lasting five years or more.

Bundled policy Life insurance policy that does not disclose to the policyowner the portions of his or her premium that are allocated to specific policy elements: the costs of the internal insurance charges, interest crediting rates, and loadings for expenses, taxes, profits, and contingencies.

Business continuation agreement. See **buy/sell agreement**.

Business overhead expense insurance Type of disability income insurance that covers the monthly expenses of a business owner or professional in private practice if he or she is disabled. Also called **overhead expense insurance**.

Buy/sell agreement Pre-death arrangement for the disposition of a business ownership interest on the death of its owner. Also called **business continuation agreement**.

Buyer ignorance An asymmetric information problem in which the seller knows more than the buyer about the seller's situation and can use that fact to the buyer's detriment. Also called **lemons problem**.

Buyer's Guide Document required to be provided to prospective life insurance buyers by the NAIC *Life Insurance Disclosure Model Regulation*, intended to assist prospective purchasers in deciding how much and what type of life insurance to buy and comparing the costs of similar policies.

Buy-term-and-invest-the-difference Strategy under which an individual who has sufficient funds to purchase cash value life insurance instead purchases a lower-premium term policy and separately invests the difference between the two policies' premiums.

Cafeteria plans Employer-sponsored benefits plans under which participants may select from a variety of benefits based on an employer-provided budget.

Call Option to buy.

Capital In general finance, financial wealth used to start and/or maintain a business.

Capital allocation Asset-liability risk management practice of attributing operational and risk capital to specified projects for risk management and performance measurement purposes.

Capital bonus See **terminal bonus**.

Capital cost Return required by those who provide financial capital plus the cost of hedging.

Capital liquidation approach Method of life insurance need determination that derives a life insurance amount by assuming that both the life insurance death benefit (capital) and interest earned thereon are liquidated to meet an income objective.

Capital retention approach Method of life insurance need determination that derives a life insurance amount by assuming that interest earned on the life insurance death benefit (capital) alone will be used to meet an income objective, with the insurance death benefit retained and ultimately transferred to heirs when its income-producing role has been fulfilled.

Capital stock and surplus Excess of assets over liabilities.

Capitation fee Amount paid per person or family by a health maintenance organization to a physician and hospital in return for the provision of health care services to that person or family.

Captive agent See **career agent.**

Capture theory of regulation Positive economic theory holding that special interest groups within the regulated industry, being well organized and well financed, influence legislation and regulation for their own benefit.

Care risk Possibility that an individual will be unable to care for him- or herself due to a physical or mental impairment.

Career agent Individual producer engaged full time in the sale of insurance exclusively or primarily for a single insurer or affiliated group of insurers. Also called **captive agent, exclusive agent**, and **tied agent.**

Cascading failure Type of systemic risk in which the failure of one financial institution is the cause of the failure of others, with the result that harm occurs elsewhere within the economy.

Cash accumulation method Cost comparison method used for comparing a term life insurance policy with a cash value life insurance policy, involves observing differences in resulting cash surrender values or side fund accumulations for the policies after setting cash outlays and death benefits to the same levels for all policies.

Cash flow statement Financial statement showing the net change in a cash position over a reporting period.

Cash matching Technique wherein a portfolio is constructed whose interest and principal payments exactly match a set of liability cash flows.

Cash refund annuity Fixed life annuity that promises a single sum payment to a beneficiary on the annuitant's death, equal to the difference, if any, between the annuity purchase price and the simple sum of previously made payments.

Cash surrender value Amount payable to the policyowner on voluntary policy termination, ignoring policy loans, and less any surrender charges. Also called the **surrender value** and sometimes the **cash value**, especially if the policy has no identifiable surrender charges.

Cash value Life insurance policy's internal savings before deduction of any surrender charges or policy loans. Also called the **policy value, account value**, and **accumulated value**, especially with unbundled policies, and the **gross cash value.**

Cash value accumulation test One method of qualification under *Internal Revenue Code* §7702 to be met by a life insurance policy for favorable income tax treatment; the policy's cash surrender value cannot at any time exceed the net single premium that would be required to fund future contract benefits provided under the policy. Typically used with bundled whole life policies.

Cash value corridor limitation One of the two prongs of the guideline premium/cash value corridor test method of qualification under *Internal Revenue Code* §7702 used for determining whether a life insurance policy qualifies for favorable income tax treatment; promised benefits at all times must be at least equal to certain percentage multiples of the policy's cash value. Typically used with unbundled life policies.

Cash value life insurance Policies that combine term insurance and internal savings – called the cash value – within the same contract; that is, they accumulate funds that are available to the policyowner. Also sometimes called **permanent life insurance.**

Catastrophic illness coverage Life insurance policy provision that promises to pay up to a specified percentage (e.g., from 25 to 100 percent) of the policy's face amount if the insured has been diagnosed as having one of several listed catastrophic illnesses, often subject to an overall maximum payment (e.g., $250,000). Also called **dread disease coverage.**

Catastrophic reinsurance Nonproportional reinsurance designed to protect a ceding company against adverse results occurring from a specific event that affects multiple policies simultaneously.

Catch-up provision Feature under a no lapse guarantee universal life policy that permits payment of additional premiums to restore the guarantee if the minimum premium requirement was not met.

Centers of influence Persons who have an opportunity to recommend agents because of their status in a community or their role as an advisor, such as an attorney or accountant.

Certificate of annuity Single premium deferred fixed annuity that guarantees an interest rate for a set period of time, typically three to 10 years, but with no withdrawals permitted during the accumulation period.

Certificate of participation Written evidence of an employee's participation in a group deferred annuity plan, which provides details of plan benefits.

Change in reserves Marginal amount allocated each period to a life insurer's reserves (whether SAP, GAAP, or economic).

Charitable remainder trust Irrevocable trust funded with a split-interest gift by a grantor, which (1) pays an income to a named non-charitable beneficiary for life or a specified term of up to 20 years and (2), at the end of the term, pays the remaining assets to the charitable beneficiary.

Charitable split-interest gift Gift shared by charitable and non-charitable beneficiaries according to the wishes of the donor.

Chose in action Ownership right in personal property that is evidenced by a legal right; e.g., an insurance policy, rather than the possession of something tangible.

Chose in possession Ownership right in tangible personal property.

Churning Systematic and indiscriminate replacement of existing life insurance policies.

Close corporation See **closely held corporation.**

Closed block In a demutualization, a specified group of policies with participation rights protected by the allocation of specific investment, expense, and mortality results to such policies.

Closed corporation See **closely held corporation.**

Closely held business Any business typically owned and managed by a small number of investors, often family members, and whose ownership interest has no ready market.

Closely held corporation Closely held business whose shares of stock are not listed on any organized exchange. Also called **close corporation** and **closed corporation.**

Codicil Amendment that adds provisions or amends a part of a will but does not replace the will.

Coinsurance (1) Specified proportion of the excess of incurred medical expenses over the deductible that is payable by the insured. (2) Proportional reinsurance under which the ceding company pays the assuming company a proportionate part of the gross direct premium less commissions and other allowances, premium taxes, and overhead allocable to reinsured policies and the assuming company assumes a proportionate share of the risk according to the terms that govern the original policy.

Coinsurance with funds withheld Coinsurance under which the ceding company retains premiums normally paid to the assuming company, while the assuming company keeps the allowances normally paid to the ceding company.

Collateral assignment Temporary transfer by a policyowner of partial rights in a policy to another person or entity, commonly to secure a loan to the policyowner.

Collateral assignment approach Split dollar life insurance plan under which the insured employee applies for the policy and is primarily responsible for premium payments, with the policy collaterally assigned to the employer to secure amounts it advanced to the employee for premiums.

Combination distribution system See **home service distribution**.

Combination plan Life insurance or annuity contract that includes a long term care insurance rider commonly providing for an acceleration of a policy's death benefit payment in the form of monthly payments for qualified expenses.

Commercial insurance Any insurance designed for organizations, such as businesses. Commercial life, health, and retirement insurance coverages are more commonly referred to as **group insurance** in the U.S.

Commissioner's reserve valuation method Modified reserve method permitted under statutory accounting principles that allows deferred reserve funding by dividing policies into two groups: (1) those for which the net level premium for the second and subsequent policy years do not exceed the corresponding modified net premium for a 20-payment whole insurance policy, in which case the full preliminary term method is applied, and (2) those with higher premiums, in which case the additional amount for expenses is limited to that amount permitted under the full preliminary term method for a 20-payment whole life policy.

Community property Joint interest property under which all property acquired during marriage is joint property of the spouses.

Commutative Characteristic of contracts involving an approximately equal exchange of value between contracting parties.

Comparative interest rate Cost comparison method used for comparing a term life insurance policy with a cash value life insurance policy that solves for the interest rate that causes the accumulated value of the annual differences in policy premiums (the side fund) to be equal to the higher premium policy's cash surrender value at the end of the period of analysis after setting cash outlays and death benefits to the same levels for both policies. Also called **Linton yield.**

Complete financial market Theoretical market construct in which users and providers of funds have complete information about each other, borrowing/lending functions are frictionless, and monitoring is costless.

Component risk Life insurer risk associated with its internal operations, in contrast to those stemming from external social, competitive, economic, and other factors.

Composite mortality table Mortality table whose death rates include experience from both smokers and nonsmokers.

Compound interest Interest credited on both the principal amount and the interest credited thereon.

Compound probability Likelihood of the occurrence of two independent events calculated by taking the product of the simple probability of the occurrence of each event.

Comprehensive medical insurance Medical expense benefit coverage of a wide range of medical care charges with few internal limits and a high overall maximum benefit.

Comprehensive Medicare supplement policy Medicare supplemental insurance that generally has high maximum benefit limits or is unlimited with respect to the duration of confinement in a hospital or skilled nursing facility.

Concealment Withholding of information.

Conditional Characteristic of insurance contracts providing that the insurer's obligation to pay a claim depends upon the performance of certain acts by the owner or beneficiary, such as payment of premiums and furnishing proof of death.

Conditional tail expectation Refinement of value at risk that takes the average of the worst cases occurring outside the group specified by the value at risk probability or confidence level. Designed to capture the expected value of a loss, given a loss; i.e., the occurrence of an event with probability less than the confidence level. Also called **tail VaR**.

Conflict of interest Situation in which an individual or corporation has an interest in promoting one product or service over another that does not necessarily align with the customer's interest; can arise when a financial institution offers multiple financial services and promotes proprietary products of subsidiaries through formal or informal coercion.

Consanguinity Blood relationship.

Conservation Typically a customer service function undertaken to minimize policy lapses and surrenders.

Consideration clause Provision summarizing the factors that led the insurer to agree to issue a requested policy, ordinarily a simple statement that the applicant has completed an application and paid a premium in exchange for the company's promise to provide insurance.

Constant returns to scale Condition associated with the size of a firm in which further growth neither adds to nor detracts from firm efficiency; i.e., average costs are constant.

Constructive receipt Income deemed received by a taxpayer irrespective of whether it is taken in cash.

Consumer report As defined by the U.S. *Fair Credit Reporting Act*, a written, oral, or other communication of any information by a consumer reporting agency that has a bearing on the consumer's creditworthiness, credit standing, credit capacity, character, general reputation, personal characteristics, or mode of living, and that is used or expected to be used in whole or in part to establish eligibility for credit, personal insurance, employment, or certain other purposes.

Consumer reporting agency See **inspection company.**

Contagion Arises when financial distress in one unit of a financial services conglomerate becomes a source of distress throughout the group. Also called **financial infection.**

Contagion risk Possibility of cascading failures because of financial intermediaries being highly connected.

Contingency risk System devised by U.S. actuaries and used by them and insurance regulators to classify the risks faced by insurers, to include the following categories: C-1 or asset risk that arises from the possibility of defaults and changes in market values of investments; C-2 or pricing risk that arises from the possibility of inadequate risk and expense charges; C-3 or non-market interest rate risk that arises from the correlation of asset and liability cash flows; and C-4 or miscellaneous business risks that are not easily amenable to actuarial prediction.

Contingent deferred annuity Life-insurer-issued guaranteed lifetime withdrawal benefit attached to a mutual fund or managed investment account. Also called **stand alone living benefit**.

Continuation rider Provision of or a rider attached to a life insurance policy that promises to provide long term care benefit payments for a specified period after benefit payments under the provision or rider would otherwise be exhausted. Also called **extension of benefits rider**.

Continuing care center Facility providing a range of sensitive living arrangements and services that reflect each person's level of needed care and assistance under which individuals purchase for an initial, large single amount plus monthly payments, the right to live and receive support from the center. Not commonly covered by long term care insurance policies. Also called **life-care center**.

Contra proferentum Legal doctrine emanating from the notion that insurance policies are contracts of adhesion, and, therefore, any ambiguities in contract language are construed strictly in favor of the party not drafting the contract (policyowner and/or insured). Corollary is that a contract will be construed precisely as written, in the absence of any ambiguity.

Contributed surplus Amount paid for shares in excess of their par value.

Contribution principle Precept holding that divisible surplus should be distributed under participating policies in the same proportions as the policies are considered to have contributed to surplus.

Contribution to surplus Amount contributed each period to surplus capital after claims, expenses, and any required increase in reserves are satisfied.

Contributory plan Employee benefit plan in which both the employer and employees make contributions toward plan costs.

Conversion feature Life insurance policy provision that affords the owner of a term policy the option of exchanging the policy for a cash value insurance policy of a form currently being issued by the insurer, without having to provide evidence of insurability.

Coordination of benefits Provision within some health benefit plans and insurance policies setting forth guidelines to determine the order in which two insurers covering the same claim will pay.

Corporate governance Set of factors that affect the direction, administration, and control of a corporation, with particular application to the nature and extent of accountability of management.

Corporation Business entity legally separate and distinct from its owners and characterized by owners' limited liability for corporate obligations, ability to transfer owners' interests by the sale of their stock, and owners' deaths having no effect legally on the its continued existence.

Corpus Property held in a trust.

Corrective order. Provision in state insurance law that permits the insurance regulator to seek court approval to require an insurer to (1) obtain state approval before undertaking certain transactions, (2) limit or cease its new business writings, (3) infuse capital, and/or (4) cease certain business practices.

Cost accounting Convention employed to make discrete expense analyses across different product lines, services, and operations.

Cost basis See **basis**.

Cost of insurance The internal age-based rates assessed against each life insurance policy and based on its net amount at risk to cover its share of mortality charges for the period.

Cost of living adjustment Feature of some disability income policies providing for adjustments of benefits each year during a long term claim to reflect changes in the cost of living from the time that the claim began.

Cost recovery rule Under the *Internal Revenue Code*, general rule for taxation of lump sum cash surrender value payments under life insurance and annuity policies under which the amount included in the policyowner's gross income is the excess of the gross proceeds over the cost basis.

Cost-of-living-adjustment rider Term insurance rider that automatically increases a policy's death benefit each year in accordance with increases in inflation as measured by a national cost-of-living index, such as the *Consumer Price Index* in the U.S.

Creator See **grantor**.

Credit default swaps Financial instruments bought by investors to protect against defaults on bonds.

Credit insurance Special class of life and health insurance that pays off a debtor's outstanding loan balance if he or she dies or becomes disabled during the loan term.

Credit life and health insurance Life and health insurance provided through financial institutions to cover debtors' obligations if they die or become disabled.

Credit risk Category of risk specified by the *International Actuarial Association/Association Actuarielle Internationale*, possibility that obligations due a life insurer may not be paid as due, the most important of which are bond defaults and reinsurer insolvency.

Cross purchase buy/sell agreement Arrangement under which each owner of an interest in a business obligates his or her estate to sell and the other owners are obligated to purchase any owner's interest at his or her death.

Crummey power See **Crummey trust**.

Crummey provision See **Crummey trust**.

Crummey trust Irrevocable, living trust in which gifts to the trust qualify as present interest gifts and thus the annual gift exclusion, by providing trust beneficiaries a reasonable opportunity to demand distribution of amounts contributed. Also referred to as a **Crummey provision** or a **Crummey power** (within an irrevocable trust).

Current assumptions See **nonguaranteed policy elements**.

Current assumption policy Unbundled life insurance policy containing nonguaranteed policy elements.

Current assumption whole life insurance Unbundled, nonparticipating whole life insurance with nonguaranteed elements. Also called **interest sensitive whole life** and **fixed premium universal life**.

Custodial care Basic non-skilled care excluded from Medicare, typically in the form of assistance with the activities of daily living and commonly covered by long term care insurance policies.

Death benefit See **face amount**.

Death benefit internal rate of return Cost comparison method that solves for the interest rate that causes accumulated scheduled premiums (net of dividends, if appropriate) at selected policy durations to equal that duration's death benefit.

Death benefit only plan Nonqualified deferred compensation arrangement that promises to pay an income benefit to a named person on the employee's death.

Death benefit provision Universal life policy provision that sets out the various death benefit options and explains the method of determining the policy death benefit.

Death benefit solve Value solve measure that solves for the death benefit that a particular premium amount, pattern, and duration and, if applicable, attainment of a target cash surrender value by a specified policy year will support.

Death benefit universal life Universal life policy that emphasizes death benefits and provides for very low premiums per $1,000 of face amount but typically also offers low cash value accumulation and/or has heavy surrender charges. Also called **protection universal life**.

Debit Geographical territory assigned to a commissioned exclusive agent of a home service life insurer.

Debit distribution system See **home service distribution**.

Debit insurance See **industrial insurance**.

Decreasing returns to scale Condition associated with the size of a firm in which further growth diminishes firm efficiency; i.e., average costs increase.

Decreasing term life insurance Term life insurance whose face amount decreases with policy duration.

Deductible Specified incurred amount of loss to be paid by the insured before any costs are paid by an employee benefit plan or insurer.

Default risk Possibility that an insurer will become insolvent and unable to perform its contractual obligations. Also called **ruin risk**.

Deferred acquisition costs Asset under generally accepted accounting principles representing that portion of first year policy expenses incurred by an insurer not charged against income in that year and amortized, usually over the premium paying period, via a charge to income in those later years.

Deferred dividends Divisible surplus payable only at the close of a stipulated number of years, such as 5, 10, 15, and 20.

Deferred income annuity See **longevity annuity**.

Deferred life annuity Life annuity for which payments begin more than one period hence.

Deficiency reserve Used in the past in the U.S., a supplemental reserve required to be maintained if a policy's gross premiums were less than valuation net premiums.

Defined benefit pension plan Retirement plan under which income benefits to be received by each participant are specified. Contribution requirements are implicit and vary according to plan investment performance and employee eligibility.

Defined contribution pension plan Retirement plan under which contributions to be made on behalf of each participant are specified. Benefits are distributed in cash to the participant at retirement (or applied to an employer-sponsored postretirement option).

Delay clause Required life insurance policy provision that grants the insurer the right to defer cash surrender value payments, withdrawals, and the granting of policy loans (except for purposes of paying premiums) for up to six months following the request.

Demutualization Conversion of a mutual insurance company to a stock insurance company or upstream holding company.

Deposit taking institution Financial intermediary that takes deposits from and makes loans to consumers.

Derivatives Traded securities or contractual agreements whose cash flows depend on the value of other specified securities or indices.

Direct expenses Those expenses directly attributable to a specific product (e.g., agent's commission).

Direct insurance Insurance sold to the public as opposed to reinsurance.

Direct premiums Premiums written on direct insurance.

Direct response Distribution channel that serves purchasers directly without the initial intervention of an individual or institutional intermediary.

Direct writing insurer Insurer that sells direct insurance. Also called **primary insurer**.

Directive Legislation adopted by the European Parliament instructing member states to enact laws or regulations consistent with the legislation to ensure harmonization of law and regulation throughout the union.

Disability income insurance Health insurance that pays a stated, usually monthly benefit, if illness or injury prevents the insured from working.

Discharge planning Managed care function designed to limit the length of hospital stays to the medically necessary minimum.

Disciplined current scale That schedule of current nonguaranteed values shown in a basic illustration for which each set of implicit assumptions is based on the insurer's actual recent current, determinable, and credible experience.

Disintermediation Withdrawal of funds from a financial intermediary for purposes of investing elsewhere, commonly for a higher expected return.

Distributable surplus provision See **participation provision**.

Diversifiable risk That particular to a given company, usually measured by its beta. Also called **unsystematic risk** and **specific risk**.

Dividend Pro-rata share of divisible surplus paid by an insurer to the owner of a participating policy. Also called **bonus**.

Dividend history Schedule of dividends actually paid under a particular participating policy or policy form.

Dividend illustration Shows dividends that would be paid in the future under a policy if the investment, mortality, and loading factors implicit in the currently payable dividends were to remain unchanged in the future.

Dividend options Alternative applications of dividends paid under participating life insurance policies, including most or all of the following: (1) cash – pay in cash to the policyowner, (2) apply toward premium payment – credit toward premiums due, (3) accumulate at interest – held by the insurer on deposit at interest, (4) purchase paid up additional insurance – apply as a net single premium at the insured's attained age to purchase life insurance of the same type as the policy, (5) purchase one year term life insurance – either in an amount equal to the cash value or for the maximum amount that the dividend will purchase, or (6) add-to-cash-value – accumulate as additional cash value only, with no additional net amount at risk.

Dividends actually paid Amounts paid in the past under a particular participating policy or policy form. See **dividend history**.

Divisible surplus That portion of an insurer's surplus that its board of directors decides to share with owners of its participating policies.

Do not resuscitate order Advance directive requesting no cardiopulmonary resuscitation intervention if one's heart stops or one stops breathing.

Doctrine of substantial compliance Legal concept that a change of beneficiary will have been deemed effectuated even if the policyowner did not follow prescribed procedure if he or she did all that he or she could to effect the change but factors beyond his or her control precluded such.

Domestic insurer In U.S. terminology, an insurance company domiciled (incorporated) in the state in which it is licensed to do business,

Donee Person receiving a gift.

Donor Person making a gift.

Double gearing Accounting twice for subsidiary capital; once within the subsidiary and again at the conglomerate level.

Double indemnity See **accidental death benefit**.

Dread disease coverage See **catastrophic illness coverage**.

Dread disease insurance policy See **specified disease insurance policy**.

Due care Process suggesting that those offering life insurance advice conduct their business affairs with diligence, prudence, and competence, such that recommended insurance is suitable for the individual's circumstances, reasonably expected to offer good value, and procured from insurers that are financially sound.

Due diligence As applied to variable products and other securities, process by which a broker/dealer ensures that an investment is as represented.

Durable power of attorney Advance directive designating an individual to make financial and other decisions for a person who becomes incapacitated or is declared incompetent to conduct his or her own affairs; survives the person's incapacity, unlike some nondurable powers.

Duration Weighted average time to maturity of a fixed income asset or liability or portfolio of fixed income assets or liabilities.

Duration matched Property of a portfolio such that changes in asset values will be exactly offset by changes in liability values when market interest rates change.

Dynamic financial analysis Stochastic-based projection of an insurance company's cash flows and financial condition over time, taking account of a full range of economic scenarios, asset and liability cash flows, the interrelationships of the cash flows, and the factors that affect cash flows individually and collectively.

Economic capital Amount of financial capital required to absorb a maximum expected loss occurring with a specified probability over a specified time horizon.

Economic wealth Sum of human and investment capital at any point in life.

Economies of scale Marginal cost savings associated with the size of a firm in which output increases at a rate faster than attendant increases in production costs, holding product mix constant; i.e., average costs decrease.

Economies of scope Condition in which a firm's average production costs decline as it produces a greater number of different products or services.

Economizing problem Condition of unlimited wants and limited resources.

Effective date Time insurance protection begins.

Eligibility period Under a contributory employee benefit plan, the period of time that an employee is given during which he or she is entitled to apply for insurance without submitting evidence of insurability.

Elimination Period With disability income insurance, the length of time at the start of disability during which no benefits are paid. Also called the **waiting period.**

Emancipation Time at which a young person leaves the family and its authority.

Embedded value Measure of the expected value of a book of business (e.g., a product line) derived by taking the present value of projected future net cash flows and changes in reserves.

Employee Stock Ownership Plan Noncontributory qualified defined contribution retirement plan that permits shares of the employer-sponsor stock to be contributed to the plan and assets of the plan to be invested in the stock of the employer-sponsor.

Employer owned life insurance Under the *Internal Revenue Code*, life insurance on an employee's life payable to his or her employer; unless certain conditions are met, benefits in excess of the employer's basis are taxable as ordinary income.

Endorsement approach Split dollar life insurance plan under which insurance on the employee's life is applied for and owned by the employer, which is primarily responsible for premium payments.

Endow Condition under which a maturity value becomes payable under a life insurance policy upon the insured surviving to a specified date or number of years.

Endowment insurance Life insurance that makes two mutually exclusive promises: to pay a stated benefit if the insured dies during or survives the policy term.

Enhanced cash value rider Eliminates or reduces surrender charges applicable to qualified policies during the first few policy years.

Enter onto an annuity Point at which annuitization commences.

Enterprise risk management Range of processes and techniques designed to protect and create value by assisting companies uncover hidden risks, improve the stability of earnings, identify opportunities in assuming risk and risk arbitrage, and discovering natural synergies across business lines.

Entire contract clause Required life insurance policy provision stating that the policy itself and the application, if a copy is attached to the policy, along with amendments and riders, constitute the entire contract between the parties.

Entity buy/sell agreement Arrangement under which an owner of an interest in a business obligates his or her estate to sell and the business entity obligates itself to purchase that interest on the owner's death.

Equal outlay method Cost comparison method that involves observing differences in resulting cash surrender values or side fund accumulations for two or more policies by setting cash outlays and initial death benefits to the same level for all policies.

Equity-indexed annuity Fixed annuity contract whose interest crediting rate is the insurer's current crediting rate and/or a specified external index, such as the *Standard & Poor's 500 Index*.

Equity-indexed universal life Universal life policy under which the owner elects the proportion of account value to be allocated to the insurer's fixed, general account-based interest crediting rate and to an indexed account whose crediting rate is tied directly to some external index, such as the *Standard & Poor's 500 Index*. Also called **indexed universal life**.

Escheat Condition under which unclaimed property passes to the state.

Estate conservation Term used to describe the use of life insurance death proceeds to cover some or all of one's estate obligations, the most relevant of which typically are estate taxes. Also referred to as providing **estate liquidity**.

Estate tax credit Under federal tax law, credit allowed against the tentative federal estate tax for the lesser of death-related taxes paid to a state or a maximum permitted federal credit.

Estoppel Principle that prevents an individual from denying or asserting any position contrary to that established by the individual's own conduct or by previous legal determinations.

Excess of retention Proportional reinsurance whereby specified amounts of claim are shared between ceding and assuming companies.

Excess SERP Supplemental executive retirement plan providing a benefit amount equal to the difference between (1) the amount that would be paid to the executive under the employer's qualified retirement benefit formula ignoring any ERISA-imposed limits and (2) the actual retirement benefit payable to the executive under the qualified retirement plan and Social Security.

Exclusion ratio Ratio of the investment in an annuity contract to the expected return under the contract, which determines the proportion of each annuity payment excluded from taxable income.

Exclusion rider Policy endorsement excluding from coverage any loss arising from the peril named in the rider.

Exclusive agent See **career agent**.

Executive bonus plan Arrangement under which an employer pays premiums on a life insurance policy for a selected executive who owns the policy. Also called **Section 162 plan**.

Executor Individual or institution responsible for the execution of a will's provisions and the administration of the estate.

Exempt income That which is excluded from taxable income based on its character or the status of the recipient.

Exempt property By law, property excluded from the claims of creditors.

Exhaustive Condition wherein events under consideration cover all possibilities; e.g., a person will either live or die during a given year.

Expectancy interest With revocable life insurance beneficiaries, an expectation of receiving policy death proceeds but with no current vested interest or rights prior to claim maturity.

Expected return Used for determining the income tax treatment of payout annuities, the amount of the annuity payment multiplied by prescribed expected return multiples for life annuities or by the number of payments for annuities certain.

Expense margin In insurance policy pricing, amounts added to anticipated expenses and taxes intended to provide for contingencies, profits, surplus accumulations, and to cover losses associated with early policy lapses. Also called **safety margin**.

Experience factors Actual results experienced by an insurer on a block of policies as to mortality, investment returns, expenses, taxes, and persistency.

Experience rating Method of adjusting charges under an employee benefit plan by considering past financial results of the group.

Expire Termination of an insurance policy without maturity value at the end of its specified contractual duration.

Exposure unit In insurance practice and theory, a person, place, or thing exposed to the possibility of loss or other insured event.

Express authority See **actual authority**.

Extended care benefits Health care benefits paid for active nursing and other skilled care when required in an extended care facility or at home.

Extension of benefits rider See **continuation rider**.

Externality Type of market failure in which a firm's production or an individual's consumption has direct and uncompensated effects on others.

Face amount Sum of money that a life insurance policy promises to pay on the death of the insured. Also called the **sum assured** and the **death benefit**.

Facultative reinsurance Reinsurance on a policy-by-policy basis under which applications received by a primary insurer are submitted to an assuming company that chooses whether to accept the risk based on its own underwriting standards.

Fair market value Under federal tax law applicable to gifts of life insurance and annuities, the approach used to place a value on a gifted policy.

Family income policy/rider Decreasing term policy or rider that pays a death benefit to the beneficiary (usually the surviving spouse) as a monthly income until the beneficiary attains a certain age or for a set period of from 10 to 20 years from the date of policy issuance.

Family policy/rider. When issued as a policy, provides whole life insurance on one parent and term insurance generally on the spouse and children. When issued as a rider, provides level term insurance on the spouse and children.

Federal estate taxes owed Under federal tax law, net amount owed to the government after applying applicable credits against the tentative federal estate tax.

Fiduciary With regard to trusts, standard of care requiring a trustee to act solely in the beneficiary's interest.

Financial capital Funds provided to companies by investors either directly or through retained earnings, which are necessary to finance the production of goods and services.

Financial infection See **contagion**.

Financial questionnaire Supplement to a life insurance application that elicits additional financial information about and from a proposed insured or applicant who applies for a comparatively large amount of insurance.

Financial reinsurance Reinsurance transacted primarily to achieve financial goals, such as capital management, tax planning, or the financing of acquisitions.

Financially impaired insurer As defined by *A.M. Best*, insurer for which its ability to conduct normal operations is impaired, capital and surplus have been determined to be insufficient to meet legal requirements, and/or financial condition has triggered regulatory concern.

First year expense allowance Maximum allowance permitted under the *Standard Nonforfeiture Law* to derive the adjusted premium, defined as the sum of (1) 1.0 percent of the average amount of life insurance over a policy's first 10 years (or $10 per $1,000) and (2) the lesser of 125 percent of the nonforfeiture net level premium or $40 per $1,000.

First-to-die life insurance See **joint life insurance**.

Fixed annuity Annuity contract that credits investment returns based indirectly on the performance of the insurer's general account investments or directly on changes in a specified inflation or equity index, subject to a guaranteed minimum crediting rate.

Fixed premium universal life See **current assumption whole life**.

Flat extra premium method Method used in rating substandard risks in life insurance under which a constant extra premium is charged to provide for expected additional mortality.

Flexible premium deferred annuity Fixed or variable annuity contract purchased with owner-determined periodic premiums, whose benefit payments are deferred until annuitization following the accumulation period.

Flexible spending account As part of an employer-sponsored cafeteria plan, permits accumulation of pretax salary reductions for reimbursement of a variety of participant health care, dependent care, and other benefits.

Foreign insurer (1) In U.S. terminology, an insurance company domiciled (incorporated) in a state different from that in which it is licensed to do business. (2) In international terminology, an insurer organized in another country.

Form 8-K Filing required by the U.S. *Securities and Exchange Commission* between filings of its 10-K and 10-Q if significant material events occur, such as the sale of an affiliate or change of independent auditors or CEO.

Form 10-K Filing required annually by the U.S. *Securities and Exchange Commission* for companies greater than a certain minimum size whose stock is traded in public markets, which provides detailed information related to the company's history, nature of its business, organizational structure, risk factors, equity, subsidiaries, and audited financial statements, among other information.

Form 10-Q Abbreviated version of a Form 10-K filing required quarterly by the U.S. *Securities and Exchange Commission* for companies above a certain size whose stock is traded in public markets.

Fractional premium See **modal premium**.

Fraternal benefit society Entity organized under specific state law, which operates under a lodge system through which social and insurance benefits are provided to members and their family members.

Fraud Intentional deception or misrepresentation made for personal gain.

Fraudulent conveyance See **fraudulent transfer**.

Fraudulent transfer Under the *Uniform Fraudulent Transfer Act*, payment made with the actual intent to hinder, delay, or defraud a creditor. Also called **fraudulent conveyance**.

Free capital See **unassigned surplus**.

Free look provision See **right to return provision**.

Free rider problem Type of market failure in which goods or services supplied to one person are available to others at no extra cost.

Free withdrawal corridor Maximum stated proportion of annuity cash value that can be withdrawn without incurring a surrender charge, such as 10 percent.

Front-end load Explicit amount deducted from premium payments to cover some or all of an insurer's expenses, taxes, contingencies, and sometimes profits.

Full costing Allocation of both direct and indirect expenses to specific product lines.

Full preliminary term method Modified policy reserve method permitted as part of the Commissioner's reserve valuation method under U.S. statutory accounting principles that allows an insurer to assume that the first year's premium under some policies pays only for term insurance for the first policy year and that the actual policy for reserve purposes comes into operation one year later than the age of issue and will have a one year shorter premium payment and coverage period.

Funded nonqualified retirement plan Arrangement under which the employer establishes and maintains assets in an escrow account or trust fund as security for its promise to make future payments to one or more employees.

Future increase option See **guarantee of future insurability**.

Future interest Condition such that a person has possession and enjoyment of property only in the future.

General account Location of assets that support guaranteed interest-crediting contractual obligations, such as those arising from traditional and many contemporary life insurance policies, including whole life and universal life.

General agency Individual business managed by a general agent who recruits, trains, houses, and supervises individual intermediaries.

General agent Agent whose powers are identical to those of its principal within the limit of the particular business or territory in which the agent operates.

General counsel memorandum U.S. *Treasury Department* detailed analysis prepared to explain the reasoning underlying a regulation, revenue ruling, or private letter ruling.

General insurance See **nonlife insurance**.

General partnership One in which partners are actively involved in the management of the firm and fully liable for partnership obligations.

General power of appointment Right to dispose of property not owned by the person holding the power, including giving it to him- or herself.

Generation skipping transfer tax Under federal tax law, tax levied when a property interest is transferred to persons who are two or more generations younger than the transferor.

Gift splitting Under federal tax law, condition under which a spouse joins in making a gift.

Gift tax marital deduction Under federal tax law, the value of property gifted to a surviving spouse that is exempt from gift taxation and from filing a federal gift tax return.

Gompertz–Makeham law of mortality Contemporary version of the law of mortality that holds that death rates can be considered to be the sum of the traditional age-dependent exponential component (Gompertz part) and a component that works independent of age (Makeham part) that takes into consideration life shortening situations such as poor sanitation, malnourishment, and poor health or health care.

Good faith and fair dealing Implied covenant or duty that requires insurers to make prompt and full settlement with insureds and beneficiaries and to consider the insured's interest in settling claims.

Grace period provision Required life insurance policy provision that prevents its termination and requires the insurer to accept premium payments for a certain period (usually 30 or 31 days) after a premium due date or if the policy has insufficient account value to permit it to continue in force.

Graded premium whole life insurance Whole life insurance under which initial premiums are substantially (e.g., 50 percent) less than those of a comparable ordinary life policy and which increase annually for a period of from five to 20 years and remain level thereafter.

Graduation Smoothing of a mortality curve, performed to eliminate irregularities in observed data that are believed not to be true characteristics of the universe from which the sample experience was extracted.

Grantor Person who establishes a trust. Also called **creator** or **settlor**.

Gross estate Under federal tax law, value of all property and interests in property owned or controlled by at deceased person.

Gross premium (1) Net premium plus loading. (2) Premium paid to an insurer for an insurance policy.

Gross proceeds Under the *Internal Revenue Code*, amounts paid on life insurance policy surrender, including the cash value of any paid up additions and the value of dividends accumulated at interest.

Group deferred annuity Under an employer-sponsored pension plan, the purchase by the employer of units of single premium deferred annuities to provide specified amounts of life income to be paid to participants at retirement.

Group insurance Type of commercial insurance in which a group of persons who usually have a business or professional relationship to the contract owner are provided coverage under a single master contract.

Group sales representative Insurer's salesperson who generates personal group insurance sales or promotes commissioned sales by others or both.

Group term carve out Arrangement under which older, higher-paid employees are "carved out" of a group plan and provided with cash value life insurance.

Growth cap Under an equity-indexed universal life policy or annuity, the maximum possible interest crediting rate.

Growth floor Under an equity-indexed universal life policy or annuity, the guaranteed minimum interest crediting rate.

Growth rate Under an equity indexed universal life policy or annuity, the product of the index performance rate and the participation rate.

Guarantee of future insurability Feature of some disability income policies typically available for an additional premium guaranteeing that an insured can purchase additional disability income insurance in future years without having to provide evidence of insurability. Also called **future increase option**.

Guaranteed insurability option Life insurance policy rider that grants the insured the right to purchase additional life insurance at specified future periods and on the occurrence of specified events (e.g., marriage) without having to provide evidence of insurability. Also called **additional** or **guaranteed purchase option**.

Guaranteed investment contract Investment instrument offered by life insurers that promises to credit a specified interest rate for a specified period much like a certificate of deposit at a bank.

Guaranteed lifetime withdrawal benefit Under a variable or fixed annuity, promise of a lifetime minimum income benefit if the cash value is exhausted due to withdrawals or investment losses, while providing access to a substantial part of the cash value throughout the deferral and life income benefit period.

Guaranteed lifetime withdrawal benefit base With a guaranteed lifetime withdrawal benefit provision or rider, the amount which together with a distribution factor determines the annual guaranteed withdrawal amount.

Guaranteed living benefits Accumulation, income, and withdrawal guarantee features of annuities.

Guaranteed minimum accumulation benefit Rider offered under a variable annuity contract promising that the cash value will not be less than the simple sum of premiums paid.

Guaranteed minimum death benefit (1) Under a variable universal life policy, feature or rider that, for an additional premium, guarantees that a specified minimum death benefit will be paid irrespective of whether the policy account value is positive, provided benchmark premiums have been paid. (2) Under a variable annuity contract, guarantee that the amount paid on death will be the greater of the cash value or the amount invested in the contract.

Guaranteed minimum income benefit Rider offered under a variable annuity contract promising a minimum amount of retirement income based on assumptions in effect at purchase.

Guaranteed minimum withdrawal benefit Under a variable or fixed annuity, promise of a minimum income benefit for a stated period or amount if the cash value is exhausted due to withdrawals or investment losses, while providing complete access to a substantial part of the cash value throughout the deferral and income benefit period.

Guaranteed minimum withdrawal benefit base Under a guaranteed lifetime withdrawal benefit, the total amount available for withdrawal, determined as the sum of premiums paid or the sum of premiums paid and a stated interest rate to the date of determination (sometimes termed premium roll up) or periodically based on the cash value at specified contract anniversary dates (sometimes termed account value step up) until the date of determination.

Guaranteed policy elements Those policy components that are fixed and guaranteed and that the insurer may not change, commonly including mortality and loading charges, interest crediting rate, premiums, and death benefits.

Guaranteed purchase option See **guaranteed insurability option**.

Guaranteed renewable The contractual right within a health insurance policy to continue the policy by the timely payment of premiums, usually to a specified age such as 65, but with no guarantee as to the magnitude of future premiums.

Guaranteed withdrawal amount With a guaranteed lifetime withdrawal benefit provision or rider, the dollar amount of guaranteed withdrawals determined by multiplying the guaranteed lifetime withdrawal benefit base by the distribution factor for the age and sex of the annuitant.

Guaranteed withdrawal phase With a guaranteed lifetime withdrawal benefit provision or rider, the phase of the liquidation period when the account value has been depleted and the guaranteed withdrawal amount is paid by the insurer.

Guaranteed-cost, nonparticipating life insurance Nonparticipating life insurance under which all policy elements are guaranteed and fixed at policy issuance.

Guideline level premium limitation One of the two guideline premium limitations of the guideline premium/cash value corridor test that is met by a life insurance policy if cumulative premiums paid under the contract do not at any time exceed the level annual premium payable at least to age 95 that would be required to fund future insurance benefits under a contract at the insured's attained age and based on certain required assumptions.

Guideline premium test Greater of the guideline level premium and the guideline single premium as defined in *Internal Revenue Code* §7702. One of the two prongs of the guideline premium/cash value corridor method of qualification used for determining whether a life insurance policy qualifies for favorable tax treatment.

Guideline premium/cash value accumulation test One of two tests under *Internal Revenue Code* §7702 used for determining whether life insurance policies qualify for favorable tax treatment; a two-pronged test that provides (1) cumulative premiums paid under a contract may not at any time exceed the greater of a guideline single premium or a guideline level premium and (2) the cash value may not exceed the cash value corridor limitation.

Guideline single premium limitation One of the two guideline premium limitations of the guideline premium/cash value corridor test that is met by a life insurance policy if cumulative premiums paid under the contract do not at any time exceed the gross single premium that would be required to fund future insurance benefits provided under a contract at the insured's attained age and based on certain required assumptions.

Health insurance (1) Insurance that indemnifies the insured for costs incurred or wages lost because of illness, injury, and/or incapacity. (2) Insurance to cover medical expenses incurred to treat an insured's sickness or injury.

Health maintenance organization Health care financing and delivery corporation that contracts with physicians, hospitals, and other providers to provide services to beneficiaries, rather than to provide cash reimbursement.

Health reimbursement account Qualified, noncontributory employer-sponsored arrangement under which employer contributions may be used as tax-free reimbursements to employees for incurred qualified medical expenses not reimbursed under the employer's specified standard plan(s), up to specified maximums.

Health risk Possibility that an individual loses his or her ability to work or incurs medical expense because of illness or injury.

Health savings account Permits individuals to accumulate pretax contributions to pay qualified medical expenses associated with a high deductible health plan.

Hedge capital Risk management asset cash flow that substitutes for and complements surplus capital.

Hedging Strategy of acquiring securities whose gains and losses offset losses and gains in other securities or portfolios of securities, often achieved through the purchase of derivatives.

High deductible health plan Health plan carrying an annual deductible of at least specified amount ($1,250 for an individual, $2,500 for a family as of 2014) and providing for a maximum out-of-pocket expenditure of a specified amount ($6,350 for an individual, $12,700 for a family as of 2014). Health savings accounts are often combined with these plans.

High-water mark method Equity index annuity indexing method that determines index-linked interest by retrospectively selecting the highest index value recorded at specified dates, usually policy anniversaries

Holding company Corporation that owns the outstanding stock of other companies and usually does not produce goods or services itself.

Home health care Skilled nursing care, physical therapy, related professional services, and/or personal services such as assistance with the activities of daily living, with care provided in the patient's home or community, typically on a part-time basis. Commonly covered by long term care insurance policies up to a percentage (e.g., 50 percent) of the full nursing home benefit.

Home service distribution system System of commissioned exclusive agents who are assigned a geographic territory. Also known as the **combination distribution system** or **debit distribution system.**

Home service life insurance Encompasses industrial and monthly debit ordinary insurance.

Homogeneous See **identically distributed**.

Hospice care Special care and emotional support for persons diagnosed with terminal illness and imminent death, provided in a facility or in the person's home. Commonly covered by long term care insurance policies up to a percentage (e.g., 50 percent) of the full nursing home benefit.

Hospital confinement indemnity Individual health insurance policy that pays a fixed sum for each day of hospital confinement.

Hospital expense benefits Medical expense benefits paid in connection with use by a consumer of hospital services, usually distinguished between (1) room and board charges which cover the daily room charge, meals, and routine nursing care and (2) other hospital services that include charges for medical testing related to the hospitalization, operating room charges, and ambulance services.

Human capital (1) Productive capacity within each person, considered to be the driving force in economic growth. (2) Present value of an individual's future earnings.

Human life value Measure of the future earnings or value of services of an individual; i.e., the capitalized value of an individual's future earnings less self-maintenance costs such as food, clothing, and shelter.

Hurdle rate Minimum acceptable investment return an insurer expects from a product line.

Identically distributed Random variables whose probability distributions prescribe the same probability to each potential occurrence, which renders the distributions' expected values and variances equal. Also called **homogeneous**.

Illustration actuary Person designated by an insurer's board of directors to make annual certifications to the insurance regulator and the insurer's board of directors that the insurer's illustration practices comply with the requirements of the NAIC *Life Insurance Policy Illustration Model Regulation*, including that nonguaranteed values within basic illustrations rely on a disciplined current scale.

Immediate life annuity Life annuity for which payments are made at the end of the first and succeeding periods

Immunization Practice of structuring assets and liabilities such that a change in interest rates affects asset and liability values equally.

Implied authority That authority implicitly possessed by an agent associated with common duties, such as the cashier's authority to take payment for merchandise at a checkout counter.

Inactive guaranteed living withdrawal benefit phase With a guaranteed lifetime withdrawal benefit provision or rider, the initial period of the annuity deferral stage preceding the withdrawal benefit determination period when no fees are charged for the benefit provision or rider and the account accumulates as with any deferred EIA or variable annuity.

Income elasticity of insurance premiums Relative change in insurance premiums written for a given change in national income.

Income replacement ratio Gross earned income after retirement divided by gross income before retirement.

Incontestable clause Required life insurance policy provision stating that the validity of an insurance contract cannot be contested after it has been in force for a period of time, commonly two years.

Increasing premium term See **yearly renewable term**.

Increasing returns to scale Condition associated with the size of a firm in which further growth increases firm efficiency; i.e., average costs decrease.

Indemnity Payment of an amount not greater than that which would be necessary to place the insured in the same pre-loss financial position.

Indemnity reinsurance Reinsurance that indemnifies the ceding company for some or all of its reinsured underwriting losses.

Independent Relationship between random variables (e.g., exposures units) such that the occurrence of an event affecting one has no affect on the other variables.

Independent distribution channel Distribution system not owned or directed by the insurer and that relies on individual producers, usually called **brokers**, who are independent salespersons who are not required to sell insurance exclusively or primarily for a single insurer or affiliated group of insurers. Also called **non-agency building system.**

Independent practice association Health maintenance organization that relies on non-exclusive contracts with independent providers for health care services for its members.

Independent property/casualty agent Commissioned agent whose primary business is the sale of property and casualty insurance for several insurers; may also sell life insurance products to property/casualty customers.

Indeterminate premium Life insurance policy premium charged the policyowner that can be less than that guaranteed in the contract.

Index account That portion of the equity indexed universal life policy or annuity account value for which the crediting rate is determined by changes in an equity index.

Index crediting rate Under an equity indexed universal life policy or annuity, the crediting rate applied to the index account, which is the growth rate adjusted to take account of the segment growth floor and growth cap.

Index performance rate Under an equity indexed universal life policy or annuity, the change in the index's market value, typically excluding dividend income.

Index term For an equity index annuity, the specified period of time over which the performance of the equity index and the annuity guarantee determine the amounts credited to the account value.

Indexed universal life See **equity indexed universal life**.

Indexed whole life insurance Whole life insurance under which the face amount increases with increases in the inflation rate as measured by some national price index, such as the CPI in the U.S.

Index-linked interest Amounts credited to an equity index annuity based on the performance of a specified equity index.

Indirect expenses Those expenses attributable to general insurer operations that cannot be directly attributed to a specific product line.

Individual health insurance Generic term to describe any arrangement in which health-related coverage is provided to a specific individual under a policy issued to individuals (and sometimes covering multiple family members).

Individual intermediary Business person who sells insurance products on an interpersonal level and is compensated by commission for each policy sold. Also called **producers.**

Individual Retirement Account Tax-advantaged retirement plan available for individuals. Contributions are tax deductible only for those not participating in any other qualified pension, profit sharing, or Keogh plan.

Industrial life and health insurance Type of personal insurance in which policies of modest benefit amounts are sold to individuals of low to modest incomes and whose premiums are collected weekly or monthly at the insured's residence or place of employment. Also called **debit insurance**.

Inflation protection Included in some long term care insurance policies for an additional premium, coverage designed to ensure that the benefit amount more or less increases with the cost of living.

Inflation risk Possibility that an individual's cost of living will exceed that anticipated.

Informal funding The establishment of a reserve fund by an employer to meet future nonqualified retirement plan obligations but with the fund not formally linked to the obligation and that remains a general asset of the business subject to attachment by its general creditors.

Initial capital and paid-in surplus Minimum amount required by a state to establish a domestic insurer.

Initial reserve Value of a policy reserve at the beginning of a policy year, equal to the terminal reserve for the preceding year increased by the net level annual premium for that policy year.

Injury With disability income insurance, accidental bodily injury whose results were unforeseen or unexpected occurring while the policy is in force.

Inside interest buildup Interest credited to cash values under tax-qualified life insurance policies that is not subject to current taxation.

Insolvency Inability to pay one's debts.

Inspection company Industry term for a consumer reporting agency, which is an organization that collects and sells information about individuals' employment history, driving record, financial situation, creditworthiness, character, personal characteristics, mode of living, and other possibly relevant personally identifiable information.

Inspection report Industry term for a consumer report used by underwriters and prepared by an inspection company, which is intended to verify and/or supplement mainly nonmedical information provided by a proposed insured and/or applicant.

Installment refund annuity Fixed life annuity that promises continuation of income payments to a beneficiary on the annuitant's death, until total payments equal the annuity purchase price.

Institutional intermediary Deposit taking, investment intermediary, and other financial firm that sells insurers' products.

Insurability conditional premium receipt Formal acknowledgement that the applicant has tendered the first policy premium and that provides insurance coverage from the later of the application date or physical exam date, provided the proposed insured is found insurable on a basis at least as favorable as that shown in the insurance application.

Insurable interest Public policy and legal requirement that an applicant (or sometimes beneficiary) possess a lawful and substantial economic interest in the continued life, health, or bodily safety of the insured person or, for persons closely related by blood or law, a substantial interest engendered by love and affection.

Insurance (1) From an economic perspective, a financial intermediation function under which insureds each contribute to a insurance pool from which payments are made to them or on their behalf if specified contingencies occur; a contingent claim on the pool's assets. (2) From a legal perspective, an agreement (insurance policy or contract) by which one party (policyowner) pays a stipulated consideration (premium) to the other party (insurance company) in return for which the insurance company agrees to pay a defined amount or provide a specific service if specified contingencies occur during the policy term.

Insurance agent Sales person licensed by the state and under contract to sell at least one insurer's products, typically for a commission and on a face-to-face basis. Also called **producer**.

Insurance code Statutory law that specifies the scope and standards that govern the administration of the jurisdiction's insurance law and related requirements, procedures, standards, and enforcement mechanisms.

Insurance density Average annual per capita direct premium written within a market.

Insurance penetration Ratio of yearly direct premiums written to gross domestic product within a market.

Insurance pool Grouping together of similar exposure units. Also called **risk pool** and **risk class**.

Insured Person whose life or health is the object of an insurance policy.

Insuring agreement See **insuring clause**.

Insuring clause Required life or health policy provision stating the insurer's promise to pay the death or health benefits due, subject to policy conditions. Also called **insuring agreement**.

Intentionally defective grantor trust See **intentionally defective irrevocable trust**.

Intentionally defective irrevocable trust Deferred sale arrangement between a grantor and an irrevocable trust that allows the grantor to make transfers of appreciated income producing property to junior generations free of gift tax. Also called an **intentionally defective grantor trust**.

Inter vivos trust One created during life. Also called **living trust**.

Interest The price paid for the use of money.

Interest Maintenance Reserve Accounting mechanism required by regulators designed to minimize volatility in an insurer's statutory surplus by earmarking portions of it to absorb realized capital gains and losses attributable to changing market interest rates.

Interest margin Difference between the insurer's actual investment return and its interest crediting rate. Also called **investment margin** and **spread**.

Interest rate cap Specified interest rate of an interest option above which an interest rate index results in payment to its holder.

Interest rate floor Specified interest rate of an interest option below which an interest rate index results in payment to its holder.

Interest sensitive whole life See **current assumption whole life**.

Intermediate nursing care Non-continuous skilled nursing care, commonly covered by long term care insurance policies.

Intermediation Process of policyowners making payments to an insurer for investment, ordinarily in the form of premiums, policy loan interest payments, or policy loan repayments.

Internal rate of return Measure of insurer profitability derived as that rate of interest that causes the present value of positive and negative cash flows to be zero.

Interpleader Payment of disputed insurance policy proceeds to a court for it to decide the rightful recipient.

Intestate Condition of dying without a valid will or having made a complete disposition of property and debt.

Intestate succession statute State law that determines the identity of heirs and their shares of distributed property of a person who dies intestate.

Investigative consumer report Consumer report in which information on a consumer's character, general reputation, personal characteristics, or mode of living is obtained from personal interviews with the consumer's neighbors, friends, or associates.

Investment asset risk Possibility of poor relative investment performance.

Investment bank Financial institution that brings together investors and firms that issue securities; some investment banking activities involve the underwriting of securities and some are strictly sales intermediary activities; may engage in the sale of life insurers' products.

Investment capital Income from financial and real assets.

Investment expenses Costs of making, processing, and protecting an insurer's investments.

Investment generation method Technique by which an insurer determines the interest crediting rate applicable to blocks of policies by allocating segmented investment portfolios to the blocks of policies, based on the timing of investment acquisitions.

Investment in the contract See **basis.**

Investment margin See **interest margin.**

Investor owned life insurance See **stranger-originated life insurance.**

Irrevocable beneficiary designation One that can be changed only with the beneficiary's express consent.

Irrevocable life insurance trust Living trust created to own and be beneficiary of life insurance that is not part of the grantor's gross estate yet with proceeds typically available to provide estate liquidity.

Irrevocable trust One in which the grantor permanently relinquishes ownership and control of donated property.

Issue and participation limit Underwriting limitation imposed by insurers as to the maximum amount of disability income coverage that they will issue to an applicant, such that the total of all monthly benefits does not exceed 85 percent or so of earned income for insureds with low incomes, grading downward to 65 percent or less for those with the highest incomes.

Issue date Sometimes included within life insurance contracts to indicate the date of policy issuance, with contestable and suicide periods sometimes running from this date. See also **policy date.**

Joint and last survivor annuity Life annuity whose payments are determined with reference to two (or more) annuitants, providing payments for as long as either of them lives.

Joint interest property Property owned jointly by two persons.

Joint life insurance Life insurance that promises to pay the face amount on the first death of two (or more) insureds. Also called **first-to-die life insurance.**

Joint tenancy with right of survivorship Joint interest property in which a decedent's interest passes automatically to survivor owners.

Judgment method In life insurance underwriting, process under which an insurance company relies on the combined judgment of underwriting, medical, and actuarial personnel to make underwriting decisions.

Juvenile endowment insurance Endowment insurance sold on the lives of juveniles, maturing at specified ages or events associated with a child's education, marriage, or independence.

Key employee disability insurance Disability income insurance purchased to indemnify a business for a decrease in earnings brought about by the disability of a key person.

Key employee insurance See **key person insurance.**

Key man insurance See **key person insurance.**

Key person insurance Life insurance purchased to indemnify a business for a decrease in earnings brought about by the death of a key person. Also called **key employee** and **key man insurance.**

Lapse Termination of a life insurance policy and the insurer's obligations after expiration of its grace period for failure to pay a premium necessary to maintain it in full effect.

Lapse-supported policy One in which later policy values rely on gains from policy lapses and surrenders to support those values.

Lapse-supported pricing Practice of pricing a product such that gains from lapses and surrenders are allocated to subsidize later policy benefits.

Last-to-die life insurance See **second to die life insurance**.

Law of large numbers Rule or theorem that holds that, as the number of units or trials becomes large, (1) the variation of actual from probable experience decreases and (2) each additional unit lowers the variation in outcome, *ceteris paribus*.

Law of mortality Concept first put forward by Benjamin Gompertz in 1825 that the death rate increases exponentially with age, as the body at first slowly then more rapidly deteriorates or fails. See also **Gompertz-Makeham law of mortality**.

Ledger pages See **tabular detail**.

Leeway clause See **basket clause**.

Legal capacity Competency of an individual or business entity to enter an enforceable contract.

Legislative history Testimony and documents considered by the U.S. Congress during its deliberations in enacting a law.

Lemons problem See **buyer ignorance**.

Level-premium whole life See **ordinary life**.

Life annuity Any annuity whose payments are contingent on whether the annuitant is alive.

Life annuity certain and continuous The combination of an annuity certain followed by a pure life annuity. Also called **life annuity with installments certain.**

Life annuity with installments certain See **life annuity certain and continuous**.

Life assurance See **life insurance**.

Life cycle hypothesis Normative explanation of consumer financial behavior proposing that individuals can be expected to maintain a more or less constant or increasing level of consumption over their lifetimes. Earned income will be low in the beginning and end stages of life and high during the middle stage of life.

Life insurance (1) Classification of insurance providing protection against the risks associated with mortality, longevity, and/or morbidity. (2) Type of insurance that pays a benefit to a named beneficiary on the death of the insured. Also called **life assurance**.

Life insurance company Corporation authorized under the law of its sovereign state to sell products that involve life and/or health contingencies.

Life settlement Sale of an existing life insurance policy in the secondary life insurance market. Also called **viatical**.

Life-care center See **continuing care center**.

Limited liability company Form of business combining features of partnerships and corporations, whose governance and owners' rights are defined more by the operating agreement of its members than by statute, featuring limited liability and flexibility in the tax status of participants.

Limited partnership One having at least one general partner and one or more limited partners who are not actively engaged in partnership management and who are liable for partnership obligations only to the extent of their investment in the partnership.

Limited-payment whole life insurance Type of whole life insurance with uniform premiums payable over some period shorter than the insured's entire possible lifetime, such as to age 65, after which the policy guarantees that no further premiums will be due.

Lingering implied authority Condition existing when a customer has no reason to believe that an agency relationship has ended.

Linton yield See **comparative interest rate**. Named after M. A. Linton of the Provident Mutual Life Insurance Company, who devised it.

Liquid withdrawal phase With a guaranteed lifetime withdrawal benefit provision or rider, the initial phase of the liquidation period when withdrawal amounts are made from the policy account value.

Liquidation Complete and final termination of an insolvent insurer's operations under provisions of state insurance law that permit the insurance regulator under court approval to entirely dispose of all assets and liabilities in accordance with state law.

Liquidation period Time during which annuity benefits are paid.

Liquidity risk (1) Category of risk specified by the *International Actuarial Association/ Association Actuarielle Internationale*, possibility of policyowners and borrowers making unexpected payments or withdrawals in response to changing interest rates. (2) Possibility that a security or asset transaction cannot be completed quickly enough to capture a gain or prevent a loss.

Living benefit feature/rider Life insurance policy provision or rider that promises to pay some or all of a policy's face amount prior to the insured's death if the insured suffers specified adverse health conditions. Also sometimes called **accelerated benefit rider**.

Living will Advance directive setting forth an individual's wishes as to the use of life sustaining measures in case of terminal illness, prolonged coma, or serious incapacitation.

Loading Amount added to a net premium to derive a gross premium and designed to cover an insurer's expenses of operation, taxes, profits, and a margin for contingencies.

Loading charge Policy element within an unbundled policy designed to cover some or all of an insurer's future expenses, taxes, profits (or surplus accumulations), and contingencies. Also called **expense charge**, **fee**, and **policy load**.

Long straddle Position established by an options speculator through the simultaneous purchase of a put and a call on the same asset.

Long term care Broad range of supportive medical, personal, and social services needed by individuals who are unable to meet their basic living needs for an extended period of time because of accident, illness, or frailty.

Long term care insurance Type of health insurance that pays a stated, usually monthly, benefit if incapacity of the insured prohibits him or her from engaging in specified activities of daily living.

Long term care insurance rider Attachment to a life insurance policy that promises to pay up to a specified (e.g., 2.0 percent) of the policy's face amount monthly if the insured is unable to perform specified activities of daily living because of accident, illness, or frailty, subject often to a maximum monthly payment amount.

Longevity annuity Single premium deferred annuity contract that guarantees future income payments based on current rates, typically commencing a decade or more into the future and providing no death benefit or surrender value during the accumulation period. Also called **deferred income annuity**.

Longevity risk Possibility of outliving one's financial resources.

Managing general agent Individual, partnership, or corporation that holds at least one direct brokerage contract with a life insurance company registered to do business in Canada.

Marginal costing Allocation of only direct expenses to specific product lines.

Margins Additional deaths added to a basic mortality table to develop a valuation mortality table.

Marital deduction Under federal tax law, the value of property left to a surviving spouse, which may be deducted from the gross estate in determining the taxable estate.

Market A system of exchange where goods or services are bought and sold.

Market conduct Practices associated with agents' and insurers' advertising, sales, counseling, and servicing activities.

Market consistent embedded value Present value of future profits attributable to in-force business and the value of surplus, based on market-derived asset and liability values (as opposed to statutory values).

Market failure See **market imperfection**.

Market imperfection Market-based (as opposed to governmental) deviation from the conditions for perfect competition, which leads to an inefficient allocation of resources. Also called **market failure**.

Market power Market failure in which one or a few sellers or buyers has the power to influence the price of a product or service. Conditions giving rise to market power include: (1) barriers to entry or exit, (2) economies of scale or scope, and (3) product differentiation/price discrimination.

Market risk (1) Category of risk specified by the *International Actuarial Association/Association Actuarielle Internationale*, possibility of volatile values and uncertainty in financial markets that can affect expected cash flows. (2) Possibility that an investment will decrease in value due to changes in market risk factors, the four standard such factors being stock prices, interest rates, foreign exchange rates, and commodity prices.

Market value Amount that an asset would realize in a current market sale.

Market value adjusted annuity Single premium deferred fixed annuity that permits contract owners to lock in a guaranteed interest rate over a specified maturity period, typically from three to 10 years. Also called a **market value annuity**.

Market value annuity See **market value adjusted annuity**.

Marketing mix Aggregation and coordination of product origination and development, distribution, compensation, and promotion of a specific product.

Marketing program Tactical plan that deals primarily with the product, price, distribution, and promotion strategies that a company will follow to reach its target markets and to satisfy their needs.

Material misrepresentation Inaccurate statement by a proposed insured or applicant that induces an insurer to issue a policy on more favorable terms or at a more favorable price than would have been the situation had the insurer possessed the accurate information.

Materiality Property of information or of a representation that has a natural tendency to influence or be capable of influencing the decision of a decision maker to which it was addressed. In an insurance context, quality of concealed or misrepresented information such that an insurer would have refused to issue requested insurance, charged a higher premium, or issued a more limited policy had it known the truth.

Mature Final performance event of a life insurance policy that terminates upon payment of the death or endowment benefit.

Mean reserve Value of a mid-year policy reserve, equal to the arithmetic average of the initial reserve and the terminal reserve for the year of valuation.

Medical expense insurance Health insurance that indemnifies the insured for costs incurred because of sickness or injury. Also called **health insurance**.

Medical Information Bureau Membership-sponsored corporation that collects personally identifiable information from and supplies such information to its members about individuals who have applied for life or health insurance from them and who have certain medical and other conditions that might affect their insurability.

Medical necessity Health care services that generally are considered to be reasonable, necessary, and appropriate based on accepted clinical standards of care.

Medical power of attorney Advance directive designating an individual, referred to as the individual's health care agent or proxy, to make medical decisions for the person if he or she is unable to do so.

Medicare U.S. social insurance program providing health insurance coverage for the elderly, defined as anyone age 65 and over.

Medicare Advantage Plan See **Medicare Part C**.

Medicare Part A Under Medicare, covers (1) hospital stays of up to 90 days subject to cost sharing provisions, with a lifetime reserve of 60 additional days and (2) up to 100 days in a skilled nursing facility, subject to daily cost sharing.

Medicare Part B Under Medicare, optional coverage subject to an additional premium payment that covers physician, nursing, and testing services as well as durable medical equipment such as mobility devices (e.g., canes or wheelchairs), prosthetic devices, and oxygen supply machines, subject to cost sharing.

Medicare Part C Under Medicare, optional coverage that provides the option of receiving Medicare benefits under private insurance plans for beneficiaries with both Part A and B coverages under which benefits are more liberal than standard Medicare benefits and may require supplemental premiums by policyowners. Also called **Medicare Advantage Plan**.

Medicare Part D Under Medicare, optional prescription drug coverage available only through private insurers and subject to an additional premium, providing benefits distinct from Medicare Parts A, B, and C.

Medicare supplemental insurance Individual health insurance policy that pays benefits not covered under Medicare.

Minimum continuation premium Specified minimum premium amount that must be paid under a universal life policy for its no lapse guarantee to remain in effect.

Minimum efficient scale Condition at which a firm's long-run average costs are at a minimum, with further growth yielding no additional efficiencies thus exhibiting decreasing returns to scale.

Minimum premium plan Partially self funded medical expense plan that has premium tax savings as the primary objective under which the employer deposits funds into a bank account to cover employee claims, with an insurer paying claims first from this account then from its own resources after a set limit.

Misrepresentation Giving of false information.

Misstatement of age provision Required life insurance policy provision stipulating that, if the insured's age is found to have been misstated, adjustment will be made in policy values to reflect the true age.

Modal premium Premium paid other-than-annually. Also called **fractional premium**.

Modified coinsurance Proportional reinsurance under which the ceding company pays the assuming company a proportionate part of the gross premium, as under the conventional coinsurance plan, but at year's end, the reinsurer pays to the ceding company a reserve adjustment equal to the net increase in the reserve during the year, less one year's interest on the total reserve held at the beginning of the year.

Modified endowment contract Life insurance policy entered into after June 20, 1988 that meets the *Internal Revenue Code* §7702 definition of life insurance but that fails to meet the seven-pay test and therefore is not entitled to favorable income tax treatment of distributions.

Modified endowment insurance Term used outside the U.S. describing endowment insurance that provides periodic payments of a set percentage of the insured amount over the policy term, as well as a maturity amount. See **modified endowment contract** for the different U.S. usage.

Modified life insurance Whole life insurance under which premiums are less than those of a comparable ordinary life policy during the first three to five policy years then somewhat higher thereafter.

Monopolistic competition Market condition under which a large number of firms produce similar but not identical products, which gives the firms an element of market power in the short run.

Monte Carlo method Technique of applying randomly selected values to variables in a deterministic cash flow model that is repeated thousands of times to produce a range of possible results and their probabilities.

Monthly debit ordinary insurance Ordinary insurance in the $5,000 to $25,000 range whose premiums can be collected by the agent.

Moral hazard Asymmetric information problem resulting from the presence of insurance causing a change the loss prevention behavior – called *ex ante* moral hazard – or loss minimization behavior – called *ex post* moral hazard – of the insured.

Morbidity risk Possibility that injury, illness, or incapacity creates unacceptable financial consequences for an individual.

Morbidity table Tabulation showing periodic probabilities and durations of incapacity, sickness, or injury by age (or age brackets) and often by other factors, such as smoking status.

Mortality margins Amounts added to underlying mortality rates to develop actual mortality charges under a policy.

Mortality risk (1) Possibility that one's death creates undesirable financial consequences for others. (2) Possibility that a budgeting and savings program designed to support an individual or family to and through retirement is not completed due to the death of a breadwinner during his or her working life.

Mortality table Tabulation showing yearly probabilities of death by age and usually other variables such as sex and smoking status.

Mortality table with projection Mortality table whose yearly probabilities of death decrease with each calendar year, often using projection factors.

Mortgage protection term Term life insurance whose face amount decreases to match the projected decreases in the principal amount owed under a mortgage loan.

Mudarabah In Islam, form of partnership for which one party provides the funds while another provides the expertise and management.

Multiple table extra method Most common method used to classify substandard life insurance risks, it divides them into groups according to their numerical ratings for which additional charges or premiums are levied.

Multiple-line exclusive agent Commissioned exclusive agent who sells the life and health and property and casualty insurance products of a single group of affiliated insurers.

Mutual life insurance company Limited liability corporation authorized to sell life insurance, which is operated for the benefit of its policyowners who have an ownership interest in the company.

Mutually exclusive Condition wherein the occurrence of one event precludes the possibility of the occurrence of another.

Narrative summary Component of the basic illustration required by the NAIC *Life Insurance Policy Illustration Model Regulation* to be provided to prospective policyowners, which contains information about the illustrated policy including descriptions of its benefits and mechanics, available riders and options, and identification and descriptions of column headings and key terms used in the illustrations.

Natural monopoly Condition that exists when efficiency increases (i.e., average costs decrease) over an industry's entire relevant output range and fixed costs are high and cannot be recouped on exit.

Necessaries Those things reasonably necessary for the condition in life of a minor, including necessities such as food, clothing, and shelter but also items appropriate for the minor's social position and financial status.

Negative externality Condition in which a firm's or individual's activities impose costs on others without their being compensated.

Net amount at risk Difference between the policy death benefit and the cash value or policy reserve.

Net cash surrender value Gross cash value less surrender charges and the value of any outstanding loans plus the cash value of any paid up additional insurance and dividends held on deposit.

Net GAAP reserves Policy reserves reduced by deferred acquisition costs under generally accepted accounting principles; similar to modified statutory reserves with both reflecting the need to ease surplus strain.

Net interest margin Difference between the return earned on investments and the interest credited on customer savings.

Net level premium Periodic premium equivalent to the net single premium, annualized over a specified premium payment period derived by dividing the net single premium by the present value of a life annuity due for the premium payment period.

Net level premium reserve Policy reserve established for certain life insurance policies in recognition that early net level premiums are intended to prefund future insurance charges, derived for any policy year as the present expected value of future benefits less the present expected value of future premiums.

Net payment cost index Cost comparison method required by the NAIC *Life Insurance Disclosure Model Regulation* intended to inform a prospective life insurance buyer of the estimated average annual net payment or outlay per $1,000 of insurance over selected time periods (ordinarily 10 and 20 years) taking into consideration only the policy's premiums and illustrated dividends, if any, and adjusting them for the time value of money.

Net rates Insurance rates calculated to recognize the probability of the insured event, the time value of money, and the benefits promised, with no allowance for loading.

Net single premium Present value of future benefits promised under a life insurance policy.

No lapse guarantee Rider attached to or provision of some universal life policies under which the insurer guarantees that the policy will not lapse for a stipulated period of time or for life if at least a minimum continuation premium is paid. Sometimes called **guaranteed minimum death benefit rider** if coverage is guaranteed for less than the whole of life.

Non-admitted assets Those that may not be counted in meeting an insurer's statutory solvency requirements.

Non-agency-building system See **independent distribution channel.**

Noncan See **noncancellable.**

Noncancellable Health insurance policy under which premiums are guaranteed and the insured has a contractual right to continue the policy by the timely payment of premiums, usually to a specified age such as 65.

Noncontributory plan Employee benefit plan in which only the employer makes contributions toward plan costs.

Non-disabling injury benefit Provision within some disability income insurance policies that will pay up to a specific sum (e.g., one quarter of the monthly benefit) to reimburse the insured for medical expenses incurred for treatment of an injury that did not result in total disability.

Nondiversifiable risk That applicable to an entire market or class of assets or liabilities, which cannot be reduced by diversification. Also called **systematic risk**.

Nonforfeiture factor Adjusted premium when it is amortized over a period shorter or at an uneven rate than that permitted.

Nonforfeiture options Required options usually stated within the nonforfeiture provision, which are activated automatically on policy lapse or can be elected by the policyowner who chooses to terminate his or her policy. The three options ordinarily provided are (1) cash – the policy's net cash surrender value is paid in cash (e.g., check) to the owner, (2) reduced paid up insurance – the policy's net cash surrender value is applied as a net single premium to purchase a reduced amount of paid up insurance of the same type as the basic policy, and (3) extended term insurance – the policy's net cash surrender value is applied as a net single premium to purchase paid up term insurance for the policy face amount less policy loans for whatever duration that value will carry the policy.

Nonforfeiture provision Required provision of cash value life insurance policies stating the nonforfeiture options available if the policy is terminated or lapses and giving the mortality table, rate of interest, and method used in calculating the values of those options.

Nonguaranteed policy elements Those policy elements that are not guaranteed and that the insurer may increase or decrease as long as policy guarantees are respected, commonly including mortality and loading charges, interest crediting rate, dividends, and sometimes the policy premium. Also called **current assumptions**.

Nonguaranteed renewable health insurance Policy under which the insurer may unilaterally refuse to renew it, sometimes subject to restrictions.

Nonlife insurance Insurance that involves other than life or health contingencies; ordinarily insurance against property and liability losses. Also called **property/casualty insurance** and **general insurance**.

Nonmedical insurance Life or health insurance that can be written without a medical or paramedical examination, although medical questions usually are included in the application and the insurer reserves the right to request an examination.

Nonparticipating Insurance policies that are not entitled to receive dividends declared by an insurer. Also called **without bonus** policies.

Nonparticipating provision Within nonparticipating life insurance policies, provision stating that the policy is not eligible to participate in any divisible surplus and/or that the policy does not pay dividends.

Nonproportional reinsurance Reinsurance under which risk is shared on aggregate losses attributable to a specified group of policies and not to individual policies.

Nonqualified deferred compensation plan Contractual arrangement between an employer and an employee under which compensation for services rendered to an organization is postponed, usually until retirement.

Normal profit (1) Opportunity cost of enterprise. (2) Minimal profit that firms must acquire to remain in operation. (3) Maximum profit achievable in a perfectly competitive market.

Notional amount Value of capital hedged.

Numeric summary Component of the basic illustration required by the NAIC *Life Insurance Policy Illustration Model Regulation* to be provided to prospective policyowners, which is a one-page synopsis of illustrated policy values for at least policy years five, 10, and 20 and at age 70, if applicable, based on guaranteed policy elements, current nonguaranteed elements, and a midpoint set of assumptions.

Numerical rating system In life insurance underwriting, process under which an insurance company relies on a system of debits and credits representing adverse and positive expected marginal mortality rates to derive an expected mortality classification for a proposed insured.

One-way buy/sell agreement Arrangement under which the sole owner of a business obligates his or her estate to sell and another party is obligated to purchase the owner's interest on his or her death.

Operating capital That required to meet expenses, fund required reserves, and pay expected claims.

Operating expenses Costs incurred by an insurer in normal business operations, other than investment operations, usually recorded as acquisition, development, maintenance, and overhead expenses.

Operational risk Category of risk specified by the *International Actuarial Association/ Association Actuarielle Internationale*, possibility of internal or external failure of people, processes, or systems to function as intended.

Option buy/sell agreement Arrangement under which an owner of an interest in a business obligates his or her estate to sell and another party has the option but not obligation to purchase that interest on the owner's death.

Ordinary insurance Individually issued life, health, and retirement coverages, other than industrial insurance.

Ordinary life insurance Type of whole life insurance with uniform premiums payable for the entirety of the insured's life. Also called **level-premium whole life.**

Original-age conversion Exercise of a term life policy's conversion feature via a retroactive conversion, with the whole life or other cash value policy bearing the original issue date and premium rate that would have been paid had the cash value policy been taken out originally instead of a term policy.

Out-of-network provider Health care services offered through a provider not affiliated with the patient's health maintenance organization or preferred provider organization, which are reimbursed in cash by the network plan.

Out-of-pocket maximum Specified maximum incurred amount of medical expenses (generally total expenses less deductibles and coinsurance paid by the participant) that is to be paid by the insured.

Overhead expense insurance See **business overhead expense insurance**.

Overloan protection rider Guarantees that a policy will not lapse if policy loans equal or exceed the policy account value.

Override commission Compensation paid to a general agency based on an agency's first-year and renewal premiums.

Own occupation With disability income insurance, clause that deems an insured to be totally disabled if he or she cannot perform the major duties of his or her regular occupation, which is the one in which the insured was engaged at the time disability began.

Owners' equity See **capital and surplus**.

Ownership provision Life insurance policy provision stating that the policyowner can exercise all rights under the policy, unless a beneficiary is named irrevocably.

Paid-up Condition under which a policy is guaranteed to remain in effect with no further premium payments due, in accordance with the terms of the contract.

Partial disability benefit Reduced disability income benefit payable if an insured has returned to work on a limited basis after a period of compensable totally disability, commonly equal to 50 percent of the monthly total disability benefit, payable for up to six months.

Participating Insurance policies that are entitled to receive dividends declared by the insurer. Also called **with bonus** policies.

Participation Retrospective allocation to policyowners of favorable experience that develops when mortality, investment, and expense assumptions used to calculate premiums is more than sufficient to provide policy benefits.

Participation provision Required provision of participating life insurance policies stating that the policy is eligible to participate in any divisible surplus. Also called **distributable surplus provision**.

Participation rate Under an equity indexed universal life policy or annuity, the proportion of the index performance rate that is counted in deriving the growth rate.

Partnership Voluntary association of two or more individuals or entities for the purpose of conducting a business for profit as co-owners.

Payor benefit Decreasing term rider insuring the life of the premium payor under a policy insuring the life of a juvenile, which pays a death benefit earmarked to cover policy premiums remaining until the juvenile attains a certain age.

Pension Benefit Guaranty Corporation Independent agency of the U.S. government created by the *Employee Retirement Income Security Act* to insure the benefits of participants of defined benefit pension plans against employer default.

Pension maximization strategy Election by a retiree of a single life income option in lieu of a joint and survivor life income option, using the income difference to purchase life insurance on the annuitant's life for the benefit of the survivor.

Perfectly competitive market In economic theory, one with no imperfections and, therefore, in which societal welfare is maximized.

Permanent disability Defined under a disability income policy and waiver of premium features/riders as any total disability lasting longer than the waiting period specified in the policy, often six months.

Permanent life insurance See **cash value life insurance**.

Persistency Percentage of a block of life insurance policies not terminated by lapse or surrender during a given time period.

Personal insurance (1) Any insurance purchased by individuals for non-commercial purposes. (2) Life, accident, and other insurance covering a person, in contrast to insurance covering property and liability losses.

Personal-producing general agent Independent commissioned insurance producer who generally works alone, is not housed in one of an insurer's field offices, engages primarily in the sales of new policies, holds contracts with several insurers, and usually focuses on personal production as opposed to the recruitment and management of career agents.

Planned premium Amount of periodic premium that the owner of a universal life policy intends to pay and instructs the insurer to bill.

Point-of-service preferred provider organization Hybrid preferred provider organization under which beneficiaries typically are treated by an in-network primary care physician who may make referrals to in-network or out-of-network specialists as the beneficiary chooses.

Point-to-point method Equity index annuity indexing method that is based on the simple difference in the index value at the beginning and end of the index term.

Policy date Date appearing on an insurance policy that often determines period of suicide exclusion and period of incontestability. See also **issue date.**

Policy elements The pricing components of life insurance policies, including premiums, benefits, values, credits, and charges.

Policy loan provision Cash value life insurance policy provision requiring the insurer to make requested loans to policyowners on the sole security of the policy's cash value.

Policy reserves Liabilities representing the present amount that, with future premiums and interest earned, is expected to cover future benefit payments under existing policies.

Policy Summary Document required to be provided to prospective life insurance buyers by the NAIC *Life Insurance Disclosure Model Regulation*, intended to help prospective purchasers understand the specific policy being considered for purchase and which contains illustrated and guaranteed policy values along with other policy information.

Policy value See **cash value**.

Policy value provision Provision of nonparticipating life insurance policies that contain nonguaranteed policy elements, which explains the nature of the policy's nonguaranteed elements and the determination of cost of insurance charges, loading charges, and interest crediting rates, with guaranteed maximum charges and, for non-variable contracts, the guaranteed minimum interest crediting rate. Also called **account value provision**.

Policyholder See **policyowner**.

Policyowner Person who has the contractual right to exercise all policy options and with whom the insurer deals. Also called **policyholder**.

Pooled rates Used for small group cases, method of rating under which a uniform rate is applied to all groups; no experience rating.

Pooling of resources Rule that, the larger the number of fairly priced exposure units in an insurance pool, the greater the likelihood that the insurer's premium receipts and investment income will be sufficient to pay all claims that arise during the coverage period, *ceteris paribus*.

Portability Under federal estate tax law, allows any unused exemption amount following the death of a spouse to be added to the exemption amount of the surviving spouse on his or her death.

Portfolio average method Technique by which an insurer determines the interest crediting rate applicable to policies based on the investment return of its entire general account investment portfolio.

Positive externality Condition in which a firm's or individual's activities carry benefits for others without their having to pay for them.

Postmortem dividend Divisible surplus payable on the death of an insured in an amount in proportion to the part of the policy year of death for which premiums have been paid or as a one-time distribution of surplus, mainly on term insurance, in lieu of dividends on each policy anniversary while the insured was living.

Precertification Prior approval of procedures, hospital admission, and length of stay that stipulates benefits will be paid.

Predatory pricing Lowering of prices to unprofitable levels to weaken or eliminate competition with the idea of raising prices after competitors are driven from the market.

Preexisting condition With disability income insurance, exclusion of benefits, commonly during the first two policy years, for any loss that results from a condition that the insured misrepresented or failed to disclose in the insurance application.

Preferred provider organization Health care intermediary between sponsors and physicians and other health care providers who agree to provide services at discounted rates.

Premium provision Required life insurance policy provision stating that, for fixed-premium policies, premiums are due and payable as indicated elsewhere in the policy, and, for flexible premium policies, that premiums may be paid at any time, subject to insurer minimums and tax-constrained maximums. The provision also may state that premiums can be paid monthly, quarterly, semi-annually, or annually by check, automatic draft, or electronic funds transfer.

Premium solve Value solve measure that solves for the premium necessary to support a particular death benefit amount, pattern, and duration and, if applicable, attainment of a target cash surrender value by a specified policy year.

Premium waiver feature/rider See **waiver of premium feature/rider**.

Preneed funeral insurance Whole life insurance that pays death proceeds specified by the details of the goods and services to be delivered by a funeral provider.

Present interest Interest in property such that an individual has immediate possession and enjoyment of property.

Present value Value today of a future payment or payments discounted for interest.

Presumptive disability With disability income insurance, clause that deems an insured to be totally disabled if sickness or injury results in the loss of the sight of both eyes, the hearing of both ears, the power of speech, or the use of any two limbs, irrespective of whether the insured can work.

Price discrimination Offering of identical products at different prices to different groups of customers.

Price elasticity Percentage change in demand for a good or service resulting from a given percentage change in price.

Price taker Buyers and sellers that cannot influence the price of a product; trait of a perfectly competitive market.

Primary insurer See **direct writing insurer**.

Primary life insurance market Market in which new life insurance policies are bought and sold.

Principal amount Value of original investment. Also called **principal**.

Principal sum benefit Lump sum amount payable under some disability income and other insurance policies if the insured's death results from an accident.

Private letter ruling U.S. Treasury Department interpretation of a specific fact situation deemed not to be of general interest.

Private placement The negotiation of the terms of a loan offering directly between the borrower and the buyer, in contrast to securities traded on public exchanges.

Private placement life insurance Individually tailored variable life insurance designed specifically for and available only to qualified investors and not subject to *Securities and Exchange Commission* registration requirements.

Probate property That which passes by will or state intestacy laws.

Probationary period Period of time (usually one to six months) after being hired when the employee becomes eligible to participate in an employee benefit plan.

Producer See **insurance agent**.

Product differentiation Condition occurring because product quality, service, location, reputation, or other attributes of one firm's products are preferred by some buyers over rivals' products.

Product homogeneity Condition in which competing products are perfect substitutes in the minds of buyers.

Product implementation Final determination of rates, values, and other policy elements; the design of policy and application forms; the filing of these forms with regulatory authorities; the creation of supporting marketing materials and administrative systems that facilitate effective distribution and administration of the product; and the actual introduction of the product.

Product life cycle Theoretical marketing construct that describes the approximate key turning points and stages in the life of a product from introduction to decline. The four stages of the product life cycle are introduction, growth, maturity, and decline.

Product margin Total of expense, mortality, and interest margins.

Professional reinsurer Insurer that specializes in writing reinsurance.

Profit account Mechanism for capturing accumulated book profits under the accumulated book profits model.

Profit margin Measure of insurer profitability calculated as the present value of profits divided by the present value of premiums.

Profit-sharing plan Noncontributory qualified defined contribution retirement plan that does not require but allows annual contributions by the employer.

Program sales Sales efforts targeted at a limited, particular need that can be addressed with a particular product.

Projection factors Values applied to static mortality tables to account for estimated future changes in death probabilities.

Property Ownership rights of possession, control, and disposition in property, which can be real property (ownership rights associated with land and objects permanently attached to land) or personal property (ownership rights in movable property or choses in action).

Property/casualty insurance See **nonlife insurance**.

Proportional reinsurance Reinsurance under which the assuming and ceding company share risk on a per policy basis.

Proprietary life and health insurance Life and health insurance targeted and priced for a specific market and available to be sold exclusively by a cohesive group of agents.

Prospective bonus Provision under some cash value policies providing that, after a predefined time period, future interest crediting rates will be augmented by a bonus rate.

Protection universal life See **death benefit universal life**.

Provider Individual or organization providing health care services.

Provider network Health care services offered through providers affiliated with a patient's health maintenance organization or preferred provider organization.

Public good Good or service exhibiting a free rider problem or an extensive positive externality.

Public interest theory of regulation Normative economic theory holding that government regulation should be practiced in the public interest, correcting market imperfections and promoting allocative efficiency and social welfare.

Pure endowment Promise to pay a maturity amount if the insured is living at the end of a specified period, with nothing paid in case of prior death or surrender.

Put Option to sell.

Qualified family-owned business interest Under federal tax law, any trade or business with its principal place of business in the U.S., which is owned at least 50 percent by one family, 70 percent by two families, or 90 percent by three families provided the decedent's family owned at least 30 percent.

Qualified plan Retirement plan that satisfies the requirements of the U.S. *Employee Retirement Income Security Act* and *Internal Revenue Code*. The main requirements are (1) the plan must be written, legally binding, and communicated to participants in accordance with regulations; (2) participants' benefits must vest according to schedules specifying participants' lengths of service; and (3) plans must not discriminate in favor of highly compensated employees.

Qualified purchaser Under *Securities and Exchange Commission* requirements, individual or family organization with net investments of $5.0 million or more.

Qualified terminable interest property Under federal tax law, property qualifying for the marital deduction but for which the surviving spouse's interest terminates on death.

Quota share Proportional reinsurance whereby premiums and claims are shared between ceding and assuming companies. The premium share is adjusted to reflect the direct writer's expenses.

Rabbi trust One under which trust assets remain subject to the claims of the employer's general creditors if the employer becomes insolvent, but, in the absence of such claims, trust assets must be used solely to provide promised deferred compensation benefits.

Radix With a mortality table, arbitrary number of persons assumed to be alive at the youngest age for which death rates are shown.

Ratchet guaranteed minimum death benefit Type of guaranteed minimum death benefit under which a new minimum death benefit is set periodically or set to equal premiums paid accumulated at a stated interest rate, but never an amount less than the highest previously calculated amount.

Rating agency Business that provides commentary and opinions about and ratings of the ability of financial firms to meet their obligations.

Rating agency capital Amount of surplus capital required to receive the quality rating an insurer desires from a rating agency.

Reasonable expectations doctrine Viewed by many legal authorities as an extension of the *contra proferentum* doctrine, requires that the objectively reasonable expectations of applicants and intended beneficiaries regarding the terms of insurance contracts be honored even if policy provisions negated those expectations.

Rebating Practice by an agent (or insurer) of giving something of value (e.g., a portion of the agent's commission) not specified in the insurance contract to an applicant in return for the purchase of a policy.

Recurrent periods of disability With disability income insurance, provision that a new period of total disability will be considered to be one continuous period of disability unless each period is separated by a recovery of six months or more.

Reentry feature Provision within some term life policies that allows for the payment of premiums lower than guaranteed renewal premiums and sometimes lower than indeterminate renewal premiums if the insured can demonstrate that he or she meets continuing insurability criteria.

Referral Customer of an individual intermediary arising from the recommendation of another person that the customer establish a relationship with the intermediary.

Regulation Government agency's interpretation for proper implementation of a law.

Regulatory arbitrage Shifting of activities within a financial group to take advantage of different regulatory approaches in different financial sectors; e.g., insurance and banking.

Regulatory capital Legally required amount of reserves and risk-based capital and the implicit premium income necessary to fund the reserves.

Rehabilitation Provision in state insurance law that permits the insurance regulator to seek court approval to become an insurer's receiver and be granted title to its assets and the authority to carry on its business until the insurer either is returned to private management after the grounds for issuing the order have been removed or is liquidated.

Rehabilitation benefit Provision within some disability income insurance policies that generally allows a specific sum (e.g., 12 times the monthly benefit) to cover costs not paid by other insurance or public funding if the insured enrolls in a formal retraining program that will help him or her return to work.

Reinstatement clause Required life insurance policy provision stating that the policyholder has the right to reinstate a lapsed policy under certain conditions, the two most important of which are furnishing evidence of insurability and paying past due premiums or charges.

Reinsurance Insurance for insurers written by an assuming company to hedge a direct insurer's portfolio of underwriting or financial risks.

Reinsurance premiums Premiums paid for reinsurance.

Reinsurer Professional reinsurer or a direct writing insurer that writes reinsurance

Reinvestment risk Possibility that policyowners will repay loans and increase flexible premiums when interest rates fall; occurs when insurers' interest crediting rates are higher than those policyowners otherwise generally would earn.

Renewable Right of the policyowner to continue an insurance policy for one or more specified periods merely by paying the billed premium. For life insurance, the premium ordinarily increases at each renewal.

Replacement Purchase of a new life insurance policy and, in connection with that purchase, termination of an existing policy or values extracted from it.

Replacement cost Under federal tax law applicable to gifts of paid up insurance, its fair market value deemed to equal the single premium that an insurance company would charge for a comparable contract issued at the insured's/annuitant's attained age.

Representation Statement made to induce an insurer to accept a risk.

Repudiation Express act of voiding a contract.

Reserve Actuarially determined amount representing an insurer's liability attaching to the payment of future policy benefits. Assumptions used in the reserve calculation may be statutory (SAP reserves), accounting (GAAP reserves), or economic (economic reserves) depending on context. Also called **reserve capital**.

Reserve capital See **reserve**.

Reset provision Feature under a no lapse guarantee universal life policy that permits the guaranteed duration or the amount of guaranteed coverage to be reset based on future adjusted specified premiums.

Residual disability benefit Provision within some disability income insurance policies providing for a reduced monthly benefit in proportion to the insured's loss of income resulting from disability when he or she has returned to work at reduced earnings.

Respite care Temporary, short term placement of an individual needing long term care in a long term care facility for purposes of providing temporary relief for family members providing care in the individual's home or having someone stay with the individual in his or her home temporarily. Commonly covered by long term care insurance policies up to a percentage (e.g., 50 percent) of the full nursing home benefit.

Retained asset account Option granted beneficiaries to have death benefit payments retained in an interest bearing account on which drafts may be written.

Retaliatory tax law Requires out-of-state insurers to pay the higher of the tax due using their home state's and the host state's laws.

Retention Dollar amount or percentage of an insurance policy's risk that a ceding company retains for its own account.

Retirement income insurance Endowment insurance commonly used in insured pension plans under which the amount payable at death is the greater of the face amount or cash value.

Retirement tail risk Possibility of having insufficient resources at retirement to cover an individual's entire life span.

Retroactive bonus Provision under some cash value policies providing that, after a predefined time period (e.g., 10 years), a bonus interest rate will be retroactively applied to policy cash values for all previous periods.

Retrocession Ceding of an assuming company's reinsurance to another assuming company.

Retrocessionaire Insurer or reinsurer accepting a retrocession.

Retrospective premium arrangement Within employee benefit plans, type of experience rating providing for lower initial premiums than normal but with the insurer reserving the right to collect additional premiums at the end of the contract period to cover unexpected claims and expenses.

Return on assets Measure of insurer profitability calculated as the ratio of profits to the assets that result from a product for a set period of time.

Return on equity Measure of insurer profitability calculated as the ratio of profits to surplus generated for a product for a set period of time.

Return on investment Measure of insurer profitability calculated as the ratio of the present value of profits to the initial surplus employed to support the product for a set period of time.

Return-of-premium feature/rider Increasing term insurance provision or rider stipulating that, if the insured dies within a set number of years (e.g., 20 years) from the policy issue date, the death benefit will be augmented by an amount equal to the sum of all premiums paid to that point.

Return-of-premium term policy/rider (1) Increasing cash value feature of a term or other policy that promises to provide a cash value at the end of a term of from 10 to 30 years in an amount equal to the sum of premiums paid for the policy if the insured survives to that period. (2) Under a disability income insurance policy, rider providing a benefit amount after a specified number of policy years equal to the sum of premiums paid if no claims have been made for benefits.

Revenue ruling U.S. Treasury Department interpretation of a specific fact situation deemed to be of general interest.

Reversionary bonus In U.K. and Commonwealth terminology, the use of divisible surplus (bonus) to increase a policy's face amount (sum assured) and its surrender value.

Revocable beneficiary designation One that may be changed by the policyowner without the beneficiary's consent.

Revocable trust One that may be altered or terminated by the grantor and ownership of the corpus regained.

Rider Amendment attached to an insurance policy that provides supplemental benefits or options, usually requiring an additional premium payment.

Right-of-return policy provision Required life insurance policy provision that affords its policyowner an unconditional right to return a policy to the insurer within a certain number of days of its receipt, such as 10, and to receive a refund of all premiums paid. Also called a **free look provision**.

Risk capital Unencumbered funds set aside to pay unexpected claims and benefits, which are expected to remain idle and is necessary to provide confidence to policyowners and their advocates (regulators and rating agencies) that an insurer will remain solvent under reasonably extreme circumstances.

Risk class See **insurance pool**.

Risk discount rate Hurdle rate sometimes selected for application to the policy account in the accumulated book profits model, which is the rate that market investments of comparable risk command.

Risk pool See **insurance pool**.

Risk premium Additional amount that rational risk-averse individuals will pay to purchase insurance in excess of the expected value of the loss.

Risk-adjusted return on capital Project's net economic income divided by its economic investment.

Rollover Transfer of funds from one qualified retirement plan to another.

Roth Individual Retirement Account Individual Retirement Account for which contributions are not deductible but whose investment returns and distributions are received tax free, subject to limitations.

Ruin When total insured losses exceed total premiums and investment returns received by an insurance pool.

Ruin risk See **default risk**.

Run Policyowners or depositors demanding their money at once. Can lead to systemic risk.

Safety margin See **expense margin**.

Savings risk Possibility that unexpected expense, a lack of planning, or carelessness impedes or interrupts an individual's planned conversion of human capital to investment capital.

Secondary life insurance market Market in which existing life insurance policies are bought and sold.

Second-to-die life insurance Life insurance that promises to pay the face amount on the death of the second (or last) insured to die. Also called **survivorship life insurance** and **last-to-die life insurance**.

Section 1035 exchange *Internal Revenue Code* provision permitting a tax free exchange of certain types of life insurance policies and annuities for others. Also called a **1035 exchange**.

Section 162 plan See **executive bonus plan**.

Section 2503 (b) and (c) trusts One established for the benefit of a minor, which, by meeting certain requirements, permits a gift of a future interest to qualify for the annual exclusion.

Section 303 stock redemption *Internal Revenue Code* provision permitting an income-tax-free redemption of shares of stock by qualifying estates in an amount up to federal and state death taxes due, funeral expenses, and estate administration expenses.

Secular trust One under which trust assets are not subject to the claims of the employer's general creditors.

Securitization Selling of asset-backed bonds that will be repaid regularly from the cash flows of specified assets backing the securities.

Segment term Under an equity indexed universal life policy, the specified duration associated with each new transfer of funds into the index account, often from one to three years in length.

Select and ultimate mortality table Mortality table that shows probabilities of death by both age and duration of insurance.

Select mortality table Mortality table showing probabilities of death by age, duration of insurance for newly insured lives only, and other possible criteria such as sex of insureds.

Self funded plan Employee benefit plan under which large employers pay claims in cash as they arise with no funding via commercial insurance. Also called **self insured plan**.

Self insured plan See **self funded plan**.

Semi-endowment insurance Endowment insurance that pays upon survival one-half the sum payable on death during the endowment period.

Separate account Mutual fund-type account maintained by a life insurer to receive premiums and other payments from its contract holders who bear 100 percent of the investment risk.

Settlement options Provision under a life insurance policy that grants policyowners and beneficiaries the right to elect to have death and usually surrender value proceeds paid under modes of settlement other than a lump cash sum, including (1) interest option under which proceeds remain with the company and only the earned interest is paid to the beneficiary, (2) fixed period option under which proceeds are systematically liqui-dated as an annuity certain over a defined period of months or years, (3) fixed amount option under which proceeds are systematically liquidated as an annuity certain via fixed, periodic amounts, and (4) life income options under which death proceeds are systemati-cally liquidated as a pure life annuity, life annuity with refund feature, or life annuity with period certain, based on a single life or joint and survivor life configuration.

Settlor See **grantor**.

Seven-pay test Determines whether a life insurance policy is a modified endowment contract, which it is if cumulative amounts paid under the contract at any time during the first seven contract years exceeds the cumulative amount that would have been paid had the policy's annual premium equaled the net level premium for a seven-pay life policy of the same type, using certain required assumptions.

Shadow account Used for ensuring that a no lapse guarantee is in effect; derived from a modified universal life account value calculation using a set of guaranteed policy ele-ments different from the set applicable to the regular account value calculation.

Shared benefit long term care Long term care insurance policy insuring two lives with the total benefit available for one or both lives.

Short straddle Position established by an options speculator through the simultaneous sale of a put and a call on the same asset.

Sickness With disability income insurance, sickness or disease that first manifests itself while the policy is in force.

Silo risk Segregation of mortality, investment, and asset/liability risk from each other, with each having its particular risk management methods.

Simple interest Interest credited or paid on the original or unpaid principal balance amount only and not on the interest itself.

Simple probability Likelihood of the occurrence of an event calculated by dividing the number of events satisfying a stipulated condition (e.g., death) by the total number of events or exposures (e.g., lives).

Single life annuity Life annuity whose payments are determined with reference to one annuitant only.

Single market Principal existential purpose of the European Union, with the objective of presenting the union as a common entity externally and to maintaining nondiscrim-inatory relations between its members. Characterized by the free circulation of goods, capital, people, and services within the union.

Single premium deferred annuity Fixed or variable annuity contract purchased with a single premium, whose benefit payments are deferred until annuitization following the accumulation period.

Single premium immediate annuity Fixed or variable annuity contract purchased with a single premium, whose benefit payments commence one period (e.g., month) later.

Single premium whole life insurance Limited-payment whole life insurance under which only one premium payment is made.

Skilled nursing care Highest level, 24-hour nursing care ordered by a physician and pro-vided by a registered nurse, licensed practical nurse, or licensed therapist. Commonly covered by long term care insurance policies.

Skip person Under federal tax law, heir beyond those of the immediately following generation.

Social insurance substitute See **social insurance supplement**.

Social insurance supplement Supplemental disability income insurance benefit that approximates the amount an insured might reasonably expect to receive in Social Security disability benefits but which is payable only if the insured meets the policy's definition of total disability and does not qualify for any social insurance disability income benefit. Also called **social insurance substitute**.

Sole proprietorship Unincorporated business owned by an individual who usually also manages it.

Special agent Agent whose powers are limited, extending only to acts necessary to accomplish particular transactions for which it is engaged.

Special power of appointment Right to dispose of property to anyone except the person holding the power.

Special surplus funds Voluntarily earmarked surplus designated to meet general contingencies.

Specific risk See **diversifiable risk**.

Specified disease insurance policy Individual health insurance policy that pays up to substantial maximums solely for the treatment of a disease named in the policy, including most typically cancer and heart disease. Also sometimes called **dread disease insurance policy**.

Specified premium test Used for ensuring that a no lapse guarantee is in effect; if actual premiums paid equal or exceed a cumulative minimum premium requirement to date, the guarantee remains in effect.

Spendthrift trust clause Provision within a trust or life insurance settlement option stating that the beneficiary has no power to assign, transfer, or otherwise encumber installment payments to which he or she is entitled.

Spinlife See **stranger-originated life insurance**.

Split dollar life insurance Arrangement under which one party, commonly an employer, pays portions of the premiums of a life insurance policy insuring another party, commonly an employee, with policy benefits and premium payments shared between the two parties.

Split option Under a survivorship policy, option to divide the policy into two individual policies of the same generic type as the survivorship policy, one on the life of each insured life, under specified circumstances such as divorce.

Spousal lifetime access trust Irrevocable life insurance trust that can preserve the favorable estate tax treatment of insurance death proceeds while allowing indirect access to policy cash values.

Spread See **interest margin**.

Spread loss reinsurance Nonproportional reinsurance designed to smooth claim volatility experience of a ceding company.

Staff model health maintenance organization One with its own health care providers.

Stand alone living benefit See **contingent deferred annuity**.

Standard nonforfeiture value method Descriptor indicating that nonforfeiture values are higher than required minimums because of the use of nonforfeiture factors.

Stated value basis With any insurance policy, stated policy benefit payable without regard to the actual economic loss suffered. Also called **valued policy**.

Static mortality table Mortality table whose probabilities of death do not change as a function of the calendar year.

Stock life insurance company Limited liability corporation authorized to sell life insurance, which is owned by and operated for the benefit of shareholders who seek an adequate return on the capital they risk.

Stock redemption buy/sell agreement Entity buy/sell agreement under which the corporation is to purchase a deceased owner's shares.

Stop loss reinsurance (1) Reinsurance that reimburses an employer for large claims incurred in a self funded medical expense plan. (2) Nonproportional reinsurance that reimburses a ceding company for aggregate claims above a fixed amount, a percentage of premiums, or a percentage of expected mortality.

Stranger-originated life insurance Policy purchased with the intent at inception that it will be sold in the secondary life insurance market to those with no insurable interest, almost always involving material misrepresentations. Also called **stranger-owned life insurance, investor-owned life insurance,** and **spinlife**.

Stranger-owned life insurance See **stranger-originated life insurance**.

Stress test (1) In life insurer risk management, method of applying a set of extreme assumptions to a deterministic model to ascertain financial results under a limited set of economic scenarios. (2) In life insurance policy evaluations, running illustrations with reduced crediting rates and/or at less favorable charges to provide an idea of potential downside policy performance.

Structured settlement annuity Single premium deferred annuity contract issued by a life insurer on behalf of a defendant under which the plaintiff (the injured party) in a personal injury lawsuit receives periodic payments rather than a lump sum payment.

Subrogation Transfer of one party's legal rights against a third party to another.

Subrogation provision Within comprehensive medical plans, provision that gives the employer or insurer that pays a claim the rights that a covered employee or insured might have against a third party.

Substandard Higher-than-average mortality or morbidity risk classifications.

Substandard risks Insureds who are expected or do exhibit higher than average mortality or morbidity experience.

Substantial risk of forfeiture Condition under which deferred income is not considered constructively received because either (1) it is subject to the claims of the employer's creditors or (2), if the employee's rights are nonforfeitable, the deferred compensation agreement was entered into before the compensation was earned and the employer's promise to pay is unsecured.

Suicide clause Optional life insurance policy provision that excludes payment of claims if the cause of the insured's death is suicide occurring within the first two policy years.

Sum assured. See **face amount**.

Summary of operations Insurer's income statement providing a summary of income and its disposition.

Supplemental executive retirement plan Nonqualified retirement plan providing retirement benefits to selected employees only.

Supplemental illustration Optional tabulation under the NAIC *Life Insurance Policy Illustration Model Regulation* that may be provided to prospective policyowners, which is intended to augment the data and information contained in the basic illustration.

Supplier induced demand With regard to paying for health care services, the incentive of reimbursable providers to recommend and perform more health services than they would in the absence of insurance.

Surgical expense benefits Medical expense benefits for surgery paid either (1) in accordance with a schedule particular to the insurer or plan, which states amounts payable per procedure, or (2) on a usual and customary basis.

Surplus See **surplus capital**.

Surplus capital Difference between the values of an insurer's assets and liabilities as defined by a particular accounting convention.

Surplus strain Condition that occurs when a life insurance policy is surrendered and its asset share is less than its cash surrender value.

Surrender Voluntary termination of a life insurance policy by its owner for its cash surrender value.

Surrender charge Amount assessed against a policy's cash (account) value as a type of penalty for early policy termination. Also called **back-end load**.

Surrender cost index Cost comparison method required by the NAIC *Life Insurance Disclosure Model Regulation* intended to inform a prospective life insurance buyer of the estimated average annual net cost per $1,000 of insurance over selective time periods (ordinarily 10 and 20 years) taking into consideration the policy's premiums, illustrated dividends or other nonguaranteed policy values (if any), and cash surrender values and adjusting these values for the time value of money.

Surrender gain Condition that occurs when a life insurance policy is surrendered and its asset share is greater than its cash surrender value.

Surrender value See **cash surrender value**.

Surrender value internal rate of return Cost comparison method that solves for the interest rate that causes accumulated scheduled premiums (net of dividends, if appropriate) at selected policy durations to equal that duration's cash surrender value.

Surrender value solve Value solve measure that solves for the cash surrender value that a particular premium and death benefit amount, pattern, and duration will develop.

Survivorship clause Condition elected by the owner of a life insurance policy under which the beneficiary must survive the insured by a fixed period, such as 60 days, after the insured's death to be entitled to the proceeds. Also called a **time clause**.

Survivorship life insurance See **second-to-die life insurance**.

Systematic risk See **nondiversifiable risk**.

Systemic risk Possibility that, because of linkages and interdependences, the difficulties of a financial system or market, as opposed to those of individual institutions, have significant adverse effects elsewhere within an economy.

Tabular detail Component of the basic illustration required by the NAIC *Life Insurance Policy Illustration Model Regulation* to be provided to prospective policyowners, which includes policy values on a guaranteed and nonguaranteed basis for at least each policy year from one to 10 and for every fifth year thereafter, ending at the policy's terminal age. Also called **ledger pages**.

Tail risk Outlier risk associated with low frequency/high severity losses.

Tail Var See **conditional tail expectation**.

Takaful In Islam, type of solidarity or mutual fund separate from the management operation, which relies on a pact among participants to guarantee each other.

Target premium Amount of periodic premium under a universal life policy on which an agent can receive the maximum commission rate and which the insurer may believe provides reasonable policy funding.

Target return See **assumed interest rate**.

Target SERP Supplemental executive retirement plan intended to replace retirement benefits lost by ERISA-imposed limits and to counteract the bias in Social Security retirement benefits that favors low income workers.

Tax basis See **basis**.

Taxable estate Under federal tax law, portion of estate on which taxes are computed, derived by subtracting allowable deductions from the gross estate.

Taxable gift Gift of more than the annual exclusion amount made to any one person during a calendar year.

Technical advice memorandum U.S. Treasury Department statement prepared after the fact in response to a tax issue, usually in connection with a taxpayer audit.

Temporary life annuity Life annuity payable for the lesser of a set number of years or until the annuitant dies.

Tenancy by the entirety Joint interest property between spouses in which a decedent's interest passes automatically to the surviving spouse.

Tenancy in common Joint interest property in which each person owns his or her share outright, which share passes to the person's heirs.

Tentative federal estate tax Under federal tax law, product of the appropriate tax rate and the tentative tax base; estate tax before application of credits.

Tentative tax base Under federal tax law, sum of adjusted taxable gifts and the adjusted gross estate.

Term blending Rider providing term life insurance that replaces portions of a cash value policy's death benefit. Also called **blending**.

Term life insurance Policy that pays a prescribed death benefit if the insured dies during the policy term, which is a specified number of years, such as 10 or 20 years, or to a specified age, such as age 85.

Terminal bonus In U.K. and Commonwealth terminology, the payment of a supplemental bonus on policy maturity as an endowment or death benefit, the intent of which is to allow the policyowner or beneficiary to share more equitably in the favorable operations of the insurer. Also called **capital bonus**.

Terminal dividend Supplemental dividend payable when a policy terminates by death or surrender, the purpose of which is to return to terminating policyowners or beneficiaries part of the general surplus to which they have contributed or adjusting for a guaranteed cash value less than the asset share.

Terminal illness coverage Life insurance policy promise to pay up to a specified percentage (e.g., from 25 to 100 percent) of the policy's face amount if the insured is diagnosed as having a terminal illness, often subject to an overall maximum payment (e.g., $250,000). Also called **accelerated death benefits**.

Terminal reserve Value of a policy reserve at the end of a policy year, equal to the present value of future expected benefits less the present value of future expected premiums.

Testamentary trust One created through a decedent's will.

Testator Person making a will.

Third party marketer Organization that specializes in the distribution of insurance products in a banking system; may provide sales staff or support a bank's affiliation with a more traditional agency.

Three factor contribution formula Method of implementing the contribution principle of surplus distribution which recognizes that surplus derives from three main sources or factors which are (1) gains from investment earnings; i.e., actual investment returns that exceed the policy guaranteed crediting rate, (2) gains from loadings; i.e., actual expenses that are less than those implicit in policy pricing, and (3) gains from mortality; i.e., actual mortality experience that is more favorable than that implicit in policy pricing.

Tied agent See **career agent**.

Time clause See **survivorship clause**.

Tontine Any arrangement under which amounts are paid into a fund by participants who receive payments from the fund only for as long as they live, with a portion of the forfeited funds of deceased participants being used to augment payments to survivors.

Total adjusted capital Within the state-mandated risk-based capital system, value equal to statutory capital, paid-in surplus, Asset Valuation Reserve, and, in the case of mutual companies, 50 percent of any declared and unpaid dividend.

Total disability Under a disability income policy and waiver of premium features/riders, the inability of the insured, because of illness or injury, to perform either (1) the duties of his or her own occupation or (2) the duties of any occupation for which he or she is reasonably suited by reason of education, training, or experience, with the two definitions sometimes combined to provide that the first definition applies for the first few (e.g., two) years of disability, with the second definition applying thereafter.

Transfer for value rule *Internal Revenue Code* §101(a)(2) which provides that death proceeds under a life insurance policy are included in gross income to the extent of the excess of gross policy death proceeds over the policy's cost basis if the policy or any interest in it was transferred to another person for a valuable consideration.

Transfer pricing Pricing of goods and services between related parties.

Transferor Person who transfers a property interest; for estate tax, the decedent and, for gift tax, the donor.

Transplant benefit Provision within some disability income insurance policies that, if the insured is totally disabled because of the transplant of an organ from his or her body to the body of another individual, the insurer will deem him or her to be totally disabled as a result of sickness.

Treaty reinsurance See **automatic reinsurance**.

Trigger point Date designated in a formal buy/sell agreement at which a disabled owner's business interest must be purchased.

Trust Legal arrangement whereby one party transfers property to another who holds legal title and manages the trust property for the benefit of others as a fiduciary.

Trustee Person or institution receiving legal title to and managing the property of a trust.

Twisting Practice by an agent of inducing a policyowner through misrepresentation to replace an existing life insurance policy with another one.

Ultimate mortality table Mortality table showing probabilities of death by age and other possible criteria such as the sex of insureds after the select mortality period.

Unassigned surplus Surplus amounts not earmarked for special purposes. Also called **free capital**.

Unbundled policy Life insurance policy that discloses to the policyowner the portions of his or her premium that are allocated to specific policy elements: the internal insurance charges, cash values, and loadings for the insurer's expenses, taxes, profits, and contingencies.

Underwriting Process by which an insurer decides whether to issue insurance and on what terms and at what price.

Underwriting guidelines Set of recommended courses of action that underwriters generally follow in underwriting.

Underwriting risk Category of risk specified by the *International Actuarial Association/Association Actuarielle Internationale*, possibility of inadequate pricing arising from assumptions made with respect to claims and expenses and to policyowner behavior such as persistency and loan activity.

Unfunded nonqualified retirement plan Arrangement under which the employer does not formally earmark assets to fund the plan; the employee must rely exclusively on the employer's unsecured promise to make payments.

Unified credit Under federal tax law, tax credit that can be applied to offset estate and gift taxes; for deaths occurring in 2014, the credit is $2,081,800.

Unilateral Characteristic of insurance contracts providing that only one party, the insurer, gives a legally enforceable promise.

Unique risk See **diversifiable risk.**

Unit cost Measure of operating expenses allocated to some measured unit, such as face amount per thousand.

Unit linked annuity See **variable annuity**.

Unit linked life insurance See **variable life insurance**.

Universal life insurance Unbundled life insurance policy characterized by flexible premium payments and adjustable death benefits whose cash values and coverage period depend on the premiums paid into it.

Unsystematic risk See **diversifiable risk.**

Utility A measure of consumer satisfaction derived from economic goods.

Utilization management See **utilization review**.

Utilization review Determination of the medical necessity of procedures and treatments, including precertification and discharge planning. Also termed **utilization management.**

Utmost good faith Principle holding that parties to an insurance contract are entitled to rely in good faith upon the representations of the other, and each is under an obligation not to attempt to deceive or withhold material information from the other.

Valuation Practice of estimating future revenues, expenses, and reserves; central to reporting of both solvency and profitability.

Valuation mortality table Tabulation that displays yearly probabilities of death used in the calculation of minimum reserves and cash surrender values; usually contains margins.

Value at Risk Maximum acceptable loss associated with an asset or liability or portfolio of assets and liabilities over a specified time period with a specified probability or confidence level.

Value solve measure Comparison method commonly used to discern differences in the illustrated performance of life insurance policies, which solves for one element (e.g., premiums, death benefits, or cash values) by setting the remaining elements to identical values.

Valued policy See **stated value basis**.

Variable annuity Annuity whose cash values and benefit payments vary directly with the investment performance of assets held in one or more separate accounts. Also called **unit linked annuity**.

Variable life insurance Either bundled or unbundled life insurance under which the policyowner allocates premium payments to separate accounts offered by the insurer, with the cash values and usually death benefits directly determined by the investment performance of the assets held in these accounts, which are separate from the insurer's general account assets. Also called **unit linked life insurance**.

Variable universal life Variable life insurance configured as a universal life policy with its transparency, premium flexibility, and death benefit adjustability. Also called **flexible premium variable life** and **unit linked life insurance**.

Vesting Legal event that perfects ownership rights by an employee in retirement account balances or benefits contributed by or promised by an employer on the employee's behalf by making them nonforfeitable. Vesting may occur at any time according to the retirement plan provisions, but must occur no later than dates specified in the *Employee Retirement Income Security Act*. Employee contributions are never forfeitable.

Viatical See **life settlement**.

Void Agreement that has no legal force or effect.

Voidable Agreement that can be made void at the option of the innocent party.

Volatility Deviation of actual from average returns.

Wage risk Possibility that an individual's earnings from employment decline by more than expected.

Wait-and-see buy/sell agreement Arrangement under which shareholders and the corporation postpone the decision between a cross purchase and stock redemption agreement until the death of a stockholder.

Waiting period See **elimination period**.

Waiver of premium feature/rider Provision of or a rider attached to an insurance policy providing disability income coverage earmarked to pay ("waive") (1) premiums otherwise due under fixed-premium products or (2) premiums of a specified amount (often called wavier of a specified premium rider) or the monthly cost of insurance and expense charges (often called wavier of monthly charges rider) under flexible-premium policies. Also called **premium waiver feature/rider**.

War exclusion Optional clause within a life insurance policy that excludes claims arising from or while the insured is serving in the armed forces.

Warranty Attestation that a statement is absolutely and literally true.

Wealth replacement trust Irrevocable life insurance trust designed to provide a death benefit to beneficiaries roughly equivalent in value to property transferred by the donor/grantor to a charitable remainder trust or others.

Whole life annuity Life annuity payable for as long as the annuitant lives.

Whole life insurance Typically a bundled life insurance policy characterized by fixed death benefits and fixed uniform premiums designed to enable the policy to remain in effect for the entirety of the insured's life.

Will Legal declaration of an individual's wishes as to the disposition of his or her property on death.

With bonus In U.K. and Commonwealth terminology, a participating policy.

Without bonus In U.K. and Commonwealth terminology, a nonparticipating policy.

Yearly price per $1,000 of protection Cost comparison method that derives year-by-year measures for a policy's implicit mortality charges per $1,000 of net amount at risk.

Yearly rate of return Cost comparison method that derives year-by-year measures for the implicit rate of return on the savings component of a cash value policy.

Yearly renewable term Term life insurance whose premiums increase yearly. Also called **annual renewable term**.

Yearly renewable term reinsurance Proportional reinsurance under which the assuming company assumes the reinsured policy's net amount at risk in excess of the ceding company's retention, with premium rates varying by the age, sex, rating, and other underwriting factors.

INDEX

Page numbers followed by *t* indicate tables, charts, or graphs.

Residual disability
  benefit, 215–216
Respite care, 226
Results clauses, 125, 209
Retained asset accounts, 128,
    559–560
Retained interest, 679
Retained risk, 321
Retaliatory tax laws, 348
Retention, 321
Retirement age, 701
Retirement income insurance, 107
Retirement planning, 687–717
  current environment
    for, 687–690
  features of employer-provided
    plans, 712t–717t
  personal savings for, 696–711
  personal savings through life
    insurance, 708–711
  personal savings through non-
    qualified annuities, 703–708,
    703t–705t
  process of, 693–695
  psychological dimensions
    of, 690–693
  risk management, 695–702
  standard of living in
    retirement, 702
Retirement plans, 168–170
Retirement risk, 143–144, 144t
Retirement tail risk, 696
Retroactive bonuses, 502
Retrocession, 319
Retrocessionaire, 319
Retrospective policy reserve
    calculation, 470
Retrospective premium
    arrangements, 190
Return-of-premium feature/
    rider, 66, 217
Return-of-premium term policy/
    rider, 67
Return on assets (ROA), 498
Return on equity (ROE), 498
Return on investment (ROI), 498
Revenue rulings, 560, 634
Reversionary bonus, 501
Revocable beneficiary
    designations, 127
Revocable trusts, 676–677

Riders, 134–141. *See also specific
    riders*
  defined, 134
  enhanced cash value, 141
  for life insurance
    coverage, 134–137
  living benefit, 137–139
  to protect against policy
    lapse, 140–141
  in term insurance, 65
Riedner, H. L., 70
Right-of-return policy provi-
    sions, 118, 125
Risk
  capital and, 389–390
  defined/measured, 421
  diversification and, 421
  redefining, for financial
    intermediaries, 245–246
Risk-adjusted return on capital
    (RAROC), 412
Risk adjustment program, 185
Risk-based capital (RBC), 339,
    369
Risk-based capital (RBC)
    ratio, 530
Risk-Based Capital (RBC)
    Report, 363
Risk capital, 241, 387, 390–391
Risk classes, 49. *See also* Insur-
    ance pools
Risk discount rate, 500
Risk intermediation, 245
Risk management
  in 1990s, 248
  financial (*See* Financial risk
    management)
  future issues, 382
  personal financial planning
    and, 608–619
  in post-WWII era, 248
  reinsurance and, 320–322
  for retirement
    planning, 695–702
Risk pooling, 294
Risk premium, 53
Risks, 256–257
Risk selection, 185
ROA (return on assets), 498
ROE (return on equity), 498
ROI (return on investment), 498
Rollover, 698
Rome, ancient, 2

Roth Individual Retirement
    Account, 698–699
Royal Exchange, 3
RPNA (Required Policy Nonfor-
    feiture Account), 485
Ruin, 51, 52t
Ruin risk, 389
Runs (bank runs), 17

Safety margins, 491. *See also*
    Expense margins
Sales promotions, 283
SAP. *See* Statutory Accounting
    Principles
"satisfactory to the company," 121
Savings
  life insurance as motivator
    for, 10–11
  means of dealing with financial
    consequences of death, 36
  and retirement
    planning, 696–701
  risks in accumulation of, 607
Savings bank life insurance
    (SBLI), 236–237
Savings risk, 609
Scheduled premium policies, 98
SCIs (surrender cost indices), 585
Scope of authority, 554, 555
SEC. *See* Securities and Exchange
    Commission
Secondary beneficiaries, 126
Secondary life insurance
    market, 709–711
Second-to-die life
    insurance, 103–104
Section 162 plans, 735. *See also*
    Executive bonus plans
Section 303 stock
    redemptions, 731
Section 409A nonqualified retire-
    ment plans, 739–740
Section 1035 exchange, 647
Section 2503 (b) and (c)
    trusts, 677
Secular trusts, 740
Securities. *See* Stock(s)
Securities Act (1933), 334
Securities and Exchange Commis-
    sion (SEC)
  agent information from, 514
  and annuities, 161
  derivatives regulation, 334

9 780985 876517